FIRST CORINTHIANS

Sacra Pagina Series

Volume 7

First Corinthians

Raymond F. Collins

Daniel J. Harrington, S.J.
Editor

A Michael Glazier Book
THE LITURGICAL PRESS
Collegeville, Minnesota

Cover design by Don Bruno.

A Michael Glazier Book published by The Liturgical Press.

1   2   3   4   5   6   7   8

Library of Congress Cataloging-in-Publication Data

Collins, Raymond F., 1935–
    First Corinthians / Raymond F. Collins ; Daniel J. Harrington,
 editor.
      p.   cm. — (Sacra pagina series ; vol. 7)
    "A Michael Glazier book."
    Includes bibliographical references and indexes.
    ISBN 0-8146-5809-1 (alk. paper)
    1. Bible. N.T. Corinthians, 1st—Commentaries. I. Harrington,
 Daniel J. II. Title. III. Series: Sacra pagina series ; 7.
 BS2675.3.C645   1999
 227'.2077—dc21   98-51063
                                                                 CIP

In Memory of

Raymond E. Brown, S.S.

Priest, Scholar, Friend

CONTENTS

Editor's Preface   xi

Author's Preface   xiii

Note on References   xvii

Abbreviations   xix

Introduction

1. A Real Letter   1

2. A Hellenistic Letter   6

3. A Long Letter   8

4. A Single Letter?   10

5. A Stylistic Feature   14

6. Problems at Corinth   16

7. Paul's Rhetoric   17

8. The Issues   20

9. Corinth   21

10. A Theological Perspective   25

11. Outline of the Structure of the Letter   29

General Bibliography   31

Translation, Interpretation, Notes

INTRODUCTION (1:1-9)

A. Epistolary Opening (1:1-3)   41

B. Thanksgiving (1:4-9)   55

BODY OF THE LETTER (1:10–15:58)

A. Theme and Occasion (1:10-17)   67

B. First Rhetorical Demonstration (1:18–4:21)   86

   1. Wisdom and Power (1:18-31)   89

   2. Paul's Mission (2:1-5)   115

   3. God's Wisdom (2:6-16)   121

   4. Mother and Farmer (3:1-9)   139

   5. The Construction (3:10-17)   148

   6. Slogans Reversed (3:18-23)   162

   7. The Ultimate Tribunal (4:1-5)   167

   8. The Lesson of Paul and Apollos (4:6-7)   175

   9. Filled and Hungry (4:8-13)   182

   10. A Letter of Admonition (4:14-16)   192

   11. Recommendation of Timothy (4:17-21)   195

C. Second Rhetorical Demonstration (5:1–7:40)   203

   1. A Purified Community (5:1-8)   205

   2. Shunning Evil (5:9-13)   216

   3. Use of the Courts (6:1-11)   224

   4. Embodied Existence (6:12-20)   239

   5. Sex Within Marriage (7:1-7)   251

   6. Special Situations (7:8-16)   262

   7. Remain As You Were Called (7:17-24)   273

   8. Advice for the Unmarried (7:25-35)   287

   9. To Marry or Not to Marry (7:36-40)   298

D. Third Rhetorical Demonstration (8:1–11:1)   304

   1. Food Offered to Idols (8:1-3)   308

   2. The Monotheistic Confession of Faith (8:4-6)   313

   3. Eating and Freedom (8:7-13)   321

   4. Apostolic Rights (9:1-14)   327

   5. Christ's Slave (9:15-18)   343

   6. For the Sake of the Gospel (9:19-23)   349

7. The Games (9:24-27)   357

8. Learning from Scripture (10:1-13)   363

9. Avoid Idolatry (10:14-22)   375

10. Summing Up (10:23–11:1)   382

E. THE FOURTH RHETORICAL DEMONSTRATION (11:2-34)   392

1. Let Men Be Men and Women Be Women (11:2-16)   393

2. The Lord's Supper? (11:17-22)   416

3. The Lord's Supper (11:23-26)   425

4. Judgment (11:27-34)   435

F. FIFTH RHETORICAL DEMONSTRATION (12:1–14:40)   441

1. A Matter of Principle (12:1-3)   445

2. Allotment of Gifts (12:4-11)   448

3. The Body (12:12-26)   457

4. Christ's Body (12:27-31a)   466

5. Not to Have Love (12:31b–13:3)   471

6. Love's Rhythm (13:4-7)   478

7. A Unique Gift (13:8–14:1a)   483

8. The Greater Gift of Prophecy (14:1b-5)   489

9. A Trilogy of Cultural Analogies (14:6-12)   494

10. Praying with Full Participation (14:13-19)   500

11. Outsiders and Unbelievers (14:20-25)   504

12. Order in the Assembly (14:26-40)   511

G. SIXTH RHETORICAL DEMONSTRATION (15:1-58)   525

1. The Creed (15:1-11)   528

2. If Christ Has Not Been Raised (15:12-19)   540

3. Ultimate Victory (15:20-28)   546

4. An Exhortation (15:29-34)   556

5. How Can the Dead Be Raised? (15:35-44a)   562

6. The Last Adam (15:44b-49)   568

7. Victory over Death (15:50-58)   573

CLOSING (16:1-24)

1. Collection for the Holy Ones (16:1-4)   585

2. Travel Plans (16:5-9)   590

3. Timothy and Apollos (16:10-12)   594

4. Goodbye (16:13-14)   599

5. Commendation of Stephanas (16:15-18)   602

6. Greetings (16:19-21)   607

7. Solemn Farewell (16:22-24)   613

Indexes

Index of Scripture References   619

Index of Classical, Jewish, and Patristic Sources   661

Index of Modern Authors   676

Index of Topics   686

EDITOR'S PREFACE

Sacra Pagina is a multi-volume commentary on the books of the New Testament. The expression *Sacra Pagina* ("Sacred Page") originally referred to the text of Scripture. In the Middle Ages it also described the study of Scripture to which the interpreter brought the tools of grammar, rhetoric, dialectic, and philosophy. Thus *Sacra Pagina* encompasses both the text to be studied and the activity of interpretation.

This series presents fresh translations and modern expositions of all the books of the New Testament. Written by an international team of Catholic biblical scholars, it is intended for biblical professionals, graduate students, theologians, clergy, and religious educators. The volumes present basic introductory information and close exposition. They self-consciously adopt specific methodological perspectives, but maintain a focus on the issues raised by the New Testament compositions themselves. The goal of *Sacra Pagina* is to provide sound critical analysis without any loss of sensitivity to religious meaning. This series is therefore catholic in two senses of the word: inclusive in its methods and perspectives, and shaped by the context of the Catholic tradition.

The Second Vatican Council described the study of the "sacred page" as the "very soul of sacred theology" (*Dei Verbum* 24). The volumes in this series illustrate how Catholic scholars contribute to the council's call to provide access to Sacred Scripture for all the Christian faithful. Rather than pretending to say the final word on any text, these volumes seek to open up the riches of the New Testament and to invite as many people as possible to study seriously the "sacred page."

DANIEL J. HARRINGTON, S.J.

AUTHOR'S PREFACE

First Corinthians is one of the longest of the apostle's letters and has duly merited the attention paid to it by commentators from Chrysostom to the end of this twentieth century. In many ways 1 Corinthians is one of the most exciting of Paul's letters. It introduces us to a number of people, Stephanas, Fortunatus, Achaicus, and Gaius among them, who belonged to the church at Corinth. These individuals belonged to a flesh-and-blood community whose humanness was all too apparent. Sex, death, and money were among the issues they had to face. Social conflicts and tension within their Christian community were part of their daily life. It was to a very real community with very real issues that Paul wrote his first letter to the Corinthians.

The letter is remarkable in many respects, not the least of which is the way in which Paul constantly alludes to the social location of his addressees. He responds to their concerns with due respect to their situation in a mid-first century C.E. Hellenistic metropolis. To a large extent his letter affects the language of contemporary philosophers as they address issues similar to those treated by Paul. This commentary approaches 1 Corinthians as a Hellenistic letter written to people dealing with real issues in the Hellenistic world. It cites other extant Hellenistic letters to show that Paul was truly a letter writer of his own times. It makes frequent reference to the writings of the philosophic moralists to help clarify the way in which Paul spoke to his beloved Corinthians. It also comments on some aspects of the social circumstances in which the Christians of Corinth actually lived.

In the Hellenistic world the art of letter writing was taught in rhetorical schools. While one can hardly make the case that Paul attended a rhetorical school, it is clear that he knew a great deal about the art of letter writing. It is no less true that Paul was a great preacher. His rhetorical skill has made its impress upon this first letter to the Corinthians. This commentary takes the tack of dealing with the letter as a kind of speech that is conveyed in the form of a letter. It focuses on Paul's manner of communicating with the Christian community at Corinth. Writing to them, Paul is serving them as their apostle (1:1; 9:1-2). The community is struggling with various issues as it strives to become what it is, namely, the church of God at Corinth. The commentary is intended to engage their struggle as Paul speaks to them, urging them to be of the same mind (1:10), putting on the mind of Christ (2:16).

No more than Paul wrote his letter in a vacuum was this commentary written in a vacuum. As Paul was reliant upon the traditions he had received, so this commentary is indebted to those who have gone before. The demands of space have made it impossible for me regularly to cite the major commentaries that have preceded my own. It is, nonetheless, appropriate that I prefix to my effort an acknowledgment particularly of the work of Johannes Weiss, Ernest-Bernard Allo, Hans Lietzmann, Archibald Robertson and Alfred Plummer, Hans Conzelmann, Charles Kingsley Barrett, Gordon D. Fee, and Wolfgang Schrage. Without their efforts my own would not have come to pass. Three other authors deserve particular mention. They are Jerome Murphy-O'Connor, for his innovative and probing remarks, Margaret M. Mitchell, for applying the insights of rhetorical criticism to 1 Corinthians, and Ben Witherington III, for his recent socio-rhetorical commentary on the letter.

My debt of gratitude extends beyond those who have written commentaries on Paul's letter or who have otherwise worked extensively on the letter. I am especially grateful to Michael Glazier, who asked me to contribute a commentary in the Sacra Pagina series that he so successfully launched. I am grateful to Wilhelm Wuellner and Abraham Malherbe, whose insights into rhetorical criticism and epistolary analysis, respectively, have largely inspired my own. I am most thankful to Jan Lambrecht, who has sustained me with his friendship and his fraternity throughout my exegetical efforts.

In making his plea for the unity of the Christian community at Corinth Paul made use of three powerful images: the field, the building, and the body. I sometimes wonder whether this skillful writer and great communicator would have made use of yet another striking image of corporate endeavor had he lived in our day. I suspect that he who was supremely conscious of the role of the many in constituting the one would also have used the image of the book. No book comes into print without the contributions of the many.

Many, in fact, have contributed to this particular book. With heartfelt gratitude I acknowledge their contributions. Among them are Mrs. Marie Vignali and Ms. Mary Dancy, assistants in the office of the Dean of the School of Religious Studies at The Catholic University of America. When I arrived at CUA as dean in the fall of 1993 these valiant ladies had to learn not only to cope with the idiosyncrasies of a new dean, they also had to learn to deal with a dean who wanted to teach and to write. I thank them for their patience and their support.

I have learned much from my students, those in my seminar on 1 Corinthians at the Catholic University of Leuven in the spring of 1991 and those doctoral students at The Catholic University of America whom I value as colleagues and coworkers, particularly Mario Barbero, Mary Kate Birge, Margaret Christi Karwowski, and Thomas Song. Colleagues far and wide have assisted me in gathering material that was not otherwise readily accessible to me. Among these are Reimund Bieringer, Susan Calef, Chrys Caragounis, Otis Coutsoumpos, Will Deming, Jack Dick, Wilfred Sebothoma, Elaine Wainwright, and Gilbert van Belle.

I owe a very special word of thanks to John Smolko, whose technical skills and many hours of labor rescued the results of almost two years of research from the destruction to which a computer virus had doomed them. Lee Dudek helped greatly by printing the manuscript in its various stages. Mary T. Burns and Joan Fricot, the first in an earlier stage, the latter in the final stage, were invaluable proofreaders. James Rhodes performed a yeoman task in preparing the indices. Dan Harrington, the general editor of the Sacra Pagina series, offered judicious remarks, helpful comments, and careful criticism. Joseph Jensen, my graduate assistant during these past five years, has worked with me throughout this project. Without his generous dedication to our project, his linguistic and bibliographic skills, and his many and diverse efforts this commentary on 1 Corinthians would have forever remained a hope rather than the book that it has become. To him I owe a most special thanks. He has been my Timothy.

NOTE ON REFERENCES

References to the Old Testament are given according to the New Revised Standard Version. Where the LXX numbering is different and it seems appropriate to call attention to this, the LXX reference is given in brackets [LXX . . .] following the primary reference. When the reference is directly to the LXX, the Hebrew numbering, if different—as is usually the case in the Psalms—is indicated in brackets following the LXX reference.

References to Pseudepigrapha of the Old Testament are given according to the collection edited by James H. Charlesworth, *The Old Testament Pseudepigrapha*. 2 vols. (Garden City, N.Y.: Doubleday, 1983, 1985). References to Qumran material (though not necessarily the translation) follow the edition of Florentino García Martínez, *The Dead Sea Scrolls Translated* (Leiden: Brill, 1994), except that in the case of the "Thanksgiving Psalms" (1QH) the more traditional column numbering has been retained.

ABBREVIATIONS

Biblical Books and Apocrypha

Gen	Hag	Wis
Exod	Zech	Matt
Lev	Mal	Rom
Num	Ps (*pl.:* Pss)	1–2 Cor
Deut	Prov	Gal
Josh	Cant	Eph
Judg	Qoh	Phil
1–2 Sam	Lam	Col
1–2 Kgs	Esth	1–2 Thess
Isa	Dan	1–2 Tim
Jer	Neh	Phlm
Ezek	1–2 Chr	Heb
Hos	Bar	Jas
Obad	1–2 Esdr	1–2 Pet
Mic	Jdt	1–2–3 John
Nah	1–2–3–4 Macc	Rev
Hab	Sir	
Zeph	Tob	

Pseudepigrapha

2–3 Apoc. Bar.	Syriac, Greek Apocalypse of Baruch
Apoc. Mos.	Apocalypse of Moses
1–2–3 Enoch	Ethiopic, Slavonic, Hebrew Enoch
Ep. Arist.	Epistle of Aristeas
Gos. Thom.	*Gospel of Thomas*
Jub.	Jubilees
Sib. Or.	Sibylline Oracles
T. Abr.	Testament of Abraham
T. Asher	Testament of Asher
T. Dan	Testament of Dan
T. Gad	Testament of Gad

T. Job	Testament of Job
T. Jos.	Testament of Joseph
T. Judah	Testament of Judah
T. Levi	Testament of Levi
T. Mos.	Testament of Moses
T. Naph.	Testament of Naphtali
T. Reub.	Testament of Reuben
T. Simeon	Testament of Simeon

Qumran and Related Literature

CD	Cairo (Genizah text of the) Damascus (Document)
1 QH	*Hôdāyôt (Thanksgiving Hymns)* from Qumran Cave 1
1 QM	*Milḥāmâ (War Scroll)*
1 QpHab	*Pesher on Habakkuk* from Qumran Cave 1
1 QS	*Manual of Discipline*
1QSa	Appendix A *(Rule of the Congregation)* to 1 QS
4 QD^e	Fifth copy of the Damascus Document from Qumran Cave 4
4 QM^a	First copy of the *War Scroll* from Qumran Cave 4
4 QpNah	*Pesher on Nahum* from Qumran Cave 4
11 Q Temple	*Temple Scroll* from Qumran Cave 11

Mishnaic and Related Literature

1. Babylonian Talmud *(b.)*

b. B. Bat.	*Baba Batra*
b. B. Meṣ.	*Baba Meṣiʿa*
b. ʿErub.	*ʿErubin*
b. Ketub.	*Ketubot*
b. Menaḥ	*Menaḥot*
b. Qidd.	*Qiddušin*
b. Sanh.	*Sanhedrin*
b. Yebam.	*Yebamot*
b. Yoma	*Yoma*

2. Mishna *(m.)*

m. ʾAbot	*ʾAbot*
m. B. Qam.	*Baba Qamma*
m. Ber.	*Berakot*
m. Beṣa	*Beṣa*
m. Giṭ.	*Giṭṭin*
m. Ker.	*Keritot*
m. Ketub.	*Ketubot*

m. Ned.	Nedarim
m. Pesaḥ.	Pesaḥim
m. Qidd.	Qiddušin
m. Sanh.	Sanhedrin
m. Yad.	Yadayim

3. Tosepta *(t.)*

t. Ber.	Berakot
t. Ned.	Nedarim
t. Qidd.	Qiddušin
t. Šabb.	Šabbat
t. Sanh.	Sanhedrin

4. Jerusalem Talmud *(y.)*

y. Ber.	Berakot
y. Ker.	Keritot
y. Ketub.	Ketubot
y. Kil.	Kilʾayim
y. Pesaḥ.	Pesaḥim

Other Jewish Literature

Gen. Rab.	Genesis Rabbah
Pesiq. R.	Pesiqta Rabbati
Pirqe R. El.	Pirqe Rabbi Eliezer
Qoh. Rab.	Qoheleth Rabbah
Sipre Deut.	Sipre Deuteronomy
Tg. Isa.	Targum of Isaiah

Early Patristic Literature

Barn.	Barnabas
1–2 Clem.	1–2 Clement
Did.	Didache
Herm. Man.	Hermas. Mandates
Herm. Sim.	Hermas. Similitudes
Herm. Vis.	Hermas. Visions
Ign. *Eph.*	Ignatius, Letter to the Ephesians
Ign. *Magn.*	Ignatius, Letter to the Magnesians
Ign. *Phld.*	Ignatius, Letter to the Philadelphians
Ign. *Pol.*	Ignatius, Letter to Polycarp
Ign. *Rom.*	Ignatius, Letter to the Romans
Mart. Pol.	Martyrdom of Polycarp

Papyri

P. Bononiensis	*Papyri Bononienses.* Pubblicazioni dell' Università Cattolica del Sacro Cuore 42. Orsolina Montevecchi, ed. Milan: Vita e pensiero, 1953.
P. Elephantine	BGU Supplement. *Elephantine Papyri.* Otto Rubensohn, ed. Berlin: Weidmann, 1907.
P. Hamburg	*Griechische Papyrusurkunden der Hamburger Staats- und Universitätsbibliothek,* I/3. P. M. Meyer, ed. Leipzig and Berlin: B. G. Teubner, 1924.
P. London	*Greek Papyri in the British Museum.* 5 vols. and 3 portfolios. F. G. Kenyon and H. I. Bell, eds. London: British Museum, 1898–1917. Reprint Milan: Cisalpino-Goliardica, 1973.
P. Michigan	*Papyri and Ostraca from Karanis.* Michigan Papyri 8. H. C. Youtie and J. G. Winter, eds. Ann Arbor: University of Michigan Press, 1951.
P. Nessana	*Excavations at Nessana III: Non-Literary Papyri.* C. J. Kraemer, Jr., ed. Princeton: Princeton University Press, 1958.
P. Oxyrhynchus	*The Oxyrhynchus Papyri.* B. P. Grenfell and A. S. Hunt, eds. London: Egypt Exploration Fund, 1898.

Classical Literature

Corp Herm	*Corpus Hermeticum*
JosAs	*Joseph and Aseneth*
Ap.	Flavius Josephus, *Against Apion*
Ant.	Flavius Josephus, *Antiquities of the Jews*
Bell.	Flavius Josephus, *The Jewish Wars*

Periodicals, Reference Works, and Serials

AB	Anchor Bible
ABD	David N. Freedman et al, eds., *Anchor Bible Dictionary*
ABR	*American Benedictine Review*
ACNT	Augsburg Commentary on the New Testament
AKG	Arbeiten zur Kirchengeschichte
AGJU	Arbeiten zur Geschichte des antiken Judentums und des Urchristentums
AJA	*American Journal of Archaeology*
AnBib	Analecta biblica
AnCr	*Analecta Cracoviensia*
AnJBI	*Annual of the Japanese Biblical Institute*
ANRW	*Aufstieg und Niedergang der römischen Welt*
ASCS	American School of Classical Studies
ASNU	Acta seminarii neotestamentici upsaliensis

AThANT	Abhandlungen zur Theologie des Alten und Neuen Testaments
ATR.S	*Anglican Theological Review,* Supplement Series
Aug	*Augustinianum*
AusBR	*Australian Biblical Review*
AV	Authorized Version
BA	*Biblical Archaeologist*
BAG(D)	Walter Bauer, William F. Arndt, and F. Wilbur Gingrich (2nd ed.: and Frederick W. Danker), *Greek-English Lexicon of the New Testament.* 2nd ed. Chicago: University of Chicago Press, 1979.
BARev	*Biblical Archaeology Review*
BDF	Friedrich W. Blass, Albert Debrunner, and Robert W. Funk, *A Greek Grammar of the New Testament.* Chicago: University of Chicago Press, 1961.
BeO	*Bibbia e oriente*
BEThL	Bibliotheca Ephemeridum theologicarum Lovaniensium
BFCT	Beiträge zur Förderung christlicher Theologie
BGU	*Ägyptische Urkunden aus den königlichen Museen zu Berlin. Griechische Urkunden.* 4 vols. Ulrich Wilcken, et al, eds. Berlin: Weidmann, 1907–
BHTh	Beiträge zur historischen Theologie
Bib.	*Biblica*
BibBH	*Bible Bhashyam*
Bijdr	*Bijdragen*
BiKi	*Bibel und Kirche*
BiTr	*Bible Translator*
BJRL	*Bulletin of the John Rylands University Library of Manchester*
BLE	*Bulletin de littérature ecclésiastique*
BR	*Biblical Research*
BSac	*Bibliotheca Sacra*
BTB	*Biblical Theology Bulletin*
BWA(N)T	Beiträge zur Wissenschaft vom Alten (und Neuen) Testament
BZ	*Biblische Zeitschrift*
BZNW	Beihefte zur *ZNW*
CBET	Contributions to Biblical Exegesis and Theology
CBG	*Collationes Brugenses et Gandavenses*
CBQ	*Catholic Biblical Quarterly*
ChiSt	*Chicago Studies*
CJ	*Concordia Journal*
CJT	*Canadian Journal of Theology*
ConBNT	Coniectanea biblica, New Testament
CorC	*The Corinthian Correspondence.* Reimund Bieringer, ed. BEThL 125. Leuven: Leuven University Press, 1996.
CorpH	Corpus Hermeticum
CRINT	Compendia rerum iudaicarum ad Novum Testamentum
CStor	*Cristianesimo nella Storia*

CTJ	*Calvin Theological Journal*
CTQ	*Concordia Theological Quarterly*
CTR	*Criswell Theological Review*
CV	*Communio Viatorum*
DBM	*Deltion Biblikon Meleton*
DRev	*Downside Review*
EDNT	*Exegetical Dictionary of the New Testament* (English translation of *Exegetisches Wörterbuch zum Neuen Testament*)
EKKNT	Evangelisch-katholischer Kommentar zum Neuen Testament
EpRev	*Epworth Review*
EstBib	*Estudios biblicos*
EstEcl	*Estudios eclesiásticos*
EtB	Etudes bibliques
EThL	*Ephemerides theologicae Lovanienses*
EThR	*Etudes théologiques et religieuses*
EThSt	Erfurter theologische Studien
EvQ	*Evangelical Quarterly*
EWNT	Horst Balz and Gerhard Schneider, eds., *Exegetisches Wörterbuch zum Neuen Testament*
ExpT	*Expository Times*
FNT	*Filologia Neotestamentaria*
FRLANT	Forschungen zur Religion und Literatur des Alten und Neuen Testaments
GNS	Good News Studies
GNT[4]	Barbara Aland et al, eds., *The Greek New Testament*. 4th ed. Stuttgart: Deutsche Bibelgesellschaft; United Bible Societies, 1994.
Greg	*Gregorianum*
GTA	Göttinger theologische Arbeiten
GTJ	*Grace Theological Journal*
HAR	*Hebrew Annual Review*
HBT	*Horizons in Biblical Theology*
HCNT	M. Eugene Boring, Klaus Berger, and Carsten Colpe (eds.) *Hellenistic Commentary to the New Testament*. Nashville: Abingdon, 1995.
HDR	Harvard Dissertations in Religion
HeyJ	*Heythrop Journal*
HNT	Handbuch zum Neuen Testament
HR	*History of Religions*
HThR	*Harvard Theological Review*
HTS	*Hervormde Teologiese Studies*
HUT	Hermeneutische Untersuchungen zur Theologie
IBS	*Irish Biblical Studies*
ICBS	International Congress on Biblical Studies
ICC	International Critical Commentary
IDB	George A. Buttrick, ed., *Interpreter's Dictionary of the Bible*
IDBSup	Supplementary volume to *IDB*

ILS	*Inscriptiones latinae selectae.* 5 vols. Hermann Dessau, ed. Berlin: Wiedmann, 1892–1914. Reprint Chicago: Ares, 1979.
Interp.	*Interpretation*
ISA	Stobaeus, *Anthology.* Curt Wachsmuth and Otto Hense, eds. *Ioannis Stobaei Anthologium.* 5 vols. Reprint Berlin: Weidmann, 1974.
JAAR	*Journal of the American Academy of Religion*
JAARSup	*Journal of the American Academy of Religion Supplement*
JAC	*Jahrbuch für Antike und Christentum*
JB	Jerus. lem Bible
JBL	*Journal of Biblical Literature*
JETS	*Journal of the Evangelical Theological Society*
JNES	*Journal of Near Eastern Studies*
JQR	*Jewish Quarterly Review*
JSNT	*Journal for the Study of the New Testament*
JSNT.S	*JSNT* Supplement Series
JSOT	*Journal for the Study of the Old Testament*
JSSt	*Journal of Semitic Studies*
JThS	*Journal of Theological Studies*
KEK	Kritisch-exegetischer Kommentar über das Neue Testament (Meyer-Kommentar)
LB	*Linguistica biblica*
LeDiv	Lectio divina
LouvSt	*Louvain Studies*
LSJ	Liddell-Scott-Jones, *Greek-English Lexicon*
LTJ	*Lutheran Theological Journal*
LTP	*Laval théologique et philosophique*
LXX	The Greek Bible (the Septuagint)
MM	James H. Moulton and George Milligan, *The Vocabulary of the Greek Testament*
MNTC	Moffatt New Testament Commentary
MSSNTS	Society for New Testament Studies Monograph Series
MT	Masoretic Text
N-A[27]	Kurt Aland, et al, eds., *Novum Testamentum Graece: post Eberhard et E. Nestle,* 27th ed. Stuttgart: Deutsche Bibelgesellschaft, 1993.
NBl	*New Blackfriars*
Neotest.	*Neotestamentica*
NIC	New International Commentary
NICNT	New International Commentary on the New Testament
NIGTC	New International Greek Testament Commentary
NIV	New International Version
NJB	New Jerusalem Bible
NovT	*Novum Testamentum*
NovT.S	*Novum Testamentum* Supplements
NRSV	New Revised Standard Version
NT	New Testament

NTA	Neutestamentliche Abhandlungen
NTD	Das Neue Testament Deutsch
NTL	New Testament Library
NTMes	New Testament Message
NTS	*New Testament Studies*
NTTS	New Testament Tools and Studies
Numen	*Numen: International Review for the History of Religions*
OT	Old Testament
ÖTKNT	Ökumenischer Taschenbuchkommentar zum Neuen Testament
PG	J.-P. Migne, ed., *Patrologia graeca*
Phil.S	Philologus Supplement Series
PL	J.-P. Migne, ed., *Patrologia latina*
PNTC	Pelican New Testament Commentaries
PRS	*Perspectives in Religious Studies*
PSB	*Princeton Seminary Bulletin*
QD	Quaestiones disputatae
RAT	*Révue africaine de théologie*
RB	*Revue biblique*
RBR	*Richerche bibliche e religiose*
REB	Revised English Bible
RefR	*Reformed Review*
ResQ	*Restoration Quarterly*
RExp	*Review and Expositor*
RevB	*Revista biblica*
RevScR	*Revue des sciences religieuses*
RivBib	*Rivista biblica*
RNAB	Revised New American Bible
RNT	Regensburger Neues Testament
RSR	*Recherches de science religieuse*
RSV	Revised Standard Version
RTR	*Reformed Theological Review*
Salm	*Salmanticensis*
SBFLA	*Studii Biblici Franciscani Liber Annuus*
SBL	Society of Biblical Literature
SBL.DS	SBL Dissertation Series
SBL.MS	SBL Monograph Series
SBL.SBS	SBL Sources for Biblical Study
SBL.SP	SBL Seminar Papers
SBL.SS	SBL Semeia Studies
SBS	Stuttgarter Bibelstudien
SBT	Studies in Biblical Theologie
ScEs	*Science et esprit*
SCHNT	Studia ad corpus hellenisticum Novi Testamenti
ScrB	*Scripture Bulletin*
SEÅ	*Svenks exegetisk årsbok*

SJOT	*Scandinavian Journal of the Old Testament*
SJTh	*Scottish Journal of Theology*
SNT	Studien zum Neuen Testament
SNTU	Studien zum Neuen Testament und seiner Umwelt
SP	Sacra Pagina
SPC	*Studiorum paulinorum congressus internationalis catholicus 1961* (2 vols.)
SR	*Studies in Religion/Sciences religieuses*
ST	*Studia theologica*
StBT	*Studia Biblica et Theologica*
StEv	*Studia evangelica*
Str-B	[Hermann Strack and] Paul Billerbeck, *Kommentar zum Neuen Testament aus Talmud und Midrasch*
SVF	*Stoicorum Veterum Fragmenta*, Hans Friedrich August von Arnim, ed. 4 vols. Leipzig: Teubner, 1903–1924; reprint Stuttgart: Teubner, 1964.
TBT	*The Bible Today*
TD	*Theology Digest*
TDNT	Gerhard Kittel and Gerhard Friedrich, eds., *Theological Dictionary of the New Testament* (translation by Geoffrey Bromiley of *Theologisches Wörterbuch zum Neuen Testament*)
ThBeitr	*Theologische Beiträge*
ThH	Théologie historique
ThHKNT	Theologischer Handkommentar zum Neuen Testament
ThQ	*Theologische Quartalschrift*. Tübingen
ThZ	*Theologische Zeitschrift*
TJT	*Toronto Journal of Theology*
TLNT	Ceslaus Spicq, *Theological Lexicon of the New Testament*. 3 vols. Peabody, Mass.: Hendrickson, 1994.
TLZ	*Theologische Literaturzeitung*
TrJ	*Trinity Journal*
TS	*Theological Studies*
TThZ	*Trierer theologische Zeitschrift*
TU	Texte und Untersuchungen zur Geschichte der altchristlichen Literatur
TvT	*Tijdschrift voor theologie*
TynB	*Tyndale Bulletin*
USQR	*Union Seminary Quarterly Review*
VC	*Vigiliae christianae*
VT	*Vetus Testamentum*
WuD	*Wort und Dienst*
WdF	Wege der Forschung
WMANT	Wissenschaftliche Monographien zum Alten und Neuen Testament
WThJ	*Westminster Theological Journal*

WUNT	Wissenschaftliche Untersuchungen zum Neuen Testament
ZNW	*Zeitschrift für die neutestamentliche Wissenschaft*
ZThK	*Zeitschrift für Theologie und Kirche*
ZWTh	*Zeitschrift für wissenschaftliche Theologie*

INTRODUCTION

Paul was well aware of what he was doing and why he was doing what he was doing when he wrote to the church of God at Corinth (1:2). On four occasions he refers to what he is doing as "writing" (4:14; 5:11; 9:15; 14:37). The first three times Paul speaks about writing he gives his reasons for writing. "I am writing these things," he says in 1 Cor 4:14, "not to make you ashamed, but to admonish you as my beloved children." Turning his attention to a specific situation in 5:11, he writes "Now I write to you not to be associated with someone who bears the name of brother or sister and who is sexually immoral or avaricious or idolatrous or slanderous or a drunkard or greedy."

Paul's purpose in writing to the Corinthians is clearly admonitory. He is concerned with the assembly and wants them to know what they should do and what they should not do. In 9:15 he tells them that he is not writing to them in order to gain some advantage for himself. Then, after a long exhortation in which he tells the community many things about their coming together for worship Paul concludes his reflection with a remark that attempts to put his entire exhortation into the proper perspective. What he is writing "is a command of the Lord" (14:37).

1. A Real Letter

Paul obviously knew what a letter was (16:3). He makes a point of comparing what he is writing with a letter he had previously written to the Corinthians (5:9, 11). The way in which he begins writing to the Corinthians closely resembles the way that letters began in the Greco-Roman world of the first century. People of those times typically began their letters with "so-and-so to so-and-so, greetings." Paul begins his writing to the Corinthians with "Paul and Sosthenes to the church of God at Corinth, grace to you and peace." Admittedly Paul's salutation is a bit more complex than that, but we recognize in 1 Cor 1:2-3 words that indicate that Paul was writing a real letter to the Corinthians.

In his day, as now, it is the opening salutation and the complementary close that clearly identify documents as letters. Paul's opening salutation

1

is similar to the way Hellenistic writers began their letters. Many features of the closing verses of 1 Corinthians (16:13-24) are comparable to the way in which Hellenistic letters were brought to conclusion. Paul signed his letter (16:21) and expressed his best wishes (16:23). He also added a brief postscript (16:24). In passing he conveyed greetings to the Corinthians on behalf of a variety of folks (16:19-20a) and asked that they pass along his greetings to others (16:20b). This is the kind of thing that modern letter writers do as they bring to closure their own personal letters.

A remarkable feature of Paul's letter closing is his signature, or at least the way Paul has added his signature at the end of his letter. "A greeting in my own hand, the hand of Paul," he writes (16:21). The signature comes not at the very end of his letter, just before his postscript, but before his complementary close (16:23). We moderns expect a signature to be in one's own hand. Anything other than that is rather unusual. At the very least we expect the secretary who signs a dictated letter to add initials in order to verify the extraordinary circumstances in which a letter was signed and sent. Rarely, however, did Hellenistic letter writers "sign" their letters. They identified themselves at the beginning of their letters, not at the end.

It was not uncommon for Hellenistic letter writers to dictate their letters to professional scribes (amanuenses). Sometimes this was done because the letter writers themselves were illiterate. Not being able to read or write, they had to make use of professional scribes. Some of the extant Hellenistic letters on papyrus actually state that the scribe was writing a letter on behalf of a person who did not know how to write. Writing a letter was a long and tedious process. As a result people of means or of political importance often used scribes to transcribe their epistolary dictation. Cicero tried to save time by sometimes dictating as many as four letters at a time, using four different scribes to do so.

When letters were dictated by people who could read and write it was not unusual, but not altogether common, for them to add personal greetings to letters they had written and to do so in their own hand. The practice was not so very different from current letter-writing practice when an author adds a few personal words of greeting to a letter that has been computer generated. A difference in calligraphy between the body of the letter and the greetings at its end in many of the papyrus letters shows that the letters were actually written by scribes and that the real authors took reed in hand only to add a few words at the end. Those who saw the letter could clearly recognize the difference in handwriting styles between the final greetings and the body of the letter that had preceded them.

That Paul made a point of signing his letter in 16:21 (cf. Phlm 19; Gal 6:11; Col 4:18; 2 Thess 3:17) shows that Paul dictated this first letter to the

Corinthians. In addition to his signature Paul added a final farewell and a postscript (16:21-24). An otherwise unknown Tertius was the scribe who penned Paul's letter to the Romans (Rom 16:22; cf. 1 Pet 5:12), but we do not know the name of the person who transcribed 1 Corinthians. The unusual way in which Paul draws attention to his signature is an indication that the letter Paul had written was to be read aloud to the Corinthians. Addressed to an assembly (1:1), it was read by a single person (see 1 Thess 5:27). Most people in the gathering would not see the actual text of the letter so they would not have been able to differentiate between the hand of Paul and that of the anonymous scribe.

It is likely that whoever brought the letter to Corinth read it to the group that had gathered. Paul's signature and his postscript expressed his affection for the community at Corinth (cf. 4:14; 10:14; 15:18). For Hellenistic letters of the friendly type, Pseudo-Demetrius' *typos philikos,* the addition of a handwritten signature served as a token of the particularly close relationship that existed between the letter writer and the addressee.

Hellenistic letters, like modern letters—although we more commonly use the phone or electronic communication for this purpose today—were a way of extending one's presence when one is unable to be present. Presence and absence, like two sides of a coin, are themes that run throughout letters. In his classic study of Hellenistic letters (1956) Heikki Koskenniemi showed that "presence" *(parousia)* was one of the principal functions of a Hellenistic letter. A reading of Paul's first letter to the Corinthians shows that Paul was keenly aware of his absence from the Corinthian community. Using the very language that is found in some of the ancient letters, Paul writes to the Corinthians about his being "present in spirit although absent in body" (5:3). Three times he writes about what he will do when he visits the Corinthians (4:19-21; 11:34; 16:3-4). He even tells them about his travel plans. After he has completed his work in Ephesus and has made a pastoral visit to Macedonia he will go to Corinth (16:5-9). His travelogue speaks of his desire to spend some time with the Corinthians (16:7). In the meantime Paul sent Timothy to the Corinthians to represent him and act on his behalf (4:17; 16:10-11).

The arrival of Stephanas, Fortunatus, and Achaicus from Corinth brought joy to Paul's heart (16:17-18; cf. Phil 4:10, 18). Their presence *(parousia)* partially compensated for the absence of the Corinthians. Just as people today write about their happiness in receiving a letter from a friend, people in the Hellenistic world expressed their joy on the receipt of a letter (see P.Elephantine 13.2-3; P.Hamburg 1.88.3).

It is not unlikely that Stephanas and his fellow travelers provided the delivery service for Paul's exchange of correspondence with the Corinthians. The Emperor Augustus had established a kind of imperial mail service, but use of this postal service was restricted to the government and its military. The emperor created a series of relay stations along the major trade routes somewhat similar to the relay stations that formed the backbone of the American Pony Express system. Private individuals were left to their own devices to ensure the delivery of their correspondence. Paul was fortunate that Christian missionaries and evangelists traveled as they did—hence the importance of hospitality as a Christian virtue (see Rom 12:13; Heb 13:2)!—and that he was able to make use of their services for the delivery of his letters. The comings and goings of Stephanas and his companions provided Paul with an opportunity for at least one exchange of correspondence with his beloved brothers and sisters at Corinth.

Paul does not actually say that Stephanas, Fortunatus, and Achaicus brought a letter from the Corinthians, but we do know that Paul had received a letter from there (7:1). The group was to return to Corinth. Paul strongly commends them to the Corinthian assembly (16:16, 18). The epistolographic conventions found in the passage where they are commended suggests that they were the ones charged with delivering Paul's letter to Corinth. Letters of recommendation (Pseudo-Demetrius' *typos systatikos*) were well known in the Hellenistic world. They were frequently written on behalf of those who were carrying correspondence from a letter-writer. So the commendation of Stephanas and his companions in 16:15-18 gives credence to the suggestion that it was this group that carried Paul's letter to the Corinthians. Were they the ones who did so, it is likely that Stephanas or one of his companions read Paul's letter to the Corinthian assembly.

Paul's letter to the Corinthians was part of a continuing correspondence between himself and the Christians of Corinth. Although it is called the first letter to the Corinthians it was not the first letter Paul had written to that assembly (see 5:9), nor would it be the last. The NT canon contains another letter of Paul to the Corinthians, our canonical 2 Corinthians. Traditionally this first letter to the Corinthians is called first in comparison with the second letter to the Corinthians. According to the stylometric principle of compiling the NT texts, longer texts are called "first" (1 Corinthians, 1 Thessalonians, 1 Timothy, 1 Peter, 1 John) with respect to the shorter texts that are called "second." Paul's so-called second letter to the Corinthians is not, however, his third letter to that community (see 5:9; 2 Cor 2:3-4, 9). Second Corinthians is at least Paul's fourth letter to that community, unless perhaps 2 Corinthians is not a single letter but some sort of a composite of letters, as many scholars hold. On the other hand, 1 Cor 7:1 (cf. 16:17-18) provides the only sure evidence that Paul had received any correspondence at all from the Corinthians. We simply do not know how much correspondence Paul might have received from the community at Corinth.

As part of an ongoing exchange of correspondence Paul's first letter to the Corinthians contains a response to the letter he had received. One of the issues raised in that letter was the implications of a popular slogan, "it is good for a man not to touch a woman." Paul takes up this issue in 7:1, "Concerning the matters about which you wrote: 'it is good for a man not to touch a woman.'" "Concerning" *(peri de)* is a common expression in ancient letters (e.g., P.Elephantine 13). Paul's use of the epistolographic formula has led some commentators to suggest that as often as this formula occurs in 1 Corinthians Paul is taking up another topic about which the Corinthians had written to him (7:25; 8:1, 3; 12:1; 16:1, 12), but the suggestion cannot be accepted without further reflection.

"Concerning" is a stock phrase in Hellenistic letters, but it was used in a variety of ways. Sometimes it served merely as an introduction to another topic; at other times it was used to introduce the letter-writer's answer to a written request; at still other times it introduced a reply to an oral report. Paul had received a letter from the Corinthians (cf. 7:1), but he did not lack other sources of information about the situation in Corinth. Among those sources were undoubtedly Stephanas, Fortunatus, and Achaicus, the conveyors of the correspondence (16:15-18). Chloe's people, who gave Paul an oral report about the tensions within the community (1:11), provided another source of information.

Notwithstanding the ambiguity attending the precise interpretive nuance to be attached to Paul's "concerning," there is no doubt that "concerning" is an epistolary cliché. So, too, is an expression of joy upon someone's arrival (16:17). Yet another epistolary convention employed by Paul is the use of "therefore" *(oun)* to mark a transition between background material and a request that he was going to make (4:16; 10:31; 16:18). This is the very expression Hellenistic letter-writers used as they moved from making their case to making a specific request.

Paul's first use of "therefore" as an epistolary transitional formula is in 4:16. The request follows in the form of an exhortation with the verb *parakaleō,* whose meaning is "to encourage" or "to exhort." This is not so much an epistolary cliché used in friendly letters as it is the language of diplomatic letters. In these official letters the verb was used to phrase tactfully an order that was being conveyed by an official acting on behalf of someone else. Paul was conscious that his own appeal was not based on his personal authority but on that of the Lord Jesus Christ (1:10). The language of the diplomat was appropriate for him (Rom 12:1; 15:30; 16:17; 2 Cor 2:8; 6:1; 10:1; Phil 4:2; 1 Thess 4:1, 10; 5:14; Phlm 9). He identifies himself as one who was named apostle (1:1; cf. 15:9), and he tells the Corinthians that they are to consider what he was writing to them as a command of the Lord (14:37). True envoy that he was, having satisfied the requisite conventions of the salutation (1:1-3) and an expression of a heartfelt thanksgiving (1:4-9) Paul begins the body of his letter in the language of the diplomat: "I exhort you *(parakalō hymas)* in the name of our Lord Jesus Christ that all of you be in agreement and that there be no divisions among you" (1:10).

Paul's letter contains the formal structural elements of the Hellenistic letters of his day and many phrases that were virtually clichés in Hellenistic letters. Nonetheless, Paul's letter must be seen as having a literary form somewhat different from that of the personal letters of the Hellenistic period discovered during late nineteenth- and early twentieth-century archaeological excavations. His sixteen-chapter-long letter to the Corinthians has some features that type it as belonging to a genre akin both to literary letters and to diplomatic correspondence. It is not without some justification that Paul's letter to the Corinthians can be styled an apostolic or ecclesial letter.

2. *A Hellenistic Letter*

Paul's letter was intended to persuade and dissuade the Corinthian Christians with regard to various forms of behavior (1:10). So it is to be expected that Paul's letter to the Corinthians manifests some affinity with the correspondence of the Hellenistic moralists. Michael Bünker (*Brieffor-mular* 41–47) has compared various features of Paul's letter with features found in the literary letters of Seneca, the Stoic moralist. The similarity lies not so much in their use of common epistolary jargon—although they do share many epistolary clichés—as in the way both authors develop an ethical appeal in a formal letter.

As does the philosopher, Paul has developed his argument using syllogisms (2:1-5; cf. Seneca, *Epistles* 76.10). Both authors used enthymemes, those incomplete syllogisms used by ancient rhetors who usually omitted the major premise, to good advantage, presumably because it could be readily supplied by the audience (15:13-19; 11:3-15; cf. Seneca, *Epistles* 13.9; 22.11-12; 45.11; 85.19-20, 24). When Paul writes, as he does in 5:6, "Do you not know that a little yeast leavens the entire mound of dough?" or "Bad company corrupts good morals" (15:33), the latter a saying similar to one found in Menander's *Thais,* he is appealing to utterances of gnomic wisdom similar to those found in Seneca, *Epistles* 14.10; 40.4; 42.7; 47.19 and 77.15. Besides his occasional appeal to popular wisdom Paul cites sayings attributed to Jesus. He carefully distinguishes the word of "the Lord" from his own words (7:10). He invokes an ordinance of the Lord to the effect that those who preach the gospel should be provided with sustenance (9:14).

More often than he has recourse to the "word of the Lord" Paul cites the Jewish Scriptures, frequently introducing them with a characteristic lemma, "it is written." Paul cites the Scriptures twenty times in all. He quotes from Genesis (2:24 in 6:16; 2:7 in 15:45); Exodus (32:6 in 10:7); Deuteronomy (17:7 in 5:13; 25:4 in 9:9); the Psalms (8:7 [LXX] in 15:27; 24:1 in 10:26; 93:11 [LXX] in 3:20; 110:1 in 15:25); Job (5:12 in 3:19); Isaiah (45:14 in 14:25; 22:13 in 15:32; 25:8 in 15:54; 28:11-12 in 14:21; 29:14 in 1:19; 40:13 in 2:16); Jeremiah (9:22-23 in 1:31); Hosea (13:14 in 15:55); Sirach (6:19 in 9:10); and the Apocalypse of Elijah (see the note at 2:9).

Paul's authorities are those revered within his Christian-Jewish experience. Seneca, on the other hand, quotes various poets, including Homer (*Epistles* 40.2), Virgil (*Epistles* 41.2; 78.15; 85.4; 105.33, 68; 108.24, 25), Terence (*Epistles* 105.53), Lucretius (*Epistles* 105.11), Horace (*Epistles* 119.14), and Ovid (*Epistles* 90.20). He also cites philosophers, including Epicurus (*Epistles* 12.10; 26.8; 66.18, 45-48; 78.7; 85.19), Aristotle (*Epistles* 65.4), Plato (*Epistles* 44.4), Socrates (*Epistles* 104.21), Zeno (*Epistles* 104.21), Xenocrates (*Epistles* 85.18), and Speusippus (*Epistles* 85.18), along with a selection of wise sayings (*Epistles* 7.11; 24.26; 67.7; 71.8; 94.27; 95.70; etc.).

Writing to the Corinthians, Paul is clearly aware of his personal authority and his prestige. He has been named an apostle (1:1) and possesses the Spirit (7:40). He appeals to his own authority as he deals with issues relating to sex and marriage (7:12, 25; cf. 6:3). In invoking his authority as he does, Paul's fashion of exhorting the Corinthians is similar to the way Seneca appeals to what Bünker has called the authoritative "I" (*Epistles* 12.11; 29.12; 59.6; 78.5; 80.1, 7; 83.13; 95.65-66; etc.). Paul's letter to the Corinthians is liberally sprinkled with the example of himself as a model for his addressees to emulate. Not only does he exhort them to imitate himself (4:16; 11:1), he also cites his own example throughout the letter (2:1-4; 8:13; 9:1-27; 13:1-3, etc.).

Self-praise was a classical topos, a subject of discussion in schools of rhetoric. Plutarch notes that it is useful to mention one's character and accomplishments to humble and subdue the headstrong and rash ("On Inoffensive Self-Praise," *Moralia* 544F) or to inspire others to imitation when some advantage accrues to the audience ("On Inoffensive Self-Praise," *Moralia* 544D-E). This is the case in 1 Corinthians where Paul's self-reference serves to confound the strong and enhance his *ethos* appeal.

In writing the moral epistles Seneca drew his examples from Roman history. He tells about the death of Cato (*Epistles* 24.6-8) and offers this example "not for the purpose of exercising my wit, but for the purpose of encouraging you" (*Epistles* 24.9). Seneca tells stories about Scipio Africanus (*Epistles* 86.1-2), Caesar, Pompey, and Cato (*Epistles* 14.12-13). The names of these and other figures in Roman history are laced throughout Seneca's moral epistles. Paul draws his examples from the experience of the people of God wandering through the desert (1 Cor 10:1-13) and cites a traditional story about Jesus' last meal (11:23-26).

As does Seneca (*Epistles* 13.1-3; 59.6; 78.16), Paul effectively uses similes and metaphors in his argument. The "fable" (*fabula*) of the human body was a classical rhetorical topos, employed alike in the letters of Seneca (Epistles 95.52) and Paul (12:12-26). Paul cites examples drawn from the construction industry (3:10-17), the world of athletics (9:24-27; cf. Seneca, *Epistles* 78.16), and the farmer's field (3:6-9; 9:8-10; 15:36-41). His letter is full of imagery. His metaphors are drawn from the family (3:1-2; 4:14-17) and the sea (4:1; 12:28). The sounds of music come to the ears of his audience (13:1; 14:7-8; 15:52).

These and other features of Paul's letter suggest that it is not only useful to compare what Paul has written to the Corinthians to Seneca's moral epistles but that some profit is to be gained by considering Paul's letter in the light of the various kinds of letters written in the Hellenistic world. His language, style, and purpose are comparable to these in many different respects.

3. *A Long Letter*

Paul's letter to the Corinthians is one of the longest extant Hellenistic letters. Given the length of the letter and its purpose, to exhort a divided community to greater unity (1:10), it would be surprising were Paul not to address various subgroups within "the church of God which is at Corinth" (1:2). At times he addresses the unmarried and widows (7:8), the married (7:10), the rest (7:12), and those who appear to be sensible or claim to be so (10:15). His use of various different datives of address shows that he was well aware of the diversity of his audience. At any given moment he was not directly addressing the entire group of those who were listening to the reading of his words.

Because Paul directly addressed various audiences within the Corinthian assembly his lengthy composition affects various tones. Different parts of the letter have traits comparable to those of various letter types identified by the Pseudo-Demetrius. Pseudo-Demetrius' *Epistolary Types*, one of two extant classical manuals on letter writing (cf. Pseudo-Libanius in the 4th–6th c. C.E.), cannot be dated with certainty but it may well come from pre-Christian times (see Klaus Thraede, *Grundzüge* 26). Ostensibly addressed to Heraclides, it treats the "theory" of letter writing. Pseudo-Demetrius initially observes that letters can be composed in a great variety of styles but that they ought to fit the particular circumstances to which they are addressed. For him and most classical authors the friendly letter was the ideal type of personal letter.

Pseudo-Demetrius observes that friendly letters are frequently written by people in prominent positions to those who are their inferiors or their equals. Writing to the Corinthians, Paul constantly mentions the bonds of affection he had for the community and the relationship he enjoyed with them. Twenty times he addresses the Corinthians as his "brothers and sisters" (*adelphoi;* 1:10, 11, 26; 2:1; 3:1; 4:6; 7:24, 29; 10:1; 11:33; 12:1; 14:6, 20, 26, 39; 15:1, 31, 50, 58; 16:15; see the discussion on Paul's use of kinship language, pp. 70–71), culminating in "my beloved brothers and sisters" in 15:58 (cf. 1:11; 11:33). In a stirring passage Paul varies his choice of kinship language when he calls the Corinthians "my beloved children" (4:14) and explains that he is their only father (4:15). Paul does not usually add a postscript to his letters, but he does so in this first letter to the Corinthians. The postscript speaks of his love for the entire assembly (16:24).

Pseudo-Demetrius identifies and describes twenty-one types of letters, each adapted to the circumstances in which it was written. He also provides a sample of each type of letter. Pseudo-Demetrius' model of a friendly letter is one that speaks of physical separation from the friend, expresses the letter-writer's concern for that friend, talks about the letter-writer's expectation that the friend will respond to his request, and voices a request that the friend take care of the absent letter-writer's own household. All the elements that appear in Pseudo-Demetrius' sample friendship letter are to be found in Paul's letter to the Corinthians. His physical absence is noted at 5:3. His concern is evident as he writes about admonishing his beloved children (4:14) and about their salvation (1:18; 5:5; 9:22; 10:33; 15:2). He recommends Timothy to the Corinthians, expecting that the community will send him back just as Paul requests (16:10-11). The way in which Paul urges the Corinthians to treat the household of Stephanas evokes something of the typical letter-writer's request that his family be taken care of during the time of his own absence. With so many features that allow it to be favorably compared with the friendly letters of his day, Paul's letter is characterized by its expression of friendship (*philophronēsis*), the second major function of a Hellenistic letter (see Koskenniemi, *Studien* 128–154). Some portions of Paul's are, nonetheless, crafted in language similar to that of other types of letters identified by Pseudo-Demetrius.

Pseudo-Demetrius' second type of letter is the letter of recommendation (*typos systatikos*). It is one "which we write on behalf of one person to another, mixing in praise, at the same time also speaking of those who had previously been unacquainted as though they were [now] acquainted." Paul speaks about letters of recommendation in 16:3 and in 2 Cor 3:1, where he uses some of the very language found in Pseudo-Demetrius. In the final chapter of 1 Corinthians Paul speaks about Timothy (16:10-11; cf. 4:17) and Stephanas and his companions (16:15-18) in a way that evokes the classical letter of recommendation. Paul's way of talking about Stephanas, Fortunatus, and Achaicus is such that this group of travelers can be presumed to have provided Paul with the postal service needed to carry his letter to the Corinthian assembly.

Pseudo-Demetrius' seventh kind of letter is the letter of admonition *(typos nouthetētikos)*. This is "one which indicates by its name what its character is. For admonition *(nouthetein)* is the instilling of sense in the person who is being admonished, and teaching him what should and should not be done." The model provided by Pseudo-Demetrius is one that speaks about kinship and relationship. When Paul first tells the Corinthians exactly why he is writing to them he says, "I am writing these things, not to make you ashamed, but to admonish *(noutheton)* you as my beloved children" (4:14). In the passage that follows Paul uses kinship language of a sort and an intensity otherwise found in the letter. The entire passage (4:14-21) is one that echoes the letter of admonition and expresses the length to which Paul will go in order to bring his beloved children to their senses and teach them the ways they should follow.

Among the other kinds of letters on Pseudo-Demetrius' list are the letter of response and the letter of apology. "The responding type *(typos apophantikos),"* says the manual, "responds to the person making an inquiry." "The apologetic type *(typos apologētikos)* is that which adduces, with demonstration, arguments which contradict charges that are being made." The author of the manual provides only a very short example of a letter of response. His sample apologetic letter is much longer. For his part Paul responds to the written inquiry of some members of the community (7:1). In ch. 9 he expresses a kind of apology (see 9:3).

4. *A Single Letter?*

Late nineteenth- and early twentieth-century archaeological excavations of ancient tombs and cemeteries, rubbish heaps and ruined buildings unearthed a fair number of papyri containing either literary or personal letters. For the most part these troves come from excavations that took place in some of the small provincial towns in Egypt. Unfortunately we do not have any such discoveries from Corinth, nor for that matter from any of the other great centers of Hellenistic culture. We do not have, nor can we realistically expect to have, the autograph copy of the letter Paul dictated.

The oldest more or less complete copy of this letter available to us is preserved on a number of papyrus sheets housed in the Chester Beatty museum, not far from Dublin, Ireland. In the museum they are classified as Papyrus Chester Beatty II, but in the scholarly literature they are identified as $\mathfrak{P}^{46}$. These sheets of papyrus contain virtually the entire letter; only three verses of the letter (9:3; 14:15; 15:16) are not found at all among the papyrus sheets. The Beatty papyrus dates from about 200 C.E., approximately 150 years after Paul wrote the letter. This is remarkable. Our oldest more or less complete copy of any one of the gospels, for example, dates back only to the fourth century.

The archaeologists' discovery of letters on papyrus has proven to be a boon for Pauline scholars. These letters enable us to compare what Paul has written in his letters with what his contemporaries wrote in theirs. One striking feature is that by and large—and with the exception of Paul's letter to Philemon—Paul's letters are much longer than those of his contemporaries. Some of the letters written by philosophers such as Epictetus and Seneca were relatively long, as were some of the apologetic letters, but the letters that appear among the extant papyri are relatively short, especially letters of the "friendly type." Paul's letters are long; his first letter to the Corinthians is especially long.

The length of this letter, coupled with the variety of subjects treated in 1 Corinthians and the different ways he treats some of his topics, have led many scholars to question whether 1 Corinthians as it presently exists was written by Paul in the form of a single letter. The question was first raised in Holland in 1876 by H. Hagge. The early discussion of the issue was surveyed in Carl Clemen's 1894 monograph.

The twentieth-century discussion essentially begins with Johannes Weiss. Weiss's commentary (1910) argued that canonical 1 Corinthians is the work of an editor who compiled the text from pieces of two different letters Paul had written to Corinth. One letter, to which 5:9 refers, was from Ephesus (cf. 16:8) and provides material for 10:1-23; 6:12-20; 9:24-27; 11:2-34; 16:7b-9, 15-20; and 2 Cor 6:14–7:1. The other was from Macedonia. It provides 1:1–6:11; 7:1–8:13; 13; 10:24–11:1; 9:1-23; 12; 14:1–16:7a; 16:10-14, 21-24. In assembling the canonical letter the anonymous editor would have added a few explanatory and transitional elements that gave the new "letter" a more general or catholic character (1:2; 4:17; 7:17; 10:29-30; 11:11-12, 16; 14:34-35).

Shortly before his death Weiss revised his suggestion. In his posthumous *Urchristentum* (Rudolf Knopf, ed., Göttingen: Vandenhoeck & Ruprecht, 1917), Weiss suggested that three Pauline letters constituted the raw material out of which an anonymous editor has created "1 Corinthians." Prior to that there existed a letter A (= the letter from Ephesus), a letter B1 (7:1–8:13; 13; 10:24–11:1; 9:1-23; 12; 14:1–16:7a; 16:10-14, 21-24), and a letter B2 (1:1–6:11). In this reconstruction Weiss apportioned sections of the canonical letter's epistolary closing (16:10-24) to each of the three hypothetical letters: vv. 20-21 to A, vv. 15-19 to B1, and vv. 10-14, 22-24 to B2.

These provocative suggestions were taken up in earnest by Walter Schmithals who, in a series of writings beginning with his 1956 doctoral dissertation, vigorously argues that both 1 Corinthians and 2 Corinthians are composite texts. Schmithals initially argued that extant 1 Corinthians was compiled from two earlier letters, letter A (= 6:12-20; 9:24–10:22; 11:2-34; 15; 16:13-24; and 2 Cor 6:14–7:1) and letter B (= 1:1–6:11; 7:1–9:23; 10:23–11:1; 12:1–14:40; 16:1-12). By 1984 Schmithals had concluded that elements of thirteen different letters from Paul to the Corinthians at Corinth have been gathered together in the two canonical letters to the Corinthians. In his opinion five of the original letters were used to assemble canonical 1 Corinthians.

Similar but not always identical opinions as to the origin of canonical 1 Corinthians have been offered by other literary critics as well. Erich Dinkler (1960), Johannes Müller-Bardorff (1958), Robert Jewett (1971), Hans-Martin Schenke and Karl Martin Fischer (1978), Alfred Suhl (1975), Jean Héring (1959), Hans-Josef Klauck (1984) and Philipp Vielhauer (1975) claim that two original letters lie behind 1 Corinthians. Having originally opined that 1 Corinthians was a single composition, both Günther Bornkamm (1971) and Willi Marxsen (1978) later joined the ranks of those who hold that extant 1 Corinthians is a composite of two earlier letters. Like the later Weiss, the French critics Alfred Loisy (1922) and Maurice Goguel (1926) suggested three original letters. The idea that more than three letters were used by a hypothetical compiler has been advanced by Wolfgang Schenk (1969), Christophe Senft (1979), and Martin Widmann (1978).

Various commentators continue to argue that extant 1 Corinthians is a composite. Gerhard Sellin, for example, has contended (1987, 1991) that 1 Corinthians is a composite of three letters: the letter mentioned in 1 Cor 5:9, letter A (= 11:2-34; 5:1-8; 6:12-20; 9:24–10:22; 6:1-11); letter B, a response to the Corinthians' letter (= 5:9-13; 7:1–9:23; 10:23–11:1; 12:1–16:24); and letter C (= 1:1–4:21). Rudolph Pesch (1986), Miguel de Burgos Núñez (1993), and Khiok-Khng Yeo (1995) have suggested that 1 Corinthians contains elements of four letters. For Pesch the four letters are an antecedent letter (= 1:1–5:8; 6:1-11), an interim letter (= 5:9-13; 6:12-20; 10:1–11:34), a resurrection letter (= 15:1-58), and an answer letter (= 7:1-40; 8:1–9:27; 12:1–14:40; 16:1-24). For Yeo letter A was a short letter on apostolic authority (= 11:2-34), letter B a letter on paganism and resurrection (= 9:24–10:22; 15:1-58; 16:13-24; and 2 Cor 6:14–7:1), letter C a letter on various issues raised by the Corinthians (= 1:1–6:11; 7:1–8:13; 9:19-23; 10:23–11:1; 12:1-31a; 14:1c-40; 12:31b–13:13; 16:1-12), and letter E a kind of apology (= 1 Cor 9:1-18; and 2 Cor 10:1–13:13; Yeo holds that six original letters provide material for the two canonical letters). Following a chronology of Paul's activity developed by Gerd Lüdemann, Norbert Baumert (*Woman and Man* 3) suggests that the different parts of Paul's first letter to the Corinthians may have been written over a span of fifteen years (41–55).

No manuscript evidence exists to suggest that 1 Corinthians once existed in a form other than that in which it exists today (see the discussion on 14:34b-38, considered by some an interpolation). The suggestion that 1 Corinthians is a composite document is not, however, entirely arbitrary. There were at least four letters to the Corinthians (cf. 5:9; 2 Cor 2:3-4, 9) and we have only two. Paul's letter of response to the Corinthians (7:1) appears to address issues raised in a letter that had been sent to him (with a repeated "concerning," *peri de,* 7:1, 25; 8:1; 12:1; 16:1, 12), but it may be that the denial of the resurrection was not among them (it lacks the *peri de*; cf. 15:12). Another observation is that Paul appears to treat the issue of food offered to idols in two different ways. He urges a prudential concern for the sensitivities of the members of the community who have a weak consciousness in 8:1-13 and 10:23–11:1. He calls for complete avoidance of idolatry in 9:24–10:22. Harsh transitions often serve as textual indications that a text is a composite document and 1 Corinthians contains a number of such connections (6:12-13; 8:13–9:1; 9:23-24; 10:22-23).

If an early letter called for a severance of association with immoral people, then 5:1-8 and 6:1-20 may have been part of the early letter. The immoral are those who are sexually immoral, avaricious, idolatrous, slanderous, drunkards, or greedy (5:11). Since idolatry is treated in 9:24–10:22 (see 10:14-22) and drinking in 11:2-34 (v. 21), Sellin argues that these passages too must have belonged to the early letter. Some argue that the root problem in ch. 15 is a misunderstanding of the resurrection coupled with a kind of "spiritualism" whose appreciation of the human body betrays a false anthropology. Since Paul's disquisition on the resurrection is not introduced by the *peri de* formula (also absent as an introduction to the discussion on worship in 11:2-34), as are the other topics treated in 7:1–16:12, some authors propose that ch. 15 must have come from an early letter.

The fact that Weiss and Schmithals, two of the major proponents of the partition theory, changed their mind as to precisely how 1 Corinthians is to be divided up into component parts militates against the validity of the opinion that Paul's extant "first letter to the Corinthians" is a composite work. So too does the fact that those who argue against the original unity of the letter do not agree among themselves as to how the canonical letter is to be divided. Sustained arguments in favor of the literary unity of 1 Corinthians have been developed by John C. Hurd in English (1983) and by Helmut Merklein and Dieter Lührmann in German (1984). Margaret M. Mitchell's more recent (1989, 1991) rhetorical analysis of the text led to the conclusion that 1 Corinthians is a single rhetorical unit in which 1:10 is a rhetorical proposition that is then developed in four proofs.

Eduardo de la Serna (1991) and Martinus De Boer (1994) adopt a *via media* position. They argue that Paul had substantially drafted his observations on the situation at Corinth—a situation about which he had been apprised in an oral report (by Stephanas' household according to de la

Serna; by Chloe's people according to De Boer)—when a second delegation arrived from Corinth. The arrival of the new group provided Paul
with additional information and prompted Paul to extend the letter
which he had virtually completed (De Boer views chs. 5–16 as the expansion; de la Serna considers chs. 1–4 to be the additional material). For
these authors our extant 1 Corinthians is virtually a two-in-one letter, the
circumstances of its composition having contributed substantially to its
unusual length.

The length of the letter is in any case such that it would have taken the
apostle some time to dictate. It is not impossible that people arriving from
Corinth would have provided Paul with additional information about the
Christian community there and led him to extend his earlier letter. The
language of the letter is such that it must be viewed as a single composition, even if it was composed over a somewhat extended period of time.
The letter was written by Paul during one of his Ephesian stays (16:8; cf.
15:32).

5. *A Stylistic Feature*

The identification of 1 Cor 1:10, "I exhort you in the name of our Lord
Jesus Christ that all of you be in agreement and that there be no divisions
among you, but that you be of a same mind and of a same opinion," as
the formal expression of Paul's thesis allows the letter to be seen as a plea
for the unity of the community. That a variety of topics should be treated
in a composition whose main theme is harmony within the community
would not have been exceptional. Already in the fifth century the Athenian sophist Antiphon treated of the burdens of wife and children in his
work *Harmony*.

An important feature of Paul's style is the use of chiastic presentations
in a familiar A-B-A' pattern. To a large extent the letter as a whole is constructed according to a pattern of chiastic parallelism. Paul offers some
general considerations (A), then a digression that supports his argument
(B), and finally a further reflection that specifies the general reflection and
responds to the particular issue at hand (A'). Paul's use of digression in
support of his argument is consistent with the ancient rhetoricians'
understanding of digression. Quintilian avers that digression can serve a
variety of purposes. It is used to amplify an argument's principal point,
to abridge an argument, to make an emotional appeal, or to introduce
such topics as would add charm and elegance to the composition (see
Training of an Orator 4.3.15; cf. Cicero, *De inventione* 1.19.27; *De oratore*
2.19.80).

Paul's use of digression within an encompassing chiastic structure is
to be seen in chs. 1:10–3:23; 5–7; 8–10; 12–14, where he deals respectively

with unity in the community, the responsible use of sexuality, food offered to idols, and spiritual gifts. In dealing with the issue of unity within
the community Paul treats the issue in general fashion in 1:10–2:5 (A), digresses in 2:6-16 (B), and returns to his initial topic in 3:1-23 (A'). Treating
the responsible use of sexuality, Paul writes about a problem in Corinth
in ch. 5 (A), digresses about the Christian's use of secular courts in ch. 6
(B), and returns to sexual responsibility in ch. 7, using the guise of a response to a letter he had received from the Corinthians (A'). Even ch. 7 is
organized according to a chiastic pattern. Having treated a variety of issues relating to the sexual life of those who are or had been married (7:1-
16, A), Paul speaks of social stability (7:17-24, B) before returning to his
discussion of human sexuality, this time insofar as it relates to those who
are not yet married (7:25-40, A'). In treating the matter of food offered to
idols (chs. 8–10) Paul responds in general to the concern expressed by the
Corinthians in regard to the issue (ch. 8, A), then offers himself, a classical topos using the *agōn* motif, and an episode from Israel's history as examples (9:1–10:13, B), finally returning to the issue at hand, food offered
to idols, in 10:14–11:1 (A').

Paul's disquisition on spiritual gifts begins in ch. 12 (A). He then
writes a paean on *agapē* (ch. 13, B) and returns to a specific consideration
on the relative value of the gifts of prophecy and speaking in tongues in
ch. 14 (A'). In this instance the first part of his disquisition is itself characterized by a chiastic pattern, for having begun his exposition (12:1-11,
A), he resorts to an argument based on a classical topos, the image of the
body (12:12-26, B), only to return to the spiritual gifts in vv. 27-31 (A'). Talbert (*Reading Corinthians* 66, 81) has suggested that the chiastic pattern
found in chs. 12–14 is part of a still larger chiasm. He identifies these
chapters as element A' in a chiasm that focuses on prayer and prophecy
(11:2-16, A; 12–14, A') around a presentation of the Lord's supper (11:17-
34, B).

The use of chiasm to structure large epistolary units is chiasm on the
macro level (cf. Ian H. Thomson, *Chiasmus in the Pauline Letters* [JSNT.S
111; Sheffield: JSOT, 1995] 34–36; Mitchell Dahood, "Chiasmus," *IDBSup*
145). It is a structuring device and is to be distinguished from Paul's use
of chiasm at the micro level, that is, within a single sentence (Lausberg's
Klein-Chiasmus) or small group of sentences (Lausberg's *Gross-Chiasmus*).
It is likely that Paul's extensive use of chiastic structure represents a Semitic influence on the expression of his thought. In concert with biblical
authors who preceded him, Paul uses chiasm to provide his argument
with verve and emphasis. Like his predecessors Paul sometimes used a
chiastic pattern with three members (chiastic tricolon, A-B-A') and sometimes a chiastic pattern with four members (chiastic tetracolon, A-B-B'-
A'). Chiasms are recognized by the phenomenon of *inclusio,* the literary

device of ring construction, in which the final element of the exposition corresponds to the first.

Along with the recognition that 1 Corinthians is a letter composed in the deliberative mode of rhetoric, the insight that Paul has organized his thought along the lines of a chiastic pattern of exposition goes a long way to resolving some of the problems raised with respect to the unity of the letter. The digressive central element of the chiasm (B) serves the rhetorical purpose of the whole unit by providing a perspective from which the issue, set out in A and specified in A', is to be judged. The use of chiasm as a structuring device imposes a kind of organization on elements that might otherwise seem to be disparate. For example, the A and A' units within ch. 7 (vv. 1-16; 25-40) treat two related but obviously distinct topics that Paul has clearly identified by an enumerative *peri*/concerning, namely sexuality and the married, sexuality and the unmarried. A digressive interlude concerns the use of freedom and remaining in the condition in which one was called. As the A' unit in the broader chiastic pattern of chs. 5–7, ch. 7 corresponds to the earlier unit in which Paul offers his response to an issue dealing with human sexuality about which he had heard an oral report (5:1).

6. *Problems at Corinth*

It is obvious that there were problems at Corinth and that Paul had been apprised of these problems by the people who came to him from Chloe's household (1:11). It may be that these people brought a letter with them, telling Paul about the difficulties in the community he had evangelized (3:10-15; 9:2; 15:1-2), but it is more likely that the letter he received (7:1) was brought by Stephanas, Fortunatus, and Achaicus (16:17). Whether or not these people came to Paul to report on the situation at Corinth is a moot point. No matter what, their presence with Paul would have afforded him an additional source of information about the situation of the fledgling Christian community in the Achaian metropolis.

Early twentieth-century commentators often expressed the view that the basic problem in Corinth was factionalism, with various segments of the Christian community rallying around the name of one or another Christian hero—Apollos or Cephas, Paul, or even Christ himself (see 1:11-12). Paul, however, does not seem so much to have addressed himself to particular groups as to have dealt with particular issues as he developed the argumentation of his letter. Hence, an understanding of 1 Corinthians based on the hypothetical existence of factions in the community has been largely abandoned in late twentieth-century exegesis.

Instead of factionalism many commentators in the second half of the twentieth century pointed to some form of Gnosticism as the background against which problems arose in the church of Corinth. Among the authors who have taken this approach to an understanding of 1 Corinthians are John Dominic Crossan, Helmut Koester, Stephen J. Patterson, and Ulrich Wilckens. Frequently reference has been made to the Gnostic *Gospel of Thomas,* a copy of which was found at Nag Hammadi in Upper Egypt in 1945. The document, an anthology of 114 sayings of Jesus, reflects a type of early Christianity with some similarity to the situation at Corinth. For example, the seventeenth saying in the collection is "I shall give you what no eye has seen and no ear has heard and no hand has touched and what has not entered the heart of man" (*Gos. Thom.* 17). This logion is remarkably similar to the problematic "scripture" cited by Paul in 2:9.

Thomas's Christianity features Jesus as one who speaks as Wisdom (cf. *Gos. Thom.* 28). It is reserved with regard to consequent eschatology and adopts an anti-apocalyptic stance (*Gos. Thom.* 3, 18, 24, 51, 113). It is, moreover, characterized by a kind of social critique directed against material possessions and financial matters (*Gos. Thom.* 36–37, 63, 64, 76, 81, 85, 95, 109, 110) and human sexuality (*Gos. Thom.* 11, 22, 106, 114). Paul's letter to the Corinthians, however, reflects an apocalyptic worldview that contrasts sharply with the immediacy of a salvific possession of wisdom. Paul takes issue with those in the Corinthian community who disparage or disdain the weak. He takes a realistic attitude toward human sexuality. In sum, Paul deals with many of the issues addressed in the *Gospel of Thomas,* but he takes a different tack from that of the anonymous compiler of the Gnostic gospel.

This commentary proceeds on the assumption that there were indeed various problems in the community at Corinth. Paul treats them insofar as they were divisive of a community that was called to unity (1:10) as God's holy people (1:2). Rather than pursue the quest of the ideological source(s) from which the issues arose, the commentary will treat them from the vantage point of Paul's own response to the problems. The problems appear to have been of two sorts. Some were of a more ideological (philosophical or theological) nature; some were more practical. Paul takes on the ideological issues in a straightforward manner. He argues in an appropriate and logical fashion. He puts the behavioral issues in a communitarian and theological context. Throughout the letter Paul argues that thought and behavior are closely linked. For him there is an indissoluble tie between the theology of the community and its behavior.

7. Paul's Rhetoric

Although Paul was self-consciously aware that he was writing a letter (4:14; 5:11; 9:15; 14:37), he also realized that through his letter he was actually speaking to the Corinthians. Fifteen times in the course of the letter, using three different verbs—"to say" *(legō)* in 1:12; 6:5; 7:6, 8, 12, 35; 10:15, 29; 15:12; "to speak" *(laleō)* in 9:8; 15:34; "to assert" *(phēmi)* in 7:29; 10:15, 19; 15:50—Paul affirms that he is speaking to the Corinthians. Paul's communication with the Corinthians is a kind of "speech act." For Paul to have considered his letter to the Corinthians as a kind of oral communication in writing was not a new idea. In the first of his extant letters, 1 Thessalonians, Paul gave specific instructions that his letter should be read to all the members of the community (1 Thess 5:27). The point of his instruction was that all the members of the church of Thessalonica should be aware of the content of his letter. In order for this to happen it was necessary for the letter to be read aloud to the community in some sort of gathering. Paul's realization that his letter would be read aloud so that all members of the community might hear it serves as an indication of an awareness that the vast majority of people in his day could neither read nor write. In the Hellenistic world of Paul's day reading was generally an oral proclamation. It was not a merely visual experience as it generally is today. For Paul and his contemporaries a letter was an oral communication in written shape, a speech in epistolary form.

Hellenists considered a letter to be part of a dialogue. The art of letter writing was taught as a rhetorical art in schools of rhetoric. Demetrius, a classic epistolary theorist more or less contemporary with Paul wrote: "The epistolary style *(ho epistolikos charaktēr)* should be plain *(ischnotētos)*. Artemon, the editor of Aristotle's *Letters,* says that a letter ought to be written in the same manner as a dialogue, a letter being regarded by him as one side of a dialogue *(to heteron meros tou dialogou)*. There is perhaps some truth in what he says, but not the whole truth. The letter should be a little more studied than the dialogue since the latter reproduces an extemporary utterance while the former is committed to writing and is sent as a gift" (Demetrius, *On Style* 223–224). Realization that the ancients considered the letter to be part of a dialogue, that Paul expected his letter to be read to the people, and that he considered what he was writing to be a kind of speech act implies that 1 Corinthians must be considered as a rhetorical act. That it be so considered is all the more important because Paul was a preacher (1:17) who occasionally wrote letters.

To what extent is it useful to consider Paul's first letter to the Corinthians from the standpoint of the canons of classical rhetoric? Does the practice of ancient rhetoric shed any light on Paul's letters? These kinds of questions have been raised by different commentators in recent years. One of the first issues to be considered is the determination of the kind of rhetoric used by Paul. This provides an indication of how one ought to look at the letter as a whole.

Following a tradition going back to Aristotle (384–322 B.C.E.), both Greek and Latin authorities considered that there were three kinds *(gen-*

era) of rhetoric: forensic, demonstrative, and deliberative. Forensic rhetoric basically concerned the past. Its purpose was to lead the audience to make a judgment. Its proper venue was the courtroom. Demonstrative rhetoric essentially concerned the present. Its purpose was to offer praise or blame. Its proper venue was a celebration, typically the celebration of a funeral. Deliberative rhetoric essentially concerned the future. Its purpose was to lead the audience to make a decision. Its typical venue was the public political assembly. An important subset of deliberative rhetorical speeches were *homonoia* speeches, in which political concord *(homonoia)* or the unity of the political group was the principal theme.

In his classic manual on rhetoric Quintilian, a Latin author born about the time Paul became a Christian, gave a description of deliberative rhetoric. "The deliberative department of oratory (also called the advisory department)," he wrote, "while it deliberates about the future, also inquires about the past. Its functions are twofold and consist in advising and persuading" *(Training of an Orator* 3.8.6). Again, "The objective of the deliberative orator is advantage or harm. To exhort is to urge as being more advantageous. To deter is to dissuade as being more harmful. Other aspects such as justice or nobility are ancillary" *(Training of an Orator* 1.2.3).

Quintilian's opinions on deliberative rhetoric, while written some few years after Paul wrote his first letter to the Corinthians, basically represented the common opinion of Greco-Roman orators in Paul's day. With Quintilian as a guide we can fairly easily identify Paul's first letter to the Corinthians as a composition whose form is that of deliberative rhetoric. Immediately after his expression of thanks to God, Paul directs a clearly stated exhortation to his readers: "Brothers and sisters, I exhort you in the name of our Lord Jesus Christ that all of you be in agreement and that there be no divisions among you" (1:10). Throughout the letter, and especially from the point at which he treats the matter of the man who was sleeping with his father's wife (5:1), Paul urges the Corinthians to make decisions about their way of life, to adopt certain manners of conduct and to avoid others.

In his appeal to the Corinthians Paul reminds them that following the behaviors he is urging redounds to their own advantage. John Chrysostom, arguably the most important commentator on the NT among the Greek Fathers, draws attention to this feature of Paul's letter in his homily on it (cf. *On the First Epistle to the Corinthians, Homily* 17.1; *PG* 61, 139). Paul uses classic terminology to talk about the advantage that can accrue to the Corinthians *(sympherein,* 6:12; 10:33; 12:7; the substantivized *sympheros* in 7:35; 10:23). He also uses a variety of synonyms to make a similar point (cf. 9:18, 20; 13:3; 14:6; 15:32, 58). In his letter Paul joins to the motif of advantage that of building up the community (8:1, 10; 10:23;

14:4, 17; cf. 3:9; 14:3, 5, 12, 26). For the apostle the upbuilding of the community is of the essence of *homonoia*.

From the time of Aristotle the arrangement of the argument, its *taxis* or *dispositio*, was very important. Aristotle (*Art of Rhetoric* 3.13.4) held that there were two essential parts of a speech, the statement of the case (*prothesis*) and its proof (*pistis*). A fully developed forensic speech had several parts: the proemium, the narration, the proposition, the proof, (the counter-proof or apology), and an epilogue. The art of forensic rhetoric was more fully refined and is more completely described in the manuals than were either of the other two types of rhetoric. Aristotle thought it was foolish to include all the parts of a rhetorical speech in a demonstrative or deliberative speech. According to Aristotle, "narrative (*diēgēsis*) is very rare, because no one can narrate things to come; but if there is narrative, it will be of things past, in order that, being reminded of them, the hearers may take better counsel about the future" (*Art of Rhetoric* 3.16.11).

1 Corinthians is a speech in the framework of a letter. Its thanksgiving period (1:4-9) functions as does the proemium (*exordium*) of a speech. After that, 1:10 provides Paul's statement of his case. There is no narration (*diēgēsis*), as is appropriate in deliberative rhetoric. Such rehearsal of facts as is necessary has been incorporated into the epistolary thanksgiving (1:4-9). Paul's final exhortation (15:57-58) provides his letter with its rhetorical peroration (*epilogos*). It is an exhortation, as is fitting in a piece of deliberative rhetoric.

8. *The Issues*

The recognition that 1:10 expresses the thesis or *propositio* of Paul's letter implies that the letter should be read as an extended exhortation. It is addressed to the Christians at Corinth, urging them in the name of the Lord Jesus to have no divisions among them. Rather they ought to be in agreement with one another. At issue is the nature of the Christian community itself. Concern for the community as a community called to be holy pervades the entire letter.

Paul's choice of the image of the human body in 12:12-26 graphically represents the situation. In developing his reflection on the image of the body, identified as the body of Christ (12:12, 27), Paul focuses on the unity-in-diversity and diversity-in-unity of the community. The body is one's own space. People are concerned about the boundaries of the body. Today these concerns are expressed in regard to privacy and dignity; in more traditional societies, they are expressed in traditions revolving around purity. Identity issues concern integrated unity from within and clear distinction from without. The human body graphically bespeaks the unity of its members and its distinction from others.

Paul's use of the image gives dramatic expression to his concern for the integrity of the Corinthian community, its unity in diversity. He is no less concerned with the distinctness of the community. From the very outset of his letter he addresses the community as holy (1:2), that is, as set apart from others. These two aspects of the social identity of the Christian community at Corinth provide two foci of Paul's letter. How is the community one? How is the community distinct? How can it be one and distinct?

Language that distinguishes the Christian community at Corinth from other people in Corinth permeates the letter. Paul's most common way of addressing the Corinthians is "brothers and sisters" (*adelphoi*, 1:10 and following). This use of family language not only bespeaks the ties that bind the Corinthians to Paul; it also indicates the bonds that exist among the Corinthians themselves and distinguishes them from those who do not belong to the family.

Other descriptive language that serves to set the church of God at Corinth apart from those who are not Christian includes "church," literally, "the gathering." The language of "sanctification" identifies the Corinthians as those set apart and belonging to God (*hagioi*, "holy ones"; *hagiazō*, "to make holy"). Christians are "beloved" (*agapētoi*, 10:14). They are "believers" (*pisteuontes*, 1:21) and "insiders" (*hoi esō*, 5:12). In contrast, those who do not belong to the church of God are "non-believers" (*apistoi*, 6:6; 7:12-15; 10:27; 14:22-24) and "outsiders" (*hoi exō*, 5:12, 13). They are "unjust" (*adikoi*, 6:1), "those who have no standing in the church" (6:4).

Paul's shock, perhaps feigned, that Christians would bring their petty disputes for adjudication before unjust judges (6:1-11) and his rejoinder that the Corinthians countenance sexual immorality in a way that Gentiles would not (5:1) serve to reinforce his conviction that the Corinthian Christians were a community set apart. A distinction is to be made between the holy people of God and heathens (*ethnē*, 5:1; 10:20; 12:2). Repeatedly he reminds the community not to associate with evil people (5:9). The statement of purpose that Paul expresses in 1:10 is that the community at Corinth be united as God's holy people (cf. 1:2). This is its basic message, its *homilia*. Having a specific message to convey was the third function of the Hellenistic letter (see above on presence and friendship).

For Paul the "conversation" or specific message of his letter was an exhortation to unity within the community. This is the overarching and unifying theme of the letter. Paul's consideration of the various issues that divide the community contributes to the development of the theme.

9. Corinth

Paul's letter is addressed to the church of God at Corinth (*en Korinthō*). The history of the city of Corinth can be neatly divided into two periods, that of the Greek city-state which flourished in the fifth century B.C.E. and was destroyed by the Roman Consul Lucius Mummius in 146 B.C.E., and that of the Roman city, the thriving political and mercantile community founded in 44 B.C.E. by Julius Caesar. At that time the name of the old city, Ephyra, was changed to Colonia Laus Julia Corinthiensis (cf. Strabo, *Geography* 8.2.1-3; 8.4.8; 8.6.20-23). While one should not visit the sins of the ancient city on the Roman colony as earlier generations of commentators on Paul's letter were inclined to do, neither should one think that the site was completely dead during the century that lies between the destruction of the ancient city and the Roman foundation. Archaeological finds provide evidence of some settlement on the site in the time between its two thriving periods.

From the time of the establishment of the Roman colony the city was organized according to Roman customs. Epigraphic and numismatic evidence bears witness to this. Following the Roman practice the highest magistrates were the duoviri (the "two men"). Strabo claims that many in the population were freedmen. The fact that both Greek and Latin appear on the local coinage indicates that the population consisted of both Greek- and Latin-speaking people. A compilation of the known names of first-century Corinthian Christians reveals that the community was a composite of Greeks and Romans.

Considerable archaeological evidence attests to the existence of various pagan cults in Corinth. Pausanias (*Description of Greece* 2.2) affirms that two statues of Dionysus had been erected in the *agora*, one known as the Lysian Dionysus, the other as Dionysus the Reveler. Corinth was also a major center for the cult of Isis, the Egyptian goddess. The Romans reestablished or refurbished the sanctuary of Demeter and Persephone, with its orientation to the underworld and the dead (cf. 15:29). In the same period the temples dedicated to Asklepios and Poseidon were refurbished and temples were constructed in honor of traditional Hellenic deities such as Apollo and Hermes.

One bit of archaeological evidence that is frequently mentioned in the literature on first-century Corinth is a fragmentary inscription, "Synagogue of the Hebrews," *[Syna]gōgē Hebr[aiōn]*. When the inscription was discovered in 1898 it was hailed almost immediately by biblical scholars as providing evidence for the existence of a Jewish synagogue in Corinth at the time of Paul's visit (see Acts 18:4). The inscription is, however, of rather late origin. Most probably it dates from the latter part of the second century C.E. The epigraph was, moreover, not found on the site of the original building. That this archaeological trove does not provide evidence of a Jewish synagogue in first-century Corinth does not mean that no Jewish synagogue existed in Paul's day. Literary evidence amply attests to the existence of a significant Jewish colony at this crossing of the trade routes. Philo writes about a Jewish colony being sent to Corinth (*Gaius* 281). With Jewish settlers there would have been a synagogue (cf. Acts 18:4), and probably more than one.

Another archaeological finding is of an area located between the city's ancient theater and its agora. It is paved with Acrocorinthian limestone. A Latin inscription reads *Erastus pro aedilit[at]e s[ua] p[ecunia] stravit*, "Erastus in return for his aedileship laid [the pavement] at his own expense." The inscription bears witness to the link between patronage and civic status in first-century Corinth, more or less at the time when Paul visited the city. In a letter written to Roman Christians from Corinth Paul extends greetings on behalf of an Erastus, identified as the city manager or treasurer (*oikonomos tēs poleōs*, Rom 16:23). The peculiarity of this being Paul's only mention of any individual Christian's social status and the relative rarity of the name Erastus have led many commentators to assume that the inscription and Paul's epistolary salutation refer to one and the same individual. If so, Erastus (cf. Acts 19:22; 2 Tim 4:20) would have been one of that group of Corinthian Christians that allowed Paul to describe the community as he does in 1:26. Objections to the likelihood of the Christian Erastus and Erastus, the aedile, being one and the same person have, however, been raised by Justin J. Meggitt ("The Social Status of Erastus [Rom 16:23]," *NovT* 38 [1996] 218–223).

Paul visited the city of Corinth during its Roman period. A brief and stylized account of that visit is given by Luke in Acts 18:1-18. That account mentions that Paul stayed with a couple by the name of Aquila and Priscilla (cf. 1 Cor 16:19), expelled from Rome at the time of the Emperor Claudius' ban of Jews (Acts 18:2). Suetonius Tranquillus, the Roman historian (ca. 69–after 122 C.E.), mentions that Jews had been expelled from Rome because they had rioted "at the instigation of Chrestus" (*Claudius* 25). Orosius, a fifth-century church historian, places the expulsion in the year 49 C.E., the ninth year of the emperor's reign. Paul stayed with Aquila and Priscilla, whom he calls Prisca (1 Cor 16:19), and plied the leatherworker's trade in their shop. They were his patrons. Exercising his trade with them gave Paul the opportunity to evangelize (cf. 1 Thess 2:9). The shop on the *agora* gave him the chance to speak about Jesus Christ to customers and passersby. Visits to the synagogue in Corinth also gave Paul the opportunity to preach the gospel (Acts 18:4).

In his account about Paul's visit to Corinth Luke cites Paul's judicial appearance before Gallio, a Roman proconsul (Acts 18:12). Reconstructed epigraphic inscriptions from Delphi show that Gallio was proconsul from 50 to 51 or from 51 to 52. A proconsul normally held office on site from early June to mid-April (cf. Dio Cassius, *Roman History* 57.14.5), but Seneca, Gallio's younger brother, reports that Gallio "began to develop a fever in Achaia and took ship at once, insisting that the disease was not

of the body but of the place" (*Epistles* 104.1). It is likely that Gallio left
Corinth by the end of 51 C.E. Luke reports that Paul stayed in Corinth for
eighteen months (Acts 18:11). His stay would have spanned the greater
part of 51–52 C.E., although some would place it in 49–51. Slingerland
cautiously suggests that Paul's initial visit to Corinth took place at some
point between December of 47 and April of 54. At the time of his visit the
city had a population of about 100,000 (see James Wiseman, *Ancient
Corinth* 11–12). Paul's letter was written from Ephesus (16:8) to Christians
living in Corinth, sometime after his visit, certainly no later than 57, perhaps as early as 53–54.

The allusions to Claudius and Gallio are among the few NT references
to external history. Even these, however, do not allow for a precise dating
of Paul's visit to Corinth. Luke's narrative about Paul's visit to the Achaian metropolis may be a conflation of various traditions, as are many of
his accounts. Acts 18:2 may in fact provide a hint that this is indeed the
case. Some scholars question Orosius's dating of the Claudius incident.
Suspicious of the traditional dating of Paul's visit to Corinth, some scholars now consider that Paul's first visit to Corinth took place in the early
forties. Gerd Lüdemann, for example (*Paul* 262), suggests that the Clau-
dian edict was issued in 41 C.E. and that Paul's visit occurred shortly
thereafter.

Paul's first letter to the Corinthians is the only extant literary piece of
some substance to say something about the life and ethos of the mid-first-
century metropolis. Little is to be gleaned from Luke's account in Acts 18.
Strabo's *Geography* was written some time earlier and is largely concerned
with the ancient city state. Pausanias' *Description of Greece* dates from the
middle of the second century. Paul's letter tells us something about the social situation in mid-first-century Corinth. The city had a social mix (1:26);
dinners were part of its social life (10:27; 11:20-21, 34). Paul's references to
the comings and goings of Christians (1:11; 4:17-21; 16:1-12, 17-18) and the
market (10:25) suggest the hustle and bustle of a busy commercial center
with easy access to the trade routes. Mention of the games (9:24-27) and of
the theater (4:9) says something about the size and importance of the city.
His references to the city's many gods and lords (8:5, 10; 12:2) are an indication of the various cults that were celebrated.

These many allusions to the social situation of the city serve to confirm that 1 Corinthians is a real letter. It was written to people caught up
in the ebb and flow of day-to-day existence in an important metropolitan
center in the Hellenistic world. The point of view adopted in this commentary is that Paul's letter must be allowed to speak for itself. Its first
and last chs. show that it was clearly a letter. Its language shows that it
was written so that Paul might be able to speak to the beloved kin from
whom he was physically separated.

10. *A Theological Perspective*

To a large extent the language Paul speaks in 1 Corinthians is the same as that used by other Hellenistic authors who dealt with issues similar to those faced by the Christians of Corinth. Some considerable part of his language is, nonetheless, language that reflects the Greek Bible. Paul addresses the community as the church of God at Corinth. The community consists of people who have been made holy in Christ Jesus (1:2). With this descriptive language of his *intitulatio* Paul inserts the Christian community of Corinth within the perspective of salvation history as he brings his Christian Jewish faith to bear upon them.

Paul's overriding concern is that the Corinthians be the holy people God has called them to be. From this perspective several dominant themes that echo throughout the letter can be gathered together. Particularly important is the realization that the Corinthian Christians belong to the one God. Imaginatively Paul describes them as God's field, God's building, and God's temple (3:9, 16-17). The Corinthians have been called by God (1:2, 26; 7:17-24). God, who has called the Corinthians to be his holy people, is the God through whom all things exist (8:6; cf. 12:6). It is the one and jealous God who has called the Corinthians to belong to him. Hence they must flee idolatry (10:14; cf. 10:7). They belong exclusively to the one God.

The concern that the Corinthians avoid idolatry dominates Paul's discussion of the matter of food that had been offered to idols (chs. 8, 10). As God's holy people the Corinthians are to learn from the example of their ancestors in God's plan of salvation, Israel at the time of the Exodus (10:1-13). In his most extensive use of scripture in 1 Corinthians Paul develops a kind of midrash on Numbers 11 as he exhorts the Corinthians to avoid idolatry. The one God of Israel to whom the Corinthians belong is not like the many gods and many lords with whom the Corinthians are familiar (8:5) and after whom they had once followed (12:2). The call of the Corinthians as God's holy people requires their total allegiance and appropriate behavior. They are to participate in normal social engagements but they must avoid anything that deters from their commitment today to the one and only God.

Paul's use of the Jewish Scriptures, especially as a warrant for his many exhortations, underscores the Corinthians' relationship with Israel and the claims God makes upon them. The apostle's understanding of creation is dependent on Jewish tradition and the Jewish Scriptures that attest to the tradition (Genesis 1-2). He uses creation motifs when he writes about the relationship between men and women (6:16; 11:7-9). He draws a lesson from creation in order to speak meaningfully about the as-yet-unexperienced (2:9) age to come (15:35-50). The first and last things go together: protology is related to eschatology and eschatology to protology (8:6). Eschatology serves as a corrective to a naïve understanding of protology (11:11-12); protology provides a model for understanding "the end," when Christ will hand over the kingdom to the Father (15:24).

Jesus Christ is the mediator of the Corinthian Christians' relationship with God. The Corinthians belong to God through Jesus Christ (3:23; cf. 1:2; 8:6; 15:24). Redeemed (1:30), the Corinthians have been "bought and paid for" (6:20; 7:23). Christ is now their Lord. The message of the cross of Christ makes the wisdom of this world mere foolishness (1:18-23). In most of his letters the *Kyrios* title is Paul's preferred christological epithet. In 1 Corinthians Paul uses the title to good advantage particularly in his paraenesis. From the outset of his letter Paul urges the Corinthians to be what they are, God's holy people in Christ Jesus (1:2). The realization that individual Christians belong to Christ the Lord should inform their patterns of sexual behavior (5:1-8; 6:12-20). The community gathers in a kind of fellowship meal that is supposed to be the Lord's supper (11:20). Social divisions that gnaw at the unity of the community make of this festal gathering something less than that. Christians must remember the tradition of the Lord's supper (11:23-26). They are to remember that it is the Lord's death that they proclaim when they gather together for their common meal.

The Corinthians considered themselves to be spiritual people (3:1), but Paul corrects the misunderstanding that resulted from their naïve claim to possess the Spirit (2:6-16). The Corinthians' incorrect understanding of the role of the Spirit in their lives was most apparent when they came together in a common assembly. In these gatherings some of the Corinthians had a tendency to value the ecstatic gift of speaking in tongues above all other gifts. Accordingly Paul reminds them that speaking in tongues is but one among the many gifts that God gives to the members of the community through the divine Spirit. The entire community was richly endowed with spiritual gifts (1:5-7; 4:8). Each and every member of the community had his or her own gift according to the measure of the Spirit's gift (12:4, 7, 11). There is one Spirit, but there are many gifts of the Spirit. The good of the entire church is the criterion to be used for the proper exercise of the charisms. Through the gifts of the Spirit the church is to be built up as the body of Christ (12:12-26).

In a detailed argument Paul teaches the Corinthians about the relative value of the gift of tongues (ch. 14), particularly in comparison with the gift of prophecy. Prophecy is the one charismatic gift that Paul appears to value most highly (14:1, 5, 18-19); it appears to be the one gift that is necessary for the continued existence of a Christian community. Paul himself enjoyed the gift of prophecy (13:2; 14:6, 18-19), but without love, he confesses, he would be nothing. Love is the fundamental gift, the basis of all other gifts, and the paradigm against which all other gifts are to be measured (13:4-13).

The eschatological perspective that Paul brings to bear upon the charisms in ch. 13 provides the horizon against which he writes his entire letter. He describes the Corinthians as those who await the revelation of the Lord Jesus Christ (1:7). Eschatological motifs provide the judgment theme that is integral to Paul's paraenesis (1:18; 3:13-17; 4:1-5; 5:3-5; 6:2-4; 11:27-34), and the eschatological perspective dominates Paul's anthropology (2:11-16; 15:35-57). It is the context within which decisions about marriage are to be made (7:29-31).

Eschatology is the perspective from which Paul addresses the fate of the dead, a matter of concern for many first-century Corinthians. Some who belonged to the community denied the resurrection of the dead (15:12). Paul addresses this issue in systematic fashion, dividing the question and developing a tightly knit and multifaceted argument. Using a traditional credal formula (15:3-5), he affirms that the resurrection of Jesus from among the dead is central to the Christian faith. He appeals to the experience of the Corinthians and to his own experience (15:29-32) as he argues that Christians who have died will be raised from the dead. The sophistry that would lead people to question how a future resurrection from the dead is possible (15:35) is to be put aside in the light of what God has done in creation (15:35-49). Christ is the firstfruits of those who have died; through him comes the resurrection of the dead (15:21-24). The resurrection of Christ provides a warrant for the resurrection of those who die in Christ.

In 1 Corinthians the thoughts that Paul expresses proceed from a profound theology strongly rooted in the Jewish tradition and enriched by a Christian faith. The apostle acknowledges that the Corinthians are familiar with the rituals of baptism and eucharist (1:13-17; 10:1-5, 14-22; 11:23-26). In his letter, however, Paul does not attempt to make a systematic exposition of his theology nor does he offer a theological rationale for the celebration of the rituals. His is a letter that urges the community to be one in heart and mind (1:10). His apostolic letter addresses a variety of issues that were sources of division within the community. Paul treats these issues from the perspective of his theological insights and his Christian faith. He examines them on the basis of the Corinthians' own experience and offers himself as an example for the Corinthians to imitate (4:16; 11:1). He uses the experience of the Christian liturgy as an argument for the unity of the community (1:13-17; 11:23-26).

The basic issue in 1 Corinthians is ultimately ecclesiological. What does it mean for the Christians of Corinth to be God's one holy people at Corinth? One after another Paul treats the divisive issues that confront the community. He brings his own rich theological insights to bear on the various aspects of their real situation. Rather than develop a theological exposition Paul offers repeated exhortations from his insightful theological perspective. Written almost two millennia ago, Paul's first letter to the Corinthians continues to whet the interest of contemporary readers and to maintain its theological significance. His letter to a church has become a letter for the church.

The problems of the contemporary Church are quite different from those of the church in ancient Corinth, but there is a remarkable similarity between the issues facing Christians today and the issues that faced the church of God at Corinth. Today, as then, people are fascinated with knowledge. Contemporary readers of Paul's first letter to the Corinthians are challenged to hang onto the gospel message, allowing it to form their lives even as the knowledge explosion bursts upon them. Those who have any of the various kinds of knowledge available in the world of today are challenged not to look down on people who are less intellectually gifted or do not possess a specific kind of expertise or intellectual knowledge. A kind of gnostic fascination with education and gifts of intellect continues to be problematic in the world in which we live. All too often the haughty claims of those "in the know" appear to denigrate the dignity of the "have nots" of this world. The pious who possess the Spirit sometimes disdain activist Christians. Conversely some activists claiming empowerment by the Spirit denigrate the religiosity of the pious.

Sexuality, marriage, and gender issues are addressed in Paul's letter to the Corinthians. The solutions the apostle offered may not be adequate for those who face similar issues at the present time. Paul's manner of approaching these issues remains nonetheless a valid one. He urges that issues of sexuality, marriage, and gender be resolved on the basis of a theological anthropology rooted in the biblical tradition, the Christian's union with and existence in Christ, and the coming eschaton. This triple perspective continues to inform a truly Christian attitude in matters of sexuality, marriage, and gender in contemporary society.

While idol worship *per se* may not be a problematic issue for the contemporary reader of Paul's letter to the Corinthians, today's reader exists in a world characterized by cultural diversity and religious pluralism. A Christian reader of Paul's letter is challenged to maintain a faithful commitment to the one God and the one Lord even as he or she maintains a wide variety of commercial and social relationships with people of different cultures and with people of different or no faith. Like the Corinthian Christians, the contemporary reader should learn from the experience of those who are our ancestors in faith even if it is impossible to repeat anew the experience of Israel of old or the ministry of Paul in the contemporary world.

As a social community the Church of today must appreciate the centrality of the Eucharist in its life. The social community that is the Church must learn to live with and appreciate the different gifts given to each and every member of the community. What Paul has to say about the spiritual gifts given to each and every one provides a kind of paradigm for all ecclesial communities that seek to be built up as the body of Christ. Paul's words on charisms and on the centrality of love, the foundation of all the individual charisms, offer a perspective for the individual parish community that is seeking to live as a church. It offers a perspective to the larger Church that is called to recognize the different Spirit-endowed gifts of the laity and of the clergy, of the hierarchy and theologians, of the several religious orders and the new forms of apostolic life. Indeed the unity-in-diversity and diversity-in-unity of the Church about which Paul writes offer a vantage point from which the contemporary reader of 1 Corinthians can reflect on the unity and diversity of the different Christian churches.

The reality of people without hope and the issue of death with dignity are part of the world in which the contemporary reader of Paul's letter lives. Paul's words about the reality of Jesus' resurrection, the ground of Christian hope, are pertinent to those who are without hope and to those who seek to find meaning in death. Physical life is not all that there is and death is not the end. The Christian is called to look back to what God did in raising Jesus from the dead and to hope for the future resurrection in which all who have died in Christ will live with him.

Finally, one should not overlook the fact that Paul wrote his first letter to the Corinthians to a community that consisted of real individuals, that was socially engaged in its own world, and that was in the midst of a cultural transformation. Paul's first letter to the Corinthians offers the contemporary reader a view of a real and struggling flesh-and-blood community such as is offered by no other New Testament text. His letter challenged the Corinthians to allow the gospel to engage them in the warp and woof of their daily lives. The contemporary reader of Paul's first letter to the Corinthians is likewise challenged to allow the gospel message to engage him or her in the very realities of daily life and to celebrate our oneness in Christ when the church gathers for Eucharist and Spirit-inspired discourse.

11. OUTLINE OF THE STRUCTURE OF THE LETTER

Introduction (1:1-9)
  A. Epistolary Opening (1:1-3)
  B. Thanksgiving (1:4-9)

Body of the Letter (1:10–15:58)
  A. Theme and Occasion (1:10-17)
  B. First Rhetorical Demonstration (1:18–4:21)
      1. Wisdom and Power (1:18-31)
      2. Paul's Mission (2:1-5)
      3. God's Wisdom (2:6-16)
      4. Mother and Farmer (3:1-9)
      5. The Construction (3:10-17)
      6. Slogans Reversed (3:18-23)
      7. The Ultimate Tribunal (4:1-5)
      8. The Lesson of Paul and Apollos (4:6-7)
      9. Filled and Hungry (4:8-13)
      10. A Letter of Admonition (4:14-16)
      11. Recommendation of Timothy (4:17-21)
  C. Second Rhetorical Demonstration (5:1–7:40)
      1. A Purified Community (5:1-8)
      2. Shunning Evil (5:9-13)
      3. Use of the Courts (6:1-11)
      4. Embodied Existence (6:12-20)
      5. Sex Within Marriage (7:1-7)
      6. Special Situations (7:8-16)
      7. Remain As You Were Called (7:17-24)
      8. Advice for the Unmarried (7:25-35)
      9. To Marry or Not to Marry (7:36-40)
  D. Third Rhetorical Demonstration (8:1–11:1)
      1. Food Offered to Idols (8:1-3)
      2. The Monotheistic Confession of Faith (8:4-6)
      3. Eating and Freedom (8:7-13)
      4. Apostolic Rights (9:1-14)
      5. Christ's Slave (9:15-18)
      6. For the Sake of the Gospel (9:19-23)
      7. The Games (9:24-27)
      8. Learning from Scripture (10:1-13)
      9. Avoid Idolatry (10:14-22)
      10. Summing Up (10:23–11:1)
  E. Fourth Rhetorical Demonstration (11:2-34)
      1. Let Men be Men and Women Be Women (11:2-16)
      2. The Lord's Supper? (11:17-22)
      3. The Lord's Supper (11:23-26)
      4. Judgment (11:27-34)
  F. Fifth Rhetorical Demonstration (12:1–14:40)
      1. A Matter of Principle (12:1-3)
      2. Allotment of Gifts (12:4-11)

3. The Body (12:12-26)

4. Christ's Body (12:27-31a)

5. Not to Have Love (12:31b–13:3)

6. Love's Rhythm (13:4-7)

7. A Unique Gift (13:8–14:1a)

8. The Greater Gift of Prophecy (14:1b-5)

9. A Trilogy of Cultural Analogies (14:6-12)

10. Praying with Full Participation (14:13-19)

11. Outsiders and Unbelievers (14:20-25)

12. Order in the Assembly (14:26-40)

G. Sixth Rhetorical Demonstration (15:1-58)

1. The Creed (15:1-11)

2. If Christ Has Not Been Raised (15:12-19)

3. Ultimate Victory (15:20-28)

4. An Exhortation (15:29-34)

5. How Can the Dead Be Raised? (15:35-44a)

6. The Last Adam (15:44b-49)

7. Victory over Death (15:50-58)

Closing (16:1-24)

1. Collection for the Holy Ones (16:1-4)

2. Travel Plans (16:5-9)

3. Timothy and Apollos (16:10-12)

4. Goodbye (16:13-14)

5. Commendation of Stephanas (16:15-18)

6. Greetings (16:19-21)

7. Solemn Farewell (16:22-24)

GENERAL BIBLIOGRAPHY

Note: Works listed here are subsequently cited by short title only in the Notes and For Reference and Further Study sections following the individual sections of the commentary. In addition to the works listed in the For Reference and Further Study sections following the individual pericopes of Paul's letter there are separate bibliographies for each of the rhetorical demonstrations identified in the outline of the letter.

A. *Letter Writing*

Belleville, Linda L. "Continuity or Discontinuity: A Fresh Look at 1 Corinthians in the Light of First Century Epistolary Forms and Conventions," *EvQ* 59 (1987) 15–37.

Borse, Udo. "'Tränenbrief' und 1. Korintherbrief," SNTU. ser. A. 9 (1984) 175–202.

Collins, John J. "Chiasmus, the 'ABA' Pattern and the Text of Paul," *SPC* 2, 575–584.

Collins, Raymond F. "Reflections on 1 Corinthians as a Hellenistic Letter," *CorC* 39–61.

Jeremias, Joachim. "Chiasmus in den Paulusbriefen," *ZNW* 49 (1958) 145–156. Reprinted in idem, *Abba. Studien zur neutestamentlichen Theologie und Zeit-geschichte.* Göttingen: Vandenhoeck & Ruprecht, 1966, 276–290.

Koskenniemi, Heikki. *Studien zur Idee und Phraseologie des grieschischen Briefes bis 400 n. Chr.* Suomalaisen Tiedeakatemian Toimituksia/Annales Academiae Scientiarum Fennicae B, 102,2. Helsinki: Akateeminen Kirjakauppa, 1956.

Lührmann, Dieter. "Freundschaftsbrief trotz Spannungen. Zur Gattung und Auf-bau des Ersten Korintherbriefes" in Wolfgang Schrage, ed., *Studien zum Text und Zur Ethik des Neuen Testaments. Festschrift zum 80. Geburtstag von Hein-rich Greeven.* BZNW 47. Berlin: Walter de Gruyter, 1986, 298–314.

Malherbe, Abraham J. *Ancient Epistolary Theorists.* SBL.SBS 19. Atlanta: Scholars, 1988.

Mitchell, Margaret M. "Concerning *peri de* in 1 Corinthians," *NovT* 31 (1989) 229–256.

Murphy-O'Connor, Jerome. "Co-Authorship in the Corinthian Correspondence," *RB* 100 (1993) 562–579.

_____. *Paul the Letter-Writer: His World, His Options, His Skills.* GNS 41. Col-legeville: The Liturgical Press, 1995.

Richards, E. Randolph. *The Secretary in the Letters of Paul.* WUNT 2nd ser. 42. Tübingen: J.C.B. Mohr, 1991.

Schnider, Franz, and Werner Stenger. *Studien zum neutestamentlichen Briefformular.* NTTS 11. Leiden: Brill, 1987.

Stowers, Stanley K. *Letter Writing in Greco-Roman Antiquity.* Library of Early Christianity. Philadelphia: Westminster, 1986.

Terry, Ralph Bruce. "Patterns of Discourse Structure in I Corinthians," *Journal of Translation and Textlinguistics* 7 (1996) 1–32.

Thraede, Klaus. *Grundzüge griechisch-römischer Brieftopik.* Zetemata 48. Munich: Beck, 1970.

White, John Lee. *The Form and Function of the Body of the Greek Letter: A Study of the Letter-Body in the Non-Literary Papyri and in Paul the Apostle.* Missoula: Schol-ars, 1972.

_____. *Light from Ancient Letters.* Foundations and Facets. Philadelphia: Fortress, 1986.

_____. "Saint Paul and the Apostolic Letter Tradition," *CBQ* 45 (1983) 433–444.

_____. "New Testament Epistolary Literature in the Framework of Ancient Epistolography," *ANRW* II, 25, 2 (1984) 1730–1756.

B. *Unity of the Letter*

Boer, Martinus C. de. "The Composition of 1 Corinthians," *NTS* 40 (1994) 229–245.

Burgos Núñez, Miguel de. "La Correspondencia de Pablo con las Comunidades de Corinto," *Communio* 26 (1993) 33–67.

Clemen, Carl. *Die Einheitlichkeit der paulinischen Briefe an der Hand der bisher mit Bezug auf sie aufgestellten Interpolations- und Compilationshypothesen.* Göttin-gen: Vandenhoeck & Ruprecht, 1894.

Hagge, H. "Die beiden überlieferten Sendschreiben des Apostels Paulus an die Gemeinde zu Korinth," *Jahrbücher für protestantische Theologie* 2 (1876) 481–531.

Hurd, John C. "Good News and the Integrity of 1 Corinthians," in L. Ann Jervis and Peter Richardson, eds., *Gospel in Paul. Studies on Corinthians, Galatians and Romans for Richard N. Longenecker.* JSNT.S 108. Sheffield: Sheffield Academic Press, 1994, 38–62.

————. *The Origin of I Corinthians.* London: S.P.C.K., 1965. New ed. Macon, Ga.: Mercer University Press, 1983.

Merklein, Helmut. "Die Einheitlichkeit des ersten Korintherbriefes," *ZNW* 75 (1984) 153–183.

Pesch, Rudolf. *Paulus Ringt um die Lebensform der Kirche. Vier Briefe an die Gemeinde Gottes in Korinth. Paulus—neu gesehen.* Herderbücherei 1291. Freiburg: Herder, 1986.

Sellin, Gerhard. "1 Korinther 5–6 und der 'Vorbrief' nach Korinth: Indizien für eine Mehrschichtigkeit von Kommunikationsakten im ersten Korintherbrief," *NTS* 37 (1991) 535–558.

Serna, Eduardo de la. "Los orígenes de 1 Corintos," *Bib.* 72 (1991) 192–216.

C. *Archaeology and History*

Broneer, Oscar. "Paul and the Pagan Cults at Isthmia," *HThR* 64 (1971) 169–187.

Harding, Mark. "Church and Gentile Cults at Corinth," *GTJ* 10 (1989) 203–223.

Kent, John Harvey. *Corinth: Results of Excavations Conducted by the American School of Classical Studies at Athens.* Vol. 8, 3: *The Inscriptions 1926–1950.* Princeton: The American School of Classical Studies at Athens, 1966.

Klauck, Hans-Josef. *Herrenmahl und hellenisticher Kult. Eine religionsgeschichtliche Untersuchung zum ersten Korintherbrief.* NTA n.s. 15. Münster: Aschendorff, 1982.

Lang, Mabel L. *Cure and Cult in Ancient Corinth: A Guide to the Asklepieion.* Princeton: American School of Classical Studies at Athens, 1977.

Lisle, Robert. "The Cults of Corinth." Ph. D. Dissertation, Johns Hopkins University, 1955.

Murphy-O'Connor, Jerome. "The Corinth that Saint Paul Saw," *BA* 47 (1984) 147–159.

————. *St. Paul's Corinth: Text and Archaeology.* GNS 6. Wilmington, Del.: Michael Glazier, 1983.

O'Mahony, Kieran. "Roman Corinth and Corinthian Christians," *Scripture in Church* 27 (1997) 115–124.

Oster, Richard E., Jr. "Use, Misuse and Neglect of Archaeological Evidence in Some Modern Works on 1 Corinthians (1 Cor 7,1-5; 8,10; 11,2-16; 12,14-26)," *ZNW* 83 (1992) 52–73.

Slingerland, Dixon. "Acts 18:1-18, the Gallio Inscription, and Absolute Pauline Chronology," *JBL* 110 (1991) 439–449.

Wiseman, James. "Corinth and Rome I: 228 B.C.–A.D. 267," *ANRW* II, 7, 1 (1979) 435–548.

_____. *The Land of Ancient Corinth: Studies in Mediterranean Archaeology.* Göteberg: P. Artiömis, 1978.

D. *Rhetorical Approach*

Anderson, R. Dean, Jr. *Ancient Rhetorical Theory and Paul.* CBET 18. Kampen: Kok Pharos, 1996.

Bünker, Michael. *Briefformular und rhetorische Disposition im 1. Korintherbrief.* GTA 28. Göttingen: Vandenhoeck & Ruprecht, 1983.

Eriksson, Anders. *Traditions as Rhetorical Proof: Pauline Argumentation in 1 Corinthians.* ConBNT 29. Stockholm: Almqvist & Wiksell, 1998.

Fiore, Benjamin. *The Function of Personal Example in the Socratic and Pastoral Epistles.* AnBib 105. Rome: Biblical Institute Press, 1986.

_____. "'Covert Allusion' in 1 Corinthians 1–4," *CBQ* 47 (1985) 85–102.

Hester, James. "Re-Discovering and Re-Inventing Rhetoric," *Scriptura* 50 (1994) 1–22.

Mitchell, Margaret M. *Paul and the Rhetoric of Reconciliation: An Exegetical Investigation of the Language and Composition of 1 Corinthians.* Louisville: Westminster/John Knox, 1991.

Probst, Hermann. *Paulus und der Brief: Die Rhetorik des antiken Briefes als Form der paulinischen Korintherkorrespondenz (1 Kor 8–10).* WUNT 2nd ser. 45. Tübingen: J.C.B. Mohr, 1991.

Reinmuth, Eckart. "Narratio und argumentatio—zur Auslegung der Jesus-Christus-Geschichte im Ersten Korintherbrief. Ein Beitrag zur mimetischen Kompetenz des Paulus." *ZThK* 92 (1995) 13–27.

Terry, Ralph Bruce. *A Discourse Analysis of First Corinthians.* Summer Institute of Linguistics and the University of Texas at Arlington Publications in Linguistics 120. Dallas: Summer Institute of Linguistics, 1995.

Wuellner, Wilhelm. "Paul as Pastor: The Function of Rhetorical Questions in First Corinthians" in Albert Vanhoye, ed., *L'Apôtre Paul. Personnalité, style et conception du ministère.* BEThL 73. Louvain: Louvain University Press/Peeters, 1986, 49–77.

_____. "Greek Rhetoric and Pauline Argumentation" in William R. Schoedel and Robert L. Wilken, eds., *Early Christian Literature and the Classical Intellectual Tradition: in honorem Robert M. Grant.* Paris: Beauchesne, 1979, 177–188.

Yeo, Khiok-Khng. *Rhetorical Interaction in 1 Corinthians 8 and 10: A Formal Analysis with Preliminary Suggestions for a Chinese Cross-Cultural Hermeneutic.* Biblical Interpetation Series 9. Leiden: Brill, 1995.

E. *Social Situation of the Corinthian Church*

Baird, William. "One Against the Other: Intra-Church Conflict in 1 Corinthians" in Robert T. Fortna and Beverly Roberts Gaventa, eds., *The Conversation Continues: Studies in Paul and John.* Nashville: Abingdon, 1990, 116–136.

Barton, Stephen C. "Paul's Sense of Place: An Anthropological Approach to Community Formation in Corinth," *NTS* 32 (1986) 225–246.

————. "Christian Community in the Light of 1 Corinthians," *Studies in Christian Ethics* 10 (1997) 1–15.

Chow, John K. *Patronage and Power: A Study of Social Networks in Corinth.* JSNT.S 75 Sheffield: JSOT Press, 1992.

Clark, Gillian. "The Women at Corinth," *Theology* 85 (1982) 256–262.

Clarke, Andrew D. *Secular and Christian Leadership in Corinth: A Socio-Historical and Exegetical Study of 1 Corinthians 1–6.* AGJU 18. Leiden: Brill, 1993.

Engberg-Pedersen, Troels. "The Gospel and Social Practice According to 1 Corinthians," *NTS* 33 (1987) 557–584.

Gill, David W. J. "In Search of the Social Élite in the Corinthian Church," *TynB* 44 (1993) 323–337.

Horsley, Richard A. "1 Corinthians: A Case Study of Paul's Assembly as an Alternative Society" in idem, ed., *Paul and Empire: Religion and Power in Roman Imperial Society.* Harrisburg: Trinity Press International, 1997, 242–252.

Klauck, Hans-Josef. "Gemeindestrukturen im ersten Korintherbrief," *BiKi* 40 (1985) 9–15.

Marshall, Peter. *Enmity in Corinth: Social Conventions in Paul's Relations with the Corinthians.* WUNT 2nd ser. 23. Tübingen: J.C.B. Mohr, 1987.

Meeks, Wayne A. *The First Urban Christians: the Social World of the Apostle Paul.* New Haven and London: Yale University Press, 1983.

Sanders, Jack T. "Paul between Jews and Gentiles in Corinth," *JSNT* 65 (1997) 67–83.

Theissen, Gerd. *The Social Setting of Pauline Christianity: Essays on Corinth.* Philadelphia: Fortress, 1982.

F. *Theological and General Studies*

Bailey, Kenneth E. "The Structure of 1 Corinthians and Paul's Theological Method with a Special Reference to 4:17," *NovT* 25 (1983) 152–181.

Balch, David L., Everett Ferguson, and Wayne A. Meeks. *Greeks, Romans, and Christians: Essays in Honor of Abraham J. Malherbe.* Minneapolis: Fortress, 1990.

Bieringer, Reimund, ed. *The Corinthian Correspondence.* BEThL 125. Leuven: Leuven University Press, 1996. [= *CorC*]

Boring, M. Eugene, Klaus Berger, and Carsten Colpe, eds. *Hellenistic Commentary to the New Testament.* Nashville: Abingdon, 1995.

Carter, Timothy L. "'Big Men' in Corinth," *JSNT* 66 (1997) 45–71.

Collins, Raymond F. "'It was indeed written for our sake' (1 Cor 9,10). Paul's Use of Scripture in the First Letter to the Corinthians," *SNTU.* ser. A. 20 (1995) 151–170.

Crofts, Marjorie. "Some Considerations in Translating 'Body' in 1 Corinthians," *Notes on Translation* 119 (1987) 40–49.

Dewey, Joanna. "Textuality in an Oral Culture: A Survey of the Pauline Traditions," *Semeia* 65 (1995) 37–65.

Donfried, Karl P. "Paul as *Scēnopoios* and the Use of the Codex in Early Christianity" in Karl Kertelge, Traugott Holtz, and Claus-Peter März, eds., *Christus bezeugen. Festschrift für Wolfang Trilling zum 65. Geburtstag,* 1. EThSt 59. Leipzig: St. Benno, 1989, 249–256.

Dungan, David L. *Sayings of Jesus in the Churches of Paul: The Use of the Synoptic Tradition in the Regulations of Early Church Life.* Philadelphia: Fortress, 1971.

Dunn, James D. G. *Unity and Diversity in the New Testament: An Inquiry into the Character of Earliest Christianity.* 2nd ed. London: SCM, and Philadelphia: Trinity Press International, 1990.

_____. "In Search of Wisdom," *EpRev* 22 (1995) 48–53.

_____. *1 Corinthians.* New Testament Guides. Sheffield: Sheffield Academic Press, 1995.

Ellis, E. Earle. *Prophecy and Hermeneutic in Early Christianity. New Testament Essays.* WUNT 18. Tübingen: J. C. B. Mohr, 1978.

_____. "Traditions in 1 Corinthians," *NTS* 32 (1986) 481–502.

Fee, Gordon D. "Toward a Theology of 1 Corinthians" in David M. Hay, ed., *Pauline Theology, 2: 1 & 2 Corinthians.* Minneapolis: Fortress, 1993, 37–58.

Feuillet, André. *Le Christ Sagesse de Dieu d'après les épîtres pauliniennes.* EtB. Paris: Gabalda, 1966.

Fredrickson, David E. "No Noose is Good News: Leadership as a Theological Problem in the Corinthian Correspondence," *Word & World* 16 (1996) 420–426.

Furnish, Victor P. "Theology in 1 Corinthians" in David M. Hay, ed., *Pauline Theology, 2: 1 & 2 Corinthians.* Minneapolis: Fortress, 1993, 59–89.

Genest, Olivette. "L'interprétation de la mort de Jésus en situation discursive. Un cas-type: L'articulation des figures de cette mort en 1–2 Corinthiens," *NTS* 34 (1988) 506–535.

Gillespie, Thomas W. *The First Theologians: A Study in Early Christian Prophecy.* Grand Rapids: Eerdmans, 1994.

Harvey, Anthony Ernest. "The Opposition to St. Paul" in Frank Leslie Cross, ed., *Studia Evangelica IV.* TU 102. Berlin: Akademie-Verlag, 1968, 319–332.

Hays, Richard B. *The Moral Vision of the New Testament: Community, Cross, New Creation: A Contemporary Introduction to New Testament Ethics.* San Francisco: HarperSanFrancisco, 1996.

_____. "Ecclesiology and Ethics in 1 Corinthians," *Ex Auditu* 10 (1994) 31–43.

Hollander, Harm W. "The Meaning of the Term 'Law' *(NOMOS)* in 1 Corinthians," *NovT* 40 (1998) 117–135.

Hübner, Hans. *Biblische Theologie des Neuen Testaments, 2: Die Theologie des Paulus und ihre neutestamentliche Wirkungsgeschichte.* Göttingen: Vandenhoeck & Ruprecht, 1993.

Jewett, Robert. *Paul's Anthropological Terms: A Study of Their Use in Conflict Settings.* AGJU 10. Leiden: Brill, 1971.

_____. "The Redaction of I Corinthians and the Trajectory of the Pauline School," *JAARSup* 44 (1978) 389–444.

Koester, Helmut. *Ancient Christian Gospels: Their History and Development.* Philadelphia: Trinity Press International, 1990, 55–62.

_____. "Apocryphal and Canonical Gospels," *HThR* 73 (1980) 105–130, 113–119.

Koet, Bart J. "As Close to the Synagogue as Can Be. Paul in Corinth (Acts 18, 1-18)," *CorC* 397–425.

Kraus, Wolfgang. *Das Volk Gottes: zur Grundlegung der Ekklesiologie bei Paulus.* WUNT 85. Tübingen: J. C. B. Mohr, 1996.

Krentz, Edgar. "Preaching to an Alien Culture: Resources in the Corinthian Letters," *Word & World* 16 (1996) 465–472.

Lambrecht, Jan. *Pauline Studies.* BEThL 115. Louvain: Louvain University Press/Peeters, 1994.

Lüdemann, Gerd. *Paul, Apostle to the Gentiles: Studies in Chronology.* London: SCM, 1984.

Malan, François S. "The Use of the Old Testament in 1 Corinthians," *Neotest.* 14 (1981) 134–170.

Martin, Dale B. *The Corinthian Body.* New Haven: Yale University Press, 1995.

Martin, Ralph P. *1, 2 Corinthians.* Word Biblical Themes. Dallas: Word Books, 1988.

Martyn, J. Louis. "The Covenants of Hagar and Sarah" in John T. Carroll, Charles H. Cosgrove, and E. Elizabeth Johnson, eds., *Faith and History. Essays in Honor of Paul W. Meyer.* Atlanta: Scholars, 1990, 160–192.

Mearns, Christopher L. "Early Eschatological Development in Paul: the Evidence of I Corinthians," *JSNT* 22 (1984) 19–35.

Meeks, Wayne A. "The Circle of Reference in Pauline Morality" in David L. Balch, Everett Ferguson, and Wayne A. Meeks, eds., *Greeks, Romans, and Christians. Essays in Honor of Abraham J. Malherbe.* Minneapolis: Fortress, 1990, 305–317.

Miranda, Americo. "L'uomo spirituale *(Pneumatikos anthrōpos)* nella Prima ai Corinzi," *RivBib* 43 (1995) 485–519.

Müller, Ulrich B. *Prophetie und Predigt im Neuen Testament.* SNT 10. Gütersloh: Gerd Mohn, 1975.

Murphy-O'Connor, Jerome. *Paul: A Critical Life.* Oxford: Clarendon Press, 1996, 252–322.

Omanson, Roger L. "Acknowledging Paul's Quotations," *BiTr* 43 (1992) 201–213.

Paige, Terence. "Stoicism, *Eleutheria,* and Community at Corinth" in Michael J. Wilkins and Terence Paige, eds., *Worship, Theology and Ministry in the Early Church: Essays in Honor of Ralph P. Martin.* JSNT.S 87. Sheffield: Sheffield Academic Press, 1992, 180–193.

Patterson, Stephen J. "Paul and the Jesus Tradition: It is Time for Another Look," *HThR* 84 (1991) 23–41.

Pearson, Birger A. *The Pneumatikos-Psychikos Terminology in I Corinthians; A Study in the Theology of the Corinthian Opponents of Paul and Its Relation to Gnosticism.* SBL.DS 12. Missoula: Scholars, 1973.

Penna, Romano. *Paul the Apostle: A Theological and Exegetical Study.* 2 vols. Translated by Thomas P. Wahl. Collegeville: The Liturgical Press, 1996.

Pfitzner, Victor C. "Proclaiming the Name: Cultic Narrative and Eucharistic Proclamation in First Corinthians," *LTJ* 25 (1991) 15–25.

Pickett, Raymond. *The Cross in Corinth: The Social Significance of the Death of Jesus.* JSNT.S 143. Sheffield: Sheffield Academic Press, 1997.

Richardson, Neil. *Paul's Language about God.* JSNT.S 99. Sheffield: JSOT, 1994.

Rosner, Brian S. *Paul, Scripture and Ethics: A Study of 1 Corinthians 5–7*. AGJU 22. Leiden: Brill, 1994.

Schmithals, Walter. *Gnosticism in Corinth*. Translated by John E. Steely. Nashville: Abingdon, 1971.

Schüssler Fiorenza, Elisabeth. "Rhetorical Situation and Historical Reconstruction in I Corinthians," *NTS* 33 (1987) 386–403.

Sellin, Gerhard. "Hauptprobleme des Ersten Korintherbriefes," *ANRW* II, 25, 4 (1987) 2940–3044.

Söding, Thomas. "Das Geheimnis Gottes im Kreuz Jesu (1 Cor). Die paulinische Christologie im Spannungsfeld von Mythos und Kerygma," *BZ* 38 (1994) 174–194.

_____. *Das Liebesgebot bei Paulus. Die Mahnung zur Agape im Rahmen der paulinischen Ethik*. NTA 26. Münster: Aschendorff, 1995.

_____. *Das Wort vom Kreuz. Studien zur paulinischen Theologie*. WUNT 93. Tübingen: Mohr-Siebeck, 1997.

Spilly, Alphonse P. "The Church in Corinth," *ChiSt* 24 (1985) 307–321.

Stanley, Christopher D. *Paul and the Language of Scripture: Citation Technique in the Pauline Epistles and Contemporary Literature*. MSSNTS 69. Cambridge: Cambridge University Press, 1992.

Sterling, Gregory E. "'Wisdom among the Perfect': Creation Traditions in Alexandrian Judaism and Corinthian Christianity," *NovT* 37 (1995) 355–384.

Tomson, Peter J. *Paul and the Jewish Law: Halakha in the Letters of the Apostle to the Gentiles*. CRINT III, 1. Assen: Van Gorcum; Minneapolis: Fortress, 1990.

_____. "La première épître aux Corinthiens comme document de la tradition apostolique de Halakha," *CorC* 459–470.

Ward, Richard F. "Pauline Voice and Presence as Strategic Communication," *Semeia* 65 (1995) 95–107.

Weiss, Johannes. "Beiträge zur paulinischen Rhetorik" in C. R. Gregory, Adolf Harnack, et al, eds., *Theologische Studien. Herrn Wirkl. Oberkonsistorialrath Professor D. Bernard Weiss zu seinem 70. Geburtstage dargebracht*. Göttingen: Vandenhoeck & Ruprecht, 1897, 165–247.

Wenham, David. "Whatever Went Wrong in Corinth?" *ExpT* 108 (1977) 137–141.

Wilson, Robert McLachlan. "Gnosis at Corinth" in Morna D. Hooker and Stephen G. Wilson, eds., *Paul and Paulinism: Essays in Honour of C. K. Barrett*. London: SPCK, 1982, 102–114.

_____. "How Gnostic were the Corinthians?" *NTS* 19 (1972) 65–74.

Winter, Bruce W. *Philo and Paul among the Sophists*. MSSNTS 96. Cambridge: Cambridge University Press, 1996.

Wire, Antoinette C. *The Corinthian Women Prophets: A Reconstruction through Paul's Rhetoric*. Minneapolis: Fortress, 1990.

G. *Commentaries*

Allo, Ernest-Bernard. *Saint Paul. Première Épître aux Corinthiens*. EtBib. 2nd ed. Paris: Gabalda, 1956.

Barbaglio, Giuseppe. *La Prima lettera ai Corinzi. Introduzione, versione, commento. Scritti delle origini cristiane 7.* Bologna: Dehoniane, 1995.

Barclay, William. *The Letters to the Corinthians.* Philadelphia: Westminster, 1956.

Barrett, Charles Kingsley. *The First Epistle to the Corinthians.* Harper's New Testament Commentaries. New York: Harper, 1968.

Baudraz, François. *Les Épîtres aux Corinthiens.* Geneva: Labor et Fides, 1965.

Bruce, Frederick Fyvie. *1 and 2 Corinthians.* New Century Bible. London: Oliphants, 1971.

Conzelmann, Hans. *Der erste Brief an die Korinther.* KEK 5. 11th ed. Göttingen: Vandenhoeck & Ruprecht, 1969. ET: *1 Corinthians: A Commentary on the First Epistle to the Corinthians.* Translated by James W. Leitch. Hermeneia. Philadelphia: Fortress, 1975.

Ellingworth, Paul, and Howard A. Hatton. *Paul's First Letter to the Corinthians.* UBS Handbook Series. New York: United Bible Societies, 1994.

Evans, Ernest. *The Epistles of Paul the Apostle to the Corinthians.* The Clarendon Bible. Oxford: Clarendon Press, 1930.

Fascher, Erich. *Der erste Brief des Paulus an die Korinther, 1: Einführung und Auslegung der Kapitel 1–7.* ThHKNT 7/1. Berlin: Evangelische Verlagsanstalt, 1975.

Fee, Gordon D. *The First Epistle to the Corinthians.* NICNT. Grand Rapids: Eerdmans, 1987.

Grosheide, Frederik Willem. *Commentary on the First Epistle to the Corinthians.* NIC. Grand Rapids: Eerdmans, 1953.

Harrisville, Roy A. *I Corinthians.* ACNT. Minneapolis: Augsburg, 1987.

Hays, Richard B. *First Corinthians.* Interpretation. Louisville: John Knox, 1997.

Heinrici, Carl Friedrich Georg. *Der erste Brief an die Korinther.* KEK 5. 8th ed. Göttingen: Vandenhoeck & Ruprecht, 1896.

Héring, Jean. *La première épître de Saint Paul aux Corinthiens.* Commentaire du Nouveau Testament 7. 2nd. rev. ed. Neuchâtel: Delachaux & Niestlé, 1959. ET: *The First Epistle of St. Paul to the Corinthians.* Translated by A. W. Heathcote and P. J. Allcock. London: Epworth, 1962.

Kremer, Jacob. *Der Erste Brief an die Korinther.* RNT 7. Regensburg: Pustet, 1997.

Lambrecht, Jan. *1 Korintiërs. Belichting van het Bijbelboek.* 's-Hertogenbosch: Katholieke Bijbelstichtingl Bruges: Tabor, 1997.

Lang, Friedrich. *Die Briefe an die Korinther.* NTD 7. Göttingen: Vandenhoeck & Ruprecht, 1994.

Lietzmann, Hans. *An die Korinther I/II.* HNT 9. 4th. ed. Tübingen: J. C. B. Mohr, 1949.

Merklein, Helmut. *Der erste Brief an die Korinther. Kapitel 1–4.* ÖTKNT 7/1. Gütersloh: Gerd Mohn, 1992.

Meyer, Heinrich August Wilhelm. *Kommentar über den ersten Brief an die Korinther.* KEK 5. 5th ed Göttingen, Vandenhoeck & Ruprecht, 1870. ET: *Critical and Exegetical Handbook to the Epistles to the Corinthians.* 2 vols. Edinburgh: T & T Clark, 1883–1884.

Moffatt, James. *The First Epistle of Paul to the Corinthians.* MNTC. New York: Harper, 1938.

Morris, Leon. *The First Epistle of Paul to the Corinthians.* Tyndale New Testament Commentaries. 2nd ed. Leicester: Intervarsity Press; Grand Rapids: Eerdmans, 1985.

Murphy-O'Connor, Jerome. *1 Corinthians.* NTMes 10. Wilmington, Del.: Michael Glazier, 1979.

Orr, William F., and James A. Walther. *I Corinthians.* AB 32. Garden City, N.Y.: Doubleday, 1976.

Robertson, Archibald, and Alfred Plummer. *The First Epistle of St Paul to the Corinthians.* ICC. 2nd ed. Edinburgh: T & T Clark, 1958.

Ruef, John S. *Paul's First Letter to Corinth.* PNTC. Baltimore: Penguin, 1971.

Schrage, Wolfgang. *Der Erste Brief an die Korinther.* EKKNT 7/1: 1 Kor 1,1–6,11; 7/2: 1 Kor 6,12–11,16. Neukirchen-Vluyn: Neukirchener Verlag, 1991–1995.

Senft, Christophe. *La première Épître de Saint-Paul aux Corinthiens.* Commentaire du Nouveau Testament, 2nd ser. 7. Neuchâtel: Delachaux & Niestlé, 1979; 2nd corrected and augmented ed. Geneva: Labor et Fides, 1990.

Talbert, Charles H. *Reading Corinthians: A Literary and Theological Commentary on 1 and 2 Corinthians.* New York: Crossroad, 1989.

Thrall, Margaret E. *I and II Corinthians.* The Cambridge Commentary on the New English Bible. Cambridge: Cambridge University Press, 1965.

Watson, Nigel M. *The First Epistle to the Corinthians.* London: Epworth, 1992.

Weiss, Johannes. *Der erste Korintherbrief.* KEK 9. Göttingen: Vandenhoeck & Ruprecht, 1910.

Witherington, Ben III. *Conflict & Community in Corinth: A Socio-Rhetorical Commentary on 1 and 2 Corinthians.* Grand Rapids: Eerdmans, 1995.

Wendland, Heinz-Dietrich. *Die Briefe an die Korinther.* NTD 7. 12th ed., revised and expanded, Göttingen: Vandenhoeck & Ruprecht, 1968.

Wolff, Christian. *Der erste Brief des Paulus an die Korinther, 2: Auslegung der Kapitel 8–16.* ThHKNT 7/2. Berlin: Evangelische Verlagsanstalt, 1982.

TRANSLATION, INTERPRETATION, NOTES

INTRODUCTION (1:1-9)

A. EPISTOLARY OPENING (1:1-3)

1. Paul, called apostle of Christ Jesus through the will of God, and brother Sosthenes 2. to the church of God that is at Corinth, those made holy in Christ Jesus, called the holy ones, together with all those in every place who invoke the name of our Lord Jesus Christ, that is, their Lord and ours. 3. To you be grace and peace from God our Father and the Lord Jesus Christ.

Although many scrolls containing the papyrus letters of the Hellenistic world had an external address, it was customary for Hellenistic letters to begin with a simple but formal address such as "Apollonius to Serapion, greetings" or "Claudius Lysias to his Excellency the governor Felix, greetings" (Acts 23:26). Essentially the salutation of Paul's first letter to the Corinthians is similar to the epistolary greeting of the typical Hellenistic letter with its three parts: the identification of the sender, the identification of the addressee, and a greeting.

Epistolary Function. As the philosopher Epictetus and others had done before him, Paul has considerably expanded upon and modified the standard greeting, making it his personal formula of address. Each of his extant letters has an appropriate formula of address, but the salutation of his letter to the Corinthians is the most lavish among the letters written by Paul to communities he had personally evangelized. The salutation of the letter to the Romans is longer than is the salutation of this letter to the Corinthians, but that letter was intended for a community Paul had not founded and of which he had not had a personal experience at the time of writing.

41

Hellenistic letters typically began with the name of the sender. It was rare but not unknown (six instances in the 645 papyrus letters studied by Richards, *The Secretary in the Letters of Paul* 47 n. 138) for Hellenistic letters to join to the name of the principal author the name of another person or persons. Those cited in the salutation alongside the principal author generally had a specific relationship with the recipients of the letter. Cicero, who wrote letters in Latin about a century before Paul wrote in Greek, occasionally mentioned his son Marcus in the greeting of letters to members of his family and his friends (*Letters to his Friends* 14.14, 18; 16.1, 3, 4, 5, 6). Except in the letter to the Romans Paul associates others with himself in the sending of his letters. Sosthenes is Paul's associate in the greetings of this letter; Timothy is his associate in the salutation of the second canonical letter to the Corinthians. Mentioned in the salutation but in no other place in the letter, Sosthenes must have been someone with whom the community at Corinth was familiar. Neither this letter nor the account in Acts 18:17 suggests that Sosthenes had a role in the evangelization of Corinth. That he is mentioned in the salutation is an indication that he was with Paul in Ephesus when the letter was written, but the letter gives no further indication that Sosthenes was a preacher of the gospel.

That the letter is composed, for the most part, in the first person singular suggests that Sosthenes was not involved in the composition of the letter but that Paul mentions him in the opening salutation simply because of his presence in Ephesus and his significance for the community at Corinth. The singular is used eighty-six times, the plural only fifty-four times and most of these (thirty-three cases) are instances in which the first person plural refers to the entire body of Christians, as in the confessional expression "our Lord Jesus Christ." Michael Prior has suggested that Sosthenes may have served as Paul's scribe in writing the letter (*Paul the Letter-Writer* [JSNT.S 23; Sheffield: JSOT, 1989] 39–42), but extant Hellenistic correspondence does not in any way suggest that scribes would insert their names in the epistolary greeting (cf. Rom 16:22). Jerome Murphy-O'Connor ("Co-authorship"), however, opines that the plural verbs in 1:18-31 and 2:6-16—two passages that are followed immediately by an emphatic *kagō*, "I myself"—may indicate that Sosthenes had a greater contribution to make in the formulation of 1 Corinthians than is generally assumed. The emphatic *kagō*, he argues, indicates Paul's impatient desire to state his own position clearly.

The simplest of the Hellenistic papyrus letters begin only with the name of the sender. In the salutation of his first letter, that to the Thessalonians, Paul associated Silvanus and Timothy with himself. All three are cited only by name in the salutation of the letter. In his later letters Paul follows the Hellenistic custom of adding an *intitulatio*, a characteristic epithet, to his name. The *intitulatio* is akin to the signature block of a modern letter, which identifies a title of the person who is writing and suggests the capacity in which the person is writing the letter, that is, the quality of the presence he or she wants to convey to the addressee. Most commonly (cf. Rom 1:1; 2 Cor 1:1; Gal 1:1) Paul designates himself as an apostle, as he does here.

One of the principal functions of a Hellenistic letter was that of *parousia*. The letter was the way by which the letter writer could make him- or herself present to those to whom he or she was writing. The *intitulatio* defines the modality of this presence. The *intitulatio* Paul has chosen for himself is that of apostle. It is in his capacity as an apostle that Paul writes as he does. His letter is not just a substitute for his personal presence nor is it merely a substitute for his presence as a fellow Christian. It is a substitute for his apostolic presence. Paul's letter can therefore be appropriately called an "apostolic letter."

In his epistolary salutations Paul customarily adds an *intitulatio* to the names of those he cites as co-greeters. In his letter to the Philippians Paul identifies himself and Timothy as "servants of Christ Jesus" (Phil 1:1). In 1 Corinthians Sosthenes is identified simply as "brother," the designation by which Timothy is identified in the salutation of Paul's second letter to the Corinthians and his letter to Philemon (2 Cor 1:1; Phlm 1).

The second element in the salutation of the Hellenistic letter is the *adscriptio*, the identification of the one to whom the letter is being sent. Typically letters were sent to individuals cited by name in the epistolary address. In some instances a noun identifies the relationship between the sender and the addressee ("Hilarion to his sister Alis"). Sometimes the relationship is further specified by means of an adjective appended to the name of the addressee. Each of Paul's extant letters (Romans, 1–2 Corinthians, Galatians, Philippians, 1 Thessalonians, Philemon) has been sent to a group of people. Paul characterizes those to whom he is writing as a "gathering" (*ekklēsia*). This group seems to have come together for the reading of the letter.

The designation of the recipients of the letter as a "church" (*ekklēsia*) indicates that the letter is, from the outset, a church or ecclesial letter. Pseudo-Demetrius, one of the most important classical epistolary theorists (ca. 2nd c. B.C.E.–3rd c. C.E.), identified twenty-one epistolary genres (*typoi epistolikoi*), the first of which was the friendly letter (*typos philikos*). Paul created a new epistolary genre, the ecclesial letter, characterized by what has been called "church rhetoric" (Olbricht, "Aristotelian Rhetorical Analysis," 226). His first letter to the Corinthians clearly belongs to this new genre.

Paul commonly identifies those to whom he is writing by mentioning the place where they gathered. This letter is addressed to a gathering in the city of Corinth. Corinth was a cosmopolitan trade center located at the intersection of the major trade route between East and West and a trade route that extended from mainland Greece to the Peloponnesian peninsula in the south. It was situated on the Isthmus of Corinth where it controlled the port of Lechaion on the Gulf of Corinth to the west and the port of Cenchreae (Rom 16:1) on the Saronic Gulf to the east. At the time of Paul's letter Corinth was also the capital of the Roman province of Achaia. Making use of the imperial trade routes, Paul had visited Corinth during one of his missionary journeys (see Acts 18:1-18). In place of an *intitulatio* Paul offers a dense description of the group to whom he is sending the letter. The characterization of the community is made in theological rather than in sociological terms.

The Hellenistic letter always begins with the identification of the sender and the intended recipient of the letter. This is usually followed by a brief greeting, typically *chairein* in Greek or *salus* in Latin, the *salutatio*. The greeting is absent from some extant Hellenistic letters and abbreviated in others (*cha* or *s*; cf. P.Oslo Inv 1460; Cicero, *Letters to his Friends* 7.14-15), but it is as much a part of ancient letter writing as is the complimentary close, a feature of contemporary letter writing. None of Paul's extant letters omits the greeting, not even the letter to the Galatians in which Paul's negative feelings are so apparent. Paul's greeting is not the conventional *chairein* but an expanded formula that has a liturgical ring, "To you be grace and peace from God our Father and the Lord Jesus Christ." In Greek the beginning of Paul's greeting, *charis* ("grace") was assonant with the familiar *chairein* of the Hellenistic letter. White ("Apostolic Letter Tradition," 437) notes that the more simple form of Paul's greeting, found in 1 Thess 1:1, is akin to the opening blessing in some Near Eastern letters and is roughly equivalent to the health wish of the Hellenistic papyri letters.

Paul and Sosthenes. The *intitulatio* describes Paul as one who is called an apostle of Jesus Christ through the will of God. It identifies Paul as the plenipotentiary envoy of Jesus Christ, appointed to this role according to the very will of God. Paul is obviously a person of authority who ought to be accepted as such by the Corinthian community to which he is writing. Paul returns to the theme of the apostolate in several passages of his letter. The apostolate is the first (*prōton*) among the gifts the Spirit has given to the Church (12:28, cf. v. 29). Using the term *apostolos*, Paul reflects on what it means for him to be an apostle in 9:1-2 and 15:1-11. The letter has several additional passages in which Paul offers extended reflection on the fashion in which he conducted his apostolate.

By identifying himself as he does Paul shows that he considers his letter to the Corinthians to be something other than a friendly letter. His writing to the Corinthians is, in fact, an exercise, albeit from a distance, of the apostolate to which he had been called by God. Paul admits that he was unworthy to have been called an apostle, but he has, nonetheless, been called apostle (15:9). The mention of Paul's calling as an apostle in the salutation of the letter anticipates one of the major themes of the letter, namely, that Christians as individuals and as a community have been called. They should be faithful to the calling that is theirs (1:9, 24, 26; 7:15, 17, 18, 20, 21, 22, 24; 15:9). This theme appears in v. 2 when Paul identifies the recipients of his letter as those who are called holy. As Paul fulfills his vocation by the very writing of his letter, so they are challenged to fulfill their vocation by living as God's holy people.

"Brother" *(ho adelphos)* is the *intitulatio* Paul ascribes to Sosthenes. By means of this epithet Sosthenes is identified as Paul's fellow Christian. With the *intitulatio* Paul has done more than merely identify Sosthenes for the benefit of his addressees. He has also introduced kinship language, the language of belonging, into the letter from its outset. Use of kinship language occurs frequently throughout the letter, most commonly when Paul addresses the members of the community as "brothers and sisters." He does this more often in 1 Corinthians than in any of his other letters: some twenty-one times in all, first in 1:10 and finally at the very end of the letter in 16:20. Paul's use of kinship language emphasizes the bonds that bind Christians to one another as members of the same family. The language is particularly appropriate to a community that is divided (1:10-11). Paul makes effective use of family and household language throughout the letter, especially when he deals with the scandal of a Christian bringing a fellow Christian before the secular judiciary (ch. 6); with sexual and family issues (ch. 7); and with table fellowship, the issue of food that has been offered to idols as well as behavior that is appropriate for the community when it gathers to celebrate the Eucharist (chs. 8, 10, 11).

The Recipients: The Church at Corinth. Paul's letter is addressed to the church of God at Corinth. It seems to have been at least his second letter to this community (see 5:9, 11). The way Paul addresses those to whom he writes evokes some of the themes he will develop later in the letter. A first theme is that the community has been assembled by God and belongs to God. God took the initiative in calling the Corinthians together as church, just as God had taken the initiative in naming Paul an apostle. The idea that the church at Corinth belongs to God is immediately expanded and clarified as Paul writes about the Corinthians being sanctified in Christ Jesus and their being God's holy people. Paul's words about the Corinthians being holy are in the plural number; his description of the Corinthians as the church of God is in the singular. This juxtaposition of singular and plural anticipates Paul's treatment of the issues at hand, specifically that of the relationship of the several members of the community to the one community. The relationship between the one and the many is treated negatively in 5:1-13, where the holiness of the community is at issue and provides a warrant for the excommunication of a deviant member. The relationship between the one and the many is treated positively in ch. 12, where Paul speaks of individual spiritual gifts and the unity of the body of Christ.

The language Paul uses to describe the community at Corinth, "being sanctified" and "holy," is biblical. It is not typical of the jargon found in Hellenistic letters. To be holy is to be set apart from the profane so as to be in the service of the living God. Both terms belong to the semantic domain of the cult but there is a difference between them. The perfect passive participle *hēgiasmenois*, "being sanctified," suggests an action in the past, with Christ Jesus as the agent and with a continuing effect in the present. The past event is the baptism of the Corinthian Christians. The adjective *hagiois*, "holy," indicates the result of the process of sanctification. The process itself is indicated by means of the participle. Because they have been sanctified in Christ Jesus, God, as it were, has pronounced (*klētois*, "called") them holy, that is, God's very own.

Having entered into the linguistic register of the cult in his formula of address, Paul will devote a major portion of his letter to issues that pertain to the cultic activity of the Christians of Corinth (chs. 8–14). "The church of God" is a biblical expression, principally used of Israel at the time of the Exodus. Paul writes about the experience of Israel in the desert in 10:1-13, noting that the biblical tale had been written down for our instruction (10:11). Paul talks about the church of God in 11:17-22, a passage in which he calls the Corinthians to reflect on what it means for them to assemble as a church (11:18). That Paul persecuted the church of God underscores his own unworthiness to be called as an apostle (15:9; cf. Gal 1:13). The description of the group as "the church of God" (1:2; 10:32; 11:16, 22; 15:9) highlights the assembly as a gathering. It places the existential gathering at Corinth within the context of the history of salvation of Israel. It underscores the fact that the assembly at Corinth belongs to God and is therefore as subservient to God as is Paul, who is what he is as apostle because of God's will. Finally, it reinforces the notion that this is an assembly that is and is called to be holy, as God's own people.

The Christian assembly at Corinth does not exist in isolation; that it is not a solitary entity is suggested by Paul's describing it as the church that is at Corinth. The Corinthian church's solidarity with other churches becomes an explicit theme when Paul describes those to whom he was writing as "together with all those in every place who invoke the name of our Lord Jesus Christ, that is, their Lord and ours." The double use of the universal, "with all *(pasin)* . . . in every place *(panti topǭ)*," and the formal explanation of "ours," that is, "theirs and ours," bespeak the Corinthians' relationship with other Christian communities. This outreach foreshadows Paul's use of the ecclesiastical argument in his exhortation to the community (see 4:17; 7:17; 11:16; 14:33; 16:1; cf. 16:19).

"The name of our Lord Jesus Christ" will also be an important feature of Paul's argument. The phrase occurs four times in the letter, in the salutation and then in 1:10; 5:4, and 6:11. Paul will cite the name of the Lord Jesus Christ as the authority on the basis of which he is making the appeal to follow when he formulates his proposition in 1:10. It is in the name of the Lord Jesus Christ that judgment is pronounced (5:4). Then, in 6:11, Paul reminds the Corinthians that even though they had been sinners and thereby excluded from the kingdom of God, now they have been redeemed, made holy, and justified in the name of the Lord Jesus Christ.

The phrase "those in every place who invoke the name of our Lord Jesus Christ," continues Paul's appropriation of biblical motifs to describe the Corinthian community. "The name of the Lord" occurs more than a thousand times in the Hebrew Scriptures. In the biblical tradition there is a close connection between the name and the person, so much so that the name was almost a manifestation or representation of the person, an icon. The name of someone is almost tantamount to the person himself or herself. To know the name of someone is to know the person. To know the name of God is to know God insofar as God has revealed himself. To know the name of God is to have had an experience of God. Early Christians applied various biblical passages that spoke of the Lord (*Kyrios*) to Jesus who had become Lord in virtue of his being raised from the dead. The phrase that Paul has appropriated for the address of his letter is one in which the biblical phrase "name of the Lord" has been christianized with the confession that Jesus is Lord. "To invoke the name of our Lord Jesus Christ" is not to call upon Jesus in prayer. Paul's prayers are addressed to God (note the report of Paul's prayer of thanksgiving in 1:4). To invoke the name of the Lord Jesus Christ is to confess Jesus as Lord. Those who invoke the name of the Lord Jesus Christ are Christians.

The Salutation: Grace to You and Peace. In the typical Hellenistic letter a brief greeting, usually, *chairein,* "greetings" (cf. Acts 15:23; Jas 1:1) followed the identification of sender and receiver. Paul's own greetings are somewhat longer and very Christian, "to you be grace and peace from God our Father and the Lord Jesus Christ." This formula of greetings is found in all Paul's letters (Rom 1:7, Gal 1:3; Phil 1:2; 2 Cor 1:2; Phlm 3; cf. 2 Thess 1:2; Col 1:2; Eph 1:2; Rev 1:4), with the exception of his earliest letter, 1 Thessalonians, which has a simple "grace to you and peace." The formula of greeting may have been of Pauline coinage, perhaps reflecting the influence of the Aaronic blessing (Num 6:24-26). It is a prayer that the fullness of God's blessing descend on the community at Corinth. "Grace" (*charis*) represents God's covenantal love (*ḥēn*); "peace" (*eirēnē*) represents the fullness of God's benefaction to God's people, the biblical *šālôm*.

Paul identifies a double source of this fullness of grace and peace, God the Father and the Lord Jesus Christ. For Paul, God (*theos*) is always the God of the biblical tradition. God has manifested himself as Father insofar as he has raised Jesus from the dead (Rom 1:4; cf. Rom 15:6; 2 Cor 1:3). Paul typically writes about God as Father in a context that calls forth mention of Jesus. There is a close relationship between the designation of God as Father and Jesus as Lord. Almost all of the references to God the Father and to Jesus are found in the salutations of his letters and doxological contexts (Rom 6:4; 8:15; 15:6; Gal 1:3-4; 4:6; Phil 2:11; 4:20; 1 Thess 3:11, 13). In Rom 8:15, Paul explains how God, who is Father of our Lord Jesus Christ, is also our Father.

In designating the Lord Jesus Christ as the correlative source of the fullness of grace and power, Paul has used a proper name, Jesus [= Joshua], and two titles, "Christ" and "Lord." The Christ title (*christos*) is a kind of substantivized verbal adjective, derived from the root *chri-*, to rub or anoint with oil. In form the Greek *christos* is similar to the Semitic "messiah," "the anointed one." The Christ title appears sixty-four times in Paul's first letter to the Corinthians. Most often it is used alone as a proper noun either with the article (15x) or without it (30x). At other times it is used in apposition to the name of Jesus, with or without the "Lord" title. The title of Lord is applied to Jesus sixty-six times in the letter, that is, with greater frequency than in any other of Paul's letters.

References to both Jesus Christ and God abound throughout the letter. The four references to Christ and three to God in the opening salutation give initial expression to a christological and theological frame of reference that will pervade the entire discourse and provide a thematic link between the salutation and the thanksgiving, with its six references to Christ and three to God.

Rhetorical Function. The epistolary opening and the closing epistolary conventions of Paul's letters enclose communications whose development may profitably be analyzed from the standpoint of Hellenistic rhetoric. Rhetorical analysis often leads commentators to conclude that Paul's letters are rhetorical compositions within an epistolary envelope, as it were. Paul's letters are addresses in the form of letters. This kind of observation is apropos in the analysis of 1 Corinthians. Its epistolary opening, salutation, and thanksgiving (1:1-9), and closing formulae (16:13-24), encompass a lengthy message (*homilia*) replete with the idiom and logic of Hellenistic rhetoric.

Less frequently is it observed that Paul's epistolary openings fulfill the functions of the prologue (*proemium*) and the rehearsal of facts (*diēgēsis*) of the typical rhetorical composition. One of the most important functions of the prologue and rehearsal is preparation for the argument that is to be developed. A good speaker is one who prepares the ground for what he or she intends to say later. The total composition is in mind as he or she begins to speak. Insofar as it identifies sender and receiver Paul's salutation has a precise epistolographic function. It has an important rhetorical function insofar as it foreshadows the argument Paul will develop in the course of a very long letter. That the salutation is a harbinger of things to come is clearly the case with the formal salutation of 1 Corinthians (1 Cor 1:1-3). Paul anticipates the line of thought he will pursue in the letter to follow.

The address of the letter succinctly describes what it means for the Corinthians to be assembled as a church. Much of Paul's ecclesiology, his understanding of church, is contained *in nuce* in v. 2. Paul describes the church as a gathering. He describes it in biblical terms as God's very own. He describes it as one and many. He describes it as a community that is related to other communities that similarly confess the name of the Lord Jesus Christ. This polyvalent description anticipates some of the major themes of the letter. What follows in the letter is Paul's challenge to the community to become what they already are.

In Hellenistic rhetoric the *proemium* establishes the moral authority of the rhetor. The address of a letter, especially when titles are used, identifies the capacity of the sender of the letter as well as his or her relationship to those who will receive it. The *intitulatio* Paul uses of himself is one that establishes his moral character and his authority vis-à-vis the Corinthians. From the outset he has established the *ethos* that will serve as a powerful argument in the communication to follow.

In deliberative rhetoric the argument from example *(paradeigma)* is particularly important. Paul will use this argument to good advantage in the letter. Among the examples he cites perhaps none is more important than the example of himself. In 13:1b-3 he offers himself as an example to be imitated by the Corinthians. In 4:16 and 11:1 he tells the Corinthians to follow his example. In setting himself up as an example to be followed he identifies himself as an apostle and cites the way in which he has conducted himself as an apostle. He is faithful to his calling as apostle (1:1). By establishing his moral character and authority from the outset of the letter he has projected an *ethos* that will serve as a powerful rhetorical argument in the appeal that is to come.

NOTES

1. *Paul:* It was typical of Hellenistic letters to begin with the name of the sender. Shorter letters, virtually only notes, were sometimes written on bits of leather or pieces of earthenware (ostraca); longer letters were written on papyrus or

parchment. When parchment letters were unrolled for reading the first word to appear was that of the sender. In Hellenistic letters it was rare for the name of the sender to appear in the letter after the opening salutation. In this regard Paul's first letter to the Corinthians is an oddity among Hellenistic letters— including Paul's own—in that his name is frequently reprised throughout the letter (1:12, 13; 3:4, 5, 22; 16:21). In Paul's other extant letters his name appears after the opening salutation only six times (2 Cor 10:1; Gal 5:2; 1 Thess 2:18; Phlm 9, 19).

In his letters Paul always identified himself as "Paul," never by the Jewish name "Saul," the name of the great king of the tribe of Benjamin, the tribe to which he belonged (Phil 3:5). Both names appear in the Acts of the Apostles but there is no record either in Acts or in the letters that Paul's name was changed as a result of some christophany or theophany. It is likely that Paul, like many Hellenistic Jews, used two names with similar sounds, one in Jewish circles, the other in Hellenistic circles. The name Paul *(Paulos)* is the Greek form of *Paulus,* a common Roman name used especially by members of the Aemilian clan.

called: In Hellenistic letters the sender frequently identified himself by means of one or another title. Paul begins this letter by identifying himself as an apostle. He provides legitimacy to the title by indicating that he had been named to the function of apostle *(klētos apostolos).* In 1 Corinthians the verbal adjective "called" *(klētos)* is found only in 1:1, 2, 24. God does the calling (see 7:15, 17, and the divine passives in 1:9; 7:18, 20, 21, 22, 24; 15:9). One who has been called by God really is what God calls the person to be (cf. Matt 5:9). The juxtaposition of Paul's having been called (v. 1) with the Corinthians having been called (v. 2) identifies a similarity between them. Implicitly it provides a challenge to the Corinthians. In 1 Corinthians Paul uses the verb "to call" *(kaleō)* and its cognates, the word group to which *klētos* belongs, with unusual frequency: the verb twelve times (1:9; 7:15, 17, 18[2x], 20, 21, 22[2x], 24; 10:27; 15:9; fifteen times in the other six letters); the noun twice (1:26; 7:20; twice elsewhere); the verbal adjective three times (1:1, 2, 24; four times elsewhere). A comparable intensity of usage of this word group appears only in Paul's letter to the Romans.

apostle of Christ Jesus: The "title" Paul has chosen for himself is that of "apostle of Christ Jesus." This is the first letter in which he does so. Paul also identifies himself as an apostle in the salutations of his letters to the Romans, Galatians, and his second letter to the Corinthians (cf. Eph 1:1; Col 1:1; 1 Tim 1:1; 2 Tim 1:1; Titus 1:1). In other letters Paul identifies himself as a servant of Jesus Christ (Phil 1:1) or a prisoner of Jesus Christ (Phlm 1). The title Paul gives to himself describes a function in the early Christian church, one similar to the Jewish institution of the *šālîaḥ,* an emissary (cf. 9:2) designated by a congregation for a particular purpose. Such emissaries acted on behalf of and with the authority of those who sent them on their way. The author of Luke-Acts calls Paul and Barnabas apostles (Acts 14:14) but otherwise reserves the nomenclature for the group of twelve, whose characteristics are described in Acts 1:21-22. Paul uses the term "apostle" in a broader sense (see 15:5, 7; Rom

16:7; 2 Cor 8:23 [11:13]; Phil 2:25; 1 Thess 2:6). The apostle is one who has been sent on a mission. In v. 17 Paul explains that he was sent to preach the gospel.

through the will of God: Paul did not consider his apostolate to have resulted from a commissioning by some human agency. He was commissioned by God and is an envoy of Jesus Christ (15:8-10; Rom 1:1; Gal 1:1). It is from God and his Christ that Paul's authority is derived. That it was God's will that established Paul as an apostle made an impression on later generations of his disciples (see 2 Tim 1:1; cf. 1 Tim 1:1).

and brother Sosthenes: In the salutation Paul did not include all those with him in Ephesus who were known to the Corinthians (see 16:19). He does, however, mention Sosthenes, as he mentioned Silvanus and Timothy in 1 Thessalonians and will mention Timothy in 2 Corinthians, Philippians, and Philemon. It is likely, but not altogether certain, that the Sosthenes of Acts 18:17 is the individual who is cited in Paul's salutation. Sosthenes, a ruler of the synagogue *(archisynagōgos),* was seized and beaten during the disturbance that followed Gallio's transfer of jurisdiction in the case of Paul, who had been brought before him. As the *archisynagōgos* Sosthenes was probably a colleague of Crispus (1 Cor 1:14; cf. Acts 18:8).

Sosthenes is identified as a "brother" *(adelphos;* cf. 2 Cor 1:1; Phlm 1; Col 1:1). At a time when the adjective "Christian" *(Christianos)* had not yet come into common use (cf. Acts 11:26), "brother" had the connotation of fellow Christian. Sosthenes and Apollos (16:12) are the only "brothers" identified by name in 1 Corinthians. Paul, however, commonly uses the term in the vocative plural when addressing the community (1:10, 11, 26; 2:1; 3:1; 4:6; 7:24, 29; 10:1; 11:33; 12:1; 14:6, 20, 26, 39; 15:1, 31, 50, 58; 16:15, 20). He often uses the term in the singular to identify a Christian in some of his case studies (5:11; 6:5, 6; 7:12, 14, 15; 8:11, 13 [twice]); cf. 7:15; 9:5 [feminine singular]; 6:8; 8:12; 15:6 [masculine plural]). Members of the Jewish synagogue were similarly called brothers by their confreres. Paul's use of kinship language highlights the bonds with which Christians were united to one another. The absence of the qualifying pronoun "my" *(mou;* cf. 2 Cor 1:1; Phlm 1) implies that Sosthenes is bound by kinship ties not only to Paul but also to the Corinthians, all of whom are members of a single family unit. The sociological implications of Paul's use of kinship language should not be overlooked. Christians gathered in the home of one of their number (see 16:19). In this setting kinship language was very much "at home."

2. *to the church of God:* The church *(ekklēsia),* literally, "the assembly," is a term Paul always uses to describe a local gathering of Christians (see 11:18). In the golden days of Athens *"ekklēsia"* was used of the assembly of citizens who gathered to make civic decisions. It was used by Paul in the salutations of all his letters, with the exception of his letter to the holy ones at Rome (Rom 1:7) whose assembly Paul had not yet encountered. It evokes the idea of a gathering of people in a free city, assembled as God's holy people.

Paul describes the assembly at Corinth as "the church of God" (see 10:32; 11:22; 15:9; 2 Cor 1:1; Gal 1:13; cf. the "churches of God" in 11:16; 1 Thess 2:14). His expression evokes the biblical description of Israel as the assembly *(qāhāl/*

ekklēsia; see Deut 4:10; Judg 20:2; 1 Kings 8:14; Ezra 2:64; etc.). *"Qěhal-yhwh/Hē ekklēsia tou Kyriou"* is an epithet that evokes the memory of the nation gathered together in the wilderness during the time of the Exodus, Israel's preeminent experience of redemption and salvation (Deut 23:1-8; Judg 20:2, etc.). Deuteronomy 32 in particular recalls the holiness of the assembly.

Deuteronomy speaks of the "day of the assembly" *hē hēmera tēs ekklēsias* (LXX, Deut 4:10; 9:10; 18:16). The assembly is an event that takes place in time and space. The salutations of Paul's letters identify the political space, the city or region in which the Christian gathering takes place, but not the architectural space, that is, the specific venue of the gathering. Early Christian gatherings were held in the homes of the most prominent Christians in the community (see 1 Cor 16:19; Rom 16:23; Phlm 2). Since Christians gathered not in palaces but in the homes of ordinary citizens, an early Christian "church" could not have consisted of a very large number of people. Jerome Murphy-O'Connor suggests that a reasonable figure would probably be between thirty and forty (*St. Paul's Corinth* 156).

that is at Corinth: Only in the Corinthian correspondence (2 Cor 1:1; cf. Acts 13:1) does Paul use a participial clause to identify the recipients of his letter as an assembly that is located in a given city. The distinctive address suggests that the participial form of the verb "to be" *(ousē)* is not merely a copulative; it is a statement of existence as such. The church of God actually exists in Corinth. Paul's use of the singular noun with the participle is striking. The "church at Corinth" seems to have consisted of several smaller groups that occasionally came together (see 11:17-20, 33). Throughout his letter Paul will urge the unity of the church. Corinth was a major city, a crossroads of the ancient world (see Strabo, *Geography* 8.6.2). It was located at the intersection of the great trade route from the East to Rome and the trade route that linked Macedonia to the Peloponnese. Following the East-West trade route in his missionary voyages, Paul had preached the gospel in Corinth (15:1-2) before he wrote this letter. On Paul's evangelization of Corinth see Acts 18:1-17 and pp. 23–24.

those made holy in Christ Jesus, called the holy ones: See Rom 1:7. As Paul has been named an apostle of Christ Jesus by the will of God, so the Corinthians have been designated as the holy ones, presumably by the will of the same God. "Holy" characterizes the community as such and evokes the early Christian community in Jerusalem. Rather than being ethical in its emphasis, the term has cultic or political connotations. It describes the community insofar as it belongs to the Holy One, God. In Paul's biblical tradition the epithet "holy" was especially used of Israel (Lev 11:44; 20:26), a people in a special covenanted relationship with YHWH, a nation set apart to be holy as YHWH was holy (Lev 19:2).

together with all those in every place: Some authors (e.g., Franz Schnider and Werner Stenger) consider this expansion of the addressees to be a post-Pauline addition to the letter, added to its original text when Paul's letters began to be collated into codices and circulated among the Christian churches. This idea goes back to Johannes Weiss (1910), who considered that 4:17, 7:17,

11:16 and 14:33, along with 1:2, beginning at "together" *(syn pasin . . .)* were added to provide a "catholic element" to the letter at the time when Paul's letters were gathered together as a collection for the churches. Second Peter 3:16 and 𝔓⁴⁶, a papyrus manuscript of Paul's letters dating from around 200 C.E. (see Jerome D. Quinn, "𝔓⁴⁶—the Pauline Canon?" *CBQ* 36 [1974] 379–385), attest to the existence of an early ecclesiastical collection of Paul's letters. There is, however, no manuscript evidence to support the suggestion of catholicizing interpolations into the text of Paul's letters. The phrase does, nonetheless, seem to be out of place in a letter that is clearly concerned with the problems of a specific local community. It may be that Paul intended to draw the Corinthians' attention to the example of other Christian congregations from the very beginning of his letter (see 4:17; 7:17; 11:16; 14:33; 16:1; cf. 16:19; 2 Cor 1:1). Werner Georg Kümmel opines that Paul's reference to "every place" is a customary expression that Paul has borrowed from the Jewish liturgical tradition.

who invoke the name of our Lord Jesus Christ, that is, their Lord and ours: Calling on the name of the Lord is a traditional biblical motif (e.g., Joel 2:32, cited by Paul in Rom 10:13; cf. Acts 2:21). Gordon J. Wenham (*Genesis 1–15*, 117) suggests that the theme of calling upon the name of the Lord was linked, in the biblical tradition, to the line of Seth (cf. Gen 4:26). It would thus have universal import since Seth was, through Noah, the common ancestor not only of the patriarchs who are said to have called on the name of the Lord (Gen 12:8; 13:4; 21:33; 26:25) but also of all postdiluvian humanity (Gen 5:1-32; Num 24:17). The biblical formula also occurs in Ps 99:6; 105:1; and Joel 2:32. Paul has added a precision—and a development—to the traditional motif. For Paul "the Lord" is the Lord Jesus Christ. Paul's description of Christians as those who call on the name of the Lord Jesus Christ may not only indicate what is specific to Christians, thereby distinguishing them from other groups, but may also characterize what Christians do when they come together as a worshiping assembly. *Epikaleō*, "invoke," suggests the invocation of the name of God. The verb is aptly used of all Christians who invoke the name of Jesus Christ as Lord. Manuel Guerra ("Los *'epikaloúmenoi'* de 1 Cor 1,2, directores y sacerdotes de la comunidad cristiana en Corinto," *Scripta Theologica* 17 [1985] 11–72) takes "place" *(topō)* to be an indication of a ministerial position and interprets Paul's phrase as if it were a reference to a cadre of cultic leadership at Corinth, but there is no need to give a restrictive, cultic sense to the verb. Paul is writing generally about Christians who live in places other than Corinth.

Throughout Paul's correspondence the interplay of personal pronouns is very important. Lest there be any misunderstanding of what he means by *"our* Lord Jesus Christ" Paul indicates that "our" refers not only to those who stand with Paul in the disputed Corinthian situation but to all who acknowledge Jesus Christ as their Lord ("ours" [*hēmōn*] = "theirs and ours and yours" [*autōn kai hēmōn*]).

3. *To you be grace and peace from God our Father and the Lord Jesus Christ:* The formula is the standard salutation in Paul's letters (cf. Rom 1:7; 2 Cor 1:2; Phil

1:2; Phlm 3), but it is different from the typical Greco-Roman epistolary greeting, *chairein*, "rejoice" (cf. 2 Cor 13:11). Paul's formula identifies grace and peace as gifts from *(apo)* God our Father and the Lord Jesus Christ. "To you" is redundant with the identification of the designated recipients of the letter in v. 2. This redundancy and the solemnity of the formula have led several commentators to suggest that Paul's words of greeting are derived from a liturgical greeting (thus Ernst Lohmeyer, Béda Rigaux). If so they may have originated in a bicultural community. Grace *(charis)* has a sound similar to "greetings" *(chairein)* and peace *(eirēnē)* is the Greek equivalent of the typical Semitic greeting *(šālôm)*. Paul used a more simple form of his greeting, "grace and peace to you," in 1 Thessalonians. The fuller form, as here, subsequently became a standard epistolary greeting (cf. 1 Pet 1:2; 2 Pet 1:2; 2 John 3; Rev 1:4).

For Reference and Further Study

Collins, Raymond F. "Glimpses into Some Local Churches of New Testament Times," *LTP* 42 (1986) 291–316.

Klein, William W. "Paul's use of *Kalein:* A Proposal," *JETS* 27 (1984) 3–64.

Koester, Helmut. "I Thessalonians—Experiment in Christian Writing" in F. Forrester Church and Timothy George, eds., *Continuity and Discontinuity in Church History: Essays Presented to George Hunston Williams.* Studies in the History of Christian Thought 19. Leiden: Brill, 1979, 34–44.

Lieu, Judith M. "'Grace to You and Peace': The Apostolic Greeting," *BJRL* 68 (1985) 161–178.

Murphy-O'Connor, Jerome. "Co-Authorship in the Corinthian Correspondence," *RB* 100 (1993) 562–579.

Olbricht, Thomas H. "An Aristotelian Rhetorical Analysis of 1 Thessalonians" in David L. Balch, et al, eds., *Greeks, Romans and Christians: Essays in Honor of Abraham J. Malherbe.* Minneapolis: Fortress, 1990, 216–236.

Palliparambil, Jacob. "The Will of God in Paul: A Commitment to Man: An Exegetico-Theological Study of *'theo-thelema'* Vocabulary in the Writings of Paul." STD Dissertation, Gregorian University, Rome, 1986.

Steyn, Gert J. "Reflections on *to onoma tou kyriou* in 1 Corinthians," *CorC* 479–490.

Verhoef, Eduard. "The Senders of the Letters to the Corinthians and the Use of 'I' and 'We,'" *CorC* 417–425.

B. THANKSGIVING (1:4-9)

4. I always thank my God for you because of the grace of God given to you in Christ Jesus, 5. since you have been thoroughly enriched in him, in every word and in all knowledge, 6. insofar as the testimony to Christ was confirmed among you, 7. with the result that you are not lacking in any gift, you who are eagerly awaiting the revelation of our Lord Jesus Christ, 8. who will maintain you blameless until the end, on the day of our Lord Jesus Christ. 9. Faithful is God, by whom you have been called into the fellowship of his Son, Jesus Christ our Lord.

INTERPRETATION

The Epistolary Form and Function of the Thanksgiving Period. In Hellenistic letters it was customary for an expression of thanksgiving to the deity to follow after a health wish (cf. 3 John 2). For example, in the second century C.E. a young sailor wrote to his father, "Apion to his father and lord, Epimachos, very many greetings. Before all else I pray that you are well and that you may prosper in continual health together with my sister and her daughter and my brother. I give thanks to the lord Serapis because when I was endangered at sea, he rescued me immediately. When I arrived at Misenum I received three gold pieces from Caesar for traveling expenses . . ." (BGU 2.423). In some Hellenistic letters, particularly those that Heikki Koskenniemi has called "family letters," mention is made of a prayer of supplication, using a *proskynēma* ("making obeisance") formula. Dating from the same era (early second century C.E.) as Apion's letter is a letter that begins, "Claudius Terentianus to his lord and father, Claudius Tiberianus, very many greetings. Before all else I pray that you are well and prospering, which is my desire. I myself am also well, making obeisance on your behalf *(poioumenos sou to proskynēma)* daily before the lord Serapis and the allied gods" (P.Michigan 8.476).

There is some formal similarity between Paul's expression of thanksgiving and that of the young recruit who had been sent abroad. Apion wrote, "I give thanks to the lord Serapis because . . ." *(tǭ kyriǭ Serapidi hoti . . .)*. Paul shares with Apion the use of the verb *eucharistō*, a reference to the deity, and a *hoti* clause that indicates the reasons for thanksgiving. Whereas Apion addressed his thanksgiving to Serapis, one of the gods of his native Egypt, Paul's thanksgiving is addressed to God, that is, God the Father, whom he identifies as *theos* (see vv. 1, 3). This is customary in the Pauline correspondence. All of his prayer formularies and the reports on his prayers of thanksgiving are addressed to God the Father.

Apion's personal relationship with the divine Serapis is based on their common tie to Egypt and the benefaction Serapis has bestowed on Apion. Paul expresses his personal relationship with God by means of the personal pronoun *(mou)*, as is his custom (see Rom 1:8; Phil 1:3; Phlm 4). The reader of the letter already knows that Paul has a personal relationship with God. It was God who had called Paul as an apostle of Christ Jesus (1:1). Paul had, moreover, invoked the blessing of "God, our Father," on the community of Corinth (1:3). His God is also their God. They share a single and common Father. Paul's prayer of thanksgiving is implicitly addressed to God our Father.

In the report on his prayer of thanksgiving Paul employs the temporal adverb "always" *(pantote)*. Characteristic of Paul's thanksgiving periods (Rom 1:10; Phil 1:4; 1 Thess 1:2; Phlm 4), "always" is not usually found in the expressions of thanksgiving to the gods found in Hellenistic letters (see, however, White, *Letters* 102). A half a century or so after Paul wrote to the Corinthians a pair of early second century letters addressed to Tiberianus, a military veteran, one from his son Terentianus, the other from Papirius Apollinarius, an acquaintance of his son, mention, nonetheless, that "daily" *(kath' hekastēn hēmeran)* obeisance is being offered to Serapis on behalf of Tiberianus (White, *Letters*, 109–110). As the writers to Tiberianus would do, Paul explicitly mentions that he offered thanks on behalf of the Corinthians *(peri hymōn;* cf. Rom 1:8; Phil 1:4; 1 Thess 1:2).

In Hellenistic letters a *hoti* clause is occasionally used to indicate the reason for offering thanks, as it was in Apion's letter to his father. Paul employs this epistolary convention to express the reason for his gratitude. In other letters he cites the specific reasons for his gratitude by means of participial clauses (see Phil 1:3-11; 1 Thess 1:2-10; Phlm 4-7). Paul's thanksgiving period is different from those of other extant Hellenistic letters. It is addressed to God rather than to a god. Paul gives thanks to God for the benefits that have been bestowed on those to whom he is writing rather than for the benefits he himself has received. Hellenistic letter writers did, nonetheless, occasionally give thanks on behalf of those to whom they were writing when they had received specific bits of good news about their correspondents. For example, Barkaios wrote to his brother Apollonios in 156 B.C.E., "We had great thanks for you *(charin megalēn eschēkamen;* note the plural, *eschēkamen)* when you reported to us about the wretches who had escaped from the prison. You made quite clear in addition that your brother Sarapion was mistreated by Harpaesis the guard. . . ." (White, *Letters*, 39). In the early second century C.E. a young soldier, Theonas, wrote to his mother, Tetheus, "My brother, Dionytas, brought the present to me and I received your letter. I give thanks [to the gods]. . . ." (White, *Letters*, 102).

In typical fashion Paul writes in 1:4 "I always thank my God . . . since . . ." *(eucharistō tō theō mou pantote . . . hoti . . .)*. Although Paul's language appears to be and in some respects is performative, his epistolary thanksgiving is actually a report on his prayer of thanksgiving. The language is performative insofar as the very expression of his thanks in a letter is an act of thanksgiving to God. Paul's words are, however, addressed to the Corinthians. Hence the reader is to understand that Paul is reporting on his giving thanks to God rather than taking the writing of the letter as an occasion to give thanks to God.

Paul's expression of thanksgiving is in the first person singular, present tense. For the apostle thanksgiving is an ongoing activity. Thanksgiving is more than an attitude. It is expressed in prayer, which invokes the name of God and includes intercession. Paul customarily cites the fact that his thanksgiving is expressed in prayer, using a participial phrase to do so (Rom 1:9-10; Phil 1:3-4; 1 Thess 1:2-3; Phlm 4; cf. Col 1:3). He does not do so in his first letter to the Corinthians, pressing on as he does to an encomium of the gifts that have been given to them.

The use of the temporal adverb *pantote,* "always" (see Rom 1:10; Phil 1:4; 1 Thess 1:2; Phlm 4; cf. Col 1:3; 2 Thess 1:3), accentuates the continuous nature of Paul's giving thanks to God on behalf of the Corinthians. The use of the adverb is, in fact, hyperbolic. Paul's meaning is that he often gives thanks to God for the Corinthians. When he prays he gives thanks for the Corinthians. As is his custom (see Rom 1:8; Phil 1:3; Phlm 4), Paul reports on his thanksgiving in the first person singular, but he does not use an emphatic *egō.* The singular distinguishes him from Sosthenes, who is not mentioned again in the letter. For the most part the remainder of the letter will be written in the first person singular.

Paul's thanksgivings are always addressed to God, whom Paul typically identifies in the thanksgiving as "my God" *(tō theō mou,* Rom 1:8; Phil 1:3; Phlm 4). "My" does not appear in some of the most important textual witnesses to 1:4 (ℵ, B, Ephraem), but it is a common feature of Paul's initial expressions of thanksgiving and is well attested by the manuscript tradition (𝔓⁶¹, A, C, D, Ψ, etc., and various Eastern Fathers). Its presence in 1 Corinthians is consistent with the emphasis on the particular relationship between Paul and God that characterizes the proem of Paul's letter. Paul's highlighting of his personal relationship to God is to be seen in the light of his immediately preceding description of God as "our Father." God is the common Father of all Christians, yet Paul has a particular relationship with the God who is Father of all.

Paul expresses his gratitude for the Corinthians to whom he is writing, "for you" *(peri hymōn).* A similar referential phrase is found in his letters to the Romans (with *peri*), Philippians (with *hyper*), Thessalonians (with *peri*) and in the deutero-Pauline letters to the Colossians and the

Thessalonians. In the authentic letters, but not in the pseudepigraphical correspondence, the personal pronoun is qualified by "all" (*pantōn;* Rom 1:8; Phil 1:4; 1 Thess 1:2). As there is no need to see in Paul's use of *pantōn* an indication that the community is divided and that Paul wants to assure all the members of the community that he is offering thanks on their behalf, so there is no need to see in the omission of *pantōn* the exclusion of any of the Corinthians from Paul's prayer of thanksgiving.

In comparison with extant Hellenistic letters Paul's description of the reason for his thanksgiving in v. 3-9 is unusually long. Grammatically his *hoti* clause is in apposition to a prepositional phrase *(epi tę chariti tou theou . . .)* that cites more succinctly the motivation of Paul's thanksgiving. This thanksgiving serves Paul's epistolary style well. It functions to provide a transition to the body of his letter. In this regard his thanksgiving is similar to the use of the disclosure formula found in many Hellenistic papyri (see note on 10:1 and Terence Y. Mullins, "Disclosure," referenced there).

The Rhetorical Function. Paul's epistolary thanksgivings always cite the result of God's activity among those to whom he is writing. Because Paul gives thanks to God for the gifts given to the community his expressions of thanksgiving function rhetorically as a kind of *captatio benevolentiae.* They capture the good will of the readers and are designed to make them more attentive to what will follow in the body of the letter. In this respect Paul's expressions of thanksgiving function in a way similar to the proemium of a Hellenistic speech whose purpose was to attract the interest and good will of the audience.

One of the features of Paul's discourse is his careful use of pronouns. First (vv. 7, 8, 9) and second person (vv. 4[2x], 6, 7, 8) plural pronouns run throughout the thanksgiving with which he begins his letter to the Corinthians. These pronouns define the epistolary stasis of his letter. "We" and "us" bespeak the relationship between Paul and the Corinthians and especially their common relationship with Jesus Christ. Pronouns in the second person describe the Corinthians' relationship to God in Christ. With a skillful use of pronouns Paul identifies the set of interlocking relationships that has been effected by the call of God. It may not be coincidental that in Paul's Greek the final word of the thanksgiving period is "our."

The thanksgiving period of 1 Corinthians continues along the lines of the salutation. Anticipating themes that Paul will develop in the body of his letter, the thanksgiving presents the church at Corinth as a richly endowed community. That God himself is the source of the community's giftedness is underscored in the verbs used by Paul: given (v. 4), enriched (v. 5), confirmed (v. 6), maintain (v. 8), called (v. 9). In alluding to the spiritual gifts treated at length in chs. 12–14 Paul makes reference to the gifts of knowledge and the word (1:5). These are not only spiritual gifts (knowledge: 12:8; 13:2, 8; 14:6; word: 12:8; 14:9, 19); they also give rise to pastoral concern (8:1, 7, 10, 11). With its reference to testimony to Christ the thanksgiving announces Paul's disquisition on the proclamation of the gospel (v. 6; cf. 1:18–4:21) and prepares for his further use of the language of the court (especially in 6:1-11). In 1:18 the disquisition on the gospel is topically introduced as "the word of the cross," a motif that harkens back to the Corinthians' being gifted in word (1:5). Paul's first rhetorical demonstration addresses an epistemological issue, the basis for real knowledge and wisdom. In subtle fashion the apostle contrasts the Corinthians' epistemological basis with the knowledge with which they have been gifted (1:5).

With references to the revelation of Jesus Christ (1:7; cf. 15:20-28, 50-58), the end (1:7; cf. 10:11; 15:24), and the day of the Lord (1:8; cf. 3:13; 4:3; 5:5) Paul's thanksgiving foreshadows motifs that will recur in the body of the letter. Paul's extended treatment on the resurrection of the dead (15:12-57) puts "the end" within the perspective of the eschatological kingdom of God (15:24), when victory will accrue to believers through the Lord Jesus Christ (15:57). The ejaculatory thanksgiving with which Paul concludes his disquisition on the resurrection of the dead (15:57) brings substantial closure to the body of the letter and forms a literary inclusion with Paul's thanksgiving period. The intervening text is so full of references to the final events (4:5; 7:31b; etc.) that an eschatological perspective pervades the entire letter. With its subtle advance announcement of the major themes to be treated Paul's epistolary thanksgiving appropriates much of the function of the summary rehearsal of facts (the *diēgēsis* or *narratio*) at the beginning of a Hellenistic rhetorical composition.

The Eschatological Conclusion. The apostle typically concludes his epistolary thanksgivings on an eschatological note (cf. Phil 1:10; 1 Thess 1:10; 2:12; 3:11-13; compare 2 Thess 1:6-10). The eschatological conclusion first appears in his letter to the Thessalonians, which features two eschatological discussions (4:13-18; 5:1-11) as Paul attempts to supply what was lacking in the community's faith. First Thessalonians has a very long thanksgiving period (1:2–2:12), but its eschatological conclusion is relatively brief (2:12; cf. 1 Thess 1:10). The letter to the Philippians has a thanksgiving period (Phil 1:3-11) that is longer than that of 1 Corinthians, but its eschatological finale consists of but a single statement (Phil 1:10b-11).

The eschatological conclusion of the thanksgiving period in 1 Corinthians is particularly long. This points to the importance of eschatological considerations in the various arguments Paul will develop in the letter to follow. From the very outset of the letter Paul has given expression to the eschatological situation of the Corinthians. By so doing he has provided a perspective in the light of which his remarks on sexuality (ch. 7), the spiritual gifts (chs. 12–14), and the resurrection are to be understood. Paul's protracted description of the eschatological condition of the Corinthians serves a critical function in his letter. It is in the light of a Christian eschatology that the Corinthian Christians must judge their present situation and the factors that cause division among them.

The eschatological conclusion consists of vv. 7b-9: an expression of expectation (vv. 7b-8) and a confession (v. 9). Both parts of the eschatological coda speak of the eschaton. They anticipate Paul's reflections on the resurrection of the dead in ch. 15. Paul's language speaks of the end time in characteristic phrases, notably "waiting for the revelation (apocalypsis) of our Lord Jesus Christ" (cf. 1 Thess 1:10); "maintain you blameless until the end" (cf. 1 Thess 3:13; 5:23); and "the day of our Lord Jesus Christ." With its reference to "his Son, Jesus Christ our Lord," the confession ends on an eschatological note. The designation of Jesus Christ as "his Son" and "our Lord" employs two Pauline phrases whose christological significance is clearly eschatological.

The reference to the "calling" of the Corinthians in v. 9 calls to mind the "calling" of the salutation (v. 2). It also anticipates ch. 15, where Paul makes reference to his own calling (15:9) and reflects extensively on the relationship between Christ and those who belong to him. Paul's choice of the language of "fellowship" *(koinōnia)* is particularly significant. The fellowship into which the Corinthians have been called is that of "his [God's] Son, Jesus Christ our Lord." This eight-word (in Greek both "Son" and "Lord" are qualified by the definite article as well as by a personal pronoun) christological definition is the longest christological designation in the extant Pauline correspondence. It employs all three of the christological titles that are particularly significant in Paul's letters: "Son," "Christ," and "Lord" *(Hyios, Christos, Kyrios)*. Of these the title of "Son" occurs with the least frequency in the Pauline correspondence. It is not used at all in Philippians and Philemon, only once in 1 Thessalonians, and only three times in the Corinthian correspondence (1:9; 15:28; 2 Cor 1:19). It is a title Paul attributes to Jesus as of the resurrection (Rom 1:4), an act of God in which God manifests his fatherhood by raising Jesus from the dead as his Son. The expectation of Jesus as Son is part of Paul's apocalyptic scenario (15:28; cf. 1 Thess 1:10, where the community is described as those who are waiting for the Son). Because of Christians' fellowship with Jesus the reality of Jesus' Sonship, realized in the resurrection, is the foundation of their claim to future glory (Rom 8:29-30; Gal 4:1-7).

Concluding his thanksgiving with a mention of the Corinthians' fellowship with the Son of God, Jesus Christ our Lord, Paul not only provides his readers with a cipher for the task that they are to realize, but also provides them with a symbol of their eschatological call and destiny.

The language of fellowship *(koinōnia)* evokes participation of those who are in communion in a third reality, in this case the resurrection of the dead. Foreshadowing what Paul will write about the eschaton and evoking the memory of Jesus, the eschatological conclusion in v. 9 serves as a quite appropriate transition to the body of the letter.

NOTES

4. *I always thank my God for you:* Paul's letters, addressed to communities rather than to a specific individual, do not include a health wish. Omitting the health wish, Paul usually expresses his thanks to God immediately after having greeted the community to which he is writing. With the exception of his letter to the Galatians, with its intentional omission of the thanksgiving, and the second letter to the Corinthians which has a blessing in place of the traditional epistolary thanksgiving, Paul's letters begin with a thanksgiving expressed in stereotypical fashion, the verb *eucharistō, theos* in the articular dative, a temporal adverb, and a *hoti* clause that offers the reason for his thanksgiving.

because of the grace of God: In the NT "grace" *(charis)* is a Pauline term, but it does not occur as frequently in 1 Corinthians (10x), as it does in Romans (24x), in 2 Corinthians (18x), and, proportionately, in Galatians (7x). Grace is "God's grace" *(charis tou theou;* 3:10; 15:10[2x], 57). Paul evokes the element of salvation, which the Corinthians have already received. As in the LXX, *charis* represents the biblical *ḥēn,* God's covenantal love. The Greek term, *charis,* used to express the biblical notion, is one that has a variety of meanings. It can denote (1) a favorable attitude, (2) a favor, the result of a favorable attitude, or (3) the quality that elicits a favorable attitude in another (e.g., beauty). God's covenantal love is owing to the goodness of God himself. God's love is expressed in the election of his people and the blessings he bestows on them. Paul's salutation (v. 3; cf. 16:23) was in the form of a wishful prayer that the Corinthians be graced by God. The prepositional phrase *epi tē chariti tou theou* expresses Paul's conviction that the Corinthians have already been abundantly graced by God, as he explains in v. 5. The various charismata are expressions of the one grace that is given to all. At the time of his writing to the Corinthians Paul had not yet been involved in the controversies that had taken place before he wrote to the Romans and the Galatians. It is anachronistic and an exercise of eisegesis to read ideas refined in the heat of later controversy, specifically the antithesis between grace and works, into what Paul writes to the Corinthians.

given to you in Christ Jesus: An aorist passive participle *(dotheisē;* cf. 3:10) emphasizes that God's grace is indeed a gift and indicates that Jesus is the mediator of the blessings that have been conferred on the Corinthians. Following Jewish custom the divine passive is used to designate God as the source of these blessings (cf. 3:10; 12:7, 8). In the Corinthian correspondence when the verb *didōmi,* "give," is used in the active voice it has God as its subject (11x;

cf. 15:38, 57). That Jesus is the mediator of all God's gifts is forcefully expressed in Paul's midrash on the Shema later in the letter (8:6). Jesus' mediation of God's gifts is also expressed in Paul's farewell prayer (16:23). Mention of Jesus is unusual in a Pauline thanksgiving. Indeed, the entire clause, "because of the grace of God given to you in Christ Jesus," is redundant in the light of the *hoti* clause that is to follow. One cannot exclude the possibility that Paul has inserted this additional clause into his thanksgiving because he intends to set forth "Christ Jesus" in his subsequent argumentation. Writing about charisms in ch. 12 Paul observes that the charisms are varieties of service in the Lord. He cites the body of Christ (vv. 12-26) as a model of the charisms being given and used for the common good.

5. *since you have been thoroughly enriched in him:* Paul explains why (the *hoti* is causal) he is grateful to God, clarifying what he has had to say about the grace of God given to the Corinthians. With a thrice-repeated use of words derived from the root *pas-* (thoroughly, every, all), the clarification highlights the plenitude of God's gift. The use of paronomasia provides Paul's expression of gratitude with rhetorical flourish. "Thoroughly" (*en panti*, "in every way") anticipates the expression of his conviction that all within the community are appropriately gifted (12:6, 7, 11). Paul's critical perspective on the gifts is foreshadowed in the phrase "enriched in him" (*eploutisthēte en autō*). The use of the divine passive of *ploutizō*, "to be made wealthy," hapax in 1 Corinthians (cf. 2 Cor 6:10; 9:11), is a reminder that the Corinthians are merely the recipients of these gifts. "In him" (*en autō*) has a critical function. It echoes the "in Christ Jesus" of the preceding phrase and offers a comparable perspective on the gifts that have been given. Paul highlights his critique even before he offers significant illustrations of the giftedness of the community. If the community is gifted, it is gifted through the mediation of Christ Jesus.

in every word and in all knowledge: Paul illustrates the radical giftedness of the community by citing the gifts of speech and knowledge. This pair of gifts (12:8; 13:1-2; 2 Cor 8:7; 11:6) was highly valued in the community. The gifts were, however, used to the detriment of others within the community. Paul will return to a consideration of these gifts later in the letter, offering various critical remarks (e.g. 13:1-2; cf. 3:21b-23). In later correspondence with them Paul will describe the community as one that excels in everything, including the gifts of word and knowledge (*en panti perisseuete . . . kai logō kai gnōsei*, 2 Cor 8:7).

6. *insofar as the testimony to Christ:* In the NT "testimony" (*martyrion*) has become virtually a technical term for the proclamation of the gospel. It is, however, rarely used by Paul (cf. 2:1; 2 Cor 1:12). Taken from the forensic register, the term may anticipate Paul's treatment of judicial matters in 6:1-11 and his use of forensic rhetoric in the apology of ch. 9. Ancient rhetoricians considered *heurēsis, inventio,* to be one of the essential elements of rhetoric. This was a matter not only of determining the matters to be taken up in the appeal but also the manner in which these were to be addressed. Since 1 Corinthians is a letter in which Paul deals with the issue of Hellenistic rhetoric (see 2:1-5) and exploits a variety of rhetorical techniques in the development of his ar-

gument, it is not unlikely that the use of *martyrion* is the result of Paul's rhetorical *heurēsis.* "The testimony to Christ" (*Christou,* an objective genitive) is a cipher for the proclamation of the Gospel, similar to Paul's more frequent "gospel of Christ" (*euaggelion tou Christou,* 9:12; cf. 2 Cor 2:12; 9:13; 10:14; Rom 15:19; Gal 1:7; Phil 1:27; 1 Thess 3:2), but with a judicial nuance. The object of Paul's testimony is Christ, a title that draws attention to Christ's death and resurrection. In describing his own testimony to God in 2:1-5 Paul notes that he knows only Jesus Christ and him as one who has been crucified (2:2). Paul's phrase "insofar as the testimony to Christ was confirmed among you" is virtually an aside. A similar construction with the causal *kathōs* (BAGD 391.3; BDF 453.2) is found in 5:7. By making mention of his testimony to Christ at the very outset of the letter Paul foreshadows the argument he will develop in his first major proof, 1:10–4:16.

was confirmed among you: In Greek "to confirm," *bebaioō* along with its cognates, is frequently used with reference to *logos,* word. It suggests that the word in question is verified and confirmed. In the NT *bebaioō* belongs to early Christian missionary jargon, where it has a juridical undertone as it frequently did in secular usage (*EDNT* 2:210-211). Paul uses the verb just three times (1:6, 8; 2 Cor 1:21), but in Phil 1:7 he says that his imprisonment contributes to the defense (*apologia*) and confirmation (*bebaiēsis*) of the gospel. Here Paul is suggesting that the proclamation of the gospel of Christ has indeed been verified among the Corinthians. Their gifts serve as the confirmation of Paul's gospel.

7. *with the result that you are not lacking in any gift:* The Greek *hōste* is used with the infinitive, as it is in classical Greek, to express result. Paul's negation reiterates what he had stated positively in v. 5. In rhetorical composition hyperbole is often used to prepare for an example of litotes, thus achieving the emphasis desired by the rhetor. That the Corinthians lack no gift confirms Paul's testimony to Christ. That the gospel has been effective among the Corinthians is a verifiable reality: the array of gifts given to the Corinthians attests to the effectiveness of the gospel.

To describe these gifts Paul uses the term *charisma,* which may be a neologism to which 1:7 may be the first recorded witness. There is no unassailable earlier textual evidence of its use before Paul. In the NT the term is used only by Paul, in Romans, 1 Corinthians, 2 Cor 1:11, and in literature dependent on Paul (1 Tim 4:14; 2 Tim 1:6; 1 Pet 4:10). Paul's use of hyperbole and litotes (vv. 5, 7) to describe the giftedness of the Corinthian community anticipates the extended consideration of the charismata in chs. 12–14. There Paul distinguishes the real gifts of God, *charismata* (12:4), from mere ecstatic phenomena, the *pneumatika* (12:1).

you who are eagerly awaiting: The participle *apekdechomenous* modifies the subject of the infinitive clause (*hymas*). *Apekdechomai,* an intensive form of the verb *ekdechomai,* is rarely found in classical and Hellenistic Greek. In the NT it is a Pauline term (Rom 8:19, 23, 25; 1 Cor 1:7; Gal 5:5; Phil 3:20; Heb 9:28; 1 Pet 3:20). In his correspondence the word is almost a technical term used to connote the expectation of the parousia, often with the nuance of patient expectation despite the eagerness of waiting (cf. Rom 8:25). Paul characterizes the

Corinthians as being in a situation of eager, almost anxious, expectation (cf. 1 Thess 1:10, which uses the verb *anamenō*).

the revelation of our Lord Jesus Christ: The "revelation *(apokalypsis)* of Jesus Christ" is a formulaic expression that occurs in later NT texts (2 Thess 1:7; 1 Pet 1:7, 13; cf. 4:13). The formula is used to designate the eschatological event Paul describes as the arrival *(parousia)* of the Lord Jesus Christ (15:23; cf. 1 Thess 2:19; 3:13; 4:15; 5:23). Paul uses the term *apokalypsis* in reference to a variety of revelatory experiences, auditory or visual, enjoyed by himself or another Christian charismatic, such as his own vision of the Lord (Gal 1:12) or the experience of Christian prophets (14:6, 26; 2 Cor 12:1, 7; Rom 16:25; cf. Gal 2:2; Eph 1:17; 3:3; Rev 1:1). Apart from its use in Paul and in the literature dependent on him the term occurs in the NT only in Simeon's canticle (Luke 2:32). In the letter to the Romans Paul employs *apokalypsis* in an eschatological sense but with a specific theological focus. He writes about the day of the revelation of God's righteous judgement (Rom 2:5) and of the eagerly awaited *(apekdechetai)* revelation of the children of God (Rom 8:19). The use of *apekdechomai* in 1 Cor 1:7 and Rom 8:19 points to this revelation as an event in the future. Both the verb *apekdechomai* and the noun *apokalypsis* are part of the technical jargon used by early Christians in reference to the day of the Lord, the day of the great revelation.

In 1:7 Paul uses the full christological title "our Lord Jesus Christ" (cf. 1:2, 10; 1:3) to describe the focus of revelation on that day (see v. 8). The accumulation of christological titles points to the fullness of revelation on the day of the Lord. Each term in the title, however, has its own nuance, which must not be neglected if the full import of Paul's phrase is to be grasped. Jesus is identified as Christ, a title Paul uses to evoke the memory of the death and resurrection of Jesus (see "Interpretation" of 1:1-3 above, p. 48). An anarthrous *Christos,* used in apposition to the personal name *Iēsous,* is typical of Paul, especially in 1 Corinthians. The usage is so common that some commentators suggest that *Christos* had lost its formal significance in its use by the Hellenistic elements of the early church. Some passages in 1 Corinthians suggest that this may be so, but others, particularly those where an otherwise unqualified arthrous *Christos* appears, suggest that Paul continues to evoke the formal sense of the term, although the meaning Paul ascribes to it is somewhat different from the denotation of the word in other early Christian usage. For Paul *ho Christos* is clearly the one who has died and been raised from the dead, the focus of the faith of Christian believers.

That the personal name of Jesus is situated between the two titular expressions, "Christ" and "our Lord," indicates that "our Lord" *(tou Kyriou hēmōn)* is in apposition to the composite "Jesus Christ." Appearing sixty-six times in 1 Corinthians alone, *Kyrios* is Paul's preferred christological title. Evoking Jesus who has been raised from the dead and is awaited as the eschatological Lord, the title is particularly apropos in an eschatological passage such as this finale of Paul's thanksgiving period. By the resurrection (see 6:14) God has revealed Jesus as the one who will be God's primary agent in the end-time events (cf. 15:20-28). At the parousia Jesus will function as

"Lord," assuming a role that properly belongs to God himself. The Christian community at Corinth is waiting for Jesus, the eschatological Lord, as their Lord. Jesus Christ is our Lord (1:2, 8, 9, 10; 5:4[2x]; 9:1; 15:31, 57). The personal pronoun expresses a personal relationship between the one who is expected as eschatological Lord and the Christian community that is awaiting his arrival *(parousia)*. The community belongs to Jesus Christ who is their Lord. The personal pronoun bespeaks a claim to salvation when Jesus Christ is finally revealed as eschatological Lord.

8. *who will maintain you blameless until the end:* Hapax in Paul, "blameless" *(anegklētous;* cf. Col 1:22) is a term which comes from the catalogue of virtues (cf. 1 Tim 3:10; Titus 1:6, 7). Etymologically it designates those who have not been accused *(egkaleō;* cf. Rom 8:33) and can therefore be presumed to be blameless, having no reason to be accused. It belongs to the register of judicial terminology (cf. Xenophon, Demosthenes, and other classical authors). With his use of *bebaiōsei,* "maintain," and *anegklētous,* "blameless," Paul continues the forensic imagery he had introduced in v. 7. Use of judicial imagery is characteristic of Paul's eschatological scenario (cf. 2 Cor 5:10; Phil 1:10; 1 Thess 3:13; 5:23). In the wish prayers of 1 Thessalonians Paul expresses his hope that Christians be maintained blameless until the parousia of the Lord. In 1:8 he expresses the conviction that the eschatological Lord of the community will maintain it in a blameless condition until the time of judgment (cf. Phil 1:6). That time is "the end," the eschaton (cf. 1 Thess 2:16). In 1 Corinthians Paul describes Christians as those "for whom the ends of the ages *(ta telē tōn aiōnōn)* have arrived" (10:11). In his rebuttal of those who deny the resurrection of the dead Paul describes the eschatological sequence: first Christ, then those who belong to him, then the end *(to telos,* 15:24). The end that impinges on the Corinthians establishes them in an eschatological situation.

on the day of our Lord Jesus Christ: Paul specifies that "the end," that is, the end of the present order of things, is the day of our Lord Jesus Christ. The day of the Lord *(hē hēmera tou Kyriou)* is a biblical motif frequently used by the prophets (Isa 13:6, 9; Jer 25:33 [32:33 LXX]; Ezek 7:10; 13:5; Joel 2:1; 3:14 [4:14 LXX]; Amos 5:18, 20; Obad 1:15; Zeph 1:7, 14; Mal 4:1 [3:19 LXX]). That day is a day of judgment (Amos 5:18-20) and salvation (Joel 2:32 [3:5 LXX]). For Paul "the Lord" is always the Lord Jesus Christ. As Lord, Jesus Christ is vicegerent of God on the great day of judgment and salvation. Hence the biblical day of the Lord is really the day of the Lord Jesus Christ (cf. 2 Cor 1:14; Phil 1:6, 10, 2:16; 1 Thess 5:2). The sequence of words in Paul's Greek is such that "our . . . Jesus Christ" is appended to the formulaic expression "the day of the Lord." A few important manuscripts ($\mathfrak{P}^{46}$, B) omit "Christ" from the christological designation, but the presence of the fuller title is firmly attested by the manuscript tradition ($\aleph$, A, C, D, Ψ). The fuller title is, moreover, commonly used by Paul when he writes about the eschaton.

9. *Faithful is God:* Paul's *pistos,* "faithful," reflects the biblical *mʾmn,* from a root *(ʾmn)* that suggests strength and validity. The formulaic expression (cf. 10:13)—there is no verb!—recalls the biblical and Jewish understanding of God as the faithful one (Deut 7:9; 32:4; Isa 49:7; Ps 145:13 [144:13 LXX]). "God

who speaks to us is faithful" *(ho de theos kai legōn pistos estin)* says Philo *(Sacrifices* 93; cf. *Allegorical Interpretation* 3.228; *Heir* 93). Fidelity is one of YHWH's defining traits (see Deut 7:9). God is trustworthy and reliable, steadfast and loyal. God's fidelity is expressed in his ongoing covenantal love for his people and the abiding force and validity of his word.

by whom you have been called: God is the source of the Corinthians' call (BDF 119.2; cf. 1:2). In his letter to the Thessalonians, in an eschatological and exhortative context, Paul had written "faithful is the one who calls you" *(pistos ho kalōn hymas,* 1 Thess 5:24). In this letter, as in the earlier missive to the Thessalonians, Paul writes of the fidelity of God who calls his people (10:13; cf. Deut 7:9; 32:4; Ps 145:13 [144:13 LXX]). Paul's use of the aorist *eklēthēte* in 1:9, with its reference to a past event, presumably the call of the Corinthians expressed in baptism, contrasts with the present participle *(kalōn)* of 1 Thess 5:24 that highlights the ongoing call of God to his people. In 1 Thessalonians Paul emphasizes that God's fidelity is an active fidelity: "The one who calls you is faithful, and he will do this." Particularly significant is that in both 1 Thessalonians and 1 Corinthians Paul describes the call of God as addressed to a community largely composed of Gentiles. Deutero-Isaiah, whose vision of the salvation of Gentiles has been appropriated by Paul, speaks of the God who calls his people (Isa 42:6; 48:12) and accomplishes what he has planned for them (Isa 46:10; 49:7).

into the fellowship of his Son, Jesus Christ our Lord: God has called the Corinthians, to whom Paul is writing, into the fellowship of his Son. In the NT "fellowship" *(koinōnia)* and its cognates, "to participate" *(koinōneō),* and "sharing" *(koinōnos),* are particularly to be found in the Pauline correspondence and in literature dependent on Paul. The term *koinōnia* is an abstract form in which the emphasis may lie upon the relationship of those in fellowship (thus "partnership," "fellowship"). Alternatively the emphasis may lie on the partners' common *(koinos)* sharing in something else (thus "participation," "sharing"). Paul's use of the personal genitive, "his Son," to qualify *koinōnia* represents a relatively rare Greek construction. Paul does not further define the nature of this fellowship nor does he state how it came into existence. First Corinthians 10:16-17 suggests that eucharistic fellowship is integral to the fellowship enjoyed by the Corinthians. In any case God's call is a task. The Corinthians are called to realize the fellowship into which they have been called by God. This proves to be the burden of Paul's letter, as is equivalently expressed in the statement of purpose that follows immediately upon the conclusion of Paul's thanksgiving.

For Reference and Further Study

Malan, François S. "Die funksie en boodskap van die 'voorwoord' in 1 Korintiërs," *HThS* 49 (1993) 561–575.

O'Brien, Peter T. *Introductory Thanksgivings in the Letters of Paul.* Leiden: Brill, 1977.

Panikulam, George. *Koinōnia in the New Testament: A Dynamic Expression of Christian Life.* AnBib 85. Rome: Biblical Institute Press, 1979, 8–16.

Roberts, J. H. "The Eschatological Transitions to the Pauline Letter Body," *Neotest.* 20 (1986) 29–35.

Schnackenburg, Rudolph. "Die Einheit der Kirche unter dem *Koinonia*-Gedanken" in Ferdinand Hahn et al, eds., *Einheit der Kirche. Grundlegung im Neuen Testament.* QD 84. Freiburg, Basel, and Vienna: Herder, 1979, 52–93.

Schubert, Paul. *Form and Function of the Pauline Thanksgivings.* BZNW 20. Berlin: Töpelmann, 1939.

BODY OF THE LETTER (1:10–15:58)

A. THEME AND OCCASION (1:10-17)

10. Brothers and sisters, I exhort you in the name of our Lord Jesus Christ that all of you be in agreement and that there be no divisions among you, but that you be of a same mind and of a same opinion. 11. For concerning you it has been reported to me, my brothers and sisters, by Chloe's people that there are quarrels among you. 12. But I tell you this: that each one of you says, I am Paul's, I am Apollos's, I am Cephas's, I am Christ's. 13. Is Christ divided? Has Paul been crucified for your sake? Or were you baptized in the name of Paul? 14. I thank God that I did not baptize anyone of you except Crispus and Gaius, 15. lest anyone say that you were baptized in my name. 16. I also baptized the household of Stephanas; for the rest I do not know whether I baptized anyone else. 17. For Christ did not send me to baptize, but to evangelize, not with cleverness of speech, lest the cross of Christ be deprived of its power.

INTERPRETATION

In Hellenistic letters an expression of thanksgiving or a health wish, or both, typically provides the transition between the epistolary salutation and the body of the letter. Paul's letter, addressed to a community, lacks a health wish. He begins the body of the letter with a direct appeal (*parakalō de hymas*) to the Corinthians, whom he addresses as his brothers and sisters (*adelphoi*). The letter begins on a solemn note with a formal appeal.

Epistolary Considerations. A formula of encouragement, the *parakalō* formula, provides an opening for the body of the letter. Carl J. Bjerkelund has shown that a *parakalō* formula was typically used in official diplomatic letters, where it not only suggested the authority of the one who was writing but also tactfully served to underscore the importance of the matter at hand. The language of exhortation (*parakalō*, "urge" or "encourage") rather than the language of command was used, but the effect was the same. Those to whom the exhortation was directed were expected to respond as they would if a formal command had been addressed to them. There can be no mistaking the force of Paul's language. His diplomatic formula is apropos in a letter that purports to be from a legate of Christ Jesus according to the very will of God (v. 1).

The appeal is not ultimately based on Paul's own authority, formally articulated in the self-designation of v. 1. Paul's appeal is rather made "in the name of our Lord Jesus Christ," the name the Christians of Corinth invoke (v. 2). The invocation of the name of Jesus as Lord expresses the authority the Lord Jesus has over the community. According to Paul's biblical tradition and in the Hellenistic world the name manifests the function and status of a person. His appeal to the Corinthians in the name of the Lord Jesus suggests that in some real way Jesus is present to the community as their Lord (see 5:4).

Paul appeals to the Corinthians as his brothers and sisters *(adelphoi).* This formula of direct address will be used frequently throughout the letter, some twenty times in all, although proportionately not as frequently as in his earlier and perhaps more friendly letter to the Christians at Thessalonica where it occurs fourteen times. The familiarity of this form of direct address contrasts with the otherwise formal and solemn character of Paul's opening sentence, "I exhort you in the name of our Lord," with its epistolary convention and theological density.

In his classic treatise on epistolary types Pseudo-Demetrius proposed the friendly type *(typos philikos)* as the first of the twenty-one types of letters he describes. He says, "it is by no means only friends who write in this manner. For frequently those in prominent positions are expected by some to write in a friendly manner to their inferiors and to others who are their equals. . . . They do so, not because they are close friends and have only one choice of how to write, but because they think that nobody will refuse them when they write in a friendly manner, but will rather submit and heed what they are writing. Nevertheless, this type of letter is called friendly as though it were written to a friend" (Malherbe, *Ancient Epistolary Theorists,* 32–33). Paul's calling on the Corinthians as his brothers and sisters achieves the same purpose.

A reading of Hellenistic letters does not indicate that the composition of the body of a letter was governed by strict conventions similar to those that govern opening salutations, health wishes, and expressions of thanksgiving. Various epistolary formulae occur in the body of these letters, but there is no standard manner of opening or closing the letter-body. The choice of epistolary conventions and the letter's subject matter, its *homilia*, the *dialogos*, determine the specific nature of its epistolary character. Paul has amply prepared for the exposition of the subject matter he will pursue in the many preparatory hints he has given in the salutation and thanksgiving of this letter. The body of his letter will employ various epistolary conventions found in the Hellenistic letters of his day.

Rhetorical Function. The object of Paul's appeal is that the Corinthians come to agreement among themselves and that they banish divisions from their midst. Paul's opening gambit (v. 10) makes a statement that defines the purpose of his letter. In rhetorical terms the verse can be considered as Paul's *prothesis* or *propositio*, the statement of the case he intends to make. Aristotle (*Art of Rhetoric* 3.13.1-2) maintained that the essential feature of a rhetorical argument was the statement of the thesis to be developed and the exposition of the probatory arguments, the *prothesis* and its *pisteis*. Rhetorically the beginning of the body of Paul's letter constitutes his statement of purpose. What follows in the body of the letter is a rhetorical exposition in support of Paul's plea for unity within the community.

Since Paul's statement of purpose looks to the future, that is, to the restoration of the Corinthians to their prior situation in which there was at least a presumed unity of mind and purpose, Paul's *propositio* helps the modern commentator to characterize Paul's communication as an exercise in deliberative rhetoric. Political language abounds in the first pericope of the body of the letter. Paul pleads with the community to have a common spirit and purpose. He urges them to banish division (*schisma*) from among them. The opening plea will be echoed later in the letter when he reminds the Corinthians that the divisions among them (*schismata*, 11:18-19) allow the authentic members of the community to be distinguished from those who are not. In his plea that the charismatic gifts given to the several members of the community be used for their mutual benefit, he urges that there be no rupture in the body (*hina mē ē̜ schisma*, 12:25). In a long disquisition on the body (12:12-26) he employs a classic topos to plead for harmony within the community.

In his *prothesis*, the statement of purpose, Paul explains his intention both negatively and positively. The general intention is that the Corinthians be in agreement. This means that there should be no divisions among them; it also means that they should be restored to a same mindset and share a common opinion. "Same mind" (*nous*) and "same opinion" (*gnōmē*) are essentially synonymous. The repetition has the rhetorical effect of emphasizing Paul's point. He wants unity to replace the divisions that are adversely affecting the Corinthian assembly. Paul wants the Corinthian

Christians to have a common understanding of things. In the form of an exhortation, his statement of purpose has an anticipatory function. It prepares for the argument Paul will develop later in his letter. "Mind" *(nous)* and "opinion" *(gnōmē)* are significant lexical choices. The terms do not occur with great frequency in the body of the letter but they are the subject of strategic utterances. The one mind that Paul would have the Corinthians adopt is the mind of Christ (2:16). His opening statement is an implicit plea for a radical change in the understanding of the Corinthians, a shift in their operative epistemology. The opinion is that of Paul, inspired by the Spirit of God (7:40; cf. v. 25). Paul wants the Corinthians to share his Spirit-inspired way of seeing things.

Kinship Language. In 1:10 "brothers and sisters" *(adelphoi)* appears for the first time in 1 Corinthians as a formula of direct address. This is Paul's customary way of addressing himself to the Corinthians. He appeals to them as if we were directly addressing them. Paul's letters were a way of making himself present when in fact he was absent. Along with his contemporaries he considered that the extension of personal presence *(parousia)* was one of the principal functions of a letter (see 5:3).

His lexical choice, *adelphoi,* "brothers and sisters," suggests the nature of the relationship that binds Paul to those Christians, but it represents more than a merely conventional or metaphorical use of language. In Paul's time Christians gathered together in their homes *(oikos, oikia;* see 16:19; cf. Rom 16:23). In this context Paul's writing and other early Christian use of such kinship language as "brothers and sisters" must be seen as a reflection of the setting in which they came together. It is in the home that kinship language, the language of the family, truly belongs.

"*Adelphoi*" is a vocative form in the masculine plural, with the literal meaning of "brothers." The term should be taken in its more general connotation, "brothers and sisters," rather than as a gender-specific "brothers." In classical Greek the plural form, especially in the vocative, often connotes "brothers and sisters." In some instances *adelphoi* is used of two persons, a brother and sister. Such comprehensive usage is found as early as the fifth century B.C.E. in the writings of Euripides. See BAGD 16.1, LSJ 30, *EDNT* 1:28–30. Georg Friedrich has demonstrated that Paul's letters were directed to male and female members of the congregation ("Der erste Brief an die Thessalonicher." *Die Briefe an die Galater, Epheser, Philipper, Kolosser, Thessalonicher und Philemon.* Jürgen Becker et al. NTD 8. Göttingen: Vandenhoeck & Ruprecht [1976] 212–213). In writing to the Corinthians Paul clearly has women as well as men in mind (cf. 7:10-11; 11:2-16; etc.).

Paul is not always consistent in his appropriation of kinship language. While he normally addresses the Corinthians as his siblings he sometimes adopts a paternalistic tone, addressing them as his children. In a pericope that bears many of the characteristics of a letter of admonition (*typos nouthētikos;* 4:14-21) Paul addresses the Corinthians as his beloved children (*hōs tekna mou agapēta,* 4:14). He explains that he has engendered them through the gospel he has preached to them, alluding thereby to the role of a Jewish father whose principal task was to provide for the transmission of traditional lore to his children. Despite the profession of affection for his "beloved" children in the formula of address Paul exploits his paternal relationship with the Corinthians insofar as he has a role of admonition to fulfill (4:14-21; 3:1-4). Timothy is called Paul's "beloved and faithful child in the Lord" (*mou teknon agapēton kai piston en kyriǭ,* 4:17) insofar as he has appropriated the ways of Paul, his father.

In his frequent direct appeal to the Corinthians as his "brothers and sisters" Paul uses *pathos* as a form of rhetorical argument. He appeals to the sensibilities of the community. Paul experiences himself as one who is bonded with the community. His repeated apostrophic formula invites them to experience a similar bond with himself. In an essay, "Brotherly Love," Plutarch, a younger contemporary of Paul (46–ca. 120 C.E.), writes that nature teaches that family life is to be lived in agreement (*symphōnia*) and concord (*homonoia;* Plutarch, "Brotherly Love," *Moralia* 478D–479B; cf. 4 Macc 13:25). From this perspective Paul's repeated appeal to the Corinthians as his brothers and sisters is a significant feature of his rhetorical strategy.

On the other hand, Plutarch teaches that personal enmity engenders painful emotions. When, moreover, personal enmity exists among siblings, who share so much in common and are often neighbors, the emotional burden is heavier still (Plutarch, "Brotherly Love," *Moralia* 481B-E). Paul shares a similar understanding of the sibling relationship. The scandal of Christians' summoning one another before the secular courts is aggravated by the fact that they are brothers and sisters (6:6, 8).

Cries of Allegiance. Since the mid-nineteenth century the "slogans" of v. 12 have frequently been construed as an indication that there were various Christian factions at Corinth, rallying respectively around the authority of Paul, Apollos, Cephas, or Christ. The Tübingen critic, Ferdinand Christian Baur, was perhaps the most influential scholar urging this point of view. Influenced by Hegel, Baur had a dialectical view of the history of the early Christian church. For him the confrontation of opposing points of view led to the emergence of early Christianity, to which the later texts of the New Testament, including some that have been handed down in Paul's name, bear witness. Baur viewed the Corinthian situation almost as if it were a case study of his thesis. In his view there were four parties vying with one another for dominance within the community.

The discussion of the different ideologies espoused by the parties has, to a large extent, focused on the interpretation of *Egō de Christou,* "I'm for

Christ" (for the history of the interpretation of the phrase, see Baumann, *Mitte und Norm* 49–55; Walter Schmithals, *Gnosticism in Corinth* 117–124). The parallel with the previous three slogans led many historical-critical readers of Paul's letter to affirm that there actually was a group at Corinth that rallied round the name of Christ in opposition to those who rallied round the names of Paul, Cephas, and Apollos. Given Baur's contention that the critical antithesis in the early church was between a Pauline view and a Jewish-Christian view, many of the early historical critics considered that the Christ party was a group of Judaizers or Christian Jews who maintained an anti-Pauline stance. Later critics identified the Christ party with a group of Corinthian "enthusiasts," a group of pneumatic Gnostics who opted for the Spirit over and against tradition, the spirit over and against mere bodily existence. The classic proponent of this point of view was Wilhelm Lütgert (*Freiheitspredigt und Schwarmgeister in Korinth* [BFTh 12, 3. Gütersloh: Bertelsmann, 1908]). A similar reading of the formula was vigorously maintained by Schmithals in *Gnosticism in Corinth*, a book whose first German edition appeared in 1956. More recent scholars, such as Helmut Koester, Stephen J. Patterson, and John Dominic Crossan, who consider that Gnosticism was a real issue at Corinth, prefer to speak of proto-Gnosticism, emergent Gnosticism, or a Gnostic influence, and are loath to identify this influence simply with the "Christ party."

Others see "I am Christ's" as a response. Some take the phrase to be a response by some Christians in Corinth who proclaimed their allegiance to Christ rather than to a merely human rhetor. Still others take the words to be a rhetorical flourish on the part of the apostle (the ancient Greek manuscripts lacked punctuation). The cry, "I am Christ's," would be Paul's addition to the series of three. Attempting to reduce Corinthian factionalism to the absurd, Paul would have employed a bit of sarcasm. Alternatively "I am Christ's" is taken as Paul's own declaration of allegiance, stated in almost sarcastic fashion: You are for this one or that one; I'm for Christ! Were this the case one might have expected Paul to have employed a strongly adversative "but" (*alla*), but he does not do so.

Those who hold that "I am Christ's" is Paul's rhetorical rebuttal maintain that there were three different factions at Corinth. Apollos, to whom Paul devotes an extended comparison throughout the first part of the letter, was often considered to be the principal proponent of the kind of Jewish wisdom teaching (cf. Acts 18:24-28) to which the writings of Philo bear witness (e.g., Gerhard Sellin). Cephas, the Aramaic nickname given by Jesus to one of his disciples, Simon Peter, would have served as a rallying cry for those at Corinth who espoused a strongly conservative Christian Jewish point of view. Sometimes it is argued that Paul was not so much concerned with these figures themselves as he was with some of their followers, people who rallied around their names and perverted the

Pauline gospel (e.g., Friedrich Lang, "Die Gruppen"). Alternatively it is sometimes urged that the issue was not so much the existence of different factions at Corinth but of petty squabbles and a kind of cliquishness (esp. Johannes Munck, *Paul and the Salvation of Mankind* [London: SCM, 1989; Richmond: John Knox, 1990] 135–167).

The community was certainly divided on many issues, a number of which Paul will treat in his letter. Yet there is really no indication in the letter that there were three or four distinct factions in the community at Corinth, each with its own theological point of view, behavioral pattern, and putative authority. Throughout the entire letter Paul's argument appears to be addressed to the community as a whole. These so-called factions do not appear in the letter after the opening argument. Hence it seems best to take the dramatic language of v. 12 as a forceful piece of rhetoric on the part of Paul rather than a statement about the specific situation at Corinth. The so-called slogans are not slogans used by various groups among the Corinthians. They are caricatures created by Paul. These caricatures implicitly compare the behavior of the Corinthians to that of groups of children who are dependent on their parents or groups of slaves dependent on their masters.

The Household of Stephanas. In his letter to the Corinthians Paul twice makes reference to the household of Stephanas (1:16; 16:15), first using the noun *oikos*, then the noun *oikia*. In Greek the two terms were originally distinguishable from each other, the former indicating all that one owned, the latter only one's dwelling. Gradually, however, the terms came to be used as synonyms, as they were in NT times. The NT prefers *oikos* (115x) to *oikia* (95x), as does Paul, who uses *oikos* six times and *oikia* five times. In Paul, as in the rest of the NT, the terms are basically interchangeable. Most of Paul's uses of the terminology are in the Corinthian correspondence (*oikos* 1 Cor 1:16; 11:34; 14:35; 16:19; Rom 16:5; Phlm 2; *oikia* 1 Cor 11:22; 16:15; 2 Cor 5:1[2x]; Phil 4:22).

The recurrence of household language in the NT (see especially Luke-Acts) is undoubtedly due to the importance of the household in early Christianity. Paul writes about people eating "at home" (the formulaic *en oikō*, 11:34, cf. v. 22) and wives talking to their husbands "at home" (14:35), but he also writes about baptizing the household of Stephanas (1:16). Via Paul the church in the house of Aquila and Prisca (*syn te kat' oikon autōn ekklēsią*, 16:19) sent its warm greetings to the community at Corinth. Passages such as 11:22, 34; 14:35; and 16:19 indicate that Paul uses the terminology in the usual sense of a dwelling place, but other passages, such as 1:16 and 16:15, indicate that he uses the terminology to designate a family, a household. Both *oikos* and *oikia* are used with these two connotations. Paul's writing about his having baptized the household of Stephanas and his conveying of greetings from those who gather in the house of Aquila and Prisca constitute an acknowledgment that he was not unaware of the importance of the house and the household in the life of the church at Corinth.

The household was the basic structural unit of the early Christian church. Christians gathered in one another's homes. It was there that they came together to hear the gospel preached and explained. It was there that they gathered for the celebration of the Eucharist, their Christian family meal (11:18-22). In effect, it was there that they assembled as "church" (11:18). It was there that the church, an assembly, took place. The NT provides some evidence that the gathering of Christians regularly took place in the homes of the more wealthy and powerful Christians. These alone would have had homes large enough to accommodate even a small gathering of Christians. The owners of these homes by extending their welcome to their fellow Christians were patrons of the church that gathered in their home. The local church was called by the name of the owner of the home in which the ecclesial gathering took place. Among the patrons of the church at Corinth were Gaius (Rom 16:23) and perhaps Stephanas (1:16). Phoebe was a patron of the church in nearby Cenchreae (Rom 16:1-2). Aquila and Prisca were, in this sense, patrons of the church in Ephesus (16:19).

The household was an important instrument of evangelization in early Christianity. Along with the public forum and the workshop, evangelization took place in the homes of Christians or those who were sympathetic to the Christian gospel. The homes of Christians located along the major trade routes provided a lodging place for traveling missionaries. It would appear that Paul enjoyed the hospitality of Gaius on the occasion of his visit to Corinth (Rom 16:23). Aquila and Prisca were among Paul's special patrons (Rom 16:3-5). The couple not only provided lodging for Paul; they also gave him an opportunity to ply a trade by means of which he could be economically self-sufficient (Acts 18:3). This enabled him to preach the gospel free of charge (9:18).

In large metropolitan areas such as Rome, Ephesus, and Corinth, it is likely that there was more than one household church. In a long list of greetings (Rom 16:3-16) Paul conveys his best wishes to various groups of people in Rome. It is probable that these groups of people belonged to various Roman household churches known to Paul. It is not unlikely that the different household churches in Corinth were a source of some of the friction and social tension that divided the community, but the assertion that the different slogans of v. 12 are to be construed as the rallying cries of four independent household churches is unwarranted.

In the aside of 1:16 Paul makes reference to having baptized the household of Stephanas. In recent NT *Wirkungsgeschichte,* the history of interpretation, a debated issue has been whether the formula, "baptize a household" (cf. Acts 16:15, 33, with reference to the baptisms of the households of Lydia and the jailer at Philippi) indicates that infants and small children were baptized in the churches of NT times. Although Joachim Jeremias (*Infant Baptism in the First Four Centuries*. Library of History and Doctrine. Philadelphia: Westminster, 1962, 19–24; *The Origins of Infant Baptism: A Further Study in Reply to Kurt Aland*. Studies in Historical Theology. London: SCM, 1963) staunchly defended the position that the formula suggested that infants were also baptized, most biblical scholars contend that mere use of the formula does not provide probative evidence that this was indeed the case. Much more important is that Paul's use of the formula indicates that the conversion of Stephanas brought in its wake the conversion of at least some members of his (biological) family and probably some of his slaves as well. Such was the influence of a *paterfamilias* in his household during imperial times.

Paul and Hellenistic Rhetoric. Despite his professed disavowal of the use of rhetorical techniques in v. 17 Paul in fact uses the *ars rhetorica* to deny that his appeal is based on rhetoric. His manner of arguing his point is clearly an appeal expressed in the language of persuasive rhetoric with its conventions and rhetorical devices.

Paul's way of denying that he had used rhetorical technique is reminiscent of various ancient rhetors' depreciation of rhetoric. Notwithstanding the fact that his denunciation of rhetoricians is couched in powerful rhetoric, Plato used strong words to criticize rhetoricians. In a passage of *Phaedrus* often quoted by students of classical rhetoric Plato maintained that "in the courts . . . nobody cares for truth . . . but [only] for that which is convincing . . . paying no attention to truth" (*Phaedrus* 272E; cf. 273B–273C). Similarly, Cicero describes Roman orators criticizing professional orators, all the while admitting the benefit they had received from their own rhetorical training (*De oratore* 1.11.47).

Throughout his first letter to the Corinthians Paul shows himself to be the "compleat" rhetorician. His rhetorical skills are clearly at work in the first pericope of the body of his letter. The "each of you" who says different things (v. 12) contrasts sharply with the "each of you agree" (literally, "say the same thing," v. 10). The anaphoric gradation of the cries of allegiance in v. 12, with an emphatic and repeated "I" (*egō*), contrasts with the community implied in "a same mind and of a same opinion" of v. 10. The "I" points to the root of the problem at Corinth as located in a radical individuality rather than in substantive theological differences. Building from himself to Christ, Paul puts his apostolic function in proper perspective and highlights the singular importance of Christ.

The series of rhetorical questions that follows in v. 13 serves to put the Corinthians on the defensive. Rhetorical questions are a characteristic feature of the classic diatribe. The rhetorical questions of v. 13 create a chiastic structure with the cries of allegiance of the previous verse. They reverse the sequence of the previous *gradatio,* embracing the motifs of Paul and of the crucifixion, which serve as the focal points for Paul's first proof (chs. 1–4).

Even Paul's denial that he uses rhetorical technique, lest the cross of Christ be deprived of its power, is a rhetorical device. Ancient rhetors frequently used demurrals and veiled apologies in order to win the goodwill of their audience or disarm their opponents (e.g., Isocrates, *Nicocles, or The Cyprians* 45). In any event the language of the first paragraph in the body of Paul's letter is laced with terms and expressions that were commonly used in Hellenistic political rhetoric.

NOTES

10. *Brothers and sisters:* Paul's epistolary style is such that the text of his letters is interspersed with formulas of direct address. One of the most common of these was *adelphoi,* "brothers and sisters." As a form of direct address it occurs in all of Paul's letters, but it is more common in those letters that reflect the warmth and positive affect of Paul toward those to whom he was writing. Accordingly the formula occurs proportionately with greater frequency in his letters to the Macedonian churches (1 Thessalonians, Philippians) than it does in his letters to other churches. In 1 Corinthians this familiar form of direct address occurs with considered frequency, twenty times in all (1:10, 11, 26; 2:1; 3:1; 4:6; 7:24, 29; 10:1; 11:33; 12:1; 14:6, 20, 26, 39; 15:1, 31, 50, 58; 16:15), normally without further qualification. In 1:11 and 11:33, however, Paul addresses himself to "*my* brothers and sisters," in 15:58 to "*my beloved* brothers and sisters." These qualifications strengthen the expression of endearment in Paul's formula of direct address.

    I exhort you: "I exhort you" *(parakalō hymas)* is a standard formula in Hellenistic letters (see 4:16; 16:15). The formula was used in friendly letters; in the present instance it introduces the paraenetic theme that dominates the entire letter.

    in the name of our Lord Jesus Christ: Paul uses an idiomatic "in" *(dia* = "by;" cf. BDF 223.4). In the ancient world a "name" functioned somewhat differently from the way it does in contemporary society. In our society a name often is merely a convenient label. In the ancient world the name had a distinguishing function but it also served to manifest the person who bore the name. It was almost an expression of the person; hence the importance of giving names, changing names, and revealing names. In the NT the importance of the name of Jesus appears primarily in Acts and in the Johannine literature. First Corinthians is the first of the three letters in which Paul draws attention to the importance of the name of Jesus (see 1:2; 5:4; 6:11; Rom 1:5; 10:13; Phil 2:9-10). As Paul highlights the name of Jesus one can see a reflection of biblical onomatology. Paul's appeal is motivated by the Lord Jesus Christ (cf. Rom 15:30; compare 12:1). "The name of the Lord Jesus Christ" is, in fact, the person of the Lord who is present to the community. By alluding to the baptismal formula (see 1:13) Paul's appeal evokes the baptism through which all Christians become one with the Lord Jesus.

that all of you be in agreement: Paul's appeal is directed to the entire community *(pantes)* as he pleads positively and negatively for unity within the community. "That all of you be in agreement" means literally "that all of you say the same thing," *hina to auto legēte.* The same expression is used by Thucydides *(History of the Peloponnesian War* 5.31.6). Similarly, Dio Chrysostom urged the populace of Nicea to maintain an attitude of peace and concord, "speaking with one voice" (*mian de phōnēn aphientas, Discourses* 39.3).

and that there be no divisions among you: The divisions within the community, for whose eradication Paul pleads, are described as *schismata* (cf. 11:18; 12:25). A *schisma* is literally a rip, as of a piece of cloth. In political rhetoric *schisma* was figuratively used of a division of opinion or a cleft in political consciousness (Herodotus, *Persian Wars* 7.219). The cognate verb, *schizein,* meaning to divide, separate, rend, or tear, was, similarly, albeit rarely, used of political divisions. Diodorus describes a multitude divided *(schizomenos)* as a result of civil strife at Megara *(Library of History* 12.66.2; cf. P.London 1710.13). Some forty years after Paul wrote to the Corinthians, Clement of Rome could ask, "Why are there strifes and wraths and factions and divisions *(schismata)* and war among you?" *(1 Clem.* 46:5; PG 1, 304).

but that you be: As used in political rhetoric, *katartizō* (literally, "to restore") connoted the calming of political unrest, the appeasement of factions, and the restoration of political unity (Herodotus, *Persian Wars* 5.28). The basic meaning of the term is the restoration of something to a given condition, its adaptation to a specific purpose. Paul's choice of this term (cf. 2 Cor 13:11) suggests that there was something amiss in the community at Corinth, some kind of societal division that was preventing the assembly from realizing its nature as "the church of God" (1:2).

of a same mind and of a same opinion: The two prepositional phrases are similar in form *(en tō autō noi; en tē autē gnōmē).* "Mind" *(nous)* and "opinion" *(gnōmē)* are Pauline terms. Fourteen of the twenty-four NT occurrences of the former (seven more are in the deutero-Pauline NT texts) and five of the eight occurrences of the latter (cf. Acts 20:3; Rev 17:13, 17) are in Paul's authentic writings. A concentrated use of these terms is to be found in 1 Corinthians *(nous* in 1:10; 2:16[2x]; 14:14, 15, 19; *gnōmē* in 1:10; 7:25, 40). Inspired by principles derived from Hellenistic philosophical anthropology, many of the Fathers distinguished *nous* and *gnōmē* as respectively referring to theoretical understanding and practical disposition. Paul's Semitic anthropology did not lead him to make such a distinction. For Semites knowledge is practical and experiential. For Paul *nous* and *gnōmē* are fundamentally synonymous. Even in classical Greek *gnōmē* can be synonymous with *nous,* both designating the organ of knowing, the mind. In 1 Corinthians Paul's use of the terms is such that he employs *nous* in christological discussion (cf. 2:16), while *gnōmē* suggests his opinion as an apostle. He makes it clear that he voices his opinion because he has the Spirit of God (7:40). *Gnōmē,* "opinion," is, nonetheless, a term used in Hellenistic rhetoric (see Herodotus, Sophocles, Thucydides). That the people be of "a single opinion" *(mia gnōmē)* is part of the plea Dio Chrysostom addressed to the citizenry of Nicea *(Discourses* 39.8). It was used by Aelius Aristides in his appeal to the populace of Rhodes *(Orations* 24.37). Paul's plea that the assembly at Corinth be of a same opinion *(en tę autę gnōmę)* makes use of this rhetorical term to urge unity within the assembly. His appeal that they be of a same mind *(en tǭ autǭ noi)* suggests that they must have a similar understanding of Christ if, indeed, they are to be a single community, the church of God.

11. *For concerning you it has been reported to me, my brothers and sisters:* The rehearsal of events leading up to the sending of the letter (the rhetorical *diēgēsis)* is introduced by a postpositive *gar.* The verb in the aorist *(edēlōthē)* indicates the specificity of the report Paul had received. That report was neither hearsay nor rumor. There was a specific time when a report had been made to Paul. The report concerned the Corinthians. It had been made directly to Paul, who now appeals to the Corinthians as his brothers and sisters. Paul's formula of direct address echoes the appeal of v. 10. He underscores the fact that he is in a familial relationship with the Corinthians by using the pronoun *mou,* "my." The subject of the report Paul had received was a matter of particular concern because it had to do with those he considered to be his own siblings. For Paul it was a family matter.

by Chloe's people: Rhetorically the mention of Chloe's people gives credence to the report received by Paul. The report was not hearsay; it came directly from Chloe's people. Little is known about Chloe and her people other than that they served as Paul's informants in this instance. This is the only mention of them in the NT. Commentators generally agree that Chloe's people *(tōn Chloēs,* literally "those of Chloe"; see BDF 162.5) were members of the family, perhaps even slaves or freed persons belonging to the household.

If those who visited Paul in Ephesus were Chloe's slaves, it may be that Chloe herself was not a Christian. In the early history of the church it sometimes happened that a group of slaves belonging to a same household were Christian even if the slave owner was not. Alternatively, when the owner was Christian it was quite likely that the slaves were Christian as well. Given the fact that Paul designates those who visited him by Chloe's name it is likely that Chloe was a Christian and, most probably, the patron of a church that gathered in her house (cf. Rom 16:10-11; Acts 16:15; Col 4:15). Since the expression "those of Chloe" *(tōn Chloēs)* is different from the wording Paul uses in Rom 16:10-11, "those who belong to the family of Aristobulus *(tous ek tōn Aristoboulou) . . .* those who belong to the family of Narcissus *(tous ek tōn Narkissou),*" it has been argued that Chloe's entire household was Christian (Meeks) or that she, like Apollos (see v. 12), had her own following in Corinth (Schüssler Fiorenza, "Rhetorical Situation," 394–395).

It is not certain that Chloe lived in Corinth. On the basis of her people's knowledge of the situation at Corinth some commentators think that she lived there (Theissen, Meeks) and that her people came to visit Paul in Ephesus. Other scholars think it is more likely that hers was an Ephesian household whose members had gone to Corinth on a business trip (Fee, Gillman). If Chloe actually resided in Corinth and if she was Christian she, along with Erastus and Gaius (1:14; Rom 16:23), would have been one of the "powerful" Christians of Corinth (1:26).

that there are quarrels among you: Chloe's people brought news of hot disputes *(erides)* among the Corinthians. In Attic Greek the term *erides* was used in political discourse to designate political strife and discord (Herodotus, Plutarch). This kind of political discord stems from jealousy and rivalry (cf. 3:3, where *eris* is again used). The term itself appears in classic lists of vices (Sir 28:11) and in hardship lists (Sir 40:5, 9), such as those used by Paul and Clement in later references to the Corinthians (2 Cor 12:20; *1 Clem.* 46:5; PG 1, 304; cf. Rom 13:13; Gal 5:20). The terms used by Paul to describe the situation at Corinth, "divisions" and "quarrels," are borrowed from classic political usage. They describe a community that is at odds within itself.

12. *But I tell you this: that each one of you says:* A postpositive *de* connects Paul's exposition to his account of the report he received. The political imagery continues in the slogans used by Paul. The divisions within the assembly are underscored by Paul's *hekastos,* "each one." Each one is saying something different. Paul wishes that they would all say the same thing *(to auto legēte pantes,* v. 11), but each of them is saying something different *(hekastos hymōn legei . . .).* They are not in unanimity or harmony. In using the classical topos of the body as a metaphor for the Christian community at Corinth (12:12-26) Paul also presents the members as saying things that affirm their independence from others within the body (vv. 15, 16, 21).

I am Paul's: What they are saying evokes the political arena. In antiquity political groups were designated by the name of the person whose political interests they served. "I am Paul's" *(egō men eimi Paulou,* with an emphatic *egō)* would be similar to the political slogan, "I'm for X," heard during the election season. The different slogans uttered by the Corinthians illustrate the fact that they are not in agreement (see note on 4:6).

I am Apollos's: The second slogan cited by Paul lacks a verb and is elliptical in form *(Egō de Apollō).* Like the first slogan, with which it contrasts sharply *(men . . . de;* BDF 447.2), it contains an emphatic *egō.* Some say that they are for Paul; others say that they are for Apollos. Apollos was a well-known and almost legendary figure in the early Christian movement. Luke describes him as a native of Alexandria, well-versed in the Scriptures, catechized by Aquila and Prisca (Acts 18:24–19:1a), instructed in the way of the Lord (probably an allusion to his acceptance of Christianity, see Acts 9:2, although some take it to be a reference to his knowledge of the LXX), ardent in spirit, and an eloquent and enthusiastic speaker. Apollos spent some time in Corinth where, according to Luke, he greatly helped those who were believers and used scriptural argumentation to refute the Jews. The Western text of Acts gives an indication of the motivation for Apollos's visit to Corinth. It tells how some Corinthian Christians residing in Ephesus were so impressed by Apollos's oratory that they begged him to go with them when they returned to Corinth (Acts 18:27). Apollos seems to have been with Paul in Ephesus as Paul was writing this letter to the Corinthians (1 Cor 16:12). Paul urged him to return to Corinth but Apollos was reluctant to do so. The pseudepigraphical letter to Titus cites the name of Apollos as one of Paul's emissaries (Titus 3:13).

Peter Richardson ("Thunderbolt") has argued that some Corinthians had exploited the Q tradition, a hypothetical source used by Matthew and Luke, which features John the Baptist and a wisdom motif *(sophia),* thus preferring Apollos to Paul. Other scholars opine that under the aegis of Apollos some Corinthians had accepted the idea that the espousal of a Philonic kind of wisdom could lead to spiritual status and salvation. In his first major rhetorical argument Paul writes extensively about wisdom (1:17–4:21). In this rhetorical *pistis* Paul frequently cites the harmonious relationship between himself and Apollos (3:4, 5, 6, 22) as an example for the Corinthians. As he brings the unit to closure he explicitly states that he has cited the example of himself and Apollos for their benefit (4:6).

I am Cephas's: In form this slogan is similar to the second, "I am Apollos's." With the exception of Gal 2:7-8 Paul always refers to Peter as "Cephas" (1 Cor 1:12; 3:22; 9:5; 15:5; Gal 1:18; 2:9, 11, 14), the name used for Peter in early Christian circles. Derived from the Aramaic term for a rocky crag, the nickname was conferred upon Simon (a name not used by Paul) by Jesus (Matt 10:2; 16:18; Mark 3:16; John 1:42). That Simon's Aramaic alias was known to the Corinthians and is cited, rather than paraphrased *(Petros),* in Paul's Hellenistic composition is an indication that not only Peter but also his Aramaic nickname were widely known in early Christianity.

Since Ferdinand Christian Baur's analysis of early Christian history in terms of the Hegelian schema of thesis-antithesis-synthesis scholars have commonly opined that Paul's citation of the "I am Cephas'" slogan indicated the existence of a Jewish-Christian faction at Corinth, the Petrine party. Despite several references to Cephas in 1 Corinthians (3:22; 9:5; 15:5) there is no evidence that the one known as Cephas had visited Corinth. It is more likely that the Corinthian Christians knew of Peter only through the early tradition, in which case it is hardly likely that there was a Petrine or Jewish-Christian faction at Corinth. Moreover, the unitary address of Paul's argument militates against the existence of a separate Jewish-Christian faction at Corinth, as does the fact that Paul can write about Paul, Apollos, Cephas, and Christ, about Paul, Apollos, and Cephas (3:22), or about Paul and Apollos (3:4, where similar slogans appear). According to Chrysostom (*On the First Epistle to the Corinthians,* Homily 3.1; PG 61, 24) the citation of four names in 1:12 does not indicate that different factions in Corinth actually rallied around Paul, Apollos, and Cephas; rather it is Paul's way of tactfully alluding to those who were the cause of divisiveness at Corinth (cf. 4:6).

I am Christ's: Some influential scholars, especially C.F.G. Heinrici and Johannes Weiss in his 1910 commentary on 1 Corinthians, consider this phrase to be an addition to the series of slogans that might have been heard in Corinth. Their hypothesis is principally based on 3:22 and 1 *Clem.* 47:3; PG 1, 308, which mentions only Paul, Apollos, and Cephas, as well as on the inherent difficulty in limning an exclusive group at Corinth that would rally around the name of Christ. The latter problem led Emil R. Perdelwitz, in 1911, to suggest that the fourth member of Paul's text originally read "I am Chrispus'" (cf. 1:14), in place of which an inadvertent scribe could easily have written "I am Christ's," "Chrispus" and "Christ" being similar in sound and in Greek majuscule calligraphy. The manuscript tradition does not provide any significant evidence of a scribal addition to the text at this point, nor does it provide any warrant for Perdelwitz's ingenious conjecture.

"I am Christ's" (cf. 2 Cor 10:7) was part of the letter as written. Given the rhetorical crescendo, it is likely that it is Paul himself who has composed the entire series of slogans. They represent a dramatic expression of independence from Paul and the gospel he had preached. The series concludes with reference to Christ, testimony to whom Paul has already spotlighted (v. 6).

13. *Is Christ divided?:* Paul's *ad hominem* rejoinder to the divisions at Corinth takes the form of a series of rhetorical questions. "Is Christ divided?" is the first of these questions. In 1 Corinthians Paul makes frequent and effective use of rhetorical questions. They engage the audience in the discussion of the issues under consideration. The first of his rhetorical questions puts Christ at the focal point of the discussion. It challenges the Corinthians to make a judgment with respect to Christ.

Some manuscripts and some ancient versions ($\mathfrak{P}^{46}$, syr[P], cop[sa], arm) include a "not" and read Paul's words as an affirmation, "Christ is not divided," rather than as a rhetorical question. Ancient Greek manuscripts had no punctuation. As a result some scribes apparently misunderstood Paul's rhetorical question. Reading the text as if it made an unlikely affirmation ("Christ is divided"), rather than as posing a question ("Is Christ divided?"), they corrected the text so that it made full sense. The noetic content of the "corrected" text, the work of "intelligent" scribes, is the same as that of Paul's rhetorical question, but the syntactical change deprives Paul's argument of its rhetorical force.

Paul's question evokes the metaphor of the body of Christ. The metaphor of the body is a popular political image, effectively used by Paul in reference to the church at Corinth (12:12-26). For Paul the unity of Christ is a given (see 12:5, 12-26). *Meris* is a common Greek term for a class or political party; the cognate verb, *merizō*, has the connotation "to split into political factions" (Appian, *Civil Wars* 1.1; Polybius, *Histories* 8.21.9). In effect Paul is saying to the Corinthians, "Is the body of Christ splintered into political parties?" "Has Christ been dismembered?"

Has Paul been crucified for your sake?: Paul's first rhetorical question, evoking a negative response (the question begins with the interrogative particle *mē*, which indicates the expectation of a negative reply), may well have elicited the mental response, "No, Christ has not been divided, Christ has been crucified." In the theological and kerygmatic vocabulary of the apostle the Christ title evokes the death and resurrection of Jesus. In the first rhetorical question of his letter Paul had asked the Corinthians to reflect on Christ, put to death and raised from the dead. Now with a subtle movement of rhetorical slippage Paul asks whether he had been crucified on behalf of the Corinthians. It was virtually unthinkable for a Roman citizen to be crucified. This circumstance (cf. 9:1) only adds to the implausibility of a positive response to the question as phrased. With rhetorical inversion and by means of the succinct formula "for your sake" (*hyper hymōn; peri hymōn* in 𝔓⁴⁶, B), Paul's question effectively calls attention to the vicarious death of Jesus. The kerygma, with its focus on the death and resurrection of Jesus, will underlie Paul's argument throughout the letter. For a comparable use of a *hyper* phrase to express the vicarious character of Jesus' death see 11:24; 15:3; Rom 5:8; 8:32; 14:15 (cf. 1 Cor 8:11); 2 Cor 5:14-15; Gal 1:4; Col 1:24 (cf. Eph 3:1, 13; Col 2:1).

Or were you baptized in the name of Paul?: This question and the previous one form a single sentence in Greek. In the second part of the double question Paul continues his rhetorical inversion. Both questions are intended to elicit a strong negative response from Paul's audience. Both suggest just how preposterous it is to substitute Paul for Christ. Both appeal to the experience of the Corinthians. Paul's letter to them is laced with appeals to their experience, most clearly in his use of the rhetorical question, "Don't you know that?" (*ouk oidate*, 3:16; 5:6; 6:2, 3, 9, 15, 16, 19; 9:13, 24). Paul's first rhetorical question appeals to the Corinthians' hearing of the kerygma (cf. 15:1-3), the second to their baptismal practice.

Paul's second question implies that the Corinthians were baptized in the name of Jesus Christ (on the name, see note on 1:10). Paul's words make allusion to an early baptismal formula (cf. Acts 8:16, 19:5 [both with *eis*, as in 1:13]; Acts 2:38 [with *epi*]; 10:48 [with *en*]; compare Matt 28:19), probably derived from a Hebrew and Aramaic cultic formula, *lĕšēm*, in the name, suggesting that the baptismal ritual is fundamentally determined by the Christ event (cf. 10:2; Rom 6:3; Gal 3:27). The Semitic formula "in the name of" indicates a fundamental reference, a reason, purpose, or capacity of something. Paul's rhetorical question, with its awaited negative response, suggests that the fundamental reference for baptism among the Corinthians is not Paul but another.

With his allusive references to the death of Jesus and to baptism in his name Paul has elicited the inaugural events of the Corinthian Christians' eschatological situation. It was the death by crucifixion of Jesus that, elucidated by his resurrection, inaugurated the eschatological era to culminate in the day of our Lord Jesus Christ. It was the baptism of the Corinthian Christians in the name of the same Lord Jesus Christ that entailed their participation in this eschatological situation.

On the relationship between baptism and the death/resurrection of Jesus see Rom 6:1-11. In his first letter to the Corinthians Paul does not so much reflect on the theological meaning of baptism as on its consequences for ecclesial practice. This is the case here. That the Corinthians have been baptized in the name of Christ rather than in the name of Paul (or Apollos or Cephas) means that their existence should be normed by reference to the Christ event.

Paul's rhetorical question calls for a reflection on his ministry among the Corinthians. In the letter an appeal to the Corinthians' experience of his ministry will form a significant part of his argument, which is largely an *ethos* argument. In the verses that follow Paul will pursue the thought of his baptismal activity (vv. 14-17).

14. *I thank God:* Paul's expletive recalls the formal expression of thanksgiving with which he began his communication with the Corinthians; his thanksgiving continues to be addressed to God (see note on 1:4). Some manuscripts (A, 33, 81, and many of the ancient versions, including several of the Old Latin texts) add a qualifying "my" to "God." It may be that these scribes were influenced by 1:4 so that they made the expression in v. 14 conform with Paul's earlier expression. Other manuscripts (especially ℵ and B, which also omit "my God" from 1:4, and many Fathers, including Clement, Origen, and Chrysostom) omit any reference to the God to whom Paul's thanksgiving is directed. The omission of "God" reduces the wording of the parenthetical remark to a rather bland "I am grateful that. . . ." That Paul's epistolary thanksgivings are normally addressed to God provides an element of intrinsic probability to the reading adopted by *GNT*[4].

Paul's expression of thanksgiving functions as an aside in his rhetorical appeal, but Paul is not disinclined to make passing reference to God in his letters (e.g., 1 Thess 2:5). In 1 Corinthians God-language abounds, particularly in 1:18–3:23. The mention of God in 1:14, the eighth use of *theos* in the opening verses of the letter, prepares the way for the appeal to follow.

that I did not baptize anyone of you: The absence of a temporal adverb indicates that Paul's expression of thanksgiving is not an epistolary thanksgiving as such. Nevertheless, Paul indicates the reason for his thanksgiving by means of a *hoti* clause. The reason alleged is a negative one. Paul is grateful that he did not baptize, that is, with but a few exceptions. Paul says that he baptized, but only rarely, to preclude anyone's saying that they were baptized in his name (1:13). His disquisition on his baptismal activity is the first element of an extended *contradictio* (see v. 17). Use of the rhetorical device highlights the fact that Paul considers his own ministry to be that of evangelizing. Paul's evangelization of the Corinthians is a central issue in his letter; Rolf Baumann, in fact, holds that it is the central issue (*Mitte und Norm* 63).

except Crispus: Named before Gaius and the household of Stephanas, Crispus probably was one of the Corinthians whose support Paul could presume. Acts 18:8 identifies a Crispus, an official of the synagogue *(archisynagōgos)*, who became a believer in the Lord together with all his household. As a synagogue official this Crispus would have been responsible for the order of the service, the proper upkeep of the synagogue building, and perhaps the provision of a new synagogue. Crispus' influence appears to have been such that others came to believe in the Lord as well. His function seems to suggest that he was a man of means and if, as is likely, he is to be identified with the Crispus of v. 14 he must be ranked among the powerful Christians of Corinth (1:26). Crispus was one of the few Corinthians actually baptized by Paul.

and Gaius: Since Gaius is mentioned by name and had been baptized by Paul it is reasonable to suppose that he also was one of Paul's supporters within the Corinthian church. He appears to have been the person with whom Paul was staying when he wrote the letter to the Romans (or at least the last chapter of Romans; see Rom 16:23). Since Gaius' house was large enough to accommodate the entire Christian community at Corinth—he was host to the whole church *(ho xenos . . . holēs tēs ekklēsias)*—he must have been a man of some affluence. Since he had a Roman *praenomen* and acquaintances at Rome it may be that Gaius was a Roman colonist who had emigrated to Corinth. Some commentators suggest that he might have been the Titius Justus to whose house Paul went after he visited the synagogue in Corinth (Acts 18:7). If the suggestion could be proven to be true, Gaius' full name would have been, in good Roman fashion, Gaius Titius Justus. As Roman Gaius was probably a Gentile. Paul has apparently affirmed that he had baptized both a Jew (Crispus) and a Gentile (Gaius) at Corinth.

15. *lest anyone say that you were baptized in my name:* A consequence *(hina mē)* of Paul's having baptized so few people at Corinth is that the Corinthians were not able to say that they were baptized in Paul's name. The disclaimer continues to be marked by the hyperbole *(hina mē tis,* "lest anyone") that characterizes the opening verses of the letter. "In my name" *(eis to emon onoma)* recalls the rhetorical question of v. 13 and the Christian practice of baptism in the name of Jesus. The Corinthians' speech, the way they talked, is an issue for Paul (cf. vv. 5, 10, 12; see also chs. 12–14, with their mention of various gifts of speech, the word of wisdom, the word of knowledge, speaking in tongues, the interpretation of tongues, prophecy). Those who were baptized by Paul, Crispus and Gaius, are presumed not to claim that they had been baptized in Paul's name.

16. *I also baptized the household of Stephanas:* Unlike some other individuals whom Paul cites by name in the letter (Crispus, Gaius, Apollos, Aquila, and Prisca), Stephanas and his household are not mentioned in any NT text except this letter to the Corinthians. With the verve of his rhetoric intended to emphasize how few people he had baptized so as to preclude any claim that people were baptized in his name, Paul appears to have forgotten to mention that he had baptized the household of Stephanas. The mention of the household of Stephanas appears to be an afterthought in 1:16, the result of Paul's writing *currente calamo* and allowing his rhetoric to escape his control. Paul's omission of a reference to the household of Stephanas may, however, have been disingenuous. The family was well known to Paul and to the Corinthians. "You know the household of Stephanas," he writes in 16:15, thereby indicating that the Corinthians were acquainted with Stephanas's family. Having described them as the first fruits of his Asiatic mission and lauding them for their service to the church, Paul commends the household of Stephanas to the Corinthians and urges the Corinthians to recognize their leadership (16:15-18). As the patron of a household church and with the capacity to render service to the community, Stephanas is to be ranked among the powerful members of the community. Meeks *(Urban Christians* 57–58) opines that Stephanas probably enjoyed a stature within the community similar to that of Crispus and Gaius, even if he may not have been as wealthy as the latter. Stephanas, along with Fortunatus and Achaicus, visited Paul during his stay in Ephesus (16:17).

for the rest I do not know whether I baptized anyone else: For the third time Paul uses a negative (*oudena*, v. 14; *hina mē tis*, v. 15; *ouk oida*, v. 16) to affirm that he did not baptize. Baptizing was not his mission, as he will explain in the following verse. The triple repetition, culminating in his explanation of his apostolate (cf. 1:1), which also uses a negative, underscores Paul's fidelity to the mission that was his. *Loipon*, "for the rest" is used adverbially.

17. *For Christ did not send me to baptize, but to evangelize:* Paul offers an explanation (note the postpositive, explanatory *gar*) of why he had baptized so few at Corinth. In the *intitulatio* of his letter Paul designated himself as an "apostle of Christ Jesus" (1:1), one who had been sent. Now he clarifies the nature of his mission. Paul was sent to proclaim the good news (*euaggelizesthai*); evangelization is his mission. The use of the rhetorical device of *contradictio* allows him to highlight the proclamation of the gospel as the task for which he has been sent. Despite the occasional baptisms he performed, baptizing was not his essential task. It was not his apostolic task. In 9:16-18, the only other passage in 1 Corinthians in which he uses the verb *euaggelizesthai*, Paul explains that he preaches the gospel as a servant, a slave of Jesus Christ.

not with cleverness of speech: A second negation (*ouk en*) sharpens the focus on Paul's statement with regard to his mission of evangelizing. "Not with cleverness of speech" (*ouk en sophią logou*) is literally "not in wisdom of word." Since both Greek nouns admit of a wide range of meanings Paul's phrase could well be paraphrased, "not with rhetorical technique" (Pogoloff, *Logos and Sophia*; Martin, *Body* 47), that is, not with the skill of word. Paul denies that the persuasive force of his message derives from his clever use of rhetorical technique, a point to which he will return in 2:1-5, a passage that is virtually a commentary on v. 17b. In that pericope Paul twice (vv. 1, 4) denies the power of his own rhetoric. The negation in the first part of this implied antithesis, "not with cleverness of speech," continues in the following clause ("lest," *hina mē*, cf. 1:15). Together these two phrases point to the manner of Paul's proclamation ("not with cleverness of speech") and its content ("the cross of Christ," cf. v. 18).

lest the cross of Christ be deprived of its power: Paul suggests that his reliance on rhetoric would have deprived the cross of its power, that is, its power to save (1:18). In the second rhetorical question of the short diatribe addressed to the Corinthians (1:13) Paul had suggested that the cross was the standard against which all allegiance is to be judged. Now he suggests that the cross is at the center of his preaching. The situation is anomalous. To evangelize is to announce good news (*eu-aggelizesthai*). On the surface of things the cross is "bad news." It was the weak and powerless who were crucified in the Roman Empire (see note on v. 13), but Paul suggests that there is power in the cross of Christ, a motif he will pick up in his topical exposition on the message of the cross in v. 18. The implied antithesis between the cross of Christ and cleverness of speech is strange, yet it will serve as the focus of Paul's discourse in the considerations to follow (1:18–2:16).

FOR REFERENCE AND FURTHER STUDY

Bjerkelund, Carl J. *Parakalo: Form, Function und Sinn der Parakalo-Sätze in den paulinischen Briefen.* Reprint Oslo: Universitetsforlaget, 1985.

Cotter, Wendy. "Women's Authority Roles in Paul's Churches: Countercultural or Conventional?" *NovT* 36 (1994) 350–372.

Delling, Gerhard. "Zur Taufe von 'Häusern' im Urchristentum," *NovT* 7 (1964–65) 285–311.

Gillman, Florence M. *Women Who Knew Paul.* Zacchaeus Studies: New Testament. Collegeville: The Liturgical Press, 1992, 38–39.

Grayston, Kenneth. "A Problem of Translation: The Meaning of *parakaleō, paraklēsis* in the New Testament," *ScrB* 11 (1980) 27–31.

Hartman, Lars. "Baptism 'Into the Name of Jesus' and Early Christology: Some Tentative Considerations," *ST* 28 (1974) 21–48.

Klauck, Hans-Josef. "The House Church as a Way of Life," *TD* 30 (1982) 153–157.
_____. *Hausgemeinde und Hauskirche im frühen Christentum.* SBS 103. Stuttgart: Katholisches Bibelwerk, 1981.

Perkins, Pheme. *Peter: Apostle for the Whole Church.* Studies on Personalities of the New Testament. Columbia, S.C.: University of South Carolina Press, 1994, 111–115.

Richardson, Peter. "The Thunderbolt in Q and the Wise Man in Corinth" in Peter Richardson and John C. Hurd, eds., *Jesus to Paul: Studies in Honour of Francis Wright Beare.* Waterloo, Ont.: Wilfred Laurier University, 1984, 91–111.

Schenke, Ludger. "Zur sogennanten 'Oikosformel' im NT," *Kairos* 13 (1971) 226–243.

Vogler, Werner. "Die Bedeutung der urchristlichen Hausgemeinden für die Ausbreitung des Evangeliums," *TLZ* 107 (1982) 785–794.

Weigandt, Peter. "Zur sogennanten 'Oikosformel,'" *NovT* 6 (1963) 49–74.

B. FIRST RHETORICAL DEMONSTRATION (1:18–4:21)

In his treatise on rhetoric Aristotle compared the rhetorical statement of the case *(prothesis)* and the proof *(pistis)* to a problem and its demonstration *(to men problēma to de apodeixis).* He went on to say in regard to those who wanted to find a full and neatly articulated rhetorical order *(taxis)* in every exposition that "the division now generally made is absurd" *(Art of Rhetoric* 3.13.3). Something similar might be said about some contemporary attempts to analyze Paul's letter to the Corinthians according to the categories of ancient rhetoric. Recourse to ancient rhetoric is useful. It provides us with a way of looking at Paul's letter that offers a different and insightful vantage point, but it must not be pushed to the extreme. The somewhat artificial categories of the manuals must not be superimposed on Paul's living communication to the Corinthians. Taking a hint from Aristotle, this commentary will simply identify the major units in the body of Paul's letter as "rhetorical demonstrations."

The first rhetorical demonstration (1:18–4:21) follows upon Paul's statement of purpose (1:10). To the statement of the case were appended several verses that had principally an epistolary function (1:11-17). The statement of the case itself was characterized by its brevity, completeness, and conciseness, the very qualities that Cicero, Paul's contemporary, had identified as the hallmark of a good rhetorical *propositio* (*De inventione* 1.22.32).

The core of the first rhetorical demonstration is 1:18–3:23. The reference to wisdom and foolishness and the citation of Scripture in 3:19-20 recalls Paul's words on wisdom and foolishness and his use of Scripture in 1:18-19. Thus it is possible to speak of an *inclusio* or ring construction that identifies 1:18–3:23 as a distinct subunit within the first rhetorical demonstration. Wilhelm Wuellner ("Greek Rhetoric," 185) calls the subunit a major digression. It is encompassed between the letter body's opening unit (1:10-17), which spoke about Paul's purpose in writing and his relationship with the community, and the recurrence of these motifs in 4:6-21, where Paul speaks of the purpose of his writing (4:14-16) and reflects on his past and future relationship with the community.

Impressed by Paul's frequent recourse to Scripture, both in explicit citation and in the form of literary allusion, a number of scholars (Branick, Ellis, Peterson, Wuellner) believe that a homily, in the form of a homiletic midrash, lies at the origin of Paul's exposition on divine wisdom. Ellis has proposed two midrashic expositions with respective applications and a final conclusion as the basic outline of the midrash, thus midrash (1:18-31), application (2:1-5), midrash (2:6-16), application (3:1-17), conclusion (3:18-20).

FOR REFERENCE AND FURTHER STUDY

Adamo, David. "Wisdom and its Importance to Paul's Christology in I Corinthians," *DBM* 17 (1988) 31–43.

Aletti, Jean-Noel. "Sagesse et mystère chez Paul. Réflexion sur le rapprochement de deux champs lexicographiques" in Jacques Trublet, ed. *La Sagesse biblique de l'Ancien au Nouveau Testament*. LeDiv 160. Paris: Cerf, 1995, 357–379, 380–384.

Baumann, Rolf. *Mitte und Norm des Christlichen. Eine Auslegung von 1 Korinther 1,1–3,4*. Munich: Aschendorff, 1968.

Beatrice, Pier Franco. "Gli avversari di Paolo e il problema della Gnosi a Corinto," *CStor* 6 (1985) 1–25.

Borghi, Ernesto. "Il tema sophia in 1 Cor 1–4," *RivBib* 40 (1992) 421–458.

Branick, Vincent P. "Source and Redaction Analysis of 1 Corinthians 1–3," *JBL* 101 (1982) 251–269.

Brown, Alexandra R. *The Cross and Human Transformation: Paul's Apocalyptic Word in 1 Corinthians*. Minneapolis: Fortress, 1995.

_____. "Apocalyptic Transformation in Paul's Discourse on the Cross," *Word & World* 16 (1996) 427–436.

Cipriani, Settimio. "'Sapientia crucis' e sapienza 'umana' in Paolo," *RivBib* 36 (1988) 343–361.

Dahl, Nils A. "Paul and the Church at Corinth according to 1 Corinthians 1.10–4.21" in William R. Farmer, Charles Francis Digby Moule, and Richard R. Niebuhr, eds., *Christian History and Interpretation: Studies Presented to John Knox*. Cambridge: Cambridge University Press, 1967, 313–335.

Davis, James A. *Wisdom and Spirit: An Investigation of 1 Corinthians, 1,18–3,20 against the Background of Jewish Sapiential Traditions in the Greco-Roman Period*. Lanham, Md.: University Press of America, 1984.

Elliott, Neil. "The Anti-Imperial Message of the Cross" in Richard A. Horsley, ed., *Paul and Empire: Religion and Power in Roman Imperial Society*. Harrisburg: Trinity Press International, 1997, 167–183.

Ellis, E. Earle. *Prophecy and Hermeneutic in Early Christianity: New Testament Essays*. WUNT 18. Tübingen: J.C.B. Mohr, 1978, 147–172, 213–220.

Fitzgerald, John T. *Cracks in an Earthen Vessel: An Examination of the Catalogues of Hardships in the Corinthian Correspondence*. SBL.DS 99 Atlanta: Scholars, 1988, 117–148.

Gooch, Paul W. *Partial Knowledge: Philosophical Studies in Paul*. Notre Dame, Ind.: Notre Dame University Press, 1987.

Goulder, Michael D. "Sophia in 1 Corinthians," *NTS* 37 (1991) 516–534.

Humphries, Raymond A. "Paul's Rhetoric of Argumentation in I Corinthians 1–4." GTU Ph.D. Dissertation. Berkeley, CA, 1979.

Hyldahl, Niels. "The Corinthian 'Parties' and the Corinthian Crisis," *ST* 45 (1991) 19–32.

Kuck, David W. *Judgment and Community Conflict: Paul's Use of Apocalyptic Judgment Language in 1 Corinthians 3:5–4:5*. NovT.S 66. Leiden: Brill, 1992.

Lampe, Peter. "Theological Wisdom and the 'Word About the Cross.' The Rhetorical Scheme in I Corinthians 1–4," *Interp.* 44 (1990) 117–131.

Lang, Friedrich. "Die Gruppen in Korinth nach 1. Korinther 1-4," *ThBeitr* 14 (1983) 68–79.

Litfin, A. Duane. *St. Paul's Theology of Proclamation: 1 Corinthians 1–4 and Greco-Roman Rhetoric*. MSSNTS 79. Cambridge: Cambridge University Press, 1994.

Peterson, Erik. "1 Kor 1,18f und die Thematik des jüdisches Busstages," *Bib.* 32 (1951) 97–103.

Pogoloff, Stephen M. *Logos and Sophia: The Rhetorical Situation of 1 Corinthians*. SBL.DS 134. Atlanta: Scholars, 1992.

Pöttner, Martin. *Realität als Kommunikation: Ansätze zur Beschreibung der Grammatik des paulinischen Sprechens in 1 Kor 1,4–4,21 im Blick auf literarische Problematik und Situationsbezug des 1. Korintherbriefes*. Theologie 2. Münster: Lit, 1995.

Reese, James M. "Paul Proclaims the Wisdom of the Cross: Scandal and Foolishness," *BTB* 9 (1979) 147–153.

Schwarz, Eberhard. "Wo's Weisheit ist, ein Tor zu sein. Zur Argumentation von 1 Kor 1–4," *WuD* 20 (1989) 219–235.

Sellin, Gerhard. "Das 'Geheimnis' der Weisheit und das Rätsel der 'Christuspartei' (zu 1 Kor 1–4)," *ZNW* 73 (1982) 69–96.

Sevrin, Jean-Marie. "La gnose à Corinthe. Questions de méthode et observations sur 1 Co 1,17–3,3," *CorC* 121–139.

Söding, Thomas. "Kreuzestheologie und Rechtfertigunslehre. Zur Verbindung von Christologie und Soteriologie im Ersten Korintherbrief und im Galaterbrief," *Catholica* 46 (1992) 31–60.

Stowers, Stanley K. "Paul on the Use and Abuse of Reason" in David L. Balch, et al, eds., *Greeks, Romans, and Christians. Essays in Honor of Abraham J. Malherbe.* Minneapolis: Fortress, 1990, 253–286.

Trevijano Etcheverría, Ramón M. "El contraste de sabidurías (1 Cor 1,17–4,20)," *Salm* 34 (1987) 277–298.

Vadakkedom, J. "The Corinthian Community: A Divided Church? A Study Based on 1 Corinthians 1–4," *BibBH* 23 (1997) 27–44.

Vielhauer, Philipp. "Paul and the Cephas Party in Corinth," *Journal of Higher Criticism* 1 (1994) 129–142. ET of "Paulus und die Cephaspartei in Korinth," *NTS* 21 (1975) 341–352.

Vos, Johannes Sijko. "Die Argumentation des Paulus in 1 Cor 1,10–3,4," *CorC* 87–119.

Welborn, L. L. "On the Discord in Corinth: 1 Corinthians 1–4 and Ancient Politics," *JBL* 106 (1987) 85–111. Revised in idem, *Politics and Rhetoric in the Corinthian Epistles.* Macon, Ga.: Mercer University Press, 1997, 1–42.

Widmer, Gabriel-Philippe. "La parole de la croix et le langage du monde," *CV* 24 (1981) 109–122.

Wilckens, Ulrich. *Weisheit und Torheit. Eine exegetisch-religionsgeschichtliche Untersuchung zu 1. Kor. 1 und 2.* BHTh 26. Tübingen: J.C.B. Mohr, 1971.

Wuellner, Wilhelm. "Greek Rhetoric and Pauline Argumentation" in William R. Schoedel and Robert L. Wilken, eds., *Early Christian Literature and the Classical Intellectual Tradition in honorem Robert M. Grant.* ThH 53. Paris: Beauchesne, 1979, 177–188.

_____. "Haggadic Homily Genre in 1 Cor 1–3," *JBL* 89 (1970) 199–204.

1. *Wisdom and Power* (1:18-31)

18. For the message of the cross is foolishness to those who are perishing; but it is the power of God to us who are being saved. 19. For it is written, "I will destroy the wisdom of the wise and I will put aside the cleverness of the clever." 20. Where is the wise person? Where is the learned one? Where is the one who searches in this age? Did not God make foolish the wisdom of the world? 21. For since, in the wisdom of

God, the world does not know God through wisdom, God chose to save those who believe through the foolishness of the proclamation; 22. and since Jews are asking for signs and Hellenes are looking for wisdom; 23. we, however, proclaim Christ crucified, for the Jews a stumbling block, for Gentiles foolishness, 24. but to those who have been called, both Jews and Hellenes, Christ is the power of God and the wisdom of God; 25. for the foolishness of God is wiser than humans and the weakness of God is stronger than humans.

26. Brothers and sisters, ponder your call because not many are wise according to human standards, not many are powerful, not many of noble birth. 27. But God chose the foolish of the world in order to put the wise to shame, and God chose the weak of the world in order to put the strong to shame, 28. and God chose those of lowly birth of the world and those who are scorned, those who are nothing, in order to make ineffective those who are, 29. lest all flesh boast in the presence of God. 30. From him you are in Christ Jesus, who became wisdom from God for us, and righteousness, holiness, and redemption, 31. as it is written, "Let the one who boasts boast about the Lord."

Interpretation

Paul succinctly articulates the theme of his first demonstration (1:18–4:21) in an opening statement (v. 18) that is developed as an explanatory comment on the gospel which he has proclaimed. Paul's explanation focuses on the wisdom and power of God. The gospel is divisive. There are those who consider the message of the cross as foolishness and those who consider it as power. Those who consider it to be foolishness perish; those who consider it to be a manifestation of God's power are saved. The notion of God's power *(dynamis theou)* in vv. 18 and 24 creates an *inclusio* that constitutes 1:18-24 as a discrete literary unit. Verse 25 summarizes this unit and provides a transition to 1:26-31, a reflection on the condition of the Corinthians who have been called to believe the message of the cross.

The careful construction and skillful use of parallelism that characterize v. 25 are continued in the following section (vv. 26-31). It is circumscribed as a literary unit by an allusion to Jer 9:23 (9:22 LXX) in v. 26 and an abbreviated citation of the same scriptural passage in v. 31. Parallelism, similar to the parallelism that characterizes 1:18-24 and provides a structure for v. 25, continues to be used, especially in vv. 26-28. Paul's use of parallelism is so skillful that he is able to express his thought fully without compromising in the least the form of his construction.

Although vv. 18-24 and vv. 26-31 are two discrete literary units linked together by v. 25, they form a single larger literary unit, circumscribed by a scriptural citation introduced by the classic lemma "it is written" (vv.

19, 31). From the rhetorical point of view Paul has divided the question. Verse 18 serves as a rhetorical *partitio,* which takes up the themes of wisdom and power from v. 17. Wisdom is the focus of vv. 18-25 with their nine uses of *soph-* (wise) and five uses of *mōr-* (foolish). Power is the focus of vv. 26-31 with their commentary on the social situation of the Corinthians. Ethnicity serves as the social framework of the first unit, social division as the background of the second. Ethnicity and social division are issues to which Paul will return later in the letter, especially in 7:17-24 when he systematically treats of "the call" and in 1:26 when he asks the Corinthians to ponder their call.

Although Paul had professed that he did not use cleverness of speech in his proclamation of the gospel (v. 17) his exposition of the message of the cross is fraught with powerful literary and rhetorical devices. The passage is characterized not only by its use of consistent parallelism but also by the techniques of the rhetorical question, comparison and contrast, repetition, *paronomasia,* gradation, and irony. Its method of argumentation is that of the enthymeme. Paul's direct mode of address echoes the Stoic diatribe. In sum, the message of the cross is phrased in powerful rhetoric.

The Jewish Scriptures are an important feature of Paul's rhetorical *heurēsis (inventio).* Neither the citation of Isa 29:14 with which he begins the argument nor the citation of Jer 9:23 with which it is closed is haphazardly inserted into Paul's text. They have been deliberately chosen in view of Paul's argument. Jeremiah 9:22-23 serves as the intertextual dialogue partner of an argument Paul develops in the second unit of his blatantly rhetorical exposition. Jeremiah has strongly influenced Paul's thought and even his self-image, but it may be that there is no other passage in the Pauline correspondence in which Jeremiah has shaped Pauline rhetoric as strongly as it has in 1 Cor 1:26-31.

The Cross of Christ. Paul's summary description of the kerygma as "the message of the cross" is unique within the NT. Many passages in Paul's letters refer to the death of Jesus, but those that use crucifixion language are relatively rare (Rom 6:6; 1 Cor 1:17, 18, 23; 2:2, 8; 2 Cor 13:4; Gal 2:19; 3:1 (13); 5:11; 6:12, 14; Phil 2:8; 3:18). Paul obliquely referred to the crucifixion of Jesus in one of the rhetorical questions of 1:13, but it is only at 1:17 that he begins to write about the crucifixion. Only in vv. 17 and 18 does he actually mention the cross *(stauros).* Only in 1:17, Gal 6:12 (cf. Gal 6:14), and Phil 3:18 does he use the expression "the cross of Christ."

In the ancient world the use of crucifixion as a form of punishment was fairly widespread. In some cultures it served primarily as a form of political punishment or as a punishment for military rebellion. In the Roman world crucifixion was a type of punishment usually inflicted on the lower classes of society, particularly slaves and unruly criminals.

Accompanied by flogging and other kinds of torture, crucifixion was a particularly painful and degrading form of punishment. Cicero called it a "most cruel and disgusting penalty" and "the most extreme form of punishment" (*Orations against Verres* 2.5.165, 168; cf. Josephus, *Bell.* 7.203). The victims, generally slaves who had been flogged beforehand, were tied or nailed to the cross on which they were left to die in the sight of passersby. Sometimes death did not occur for several days. The naked victims of crucifixion were the object of public display. Often they did not even receive a proper burial.

The impact and social significance of Jesus' death by crucifixion could hardly have been lost on the Corinthians. For the Jews among them Deuteronomy's identification of one who was crucified as one "under God's curse" (Deut 21:22-23; cf. Gal 3:10-14; 11QTemple 64:6-13; 4 QpNah 1:7-8) would have added to the abhorrence of crucifixion. Despite the absence of specific reference to the crucifixion in the traditional credal formulae cited by Paul (1 Cor 15:3-5; Rom 1:3-4; 4:25; 8:34; 10:8-9; 1 Thess 1:10; 4:14; 5:10; Gal 1:3-4) and Paul's own relatively few literary allusions to the crucifixion (1 Cor 1:13, 17, 18, 23; 2:2, 8; 2 Cor 13:4; Gal 3:1; 5:11, 24; 6:12, 14; Phil 2:8; 3:18) the theme was an important one for him. He has inserted a mention of the crucifixion into the christological hymn he uses in Phil 2:5-11. In 1:18 he describes his preaching as the word of the cross. In 1:23 he identifies the crucified Christ as the object of his proclamation. With this double reference Paul has made the cross, that is, Jesus' death on the cross, a focal point of his reflection on the nature of divine wisdom.

Eschatological Division. The division of humanity into two camps by means of the message of the cross, a manifestation of the power of God, is an eschatological reality that transcends the natural social division of humanity into two "races," Jews and Gentiles. In vv. 22-24 Paul describes the message about Christ crucified in the presence of all humankind. Humankind is presented in common Jewish categories as being comprised of two groups, Jew and Gentile, the people *(ho laos)* and the nations *(ta ethnē).* Although there are cultural differences between the two groups—Jews are asking for signs while Hellenes seek for wisdom —they are as one before the gospel message, to which they are largely unresponsive. Paul's reflections on the power of the gospel vis-à-vis the division of humanity into two groups is foreshadowed by a pair of rhetorical questions, "Where is the learned one? Where is the one who searches?" that focus on those deemed to be knowledgeable by Jews and Hellenes, respectively.

The eschatological motif of the power of God that is manifest in the message of the cross and divides humanity into two groups is developed in a literary context that exploits, but is not dominated by, eschatological themes. Of these the most significant is the antithesis between "being saved" *(tois de sōzomenois)* and "perishing" *(tois apollymenois),* introduced in v. 18 and reprised in v. 21. The eschatological context of Paul's message is reinforced by his reference to "this age" (v. 20), a notion that reflects the Jewish apocalyptic understanding of time. Time, as a measure of God's activity, is divided between this age and the age to come. Also borrowed from Jewish apocalyptic is the expectation of apocalyptic signs (v. 22), the anticipation of marvelous demonstrations of God's power, with which the real manifestation of God's power, the message of the cross, stands in stark contrast. Jewish expectations of the age to come are that it will be a reversal of the present order of things. From the perspective that is his Paul introduces the theme of eschatological reversal into the letter by means of a scriptural quotation, Isa 29:14 (v. 19), which Paul has modified so that it speaks even more powerfully than the Scripture itself, albeit with the authority of the Scripture, of the destruction of human wisdom and cleverness.

God's Wisdom. In the exposition of the theme announced in v. 18, the message of the cross that is at once both folly and power, Paul divides the question. He first addresses the theme of wisdom (1:19-25); then he takes up the theme of power (1:26-31). The theme of wisdom, which Paul hardly considers in any of his other letters, is presented in negative fashion, that is, as the foolishness of those who are lost. It is obvious that Paul is trying to change the minds of those who consider themselves to be wise (see 3:18). The theme of power, on the other hand, is presented in positive fashion, that is, the power of God, which is directed to those who are saved.

In Paul's demonstration divine wisdom is contrasted with human foolishness. Using Isa 29:14, Paul explains that God himself has said that he will destroy the wisdom of the wise. The verb *apollymi*—which means "to destroy" in the active voice and "to be destroyed" or "to perish" in the passive voice—establishes the link between Paul's theme and the Scripture offered in explanation. The scriptural passage is one in which God himself is presented as speaking, that is, expressing divine wisdom. God's wisdom speaks. God's word is a judgment on the wisdom of humans. God will destroy human wisdom, rendering it null and void.

In many ways Paul's reflection on the wisdom of God, which stands in sharp contrast to human wisdom, echoes themes found in Baruch's eulogy of Wisdom, Bar 3:9–4:4. Tradition has attributed that book to Baruch, the son of Neriah, Jeremiah's secretary and scribe (Jer 36:1-32; 43:1-7), but today the book is generally considered to be of unknown authorship and unknown date. Different scholars have suggested that the book was written at various points from the sixth century B.C.E. to the early second century C.E. The pros and cons advanced for each of these suggestions do not lead to any convincing proof as to the date of Baruch.

In his praise of Wisdom the prophet reflects on the foolishness of those who are perishing: "God did not choose them, or give them the way to knowledge; so they perished because they had no wisdom, they perished through their folly" (Bar 3:27-28). Baruch's reflection on the destruction of the foolish is not explicitly cited by Paul, yet there are similarities between what Paul writes in 1:18 and what is attributed to the prophet in 3:27-28. As the prophet had done, Paul has written to the Corinthians about the foolishness of those who are perishing. In this same context Paul will also write about the way God chooses humans (1:27-28). Although Paul does not cite Baruch, there are manifest similarities between 1 Cor 10:20 and Bar 4:7 as well as between what is attributed to the prophet in Bar 3:29 and what Paul will write to the Romans in Rom 10:6-8.

Despite Paul's failure to cite Baruch verbatim his brand of Hellenistic Judaism shares with Baruch a tendency to personify wisdom. Baruch (4:1) and other forms of Judaism tend to identify wisdom with the Torah, but Paul identifies personified wisdom of God with the Christ (1:24, 30).

Paul's Use of Scripture. The quotation of Isa 29:14 in v. 19 is the first explicit citation of Scripture to appear in the rhetorical argument of 1 Corinthians. It occurs immediately after the proposition of the theme. Paul's scripturally based explanation is a harbinger of things to come. The formal fashion in which he first quotes Scripture in 1 Corinthians serves to highlight the role the scriptural tradition will play in the development of his argument. Paul's reflection is replete with citations from the Scriptures and allusions to biblical passages. These Scriptures provide material for the Pauline letter throughout, but in a variety of different ways.

In 1:18–3:23, the heart of Paul's first rhetorical proof, biblical material is cited explicitly no less than six times: Isa 29:14 in 1:19; Jer 9:22 in 1:31; Isa 64:4 (52:15) in 2:9; Isa 40:13 in 2:16; Job 5:12-13 in 3:19; and Ps 94:11 [LXX 93:11] in 3:20. The Hellenistic rhetorical tradition often used sayings of philosophers and statesmen as arguments from authority in the development of a rhetorical argument. Paul uses a popular saying attributed to Menander in this fashion (15:33), but more consistently he uses passages from the Jewish Scriptures as his personal argument from authority. He does so twenty times in the letter (see 1:19; 1:31; 2:9; 2:16; 3:19; 3:20; 5:13; 6:16; 9:9; 9:10; 10:7; 10:26; 14:21; 14:25; 15:25; 15:27; 15:32; 15:45; 15:54-55).

Isaiah is the biblical book most often cited in Paul's correspondence, as it is in 1 Corinthians, where Isaiah is cited six times (Isa 29:14 in 1:19; Isa 40:13 in 2:16; Isa 28:11-12 in 14:21; Isa 45:14 in 14:25; Isa 22:13 in 15:32; Isa 25:8 in 15:54). Paul cites the Psalms four times (Ps 8:7 [LXX] in 15:27; Ps 24:1 in 10:26; Ps 93:11 [LXX] in 3:20; Ps 110:1 in 15:25). On five occasions he cites the Torah, Genesis twice (Gen 2:7 in 15:45; Gen 2:24 in 6:16), Deuteronomy twice (Deut 17:7 in 5:13; Deut 25:4 in 9:9), and Exodus once (Exod 32:6 in 10:7). Of the other biblical books Job (Job 5:12 in 3:19), Sirach (Sir 6:19 in 9:10), Jeremiah (Jer 9:22-23 in 1:31), and Hosea (Hos 13:14 in 15:55) are verbally referenced once each in Paul's first letter to the Corinthians. In addition to these easily recognized quotations there is the problematic citation found in 2:9 (see the note *ad loc*).

The incidence of explicit scriptural citations in 1 Corinthians is comparable to Paul's general use of the Scriptures. In the extant correspondence he most frequently cites Isaiah (28x), the Psalms (20x), Deuteronomy and Genesis (15x each). In 1 Corinthians Paul introduces most of his scriptural citations in a formal and traditional Jewish fashion, using a characteristic lemma, *gegraptai*, "it is written" (1:19, 31; 2:9; 3:19; 9:9; 10:7; 14:21; 15:45). The use of *graphō* clearly indicates that Paul indeed considers the Scriptures as written texts. It is the same verb he uses in referring to the correspondence between himself and the Corinthian Christians (4:14; 5:9, 11; 9:15; 14:37). The perfect passive form of the verb implies the abiding relevance of the Scriptures—a conviction the Apostle explicitly affirms in 9:10 and again in 10:11 (cf. v. 6). When Paul uses *graphō* in reference to the Scriptures the reference is always to a specific passage in the Scriptures— that is, with the single exception of 10:11.

A classic consideration in any examination of Paul's use of Scripture is that of the provenance of his Greek text. In this regard it is frequently asserted that Paul generally quotes the Scriptures according to the LXX, often from memory or according to an oral tradition. This position, which has been almost a given in the discussion on Paul's use of Scripture since the pioneering work of Georgius Roepe (1827) and A.-F. Kautzsch (1869), needs to be revisited in the light of contemporary Septuagintal studies. In this respect Christopher D. Stanley has judiciously observed: "Though his [= Paul's] primary text is clearly that Greek translation known today as the 'Septuagint' (LXX), a number of Paul's quotations agree with readings preserved in only a minority tradition within the text-history of the LXX. In other places, Paul agrees with the majority tradition against a significant minority reading, or follows one strand of a strongly divided LXX tradition. Most interesting are those places where Paul's quotations appear to have come from a biblical text that is only weakly attested (if at all) in the extant LXX manuscripts" (*Paul and the Language of Scripture* 254– 255).

Sharing the hermeneutic of his Jewish contemporaries, Paul held that the Scriptures applied to the situation he encountered at Corinth. The Qumran *pesharim* and rabbinic *midrashim* make use of the Scriptures in an actualizing fashion. Since God's word enjoys abiding relevance it is pertinent to the situation with regard to which it is cited. Like his contemporaries, Paul does not explicate the Scriptures in a historical-critical fashion; rather he uses them with a typically Jewish contemporizing hermeneutic. From the perspective of Jesus as Messiah and Lord, Paul's contemporizing hermeneutic leads to a christological and ecclesiological reading (that is, application) of the biblical texts.

A particularly striking feature of Paul's actualizing hermeneutic is his application of the biblical texts that identify God as Lord *(Kyrios)* to Christ, the Lord *(Kyrios)* (see Lucien Cerfaux, *Christ in the Theology of St. Paul* [New York: Herder and Herder, 1959] 470–472). Use of this technique reinforces the exalted status and function that Paul attributes to Jesus. In 1 Corinthians the technique is used with regard to Jer 9:22-23 in 1:31, Isa 40:13 in 2:16, Ps 78:18 and Num 21:5-6 in 10:9; Deut 32:21 in 1 Cor 10:22, Ps 24:1 in 10:26, as well as in the application of the prophetic "Day of the Lord" to the day of the Lord Jesus Christ (1:8). A similar christological use of Scripture is found in 1 Cor 10:4 and 10:21 where Exod 17:6 and Mal 1:7 are exploited christologically even though the first of these biblical texts does not employ *Kyrios* in its Greek translation.

Paul's scriptural argument normally does not cite the Scriptures merely as proof texts, nor does he do so for the sake of literary embellishment. When Paul cites biblical passages he evokes the entire context to which they refer. Thus the Isaian Scripture (Isa 29:14) that Paul uses in 1:19 is taken from a judgment oracle at the conclusion of a speech directed against Jerusalem, which has failed to understand Yhwh's word and work. The oracle states that the wisdom of the unwise counselors who advised the king to ally with Egypt will be brought to nought.

Wisdom of the World. What is the wisdom of the world (v. 20), to which Paul opposes the wisdom of God? Paul had introduced the theme into his appeal in v. 17 with his denial that he preached the gospel "with cleverness (*sophia,* literally 'wisdom') of speech." This wisdom is, says Stanley K. Stowers, "any wisdom characterized by certain moral and epistemic vices" ("On the Use and Abuse of Reason," 258). Immediately after contrasting the wisdom of God with the wisdom of the world Paul offers two examples of how the Corinthians' lack of wisdom leads to conduct that is destructive of their existence as the church of God, sexual immorality in 5:1-13, and lawsuits against one another in 6:1-11.

Other commentators have sought to identify the worldly wisdom that comes under criticism from Paul with one or another specific current of thought. There are those who believe that the focus of his reflections is the Jewish wisdom tradition (thus Hans Conzelmann, Jacques Dupont, André Feuillet, Hans Windisch). Other authors think more specifically of the kind of wisdom tradition found in Hellenistic Judaism and reflected in the writings of Paul's contemporary, Philo of Alexandria (thus Richard Horsley, Birger A. Pearson, James A. Davis). Others think of a more complex situation. Among these some believe that it was the Jewish wisdom tradition combined with apocalyptic elements that had had an impact on the Corinthians (Robin Scroggs) while others think that a confluence of apocalyptic and philosophical elements was the source of "the wisdom" valued by the Corinthians (Alexandra R. Brown). Yet another group of authors seek the background of Paul's discussion of the wisdom of this world in Gnosticism, perhaps in some primitive form of Gnosticism (Wilhelm Lütgert, Rudolf Bultmann, Walter Schmithals, Ulrich Wilckens, Bruce W. Winter).

While something may be said in support of the arguments of the various commentators, and each of them offers insights that shed some potential light on the situation of the Corinthian Christians, it is preferable to look upon the search for a particular kind of wisdom that was specifically problematic for the community at Corinth as a quest that does not admit of resolution. The way in which Paul denies his own recourse to wisdom in 1:17 seems to suggest that he is writing about wisdom as it was taught in the rhetorical schools and exploited by popular rhetoricians, whose speech was appealing to the Hellenists of Paul's day (1:22).

Paul's letter to the Corinthians is a pastoral response to a community beset by a variety of problems. This letter does not engage in philosophical discussion *per se*; rather it deals with a community and its issues in a practical manner. That community is rather diverse. Ethnically it is composed of Jews and Gentiles. Some of the Gentiles seem to have come from among the Roman colonists of the area while others were among the natives. Some of the community belonged to the political and social elite; others did not. Some of the members of the community appear to have had their ideas formed by a philosophical ideology while others did not. The relatively small community of Corinthian Christians lived in a larger community, the metropolitan population of the provincial capital, which was marked by tremendous diversity.

Given this situation it seems unwarranted to try to identify one particular philosophical system as the "wisdom of the world" to which Paul was making reference. Many commentators speak of Gnosticism as the background of Paul's letter, but first century "Gnosticism" is more amorphous than is sometimes suggested. At best one can speak of a popular philosophical trend, common in the Mediterranean Hellenistic world, in which knowledge was highly valued and matter was demeaned in such a way that all aspects of the human situation (anthropology, ethics, cosmology) were viewed dualistically. Indeed, it is unlikely that one should even write about philosophical systems that provide relevant background for understanding Paul's letter to the Corinthians. At most Paul would be making reference to certain currents of thought that would have been shaped by a variety of philosophical influences. To the extent that these philosophical influences led various members of the community to

engage in socially disruptive behavior and to depart from the message of
the cross and the tradition Paul had imparted to the Corinthians, Paul
would raise objections, as he does in 1:18-31.

Social Status. In v. 18-25 Paul had spoken about the "wise," if only allusively. Now he describes them as powerful and well-born. All three
adjectives describe the upper class within Corinthian society. That Paul
seems to have experienced no need to defend his statement suggests that
his description of the Corinthian church was accurate. Those who were
called holy were not a socially homogeneous group. While most of them
were neither wise, powerful, nor well-born, some were. By these standards the Christians at Corinth were a representative social sampling.
Only a small portion of the population of Hellenistic cities belonged to
the well-educated and economically and politically powerful upper class.
Still fewer were of noble birth. Among Corinthian Christians those who
were well-placed might have been Paul's colleagues and patrons Aquila
and Prisca (16:19-20), the householder Stephanas (1:16; cf. 16:15-18), and
Chloe (1:11). Other persons of some prominence in the Corinthian community would have been Crispus (1:14; cf. Acts 18:8), Gaius, sometime
host to the whole church of Corinth (1:14; cf. Rom 16:23), Erastus, the city
treasurer (Rom 16:23), and Phoebe, from nearby Cenchreae (Rom 16:1-2).

That Paul could state that only some belonged to the upper class indicates that the remainder, most likely the overwhelming majority, belonged to the lower classes of society. In this first comment on the social
conditions of the Corinthian community Paul suggests that it is a community in which it is possible to recognize some social stratification. It
may well be that the social differences within the community were at the
origin of many of its problems. A reading of the letter shows that Paul frequently uses terms with a social significance, for example in ch. 7. Even
when he does not make use of language that clearly indicates social differences within the community, it seems not unreasonable to suggest that
these social differences provided the circumstances in which such problems as that of some Christians bringing other Christians to court (1 Cor
6:1-11), food offered to idols (ch. 8), and Christians coming together for a
common meal (11:17-22) may have arisen.

Paul's assertion that some of the Corinthian Christians belonged to
the social elite was exploited by Origen who quoted it to counter Celsus'
jibe that only people from the lower classes could be found in a gathering
of Christians (*Contra Celsum* 3.48; PG 11, 984). Perhaps inspired by the
very same verse, Celsus had cited Christians as saying: "Let no one edu-
cated, no one wise, no one sensible draw near. For these abilities are
thought by us [= Christians] to be evils. But as for anyone ignorant, anyone stupid, anyone uneducated, anyone who is a child, let him come
boldly" (so Origen in *Contra Celsum* 3.44; PG 11, 981).

Paul chose three terms, "wise," "powerful," and "of noble birth" to describe the social status of the "strong" and the "haves" at Corinth. Paul's choice of three terms to describe the social situation not only reflects his predilection for literary triads, but also echoes Jer 9:23 (9:22 LXX). Although Paul describes the social status of the Corinthians in 1:26, his description is not a piece of sociological analysis. It is a piece of rhetoric in the service of Paul's rhetorical appeal. He uses the description of the social status of the Corinthians, perhaps reflecting their own analysis of their social situation, in an attempt to disabuse the Corinthians of the notion that the social status they enjoy determines the quality of their relationship with Christ.

In developing his argument Paul uses the rhetorical strategy of "redefinition" (Humphries, "Argumentation," 75), an argument he employs with advantage at various points throughout the letter. The technique had been used by Jeremiah, who in Jer 9:23 redefines boasting in terms of knowledge of God. The Corinthians define themselves according to human standards; Paul will define them according to God's wisdom. By God's standards and to serve God's purposes it is the foolish, weak, and lowly born who have been chosen. Although the Corinthians may boast of their exalted status they must remember that they have a redeemer, none other than Christ who is the wisdom of God for us.

Boasting About the Lord. Paul began (v. 26) his description of the social situation of the Corinthians by echoing Jer 9:23. He concludes his reflections on their social situation with the same scriptural passage, cited in explicit, although abbreviated fashion: "Let the one who boasts boast about the Lord" (v. 31). Paul's strong perorational paraenesis finds a warrant in the Scriptures. He appears to have borrowed the verb *kauchaomai,* "to boast," from the LXX, as his syncopated citation of Jer 9:22-23 indicates. This passage from Jeremiah, which Paul quotes twice in the Corinthian correspondence, seems to have enjoyed some importance in the Jewish tradition. It appears as a gloss in some manuscripts of 1 Sam 2:10; its thought is echoed in such passages as Philo, quoted below, *T. Judah* 13:2, and Pseudo-Phocylides 53.

In the citation of Jer 9:22-23, which occurs in 1:31 and serves as the peroration of the rhetorical unit (1:18-31), Paul identifies the Lord *(Kyrios)* as the indicated object of legitimate boasting, as he does in 2 Cor 10:17, where the same citation of Jeremiah is quoted in the same syncopated fashion as in 1:31, albeit without the classic lemma "it is written." For Paul boasting about the Lord clearly contrasts with boasting about human beings, which Paul clearly eschews (3:21). Jeremiah 9:22 precludes anthropocentric boasting. For Paul and his Jewish tradition it is only boasting about the Lord that is warranted. "Let God alone," writes Philo, Paul's contemporary, "be thy boast and thy chief glory, he [= Moses in

Deut 10:21, which uses *kauchēma* rather than *auchēma*, the synonym used by Philo] continues, and pride thyself neither on riches nor on reputation nor dominion nor comeliness nor strength of body, nor any such thing, whereby the hearts of the empty-minded are wont to be filled up" (Philo, *Special Laws* 1.311).

Paul's use of Jer 9:22-23 in reference to Christ is one of several instances in his letters in which he uses biblical passages that speak of the Lord, *Kyrios* in the LXX, in reference to Christ. See also 2:16; 10:4, 9, 21, 22, 26. Paul understands the Jewish tradition about boasting in the light of the Christ event. "We boast in Christ Jesus and have no confidence in the flesh," he writes in Phil 3:3. Paul's "fool's speech" (2 Cor 11:1–12:10) is a fine rhetorical expression of his conviction that one should boast only in the Lord.

Within the NT "boasting" is a Pauline notion. Of the sixty occurrences of vocabulary belonging to the *kauch-* word group fifty-four are in the authentic letters of Paul (cf. Eph 2:9). Boasting is a major motif in Paul's second letter to the Corinthians, where the verb "to boast" *(kauchaomai)* occurs twenty times (2 Cor 5:12; 7:14; 9:2; 10:8, 13, 15, 16, 17[2x]; 11:12, 16, 18[2x], 30[2x]; 12:1, 5[2x], 6, 9), the noun "boasting" *(kauchēsis,* the act of boasting) six times (2 Cor 1:12; 7:4, 14; 8:24; 11:10, 17), and "boast" *(kauchēma,* the object of one's boasting) three times (2 Cor 1:14; 5:12; 9:3). All three words in the word group appear in 1 Corinthians, albeit not in the same frequency as in Paul's later letter to them (*kauchaomai* in 1:29, 31[2x]; 3:21; 4:7; *kauchēsis* in 15:31; *kauchēma* in 5:6; 9:15, 16). With thirty-eight of its occurrences in the Corinthian letters, "boasting" is an important issue for Paul in this correspondence.

Paul has taken this terminology over from the Jewish Scriptures. He has retained its biblical and Jewish connotations but imparts further specification to it by employing the verb in comparisons and contrasts and by qualifying it with prepositional phrases. Both kinds of specifications occur in 1:29. Paul offers "to put to shame" *(kataischynō,* v. 27) as an antonym for "to boast" *(kauchaomai).* He identifies God as the one in the presence of whom boasting takes place.

"To boast" *(kauchaomai)* can have a positive connotation, with the meaning "to take [legitimate] pride in" (see 13:3), but the term is most often used in a pejorative sense by Paul. In his letters "boasting" suggests an unwarranted kind of bragging, an undue exaltation of oneself. Accordingly Paul often uses the verb in various kinds of prohibitions (1:29; 3:21; cf. 2 Cor 10:17; Gal 6:14; see also Jas 1:9; 3:14). In 4:7 "boasting" appears to be a synonym for *physioō,* "to be inflated," an expression used by Paul only in 1 Corinthians, where it belongs to a body of rhetorical terms with which Paul characterizes the Corinthians (4:6, 18, 19; 5:2; 8:1; 13:4; cf. Col 2:18).

Negative use of the term had been common ever since the word was first attested in the writings of the sixth century B.C.E. Greek poet Sappho (P.Oxyrhynchus 1231, frag. 1, col. I, 10). Hellenists generally considered that boasting in one's own achievements was a sign of a lack of modesty and refinement. In the Jewish tradition boasting is unwarranted since all things come from God, to whom alone is due all honor and praise. It is God who should be the object of one's boasting. The Jewish tradition, to which Paul is heir, is radically rooted in the Jewish Scriptures, which offer several sayings showing the foolishness of boasting about oneself (1 Kings 20:11; Prov 25:14; 27:1). Boasting is characterized as an attitude of a foolish and evil person (Ps 52:1; 94:4).

Notes

18. *For the message of the cross:* There is a kind of anaphora as Paul picks up the motif of the cross of Christ (v. 17). He offers an explanation (the postpositive *gar*) of why it is that his having recourse to Hellenistic rhetoric would have deprived the cross of Christ of its power. His summary description of the kerygma as "the message of the cross," *ho logos . . . ho tou staurou*, literally, "the word of the cross," is unique within the NT. On the other hand Paul often describes the gospel as "the word" of God, the word of reconciliation, the word of life, or simply the word (2 Cor 1:18; 2:17; 4:2; 5:19; Gal 6:6; 1 Thess 1:8; 2:13[2x]). That word, as Paul had explained to the Thessalonians, is a powerful and effective word (1 Thess 2:13; cf. Rom 9:6). Describing the word of God as a powerful and effective word is a biblical motif (see, for example, Isa 55:10-11). It creates, as Gerhard von Rad explains, "a new historical situation" (*Old Testament Theology.* 2 vols. [New York: Harper & Row, 1962–65] 2, 87). By identifying the message of the cross as the leitmotif of his first rhetorical *pistis* Paul capitalizes on the fact that he has already captured the good will of the Corinthians whom he has characterized as a community endowed with the gift of "the word" (1:5). Given the fact that the word about the cross is spoken by one who has been sent (Paul, designated apostle, 1:1) and who has the proclamation of the gospel as his sole task (1:17), it is appropriate to translate *logos*, "word," as "message." In Greek *logos* denotes not only an individual word but also a speech, address, or oration.

   is foolishness to those who are perishing: The phrase is to be read subjectively and construed to mean that the word of the cross is considered as folly by some who perish as a result (BDF 190.1). The present participle, *tois apollymenois*, is used as a substantive, "those who are perishing." Paul uses the verb as it is used in the LXX, where it translates the Hebrew ʾbd to denote eschatological ruin. In form the verb is middle or passive. The parallelism with "we who are saved" *(tois de sǭzomenois hēmin)* suggests that *tois apollymenois* should be taken as a passive with God as the implied agent. They, as opposed to Paul's "we," are being subjected to eschatological ruin. Their judgment on the word of the cross brings about God's ultimate judgment on them.

Like Jesus' parables (see Mark 4:10-12 *par.*), the word of the cross is discriminating. It is a revelatory event (cf. 2:2) that divides humanity into two groups. In this respect it has an eschatological function. Not only is the word of the cross discriminatory, but it also overcomes the social division of humanity into two groups, Jew and Gentile. In the face of the word of the cross all humanity stands alike.

but it is the power of God to us who are being saved: The power of God is often mentioned in Paul's biblical tradition (Deut 3:24; Josh 4:24; Jer 16:21, etc.), where it is frequently evoked in the Psalms (Ps 21:2, 14; 46:2; 59:17, etc.). God's power manifests itself preeminently in God's victory over the enemies of Israel. God's power *(dynamis)* is the manifestation of God's salvific presence, of which the Exodus is the paradigmatic experience (Exod 9:16; Neh 1:10). In 1:18 the "power of God" indicates the dynamic force of the word of the cross. God's power is operative in human history and brings about salvation through the word of the cross. Second Corinthians 13:4 provides a virtual commentary on the idea that Paul states so succinctly in 1 Cor 1:18. Jesus has been crucified in weakness, but he has been raised and lives from the power of God. God's power is life-giving and salvific.

In 1:24 Paul identifies Christ as the power of God. The power of the cross is related to the power of Christ since the cross is the cross of Christ (1:17). Christ is the content of that dynamic gospel Paul has described as the word of the cross. In 1 Thess 5:9-10 with reference to the common faith of Christians Paul makes it clear that salvation comes through the Lord Jesus Christ who died for us. In a letter to the Christians at Rome written some few years after his early correspondence with the Corinthians Paul describes the gospel as "the power of God for salvation *(dynamis gar theou estin eis sōtērian)* to everyone who has faith, to the Jew first and also to the Greek" (Rom 1:16).

In 1 Cor 1:18 Paul uses the rhetorical device of *contradictio* (note the contrasting particles *men . . . de*) to emphasize the power of the word of the cross. There is formal parallelism and conceptual contrast between the two participles, *tois sōzomenois* and *tois apollymenois*, those being saved and those being lost. In both instances God is the implied agent of the action indicated by the verb. Both verbs, which have an ordinary meaning, are used in a religious and eschatological sense. "To save" *(sōzō)* is to deliver from the wrath to come (cf. 3:15; 5:5). The present participle implies that salvation is effective and will continue to be effective. See 1 Thess 1:10 where the participle *ruomenon* is used with similar meaning. The contrast between being ruined and being saved evokes a context of judgment.

The antithesis is not perfect, however. One might have expected *sophia*, wisdom, in contrast to *mōria*, the "foolishness" of the first member of the antithesis. Instead, Paul has *dynamis*. The word of the cross is not human wisdom; it is the power of God. Paul's use of *theou*, "of God," ruptures whatever remains of the *parallelismus membrorum*. Paul underscores the power of God, which is emphatically placed at the end of his sentence in Greek. The parallelism between the two members of the antithesis is further broken by the use of "us" *(hēmin*, absent from a few ancient witnesses). Paul's contrast between noetic elements on the human level and elements of salvific power on the divine level continues throughout the pericope and fleshes out the enigmatic assertion of the *hina* clause of v. 17.

By identifying the message of the cross as the power of God Paul affirms the power of the kerygma. The power of God is effective on behalf of those who have received the kerygma. Paul does not, however, further identify those who receive the kerygma other than to affirm that the "we" who receive the kerygma are those who are saved. Only in v. 21 will those who receive the kerygma be identified as believers. Thereafter a series of datives (1:23-24, 30; 2:6, 10, 14) will identify those to whom the message is addressed (see 1:24, 30; 2:6, 10, 12, 15). In the meantime Paul will underscore the salvific function of the kerygma. It is a powerful word that effects salvation, yet it is effective not only with respect to those who are saved; even those who are lost will experience its effect. This is what Paul details in the following verse with its explanatory *gar.*

19. *For it is written, "I will destroy the wisdom of the wise and I will put aside the cleverness of the clever":* Paul continues to explain (note the postpositive *gar*) the strange antithesis between worldly wisdom and the power of the gospel. To do so he cites Isa 29:14 (LXX). That the first part of this Isaian oracle also appears in Mark 7:6-7 (par. Matt 15:8-9) is an indication that use of the oracle belonged to early Christian scriptural apologetic. The apostle's citation of Isa 29:14 is the first explicit citation of the Jewish Scriptures in 1 Corinthians.

In this and subsequent passages (1:31; 3:20) Paul makes implicit reference to the context from which his citations come. In these instances the Scriptures to which Paul points by means of his quotations call for humility on the part of those who take pride in their wisdom. In the present instance the Isaian passage from which Paul quotes goes on to allude to the understanding of God and to the creation of a new order of things (Isa 29:16, 18, 24). From a literary point of view Paul's citation of Isaiah forms an inclusion with the scriptural quotation in 1:31, thereby delineating 1:18-31 as a discrete unit within his letter.

By citing Isa 29:14 Paul has not only found a proof text for the thesis he has enunciated in v. 18 but has also described the effect of the word of the cross as the activity of God himself. It is God who is active in the dynamic of the preaching of the cross. The Apostle has accentuated the thrust of the biblical text he cites by substituting "put aside" *(athetēsō)* for the LXX's "hide" *(krypsō).* In Paul's version of the citation the chiastic structure of the text highlights its synonymous parallelism. In his version of the biblical text the point is not so much that God has hidden understanding from the wise and the clever but that, in Jesus, God has done something that defies all human understanding.

20. *Where is the wise person? Where is the learned one? Where is the one who searches in this age?:* A series of rhetorical questions follows immediately after Paul's citation of Isa 29:14. The questions recall similar but isolated questions in Isaiah (Isa 19:12; 33:18). Paul's triad of parallel questions is an example of his rhetorical use of *repetitio* or *expolitio.* Each of the questions begins with "where"

(pou), the rhetorical device of anaphora (repetition of an initial expression). Use of the threefold rhetorical question, with *pou,* is also found in Epictetus *(Discourses* 3.10.17). The style is reminiscent of the Stoic diatribe.

By illustrating what he means by a "wise person" with the learned one and the searchers, well-known figures in Jewish and Gentile Hellenistic sub-cultures, Paul foreshadows the argument of v. 22 where he writes disparagingly of the false search of Jews and Greeks. "The learned one" *(grammateus)* is one who is lettered, or the scribe. In the NT the term is frequently used of the scribes associated with the various religious movements within Judaism. These scribes were not only skilled copyists who were able to transcribe biblical manuscripts; they were also versed in the Scriptures themselves. The Hellenistic Jewish book of Ben Sira speaks of the wisdom of the scribe (Sir 38:24–39:11). Sirach's scribe is compared to various skillful people *(hoi sophoi)* in the Hellenistic world. "The searcher" *(syzētētēs)* was a well known figure in the Hellenistic world. The term identifies one who searches for wisdom by means of a discursive and dialectic process. Sometimes it was used of the debater whose perorations *(controversiae)* found a place in courtroom, academy, and dinner gathering *(symposion).*

Paul describes the one who searches as belonging to this age *(tou aiōnos toutou),* but the phrase, a subjective genitive, qualifies all three of these questions. The qualification, which recurs in 2:6 (2x), 2:8, and 3:18, has an eschatological connotation. The *Testaments of the Twelve Patriarchs* and *Joseph and Aseneth* use *aiōn* principally with a future, often eschatological, meaning. The implication of "*this* age" is that there is another age. A two-age view of history, this age and the age to come, is typical of the apocalyptic world view. According to *m. ʾAbot.* 2:7 Hillel spoke of life in the age to come. In the traditional terms that early Christianity appropriated from apocalyptic Judaism via the preaching of Jesus the age to come is the kingdom of God, the eon of God's ultimate reign. The present age is being shaped and judged by the world to come. The expectation of the age to come is characterized by present revelatory experience. Paul shares with apocalyptic Judaism this two-age understanding of time (3:6, 18; 2 Cor 4:4; Gal 1:4).

Did not God make foolish the wisdom of the world?: The antithesis between wisdom and folly is classic. As used by Paul, the antithesis between the wisdom of this world *(tēn sophian tou kosmou)* and God's action in making it foolishness is particularly striking. "To make foolish" *(mōrainō;* cf. Rom 1:22) belongs to a group of words that Hellenistic rhetoricians used in a pejorative way. "Was he so foolish," writes Epictetus, "that he did not understand that this way would lead to this end?" (Epictetus, *Discourses* 2.2.16). The rhetorical question in 1:20 implies the reversal of this world's standards, a reversal dominated by Paul's apocalyptic vision. The aorist tense of the verb puts God's making this age's wisdom foolish in a specific time frame. The time when God made foolish this age's wisdom was the time of the crucifixion. In the verses that follow Paul offers an explanation of the eschatological reversal (vv. 21-25; see the explanatory *gar* in v. 21) and two examples of it. The examples are the call of the Corinthians (1:26-31) and Paul's proclamation (2:1-5).

The seventh century $\mathfrak{P}^{11}$, a few majuscules (F, G, Ψ), and correctors of some of the more important ancient manuscripts (ℵ, C, D) have added "this" to Paul's "world" *(kosmou toutou)* to make it clear that the apostle is writing not about the efforts of human rationality as such, but about what is considered wise in the age that is passing away. In 2:6 Paul describes the wisdom of the world *(tēn sophian tou kosmou)* as the wisdom of this age *(sophia tou aiōnos toutou)* and contrasts it with the wisdom of God *(theou sophia,* 2:7) imparted in mystery.

21. *For since, in the wisdom of God, the world does not know God through wisdom:* The causal "since" *(epeidē)* links the world's ignorance of God to what precedes, as if to explain God's making this age's wisdom foolish, and to the following clause, which indicates how God chose to save through the folly of the kerygma. The explanation continues the antithetical opposition between God's wisdom and the wisdom of this age. In the biblical tradition "to know God" is to experience God; conversely, those who do not know God are the godless. For Paul the wisdom of this world does not lead to the experience of God, certainly not to the experience of God who has revealed himself through Jesus Christ, the very power and wisdom of God. For all practical purposes to know God is to believe. Human wisdom does not lead to salvific belief and the experience of God.

God chose to save those who believe through the foolishness of the proclamation: Together with v. 20b, v. 21a brackets human ignorance with divine activity. In Rom 1:18-32 Paul will develop the consequences of human ignorance of God in a totally different manner. Here he affirms that since by God's design human wisdom did not lead to the saving experience of God and was accordingly rendered foolish by God, God chose to save people by means of the proclamation *(kerygma).* In contemporary Christian parlance "kerygma" has become a technical term to denote the early Christian preaching of the gospel. Used by Paul only in 1 Corinthians and in Romans (cf. 2:4; 15:14; Rom 16:25), the term evokes not only the content of Paul's preaching but also the manner in which it was preached (see 2:4). Proclaiming involves not only the activity of the preacher; it also involves the activity of the hearer. Proclamation leads to saving faith (cf. Rom 1:16; 10:14-15).

Those who accept the kerygma are described as those who believe, *tous pisteuontas,* the present participle of *pisteuō,* "to believe." When Paul wrote to the Corinthians his use of the verb *pisteuō* had not yet acquired the connotation that it will have as a result of the controversies to which allusion is made in Romans and Galatians. "To believe" is to have a strong and very positive salvific relationship with God as a result of acceptance of the kerygma. Those who believe are those in whom the word of God is at work in dynamic fashion (cf. 1 Thess 2:13). Those whom we call Christians Paul calls "believers" *(hoi pisteuontes;* cf. 14:22; Rom 1:16; 3:22; 4:5, 11; 10:4; 1 Thess 1:7; 2:10, 13).

22. *and since Jews are asking for signs:* Despite God's activity in the past (both "made foolish" *[emōranen]* and "chose to save" *[eudokēsen . . . sōsai]* are in the aorist), people continue to seek. Paul's reference to the Jews *(Ioudaioi)* who are seeking signs *(sēmeia aitousin)* is striking. Paul otherwise assiduously avoids

the use of the verb "to ask for" (*aiteō*, hapax in the extant correspondence) and uses *sēmeion* on only one other occasion in this letter, 14:22, where glossolalia is presented as a sign for unbelievers. In the NT "signs" (*sēmeia*) generally designate miraculous phenomena. That would seem to be Paul's meaning here (cf. 2 Cor 12:12).

Waiting for wondrous manifestations is here characterized as a feature of Jewish eschatological expectation. Jews are sign-seekers. Unlike Paul's letters to the Galatians and the Romans, 1 Corinthians is not concerned with the different aspects of what has been called "the Jewish question." Paul mentions the Jews (*Ioudaioi*) only in four passages of this letter (1:22-24; 9:20; 10:32; 12:13). All four passages relate to the universal appeal of the gospel message.

Paul will take up the issue of human wisdom in the letter, but he does not discuss eschatological signs *per se*. An eschatological misconception exists among the Corinthians, but it does not bear upon eschatological signs. The Corinthians' misconception is rather a misunderstanding that derives from undue reliance on human wisdom.

and Hellenes are looking for wisdom: Given Paul's simple social world, "Jews and Hellenes" represents the totality of humankind (cf. "all flesh," *pasa sarx*, 1:29) from the perspective of salvation history (1:24; 10:32; 12:13; cf. Rom 1:16; 2:9-10; 3:9; 10:12; Gal 3:28; compare Acts 19:10; 20:21). In elaborating his views on the history of salvation Paul always follows the schema of Jews first, then Gentiles (see, for example, Rom 1:16; Rom 11:11-24). Since the kerygma is an instrument of salvation (1:18) for both Jew and Gentile it is appropriate that Paul cite Jews before Gentiles. Historically the gospel was proclaimed to Jews before Christian missionaries proclaimed the gospel to Gentiles. With respect to the history of salvation, Paul typically presents himself as having had a mission to Jews and to Gentiles. In Acts, in dramatic and thoroughgoing fashion, Luke presents Paul's mission as being first to Jews, then to Gentiles. The evangelist even presents Paul's typical kerygmatic speech to a Jewish audience (Acts 13:16-31) before he offers an example of Paul's evangelical appeal to Gentiles (Acts 17:22-31).

Paul's choice of "Hellenes" (*Hellēnes*) rather than "Gentiles" (*ethnē*) to describe non-Jews may be due to his diatribal invective against dependence on Hellenistic wisdom. In the Hellenistic era it was common for *Hellēn* to be used with a sense of some social superiority. It was used of those who spoke the Greek language, had an education, and shared the Greek culture. These were in a class distinct from the barbarians (cf. Rom 1:14). The suggestion of hybris attached to "Hellenes" makes the choice of this term appropriate in a letter written to a community within which the problematic element is a group of people who are puffed up with pride as a result of the knowledge they possess (4:18, 19; 5:2; 8:1; 13:4).

Jews await wonders; Hellenes await wisdom. Paul is capable of performing miracles (2 Cor 12:12; cf. 1 Cor 13:2); he is endowed with the charism of speaking in tongues (13:1; 14:6, 18). He is capable of imparting wisdom (2:6); he is adept in utilizing the techniques of rhetorical appeal. Yet no more than he prides himself on having baptized (1:14-17) does Paul vaunt his ability to work miracles or pride himself as one who possesses wisdom. Rather he presents himself as one who is called to proclaim Christ crucified. For its strength Paul's message does not rely on its appeal to popular expectations, whether these be the expectations of the Jews or the expectations of the Hellenes (1:23).

23. *we, however, proclaim Christ crucified:* Paul uses the expression "we, however" *(hēmeis de)* to introduce a contrast between subjects as well as a shift of focus (2:12, 16; 4:10[3x]; 9:25; cf. 2 Cor 10:13; Gal 4:28; 1 Thess 2:17; 5:8, etc.). In 1:23 Paul contrasts the expectations of Jews and Hellenes with his own activity. He asserts that he and Sosthenes had proclaimed the crucified Christ to the Corinthians (cf. 1 Tim 2:7; 2 Tim 1:11, where Paul alone is designated as the "herald," *kēryx*). Earlier Paul had characterized his activity as "evangelizing" (1:17) *(euaggelizō).* Now he identifies that work as proclaiming *(kēryssō;* cf. 9:27), an activity that involves both the hearer and the one who proclaims. The object of Paul's proclamation is the crucified Christ (cf. 1:18; comp. 1:21), otherwise identified as folly, that is, specifically folly to Gentiles (cf. vv. 21, 23c). Later in the letter Paul will identify Christ who has been raised from the dead as the object of his proclamation (15:11-12). The object of Paul's proclamation is "Christ," a title Paul uses to designate Jesus who has died and has been raised from the dead.

for the Jews a stumbling block, for Gentiles foolishness: Because of their own cultural traditions with respect to knowledge Jews and Gentiles are closed to the gospel of the crucified Christ. With respect to salvation and their appropriation of the salvific word of the cross both Jews and Gentiles ultimately share a common lot. The equality with respect to salvation of both Jew and Gentile is a major theme of Paul's "last will and testament," the letter to the Romans (1:16–3:20; 9-11).

Specifically Paul's reference to the stumbling block, the only such reference in 1 Corinthians, calls to mind what he has to say about a stumbling block for Israel in Rom 9:33 and 11:1-10 (cf. vv. 11-12). In both instances Paul employs a scriptural citation, Isa 8:14 in Rom 9:33, Ps 69:23-24 in Rom 11:9, to describe Christ as a stumbling block for Israel. Israel's rejection of Christ as the crucified and risen Lord has caused it to experience Christ as a stumbling block. Through the crucified Christ, God has caused Israel to stumble and fall. Cited in Rom 11:9, Psalm 69 was often used in early Christian apologetic to elucidate the death of Christ. Paul's use of the psalm verse in Romans suggests that something that is closest to Israel, something good that it ought to relish, is the source of its stumbling and its fall. The proclamation of the gospel produces a stumbling block for Israel: this is a real outcome of the proclamation of the gospel.

Implicitly Paul identifies the Gentiles *(ethnesin; hellēsi,* "Hellenes," in some mss.) with the "Hellenes" of vv. 22, 24. For those Gentiles who did not receive the gospel of Christ preached by Paul the content of his message is folly. Had Paul allowed cultivated Gentiles to be captivated by his use of oratorical skills he would have deprived the very cross of Christ of its power (1:17). In fact the object of Paul's epistolary wrath is not so much Gentiles as such but the Hellenes, whom he now identifies as Gentiles, whose pursuit of wisdom causes the cross of Christ to be deprived of its power.

24. *but to those who have been called, both Jews and Hellenes, Christ is the power of God and the wisdom of God:* Several times already (1:1, 2, 9) Paul has alluded to the call addressed to humans and concretized in the preaching of the gospel. The call is a universal appeal even if it is not well received by all. "Jews and Hellenes" bespeaks the universal appeal of the gospel. They are called into fellowship as the single church of God (1:9).

The description of Christ as the power and wisdom of God harkens back to Christ, the object of apostolic proclamation (v. 23). Dan 2:20 (cf. 1:24 in $\mathfrak{P}^{46}$) speaks of the power and wisdom of God. For Paul the act by which the Father raised Jesus from the dead was an act that endowed him with power (Rom 1:4; Phil 3:10). So endowed, the risen Christ is succinctly described as the power of God (cf. Joseph A. Fitzmyer, "'To Know Him and the Power of His Resurrection' (Phil 3.10)," *Mélanges bibliques en homage au R. P. Béda Rigaux* [Gembloux: Duculot, 1970] 411–425, especially 417–418). Only in 1:24 does Paul explicitly identify Christ as the wisdom of God.

Paul's repeated "Jews and Hellenes" establishes contrasts between the signs and wisdom they respectively seek, the scandal and foolishness that is preached to them, and the power and wisdom of God that are given to them.

25. *For the foolishness of God is wiser than humans and the weakness of God is stronger than humans:* As Paul tries to explain (the explanatory *hoti* = "for") his terse formulation, Christ the power of God and the wisdom of God, the reader would expect Paul to speak of God's power and wisdom. He does not do so; rather he makes his point by using the rhetorical technique of litotes, rhetorical understatement, as he writes about God's foolishness and weakness.

Paul's carefully crafted sentence, offered by way of explanation, introduces a disquisition on wisdom and strength (1:25-29) which is a model example of Pauline parallelism (BDF 490). Each of the parallel members makes use of the rhetorical technique of *sygkrisis*, rhetorical comparison, to highlight God's wisdom and power. Divine wisdom and power are implicitly contrasted with human wisdom and power.

There is a contrast between God *(theos)* and humans *(anthrōpoi)*. There is also a contrast between foolishness and wisdom as well as between weakness and strength. Wisdom and strength are implicitly attributed to humans. To designate the attributes of God Paul uses the substantivized adjectives "foolish" *(mōron)* and "weak" *(asthenes)* rather than the cognate nouns "foolishness" *(mōria)* and "weakness" *(astheneia)*. God's weakness is stronger *(ischyroteron)* than humans. To speak of humans Paul uses the gender-neutral *anthrōpōn*, "humans," rather than a gender-specific *andrōn*, "men," adult males. *Anthrōpos* is used more frequently in 1 Corinthians (30x) than in any other Pauline letter. To speak of strength, that is, human strength Paul uses a comparative of the adjective *ischyros*. This term is used frequently in classical, Hellenistic, and Septuagintal Greek, but it is infrequent in Paul who uses the word group only in adjectival form and only in the Corinthian correspondence, where it clearly designates a very human quality (1:25, 27; 4:10; 10:22; 2 Cor 10:10).

In the background of Paul's argument lies the image of the wisdom and power of God; these are compared with human wisdom and power. Paul's explanatory clause forms a chiasm with the preceding clause, v. 25b, which speaks of God's power and wisdom. In the next pericope (vv. 26-31) Paul will expatiate on the wisdom and strength of human beings.

26. *Brothers and sisters, ponder your call:* As he takes up the second theme to which he had addressed the Corinthians' attention in v. 18, namely the power of God, Paul makes a direct appeal to them, addressing them in the fraternal idiom (cf. 1:10). Paul asks the Corinthians to carefully consider (*blepete*, literally "look at," used here of a mental function [BAGD 143.4]; cf. 8:9; 16:10) their call. He had previously drawn attention to the call of the Corinthians (1:2) and to his own call (1:1), which he has set forth as an example to them, but here he objectifies the call (*klēsis;* cf. 7:20; Rom 11:29; Phil 3:14).

In writing about the call that God addresses to those whom he has chosen Paul normally uses a verbal form (a verb or a verbal adjective) to underscore both the dynamic nature of the call and God as the agent of the call. Both aspects are inherent in Paul's use of the noun *klēsis* in v. 26. He asks the Corinthians to carefully ponder the fact that they have been called by God, irrespective of their social status. Paul's challenge to the community that they examine their call from God is the first imperative he addresses to the Corinthians in this letter. Although his imperative is an invitation to the Corinthians, it is phrased in the guise of an explanation of the foolishness and weakness of God (see the postpositive *gar*).

because not many are wise according to human standards, not many are powerful, not many of noble birth: Paul's construction is elliptical. He omits an expected *hymōn*, "of you" as well as the verb "to be" as he comments on the social condition of the Corinthian community. Members of the Christian community did not belong to the same social class. The church was not a socially homogenous group. Paul's choice of terminology, especially "powerful" and "well born," clearly describes an upper class of people, a social elite. Only a few of the Corinthian Christians may have been wise, rich, or well born, but some of the community did enjoy such status. The first two qualities are antithetical to the attributes of God cited in v. 25. The antithesis is underscored by the phrase "according to human standards" (*kata sarka;* cf. BAGD 744.6). This phrase contrasts with the repeated "of God" *(tou theou)* of v. 25 and with "in the presence of God" in v. 29, a formula that provides an element of criticism of judgments "according to human standards."

For Jews the "wise" were those who had practical common sense and a knowledge of God; Hellenists considered the wise to be people endowed with an understanding of science, philosophy, and culture. The "powerful" were those who wielded considerable influence or exercised authority by virtue of their wealth or political position. There were, however, some things that money could not buy. Just prior to Paul's arrival in the city Babbius Philinus was one of the richest and most powerful men in Corinth. Despite his wealth and power, and the many honors and offices he accrued, he never gained the highest honor, that of leader of the Isthmian games (see 9:24-27). The fact that he was not born as a free man is the most likely reason why he did not obtain this much sought after distinction. Being of noble birth *(eugeneis)* brought distinction and entitlement.

"Powerful" *(dynatoi)* is hapax in 1 Corinthians, but the contrast between the "powerful" *(dynatoi)* and the "weak" *(astheneis)* is not foreign to Paul (see 2 Cor 12:10; 13:9; cf. Rom 15:1). In 1 Corinthians his preferred contrast is between the "strong" *(ischyroi)* and the "weak" (cf. 1:25, 27; 4:10). Both of these terms are used with some frequency in the letter. "Well born" *(eugeneis)* is likewise hapax, not only in 1 Corinthians but also in the extant Pauline corpus.

Wilhelm Wuellner ("Sociological Implications," 672; with support from Gail R. O'Day, "Study," 263–265) takes Paul's *hoti* to be an interrogative particle. On this reading Paul's question would be another in the series of rhetorical questions addressed to the Corinthians, "are not many of you wise, powerful, and of noble birth?" Not without a touch of irony, this question calls the Corinthians to make a judgment about themselves, that is, to admit that according to the standards they accept they are generally wise, powerful, and well-born. In that case Paul's rejoinder (vv. 27-29) would be all the more powerful. Even though some parallels can be adduced in support of reading Paul's words as a rhetorical question and the reading is attractive from a rhetorical point of view, Paul does not seem to have otherwise used an interrogative *hoti,* a circumstance that makes it unlikely that the *hoti* of v. 26 introduces a rhetorical question.

27. *But God chose the foolish of the world in order to put the wise to shame:* It is tempting to read this statement and those that follow as a theological reflection on the social circumstances of the Corinthian community. In spite of the fact that most in the Corinthian community did not belong to the social elite, the Corinthian Christians have been chosen by God. However, Paul's triad has a strong rhetorical function. The adversative *(alla)* suggests that Paul is making a theological statement that is intended to challenge the Corinthians. They see themselves as wise, but in fact, God has chosen the foolish to confound the wise, the weak to confound the strong, and the lowly so that the powerful are deprived of their power. Paul's three-part construction is typical of his literary style with its predilection for triads. With the verb *eklegomai,* used in the three parallel statements but nowhere else in the correspondence, Paul emphasizes the idea of God's choice.

The action of God in choosing those who would serve his purpose is paramount in Paul's discussion. His "but" *(alla)* moves the discussion from the human categories of the Corinthians to a theological plane with a theocentric focus. The thrice-repeated *exelexato ho theos* emphasizes that it is the action of God that is at issue. The categories that are brought to bear on the Corinthians' situation are theocentric ones.

To emphasize the foolish quality of those who have been chosen by God (cf. v. 25, "God's foolishness"), Paul uses a neuter plural *(ta mōra,* a substantivized adjective, literally "the foolish things") to designate persons (BAGD 138.1; 263.4). The use of antithesis highlights God's purpose in choosing the foolish. The foolish have been chosen so that the wise (cf. vv. 20, 21b) may be put to shame. "To put to shame" (*kataischynē*, a compound verb used for emphasis' sake) has neither a psychological nor an eschatological connotation; rather it must be taken as an antithesis of *kauchaomai*, "to boast." The contrast between putting to shame and boasting is found in other Pauline passages (see Rom 5:2-5; 2 Cor 7:14; 9:2-4). In the Greek Bible "to put to shame" is an expression used to designate God's vindication over his enemies (cf. Ps 6:10; 31:17; 35:4, 26-27, etc.).

and God chose the weak of the world in order to put the strong to shame: The expression is parallel with the preceding phrase. The words "weak" and "strong" replace the "foolish" and "wise" of the previous antithesis. Paul's double focus, on wisdom and power, continues the two-pronged discourse introduced in v. 18. In each of the parallel phrases of v. 27 a substantivized adjective in the articular neuter plural is used to describe the object of God's choice. "Wise" (v. 27a) was in the masculine plural, but "strong" (*ischyra*, v. 27b) is neuter. This provides additional emphasis with good rhetorical effect.

28. *and God chose those of lowly birth of the world and those who are scorned:* Since Xenophon "of lowly birth" (*agenēs*, hapax in the NT) had been used as an antithesis of *eugenēs* "of noble birth," but in popular usage the term had the meaning of "base" or "insignificant." The antithetical sense is retained in v. 28 since Paul had employed *eugenēs* (hapax in Paul) in v. 26. Paul's unusual choice of vocabulary, two pronominal adjectives that he does not otherwise use, clearly indicates that he is commenting on the social status of the Corinthian community in these verses. He describes the Corinthians not only as coming from the lower classes of society but also as those who are scorned. The verb (*exouthenēmena*; cf. 6:4; 16:11; Rom 14:3, 10; 2 Cor 10:10; Gal 4:14; 1 Thess 5:20) suggests disdain and derision.

those who are nothing, in order to make ineffective those who are: To underscore the quality of those who are insignificant and despised Paul adds "those who are nothing" in apposition to what he has written. His idiom—underscored in the antithesis between *ta mē onta*, literally "things that are not," and *ta onta*, literally "things that are"—echoes that of Hellenistic rhetoric. Nothingness (*oudenia*) was a notion present in the old Delphic religion. It was a classic topos in Hellenistic rhetoric, where it was employed in the discourse of philosophical rhetoric. Paul's jargon (cf. 2 Cor 12:11) is roughly equivalent to the contemporary contrast between the "haves" and the "have-nots." "To make ineffective" (*katargēsē*) is used for rhetorical effect in place of the previous "to put to shame" (*kataischynē*).

29. *lest all flesh boast in the presence of God:* The formulaic "all flesh" (*pasa sarx*) is a Septuagintal phrase (representing the biblical *kol-bāśār*) that denotes all humanity insofar as it is created by God. In the NT it is found in biblical citations in Luke 3:6; Acts 2:17; 1 Pet 1:24, but also in John 17:2. Paul himself uses the phrase only negatively, here and in Gal 2:16. His use of a biblical phrase to

designate all humanity continues the universalism of the Jew-Hellene motif and introduces a creation motif, which he will further exploit when he deals with the issues of an appropriate dress code for worship (ch. 11) and the reality of the resurrection (ch. 15). Paul's counsel that created humanity not boast before God reflects the thought of his biblical tradition. Everything that created humanity possesses is but God's gift; accordingly, humankind has no right to boast before God (cf. 4:7). It is to God alone that all praise and honor are due.

Paul's "all flesh in the presence of God" *(pasa sarx enōpion tou theou)* is echoed in Rom 3:20, "all flesh in his sight" *(pasa sarx enōpion autou)*." In 1:29 "in the presence of" *(enōpion)* identifies the one or those before whom boasting takes place. "In the presence of God" *(enōpion tou theou:* Rom 14:22; 2 Cor 4:2, 7:12; Gal 1:20; cf. Rom 3:20; 2 Cor 8:21) recalls the biblical phrase *lipnê yhwh,* "in the sight of God," frequently used in a cultic sense. In the present context "in the presence of God" is in antithesis to the "according to human standards" (1:26) on which the Corinthians are wont to base their self-evaluation.

30. *From him you are in Christ Jesus:* Verses 30 and 31 constitute a single relative clause modifying "God" *(theou).* Paul continues the creation motif, to which he had alluded using the biblical phrase "all flesh." He reminds the Corinthians that God is their origin. The "in" *(en)* of "in Christ Jesus" is most likely a Semitism, reflecting the instrumental *bĕ* (BDF 4.3), used in a prepositional phrase in lieu of the classical instrumental dative. The instrumentality of Christ Jesus in creation is further expressed in the hymnic expansion of the Shema in 8:6. There, as here, Paul uses *ex* in reference to God's being the source of humanity, but in 8:6 he uses *dia* to convey the idea of christic mediation in creation.

who became wisdom from God for us: In v. 24 Paul had affirmed that Christ is the wisdom of God; now he affirms that God's wisdom has been made available to us, that is, to Christians, for whom Christ Jesus is God's wisdom. Those who seek after wisdom, namely, Hellenes (v. 22) should seek God's wisdom, now accessible to us. Wisdom is none other than Christ Jesus, who is God's wisdom for us. Christ Jesus is not simply God's wisdom; he is God's wisdom "for us" *(hēmin).* The "for us" is important, as Paul will explain in the triad that follows.

and righteousness, holiness, and redemption: The triad in apposition to wisdom recalls the triad characterizing God in Jer 9:24, "love, justice, and righteousness." "Righteousness" *(dikaiosynē)* is an element in Jeremiah's triad (Jer 9:23 LXX), as it is in Paul's. Paul reads the biblical tradition christologically. The various epithets in Paul's triad signify, individually and cumulatively, what God does for his people and what he gives to them. By applying these terms to Jesus Christ, Paul affirms that God's salvific beneficence has been mediated through him. The accumulation of terms, the rhetorical device of *repetitio,* implies that the entirety of God's salvific beneficence has been mediated to his people "in Christ Jesus."

The three soteriological epithets, "righteousness *(dikaiosynē),* holiness *(hagiasmos),* and redemption *(apolytrōsis)*" are hapax in 1 Corinthians. "Righteousness" and "holiness" are common expressions in Paul's other letters, but "redemption" occurs only in Rom 3:24 and 8:23. Righteousness bespeaks a right relationship with God, gratuitously mediated through Jesus Christ. Holiness connotes a belonging to God manifest in Spirit-empowered conduct appropriate to those who do belong to God. "Redemption" basically signifies the manumission of slaves (cf. 7:23), but Paul uses the term as a theological metaphor. Paul's idea is at once theological, soteriological, and christological (see Rom 3:23-26). In redemption the emphasis lies on the divine initiative. What God has initiated is experienced as a remission of sins. God's agent in redemption, the mediator of redemption, is Jesus Christ (cf. Rom 6:18, 22; 8:2; Gal 1:4; 3:13; 4:5; 1 Thess 1:10) who effects redemption through his salvific death and resurrection. Hence the importance of the Christ title.

The location of "redemption" as the third of the series may represent an instance of the rhetorical device of *gradatio*, in which the emphasis falls on the final element of a series arranged in ascending order. In Paul's rhetorical context the emphasis on redemption effected through Christ stands in contrast to the lowly status of most of the Corinthians. The abstract formula serves to designate Jesus as the Redeemer *(abstractum pro concreto).*

31. *as it is written, "Let the one who boasts boast about the Lord":* Urging those who boast to boast in the Lord, the Apostle confronts those who boast in their own power. He exhorts them to turn from themselves to the Lord. The exhortation is based on the Scriptures (note the use of the classic lemma "as it is written") and summarizes Jer 9:23 (9:22 LXX), cited here as it is in 2 Cor 10:17. A modification of the biblical text allows Paul to create a contrast with v. 29. The prophetic text, to which Paul had already made allusion in v. 26, criticized those who boast in their intellectual, social, and economic powers. The apostle synthesized the prophet's threefold negative exhortation and applied it to Christ. In Jeremiah the Lord is YHWH; in Paul the Lord is the risen Christ, the power of God, the wisdom of God. By identifying Christ as the one in whom the Corinthians should boast Paul has accommodated the biblical text to the situation of the Corinthians. As in v. 19 Paul cites the Scripture because of the perceived similarity between the biblical situation and his own. Through his choice of a biblical text Paul evokes the entire biblical context. He has not chosen a text of Jeremiah simply as a proof text or for the sake of literary embellishment. The Lord of whom the Corinthians should boast is Christ Jesus, our wisdom, righteousness, holiness, and redemption. No matter what the Corinthians' social status is, it is Christ who is their redeemer.

FOR REFERENCE AND FURTHER STUDY

Bender, Wilhelm. "Bemerkungen zur Übersetzung von 1 Korinther 1:30," *ZNW* 71 (1980) 263–268.

deSilva, David A. "'Let the One Who Claims Honor Establish That Claim in the Lord': Honor Discourse in the Corinthian Correspondence," *BTB* 28 (1998) 61–74.

Fitzmyer, Joseph A. "Crucifixion in Ancient Palestine, Qumran Literature, and the New Testament," *CBQ* 40 (1978) 493–513.

Genest, Olivette. "L'interprétation de la mort de Jésus en situation discursive. Un cas-type: L'articulation des figures de cette mort en 1–2 Corinthiens," *NTS* 34 (1988) 506–535.

Hengel, Martin. *Crucifixion in the Ancient World and the Folly of the Message of the Cross.* Philadelphia: Fortress, 1977.

Hübner, Hans. "Der vergessene Baruch. Zur Baruch-Rezeption des Paulus in 1 Kor 1,18-31," *SNTU* 9 (1984) 161–173.

Judge, Edwin Arthur. "Paul's Boasting in Relation to Contemporary Professional Practice," *AusBR* 16 (1968) 37–50.

_____. *The Social Patterns of the Christian Groups in the First Century: Some Prolegomena to the Study of New Testament Ideas of Social Obligation.* London: Tyndale, 1960.

Keck, Leander E. "God the Other Who Acts Otherwise: An Exegetical Essay on 1 Cor 1:26-31," *Word & World* 16 (1996) 437–443.

Lautenschlager, Markus. "Abschied vom Disputierer. Zur Bedeutung von *suzētētēs* in 1 Kor 1,20," *ZNW* 83 (1992) 276–285.

Mangan, Céline. "Christ the Power and the Wisdom of God: The Semitic Background to 1 Cor 1:24," *Proceedings of the Irish Biblical Association* 4 (1980) 21–34.

Merklein, Helmut. "Das paulinischen Paradox des Kreuzes," *TThZ* 106 (1997) 81–98.

Montagnini, Felice. "'*Videte vocationem vestram*' (1 Cor 1,26)," *RivBib* 39 (1991) 217–221.

O'Day, Gail R. "Jeremiah 9:22-23 and 1 Corinthians 1:26-31: A Study in Intertextuality," *JBL* 109 (1990) 259–267.

Pack, Frank. "Boasting in the Lord," *ResQ* 19 (1976) 65–71.

Penna, Romano. "The Gospel as 'Power of God' According to 1 Corinthians 1:18-25," in *Paul the Apostle* 1:169–180.

Sánchez Bosch, Jorge. "*Gloriarse*" *según San Pablo. Sentido y teología de kauchaomai.* AnBib 40. Rome: Pontifical Biblical Institute, 1970.

Sänger, Dieter. "Die *dynatoi* in 1 Cor 1,26," *ZNW* 76 (1985) 285–291.

Schreiner, Josef. "Jeremia 9:22.23 als Hintergrund des paulinischen 'Sich-Rühmens'" in Joachim Gnilka, ed., *Neues Testament und Kirche. Für Rudolf Schnackenburg.* Freiburg and Vienna: Herder, 1974, 530–542.

Söding, Thomas. "'Was schwach ist in der Welt, had Gott erwählt' (1 Kor 1,27). Kreuzestheologie und Gemeinde-Praxis nach dem Ersten Korintherbrief," *BiLi* 60 (1987) 58–65.

Wuellner, Wilhelm. "The Sociological Implications of 1 Corinthians 1,26-28 Reconsidered," *StEv* IV, 666–672.

_____. "Ursprung und Verwendung der *sophos-, dynatos-, eugenēs*-Formel in 1 Kor. 1, 26" in Ernst Bammel et al, eds., *Donum Gentilicum: New Testament Studies in Honour of David Daube.* Oxford: Clarendon, 1978, 165–184.

2. *Paul's Mission (2:1-5)*

1. And when I came to you, brothers and sisters, I came not with the advantage of rhetoric or wisdom, but announcing to you the mystery of God. 2. For I did not decide to know anything among you except Jesus Christ and him crucified. 3. And I was among you in weakness, fear, and with much trembling, 4. and my speech and my proclamation were not in persuasive words of wisdom, but in the demonstrative proof of the Spirit and power 5. so that your faith is not grounded in human wisdom but in the power of God.

INTERPRETATION

In the *intitulatio* of the letter Paul identified himself as one called apostle (1:1). The nomenclature implies that he deemed himself to be one who had been sent on a mission. Paul picked up the theme of his mission when he wrote about the occasion that prompted his writing to the Corinthians. In positive terms he stated that his mission was to evangelize, but not with cleverness of speech (1:17). It was for that purpose that Paul was sent. In 2:1-5 Paul returns to the theme of his mission. An emphatic *kagō elthōn pros hymas*, "and I came to you," with an emphatic and unnecessary *egō* and the redundant use of the participle *elthōn*, defines the topic. Sent by God, he went to the Corinthians.

The Mission. The term "apostle" is not used in this pericope, but the passage clearly articulates what it means for Paul to be sent on a mission. The emphatic language with which the pericope begins highlights the mission. Twice Paul mentions his "coming," that is, in the participial introduction and in the principal verb of the sentence. The redundancy highlights Paul's mission. The use of a second participle, "announcing," clarifies the nature of the mission. Paul came to the Corinthians in order to announce something to them. His word is the word of one who has been sent as a messenger.

What Paul announced to the Corinthians at the time of his missionary visit to them was the mystery of God. In the Hellenistic world "mystery" connotes something esoteric, an experience beyond the normal range of human experience. Paul has explained that he has not preached the gospel according to worldly wisdom (1:17-18) and that knowledge of God does not come through human wisdom (1:21). In Jewish apocalyptic literature "mystery" (*rāz*) has an eschatological meaning. It designates the salvific events to be revealed in the age to come, knowledge of which is entrusted to God's chosen seers. Apart from 1 Corinthians Paul uses "mystery" only in Rom 11:25 (Rom 16:25 is an interpolated text), where the term clearly has eschatological overtones. The eschatological connotation of mystery is pertinent to Paul's use of "mystery" in 2:1, as it is in 2:7; 4:1; and 15:51 (cf. 13:2; 14:2). He had explained that his message was the message of the cross, a message that had eschatological significance, as Paul expressed in the apocalyptic language of 1:18. The eschatological motif continues to play in the exposition of Paul's thought until 2:13.

Paul contrasts the apocalyptic object of his proclamation with the advantage coming from the use of rhetoric or a focus on human wisdom. The implied antithesis recalls Paul's denial that he preached with cleverness of speech (1:17). He eschewed the advantages of human learning, preferring that the power of God be manifest in the eschatological message he had been sent to proclaim. His having been sent to proclaim such a message is no mere generality. Specifically he went to the Corinthians (cf. 9:2), a point he underscores with the prepositional phrase "to you" *(pros hymas)* and the double use of "to come."

Paul's Condition. In v. 3 Paul describes his own condition when he was among the Corinthians as one of weakness, fear, and trembling. Paul's self-depreciation is part of his rhetorical appeal. Ancient rhetors such as Isocrates and Dio Chrysostom often voiced a kind of mock humility so as to win the good will of their audience. Nonetheless, Paul's description of his weakness may reflect his real situation as well as his rhetorical strategy (cf. 2 Cor 11:16-29).

In v. 4 Paul implicitly contrasts his proclamation of the kerygma with the persuasive speech of other orators. It is likely that in cosmopolitan Corinth, as in most other cities of the Hellenistic world (cf. Acts 17:17), there were orators to whom the populace listened. Eloquence in speech *(megaloprepeia)* was a trait for which the orators of the day strove, notwithstanding Plato's having taken exception to mere eloquence, that is, oratory for oratory's sake, some centuries previously (see above, p. 75). In the Hellenistic world some teachers and orators gained their livelihood by charging fees of their audience. Paul would have none of this. He claimed not to have sought rhetorical advantage or a demonstration of rhetorical eloquence. Moreover, he proclaimed the gospel free of charge (9:15-18).

Paul's rhetorical depreciation of his person and his oratory so as to highlight the power of God at work in the gospel is reflective of his view that the messenger and the message are as one in the proclamation of the gospel (see 1 Thess 1:5). The argument he advances in 2:1-5 is skillfully set forth. It rests on an antithesis for which Paul provides theological depth and an ironic twist. The superficial contrast is between Paul's proclamation, his work taken as kerygma (v. 4), and the advantageous use of rhetoric to which his threefold use of "wisdom" (vv. 2, 4, 5) points. Theological depth is provided by the fact that the word of Paul, in his making known the Crucified One, proclaims the apocalyptic mystery of

God. The ironic twist comes from the fact that although Paul professedly denies that his message is couched in wise words, it enjoys demonstrative power *(apodeixis)*. The source of its demonstrative power is not the eloquence of the human rhetor, Paul, but the Spirit and power of God. The exercise of this demonstrative power results in a proof *(pistis)* that is none other than faith. The Spirit has entered into Paul's discussion in the guise of a twofold contrast. The power of the Spirit contrasts with Paul's weakness and trembling. The demonstrative power that comes from the Spirit contrasts with the persuasive words of merely human wisdom.

"Demonstrative proof" *(apodeixis)* and "proof" *(pistis)* are words that belong to the technical jargon of Hellenistic rhetoricians (see above, p. 86). As a Jew Paul would not have attended the rhetorical schools. Moreover, he seems to deny that he had any formal scholastic training. The entire letter is, nonetheless, a rhetorical masterpiece, especially chs. 1–4, which Jean-Noël Aletti has called a "rhetorical chef d'oeuvre" ("Sagesse et mystère," 382). Despite his formal disclaimer of basing his appeal on rhetorical skill (2:1-5), Paul's letter to the Corinthians is familiar with and employs many of the rhetorical devices of the day. Like other great orators he makes use of the threefold artificial argument, *ethos, pathos, logos.* He appeals to his own person and frequently sets forth the example of his own *persona* (the argument from *ethos*). He elicits the interests and passions of his addressees, whom he calls his brothers and sisters (the argument from *pathos*). Not so infrequently he works out his argument in a kind of syllogistic reasoning replete with enthymemes and explanatory statements, employing the postpositive *gar*, "for." This is his argument from *logos*. Paul's statement of principle with regard to all of this is expressed in 2:15. Whatever the appeal of Paul's argument, its demonstrative force comes from the Spirit. In the Pauline kerygma the power of God is at work.

NOTES

1. *And when I came to you, brothers and sisters:* In 1:17 Paul had reflected on the nature of his apostolic mission, that Christ had sent him to evangelize but not with cleverness of speech. Now he comments on his apostolic mission, reiterating the theme of his manner of proclaiming the gospel. Twice he uses the verb "to come" *(elthōn . . . ēlthon,* "coming, I came") and specifically notes that his apostolic mission brought him to the Corinthians (cf. 9:1), whom he addresses directly as his brothers and sisters.

   Paul begins his reflection with "and I" *(kagō,* an ellipsis of *kai,* "and" and *egō,* "I"). This emphatic expression evokes some of Paul's passion as he reflects on the preaching of the gospel. It serves to contrast the position with which Paul has taken issue in the previous pericope (1:18-31) with Paul's own stance (2:1-5). The use of "and I" *(kagō)* is a characteristic of Paul's correspondence with the Corinthians. Nineteen of the twenty-six times that Paul uses it are to be found in his two letters to the Corinthians (1 Cor 2:3; 3:1; 7:8, 40; 10:33; 11:1; 15:8; 16:4, 10; 2 Cor 2:10; 6:17; 11:16, 18, 21, 22[3x], 12:20). In the extant correspondence only in 2:1 and 3:1 is the expression found at the beginning of an epistolary unit.

I came not with the advantage of rhetoric or wisdom: "With the advantage of rhetoric or wisdom" *(ou kath' hyperochēn logou ē sophias)* is a reprise of the cleverness-of-speech motif of 1:17 *(ouk en sophią logou).* The disjunction "rhetoric or wisdom" has virtually the same meaning as "cleverness of speech," where "speech" is a genitive modifying "wisdom." "Advantage," *hyperochē,* literally "heights," is hapax in Paul. Used metaphorically it suggests not only the loftiness of one's words but even more the advantage that accrues to one who has the advantage of high ground in a battle. Paul denies that when proclaiming the gospel to the Corinthians he used his oratorical skills to gain a competitive edge.

but announcing to you the mystery of God: Paul's construction consists of the principal verb, "I came," modified by two participial clauses, "coming . . ." and "announcing. . . ." By placing the first participial clause before the principal verb, from which it is separated by the formula of direct address, "brothers and sisters," Paul indicates that he is going to be writing about his mission. His use of a negative, "not with the advantage of rhetoric or wisdom," indicates that he was suggesting an antithesis, an antithesis that is reflected in my translation, even if Paul's Greek does not include a "but" *(alla).*

Paul's choice of language, "announcing a mystery" *(mystērion)* is attested by the Beatty Papyrus, the Codex Sinaiticus, other ancient codices and versions, and a wide range of Latin Fathers, but other ancient manuscripts (B, D, G, P, Ψ, etc.) and a wide variety of Greek Fathers as well as the medieval Byzantine manuscripts take "the mystery" out of the text. They read "announcing to you the testimony *(martyrion)* of God." Other textual variants, including "gospel" in Theodoret and "salvation" in 489 and some lectionaries, confirm the difficulty scribes experienced in reading "mystery." Their difficulty may have arisen from the apparent oxymoron in "making known a secret" and the fact that *mystērion* appears to have a meaning somewhat different from the sense it otherwise enjoys in Pauline usage. "Testimony" may have been introduced from 1:6. Scrutiny of the textual witnesses and a closer reading of the text confirm, however, that "mystery" is indeed the better reading. Moreover, it makes full sense in the present context (see "Interpretation").

2. *For I did not decide to know anything among you except Jesus Christ and him crucified:* Paul offers an explanation (note the use of *gar*) of why he preached as he did. It was a decision on his part (thus the aorist tense of the verb). The object of his choice was to know nothing, with the consequence that he would make nothing known except Jesus Christ. An epexegetical *kai,* "and," (cf. 5:1; 6:6, 8, 11; BDF 442.9) specifies that the object of Paul's knowledge is Jesus Christ

insofar as he has been crucified. Effectively the crucified one is identified as the object of the gospel (1:17) and the mystery of God (2:1).

3. *And I was among you in weakness, fear, and with much trembling:* Paul's *repetitio* coupled with his feigned denial of the use of rhetorical technique (vv. 1, 4), serves to underscore the power of the gospel. "Fear" *(phobos)* and "trembling" *(tromos)* are hapax in 1 Corinthians. The binomial expression "fear and trembling" is an expression Paul uses of himself in 2 Cor 7:15 and of the Philippians in Phil 2:12 (cf. Eph 6:5). It has its origin in the LXX where the expression is typically found in a context in which it characterizes the "fear and trembling" felt by someone who is faced with the threat of an enemy's hostile and perhaps deadly assault (Exod 15:16; Deut 2:25; 11:25; Jdt 2:28; 4 Macc 4:10; Ps 54:6; Isa 19:16; cf. Gen 9:2). Paul's use of the traditional binomial is consistent with the apocalyptic atmosphere that characterizes his discourse. The binomial defines the weakness he experienced while he was among the Corinthians. His weakness *(astheneią)* was a kind of mortal dread. The use of the word group to which "weakness" belongs *(astheneia* and its cognates) is common in Paul's correspondence with the Corinthians. The word group is used in a variety of ways, one of which is to suggest that weakness is the locus of the revelation of God's power (cf. 1:27; 2 Cor 12:9).

4. *and my speech and my proclamation were not in persuasive words of wisdom:* Verses 4 and 5 recall 1:17b; 1:17b is prospective while 2:4-5 is retrospective. Paul's phrase lacks a principal verb. Its line of thought is dominated by the preceding "I was among you" *(egenomēn pros hymas,* with the verb in the aorist). Paul's speech *(logos mou)* harkens back to 1:18, where it is described as the message of the cross *(logos . . . tou staurou).* The epexegetical *kai* identifies his speech as the word of a messenger *(kērygma;* in Paul only here and 1:21; 15:14; cf. Rom 16:25, an interpolation).

The phrase "not in persuasive words of wisdom" has biblical overtones (cf. Dan 1:20 [Theodotion]; Sir 39:6), but the phraseology constitutes one of the most elusive textual problems attested by the manuscript tradition of 1 Corinthians. The manuscript tradition shows considerable variety in the reading of Paul's words. All the extant manuscripts retain *sophias* and have some form of the root *peith-.* Some manuscripts use *anthrōpinēs,* "human," to qualify *sophias.* Some, including B, D, and a corrector of ℵ, include *logois,* "words." Some manuscripts include both "human" and "words." All told, the editors of *GNT*[4] have identified eleven different combinations of these variants attested in the manuscript tradition.

"Not in persuasive words of wisdom," *ouk en peithois sophias logois,* is the reading for which Lietzmann opted and that has been adopted, albeit with some qualification, by the editors of *GNT*[4]. This reading appears in B (and in ℵ, albeit in a somewhat modified form), in some minuscules, and in the writings of some important and disparate Fathers (Origen, Eusebius, Chrysostom, Jerome, Cyril, and others). The reading includes a rare dative masculine plural form *(peithois)* of an otherwise unattested adjective *(peithos). Pithanos* is the normal and widely used form of the adjective in the word group (e.g., Aristotle, *Art of Rhetoric* 1.1).

A number of critics, however, including Johannes Weiss, Günther Zuntz, Gordon D. Fee, and Stephen Pogoloff, hold that the original wording was "not in the persuasiveness of wisdom" *(ouk en peithoi sophias)*. This reading is not found in the Greek manuscript tradition, but it seems to lie behind some Old Latin versions of the text (it[b,f,g]). It could also be the source of the reading adopted by the editors of *GNT*[4] insofar as the final sigma of *peithois* might be an instance of dittography. Sigma is the first letter of the following word, *sophias*. On this reading Paul's phrase would balance nicely with "in the demonstrative proof of the spirit" *(en apodeixei pneumatos)*. Both "persuasive" *(peithos)* and "demonstrative proof" *(apodeixis)* are hapax not only in 1 Corinthians but also in the entire Pauline corpus.

but in the demonstrative proof of the Spirit and power: Contrasted with the "persuasive words of wisdom" is the demonstrative proof of the Spirit. Despite his own lack of formal rhetorical training (cf. 2 Cor 11:6), Paul is using the technical language of the rhetorical schools *(apodeixis)*. His is the language of rhetorical appeal, the language of persuasion, demonstration, and power. Aristotle had described rhetoric as the faculty of discovering the possible means of persuasion in reference to any subject whatsoever (see *Art of Rhetoric* 1.1, specifically 1.1.14). Aristotle explained that "proof *(pistis)* is a sort of demonstration *(apodeixis tis)* since we are most strongly convinced when we suppose anything to have been demonstrated *(apodedeichthai)*" (*Art of Rhetoric* 1.1.11; cf. Longinus, *On the Sublime* 11.1; Plutarch, "The E at Delphi," *Moralia* 387A).

Isocrates and other Sophists spoke of the power *(dynamis)* of speech (cf. Gorgias' ode to the *dynamis logou*). Quintilian's rhetorical handbook speaks of the power *(vis)* of the spoken word (*Training of an Orator* 2.15.3-4). In contrast with the power of the rhetoricians' spoken word, Paul's gospel has come to the Corinthians in "spirit and power." The phrase "in the demonstrative proof of the Spirit and power" attributes the demonstrative force of Paul's message not to his own words, but to the Spirit. The Spirit is the powerful rhetor; Paul is but the spokesperson. His word is the word of the messenger. "Spirit and power" *(pneumatos kai dynameōs)* is a classic Pauline hendiadys (1 Thess 1:5; cf. Acts 1:8) in which the epexegetical "and power" identifies "the spirit" as the powerful Spirit of God. The hendiadys identifies the supernatural conviction and force with which Paul has made his appeal (so Barrett, *Commentary* 65). Richard, however, considers that "spirit" indicates the source of divine power and "power" the effect of the Spirit's manifestation of power in the apostolic ministry (see Earl J. Richard, *First and Second Thessalonians* [SP 11. Collegeville: The Liturgical Press, 1995] 65).

5. *so that your faith is not grounded in human wisdom but in the power of God:* "Human wisdom" and "the power of God" are contrasted with one another. This continues the series of contrasts with which Paul has played since 1:17. Both "human wisdom" and the "power of God" are the object of the preposition *en*, reflecting the Semitic *bĕ* and having an instrumental sense. It is not human rhetoric that leads to faith, but the power of God.

It is quite conceivable, however, that Paul is not using *pistis*, "faith," in its usual theological sense. *Pistis* is a technical rhetorical term. Used to designate a rhetorical demonstration, it is the Greek equivalent of Quintilian's *probatio*, "proof." In 2:1-5 Paul is dealing with rhetoric and shows his knowledge not only of rhetorical skills but also of classic rhetorical terms. In this context what he affirms is that he spoke in the way he did with the result (*hina* with subjunctive; BDF 369.3) that the proof of his argument to the Corinthians derived not from human wisdom but from the very power of God. This represents a singular use of *pistis* in 1 Corinthians, but "faith in God's power" would likewise be an unusual expression for Paul.

For Reference and Further Study

Bullmore, Michael A. *St. Paul's Theology of Rhetorical Style: An Examination of I Corinthians 2.1-5 in Light of First Century Greco-Roman Rhetorical Culture.* San Francisco, London, and Bethesda: International Scholars Publications, 1995.

Horsley, Richard A. "Wisdom of Word and Words of Wisdom in Corinth," *CBQ* 39 (1977) 224–239.

Koperski, Veronica. "Knowledge of Christ and Knowledge of God in the Corinthian Correspondence," *CorC* 377–396.

Lim, Timothy H. "'Not in Persuasive Words of Wisdom, but in the Demonstration of the Spirit and Power,'" *NovT* 29 (1987) 137–149.

Litfin, A. Duane. *St. Paul's Theology of Proclamation: 1 Corinthians 1–4 and Graeco-Roman Rhetoric.* MSSNTS 79. Cambridge: Cambridge University Press, 1994.

3. *God's Wisdom* (2:6-16)

6. We utter wisdom among those who are all that they can be, but not the wisdom of this age or of the rulers of this age who are passing away; 7. rather we speak the wisdom of God hidden in mystery, which God pre-ordained before the ages for the sake of our glory, 8. which not one of the rulers of this age knew; for if they had known they would not have crucified the glorious Lord. 9. But, as it is written, "Eye has not seen and ear has not heard, nor has it penetrated into the human heart what God has prepared for those who love him." 10. God revealed to us through the Spirit; for the Spirit searches everything, even the depths of God. 11. For what human person knows about a person except the spirit of the person, which is in that person? Thus no one knows about God except the Spirit of God. 12. We, however, did not receive the spirit of the world, but the Spirit that is from God, in order that we might know those things that have been graciously given to us by God; 13. things about which we

also speak in words taught not by human wisdom, but taught by the Spirit, interpreting spiritual things for the spiritual. 14. The natural person does not receive the things of God's Spirit, for they are foolishness to that one. He or she is incapable of understanding because he or she is spiritually judged; 15. but the spiritual person judges all things, and is judged by no one. 16. "For who knows the mind of the Lord; who advises him?" But we have the mind of Christ.

INTERPRETATION

In many ways this passage is similar to 1:18-31. The central theme of each passage is the wisdom of God. Both begin with mention of a spoken message that is addressed to the community in such a way as to be of ultimate benefit to them. Those to whom the word is beneficial are contrasted with those who have not understood the wisdom of God. The subsequent exposition is similar in form to that of the homiletic midrash. The exposition begins with a scriptural text that is identified as Scripture and continues with an exposition that is linked to the lemma in content and by catchwords. It concludes with another passage of Scripture. In this instance the scriptural proem (v. 9) is an enigmatic passage Origen believed to have been derived from the Apocalypse of Elijah but that has, in any case, similarity with various passages from the trito-Isaiah. The concluding Scripture is Isa 40:13, cited according to the Septuagint (LXX). To his citation of Isaiah Paul appends a rousing "but we have the mind of Christ." Paul frequently brings the arguments of 1 Corinthians to closure with this kind of summative statement that invokes the name of God or his Christ (cf. 3:23; 4:5; 6:11). As a feature of Paul's rhetorical style his use of this kind of summative closure is similar to the kind of closure used by poets and orators.

We Utter Wisdom. The opening words of this passage, "we utter wisdom" *(sophian de laloumen)* contrast with the previous pericope in which Paul had focused on his mission and his own proclamation of the gospel (see the emphatic *kagō* in 2:1). With the use of a verb in the plural Paul indicates that the proclamation of divine wisdom is not restricted to himself and his companions. It is a common activity within the community. What the community speaks is the leitmotif of the pericope. Paul repeats the initial *laloumen* in vv. 7 and 13. A striking feature of Paul's exposition is his use of the first person, both in pronominal form (vv. 7, 10, 12[2x], 16) and as the subject of his verbs (vv. 6, 7, 12[2x], 13). The "we" style is so distinctive that Martin Widmann ("1 Kor 2:6-16: Ein Einspruch gegen Paulus," *ZNW* 70 [1979] 44–53) has used it as an argument to support his unsuccessful claim that 2:6-16 is a later interpolation into Paul's text.

Paul's exposition concludes with an emphatic "we" *(hēmeis):* "but we have," says Paul, "the mind of Christ." In the following verse he begins again with an emphatic *kagō* as he returns to a consideration of his ministry in the first person singular. In effect the first person plural exposition of 2:6-16 is sandwiched between two sections of the letter in which Paul reflects on himself and his ministry. Each of these sections, 2:1-5 and 3:1-9, begins with the emphatic *kagō.*

With his emphasis on "we" in 2:6-16 Paul aligns himself with the community. Linguistically this is reflected not only in the use of the first person plural but also in the absence of the apostrophic *adelphoi,* "brothers and sisters," the common form of address that pervades Paul's letter. In this passage Paul adopts a quasi-logical form of argument, the rhetorical argument from *logos.* He articulates the experience that is common to himself and his addressees rather than the arguments from *ethos* or *pathos* that in different fashions set the rhetor over and against the addressees.

Paul's word is an intra-community word; it is spoken among those who, by the grace of God, are all that they can be, the *teleiois* of v. 6. These are those who have the mind of Christ (v. 16). The verb he uses in this pericope is *laleō,* "utter," rather than *kataggellō,* "announce," used in the preceding pericope (v. 1) to characterize Paul's kerygmatic proclamation. In vv. 6-16 he is dealing with the word spoken within the community and preparing the way for the reflections on prophetic speech that will occur later in the letter, especially in ch. 14.

The Wisdom of God. In his first reprise of the theme of the spoken word Paul specifies that what is spoken is the wisdom of God (v. 7). Mention of the wisdom of God links this passage to 1:18-31, where Paul twice mentions the wisdom of God (vv. 21, 24) and identifies the wisdom of God with Christ (vv. 24, 30). "God-talk" abounds in this passage. The ten uses of *theos* recall the concentration of specifically theological language in 1:18-31.

A particular feature of the passage at hand is the contrast that Paul makes between *theos* and *anthrōpos,* between God and the human being, between the Spirit of God and the spirit of the human. Both *theos* and *anthrōpos* are found in the scriptural argument cited in v. 9. The two terms provide the catchwords by means of which Paul develops his subsequent exposition. The contrast between God and a human being is particularly important in the antithetical argument of v. 11, where *anthrōpos* appears three times and *theos* twice.

Paul's words underscore not only the otherness of God but also the action of God and the divine initiative. God is one who has preordained before the ages (v. 7). God is one who has revealed (v. 10). God has prepared untold things for those who love him (v. 9). God has graciously given gifts of wisdom to those who are chosen (v. 12). The agent of God in all this activity is the Spirit of God. It is by the Spirit that revelation is communicated to human beings (v. 10). It is by the Spirit that Paul and the members of the community have been taught the things that they have been able to speak out (v. 12). This is the Spirit who alone knows the things of God (v. 11). This is the Spirit of God (vv. 11, 14); it is the Spirit from God (v. 12).

What is spoken within the community, Paul says, results from their having been gifted by God (see 1:4-5; 10, 12, 13, 15). What is spoken is the wisdom of God, communicated by the Spirit. The emphasis lies not on the preacher but on the word of wisdom that is proclaimed. Having introduced wisdom *(sophia)* as the topic of his proclamation in v. 6, Paul describes what wisdom is and what it is not. It is not the wisdom of this age or of the rulers of this age (vv. 6, 8). It is hidden in mystery . . . that God preordained before the ages . . . that eye has not seen nor ear heard . . . what God has prepared for those who love him . . . everything, even the depths of God . . . those things that have been graciously given to us by God . . . things about which we also spoke . . . things taught not by human wisdom, but by the Spirit . . . the things of God's Spirit . . . all things . . . the mind of the Lord . . . the mind of Christ.

Hidden in Mystery. The language employed by Paul in this passage represents a decided shift in his choice of vocabulary. He uses words and expressions such as "perfect" (v. 6), "mystery" (v. 7), "hidden" (v. 7), "to know" (vv. 8, 11, 12), "reveal" (v. 10), "receive the spirit" (v. 12), and the language of discernment ("search," v. 10; "judge," vv. 14, 15). This vocabulary is not only different from the language Paul has hitherto used in his letter, it also represents a choice of terminology that is rarely attested in his extant correspondence. The shift of vocabulary, particularly in a passage with an emphasis on "we," seems to suggest that Paul is dealing with the claims of some members of the community and has adopted their language in order to confront them.

On the other hand, the use of such terms is typical of apocalyptic vocabulary. Other expressions, such as "rulers of this age" (v. 6) and "glory" (vv. 7, 8), likewise bespeak an apocalyptic worldview. The worldview of 2:6-16 is manifestly apocalyptic. Paul uses apocalyptic language to articulate his views. The apocalyptic vision is generally characterized by a cosmic and anthropological dualism as well as by a view of history that sees history according to a time line that God alone has determined. To articulate this vision apocalyptic literature frequently speaks of the eons that follow upon one another in God's plan. Paul's own apocalyptic vision is clearly reflected in 2:6-16. A kind of apocalyptic dualism sets the rulers of this age over and against the glorious Lord. He views the death of Jesus as an event of cosmic proportions. The temporal determinism of the apocalyptic worldview is represented by the way Paul speaks of God preordaining before the ages (v. 6) and of God preparing untold realities for those who love him (v. 9).

According to Nils Dahl ("Formgeschichtliche Beobachtungen") the literary form of vv. 7-10 is a "revelation schema." Characterized by the use of "mystery" *(mysterion)*, "to hide" *(apokryptō)*, and other characteristic expressions, it also appears in Rom 16:25 (cf. Col 1:26-27; Eph 3:4-5). It was adapted by later Christian literature (cf. 2 Tim 1:9-10; Titus 1:2-3; 1 Pet 1:20-21; 1 John 1:1-3; Ign. *Eph.* 19:1-2; *Magn.* 6:1; 8:2; *Herm. Sim.* 9.12.2-3), but its use in 2:7-10 is singular in that the mystery is linked to the folly of the cross.

Paul carefully develops his argument in a twofold movement of thought (vv. 6-9; 10-16). Each movement of thought culminates in a reference to the Scriptures. The first movement of thought focuses on wisdom (*sophia*, 3x in vv. 6-9), expressed in apocalyptic language, the second on the spirit (the *pneuma*-word group appears twelve times in vv. 10-16). This two-part exposition is characteristic of prophetic speech. Paul will use a similar two-part schema in his exposition of the mystery in 15:50-57. There he first proclaims the mystery, then explains it. Similarly in 2:6-16 Paul proclaims the wisdom of God hidden in mystery, then proceeds to explain it. The two-part schema is classic in revelatory discourse, especially when the prophetic utterance is couched in esoteric language. Other examples of the two-part schema are the dreams interpreted by Daniel and the visions interpreted by a divine emissary in the book of Daniel (Daniel 2, 4, 5, 7, 8, 10–12) and some of the kingdom parables proclaimed and interpreted by Jesus (Matt 13:1-23, 24-30 & 36-43; Mark 4:1-20; Luke 8:1-15).

As will be the case in 15:54, where Isa 25:8 and Hos 13:14 are cited as if they were a single scripture, a formally introduced passage from Scripture is a key element in Paul's argument. The provenance of the scriptural citation in v. 9 is problematic (see the notes on 2:9), but Paul clearly identifies the passage as Scripture. The passage is, moreover, part of Paul's received tradition. The Scripture cited in v. 16 is Isa 40:13 [LXX]. Jewish apocalyptic literature is characterized by a new way of rehearsing and using Scripture. To a large extent apocalyptic literature is a rereading of traditional texts. See the use of Isa 6:9-10 in Mark 4:12 (and *par.*) and the thoroughgoing use of the Jewish Scriptures in the NT book of Revelation. Paul's use of Scripture in 2:6-16 is consistent with the use made of the Scriptures in the Jewish apocalyptic tradition.

In concluding his two-part argument Paul makes a critical distinction between those who have received the spirit of God and those who have not (implied by the emphatic use of *hēmeis de* in v. 12), between the spiritual person and the unspiritual person (vv. 14-16). Apocalyptic language and literature are judgmental. They bring judgment to bear on the present situation, separating out those who are saved from those who are not. Paul's discriminating language in vv. 6, 14-15 is consonant with the judgmental function of apocalyptic discourse. Apocalyptic discourse, moreover, typically conveys hope and consolation to those to whom it is directed. Much the same can be said apropos the rousing "we have the mind of Christ" with which Paul concludes his exposition.

The Human Person. The apocalyptic discourse of 2:6-16 is used to correct the outlook of the Corinthian pneumatists. In v. 11 Paul contrasts the noetic function of the human person with the noetic function of the Spirit of God. Three times v. 11 uses *anthrōpos* to identify the human person. The term is often translated "man," but I have translated it as "human person" because it is clearly different from *anēr,* the Greek term for the adult male human. *Anthrōpos* is a term the Hellenists used to speak of all human beings. It is a term, moreover, that occurs with considerable frequency in the first letter to the Corinthians. Thirty-one of Paul's eighty-eight known uses of the term are found in this letter. It occurs twenty-seven times in Romans, eight times in 2 Corinthians, fourteen times in Galatians, three times in Philippians, and five times in 1 Thessalonians.

In his correspondence Paul uses a variety of anthropological terms, particularly in conflict settings, in passages in which he wants to introduce a corrective to his correspondents' notion of what it means to be human. The divisiveness that fractured the Christian community in Corinth was in some measure due to a misunderstanding on the part of some as to what it meant to be a human being and what it meant to be graced by God. Some within the community made an all-too-facile distinction between the haves and the have nots, between those who were in the know and those who were not. The anthropological focus of 2:6-16, to which Paul's opening *tois teleiois,* "those who are all that they can be" (v. 6) poignantly points, has an argumentative purpose. It seeks to correct the erroneous anthropology of some of the Corinthians.

Since the groundbreaking work of Rudolf Bultmann (*Theology of the New Testament,* 1 [New York: Charles Scribner, 1951], especially pp. 191–227, "The Anthropological Concepts"), it has been common for commentators on Paul's letters to note that Paul's anthropology is essentially Semitic. Rather than viewing the human person as a composite of two principles, matter and spirit, Paul views the human person as a single human being. The various anthropological terms that Paul uses designate the whole human person, not one or another of its parts. Paul's use of "body" *(sōma)* and "soul" *(psychē)* does not so much indicate that the human being is composed of a material and spiritual principle, of matter and form, as it says that the single human person can be looked at insofar as he or she is corporeal *(sōma)* or insofar as he or she is a living human person *(psychē).* Paul is quite consistent in using anthropological terms in such a way that they designate the whole human person from the perspective of one or another aspect. Essentially Paul uses his Semitic anthropology, reflected in his normative Scriptures (see the "all flesh" of 1:29), to confront Hellenistic dualism.

In 2:6-16 Paul uses, in addition to the basic anthropological term *anthrōpos*, the expressions "the spirit of the person" (*to pneuma tou anthrōpou*, v. 11), "the natural person" (*psychikos anthrōpos*, v. 14; see note on 2:14 with regard to the translation), and "the spiritual person" (*ho pneumatikos*, v. 15). The natural person and the spiritual person are contrasted with one other in vv. 14-15. The natural person is one who has a merely "natural" life; the spiritual person is one who has received the gift of the Spirit of God. The contrast is consistent with Paul's apocalyptic view of reality. He wants the Corinthians to understand what a truly spiritual person really is. There is not a little argumentative edge in his exposition. From his perspective it is only those who are really spiritual persons who are all that they can be, *hoi teleioi.*

The Mind of Christ. Paul's exposition finishes with a strong rhetorical flourish. The epistolary unit is one in which the concluding verses (vv. 14-16) enjoy something of the character of a peroration in a discrete unit of Paul's deliberative discourse. His final words contrast "we" with unnamed others and maintain the focus on "Christ," whose reality has been at the forefront of Paul's exposition since he announced his theme in 1:10. This rhetorical unit expresses the view that the Christ event must be understood in cosmic perspective, a perspective that is not grasped by the rulers of this age (v. 8).

Paul's reminder to the Christians of Corinth that "we have the mind of Christ" has a hortatory purpose. It serves the deliberative function of the entire letter. There are things that divide the community. Among them is the understanding that some members of the community have of one another. Paul urges them to correct their view and consider all things in the perspective of the Christ event (cf. Phil 2:5-11). His appeal to Christ, his apocalyptic language, and his anthropological corrective are intended to dispel the lack of harmony that has fractured the community.

Paul's rhetoric serves his paraenetic purpose. His two citations of Scripture function in his rhetorical appeal as do the maxims of the sages in secular rhetoric. In his quasi-logical argument, the argument from *logos,* they serve as an inartificial proof. With its five uses of an explanatory *gar,* "for" (vv. 8, 10, 11, 14, 16, as well as a variant reading in 2:10 [see note]), Paul's argument is clearly one that is based on *logos.* It is enhanced by an almost syllogistic kind of reasoning as well as by the use of antithesis, comparison, paronomasia, and assonance, the repetition of the same word and the recurrence of similar sounds, and is not without an appropriate touch of irony.

In the previous pericope (2:1-5) Paul had resolutely denied that his message was based on human wisdom, that the power of his words depended on his use of rhetorical technique. The denial served to explain what he had written in 1:17 where he reminded the Corinthians that he had been sent to preach the gospel, but not with cleverness of speech. He had, nonetheless, used rhetorical techniques to deny that the strength of his message was based on the use of rhetoric. A clue to understanding Paul's ambiguity may be found in v. 13. Paul reminds the Corinthians that what he and the truly spiritual persons among them speak of are things that are taught in words, words not derived from human wisdom but taught by the Spirit. The Spirit provides the content and the demonstration (2:4). In rhetorical terms Paul attributes to the Spirit both the *heurēsis* and the *pistis*. That having been said, Paul has no further need in 1 Corinthians to deny his use of rhetorical technique.

NOTES

6. *We utter wisdom among those who are all that they can be:* After all his denials Paul acknowledges that he and his companions do impart wisdom. This wisdom is for those who are all that they can be. Paul's notion of wisdom, suggests Aletti ("Sagesse et mystère," 369), derives from Daniel 2, where we also find the antithesis between divine wisdom and worldly wisdom, the notion that true wisdom comes from God, and the idea that wisdom is given not to the arrogant, but to the poor and oppressed. Paul has, of course, already defined wisdom; it is Christ, the wisdom and power of God (1:24).

   Paul's reference to those who are all that they can be is one in the series of datives (see 1:18, 23-24, 30; 2:10, 14) he uses to identify those to whom his proclamation of the gospel is addressed. Those who are all that they can be are *tois teleiois,* literally "the perfect" (see Johannes DuPlessis, *Teleios: The Idea of Perfection in the New Testament* [Kampen: Kok, 1959], 176–205). Notwithstanding the opinion of those authors who hold that Paul's "wisdom" is esoteric teaching reserved for the few or is some sort of mysterious eschatological teaching (e.g., Robin Scroggs, "Paul: *Sophos* and *pneumatikos* [1 Cor 2:6-16; Wis 9:9-18]," *NTS* 14 (1967–68) 33–55; Gooch, *Partial Knowledge* 44–45; Stowers, "On the Use and Abuse of Reason," 260–261), Paul has not suggested that the wisdom he proclaims, his message, is reserved to some group of elite persons. He does not espouse a two-tier view of the Christian community with an eschatological message being addressed to the perfect and the basic teachings essential for Christian life being addressed to others. Such a division of the community would be inconsistent with the genre of the entire letter, which is a rhetorical plea for unity within the community.

   The adjective *teleios* has more the connotation of fulfillment than of perfection. In the context of the mystery religions the term was used to describe those who had completed the cycle of ritual initiation. In philosophical circles it was applied to those who are truly wise. Otherwise the term can be used of those who are accomplished in rhetoric or some other skill. In the Semitic world "perfect" contained the idea of completion; hence it was an appropriate description of God and those who belong to God (cf. Matt 5:48). This idea of having being brought to fulfillment is present in Paul's use of *teleios* except in those passages where Paul uses the adjective in a derogatory fashion to describe those who consider themselves to be perfect. According to Paul the gospel is wisdom to all those who, under the grace of God, realize their full potential. These are those who are saved (1:18). In Paul's exposition they are equivalently identified with those who love God (v. 9). The spiritual person (*ho pneumatikos,* v. 15) is the one who is all that he or she can be.

but not the wisdom of this age or of the rulers of this age who are passing away: Paul explains (the explanatory *de*; BDF 447.8) what he means by the wisdom that he and his associates impart. With regard to Paul's repeated use of "this age" (*tou aiōnos toutou*) see the note on 1:20. Paul is making use of a traditional apocalyptic motif as he contrasts the eschatological wisdom of God, which he and his companions impart, and the wisdom of this age. Paul's thought may have been inspired by Baruch, where in a prophetic paean on divine wisdom (Bar 3:9–4:4) mention is made of the rulers of the nations (*hoi archontes tōn ethnōn,* Bar 3:16). The hymn speaks of those who have not followed the way of wisdom (3:23) and those who perished (*apōlonto*) through their folly because they had no wisdom (3:28).

Since patristic times interpreters have disputed with one another as to the meaning and origin of "the rulers of this age" (*tōn archontōn tou aiōnos toutou*). Who are the rulers of this age? The expression "of this age who are passing away" postulates an apocalyptic frame of reference. The NT uses of the term "rulers" (apart from Rev 1:5, with reference to Christ) are divided between passages in which the term refers to political authorities and those in which the term refers to cosmic powers who control the physical universe. The apocalyptic character of this epistolary unity with its reprise of biblical motifs makes it likely that Paul has superhuman forces, angelic, demonic, or astral, in mind as he writes about the rulers of this age (cf. 2 Cor 4:4; compare Gal 1:4). Various terms are used in the NT to designate the cosmic forces popularly believed to hold sway over the universe (see 1 Cor 15:24; Rom 8:38, etc.). Among them are *archōn,* "ruler" (singular) or the related *archai,* "elementary principles" (plural). In 2:6 Paul uses *archontōn,* the genitive plural of *archōn,* to designate the cosmic powers (cf. *EDNT* 1:168). Paul's apocalyptic worldview was such that he saw the human drama as one that was played out under the influence of supernatural forces (see 1 Thess 2:18). That the rulers of this age are passing away (*katargoumenōn;* cf. 15:24-26) suggests that their power is already in the process of being destroyed.

7. *rather we speak the wisdom of God hidden in mystery:* With a strong adversative (*alla*) and a reprise of the verb "to speak" (*laloumen*) Paul continues his explanation of the wisdom he imparts. It is divine wisdom, conceived in apocalyptic and salvific terms. Two qualifying expressions describe the eschatological wisdom of God: it is hidden in mystery and it is preordained by God before the ages for the sake of our glory.

Divine wisdom is "hidden in mystery" ("in the form of a mystery"; BDF 220:2). This is not mysterious wisdom with the connotations that "mystery" has in the mystery religions of the Hellenistic era. Paul resolutely avoids the use of the various adjectives derived from the *myster-* root. His view of wisdom is consistent with his Jewish and biblical tradition. Its object is ultimate, eschatological reality. The idea of that which is hidden is important in the Jewish mystical tradition. That which is hidden has not yet been identified. For Paul wisdom that has long been hidden, especially from the wise of this world, is now revealed to those whom God has chosen (cf. Bar 3:27, *ou toutous exelexato ho theos;* cf. 1:27).

which God preordained before the ages for the sake of our glory: A relative clause, "which God preordained before the ages for the sake of our glory," adds a second qualification to "divine wisdom." The clause speaks of a divine plan of salvation accomplished within a predetermined apocalyptic time frame. *Proorizō,* "preordain," a rarely used intensive verb (only three times in Paul; cf. Rom 8:29-30), bespeaks divine predestination in regard to those whom God has chosen. "Before the ages" (cf. Gal 1:4) places the divine initiative before creation itself. "For the sake of our glory" is "for the sake of our salvation." "Glory" *(doxa)* is a divine quality associated with God's self-revelation; that self-revelation concerns the salvation of those whom God has created to share in his glory (15:43; cf. 11:7; 15:40-41).

8. *which not one of the rulers of this age knew:* A second relative clause describing the divine wisdom hidden in mystery reintroduces the rulers of this age (v. 6). In v. 8 these rulers were those who crucified the glorious Lord (v. 8b), the political powers responsible for Jesus' death. Paul's eschatological outlook is such that he views the death of Jesus as part of a cosmic drama. In his apocalyptic worldview the world is subject to cosmic forces (see 15:24-26). Ever the realist, Paul knew that human agents were responsible for the death of Jesus (see 1 Thess 2:15). Those political leaders responsible for Jesus' death were, in his view, instruments of the cosmic forces opposed to God. Accordingly they merit the same qualifying epithet, "the rulers of this age," *tōn archontōn tou aiōnos toutou.* In *The Jewish War* Josephus tells about a man named Jesus, son of Ananias, who created a public disturbance in the temple and was subsequently punished by the magistrates *(archontes),* scourged in the presence of the procurator, and finally killed by a Roman missile (*Bell.* 6.300-309).

for if they had known they would not have crucified the glorious Lord: Paul uses a verb in the indicative ("had known," *egnōsan*) to express an unreal condition (cf. 11:31; 12:19; Gal 1:10; 3:21; 4:15; see BDF 360.4). The conditional sentence provides a commentary on the ignorance of the rulers of this age. Not having understood the wisdom of God, these rulers have crucified the glorious Lord. The rulers of this earth, excluded from the wisdom of God according to the wisdom of God (1:21), have perpetrated the crucifixion of Jesus. They did not recognize God's eschatological and salvific intervention in the death of Jesus. There is not a little irony in what Paul has to say. The Corinthians aspire to wisdom, knowledge, and status; Paul observes that those who have status in this age are not "in the know."

Paul's juxtaposition of "glory" and "crucified" *(ton kyrion tēs doxēs estaurōsan)* is jarring. Glory speaks of honor, crucifixion of shame. The expression "the glorious Lord" *(ton kyrion tēs doxēs,* literally "Lord of glory") is a Semitism in which the genitive functions as a modifier. Hapax in the NT (cf. Jas 2:1; Eph 1:17), the descriptive epithet is found in one of the seer's throne visions in the Apocalypse of Enoch (*1 Enoch* 63:2; cf. 22:14; 25:3, 7; 27:3, 5, etc.) where, juxtaposed with "Lord of Wisdom," it characterizes an angelic figure. Paul's striking description of the crucified Jesus is appropriate in the present context. His language is manifestly apocalyptic. The descriptive epithet highlights the significance of Jesus as Lord in God's eschatological plan of salvation. In Jewish apocalyptic literature "glory" is used to describe those who share in God's glory, those who participate in eschatological salvation (e.g., 4 Ezra 7:91-101; *2 Apoc. Bar.* 51:10; *1 Enoch* 62:15). That Jesus is now the glorious Lord is something that has been revealed to Paul. The reality is an essential component of the wisdom of God, previously hidden in mystery, now spoken by Paul and his associates but not understood by the rulers of this age.

9. *But, as it is written, "Eye has not seen and ear has not heard nor has it penetrated into the human heart what God has prepared for those who love him":* Paul uses a classic lemma, "as it is written," *kathōs gegraptai,* to introduce a citation that is not a quotation of the Jewish Scriptures. The usage is exceptional since Paul otherwise uses the lemma only to introduce a citation of Scripture. What Paul has identified as a quotation has wording that is similar to the Greek text of Isa 52:15 and 64:3, but Paul cites neither of these passages. In rabbinic literature a saying similar to that cited by Paul is attributed to R. Yohanan: "Except for you, O God, the eye has not seen what God has prepared for him who waits for him" (*b. Sanh.* 99a; cf. Str-B, 3, 328–329). This rabbinic adage seems to be the result of a free association of Isa 64:3 with Ps 31:20. In the Gnostic *Gospel of Thomas* a comparable saying is attributed to Jesus: "Jesus said, 'I shall give you what no eye has seen and no ear has heard and no hand has touched and what has not entered the heart of man'" (*Gos. Thom.* 17).

Various opinions have emerged as to the origin of Paul's citation. Similar sayings are found in the *Ascension of Isaiah,* where Pauline influence is to be discerned, and in the Ethiopic *Apocalypse of Ezra,* the Syriac *Apocalypse of Daniel, Apocalypse of Pseudo-Hippolytus, Apocalypse of Peter,* the Arabic *Gospel of Pseudo-John,* the Ethiopic *Apocalypse of Mary,* and the *Letter of Pseudo-Titus.* Similar sayings are also found in such philosophical writings as those of Empedocles (frag. 1.2) and in Pseudo-Philo (*Biblical Antiquities* 26:13). Origen (PG 13, 1769) ascribes the quotation to the *Apocalypse of Elijah.* Jerome, who knew of both the *Ascension of Isaiah* and the *Apocalypse of Elijah,* disputes the claim that Paul actually quoted an apocryphal work (PL 24, 622). The extant Coptic and Greek fragments of what appears to be an *Apocalypse of Elijah* do not contain the saying quoted at 2:9, but it may well be that more than one apocalyptic work associated with the name of Isaiah was in existence. It is likely that Paul's source is an anonymous apocalyptic saying that the apostle took to be Scripture.

Apocalyptic dicta frequently consist of a pastiche of biblical allusions. Isaiah 64:3 (cf. Isa 6:10; Jer 5:21-23 [LXX]), with allusion to the Exodus tradition, announces that when YHWH comes to save Israel he will do things that humankind had never previously experienced. In his rehearsal of the Exodus events the Deuteronomist had spoken of the human incapacity to see and hear unless the capacity be given by God (Deut 29:2-4; cf. Sir 17:6), but also of what is given to those whom God loves (Deut 4:37; 7:8). In turn the *Shema* proclaims the singular importance of loving God (Deut 6:4; cf. 30:6, 20).

The adage cited by Paul, with a relatively unusual Pauline reference to the love of God, underscores the radical divide between what humans can know *kata anthrōpon* and the divine mystery, known only to God and those to whom God chooses to reveal it (see 8:2-3). Rhetorically the citation functions as do the other scriptural arguments employed by Paul. It provides an "artificial" warrant within a logical argument (the argument from *logos*).

10. *God revealed to us through the Spirit:* Paul continues his rhetorical argument with a comment on the role of the Spirit. This comment serves to qualify what he has written in vv. 7-10 as a "revelation schema": what has been unknown is now revealed. A similar use of the schema, using the same characteristic vocabulary, "mystery" *(mystērion)*, "to reveal" *(apokalyptō)*, and "the Spirit" *(pneuma)* appears in the deutero-Pauline Eph 3:3-5.

There is some variation in the textual tradition of this verse. Several ancient manuscripts (D, F, G, Ψ, and the majority of medieval manuscripts) add a qualifying "his" *(autou)*, that is, God's, to "Spirit," but even without this clarification it is clear that Paul is writing about the Spirit of God, the prophetic spirit. According to some witnesses ($\mathfrak{P}^{46}$, B, several minuscules, some Fathers including Clement of Alexandria, Basil, and Origen), Paul's comment is introduced by a post-positive *gar*, "for." The use of this connective particle is common in logical rhetorical argument, but the relatively weak connective particle "and" *(de*, not translated in my version) enjoys the overwhelming support of the manuscript tradition and appears to be the preferable reading. In 2:16 Paul similarly uses *de* to introduce the application of his citation.

Verse 2:10a affirms not only that revelation comes from the Spirit (cf. Isa 61:1; Ezek 8:3) but also that it has been given. It has been given not only to Paul and his associates but also to the Corinthians ("to us," *hēmin*). Having received the revelation given by the Spirit (cf. 7:10; 14:6; 2 Cor 12:1, 7), Paul is able to proclaim the mystery of God (2:7). The Spirit, to whom Paul had made reference in 2:4, is a major theme of Paul's letter to the Corinthians. Verses 10-16 of this chapter make up his first sustained reflection on the Spirit, one in which he focuses on the Spirit as the source of divine revelation, that is, of divine wisdom imparted to human beings. In ch. 14 he will consider the gift of prophecy, contemplating those who, like Paul (14:6), have received a gift of the Spirit enabling them to speak revelation and knowledge.

for the Spirit searches everything, even the depths of God: Paul uses an explanatory *gar* to explain why it is that the Spirit of God is the one who has revealed the mystery and divine wisdom. His verb, "to search" (*eraunaō*, elsewhere in Paul only in Rom 8:27, where it is used of God who searches human hearts; cf. Rev 2:23), is a late classical form of the verb *ereunaō* (see BDF 30.4), used especially by Philo in his musings on inspiration and the quest for the divine mind. Dio Chrysostom (*Discourses* 35.5) uses the language to describe one who is searching (*zēteō*; cf. 1:20c) for someone who can share a revelation (*apokalyptō*; cf. 2:10a). Paul counters the human search for divine wisdom with an affirmation that the Spirit is the one who searches. For Paul God's Spirit alone can fathom the full reality of God (cf. Rom 11:33-34, where *bathos* is also used). Since the idea of the Spirit searching everything is not otherwise found in ancient literature (see Reiling, "Wisdom and the Spirit," 205–206), it may be that the idea was one that had some currency in first-century Corinth and that Paul then used the idea as a point of departure for his argument that revelation takes place only through the power of the Spirit.

11. *For what human person knows about a person except the spirit of the person, which is in that person?:* Paul uses a kind of syllogistic reasoning (note the postpositive *gar*) to explain why it is that the Spirit (alone) can fathom the depths of God. To engage the reader and invite her or him to a judgment about connatural knowledge of the self Paul offers his premise in the form of a rhetorical question (cf. Rom 11:34) that suggests a negative response. The rhetorical question—Paul's first use of this rhetorical technique since 1:21—is characterized by its threefold use of *anthrōpos*, "human being." The repetition is clearly intentional. Paul's rhetorical question could have been introduced by a simple "who" *(tis)*; instead Paul wrote which "human being" *(tis. . . anthrōpōn*, literally "who among human beings"). The final reference to the human being is in a phrase, "the human spirit" *(to pneuma tou anthrōpou)*, that introduces a notion that is antithetical to the Spirit (of God), to whom Paul has twice referred in v. 10 and whom he specifically describes as "the spirit of God" *(to pneuma tou theou)* in v. 11b. The final relative clause, "which is in that person" *(to en autǫ)*, adds to the element of connaturality the element of specificity.

Thus no one knows about God except the Spirit of God: The implicit antithesis of v. 11a becomes explicit in v. 11b, the quasi-syllogistic conclusion to Paul's argument. Each element in the conclusion corresponds exactly to the elements of the rhetorical question: "no one" *(oudeis)* to "who" *(tis);* "about God" *(ta tou theou,* literally "the things of God") to "about the person" *(ta tou anthrōpou,* literally "the things of the person"); "except the Spirit of God" *(ei mē to pneuma tou theou)* to "except the human spirit" *(ei mē to pneuma tou anthrōpou).* "Thus" *(houtōs)* draws the analogy and sets up the conclusion. While Paul's argument from the lesser to the greater is reminiscent of rabbinic argument *(qal wa-ḥomer)*, his quasi-syllogistic reasoning constitutes a strong argument for Hellenists. Aristotle had written that "rhetorical demonstration *(apodeixis rētorikē)* is an enthymeme, which, generally speaking, is the strongest of rhetorical proofs; and . . . the enthymeme is a kind of syllogism" *(Art of Rhetoric* 1.1.11).

With this conclusion Paul completes his explanation (vv. 10b-11) of the role of the Spirit in revelation (v. 10a). The Spirit is alone capable of revealing the mystery of God since only the Spirit has connatural knowledge of God.

12. *We, however, did not receive the spirit of the world, but the Spirit that is from God:* Paul continues his commentary on v. 10a. Having reflected on the Spirit through whom God reveals in vv. 10b-11, Paul turns his attention to those to whom the revelation is given (*hēmin*, v. 10a). His *hēmeis de*, "we, however" (cf. 1:23), contrasts the intellectual exercise of vv. 10b-11 with a reflection on the experience that is common to himself and the Corinthians. The use of a strong antithesis emphasizes that Paul and the Corinthians have received the Spirit from God. This Spirit is contrasted with the "spirit of the world," an expression that does not otherwise appear in the NT or even in the LXX. Paul has, however, spoken of the world in such a way as to imply that its wisdom and its standards are not those of God (1:21, 25, 27; cf. 3:19). In 2:12 Paul's apocalyptic worldview suggests that the contrary world is moved by a spirit other than God's Spirit.

in order that we might know those things that have been graciously given to us by God: In writing about the knowledge that results from the gift of the Spirit Paul uses the verb *oida*, the perfect tense of *eidon*, "to see." In NT and classical usage *oida* means "know" in the sense of "have knowledge" rather than in the sense of "acquire knowledge," for which classical and NT authors alike tend to use *ginōskō*. Paul urges not only the divine initiative in the bestowal of the Spirit but also the graciousness of the gift as he describes the purpose of the gift of the Spirit to the Corinthians. Paul's use of the verb "to give graciously" (*charizomai*) is hapax in 1 Corinthians. It is, however, related to the noun *charis* (see 1:3-4). In the thanksgiving of his letter Paul had written about the full measure of the gifts given to the Corinthians.

13. *things about which we also speak:* In the epistolary thanksgiving Paul cited his gratitude for the gift that God had given to the Corinthians, citing not only its fullness but also that it was a gift in word and knowledge (1:4). Now he affirms that those to whom knowledge of divine realities has been given through the Spirit have spoken of the things they know. With this he returns to the notion with which the pericope had begun, namely, that Paul and his companions—ultimately the Corinthians as well—had spoken the wisdom of God. They were able to do so because they had received the gift of the Spirit that enabled them to know things about God. Because of this gift they could articulate the wisdom of God.

in words taught not by human wisdom, but taught by the Spirit: Paul qualifies his manner of speaking by means of two clauses: the first is an antithetical construction of prepositional phrases, the second a participial clause. The antithesis is clear, its construction less so. The antithesis contrasts the utterances of human wisdom with those prompted by the Spirit of God. The emphasis clearly lies on the teachings of the Spirit. The reference to the utterances of human wisdom might be an implicit reference to such Corinthian "slogans" as are cited in 6:12; 10:23; and 7:1. A similar contrast between merely human speech and that which comes from God is also found in Philo (see *The Worse Attacks the Better*, 39, 44, 133).

In the second member of his antithesis Paul uses a classical construction (see BDF 183), a substantivized verbal adjective with a designated agent in the genitive: *en didaktois pneumatos,* literally "in the things taught by the Spirit." The first part of the antithesis is more complex: *en didaktois anthrōpinēs sophias logois,* "in the things taught by human wisdom, the words." Had Paul written only *en didaktois anthrōpinēs sophias,* "in the things taught by human wisdom" his antithesis would have been linguistically balanced. He has, however, added "the words" *(logois),* almost as if the verbal adjective, *didaktois,* "things taught," had not been used. One result is that this use of *didaktois* is the only NT occurrence of a non-substantivized verbal adjective. Another result is the highlighting of the phrase *anthrōpinēs sophias logois,* "words of human wisdom," an emphasis consistent with Paul's emphatic denial that the power of the proclamation depends on the force of his rhetoric. Despite the complexity of the construction the textual tradition is quite consistent in its witness to what Paul wrote. An occasional addition of "holy" *(hagiou)* to "Spirit" is the only significant variant attested in the manuscript tradition.

interpreting spiritual things for the spiritual: Paul's qualifying participial clause is linked to the antithesis by means of paronomasia, three uses of *pneuma-,* following immediately after one another, *pneumatos pneumatikois pneumatika,* "of the spirit, for the spiritual, spiritual things." The clause poses two interrelated semantic problems (see BAGD 774.2-3). The first concerns the gender of the plural form, *pneumatikois,* "the spiritual." Is it masculine or neuter? The second concerns the meaning of the participle *sygkrinontes,* "interpreting."

Despite Paul's predilection for compound verbs with the prefix *syn,* his only other use of this verb is in 2 Cor 10:12. Of itself the verb admits of a variety of meanings: "link with," "compare," "explain," and so forth. In rhetorical jargon the verb was used in reference to the use of the technique of comparison, *sygkrisis.* Accordingly some commentators opt for "compare" as the meaning of Paul's verb. They suggest that with his clause Paul is summarizing what he has said. He has compared spiritual things *(pneumatika)* with other spiritual things *(pneumatikois,* taken as a neuter).

The verb *sygkrinō* is, however, used in the LXX for the interpretation of dreams (Gen 40:8, 16, 22; etc.). In this usage it seems to enjoy the status of a *terminus technicus* to connote the interpretation of revelation (cf. Dan 5:7). If the verb were to be taken in this sense Paul's use of it would be consistent with the apocalyptic and often unusual language that characterizes 2:6-16. What are interpreted are *pneumatika,* that is, the things God has revealed through the Spirit (v. 9), those things that have been graciously given by God (v. 12). These have been interpreted for the benefit of spiritual persons (see v. 15), that is, those who are all that they can be (v. 6). The final words of v. 13a serve as an effective commentary on v. 6, the first words of the epistolary unit.

14. *The natural person does not receive the things of God's Spirit:* This may be the first of the slogans bandied about by the Corinthian pneumatists to be cited by Paul (cf. Ulrich Wilckens, *Weisheit* 88–89 [96]; Robert Jewett, *Paul's Anthropological Terms* 354). Natural persons *(psychikos anthrōpos)* are not yet all that they can be; they do not belong to the eschatological age. They enjoy only ordinary human vitality *(psychē).* Those who do belong to the eschatological age are those to whom the gifts of the Spirit are given. Philo and other

Hellenistic Jews distinguished two levels of human existence with respect to the divine but they use the language of child-adult, imperfect-perfect rather than that of natural-spiritual to describe the contrast.

For Paul the natural person is one who has not received the gifts of the Spirit; the natural is "unspiritual." Some authors view *psychikos* as a "neutral" term (so Allen Rhea Hunt, *The Inspired Body* 82), but the term functions as the antithesis of *pneumatikos* in 2:14-15 and again in 15:44-46, the only passages in the extant correspondence in which Paul uses *psychikos*. It is likely that Paul uses *psychikos* in 2:14 with a touch of irony. The pneumatists among the Corinthians might have disparaged others in the community by calling them *psychikoi*, thereby implying a lesser status. Paul appropriates the term and applies it to the so-called *pneumatikoi* themselves. Vaunting their possession of the spirit, they nonetheless do not possess the wisdom of God, which comes from the Spirit of God.

Given the antithesis between *psychikos* and *pneumatikos* it is appropriate to translate *psychikos* as "unspiritual." In the following passage, however, Paul uses *sarkinos* (3:1; cf. Rom 7:14; 2 Cor 3:3) as an antithesis to *pneumatikos*. Both *psychikos* and *sarkinos* might be appropriately rendered "unspiritual." To preserve the distinction between the two terms I have chosen "natural" and "carnal" as appropriate translations.

The natural person does not receive the gifts of the Spirit of God. Some textual witnesses, various minuscules, and some Fathers including Clement, Tertullian, Origen, Athanasius, Jerome, and Chrysostom omit the explanatory "of God" *(theou)*, but a broad range of manuscripts ($\mathfrak{P}^{11}$, $\mathfrak{P}^{46}$, $\aleph$, A, B, C, D, Ψ) include the qualifier. "God-language," however, pervades 2:6-16. Moreover, Paul introduced the antithesis between the human person *(anthrōpos)* and God *(theos)* in v. 11. With the use of "of God" Paul reprises the earlier antithesis.

for they are foolishness to that one. He or she is incapable of understanding: With this clarification (note the postpositive *gar*) Paul endorses, all the while reinterpreting, the Corinthians' slogan. For the natural person, the unspiritual person, the things of God's Spirit are foolishness. The eschatological mystery revealed by the Spirit is foolishness. To those who have not received the Spirit of God, God's wisdom, revealed in the cross of Christ (see 1:18, 23-24), is so much foolishness. They are simply incapable of understanding the wisdom of God (this clause is joined to the preceding clause by "and," *kai*, omitted in the present translation for stylistic reasons.

because he or she is spiritually judged: Grammatically the verb *anakrinetai*, in the third person singular, may refer to the things of the Spirit of God (so RSV, Mathias Rissi in *EDNT* 2:321) or to the natural person. Given the parallelism with v. 15b a personal reference seems to be the better reading of the text. Paul's hapax use of the adverb "spiritually" *(pneumatikōs;* a variant reading of v. 13's *pneumatikois* in B, 33) suggests that the natural person is judged according to the Spirit. In contrast a spiritual person can be judged by no human person (v. 15b).

15. *but the spiritual person judges all things, and is judged by no one:* Verse 15 contrasts the situation of the spiritual person *(ho pneumatikos*, without *anthrōpos)*

with the natural person *(psychikos anthrōpos)* described in v. 14. The use of a rhetorical assonance (see BDF 488.1) leads Paul to play with the verb "to judge," *anakrinō* (an intensive form of the verb *krinō*, "to judge;" cf. 4:3[2x], 4; 9:3; 10:25, 27; 14:24), used in the passive in v. 14, then in the active, and again in the passive in v. 15. Having received the Spirit who searches everything *(panta,* 2:10), the spiritual person is capable of testing all things—and all persons (cf. 14:24). On the other hand the spiritual person, to whom Paul draws attention by means of an untranslated *autos,* "that one" can be properly judged by no human being.

The manuscript tradition gives evidence of some divergence with regard to "all things" *(ta panta,* adopted by *GNT*[4] and found in 𝔓[46], A, C, D, and some passages in the writings of Origen and Clement). Other manuscripts, with no substantive difference of meaning, read *men panta, panta,* or *men ta panta.*

16. *For "who knows the mind of the Lord; who advises him?":* Paul's rhetorical question is a citation of Isa 40:13 [LXX]. The scriptural phrase "mind of the Lord" picks up the theme of the hidden wisdom of God (v. 7) and harkens back to the idea that God's thoughts cannot be plumbed by a mere human being (v. 11). Paul has sharpened the rhetorical impact of the prophetic cry by omitting the third parallel question, "who has become his counselor?" (Isa 40:13b). The prophet's third question is, however, reflected in Paul's truncated use of the same passage of Isa 40:13 in Rom 11:34, a verse that belongs to an epistolary unit (Rom 11:25-36) that is not lacking in verbal and thematic parallels with 2:6-16.

But we have the mind of Christ: The deutero-Isaian "mind of the Lord" is implicitly defined by Paul as the mind of Christ. Paul frequently uses biblical passages that speak of YHWH, *Kyrios* ("Lord") in the LXX, and applies them to Christ. Such usage is a key element in Paul's christological use of the Scriptures. Functions traditionally attributed to God were attributed by Paul to Christ, God's agent *par excellence.* Paul identifies Christ as "the Lord." Paul's actualizing hermeneutic is similar to that of other Jewish hermeneutical endeavors (Qumran, the rabbis). What is proper to Paul's use of the Scriptures is his blatant application of the text to Christ (and even to the church). Paul employs a scriptural hermeneutic to interpret the reality of Jesus and his work (see the "according to the scriptures" *[kata tas graphas]* formula of 15:3-4). By so doing he affirms the role of Christ in the eschatological work of salvation and attributes to him an exalted status succinctly evoked in the designation "Lord" *(Kyrios).*

Unlike other instances in which his scriptural hermeneutic leads to an implicit christological appropriation of the biblical text, Paul specifically redefines "the mind of the Lord" as "the mind of Christ." "Christ" is a christological epithet by means of which Paul customarily refers to the death and resurrection of Jesus. By redesignating the mind of the Lord as "the mind of Christ" Paul alludes to the revelation of divine wisdom in the crucifixion, albeit noting that it must be understood in otherworldly terms (see "the glorious Lord" in v. 8). Within a history-of-religions' perspective Richard Reitzenstein *(Hellenistic Mystery-Religions: Their Basic Ideas and Significance* [translated from the the the 3rd. German edition of 1926 by John E. Steely; Pittsburgh: Pickwick, 1978] 431–432) suggested that in the Hellenistic mystery religions and in Gnosticism union with the deity is achieved by means of the gift of *nous* ("mind"), which brings knowledge of the saving mysteries. Using the technique of redefinition, Paul clearly affirms that wisdom is not to be dissociated from the crucifixion. Paul's emphasis on "Christ" is consistent with the emphasis he first introduced in 1:12.

Paul's use of the Isaian text is not only christological in its application; it is also of ecclesiological import. He affirms that spiritual people, "we" (note the use of an emphatic *hēmeis*), who constitute God's holy people, have the mind of Christ. The term *nous* suggests a constellation of thoughts and beliefs that provide criteria for judgment and action. Paul is stating that the members of the assembly share the thinking or plans of Christ (cf. Fee, *1 Corinthians* 53, n. 29). In contrast to the divisiveness that characterizes the Corinthian community Paul is urging an ethical outlook, attitudes and a consequent pattern of behavior that are shaped by attentiveness to Christ. On the mind of Christ see also Paul's letter to the Philippians (Phil 1:27, 2:5), which, however, does not use the cipher "mind of the Lord/mind of Christ."

For Reference and Further Study

Beker, Johan Christiaan. *Paul the Apostle: The Triumph of God in Life and Thought.* Edinburgh: T & T Clark; Philadelphia: Fortress, 1980, 182–212.

Berger, Klaus. "Zur Diskussion über die Herkunft von I Kor. ii. 9," *NTS* 24 (1978) 270–283.

Dahl, Nils A. "Formgeschichtliche Beobachtungen zur Christusverkündigung in der Gemeindepredigt" in Walther Eltester, ed., *Neutestamentliche Studien für Rudolf Bultmann.* BZNW 21 (1954) 3–9.

Ellis, E. Earle. *Prophecy and Hermeneutic* 213–220.

Funk, Robert W. "Word and Work in 1 Corinthians 2:6-16" in idem, *Language, Hermeneutic, and the Word of God: The Problem of Language in the New Testament and Contemporary Theology.* New York: Harper and Row, 1966, 275–305.

Kovacs, Judith. "The Archons, the Spirit, and the Death of Christ: Do We Need the Hypothesis of Gnostic Opponents to Explain 1 Corinthians 2:6-16?" in Joel Marcus and Marion L. Soards, eds., *Apocalyptic and the New Testament: Essays in Honor of J. Louis Martyn.* Sheffield: JSOT, 1989, 217–236.

Newman, Carey C. *Paul's Glory-Christology: Tradition and Rhetoric.* NovT.S 69. Leiden: Brill, 1992.

North, J. Lionel. "'Human Speech' in Paul and the Paulines: The Investigation and Meaning of *anthrōpinos ho logos* (1 Tim. 3:1)," *NovT* 37 (1995) 50–67.

Pesce, Mauro. *Paolo e gli Arconti a Corinto: Storia della Ricerca (1888-1975) ed esegesi di 1 Co 2, 6.8).* Brescia: Paideia, 1977.

Ponsot, Hervé. "D'Isaïe LXIV, 3 à I Corinthiens II, 9," *RB* 90 (1983) 229–242.

Reiling, J. "Wisdom and the Spirit: An Exegesis of 1 Corinthians 2,6-16" in Tijtze Baarda et al, eds., *Text and Testimony: Essays in Honor of A. F. J. Klijn.* Kampen: Kok, 1988, 200–211.

Sterling, Gregory E. "'Wisdom among the Perfect': Creation Traditions in Alexandrian Judaism and Corinthian Christianity," *NovT* 37 (1995) 355–384.

Stuhlmacher, Peter. "Zur hermeneutischen Bedeutung von 1 Kor 2,6-16," *ThBeitr* 18 (1987) 133–158.

Verheyden, Joseph. "Origen on the Origin of 1 Cor 2,9," *CorC* 491–511.

Willis, Wendell Lee. "The 'Mind of Christ' in 1 Corinthians 2,16," *Bib.* 70 (1989) 110–122.

4. *Mother and Farmer* (3:1-9)

1. And I, brothers and sisters, was able to speak to you not as spiritual people, but only as carnal people, as infants in Christ. 2. I gave you milk to drink, not substantial food, because you were not yet capable, nor are you capable until now, 3. for you are still fleshy people. Insofar as there is jealousy and rivalry among you, aren't you fleshy people? And aren't you behaving according to merely human standards? 4. For when someone says "I am Paul's," and another "I am Apollos's," aren't you merely human? 5. What, after all, is Apollos? And what is Paul? Servants through whom you have come to faith, as the Lord has assigned to each. 6. I planted, Apollos watered, but God provided the growth; 7. so neither is the one who plants anything nor the one who waters, just God who provides the growth. 8. The one who plants and the one who waters are one and the same, and each one will receive compensation according to his or her own labor, 9. for we are God's coworkers; you are God's field, God's construction.

INTERPRETATION

For a third time in this letter Paul writes about his ministry among the Corinthians (cf. 1:13-17; 2:1-5). As in the earlier epistolary units Paul writes in the first person singular, thereby developing the *ethos* aspect of his rhetorical argument. He returns to a reflection on the quality of his discourse among the Corinthians after the rhetorical digression of 2:6-16. His initial and emphatic "and I, brothers and sisters," recalls the use of a similar phrase in 2:1.

Paul's tone is ironically confrontational. The chapter is encompassed by allusions to the Corinthians' choice of descriptive epithets for themselves. They might consider themselves to be perfect (see 2:6) but Paul considers them mere infants (3:1). They might consider themselves wise, but Paul will exhort them to be fools (3:18).

Carnal People. Not only do some of the Corinthians consider themselves perfect; they also consider themselves spiritual persons. Paul's opening antithesis draws a sharp contrast between those who are spiritual and those who are carnal. The antithesis is based on the anthropology Paul had developed in the preceding digression. In light of those considerations Paul can only consider the pneumatists at Corinth to be carnal persons, not the spiritual persons they claim to be. That these Corinthians are flesh is the dominant motif in Paul's first movement of thought (vv. 1-4). Three times Paul draws attention to the fact that they are carnal: in the opening antithesis (v. 1), in an explanatory affirmation (v. 3a), and in a rhetorical question (v. 3b).

In Paul's anthropology flesh *(sarx)* is antithetical to spirit *(pneuma)* and generally has a negative connotation. It denotes the human being insofar as the human, mere creature that he or she is, is weak, capable of being subject to forces hostile to God, and therefore prone to sin (cf. 1:29). In the Greek Bible both "flesh" *(sarx)* and "body" *(sōma)* render the single Hebrew term *bāśār,* flesh or body. Both designate the human insofar as the human is corporeal and in relationship with other humans, but Paul has a tendency to use "flesh" when he wants to refer to the human as weak and potentially sinful and "body" when he wants to describe the human as creature and open to the power of God's Spirit.

The engaging rhetorical question of v. 3b constitutes a direct appeal to the Corinthians. It challenges them to realize that they are carnal people inasmuch as there is rivalry among them. That there is rivalry had been reported by Chloe's people (1:11). As he did in the beginning of the letter (1:12) Paul uses slogans to caricature the divisiveness that exists. In 3:4 he uses two of the slogans to highlight the disunity of the community. Saying "I am for Paul" or "I am for Apollos" indicates that the community does not have the unity it ought to have and that its members are hardly spiritual people. Their conduct is based on merely human standards. They do not walk *(peripateō)* along the ways of God. The reflections of vv. 3-4 bring an anthropological evaluation to bear upon the divisiveness of the community that had prompted Paul's letter (1:10-17) and place this rivalry under the scrutiny of eschatology developed in the rhetorical digression of 2:6-16.

Milk to Drink. Paul uses both simile (infants) and metaphor (the nurturing mother) to describe his relationship with the Corinthians. C. H. Dodd once claimed that Paul "lacks the gift for sustained illustration of ideas through concrete images (though he is capable of a brief illuminating metaphor)" (*The Epistle of Paul to the Romans* [London: Hodder and Stoughton, 1932] 121), but the use of metaphor is characteristic of Hellenistic rhetoric and Paul uses metaphor to good rhetorical effect throughout 1 Corinthians.

The rhetorical handbooks urged the use of metaphor in the development of a logical argument. Aristotle considered that similes were a kind of metaphor (*Art of Rhetoric* 3.2.13) and noted that metaphors are a useful rhetorical argument, as are the use of antithesis and balanced phrases (see *Art of Rhetoric* 3.2.10). In 3:1-9 Paul's argument makes use of balanced phrases (vv. 4, 5, 6, 7, 8) and antithesis (vv. 2, 3, 6, 7, 9), but it is built on the effective use of simile and metaphor. Seneca similarly used simile and metaphor to develop a moral argument (e.g., *Epistles* 13.1-3; 59.6; 78.16). He wrote, for example, "our ancient prose writers . . . whose eloquence was simple and directed only towards proving their case, are full of comparisons; and I think that these are necessary, not for the same reason which makes them necessary for the poets, but in order that they may serve as props to our feebleness, to bring both speaker and listener face to face with the subject under discussion" (Seneca, *Epistles* 59.6).

Despite Dodd's demurrer Paul appears to be no less skilled in this type of epistolary argumentation than was Seneca. Immediately after addressing the Corinthians as brothers and sisters Paul characterizes them as "infants in Christ." His metaphor is mixed (cf. 1 Thess 2:7, 11), but deliberately so. The clash of the metaphors brings sharp focus to the situation of the Corinthians. They may be Paul's siblings but they are, nonetheless, mere infants. Paul calls the Corinthians babies in order to call them to task (cf. 4:14). They consider themselves to be perfect yet they are but infants. They need to be fed as infants since they are not yet capable of ingesting solid food. They are just children, not yet the mature adults they consider themselves to be. The irony is only too readily apparent.

Paul's use of an image of the nurturing mother to illustrate the relationship that existed between himself and the Corinthians is not unique in his correspondence. See 1 Thess 2:7-8, where Paul compares himself to a nursing mother or a wet nurse, and Gal 4:19, where he compares himself to a mother in labor. Paul also uses a paternal image to describe the relationship between himself and his addressees (see 4:14-21; 1 Thess 2:11-12; Gal 4:19; cf. Phlm 10). These parental metaphors describe the relationship between himself and those he has evangelized. They bespeak Paul's affection for his correspondents, but the images are not used in exactly the same fashion. The paternal image draws attention to Paul's ministry of evangelization, his having engendered children in Christ (1 Cor 4:16; Phlm 10). The maternal image evokes Paul's pastoral care, his devoted nurture of those he has evangelized (cf. 1 Thess 2:11-12).

Planting and Watering. Almost immediately after using the image of a nurturing mother to describe his ministry Paul uses the image of the farmer (see 15:36-41). Philo similarly juxtaposes the images of giving milk and planting a field (see Philo, *Husbandry* 9). Paul used the maternal image to highlight the singularity of his ministry vis-à-vis the Corinthians and to characterize his work among them as a nurturing ministry (vv. 1-2). The agricultural image permits him to focus further on his original role in the Corinthians' coming to faith (cf. 4:15), but it also allows for the development of other ideas. One such idea is that he and Apollos worked together in a common enterprise for the benefit of the Corinthians. Another is that the entire enterprise is God's enterprise (v. 9), for which Paul uses the metaphor of the field. Within the biblical tradition agricultural imagery evokes the image of growth in the realm of creation (e.g., Genesis 2) and of Israel as the vineyard (e.g., Isa 5:1-7). The seed parables of the synoptic tradition (Matt 13:3-9, 24-30, Mark 4:2-9, 26-32; Luke 8:5-8) reflect similar imagery. Paul's emphasis on God and the divine initiative is a dominant theme, perhaps *the* dominant theme of 1:18–4:5.

In the balanced phrases of his rhetoric Paul juxtaposes himself with Apollos three times in this pericope: first in the reprise of the slogans of 1:12 (v. 4), then in a brace of rhetorical questions (v. 5), and finally in the nuanced metaphor of v. 6, where the name of Paul is replaced by the emphatic pronoun "I" *(egō)*. Both Paul and Apollos were known to the Corinthians. In 1 Corinthians Paul often cites his own example in the pursuit of his rhetorical argument. Now he cites the complementary example of Apollos so that the Corinthians might learn from it (4:6). Paul and Apollos have worked side by side but the power comes from God and the enterprise belongs to God. That is something from which the Corinthians should learn rather than conforming their behavior to merely human norms.

NOTES

1. *And I, brothers and sisters:* The emphatic and resumptive "I" *(kagō)* with which this pericope begins, along with the apostrophic "brothers and sisters" (see the similar construction in 2:1) indicates that Paul is returning to the discussion of his own ministry in Corinth, a discussion that he had temporarily abandoned in the rhetorical digression of 2:6-16. His "I-you" language contrasts sharply with the "we" language of 2:6-16. Despite the rebuke the "I-you" implies, Paul addresses the Corinthians in familial terms. The appeal to family unity is congruous with the deliberative purpose of the letter and serves as a background for the imagery used in 3:1-2.

   was able to speak to you not as spiritual people but only as carnal people: To describe his earlier discourse to the Corinthians Paul makes use of a strong antithesis that probably echoes the language of those Corinthians who considered themselves spiritual people. Paul rejects their self-description and indicates that he spoke to them as people who had not yet received the Spirit—and that was all he was able to do.

as infants in Christ: The description of the Corinthians as carnal people is not entirely negative. They are "infants in Christ" *(nēpioi en Christō).* Elsewhere in his correspondence Paul describes Christians as "infants" only in Gal 4:3 (cf. Gal 4:1) and 1 Thess 2:7 (at which there is a widely attested variant, *ēpioi,* "gentle"). The term evokes a kind of maternal relationship between Paul and those to whom he spoke. Infants need to be cared for and taught (Rom 2:20). Paul's ministry among the Corinthians was a nurturing ministry.

There is, nonetheless, some irony in Paul's use of this term to describe the Corinthians. In the Hellenistic world "infants" was metaphorically used in the sense of foolish or silly. The Corinthians thought that they were very mature (2:6); in Paul's eyes, and from a Christian perspective, they were very childish (cf. 13:11; see note on 10:7).

2. *I gave you milk to drink, not substantial food, because you were not yet capable, nor are you capable until now:* Paul's use of a single verb, "to give to drink" *(potizō),* in the principal clause is an example of *zeugma,* that type of ellipsis in which a verb inappropriately serves a double purpose. Perhaps Paul's expression reflects a Semitic construction, where such double use of a single verb is fairly common. Only in 3:2 does Paul use "milk" *(gala)* as a metaphor (cf. 9:7). The provision of milk for those who were as yet infants serves to describe his pastoral care. Philo and Epictetus, along with other ancient authors (e.g., Heb 5:12-13; 1 Pet 2:2), occasionally distinguished milk-drinking infants from meat-eating adults (Philo, *Every Good Man is Free* 160; *Preliminary Studies* 19; *Migration of Abraham* 29; *Dreams* 2.10; Epictetus, *Discourses* 2.16.39; 3.24.9). Philo contrasts infants who drink milk *(nēpiois . . . gala)* with adults who eat wheat bread *(teleiois de ta ek pyrēn pemmata)* (*Husbandry* 9). Like Philo, Paul distinguishes the mature *(hoi teleioi,* 2:6) from infants *(nēpioi).* Unlike Philo, Paul does not project two stages of Christian development (see note on 2:6). Rather he confronts the Corinthians by reminding them of their need to be nurtured and of his own role in their nurturing.

Neither at the time of Paul's visit nor at the time of his writing were the Corinthians capable of sustaining themselves. In vv. 1 and 2 Paul writes about the respective capabilities of himself and the Corinthians, using the verb *dynamai* to describe what they were and were not able to do. In 1 Corinthians the issue of capability is important. In his initial exposition of the message of the cross Paul had spoken about the power *(dynamis)* of God. One of the principal leitmotifs of 2:6–3:23 is the relationship between God *(theos)* and the human being *(anthrōpos).* Now 3:1-4 functions as a transition between 2:6-16, where Paul considers the human being and how the human being becomes a spiritual person *(pneumatikos),* and 3:5-17, where he reflects on God *(theos)* as the source of the effectiveness of his own ministry.

3. *for you are still fleshy people:* The Greek language has two adjectives derived from the noun *sarx,* "flesh," *sarkikos* and *sarkinos.* The two terms are virtually synonymous, the nuance of *sarkikos* being "having a fleshy nature," of *sarkinos* "being made of flesh" (see BDF 133.2). In v. 3 Paul twice uses *sarkikos* (cf. 9:11; 2 Cor 1:12; 10:4; Rom 15:27; in v. 1 he had used *sarkinos* (cf. 2 Cor 3:3; Rom 7:14). To distinguish the two terms, both of which are used substantively by

Paul, *sarkikoi* is here translated as "fleshy people," while *sarkinoi* is rendered as "carnal people." The textual tradition gives evidence of the alternate spelling in each of the three uses of the *sark-* adjectives in 3:1-3.

Insofar as there is jealousy and rivalry among you: That there was contention at Corinth had been reported to Paul by the group of Chloe's people who visited him in Ephesus (1:12; cf. 2 Cor 12:20). For Paul this anti-social behavior is infantile conduct, the result of the Corinthians' immaturity and lack of progress.

On the pairing of jealousy and rivalry see Rom 13:13; 2 Cor 12:20; Gal 5:20. These are catalogues of vices in which jealousy and rivalry are cited as typical examples of antisocial behavior. Most of the ancient manuscripts ($\mathfrak{P}^{11}$, $\aleph$, B, C, P, Ψ), many of the medieval manuscripts (81, 181, 630, etc.), many of the ancient versions (Old Latin, Armenian, Coptic, Ethiopic), and many Fathers of the East and West (Clement, Origen, Ambrosiaster, etc.) offer a reading of 3:3 in which Paul uses two words, "jealousy and rivalry" (*zēlos kai eris*) to describe the lack of harmony within the Corinthian community. A large number of medieval manuscripts (33, 88, 104, 181, 326, 330, etc.) add a third element to the description, "and dissension" (*kai dichostasiai*). This reading finds support in such earlier manuscripts as $\mathfrak{P}^{46}$, D, and G and is reflected in the writings of some Greek Fathers (Origen and Chrysostom on occasion, John Damascene), several Latin Fathers (e.g., Irenaeus, Cyprian, Ambrose), an occasional Latin translation of a Greek Father, and a few ancient versions (the Syriac Peshitta, the Slavonic, and a Georgian version). A few other manuscripts have an anacoluthic "contention and dissension" (*eris dichostasiai*). The triadic reading appears to be the result of scribal clarification, perhaps under the influence of Gal 5:20. There is no obvious reason that explains why the third element, if original, would have been dropped within the manuscript tradition.

aren't you fleshy people? And aren't you behaving according to merely human standards? With his use of the rhetorical question—Paul's Greek is a single question with two parts—Paul returns to the use of a diatribal style, which had characterized much of the earlier part of the letter. The question calls for the Corinthians to make a judgment about themselves, that is, to acquiesce in Paul's characterization of them as "carnal" rather than hold to the "pneumatic" condition they had attributed to themselves. In the second part of his question Paul evokes the anthropology he had developed in 2:6-16. The divisiveness of the community is seen as indicative of conduct (*peripateite*, literally, "aren't you walking?") that has the merely human as its norm. Paul is of the opinion that the conduct of Christians ought to be according to the Spirit (*kata pneuma*, Rom 8:4; cf. 1 Cor 3:10), rather than being based on merely human standards (*kata anthrōpon*).

Paul's use of the metaphor "to walk" (*peripateō*) to describe human conduct is not only an example of synecdoche. It is also typical of Paul when he evokes norms of conduct. In the Jewish tradition *halakah*, from the Hebrew verb "to walk," describes the rabbinic jurisprudence that is drawn from the Torah.

4. *For when someone says "I am Paul's," and another "I am Apollos's," aren't you merely human?* To characterize and perhaps caricature the divisiveness of the community Paul evokes the slogans he had cited in 1:12. The kind of divisiveness to which such slogans point is inconsistent with the anthropology Paul had elaborated in 2:6-16. It is merely human; it is not a result of the action of the Spirit of God. Only two of the slogans cited in 1:12 are reprised in 3:4 (cf. 3:22). The respective roles of Paul and Apollos will serve as a focus of the next few verses. Paul hopes that their example will be beneficial to the Corinthians (see 4:6).

5. *What, after all, is Apollos? And what is Paul?* Paul continues his barrage of rhetorical questions by asking about the status of Apollos and himself. Several witnesses in the manuscript tradition introduce these questions with the personal interrogative pronoun "who" (*tis*, $\mathfrak{P}^{46}$, C, D, F, G, Ψ), but the neuter what *(ti)* is better attested. The effect is the same. On either reading Paul is asking about the status and role of Apollos and himself. An epistolary *oun* ("after all") links these questions to the preceding exposition.

Servants through whom you have come to faith: Departing from the classical pattern of leaving rhetorical questions unanswered, Paul provides a response to his own questions. Apollos and he are "servants" (*diakonoi*, an expression enhanced by the *all' ē*, "except," interpolated in a few ancient manuscripts [D*, Ψ] and the majority of the medieval manuscripts). Jürgen Roloff considers that the image of the servant is central to Paul's self-understanding (see *Apostolat—Verkündigung—Kirche. Ursprung, Inhalt und Funktion der kirchlichen Apostelamtes nach Paulus, Lukas und den Pastoralbriefen* [Gütersloh; Mohn, 1965] 121), but this is the only place in this letter in which Paul describes himself (and Apollos) in this manner (cf. 4:1). Servants have a specific role and Paul indicates that the role that fell to himself and Apollos was instrumental in the Corinthians' coming to faith. "You have come to faith" (*episteusate*) is an ingressive aorist, indicating that the Corinthians' embrace of the kerygma is the decisive event.

as the Lord has assigned to each: "Servant" connotes a relationship with a lord and master. In the case of Paul and Apollos the Lord *(kyrios)* is Jesus Christ (1:1). The Lord not only assigns the task, but also enables the task to be fulfilled (*edōken*, literally "gave," without a specified object). Paul emphasizes that the task is individually assigned, "to each of them" (*hekastō*), stressed by means of emphatic *kai* (not translated). The emphasis on each one is maintained throughout the subsequent development (see the use of *hekastos* in vv. 8, 10, 13[2x]; cf. 7:7, 17, 20, 24; 12:7, 11, 18). The use of "each" highlights the particularity of the task assigned by God (cf. 12:7, 11). In a moment Paul will note that the construction of a building is a collaborative effort in which each has a contribution to make. Each will receive a reward according to the work done (3:8; cf. 3:13-14).

6. *I planted, Apollos watered, but God provided the growth:* Paul's use of an emphatic "I" (*egō ephuteusa*) allows him to continue the complementary presentation of himself and Apollos. Paul suggests that he and Apollos are like workers in a

field (see v. 9). The agricultural metaphor allows Paul to reflect further on the subordinate roles that he and Apollos have with respect to the faith of the Corinthian community. It provides an illustration of how servants have different roles according to their assignment. The image highlights the complementarity of Apollos' role to Paul's ministry and suggests the truly seminal nature of Paul's ministry. Paul had a role in the foundation of the community.

The verbs "to plant" *(phuteuō)* and "to water" *(potizō,* literally "give to drink," cf. 3:2), are juxtaposed in each of the three verses (vv. 6, 7, 8). These verbs belong to the world of husbandry as does the verb "to provide growth" *(auxanō)* that Paul uses to attribute the effect of their ministry to God. Behind his use of the verb, as in the rest of the NT, is the image of growth in the realm of creation. The use of a contrary "but" *(alla)* underscores the singular and overarching role of God (see BDF 448.2).

7. *so neither is the one who plants anything nor the one who waters, just God who provides the growth:* Paul moves the discussion from the application of the metaphor to the situation of himself and Apollos to a generic statement about agricultural growth seen from the perspective of Jewish monotheism. The final, contrasting clause is verbally identical to the final clause of v. 6 except for the tense of the verb.

8. *The one who plants and the one who waters are one and the same, and each one will receive compensation according to his or her own labor:* Using a classical turn of phrase, *hen* to mean "one and the same" (similarly Plato), Paul affirms that he and Apollos are as one in their common task. Although theirs is a common endeavor each one will be paid according to the work that has been done. This is the first of four references to judgment in 1:10–4:21 (cf. 3:12-15, 17; 4:5). The underlying image is that of the paymaster who pays the workers appropriately. Paul's use of "compensation" *(misthos)* to speak of divine recompense is consistent with the usage of Hellenistic moralists and Jewish authors (Plutarch, "Sayings of Kings and Commanders," *Moralia* 183D; Lucian, *Philosophies for Sale* 24; Josephus, *Ant.* 1.183; 18.309). In the passages in 1:10–4:21 that speak of final judgment that judgment is individualized. Not even Paul and Apollos are beyond being held accountable for their work.

9. *for we are God's coworkers:* Verse nine introduces, albeit without use of emphatic pronouns, a contrast between Paul and Apollos on the one hand and the Corinthians on the other. A thrice-uttered "God's" *(theou)* underscores the fact that the worker and the results of the work belong to God. Displaying his predilection for compounds with *syn,* "with," Paul describes himself and Apollos as coworkers *(synergoi).* In classical usage the term was used to designate fellow workers, sometimes helpers or accomplices. In the NT the term is especially Pauline. For the apostle *ergon* is virtually a technical term to connote the work of evangelization (see 15:58; 16:10). Hence the term "coworkers" designates those who are involved with Paul in the mission of evangelization (Rom 16:3, 9, 21; 2 Cor 1:24; 8:23; Phil 2:25; 4:3; 1 Thess 3:2; Phlm 24). Could the use of the term in 3:9 indicate that Paul considers himself and Apollos to be coworkers with God? This does not seem to be what

Paul is saying. The location of the possessive genitive "God's" *(theou)* before each of the nouns along with the parallelism between the two clauses in his sentence militates against a synergistic reading of the term in this verse. "God's coworkers" implies that Paul and Apollos are coworkers who work with one another and for God. They belong to God just as the field and construction of v. 9b belong to God.

you are God's field, God's construction: Paul brings his exploitation of the agricultural metaphor, which he had previously been using to comment on the ministry of himself and his coworker, to closure by describing the Corinthian community as God's field (*geōrgion*, hapax in the NT). The summary statement serves Paul's deliberative rhetoric insofar as it designates a single entity (whose diversity is only to be imagined) and one that belongs to God. With this statement Paul abandons the agricultural imagery in order to exploit a construction metaphor (3:10-15 + 16-17). The juxtaposition of agricultural and architectural images is common in Hellenistic and biblical literature. See, for example, Plato, *Laws* 1.643B; Dio Chrysostom, *Discourses* 71.5; Philo, *Allegorical Interpretation* 3.48; *Cherubim* 100-102; Deut 20:5-6; Jer 1:10; 18:7-10; 24:6; 31:28; 42:10; Sir 49:7; Luke 17:28. In Qumran's *Manual of Discipline* the community is called "an eternal plant, a holy house" (1QS 8:5) and "a house of holiness for an eternal plant" (1QS 11:5).

In calling the Corinthians God's field and construction Paul underscores that the Corinthian community belongs to God. It is God's possession, as it were, but also it is God's work. It is God, who, through Paul and Apollos, has cultivated the field and constructed the building.

FOR REFERENCE AND FURTHER STUDY

Byrne, Brendan. "Ministry and Maturity in 1 Corinthians 3," *AusBR* 35 (1987) 83–87.

Francis, James. "'As babes in Christ'—Some proposals regarding 1 Corinthians 3.1-2," *JSNT* 7 (1980) 41–60.

Gaventa, Beverly Roberts. "Our Mother St. Paul: Toward the Recovery of a Neglected Theme," *PSB* 17 (1996) 29–44.

———. "Mother's Milk and Ministry in 1 Corinthians 3" in Eugene H. Lovering, Jr., and Jerry L. Sumney, eds., *Theology and Ethics in Paul and His Interpreters. Essays in Honor of Victor Paul Furnish.* Nashville: Abingdon, 1996, 101–113.

Grundmann, W. "Die *nēpioi* in der urchristlichen Paränese," *NTS* 5 (1958–59) 188–205.

Hooker, Morna D. "Hard Sayings: 1 Corinthians 3:2," *Theology* 69 (1966) 19–22.

Yarbrough, O. Larry. "Parents and Children in the Letters of Paul" in L. Michael White and O. Larry Yarbrough, eds., *The Social World of the First Christians: Essays in Honor of Wayne A. Meeks.* Minneapolis: Fortress, 1995, 126–141.

5. *The Construction* (3:10-17)

10. According to the grace of God given to me I, as a wise builder, have laid the foundation, but another builds on it. Let each one look at the way in which he or she builds. 11. For no one can lay a foundation other than that which has been laid, which is Jesus Christ. 12. If anyone builds on the foundation with gold, silver, precious stones, wood, straw, reeds, 13. each one's work will be visible, for the day will make it clear, because it will be revealed in fire; and the fire will test each one's work such as it is. 14. If anyone's construction work survives, that one will receive wages; 15. if anyone's work burns, that one will suffer a penalty; the person will, however, be saved, in similar fashion, as if through fire.

16. Don't you know that you are the temple of God and that the Spirit of God dwells in you? 17. If anyone ruins the temple of God, God will bring that one to ruin. For the temple of God is holy, which you are.

INTERPRETATION

This pericope could be entitled "God's construction" (3:9). It is readily divided into two parts, vv. 10-15, which describe the construction, and vv. 16-17, which identify the construction as God's temple. To a large extent Paul's exposition of the construction metaphor parallels his exploitation of the agricultural metaphor (vv. 5-9b). In both reflections Paul develops the idea of the complementary roles of those who work together in the building up of the community. In both he provides an eschatological horizon (vv. 8b, 13, 15). In each instance Paul concludes the development of the metaphor by indicating its referent, the Corinthian community (vv. 9, 16). In each instance a theological component is inserted into the exposition of the metaphor (vv. 5-9, 10, 11) and its denouement (vv. 9b-c, 16). Paul's development of the construction metaphor allows him to explore further the thoughts expressed in his exposition of the agricultural metaphor and to move beyond them. The expectation of future judgment is set out before the community as a warrant for behavior appropriate to building up the community (cf. 11:27-32).

God's Grace. Paul's role in the construction is to lay the foundation. This is a charismatic function (12:28). Continuing the focus on the activity of God as the chief agent in building up the Christian community at Corinth (3:6-8), Paul begins his development of the construction metaphor with a reference to the grace of God that had been given to him. Paul's work is the result of God's gift to him and the task that is assigned to him (cf. 3:5).

The letter began with a mention of the many gifts given to the Corinthians (1:7). Now Paul reminds them that he, too, has been gifted by God (cf. 7:7, 40). His particular task was to lay the foundation for the construction. Describing his role in charismatic terms (*charis*, "grace," v. 10; cf. 15:10), Paul distinguishes his work from the tasks to be done by others and establishes the complementarity of the various roles. The variety of roles within the community is a theme to which he will return and one he will systematically exposit in ch. 12.

In developing the construction metaphor Paul states that he himself had received a grace of God but he does not mention the grace given to other workers. The rhetorical force of his self-description should not, however, be overlooked. The image of himself as a skillful builder by the grace of God is a component of his *ethos* appeal. Paul places himself before his correspondents as an example to them. The description of himself as a master builder (*sophos architektōn*) is a literary coup. It exploits the wisdom motif (*sophia*) that pervades the argument of 1:18–3:23.

Paul's description of himself as having laid the foundation is a way of imaging the apostolic and foundational role of preaching the gospel (cf. Rom 15:20). The metaphor draws attention to the single foundation and thereby to the uniqueness of the gospel that is preached (cf. Gal 2:7). There is but one foundation and that is Jesus Christ (see 1:17; 2:2). Paul's imaginative reference to Jesus Christ provides a specifically christological reference for an exposition that otherwise has a theological focus (vv. 6, 7, 8, 9, 10, 16, 17). No other foundation can be laid because the one foundation has ultimately been laid by God (v. 11). Verse 11 is integral to Paul's argument. Highlighting the example of Paul as one who has acted in accordance with the grace given to him, it serves as a reminder that there is but one church of God at Corinth, a theme to which Paul continually returns throughout the letter.

Building on the Foundation. An Arcadian epigraph from the fourth century B.C.E. sheds significant light on Paul's construction metaphor (see C. D. Buck, *Greek Dialects* [Chicago: University of Chicago Press, 1955] 201–203). This inscription describes the building and repair of the temple of Athena. Several individuals, roughly comparable to modern-day subcontractors, were involved in various phases of construction. Each had a specific task to perform. The inscription repeatedly mentions their "work" (*ergon*), using the same vocabulary as does Paul in vv. 13, 14, and 15. The epigraph refers to the penalties meted out to contractors for various infractions, such as delaying the construction by failing to finish their work on time, harming workers, and damaging property. The vocabulary is similar to that of Paul, who contrasts the wages (*misthon lēmpsetai*) paid to those whose work is satisfactory (v. 14) with the penalty (*zēmiōthēsetai*) incurred by those whose work does not pass inspection (v. 15).

Paul carefully distinguishes between two phases of construction: laying the foundation and building the superstructure. These two phases of construction allow him to distinguish various functions as he did in his use of the agricultural metaphor. Paul's perspective is, however, no longer restricted to the complementary roles of himself and Apollos as it was in vv. 6-9. His use of "another" (v. 10), "each" (vv. 10, 13), and "anyone" (vv. 12, 14, 15) clearly shows that he is thinking about all those who have a role to play in the building up of the community as the edifice of God. The roles of these anonymous others are different from Paul's role but they presuppose that Paul's work has been done.

Quality Control. The purpose and focus of Paul's exposition is clearly paraenetic. Having distinguished the construction of the superstructure from the laying of the foundation, Paul exhorts each of the construction workers to examine the quality of their work (v. 10c). Paul devotes a single verse (v. 11) to the laying of the foundation but he develops the construction metaphor to some length (vv. 12-15). Verses 13-15 describe the inspection and testing of the construction by an anonymous inspector. Those whose work passes inspection will be paid; others will be assessed penalties. For those familiar with Jewish apocalyptic Paul's reference to "the day" (v. 13) suggests that God is the silent assessor.

Paul's use of the imperative in the friendly warning of v. 10c puts the paraenetic motif up front in his development of the construction metaphor. A much stronger exhortation is added when Paul identifies the building as the temple of God in v. 16. The exhortation in v. 17 has the form of a sentence of holy law, a kind of eschatological law of talion. If anyone ruins God's temple, says Paul, that very one will be brought to ruin by God. This is the most judicial of the four passages in 1 Cor 1:18–4:21 that speak of God's eschatological judgment (cf. 3:8, 12-15; 4:5).

Building Materials. Paul's distinction between the foundation and the superstructure of the building not only serves to underscore his essential and complementary role in the building up of the community at Corinth but also to emphasize the uniqueness of the edifice under construction. There is but one building that is built, the one built on the foundation that is Jesus Christ. To return to the metaphor, various materials are used in most types of construction. In v. 12 Paul distinguishes among six kinds of possible building materials: gold, silver, precious stones, wood, straw, and reeds. Some of these are flammable (wood, straw, reeds) and some are not (gold, silver, precious stones).

The nonflammable materials listed by Paul recall the kinds of materials used for the construction of the Jewish Temple (1 Chr 22:14-16; 29:2; 2 Chr 3:6; cf. Exod 25:3-7; 31:4-5; 35:32-33). It almost appears as if Paul is anticipating the identification of the community as the temple of God (v. 16), perhaps suggesting that it is the eschatological temple (cf. Rev 21:18-19). Indeed, much of Paul's vocabulary (master builder, wise, gold, silver, stones, wood, work, and the reference to God's gift of the Spirit) recalls

Exod 31:1-5, a description of the Lord's instruction to Bezalel relative to the construction of the meeting tent (cf. Exod 35:30–36:1; compare further Exod 31:6 with Isa 29:14, cited by Paul in 1:19). Paul's thought is admittedly complex and his use of metaphors more than occasionally mixed. Indeed, he mixes his metaphors to good rhetorical advantage (e.g., 3:1). The point of v. 12 seems not so much to foreshadow the motif of the temple as to imply a distinction between two kinds of building materials, fire-resistant and flammable. Gold and silver are a well-known pair of precious metals. Their resistance to fire—a quality exploited to advantage in the refinement process!—is a common motif in Jewish and Hellenistic literature, including the NT. Straw and reeds, on the other hand, were well known for their susceptibility to destruction by fire. The contrast between gold and silver on the one hand and straw and reeds on the other is powerful.

The various materials are figures for the contributions each member of the community makes to the upbuilding of the community as the church of God (1:2). The list is far from exhaustive. It does, however, enable Paul to make two points. First of all, the variety of building materials suggests that the various members of the community have distinctive contributions to make, a point on which Paul does not expatiate in this exposition but to which he will return and to which he will devote considerable attention in ch. 12. Paul's second point is that the contribution which each one has to make must be evaluated in the light of the coming eschaton.

Visibility of the Work. To make the point that everyone's work must be evaluated in the light of the eschaton Paul appeals to traditional apocalyptic motifs, specifically the notion of a testing by fire. In effect the metaphorical motif of the building inspection is interpreted by means of apocalyptic motifs. In his epistolary thanksgiving Paul had written about the gifted circumstances of the Corinthians that, however, he had placed under an eschatological reservation. "You are not lacking in any gift," he wrote, "you who are eagerly awaiting the revelation of our Lord Jesus Christ, who will maintain you blameless until the end, on the day of our Lord Jesus Christ" (1:7-8). As he began to develop the construction metaphor Paul spoke of his own gift, cited as an example for the Corinthians (3:10). When he calls upon them to scrutinize their own work in the light of the eschaton he returns (see v. 13) to the motifs of revelation (cf. 2:10) and the day, which he had introduced in the opening thanksgiving. Revelation and "the Day" are classic apocalyptic motifs as are some other elements in 3:10-17 that serve the paraenetic thrust of Paul's argument.

Among the other apocalyptic motifs employed by Paul for the sake of his paraenesis are the motifs of testing, fire, receiving a reward, salvation, and the sentence of holy law found in v. 17. The motif of fire is particularly apropos with respect to the way Paul has developed the image of the building. Some building materials withstand fire; others do not. The activities of each member of the community are subject to divine scrutiny, for which fire serves as a symbol. With the fire motif Paul exhorts the community to consider that each of its members stands under eschatological judgment.

In his writings on Paul's "eschatological reservation" Ernst Käsemann has developed the idea that Paul uses eschatological motifs, particularly in 1 Corinthians, as a polemical device to counter the aberrations of some Corinthian pneumatists, enthralled by a kind of Corinthian "enthusiasm." Käsemann stressed the central place that eschatology and an apocalyptic vision occupy in Paul's *Weltanschauung*. There can be little doubt that Paul employs eschatological motifs to serve a paraenetic function in 3:10-17. The contractual motif of the payment of wages is, as it were, reread by Paul as an apocalyptic theme (see note on v. 14).

Salvation by Fire. The image of construction workers dominates Paul's exhortation. Those whose works withstand the testing by fire will receive a reward, literally their "wages"; those whose works are destroyed by fire will be penalized. Paul does not say that these workers will be destroyed. Their work suffers destruction. The work will not last. The workers will be penalized. They will, nonetheless, be saved (v. 15). Paul does not tell his readers the grounds for this amazing affirmation. Despite the fact that he has used the apocalyptic imagery of a destructive fire in his exhortation the apostle remains convinced that those who belong to God's holy people (1:2) will be saved.

Having expressed his conviction as to the salvation of those who have worked in the construction of the building, Paul proceeds to identify the nature of the construction. This identification is introduced by the rhetorical formula, "Don't you know?" This disclosure formula Paul addresses directly to the Corinthians. It calls upon them to recall what they are presumed to know to be true about themselves. The direct appeal is consistent with Paul's rhetorical style. The construction metaphor was written in the third person (vv. 10-15); the exhortation of vv. 16-17 is a direct appeal in the second person: "Don't you know that . . . dwells among you . . . which you are?" The disclosure formula introduces a rhetorical digression. The digression identifies the nature of the construction and explicates the paraenetic function of Paul's metaphor. The apparent digressions in the rhetorical argument of 1 Corinthians normally provide a more profound reflection on the topic at hand and a foundation for Paul's argument. This is certainly the case for the rhetorical digression of 3:16-17.

The disclosure formula highlights something Paul's audience is presumed to know: that they are the temple of God and that the temple of

God, which they are, is holy (vv. 16-17). The idea of the holiness of the community reprises a theme that Paul had introduced in his epistolary salutation. There the Corinthian assembly was described as being made up of those who are made holy in Christ Jesus, those who are called the holy ones (1:2). In his epistolary thanksgiving, as he draws upon apocalyptic motifs, Paul affirms that the Corinthian community is one that eagerly awaits the revelation of our Lord Jesus Christ who will maintain them blameless until the end, on the very day of our Lord Jesus Christ (1:7-8).

The affirmation of v. 15b is a kind of theological reflection added to Paul's paraenetic development of the construction metaphor. There is no need to see in it—nor is there any exegetical warrant for seeing in it!—a reference to the Christian idea of purgatory (see Joachim Gnilka, *Ist 1 Kor 3,10-15 ein Schriftzeugnis für das Fegfeuer? Eine exegetisch-historische Untersuchung* [Düsseldorf: Triltsch, 1955]). The concept of purgatory was developed at a much later time in the history of Christianity.

God's Temple. With the disclosure formula the Corinthian Christians are identified as "the temple of God." This identification is consistent with Paul's construction metaphor. The building that is being built is God's temple. It is the community as such that is the temple of God (see note on v. 16). Identifying the construction (v. 9) with the temple of God and equating the temple with the community enables Paul to specify his metaphor and to underscore the radical unity of the community.

In the biblical tradition there was but one Temple. It provided a focal point for the unity of the people of God. It served as a symbol of the uniqueness of YHWH and as the cosmic center of the universe he had created. By equating God's construction at Corinth with the Temple Paul was able to emphasize the idea that the Corinthians were called to be one (see 1:10).

The Temple was God's dwelling place. The temple was the "house of YHWH," the "house of God" (cf. Mark 2:26, *par.*). The temple of which Paul writes is a temple in which the Spirit of God dwells. The Spirit of God dwells (*oikei*, v. 16) in God's own building (*oikodomē*, v. 9). Judaism was familiar with the idea that the Spirit of God dwells in the Temple (see note on v. 16), but the motif is particularly apropos in 1 Corinthians as Paul attempts to counter the claims (see 2:14-16; 7:40) of those Corinthians who consider themselves to be spiritual persons (3:1; cf. 14:37).

The Spirit is the eschatological power of God, a power tradition frequently associates with fire (cf. the Q saying found in Luke 3:16 = Matt 3:11). With the motif of the Spirit of God Paul maintains the eschatological perspective introduced by the motifs of the day and the fire (v. 13). The eschatological horizon continues in v. 17. In the apocalyptic period of 2:6-16 Paul had similarly focused on the role of the Spirit.

The Destruction of the Temple. Paul continues his paraenesis by invoking an eschatological sanction, "if anyone ruins the temple of God, God will bring that one to ruin" (v. 17). Paul is writing about the eschatological loss to be suffered by those who inflict severe damage on the temple. There is parallelism between the two members of the clause, reflecting a kind of tit-for-tat situation. Paul picks up on the thought of v. 15a but moves it to a new level and applies it explicitly to the members of the community.

A kind of eschatological law of talion is at work. The *lex talionis,* the law of equal retaliation, an eye for an eye, a tooth for a tooth, is well known in Paul's Jewish tradition (Gen 9:6; Exod 21:23-25; Lev 24:20; Deut 19:21; cf. Matt 5:38). Paul argues that eschatological punishment will be equal to the crime that has been perpetrated. Although the punishment will not be received until the Day of the Lord there is a kind of *quid pro quo* retributive justice at work.

Ernst Käsemann, followed by Robert Grant, has described this kind of literary formula as a sentence of holy law (cf. 1 Cor 14:38; compare 1 Sam 15:26; Mark 8:38). The introductory formula of v. 17, "if anyone," a telltale indication of case law, and the presence of the verb *phtheirō,* "ruin," in both the protasis and the apodosis of the conditional sentence confirm that Paul is indeed using this literary form (cf. Josh 7:25). Use of the literary form expresses the conviction that God rewards people according to their activity. With his use of the form Paul verbalizes Christian belief about the eschaton (the eschatological correlation) and affirms a close connection between human misdeed and divine judgment. Demurring from the opinion that Paul's words are a sentence of holy law, Klaus Berger opines that Paul's exhortation is in the form of sapiential apocalyptic instruction that has origin in early Christian prophecy: every human misdeed has its recompense, even if the punishment is delayed until the eschaton.

Which You Are. Paul brings his two-part exhortation to closure with an explanation that leaves no doubt about the addressees of his paraenesis: "for the temple of God is holy, which you are." The formula echoes Paul's rhetorical question in v. 16 and recalls the conclusion of the agricultural metaphor in v. 9, thereby forming a ring construction around vv. 10-17.

From the outset of his letter Paul had reminded the Corinthians that they were holy (1:2). They belong to God. The apostle reiterates the idea as he concludes the paraenesis he has developed on the basis of the construction metaphor. Paul's conviction that the Corinthians are holy has practical consequences (cf. 7:14-15). It may well be that the holiness of the community is the most basic reason why Paul is aghast that the Corinthians have not expelled the wanton sinner whose case is discussed in 5:1-13.

NOTES

10. *According to the grace of God given to me:* As Paul shifts his imagery from agriculture to construction he focuses on himself and others but does not specifically mention Apollos by name. His perspective is much as it was in the
digression of 2:6-16 in which Paul's focus was on the community of believers,
including himself. The focus on himself is consonant with the *ethos* appeal
that pervades the entire letter. That he was graced by God (*kata tēn charin tou
theou tēn dotheisan moi*, "grace given to me") reprises the theme of 3:5d, applying it to the construction Paul is about to undertake, but the expression itself has a broader referent. In 3:10 Paul writes of God's grace, that is, God's
gift, at one and the same time a task and the capacity to fulfill the task. Paul
gave thanks to God for the Corinthians because of the grace of God given to
them (*epi tē chariti tou theou tē dotheisē hymin*, 1:4). Aristotle had underscored
the gratuitous nature of "grace" (see *Art of Rhetoric* 2.7).

$\mathfrak{P}^{46}$ and a relatively few late manuscripts along with a limited number of
Fathers read the text without a qualifying *tou theou*, "of God," but the qualifying phrase is found in the most ancient majuscules and is well attested by
the ancient versions. For the apostle to have qualified *charis*, "grace," with "of
God" is consistent with his style.

I, as a wise builder, have laid the foundation: Paul is using a well-known idiom in
self-conscious fashion (see the use of "as," *hōs*). Among others Euripides (*Alcestis* 348), Maximus Tyrius (*Dissertations* 6.4), and Philo (*Dreams* 2.8) wrote
about the master or skillful builder. Aristotle wrote about the master sculptor
(*Nicomachaean Ethics* 6.7) and Pindar (*Nemean Odes* 7.25) about the experienced
steersman. Use of the adjective *sophos*, literally "wise," is a classic feature of
the idiom. In this idiomatic use *sophos* has the sense of "master," "skillful," or
"experienced." In 3:10 the idiom functions as a pun used ironically. Some of
the Corinthians think that they are wise (3:18), but it is Paul who is "wise."
His adjective evokes the theme of (divine) wisdom, which has thus far pervaded his exposition (1:18–4:21). The simile of the master builder (cf. Isa 3:3
[LXX]) is the third in a series of metaphors that Paul uses to describe his role
in the foundation of the church at Corinth as a community of faith. He is a
mother, a planter, one who has laid the foundation (cf. Eph 2:20). All three
metaphors focus on a new beginning. As such they provide an imaginative
description of Paul's role as an apostle (1:1), the first of the charismatic min-
istries (12:28).

but another builds on it: "Builds on," *epoikodomei*, belongs to the *oiko-* group
of words, which are used with some frequency in Paul's correspondence.
The compound verb is cognate with the simple verb *oikodomeō*, "to build,"
used metaphorically in Paul's paraenesis with the meaning of "edify" (8:1,
10; 10:23; 14:4, 17; cf. 1 Thess 5:11). The related noun, *oikodomē*, "construction" (v. 9), recurs four more times in 1 Corinthians (14:3, 5, 12, 26), in each
instance with edification as the connotation. Paul's regular use of the
oikodom- word group in contexts of moral exhortation insinuates that his use
of the construction metaphor has a paraenetic purpose. The compound

epoikodomeō appears only in the present context (3:10-15; see 10, 12, 14; cf. Eph 2:20; Col 2:7). In the context of the construction metaphor the compound form of the verb is particularly appropriate. It enables Paul to distinguish the construction of the superstructure from the laying of the foundation. He has his work; others *(allos)* have theirs, each according to his or her assignment.

Let each one look at the way in which he or she builds: The paraenetic purpose is expressed in a warning (the imperative *blepetō*) that Paul addresses to the construction workers. Each worker must carefully examine the quality of her or his work. Paul is exhorting the workers to individual responsibility and quality control. In Paul, certainly in 1 Corinthians, "to see" *(blepō)* is used in paraenetic contexts (see 1:26; 8:9; 10:12, 18; 13:12; 16:10).

11. *For no one can lay a foundation other than that which has been laid:* With this clause Paul begins an explanation (see the postpositive *gar*) of the paraenetic exhortation in v. 10d. The explanation continues until the end of v. 15. Paul suggests that there is a single foundation for the construction and that the foundation has already been laid. The workers (see v. 10c) are expected to build on this single foundation. Paul admits of no other possibility. Formally v. 11 constitutes a kind of parenthesis in Paul's argument, but it serves his paraenetic purpose by highlighting the one construction and providing an important reference to Jesus Christ.

   In his use of the image of the foundation Paul's language does, however, admit of some ambiguity with regard to who it is who has laid the foundation. Paul considers himself to have been the one who has laid the foundation (v. 10b). In his letter to the Romans he indicates that preaching the gospel *(euaggelizesthai)* is the act of laying the foundation (Rom 15:20). Nonetheless a case can be made that the present passive participle of v. 11 *(keimenon,* "which has been laid") is a theological passive in which God is the implied agent. An implied reference to God fits the context. Paul has already mentioned that God provides growth to plants (vv. 6, 7), that Paul and Apollos are God's coworkers (v. 9a), and that he himself is what he is and has done what he has done according to the grace of God given to him (v. 10a). An implied reference to God's having laid the foundation serves to explain and clarify why it is impossible to lay a foundation other than that which has been laid. This does not preclude the possibility of Paul's being the servant of God in the laying of the foundation for the construction.

   which is Jesus Christ: For the third and final time in his letter Paul writes of "Jesus Christ." The single title appended to the name continues the focus on Christ that Paul has maintained since 1:17. "Jesus Christ," identified as the foundation of the building, is undoubtedly a cipher for the preaching of Jesus Christ. Earlier references to Jesus Christ in this letter (1:1; 2:2) evoke Paul's work as an apostle who knows and preaches Jesus Christ. The deutero-Pauline epistle to the Ephesians reprises and transforms the image of the foundation. Jesus Christ having been relocated to the cornerstone (Eph 2:20), the apostles and prophets are identified as the foundation.

12. *If anyone builds on the foundation with gold, silver, precious stones, wood, straw, reeds:* The conditional clause reprises the motif of v. 10c, fleshing it out with reference to a variety of building materials. Paul's lack of connectives in the series (asyndeton) lends rhetorical effect to the metaphor insofar as the building materials are listed in an order of descending worth (see BDF 460.3). Paul obviously does not intend to give a complete list of materials that might be used in the construction of a building. Literary lists are often indicative rather than exhaustive (e.g., the catalogues of virtues and vices, hardship catalogues, Paul's list of charisms, etc.). Paul cites a representative selection of materials for the purposes of his rhetorical argument. The various building materials represent in generic fashion the contributions the different members of the community make to its upbuilding.

That precious metals, especially gold and silver, are tested, purified, or refined by fire (cf. 3:13) is a familiar motif in biblical, Jewish, and early Christian literature. See Num 31:22-23; Job 22:25; Ps 12:7; 66:10; Ezek 22:18-22; Zech 13:9; Mal 3:2-3; Wis 3:4-6; 1 Pet 1:7; 4:12; Rev 3:18; Philo, *Sacrifices* 80, and *Decalogue* 48; *Did.* 16:5; *Herm. Vis.* 4.3.4; *Mart. Pol.* 15:2. In Hellenistic literature the verbs "to heat" *(pyroō)*, "to purify" *(katharizō)*, and "to test" *(dokimazō)* are used to describe the refinement process. Paul mentions the process of testing by fire *(to pyr . . . dokimasei)* in v. 13. His reference is to a testing of each person's contribution to the construction.

"Precious stones" *(lithous timious)* is an expression similar to the language used by Diodorus Siculus and Josephus to describe the costly stone (e.g., marble) that was sometimes used in the construction of important buildings. Ancient literature gives no indication that precious stones were tested by fire. Precious stones probably appear on Paul's list because precious stones were often listed together with gold and silver (see 2 Chr 32:27; Prov 8:10-11, 19 [LXX]; Dan 11:38 [Theodotion]; Rev 18:12; *Apocalypse of Pseudo-Methodius* 11:14). All three elements are fire-resistant (cf. *1 Enoch* 14:9-10). Ancient metallurgy used fire-generated heat both in the refinement process and in the production of precious metal artifacts.

To the modern reader gold, silver, and precious stones evoke images of the elaborate ornamentation of a building. Wood, straw, and reeds are typical but elementary building materials. In ancient inscriptions "wood" *(xyla)* designates the heavy construction timbers used as roof beams or upright supports. Straw and reeds were used in huts and the homes of the poor. Such huts were easily and rapidly destroyed by fire. "Since the huts were made of reeds and straw," wrote Diodorus Siculus, "and the fire was forcibly fanned by the breeze, the aid brought by the soldiers came too late" (*Library of History* 20.65.1).

Paul describes himself as a skillful builder but one must not presume that he had a degree in engineering. In contrasting materials that are resistant to fire with those that are flammable Paul cites a couple of well-known fire-resistant materials (gold, silver) and two easily inflammable materials (straw, reeds). Each pair is expanded by a significant construction item (stone, wood) that is readily assimilated to the classic fire-resistant and fire-susceptible materials.

13. *each one's work will be visible:* The visibility of the contribution of the various subcontractors is readily apparent. Some commentators enter into discussion as to whether "work" (*ergon*) refers to a person or a person's activity. Sometimes "work" is assumed to be a metaphor for "doctrine" or "teaching," as if Paul were making a distinction between some kind of orthodoxy and heterodoxy. The language of "work" belongs to Paul's image. In the fourth-century Arcadian inscription (see "Interpretation") *ergon* designates the "job" of the various subcontractors. In Paul's metaphor "work" is a reference to the activity of the various members of the community. Elsewhere Paul uses *ergon* symbolically to describe, almost in technical fashion, apostolic and other activity that contributes to the upbuilding of a community (e.g., 1 Thess 5:13).

The members of the community build up the community in various ways. See 12:6, where the charisms accorded to the various members of the community are identified as "works" or "activities" (note the use of *energēmata* and *energeō*). No more than he attempts to offer a complete listing of the building materials used in the Greco-Roman world in 3:12 does Paul attempt to offer an exhaustive list of the charisms in any of his three lists (1 Cor 12:7-10, 28, 29-30; cf. Rom 12:6-8; Eph 4:11; 1 Pet 4:10-11).

for the day will make it clear: The postpositive *gar* suggests that Paul is explaining (v. 13b-d, with a verb of disclosure in each clause, "make clear," "reveal," "test") why it is that the results of the various workers are so readily apparent: the light of day makes their work quite visible. Paul has not, however, suggested that the construction had taken place in the night or that the building had been visited by night. The day to which he refers should be understood as the "day of the Lord" (cf. Rom 13:12; 1 Cor 5:5; 1 Thess 5:4; cf. Phil 2:16). The day of the Lord is a common motif in Jewish prophetic literature (e.g., Isa 10:20; 13:6, 9; Amos 9:11; Zeph 1:14-16, 18; 2:3; Zech 12:3-4; Mal 4:1-6), whence it entered into the apocalyptic tradition. Various Jewish texts use "the day"—generally with a qualifier, such as "of the Elect One," "of the Mighty One," "your," or "of tribulation and pain"—as a cipher to speak of the planned and decisive judgment of God. The day of the Lord will bring the present era of human existence to a close. It is the time of the ultimate manifestation of YHWH as Lord. It is commonly construed as a time of discrimination, when the just and unjust will suffer different fates. In some of the literature the indicative expression is simply "that day" (see *1 Enoch* 45:3; 51:2; 62:13; 60:6; *Sib. Or.* 3.55, 741).

because it will be revealed in fire: With a causal clause (*hoti*) Paul continues to clarify his remark on the visibility of the work. In Lucian's satire *The Downward Journey* (13, 23-27) the wicked Megapenthes is said to be revealed (*apokalypsō*) and shown plainly (*deixō phanerōteron*). There is some discussion as to the implied subject of Paul's verb (*apokalyptetai*). A third person singular subject is indicated by the declension of the verb. Grammatically the intended referent could be either "the work" (v. 13a) or "the day" (v. 13b). Commentators are divided among themselves. Most (Johannes Weiss, Archibald Robertson and Alfred Plummer, Hans Conzelmann, Gordon Fee, David Kuck, etc.) opine that the implied subject is "the day." This is the noun closest to the verb *apokalyptetai,* but "the day" *(hē hēmera)* does not otherwise appear in the extant literature as a subject of "to reveal," *apokalyptō. Apokalyptō* is, on the other hand, linked with "work," *ergon,* in Sir 11:27. Moreover, 3:13d speaks of fire testing each one's work.

"Fire" is frequently associated with the eschatological appearance of the Lord in biblical and Jewish apocalyptic literature. See Dan 7:9; Joel 2:3, 30; Mal 4:1; cf. Matt 3:10, 11, 12; 5:22; 10:28; 13:40, 42, 50; 18:8, 9; 25:41; Mark 9:43, 45, 47; Luke 3:9, 16, 17; 12:49; 2 Thess 1:8; Heb 12:29; Jas 3:6; 1 Pet 1:7; 2 Pet 3:10, 12; and frequent references in the book of Revelation.

and the fire will test each one's work such as it is: In no other place in Paul or in the NT is there as much emphasis on individual eschatological scrutiny as there is in 3:13 (cf. 4:5). Words similar to those of 3:13d are found in a well-known passage of the *Testament of Abraham* (first or second c. B.C.E.): "he tests the work of men through fire. And if the fire burns up the work of anyone, immediately the angel of judgment takes him and carries him away to the place of sinners, a most bitter place of punishment. But if *the fire tests the work of anyone* and does not touch it, this person is justified and the angel of righteousness takes him and carries him up to be saved in the lot of the righteous. And thus, most righteous Abraham, all things in all people are tested by fire and balance" (*T. Abr.* 13:11-14; translated by E. P. Sanders; cf. J. H. Charlesworth, ed., *The Old Testament Pseudepigrapha, 1: Apocalyptic Literature & Testaments* [Garden City, NY: Doubleday, 1983] 890).

The *Testament of Abraham* attributes the testing to the angel Purouel ("God's fire") and also provides for a parallel testing with the scales of justice, but the similarity of *T. Abr.* 13:11-14 to 1 Cor 3:13-14 is manifest. It is likely that both the *Testament* and Paul were dependent on a similar Jewish apocalyptic tradition. Paul adopted the tradition and adapted it, with a paraenetic purpose, for use in his construction metaphor. H. W. Hollander ("1 Corinthians 3.10-15") has attempted to reconstruct the tradition.

14. *If anyone's construction work survives, that one will receive wages:* Paul's expression, *misthon lēmpsetai,* belongs to the image he is developing. "Wages" *(misthos)* are the appropriate payment for a "job" *(ergon;* vv. 13, 14, 15, where the expression refers to the job that has been done rather than the doing of it). "To receive wages," to get paid, is a common phrase in economy (3:8; cf. Matt 20:8, Luke 10:7 and the writings of such Hellenistic authors as Diodorus Siculus and Josephus).

From the perspective of the history of religions Seneca (*Benefits* 4.1.3; 4.33.3) and Lucian (*Philosophies for Sale* 24) use the phrase "to receive a reward" to describe a favorable judgment after death. That each one receives a reward for his or her labor is a traditional motif in the Jewish literature that speaks about judgment (Ps 61:13 [LXX]; Jer 17:10, etc.). The underlying image is the paymaster's office, not the courtroom (see Kuck, *Judgment* 42). Only in 3:8 and 14 does Paul use "wages" *(misthos)* as a metaphor for eschatological reward; elsewhere it indicates pay for a job well done (Rom 4:4; cf. 1 Cor 9:17, 18).

15. *if anyone's work burns, that one will suffer a penalty:* The conditional clause, with its apodosis, stands in antithetical parallelism with v. 14. Both belong to the metaphor Paul is developing. This aspect of the metaphor reflects the use of fire in the refinement of precious metals (see v. 12). Those whose work withstands the flames of fire will be paid (v. 14); those whose work is destroyed will not be paid. Instead they will be fined for their shoddy work. The Arcadian inscription uses the same verb (*zēmiōthēsetai*) to describe the penalty meted out to those workers whose work is not up to standards.

    the person will, however, be saved, in similar fashion, as if through fire: Paul does not offer a reason why those whose works do not pass the test of fire will be saved; he merely expresses the conviction that they will be saved. His theological reservation brings together a use of the traditional apocalyptic imagery of fire with a conviction that the members of the community belonging to God as God's holy ones (1:2) are saved by God. The comparative language (*houtōs de hōs*, "in similar fashion, as if through," see BDF 897.1) makes it clear that Paul writes of salvation by fire in a metaphorical fashion.

    "Fire" is the catchword that links the theological reservation to the metaphor that has been developed. A Jewish apocalyptic motif evokes the image of those who belong to God being saved from the destructive power of the fire in which they are tested. See Dan 3:50, 94 (LXX); Pseudo-Philo, *Biblical Antiquities* 6:16-18; 38:3-4 (see Charlesworth, *The Old Testament Pseudepigrapha* 2.312, 351). Paul had previously used apocalyptic language in 2:6-16. In 3:10-15 the apocalyptic motif of testing by fire impinges on the construction metaphor Paul had developed in order to speak of the unity of the community and of the contribution each member has to make to the community. In 1 Pet 4:12-19, with an image that seems to evoke Mal 3:2-3, reference is made to the "house of God" that is to be tested by fire (vv. 12, 17).

16. *Don't you know?* With this disclosure formula Paul makes a direct appeal to his audience. Direct appeal is a well-known rhetorical technique (apostrophe). Paul's formula "Don't you know?" occurs frequently in 1 Corinthians, particularly in ch. 6 (see 5:6; 6:2, 3, 9, 15, 16, 19; 9:13, 24). Some commentators (e.g., C. K. Barrett, Peter Marshall) opine that the formula draws attention to ideas Paul had expressed in his oral instruction of the Corinthians. In any case the formula draws attention to ideas that are shared—or presumed to have been shared!—by Paul and the Corinthians. Appeal to commonly held convictions is a crucial factor in Paul's rhetorical technique. Normally, in the ancient world as in ours, letters presuppose more than they actually state. Paul's explication of convictions shared by himself and his audience indicates that this letter to the Corinthians is not an ordinary, friendly, letter. It is a rhetorical appeal in epistolary form.

    that you are the temple of God and that the Spirit of God dwells in you? Paul's use of the verb "are" (*este*, in the plural) and of the simple prepositional phrase "in you" (*en hymin*) rather than a distributive phrase, "in each of you" (*en hekastō hymōn*), indicates that he is using the temple as a metaphor for the entire community (cf. 2 Cor 6:16). The parallelism between Paul's denouement of the construction metaphor in v. 16 and his explanation of the agricultural metaphor in v. 9 confirms the communitarian dimension of vv. 16-17. Within Hellenistic Judaism the only other group that considered itself to be the temple were the Qumranites (see 1QS 8:5-9). A "rereading" of the imagery of 1 Cor 3:10-17 in Ephesians continues to exploit the ecclesial character of the metaphor (see Eph 2:20-21; cf. 1 Pet 2:4-5). In 6:19 Paul applies the imagery of the temple to an individual Christian. The biblical tradition affirms that God dwells in the Temple. The notion that the Spirit of God dwells in the Temple was known to Josephus (*Ant.* 8:114).

17. *If anyone ruins the temple of God, God will bring that one to ruin:* With a reference to damage *(phtheirei)* done to the construction, now identified as the temple of God, Paul continues and moves beyond the imagery of vv. 10-15. Paul's point is clear. Whoever seriously harms the upbuilding of the church will suffer a severe loss. The Arcadian temple inscription (see notes on vv. 13, 15) also spoke of those who might damage *(phthērōn)* the temple. With particular casuistry the epigraph dictated that "if anyone, having signed a contract, would damage any other of the existing works, whether sacred, public or private, contrary to the agreement of the contract, let him restore the part that was damaged at his own expense (to a condition) not inferior to what it was at the time of the contract. If he does not restore it, let him pay the fines" (*epizamia,* see v. 15). With his formulation of a norm of retributive justice, for which he offers an explanation in v. 17b, Paul goes beyond the terms of the Arcadian contract. It is, however, difficult to find a single verb in English that provides a translation of *phtheirō* that is suitable for both parts of Paul's sentence. "Ruin" seems to be the most appropriate translation. The second part of Paul's sentence cannot be construed to mean that one who seriously impedes the upbuilding of the church will suffer the punishment of eschatological annihilation. Moreover, the Greek verb *phtheirō* (cf. 15:33; 2 Cor 7:2; 11:3) is not generally used of utter destruction; rather it is commonly used to describe the infliction of severe damage, as, for example, grave financial loss, the seduction of a virgin, corruption, and so forth.

For the temple of God is holy, which you are: Paul offers this reflection as an explanation for his promulgation of eschatological law. With a third mention of the temple *(naos),* Paul concludes part two of his exposition on construction. The identification of the Christian community as God's temple reinforces the idea of the rhetorical question in v. 16 and harkens back to the title of Paul's epistolary unit (v. 9). The idea of holiness (see 1:2) suggests that something or someone belongs to God and is thereby removed from the sphere of the profane. As such the notion frequently has cultic overtones and is appropriate in a description of a Christian community as God's temple.

FOR REFERENCE AND FURTHER STUDY

Berger, Klaus. "Die sog. 'Sätze heiligen Rechts' im N.T.: Ihre Funktion und ihr Sitz im Leben," *ThZ* 28 (1972) 305–330.

_____. "Zu den sogenannten Sätzen heiligen Rechts," *NTS* 17 (1970–71) 10–40.

Derrett, J. Duncan M. "Paul as Master-Builder," *EvQ* 69 (1997) 129–137.

Grant, Robert M. "Holy Law in Paul and Ignatius" in Dennis E. Groh and Robert Jewett, eds., *The Living Text: Essays in Honor of Ernest W. Saunders.* Lanham, Md.: University Press of America, 1985, 65–71.

Hollander, Harm W. "The Testing by Fire of the Builders' Works: 1 Corinthians 3.10-15," *NTS* 40 (1994) 89–104.

_____. "Revelation by Fire: 1 Corinthians 3.13," *BiTr* 44 (1993) 242–244.

Käsemann, Ernst. "On the Question of Primitive Christian Apocalyptic" in idem, *New Testament Questions of Today.* NTL. Philadelphia: Fortress, 1969, 108–137.

_____. "Sentences of Holy Law in the New Testament" in idem, *New Testament Questions of Today.* NTL. Philadelphia: Fortress, 1969, 66–81.

Lanci, John R. *A New Temple for Corinth: Rhetorical and Archaeological Approaches to Pauline Imagery.* Studies in Biblical Literature 1. New York and Bern: Peter Lang, 1997.

Proctor, John. "Fire in God's House: Influence of Malachi 3 in the NT." JETS 36 (1993) 9–14.

Shanor, Jay Y. "Paul as Master Builder: Construction Terms in First Corinthians." NTS 34 (1988) 461–471.

6. *Slogans Reversed* (3:18-23)

> 18. Do not deceive yourselves. If anyone of you thinks that you are wise in this age, become foolish so that you might be wise. 19. For the wisdom of this world is foolishness before God. For it is written, "He is the one who catches the wise in their cunning," 20. and again, "The Lord knows the thoughts of the wise that they are useless." 21. Wherefore let no one boast about humans; for all things are yours 22.—whether Paul, or Apollos, or Cephas, or the world, or life, or death, or the present, or the future—all things are yours, 23. and you are Christ's, and Christ is God's.

INTERPRETATION

The pericope in 3:18-23 brings preliminary closure to the argument of 1:10–3:23. The apostle's reference to himself, Apollos, and Cephas recalls the slogans introduced in 1:12. The pair of scriptural citations (vv. 19-20) evokes the quotation from Isa 29:14 in 1:19. Paul forms a kind of inclusion around his rhetorical development thus far. Thus 1:10–3:23 is identified as a discrete rhetorical unit within the letter.

This unit, 3:18-23, functions as a kind of peroration within the first rhetorical demonstration. It reprises and sharpens the themes of 1:10–

2:16. The motifs of wisdom, foolishness, this age, this world, boasting, humanity, and the use of Scripture appear in the body of Paul's letter prior to the extended metaphors in 3:1-17. Some of the themes of 3:18-23 specifically recall, nonetheless, motifs rehearsed in 3:1-17. Paul, Apollos, and God were named in the development of the metaphor of the field; Paul and God appeared in the metaphorical exposition of the building. The mention of the present and the future calls to mind the judgment of everyone's work that Paul had developed in the construction metaphor (3:10-17). That pericope's temple motif underscored the notion that the Corinthians belong to God. The reference to the world in v. 22 evokes the thought of God's dealing with the world (1:20, 21, 27, 28; 2:12; 3:19).

Foolishness. In a direct appeal to the Corinthians Paul urges them not to deceive themselves. Once again he challenges them to reflect on their own self-perception (1:26; 2:6; 3:1; cf. 8:2; 10:12; 11:16; 14:37). Self-deception is antithetical to true wisdom.

First Corinthians is an exercise in deliberative rhetoric, but Paul rarely resorts to the use of the imperative to make his point. The language of his paraenesis tends to be more diplomatic (see note on 1:10) as he exhorts them to follow the pattern of conduct he sets out. This unit begins, nonetheless, with a pair of direct exhortations in the imperative mood. The imperatives are in the singular. Thus they are addressed to each and every member of the community. There is no formula of direct address such as "brothers and sisters." Paul simply says: Do not deceive yourselves; become foolish to become wise.

Paul's direct and succinct paraenetic formulation brings to a climax, albeit paradoxically, the rhetorical argument that he has been developing up to this point. The tightly-knit logical argument, with its twofold use of an explanatory *gar,* "for," reprises many of the themes of the previous development. "Wise," "foolish," "wisdom," "foolishness," "this age," "God," and the use of a formal scriptural argument echo the key elements of 1:18–2:16. The rhetorical argument of 3:18-23 is similar to that of 1:18–2:16.

Directed to those who are sure of themselves and conceited in their wisdom, the double exhortation of v. 18 is one that Paul supports by a kind of logical argument. The purpose of the Corinthians becoming foolish is that they become wise. If this seems paradoxical, and it is, then Paul offers an explanation (the first *gar,* v. 19a). The wisdom of this age is foolishness in the sight of God. In support of this contention (the second *gar,* v. 19b) Paul offers an argument from authority. His argument is based on two scriptural passages treated as one. The two passages are taken from the Jewish wisdom tradition: Job 5:13 and Ps 93:11 [LXX]. They speak of the futility of human wisdom. Paul has modified the two passages in such a way that they are to be interpreted in the light of one another. The scriptural citations evoke the biblical context from which they are drawn and substantiate Paul's affirmation that in the eyes of God human wisdom is foolish.

All Things are Yours. Paul adds to the terse exhortations of v. 18 a third exhortation in v. 21, "let no one boast about humans." Similar to the previous exhortations and phrased as an imperative in the third person singular, the exhortation is presented as an inference from Paul's summary paraenesis on human wisdom. Paul urges the Corinthians not to boast about their human leaders.

Paul's exhortation requires an explanation. He offers one (a third *gar*, v. 21b) by citing a dictum of popular wisdom, "all things are yours." This popular maxim had apparently been invoked by some Corinthians as a warrant for behavior that Paul considered to be disruptive of the unity of the community. The contrast between the way Paul deals with this philosophical slogan and the way he cited Scripture as a warrant for the exhortation in v. 18 is readily apparent.

Paul treats the philosophical adage in a way similar to the fashion in which Greco-Roman rhetoricians dealt with popular maxims they wanted to refute. Paul begins to relativize the argumentative force of the maxim by first affirming its truth, namely that all things, including the leaders to whom the Corinthians appeal and the ultimate realities of human existence, time and space, life and death, belong to the Corinthians. He then forcefully asserts that the Corinthians themselves belong to Christ (cf. 1:30; 6:20; 7:23) and that Christ belongs to God.

The way in which Paul deals with himself, Apollos, and Cephas in v. 22 reverses the claims the Corinthians might have made on their behalf (1:12). The resounding "you are Christ's and Christ is God's" brings this phase of Paul's argument to a forceful conclusion. The Corinthians' relationship with Christ and God has been a focus of Paul's communication with the Corinthians from the very beginning of his letter. The reality of that relationship will continue to ground Paul's argument until the end of the letter.

NOTES

18. *Do not deceive yourselves:* In Greek the opening gambit of Paul's exhortation uses the verb "to deceive," (*exapataō;* cf. Rom 7:11; 16:18; 2 Cor 11:3) in the imperative (cf. 1:26; 3:10). The object of the verb is a masculine singular reflexive pronoun. To retain the force of Paul's rhetoric a translation is offered here in the second person plural (see the conditional clause which follows). As Paul has warned the Corinthians to examine their activity carefully (3:10), now he warns them against self-deception.

If anyone of you thinks that you are wise in this age, become foolish so that you might be wise: The conditional sentence has the force of a rhetorical question. The apodosis, with an imperative that is consistent with Paul's paraenetic purpose, expresses the paradox of the Christian situation (cf. 1:27-28; 7:22). "If anyone of you thinks that . . ." is an expression that occurs twice more in the letter (8:2; 14:37; cf. 11:16). The formula highlights various attributes the Corinthians claim for themselves: wisdom (3:18), knowledge (8:2), spiritual quality (14:37). The Corinthians' self-deception with regard to wisdom is a sign that they belong to this age and are not yet spiritual persons (see 2:6-16).

19–20. *For the wisdom of this world is foolishness before God:* Paul's comment on cosmic wisdom is offered as an explanation *(gar)* of the paraenesis of v. 18. Supported by a scriptural warrant, it recalls and forms an *inclusio* with the apocalyptic paradox of 1:19. In the eyes of God this world's wisdom is foolishness *(mōria);* in the eyes of the mere humans who belong to this age divine wisdom is foolishness.

For it is written: Using a pair of scriptural texts (Job 5:13; Ps 93:11 [LXX]) in a way that recalls the use of Isa 29:14 in 1:19, Paul provides an argument for his contention that association with the "wise" does not entail true wisdom. The two biblical passages are associated with and interpreted in the light of one another on the basis of the *gezera shawah* principle. Rabbinic tradition attributed this hermeneutical principle, the comparison of like with like (analogy), to Rabbi Hillel, a contemporary of Paul. "Wise" *(sophoi)* is the catchword that allows Paul to link Ps 93:11 with Job 5:13 and so interpret the passages by means of one another. The association of the two passages is disingenuous. Paul cites only phrases from Job 5:13 and has rendered the LXX's "our thoughts" (Ps 93:11) as "the thoughts of the wise" on the basis of the immediately preceding verse in the psalm (Ps 93:10). The brace of citations hearkens back to 1:19. It brings divine judgment to bear upon the Corinthians' self-deception. What human beings claim to be wisdom stands under divine judgment.

"He is the one who catches the wise in their cunning": The scriptural argumentation uses a passage from a speech by Eliphaz in the Book of Job. Citing Job, Paul uses "to catch" *(drassomai,* hapax in the NT) instead of the LXX's "to seize" *(lambanō).* For the sake of readability I have rendered Paul's participle *(ho drassomenos)* as "he is the one who catches." Job sees wisdom as a positive value (9:4, etc.), but Job 5:13 proclaims that God overthrows the wise, the counselors of the powerful, because of their craftiness. The weak, however, escape from the hands of those who are powerful.

20. *and again, "The Lord knows the thoughts of the wise that they are useless":* With a quotation from Ps 93:11 (LXX) Paul alludes to the scriptural distinction between good wisdom and bad wisdom. This is a major theme of Psalm 93. Paul modifies the quoted text so that it might better serve the needs of his rhetoric. Replacing the verse's "humans" *(anthrōpōn)* with "the wise" *(sophōn),* Paul is able to indict those Corinthians who claim to be wise. Their self-deception is futile.

21. *Wherefore let no one boast about humans:* From the associated Scriptures Paul draws the paraenetic inference that people should not boast about their human leaders. Boasting about humans is a carnal way of acting (see 1:29). It is contrary to the message of Scripture, which enjoins that we should boast about the Lord (1:31). As for the human beings in whom the Corinthians take pride (1:12), they are to be put in their place. Paul explains this as he refutes a maxim that sums up the Corinthians' claims.

    for all things are yours: "All things are yours" is a Stoic maxim *(gnōmē)* readily applicable to one situation and then to another (cf. 6:12; 10:23). "All things belong to the wise" *(pant' ara esti tōn sophōn),* writes Diogenes Laertius (*Lives* 6.37, cf. 6.72; 7.125). See also Seneca, *Epistles* 109.1; *Benefits* 7.2.5; 7.3.2-3; 7.4.1; 7.8.1; 7.10.6; and Cicero, *De finibus* 3.22.75; 4.27.74. The maxim, repeated again at the end of the coordinated series of realities cited in the following verse, sums up the Corinthians' claims to freedom, wisdom, and power.

22. *whether Paul, or Apollos, or Cephas, or the world, or life, or death, or the present, or the future:* Among NT authors Paul especially uses the paratactical style. Here he achieves coordination by repeating, eight times, *eite,* "or," virtually equivalent to "and" in this kind of construction (BDF 454:3). Beginning with the names of those the Corinthians presumably invoked as their authorities (1:12), Paul offers a series of eight realities in apposition to the "all" *(panta hymōn)* of the philosophical maxim (v. 21). The rehearsal, in the same order, of the same four names ("Christ" is in 3:23) found in 1:12 indicates that Paul has reached an important stage in his exposition. He reverses the situation described by the rhetorical use of the slogans of 1:12. Instead of some Corinthians belonging to Paul, Apollos, or Cephas (1:12; cf. 3:4), Paul, Apollos, and Cephas belong to the Corinthians. So, too, do the human realities that define their existence.

    all things are yours: Paul's repetition (cf. v. 21c) of the philosophical maxim forms an inclusio around the list of the eight realities in v. 22a. The repetition of the maxim in a synthetic form of just two pronouns provides summation, emphasis, and focus. Paul then deals with the maxim as did ancient rhetoricians who attempted to refute some of the popular maxims that were deemed to express common wisdom. Paul admits the truth of the maxim but then shows (v. 23) that it has been inappropriately applied or inadequately understood. Typically the ancients capitalized on the maxim itself, using some of its vocabulary in a reformulation. This is what Paul does in v. 23. The rhetorical technique of reformulation (cf. Aristotle, *Art of Rhetoric* 2.21.14) is similar to the technique of redefinition that Paul uses to good effect in 1 Corinthians.

23. *and you are Christ's, and Christ is God's:* "You are Christ's" *(hymeis de Christou)* recalls the fourth slogan of 1:12. Contrasted with the simple mention of Paul, Apollos, and Cephas in v. 22, the wording, "you are Christ's," confirms the suggestion that the slogan in 1:12 is a product of Paul's own rhetoric. Paul's reversal of the twice-repeated Stoic maxim, "all things are yours," counters the Corinthians' claim to the putative patronage of various apostolic figures. The Corinthian Christians belong to Christ, to whom all things ultimately be-

long (8:6; 15:27-28). On the relationship between Christ and God see 8:6; 11:3; 15:28. In 3:7 and 9 Paul had affirmed the subordination to God of both himself and Apollos. That the Corinthians belong to Christ and that through Christ they belong to God is a rhetorical formulation of what Paul meant when he described the Corinthians as holy (1:2). This theological characterization of the community is the foundation of much of Paul's deliberative argument in 1 Corinthians. See, for example, his statement of thesis in 1:10.

For Reference and Further Study

Plag, Christoph. "Paulus und die Gezera schawa: Zur Übernahme rabbinischer Auslegungskunst," *Judaica* 50 (1994) 135–140.
Ramsaran, Rollin A. *Liberating Words: Paul's Use of Rhetorical Maxims in 1 Corinthians 1–10.* Valley Forge: Trinity Press International, 1996.

7. The Ultimate Tribunal (4:1-5)

1. Let any human being look upon us as Christ's assistants and stewards of the mysteries of God. 2. In this regard it is expected of stewards that each one be found trustworthy. 3. To me it matters little that I be judged by you or by some human tribunal; neither do I judge myself. 4. For I know of nothing against myself, but with this I am not acquitted. The one who judges me is the Lord. 5. Hence do not judge anything before the time, until the Lord comes who will shed light upon things hidden in darkness and will make manifest the intentions of hearts; and then commendation will come to each one from God.

Interpretation

Once again (cf. 2:1-5, 6-16; 3:1-9, 10) Paul turns to a reflection on his own ministry. The passage is replete with forensic language, the language of the courtroom. "Judging" (vv. 3, 4, 5), being found trustworthy (v. 2), knowing of something that could be held against oneself (v. 4), "being acquitted" (v. 4), "bringing to light" (v. 5), "making intentions manifest" (v. 5), and "commendation" (v. 5) bespeak the setting of a courtroom. Paul is obviously making an apology (see 9:3) for his ministry, but one must not assume that his ministry has been under attack at Corinth or that some of the Corinthians had accused Paul of doing evil. It may be that this "apology," like that of ch. 9, is an element in the rhetorical strategy adopted by Paul to enhance his *ethos*.

Stewards. Paul's use of the term *oikonomos* as a descriptive metaphor for his own work in 4:1-2 is unique (cf. Rom 16:23; Gal 4:2). It belongs to the *oiko-* word group that figures prominently in the Pauline correspondence, especially in 1 Corinthians (see above, pp. 155–156). In later Christian literature the term, evocative of the chief household slave, was applied to those who had a managerial role within the church (see Titus 1:7; 1 Pet 4:10). Given the function of the household in the organization of the early church and the common use of kinship language to describe Christians, use of the term *oikonomos* as a ministerial metaphor was quite appropriate.

The steward or manager *(oikonomos)* was a well-known figure in the Hellenistic world (see *EDNT* 2:568–575). Households (cf. Gal 4:2), voluntary associations, and cities (cf. Rom 16:23) had their stewards or managers. Within a large household the steward was generally a trustworthy slave who had responsibility for the household goods and was in charge of the other household slaves (Luke 12:42; 16:1-8; Philo, *Joseph* 37; Epictetus, *Discourses* 3.22.3; etc.). Philo considered household management *(oikonomia)* to be necessary training for the statesman *(politikos;* Philo, *Joseph* 38–39).

In the various private societies, guilds, and clubs of the Greco-Roman world the *oikonomos* was someone who often had cultic duties to perform in addition to his other responsibilities. Extant pre-Christian inscriptions, papyri, and ostraca attest to this religious role. In the cults of Sarapis and Hermes-Trismegistus the *oikonomos* had a religious function. The *oikonomoi* of voluntary religious associations had cultic roles, but so too did other *oikonomoi.* Some voluntary associations were made up of people who practiced the same trade, but the various trade guilds honored one or another deity. Silvanus was honored by carpenters and woodcutters, Annona and Ceres by the grain measurers, and so forth. A monumental inscription dating from the turn of the first century C.E. shows that at least one Corinthian association offered worship to the Lares of the imperial household (cf. Allen Brown West, ed., *Latin Inscriptions, 1896–1926.* Corinth; Results of Excavations Conducted by the American School of Classical Studies at Athens 8/2 [Cambridge, Mass.: Harvard University Press for the ASCS, 1931] 29–31).

The city manager *(oikonomos)* was someone who might be described today as the city treasurer. Since virtually all public officials in the Greco-Roman world had civic religious duties to perform, city managers had a role to play in public worship. Paul was personally acquainted with at least one city manager *(hos oikonomos tēs poleōs),* Erastus, whose greetings Paul extended to the church at Rome (Rom 16:23). Since Erastus was not an altogether common name there is a good possibility that Paul's Erastus is to be identified with a freedman known to us from a mid-first-century Latin inscription on a limestone paving block found near the municipal theater of Hellenistic Corinth: ". . . Erastus in return for his aedileship laid [the pavement] at his own expense *(sua pecunia)*."

The Erastus of the inscription probably received the title of aedile after he promised to install the pavement that now bears his name. "Aedile" is a Roman civic rank whose usual Greek equivalent is *agoranomos.* Since Paul identifies Erastus as an *oikonomos* rather than as an *agoranomos,* Erastus may not have been an aedile at the time of Paul's letter to the Romans. Gerd Theissen and Wayne Meeks opine that Erastus may have had the function of quaestor when Paul was writing but that he later advanced in the municipal hierarchy because of his munificence. Henry J. Cadbury and Jerome Murphy-O'Connor hold that Paul's Erastus was a slave *(oikonomos)* who held a relatively minor bureaucratic position in the city administration. Cadbury also held that Paul's Erastus was not to be identified with the epigraphic Erastus. It would have been a source of pride for the Christian community at Corinth if one of its members were to have enjoyed political prominence.

The Tribunal. The language of vv. 3-5 is of the sort that properly belongs in the courtroom. "The day" *(hē hēmera)* is the civil day, the day designated for a specific purpose, the day of a trial in the case to which Paul alludes. Paul uses the language of judgment: *krinō,* "to judge" in v. 5 and the related compound *anakrinoō,* "to judge" in the sense of "to scrutinize or interrogate" in vv. 3[2x] and 4. To speak of a verdict he uses the passive of the verb *dikaioō* with the meaning of "being found in the right."

Juridical language is not foreign to 1 Corinthians. Paul treats of lawsuits in 6:1-8; he comes to his own defense in 9:3-14. Paul's identification of the issues of lawsuits uses the verb *krinō* (6:1). Paul's defense is directed to those who would scrutinize him *(anakrinō,* 9:3). The verb *krinō* is also apposite to 5:3-5, where Paul speaks of the judgment he has already pronounced on the incestuous man (5:3). There is no doubt that the language of 4:3-5 belongs to the semantic field of forensics.

There is, however, a question as to whether the language indicates a forensic purpose. Is every use of forensic language an indication of an exercise in forensic or judicial rhetoric? That is the question the interpreter must face in trying to understand 4:1-5. Reflecting a long exegetical tradition (Johannes Weiss, John C. Hurd, N. A. Dahl, C. K. Barrett, Christophe Senft, Michael Bünker, Rudolf Pesch, etc.), Karl Plank *(Irony of Affliction* 14) opines that "taken together, the juridical imagery and Paul's intent to undercut the power of human judgment point to his perception of a challenge to his trustworthiness as an apostle." This is, however, not necessarily the correct way of reading Paul's words. The entire letter to the Corinthians is a piece of deliberative rhetoric whose first proof is encompassed by the *parakalō* motif (1:10; 4:16). To provide a ground for his appeal Paul offers himself as an example. His presentation of himself provides a rhetorical warrant for his paraenesis. In rhetorical argument this is the *ethos* appeal. Paul offers himself as an example to the Corinthians. Indeed, in 1:18–4:21 (see 4:6, 16; cf. 11:1) he makes it clear that this is his intention. It is a typical rhetorical ploy for rhetors to portray themselves as put upon, to argue their innocence so as to make an appeal. This is Paul's rhetorical tactic in 1 Thess 2:1-12 (see A. J. Malherbe, "Gentle as a Nurse"). Paul is convinced of his innocence and so can offer the example of himself to the Corinthians.

Rather than precipitously judging others Paul refrains from judging, indeed, from judging even himself. He radically refuses to engage in the type of prejudice that leads some Corinthians to disdain others. The day in court about which Paul writes in 4:3 recalls the day of 3:13. The day on which the human court convenes (4:3) contrasts with the day of the Lord, a day of judgment (3:13). The day of the Lord is the time in which the work of each individual builder is to be made visible (*phaneron genēsetai,* 3:13). At the divine assizes the Lord will make manifest (*phanerōsei*) the intentions of human hearts. From the standpoint of Paul's rhetorical composition his words on the eschatological judgment (4:3-5) stand in relationship to the servant and steward metaphorical motif (4:1-2) much in the way that the words on judgment (3:14-17) stand in relationship to the construction metaphor of 3:10-13.

Judgment. The exhortation not to judge in v. 5 is a paraenetic inference from what Paul has previously written. Since the inference is immediately drawn from Paul's own example, some commentators suggest that it is an exhortation that brings 3:5–4:5 to closure. A broader perspective would suggest that the inference is based on all that Paul has written since the enunciation of his thesis in 1:10, even on the rhetorical rehearsal of facts in his epistolary thanksgiving (1:4-9). This section, 4:1-5, comes between two references to Paul and Apollos (3:22; 4:6), which recalls the slogans of 1:12. The apocalyptic coloring of Paul's judgment motif capitalizes on the apocalyptic motifs that have punctuated his entire exposition thus far.

Linking Paul's exhortation with what has gone before, the inferential "hence" (*hōste*) characterizes the principal purpose of 4:1-5 as paraenetic. Paul urges the Corinthians not to be judgmental, to avoid those judgments of others and of themselves (1:11-12, 29; 2:6; 3:1, 3-4; 4:3, 6) that are detrimental to the harmony of the community. With its paraenetic purpose 4:1-5 is consistent with the deliberative rhetoric of Paul's appeal since the enunciation of his thesis in 1:10.

In the development of his rhetorical argument Paul often appeals to his own prestige. He does so in vv. 1-4, where he chooses two unusual metaphors (v. 1) to describe his own ministerial task. Implying that he is to be found trustworthy, he introduces the language of the courtroom to suggest that he will receive ultimate commendation from God. The Corinthians should learn from his example. They should not judge as he did not judge. If judged by others in the community, even if judged by a human court (4:3; cf. 6:1-6), they should take heart because the Lord is the ultimate judge of humans.

Christians live and act "before the time" *(pro kairou)*. The Corinthians are under the pressure of time, that is, the time of the Lord's coming, eschatological time (see 7:29). They are people who are waiting for the revelation of our Lord Jesus Christ (1:7). This expectation should characterize their entire existence but apparently it has not. Some of the Corinthians seem to have lived and acted without a proper understanding of eschatology (4:8). Consequently Paul reminds the Corinthians of his own situation before the impending eschaton (v. 4). They should likewise realize that their own work stands under eschatological scrutiny (see 3:13-15). Their eschatological existence, in the already but not yet fully realized eschaton, should provide a corrective to the all-too-human sociological anthropology they are inclined to follow (see 2:6-16; cf. 1:18). As elsewhere in 1 Corinthians, Paul uses apocalyptic motifs to advance his paraenetic purpose.

Paul's final phrase with its distributive "each" *(hekastō)* reinforces the idea that 4:1-5 is a unit of deliberative rhetoric rather than an apologetic appeal. Every human being should expect and desire commendation from God. The expectation—a positive one!—is that each will receive his or her commendation. Whether they do so or not depends on how they fulfill the task that is assigned to them by the Lord. Paul's task was to be an assistant and a steward. The plural form of the nouns in v. 1 shows that the task was not entrusted to Paul alone. Every assistant and steward will stand before the divine tribunal.

NOTES

1. *Let any human being look upon us as Christ's assistants:* Paul continues his exhortation with an imperative that appeals directly but has a broad appeal *(houtōs hēmas logizesthō anthrōpos;* cf. 2 Cor 10:7, 11). His emphatic use of "human being" *(anthrōpos;* see 11:28; cf. Epictetus, *Discourses* 3.23.15) instead of "anyone" *(tis)* hearkens back to the contrast between the merely human and the divine (2:6-16) and the theological point he had underscored in the previous verse (3:23). "To look upon," *logizesthō,* literally "reckon" introduces a string of verbs that suggest some form of evaluation: "look upon . . . is expected . . . be found . . . be judged *(anakrinō)* . . . judge *(krinō)* . . . shed light . . . make manifest . . . commendation." Paul's use of "human being" prepares for the contrast between the human tribunal (v. 3) and the divine tribunal (vv. 4c-5) that will be the burden of his reflection.

"Assistants" (*hypēretas*, literally "under-rowers") properly designated those who were positioned on a lower deck of a trireme (cf. EDNT 3:398–402). Hapax in Paul, the term was commonly used in Hellenistic literature and in the NT (especially in John) to designate various functionaries (Luke 4:20, etc.). In Hellenistic Greek the term was used of those who were in service to others (e.g., Philo, *Sacrifices* 44), including construction workers (Philo, *Posterity* 50). Elsewhere in his writings Paul uses the language of "servant" (*diakonos*, 3:5; cf. Rom 16:1; 2 Cor 3:6; 6:4; 11:15, 23) or "slave" (*doulos*, Rom 1:1; Phil 1:1; cf. 1 Cor 7:22[2x] and 2 Cor 4:5) to describe his ministerial function. Here the term "assistant" does not apply to Paul alone. Others, presumably at least Apollos (cf. 3:5, 22), are included under the rubric. As a servant/slave Paul can be legitimately judged only by his Lord (v. 4b). Influenced by Paul, Ignatius uses the language of "assistants" (*hypēretai*) and "stewards" (*oikonomoi*) to describe Christian ministers in his letter to Polycarp (*Pol.* 6:1; *PG* 5, 724).

and stewards of the mysteries of God: In describing himself, along with Apollos (and perhaps Cephas), as stewards of the mysteries of God and Christ's assistants, Paul maintains the binomial reference of his ministry, that is, to both God and the Christ, that he had introduced in his epistolary *intitulatio* (1:1). To be an assistant of Christ is to be a steward of the mysteries of God (cf. Rom 15:16, with a cultic reference).

Paul specifies his steward's task as having reference to the mysteries of God. Given Paul's tendency to use verbs of speaking with "mysteries" (2:1, 7; 14:2; 15:51) it is probable that he has the ministry of the word in mind as he writes about being a steward of the mysteries of God. Paul describes his ministry as one of proclaiming the mysteries of God, in contexts that evoke an apocalyptic vision of eschatology (2:1, 7; 15:51). Epictetus describes the wise person as one who recognizes that he is but a "steward" (*oikonomos*) in the world of God, the *oikodespotēs*, who assigns an appropriate function to each person and thing (see *Discourses* 3.22.3-4).

2. *In this regard it is expected of stewards that each one be found trustworthy:* Trustworthiness and prudence were qualities a master would hope to find in a person appointed steward of the household (Luke 12:42). These qualities belonged, as it were, to their job description. Paul's lexicographical choice of "expected" (*zēteitai;* see BAGD 339.2c) and "each one" (*tis*) suggest the proverbial or gnomic character of Paul's utterance. A steward should be trustworthy (*pistos*) because it is to the steward that a responsible task is entrusted (*pisteuthēnai;* cf. 1 Thess 2:4). Paul considers both Timothy (4:17) and himself (7:25) to be trustworthy.

3. *To me it matters little that I be judged by you or by some human tribunal; neither do I judge myself:* The expression "to me it matters little that" (*emoi de eis elachiston estin hina*) is hapax in Paul. This relatively free construction (BDF 145.2; 393.6) says that the circumstances that Paul describes do not make a great deal of difference to him. Paul had previously stated that spiritual people are really judged by no human being (2:15). Now he states that it matters little whether or not he, who has the Spirit (7:40), is judged by any human agency, be that the Corinthians, a secular court, or even himself.

"By some human tribunal" *(hypo anthrōpinēs hēmeras)* uses the noun *hēmera*, literally "day," often a legal day or a day of special observance, to describe the day of a court session. Similar words, *anthrōpinē hēmera*, are to be found on a coin amulet dating from the second or third century C.E. Paul's expression contrasts with "the day" of the Lord in 3:13 and the divine tribunal about which Paul will speak in vv. 4c-5. As to the jurisdiction of secular courts see further 6:1-6.

4. *For I know of nothing against myself, but with this I am not acquitted:* Paul's affirmation of his own innocence clarifies his remark (note the explanatory *gar*) about his judgment on himself (v. 3c). His use of "know" *(synoida)* is hapax in the extant correspondence, but a similar construction *(synoidon* + the reflexive, frequent in popular Hellenistic usage) is found in Job 27:6 (cf. Lev 5:1 [LXX]), where Job similarly protests his innocence. Despite Theissen's psychological reading of Paul there is little reason to suggest that Paul's words intimate that the apostle had a pre-Freudian awareness of the importance of the unconscious in human behavior.

Despite Paul's avowal of innocence he admits that the final judgment does not belong to him. He is not thereby acquitted *(ouk en toutō dedikaiōmai).* Paul's juridical lexis, his choice of the language of the courtroom, provides for his use of the verb *dikaioō*, "to declare righteous." See the similar use of the related noun, righteousness *(dikaiosynē)* in Job 27:6. "To declare righteous" will acquire another connotation in the context of the issues discussed in Paul's letters to the Romans and to the Galatians, where the verb *dikaioō* appears with some frequency (15x in Romans; 8x in Galatians).

The one who judges me is the Lord: In contrast with the competency the Corinthians claim for themselves (vv. 3a, 5), the limited competency of the secular court (6:1-6), and Paul's own self-judgment, Paul affirms that it is the Lord who judges him. Whether Paul intends "Lord" as a reference to God or to Jesus, for whom "Lord" is his preferred title, is difficult to determine. In the biblical tradition it is God who judges (cf. Ps 94:1, where the LXX [Ps 93:1] has more the sense of judgment than does the Hebrew, which stresses vengeance). In Rom 2:16 Paul writes about God who judges things hidden within human beings *(ta krypta tōn anthrōpōn)* with Christ Jesus as the intermediary. Rather than seeing 4:4 as an instance of Paul's transference of *Kyrios* language and function to the resurrected Jesus it may be better to speak, as does Neil Richardson, of "overlap" (see *Language about God* 286). Paul's concern is not to focus on the relationship between God and the Christ but to underscore that he will be judged in God's court, not in some human court. Paul's insistence on the singular competence of the divine tribunal is consistent with the biblical and Jewish motif of the divine tribunal as the court of final appeal (see Kuck, *Judgment and Community Conflict* 46–50, 60–61).

5. *Hence do not judge anything before the time, until the Lord comes:* With "hence" *(hōste)* Paul brings to a conclusion the argument he has been developing thus far, presumably since 1:10 when he appealed to the Corinthians to avoid divisions within the community. Paul's urging the community to avoid judgment echoes the Q saying of Luke 6:37=Matt 7:1, which likewise has an eschatological referent.

For Paul the time of judgment is the time *(kairos)* when the Lord comes. The motif of the coming of the Lord forms an *inclusio* around the entire letter. See 1:7-8 and the "maranatha" ("come Lord") of 16:22. The Lord who will come is Jesus *Kyrios*, the parousiac Lord. All that the Corinthians do must be evaluated in the light of the coming of the Lord. Hence they must refrain from judgment, since judgment will take place at the coming of the Lord (v. 5b).

who will shed light upon things hidden in darkness and will make manifest the intentions of hearts: Paul's formulation of an early Christian apocalyptic vision (cf. 2 Cor 5:10) may be a borrowed tradition. The parallel clauses beginning with *kai,* "and," (the first of which is not translated) suggest a poetic structure. Only here in the extant correspondence does Paul use the expressions "shed light" *(phōtisei)* and "intentions" *(boulas).* The phrase "things hidden in darkness" *(ta krypta tou skotous)* is hapax in the NT. The contrast between light and darkness is, however, a well-known figure of speech and a common motif in apocalyptic literature. Paul, moreover, speaks of the coming of the Lord only when he is using traditional material (cf. 11:26; 16:22).

Paul's use of "manifest" to speak of disclosure at the final judgment is echoed in Hermas, *Sim.* 4.2-4, where *phaneroō* is used five times. Paul's reference to the manifestation of the intentions of the heart is similar to an expression he uses in 14:25 when he speaks of the manifestation of the hidden things of the heart *(ta krypta tēs kardias autou phanera ginetai).* The notion of a probing of the heart by God is a Jewish concept (Jer 11:20, etc.; cf. 1 Thess 2:4), in which "the heart" (Hebrew *lēb*) expresses the depths of the human person. Previously in this letter Paul had written of the heart only in the apocalyptic saying of 2:9. As in 2:6-16, Paul uses apocalyptic notions and biblical anthropology to confront the Corinthians: there, their claim to be perfect; here, the judgments they bring to bear on one another. Paul's emphasis on disclosure at "the time" parallels his emphasis on disclosure on "the day" in 3:13.

and then commendation will come to each one from God: "Commendation" *(epainos)* is a Pauline term, appearing in the NT only in his letters and in literature dependent on him (Ephesians, 1 Peter). Found in Hellenistic inscriptions, the term denotes the recognition conferred by civic authorities and the legal protection a person so commended can expect to enjoy. In a culture in which shame and honor are dominant factors the approval and recognition implied by *epainos* are particularly important. Paul's "from God" *(apo tou theou)* is an expression he uses in reference to the effects of God's grace (1:30; 6:19; Phil 1:28; cf. Rom 15:15, with its variant *hypo*). As used here it contrasts the verdict rendered in the divine tribunal with the findings of any human court. As in 3:13, Paul stresses that God's judgment will be meted out to each individual *(hekastō).*

For Reference and Further Study

Cadbury, Henry J. "Erastus of Corinth," *JBL* 50 (1931) 42–58.
Gillman, Florence M. "Erastus," *ABD* 2:571.

Kuck, David W. *Judgment and Community Conflict,* 196–210.

Malherbe, Abraham J. "'Gentle as a Nurse': The Cynic Background to 1 Thess 2," *NovT* 12 (1970) 203–217. Reprinted in idem, *Paul and the Popular Philosophers.* Minneapolis: Fortress, 1989, 35–48.

Reumann, John H. "*Oikonomia*-terms in Paul in Comparison with Lucan Heilsgeschichte," *NTS* 13 (1966–67) 147–167.

_____. "'Stewards of God': Pre-Christian Religious Application of *Oikonomos* in Greek," *JBL* 77 (1958) 339–349.

Theissen, Gerd. *Psychological Aspects of Pauline Theology.* Philadelphia: Fortress, 1987, 59–66.

_____. *Social Setting of Pauline Christianity,* 75–83.

Unnik, Willem C. van. "Lob und Strafe durch die Obrigkeit. Hellenistiches zu Röm 13,3-4" in E. Earle Ellis and Erich Grässer, eds., *Jesus und Paulus. Festschrift für Werner Georg Kümmel zum 70. Geburtstag.* Göttingen: Vandenhoeck & Ruprecht, 1975, 334–343.

8. *The Lesson of Paul and Apollos* (4:6-7)

6. These things, brothers and sisters, I have applied to myself and to Apollos for your sake, in order that you might learn from us how to appreciate the adage "not beyond what is written," so that no one be inflated with pride in favor of the one over and against the other. 7. For who concedes you any distinction? What do you have that you have not received? And if you have received, why do you boast as if you had not received?

INTERPRETATION

Paul quickly turns from a rhetorical appeal, in which the Corinthians were asked to sit as putative judges, to an appeal based on the family ties that bind Paul to the Corinthians. In what is almost a courtroom aside addressed to the members of his family Paul begins, "these things, brothers and sisters, I have applied to myself and to Apollos for your sake." Paul reveals that he has been using a well-known rhetorical technique in order to confront the powerful within the community. Then he tells them that they have something to learn from himself and Apollos. Finally, with an *ad hominem* kind of appeal Paul challenges the Corinthians to bring judgment to bear upon themselves and to consider that they are rich, but only because they have been gifted.

Hidden Meaning. The verb *metaschēmatizō* ("apply") literally means "to change the form of"; the context determines the precise nature of the change. On occasion Pseudo-Demetrius (*Elocution* 287; 292-294; BAGD 513) used the verb to mean "say something with the help of a figure of speech." Ancient rhetoricians were familiar with the technique of "covert allusion" *(logos eschēmatismenos)*. This was a kind of extended metaphor in which the rhetor spoke ostensibly of one reality, intending that the audience apply the speech to another. Rhetoricians used the device to admonish the powerful. The technique was characterized by hyperbole, irony, contrast, and figurative language.

Use of literary devices has pervaded Paul's exposition thus far. On first reading Paul's words in 1:10–4:5 seem to concern a disruption within the community coming from the various factions that claim for themselves the authority of one or another apostolic figure: Paul, Apollos, or even Cephas (1:12; 3:4-9, 22; 4:6). This reading may be illusory. Paul was using covert allusion, the technique used by ancient rhetoricians to confront potentates. The second century C.E. Aelius Aristides offers what he calls "a human example" *(anthrōpeion paradeigma)* to the citizens of Rhodes engaged in a class struggle. Aristides urged the Rhodians to imitate *(mimeisthai)* the example of the emperors Marcus and Verus. In similar fashion Paul writes about the situation in Corinth as if the issue were Paul and Apollos. That is not the issue; rather the Corinthians should learn from the example of Paul and Apollos how they should relate to one another and to their leaders.

By saying "I have applied all these things to myself and Apollos" Paul intends his audience to understand that he has not really been speaking about himself and Apollos. He is telling them that he has been using the rhetorical ploy of covert allusion. Without naming any names the apostle has surreptitiously addressed the issue of divisiveness in the community. Rather than naming those who were responsible for the disharmony in the community Paul cited himself and Apollos as if they were leaders and projected their cooperation as a model to be followed (3:4-9; cf. 4:16, "therefore, I urge you, be imitators *[mimētai]* of me").

At Corinth there were no parties that rallied around the names of Paul and Apollos. There was, however, division in the community (1:10-11; cf. 11:19) and various forms of disruptive leadership. The metatext of v. 6a implies that Paul's argument (1:10–4:5) is, as it were, an argument by analogy. What he has been ostensibly saying about himself and Apollos is really a commentary on how the Corinthians should view their own leaders.

Those Who are Puffed Up. Paul's critique of those who are "puffed up" *(hoi pephysiōmenoi,* 4:19; cf. 5:2) is reminiscent of a classic topos, the critique addressed by various philosophers to those who are inflated with pride as a result of their wisdom and knowledge. Plato had strong things to say about those who had a conceit of wisdom (*doxosophia, Sophist* 231B) and "high and conceited opinions about themselves" (*Sophist* 230B). For Plato, Socrates was a model of dealing with people who are puffed up with pride in their own knowledge. The consequence of intellectual conceit and arrogance is antisocial behavior. Those who are not truly wise but wise in their own conceit are difficult to get along with, says Plato (*Phaedrus* 275B).

To describe those who are conceited in this way Paul uses the verb *physioō*, "to be inflated," an expression he uses only in 1 Corinthians, where it belongs to a body of rhetorical terms used to caricature the Corinthians (cf. 4:18, 19; 5:2; 8:1; 13:4). The only other NT usage of the term is in the deutero-Pauline epistle to the Colossians, whose author criticizes those who have an appearance of wisdom (Col 2:23) and are "puffed up without cause by a human way of thinking" (*eikē physioumenos hypo tou noös tēs sarkos autou,* Col 2:18).

The word *physioō* was common in Hellenistic rhetoric where it was used to characterize those whose self-conceit was such that it led to partisanship. Xenophon, for example, describes the political extremists Alcibiades and Critias as "inflated with power" (*pephysēmenō epi dynamei, Memorabilia* 1.2.25). Philo described Gaius, whom he contrasts with the Dioscuri, imitable examples of sibling love (*philadelphia),* as "puffed up with pride" (*pephysēsai tōn paraplēsiōn, Gaius* 86; Cf. 69, 154; Demosthenes, 59.97; 19.314). Pseudo-Plato (*Alcibiades II* 145E) used the verb to describe political orators who were conceited.

Paul's phrase caricatures the conceit of those Corinthians who built themselves up at the expense of others, leading to the destruction of the unity of the community. Examples of the antisocial behavior of the Corinthians who were puffed up with conceit are their failure to deal with the issue of the man who was sleeping with his father's wife (5:1-13; see v. 2, "Are you so conceited?" *kai hymeis pephysiōmenoi este*) and their taking other members of the community to court (6:1-11). The root of the problem is their espousal of the wisdom of this world (1:20) rather than the wisdom of God.

An Enigmatic Saying. In 1 Corinthians Paul cites many popular sayings. One lesson he wishes to teach the Corinthians is summed up in a phrase, "not beyond what is written." The phrase was certainly one Paul expected the Corinthians to understand, but the allusion is difficult to capture. It may be that the meaning of the saying was something like "there is no need to go beyond the letter of the law," that is, act in accordance with the rules (cf. 2 Cor 10:13; compare Rom 12:3). Thus the *NEB,* "learn to 'keep within the rules.'" Peter Marshall thinks that Paul cites the phrase as a warning against the kind of excessive behavior that stems from *hybris*. "What is written" would mean something like the "measure" of 2 Cor 10:13. It would suggest the allusions to the Scriptures and the self-awareness to which Paul has already made reference in the letter.

Other scholars prefer to deal with the problematic phrase from the perspective of Paul's rhetoric. Martin Ebner suggests that the enigmatic passage is part of Paul's characterization of the Corinthians as children (see 3:1-2). They do not even know how to trace letters properly. Other scholars, using the same image of grammar-school children tracing letters made by a teacher, take Paul's words to be a metaphorical exhortation urging the Corinthians to follow closely his example and that of Apollos (so Heinrich Schlier, John Fitzgerald, Benjamin Fiore, David Kuck).

L. L. Welborn suggests that the phrase recalls the advice offered, in a context of arbitration, by philosophers and statesmen to people who were about to cause disharmony in a community. Paul's version of the advice is without a verbatim parallel in the extant literature, but it is presented as a saying (note the use of *to* in v. 6; cf. Rom 13:9; Gal 5:14; 6:9). Since it is offered as a maxim but is not otherwise attested, Welborn considers that "it was Paul who abstracted the admonition from its context and gave it the character of a maxim" ("Conciliatory Principle," 345). Without identifying a context the *JB* translates the phrase as a Pauline aside, "remember the maxim: 'Keep to what is written.'"

"Not to go beyond the things that are written" was a meaningful injunction for the Corinthians. Paul cited the phrase as part of his attempt to urge the Corinthians to avoid factionalism and foster reconciliation (v. 6c). Offering himself and Apollos as examples of people who work together in a common enterprise (3:5-9) and who are not self-serving (4:9-13) serves the purpose of Paul's deliberative rhetoric. It is, nonetheless, difficult today fully to appreciate exactly what is meant by the saying to which he refers.

Superiority. Many commentators think that v. 7 is key to understanding one of the major issues underlying the problems at Corinth. Social divisions may be at the root of many of these problems faced by the Corinthian community. The three verbs used by Paul in the ironic triad of 4:8—to be satiated, to be rich, and to act like kings—were used in Hellenistic literature to characterize the rich and powerful. It may well be that some of the better-off Corinthians were acting like kings, treating others with disdain, and acting as if there were no limits to their freedom. Such an attitude would have led to a divided community.

With a return to the language of the courtroom (4:3-5) and abandoning the use of covert allusion, whose purpose he, as a brother, had revealed in v. 6, Paul addresses the Corinthians directly in v. 7. With a trio of rhetorical questions he challenges them to bring judgment to bear upon themselves. It is a matter of discernment. The Corinthians are invited to discern for themselves who they really are. They may be rich, and Paul ironically concedes that they are (4:8), but Paul invites them to consider what they have received and that they have received all that they have. Three times Paul uses the verb "to receive" *(lambanō)* to underscore what the Corinthians have received.

Absent from Paul's direct rhetorical appeal (vv. 7-8) is any mention of God. This is all the more striking in that the exhortation—apart from the explanatory aside of v. 5—is embraced by explicit language about God (vv. 5, 9). Reference to God is implied by Paul's language and by the context, a context (1:10–4:16) in which God-language abounds. In their boasting the Corinthians have left God out of consideration.

NOTES

6. *These things, brothers and sisters, I have applied to myself and to Apollos for your sake:* For the first time since 3:1 Paul appeals directly to the Corinthians with an apostrophic "brothers and sisters." The vocative adds rhetorical appeal to his *di' hymas,* "for your sake."

What follows the vocative is difficult to understand. First of all, there is the matter of the antecedent of the demonstrative "these things" *(tauta),* emphatically positioned at the beginning of the sentence. A second problem is the connotation of the verb "to apply" *(meteschēmatisa),* hapax in 1 Corinthians and used in the NT only by Paul (2 Cor 11:13, 14, 15; Phil 3:21). Commentators frequently opine that Paul's *meteschēmatisa* has a connotation different from that which it normally had in common parlance (so, BAGD 513: "1 Cor 4:6 is more or less unique"). With regard to "not beyond what is written" (v. 6b) a major textual problem has long confounded textual critics.

Chrysostom *(On the First Epistle to the Corinthians, Homily* 12.1; *PG* 61, 97) held that "these things" refers to the exposition in 1:10–4:5. Johannes Vos takes "these things" to be a reference only to 3:5–4:5, but Chrysostom is probably right. The section 1:10–4:5 constitutes a single literary unit and the demonstrative normally applies to something that comes before the pronoun. "These things" refers to the extended paraenesis Paul has directed to those who were disrupting the unity of the community (1:10). "Applied" *(meteschēmatisa)* seems to indicate that all that Paul has said thus far has been said in the guise of covert allusion.

in order that you might learn from us: Since the Apostle has just spoken about himself and Apollos it is reasonable to assume that "so that in us you learn" *(hina en hēmin mathēte)* means "so that you learn from our example" (see 4:16), that is, the example of Paul and Apollos. The proximity of the pronouns "you" and "us" in a pair of short prepositional phrases *(di' hymas . . . en hēmin)* adds strength to Paul's argument. The example of Paul and Apollos is further set before the Corinthians in vv. 9-13. The contrast between "you" (the Corinthians) and "us" (Paul and Apollos) is particularly poignant in v. 10.

how to appreciate the adage, "not beyond what is written": The Greek text found in *GNT*[4], *to mē hyper ha gegraptai,* is found in virtually all the editions and is so strongly attested that it merits no comment in Metzger's *Textual Commentary.* The saying is exceptionally difficult to understand. The purpose clause literally reads, "so that in us you learn the not above what is written." One commentator began his commentary by saying, "let us confess at once that it is untranslatable." "What is written" is typical Pauline usage to introduce a scriptural quotation, but no Scripture is cited and it is difficult to imagine a particular scriptural passage that the Apostle might have had in mind as he was writing about the example Apollos and himself have offered to the Corinthians.

From the early days of NT textual criticism many scholars have been of the opinion that Paul's words have suffered severe textual corruption in the process of scribal transcription, but there is little extant textual evidence to support this view. With only meager evidence in the medieval Greek manuscripts and later "corrections" of some of the ancient manuscripts (ℵ, C [apparently], D, E [so Tischendorf]), the Textus Receptus incorporated a "how to be humble" *(phronein)* into its reading of v. 6. Humility is what the Corinthians are to learn from Paul and Apollos. This results in a translation such as that of the Authorized Version, "that ye might learn in us not to think of men above that which is written." The textual support for *phronein* is so weak that it was not accepted into Tischendorf's *Editio octava critica maior* (1869–72) nor is it accepted by contemporary editors.

Some textual critics, beginning with the 1884 doctoral dissertation of the Dutch scholar J.M.S. Baljon, have conjectured that "the not above what is written" was a scribe's marginal note. The note would have said the word "not," omitted from a previous manuscript, was to be inserted into the text (see L. Alonso Schökel, *Understanding Biblical Research* [New York: Herder and Herder, 1968] 66–69). Were this conjecture correct, Paul's text would have simply meant, "learn from our example, so that no one is puffed up to the advantage of someone and the disadvantage of another." There is, however, no support for this conjecture in the extant manuscript tradition. Nor is there any textual support for the hypothesis advanced by many scholars, including Jerome Murphy-O'Connor, that the entire verse is a later interpolation into Paul's text.

The present, problematic reading of the text best explains the variant readings found in the manuscript tradition. Hence most editors publish the text as it is in *GNT*[4]. Its enigmatic character is, however, such that the text appears in differently punctuated forms, and is therefore interpreted differently, in the various editions of the New Testament in Greek.

so that no one be inflated [with pride] in favor of the one over and against the other: For C.F.D. Moule, followed by Stephen Pogoloff, "in favor of one over and against the other" (cf. BDF 247.4) alludes to the factionalism at Corinth in that some prided themselves in their allegiance to one hero of the tradition (cf. 1:12) over and against another. This is the first mention of those who are puffed up in 1 Corinthians. The verb *physioō* is a Pauline word. Outside 1

Corinthians, where it appears in 3:6, 18, 19; 5:2, 8:1, and 13:4, it appears in the NT only in Col 2:18. Paul's use of the verb at the beginning of each of the next major sections of the letter, that is, chs. 5–7 on sexual issues, chs. 8–10 on food offered to idols, and chs. 12–14 on spiritual gifts—the three following rhetorical demonstrations in his letter—is a strong indication of its importance in Paul's rhetoric. Each of these problem areas seems to have developed from a circumstance Paul can describe as the puffed-up situation of the Corinthians.

7. *For who concedes you any distinction? What do you have that you have not received? And if you have received, why do you boast as if you had not received?* This short series of rhetorical questions returns to the line of argumentation in the mode of the judicial forum on which Paul had capitalized in vv. 1-5. From the apparently defensive and apologetic tone of vv. 2 and 3 Paul turns to the offensive. His first question is phrased in the language of the courtroom. "Concedes" (*diakrinō*, literally "to separate"), cognate with the *anakrinō* and *krinō* of vv. 3-5, was often used in ancient literature to describe judicial judgments (cf. 6:5). In 4:7 it means "who concedes you any distinction?" (BAGD 185.1b). Paul's rhetorical question awaits a negative response. No distinction is to be conceded to the Corinthians because all that they have, they have received from God. The question is phrased in the singular. Paul appeals to each one of the Corinthians (see the "each one" of v. 5) to bring judgment to bear upon himself or herself (cf. 3:10, 18). Returning to the use of judicial language in v. 7, Paul isolates v. 6 aside as an explanatory comment on the argument he had developed up to that point. Thereafter he appeals to them in plain language.

The second and third rhetorical questions—with a thrice-repeated *lambanō*, "receive"—underscore that the things of which the Corinthians boast are the very things they have received as gifts from God. Paul's line of argument is consistent with his Jewish and biblical tradition. All that humans have, they have as God's gift. Thus there is no reason for humans to boast (cf. 1:29-31). To God alone all honor and glory are due. See above, pp. 99–101. The rhetorical questions confront the boasting of the Corinthians. They also type the puffed-up Corinthians as a bunch of ingrates. Such characterization sharpens the irony of v. 8.

For Reference and Further Study

Fiore, Benjamin. "'Covert Allusion' in 1 Corinthians 1–4," *CBQ* 47 (1985) 85–102.

Hall, David R. "A Disguise for the Wise: *Metaschēmatismos* in 1 Corinthians 4.6," *NTS* 40 (1994) 143–149.

Hanges, James C. "1 Corinthians 4:6 and the Possibility of Written Bylaws in the Corinthian Church," *JBL* 117 (1998) 275–298.

Marshall, Peter. *Enmity in Corinth*, 194–218.

Plank, Karl A. *Paul and the Irony of Affliction*. SBL.SS. Atlanta: Scholars, 1987.

Vos, Johannes Sijko. "Der *metaschēmatismos* in 1 Kor 4,6," *ZNW* 86 (1995) 154–172.

Wagner, J. Ross. "'Not Beyond the Things which are Written': A Call to Boast only in the Lord (1 Cor 4.6)," *NTS* 44 (1998) 279–287.

Welborn, L. L. "A Conciliatory Principle in 1 Cor. 4:6," *NovT* 29 (1987) 320–346.
    Revised in idem, *Politics and Rhetoric in the Corinthian Epistles*, 43–75.
Winter, Bruce W. *Philo and Paul*, 196–200.
Yinger, Kent L. "First Corinthians 4:6 and Hellenistic Pedagogy," *CBQ* 60 (1998)
    97–103.

9. *Filled and Hungry* (4:8-13)

8. Already you are satiated! Already you are enriched! Independently of us you have acted royally! And would that you did reign, so that we might also reign with you! 9. For I think that God has made a show of us as the last apostles, like people sentenced to death, because we have become a spectacle to the universe, to angels and to humans alike. 10. We are fools for the sake of Christ, and you are prudent in Christ; we are weak, and you are strong; you are held in esteem, and we are without honor. 11. Until this very hour we are hungry, and we are thirsty, and we are naked, and we are beaten, and we are homeless, 12. and we toil, working with our own hands. Slandered, we bless; persecuted, we endure patiently; 13. insulted, we encourage; we have become like the refuse of the world, the scum of all until now.

Interpretation

In an attempt to change the Corinthians' outlook radically Paul had offered a lesson ("that you might learn from us," v. 6) that ultimately had a paraenetic purpose. To make his point and to continue the engagement with the Corinthians he had initiated with the trio of rhetorical questions in v. 7 Paul develops an argument that is a classic example of paradoxical irony. Ironic speech is typically characterized by the use of figurative language. Paul uses two strong and self-depreciating images to characterize himself and Apollos, one of people about to die in the amphitheater with the crowds looking on (v. 9), and the other of the dregs of the earth (v. 13). These images form an *inclusio*, a kind of ring construction that constitutes 4:9-13 as a literary unit.

A First Point. In 1 Corinthians Paul frequently concedes the (partial) accuracy of the troublemakers' contentions and then proceeds to offer a corrective (see 3:21b-23). In v. 8 he concedes that the Corinthians are gifted (cf. 1:7, a *captatio benevolentiae*). The concession of v. 8 is, however, ironically phrased, as the explanatory corrective will be (vv. 9-13). The descriptive verbs of v. 8—to be satiated, to be rich, to act in royal fashion—

were typically used in the literature of his day to describe the rich and powerful.

The Corinthians may have been acting regally but the kingdom has not yet come. There is an epistemological difference between the way Paul sees things and the way the Corinthian know-it-alls see things. This difference bears especially upon eschatological realities. The Corinthians extol the present, the "already" (*ēdē*, 2x in v. 8). Paul counters with an "until now" (vv. 11, 13) that suggests the ephemeral quality of time and speaks of the kingdom that has not yet come.

Those who have perturbed the community with their superior attitudes have done so in total independence from and disregard of Paul and his apostolic companions. In Paul's perspective when the kingdom does come they will all share together in its benefits. In the meantime things are not as they appear to be. Paul's biting irony, sharpened by the use of comparison and contrast, indicates that things really are not as they seem to be.

Paul's Difficulties. The heart of this epistolary unit consists of a twelve-item description of Paul's own situation (vv. 10-13). The list of tribulations, the peristatic catalogue (from *peristasis*, "external circumstance"), was a classic topos in first-century Hellenistic literature. Widely used in the first century, it appears in the writings of such Stoics as Plutarch ("On the Fortune or the Virtue of Alexander," *Moralia* 326 D-E, 327 A-C, etc.) and Epictetus, as well as in the works of Greek biographers and historians (e.g., Arrian's *History of Alexander and Indica* 7.10.2). Hardship lists are also found in Jewish apocalypses (e.g., *2 Enoch* 66:6) and the works of Josephus (*Bell.* 2.151-153), the Mishnah (*m. Pesaḥ.* 10:5, *m. B. Qam.* 1:1, 4; etc.), and Gnostic texts from Nag Hammadi. The lists provide a rehearsal of various external and adverse circumstances that were beyond the control of the one who was subject to them. Their literary function was paraenetic rather than biographical. They were used to demonstrate the virtue of philosophers and moralists and their ability to overcome adversity.

Paul used the literary form with good effect in several of his letters, especially in 2 Corinthians (2 Cor 4:8-9; 6:4b-5, 8-10; 11:23-29; cf. Rom 8:35; Phil 4:12). First Corinthians 4:11 is the earliest of his uses of the hardship catalogue. That Paul is using a literary convention is indicated by the number of hapax legomena, words that appear only once in his writings, in these verses. "Being thirsty" (*dipsaō*), "being naked" (*gymniteuō*), and "being homeless" (*astateō*) are vocabulary of which the Pauline letters are generally innocent. As a presumably factual description these hardships are not otherwise supported in the early literature by and about Paul. "Being beaten" (*kolaphizō*) appears in 2 Cor 12:7, where it is an item on a hardship list, but it is not otherwise used by Paul. Luke, however, does tell a tale of Paul having been beaten with rods at Philippi (Acts 16:21-23; cf. 1 Thess 2:2; 2 Cor 11:25).

The twelve items on Paul's list are organized in a chiastic pattern (A-B-A'), in which the first unit (A, v. 10) and third (A', vv. 12b-13a) consist of three elements, each of which provides a contrast between Paul and Apollos and the Corinthian troublemakers. Paul's use of comparison and contrast heightens the rhetorical power of his list. Epictetus (*Discourses* 2.19.24), Josephus (*Bell.* 4.165), and the author of the *Testament of Joseph* (*T. Jos.* 1:4-7) also used antithesis to strengthen the rhetorical impact of their list of tribulations.

The central unit (B, vv. 11-12a) is characterized by vocabulary that is typical of the tribulation lists but unusual for Paul. A repetitive, paratactic use of "and" (*kai,* 6x in vv. 11-12) binds together six different tribulations in a kind of run-on description. This central unit of the chiasm (v. 11-12a) portrays the kind of life Paul and his companion evangelists had to live. It depicts Paul and Apollos as being in a situation in which they can identify with the Corinthian have-nots. They went without food and drink; they had no clothes and no home; they were beaten and had to work. Such was their state!

An "until now," strategically placed at the end of v. 13 in Paul's Greek text, brings the unit to closure. It suggests not only that things are not as they seem to be but also that they soon will be different. The expression harkens back to the "until the present moment" of v. 11, binding closely together elements B (vv. 11-12a) and A' (v. 13) of Paul's chiasm. Despite the difficult situation portrayed in vv. 11-12a all is not lost. Despite the tribulations and their ill-treatment the apostles were able to respond positively to their condition. Despite it all they blessed, endured, and encouraged.

The last named, "encouraged" (*parakaloumen),* is a performative verb. Paul has written as he has in order to exhort the Corinthians. In the pericope that follows (4:14-21) he will explain why he has exhorted the Corinthians as he has. The philosophers of Paul's day used hardship lists to demonstrate their inner tranquility in the face of adversity. The truly wise person, the *sophos,* was one who could cope with the adversities imposed by Fate or the gods. The ability to submit to hardships was a sign of wisdom. Paul used the list of his tribulations in order to portray human weakness, despite which the gospel of God is able to achieve its effect. The hardships he and Apollos endured were a sign of their wisdom (cf. 2:6-7).

The Reversal of Roles. Paul's first antithetical triad (v. 10) suggests a reversal of roles. It rehearses the major themes of 1:26-28. With sarcastic irony Paul criticizes those Corinthians to whom he addresses his remarks as appearing to be what they really are not. In contrast, it is Paul and Apollos who manifest the qualities appropriate to those who are chosen by God. Paul's self-deprecating description echoes various themes developed earlier in the letter. In 2:1-4 he had described himself as one who had come to the Corinthians without words of wisdom (vv. 1, 4), but in weakness and with fear and trembling (v. 3).

The ironically negative description of himself and Apollos in v. 10 is continued in the list of six hardships cited in vv. 11-12a. The vocabulary is typical of the topos, but Paul's lexical choice is such that it enables him and Apollos to identify with the "weak" (4:10b; 9:22) in the community.

In his concluding triad the contrast between the actions of the superior Corinthians and his own behavior enables Paul to focus, as he has done so often in the letter, on his ministry among the Corinthians. His final word is that of encouragement, the leitmotif of the entire epistolary unit (1:10–4:21), encompassed as it is by the use of *parakaleō*, "to encourage" (v. 13a; cf. 1:10; 4:16).

Paul's Work. With reference to his manual labor (v. 12) Paul draws attention to the arduous nature of the way in which he maintained his livelihood, but he does not tell his readers what he actually did for a living. Presumably his audience would know that he was a leather-worker by trade and that at Corinth he had exercised his trade as an associate of Aquila and Prisca (16:19; cf. Acts 18:1-3). The exercise of his trade was part of Paul's missionary strategy (cf. 9:16-18); he could preach the gospel while working away in a shop on the agora (see 1 Thess 2:9; cf. 2 Thess 3:8).

Rabbis—and Paul seems to have been one, at least in a broad sense—like all law-abiding Jewish males were expected to exercise a trade (*m. ʾAbot* 2:2; 4:5; *t. Qidd.* 1:11; *b. Qidd.* 29a). In the Hellenistic world philosophers generally disdained manual labor, preferring to receive their livelihood from the support of a benefactor or fees paid by their pupils. Some Stoics and Cynics, however, preferred to support themselves by the exercise of a trade. Among Paul's contemporaries Dio Chrysostom worked as a gardener, Demetrius of Sunium as a porter, and Musonius Rufus as a farmer. The last of these considered his work to be ideal for a philosopher. "Pupils," he wrote, "would seem to be benefitted by seeing him [the philosopher] at work in the fields, demonstrating by his own labor the lessons which philosophy inculcates—that one should endure hardships, and suffer the pains of labor with his own body, rather than depend upon another for sustenance" (Musonius, frag. 11).

That Paul cites his manual labor within a hardship list (cf. 2 Cor 11:27) suggests that he may have come from the relatively well-to-do classes (cf. 9:19). It is likely that some within the Corinthian community looked down on Paul's manual labor (cf. 2 Cor 11:7-15; 12:13-18). Corinth was a community in which Paul could have found patrons—not only Aquila and Prisca, but also Justus, Crispus, Gaius, Erastus, Quartus, Stephanas, and Chloe. Paul may have refused an offer of financial support from some of the powerful within the community (thus Marshall, *Enmity in Corinth*, 218–257). That Paul provided for his own livelihood by means of manual labor makes his conduct (cf. 9:22) similar to the behavior of those Cynics and Stoics who worked for a living. Some of their ethical paraenesis is similar to Paul's, in content if not in motivation.

NOTES

8. *Already you are satiated! Already you are enriched!* An emphatic "already" (*ēdē*) at the beginning of each of the two clauses draws attention to the present condition of the Corinthians. Now they are satisfied and enriched. As Paul continues his argument he returns to a use of the second person plural. His words recall not only his epistolary thanksgiving (1:5, 7) but also the phrase "all things are yours" that Paul had twice used to describe the Corinthians' situation (3:21-22).

   The verb "to be enriched," *eploutēsate*, is used by Paul only here in this letter (cf. Rom 10:12; 2 Cor 8:9). "To be satiated" (*kekoresmenoi*) is hapax in Paul. Its common connotation is "to have one's appetite for food satisfied," but the expression was often used metaphorically of having one's every need met. Hellenistic philosophical writers see a close link between *hybris* and being sated. Philo often expresses this view. "And as so often happens satiety had begotten *hybris*" (*kai, hoper philei, koros hybrin egennēse)*, he writes (*Migration of Abraham* 228); and again, "we wax wanton through satiety" (*exybrizomen dia koron, Allegorical Interpretation* 2.29, cf. 2.70; *Husbandry* 32, 48; *Flaccus* 91; *Life of Moses* 2.13, 164; *Creation* 169; *Posterity* 98, 145; *Special Laws* 3.43; *Virtues* 162). Paul writes with paradoxical irony about the Corinthians' being satiated (cf. 2 Cor 11:19-20). His real meaning is something other than what he actually states. The irony is biting (cf. 1:26).

   In this letter Paul has much to say about the Corinthians' eating habits. They are not capable of receiving substantial food (cf. 3:2). Paul reminds them that food is meant for the stomach (6:13) and chastises them because some eat and drink to excess while others go without (11:20-21). There is a lengthy discussion on food offered to idols in chs. 8 and 10 that is not without serious implications pertinent to the social situation in Corinth. He reminds them of the idolatrous Israelites who ate and drank (10:7). Finally, the Corinthians' "full bellies" contrast with the hunger and thirst of Paul and those with whom he associates himself (4:11).

   Independently of us you have acted royally! By placing the expression "without us" (*chōris hēmōn*) in an emphatic position at the beginning of the clause, where it parallels the "already" of the previous clauses, Paul underscores the fact that the present condition of those to whom he is addressing his remarks is independent of himself and other preachers of the gospel, specifically Apollos (cf. 3:5-9). It is possible, however, to understand "us" as a reference not only to such "stewards of the mysteries of God" (4:1) as Paul and Apollos but also to the Corinthian community, with whom Paul is linked (2:6-13; 9:22).

Those who claim that all things are lawful disregard the other members of the community. Not without a touch of irony Paul characterizes those who do so as having acted like kings (*ebasileusate,* literally, "to reign," "to be a king"). Those who claim unrestricted liberty are those who are acting like kings. Kings were described by the Stoics as those to whom "all things are lawful" (*hotō panta exesti,* Dio Chrysostom, *Discourses* 3.10; cf. 3.40, 44; Seneca, apropos Nero, *cui omnia licent, Mercy* 1.8.5). This is the phrase Paul uses to characterize those who are causing the problems in Corinth (see 6:12; 10:23). The trouble-makers claim to possess wisdom. The wise man, "the most powerful and best," according to Seneca, "sees the whole human race beneath himself" (*Benefits* 7.3.2). A theme of the wise man as king appears in the writings of both Epictetus and Seneca (*Benefits* 7.2.5; cf. Plutarch, "The Stoics and the Poets," *Moralia* 1058B). Cicero would say about the wise that "if poor they are still rich; if slaves they are still kings" (*Pro Murena* 29.61; cf. *Academia* 2.44.136-137; *De finibus* 3.22.75-76). Wisdom, riches, and royalty appear as a triad in the discourse of the Stoics. Within the Jewish tradition wisdom is likewise associated with acting in a royal fashion. "Honor wisdom," writes the author of the book of Wisdom, "so that you may reign forever" (*timēsate sophian hina eis ton aiōna basileusēte,* Wis 6:21).

Those who act in such fashion, without regard for others, are those described as "hybrists" by Peter Marshall. The traits with which Paul describes them are those associated with *hybris* in philosophical writings from Aristotle to the Stoics. These are the "inspirited ones" (*pneumatikoi*) who boast of their possession of the spirit or spirit-related realities (cf. 12:1). Their situation is sometimes described as "enthusiasm" and their ideological position as a "realized eschatology." "Enthusiasm" (the German *Enthusiasmus*) is virtually a technical term, first used in NT scholarship by Wilhelm Lütgert (1908) to describe the ecstatic and spirit-filled situation of the Corinthians.

And would that you did reign, so that we might also reign with you! In classical Greek *ophelon* followed by the infinitive is used to express a wish that cannot be fulfilled; in Koine Greek the unfulfillable wish is followed by the indicative (compare with Septuagintal usage, e.g., Exod 16:3; Num 14:2; 20:3, and Epictetus, *Discourses* 2.18.15), as it is here. Paul gives emphasis to his unfulfilled and unfulfillable wish by using the emphatic particle *ge* (BDF 439.2). The wish is a corrective to those among the Corinthians who were acting like kings. With their overly realized eschatology Paul contrasts his "eschatological reservation," the "already but not yet" of the eschaton. The kingdom has not yet come (cf. 6:13; 15:12) but Paul expresses the wish that it had come. His wish is an expression of eschatological hope with the understanding that the coming of the kingdom depends neither on himself nor on the Corinthians. The coming of the kingdom of God depends only on God.

Paul wants the Corinthian hybrists to share in the kingdom of God, where they and the entire community would truly be regal. His wish stands in sharp contrast with the preceding clause. The hybrists have been acting in regal fashion but the kingdom has not yet come. They have acted "without us," but when the kingdom comes "we also" shall reign. Paul's doubly emphatic "we also" (*kai hēmeis,* with an emphatic *kai* and the use of an emphatic pronoun) underscores the communitarian dimension of eschatological existence.

To describe the Corinthians as having acted like kings and to express his wish for the coming of the kingdom Paul uses the simple verb *basileuō,* "to reign." When he speaks of the expected result of the fulfillment of his wish he uses the compound verb *symbasileuō,* "to reign together with." The language of Paul's letters is typically marked by an unusual number of compound verbs with the preface *syn,* "with" or "co." Paul himself has apparently coined some of these verbs. As a group the *syn*-verbs generally speak of the solidarity of those who share in the experience of salvation. See, for example, Rom 6:4-8, "buried with *(synetaphēmen)* . . . united with *(symphytoi)* . . . crucified with *(synestaurōthē)* . . . live with *(syzēsomen)."*

9. *For I think that God has made a show of us as the last apostles, like people sentenced to death, because we have become a spectacle to the universe, to angels and to humans alike:* Having countered the self-sufficiency (v. 7) of the Corinthians with the irony of v. 8 Paul offers a further reflection that is consistent with the *ethos* appeal of his argument but also appeals to the *pathos* of the Corinthians. His powerful image is introduced by a verbal construction that lacks the usual connecting conjunction (asyndeton, BDF 461.2).

Paul's powerful image maintains the primacy of God in the apostolate and offers a self-deprecating description of himself (and others) as an apostle (see 15:8-9). Paul's image comes from the amphitheater. To construct the image he uses vocabulary he does not otherwise employ: "make a show," *(apodeiknymi),* "sentenced to death" *(epithanatios),* and "spectacle" *(theatron).* Although Paul describes himself as one called last of all in 15:8, his use of "last" *(eschatous)* in 4:9 comes from the image he is portraying. Conquering generals returned home in triumphal procession (see the imagery of 1 Thess 4:16-17). Prisoners condemned to die in the arena brought up the rear of the parade.

In the Greco-Roman world gladiators' struggles unto death provided entertainment for the rich and the powerful in the *theatron.* These fatal contests were the final events on the program. The mortal combats actually took place in an amphitheater, an enclosed oval structure. Paul presents himself and Apollos as providing entertainment, as it were, for the entire cosmos, humans and angels (cf. 6:2; 10:11; 13:1) alike. "All the world's a stage," wrote Shakespeare (*As You Like It* 2.7.139). Paul envisioned himself on the cosmic stage. His image suggests that the Corinthians belonged, as it were, to the royal claque. The contrast between himself and the Corinthians will be further developed in the peristatic catalogue of the verses that follow.

10. *We are fools for the sake of Christ, and you are prudent in Christ; we are weak, and you are strong; you are held in esteem, and we are without honor:* Paul's first group of hardships is formed as a literary subset by a "we" (*hēmeis*) at the beginning and end of the unit. The subset contrasts the situation of Paul and his companions with the wise and strong in the community in an antithetical triad. A threefold use of the emphatic "we" (*hēmeis*) and "you" (*hymeis*) underscores the contrast. In a letter that disavows the use of rhetoric (2:1-5) Paul employs

the rhetorical device of *sygkrisis*, comparison, to discredit the powerful and confirm his own authority. The rhetorical force of this first group is heightened by its lack of any verb.

The first contrasting pair is expanded by the christological reference. Explicit with reference to the first antithetical pair, it is implied for the two following pairs as well. Given the role of the fool *(mōros)* in classical commentary on the social situation it is not impossible that the first epithet used by Paul continues to exploit the theatrical imagery introduced in v. 9 (see the "fool's speech" in 2 Cor 11:21b–12:20). In contrast with fools, the Corinthians are prudent *(phronimoi,* cf. 10:15). Prudence, a virtue that dictated a pattern of human behavior, was the first of the four cardinal virtues (Philo, *Allegorical Interpretation* 1.66-67). The prudence of the wise person was legendary (Philo, *Every Good Man is Free* 59). The prudent may do whatever they wish (Dio Chrysostom, *Discourses* 14.17).

A chiastic structure (vv. 10b-c, see BDF 477.2) brings Paul's second and third antitheses together as a subset within the first triad. Weakness is characteristic of his apostolate (9:22). The third contrast formally introduces notions of shame and honor, so important in Hellenistic society. Although he had not previously described himself as being without honor *(atimos,* cf. 12:23), Paul had presented himself as one who might be judged by the Corinthians or some human court (4:3). In the society in which he lived, more often than not it was the weak and powerless who were subject to court proceedings (see below, in the commentary on 6:1-11).

In contrast with Paul and Apollos the Corinthian hybrists are prudent, strong, and of good repute. The list of epithets recalls a series of questions raised by Simeon b. Zoma, a younger contemporary of Rabbi Aqiba, who asked, "Who is wise . . . Who is rich . . . Who is honored?" *(m. ʾAbot* 4:1). Paul's description of the Corinthians recalls and contrasts with the rhetorical utterance in 1:26-28. Then the Corinthians were portrayed as being for the most part not wise, powerful, or well-born. Such a condition qualified them for God's claim and call. Ironically they now appear to be virtually unqualified for God's call. Their inflated self-esteem earns a characterization meriting for them God's disqualification (see 1:27-28). In contrast, the epithets with which Paul describes himself and Apollos qualify them for God's call and claim. They are as the Corinthians once were.

11–12. *Until this very hour we are hungry, and we are thirsty, and we are naked, and we are beaten, and we are homeless, and we toil, working with our own hands:* The triadic contrast of v. 10 had followed a we-you, we-you, you-we order. Its final "we" provides an introduction to a rehearsal of additional hardships suffered by Paul and Apollos. The six hardships, two groups of three, are linked together by a repeated "and" *(kai).* The parataxis heightens the *pathos* of the description, providing a cumulative effect as yet another hardship continues to be added to a shorter list.

Hunger and thirst are common experiences of the poor (see 11:21-22). The hunger and thirst of Paul and Apollos contrast with the satiety of the Corinthians. Nakedness *(gymniteuomen,* hapax in the NT) is not so much total nudity (cf. 2 Cor 5:3) as it is having tattered and threadbare clothing (cf. Seneca, *Benefits* 5.13.3). Describing himself as one who is hungry, thirsty, and naked, Paul identifies with the "have nots" at Corinth. "Beaten" *(kolaphizometha)* and "homeless" *(astatoumen)* are hapax in 1 Corinthians. "To be homeless" is literally "to be unstable and unsteady." It characterizes the existence of the homeless wanderer. Toil is hard work *(TLNT* 2:322–329). This toil may recall the rewarded work in 3:8.

The sixth hardship breaks the rhythm of the list. Previously Paul used five verbs joined by a paratactic *kai.* Now he qualifies the verb *kopiōmen*, "we toil," with a participial expression "working with our own hands." Given the image of himself as a slave that he presents in the letter (9:19-23), the description of himself as one who had worked with his own hands may also be an example of his identifying with the group of people from the lower socioeconomic strata who comprised the greater part of the Corinthian Christian community (1:26).

Slandered, we bless; persecuted, we endure patiently; insulted, we encourage: Having broken the rhythmic listing of the hardships he endured with a comment on his manual labor, Paul continues the list in yet another format. This third group, consisting of another three hardships, completes the list of life's difficulties (vv. 10-13a). The antithetical triad forms a chiasm with the contrasting trio of v. 10.

Like the first group of hardships, this group makes effective use of the literary device of contrast. Using participles, Paul identifies slander, persecution, and insult as hardships he had endured (cf. 1 Thess 2:2). Peristatic catalogues typically indicate that the adverse circumstances are beyond the control of the one who is suffering from them, suggesting that they come from Fate *(Tychē)* or from a god *(theos).* Paul's passive participles seem, however, to suggest that these particular tribulations had been inflicted upon Paul by the Corinthian hybrists.

The participles Paul uses to describe himself are not otherwise used by him in self-referential fashion. "Slander" *(loidoreō)* and "insult" *(dysphēmeō;* see the related *dysphēmia* in 2 Cor 6:8) are hapax in the Pauline corpus. They attest to the typical vocabulary of the classic hardship lists. Paul uses the verb "to persecute" *(diōkō)* when he acknowledges that he has persecuted the church of God (15:9; Gal 1:13, 23; Phil 3:6). That he and others were persecuted is echoed in the peristatic catalogue of 2 Cor 4:7-12 (see v. 9). Paul may have been opposed by some at Corinth (1:12), and his travel plans were viewed with suspicion (4:18).

To each participle Paul appends a verb indicating a contrary action. The combination of *repetitio* and contrast provides an emphatic effect and prepares for Paul's strong summarizing conclusion in v. 13b. The contrasts used by Paul are echoed in the paraenesis of Rom 12:14 and the hardship list of 2 Cor 4:8-9. Paul and those associated with him bless *(eulogoumen,* 4:12; cf. Rom 12:14), bear up patiently *(anechometha;* cf. 2 Cor 11:1, 4, 19, 20), and encourage *(parakaloumen).* Like the Stoics who thought that there was a lesson to be learned by others from the hardships they had endured, Paul cites his hardships in a context of paraenesis. Although insulted, he will encourage *(parakaleō)* the Corinthian hybrists. In the following epistolary unit (4:14-21) he will encourage them to follow his example (4:16, with the *parakaleō* that forms an *inclusio* with 1:10). He will remind the Corinthians of his ways in Christ (4:17), the christological title that evokes the death of Jesus. The exhortation to learn from his example is introduced by the twelfth member of the hardship list.

13. *We have become like the refuse of the world, the scum of all until now:* "Until now" *(heōs arti)* forms an *inclusio* with "until this very hour" *(achri tēs arti hōras)* of v. 11. The image, however, forms an *inclusio* with the image of v. 9. The two images complement one another. In the exposition of each of the similes Paul uses the comparative particle *hōs* ("like") and the verb *egenēthēmen* ("have become"). He provides a cosmic perspective with the use of "world" *(kosmos)* with a comprehensive expression ("angels and humans"; "all") in apposition. In both cases divine agency is implied as the cause of the apostles' being reduced to the status of refuse and scum.

Paul's temporal phrase, "until now," also recalls the repeated "already" of v. 8. The result is a striking contrast between the hybrists, well-satisfied, prosperous, and acting like kings, and Paul, apparently condemned to death, a spectacle, the scum of the earth. Paul's forceful but figurative language employs two terms that do not otherwise appear in the NT, "refuse" *(perikatharma)* and "scum" *(peripsēma)*. These are vulgar synonyms. Etymologically they evoke what has been washed away, like dirt from dirty dishes, and what has been rubbed off and thus is to be tossed away (See Friedrich Hauck, *perikatharma, TDNT* 3:430–431; Gustav Stählin, *peripsēma, TDNT* 6:84–93; *TLNT* 3:93–95).

In Greek literature the terms "refuse" and "scum" were sometimes used figuratively as terms of insult and abuse for criminals and other persons whom society held in utter contempt. Occasionally they were used to describe expiatory scapegoats. Because of the parallelism between vv. 13 and 9 it may be that Paul is suggesting a willingness to be an expiatory victim, in which case Paul's thought would be similar to what he expresses in 1 Cor 15:31; 2 Cor 4:10-11; Gal 6:17; Phil 2:17. Even without this possible nuance— and perhaps more so without it—the graphic metaphor functions as a fitting climax to Paul's list of hardships.

FOR REFERENCE AND FURTHER STUDY

Fitzgerald, John T. *Cracks in an Earthen Vessel: An Examination of the Catalogues of Hardships in the Corinthian Correspondence.* SBL.DS 99. Atlanta: Scholars, 1988.

Gibbs, Jeffrey A. "Wisdom, Power and Wellbeing," ICBS, Studia biblica 3; JSNT.S 3. Elizabeth A. Livingstone, ed. Sheffield: JSOT, 1980, 119–155.

Hanson, Anthony T. "1 Corinthians 4:13b and Lamentations 3:45," *ExpT* 93 (1982) 214–215.

Hock, Ronald F. "Paul's Tentmaking and the Problem of his Social Class," *JBL* 97 (1978) 555–564.

_____. *The Social Context of Paul's Ministry: Tentmaking and Apostleship.* Philadelphia: Fortress, 1980.

Hodgson, Robert Jr. "Paul the Apostle and First Century Tribulation Lists," *ZNW* 74 (1983) 59–80.

Marshall, Peter. *Enmity in Corinth*, 194–257.

10. *A Letter of Admonition* (4:14-16)

> 14. I am writing these things not to make you ashamed, but to admonish you as my beloved children. 15. For even if you should have innumerable tutors in Christ you do not have many fathers; for I have sired you in Christ Jesus by means of the gospel. 16. Therefore, I urge you, be imitators of me.

Interpretation

In this section Paul reflects in rather self-conscious fashion on why it was that he was writing to the Corinthians. The tone of his words is similar to that found in the well-known Hellenistic letter of admonition. The letter of admonition, says Pseudo-Demetrius, is "one which indicates by its name what its character is. For admonition is the instilling of sense in the person who is being admonished, and teaching him what should and should not be done" (*Epistolary Types* 7).

In his brief description of the letter of admonition (*typos nouthetētikos*), Pseudo-Demetrius twice uses the verb "to admonish" (*noutheteō*), the same verb Paul uses to describe his purpose in writing. Paul underscores that this is indeed his purpose by contrasting his admonition with an attempt merely to put the Corinthians to shame (*entrepōn*). His letter takes the place of his personal presence, and Paul suggests that if the Corinthians do not change their ways it might be necessary for him to come with the rod (4:21). Paul's remarks on why he was writing to the Corinthians (cf. 5:9; 9:15; 14:37) confirm the paraenetic purpose of 1:10–4:16 and clearly type the composition as a piece of deliberative rhetoric.

Paul, the Father. To enhance the authority on the basis of which he admonishes the Corinthians Paul refers to them as his children and to himself as their only father (1 Thess 2:11-12; Phlm 10). The contrast between himself and the innumerable tutors (*paidagōgous*) of the Corinthians highlights his authority over them. Not only is there a contrast between the greater and the lesser, but also between the one and the many. In the Greco-Roman world "pedagogues" were not teachers as such. Pedagogues were lower-status slaves who accompanied children to school, disciplining them when necessary. By the time of the Hellenistic era the picture of the pedagogue had changed. No longer were pedagogues regularly portrayed as strict disciplinarians who would beat their charges to gain compliance with their orders. Rather they were revered as tutors whose role in the education of the young was truly appreciated.

Paul contrasts the many tutors available to the Corinthians with the reality of their having a single father. Paul shares first-century Judaism's understanding of paternity, in which the principal role of the father was to ensure the socialization of his sons. According to rabbinic tradition "the father is bound in respect of his son, to circumcise, redeem, teach him Torah, take a wife for him, and teach him a craft" (*b. Qidd.* 22a). In the circumcision ceremony the father manifested commitment to care for and nurture the infant son so that he would eventually learn the Torah, take a wife, and perform good deeds. To have taught the Torah to another's child was like having begotten that child (cf. *b. Sanh.* 19b). The child had become a son to him. Paul seems to share these views, but with one notable difference. The gospel replaces the Torah as the means of generation (cf. Phlm 10).

Imitation of Paul. Paul's first rhetorical proof concludes in v. 16 with a summary exhortation addressed to the Corinthians as Paul's beloved children, urging them to imitate him. This is one of two "imitation" (*mimētēs*) passages in 1 Corinthians (cf. 11:1), of which there are four all told in the extant correspondence (cf. Phil 3:17; 1 Thess 1:6).

The use of the singular in this summarizing exhortation is striking. In simple and straightforward language the exhortation affirms that Paul is placing himself before the Corinthians as an example to be followed. Essentially he has already done that by writing about himself and Apollos in an extended topos that proved to be an example of covert allusion (4:6). Paul's own example will continue to serve as a powerful rhetorical argument throughout the letter. In 7:8 he offers himself as an example to once-married persons who are facing a decision as to whether they should remarry. In ch. 9 he digresses at length on his own willingness to forego his apostolic rights in order to provide the Corinthians with an example and concludes his treatment of the food-offered-to-idols issue with another exhortation urging that the Corinthians imitate him (11:1). As he has willingly given up the use of his rights for the sake of the gospel, so those Corinthians who are sufficiently mature to realize that idols have no real existence should willingly forego their right to eat food offered to idols for the sake of their brothers and sisters within the community.

In dealing with the spiritual gifts in chs. 12–14 Paul offers himself as an example in the introduction (13:1-3) to the paean on love and speaks of his own gift of glossolalia (14:6, 14-15) when he tackles the specific issue of speaking in tongues. Paul's use of his own example is a feature of the kind of deliberative rhetoric he employs in his letter to the Corinthians. It was a key feature of his *ethos* appeal. In his moral epistles Seneca also appealed to the authority of his own example (see Bünker, *Briefformular* 44).

Thus far in his letter Paul has presented himself to the Corinthians as one who was sent to preach the gospel, as one who has eschewed the niceties of rhetoric, and as one who responded to his Christian calling by working alongside Apollos in building up the community. In the epistolary postscript that follows (4:17-21) Paul will develop another motif. His children should remember to follow his ways. The biblical tradition spoke of a father's teaching his children the ways of the Lord and the ways of wisdom. Paul will write about his children learning his own ways in Christ Jesus (4:17).

Notes

14. *I am writing these things not to make you ashamed, but to admonish you as my beloved children:* Paul's first reflection on why it was that he had chosen to write to the Corinthians places the reader in a culture of honor and shame that so characterized the Mediterranean world in his day. His language is exceptional. "To put you to shame" (*entrepō;* cf. 2 Thess 3:14; Titus 2:8) is a verb he does not otherwise use. As a formula of direct address Paul generally uses "brothers and sisters" in his letters—sixty-five times in all. Only occasionally does he refer to his addressees as his children (cf. Gal 4:19; 2 Cor 6:13; 12:14). Paul recognizes the metaphorical character of his language. The Corinthian Christians are "as" or "like" (*hōs;* cf. 3:1; 1 Thess 2:7, 11) his beloved children. For Paul to write about the Corinthians in this fashion is more than for him to make use of a common literary (epistolary) convention or a trite expression. Paul had already portrayed the Corinthians as his children, but in 3:1-2 the imagery was maternal rather than paternal as it is in 4:14-15.

      Paul's love for the Corinthians is expressed later in the letter when he addresses them as his "beloved" (10:14; cf. 2 Cor 7:1; 12:19) and as his "beloved brothers and sisters" (15:58). His love for the Corinthians is reiterated in the unusual postscript with which he closes the letter (16:24). In later correspondence Paul continues to assure the Corinthians of his love (2 Cor 8:7; 12:15). Some manuscripts of 2 Cor 8:7, including the majority of the medieval manuscripts and some of the older majuscules (א, C, F, G, Ψ) read the text as if Paul were writing of the Corinthians' love for him rather than of his love for them, suggesting that his love for them should be reciprocated (2 Cor 12:15).

15. *For even if you should have innumerable tutors in Christ you do not have many fathers:* Paul recognizes the role of the various teachers in the community. In

the Hellenistic era the "tutor" (*paidagōgos,* one who leads a child along the way; cf. Gal 3:24-25) was no longer simply the slave who accompanied a child to school; he was also a virtual instructor (see *TLNT* 3:1-3). The several (*myrious,* elsewhere in Paul only in 14:19) guides of the Corinthian community are important, but they have a lesser role than does the (one) father (cf. 3:10). After the conditional (*ean*), Paul's "but" (*alla*) has the sense of "yet, certainly, at least" (BDF 448.5), but it seems best to leave the conjunction untranslated.

for I have sired you in Christ Jesus by means of the gospel: Paul explains (*gar*) why he can call the Corinthians his children and why he can make a paternal claim on them: He has engendered them through the gospel he has preached (cf. Phlm 10). The adoption of children in this way is an expression of Paul's paternal love for the Corinthian Christians.

16. *Therefore, I urge you, be imitators of me:* The resumptive *oun* ("therefore") is one of the most commonly used Greek particles. *Oun* is also one of the most frequently used consecutive coordinating conjunctions in the NT. In Hellenistic letters the particle was used as an epistolary convention to make a transition between the background for a request and the request itself (cf. 10:31; 16:18). Paul's use of the particle in 4:16 allows him to bring his argument to closure with an appeal to the Corinthians, urging them to emulate Paul himself. "I urge you" (*parakalō . . . hymas*) hearkens back to 1:10, forming an inclusio with Paul's statement of purpose. In this fashion 1:10–4:16 is circumscribed as the first major epistolary unit in 1 Corinthians, the exposition of Paul's first rhetorical demonstration. What follows (4:17-21) is a kind of epistolary postscript added to the first rhetorical proof. Speaking of Paul's travel plans, its function is that of expressing apostolic *parousia*.

FOR REFERENCE AND FURTHER STUDY

Castelli, Elizabeth A. *Imitating Paul: A Discourse of Power.* Louisville: Westminster/ John Knox, 1991.

Gutierrez, Pedro. *La paternité spirituelle selon saint Paul.* EtB. Paris: Gabalda, 1968, 119–211.

Jenkins, Claude. "Documents: Origen on I Corinthians IV," *JThS* 10 (1909) 29–51.

Lassen, Eva Maria. "The Use of the Father Image in Imperial Propaganda and 1 Corinthians 4:14-21," *TynB* 42 (1991) 127–136.

Sanders, Boykin. "Imitating Paul: 1 Cor 4:16," *HThR* 74 (1981) 353–363.

11. *Recommendation of Timothy* (4:17-21)

17. For this reason I sent to you Timothy, who is my beloved and faithful child in the Lord, to remind you about my ways in Christ Jesus, as I teach everywhere in every church. 18. When I didn't come to you, some

became conceited. 19. I will come to you quickly, the Lord willing, and I will get to know, not the word of those who are conceited, but their power; 20. for the kingdom of God is not in word, it is rather in power. 21. What do you want? That I should come to you with a rod or with love and a spirit of gentleness?

INTERPRETATION

In the Hellenistic world the primary function of the letter was that of *parousia*, presence, specifically making oneself present when, in fact, one was absent. Paul's reflections on the purpose of his letter in 4:14-16 are immediately followed by a unit that bears the traits of a letter of recommendation. In that unit Paul explicitly writes about his absence and his expected presence in the future. In the meantime he has sent Timothy to exercise a charge on his behalf. Thus in the epistolary conclusion to the first rhetorical proof (1:10–4:21) Paul dwells on the motif of presence in person, by letter, and through an emissary.

Epistolary characteristics continue to be present in this section of Paul's letter. Some aspects of it, particularly the recommendation of Timothy, echo features of the Hellenistic letter of recommendation. Closely linked to what Paul has already written, it functions as a kind of epistolary postscript that brings to closure Paul's first rhetorical proof. From this perspective it functions as a kind of rhetorical peroration.

Paul's Emissary. Timothy (see 16:10-11) was a trusted fellow missionary with Paul and in many respects his chief lieutenant. His name appears in the salutation of several Pauline letters (1 Thess 1:1; 2 Cor 1:1; Phil 1:1; Phlm 1; cf. 2 Thess 1:1; Col 1:1). At different times Paul calls him his child (here and Phil 2:22; cf. 1 Tim 1:2; 2 Tim 1:2), his brother (1 Thess 3:2; 2 Cor 1:1; Phlm 1), and his fellow worker (1 Thess 3:2; Rom 16:21). Paul also speaks of him as God's coworker in the proclamation of the gospel (1 Thess 3:2). That Paul calls Timothy his child suggests that Timothy was evangelized by Paul. Paul describes himself as a father insofar as he had brought people to faith (4:15; Phlm 10) and had fostered their leading a Christian life.

The Acts of the Apostles notes that because of the good reputation he enjoyed among his fellow Christians Timothy, a man of mixed ethnicity, was chosen by Paul as a companion on the missionary voyages (Acts 16:2-3). On Paul's own testimony Timothy had worked with Paul in the evangelization of such communities as Philippi, Thessalonica, and Corinth (Phil 2:22; 1 Thess 3:2; 2 Cor 1:19). Paul indicates that he had no one like Timothy in his entourage (Phil 2:20) and that he could hardly bear to be without him (1 Thess 3:1). Nonetheless, Paul sent Timothy to each of these communities as his personal and trusted emissary, particularly when circumstances prevented Paul from visiting the community as he would have liked to do (4:17; Phil 2:19-24; 1 Thess 3:1-6). Later tradition honored Timothy by choosing him as the patronymic recipient of two of the pastoral epistles (1 Timothy; 2 Timothy) and revered him as the first bishop of Ephesus (Eusebius, *Ecclesiastical History* 3.4.5).

In 1 Cor 4:18 and Phil 2:22 Paul calls Timothy his child in order to recommend him to the community (see 1 Cor 16:10-11; cf. 1 Tim 1:2; 2 Tim 1:2; compare Titus 1:4). The motif of Timothy, beloved and faithful child of the Apostle, is taken up in the salutations of the NT's epistles to Timothy. The first epistle to Timothy characterizes Paul's aide as "my true child in the faith" (1 Tim 1:2), echoing Paul's "faithful child in the Lord." The second epistle characterizes him as Paul's "beloved child" (2 Tim 1:2), a phrase that harkens back to Paul's "my beloved child." These later descriptions of Timothy as Paul's faithful son indicate that Timothy had indeed learned the tradition from Paul and was faithful to it. The description thus contributes to the Pauline warrant on which is based the authority of these pastoral epistles (cf. Titus 1:4).

Although Timothy had been sent to Corinth, he had not yet arrived at the time when Paul was writing his letter (see 16:10). Many authors, both ancient and modern (e.g., Robert Funk, Linda Belleville), take Paul's aorist ("I sent") to be an epistolary aorist, with the implied possibility that it was Timothy who took Paul's letter to the Corinthians. In that case Timothy's not-yet-arrival would have been obvious. Among the Fathers both Origen and Chrysostom (*PG* 61, 12) believed that Paul sent Timothy to Corinth in order to deliver the letter he had written. On the other hand, the absence of Timothy's name from the letter's opening salutation (1:1; cf. 2 Cor 1:1) and the tenor of 16:10 serve to suggest that Timothy was not with Paul as he was writing the letter. Theodoret (*PG* 82, 228) was among the Fathers who were of the opinion that Timothy was not the carrier of Paul's letter (cf. 16:15-18). Should the canonical first letter to the Corinthians be a composite text, as some scholars hold (see above, pp. 10–14), it would be possible for Timothy to have carried one letter to the Corinthians and for Stephanas's group to have delivered another.

A Recommendation. The letter of recommendation *(typos systatikos)* was the second on Pseudo-Demetrius' list of twenty-one epistolary types. Paul was familiar with this kind of letter (see 2 Cor 3:1-2; Rom 16:1-2; cf. 1 Cor 16:3). In the personal correspondence of the Greco-Roman world the letter of recommendation was frequently a letter of introduction of the letter carrier accompanied by a request that the bearer be offered hospitality. Pseudo-Demetrius offered this textbook example:

> So-and-so, who is conveying this letter to you, has been tested by us and is loved on account of his trustworthiness *(di' hēn echei pistin agapōmenon).*

You will do well if you deem him worthy of hospitality both for my sake and his, and indeed for your own. For you will not be sorry if you entrust to him, in any matter you wish, either words or deeds of a confidential nature. Indeed, you, too, will praise him to others when you see how useful he can be in everything.

In diplomatic circles the letter of introduction followed a rather standard format: the name of the person being introduced, that person's relationship to the sender, qualifications, and assignment. These traits are to be found in Paul's description of Timothy, who has been sent to the Corinthians on Paul's behalf. Paul frequently used envoys when circumstances prevented him from returning to a community that he had evangelized and that had a need for his pastoral care (see 1 Cor 16:3; 2 Cor 8:18, 22; 9:3; 12:17; Phil 2:19, 23, 25, 28; 1 Thess 3:2; cf. Col 4:8). In Paul's world it was assumed that emissaries should be treated according to the status of the one who had sent the emissary, not on the basis of the emissary's personal qualities. It was further assumed that emissaries enjoyed a considerable amount of power. In some respects they were virtually plenipotentiary envoys. In the extant Greco-Roman diplomatic letters reference to this representative status of envoys and the power they enjoyed is explicitly expressed (e.g., the second Socratic epistle).

First Corinthians 4:17-21 has many of the characteristics of the classic letter of recommendation, including the explicit mention of the sending of Timothy, the citation of his qualities as one who is beloved and faithful, and the indication of the task that has been entrusted to him (cf. Rom 16:1-2). Paul's discourse about his not having come and now having an intention to come to the Corinthians is also an expression of an epistolary convention. Three times he uses the verb "to come" *(erchomai)*. Hellenistic letters frequently speak of the absence of the letter-writer from those to whom the letter is addressed and express the letter-writer's wish that he or she might soon be able to visit those to whom the letter is being written.

These epistolary features have led many authors to conclude that 4:17-21 was part of an earlier letter written by Paul that a later compiler put together with other Pauline correspondence to form the canonical first letter to the Corinthians. One should not, however, be overly rigorous in the interpretation of the epistolary features of Paul's composition. "There should be," wrote Demetrius, "a certain degree of freedom in the structure of a letter. It is absurd to build up periods, as if you were writing not a letter but a speech for the law courts" *(On Style* 229).

Summing Up. In the hypothesis of the unitary composition of 1 Corinthians, 4:17-21 serves as a kind of epistolary peroration that rehearses some of the principal themes of the rhetorical unit: the example of Paul, the conceit of some of those to whom he is writing, the motifs of word and power, and the eschaton in the light of which all things must be judged.

In paternal fashion Paul writes about his coming to the Corinthians. In his absence some became conceited, but he hopes soon to be able to visit with the Corinthians. The manner of his presence among them, as a strict disciplinarian or as a loving father, depends on their response to his letter. The choice is theirs.

Having thus summarized the thrust of his exhortative letter Paul can turn to one of the specifics in the report he had received from Chloe's people (1:11), namely, a case of incest in the community.

NOTES

17. *For this reason:* The *lectio brevior, dia touto,* "for this reason," is found in two of the ancient papyri ($\mathfrak{P}^{46, 68}$) and most of the major majuscules (B, C, D, G, L, Ψ, etc.). The Codex Sinaiticus, along with $\mathfrak{P}^{11}$, the Codex Alexandrinus, and several of the minuscules, had a more emphatic reading, *dia touto auto,* "for this very reason," but the emphasis has been removed from the Sinaiticus by an erstwhile corrector. The simpler reading is to be preferred, not only on the basis of Bengel's *lectio brevior* principle but also because of its widely diverse attestation. Bailey ("Structure of I Corinthians") considers the verse to be an indirect statement about Paul's theological methodology and an introduction to the following section of the letter, that he considers to have been a collection of five originally independent essays.

    I sent to you Timothy: Paul's aorist, "sent" *(epempsa),* may be a genuine aorist or it may be an epistolary aorist. If it is a genuine aorist Paul had sent Timothy to the Corinthians at some time prior to writing this letter. If the verb form is an epistolary aorist its "past tense" is relative. It would imply that Paul had sent Timothy prior to the time when the Corinthians were reading this part of the letter. In the Hellenistic world the epistolary aorist was frequently used in letters accompanying shipments of goods as well as is in letters that served to introduce the letter carrier (see "Interpretation").

    who is my beloved and faithful child: In the Pauline correspondence only Timothy and Onesimus (Phlm 10) are identified by name as being Paul's children. Onesimus was a slave whom Paul had "sired" *(egennēsa)* while in prison (Phlm 10). Fathered by Paul, Onesimus has become Paul's "beloved brother" *(adelphos agapētos,* Phlm 16). The mixture of kinship language is typical of Paul (see above on 3:1). He uses the language of siblings when he wants to identify someone who belongs to the Christian community; he uses paternal language when he wants to draw attention to his having evangelized a person with the result that they have entered into the Christian family. Onesimus was evangelized by Paul. Apparently Timothy was also evangelized by Paul. Paul has just explained (v. 15b) that he has become a father by preaching the gospel.

In the judgment of Hellenistic moralists fathers were expected to love their children. They were to be *philoteknoi,* children-lovers (see Plutarch, "Brotherly Love," *Moralia* 480A-D). Timothy's fidelity to Paul would become legendary (cf. 2 Tim 1:2). The commendation of Timothy as Paul's beloved and faithful child is, nonetheless, an epistolary convention. In Hellenistic letters of recommendation it was typical for the letter-writer to laud the trustworthiness of the one to be recommended. Among the traits that enhanced the recommendation was the author's love for the one being recommended (see Pseudo-Demetrius, "Epistolary Types," above, pp. 197–198).

in the Lord: "In the Lord," *en Kyriǭ,* is a classic Pauline phrase (e.g., Rom 16:2, 9, 11, 12[2x], 13, 22). The formula appears in a variety of forms in the Pauline letters. The simple form, "in the Lord," without further qualification, is used six additional times in 1 Corinthians (7:22, 39, 9:1, 2; 11:11; 15:58). Sometimes the formula simply means "Christian" (cf. Acts 11:26). In 4:17 use of the prepositional phrase suggests that Paul has engendered Timothy by the proclamation of the gospel of our Lord Jesus Christ. In v. 15b reference had been made to the gospel of Jesus Christ; now it is suggested that the gospel is the gospel of the Lord. Given the nuance of authority that attaches to *Kyrios* one might find in Paul's characterization of Timothy as his child in the Lord a reference to the fact that Timothy followed Paul's ways in Christ; that is, he had really accepted Christ as his Lord. In contrast, Paul chides the Corinthians for not having done so.

to remind you about my ways in Christ Jesus: A relative clause expresses the purpose of Paul's having sent Timothy to Corinth (BDF 351.1; 378). Only in 1 Corinthians does Paul use the term "way" (*hodos;* cf. 12:31) to indicate a way of life, a pattern of behavior, that he here qualifies as being "in Christ Jesus." As is often the case with the name of Jesus and his epithets the manuscript tradition offers several variants of the prepositional phrase. "Christ Jesus" is found in 𝔓⁴⁶, ℵ, C, and many of the medieval manuscripts, but a series of medieval manuscripts and some of the ancient majuscules (A, B) have "Christ" alone. "Lord Jesus" is a Western reading (D, F, G), probably under the influence of "Lord" in 17b. "Christ Jesus" is found in the most ancient witnesses and appears to be the reading from which the other readings have been derived.

A doctrine of two ways was an important feature in the Jewish ethical tradition. See *T. Asher* 1:3-5, with further elaboration in 1:6–5:4, and *2 Enoch* 30:15. A succinct biblical formulation of the doctrine is found in Jer 21:8-14 (cf. Sir 15:11-17). Roots of the idea go back to the choices set before Israel by Moses (Deut 30:15-16) and Joshua (24:15). The idea has parallels with Qumran's notion of the two spirits (e.g., 1QS 3:13–4:26). The motif of the two ways was exploited in some of the earliest of Christian writings outside of the NT, especially *Did.* 1, 5–6 and *Barn.* 18–20 (*PG* 2, 775–780), and became quite popular in post-apostolic Christian writings (*Apostolic Constitutions* 7:1; *PG* 1, 997–1000; *Pseudo-Clementine Homilies* 15.7; *PG* 2, 360–361; Clement of Alexandria, *Stromata* 5.5.60-61; *PG* 9, 53–54).

as I teach everywhere in every church: This is the first instance of Paul's use of the "ecclesiastical argument" in 1 Corinthians. His use of the ecclesiastical argument was foreshadowed in the opening salutation when Paul addressed the Corinthian community as being "together with all those in every place who invoke the name of our Lord Jesus Christ" (1:2). Paul's teaching the Corinthians is an expression of his paternal relationship with them (cf. 1 Thess 2:10-12). In the Greco-Roman world father and mother shared responsibility for educating their children, but in Judaism responsibility for children's education fell to the father (cf. Z. W. Falk, *Introduction to Jewish Law of the Second Commonwealth* [Leiden: Brill, 1978] 2.323). As with the citation of his own example (see "Interpretation" above, pp. 193–194), recourse to the ecclesiastical argument is had in each of first four rhetorical proofs of 1 Corinthians (cf. 7:17; 11:16; 14:33).

18. *When I didn't come to you, some became conceited:* "To become conceited" *(physioō)* always has a pejorative sense in Paul's writings. It refers to arrogant behavior that goes beyond the bonds of moderation (see above, p. 177). Learning from Paul's example and following his ways are antithetical to becoming conceited (cf. 4:6). Paul's absence gave occasion to some to become conceited. Those who are conceited are so because they have espoused the wisdom of this world (1:20) rather than the wisdom of God.

19. *I will come to you quickly, the Lord willing:* Absence and presence are typical epistolary motifs. Hellenistic letters frequently speak of the writer's desire to go to the one to whom he or she is writing and to do so without undue delay. On March 26, 107 C.E. a young soldier, Julius Apollinarios, wrote to his father, "just as soon as the commander begins to grant furloughs, I shall come to you immediately *(eutheōs elthin pros hymas)*" (P.Michigan 8.466). Paul's expressed desire to go to the Corinthians and his reflection on his absence, both using the verb "to come" *(erchomai,* vv. 18a, 19a; cf. 2 Cor 12:14; 13:1; Rom 15:32; see further Phlm 22), are epistolary conventions. "The Lord willing" is a conditional clause in Greek *(ean ho kyrios thelēsē;* cf. Rom 15:32), which has the same conditional meaning as the common phrase. In discussing his travel plans Paul frequently indicates that his ability to travel to those to whom he is sending a letter depends on God and the Lord (Rom 15:32; 1 Thess 3:11; Phlm 22).

    and I will get to know not the word of those who are conceited, but their power: The purpose of Paul's intended visit is that he might have a first-hand experience of the situation in Corinth. Paul uses the verb "to know" *(gnōsomai)* in its Semitic sense, "to experience." His expressed desire to experience the power of the Corinthians is, in fact, ironic. As is often the case (cf. 2:4-5), he contrasts "word" *(logos)* and "power" *(dynamis).* With the contrast Paul returns to motifs that had occupied his attention at the outset of the first rhetorical proof, words (1:5, 17, 18; 2:1, 4, 13) and power (1:18, 24; 2:4, 5). In his rhetorical rehearsal of the situation of the Corinthians he had noted that not many of the Corinthians were powerful (1:26).

20. *for the kingdom of God is not in word, it is rather in power:* The situation of the conceited Corinthians contrasts with that of the kingdom of God. "The

kingdom of God" is a well-known biblical, apocalyptic, and NT notion that appears but rarely in the Pauline writings (1 Cor 6:9, 10; 15:24, 50; Rom 14:17; Gal 5:21; cf. 1 Thess 2:12). It refers to the final coming of God as king and may be a convenient and traditional cipher used to express the coherent center of Paul's thought. In the apocalyptic tradition the coming of the kingdom of God is the ultimate manifestation of God's power. As he has done earlier in the letter, Paul uses an apocalyptic motif to confound the inflated self-esteem of the Corinthians (2:6-16; 3:17; 4:5, 8). That the kingdom of God is in power and not in word provides a further hermeneutical key to Paul's disavowal of reliance upon rhetorical technique in order to convey his message (2:1-5).

21. *What do you want? That I should come to you with a rod or with love and a spirit of gentleness?* Having concluded his first rhetorical proof and now adding an epistolary postscript, Paul engages the Corinthians with a final pair of rhetorical questions, the only such questions in the postscript. Unlike the oratorical questions of 4:7 this final pair of questions is phrased in the plural. The questions are intended to bring the Corinthians to a decision. The choice is theirs.

Paul's letter is a substitute for his personal presence. By writing as he does he hopes that he will be spared, through his intended visit, the need to use severity in relating to the Corinthians (cf. 2 Cor 13:10). Use of the rod (*rabdos*, hapax in Paul) is a motif associated with paternal correction (cf. 3:1-2, 4:15, 17). It is an instrument of *paideia*, rearing a child (cf. Prov 22:15). Even today "spare the rod and spoil the child" is an adage expressing the common wisdom of a culture. "Those who spare the rod hate their children, but those who love them are diligent to discipline them *(paideuei),*" said the author of Proverbs (Prov 13:24; cf. Prov 10:13; 23:13-14; 26:3). In the maxims on child-rearing the "rod" sometimes serves as a metaphor for discipline. Discipline was, in any case, a paternal function (cf. Heb 12:5-11).

In contrast to the rod Paul offers the possibility of his coming with love and a spirit of gentleness. Both love *(agapē)* and gentleness *(prautētos)* appear in Paul's catalogue of virtues in Gal 5:23, where they are presented as fruits of the Spirit. His love for the Corinthians is manifest in the unusual postscript appended to his letter (16:24). It is a paternal quality (4:14, 17; see note on 4:17). In 1 Corinthians Paul writes of his gentleness only in 4:21. In 2 Cor 10:1, however, he writes of his own conduct in terms of the gentleness of Christ (cf. 4:17; 11:1) and with that as his motivation addresses an appeal *(parakalō)* to the Corinthians. Second Corinthians 10:1-2 is a passage that exploits the epistolary motif of presence and absence.

FOR REFERENCE AND FURTHER STUDY

Beker, Johan Christiaan. "Recasting Pauline Theology: The Coherence-Contingency Scheme as Interpretive Model" in Jouette M. Bassler, ed., *Pauline Theology, 1: Thessalonians, Philippians, Galatians, Philemon.* Minneapolis: Fortress, 1991, 15–24.

Funk, Robert W. "The Apostolic Parousia: Form and Significance" in William R. Farmer, Charles Francis Digby Moule, and Richard R. Niebuhr, eds., *Christian History and Interpretation: Studies Presented to John Knox.* Cambridge: Cambridge University Press, 1967, 249–268; revised as "The Apostolic Presence: Paul" in R. W. Funk, *Parables and Presence: Forms of the New Testament Tradition.* Philadelphia: Fortress, 1982, 81–102.

Mitchell, Margaret M. "New Testament Envoys in the Context of Greco-Roman Diplomatic and Epistolary Conventions: The Example of Timothy and Titus," *JBL* 111 (1992) 641–662.

Schenk, Wolfgang. "Der 1. Korintherbrief als Briefsammlung," *ZNW* 60 (1969) 219–243.

Young, Norman H. "Paidagogos: The Social Setting of a Pauline Metaphor," *NovT* 29 (1987) 150–176.

C. SECOND RHETORICAL DEMONSTRATION (5:1–7:40)

To many commentators the lack of unity in this section of Paul's letter is more apparent than its unity. The reference to the letter Paul had received from the Corinthians (7:1) seems to imply a new beginning. Indeed, Paul's reference to the reception of the letter is one factor in the argument of those who dispute the unity of the letter (see Introduction).

Another issue is the relationship between Paul's observations on the recourse to the secular judiciary by some Corinthians and the other material in chs. 5 and 6. To plead for the unity of Paul's exposition some suggest that the court case may have had to do with marriage or sexual litigation. While this may have been the case, the language of 6:1-11 does not warrant this precise reading of the Apostle's words.

The basic theme of chs. 5 and 6 is the purity of the community. What does it mean for the community to be God's holy people? Two situations of which Paul was aware were their tolerance of a man sleeping with his father's wife and their recourse to the courts to settle their petty claims against one another. In each of these situations the community did not properly exercise its own responsibility. It was the community's responsibility to expel an incestuous man from its midst. It was the community's responsibility to settle disputes—which should not have occurred in the first place! (6:7)—among themselves.

The purity of the community continues to be Paul's theme as he treats a well-known Corinthian slogan urging liberty in all things (6:12). To show the fallacy of their reasoning Paul offers the example of men using prostitutes. Dealing with a sexual issue like this forms an *inclusio* around the exposition of his ideas on the use of the courts. The topic itself is a classic rhetorical *topos*. It introduces a further consideration on sexual matters, specifically on issues that arose from another popular slogan, "it is good for a man not to touch a woman" (7:1). Paul deals with the radical asceticism urged by the slogan in casuistic fashion, using as the final argument in his arsenal a well-organized reflection on various states of life (7:17-24). The argument is also circumscribed in a ring construction. In 7:25 Paul returns to a consideration of matters pertaining to marriage and sexuality. The textual marker in 7:25, "concerning the unmarried," allows him to address the situation of those who are not yet married and of those who are no longer married (7:39). People in these situations must make a decision as to whether they should marry.

The rhetorical demonstration of chs. 5–7 is stamped with the mark of Paul's authority. It opens with a remark on his judicial presence (5:3-4). It closes with an affirmation of his possession of the Spirit (7:40). Along the way Paul is careful to identify the authority on the basis of which he renders his opinion (7:10, 25).

For Reference and Further Study

Basevi, Claudio. "La dottrina di san Paolo sulla sessualità umana e la condizione della donna in 1 Cor. Studio di *1 Cor 7* e *1 Cor 11,3-15*," *Annales Theologici* 1 (1987) 51–72.

Baumert, Norbert. *Woman and Man in Paul: Overcoming a Misunderstanding.* Collegeville: The Liturgical Press, 1996.

Claudel, Gerard. "1 Kor 6,12–7,40 neu gelesen," *TThZ* 94 (1985) 20–36.

Deming, Will. *Paul on Marriage and Celibacy: The Hellenistic Background of 1 Corinthians 7.* MSSNTS 80. Cambridge: Cambridge University Press, 1995.

_____. "The Unity of 1 Corinthians 5–6," *JBL* 115 (1996) 289–312.

Fauconnet, Jean-Jacques. "La morale sexuelle chez Saint Paul: Analyse et commentaire de 1 Co 6,12 à 7,40," *BLE* 93 (1992) 359–378.

Fiore, Benjamin. "Passion in Paul and Plutarch: 1 Corinthians 5–6 and the Polemic against Epicureans" in David L. Balch, et al, eds., *Greeks, Romans, and Christians. Essays in Honor of Abraham J. Malherbe.* Minneapolis: Fortress, 1990, 135–143.

Gavrock, M. "Why Won't Paul Just Say No? Purity and Sex in 1 Corinthians 6," *Word & World* 16 (1996) 444–455.

Gundry-Volf, Judith. "Controlling the Bodies. A Theological Profile of the Corinthian Sexual Ascetics (1 Cor 7)" *CorC*, 519–541.

_____. "Celibate Pneumatics and Social Power: On the Motivations for Sexual Asceticism in Corinth," *USQR* 48 (1994) 105–126.

Laughery, G. J. "Paul: Anti-marriage? Anti-sex? Ascetic? A Dialogue with 1 Corinthians 7:1-40," *EvQ* 69 (1997) 109–128.

Minear, Paul S. "Christ and the Congregation: 1 Corinthians 5–6," *RExp* 80 (1983) 341–350.

Nejsum, Peter. "The Apologetic Tendency in the Interpretation of Paul's Sexual Ethics," *ST* 48 (1994) 48–62.

Orge, Manuel. "El próposito temático de 1 Corintios 7: Un discernimiento sobre la puesta en práctica del ideal de la continencia sexual y el celibato," *Claretianum* 27 (1987) 5–124; 28 (1988) 5–114; 31 (1991) 125–152.

Pascuzzi, Maria. *Ethics, Ecclesiology and Church Discipline: A Rhetorical Analysis of 1 Corinthians 5.* Tesi gregoriana, Serie Teologia 32. Rome: Pontificia Università Gregoriana, 1997.

Tomson, Peter J. "Paul's Jewish Background in View of His Law Teaching in 1 Cor 7" in James D. G. Dunn, ed., *Paul and the Mosaic Law.* WUNT 89. Tübingen: J.C.B. Mohr (Paul Siebeck), 1996, 251–270.

Trevijano Etcheverría, Ramón M. "A propósito del incestuoso (1 Cor 5–6)," *Salm* 38 (1991) 129–153.

1. *A Purified Community* (5:1-8)

1. It is actually reported that there is sexual immorality in your midst such as does not exist among the Gentiles, namely that someone is having sexual relations with his father's wife. 2. Are you so conceited? More than that, shouldn't you have mourned, with the result that the one who is doing this be removed from your midst? 3. To be sure, I, present in spirit although absent in body, have already judged, as if I were present, the one who has done such a thing; 4. in the name of our Lord Jesus when you and my spirit come together with the power of our Lord Jesus, 5. hand over that person to Satan for the destruction of the flesh in order that the spirit might be saved on the Day of the Lord. 6. Your boasting is not good. Don't you know that a little yeast leavens the entire mound of dough? 7. Get rid of the old yeast so that you may be a new mound of dough, because you are unleavened; for Christ, our passover, was sacrificed. 8. Hence let us celebrate the feast not with the old yeast, not with the yeast of evil and sexual immorality, but with the unleavened bread of sincerity and truth.

INTERPRETATION

To begin his second rhetorical demonstration (5:1–7:40) Paul introduces a new issue, that of sexual immorality *(porneia).* Ancient rhetoricians considered that the first element in the rhetorical *heurēsis,* the *inventio,* was the identification of the issue itself. Identification of the situation, the rhetorical *stasis (status)* preceded the determination of how the issue was to be treated. Recognition of the issue allowed the rhetor to choose a mode of rhetorical argument and to determine the kinds of proof that would be used in the resolution of the issue (see Quintilian, *Training of an Orator* 3.6.9, 12, 21).

The identification of the issue to be addressed was not so much a matter of identifying the fact of the matter as it was of determining the moral quality of the fact. In this regard Latin rhetoricians spoke about a qualitative *status,* using the term *qualitas* to characterize the rhetorical situation (see [Cicero] *Rhetorica ad Herennium* 1.14.21; Cicero, *De inventione* 1.9.12; Quintilian, *Training of an Orator* 3.6.83; 7.4). Placing the issue of sexual immorality before the Corinthians, Paul immediately raises the issue of its ethical status, remarking that such conduct was not to be found even among pagans. Having raised the issue Paul proceeds to identify the specifics of the case. It is a case of incest.

The Letter. The recourse to epistolary motifs that characterized the previous portion of Paul's letter (4:14-21) continues in 5:1-8. Ancient epistolary theorists considered a letter to be a mode of personal presence. Specifically Demetrius held that the letter should offer a reflection of the author's very soul (*eikōn tēs heautou psychēs, On Style* 227). In 5:3 Paul explicitly plays with the absence-presence (*apōn-parōn*) motif, the only time he does so in 1 Corinthians (cf. 2 Cor 10:10-11; 13:2; compare 1 Cor 5:12; 1 Thess 2:17). He couples the epistolary absence-presence theme with his own body-spirit contrast. The expanded formula—absent in body, present in spirit—was also used in other Hellenistic letters (P.London 1926; Ovid, etc.).

Although Paul is dealing with a new issue in 5:1-8 his *heurēsis* is such that he introduces motifs that link his appeal on the new topic to what he has previously written. Reference to the conceit and importunate boasting of some of the Corinthians links Paul's treatment of incest with some of the basic attitudes that led to the lack of unity with the community: conceit, 5:2 (cf. 4:6, 18, 19) and boasting, 5:6 (cf. 1:29, 31; 3:21; 4:7). Reference to the name, day, and power of the Lord Jesus link his demonstration on sexual immorality not only to the first rhetorical proof, which considered the divisions within the community, but also with the epistolary thanksgiving, which served as a rhetorical rehearsal of facts: the name, 5:4 (cf. 1:2, 10); the power, 5:4 (cf. 1:24); and the day, 5:5 (cf. 3:13). The somewhat abrupt fashion in which Paul introduces his new topic brings the reader back to the beginning of the letter when Paul told the Corinthians about the visit that prompted him to write a letter to them (1:11).

A Matter of Judgment. The case Paul wanted the community to adjudicate is one of incest. In every culture incest is considered a particularly egregious form of sexual misconduct, even if various cultures differ from one another in the determination of the specific relationships within which sexual intercourse would be a major violation of the social ethos. Within Judaism as within the Hellenistic world in general a man's sexual intercourse with his father's wife, concubine, or paramour was considered intolerable. The conceited Corinthians tolerated such misconduct.

Paul tells the community that even though he was physically separated from them he has nonetheless rendered judgment with regard to the one who had so egregiously violated social mores. He challenges the community to do the same. The scene Paul constructs is that of the courtroom. Paul's judicial language is strikingly similar to that used in Roman judicial proceedings and the deliberations of the Sanhedrin: "convene" *(synachthentōn)*, "render judgment" *(kekrika)*, "hand over" *(paradounai)*, perhaps even "day of the Lord" *(hēmera* can suggest one's day in court; cf. 4:3). Punishment is stipulated: it is banishment. The agent of the court is identified: it is Satan, one who executes divine judgment.

References to the name and the power of the Lord Jesus Christ identify the one on whose authority ("Lord") the community is to convene. The Lord is the authority on the basis of which punishment is to be meted out. The history of the textual transmission provides evidence of considerable variation in Paul's three references to the Lord (vv. 4[2x], 5). It is, nonetheless, constant in designating Jesus as "the Lord" in all three instances. The title implies ultimate authority. Reference to the day of the Lord (v. 5) brings an eschatological nuance to Paul's words on judgment. Throughout the letter judgment is always considered in the light of the eschaton (3:13-15; 4:3-5; 11:27-32).

The punishment Paul envisions for the incestuous man is that he be handed over to Satan. This consists of banishment from the community, as Paul's concluding Deuteronomic exclusionary formula clearly suggests (v. 13). Banishment from the community was a fairly common penalty in the ancient world. B. S. Rosner has suggested that there is some similarity between the course of action charted by Paul and that adopted by Ezra (see Ezra 7–10). Ezra urged that members of the community who were involved in illicit sexual relationships be excluded from the community (Ezra 7:26; 10:8, 44).

Qumran's community council, comprised of the main body of the community, convened to render judicial decisions (cf. 1QS 6:8-10). It was empowered to find guilty all those who transgressed the covenant. Paul expected the Corinthians to judge the incestuous man and impose an appropriate punishment. It is generally acknowledged that there are some structural similarities between the Qumran community and some of the early Christian communities. Paul's expectation that the community at Corinth should sit in judgment on and mete out a penalty to one of their number whose behavior was known to be egregious was one such similarity.

The excommunication of the incestuous man that Paul recommends to the Corinthian community is echoed in 1 Tim 1:18-20 (cf. Matt 18:15-18). The author of that epistle took over from Paul the notion of handing over the sinner to Satan. Paul's own recommendation pertained to a specific form of sinful conduct, but the deutero-Pauline text speaks more generally. As is customary in the Pastoral Epistles the text of 1 Tim 1:18-20 focuses uniquely on Paul as the one who has decreed the excommunication. In 1 Corinthians the excommunication is a joint endeavor of Paul and the community and relies on the authority of the Lord Jesus. Another difference is that the procedure to which 1 Timothy makes reference has as its purpose the correction of the sinner (1 Tim 1:20; cf. Matt 18:15-18). What is at issue in the excommunication Paul urges upon the community is the holiness of the community, its own eschatological salvation (vv. 5c, 6b-8).

A Little Yeast. Paul's appeal to the community to expel the incestuous man from their midst is grounded on two arguments: their ecclesial situation, for which Paul uses the simile of unleavened bread, and the death of Christ, described metaphorically as the sacrifice of the paschal lamb.

The judicial decision, in which the Corinthians are expected to concur, that the incestuous man should be banished from the community, is rooted in the holiness of the community. The community is a holy people, sanctified in Christ (1:30). The reality of this situation, an indicative, precedes Paul's imperative that the sinner be excised from the community: "On the basis of the death of Christ, the Church is the pure festal community . . . and should correspondingly keep itself pure" (Wiard Popkes, *zymē, EDNT* 2:105). The purity of the community is Paul's primary concern. Paul urged the community to act as he did because it was the temple of God—a cameo expression of the holiness of the community—an image evoked in the discussion on judgment in 3:16-17. A strong sense of the holiness of the community, together with a concern for the covenant and a sense of corporate responsibility, prompted Paul and Ezra to invoke the ban as they did.

Paul does not consider sexual misconduct to be a private matter. For him as for other NT authors everything that Christians do, including their sexual behavior, affects the entire community. His concern for the unsullied purity of the community is graphically expressed in the metaphor of the Passover ritual and in his rehearsal of the theme of a previous letter in the short passage to follow (5:9-13). Paul's allusion to the Passover custom (see also the Exodus imagery in 10:1-12) may have been prompted by the proximity of the feast (cf. 16:8).

That the correction of the incestuous man is beyond the pale of Paul's immediate consideration emerges quite clearly in the next section of the letter. Following the biblical injunction (Deut 17:7 in 5:13), the community has only to excommunicate the incestuous individual. Judgment of that individual, now a person outside the community (*exō*, v. 12), is in the hands of God.

NOTES

1. *It is actually reported that there is sexual immorality in your midst such as does not exist among the Gentiles:* Having addressed the issue of divisions in Corinth (cf. 1:10), Paul turns to another matter about which he has apparently received a report from Chloe's people (1:11). In the NT *holōs*, "actually," is an adverb used almost exclusively by Paul (5:1; 6:7; 15:29; Matt 5:34). "Sexual immorality," *porneia,* appears frequently in NT vice lists (2 Cor 12:21; Gal 5:19, etc.). A more precise connotation of the general term must be inferred from the context. Before identifying a specific kind of immoral sexual behavior Paul makes a remark, introduced by an emphatic and epexegetical *kai,* that bespeaks his sharing of the Jewish prejudice about the sexual mores of Gentiles (cf. Rom 1:14-27; compare Lev 18:3, 27). Gentiles serve as a negative reference group for Paul's moral judgment in sexual matters (cf. 1 Thess 4:5). Paul's observation that sexual immorality exists in the midst of the community (*en hymin*) indicates that he considers the matter to be a social issue. The community's failure to deal with a serious case of sexual immorality could even impair its reputation within the largely Gentile community of Corinth (cf. 14:22-25). Paul's concern for the well-being of the community continues throughout his exposition, where verbs and pronouns in the second person plural dominate the discourse.

   namely, that someone is having sexual relations with his father's wife: Paul's use of the infinitive in the present tense (*echein,* literally, "to have") indicates that he considers the incestuous affair to be an ongoing relationship. It does not necessarily suggest that the incestuous man had married the woman. "His father's wife" (*gynaika tina tou patros,* literally, "his father's woman") refers to a woman other than the man's mother. If the woman had been the man's own mother, Paul would have written *heautou mētera,* "his own mother." The woman in question may have been the man's stepmother. The phrase *gynaika tou patros* is used of a stepmother in Lev 18:8. The Greco-Roman literature frequently mentions liaisons between men and their stepmothers (e.g., Martial, *Epigrams* 4.16; see further Patricia A. Watson, *Ancient Stepmothers: Myth, Misogyny and Reality* [Leiden: Brill, 1995]). On the other hand, the woman in question might have been his father's divorced wife or concubine, legitimate or not. On any of these possibilities the relationship would have been considered incestuous and in violation of social norms.

   Incest is the most universally recognized sexual tabu. Marriage with one's stepmother was prohibited not only by Jewish law (Lev 18:7-8; 20:11; Deut 22:30; 27:20; cf. Gen 49:4; Ezek 22:10-11) but also by Roman law (see Gaius, *Institutes* 1.63). The Jew who violated the tabu on incestuous sexual intercourse was to be cut off from the people (Lev 18:29). The literature of later Judaism maintained the biblical attitude of abhorrence toward incest. The Mishnaic tractate *Keritot* ("Extirpations") identifies a man's having sexual relations with his father's wife as one of thirty-six transgressions for which extirpation is prescribed in the Torah (*m. Ker.* 1:1; cf. *m. Sanh.* 7:4; *Jub.* 33:10-13; *t. Sanh.* 10:1). "A man shall not sleep with his father's wife and shall not uncover his father's skirt," says the Temple Scroll (11Q Temple 66:11-12, citing Deut 22:30 [23:1 MT]; cf. CD 5:6-11). Philo reiterates the traditional prohibition of incest, with special reference to a man's having his father's wife (*Special Laws* 3.20-28, 20; see further Pieter Willem van der Horst, *The Sentences of Pseudo-Phocylides* [Leiden: Brill, 1978] 229–230). With obvious reference to Lev 18:8, the ban is cited as prohibition 331 among the rabbinic tradition's 613 biblical commandments.

2. *Are you so conceited?* Paul's rhetorical question is directed to the conceited members of the community, the community leaders (*pephysiōmenoi*, in the plural, with an emphatic *hymeis*) whom he had previously addressed (4:6, 18, 19). The subject of those puffed up with pride in their own knowledge was a well known topos for Hellenistic moralists (see above, p. 176). The conceited were excoriated by the philosophers because of their disruptive social behavior. In his first rhetorical unit Paul took to task the conceited members of the Corinthian community. Their conduct was socially disruptive and demeaning to others in the community. As Paul begins his second rhetorical unit he addresses them because of their scandalous tolerance of, even pride in (see v. 6) a situation that should have been of concern to them. One of their number had violated a significant and universally recognized moral norm. It is likely that the guilty person was one of the community's conceited ones (so John K. Chow, *Patronage and Power* 130–141; Andrew D. Clarke, *Leadership in Corinth* 73–88).

More than that, shouldn't you have mourned, with the result that the one who is doing this be removed from your midst? Only in 1 Cor 5:2 and 2 Cor 12:21 does Paul use the verb "to mourn" (*pentheō*). In the latter passage he expresses a fear that when he visits the community he will have to mourn because many have failed to repent of their sexual immorality (*porneia*). The LXX uses the verb "to mourn" with regard to sin, especially in reference to sorrow over another's sins (Ezra 10:6; Neh 1:4; 1 Esdr 8:72; 9:2; Dan 10:2; cf. Neh 8:9; *T. Reub.* 1:10). In mourning (see Ezra 10:6) the experience of grief is externalized, expressed, and communicated to others in various ways: weeping, not eating, not sleeping, being unconcerned about one's looks and one's clothes. Ritualized mourning in the aftermath of a disaster, especially a major national disaster, was a customary practice among the biblical peoples (see 1 Kings 21:9, 12; 2 Chr 20:3; Ezra 8:21; Est 4:16; Isa 58:3-6; Jer 14:12; Joel 1:14).

V. C. Pfitzner and several of the commentaries suggest that the community should have mourned over the proximate loss of one of their number, but it is more likely that they should have mourned for themselves, either because of the shame that the misdeed brought on the community or because of their corporate responsibility for the errant behavior (cf. 12:26). Had they mourned they would have extirpated the incestuous man from their midst.

Paul's expression "be removed from your midst" *(arthē ek mesou hymōn)* reflects a Latin construction *(de medio tollere;* see BDF 5.3b).

3. *To be sure, I, present in spirit although absent in body, have already judged, as if I were present, the one who has done such a thing:* Paul wishes to emphasize his presence to the community, albeit by means of a letter. He began his sentence with an emphatic "I" *(egō).* Twice he uses the participle *parōn,* "present": ". . . present in spirit . . . as if I were present" *(parōn de tō pneumati . . . hōs parōn).* The contrast between presence and absence adds further emphasis to the idea of Paul's presence. Paul would have learned about the situation only in the report that has prompted his letter. Having learned about the situation, he has made a judgment that is conveyed to the Corinthians in his letter. His use of the perfect ("have already judged") suggests that his judgment has a lasting effect; that is, it continues to be in force even as the Corinthians listen to the reading of his letter.

A judgment motif with an eschatological reference is fairly strong in 1 Corinthians (3:13-15; 4:3-5; 11:27-32), but this is the only passage in which Paul talks about the judgment that he has made. Even his judgment is not without an eschatological referent (vv. 4-5). Colin G. Kruse ("The Offender and the Offence in 2 Corinthians 2:5 and 7:12," *EvQ* 60 [1988] 129–139) holds that Paul mentions this wrongdoer in 2 Cor 2:5 and 7:12, but none of these texts warrants such a precise identification of the evildoer.

4. *in the name of our Lord Jesus:* The simple but somewhat unusual identification of Jesus as "our Lord Jesus" is attested by B, D, 429, 918, etc. A still more simple form, "the Lord Jesus," is found in A, Ψ, and some minuscules. An ancient lectionary (1021) has only "our Lord." The vast majority of medieval minuscules, such ancient majuscules as 𝔓⁴⁶, G, P, and a corrected D, along with such Fathers as Ambrosiaster, Basil, and Chrysostom have the full christological title, "our Lord Jesus Christ" (without "our" in ℵ and some of the ancient versions; with an inverted sequence of wording in 81). Since copyists tended to expand sacred names—for reasons of piety? or because the formula was more familiar?—the editors of *GNT*⁴ believe that the short reading found in B and D has the best chance of having been the original wording.

The phrase "in the name of our Lord Jesus" (cf. 1:2, 10; 6:11) is a Semitism that recalls the biblical phrase *běšēm yhwh,* "in the name of the Lord." It is difficult, however, to determine whether it is "judged" or "came together" that is qualified by the prepositional phrase. The ambiguity is reflected in the different punctuation found in modern English versions of the verse. If the phrase modifies "judged" (v. 3) or "hand over" (v. 5), it would have a judicial connotation. It would mean "by the authority of" or "by the commission of." Similar phrases were used in Roman judicial proceedings and in the deliberations of the Sanhedrin. If the phrase refers to the immediately adjacent participle, *synachthentōn hymōn,* "when you come together," Paul's words would evoke the idea of a Christian assembly that invokes the name of the Lord (cf. 1:2). His usage would be similar to the language describing the Sanhedrin as meeting in the name of YHWH. Perhaps it is not necessary to make too rigid a distinction in this matter. The pregnant phrase may qualify both the Christians' coming together and the action they are to take.

when you and my spirit come together with the power of our Lord Jesus: The reference to Paul's spirit *(tou emou pneumatos)* is to be understood in the light of the epistolary contrast between Paul's physical presence and his non-physical presence in spirit, of which his letter is an expression. Various commentators point to the similarities between the type of church order at Corinth and Jewish communities. At Qumran the council of the community, consisting of all of its members, rendered judicial decisions and offered its opinion on various matters under dispute (cf. 1QS 6:8-10).

Power is preeminently a divine attribute (see 1:18; 6:14, etc.). Jesus, raised from the dead, has been constituted son of God in power (Rom 1:4). Thus power is an attribute of Jesus (cf. 2 Cor 12:9), raised from the dead and given the title Lord. Early Christians performed miracles in the name of Jesus Christ (see Acts 3:6). A distinction is to be made between the acts of power performed by Jesus and disciples and the various magical spells and exorcisms of the Hellenistic world. There is, nonetheless, some superficial similarity between the invocation of Jesus' name and Hellenistic formularies in this regard (cf. 12:2). Paul's reference to Jesus' power implies that the invocation of the name (v. 4a) is a way of appealing to the power of the Lord.

5. *hand over that person to Satan:* The use of an imperatival infinitive (Rom 12:15; Phil 3:16) is a rare instance of an old grammatical construction. Paul's words recall those of Job 2:6. Satan, who appears in 7:5 as an apocalyptic source of temptation, is God's agent, not God's enemy (cf. 2 Cor 12:7; 1 Tim 1:20, where the phrase "to hand over to Satan" also occurs). In Greek literature "to hand over" *(paradidōmi)* is a judicial term suggesting either the handing over of a person for trial (e.g., Andocides, *Orations* 1.17; Demosthenes, *Private Orations* 49.9; 51.8; Lysias, *Orations* 14.17) or the handing over of someone for punishment (Antiphon, *Prosecution for Poisoning* 20; Isocrates, *Orations* 17.15; Demosthenes, *Private Orations* 45.61). Johannes Schneider (*TDNT* 5:169) holds that Paul is urging the Corinthians to pronounce a solemn curse over the incestuous man, but this is disputed by Fee (*First Epistle* 209), who correctly argues that Paul intended that the Corinthians turn the man back out into Satan's sphere. This reflects the dichotomous view of the human situation that pervades the letter (e.g., 2:14-16). The presence of Satan in Paul's judicial presentation is consistent with the apocalyptic character of his various observations on judgment (see 2:13-15; 11:27-32).

for the destruction of the flesh: Paul concludes (v. 13) his consideration of the case of the incestuous man with a Deuteronomic injunction (Deut 17:7) that suggests the death penalty. "Destruction" *(olethron;* cf. 1 Thess 5:3) is often used in the sense of "death." Within Second Temple Judaism excommunication was considered to be a kind of substitute for execution. An excommunicated person is cut off from the life-giving community. Hellenists believed that the pronouncement of a curse would be followed almost immediately by the death of the person upon whom the curse had been pronounced. "Flesh" *(sarkos)* designates the human in its weakness and sinfulness.

in order that the spirit might be saved: The purpose *(hina)* of the decree of excommunication is that the spirit might be saved. The verse should not be read as if Paul were urging, if only metaphorically, the destruction of the incestuous man's flesh so that his spirit or soul might be saved on the day of the Lord. "Flesh" *(sarx)* and "spirit" *(pneuma)* are among the more important of Paul's anthropological terms but these terms do not refer to parts of a human being as they would in a Hellenistic anthropology. Rather they refer to aspects or orientations of a person or community. Paul's anthropological dualism is not philosophical; it is soteriological. Paul, moreover, does not use the possessive pronoun. He is not writing about the incestuous man's "spirit." Paul's perspective is that of the community. His concern is for the sanctity of the church. He directs the community to excise the fleshy individual—so characterized by reason of his incestuous behavior—from its midst so that the community might live under the power of the Spirit and be preserved for the day of the Lord.

on the Day of the Lord: The day of the Lord (see notes on 1:8 and 3:13) should be a day of ultimate salvation for those who belong to the Lord (3:15). A textual problem akin to that affecting the transmission of the sacred name in v. 4 occurs in v. 5. The textual tradition attests to no less than five variant readings of the sacred name: "the Lord" ($\mathfrak{P}^{46}$, B, Marcion, Tertullian, and other Western Fathers), "the Lord Jesus" (א, Ψ, 81, 326, etc., Basil, Theophylact), "the Lord Jesus Christ" (D, 1984, Ambrosiaster), "our Lord Jesus" (cop), and "our Lord Jesus Christ" (A, F, G, P, 33, Ephraem, Ambrose, Theodoret). Some of the Fathers are not consistent in the way they cite this verse. Augustine, for example, sometimes has "the Lord" and sometimes "the Lord Jesus." Chrysostom sometimes has "the Lord Jesus" and at other times "our Lord Jesus Christ." The *lectio brevior* principle has led the editors of *GNT*[4] to opt for the simple reading, "the day of the Lord." This reading best explains the origin of the other readings.

6. *Your boasting is not good: Kauchēma,* "the object of your boasting," generally suggests something in which one can take legitimate pride. Paul normally uses the *kauch-* word group in a negative sense (see, above, pp. 100–101), but he tends to use *kauchēma* in a positive sense (cf. 9:15, 16). The one exception is here, where Paul uses the term in a way that is consistent with his general use of the word group.

This is the second time in the letter that Paul speaks of the inordinate boasting of the Corinthians. As in 4:7, the Corinthians' boasting is linked to their conceit (4:6; 5:2). There their boasting was disordered. The Corinthians boasted as if they were not creatures who had received all that they had as a gift from the Lord (see 1:31). In 5:6 their boasting is disordered because they have not yet come to grips with the problem of the incestuous person in their midst, expelling him from the community so as to have a community that can worthily call on the name of the Lord (1:2).

Don't you know that a little yeast leavens the entire mound of dough? "Don't you know" *(ouk oidate hoti)* appeals to the common experience of the Corinthians. That a little yeast yields a whole mass of dough is a maxim *(gnōmē),* an expression of common wisdom. This household adage is again used by Paul in Gal 5:9. In the rhetorical *heurēsis* of 1 Corinthians use of the domestic maxim seems to have been prompted by the reference to the Jewish feast of Passover that follows in vv. 7-8. Paul's imagery employs language he does not generally use: "yeast" (*zymē*, vv. 6, 7, 8; Gal 5:9), "mound of dough" (*phyrama,* vv. 6, 7), "get rid of" (*ekkathairō,* v. 7), "unleavened" (*azymos,* vv. 7, 8), "passover" (*pascha,* v. 7), "sacrifice" (*thyō,* v. 7; elsewhere only in 10:20), and "celebrate a feast" (*heortazō,* v. 8). Paul's use of this festal language suggests that the feast of Passover was at hand.

7. *Get rid of the old yeast so that you may be a new mound of dough, because you are unleavened:* Paul's ethical exhortation is often characterized by language that also occurs in his declarative statements about the condition of Christians. This is the situation in 5:7 where Paul affirms that Christians are unleavened dough and urges them to become a new batch. The juxtaposition of indicative and imperative is typical of Paul. Neither the indicative nor the imperative should be minimized at the expense of the other. For Paul the indicative and the imperative exist in creative tension. The Corinthians' situation requires an appropriate mode of conduct.

   Paul's image makes reference to the Jewish practice according to which leaven was removed from the household before the feast of Passover (Exod 12:15; 13:7). Only unleavened bread would be eaten during the Passover festival. According to ancient tradition the feast was called the Feast of Unleavened Bread (Exod 12:14-20). Eating unleavened bread recalled the redemptive experience of the Exodus when the Israelites ate only unleavened bread. Paul draws from his imaginative typology on the feast an exhortation to get rid of the old yeast, a metaphor for a change of conduct, specifically banishing the incestuous man. "Yeast" (*zymē*), an instrument of organic corruption, frequently serves as a symbol of evil. A targum fragment describes Abraham as "the completely unleavened one."

   for Christ, our passover, was sacrificed: Frank Matera describes the paraenesis of Paul's letter as "ethics for the sanctified community" (*New Testament Ethics* 138–160). That Christ is the principle of the Corinthians' sanctification has been noted in 1:2. Now by way of explanation of his metaphor of the dough without yeast (*kai gar,* "for also"; BDF 453.2), and *pace* Colella who argues that the reference to the Passover is only temporal ("at the time of our passover;" see Pasquale Colella, "Cristo nostra pasqua? 1 Cor 5,7," *BeO* 28 [1986] 197–217), Paul offers a midrashic interpretation of the Passover festival (cf. 10:4). His language, with the verb in the passive, reflects the biblical expression "sacrifice the passover lamb" (Exod 12:21). Use of "passover" (*pascha,* hapax in Paul) to designate the paschal lamb reflects this biblical usage (cf. Mark 14:12; Luke 22:7). Paul uses "Christ" to evoke the memory of the death of Christ, but it is only here that he interprets Christ's death in an explicitly sacrificial fashion.

8. *Hence let us celebrate the feast not with the old yeast, not with the yeast of evil and sexual immorality, but with the unleavened bread of sincerity and truth:* Paul's exhortation continues the metaphor. Having prepared for the feast by purging

the old yeast from its midst the community is encouraged to get on with the celebration. Paul's balanced antithesis contrasts his metaphorical yeast and unleavened bread. A pair of vices, evil and sexual immorality, and a pair of virtues, sincerity and truth, are offered in explanation (the genitives are epexegetical). These particular vices and virtues are classic elements in the paraenetic catalogues, but with the exception of sexual immorality *(porneia)* they rarely appear in Paul. Evil appears as an infantile vice in 14:20 (cf. 3:1), truth as an attribute of love in 13:6. The eradication of sexual immorality from the community is the burden of the entire epistolary unit (vv. 1, 13). Sincerity *(eilikrineia,* "without mixture," *TLNT* 1:420–423) is used elsewhere in the NT only as a character trait of Paul and his companions (2 Cor 1:12; 2:17).

For Reference and Further Study

Bammel, Ernst. "Rechtsfindung in Korinth," *EThL* 73 (1997) 107–113.

Cambier, Jules. "La chair et l'esprit en 1 Cor v. 5," *NTS* 15 (1968–69) 221–232.

Campbell, Barth. "Flesh and Spirit in 1 Cor 5:5: An Exercise in Rhetorical Criticism of the NT," *JETS* 36 (1993) 331–342.

Collins, Adela Yarbro. "The Function of 'Excommunication' in Paul," *HThR* 73 (1980) 251–263.

Fitzgerald, John T. "Virtue/Vice Lists," *ABD* 6:856–859.

Forkman, Göran. *The Limits of the Religious Community: Expulsion from the Religious Community within the Qumran sect, within Rabbinic Judaism, and within Primitive Christianity.* Lund: CWK Gleerup, 1972.

Harris, Gerald. "The Beginnings of Church Discipline: 1 Corinthians 5," *NTS* 37 (1991) 1–21.

Havener, Ivan. "A Curse for Salvation—1 Corinthians 5:1-5" in Daniel Durken, ed., *Sin, Salvation and the Spirit.* Collegeville: The Liturgical Press, 1979, 334–344.

Horbury, William. "Extirpation and Excommunication," *VT* 35 (1985) 13–38.

Matera, Frank J. *New Testament Ethics: The Legacies of Jesus and Paul.* Louisville: Westminster/John Knox, 1996.

Meier, John P. *A Marginal Jew: Rethinking the Historical Jesus,* 2: *Mentor, Message, and Miracles.* ABRL. New York: Doubleday, 1994, 535–616.

Pfitzner, Victor C. "Purified Community—Purified Sinner: Expulsion from the Community according to Matthew 18:15-18 and 1 Corinthians 5:1-5," *AusBR* 30 (1982) 34–55.

Rosner, Brian S. "'Ouchi mallon epenthēsate': Corporate Responsibility in 1 Corinthians 5," *NTS* 38 (1992) 470–473.

_____. *Paul, Scripture and Ethics,* 61–93.

_____. "Temple and Holiness in 1 Corinthians 5," *TynB* 41 (1991) 137–145.

South, James T. "A critique of the 'Curse/Death' Interpretation of 1 Corinthians 5:1-8," *NTS* 39 (1993) 539–561.

Thiselton, Anthony C. "The Meaning of *sarx* in 1 Corinthians 5:5: A Fresh Approach in the Light of Logical and Semantic Factors," *SJTh* 26 (1973) 204–228.

Vander Broek, Lyle D. "Discipline and Community: Another Look at 1 Corinthians 5," *RefR* 48 (1994) 5–13.

Vos, Craig Steven De. "Stepmothers, Concubines and the Case of Porneia in 1 Corinthians 5," *NTS* 44 (1988) 104–114.

Wibbing, Siegfried. *Die Tügend- und Lasterkataloge im Neuen Testament und ihre Traditionsgeschichte unter besonderer Berücksichtigung der Qumran-Texte.* BZNW 25. Berlin: Töpelman, 1959.

2. *Shunning Evil* (5:9-13)

9. In the letter I wrote to you not to associate with sexually immoral people, 10. not meaning the sexually immoral of this world in general, or the avaricious and the greedy, or the idolatrous, because then you would have to leave the world. 11. Now I write to you not to associate with someone who bears the name of brother or sister and who is sexually immoral or avaricious or idolatrous or slanderous or a drunkard or greedy. You should not even dine with someone like that.

12. Why am I to judge outsiders? Shouldn't you judge insiders? 13. God will judge outsiders. Remove the evil one from your very midst.

INTERPRETATION

The epistolary features that characterized each of the previous sections of Paul's letter, 4:14-16, so similar to Hellenistic letters of admonition, 4:17-21, resembling the Hellenistic letter of recommendation, and 5:1-8, with its absent-in-body present-in-spirit motif, continue in 5:9-13. In this passage Paul makes reference to a previous letter he had written to the Corinthians (v. 9). This earlier letter has been lost as has, apparently, the so-called letter of tears to which Paul refers in 2 Cor 2:4, 9. Paul's reference to an earlier letter indicates that his "first" letter to the Corinthians is not, in fact, his first letter to that community. Paul had an ongoing correspondence with the Corinthians. He wrote to them on several occasions and they wrote to him (7:1).

Paul makes two references to writing. In both instances he uses the aorist tense of the verb *graphō*. One must ask, however, whether the verb has the same meaning in both cases. The so-called epistolary aorist is well known in classical and Hellenistic Greek. Since a letter was written from the perspective of an orally delivered address what has been written in a letter can be phrased in the aorist, a "past tense" (cf. 4:17). Paul's reference to having written a letter in v. 9 certainly refers to his previous correspondence with the Corinthians, but his reference to writing in v. 11 may either refer to this earlier letter or to what Paul has already written in the present letter (an epistolary aorist). The difference of interpretation of Paul's aorist expression *nyn egrapsa* is reflected in the different modern versions of the NT. The *RSV* took Paul's aorist in v. 11 as a genuine aorist and offered the translation "rather I wrote to you"; the *NRSV* takes the aorist as an epistolary aorist and translates the text "now I am writing to you."

Social Concerns. Paul's concern is clearly with the integrity of the Corinthian community as a group set apart, that is, a holy community (1:2). The emphasis on the social status of the community is reflected in the language he uses. He speaks of the community's relationships, twice using the verb "to associate," *synanamignymi,* a verb he does not elsewhere use in his correspondence (cf. 2 Thess 3:14). In the past as in the present he urges the Corinthians not to mingle with people whose behavior can be described as sexually immoral. The Jews, God's holy people, had a long tradition of avoiding social contact with those whose moral conduct was not acceptable. (See, for example, Psalm 101.) They maintained standards of sexual morality that enabled them to compare themselves favorably, and prejudicially, with Gentiles whose sexual conduct was considered to be reprehensible, the result of idolatrous behavior (5:1; cf. Rom 1:24-27; 1 Thess 4:5).

Concern for the integrity and identity of the community is also expressed in v. 11 where Paul uses kinship language (*tis adelphos,* any brother or sister) and speaks of eating together *(synesthiein).* In every culture table fellowship is one of the strongest expressions of social ties. Table fellowship provides an opportunity for meaningful social discourse. A shared meal brings people together in a truly vital activity in which individual/biological and social needs are met. Table fellowship is one of the strongest expressions of and most important means of social bonding. The paradigm of the common meal is the family meal. Paul's use of kinship language underscores the social role of table fellowship. That the Corinthians should not have table fellowship with someone with whom they have ties of fictive kinship underscores the gravity of the situation addressed by Paul.

The identity of the community continues to focus Paul's discourse as he writes about insiders (*tous esō,* v. 12) and outsiders (*tous exō,* vv. 12, 13). The language speaks strongly of group identity and social boundaries. The contrast between outsiders and insiders is patent. That Paul writes about outsiders before mentioning insiders underscores the distinctiveness of the community. The community is different from those others, the outsiders, who do such things as Paul has identified in vv. 10 and 11. Distinctiveness is a significant component of identity. Individual and group alike are who they are because they are different from those whom they are not.

Paul's exposition culminates in an exhortation (v. 13b) whose language is similar to a biblical, specifically a Deuteronomic exclusionary formula (cf. Deut 17:7; 19:19; 21:21; 22:21; 24:7). The use of the traditional formula is noteworthy. Paul does not introduce the biblical quotation by means of the classic lemma "as it is written" (cf. 1:19, 31; 2:9; 3:19; 9:9; 10:7; 14:21; 15:45). The quotation does not function explicitly as a scriptural warrant for Paul's rhetorical argument. Absent the introductory lemma the scriptural language becomes Paul's own language. Phrased in the imperative and placed at the conclusion of the exposition, it provides a paraenetic thrust to the entire unit. Its concluding words, "from your very midst" *(ex hymōn autōn)*, provide a pointed rhetorical flourish that caps Paul's expressed concern for the integrity of the community.

The community about which Paul writes in such a way as to emphasize its internal bondedness and its external distinction is a community that exists in a broader social context. That goes without saying, as Paul's summary rehearsal of his earlier correspondence with the Corinthians makes clear. The community exists in "this world" (twice in v. 10). Paul's apocalyptic worldview leads him to characterize the world in which the Corinthians live as "this world" *(tou kosmou toutou)*, with connotations of some distinction from the world to come and a judgment that this world festers with evil. This world *(tou kosmou)* is, nonetheless, the context, and the reality factor, in which the Corinthians are to live their lives as a community of God's holy people.

A Catalogue of Vices. In the context of his exhortation on sexual immorality Paul cites three lists of vices. Four vices are mentioned in v. 10. These four and an additional two are cited in v. 11. The first list mentions the sexually immoral, the avaricious, the greedy, and the idolatrous. The second adds to these four slanderers and drunkards. A third list appears in 6:9-10. This third list includes the six vices of 5:10 with an additional four vices: adulterers, perverts, homosexuals, and thieves.

Listing a series of vices in this fashion was a well-known rhetorical device in the Hellenistic world. Well-attested in ancient literature, the series has a literary form identified by modern critics as a list or catalogue of vices. Use of the literary form is especially found in the writings of classic moralists in the Stoic and Cynic tradition. The list of vices described the wretched moral condition of the masses. Adapted by Hellenistic Judaism (cf. 1QS 4:9-11), the literary form was widely used in early Christian literature (1 Pet 2:1; 4:3, 15; Rev 21:8; 22:15; *Did.* 1:2–2:7; 5:1-2). Rhetor that he was, Paul used the catalogue of vices with good rhetorical effect. See, for example, Rom 1:29-31; 13:13; 2 Cor 12:20-21; Gal 5:19-21 (cf. Eph 4:31; 5:3-5; Col 3:5, 8; 1 Tim 1:9-10; 6:4-5; 2 Tim 3:2-5; Titus 1:7; 3:3; 1 Pet 4:15). The list of vices has its antithetical counterpart in the catalogue of virtues. Paul is also not unfamiliar with the use of a list of virtues (2 Cor

6:6-7a; Gal 5:22-23; Phil 4:8; cf. Eph 4:2-3, 32-5:2; 5:9; Col 3:12; 1 Tim 3:2-4, 8-10, 11-12; 4:12, 6:11, 18; 2 Tim 2:22-25; 3:10; Titus 1:8, 2:2-10; Heb 7:26). In Gal 5:19-23 Paul effectively contrasts a list of vices, the works of the flesh, with a list of virtues, the fruits of the Spirit.

As a literary form the list of vices is characterized by its sequential nature, with (polysyndeton) or without (asyndeton) the use of connective particles. The vices are cited one after the other, generally without any further qualification. The vices may be presented in a personal fashion with nouns and substantivized adjectives (e.g., the sexually immoral, *pornoi*, in 6:10 and 11), either in the singular (5:11) or in the plural (5:10; 6:10-11). Alternatively, the list may be presented in theoretical fashion with abstract nouns (e.g., *porneia*, "sexual misconduct;" Gal 5:19-21; 1 Thess 2:3), or in active fashion with verbs (e.g., *porneuō*, "to engage in sexual misconduct"). The vices that appear on the lists are classic, but the extant literature does not provide any normative list of such vices; neither was any single listing considered to be exhaustive. Since the vices are simply listed one after the other and many of them pertain to the same sphere of morality it is often difficult to determine the precise connotation of any single vice on the list.

Characterized by their typical vocabulary, the literary catalogues of vices are generally isolable from the larger literary unit into which they have been incorporated. Each of them constitutes a distinct literary topos whose form is different from that of the embedding literary context. The standard vocabulary of the lists and their literary isolability leads to the question as to what extent a rhetor's use of a vice list actually reflects the situation that is being addressed. Does the rhetor use the vice list simply to affirm that evil is rampant in the situation under consideration? Or has a list of vices been selectively chosen so that it represents with reasonable accuracy, appropriate caricature, suitable satire, or the true rhetorical stasis?

In and of itself the fact that Paul made use of such a catalogue does not imply that each of the vices mentioned in his list was rampant at Corinth. On the other hand, when citing Scripture Paul generally intends to evoke the context to which his texts refer and some similarity does exist between the vices mentioned by Paul in vv. 10 and 11 and the various sins to which the Deuteronomistic exclusionary formula (see note on 5:13) makes reference. Paul does not use scriptural texts in proof-text fashion, that is, in epistemological isolation from their biblical context.

Paul generally adapts his lists of vices to the specific situation he is addressing. His catalogues of vices are custom-made for the epistolary situation. This seems to be the case in vv. 9 and 10. The matter of sexual morality—and immorality!—is one that occupies the principal focus of chs. 5 to 7. The reality of idol worship is the background for the discussion in chs. 8 to 10. Matters of justice come to the fore in 6:1-11. The *hybris* of some Corinthians was seen by Paul to lie at the source of the divisions with which he was concerned in 1:18–4:21. Hellenistic moralists considered that slander was caused by *hybris.* Drunkenness seems not to have been a major preoccupation of Paul in writing to the Corinthians. He was, however, concerned that some of the "elite" within the community would drink to excess without regard to sharing with others when they came together for a meal that ought to have been the Lord's Supper (11:22).

While it is impossible to say that the vices of vv. 10-11 were rampant among the Corinthian Christians, it would appear that from among the many vices known to him Paul has selected for insertion in the list of vices of ch. 5 those vices that might have been particularly troublesome for the community at Corinth.

Judgment. In vv. 12 and 13 Paul writes about judgment: judgment by himself, judgment by the church, and judgment by God. The judgment motif is one that recurs throughout the letter, but Paul's use of the verb *krinō*, "to judge" is most dense in 5:1–6:11 (see 5:3, 12[2x], 13; 6:1, 2[2x], 3, 6). The verb serves as a catchword that links together the three epistolary units (5:1-8, 9-13; 6:1-11) and provides them with a common theme, judgment, that ties the units together.

Earlier in the letter Paul had noted that people endowed with the Spirit judge everything, but that they themselves are not to be judged by any human being (2:15). Paul does not dare to judge himself (4:3), but he has made a judgment with regard to the Corinthian man who had been guilty of sexual immorality (5:3-4). Paul's willingness to adjudicate the case indicates that he considers the incestuous man to have acted in a way contrary to the movement of the Spirit. Paul, on the other hand, is not willing to judge those who do not belong to the church of God.

Those who are spiritual (2:15), those who are holy (6:2) are to judge all things. All the more are they to judge those within the community whose conduct mars the community's identity and integrity. The judgment should result in such persons' being expelled from the community (vv. 2c; 4c-5; 7a, 13b). Only in this way can the community maintain its quality of being God's holy people.

Expelled from the community, evildoers are no longer insiders; they have become outsiders. The community's judgment is not, however, the final judgment. God ultimately judges outsiders just as he judges insiders (3:17; 4:4b-5).

NOTES

9. *In the letter I wrote to you not to associate with sexually immoral people:* Paul's reference to a previous letter serves as a reminder of Paul's ongoing correspon-

dence with the Corinthian community (see 7:1; 2 Corinthians). Chrysostom omits the phrase "in the letter," but it is present in virtually all extant manuscripts and so must be considered an authentic part of Paul's correspondence. Paul had previously urged the Corinthians not to mingle with those who are "sexually immoral." This term *(pornois)* is often translated as "immoral," but the word is related to *porneia*. It means those who have engaged in sexual misconduct *(porneia;* see 5:1; 6:13, 18; 7:2; cf. 2 Cor 12:21; Gal 5:19; 1 Thess 4:3). Only in 1 Corinthians' exhortation on sexual immorality does Paul use the substantivized adjective, *pornoi* (5:9, 10, 11; 6:9). In 5:10 Paul clearly distinguishes those who are sexually immoral from those whose behavior is otherwise immoral, for example, the avaricious and the greedy.

10. *not meaning the sexually immoral of this world in general, or the avaricious and the greedy, or the idolatrous:* Paul's explanatory phrase begins with the negation of a universal *(ou pantōs)*. The negative should be taken to mean "not . . . in general" (so BDF 433.2). Some commentators, however, take the phrase to mean "not at all meaning." Norbert Baumert (*Woman and Man* 156) suggests that the phrase means "not entirely," as if the immoral were to be shunned but only up to a certain point.

"This world" *(tou kosmou toutou)* has negative and apocalyptic connotations (cf. Gal 1:4, *ek tou aiōnos tou enestōtos ponērou*). This world is a world that is passing away; it is a world in which evil holds sway. To describe the presence of evil in this world Paul speaks of those who have engaged in immoral sexual behavior as well as of the avaricious *(pleonektais)*, the greedy *(harpaxin)*, and the idolatrous *(eidōlolatrais)*.

That Paul uses the disjunctive conjunction "or" *(ē)* twice and joins "avaricious" and "greedy" by "and" *(kai)* suggests that the *kai* is an epexegetical *kai* and that "avaricious" and "greedy" are essentially synonymous with one another. Both adjectives are used in the Pauline vice lists of 5:11 and 6:10 (cf. Eph 5:5); the respective word groups occur frequently in Pauline paraenesis. In the Hellenistic world, where goods were considered to exist in finite quantity, avarice *(pleonexia;* see *TLNT* 3:117-119) was a grave social offense. "Avarice," wrote Menander, "is a very great evil for humans; for those who wish to have their neighbors' goods often fail and are conquered" (fragment in Stobaeus' Anthology, see Curt Wachsmuth and Otto Hense, eds., *Ioannis Stobaei Anthologium.* Reprint ed. Berlin: Weidmann, 1974, 3.10.3). Hellenistic moralists exhorted people to flee from avarice (see Musonius, frag., 4.48.9; 6.52.18; 8.62.17; Dio Chrysostom, *Discourses* 13.32; 17.22), as Paul exhorted people to flee from sexual immorality. It could be swindlers who were considered to be "greedy" (see BAGD 109; *TDNT* 1:157).

Paul frequently couples avarice and sexual immorality. Sharing a Jewish prejudice, he considered both vices to be rampant among pagans. The vices resulted from idolatry and went together. From a Jewish perspective, moral and religious behavior go hand in hand (see, for example, the decalogue). Idolatry results in deviant social behavior, of which sexual immorality and avarice were particularly egregious forms (cf. Rom 1:19-32; Wis 12:24; *T. Levi* 18:11; Philo, *Allegorical Interpretation* 3.8; *Migration of Abraham* 69; *Names* 205).

In his paraenetic midrash on the Exodus story in 10:5-14, Paul intimates that idolatry has sexual immorality as its consequence. Idolaters engage in sexual misconduct (see 10:6-7).

because then you would have to leave the world: "Because then" (*epei ara* = "otherwise") introduces an unrealizable condition. This worldly existence is the human condition. The Corinthians lived in the real world, from which there was no escape. Were they to live in a world where there was not idolatry, with concomitant sexual immorality and avarice, they would have to leave the real world. This they were not called to do, nor was it even possible for them to do so.

11. *Now I write to you:* Paul's *nyn egrapsa* can be taken as a true aorist with the meaning "then I wrote to you," or as an epistolary aorist with the meaning "now I write to you." On balance it would appear that Paul had previously exhorted the community not to associate with evil people without necessarily specifying various categories of evil people through the use of a list of vices. First Corinthians adds a specification to what had been implicit in the earlier exhortation. Now Paul exhorts the community to shun any of its members who falls back into an egregiously sinful pattern of conduct (cf. 6:9). It is unlikely that either in his evangelizing of the community or in his epistolary paraenesis Paul had set forth community regulations. Only the community's undue tolerance of, or perhaps their pride in immoral behavior (5:6) prompts Paul to set down rule for community order such as he does in 1 Corinthians.

not to associate with someone who bears the name of brother or sister and who is sexually immoral or avaricious or idolatrous or slanderous or a drunkard or greedy: This translation tries to capture the sense of Paul's Greek, which consists of a participial clause followed by a series of six nouns or substantivized adjectives linked paratactically by a sixfold repetition of the conjunction "or" (*ē*). The cumulative effect of the paratactic construction provides emphasis to Paul's appeal.

To "bear the name of" (*onomazomenos*) resonates with Paul's previous use of "name," the *onoma* of Jesus Christ (1:2, 10, 13, 15; cf. 6:11). Only here and in Rom 15:20 does Paul use the verb "to bear the name of." Paul's reference to the name underscores the asocial and un-christian character of the evil behavior that is illustrated in the catalogue of vices (cf. 6:11).

"Slanderous" (*loidoros*) and "drunkard" (*methysos*) appear elsewhere in the NT only in the catalogue of vices at 6:10. Both terms are, nonetheless, apt descriptions of some of the Corinthians. Slander (*loidoria*) is a form of *hybris* (*TLNT* 2:407–409), an attitude for which Paul frequently reproaches the Corinthians. That some of them become drunk (*methuei*, 11:21) is one of the scandals of their coming together. The other four categories of vicious persons, the sexually immoral, avaricious, idolatrous, and the greedy, had been previously cited in the catalogue of vices in 5:9-10.

You should not even dine with someone like that: "Someone like that" (*tō toioutō*) is literally "such a one." To "dine with" (*synesthiō*, literally "to eat together") occurs five times in the NT, three times in Luke-Acts (Luke 15:2; Acts 10:41; 11:3) and twice in Paul (see Gal 2:12). Here the term should be taken in its root sense of eating together rather than in the narrow sense of eucharistic fellow-ship. Paul wishes that the community not have social interaction, of which the common meal is a most important sign, with someone whose behavior egregiously violates social mores. Such a ban includes but is not restricted to exclusion from eucharistic fellowship.

12. *Why am I to judge outsiders? Shouldn't you judge insiders?* The pair of contrast-ing rhetorical questions is neatly balanced. Paul speaks of himself and the community *(moi, hymeis)*, of judging *(krinein, krinete)*, and of outsiders and in-siders *(tous exō, tous esō)*. The first question begs a negative response, the sec-ond a positive response. The elliptical interrogative *ti gar*, "what's it to me?" with which the first question begins is common in Paul's writings (Rom 3:3; Phil 1:18, etc.).

Outsiders are those who do not belong to the Christian community (cf. 1 Thess 4:12; Col 4:5). Throughout 1 Corinthians Paul is concerned with the so-cial status of the Corinthians. His social world is divided into two parts, those inside and those outside, those who know God and those who do not (cf. 1 Thess 4:5), those who are called saints and those who are not. While Paul pro-fesses not to judge those outside he is concerned that Christians should be held in proper esteem by outsiders lest the gospel message be compromised by the behavior of those called to be saints (cf. 1 Thess 4:12; 1 Tim 3:6-7).

13. *God will judge outsiders:* Since the older Greek manuscripts ($\mathfrak{P}^{46}$, ℵ, A, B, C, D) did not use accent marks Paul's *krinei*, "will judge," can be read as a future tense or as a present tense. In the light of Paul's repeated reference to escha-tological judgment (3:13-15; 17; 4:5) it seems preferable to take the verb in the future. The Matthean parable of the wheat and the tares (Matt 13:24-30, 36-43) symbolically speaks of the coexistence of good and evil in the present age and of the future judgment that leads to definitive separation.

Remove the evil one from your very midst: Paul's concluding exhortation in-cludes a play on words; "the evil one" *(ponēron, v. 13)* resonates with "the sexually immoral" *(pornois, vv. 9, 10, 11)*. Paul's formula—except for a change in the form of the verb (from a singular future indicative to a plural aorist im-perative)—is similar to the Deuteronomic exclusionary formula (cf. Deut 17:7; 19:19; 21:21; 22:21; 24:7; see Rosner, *Paul, Scripture and Ethics* 61–68). Deuter-onomy is after Isaiah (28x) and the Psalms the biblical book most commonly cited by the apostle (see James M. Scott, "Paul's Use of Deuteronomic Tradi-tion," *JBL* 112 (1993) 645–655), but elsewhere in 1 Corinthians Deuteronomy is exploited only in 9:8-10. Paul has applied the biblical injunction to a specific situation (note the use of the aorist), one that is similar to the situation envi-sioned by Deut 22:21.

Herbert Marks ("Pauline Typology and Revisionary Criticism," *JAAR* 52 (1984) 71–92, especially 76) correctly notes that "Paul most often appeals to the authority of scripture to reinforce ethical precepts or to adjudicate specific questions of personal conduct and church policy (Rom 13:9f., 14:11; 1 Cor 5:13, 9:9; 2 Cor 8:15, 9:9; and elsewhere)." This is the case in the present in-stance, even if Paul has not specifically identified the biblical authority on the basis of which he is making his appeal. The quotation lacks the referential marker "as it is written." That Paul is nonetheless citing a text is confirmed by his use of the verb "remove" *(exairō)* and the substantivized adjective "the evil one" *(ponēron)*. "Remove" is hapax in the NT; "evil" is hapax in 1 Corinthians. "From your very midst" *(ex hymōn autōn)* is, moreover, the only NT use of *autos* in the usual reflexive manner of classical and Hellenistic Greek (see BDF 288.1).

For Reference and Further Study

Meeks, Wayne A. "Since Then You Would Need To Go Out Of The World: Group Boundaries in Pauline Christianity" in Thomas J. Ryan, ed., *Critical History and Biblical Faith: New Testament Perspectives*. Villanova, Pa.: College Theology Society/*Horizons*, 1979, 4–29.

Mussner, Franz. "'Das Wesen des Christentums ist *synesthiein*.' Ein authentischer Kommentar" in Heribert Rossmann and Joseph Ratzinger, eds., *Mysterium der Gnade. Festschrift für Johann Auer*. Regensburg: Pustet, 1975, 92–102.

Rosner, Brian S. "The Function of Scripture in 1 Cor 5,13b and 6,16" *CorC*, 513–518.

_____. "A Possible Quotation of Test. Reuben 5:5 in 1 Corinthians 6:18a," *JTS* 43 (1992) 123–127.

Wagenhammer, Hans. "'Das Wesen des Christentums ist *synesthiein*.' Bemerkungen zu einem Programmwort" in Paul-Gerhard Müller and Werner Stenger, eds., *Kontinuität und Einheit. Für Franz Mussner*. Freiburg, Basel, and Vienna: Herder, 1981, 494–507.

Zaas, Peter S. "'Cast Out the Evil Man from Your Midst' (1 Cor 5:13b)," *JBL* 103 (1984) 259–261.

_____. "Catalogues and Context: 1 Corinthians 5 and 6," *NTS* 34 (1988) 622–629.

3. *Use of the Courts* (6:1-11)

1. Does one of you, having some issue against another, have the effrontery to be judged before unjust persons, and not before holy persons? 2. Don't you know that the holy ones will judge the world? And if the world is to be judged by you, are you incapable of rendering judgment in minor cases? 3. Don't you know that we will judge angels? How much more so ordinary cases! 4. Why then, if you do have ordinary cases, do you seat as judges those who are treated with scorn in the church? 5. I say this to shame you. So is there no wise person among you who can judge between siblings? 6. Does a brother or sister take a sibling to court and this before those who have no faith?

7. In short, it's already failure for you when you receive judgments against one another. Why not rather suffer wrong? Why not rather be cheated? 8. But you yourselves wrong and cheat even your siblings. 9. Don't you know that the unjust will not inherit the kingdom? Don't go astray! Neither the sexually immoral, nor idolaters, nor adulterers, nor perverts, nor homosexuals, 10. nor thieves, nor the avaricious, not drunkards, not slanderers, not the greedy will inherit the kingdom of God. 11. And some of you were such; but you have been washed, you have been made holy, you have been justified in the name of the Lord Jesus Christ and in the Spirit of our God.

INTERPRETATION

Paul's Rhetoric. Given the importance of the chiastic pattern (the A-B-A' schema) in 1 Corinthians many commentators have sought to identify this section of Paul's letter as a rhetorical digression. As such it would undergird the thoughts on human sexuality that the Apostle has developed in ch. 5 and ch. 6, vv. 12-20. That such is the nature of 6:1-11 is not readily apparent even though there are clear links between this epistolary unit and the encompassing sections of Paul's letter. The most obvious of these links is that the list of vices Paul cites in vv. 9-10 takes up and expands the two lists of vices cited in ch. 5. Added to the previous lists are several vices involving various forms of sexual misconduct (adultery, perversion, homosexuality).

Judgment is the primary focus of ch. 5. Judgment of one of its errant members by the community is the leitmotif of 5:1-8. The rhetorical climax of ch. 5 is 5:13, where the reference to divine judgment uses the verb "to judge" *(krinō)*, the third appearance of the verb in rapid succession (5:12-13; cf. 6:1, 2, 3, 6). Judgment, albeit from a different perspective, is the focus of Paul's remarks in 6:1-11. Forensic language abounds as the apostle deals with the resolution of civil disputes by members of the community: "to judge" *(krinō,* vv. 1, 2, 3, 6), "cases" *(kritēria,* vv. 2, 4), being seated (as on a judge's bench, *kathizō,* v. 4), "before" (as before a judge, *epi,* vv. 1, 6), "judge between" *(diakrinō,* v. 5), "receive judgments" *(krimata echein,* v. 7). The judicial language makes Paul's digression a natural continuation of the topic of judgment introduced in ch. 5, although reversing the tables. In ch. 5 Paul had spoken of the judgment of outsiders by himself and the church; now he turns to the judgment of Christians by outsiders, those who are unjust (v. 1) and with no Christian faith (v. 6).

Given the linguistic and thematic links between 6:1-11 and its epistolary context some authors suggest that 5:1-8 and 6:1-11 are different sides of the same coin. The issue, they argue, is sexual and clearly identified in 5:1 as a matter of incest. Financial interests could be at issue if the sexual relationship were such that an inheritance or a dowry were involved. In a literary diptych on the matter Paul first treats of ecclesial competence to judge the matter (5:1-8), then of civil competence in the affair (6:1-11). Richardson ("Judgment") opines that the matter should have been resolved by the church itself; but, he argues, recourse was had to the civil judiciary. Deming ("The Unity of 1 Corinthians 5–6"), on the other hand, suggests that the church might have failed in its attempt to judge the matter and that some within the community, aware of the heinousness of incest, appealed to the secular courts for redress. On either of these readings Paul clearly admonishes members of the community for taking their case to court.

The Administration of Justice. Paul's reference to the Corinthians being judged before unjust persons (6:1) evokes the context of a formal legal trial. Relatively little, however, is known about the actual administration of civil justice in Corinth at the time when Paul was writing to the Corinthians. One can presume that justice was administered in much the same fashion as it was in other cities of the Roman empire. The governor himself normally heard the more important cases. "The provincial governor," Augustus had decreed, "must himself act and judge or appoint a panel or jurors [for capital cases], but with the rest of such affairs it is my wish that Greek jurors be appointed" (cf. Victor Ehrenberg and A.H.M. Jones, *Documents Illustrating the Reigns of Augustus and Tiberius* [Oxford: Clarendon, 1976] No. 311, IV ll. 66-68). Ordinary civil cases were heard by the duoviri, two citizens appointed to the magistrature. Aediles heard cases pertaining to business and the agora.

In the Roman world a powerful patronage system was not without its influence—sometimes an undue influence—on the administration of justice. The social status of petitioner or plaintiff was a major factor in the administration of "justice." In civil cases lawsuits were usually initiated by people of equal and upper social status. The poor generally did not have the wherewithal to pay a lawyer to plead their case. In practice the system was thus unfavorable to people of the lower social classes. The elder Seneca, an older contemporary of Paul, tells the story of a rich man taunting a poor man, "Why don't you accuse me, why don't you take me to court?" To this the poor man replied, "Am I, a poor man, to accuse a rich man?" Seneca's commentary was to the effect that the rich man was powerful and influential. Even as a defendant he had nothing to fear from the court (see Lucius Annaeus Seneca, *Controversiae* 10.1.2). In a similar vein Petronius told the story of a man named Ascyltos who was afraid to go to court because he was without influence. He would, moreover, have had no money with which to bribe the magistrate. Bribery (cf. P.Oxyrhynchus 2745, 7-8) and powerful cliques were only two of the sources of corruption in the administration of justice in Paul's day. When

Paul describes the secular judiciary as unjust he is simply reflecting the general opinion of people in his times.

In the Greco-Roman world various associations had their own jurisdictions with courts to judge the disputes, quarrels, and crimes of their members. In some cities Jews enjoyed the privilege of settling some legal matters that arose among themselves. In cities such as Alexandria and Sardis Jewish communities were granted the status of a "civil corporation" *(politeuma)*. Jews living in these cities had their own courts in which they could settle their civil disputes (cf. Josephus, *Ant.* 14.235), but these courts were not competent to adjudicate capital offenses. *Sipre Deut.* 17:8-9 prescribes that in difficult civil disputes the case is to be brought before the court at Yavneh. That court is legitimate even though it includes neither priests nor Levites. In the circumstances envisioned by the *Sipre* there is no court that is recognized as authoritative other than the one at Yavneh. With a reference to Qoh 7:10 the *Sipre* indicates that one ought not to pine for the judicial structures of previous eras.

There is no evidence that the Jewish community in Corinth had been recognized as a civil corporation and had its own court. On the other hand, archaeological evidence from Corinth does indicate that two men, the *duoviri*, were the highest magistrates in the metropolis. Chosen from among the leading citizens of the town, they served for a one-year term. Civil cases normally began in the courts of these magistrates.

The Effrontery of Going to Court. Paul does not intimate that the secular courts of Corinth lacked jurisdiction to hear cases involving Christians; rather he suggests that it is unseemly for Christians to bring their disputes before the secular jurisdiction. The scandals of the community should not be made known to those who do not share the faith. At issue is the community's identity as God's holy people (1:2) and the boundaries between it and those outside.

Paul's reaction to Christians' having recourse to secular courts is developed in two movements of thought. He first argues that Christians ought to be able to settle their disputes among themselves (6:1-6). Then— and more radically—he argues that Christians should not have among themselves any disputes of such a nature as to be subject to civil litigation (6:7-8). Verses 6 and 8 provide the respective climaxes for each movement of thought. The parallelism between these verses, two rhetorical questions bearing on action against a sibling, unites what Paul has to say about the use of an arbiter and his arguments against having lawsuits (see Mitchell, "1 Corinthians 6:1-11," 42; "Litigiousness," 565).

Having expressed mild shock that some Christians have appealed to the secular judiciary (v. 1), Paul develops his argument in a striking series of nine rhetorical questions. His manner of arguing recalls the Stoic diatribe. The use of contrast (vv. 3-4, 7-8, 9-11) and direct address give added force to the argument. The first and last of Paul's rhetorical questions (vv. 2, 9) appeal to the Corinthians' knowledge about the eschaton, "Don't you know that . . .?" The questions form a literary *inclusio* and provide an eschatological framework for Paul's argument. The eschatological condition of the Corinthians makes it unseemly for them to bring their civil disputes before unjust civil magistrates.

What then? Paul asks whether there is not someone within the community who is sufficiently wise (see 1:26) to be able to adjudicate disputes among members of the community (v. 5). Paul's question is phrased in such a way that it implies that surely there must be someone within the community who is competent enough to function as an arbitrator. The extrajudicial arbiter, *arbiter ex compromisso,* was a well-known figure in the imperial era. The arbiter enjoyed broad discretionary powers. Should one of their own function in this capacity when they had disputes among themselves the Corinthian Christians would be able to maintain their distinct identity as God's holy people. It would be a serious failure on the part of the community if it were not able to identify a competent and effective arbiter within its midst. From Paul's perspective the issue is not so much that some Corinthian Christians have done wrong, which would provide legitimate grounds for a judicial case; it is rather that the pursuit of a civil case in court represents a failure on the part of Christians to maintain their identity and integrity as God's holy people. Within Israel there had been a long tradition that justice should be administered by God's people themselves. Exodus 18:21-27 describes how minor judicial matters should be settled by "able men among all the people" (Exod 18:21), while the hard cases were to be brought to Moses. The Exodus narrative speaks of these able men "judging" *(krinousin)* these matters. In the biblical tradition "to judge" is to be partial, that is, to take care of the innocent and the oppressed and to punish the wicked.

With a pair of rhetorical questions (v. 7bc) Paul suggests that it is preferable to be wronged and suffer some loss than to appeal to the courts. Paul's rhetoric puts Christians who take their grievances to court in the role of wrongdoers. They are unjust, just like the corrupt judges to whom they submit their cases. The idea that people ought not to have recourse to the secular judiciary is a thought that Paul shares with Cynics and Stoics. His own ideas differ from those of the philosophers insofar as his argument is based on the nature of the community, its eschatological status, and the family ties that bind Christians to one another.

In an essay on brotherly love Plutarch asks, in diatribal fashion, what is to be done when one has a bad sibling. He answers that one must put up with the sibling. Such is the responsibility nature assigns to members of the family. He adds that we humans often bear with more serious wrongs from chance acquaintances than we do from members of our own families (Plutarch, "Brotherly Love," *Moralia* 481E-482C). The Stoic view was influenced by the Platonic conviction that doing wrong is worse than suffering it (see Plato, *Gorgias* 509C). A classic philosophical topos on the wise person included the idea that the person who is truly wise would rather be wronged than do wrong. Musonius Rufus, for example, said: "For what does the one who submits to insult do that is wrong? It is the doer of wrong who forthwith puts himself to shame, while the sufferer, who does nothing but submit, has no reason whatever to feel shame or disgrace. Therefore, the sensible person would not go to law nor bring indictments, since that one would not even consider that he had been insulted" (*Will the Philosopher Prosecute Anyone for Personal Injury?* 10.15-23; cf. Epictetus, *Discourses* 3.22.55-56; Plutarch, "Precepts of Statecraft," *Moralia* 814E–816A; Seneca, *Epistles* 95.52).

The Kingdom of God. Returning to the eschatological perspective with which he began his appeal (6:1-3a), Paul reminds the Corinthians that those who are unjust do not inherit the kingdom of God (v. 9). The remark is primarily intended for rhetorical effect. "Don't you know that?" recalls Paul's previous teaching, but the formula does not imply that Paul had specifically taught that anyone whose *persona* could be described in terms of any of the vices on the list was actually excluded from the kingdom. His rhetoric may simply imply that he had previously taught the Corinthians about the radical incompatibility between certain forms of behavior and the call to the kingdom of God. Galatians 5:21 and 1 Thess 5:12 suggest that some form of catechesis along these lines was an integral part of Paul's instruction of neophyte Christian communities.

Being unjust should have been a matter of past history for the Corinthian Christians (v. 11). They had been redeemed, made holy, and justified "in the name of the Lord Jesus Christ and in the Spirit of our God." Having been exhorted to shun one of their number who persists in immoral behavior (5:9-13), the Corinthians should not become backsliders, returning to their old ways. That old way of life is depicted in the form of a list of vices, inserted amidst the rhetoric of vv. 9 and 11. These verses are characterized by their direct rhetorical appeal (Paul's use of the second person plural) and their eschatological perspective. Verse 11 provides a powerful rhetorical climax to Paul's appeal.

Vices and Paul's Rhetoric. Paul's use of a list of vices adds insult to injury as he takes the Corinthians to task. The philosophical moralists typically used catalogues of vices to caricature the woeful behavior of the unlettered masses; Paul uses a list of vices to confront the *hybris* of the know-it-alls in the community. Those whose lives are characterized by any one of these vices will not inherit the kingdom.

The list of ten vices reprises the six vices of 5:11, an expansion of the list of four in 5:10. The first two forms of immoral behavior cited by Paul in 6:9-10 are sexual immorality and idolatry (cf. 5:10, 11). Idolatry is a significant feature of several early Christian catalogues of vices (cf. Gal 5:20; 1 Pet 4:3; Col 3:5; Eph 5:5; Rev 9:20; 22:15). The linking of idolatry with sexual immorality is consistent with the Jewish teaching of the times. The Sibylline Oracles, for example, exhort, "Shun unlawful worship; worship the Living One. Avoid adultery and indiscriminate intercourse with males" (*Sib. Or.* 3.764-766; cf. Rom 1:24-27).

Three additional categories of those exhibiting sexual vices (adulterers, perverts, and homosexuals) appear on Paul's list immediately after his mention of idolatry. The three do not appear on the list of six vices in 5:11. In fact the descriptive terms, "adulterers" *(moichoi)*, "perverts" *(malakoi)*, and "homosexuals" *(arsenokoitai)*, are hapax in the extant Pauline correspondence. The string of *hapax legomena* suggests that Paul is using a classic topos for the sake of his argument. They illustrate a range of behavior that could be encompassed under the generic rubric "sexually immoral" *(pornoi)* and provide a sexual emphasis in the vice list of 6:9-10. An unusual emphasis on sexual immorality distinguishes this particular list of vices from other Pauline catalogues of vices (cf. Rom 13:13; 2 Cor 12:20; Gal 5:19-21; 1 Pet 4:15; compare Rom 1:29-31; 2 Cor 12:21). Rhetorically it appeals to innate sensibilities and prejudices and serves to link Paul's digression on Christians before secular courts of law with the encompassing sections dealing with issues of sexual immorality (5:1-13; 6:12-20).

Some of the forms of misbehavior cited in Paul's list may allude to one or another matter that had been submitted to the unjust judges for their judgment. "Thievery" *(kleptēs)*, not cited in 5:10-11, may be such a case. Apart from 5:11 Paul uses the noun only in the similes of 1 Thess 5:2, 4 (cf. Matt 24:43; Luke 12:39). Thievery is a standard feature of vice lists (cf. 1 Pet 4:15) but Paul's use of the cognate verb, *kleptō*, "to steal," in Rom 2:21 and 13:9 suggests that he might have added this particular vice to his list under the influence of the Decalogue where the commandments on adultery and on theft follow one another (Exod 20:14-15; Deut 5:18-19; cf. Rom 2:21-22).

In any case the vices cited by Paul generally pertain to issues with which Paul continues to be concerned throughout the letter. Paul's use of the topos is, nonetheless, such that one cannot demonstrate that any of the additional vices on the expanded list in 6:9-10 is case specific to the situation in Corinth. The list of vices is cited primarily for rhetorical effect. Indeed, it enhances Paul's rhetoric in a variety of ways. At the beginning of the exposition Paul had expressed mild outrage that some Christians at Corinth submitted their disputes to unjust persons *(adikōn,* v. 1). With his list of vices he reminds his correspondents what it means to be "unjust." Spelling out the implications of "unjust" highlights Paul's umbrage at the rash conduct of those Corinthians whose behavior implies that they are as one with those who are unjust (v. 8). His rehearsal of the various kinds of misbehavior that once characterized their behavior is an implicit invitation to them to look at their lives, claim their identity as God's holy people, and live accordingly.

NOTES

1. *Does one of you, having some issue against another, have the effrontery to be judged before unjust persons, and not before holy persons?* Aristophanes and other classical authors occasionally used "to have something" *(pragma echein)* in the negative sense of having troublesome business. "Against another" *(pragma echōn pros ton heteron)* suggests a hostile relationship (BDF 239.5), specifically, an adversarial relationship related to some particular matter. "Before [=in the presence of] unjust persons" *(epi tōn adikōn)* suggests an appeal to the courts. Paul's words evoke the legal setting of a case being heard before a judge. The case he envisions has to do with a relatively minor (v. 2) civil (v. 1) matter. Alan C. Mitchell suggests the analogy of the contemporary small claims court. Paul professes shock that relatively minor issues between Christians should be brought before civil magistrates.

    Although it is sometimes argued that "unjust" is synonymous with "unfaithful" (v. 6) and is to be taken in a religious rather than a moral sense, there is sufficient evidence of judicial corruption in the Roman world to ascribe to "unjust" *(adikōn)* its proper sense.

    Given the social divide within the Christian community at Corinth it is not impossible that only the powerful few (1:26) had recourse to the secular courts, but it is not possible to infer this conclusively from what Paul says in 1 Cor 6:1-11. In any case it is brazen for members of the community to take one another to court over trivial matters (see v. 3) when a matter such as the incestuous relationship between a man and his father's wife goes without judgment. That the judges to whom the Corinthian Christians had recourse were popularly considered to be unjust only serves to heighten the poignancy of Paul's appeal.

2. *Don't you know that the holy ones will judge the world?* Some authors (Johannes Weiss, Strack-Billerbeck, etc.) find in this passage a reference to the book of Daniel's vision of the Son of Man, in which judgment is given to the holy ones of the Most High (Dan 7:21-22); others find Wis 3:8 to be a helpful passage. Later Jewish writings commonly express a belief that God's people will participate in the final judgment (Wis 3:7-8; Sir 4:11, 15; *Jub.* 24:29; *1 Enoch* 1:9; 38:1, 5; 95:3; 96:1; 98:12; 108:12; 1QH 4:26-27; 1QpHab 5:4-5). Paul shares this eschatological outlook, all the while considering that the Corinthian Christians are among God's holy people (1:2).

    And if the world is to be judged by you, are you incapable of rendering judgment in minor cases? In the mode of rhetorical *logos* Paul's questioning has the form of an enthymeme. He argues *a maiori ad minus* (cf. Rom 5:6-9, 10; 8:32; 11:32), a procedure that some authors consider to be a reversal of the traditional *qal wa-ḥomer* hermeneutical principle, the argument from the minor premise to the major.

Paul does not indicate what he means by "minor" *(kritēriōn elachistōn)* or "ordinary cases" *(kritēria biōtika,* vv. 3, 4). The judicial term, "rendering judgment" *(kritēriōn,* in Paul in 6:2, 4) occurs in Exod 21:6. Paul's "by you" *(en hymin)* identifies the Corinthian community with (at least some of) the holy ones who will judge the world. It recalls 1:2, where the Corinthians are characterized as those "called holy." The inference, suggesting that the real issue is the community's identity as the holy ones of God, is strengthened by Paul's "incapable," *anaxioi,* literally "unworthy" (cf. 11:27).

3. *Don't you know that we will judge angels? How much more so ordinary cases!* Paul's pair of rhetorical questions (in Greek a compound rhetorical question) builds on and reinforces the pair of questions in v. 2. Both sets of questions begin with the apostrophic "Don't you know *(ouk oidate)."* There is a rhetorical *klimax* or *gradatio* in his argument. Not only will the Christians of Corinth participate in the judgment of the world, they will also participate in the judgment of the angels. The latter is probably a reference to the apocalyptic theme of the judgment of fallen angels (2 Pet 2:4; Jude 6; possibly *1 Enoch* 10:11-14; 67-68; 91:15 [corrupt]).

Paul's second question, "how much more so ordinary cases?" is elliptically phrased *(mēti ge biōtika).* The "ordinary cases" are literally "cases pertaining to life." In those jurisdictions where the Jewish community, as a civil corporation, had its own tribunals capital cases were reserved to the provincial governor. Moreover, if a Jew had a case against a Gentile the case was heard before the magistrates. It was only in lesser civil matters that a *politeuma's* court enjoyed the power of jurisdiction and that only among members of the corporation.

4. *Why then, if you do have ordinary cases, do you seat as judges those who are treated with scorn in the church?* "So" *(men oun;* BDF 450.4) is a classical construction used to intensify or correct an assertion. "To seat as judges" *(toutous kathizete,* literally "to make them sit") is found in Paul only here and in a biblical quotation in 10:7. The term is used in a technical sense where it has reference to the judicial *bēma,* the elevated bench of the magistrate. There may be a bit of irony in Paul's description of the judges as "treated with scorn *(exouthenēmenous)* in the church." For the most part the Christians of Corinth came from the lower classes of society and were scorned by the world (1:28; cf. 16:11; 2 Cor 10:10).

B. W. Winter ("Civil Litigation," 570) considers this description of the judges to be an example of rhetorical hyperbole, an instance of the *logos eschēmatismenos* device Paul had applied so effectively in chs. 1–4 (see note and interpretation of 4:6). However, the esteem in which the judiciary was held by the masses, as well as Paul's own understanding of "unjust persons" (see vv. 9-10), make it unnecessary to characterize Paul's description as an instance of effective but guarded rhetoric.

5. *I say this to shame you:* This transitional formula is the first of two instances in the letter in which Paul explicitly states that he is writing as he does in order to shame the community (cf. 15:34). In a Mediterranean society in which honor and shame were important values Paul was appealing to the self-interest of the community, most probably to its upper-class members. That believers be well regarded by those outside the community was important for Paul who considered that a positive value was to be had if Christians enjoyed a good reputation among the people (cf. 9:19-23; 10:31-32).

So is there no wise person among you who can judge: In place of Paul's "is there" (*eni*, a rare, shortened form of *enestin;* BDF 98) some manuscripts ($\mathfrak{P}^{11}$, D, F, G, etc.) read *estin.* In the secular judiciary magistrates and arbiters were chosen from among the upper classes. Not many but some Corinthian Christians belonged to that social elite; some of them were "wise" in the popular estimation (1:26). Paul suggests that Christians ought to choose one of their number, who enjoyed the reputation of being wise, to adjudicate their civil disputes. Judicial arbitration and extra-judicial arbitration were well known in imperial times (see the discussion, with references, in Mitchell, "1 Corinthians 6:1-11," 97–133, and Winter, "Civil Litigation," 568–569).

The entire procedure of bringing minor disputed matters to secular judicial authorities, rather than any specific case that had been brought for judgment before a secular tribunal, was what Paul considered to be scandalous. In dealing with the incestuous man Paul encouraged the community to take appropriate action, but he added that he himself had already judged the case (5:3). In dealing with the issue of Christians taking other Christians to a secular court Paul urges the community to find someone in their midst who can render an appropriate judgment in litigated matters. Christians should solve their disputes among themselves.

Paul is not urging the Christians of Corinth to establish their own court like those that were set up by Jewish communities in Yavneh, Alexandria, and Sardis. The strong possibility that there was no Jewish court in Corinth, the seemingly small number of Jews among the Corinthian Christians, and the constriction of time before the parousia coalesce to make it unlikely that Paul was urging the Corinthian Christians to establish a judicial system. The establishment of a Christian judicial system would have required that the Christians at Corinth be recognized as a civil corporation *(politeuma).* There is no indication that Paul ever urged or that the Corinthian Christians ever considered the possibility of such recognition. Arbitration was, however, quite feasible in the social circumstances of the first-century Corinthians.

between siblings? By introducing kinship language *(tou adelphou)* into his discussion (cf. vv. 6, 8) Paul adds another dimension to his appeal. Christians should not make use of the secular arm to resolve their disputes because they are God's holy ones. They should also not do so because they are a family. Philostratus suggested that petty disputes *(biōtika)* be settled at home (*Lives of the Sophists* 1.25.2).

Even in an era when use of the preposition *ana* was becoming obsolete Paul's "between one brother and another" *(ana meson tou adelphou autou,* literally "between his brother") was a rather unusual expression. A fuller expression would have been *ana meson tou adelphou kai ana meson tou adelphou autou* (BDF 139). Translators, both modern and ancient (the Vulgate, the Syriac Peshitta, and some manuscripts of Coptic Bohairic text, etc.) tend to rectify Paul's grammatical oddity. Paul or his scribe may have made a grammatical error but it could be the case that the linguistic peculiarity is influenced by Deut 1:16 where "to judge," "between" *(ana meson),* and "brother" are found in a sequence similar to that in which the three expressions are found in 1 Cor 1:5.

6. *Does a brother or sister take a sibling to court and this before those who have no faith?* Yet another rhetorical question punctuates Paul's appeal. The question draws the audience further into the family circle to which they had been introduced in v. 5. The adversative *alla* ("but," translated as "and") underscores the contrast between this type of behavior and family relationships. The rhetorical question "Does a brother or sister take a sibling to court?" *(adelphos meta adelphou krinetai)* evokes the temerity of family members who would dare to do such a thing. With Philostratus and Plutarch Paul shares a sense of horror that siblings should accuse one another. For Plutarch such accusations are diabolical *(diabolos kai katēgoros;* see "Brotherly Love," *Moralia* 481B).

The epexegetical *kai* introduces a phrase that characterizes the putative judges as being without faith. A contrast is to be made between siblings, presumed to be faithful, and unjust judges, presumed to be without faith *(apistōn,* used for the first time in 6:6, but see 7:12, 13, 14, 15; 10:27; 14:22, 23, 24), that is, nonbelievers. That Paul introduces the category of nonbelievers into his discussion shows that he is really dealing with the matter of group identity in this pericope, continuing thereby the discussion that began with the case of the incestuous man. It is not, however, impossible that Paul is trying to evoke a contrast between Christians who should be trustworthy and loyal to one another *(pistoi)* and judges who are simply not trustworthy *(apistoi).*

7. *In short, it's already failure for you when you receive judgments against one another:* The initial *men oun,* "in short" (see v. 4) heightens the impact of Paul's rejoinder. *Hēttēma,* "failure," is a rare word. In the extant Greek literature it is found only here, in Rom 11:12, and in Isa 31:8 [LXX]. On the basis of extant legal documents and inscriptions "receive judgments" seems to be the preferable translation of *krimata echein.* The phrase would draw attention to the conclusion of the legal process rather than to its initiation. Otherwise the phrase could be rendered "to have legal matters" or "to have lawsuits" (cf. Glenn Bowersock, *Augustus and the Greek World* [Oxford: Clarendon, 1965] 161; Mitchell, "1 Corinthians 6:1-11," 41–42).

Why not rather suffer wrong? Why not rather be cheated? The two rhetorical questions expand upon what Paul stated in v. 7a. Having told the Corinthians that accepting the rulings of the secular judiciary with its unjust judges in their civil disputes represents a failure on their part, Paul suggests that it would be better for the Christians to put up with wrong and suffer monetary loss rather than appeal to the secular arm. The first question employs the passive *adikeisthe* in the sense of "to allow yourselves to suffer wrong" (see BDF 314).

8. *But you yourselves wrong and cheat even your siblings:* Paul turns the tables on the Corinthians. With the rhetorical questions of v. 7 he had invited the Corinthians to consider the moral advantages of allowing themselves to be wronged and to be cheated. Now he affirms that the Corinthians he is addressing actually (note the emphatic *hymeis*) cheat and harm their brothers and sisters. Given the legendary injustice of the system, use of the judicial arm inflicted harm *(adikeite)* and economic loss *(apostereite)* on those who were brought to court. Social circumstances normally allowed only the rich and powerful, of whom there were some among the Corinthian Christians (1:26), to bring cases to court. Some Corinthians did make use of the unjust judiciary in relatively minor civil disputes with other Christians (6:1-6); they appealed to the secular arm. Court procedures resulted in unjust advantages for members of the upper echelon to the disadvantage of those who were taken to court. This is particularly egregious (note the emphatic and explanatory *kai*) when it is to the disadvantage of those who are one's siblings in Christ.

9–10. *Don't you know that the unjust will not inherit the kingdom?* With this observation Paul moves beyond the level of Stoic-Cynic moral discourse. It is preferable to be wronged than to do wrong not only because that is the moral thing to do but also because doing wrong has serious eschatological consequences. Paul has borrowed the formulaic expression "inherit the kingdom of God" *(theou basileian klēronomēsousin;* cf. 15:50; Gal 5:21; Matt 25:34; cf. Matt 19:29; Mark 10:17; Luke 10:25; 18:18) from the earlier tradition. In early Christian preaching "the kingdom of God" was an eschatological notion (cf. 4:20; compare 4:8), the central focus of the proclamation of Jesus (Mark 1:15). The kingdom of God was the future and ultimate manifestation of God as king.

Paul's rhetorical question, introduced by the formulaic "Don't you know?" *(ouk oidate;* 3:16; 5:6; 6:3, 9, 15, 16, 19; 9:13, 24), implies that the Corinthians know what he is talking about, presumably because he has already instructed them on this very subject. From an eschatological vantage point Paul explains the situation of the unjust. The unjust *(adikoi)* of v. 9 are the wrongdoers *(adikeite)* of v. 8. These will not inherit the kingdom of God.

The eschatological notion of the coming kingdom of God was not without an ethical component (see Frank Matera, *New Testament Ethics* 37–42). For the Apostle as for the early Christian tradition in general there was a strong connection between eschatology and ethics. The coming of the kingdom required a change in one's life, a radical conversion. This is something the Corinthians are presumed to have known. Certainly the Thessalonians did. When Paul recalled to them his initial proclamation of the gospel he reminded them that he had exhorted them to lead a life that was worthy of God, and this in the prospect of the coming of the glorious kingdom of God. Paul considered that such paraenesis was a paternal activity on his part (1 Thess 2:9-12; cf. 1 Cor 4:15).

Don't go astray! Paul's rehearsal of the traditional notion that the unjust will not inherit the kingdom issues forth in a summary paraenetic exhortation, "Don't go astray" (see 15:33; Gal 6:7). The exhortation has almost the character of an injunction. Paul's use of the expression resonates with the biblical tradition in which "going astray" is used of idol worship and its concomitant immorality, but it has its closest parallels with the Stoic diatribe where "Don't go astray" *(mē planasthe)* served as an exhortative slogan (e.g., Epictetus, *Discourses* 4.6.23; cf. *T. Gad* 3:1). In context this is an exhortation to the Corinthians to avoid the practice that renders them unjust, namely appealing to unjust judges when they have civil disputes with members of the community.

Neither the sexually immoral, nor idolaters, nor adulterers, nor perverts, nor homosexuals, nor thieves, nor the avaricious, not drunkards, not slanderers, not the greedy will inherit the kingdom of God: Using polysyndeton for rhetorical effect Paul links the first seven vices together with *oute,* "neither," but reverts to a simple negative *(ou)* to add the final three vices on the list (asyndeton). In the ten-item catalogue of vices Paul reiterates and expands the idea tersely stated in v. 9a, namely that the unjust will not inherit the kingdom. The ten-item list illustrates what Paul understands by "unjust" *(adikoi).* The resumptive "inherit the kingdom of God" forms an *inclusio* with the finale of v. 9a and indicates that an eschatological nuance is not to be excluded from the injunction not to go astray.

In 1 Thess 5:6-8a Paul underscored the incompatibility between drunkenness and the Christian eschatological condition. The inclusion of "homosexuals" on the list of vices in 6:10 is apparently the first recorded use of the term *arsenokoitai* (cf. 1 Tim 1:10; *Sib. Or.* 2.73). The neologism may derive from the prohibitions cited in Lev 18:22 and 20:13. It came to denote male homosexual activity, which was, in the eyes of Jewish authors such as Philo, Josephus, and the Pseudo-Phocylides, a sign of Gentile moral depravity. Paul apparently shared the Jewish prejudice on the sexual mores of Gentiles (see Rom 1:24-27; 1 Thess 4:5). "Perverts" *(malakoi)* is a term that was pejoratively used in Hellenistic Greek to describe passive partners, often young boys, in homosexual activity.

11. *And some of you were such; but you have been washed, you have been made holy, you have been justified:* Paul introduces a then-now schema similar to those used by the philosophical moralists in their ethical exhortation. The schema appears with some frequency in early Christian literature, typically as here in conjunction with a list of vices that illustrates and emphasizes the woeful moral condition of people before their acceptance of the gospel (cf. Rom 5:8-11; 6:15-23; 7:5; 11:30-32; Gal 1:13-17, 23; 4:3-10; Eph 2:1-10; 4:17-24; 5:8; Col 1:21-22; 2:13; 3:5-9; 1 Tim 1:12-17; Titus 3:3; Phlm 11; 1 Pet 2:10; 2:25; 4:1-4; cf. *1 Clem.* 3:2; 30:1; *Pseudo-Clementine Homilies* 1.18, PG 2, 73).

"Some of you" *(tines)* suggests nuance and realism. Paul does not intend to accuse the entire community of having previously been engaged in egregious asocial behavior but conduct of this type had been sufficiently prevalent in the previous lives of community members to enable Paul to develop a contrast between the Corinthians' previous behavior and the type of life to which they have now been called.

The initial "but" *(alla)* has the sense of "but you are so no longer; on the contrary . . ." (BDF 448.2). The conjunction is repeated before each of the other two verbs. This paronomasia, and the repetition, further emphasize the contrast between the two behavioral states. All three verbs are in the aorist, indicating a particular referent in the past. The first verb, "you had yourselves washed" *(apelousasthe)*, is hapax in the Pauline correspondence. Its only other occurrence in the NT is in Acts 22:16 where it clearly refers to baptism. Washed in the waters of baptism, the Corinthians have become God's own people; they have been made holy. Accordingly they exist in a correct relationship with God; they have been justified. For another Pauline reflection on the relationship between the removal of sin and justification see Rom 4:25.

in the name of the Lord Jesus Christ and in the Spirit of our God: Paul's reference to "the name of the Lord Jesus Christ" echoes the language of the epistolary *intitulatio* (1:2) and Paul's statement of purpose (1:10). It also recalls the use of the same formula in the putative judicial setting of 5:4. As such it serves as another indication of the similarity between Paul's treatment of the case of the incestuous man and the case of Christians' taking disputed matters before secular judges. In one and the other instance the ultimate issue is the identity and responsibility of the community as God's holy people. It has been constituted as such in Christ Jesus and it calls on the name of the Lord Jesus Christ (1:2).

The cultic nuance of the phrase "in the name of the Lord" should not be overlooked. The biblical *bĕšēm yhwh,* "in the name of YHWH" was used with verbs that suggest cultic activity—lifting one's hands (Ps 62:5 [LXX]), praising (Ps 104:3 [LXX]), blessing (Ps 128:8 [LXX]), and so forth. This biblical phrase is reflected in the Septuagintal and Pauline phrase "in the name of the Lord" *(en tǭ onomati tou kyriou).* Paul, as is his custom, identifies "the Lord" with Jesus Christ.

The manuscript tradition gives evidence of some variety in the textual tradition of Paul's christological formula. The reading without "our" *(hēmōn)* adopted by the editors of *GNT*[4] is found in 𝔓[11], 𝔓[46] (the papyri have limited legibility), ℵ, D, and a series of Western Fathers, especially Tertullian, Ambrosiaster, and Didymus, and some Eastern Fathers. The full christological formula, "our Lord Jesus Christ," is found in B, C, a wide range of minuscules, various ancient versions, and an impressive array of patristic witnesses (Cyprian, Chrysostom, etc.). Less impressive evidence can be cited in favor of two shorter formulae, "the Lord Jesus" (A, Ψ, 88, etc.) and "our Lord Jesus" (cop[sa]). Between the two more widely attested readings an option can be made for the first on the basis of the antiquity of the evidence and the *lectio brevior* principle. The "our" *(hēmōn)* found in the longer reading may have resulted from scribal accommodation to the parallel formula, "the spirit of our God."

Identifying the Lord of the biblical formula with Jesus, early Christian tradition appropriated the formula and used it of its own cultic acts, including baptism and bending of the knee (Acts 2:38; 10:48; Phil 2:10; cf. Eph 5:20; Col 3:17). With a paired reference to Jesus and to the Spirit of God (the *kai* is epexegetical; see BDF 442.9) Paul's formulation evokes the specificity of God's salvific work on behalf of his people in Jesus Christ as well as God's continuing dynamic presence among the Corinthians. Allusion is made to an early Christian baptismal formula (cf. 1:13) and the ongoing active presence of God (the Spirit of our God) among the people who belong to him. For Paul the Christian community has not only been made holy in Christ Jesus (1:2); it is also a community in which the Spirit of God is generously active (12:4-13).

For Reference and Further Study

Delcor, Mathias. "Les tribunaux de l'église de Corinthe et les tribunaux de Qumran," *SPC* 2:535–548. English: "The Courts of the Church of Corinth and the Courts of Qumran" in Jerome Murphy-O'Connor, ed., *Paul and Qumran.* London: Chapman, 1968, 69–84.

Derrett, J. Duncan M. "Judgement and 1 Corinthians 6," *NTS* 37 (1991) 22–36.

Dinkler, Erich. "Zum Problem der Ethik bei Paulus: Rechtsnahme und Rechtsverzicht (I Kor. 6:1-11)," *ZThK* 49 (1952) 167–200.

Kinman, Brent R. "'Appoint the Despised as Judges!' (1 Corinthians 6:4)," *TynB* 48 (1997) 345–354.

Malick, David E. "The Condemnation of Homosexuality in 1 Corinthians 6:9," *BSac* 150 (1993) 479–492.

Mitchell, Alan C. "Rich and Poor in the Courts of Corinth: Litigiousness and Status in 1 Corinthians 6.1-11," *NTS* 39 (1993) 562–586.

_____. "I Corinthians 6:1-11: Group Boundaries and the Courts of Corinth," Ph.D. Dissertation, Yale University, 1986.

Petersen, William L. "Can *arsenokoitai* be translated by 'Homosexuals'? (I Cor. 6.9; I Tim. 1.10)," *VC* 40 (1986) 187–191.

Richardson, Peter. "Judgment in Sexual Matters in 1 Corinthians 6:1-11," *NovT* 25 (1983) 37–58.

Rosner, Brian S. "The Origin and Meaning of 1 Corinthians 6, 9-11 in Context," *BZ* 40 (1996) 250–253.

Scroggs, Robin. *The New Testament and Homosexuality.* Philadelphia: Fortress, 1983.

Winter, Bruce W. "Civil Litigation in Secular Corinth and the Church: the Forensic Background to 1 Corinthians 6.1-8," *NTS* 37 (1991) 559–572.

_____. *Seek the Welfare of the City: Christians as Benefactors and Citizens.* Grand Rapids: Eerdmans; Carlisle: Paternoster, 1994, 105–122.

Wright, David F. "Homosexuals or Prostitutes? The Meaning of *arsenokoitai* (1 Cor. 6:9, 1 Tim. 1:10)," *VC* 38 (1984) 125–153.

_____. "Translating *arsenokoitai* (1 Cor. 6:9, 1 Tim. 1:10)," *VC* 41 (1987) 396–398.

Zaas, Peter S. "1 Corinthians 6:9ff: Was Homosexuality Condoned in the Corinthian Church?" SBL.MS 1979. Paul J. Achtemeier, ed. Missoula: Scholars, 1979, 2:205–212.

4. *Embodied Existence* (6:12-20)

12. All things are lawful for me, but all things are not advantageous; all things are lawful for me, but I will not be made subject by anyone. 13. "Food for the stomach and the stomach for food; God will destroy the one and the other," you say. But the body is not for sexual immorality; it is for the Lord, and the Lord is for the body. 14. God raised the Lord and God will raise us through his power.

15. Don't you know that your bodies are members of Christ? Taking the members of Christ, shall I make them members of a whore? Never! 16. Don't you know that the one who is joined to a whore is one body? For the two are, it is said, one flesh. 17. The one who is joined to the Lord is one spirit. 18. Flee from sexual misconduct. Every sin a person commits is outside the body; but the one who commits a sexual transgression sins with respect to his or her own body. 19. Don't you know that your body is the temple of the Holy Spirit, which you have received from God, dwelling within you, and that you are not your own? 20. You have been bought and paid for. Therefore glorify God in your body.

INTERPRETATION

Stanley Stowers has described this passage as a "deliberative argument from expediency" (*Letter Writing* 108). Paul's argument consists of three closely-knit units in which he respectively treats the notion of unlimited freedom (vv. 12-14), reflects on sexual intercourse with a prostitute (vv. 15-17), and makes a strong plea to the Corinthians to avoid sexual immorality (vv. 18-20). The way in which Paul introduces the discussion on freedom links the passage to the previous passage, which dealt with an appeal to the secular judiciary. The slogan "all things are lawful for me" (v. 12), has a legal ring. Slogans such as this figured strongly in the discourse of Stoic moralists as they attempted to make a distinction between what was legal and what was morally good. Paul talked about the legal system in 6:1-11, urging Christians to look elsewhere, that is, within the community in order to resolve their disputes. Now he will introduce them to an understanding of Christian anthropology on the basis of which he can discuss the moral issues that arise from embodied sexual existence.

The issue of sexual misconduct is the rhetorical *stasis* of the passage. Paul introduces the topic in the first unit of his development (v. 13) and returns to it in the third unit, where he strongly urges the Corinthians to shun sexual immorality. The topic, sexual misconduct *(porneia)*, is linguistically linked to the "whore" *(pornē)* of vv. 15 and 16 and "committing sexual transgression" *(porneuōn)* in v. 18. The heart of Paul's argument is, however, the importance of the human body, *sōma*. Paul first refers to the body in v. 13. All told, "body" language appears eight times in this relatively short section of 1 Corinthians (vv. 13[2x], 15, 16, 18[2x], 19, 20).

The Function of this Unit within the Letter. 1 Corinthians 6:12-20 constitutes an isolable topos within the letter. Commentators are divided among themselves as to whether there was a real problem with some of the men in the Christian community at Corinth consorting with prostitutes. The older literature on the epistle generally assumed that this was the case. This assumption was largely based on the idea that sexual immorality was rampant in first-century Corinth. That idea was derived from literature that described ancient, pre-imperial Corinth, not the Hellenistic metropolis Paul visited in the mid-first century. Paul's letter does not give any indication that some Corinthian Christian men were actually visiting prostitutes. The sexual problem at Corinth seems to be quite different from that, namely an avoidance of sexual activity (7:1).

Choosing sexual misconduct as a rhetorical *stasis* enables Paul to develop a theological basis for his later reflections on human sexuality. This section, 6:12-20, is a transitional unit that provides an introduction for what follows, particularly in ch. 7 where Paul responds to the truly problematic issue with regard to sexuality, namely an undue desire for sexual abstinence. The issue of sexual intercourse with prostitutes was one that several of the philosophical moralists considered in their discussion of the relationship between law and morality. From this perspective it would appear that Paul chose a classic topos on the basis of which he could develop his discussion on sexuality with respect to the very issues the Corinthians had raised in their letter to him (7:1).

In a discussion with an interlocutor who claims to be free to do what he would like, "the one to whom it is permitted to do what he wishes" *(hotq men exestin ho bouletain prattein),* the Stoic Dio Chrysostom treats the issue with reference to a brothel *(Discourses* 7.136-140; 14.14). In their own discussions on the relationship between law and morality Seneca *(Epistles* 1.69, 71) and Musonius ("On Sexual Relations," frag. 12.84.32-86.1, 6-8,10-15; 88.6) raise various issues with regard to sexual behavior. So, too, does Musonius' disciple Epictetus. Epictetus appears to make a distinction between a lowest-common-denominator type of morality determined by law *(Discourses* 3.7.21; *Encheiridion* 33.8) and a higher moral standard incumbent on the Stoic *(Discourses* 2.18.15-26; 3.22.13, 95; cf. 4.1.143).

Paul's epistolary unit, although isolable, is rhetorically linked with the rest of the letter in many ways. The specific topic at hand, sexual misconduct *(porneia)* recalls the sexually immoral person *(pornos)* whom Paul had cited in the catalogues of vices in the immediately preceding sections of his letter (5:10, 11; 6:9). He had even suggested the possibility that someone who bore the name of Christian might be among those who could be considered sexually immoral (*pornoi*, 5:11). Moreover, Paul reminded the Corinthians that in his early correspondence to them he had warned them not to associate with those who were sexually immoral (5:9).

The Corinthian slogan "all things are lawful" (v. 12) is echoed in 10:23. The *inclusio* that is thus formed encompasses a multifaceted and complex development of thought in which Paul deals with the issue of human freedom. Within that complex the thoughts Paul develops in 6:12-20 provide a theological-anthropological basis for his response to a variety of considerations on sexual relationships in ch. 7.

Paul urges the Corinthians to avoid sexual immorality (6:18). Avoidance of sexual immorality is something to be considered when husbands and wives ponder the conduct of their own sexual relationships (7:2). Paul is subject to no one (*exousiasthēsomai*, 6:12). This verb recurs again in 7:4 when Paul writes about the body of the wife being subject to her husband and the body of the husband being subject to his wife. This verse focuses on the reality of the body (*sōma*), the leitmotif of 6:12-20.

The priority Paul gives to the resurrection as the ground for a truly Christian anthropology (v. 14) anticipates the extensive treatment of the correlative themes of the resurrection of Jesus and the resurrection of the body in ch. 15. The crux of Paul's anthropological argument is to be found in vv. 13c-14. His theological affirmation on the destiny of the human body might suggest that some people at Corinth thought that the future consummation would involve the destruction of the body (see 15:12).

Paul's reference to the body of Christ anticipates the extended use of the metaphor of the body of Christ in 12:12-26. The temple theme he uses in 6:19 reprises the temple motif of 3:16-17. In both passages theological and pneumatological language comes into play even though Paul's perspective in 3:16-17 is the community as the temple of God whereas in 6:19 his point of reference is the body of the Christian. Paul's reference to the Holy Spirit that comes from God (v. 19) anticipates his reflections on the gift of the Spirit in chs. 12–14 even as it recalls Paul's previous exposition on anthropology (2:6-16). Together these two passages, 2:6-16 and 6:12-20, offer a profound theological anthropology.

Theological Anthropology. In 6:12-20 Paul develops a theological anthropology in response to the Corinthians' contention that everything is legitimate. An earlier section of the letter provided him with an opportunity to develop elements of a theological anthropology in response to the Corinthians' claim that they were perfect (2:6-16). Key to the anthropology developed in 6:12-20 is Paul's understanding of *sōma*, the cipher of embodied human existence.

An anthropological dualism that separated body from spirit had been accepted by some of the Christians at Corinth. That dualism underestimated the value of the body and affirmed its transience. With a slogan that proclaimed that "anything goes" ("all things are lawful") and the conviction that the body was destined for destruction those infected by this dualism did not believe that the satisfaction of physical instinct, cravings for food or sexual desire, had any long-term consequences.

In response Paul offers a biblical understanding of the human person with its holistic anthropology and a futuristic point of view. With reference to the Yahwist's story of the creation of man and woman (v. 16), which celebrated their bodily existence and their physical unity, Paul embraced traditional biblical anthropology. From a specifically Christian perspective, that of bodily resurrection, Paul offers the gist of his response in vv. 13-14. It is the resurrection of the body that imparts ultimate significance to the human body.

Paul develops his anthropology in a religious perspective. There are frequent references to God (4x), Lord (4x), Christ (2x), and the Holy Spirit (1x). The real issue is: to whom does the body belong? Who has ultimate rights over it? Paul gives a pointed answer to this crucial question in vv. 19b-20a: "you are not your own; you have been bought and paid for."

Paul's response represents a masterful use of the indicative-imperative schema, which he uses with profit in the exposition of paraenesis throughout the letter. In 16:19 the indicative, that "your bodies are not your own," derives from God's previous action in Christ. The bodies of Christians are not their own. They are "for the Lord and the Lord is for them," a Pauline phrase that bespeaks their future destiny and its proleptic implications.

Paul's Rhetoric. Paul adopts the dialogical style of the diatribe. His argument is characterized by four rhetorical questions, three of which are introduced by his reaching out to his audience and asking "Don't you know that . . .?" (*ouk oidate hoti*, vv. 15, 16, 19). The fourth rhetorical question (v. 15b) is answered with a strong denial from Paul: "Never!"

Paul's dialogue is with a putative interlocutor (cf. 15:35) who argues the case for unrestricted freedom. Paul takes up the argument with an opening statement, a kind of buzz word that summarizes some of the Corinthian attitudes, "all things are lawful" (see 10:23). The slogan represents a popular catchcry of people of importance. It is tantamount to a declaration of independence from others, especially from those whose needs and rights might be perceived as limiting the autonomy of the rich and powerful.

To respond to the antisocial attitude implied in the slogan Paul divides the question. He first takes up the issue of "all things" being legitimate. To the Corinthians' self-serving argument from universal legitimacy Paul opposes the argument of selective advantage, "not everything is advantageous." Then he takes up the slogan's egocentric "for me," juxtaposing that with his own position in life. Throughout his letter he constantly offers his own behavior as an example to the Corinthians. Here the contrast between his behavior and theirs is sharpened by the use of an emphatic "I."

Other features of Paul's rhetoric are his use of Gen 2:24 as a *testimonium* and an enthymeme in v. 20. The citation enables Paul to counter the dualistic anthropology of the Corinthians with a Semitic and biblical anthropology with its distinct appreciation for the unitive aspect of human sexuality. The enthymeme is particularly significant insofar as it provides an explanation for the answer anticipated for the second part of Paul's final rhetorical question (v. 19). Using a kind of argument from logic, Paul locates the radical origin of his anthropological vision in the redemption effected by Jesus Christ (v. 20).

Notes

12. *All things are lawful for me:* "All things are lawful" *(panta moi exestin)* was most probably a slogan bandied about among some of the Christians in Corinth and used by them to justify an indiscriminate exercise of their rights *(exousia;* see 8:9). Paul's fourfold repetition of the slogan (cf. 6:12b, 10:23a-b) serves to confirm its formulaic nature. The slogan has a legal ring to it. The impersonal verb *exestin,* "it is lawful," is a technical term used of conduct that is sanctioned by a legal system. The slogan is roughly equivalent to contemporary jargon that proclaims that "it's my right to do what I want." In a discourse on freedom Epictetus opined, "He is free who lives as he wills, who is subject neither to compulsion, nor hindrance, nor force, whose choices are unhampered, whose desires attain their ends, whose aversions do not fall into what they would avoid" (*Discourses* 4.1.1). Dio Chrysostom, in turn, described the wise person as one "to whom all things are permissible" (*Discourses* 3.10).

    In the freedom slogan cited by Paul the expression "for me" *(moi)* indicates an extreme individualism that undermines social existence and ultimately subordinates all others to the one who justifies his or her conduct with the slogan. In the Hellenistic world the attitude of being above the law and having unrestricted freedom was typical of kings such as Caligula and Nero who could do what they liked to anyone at all (see note on 4:8). The moral voice of the Stoic Musonius Rufus argued against such an attitude. He warned that a king could not long justify his actions by saying "it's lawful for me" *(exestin moi);* rather the king should say "it's appropriate for me" *(kathēkei moi).* Similarly Dio Chrysostom taught that even though a person has power to do as he likes it is not permissible *(ouk exestin)* to do mean and unprofitable things (*Discourses* 14.13-16).

    In the rhetoric of 1 Corinthians Paul's argument is often developed on the basis of an *ethos* appeal, a reference to his personal prestige and example. From this vantage point the "for me" of the freedom slogan suggests that one might look to how Paul makes use of the freedom that is his. The emphatic *egō,* "I" of v. 12d, "I will not be made subject by anyone," confirms that the "for me" of v. 12a is not merely formulaic; it is rather an integral element of Paul's rhetoric. In ch. 9 Paul directly addresses the issue of his freedom (*eleutheria,* 9:1) and the use of his rights (*exousia,* 9:5, 6, 7). As the central element in a chiastic structure ch. 9 provides a directive motif for Paul's long consideration on food that has been offered to idols (8:1–11:1). Paul presents himself as one who does what he does for the benefit of others and the sake of the gospel (9:22-23). As an introduction to his final considerations on food offered to idols (10:23-11:1) he will twice repeat the freedom slogan, albeit without the qualifying "for me."

but all things are not advantageous: Paul argues (cf. 10:23) that the exercise of freedom should be such that real advantage accrues. Here as so often in 1 Corinthians Paul's moral discourse is dictated by an appeal to rational considerations rather than by an appeal to heteronomous authority. Paul's normal approach to slogans exploited by the Corinthians (cf. 6:13a; 7:1; 8:1, 7; 10:23a-b; 14:34a) is to make some concession to the truth of a slogan and then take some reflective and critical distance from the range of its possible applications. With his contrasting statement (*alla,* "but") "not everything is advantageous" Paul sets out his own position in an antithetical argument similar to that of 10:23. He uses an argument from advantage, the first time that he does so in this letter. This type of argument is a feature of Paul's correspondence with the Corinthians (cf. 7:35; 12:7; 10:23, 33; 2 Cor 8:10 [cf. 2 Cor 12:1]). The argument appeals to the audience by putting before them what is best for them (see Margaret Mitchell, *Rhetoric of Reconciliation* 25–38). The argument is characteristic of deliberative rhetoric, as it is of symbouleutic advice (see Stowers, "Debate," 64–67).

all things are lawful for me, but I will not be made subject by anyone: To advance his argument Paul divides the question. He repeats the freedom slogan and again offers a contrasting clause for the Corinthians' buzzword. A similar technique is employed in 10:23-24. There the question is similarly divided, but the second contrasting phrase is "not everything builds up." In 6:12 Paul's first rejoinder (v. 12b) responded to the formulaic "all things are lawful." The second rejoinder (v. 12d) focuses on the slogan's "for me." Paul's emphatic "I" (*egō*) is juxtaposed with the slogan's self-centered "me" (*moi*). As he does so often throughout the letter, Paul offers himself as an example to the Corinthians. They proclaim unlimited freedom; he will not be enslaved by any one. He is truly free and will not be subjected to anyone (*ouk egō exousiasthēsomai;* the verb [cf. 7:4] belongs to the same linguistic field as *exestin,* "is lawful," and *exousia,* "right/authority"). Paradoxically, however, Paul is a slave of Christ (7:22; cf. 9:16-18). He has even made himself a slave to everyone (*emauton edoulōsa,* 9:19; cf. 2 Cor 11:7). In the later passage, 9:19 speaks of the "gain" Paul derives from his self-enslavement. In the argument of deliberative rhetoric "gain" (*kerdos;* see Paul's use of the related verb "to gain," *kerdainō,* in 9:19-22) was used in the same way as was "advantage."

13. *"Food for the stomach and the stomach for food":* This phrase may also have been a Corinthian "slogan" (cf. 8:8; see C. K. Barrett, *1 Corinthians* 146; Jean Héring,

First Epistle 46; J. B. Hurley, "Man and Woman in 1 Corinthians" [Cambridge University, Ph.D. dissertation, 1973] 87–88; Jerome Murphy-O'Connor, "Slogans," 394). If so it may have developed as a result of an exaggerated interpretation of the Gentile Christian position that Jewish dietary laws were not incumbent upon Gentile Christians (cf. Matt 15:17; Mark 7:9).

"God will destroy the one and the other," you say: Since "destroy" *(katargēsei)* is a Pauline term, one frequently used in 1 Corinthians with an eschatological nuance (1:28; 2:6; 6:13; 13:8[2x], 10, 11; 15:24, 26), it is tempting to read this phrase as if it were a Pauline qualification of the Corinthians' buzzword. It is, however, more likely that the phrase should be taken as part of their slogan that Paul then counters with the competitive slogan of v. 13c. The complete slogan presents something of an Epicurean idea of human corporeal existence or a kind of anthropology that considers the body as being somewhat independent of the spirit. Bodily existence is for this world only. This kind of anthropology may lie behind "the denial of the resurrection" to which Paul makes reference in 15:12. "You say" is not in Paul's Greek text. It is incorporated into this translation to establish the contrast between the Corinthians' slogan and Paul's counterslogan.

But the body is not for sexual immorality; it is for the Lord, and the Lord is for the body: The reference to sexual immorality suggests that the Corinthians attempted to justify sexual immorality *(porneia;* see 5:1-8) on the basis of an analogy with the eating of food. If the body is to be destroyed why not do with it as one might be inclined to do? Paul counters this attitude with a slogan that captures the rhythm of the first part of the Corinthians' slogan, "the body for food, and food for the body." Paul's own slogan is "the body for the Lord, and the Lord for the body."

In English it is difficult to render the way in which Paul's rhetoric plays the two slogans off against one another. In Greek neither Paul's rendition of the Corinthians' slogan nor his own slogan contains the verb "to be." Paul's statement contains two adversative conjunctions, *de* and *alla,* both of which can be translated as "but." The first conjunction *(de)* is used to contrast Paul's own statement with the Corinthians' slogan. The second *(alla,* a stronger adversative) is used in the antithesis *ou tē porneią alla tǫ kyriǫ,* "not for sexual immorality, but for the Lord." I have tried to capture the sense of Paul's two contrasts by using a semicolon to reflect the *alla* ("but").

With a formulaic affirmation that the body is for the Lord and the Lord is for the body Paul underscores that Christ's lordship is exercised over Christians in their bodily existence. The reference to the Lord is key to Paul's theological anthropology, in this instance his understanding of the meaning of embodied human existence. Reference to the Lord determines what is truly beneficial (cf. v. 12b) for human beings.

Paul's pithy slogan suggests that beneficial use of one's corporeality is not determined by one's sexual drive *(porneia).* Rather the embodied person is subservient to the Lord (cf. v. 12d); the body is for the Lord. Subservience to the Lord pervades the Christian ethos with regard to bodily existence, including its sexual function (cf. 7:40). The destiny of the embodied human being is related to "the Lord," a rubric Paul typically employs to make reference to the resurrected Lord on the one hand and to refer to the parousiac Lord on the other. With the terse formula of 6:13c Paul argues that embodied human existence must be understood in the light of human solidarity with the risen and awaited Lord. Bodily existence *(sōma)* undergirds human solidarity with the risen and awaited one. The human being's eschatological destiny ultimately determines what is beneficial but it is the embodied human being that has an eschatological destiny (15:35-49).

14. *God raised the Lord and God will raise us through his power:* The apparent tension between v. 14 and 1 Cor 15:51-52, the structure of 1 Corinthians 6, and the line of thought in 1 Cor 6:13-16 led Udo Schnelle to argue that v. 14 is a post-Pauline gloss ("1 Kor 6:14—eine nachpaulinische Glosse," *NovT* 25 [1983] 217–219). The textual tradition does not warrant such a radical hypothesis. That tradition does, however, show considerable variation with respect to the tense of the verb "will raise," *exegerei,* a compound verb found in the NT only in 6:14 and Rom 9:17, where it appears in a citation of Exod 9:16. The future tense *(exegerei),* the preferable reading, is found in ℵ, C, K, L, most of the minuscules, and most of the ancient versions. It is also found as a correction in 𝔓⁴⁶ and D. The future tense is required by the meaning of the text and its antithetical parallelism with v. 13 *(katargēsei,* "will destroy"). Some manuscripts, however, have the verb in the present *(exegeirei,* 𝔓¹¹, A, P, and the uncorrected D). Others have the verb in the aorist *(exēgeiren,* B, some minuscules, Origen, and various Latin witnesses). The aorist reading, which suggests a baptismal interpretation, seems to have been induced from the preceding "raised" *(ēgeiren).* A singular oddity in the history of the textual transmission of 6:14 is that 𝔓⁴⁶ first had a reading in the present that was subsequently corrected to the future and then corrected again, this time to the aorist.

The first part of 6:14 echoes the early church's credal tradition (cf. 1 Thess 1:10). Paul consistently speaks of the resurrection as an action of God and uses the verb *egeirein* to describe the resurrection (cf. 15:4). Jesus is one who has been raised. He has been raised as Lord. This honorific title evokes the personal and functional association of the risen Jesus with God. That Paul uses the title Lord absolutely, rather than as an appositive to the personal name of Jesus (cf. 2:8), appears to be dictated by the demands of Paul's rhetoric.

Paul considers the resurrection of Jesus as Lord to be the foremost manifestation of God's power (Rom 1:4; 2 Cor 13:4; Phil 3:10; cf. Eph 1:19) and an eschatological act. With his reference to the power of God in v. 14 Paul reprises the theme of 1:18, where the power of God is related to the message of the cross and human salvation. Paul does not consider the resurrection of Jesus to be an isolated event. The singular event of Jesus' resurrection "from the dead" (in the plural, see 15:12, 20) inaugurates the eschatological reality and implies the future resurrection of those who belong to Jesus (15:20). The resurrection of Jesus is completed in the resurrection of those for whom he is the Lord. In 1 Thess 4:14-16 Paul similarly sets forth an argument based on the parallel and interconnected resurrections of Jesus and those who belong to him.

15. *Don't you know that your bodies are members of Christ?* Having corrected the Corinthians' anthropology with his own resurrection-dominated anthropology Paul adopts the style of the diatribe as he turns to an issue at hand, sexual immorality, *porneia*. This term is related to the verb *pernēmi*, "to sell," and suggests some form of paid sex. The shift in christological titles, "Christ" rather than "Lord," indicates a movement of Paul's thought away from the eschatological destiny of Christians to the present and their corporate existence in Christ. Paul's blunt *ouk oidate*, "don't you know?" (6:16, 19)—the first of a series of three rhetorical questions—presupposes that the Corinthians know the meaning of the body of Christ. Paul dwells extensively on this motif in 12:12-31, when he uses the body metaphor to plead for the unity of the community.

Taking the members of Christ, shall I make them members of a whore? In the extant correspondence Paul uses the noun "whore," (*pornē*, cognate with *porneia*) only in 6:15-16. "Members" (*melē*), used three times in v. 15, suggests a real belonging. Paul's language is not merely figurative. Graphic realism is present in Paul's diatribe against sexual misconduct. He considers that Christians are members of Christ's body (cf. 12:27) and that sexual commerce with a prostitute makes the paramour one with her. "Taking" (*aras*, but some mss. read the particle *ara*, "then") suggests a "taking away," as if by force. The idea of the mutilation of the body is to be found in the Hellenistic rhetorical use of the body metaphor (see notes and interpretation for 12:12-26). That the mutilated body is the body of "Christ" makes the offense all the more egregious.

Never! Having asked a rhetorical question, Paul forcefully replies to his own question with a strong negative. He precludes any unwarranted conclusion being drawn from his question. Only then will he proceed to offer an argument for the stance that he has adopted. The use of "never!" (*mē genoito*), without its being part of a longer sentence, is a feature of Paul's rhetorical style (see Rom 3:4, 6, 31; 6:2, 15; 7:7, 13; 9:14; 11:1, 11; Gal 2:17; 3:21; 6:14). The same rhetorical formula was also used by Epictetus, his younger contemporary (see A. J. Malherbe, "*MĒ GENOITO* in the Diatribe and Paul," *HThR* 73 [1980] 231–240).

16. *Don't you know that the one who is joined to a whore is one body?* Paul develops his argument with a second rhetorical question. The verb *kollaō*, "to cling or adhere to" is used in the NT only in the passive. Used three times by Paul (6:16, 17; Rom 12:9), its appearance here appears to be dictated by Paul's allusion to the text of Gen 2:24, "Therefore a man leaves his father and his mother and clings to his wife, and they become one flesh" (NRSV; *proskollēthēsetai pros tēn gynaika autou, kai esontai hoi duo eis sarka mian*, LXX). Paul's elliptical language—his expression lacks the expected "with her," *syn autē*—seems also to have been influenced by the Genesis text.

For the two are, it is said, one flesh: In the development of his logical argument Paul has recourse to the *testimonium* of Scripture (Gen 2:24). Paul's is an argument from authority. The biblical citation not only serves as an argument against sexual relations with a prostitute; it may also allude to the idea that the believer is united with Christ in a nuptial relationship (See Rosner, *Paul,*

Scripture and Ethics, 134–136). The location of the interpretive aside "it is said" *(phēsin)* in the course of a biblical citation is a unique stylistic feature of this passage. Elsewhere Paul typically uses the classic lemma "it is written" *(gegraptai)* to introduce biblical citations. The Greek Bible speaks of "flesh" *(sarx);* Paul himself tends to use "body" *(sōma)* language. Both "flesh" and "body" render a single Hebrew term, *bāśār,* "flesh" or "body."

17. *The one who is joined to the Lord is one spirit:* The clause is introduced by the adversative particle *de* (not translated). The clause has been so constructed by Paul as to provide a contrast with v. 16a. The graphic realism of Paul's language is difficult for the modern reader to grasp. His clause contrasts union with the Lord and union with a whore, bodily existence and "spiritual" existence. Paul typically contrasts "flesh" *(sarx)* and "spirit" *(pneuma).* "Flesh" describes humanity or the human in its weakness and proneness to sin; "spirit" describes humanity or the human in its openness to God and its readiness for salvation. Paul's allusion to Gen 2:24 appears to have caused him to depart from his usual lexical usage. Since the Spirit is the power of the future eschaton and Lord is eschatological terminology one should understand by Paul's reference to union with the Lord a harbinger of ultimate salvation.

18. *Flee from sexual misconduct:* Paul gives a similar charge with regard to idolatry in 10:14. The Hebrew Scriptures warn against sexual relations with a "loose woman" *(pornē;* Prov 5:3; 6:23–7:27; Sir 9:6; 19:2). Warnings against sexual misconduct are common in the testamentary literature, particularly in the Testaments of Reuben and Judah (see also *T. Levi* 9:9). Paul's own phraseology is similar to that of *T. Reub.* 5:5, "Flee, therefore, fornication." Given the parallelism between Paul's references to God's indwelling (6:19; cf. *T. Jos.* 10:1-3) and the exhortation to glorify God (6:20; cf. *T. Jos.* 8:5), it is not unlikely that there may be some intertextual allusion to the biblical story of Joseph fleeing Potiphar's wife (Genesis 39) in Paul's exhortation.

Every sin a person commits is outside the body: In its expression of one aspect of the Corinthians' erroneous anthropology v. 18b is akin to the slogans of vv. 12 and 13. Considering the body *(sōma)* to be merely physical and without ultimate value, the Corinthians held that the domain of sin lies beyond the merely physical. What is merely physical, including irregular sexual intercourse, is not sinful, they reasoned.

but the one who commits a sexual transgression sins with respect to his or her own body: As is his custom Paul corrects the erroneous views succinctly expressed in the Corinthians' slogans with a view of his own. He highlights the specificity of the sexual transgression. Commentators disagree as to what Paul specifically had in mind when he singled out sexual transgression as a sin of the body. Is he reflecting the Jewish attitude that had well-defined views with regard to human sexuality (cf. Prov 6:25-28 on union with a whore) and considered Gentiles to be particularly remiss in this regard (cf. 1 Thess 4:5)? Some Hellenistic moralists suggest that even if sexual misconduct violates no laws it does harm to the body. It may well be that Paul has simply pointed out the obvious in order thereby to make the point that one who commits a sexual transgression has misused the very body that belongs to the Lord, the body in which the Spirit dwells. In Paul's holistic anthropology "body" is not only a cipher for the self; it also highlights the physicality of human existence and its possibility of relationship and communication. Sinning against one's own body *(to idion sōma)* is a deterrent to one's communication with the Lord.

19. *Don't you know that your body is the temple of the Holy Spirit, which you have received from God, dwelling within you:* In v. 19 Paul appeals directly to the Corinthians. His rhetorical question urges them to share a view of sanctified and embodied human existence. In 3:16 temple language had been used of the community; here it is used of the individual. An analogous use of cultic language is found in Rom 12:1 when Paul urges the holy ones at Rome to present their bodies as a living sacrifice, holy and acceptable to God. In Romans Paul's cultic exhortation serves as a preamble to a lengthy paraenetic unit (Romans 12–15). The succinct articulation of Paul's anthropology in 6:19 prepares for lengthy discussion of human sexuality in ch. 7. "Which you have received from God" might appear to be redundant were it not for the fact that the Corinthian hybrists took pride in their "spiritual" condition. Paul would remind them that the Holy Spirit within them is the gift of God (see 1:7; 12:3).

    and that you are not your own? The second part of Paul's rhetorical question responds to the exaggerated claim to freedom with which the pericope began (6:12). Christians do not belong to themselves; they belong to the Lord (cf. 3:23). With this reminder Paul anticipates an argument he will later develop in a rhetorical aside (7:22-23) within a longer discussion on human sexuality.

20. *you have been bought and paid for:* Paul offers an explanation (the explanatory *gar,* "for," is not translated) as to why Christians do not own their own bodies, that is, themselves (v.19b). His words literally mean "you have been bought with a price." The mention of the payment is important. In the Hellenistic world sales were considered to be finalized only with the payment of the purchase price, or at least of a sufficiently large down payment to preclude the buyer's withdrawal from the sales agreement. Many contracts dating from that era mention that the purchase price has, in fact, been paid. The use of the aorist tense indicates that Paul considers the affair to have been finalized and that he has a specific event in mind. His expression, "bought and paid for," evokes the sacral freeing of slaves (1:30). The image recurs in 7:23 (see note), with the same wording and a similar function.

    Therefore glorify God in your body: "Glorify God" is a Pauline expression (Rom 1:21; 15:6, 9; 2 Cor 9:13; Gal 1:24), but only here does the expression occur in the imperative aorist. With a final reference to the body Paul brings his anthropological reflection to closure. What he has to say about embodied human existence (6:13c-20) is his response to the Corinthians' claims to unrestricted freedom. "In your body" *(en tǭ sōmati hymōn)* expresses the manner in which the Corinthian Christians are expected to glorify God. Their cultic activity (cf. v. 19) takes place in and by means of their embodied existence. Far from being irrelevant to ultimate salvation, the body is the means whereby God is glorified. Throughout the letter Paul demonstrates his adamant opposition to any anthropology that separates spirit from body. His is a holistic anthropology in which body and spirit constitute one embodied existence that for the Christian has been incorporated into the one body of Christ.

The inferential "therefore" (*dē*, rarely found in the NT and hapax in Paul) is absent from some of the Western textual witnesses. The conjunction appears, nevertheless, in an impressive number of uncials ($\mathfrak{P}^{46}$, $\aleph$, A, B, C, D, F, G, etc.), various ancient versions (Latin, Coptic, and Ethiopian), and such Fathers of the Church as Tertullian, Origen, Cyprian, Epiphanius, and Cyril.

A longer reading of Paul's final injunction, "glorify God in your body and in your spirit, which is from God," appears in K, L, P, Ψ, Chrysostom, and many minuscules. Without the relative clause the expanded form appears in the ancient Armenian version. This long form includes a classic Pauline pairing (body-spirit) that is so typical of Paul that one is virtually at a loss to identify any reason why it should have been dropped by the scribal tradition had it appeared in their working manuscripts. The shorter reading (*lectio brevior*) has the rhetorical strength of the punctiliar Pauline exhortation and is well attested by the more ancient manuscripts. Hence it must be judged to be the preferable reading.

For Reference and Further Study

Bailey, Kenneth E. "Paul's Theological Foundation for Human Sexuality: I Cor. 6:9-20 in the Light of Rhetorical Criticism," *Near East School of Theology Theological Review* 3 (1980) 27–41.

Byrne, Brendan. "Sinning Against One's Own Body: Paul's Understanding of the Sexual Relationship in 1 Corinthians 6:18," *CBQ* 45 (1983) 608–616.

_____. "Eschatologies of Resurrection and Destruction: The Ethical Significance of Paul's Dispute with the Corinthians," *DRev* 104 (1986) 288–298.

Derrett, J. Duncan M. "Right and Wrong Sticking (1 Cor 6,18)?" *EstBib* 55 (1997) 89–106.

Dodd, Brian J. "Paul's Paradigmatic 'I' and 1 Corinthians 6.12," *JSNT* 59 (1995) 39–58.

Fisk, Bruce N. "*PORNEUEIN* as Body Violation: The Unique Nature of Sexual Sin in 1 Corinthians 6.18," *NTS* 42 (1996) 540–558.

Kirchhoff, Renate. *Die Sünde gegen den eigenen Leib. Studien zu pornē und porneia in 1 Kor 6,12-20 und dem sozio-kulturellen Kontext der paulinischen Adressaten.* StUNT 18. Göttingen: Vandenhoeck & Ruprecht, 1994.

Klein, George L. "Hos 3:1-3—Background to 1 Cor 6:19b-20?" *CTR* 3 (1989) 373–375.

Miller, J. I. "A Fresh Look at I Corinthians 6. 16f.," *NTS* 27 (1980) 125–127.

Murphy-O'Connor, Jerome. "Corinthian Slogans in 1 Cor 6:12-20," *CBQ* 40 (1978) 391–396.

Porter, Stanley E. "How Should *kollōmenos* in 1 Cor 6,16.17 Be Translated?" *EThL* 67 (1991) 105–106.

Radcliffe, Timothy. "'Glorify God in your bodies': 1 Corinthians 6,12-20 as a sexual ethic," *NBl* 67 (1986) 306–314.

Stowers, Stanley K. "A 'Debate' over Freedom: 1 Corinthians 6.12-20" in Everett Ferguson, ed., *Christian Teaching: Studies in Honor of Lemoine G. Lewis.* Abilene, Tex.: Abilene Christian University Press, 1981, 59–71.

Winter, Bruce W. "Gluttony and Immorality at Elitist Banquets. The Background to 1 Corinthians 6:12-20," *Jian Dao* 7 (1997) 77–90.

5. *Sex Within Marriage* (7:1-7)

1. Concerning the matters about which you have written, "it is good for a man not to touch a woman." 2. But because of sexual immorality, let each man have his own wife and each wife her own husband. 3. Let a man give to his wife what is her due; similarly, a wife to her husband. 4. A wife does not have authority over her own body, her husband does; similarly, a husband also does not have authority over his own body, his wife does. 5. Do not deprive one another, except perhaps by mutual agreement and for a period of time, in order that you have opportunity for prayer; then be together again, lest Satan tempt you because of your lack of self-control. 6. I say this to you by way of concession, not by way of command. 7. I wish that all people would be as I am; but each one has his or her own gift from God, one of one kind and another of another kind.

INTERPRETATION

Paul's Correspondence. Paul was not the only letter-writer in the early church. Some people in the community at Corinth had written (*egrapsate*) a letter to Paul about various issues that were troubling the community. Nils Dahl ("Paul and the Church at Corinth") suggests that the letter may have aggravated the divisions at Corinth. Some within the community may have wanted to appeal to Apollos or Cephas, with others suggesting that with having Christ's Spirit among them there was no need for recourse to an outside authority (cf. 1:12). The letter was probably brought to Paul by a delegation consisting of Stephanas, Fortunatus, and Achaicus (16:17). Stephanas, a leader and patron of the church at Corinth (16:15-16), may have been one of those who urged the sending of the letter to Paul. Paul's response, his "first" letter to the Corinthians (cf. 5:9, 11), is thus part of an ongoing correspondence.

One of the issues raised in the Corinthians' letter to Paul was asceticism with regard to sex. If the formula "about which" (*peri de;* cf. 7:25) always points to an issue mentioned by the Corinthians, their letter may also have been concerned with food offered to idols (8:1, 4), spiritual gifts (12:1), the collection for Jerusalem (16:1), and Apollos (16:12). "About which" is an epistolary formula. It also served as a simple formula for purposes of enumeration. Hence one cannot be sure that each of the topics identified by means of the formula was mentioned in the letter sent to Paul. Most commentators, nonetheless, continue to maintain that each of these issues appeared in that correspondence.

The manner in which Paul treats these issues is reminiscent of the style and rhetoric of the Hellenistic letter of advice. Pseudo-Demetrius describes the letter of advice *(typos symbouleutikos)* as one in which "by offering our own judgment, we exhort to something or dissuade from something." Pseudo-Demetrius' textbook example of the letter of advice begins, "I have briefly indicated to you those things for which I am held in high esteem by my subjects" (Malherbe, *Ancient Epistolary Theorists*, 36–37). In keeping with this classic model Paul frequently offers himself as an example, a *paradeigma*, in chs. 7–14. He puts his own prestige on the line as he responds to the Corinthians' concerns.

Corinthian Slogans. "It is good for a man not to touch a woman" was until recent years generally considered to be an expression of Paul's own thought. The apostle was thought to have been a celibate who urged the Corinthian men to espouse a fairly strong sexual asceticism. The thought summarized in the opening phrase then served as the interpretive key for the entire chapter. Marriage was permissible, allowed as a concession (7:6) lest people succumb to their passions and become involved in sexual misbehavior (7:2) with a consequence of eternal punishment (7:9). Paul's own celibacy (7:7a, 8b) could be cited as an example to be followed.

More recently scholars have become convinced that this traditional exegesis of Paul's words represents an anachronistic reading of his letter. The clause "it is good for a man not to touch a woman" is a kind of slogan. It encapsulates a type of sexual asceticism that some people at Corinth found to be so problematic that they wrote to Paul about it. The apostle's response begins in 7:2. When the attitude summed up in the slogan is seen to be the problem at Corinth rather than Paul's response to the problem the entire chapter, and certainly vv. 1-7, is read in a different light from what had previously been the accepted interpretation of Paul's words.

The idea that 1 Cor 7:1b represents the viewpoint of some Corinthians rather than that of Paul is one that goes back to the time of Origen (see the catena fragment, No. 121, published in Claude Jenkins, "Origen on I Corinthians. III," *JThS* 9 [1908] 500–514, especially 500). A number of factors confirm that "it is good for a man not to touch a woman" is a summarizing slogan. First of all, the expression "about which" *(peri de)* is a textual marker that serves as an enumerative device in each of the other instances in Paul's letter in which this formula is used (7:25; 8:1; 12:1; 16:1, 12). In keeping with usual Hellenistic and Pauline usage one should expect that a specific topic would be introduced in 7:1. The topic is cited in the form of a slogan. That the phrase is a slogan is indicated by the formulaic nature of the expression, "it is good for a man to . . ." (*kalon anthrōpǭ;* cf. 7:26) and by the fact that the verb "to touch" (*haptesthai*) is not otherwise used by Paul, except in the quotation found in 2 Cor 6:17.

In his letter Paul has already considered two Corinthian slogans (6:12, 13). As the letter continues he will cite other slogans that had been bandied about the metropolis (8:1, 4, 8; 10:23; 13:2; 15:12). Typically Paul concedes some measure of truth to the slogan and then proceeds to give a critical response. In 7:1-7 Paul counters the plea for sexual asceticism with an attitude toward sexuality reflecting that of his own Jewish tradition (cf. 1 Thess 4:3b-6).

What circumstances might have prompted some Corinthians to promote the kind of radical sexual asceticism summarized in the slogan? Did the attitude arise from a disordered religious enthusiasm that might have affected some Christian neophytes? Was it found among those whom some commentators describe as the "eschatological women" of Corinth? Was sexual asceticism urged on Christians because of the impending eschaton? Was there a particular set of social circumstances that might have given rise to the posture?

It may well be that sexual asceticism was "in the air" in first-century Corinth. Literary and artifact evidence suggests that the cult of Isis, the Egyptian goddess, was celebrated in metropolitan Corinth during the imperial era. The cult of Isis was certainly practiced in the Corinthian port of Cenchreae (cf. Rom 16:1-2). The Latin poets Ovid and Propertius tell us that worship of the deity implied sexual abstinence. The satirist Juvenal writes about women who must seek forgiveness from Isis because they had engaged in sexual intercourse with their husbands (*Satires* 6.535-537). In regard to women who abstained from sexual intercourse Ovid writes, "let the goddess Isis give you a pretext for denying your sexual favors" (*Amores* 1.8.74). Propertius suggests "that you pretend that the days of Isis have come and require abstinence" (*Elegies* 4.5.28-34). Worshipers of Isis and other Egyptian deities had no monopoly on sexual abstinence for religious motives, but archaeological evidence attests to the presence of these Egyptian cults in mid-first-century Corinth. Some of them were well known for their promotion of sexual abstinence.

First Corinthians contains frequent hints that Paul was generally familiar with some forms of philosophic discourse. Among the issues at Corinth was the pursuit of wisdom, to the neglect of the message of the cross. A classic philosophic topos was the discussion on marriage. Paul's fellow Tarsan, the Stoic philosopher Antipater (ca. mid-second-century

B.C.E.) wrote a treatise "On Marriage" (*SVF* 3.255.5–6) in which he taught that marriage was "among the primary and most necessary of those things which are fitting." Closer in time to Paul's visit to Corinth was an ongoing discussion between Stoic philosophers and the more radical Cynics on the nature and purpose of marriage. While urging the avoidance of sexual promiscuity the Stoics generally considered marriage to be of benefit to the polis and in that way to have a cosmic purpose. The Cynics, on the other hand, were more inclined to urge sexual abstinence so that greater attention could be paid to the pursuit of philosophy. The "debates" between the Stoics and the Cynics in this regard were frequently linked to a discussion of freedom. Paul's consideration of the issues of sexual abstinence (7:1-16) and marriage (7:25-40) is likewise embedded in a lengthy section of his letter in which he treats various issues pertaining to freedom. (See 6:12 and 10:23, the encompassing "bookends" of a literary unit, and 7:21-24, an emphatic statement on freedom in the B unit of his chiastically structured ch. 7.)

Marital Sexuality. What Paul writes about sexual relationships in marriage has been prompted by a particular situation at Corinth and the questions raised in the Corinthians' letter to the apostle. In this respect his teaching on marriage and sexuality is very much occasional and *ad hoc*. On the other hand, what Paul has written about the use of sexuality within marriage is quite consistent with the Jewish tradition, as it is with Hellenistic philosophic discourse.

Within the Jewish tradition it was expected that men and women should marry (cf. Gen 1:28). The testamentary literature, especially *The Testaments of the Twelve Patriarchs,* suggests that one of the reasons why men and women should marry is so that they might avoid succumbing to the temptation of sexual immorality (see *T. Levi* 9:9-10). Paul says something similar in v. 2. The Jewish tradition had a healthy attitude toward human sexuality. This is reflected in what Paul writes. Despite its patriarchalism one aspect of the Jewish tradition that manifested relative equality between men and women was its attitude toward sexual relationships within marriage. Divorce was generally the prerogative of the male but the rabbis allowed a woman to initiate divorce proceedings if her husband refused to have sexual intercourse with her. The tradition admitted of abstinence from sexual intercourse during the menstrual period for reasons of cultic purity but it was otherwise loath to tolerate the absence of sexual relationships within marriage except for a limited time and for purposes of prayer (see *T. Naph.* 8:8). In his treatment of the role of sexuality within marriage Paul does not make explicit use of biblical warrants nor does he invoke rabbinic authority. That his views on human sexuality derive from a biblical anthropology is, however, indicated by his contextual use of Gen 2:24 in 6:12-20. That passage articulates a holistic anthropology on the basis of which Paul is able to respond as he does in ch. 7. The pericope began with a consideration of claims to freedom (6:12).

In the Hellenistic world, particularly among the Stoics and Cynics, sexuality and marriage formed a classic topos. A typical thesis used as an exercise in the rhetorical schools was whether to marry (*ei gamēteon;* cf. Hermogenes, *Progymnasmata* 11; [Dionysius of Halicarnassus], *Ars rhetorica* 2.1-2). The exposition of the topos frequently focused on the use of freedom. Some urged that marriage be avoided so as to provide time for the pursuit of philosophy: thus Epictetus, who in his presentation of the ideal philosopher, a Cynic, wrote "Look at me . . . I am without a home . . . I have neither wife nor children . . . Yet, what do I lack? Am I not free?" (*Discourses* 3.22.47-48). On the other hand there were those who considered not only that marriage for the sake of the common weal of the city-state was incumbent upon the good citizen but also that a wife and children lighten a man's burdens and make his life more pleasant. This is the position espoused by Antipater and Hierocles in their respective treatises "On Marriage" (Hierocles, frag. 52.26-27; 53.3, 11; Antipater, *SVF* 3.256.32-33).

What Paul writes about marriage and sexuality in 7:1-7 resonates with the moralists' discussion of sexuality. Some of his linguistic usage, particularly the expressions "good for a man" (*kalon anthrōpǭ*) and "similarly" (*homoiōs de kai),* echoes the language of the Stoics and Cynics. Marital responsibility and mutuality within the relationship are two of the motifs frequently raised in the philosophic discourse. Duty and responsibility are very important for the Stoics, but so too is mutuality in marriage. Hierocles praises the matrimonial partnership in which husband and wife hold all things in common, even one another's body and soul (frag. 54.14-27). According to Antipater spouses "not only share a partnership of property, and children . . . and the soul, but these alone also share their bodies (*alla kai tōn sōmatōn houtoi monoi koinonousi; SVF* 3.255.12-18).

Paul's own exposition "On Marriage" likewise focuses on mutuality and on physical communion. Verses 2-4 contain three parallel statements on marriage and sexuality. These pertain to the importance of being married, the right to sexual intercourse, and physical autonomy. In each instance Paul talks about women in the same way that he talks about men. In the first two cases he writes first about men and then about women. This may reflect his patriarchal situation. In the third of his balanced statements he first writes of women and then of men. Strikingly, this statement addresses the issue of the submission of one spouse to the other. Paul's words in this regard urge the spouses' mutual submission to one another. Equality within the sexual relationship is the norm. Paul's plea for mutuality in the relationship is underscored by the use of such telling expressions as "similarly" (*homoiōs de kai*, vv. 3, 4) and "by mutual agreement" (*ek symphōnou*, v. 5).

Motives for Marriage. While it may appear that Paul's words with regard to sexual immorality (v. 2) imply that marriage is the lesser of two evils, both Jewish and Hellenistic sources cite similar thoughts in their discussion of marriage. The motif occurs even within passages that plead the case of a person's responsibility to marry. In modern terms one might suggest that what the sources had to say about the avoidance of sexual immorality is an indication of their healthy regard for the force of the sexual drive. On the other hand it is clear that both Jewish sources and the philosophic discourse held that the rightful place for sexual intercourse was within marriage. This is in keeping with a view that strongly favored social order. Sexual misconduct was considered to be detrimental to the common good.

By way of summative conclusion to his exposition on sexuality and marriage Paul writes about the gift that each one receives from God (*hekastos idion echei charisma ek theou*, v. 7). That each one has his or her own gift from God is an important theme in 1 Corinthians, one developed at length in ch. 12. Some interpreters have suggested that the gift of God of which Paul writes in v. 7 is the a-marital state. It would appear that Paul was no longer married (see v. 8) when he wrote 1 Corinthians. There is, however, no reason to restrict "the gift from God" to celibacy. Every person has his or her own gift from God. Paul has been writing about himself and the entire community (cf. v. 6). The burden of his exposition has been on marriage. Paul considers both marriage and the nonmarital state as gifts from God. Each bears with it power from God. Each demands responsibility to God and God's people.

Sexual Abstinence. Paul's tolerance of husband and wife refraining from the use of sex for a while so as to devote themselves to prayer reflects an attitude similar to one found in Judaism. Traditions of abstinence in preparation for cultic activities (Exod 19:15) and the priestly practice of sexual abstinence during periods of service in the Temple are found in the Hebrew Bible. Considering themselves a priestly group, the Qumran sectarians took a seemingly rigid position with regard to sexual abstinence. The *Manual of Discipline* does not mention women except in the phrase "one born of a woman" (1QS 11:21). It required the Qumranites "not to follow a sinful heart and lustful eyes, committing all manner of evil" (1QS 1:6). In similar fashion the Damascus covenant urged that "you may walk perfectly in all His ways and not follow after thoughts of the guilty inclination and eyes of lust. For through them, great men have gone astray and mighty heroes have stumbled from former times till now" (CD 2:14-16). In preparation for the end time's holy war the *Messianic Rule* enjoined that "they shall sanctify them for three days that every one of its members may be prepared" (1QSa 1:25-26).

Paul's teaching is more like that of the rabbis than like the practices of the Qumran sectarians. The Mishnaic tractate on marriage, *Ketubot,* discusses the length of time in which it is permitted for couples to practice sexual abstinence: "If a man vowed to have no intercourse with his wife, the School of Shammai say: [She may consent] for two weeks. And the School of Hillel say: For one week [only]. Disciples [of the Sages] may continue absent for thirty days against the will [of their wives] while they occupy themselves in the study of the Law; and laborers for one week" (*m. Ketub.* 5:6; cf. *t. Ned.* 5:6).

Without casuistry the *Testament of Naphtali* states simply, "There is a time for having intercourse with one's wife *(kairos gar synousias gynaikos autou),* and a time to abstain for the purpose of prayer *(kairos egkrateias eis proseuchēn autou)"* (*T. Naph.* 8:8). Like the *Testament of Naphtali* Paul suggests a limited time *(pros kairon)* in which he would concede marital abstinence. He is clearly concerned with the limitation of time. The verb "to have opportunity" *(scholazō,* literally "to have leisure") is hapax in his writing, but the cognate noun *scholē,* "spare time" or "leisure" frequently appears in the Stoic-Cynic discussion on marriage where it figures in the debate about the legitimacy of marriage when "free time" *(scholē)* is needed for the pursuit of philosophy.

On the whole Paul urges a realistic attitude toward human sexuality. With regard to sexual abstinence he offers advice on his own authority, perhaps reflecting a Jewish tradition to which he and the rabbis were heir. Paul can abide sexual continence within marriage, but only if three conditions are fulfilled: 1) that the abstinence be mutually agreed upon by husband and wife; 2) that it be limited to a relatively short period of time; and 3) that its purpose be prayer.

Notes

1. *Concerning the matters about which you have written:* "Concerning" *(peri de)* is a classic formula used to identify a topic that is about to be considered. The formula was frequently used in Hellenistic letters to point to the matters raised in previous correspondence. Here Paul indicates that he is responding to a letter he had received from the Corinthians. This is the only time in the extant Pauline corpus in which the apostle mentions his having received a letter from those to whom he was writing.

   "it is good for a man not to touch a woman": "Good for a man" *(kalon anthrōpǭ)* is a formulaic expression similar to one cited by Musonius Rufus, "a protector and benefactor must know what's good for a man *(agathon anthrōpǭ)* and what is bad" (frag. 8.60.6-10). The slogan obviously has to do with sexual

intercourse. The verb "to touch" (*haptō*, used elsewhere by Paul only in a citation of Isa 52:11; cf. 2 Cor 6:17) served as a euphemism for sexual intercourse in Hellenistic literature (*T. Reub.* 3:5; Josephus, *Ant.* 1.163; Plutarch, *Alexander* 21.5; cf. Aristotle, *Politics* 7.12; Plato, *Laws* 8.840A; Gen 20:6; Prov 6:29 [LXX]; see also Gordon D. Fee, "1 Corinthians 7:1 in the *NIV*," *JETS* 23 [1980] 307–314). This would seem to be the connotation of the verb in the slogan. Apparently some members of the community were urging rigorous sexual asceticism as a way of life. For others in the community this was problematic. They addressed their concern to Paul, who, as he commonly does in this letter, concedes the grain of truth that is found in the slogan and then addresses a radical critique to the position summed up in the slogan. His way of dealing with issues is one Paul shares with some of the philosophical moralists. See, for example, the way that Musonius Rufus deals with the issue of obedience to one's father in the diatribe, "Must One Obey One's Parents Under all Circumstances?" (frag. 16).

2. *But because of sexual immorality, let each man have his own wife and each wife her own husband:* The postpositive connective particle *(de)* has an adversative sense. It introduces Paul's rebuttal of the position espoused in the slogan. The verb "to have" *(echō)* connotes (sexual) possession (see 5:1). With the reflexive pronoun "his own" *(heautou)* and the adjective "her own" *(ton idion)* Paul clearly implies that what he is talking about is marriage. Jewish tradition not only exhorted men to have sexual relations only with their wives (Prov 5:15, 18; etc.). It also urged marriage as a means to avoid sexual misconduct *(porneia)*. See, for example, Tob 4:12 and *T. Levi* 9:9-10, "Be on guard against the spirit of sexual immorality. . . . Therefore take for yourself a wife while you are still young, a wife who is free of blame or profanation, who is not from the race of alien nations." Rabbinic Judaism attributed a positive value to sexual desire: "Were it not for the evil inclination *(yēṣer ha-raʿ)* no man would build a house, marry a wife, or beget children" (*Gen. Rab.* 9:7). The statement of principle (v. 2) that Paul contrasts with the Corinthian slogan (v. 1) is one that not only reflects his Jewish attitude toward sexuality (cf. 6:16) but bespeaks an attitude of parity with regard to human sexuality: what he says about sex and marriage in 7:1-16 applies equally to both men and women.

3. *Let a man give to his wife what is her due; similarly, a wife to her husband:* The motif of parity and mutuality in sexual relationships, introduced in v. 2, is continued. "Similarly" *(homoiōs de kai,* literally "and likewise also"), used in both v. 3 and v. 4, stresses the equality of the sexual roles in marriage. The same phrase is found in two consecutive verses in Musonius' treatise "That Women, too, Should Pursue Philosophy" (see frag. 3.38.30, 31) to underscore the equality that exists between men and women.

Paul writes about giving what is due, *opheilēn apodidotō*. Paul uses the expression elsewhere only in Rom 13:7, where it has to do with taxes or the respect due to legitimate civil authority. Clement of Alexandria interpreted "what is due" of progeny. He also considered children to be the unstated object of "deprive" in v. 5. His exegesis of v. 8 implies that it is the avoidance of the encumbrance of responsibility for children that makes the single state desirable (*Stromata* 3.10.22-23; 3.15.18; 3.18.68-70; *PG* 8, 1169, 1196, 1212). So far in the discussion, however, there has been no mention whatever of children (see v. 14). Paul's exhortation reflects the Jewish tradition that considered cohabitation with sexual intercourse to be an obligation of customary law (*b. ʿErub.* 100b).

4. *A wife does not have authority over her own body, her husband does; similarly, a husband also does not have authority over his own body, his wife does:* Using the same verb, "to have authority over," Paul has previously affirmed that he was subject to no one (6:12). Paul's anthropology is holistic. He does not claim that the physical body of the wife belongs to the husband, or that the body of the husband belongs to the wife. He is talking about the whole person with its physical and sexual characteristics. He is asserting that a wife does not enjoy complete self-determination any more than her husband does. In marriage what is most appropriate is the mutual submission of spouses to one another (cf. Eph 5:21).

5. *Do not deprive one another, except perhaps by mutual agreement and for a period of time:* Paul offers a concession (v. 6), limited in its scope, to those who would choose abstinence over and against an active sexual life. His language continues to reflect a sense of mutual obligation in marriage. In classical and Hellenistic Greek "deprive" (*apostereite*) generally connotes stealing or defrauding (6:7-8; cf. Mal 3:5; Sir 4:1; 34:21-22; Mark 10:19; 1 Tim 6:5). Within marriage abstention from sexual intercourse is a departure from the norm; it is a failure to render to one's spouse his or her due (cf. Exod 21:10 [LXX, where the verb *apostereō* is used with this meaning]). Hence Paul suggests limits on the exercise of the concession. The conditions ("except perhaps," *ei mēti*; see BDF 376) are two: mutual agreement and a limited time. *Ek symphōnou,* "by agreement," is hapax in Paul, but the expression has many parallels among the papyrological finds (P.Bononiensis 24a; P.Oxyrhynchus 1673, 20; P.Nessana 21, 26) where it is a contractual formula implying conformity, correspondence, and coincidence (*TLNT* 3:327). In Paul's use of the expression there is a nuance of moral delicacy and human consideration. "For a period of time" (*pros kairon*) is a formulaic expression used by Sophocles among others.

in order that you have opportunity for prayer: To give themselves a greater opportunity for prayer is a reason that might permit a couple to refrain from an active sexual life "for a time." A wide variety of textual witnesses cite prayer as the only warrant for this temporary abstinence ($\mathfrak{P}^{11,46}$, ℵ, A, B, C, D, G, P, Y, 33, 104, 81, 181, it, vg, cop, arm, eth, Origen, Ambrosiaster, Augustine, etc.), but a corrector of the Codex Sinaiticus and most of the medieval manuscripts have an additional phrase, *nēsteia kai tē,* before "prayer," thus producing the classic pair, prayer and fasting (cf. Luke 2:37; Acts 14:23). The longer reading was known to Chrysostom whose comments are, nonetheless, based on the shorter form of the text. The longer reading is found in a large number of medieval minuscules (88, 326, 436, 614, etc.) as well as in a few majuscules (K, L). In the inverted form "prayer and fasting" the longer reading appears in an occasional minuscule and the writings of John of Damascus. The longer reading is probably the result of scribes transcribing the text under the influence of the well-known classic expression.

then be together again, lest Satan tempt you because of your lack of self-control. The subjunctive form of the verb "to be" has the force of an imperative (see BDF 98). $\mathfrak{P}^{46}$, Ψ, and the majority of medieval manuscripts offer a clarifying "come together" *(synerchēsthe, synerchesthe)* in place of Paul's copulative verb. Paul is clearly urging Christian couples to cohabit and to have a normal sexual relationship. The reason? The temptation to self-indulgence. "Lack of self-control" *(akrasian,* literally "lack of power") is hapax in Paul. Its contrary, "self-control" *(egkrateia;* cf. 7:9; Philo, *Rewards* 116), frequently appears in Hellenistic catalogues of virtues, but only twice in the NT catalogues (Gal 5:23; 2 Pet 1:6). "Self-control" is frequently opposed to various forms of sexual promiscuity. Second Timothy 3:3 suggests that lack of self-control will be in evidence in the end times. Paul attributes lack of self-control to Satan (7:5), an end-time figure, the tempter *par excellence* (Mark 1:13 *par.*). K. N. Papadopoulos has, however, suggested that *akrasia* is derived from the verb *kerannymi* and would therefore suggest "lack of sexual relations" rather than a lack of self-control *("Hē sēmasia tēs lexeōs 'akrasia' en 1 Kor. 7,5," DBM* 8 (1979) 135–137.

6. *I say this to you by way of concession, not by way of command:* Paul's antithetical construction places the emphasis on "not by way of command" (cf. 2 Cor 8:8). His other uses of the "command" *(epitagē),* in 7:25; Rom 16:26; and 2 Cor 8:8, suggest that Paul knows of no command of the Lord (cf. 7:10, 12) that would warrant even limited sexual abstinence. At most his Jewish tradition allows him to tolerate *(syggnōmēn,* "concession," hapax in the NT) marital sexual abstinence under the stated conditions.

7. *I wish that all people would be as I am:* Used with an accusative and an infinitive, Paul's verb *(thelō)* expresses a wish. At the time of his writing to the Corinthians Paul seems to have been unmarried (7:8; cf. 9:5). Since he was a law-abiding Jew (cf. *m. Yebam.* 6:6; *b. Yebam.* 62b-64a) it is likely that Paul would have been married at some point in his life. Had Paul been a rabbi of some sort it would have been virtually impossible for him not to have been married (cf. Joachim Jeremias, "War Paulus Witwer?" *ZNW* 25 [1926] 310–312; idem, "Nochmals: "War Paulus Witwer?" *ZNW* 28 [1929] 321–323). The wish expressed in 7:7 may have been prompted by the idea that the unmarried person is able to devote undivided attention to the Lord (7:32b-35).

The postpositive connective particle *(de)* has not been translated. Modern translators frequently decline to translate this particle, which sometimes has a connective and sometimes an adversative sense. If vv. 1b-7 are construed as a paraenetic unit urging sexual asceticism, as has often been the case in the history of the interpretation of this material, v. 7 might be construed as argument from his own personal example, providing additional rationale for Paul's exhortation. Some scribes understood Paul's text in this fashion and have substituted an explanatory *gar,* "for," (B, Ψ, and the "corrected" ℵ and D; cf. K, P) for Paul's *de* ($\mathfrak{P}^{46}$, ℵ, A, C, D, the Vetus Latina, and various Fathers, including Jerome and Augustine).

but each one has his or her own gift from God, one of one kind and another of another kind: As in the previous sentence (v. 6), the use of antithesis provides a contrast between Paul and God. Here the adversative conjunction "but" *(alla)* places the emphasis on the gift of God. It is not Paul's wish but God's gift that is normative in these matters. Paul is well aware that each person in the community has his or her own *(hekastos idion)* gift from God. The individual distribution of God's gifts, dependent on God's will, is the dominant motif of 12:4-11, but the theme is echoed elsewhere in Paul's letter (3:5-9, 10-13; 7:17-24; cf. 1:7). For Paul the gift of God *(charisma ek theou)* implies power and responsibility.

FOR REFERENCE AND FURTHER STUDY

Caragounis, Chrys C. "'Fornication' and 'Concession'? Interpreting 1 Cor 7,1-7," *CorC* 543–560.

Collins, Raymond F. "The Unity of Paul's Paraenesis in 1 Thess 4.3-8 and 1 Cor 7.1-7, a Significant Parallel," *NTS* 29 (1983) 420–429. Reprinted in idem, *Christian Morality: Biblical Foundations.* Notre Dame, Ind.: University of Notre Dame Press, 1986, 211–222.

Garland, David E. "The Christian's Posture Toward Marriage and Celibacy: 1 Corinthians 7," *RExp* 80 (1983) 351–362.

MacDonald, Margaret Y. "Women Holy in Body and Spirit in the Social Setting of 1 Corinthians 7," *NTS* 36 (1990) 161–181.

Phipps, William E. "Is Paul's Attitude toward Sexual Relations Contained in 1 Cor 7.1?" *NTS* 28 (1982) 125–131.

Poirier, John C., and Joseph Frankovic. "Celibacy and Charism in 1 Cor 7:5-7," *HThR* 89 (1996) 1–18.

Schrage, Wolfgang. "Zur Frontstellung der paulinischen Ehebewertung in 1 Kor 7,1-7," *ZNW* 67 (1976) 214–234.

Scroggs, Robin. "Paul and the Eschatological Woman," *JAAR* 40 (1972) 283–303.

Stowers, Stanley K. *Letter Writing* 91–112.

Ward, Roy Bowen. "Musonius and Paul on Marriage," *NTS* 36 (1990) 281–289.

Winter, Bruce W. "1 Corinthians 7:6-7: A Caveat and a Framework for 'the Sayings' in 7:8-24," *TynB* 48 (1997) 57–65.

Yarbrough, O. Larry. *Not Like the Gentiles: Marriage Rules in the Letters of Paul.* SBL.DS 80. Atlanta: Scholars, 1985.

6. *Special Situations* (7:8-16)

8. And I say to men who are not married and to widows that it is good for them to remain as I am. 9. If they cannot exercise self-control they should marry, for it is better to marry than to be on fire with passion.

10. To those who are married I command—not I, but the Lord—that a wife is not to separate from her husband 11.—should she separate, let her remain unmarried and be reconciled to her husband—and a husband should not divorce his wife.

12. To the rest, I say—I, not the Lord—if any brother has an unbelieving wife and she consents to live with him, let him not divorce her; 13. and if a woman has an unbelieving husband and he consents to live with her, let her not divorce her husband. 14. For the unbelieving husband is made holy through his wife and the unbelieving wife is made holy through the brother; for otherwise your children would be unclean, but now they are holy. 15. And if the unbeliever separates, let him or her separate. The brother or sister is not subservient in these cases. God has called you in peace. 16. Wife, do you know if you might save your husband? Husband, do you know if you might save your wife?

INTERPRETATION

In the fashion typical of Hellenistic moralists Paul raised the issue of human sexuality by citing the case of a man's sexual liaison with a prostitute (6:12-20). The discussion allowed Paul to share some of the basic insights of his holistic and eschatological anthropology. Thereafter he turned his attention to an issue that was of concern to the Corinthians who had written to him, namely a kind of asexual existence in which men and women would not have sexual intercourse. Paul's own view of marriage, a view he shares with Judaism, was one in which sexual communion has an important role to play. Having considered and generally rejected the practice of sexual abstinence within marriage (7:2-7), he now turns his attention (7:8-16) to a number of special cases: (1) those who are no longer married (vv. 8-9); (2) those who are married (vv. 10-11); (3) and those who are married to nonbelievers (vv. 12-16).

As he proceeds with his mini-treatise "On Marriage," Paul continues to maintain the gender parity that characterized 7:2-4. In every instance what he says about a man is paralleled with a similar statement about a woman. The directive motive of Paul's exhortation is that, no matter one's marital situation, all should remain as they are (vv. 8-9, 10-11, 12-13; cf. 17-24). Otherwise a kind of casuistry pervades Paul's treatment. He treats the three cases in turn, respectively and directly addressing each group (note the series of datives: *tois agamois kai tais chērais, . . . tois gegamēskosin, . . . tois loipois,* each being joined to the preceding consideration by the connective *de*). His exposition is, moreover, characterized by the use of "if" (*ei* in vv. 9, 12, 13, 15; *ean* in v. 11).

In each of the three cases Paul treats the specific marital situation with respect to the question with which he began his exhortation on marriage, namely the desirability of avoiding sexual intercourse. Is shunning marriage altogether a proper way to avoid sexual intercourse? The various cases are different from one another, and Paul treats them differently. He devotes his longest treatment to the question of mixed marriage and carefully distinguishes the case of a believer who might contemplate divorcing a non-Christian spouse (vv. 12-14, 15c-16) from the case of the nonbeliever who might divorce a Christian spouse (v. 15ab).

Widowers and Widows. The first group Paul addresses consists of the community's widowers and widows. Presumably Paul considers the case of widowers and widows before the other cases because his *ethos* appeal had cited his own example (v. 7; see above, p. 260). He continues to cite his own example as he addresses those who once had been married. Given the patriarchalism of contemporary Hellenistic and Jewish society, Paul addresses the men before the women. Paul's remarks with regard to those whose spouses have died is closely linked with the preceding unit of his letter. With a comparative *hōs* ("as") he cites his own example in v. 8, as he did in v. 7. His discourse continues to reflect the discourse of the Hellenistic world in which the self-control/lack of self-control antithesis appears in Stoic discussions about sexual desire and passion.

In addressing widowers and widows Paul directs them to follow his own example and not marry again (cf. 7:27b), but Paul is a realist. He realizes that the gift of post-marital celibacy is not given to everyone (7:7). Accordingly he urges widowers and widows who experience a strong passionate love to marry. It is better to marry than to be afire with passion (cf. 7:2, 28, 36, 38, 39).

Married Couples. Having already considered the matter of sexual abstinence within marriage (7:2-7), Paul addresses further remarks to those who are married. He strongly urges them not to divorce their spouses. It is likely that Paul was aware of a situation in which a Corinthian Christian woman had divorced or was about to divorce her husband. In a departure from his normal manner of presentation Paul first addresses the situation of the woman. What he says with regard to the woman who might contemplate divorce is expanded with a casuistic parenthesis (v. 11ab). What he has to say about a man not divorcing his wife is simply stated and follows upon Paul's remarks on the divorcing woman.

That Paul begins his address "to those who are married" with words to the effect that a woman should not divorce her husband suggests that Paul is addressing a real case in Corinth. Unlike women in the Jewish world who were generally not permitted to divorce their husbands, women in the Hellenistic world had the possibility of divorcing their spouses. The case Paul envisions may have been reported to him in the letter he received; alternatively he may have learned about the situation from one or another of his visitors (cf: 1:11; 16:17). The casuistic aside of v. 11 confirms that he has a particular case in mind. He does not offer to the woman who would divorce her husband the option of remaining unmarried or of returning to her husband. Were he to have done so Paul would have offered an exhortation contrary to that of the tradition. Rather Paul urges the woman to remain unmarried so that she can be reconciled to her husband. Paul's exhortation reflects a Jewish view of marriage, as does much of what he writes about marriage in ch. 7. According to the traditional Jewish view a woman who had sexual intercourse with another man was forbidden to her husband (cf. 2 Sam 16:21-22; 20:3). Among other things this implied that a woman who had been divorced and was legitimately remarried was not permitted to be married again to her first husband should the second husband die or divorce her (see Deut 24:3-4).

Jesus' saying on divorce is the most widely attested of all his sayings in the NT. It appears in each of the synoptics and twice in Matthew, albeit in four different versions (Matt 5:32; 19:9; Mark 10:11-12; Luke 16:18). Each of the synoptics' versions of the saying addresses the situation of a man who would divorce his wife. Only Mark, in what is clearly a Markan addition to the tradition, speaks of a wife divorcing her husband. Paul's reference to the command of the Lord harkens back to the tradition of Jesus' saying on divorce, but unlike the rabbis Paul does not worry about citing his authoritative source verbatim. At best he offers a paraphrase of the tradition. He first addresses the matter of a divorcing wife, using language that is appropriate to his context (see vv. 12-13, 15) rather than the vocabulary of the synoptics.

The content of Paul's paraenesis is traditional. The authority on which he relies is not so much tradition as such as it is the risen Lord who reigns sovereign over his people (1:2). The reference to the command of the Lord is unique in the extant correspondence (cf. 11:23-26; 14:37; 1 Thess 4:15). "Command" (*paraggellō*, elsewhere in Paul only in 11:17 and 1 Thess 4:11) has a ring quite different from the "say" of vv. 8 and 11. The command is the command of the Lord, whom Paul carefully distinguishes from himself (vv. 10, 12). Here, as elsewhere in 1 Corinthians, the Lord is the risen Lord who enjoys sovereignty over the community of believers. Believers acknowledge the risen Christ to be their Lord, the one who has authority over them. In 14:37 Paul will refer to a commandment (*entolē*) of the Lord and in 1 Thess 4:15 to the word (*logō*) of the Lord. In 11:24-25 he will cite traditional words of the Lord, but this is the language of liturgical narrative rather a logion invoked as a behavioral norm. Only in 7:10 does Paul intimate that he is conveying a command of the Lord, using a tradition that is clearly reflected in the synoptic gospels.

Mixed Marriages. The third group of people to whom Paul addresses specific remarks in his treatise on marriage are "the rest" *(tois loipois)*. These are those who are involved in a marriage with a nonbeliever. Their situation is somewhat anomalous; Paul considers that Christians ought to marry "in the Lord" (7:39), an expression that suggests that a Christian ought to marry another Christian. Given the expectation that Christians were to marry other Christians, it is probable that "the rest" are neophyte Christians who had been married to non-Christians before becoming Christian. Paul's remarks are addressed to the new Christian, one of the brothers or one of the sisters, rather than to the non-Christian spouse.

Paul's remarks "to the rest" (vv. 12-16) constitute the longest of the three subunits within this section of the letter. The argument is discursive, with a repeated "for" *(gar)* in vv. 14 and 16 and a "for otherwise" *(epei ara),* and direct, with a pair of rhetorical questions in v. 16. Paul's treatment of mixed marriage is characterized by the rhetoric of logical argumentation *(logos)* and appeal to the audience *(pathos).* The extent and manner of his argument is striking. It is almost as if Paul had to prove his case. Having neither an adage of common wisdom (v. 9) nor a word of the Lord (v. 10) on which to rely, Paul must make use of his own rhetorical skills in order to convince those Christians who are involved in mixed marriages in their commitment to their spouses.

The case needs to be made not only because there were at Corinth some neophyte Christians whose spouses had not converted to Christianity but also because in virtually all cultures exogamous marriage is anomalous. Intermarriage flies in the face of expected mores and accepted social convention. People are expected to marry within their own group whether "the group" be defined racially, ethnically, socially, or religiously (cf. Deut 7:3; Neh 13:25). In Judaism mixed marriages were considered invalid (*b. Qidd.* 68b; *b. Yebam.* 45a). A proselyte was considered "a newly born child"; all previous family ties were terminated with the proselyte's conversion to Judaism. The customary mores of the Hellenistic world were such that a wife, in particular, was expected to worship the gods of her husband. Thus Plutarch is often quoted as having said, "It is becoming for a wife to worship and to know only the gods that her husband believes in, and to shut the front door tight upon all queer rituals and outlandish superstitions. For with no god do stealthy and secret rites performed by a woman find any favor" ("Advice to the Bride and Groom," *Moralia* 140D).

Within a context of the common reluctance to accept exogamous marriage and the fact that sexual abstinence was in the air (7:1) Paul must develop a case to prove that *ex post factum* mixed marriages are a reality from which a Christian spouse should not seek to escape. Paul begins his argument with a balanced statement of principle: a Christian man should not divorce his non-Christian wife; a Christian wife should not divorce her non-Christian husband.

Paul develops his argument (see the explanatory *gar*, "for," in v. 14) with a series of rationalizations. The first concerns the holiness of the non-Christian spouse. Paul's affirmation about the sanctification of the non-Christian spouse is, in some respects, a mirror image of 6:15-18. Paul's language reflects the Jewish understanding of marriage. At about the same time that Paul was writing to the Corinthians a Jewish marriage document *(kĕtûbâ)* was being developed that made use of the language of sanctification. During the ceremony the groom was to say to the bride, "you are made holy to me" *(qiddûšîn)*. Even if the expression were not used, as in those instances where the older covenantal formula, "you are wife to me" or "you are joined to me" was used, the wife was considered to be sanctified to her husband. By the formula was meant something more than the mere fact that the wife belonged to her husband; it also implied that by marriage the wife shared in the groom's covenanted status. Prior to marriage a woman participated in the covenant ("was sanctified") through her father; upon marriage she was sanctified through her husband.

In v. 14a-b Paul expresses something akin to the biblical tradition of holiness by association (cf. Exod 29:37; Lev 6:18; Rom 11:16; see F. F. Bruce, *1 and 2 Corinthians* 69). Through the marital relationship the unbelieving spouse has been brought into the sphere of the Christian community. Paul uses the verb "made holy," *hēgiastai*, in the perfect tense, suggesting an action in the past, the baptism of the Christian (possibly a Christian's marriage to a non-Christian, but see 7:39), that has continuing effects in the present. Rather than Christian spouses being defiled or contaminated by their non-Christian partners, the non-Christian spouses are made holy through their Christian partners. Some at Corinth might have feared that a mixed marriage would involve the defilement of a Christian; Paul suggests that the real situation is just the opposite. The reality is that marriage with a Christian involves the holiness of the non-Christian partner.

According to the Jewish tradition the wife participates in the covenanted people through her husband. Paul's two-part statement of explanation is a reflection of his own radical understanding of the mutuality of spouses, one that he shares with Stoic moralists. For Paul an unbelieving wife participates in the covenantal status of her husband; an unbelieving husband participates in the covenantal status of his wife. Because the non-Christian spouse has been made holy there is no reason for a Christian husband or wife to reject a non-Christian spouse. They are one flesh (Gen 2:24, reprised in 6:16) and share together in God's holy people.

To this idea Paul adds, as a supportive argument, the holiness of the children of a mixed marriage (v. 14c). If the marital partners were not holy their children would be unclean. As it is, they are holy. Children participate in the holy people of God, presumably because of their filial relationship with the Christian parent. In Judaism the children of proselytes were likewise considered to be bona fide members of the people of God (*m. Qidd.* 1:2; *m. Ketub.* 4:4). Were the children of the Corinthian neophytes not to participate in the holy condition of their parents they would be "unclean," that is, ritually impure. Use of this term implies that Paul's idea of the "holiness" of mixed marriage retains the cultic overtones of holiness language that has been present in his letter since 1:2. Holiness means belonging to God. It describes what is according to God's plan and design.

A second reason why Christian spouses should remain committed to their non-Christian partners is their own call in peace. Paul uses the verb "to call" *(kaleō)* of the Christian vocation. (See note on 1:2.) God has called the Christian in peace *(en eirēnē)*; that call has lasting effects *(keklēken,* in the perfect). Peace is God's gift (1:3; 14:33). Paul's understanding of "peace" is one in which the biblical notion of *šālôm* has been assumed into a Christian context. The biblical notion of peace includes the marital well-being of those whom God has blessed with divine peace. Peace is the order of creation brought to fulfillment (see Gerhard von Rad, "*Eirēnē,*" *TDNT* 2:400–422, at 402–404; J. P. Healey, "Peace," *ABD* 5:206–207). God's call includes the component of marital well-being and stability.

Finally Paul uses the rhetorical flourish of a diatribal rhetorical question to posit the possible conversion of the non-Christian spouse as the ultimate argument in his arsenal. The "salvation" *(sōseis)* of non-Christian spouses is different from their "holiness" (cf. v. 14). The non-Christian spouse, like the children of the marriage, is holy because of association with the Christian spouse who belongs to the holy people of God (1:2). There is, however, something beyond the holiness of his or her spouse to which the Christian in a mixed marriage can aspire and that is the salvation of the non-Christian spouse, his or her coming to the Christian faith. The direct address of Paul's rhetorical questions involves a challenge in this regard to Christians whose spouses have not yet embraced the faith.

A Casuistic Aside. Paul's words to "the rest" are addressed directly to the Christian husbands and wives of non-Christian spouses. With regard to their marital situation Paul has no word of the Lord (7:12). He therefore develops a carefully sustained and complex argument pleading the case for marital stability.

Paul's letter does not give any indication that he intends to limit the scope of the Lord's word to marriages between Christians. He is, however, a realist. In a marriage between a Christian and a non-Christian the non-Christian spouse presumably does not recognize the authority of "the Lord." If he or she does not consent to live with the Christian partner (vv. 12, 13) he or she may decide to divorce the Christian. In such a case there is nothing that the Christian can do. "If the unbeliever separates, let that one separate," says Paul (v. 15).

The "exception" to Paul's exhortation to stability within mixed marriages is limited to this realistic aside. Paul does not address his words to the non-Christian nor does he provide any warrant for the non-Christian to divorce his or her Christian spouse. The argument Paul develops in vv. 15c-16 continues the main thrust of the epistolary subunit. These verses do not provide justification for a non-Christian to initiate a divorce against his or her neophyte Christian spouse.

NOTES

8. *And I say to men who are not married and to widows that it is good for them to remain as I am:* A connective "and" *(de)* links this section, dealing with three specific cases, with Paul's response to a claim for sexual abstinence in marriage (7:2-6). The first case taken up by the apostle is that of widowers and widows. With his mention of both groups who have suffered the loss of a spouse Paul continues to discuss matters of sexuality and marriage in such a way that his exhortations pertain to people of either gender. Were "unmarried" *(tois agamois)* not juxtaposed with "widows" the noun might designate those who were divorced (see v. 11) or those not yet married (see vv. 32, 34). Paralleled with "widows" the term connotes a specific group of unmarried men, namely widowers. With regard to widowers and widows Paul states that it is good for them to remain as they are *(kalon autois ean meinōsin)*. There is no reason to take "good" *(kalon)* as if it were a comparative, "better." Continuing the *ethos* argumentation of his letter, Paul offers himself as an example *(hōs kagō,* with no verb). The sense of the text is that Paul was not married at the time when he was writing. Most likely he was a widower (see above, p. 260). The care of widows was a matter of concern for the early church (Acts 6:1; 9:39-41; Jas 1:27; 1 Tim 5:3-16; see Bonnie B. Thurston, *The Widows: A Women's Ministry in the Early Church* [Minneapolis: Fortress, 1989]), but this is the only time in his correspondence that Paul mentions widows.

9. *If they cannot exercise self-control they should marry, for it is better to marry than to be on fire with passion:* What Paul says about widowers and widows is a development of his concessive remarks in vv. 5-7. In both cases there is a reference to Paul's own example (vv. 7, 8); the "exercise of self-control" *(egkrateuontai)* of v. 9 contrasts with the "lack of self-control" *(dia tēn akrasian)* of v. 5. The conditional clause is consistent with Paul's casuistry, as he con-

siders one case after another. The condition is in the present indicative, the apodosis in the imperative. Despite Paul's preference that widowers and widows remain unmarried he offers a reason why widowers and widows should marry: it is better to marry than to be on fire with passion. Paul uses the verb *pyroomai* only in a metaphorical sense (cf. 2 Cor 11:29). Here the connotation is "to be aflame with erotic desire" (thus R. B. Ward, "Musonius and Paul," 284; cf. Friedrich Lang, *"pyroō," TDNT* 6:948–950; compare Sir 23:16). In a Greek anthology cited by Lang the verb appears in an epigram on *erōs* with the meaning "to burn with love for someone."

10. *To those who are married I command—not I, but the Lord—that a wife is not to separate from her husband:* Paul continues his casuistic treatment with a consideration on divorce. The category is "the married." His "command" moves the level of his paraenesis to a higher level. The verb *paraggellō* is found in Paul only in 1 Cor 7:10 and 11:17. In both cases Paul's "command" is supported by a reference to the tradition, for which "the Lord" *(ho kyrios)* is the source and the authority. The Lord is the Jesus who has been raised and to whom the members of the community owe allegiance. Paul's command on divorce is similar to the Jesuanic logion of Matt 5:32; 19:9; Mark 10:11-12; Luke 16:18, but Paul makes no attempt to cite the words of the historical Jesus. The traditional logion essentially focused on a man divorcing his wife. Only in Mark is there reference to the parallel case of a wife divorcing her husband. That Paul first addresses himself to the wife divorcing her husband—a departure from the male-female sequence that has thus far dominated his gender-equal exhortations, and different from the traditional logion—would seem to indicate that Paul was aware of a situation in Corinth in which a woman had divorced her husband or was about to do so. On the authority of the Lord Paul commands that she not do so, that she not divorce her husband. The situation is that of the Hellenistic world, in which it was possible for a woman to divorce her husband. To speak of her divorce Paul uses the verb *chōristhēnai* (see vv. 11, 15), which means "to divorce" in Hellenistic legal texts. I have translated the verb as "separate" so as to distinguish it from the synonymous *aphienai* of vv. 11c, 12, 13. In the Synoptic version of Jesus' logion the verb *apolyein* is used. If there is any distinction to be made between "to separate" *(chōristhēnai)* and "to divorce" *(aphienai)* it may be that Paul is reflecting his traditional Jewish understanding of marriage that calls for active verbs to be used of men and passive verbs to be used of women.

11. *should she separate, let her remain unmarried and be reconciled to her husband:* Paul's casuistic treatment of various possible situations leads him to offer a directive on the case of a woman who does initiate divorce proceedings against her husband, almost as if it were an aside (cf. 7:21b). Paul does not suggest that she have two possibilities (a possible interpretation of the conjunction *ē,* literally "or"), either remain unmarried *(agamos)* or be reconciled to her husband. Rather Paul's exhortation implies that the woman is to remain unmarried in order that she be reconciled to her husband. Her remaining unmarried is the condition for her reconciliation with her spouse. In his Jewish tradition a divorced woman who had remarried is forbidden to her

former spouse (Deut 24:4; cf. *Hermas, Man.* 4.1.8). Paul's paraenesis is not in opposition to the early Christian tradition on divorce, as if the word of the Lord pertained to remarriage after divorce rather than to divorce itself. In the Synoptic tradition of the Jesuanic logion on divorce (Matt 5:32; 19:9; Mark 10:11-12; Luke 16:18) the emphasis lies on the exhortation to avoid divorce. Paul, like the Jesus of the Synoptic tradition, urges commitment to one's spouse.

and a husband should not divorce his wife: Even though it would appear that the issue at Corinth was that of a wife divorcing her husband, the gender parity that characterizes Paul's entire exhortation on marriage leads him to add that a husband should not divorce his wife. To speak of the divorce of a wife by her husband Paul uses the verb *aphienai* (cf. vv. 12, 13).

12–13. *To the rest, I say—I, not the Lord:* Having considered "widowers and widows (v. 8) and the married (v. 10), Paul comes to his third case, "the rest" *(tois loipois).* His *egō,* "I," is not emphatic, as if Paul intended to underscore his apostolic authority. Rather he uses the pronoun in order to affirm that the directive he is about to give, unlike the paraenesis of vv. 10-11, stems from himself (cf. v. 40), not from the Lord. Rabbis would typically distinguish their own teaching from the teaching of the authorities who had preceded them. The "rest" are those who are married to non-Christians, a situation that Paul considers to be somewhat anomalous (cf. 7:39b).

if any brother has an unbelieving wife and she consents to live with him, let him not divorce her; and if a woman has an unbelieving husband and he consents to live with her, let her not divorce her husband: Paul continues to speak of both men and women as he considers the case of the mixed marriage. Paul is presumably speaking of a marriage between non-Christians, one of whom later becomes a Christian. In such cases the Christian spouse is not permitted to initiate divorce proceedings as long as the non-Christian spouse is willing to remain in the marriage *(syneudokei oikein).* Since the non-Christian would presumably not acknowledge the authority of "the Lord" (cf. v. 10), the consent of the non-Christian (cf. v. 15a) is the condition for the continuation of the marriage.

Although Paul treats of a Christian man married to a non-Christian wife and a Christian wife married to a non-Christian husband in parallel fashion, his two-part exhortation has some linguistic variation. The Christian husband is called "a brother" *(adelphos);* the Christian wife is called "a woman" *(gynē).* As the object of the potential divorce Paul writes of "her" *(autēn)* and "her husband" *(ton andra,* even if later manuscripts read a balanced "him," *auton).*

In both parts of his balanced exhortation Paul refers to the non-Christian spouse as an "unbeliever" *(apiston,* masculine in form with respect to the unbelieving wife as well as with respect to an unbelieving husband). Will Deming *(Paul on Marriage and Celibacy* 144–146) suggests that the adjectives "faithful" *(pistos)* and "lacking in faith" *(apistos)* may have been used by the Corinthians to distinguish themselves from those who were not Christian. Among the Hellenistic moralists to be faithful *(pistos)* was a quality expected in one's friend. As such the adjectives may connote a sense of bonding rather than a sense of belief. With the exception of Gal 3:9 where it refers to Abraham, Paul does not use the adjective "faithful" *(pistos)* to refer to a believer. He uses "unfaithful" *(apistos)* only in the Corinthian correspondence (1 Cor 6:6; 7:12, 13, 14, 15; 10:27; 14:22, 23, 24; 2 Cor 4:4; 6:14, 15).

14. *For the unbelieving husband is made holy through his wife and the unbelieving wife is made holy through the brother:* Having spoken about an unbelieving husband, Paul offers an explanation (note the postpositive *gar*) of why a woman should not divorce a nonbelieving husband. The logical sequence of Paul's argument, in which he consistently mentions men before women, and when he has just mentioned a nonbelieving husband (v. 13), requires that Paul first address the issue of a husband who is a nonbeliever. The first reason why a Christian wife should not divorce her non-Christian husband is that he is sanctified through her. He participates in God's covenanted people (see 1:2) through her.

At v. 14 the manuscript tradition offers evidence of some textual variation. *Adelphos,* "brother," is usually found in the older majuscules ($\mathfrak{P}^{46}$, ℵ, A, B, C, D, F, G, P, Ψ), but some majuscules and most minuscules read "husband" *(andri),* apparently for the sake of greater balance. Various manuscripts add a qualifying "faithful" *(tē pistē, tō pistō)* to "wife" and to "husband." These variations are stylistic and do not affect the overall sense of the text.

for otherwise your children would be unclean, but now they are holy: Closely linked ("for otherwise," *epei ara*) with the preceding statement is Paul's reflection on children, offered in support of his argument that the non-Christian spouse has been made holy through the Christian spouse. The contrast with "holy," a cultic term, is "unclean," *akatharta,* a word that occurs elsewhere in the Pauline corpus only in a quotation of Isa 52:11 (2 Cor 6:17). Paul's notion of "holiness" is cultic rather than ethical.

15. *And if the unbeliever separates, let him or her separate:* In a casuistic aside (cf. vv. 11, 21) Paul addresses a remark to the Christian spouse whose non-Christian partner *(apistos,* in the masculine, denoting either an unbelieving husband or an unbelieving wife; cf. v. 14) is not willing to remain married to the neophyte Christian. In such cases the Christian spouse is directed to let the non-Christian partner go. Paul's condition in the present is a simple one. His advice needs no justification, but Paul offers a further reflection in the following clause.

The brother or the sister is not subservient in these cases: The relative pronominal phrase *(en tois toioutois)* implies a reference to what Paul has already said. Most commentators suggest that Paul is stating that a Christian spouse is not bound to an unwilling spouse or to a marriage that the non-Christian partner does not want. They read the apostle's words as if he had used the verb *deō,* "to bind," which he normally uses with regard to marriage (7:27, 39; cf. Rom 7:2). Paul's verb, however, is *dedoulōtai,* literally, "to be enslaved" (9:19; cf. Rom 6:18, 22; Gal 4:3). The verb belongs to the same semantic field as *exousiazō* (6:12; 7:4). It belongs to a context of discourse on freedom, the overarching theme of this epistolary unit (6:12–10:23; cf. 7:17-24). Each of the three asides in 1 Corinthians 7 (vv. 11, 15, 21) deals with the exercise of freedom. Christian spouses are to be mutually submissive to one another (7:4), but in principle a Christian is subservient to no one (6:12). A Christian whose non-Christian spouse departs is free. Paul does not say that such a Christian is free to remarry. The social circumstances of his day in both Hellenistic and Jewish circles were, however, such that remarriage was a likely possibility.

God has called you in peace: With this aphorism Paul returns to the main train of thought, the reasons why a Christian should not reject a non-Christian spouse. That Paul's words affect the character of an aphorism has created a textual problem. Many of the ancient witnesses and many of the Fathers, including Chrysostom and Jerome, read "us" (*hēmas;* see $\mathfrak{P}^{46}$, B, D, F, G, Ψ) rather than "you" (*hymas;* see ℵ, A, C, K, 81, 181, etc.). On external grounds alone "us" would appear to be the preferred reading, but scribes have a tendency to generalize aphoristic sayings. It is more likely that a "you" would have been generalized by the scribal tradition rather than that an "us" would be limited to "you." The "you," moreover, corresponds to Paul's general epistolary style as well as to the direct appeal of the following verse, the final argument in Paul's arsenal of arguments on behalf of marital stability within a mixed marriage.

16. *Wife, do you know if you might save your husband? Husband, do you know if you might save your wife?* Paul shifts from a style of logical argument in the third person to the style of the diatribe with a pair of rhetorical questions. The brace of questions joined by *ē* (literally "or") reflects the constant mutuality of Paul's perspective in treating issues of sexuality and marriage. That the first question is addressed to the Christian wife (cf. v. 13) might suggest that Christian women at Corinth were particularly prone to seek divorce from their spouses (cf. v. 10).

The recent history of the interpretation of v. 16 indicates a division of opinion between those authors who opt for an optimistic reading of the text and those who opt for a pessimistic reading of Paul's words. On the former reading Paul's questions suggest that a Christian married to a non-Christian should remain committed to his or her spouse on the grounds of a well-founded hope of their conversion. After all, says Paul to the Christian spouse, you might be God's instrument in the salvation of your spouse.

A pessimistic reading of the text is generally adopted by those who take vv. 15c-16 to be Paul's explanation as to why a Christian should allow the non-Christian spouse who does not want to cohabit with the Christian to depart. On this reading the text would imply that hope for the unbelieving spouse's conversion is not a sufficient reason for remaining in a mixed marriage. After all, says Paul, you can never be sure whether your non-Christian spouse will ever become a Christian.

Paul's grammar allows for either the optimistic or the pessimistic reading of his words. Modern English translations reflect each of the possibilities. The *NRSV* optimistically reads "Wife, for all you know, you might save your husband," in place of the *RSV's* pessimistic "Wife, how do you know whether you will save your husband?" The thrust of Paul's overall argument (7:10-24) and the semantic difference between "saving" (v. 16) and "making holy" (v. 14) suggest that the optimistic reading of the text is the preferable reading.

FOR REFERENCE AND FURTHER STUDY

Best, Ernest. "1 Corinthians 7:14 and Children in the Church," *IBS* 12 (1990) 158–166.

Collins, Raymond F. *Divorce in the New Testament.* GNS 38. Collegeville: The Liturgical Press, 1992.

Daube, David. "Pauline Contributions to a Pluralistic Culture: Recreation and Beyond" in Donald G. Miller and Dikran Y. Hadidian, eds., *Jesus and Man's Hope*, 2. Pittsburgh: Pittsburgh Theological Seminary, 1970, 223–245.

Delling, Gerhard. "Nur aber sind sie heilig" in idem, *Studien zum neuen Testament und zum hellenistischen Judentum. Gesammelte Aufsätze 1950–1968.* Göttingen: Vandenhoeck & Ruprecht, 1970, 257–269.

Laney, J. Carl. "Paul and the Permanence of Marriage in 1 Corinthians," *JETS* 25 (1982) 283–294.

Lindemann, Andreas. "Die Funktion der Herrenworte in der ethischen Argumentation des Paulus im ersten Korintherbrief" in F. Van Segbroeck et al, eds., *The Four Gospels 1992.* BEThL 100. Louvain: University Press/Peeters, 1992, 677–688.

Martens, M. P. "First Corinthians 7:14: 'Sanctified' by the Believing Spouse," *Notes on Translation* 10 (1996) 31–35.

Merklein, Helmut. "'Es ist gut für den Menschen, eine Frau nicht anzufassen.' Paulus und die Sexualität nach 1 Kor 7" in Josef Blank et al, eds., *Die Frau im Urchristentum.* QD 95. Freiburg, Basel, and Vienna: Herder, 1983, 225–253.

Moiser, Jeremy. "A Reassessment of Paul's View of Marriage with Reference to 1 Cor 7," *JSNT* 18 (1983) 103–122.

Murphy-O'Connor, Jerome. "Works without Faith in I Cor., VII, 14," *RB* 84 (1977) 349–361.

Neirynck, Frans. "The Sayings of Jesus in 1 Corinthians," *CorC* 141–176.

Russell, Kenneth C. "That Embarrassing Verse in First Corinthians," *TBT* 18 (1980) 338–341.

Zimmermann, M. and R. "Zitation, Kontradiktion oder Applikation? Die Jesuslogien in 1 Kor 7,10f. und 9,14: Traditionsgeschichtliche Verankerung und paulinische Interpretation," *ZNW* 87 (1996) 83–100.

7. *Remain As You Were Called* (7:17-24)

17. But as the Lord has apportioned to each one, as God has called each one, so shall that person lead his or her life. So also have I ordered in all the churches. 18. Was any one circumcised called? Let him not remove the marks of circumcision. Was any one called without being circumcised? Let him not be circumcised. 19. Circumcision is nothing and lack

of circumcision is nothing, but keeping the commandments of God. 20.
Let each one remain in the calling in which he or she was called. 21. Were
you called as a slave? Never mind. But if you really are able to be free,
take advantage. 22. For the slave who was called in the Lord is a freed
person of the Lord; similarly the freed person who was called is a slave
of Christ. 23. You have been bought and paid for; do not become slaves
of human beings. 24. Brothers and sisters, let each one remain with God
in that calling in which he or she was called.

INTERPRETATION

Within Paul's letter 7:17-24 constitutes a distinct literary unit set off by
the literary device of *inclusio* or ring construction. The contents of this discrete topos are different from those of the encompassing units that treat
of marriage and sexuality. In the light of the chiastic pattern by means of
which Paul has organized his thought throughout the letter, vv. 17-24 can
be recognized as the B element within an A-B-A' structure. Urging each
one to remain in the social situation in which he or she has been called,
the rhetorical digression serves as a supporting argument for the paraenesis Paul has offered to the married in vv. 1-16 and for the exhortation he
will address to the unmarried in vv. 25-40.

The basic thrust of Paul's argument is that each one should remain in
the social situation in which he or she has been called. This pastoral principle of the status quo is enunciated in v. 17, reiterated in v. 20, and repeated yet again in v. 24. Enunciation of the principle gives voice to the
conviction that salvation is a pure gift that does not depend on personal
effort. With respect to salvation no social situation is more advantageous
than another. A Christian's identity and value do not derive from social
conditions but from the call of God in Christ.

God's Call. From the very outset of the letter Paul had placed the Christian vocation before the Corinthians. In the opening salutation he had reminded them of his vocation (1:1) and of their own calling (1:2). The
opening thanksgiving concluded with reference to the Corinthians' call to
the fellowship of our Lord Jesus Christ (1:9). In all three instances the call
comes from God and is related to the Lordship of Jesus Christ. With their
repeated reference to the call of the Christian these verses anticipate the
exposition on the Christian vocation that Paul elaborates in 7:17-24.

"As God has called each one" (v. 17) is key to Paul's theology of vocation and is important for the chiastic structure of the argument in 7:17-
24. The three terms "God" (*ho theos*), "call" (*kaleō*), and "each" (*hekastos*)
are repeated in v. 24. In this way the pericope is brought to closure and
constituted as a unity. Paul's mention of the call with a verb in the active

voice introduces the theme that undergirds his argument for social stability. His theme is the call of God. God calls each and every Christian (cf. 1:9).

In his disquisition Paul uses the verb "to call" *(kaleō)* eight times (vv. 17, 18[2x], 20, 21, 22[2x], 24) and the cognate noun "calling" *(klēsis)* once (v. 20). This striking example of the literary and rhetorical device of paronomasia, the repetition of words from the same root in close proximity (cf. BDF 488.1), provides focus and emphasis for Paul's exposition. Apart from these eight instances "to call" occurs in only four other passages of 1 Corinthians (1:9; 7:15; 10:27; 15:9), "calling" only once (1:26), and "called" *(klētos)*, the cognate verbal adjective, three times (1:1, 2, 24).

Paul mentions God explicitly only in vv. 17 and 24, the encompassing elements of the literary unit. God is, nonetheless, implied throughout the exposition. Reference to God is especially implied in Paul's repeated use of the theological passive. Apart from the opening and thematic exhortation in v. 17 each use of "to call" is in the theological passive. Paul provides a focus for the fact that God's call is addressed individually to each Christian by repeating "each" in v. 17. Subsequently the adjectival pronoun occurs only in vv. 20 and 24. The focus on "each one" found in this exposition of Paul's theology of calling echoes the emphasis on the individual in 3:1-17 and anticipates 12:4-26, two passages in which Paul similarly emphasizes God's gift and call (cf. Eph 4:1).

Paul's understanding of the Christian vocation provides a basis for his plea for social stability. His exposition provides rhetorical support for his current paraenesis on marital stability. This theological basis distinguishes Paul's vision of social stability from that of the philosophical moralists. Among these was the asocial Cynic Tales, who wrote ". . . one should not try to change circumstances, but rather to prepare oneself for them as they are. . . . You have grown old; do not seek the things of a young man. Again, you have become weak; do not seek to carry and submit your neck to the loads of a strong man. Again, you have become destitute; do not seek the rich man's way of life . . ." (*HCNT* 412–413).

Function and Structure of the Argument. Paul has developed this reflection on the call of God to bolster his plea to Christians that they remain committed to their marriages (7:1-17) even if they are married to non-Christians (7:12-16). He begins by affirming as a matter of principle that each Christian should conduct his or her life according to the life situation the Lord has meted out to each. The real life situation of any human being is characterized by gender, ethnicity, and social status. These are the major social factors that differentiate one human from another. Paul is aware of the importance of all three in the social mix. For Paul divisions based on gender, ethnicity, and social class have been transcended by God's call in Christ. The call of God in Christ relativizes all social conditions.

To support his argument that Christians should maintain stability in their marriage relationships (see Collins, *Divorce* 55–57), a way of responding to one's gender, Paul reflects on ethnicity and social status. His rhetorical digression (7:17-24) specifically addresses these two bases of social discrimination, ethnicity in vv. 18-19, social status in vv. 21-23. Ethnicity is considered from the relatively simple Jewish *Weltanschauung*, a worldview that divides humanity between Israel and the nations (cf. 1:22-24). From the social perspective of Judaism ethnic distinction was, like gender and social status, an either-or situation. For the Jew there were simply the people *(ho laos)* and the nations *(ta ethnē)*. With various references to the practice of the manumission of slaves Paul reflects on the relative status of slaves and freed persons (vv. 21-23) in the light of the social conditions of first-century Corinth. His overarching theme is the significance of God's call in Christ the Lord. The opening sentence affirms that God has called (active voice) each one; vv. 20 and 24 proclaim that each one has been called.

The pericope, a digression embedded as element B within the A-B-A' structure of ch. 7, is itself chiastically structured. The encompassing sentences (vv. 17, 24) and the intersection of the chiasm (v. 20) focus on the call of God that is addressed to each and every one. Paul's repeated rehearsal of the pastoral principle of social stability constitutes the digression as a discrete rhetorical unit (vv. 17, 24) and provides the central element of the chiastically structured argument (v. 20). In this fashion the digression articulates in comprehensive fashion and underscores the pastoral principle.

The directive function of the rhetorical digression is such that the principle of social stability is brought to bear on the issue of gender relationships (cf. 11:2-16) that constitutes the principal focus of the entire chapter. The principle of social stability is as applicable to the various situations of those who have been married (7:1-16) as it is to the various situations of those who have not been married (7:25-38).

With a slightly different reading of the text the threefold repetition of the principle of the status quo can be taken as a hortatory conclusion to three discussions on social distinction: gender (7:1-16), ethnicity (7:18-19), and social status (7:21-23). Relative to each distinction Paul affirms that with respect to Christ neither element of the distinction is specifically advantageous. All social conditions are mutually equal in the Lord. Therefore the Christian is to remain in the social condition in which he or she has been called as a Christian.

The Christian Difference. Paul begins his reflection with the idea that God has assigned to each person a given social condition. The call of God is addressed to each individual within the social condition to which he or she has been assigned. Each person should conduct his or her life appropriately ("so lead life," v. 17; cf. "keeping the commandments of God," v. 19; "with God," v. 24) according to the social condition to which they have been assigned by God. This, says Paul, is his general rule, one that he has proclaimed in all the churches.

After the general exhortation of v. 17 Paul addresses himself to the ethnicity of those who have been called by God. These people are either Jews or Gentiles. Paul, a Jew by birth, shares the social vision of his people in which the world is neatly divided into Jews and non-Jews, those who know God and those who do not (cf. 1 Thess 4:5). At Corinth some Christians were ethnic Jews; others, apparently the majority, were not. Paul addresses himself to the members of each group, Jew and Gentile alike, with an exhortation in two parts (rhetorical question + exhortation) and a two-part explanation. His style continues to reflect the parallelism and balance that characterizes the entirety of ch. 7, where Paul is dealing with social issues. He urges those men who have been called as ethnic Jews not to change their physical condition, the mark of circumcision. He exhorts those who were not ethnic Jews not to seek circumcision. The ground for this double exhortation is that from the perspective of salvation and God's call circumcision ultimately counts for nothing.

Having urged the Christians of Corinth to remain as they were, no matter their ethnicity, Paul similarly exhorts those who were on either side of the barrier of social status to remain in their social condition. Paul's exhortation contains some elements of his understanding of what it means to be free—from his Christian perspective. Paul presents both slavery and freedom in a paradoxical way. Christian slaves are freed persons who belong to the Lord. Ultimately they belong to the Lord because it is the Lord who has freed them. He is their redeemer who has become their patron. On the other hand those who possess socio-political freedom are slaves of Christ. These are exhorted not to enslave themselves to any human being. In a virtual aside (cf. v. 15) within the paraenesis directed to slaves Paul considers the case of slaves who are manumitted, urging them too to maintain social stability.

Paul's advocacy of the principle of social stability is similar to the stance of some Cynics, but it is radically different from that of the various Persians, Greeks, and Jews who held that social status was all-important. The well-known prayer attributed by Jewish tradition to R. Judah, disciple of Aqiba, epitomizes this latter point of view: "Blessed are thou . . . who has not made me a heathen . . . who has not made me a woman . . . who has not made me a slave" (*b. Menah.* 43b; cf. *t. Ber.* 7:18; *y. Ber.* 9:1). The three contrasts evoked in this prayer pertain to the classic social distinctions: ethnicity (Jew-Gentile), gender (male-female), social class (free-slave) considered by Paul in 7:17-24. Some commentators maintain that the baptismal formula of Gal 3:28, "There is no longer Jew or Greek, there is no longer slave or free, there is no longer male and female, for you are all one in Christ," was formulated in opposition to the view that postulates superiority on the basis of ethnicity, gender, or class. The baptismal formula proclaims that the Christian's new existence in Christ transcends all social divisions.

Although he has argued for stability in the spousal relationship and will use stability with regard to ethnicity and social state as an argument in favor of this stability, Paul is not pleading on behalf of some form of early Christian quietism. Far from urging passive withdrawal or a simple affirmation of the status quo, Paul urges an active lifestyle that is in accordance with the social condition in which each Christian has been called (cf. 1 Thess 4:10b-12). That is the burden of his command, "conduct yourselves accordingly," supported by his affirmation that each one is to keep the commandments of God (v. 19) and remain with God (v. 24).

Paul's rhetorical digression is brought to closure with a final exhortation, a summary argument, almost a kind of peroration. It is addressed to the entire community (note the apostrophic "brothers and sisters") rather than to its individual members. The apostle urges them to remain faithful to the calling in which they have been called and thus remain "with God."

Slavery in the Hellenistic World. In the Hellenistic world the institution of slavery was an accepted part of the social and economic fabric of the times. So difficult was it for people of Paul's time to imagine what life would be like without slavery that Aristotle and Athenaeus, trying to imagine what a world without slavery would be, conjured up a science-fiction vision of an automated world. Slavery was not considered to be a social ill; it was dependent labor.

Slavery was otherwise difficult to define, either legally or socially. The slavery of the Greco-Roman world was different from slavery in nineteenth-century America. In Paul's day there was no abolitionist movement. The abolition of slavery seems not even to have been an aim of the revolt of slaves in 140–70 B.C.E. Those who had been slaves, like Epictetus, did not decry their previous social condition. Slaves sometimes rose to positions of prestige and power. There are even some recorded instances of people entering into slavery in order to gain such privileges. Among some of the more famous slaves were philosophers (Epictetus, Cornutus), scholars (Verrius Flaccus, Polybius), writers (Phaedrus), governors (Felix; cf. Acts 24), and doctors. Neither race nor clothing distinguished the slave from the freed person. Slaves could own property and were allowed to have savings (*peculia*, which technically belonged to the master). They could increase their personal resources by means of additional jobs. The one thing that characterized a slave was the simple fact that he or she was not his or her own master. The Roman jurist Florentinus defined a slave as "someone who is subject to the dominion of another person, contrary to nature" (*Digest* 1.5.4).

The lot of a slave was often better than that of a lower-class free person. The master stood to derive economic benefit from treating slaves fairly. The freed person was more subject to the vicissitudes of life than was the slave whose sustenance and protection were provided by the master. Epictetus bemoans the fate of a freedman whose situation was worse than it had been before: "'Someone else kept me in clothes, and shoes, and supplied me with food, and nursed me when I was sick; I served him in only a few matters. But now, miserable man that I am, what suffering is mine, who am a slave to several instead of one!" (*Discourses* 4.1.37).

In the Roman world, somewhat different in this respect from traditional Greek society, slaves expected to be freed in due course (ten to twenty years). Freed slaves owed allegiance and various forms of service to their masters. The conditions of freedom were often stipulated in a contract (*paramonē*), sometimes of a temporally limited validity (two to ten years), the non-fulfillment of which could result in punishment (*anagkē*) or a return to slavery. Epigraphic inscriptions in the sanctuary at Delphi indicate that in approximately one quarter of the cases the contract limited the freed person's freedom to have a job and his or her freedom of movement. On the basis of analogies with other cities in the Greco-Roman world Scott Bartchy suggests that perhaps one third of the population of Corinth were slaves and that another third had experienced slavery at some time in their lives.

The Paradox of Freedom. The structured argument of vv. 21-23 is similar to but more complex than the parallel argument in vv. 18-19. In dealing with the fact that God's call is addressed to people with different ethnic backgrounds Paul distinguishes the situation of Jews and Gentiles. He urges the members of both ethnic groups not to attempt a change in their ethnicity because of the call of God (v. 18). In v. 19 Paul offers a simple explanation for his exhortation and concludes the exposition with a general exhortation.

Dealing with God's call addressed to people of different social and political status, Paul distinguishes the situation of slaves and freed persons. He urges each member of either social status not to bother about their social condition. Thereafter he offers a formal explanation (note the *gar* in v. 22) in two parts, one devoted to slaves, the other to freed persons. In addition Paul inserts an explanatory comment that pertains to people in either social condition. Only then does he offer a general exhortation: "do not become slaves of human beings."

Paul's more developed exposition with regard to those who have been called in different social conditions suggests that this issue was more problematic at Corinth than was the fact that people of different ethnicity had been called by God. Moreover, the conditional "if" *(ei)* of v. 21 suggests that Paul is speaking about a real situation in Corinth. That the relationship between slaves and freed persons and their relative importance within the community was a real issue for the Corinthians is confirmed in other passages of the letter. One of Paul's initial rhetorical appeals to the community addressed the issue of their social status (1:26). In offering himself as an example for the community—another appeal to his personal prestige in the argument from *ethos*—Paul likens himself to a servant (3:5) and a slave (9:15-18). That some within the Corinthian community were slaves is suggested by the fact that some came late for the fellowship meals while others went ahead to eat and drink to satiety and beyond (11:21-22).

Confronting the perennial issue of a community marked by difference of social status, Paul responds with a paradoxical statement on Christian freedom. The slave is really free; the freed person is really a slave. Paul's use of the technical term "freedman" or "freed person" *(apeleutheros,* hapax in the NT) in v. 22 serves as an indication that he is aware of the social situation in first-century Corinth. Among the various procedures for freeing slaves in the Greco-Roman world was sacral manumission, a custom whereby slaves were freed by means of a fictive sale to a god (cf. v. 23). The classic case of the process is the ritual that took place in the sanctuary of the Pythian Apollo at Delphi. The priest, who had previously received the amount of the purchase price from the slave or friends of the slave, "paid" the owner of the slave, thereby obtaining the slave's freedom. A record of the emancipation was then inscribed on the walls of the temple. Thereafter the slave was known as "sacred" or as a "slave of the god/goddess."

The technical term "freed person" reflects Paul's awareness of the customs and social situation. So, too, does Paul's use of the title "Lord." Admittedly "Lord" *(Kyrios)* is Paul's preferred christological title, one that he uses in theological and paraenetic contexts. In the theological contexts the title evokes the One who has been raised and whose parousia is awaited; in paraenetic contexts it evokes the Lord's authority over his people. In 7:17-24 the social significance of the term must not be overlooked. A lord *(kyrios)* was someone who had slaves *(douloi)*. "Lord" and "slaves" are socially correlative terms.

In the social situation of Greco-Roman Corinth Paul's paradoxical statement on slavery and freedom in vv. 22-23 makes abundant sense. His two-part assertion is chiastically arranged: the slave is free; the freed person is a slave. Key to understanding the paradox is Paul's use of the metaphor of sacral manumission (v. 23; cf. 6:11, 19). The metaphor evokes the redemption and salvation of Christians. Paul's first affirmation, that "the one called in the Lord as a slave is a freed person of the Lord," reflects the customary law—in this instance both custom and law—of the Greco-Roman world that required a freed person to maintain legal ties with his or her former master. His second, that "the one called as a free person is a slave of Christ," reflects the fact that lords were expected to have slaves. Ironically the Lord who has freed persons as his slaves is identified as "Christ," a title that evokes the crucifixion of Jesus, a form of death to which only the meanest of slaves were generally subject (see interpretation of 1:17).

Paradoxical as may be Paul's interpretation of the freedom of Christians, ultimately all Christians are freed persons. Their status as freed persons gives poignancy to Paul's exhortation that they not become slaves to (mere) human beings. The situation of the freed person of the Lord is antithetical to that of slaves of mere mortals. "Freed person" *(apeleutheros)* and "slaves" *(douloi)* are contrasting terms, as are "Lord" *(Kyrios)* and "human beings" *(anthrōpoi)*. In 6:12 Paul had offered himself as an example that Christians are not subjected to anyone, despite the fact that he was a slave of the Lord (9:15-18; cf. 3:5; 4:1).

An Exceptional Case. The conditional clause of v. 21c, "but if you really are able to be free," breaks the pattern of Paul's exposition. He had used three rhetorical questions (vv. 18a, 18c, 21a) to address different social situations; now he uses a conditional clause for a similar semantic purpose. It is seemingly inconsistent with the diatribal style of 7:17-24 (see Deming, "A Diatribe Pattern"). On the other hand, conditional clauses that break the rhythm of Paul's balanced argumentation had previously appeared in 7:11 and 15. The intrusion of these conditions appears to reflect the realism of Paul's consideration of the situation at Corinth.

The conditional sentence in v. 21 has been a perennial crux for interpreters. To a large extent the difficulty encountered by those who interpret the verse is compounded by the fact that the apodosis is an elliptical phrase. Its transitive verb is qualified by an adverbial expression but lacks a direct object. The difficulty of interpreting the verse is compounded by some ignorance of social conditions at Corinth and by the tendency of some commentators to read the verse from their own social location.

In the social circumstances in which Paul was writing, the situation to which Paul was referring was one over which a Christian slave had no control (cf. v. 15). Paul's words do not envision a runaway slave; they have reference to the practice of manumission. The freeing of slaves was not an unusual practice in first-century Corinth. Most slaves could expect to be freed after a period of some ten to twenty years of service to their masters. Although there were various procedures for manumission, including sacral manumission, it was not a slave's choice to become free or not; the decision was the master's. Once a master decided to free a slave there was no way for the newly constituted freedman to remain in slavery. Some slaves took the initiative in obtaining their freedom. To achieve freedom some slaves offered money to their masters. This was occasionally of economic advantage to the master since some slaves could offer more money than would be gained by the master were he to sell the slave in the marketplace. Sometimes a slave might ask a third party or a group, such as a *collegium* to which he might belong, to intervene so that he could obtain his freedom. The latter situation is envisioned by Ignatius of Antioch, who wrote "let them [slaves] not desire to be set free out of the common fund, that they may not be found slaves of lust" (*Pol.* 4:3; *PG* 5, 724). What was at issue is the expectation that a house church might use monies from the community chest to obtain the freedom of slaves who had become Christian. In writing as he did Ignatius was not so much opposed to the freeing of slaves as he desired to strengthen the authority of the bishop. He seems to have opposed the practice of manumission as a means of evangelism.

Viewed from the standpoint of social realities in the Greco-Roman world, Paul's elliptical phrase ought to be seen as a complement to his argument in favor of social stability rather than as an exception to it. Neither slaves nor freed persons have an advantage with respect to salvation. Slaves have no reason to rue their situation; freed persons should take advantage of theirs. Paul considers both situations, just as he does with regard to ethnicity in v. 18.

NOTES

17. *But as the Lord has apportioned to each one, as God has called each one:* The thrust of Paul's argument is clear but his grammatical construction is complicated. The verse begins with "but" (*ei mē,* rather than *alla,* cf. BDF 376, 448:8), followed by four correlative clauses. The first two correlative clauses (with "as," *hōs*) are in apposition to one another, "as the Lord has apportioned to each one and as God has called each one." The emphasis is on "each one" (*hekastō, hekaston*). The third clause (with "so," *houtōs*) serves as the comparative element, "so shall that person lead his or her life." The fourth correlative clause (with *houtōs*), "so also have I ordered in all the churches," relates to the entire unit with its three correlative clauses.

Although the two clauses of v. 17a-b are in apposition to one another they are not synonymous with one another. From the outset of the letter (1:1-9) Paul had related the call of himself and the community to both God and the Lord Jesus Christ. The call originates from God. Those who respond to the call do so in subjection to the Lord Jesus Christ. Some few manuscripts, including א, B, and a corrected 𝔓⁴⁶, read the verb "apportioned" in the perfect *(memeriken)*, but this reading would appear to be a scribal correction under the influence of the perfect, *keklēken*, "called." The call has ongoing implications, but Paul wants also to stress the situation at the time of one's call, when Christians accepted the Lordship of Jesus. The use of the aorist *(emerisen)* does just that. The verb "to apportion" *(merizō)* together with the pronomial adjective, "each," stresses the individuality of each Christian's social role. The entire social structure, in which each person has a specific social location with respect to gender, ethnicity, and status, stands under the lordship of Jesus.

so shall that person lead his or her life: The thrust of Paul's simply phrased imperative is clearly "conduct yourselves accordingly." The imperative clause is the principal clause in the sentence. Its present tense implies that Paul is talking about the ongoing conduct of life rather than a single act; its singular number continues the emphasis on individual responsibility. The initial and coordinating "so" *(houtōs)* evokes the various life situations of the members of the community. They are to conduct their lives in accordance with the social condition meted out to them.

"Conduct yourselves" *(peripateitō,* literally "walk") is an expression Paul uses to describe human behavior, but in 1 Corinthians this verb is used elsewhere only in 3:3. Paul's choice of verb reflects Jewish usage in which the verb "to walk" *(hlk,* hence, *hălākâ)* is typically used for human behavior, particularly for behavior that is in accordance with the law of God (cf. 1 Thess 2:12; 4:1; Gal 5:16). Paul's use of this verb prepares for his reference to the commandments of God (v. 19) and for his own authoritative pronouncements on how one ought to live (7:17d).

So also have I ordered in all the churches: Paul's explanation that the exhortation he is addressing to the Corinthians is consistent with that which he has given to other Christian communities pleads his own consistency and appeals to the practice of other Christian churches (cf. 1:2; 4:17; 7:17; 11:16; 14:33; 16:1). His language speaks of an authoritative order (cf. 9:14 with regard to the Lord, and 11:34; 16:1 with regard to Paul's directives). Paul implicitly appeals to his status as an apostle, with the consequent claims that he can make upon those he has evangelized. As such his language is consistent with v. 19 where he recalls the importance of keeping the commandments of God.

Paul's proclamation of the gospel was accompanied by moral exhortation that urged those who accepted his message to lead their lives in accordance with the will of God who had called them into his kingdom. In 1 Thess 2:12, where the verbs *peripateō* and *kaleō* also appear, Paul reminded the community of how he had exhorted them to conduct their lives in a way that was worthy of God who had called them into his kingdom.

18. *Was any one circumcised called? Let him not remove the marks of circumcision:* Paul's rhetorical question (cf. vv. 18c, 21a) produces a stronger effect than would have been achieved by a conditional clause (BDF 494). Epispasm (cf. *mē epispasthō,* "let him not remove the marks of circumcision"; the verb is hapax in the NT), removing the marks of circumcision, was a kind of operation intended to restore the foreskins of those who had been circumcised (cf.

Celsus, *Medicine* 7.25.1). After Antiochus IV Epiphanes' (175–164 B.C.E.) attempt to impose Hellenistic culture on Jews, references to Jews who under-
went epispasm so as to accommodate themselves to the Gentiles begin to
appear in Jewish literature. It was especially young Jewish men who desired
to participate in Greek athletic events, where nudity was the norm, who had
the operation. The biennial Isthmian games were held in Corinth.

First Maccabees 1:15 refers to the practice as "making themselves uncircumcised *(akrobystias)*. See also Josephus, *Ant.* 12.241; Babylonian Talmud,
passim; Epiphanius, *Treatise on Weights and Measures* 16; Martial, *Epigrams* 7.35,
82. For Jews to remove the marks of circumcision was tantamount to the rejection of the covenant that God had made with his people (*t. Šabb.* 15:9; cf. *m.
Ned.* 4:11). According to the *Testament of Moses* one of the tortures the king of
earthly kings will inflict upon Jews is that "their young sons will be cut by
physicians to bring forward their foreskins" (*T. Mos.* 8:3).

Was any one called without being circumcised? Let him not be circumcised: Having
talked about Jews in v. 18a-b, Paul formulates a parallel statement with regard
to Gentiles. The one called without circumcision (*en akrobystią,* literally "with
a foreskin," found only in the Greek Bible and the NT, especially in Romans
2–4) is the Gentile. The Mishnah indicates that "uncircumcised" is "used as a
name for the Gentiles" (*m. Ned.* 4:11, with reference to Jer 9:26; 1 Sam 17:36).
Elsewhere Paul will affirm the advantages accruing to the Jewish people who
are circumcised (Rom 3:1-2; cf. Rom 9:4-5). He also argues that it is circumcision of the heart that is important and that those who have been circumcised
are bound to observe the entire Torah (Rom 2:25-29; Gal 5:2). He would also
argue that Gentile Christians had no need of circumcision (cf. Acts 15:1-2), but
that argument is for another day and another place (Paul's letter to the Galatians and his letter to the Romans).

19. *Circumcision is nothing and lack of circumcision is nothing:* Paul's basic posture
is that of itself neither circumcision nor the lack of circumcision has ultimate
bearing on salvation. "In Christ Jesus neither circumcision nor uncircumci-
sion counts for anything" (Gal 5:6; cf. 6:15). What does count is "faith working through love" (Gal 5:6). Later in the letter to the Galatians he will note
that in comparison with circumcision the "new creation is everything" (Gal
6:15). In the letter to the Romans, treating matters of Jewish concern, Paul will
develop a sustained argument to show that circumcision is irrelevant in matters that pertain to salvation (Rom 3:27–4:12).

but keeping the commandments of God: "Keeping the commandments of God" is
similar to the exhortation that the Corinthians conduct their lives in a way
that is in accordance with their call from God (v. 17) and Paul's subsequent
urging that they not become slaves of human beings (v. 23). "Keeping the
commandments of God" is a technical expression not otherwise used by Paul
(cf. 1 Tim 6:14; Matt 19:17; John 14:15, 21, 24; 15:10; 1 John 2:3, 4; 3:22, 24; Rev
12:17; 14:12). Apart from Rom 7:13-20; 13:9, where "the commandments" are
preeminently the precepts of the Decalogue, Paul does not write about the
commandments. According to Paul keeping the commandments is appropriate conduct for the Jew.

20. *Let each one remain in the calling in which he or she was called:* Manuel Orge calls this the pastoral principle of the status quo ("El própósito temático," 125). For Joël Delobel "this 'principle of stability' expresses the conviction that salvation is a pure gift which does not depend on personal effort" ("1 Cor 11, 2-16," 389). Although "calling" *(klēsis)* and the cognate verb "to call" *(kaleō)* are typically used by Paul of a religious invitation, that is, the call of God in Christ through the medium of the proclamation of the gospel (BAGD 399.2), many commentators suggest that the connotation of "calling" is one's station in life (BAGD 436.2). This would be a singular exception to the usual NT meaning of the word (BAGD 436.1). It is preferable to accord the noun the same meaning it has elsewhere in Paul's letters (1:26; Rom 11:29; Phil 3:14). Paul urges the Christians of Corinth to remain committed to the (Christian) calling to which they were called. That call is addressed to Christians in different social conditions.

21. *Were you called as a slave? Never mind:* Paul's construction is similar to that of v. 17. The rhetorical question functions as a subordinate clause. In vv. 17-18 Paul used two rhetorical questions to contrast two different ethnic conditions. In v. 21 he uses a rhetorical question and a subordinate clause to contrast two different social conditions. The shift in construction might lead one to translate the rhetorical question of v. 21 as a condition in order to emphasize the contrast between the situation of the slave and that of the freed person.

Paul's rejoinder, "never mind" *(mē soi meletō)*, has as its meaning "don't worry about that," "don't let it bother you." In the extant correspondence he uses the verb *melō* elsewhere only in 9:9.

But if you really are able to be free, take advantage: The protasis of Paul's sentence corresponds to the rhetorical questions of vv. 18a, 18c, 21a. The apodosis, "take advantage," *mallon chrēsai* (literally "use all the more") is an elliptical phrase that has been and continues to be a perennial crux. The verb has no direct object. Technically Paul's construction is an example of brachylogy, the omission, for brevity's sake, of an element that is necessary for the thought. Hence the question: does Paul urge slaves to take advantage of their freedom (with *eleutheria* as the implied object of the verb, thus the *RSV*) or does he urge slaves to make use of their slavery and refuse to go free (with *douleia* as the implied object, thus the *NRSV*)?

Paul's grammar seems to imply the former (cf. Max Zerwick and Mary Grosvenor, *A Grammatical Analysis of the Greek New Testament* [Rome: Biblical Institute, 1979] 2.510). Moreover, since Paul has just written about freedom (v. 21a), "freedom" may be his implied antecedent. On the other hand, the context seems to require the latter interpretation: freed persons should be content with their freedom, slaves with their slavery (cf. 1 Tim 6:2). In this case *mallon* connotes "for a better reason" (BAGD 489.2). The earliest evidence of the use of the verb "to use" with reference to slavery, independent of Paul, is in an apocryphal Jewish biography dating from the first to the third century C.E. It describes Joshua who, as a member of his race, was not a slave, but "used *(chrēsthai)* his servitude, knowing him [Moses] whose servant he was" (see Eric Otto Winstedt, "Some Coptic Apocryphal Legends," *JThS* 9 [1908] 372–386, at 377; *HCNT* 412).

The verb *chraomai* is used without a grammatical object by Paul only in 7:21. It sometimes means "to live in accordance with" (thus 27x in Josephus). Arguing from this connotation of the verb and the parallelism between v. 20c and v. 19c, Bartchy has suggested that Paul's elliptical phrase means "by all means live according to God's call" (see *First-Century Slavery* 155–159).

22. *For the slave who was called in the Lord is a freed person of the Lord; similarly the freed person who was called is a slave of Christ:* Paul's chiastic structure results in a clever paradox. Only at the conclusion of his paradox does he identify the Lord as Christ. The expression "slave of Christ" is hapax in the New Testament. On the other hand Paul often writes about serving God (Rom 1:25; 12:11; 14:18 [cf. 7:6; 16:18]; 1 Thess 1:9). It is to be noted that in Paul's social world, where most people were slaves, the fact that one was a slave was not so important. What was important was whose slave one was.

23. *You have been bought and paid for:* Paul alludes to the practice of manumission as he makes reference to a complete sale. In 6:20 he uses the same expression, *timēs ēgorasthēte* (see the similar use of the compound *exagorazō* in Gal 3:13; 4:5). There he had argued that since Christians have been bought and paid for they cannot use their bodies as they would like, specifically by having sexual relations with a prostitute. Paul's allusion to the rite of the sacral manumission gives poignancy to the exhortation, "do not become slaves of human beings." As is his wont, Paul grounds the imperative of his exhortation on the indicative of an act of God.

do not become slaves of human beings: The exhortation suggests a twofold contrast. Christians are not slaves; they are free. They do not belong to other humans; they belong to the Lord. "Do not become slaves of human beings" reminds the Christians of Corinth of their new condition in the Lord. They are not to conduct themselves as fleshy beings subject to merely human standards (cf. 3:3).

In Greco-Roman culture some free persons sold themselves into slavery. Sometimes this was done in order to secure the beginnings of a *peculium (to pekoulion)* that the slave could later use to ensure a better economic situation once he or she became a freed person. In other cases self-enslavement was a means to obtain a particular position (e.g., that of *oikonomos*) or social status (see Petronius, *Sartyricon* 57.4). Clement of Rome knew the practice of self-enslavement and regarded at least one such practice as noble: "We know that many among ourselves have delivered themselves to bondage, that they might ransom others. Many have sold themselves to slavery, and receiving the price paid for themselves have fed others" (*1 Clem.* 55:2; *PG* 1, 320).

24. *Brothers and sisters, let each one remain with God in that calling in which he or she was called:* Paul's final exhortation brings the digression to closure by harkening back to v. 17, with which it forms an *inclusio*. The apostrophic "brothers and sisters," unusually placed at the end rather than at the beginning of the exhortation, lends additional emphasis to the final exhortation. In some wise, by inserting the use of a plural it gives to the final exhortation the character of a summary exhortation. Each and every Christian should remain in the

calling to which he or she was called (see v. 20). Paul's reference to God *(theos)* recalls the mention of God in v. 17 but provides, nonetheless, a contrast with the mere humans of v. 23.

FOR REFERENCE AND FURTHER STUDY

Bartchy, S. Scott. *Mallon chrēsai: First-Century Slavery and the Interpretation of 1 Corinthians 7:21.* SBLDS 11. Missoula: Published by the Society of Biblical Literature for the Seminar on Paul, 1973.

Baumert, Norbert. *Woman and Man* 63–80.

Benanti, O. "'Se anche puoi divenire libero . . .' (1 Cor 7,21)," *RBR* 16 (1981) 125–129.

Boucher, Madeleine. "Some Unexplored Parallels to 1 Cor 11,11-12 and Gal 3,28: the NT on the Role of Women," *CBQ* 31 (1969) 50–58.

Dawes, Gregory W. "'But if you can gain your freedom' (1 Corinthians 7:17-24)," *CBQ* 52 (1990) 681–697.

Deming, Will. "A Diatribe Pattern in 1 Cor. 7:21-22: A New Perspective on Paul's Directions to Slaves," *NovT* 37 (1995) 130–137.

Fischer, James A. "Pauline Literary Forms and Thought Patterns," CBQ 39 (1977) 209–223.

Harrill, James A. *The Manumission of Slaves in Early Christianity.* HUT 32. Tübingen: J.C.B. Mohr, 1995.

————. "Paul and Slavery: The Problem of 1 Corinthians 7:21," *BR* 39 (1994) 5–28.

Jones, F. Stanley. *"Freiheit" in den Briefen des Apostels Paulus: Eine historische, exegetische und religionsgeschichtliche Studie.* GTA 34. Göttingen: Vandenhoeck & Ruprecht, 1987.

Martin, Dale B. *Slavery as Salvation: The Metaphor of Slavery in Pauline Christianity.* New Haven: Yale University Press, 1990.

Thielman, Frank. "The Coherence of Paul's View of the Law: The Evidence of First Corinthians," *NTS* 38 (1992) 235–253.

Winter, Bruce W. *Seek the Welfare of the City* 145–164.

8. *Advice for the Unmarried (7:25-35)*

25. Concerning the unmarried I do not have a command of the Lord; however, as one to whom the Lord has given the favor of being trustworthy I offer an opinion. 26. I think that in view of the present distress this is good, namely, it is good for a person to remain as he or she is. 27. Are you bound to a wife? Do not seek release. Are you free from a wife? Do not seek a wife. 28. If, however, you marry, you do not sin; and if a virgin marries she does not sin; but these suffer affliction in their physical relationship, and I would spare you that.

29. I tell you, brothers and sisters, the time is growing short. Henceforth let those who have wives be as those who have not 30. and those who weep as those who do not weep, and those who rejoice as those who do not rejoice, and those who buy as those who are without, 31. and those who make use of the world as those who do not make full use of it; for the configuration of this world is passing away.

32. I wish you to be free from anxiety. The one who is unmarried is concerned about the things of the Lord, how he might please the Lord; 33. the married man is concerned about the things of the world, how he might please his wife, 34. and he is torn. And the unmarried woman, the virgin, is concerned about the things of the Lord, so that she might be holy in body and in spirit; and the married woman is concerned about the things of the world, how she might please her husband. 35. I am saying this for your very own advantage, not to impose a burden on you, but for the sake of good order and unreserved constancy to the Lord.

INTERPRETATION

Having discussed at length the condition of married Christians in 7:1-16, with supporting considerations in 7:17-24, Paul turns his attention to a consideration of the situation of Christians who have not yet married. The matter may have been raised in the Corinthians' correspondence with Paul (see the opening *peri*, "concerning" in v. 25). Even if "concerning" does not necessarily indicate that Paul is responding to a concern about which he had received a written inquiry, the preposition serves as a textual marker to indicate a variety of practical matters to which Paul wishes to respond.

The Rhetorical Unit. The "concerning" of 7:25 is a textual marker that indicates the beginning of a new unit; the "concerning" of 8:1 has a similar function. Thus 7:25-40 is delineated a discrete rhetorical unit within Paul's letter. The unit is further identified by means of an inclusio. "Opinion" *(gnōmē)* appears in vv. 25 and 40, thus setting the pericope apart from the surrounding epistolary units. Within this unit Paul offers his "opinion" with regard to the unmarried. Within the larger unit vv. 25-35 constitute a distinct subunit. The subunit is characterized by its topic, *peri de tōn parthenōn,* the unmarried, both men and women. The noun "unmarried" *(parthenōn)* is used six times in the unit (vv. 25, 28, 34, 36, 37, 38), but it does not appear elsewhere in the letter. The subunit is further delimited by an *inclusio* consisting of the use of the first person singular (emphatic in 25) and "Lord" in vv. 25 and 35.

The substance of Paul's advice to the unmarried is contained in 7:25-28. This is supported by an exhortation (7:29-31) and an explanation (7:32-35). Both the exhortation and the explanation are constituted as distinctive units by means of striking literary devices. The exhortation consists of five parallel expressions linked to one another by parallelism, polysyndeton (the multiplication of conjunctions), and anaphora (the repetition of the initial word). These verses offer advice to those who are aware of the impending eschaton and highlight the tension of eschatological existence. The explanation is characterized by parallelism (male, female) and by antithesis (unmarried, married). Its unity is reinforced by a unique play on words, the literary device of *paronomasia*. The sixfold repetition of the same sound in the pericope, *merim* in vv. 32[2x], 33, 34[3x], helps to weave the elements of the explanation together in a harmonious whole.

Paul's Opinion. Paul is wont to make a careful distinction between what he says on the authority of the Lord and what he says on his own authority (cf. 7:10, 12). He also makes a sharp distinction between what is said by way of command (*epitagēn;* cf. 7:6; Rom 16:26; 2 Cor 8:8) and what is said on the basis of some other authority. In 7:25 Paul states that the advice he is about to give is his *gnōmē,* "opinion."

In rhetorical usage "opinion" was clearly distinct from merely personal opinion *(doxa).* The two terms, *gnōmē* and *doxa,* designated different kinds of rhetorical proof (see *Rhet. ad Alex.* 1430b.1-25; 1431b.9-15). The *gnōmē* was a concisely expressed principle or rule of conduct, the Latin *sententia.* As used by Thucydides and other Hellenistic authors *gnōmē* connotes a decision made with a certain degree of stick-to-itiveness, a proposal plus a commitment. Maxims formulating rules of conduct were so formulated as to be easily memorized in the schools. In rhetoric they served as a kind of proof.

In 7:25, as in 7:40, Paul underscores the authority of his maxim by appealing to his own prestige (the argument from one's personal *ethos*). Paul is one to whom the Lord has given the favor of being trustworthy (v. 25). Paul's contemporary, Epictetus, describes the philosopher as trustworthy (*Discourses* 1.4.18, 20; 2.14.13; 2.22.26-27, 29-30; 3.20.5; 3.23.18; 4.1.133; 4.9.17; 4.13.17-24).

The topic is the unmarried. Paul's opinion is that it is good for them to remain as they are. His opinion is stated in the form of the maxim offered in v. 26. The rest is offered by way of explanation. The formulaic expression of v. 26, "it is good for a person," is parallel with the expression found in 7:1, "it is good for a man not to touch a woman." The parallel phrases identify vv. 1-16 and 25-40 as complementary passages. In 7:1-16 Paul discusses what is good for the married; in 7:25-40 what is good for those who are not married.

In addition to their similar topics some features of Paul's argumentation are to be found in both passages. In each of the expositions Paul presents a complementary argument for men and women (vv. 2-4, 10-11,

12-14, 16, 32b-34, 38-39). In each passage an important issue is the authority on the basis of which Paul is making his exhortation. In each case Paul carefully distinguishes his authority from that of the Lord (vv. 10, 25). The authority of the Lord is paramount throughout the diptych. Paul consistently refers to "the Lord" (without "Jesus" or "Christ;" see vv. 10, 12, 17, 22, 25, 32, 34, 35, 39). Of itself "lord" is a term that connotes authority. Its rhetorical use by Paul in this context suggests that Christians must obediently respond to the one they acknowledge to be their Lord.

Writing about the unmarried, Paul recognizes that he does not have a command of the Lord to offer to the Corinthians, as he had in the previous discussion (7:10). So from the outset he underscores his authority as he issues his authoritative opinion. His opinion is given in a concise formula in the form of an ethical maxim, "it is good for a person to remain as he or she is" (cf. vv. 17, 20, 24). The wisdom contained in this pithy statement is as valid for those who are married, as Paul has just demonstrated (vv. 10-24), as it is for the unmarried. Since it is the unmarried who are the object of his present concern, Paul explains at length why it is good for the unmarried to remain as they are. His explanation, broken only by an aside explaining that those who do marry have not sinned (v. 28), follows the rhetorical pattern of citing a maxim (*gnōmē*) as a kind of proof, followed by a demonstration of its validity and application. Having given his authoritative opinion in v. 26, Paul offers an explanation and an exhortation. The impending eschaton and undivided attention to the Lord are the key elements in his exposition.

"It is good for a person to remain as he or she is." The maxim Paul sets out for the Corinthians is most likely one that he has created himself (cf. Rom 14:21; Gal 4:18). The formulaic "it is good for a person" parallels the slogan of 7:1. The apostle has created a maxim as a kind of counter-slogan to the troublesome slogan of the Corinthians. Their slogan had to do with the sexual relationship between a man and a woman. Paul urged those who were married and those who had been married (vv. 8-9) to remain as they are (cf. vv. 17, 20, 24). His terse maxim sums up his opinion on the matter. He now applies his insight to the unmarried. The rhetorical questions in v. 27 distinguish the situation of the married from the situation of the unmarried. In each instance Paul urges that people not look for a social situation other than the one in which they are presently found.

Paul's maxim implies that those who are unmarried should remain in the unmarried state. There are, nonetheless, situations in which some might chose to marry. Paul is a realist with regard to human sexuality. For him marriage is good; with it should come a healthy and active sexuality (cf. vv. 2, 9). Lest the Corinthians misunderstand Paul he makes the point that those who marry do not sin. This is equally true of both a man and a woman (v. 28). Here as elsewhere in ch. 7 Paul maintains that men and women are in a similar situation with regard to marriage and sexuality.

Let those who have . . . be as if they had not. To some extent Paul's paraenesis is similar to the advice given by Stoic and Cynic moralists. For the Stoics it was imperative that a person distance himself or herself from the world in order to gain an internal sovereignty *(logos)* and live in freedom and in harmony with the universal Logos. Cynics went still further in their rejection of the world. Similar in content to the exhortations of Stoics and Cynics, Paul's paraenesis has a different basis. It is grounded in his eschatological conviction: "the time is growing short . . . the present form of this world is passing away" (see Rom 13:11-12; 1 Thess 5:1-11).

Paul's eschatological perspective is such that he recognizes that the Corinthians must face the everyday realities of life. He nonetheless urges them to take some distance from these realities. In five parallel clauses (vv. 29-31) he highlights the idea that the Corinthians are to live their everyday lives in security and serene tranquility, all the while realizing that the aspects of their lives to which the verbs point are but penultimate reality. The fivefold use of *hōs mē*, "as if not," an expression found in Stoic writings (e.g., Diogenes) and apocalyptic literature (4 Ezra 16:42-45, etc.) indicates that Christian existence is existence in a situation of creative tension between the present and the future yet to come. With Christ's death and resurrection the eschatological future has already begun. His rule is not yet complete (cf. 15:25). In the meantime Christians live in a situation of eschatological tension (cf. 1 Thess 5:1-11). This tension affects various dimensions of ordinary life in this world, as the series of contrasting clauses makes clear. The first of these is marriage (v. 29), the overall subject of the mini-treatise in ch. 7.

Freedom from Anxiety. Paul's treatise on marriage is embedded in a long discussion on freedom in a variety of situations (6:12–10:23). In 7:32 he says a few words on freedom. These words are reminiscent of a traditional philosophical topos. One of Aristotle's students, Theophrastus (ca. 370–285 B.C E.), claimed that the cares, concerns, and responsibilities of marriage made marriage and the pursuit of philosophy incompatible with one another. Later Cynics avoided marriage so that they could devote themselves to philosophy. In his discussion on whether or not the (ideal) Cynic should undertake marriage and have a family Epictetus mused, "it is a question, perhaps, if the Cynic ought not to be free from distraction *(aperispaston)*, wholly devoted to the service of God, free to go about among men, not tied down by the private duties of men, or involved in relationships that he cannot violate and still maintain his role as a good and excellent man, whereas, on the other hand, if he observes them, he will destroy the messenger, the scout, the herald of the gods, that he is" *(Discourses* 3.22.69).

Paul's recourse to this traditional topos may have been prompted by some women among the Christian community in Corinth who desired to be "holy in body and spirit." The phrase "holy in body and spirit" interrupts the otherwise balanced exposition of vv. 33-34. The description is likely to have been a Corinthian buzz word used to describe a specific group of well-intentioned and zealous unmarried women in Corinth. The virgins who aspire to be holy in body and spirit might have been akin to vestal virgins, even if there was not a formally constituted group of such virgins in Corinth.

That the description derives from the situation at Corinth is suggested by the anthropology implied in the expression "body and spirit." A "body and spirit" dualistic anthropology is different from Paul's holistic anthropology. "Body" contrasts with "spirit"—today we might say "body and soul,"—but Paul does not make such a contrast. The concept of holiness implied by the phrase's use of "holy" is also different from the apostle's understanding of holiness. For him there is no opposition between the sexual engagement of marriage and holiness. In 7:14 he had argued for stability in a mixed marriage precisely because of its "holiness."

Because of the situation at Corinth Paul makes use of the traditional rhetorical topos on freedom. He adapts it to the eschatological condition of Christians and the good order of the community (v. 35). The antithesis between the Lord and the world recalls vv. 29-31 where Paul wrote about the demands of Christian life in a real situation of eschatological tension and had characterized the world (*kosmos*) as a world that was passing away (v. 31). References to the Lord (*Kyrios,* vv. 25-35) encompass the entire pericope in which Paul offers his advice to the unmarried (7:25-35). In fact reference to the Lord pervades Paul's discussion on sexuality, beginning with the topos on sex with a prostitute (6:12-20). See 6:11, 13, 14, 17; 7:10, 12, 32, 34, 39. One's relationship to the Lord must be the determinant factor with regard to how one should live out one's sexuality. Reference to the Lord evokes the eschatological situation of Christians. The Lord to whom they are subject is the eschatological Lord.

Paul's exposition does not imply that the unmarried state is better than the married state. His "opinion" is that people should remain as they are, especially in light of their eschatological situation (v. 26). He concludes the pericope by citing the overall reasons why people should remain as they are. Using the literary technique of antithesis to emphasize his point he argues that the well-being of the community and its devotion to the Lord urge that people should remain as they are. As Paul speaks of the advantage (*symphoron,* v. 35) accruing to those who would remain as they are he uses the language of deliberative rhetoric. The argument from advantage is used in Hellenistic rhetoric that pleads for the well-being of the community. Paul's references to the advantage of the community belie the social perspective of his observations, but that perspective is emphasized by the expression "for your very own advantage" (v. 35), and by Paul's anaphoric use of *eu-*, a prefix meaning "well," in the expression "good order and . . . constancy" *(euschēmon kai euparedron)*.

NOTES

25. *Concerning the unmarried:* The next group of people Paul wants to consider are those who are not married *(peri de tōn parthenōn)*. The substantivized adjective "the unmarried" occurs six times in 7:25-40 but is used by Paul on only one other occasion (2 Cor 11:2). The term *parthenos* (literally "virgin") generally referred to an unmarried woman, her biological virginity being presumed. The NT (Rev 14:4) and other literature (e.g., *JosAs.* 4:9, 8:1) also used *parthenos* in reference to a man who had not had sexual intercourse (see BAGD 627.2; *EDNT* 3:44-52, at 50; J. Massyngberde Ford, "The Meaning of 'Virgin,'" *NTS* 12 [1966] 293–299).

    Paul uses *parthenos* with reference to a woman in vv. 28, 34, 36, 37, and 38. In these passages the noun is always used in the singular and with a definite article in the feminine. In the pericope as a whole (vv. 25-40), however, Paul discusses matters that pertain to unmarried men as well as those that have relevance for unmarried women. Indeed, the first case that he takes under consideration in his epistolary casuistry is that of the unmarried man (vv. 27b-28).

    I do not have a command of the Lord; however, as one to whom the Lord has given the favor of being trustworthy I offer an opinion: On the nature and authority of Paul's opinion *(gnōmē*, cf. 1:10; 2 Cor 8:10; and Phlm 14) see "Interpretation." Paul considers that his own ministry, like that of his coworkers, is grounded in an ongoing act of divine mercy (cf. 2 Cor 4:1; 1 Tim 1:13, 16). Paul's affirmation that he is faithful is unusual (cf. 4:2), but the description contributes to the quality of his *ethos*.

26. *I think that in view of the present distress this is good:* "Distress" *(anagkē)* is not necessarily a term with eschatological connotations. Paul uses the term to indicate a variety of stressful situations (7:37; 9:16; cf. Rom 13:5; 2 Cor 6:4; 9:7; 12:10; 1 Thess 3:7). Bradley B. Blue interprets it of the mid-century famine in Corinth ("The House Church at Corinth and the Lord's Supper: Famine, Food Supply, and the *Present Distress*," *CTR* 5 [1991] 221–239); O. Larry Yarbrough of the inability to control sexual desire (cf. 7:2, 9; *Not Like the Gentiles* 103). So Paul may simply be giving the unmarried Christians of Corinth a bit of practical advice in the midst of life's difficulties. Because of the troubles of the moment it is preferable not to marry. Since, however, Paul speaks of the impending parousia in v. 29 most commentators are of the opinion that the "present distress" to which Paul refers in v. 26 is the eschatological woes.

    Paul's "this" *(touto)* suggests that he is referring to something that is well known to the Corinthians (BDF 399.1); "I think" suggests a well-grounded opinion. The language reflects the gnomic character of the adage in v. 26b.

namely, it is good for a person to remain as he or she is: Paul uses a formulaic *kalon,* "it is good," here and in 5:6; 7:1, 8; 9:15 (cf. Rom 14:21; Gal 4:18). The recitative *hoti* may be rendered "namely" insofar as the phrase it introduces is apposite to "this is good" in v. 26a. Paul's adage, created as a counter-slogan to the slogan of 7:1, is literally "it is good for a person to be such" *(kalon anthrōpō to houtōs einai).* The language of the Corinthians' slogan was such that it was clear that the gender-neutral *anthrōpos,* "person," referred to a man. In response to the slogan Paul expounded an ethic of mutual and similar responsibility in marriage for both husband and wife. In reprising the expression of 7:1 in v. 25 Paul begins his demonstration of the validity of his maxim with the case of a man. In consideration of Paul's consistent pattern of urging similar responsibilities for men and women with regard to marriage and sexuality and the fact that both men and women are considered in vv. 25-35 it seems preferable to render Paul's *anthrōpō* by the gender-inclusive "person."

27. *Are you bound to a wife? Do not seek release. Are you free from a wife? Do not seek a wife:* As in vv. 18 and 21, Paul's asyndetic style produces a powerful rhetorical effect (cf. BDF 494). The lack of connective particles imparts force to his words. The two parts of the balanced appeal are linked together by similar terminology. This is the rhetorical device of anastrophe. Words from the same root conclude the first part of Paul's double exhortation *(lysin,* "release," hapax in the NT) and introduce the second part *(lelysai,* "are you free"). Since Paul has already written about divorce in 7:11b it may be that in v. 27b he is particularly urging men who are betrothed to remain faithful to their betrothal commitment *(EDNT* 2:364). "Wife" is *gynaiki,* that is, an adult woman regardless of her marital status. That this may be the import of Paul's word is also suggested by the fact that the topic at hand is "the unmarried" (v. 25).

28. *If, however, you marry, you do not sin; and if a virgin marries she does not sin:* The conditional clauses reflect Paul's casuistic approach to matters of marriage and sexuality. It is an aside in the overall argument (cf. vv. 9a, 15a; 21b). The second person singular of the first clause continues the apostrophe, the direct approach of v. 27. People who marry do not sin, but men who make use of prostitutes do sin, and that against their own bodies (6:18). In 7:2, 9 Paul mentioned sexual passion as a reason why people should marry.

   Mention of the unmarried woman in the second clause continues Paul's balanced treatment of sexuality (7:2-4, 8-14, 32-35). That he speaks of a woman as "marrying" rather than "being married" (in the passive; cf. Luke 20:34-35) is socially significant.

   but these suffer affliction in their physical relationship, and I would spare you that: Paul often writes about "affliction" *(thlipsis),* most frequently in reference to eschatological tribulations. The term is hapax in 1 Corinthians, where it is qualified by *en sarki,* literally "in the flesh," that is, in reference to their physical union (cf. 6:16). An emphatic *egō* underscores the persona of Paul who would spare *(pheidomai,* hapax in 1 Corinthians) the Corinthians that pain.

29. *I tell you, brothers and sisters, the time is growing short:* The emphatic formula *touto de phēmi adelphoi,* "I tell you, brothers and sisters," recurs in 15:50 where

it is also used to highlight an eschatological pronouncement. The "time" *(kairos)* is the time remaining until the day of the Lord (cf. vv. 26, 31). That time is growing short. Paul's verb *(synestalmenos),* used only here in his correspondence, normally connotes shrinking or compression *(EDNT* 3:313).

Henceforth let those who have wives be as those who have not: The initial *to loipon* is temporal ("henceforth") rather than epistolary (in which case it would imply that the writer was coming to the end of the letter, hence "finally" as in 2 Cor 13:11), but it could be inferential ("for this reason" BAGD 480:3). The first of Paul's five parallel phrases is in the form of a *hina* clause with the subjunctive. The construction has the rhetorical force of an imperative (BDF 387.3). The verb "to be" occurs in the first phrase only; the other four phrases are elliptical. In each of the five parallel exhortations, apart from some minor variants—a different verb in the fourth exhortation (buying, having), a compound form of the same verb in the fifth *(chrōmenoi, katachrōmenoi)*—the same participial form of the verb appears in both parts of the exhortation.

Despite the opinions advanced by Dennis R. MacDonald *(The Legend and the Apostle: The Battle for Paul in Story and Canon* [Phila.: Westminster, 1983]) as to the similarity between Paul's thought and that of the apocryphal *Acts of Paul and Thecla,* what Paul suggests by his "eschatological reservation" is not like the ideas expressed in the apocryphal work. Paul is not urging married Christians to embrace the celibate state (cf. 7:1-6). To the contrary, the position espoused in *Thecla* is similar to the ideas that Paul opposes in 1 Corinthians 7. What Paul is describing in v. 29 is the tension inherent in penultimate existence.

30–31. *and those who weep as those who do not weep, and those who rejoice as those who do not rejoice, and those who buy as those who are without, and those who make use of the world as those who do not make full use of it:* Paul continues his exhortation to live in the midst of eschatological tension by means of four additional contrasts. Each contrast is introduced by *kai,* "and" *(polysyndeton).* Weeping, rejoicing, buying, and using this world, as well as marrying, are part and parcel of ordinary human existence. In this context "world" does not have any negative connotation; it is a term to describe the physical universe in which people live. Weeping and rejoicing are a natural pair (cf. Rom 12:15).

for the configuration of this world is passing away: The "world" *(kosmos)* denotes the structured and orderly world. Apart from Phil 2:7 "configuration" *(schēma)* is hapax in the NT. The "configuration of this world" is the world as we know it, the world in the configuration of its present structural arrangement. Paul's intransitive verb is in the present tense *(paragei),* suggesting that the transformation of the world is in process. A similar eschatological qualification on the present order of reality is found in 4 Ezra 4:26, "the age is hastening swiftly to its end" (cf. 4 Ezra 2:34).

32. *I wish you to be free from anxiety:* This expression of Paul's wish *(thelō;* cf. 7:7, but also 10:1, 20; 11:3; 12:1; 14:5, 16:7) reprises the thought of v. 28b. Picking up the thought of that verse provides Paul with an opportunity to clarify his wish. His stated desire that the Corinthians be "free from anxiety" *(amerimnous,* hapax in the Pauline corpus) introduces a short passage in which he

gives another demonstration of his literary skill. Employing the literary device of *paronomasia*, that is, use of words with the same root (here *merim-*), to good advantage, Paul writes of the concerns of the unmarried man, the married man, the unmarried woman, and the married woman.

The one who is unmarried is concerned about the things of the Lord, how he might please the Lord: "Is concerned" *(merimnā)* echoes the sound of *merim-* (see "Interpretation"). The man who is not married *(agamos,* cf. 7:8) is any unmarried man, whether not yet married or no longer married. Paul's presumption is that this single-minded person (cf. Matt 5:8), obviously a Christian, is fully attentive to the Lord. The Pauline verb "to please" *(aresē;* thirteen of its seventeen NT occurrences are in Paul) was a legal term that later developed aesthetic connotations. As used by Paul the verb suggests obedience. Paul's statement should not be understood moralistically or psychologically. It reflects a social situation in which an individual is fully subservient to the lord.

33–34. *the married man is concerned about the things of the world, how he might please his wife, and he is torn:* Verse 33 is antithetically parallel with v. 32b and parallel with v. 34b. For Paul marriage is a reality that belongs to the present order of things (cf. 7:32a) and bears with it various social obligations. The married man has obligations toward the wife to whom he is bound in a relationship of mutual submission (cf. 7:3-4). With obligations toward his wife, the married man is a man who is divided *(memeristai,* with the echoing root *merim-*).

And the unmarried woman, the virgin, is concerned about the things of the Lord, so that she might be holy in body and in spirit: There is considerable variation in the textual tradition with regard to "and he is torn. And the unmarried woman, the virgin." No less than eight different forms of the text are found in the manuscript tradition. For the most part the variants concern the placement of the conjunctions and the adjective "unmarried" and do not substantially impinge upon the general meaning of Paul's words. The editors of *GNT*[4] have opted for a reading that is supported by ancient Alexandrian and Western texts (see Metzger, *Textual Commentary* 490).

Verse 34b is parallel with 7:32b. What Paul has said about a man is repeated with regard to a woman. The appositive "virgin" is an additional expression in the otherwise balanced exposition, perhaps a repetition intended to make it clear that he is referring to a specific issue within the community, namely that of virgins who were aspiring "to be holy in body and in spirit." The parallelism between vv. 32b and 34b suggests that trying to be holy in body and spirit is a way of trying to please the Lord (v. 32b). Implicitly this single-minded aspiration to be holy in body and spirit contrasts with being torn (v. 34a).

and the married woman is concerned about the things of the world, how she might please her husband: Among the Stoics (e.g., Antipater of Tarsus, *SVF* 3.255.22-23) and the Neo-Pythagoreans (e.g., *Letter to Kleareta* 116.4-12), it was expected that a wife should please her husband *(areskein andri).* Paul's statement is parallel with v. 33. What he said there about a husband is now said about the wife.

35. *I am saying this for your very own advantage:* The intensive *autōn,* "very own," is absent from 𝔓¹⁵, a third-century papyrus containing only 1 Cor 7:18–8:4. The argument from advantage is one that Paul employs from time to time throughout the letter (cf. 10:33). The argument is characteristic not only of public political discourse, which pleaded for concord among the populace for their own good, but also of symbouleutic rhetoric, the rhetoric of advice sometimes found in personal letters. Paul explains what he means by advantage *(pros to hymōn autōn symphoron)* in the following antithesis (v. 35b-c). The Stoics considered that among the advantages of marriage were that a wife could take care of the household chores and thus free her husband for philosophical pursuits and that children could provide for their parents in their advanced age (see Yarbrough, *Not Like the Gentiles* 32–41).

not to impose a burden on you: "Burden" *(brochos,* hapax in the NT) is literally a "noose" or "snare." Paul's use is one of a relatively few known metaphorical usages. The expression is similarly used by the Cynic Crates who said that when neither hunger nor time have quelled the strength of the flame of love the "burden" is the only remaining remedy (*Greek Anthology* 9.497).

but for the sake of good order and unreserved constancy to the Lord: In apposition to "for your advantage" *(pros to hymōn autōn symphoron)* and in antithesis to "not to impose a burden on you" *(ouk . . . alla),* the clause is marked by alliteration *(pros to euschēmon kai euparedron).* Its two verbal adjectives are rare in Paul. The first *(euschēmon,* "of good order") occurs only here and in 12:24; the second *(euparedron,* "constancy") is hapax in the NT and not attested before Paul. The first adjective denotes a universally recognized Greek moral ideal that includes aesthetic elements. As used by Paul it denotes not only what is morally appropriate but also a certain dignity and honorableness, an inclination to be steadily devoted to the Lord *(TLNT* 2:139–142). The latter term explicitly picks up on the theme of devotion to the Lord introduced in vv. 32 and 34 with respect to man and woman alike.

Paul's grammar is a bit difficult. The rare adverb "unreserved" *(aperispastōs,* hapax in the NT), emphatically placed at the end of the sentence, appears to modify "constancy." 𝔓¹⁵ solved the dilemma by supplying the verb "to be," Chrysostom by deleting the errant adverb.

FOR REFERENCE AND FURTHER STUDY

Balch, David L. "1 Cor 7:32-35 and Stoic Debates about Marriage, Anxiety, and Distraction," *JBL* 102 (1983) 429–439.

Chmiel, Jerzy. "Die Interpretation des paulinischen *hōs mē* im 1 Kor 7,29-31," *AnCr* 18 (1986) 197–204.

Dolfe, K. G. E. "1 Cor 7,25 Reconsidered (Paul a Supposed Adviser)," *ZNW* 83 (1992) 115–118.

Genton, Philippe. "1 Corinthiens 7/25-40. Notes exégétiques," *EThR* 67 (1992) 249–253.

Glenny, W. Edward. "1 Corinthians 7:29-31 and the Teaching of Continence in *The Acts of Paul and Thecla,*" *GTJ* 11 (1990) 53–70.

Gramaglia, Pier Angelo. "Le fonti del linguaggio paolino in 1 Cor. 7,35 e 7,1," *Aug* 28 (1988) 461–501.

MacDonald, Margaret Y. "Women Holy in Body and Spirit: The Social Setting of 1 Corinthians 7," *NTS* 36 (1990) 161–181.

Moiser, Jeremy. "A Reassessment of Paul's View of Marriage with reference to 1 Cor. 7," *JSNT* 18 (1983) 103–122.

Navarro Puerto, Mercedes. "La parthenos: Un futuro significativo en el aquí y ahora de la comunidad (1 Cor 7,25-38)," *EstBib* 49 (1991) 353–387.

Ramsaran, Rollin A. "More Than an Opinion: Paul's Rhetorical Maxim in First Corinthians 7:25-26," *CBQ* 57 (1995) 531–541.

Winter, Bruce W. "Secular and Christian Responses to Corinthian Famines," *TynB* 40 (1989) 86–106.

9. *To Marry or Not to Marry* (7:36-40)

36. If someone thinks that he is acting improperly with regard to his betrothed, if he has strong passions and thus it must be, he should do what he wants; he does not sin. They should marry. 37. The one who, experiencing no constraint, stands steadfast in his heart, has self-control, and has made a judgment on this matter within his own heart will do well to keep her as she is. 38. So therefore the one who marries his betrothed does well; the one who does not marry does better.

39. A wife is bound while her husband lives. If the husband dies she is free to marry whom she wants, only let it be in the Lord. 40. In my opinion she will be more blessed if she remains such; and I think that I too have the Spirit of God.

INTERPRETATION

In 7:1-16, after having addressed himself directly to the Corinthians' slogan in vv. 2-7, Paul offered his opinion on a number of related and specific topics. He does something similar in 7:25-40. In v. 26 he had offered his own maxim whose implications he then proceeded to clarify (vv. 27-31). In vv. 36-40 he turns his attention to two other cases, that of a man who is not yet married but is in a committed relationship to a woman, and that of the woman whose husband is deceased. If the two cases are read together, as well they might be, Paul will have continued the balanced treatment he has maintained throughout the chapter, treating first a case that concerns a man (vv. 36-38), then a case that concerns a woman (vv. 39-40).

In some ways the pericope with its reference to sin (*hamartanei*, v. 36, cf. vv. 27-28) and its sequence of the case of a man and a woman is a kind of commentary on v. 27. The pericope is linked to the preceding discussion by means of the noun *anagkēn* ("constraint" in v. 37, "present distress" in v. 26) and catchwords that Paul had used in the presentation of his maxim in vv. 25-26. These are the verb to "think" (*nomizei*, vv. 36, 26) and the noun "opinion" (*gnōmēn*, vv. 40, 25). The latter term serves to form the *inclusio* that defines 7:25-40 as a distinct literary unit. The reference to Paul's possession of the Spirit (v. 40) is an element of the *ethos* appeal of his letter. Paralleled with the appeal to himself as the beneficiary of divine mercy in v. 25, the reference to Paul's having the Spirit also helps to define 7:25-40 as a discrete unit.

His Betrothed. The first case (*ei de tis*, "if anyone") considered by Paul is that of a man who is not acting properly toward his "betrothed" (*tēn parthenon autou*, literally "his virgin"). Although there are no major text-critical problems with regard to Paul's Greek text, the language is ambiguous enough to admit of a variety of interpretations. The crucial issue is the nature of the relationship between the man and the unmarried woman. In addition there is the issue of what is meant by "acting improperly" (*aschēmonein*).

That there is a bonded relationship between the man and the unmarried woman is indicated by Paul's use of the pronouns "his" (*autou*, v. 37) and "his own" (*heautou*, vv. 37, 38), but Paul does not otherwise indicate the man of whom he is thinking when he writes "if anyone." The man could be a father who is faced with a decision as to whether he should give his daughter in marriage (cf. v. 34c). He could be a slaveowner who was free to marry a female slave or to give her in marriage to someone else (cf. Exod 21:7-11). He could be one who has entered into a committed but platonic relationship with an unmarried woman. Many commentators have written about spiritual brides (*virgines subintroductae*) in this regard. The man could be someone who was weighing the applicability of the practice of the levirate law (Deut 25:5-10; cf. Matt 22:23-33; Mark 12:18-27; Luke 20:27-40) to his own situation. Finally, he could be someone who was committed to marry a woman but was having second thoughts about the marriage because of the push for sexual asceticism within the community at Corinth.

On balance and in the light of v. 27c-d it is likely that Paul is writing about a man who is in a committed relationship but is as yet free from marriage. Paul had already advised such men that they would not sin were they to marry. He reiterates his advice in 7:36-38, perhaps because of his general conviction that marriage is good and the possibility that his opinion (7:26) might be misconstrued.

Better Not to Marry. Although Paul's words admit of some ambiguity with regard to the specific situation he has in mind, his advice is unambiguous. He presents his opinion in two contrasting statements. He first affirms that the man is free to marry the unmarried woman. This is not sinful at all. Then he affirms that it would be good were the man not to marry. Paul's discussion of the case concludes with a summarizing statement in which he affirms that in the case at hand foregoing marriage is better than marrying.

Paul treats the case of the unmarried woman in similar fashion. The case is unambiguous; it is that of the widow. As in the case of the man faced with the decision whether to marry or not, Paul affirms that a widow is free to marry but that it would be better for her not to do so (v. 40a; cf. v. 38). Paul's taking up the case of the widow for the second time (cf. 7:8-9) allows him to reaffirm the principle of stability in marriage (cf. 7:10-11). The explicit affirmation that a wife is bound to her husband strengthens the suggestion of some commentators that it was Christian women in Corinth (cf. 7:10-11a, 34) who most readily succumbed to the attraction of the *ethos* suggested by the slogan of 7:1.

The Literary Context. Some of the language Paul uses in expressing his judgment on the two cases, especially with regard to the man in v. 37, is similar to language employed by Philo in *Every Good Man is Free* 59-61:

> He who always acts sensibly, always acts well; he who always acts well, always acts rightly; he who always acts rightly also acts impeccably, blamelessly, faultlessly, irreproachably, harmlessly, and therefore will have the power to do anything, and to live as he wishes, and he who has this power must be free. But the good man always acts sensibly, and therefore he alone is free. Again, one cannot be compelled to do anything or prevented from doing anything, cannot be a slave. . . .

The philosopher writes about someone who behaves well, literally "does well," *eu poiōn,* comparable to Paul's "do well" (*kalōs poiēsei,* v. 37). He describes the one who behaves well as being without sin (*anamartētōs,* "impeccably"), having power (*exousian*), doing as he wants (*hōs bouletai*). He says that the good man is free (*eleutheros*) and is not under compulsion (*mēt'anagkasai*). He uses various forms of the root *anagk-,* "compulsion," six times in speaking about good behavior in the context of freedom.

Paul's discussion of the two cases falls within a broad discussion on freedom (6:12–10:23) in which his *ethos* appeal is paramount. Speaking about the case of a man with his betrothed Paul writes about his doing what he wants (*ho thelei poieitō,* v. 36) and being under no constraint (*mē echōn anagkēn,* v. 37). In discussing the case of the widow Paul explicitly mentions her freedom (v. 39). His counsel that she remain as she is (*houtōs meinē*) recalls his thrice-repeated exhortation that the Corinthians remain as they are (7:17, 20, 24). Paul's plea for social stability used the language of freedom (*eleutheros* in vv. 21, 22; *apeleutheros* in v. 22). In the context of human freedom Paul pleads for social stability, but there are contingencies (vv. 9, 21b, 28, 36, 39).

The similarity between Philo's discourse and Paul's words is striking, but Philo's discourse lacks reference to the human heart (*kardia*, twice in v. 37). In traditional Jewish anthropology the heart *(lēb)* is the core of one's being. From the heart comes a person's essential orientation. It may be that Paul has introduced the language of the heart into the exposition in order to provide the holistic anthropology of his tradition as an overarching perspective, even as he adopts the classic language of the discourse on freedom to speak of someone's freedom to marry his betrothed. Paul's discourse on human sexuality began with a reminder that he considered human sexuality from the standpoint of his biblical tradition (Gen 2:24 in 6:16). From the beginning of his discussion on freedom and sexuality (6:12-20) Paul referred to the Spirit and to the Lord, motifs that recur as he brings his discourse to closure in v. 40.

NOTES

36. *If someone thinks that he is acting improperly with regard to his betrothed:* "His virgin" *(tēn parthenon autou)* has been understood in a variety of ways: a nubile daughter, a sister-in-law whose husband had died, a fiancée, or a spiritual bride *(virgo subintroducta).* Capitalizing on suggestions by Karl Heinrich von Weizsäcker (1876, 1886) and Eduard Grafe (1899), Hans Achelis wrote a history of spiritual marriage (*Virgines Subintroductae: Ein Beitrag zum VII. Kapitel des. I. Korintherbriefs* [Leipzig: J. C. Hinrichs, 1902]). Achelis studied several cases of Christian men living with women without having a sexual relationship with these women. He argued that this was the practice to which Paul was referring in vv. 36-38. All of his cases, however, date from the patristic era. The oldest is found in *Hermas Sim.* 9.10-11, an account of a vision in which the seer spends the night, "as a brother, not as a husband," with twelve virgins. This vision, however, does not represent an actual practice of a man having a spiritual bride. The virgins are described as spirits in *Hermas Sim.* 9.13. In *Hermas Sim.* 9.15, they are endowed with the names of the virtues. There is no evidence to suggest that a practice of "spiritual marriage" was in existence at the time of Paul.

In the patristic era "his virgin" (v. 36) was generally taken to be a marriageable daughter, but the context and language of Paul's text make it difficult to sustain this as being the correct interpretation. Both v. 27c-d and v. 37 suggest that "his unmarried woman" is, in fact, a man's betrothed. "To act improperly" is to act contrary to social custom. The custom may be the practice urged by the proponents of the slogan in 7:1; alternatively, and perhaps better, it may be general social convention. In the latter case the anomaly would be betrothal that does not lead to marriage. Paul's verb *(aschēmonein)* and its cognate adjective, *aschēmōn,* are used only by Paul in the NT, the former in 7:36; 13:5; the latter in 12:23. The word group is, however, used frequently by Stoic and Cynic authors (Musonius Rufus, Dio Chrysostom, Epictetus, the *Cynic Epistles*) in their various disquisitions on human sexuality.

if he has strong passions and thus it must be, he should do what he wants; he does not sin. They should marry: Paul has added a second, cryptic conditional clause. The rare adjective *hyperakmos,* "having strong passions," from *hyper* and *akmē,* is hapax in the NT. Some patristic authors took it as an adjective describing the unmarried woman, that is, as *superadulta,* beyond the age for marriage, but it most likely refers to sexual passion (see BAGD 839). "Thus it must be" *(houtōs opheilei ginesthai)* is a concession to reality. See 7:2, 9, where sexual passion is cited as a reason to marry. Epictetus likewise justified marriage on the basis of passionate love *(ex erōtos; Discourses* 3.22.76). In such circumstances a man should do *(poieitō,* an imperative) what he wants. Reiterating his earlier dictum that it is not a sin to marry, Paul urges that he and his betrothed marry *(gameitōsan,* an imperative plural, presumably referring to the man and the woman; cf. BDF 101).

37. *The one who, experiencing no constraint, stands steadfast in his heart, has self-control, and has made a judgment on this matter within his own heart:* Yarbrough *(Not Like the Gentiles* 103) takes *anagkēn* as an inability to control sexual desires, but it is best to take the noun in a sense somewhat akin to that of its meaning in v. 26. Within the context of Paul's discussion on freedom *anagkēn* seemingly connotes constraint or external force. Apart from this participial clause, Paul uses *polysyndeton (de . . . kai)* to link together the three other clauses. "Has self-control" is literally "has power over his will" *(exousian . . . peri tou idiou thelēmatos).* Some take "will" to mean sexual desire; cf. *EDNT* 2:136; RSV, NRSV. The double use of "heart" *(kardia)* underscores Paul's holistic anthropology. Robert Jewett *(Paul's Anthropological Terms* 328, 386) acknowledges that Paul's use of the noun reflects traditional Judaic anthropology, observing that "heart" is used instead of "mind" *(nous).* Paul writes of a decision that is embedded in the depths of one's being (cf. 4:5).

will do well to keep her as she is: "To do well" is a colloquial expression used but rarely by Paul (7:37, 38; Phil 4:14; cf. Matt 12:12; Mark 7:37; Luke 6:27; Acts 10:33; Jas 2:8, 19; 2 Pet 1:19; 3 John 6). "To keep her as she is" is literally "to keep his own betrothed" *(tērein tēn heautou parthenon).* The verb, with a primary meaning of "keep watch over," may have the meaning of "support," but most interpreters opine that the sense of Paul's expression is that of maintaining her unmarried status (so, BAGD 815.2b, "keep his virgin inviolate"). Such an understanding is consonant with the "stay as you are" thrust of ch. 7.

38. *So therefore the one who marries his betrothed does well; the one who does not marry does better:* An inferential *hōste* introduces Paul's conclusion. Using two participial constructions, the second of which is elliptical, Paul compares *(kalōs . . . kreisson)* two possible solutions for the case of the betrothed man. This is the only time in the extant correspondence that Paul explicitly writes of what

is good and what is better. Together with its parallel in v. 40 this is the only place in the extant correspondence in which he affirms the superiority of remaining unmarried vis-à-vis being married, a condition whose sinlessness he has steadfastly maintained (vv. 28, 36).

39. *A wife is bound while her husband lives:* In both Jewish and Hellenistic cultures, a woman *(gynē)* was considered to be bound to her husband (cf. Rom 7:2). Some manuscripts (including the majority of medieval mss., D, F, G, Ψ, and the "corrected" ℵ), perhaps under the influence of Rom 7:2, read the text with a qualifying *nomō,* "by law," a form of the text with which Tertullian seems to have been familiar (see Johannes B. Bauer, "Was las Tertullian 1 Kor 7:39?" *ZNW* 77 [1986] 284–287). Manuscript K and the Coptic Bohairic read the text as if the woman were bound to her marriage *(gamō)* rather than to her husband.

If the husband dies she is free to marry whom she wants: Using anastrophe, Paul considers the case of a woman whose husband *(anēr,* literally "man") has died *(koimēthē,* literally "has gone to sleep," a common metaphor for death; cf. 11:30; 15:6, 18, 20, 51). In antiquity the affirmation that a once married woman was free to marry whomever she wants was a standard feature of divorce documents. "The essential formula in the bill of divorce," says the Mishnah *(m. Git.* 9:3) "is, 'Lo, thou art free to marry any man.' R. Judah says: 'Let this be from me thy writ of divorce and letter of dismissal and deed of liberation, that thou mayest marry whatsoever man thou wilt.'"

only let it be in the Lord: Paul's elliptical phrase lacks a verb. "In the Lord" *(en kyriō)* is frequently found in paraenetic contexts, where it evokes the authority of the risen Lord (cf. 1 Thess 3:8; Rom 16:2). In 7:40 the phrase indicates that Paul is placing a restriction on those who are free to marry, namely that they marry other Christians. In virtually all cultures endogamy, based on race, clan, or creed, is a common social norm. Among Jews marriage to a non-Jew was generally forbidden (Deut 7:3; Ezra 9:2). The ban continued into rabbinic times, when it was cited among the 613 Commandments. See also *m. Git.* 9:2, "thou art free to marry any man excepting . . . a slave or a Gentile." Similarly a divorce decree *(get)* from the time of Bar Kokhba affirms "you may go and be married to any Jewish man you want."

40. *In my opinion she will be more blessed if she remains such:* Paul rarely uses the adjective "blessed." Apart from a beatitude in Rom 14:22 it is found only in two biblical citations (Rom 4:7, 8). In v. 40 the adjective has the ordinary sense of good; it is commonplace in popular sayings about marriage. Menander, for example, says ". . . and a thing which they call blessed *(makarion),* I take no wife" (frag. 3K). Similarly Euripides is quoted as saying "Blessed *(makarios)* is he, whoever marries and obtains a good wife; and he who does not marry" *(ISA* 4.525.16–526.1).

Paul's comparative, *makariōtera,* is parallel with the use of a comparative in his case study of the male (v. 38). In each instance he has summed up the alternatives he has exposited in a comparative statement. Reference to Paul's opinion *(gnōmēn)* and his use of "such" *(houtōs)* are part of the *inclusio* whereby 7:25-40 is constituted as a literary unit.

and I think that I too have the Spirit of God: Paul reaffirms the argument from his own prestige (a kind of thematic *inclusio* with 7:25) with an appeal to his possession of the Spirit (see 12:7). The *ethos* appeal is joined to the preceding argument by the connective *de* and an emphatic *kagō* ("I too"). The translation is intended to reflect both the emphatic ellipsis itself and Paul's conviction of his own authority over and against that of the "pneumatics" in Corinth. "Spirit of God" is found in the overwhelming majority of ancient manuscripts, but a variant, "Spirit of Christ," perhaps influenced by v. 39's reference to the Lord, is found in 𝔓[15] and one important ninth-century minuscule (33).

FOR REFERENCE AND FURTHER STUDY

Baumert, Norbert. *Woman and Man* 117–129.

Collins, John J. "Bulletin of the New Testament: the Pauline Epistles," *TS* 17 (1956) 531–548.

Kümmel, Werner Georg. "Verlobung und Heirat bei Paulus (I. Cor 7, 36-38)" in *Neutestamentalische Studien für Rudolf Bultmann zum siebzigsten Geburtstag.* BZNW 21. Berlin: Töpelmann, 1954, 275–295.

Papadopoulos, Konstantinos Nicolaou. "*Sēmeiōma gia to* 1 Kor. 7,36-38" ["The Meaning of 1 Cor 7:36-38"] *DBM* 19 (1990) 10–12.

D. THIRD RHETORICAL DEMONSTRATION (8:1–11:1)

Paul introduces a new topic in 8:1. The subject is food once offered to idols and now served at a meal: in one's own home (10:25-26), when one is a guest (10:27-31), as a festive meal in a temple (8:10), or in the context of a cultic celebration (10:14-21). The formal introduction of the topic, "concerning" *(peri de)*, suggests that the issue might have been one about which some Corinthians had written to Paul (see 7:1).

At issue in the discussion is the matter of Christian identity in the midst of a syncretistic culture. What is at stake is ecclesial communion and an authentic theology. At bottom the theological issues are idol worship and religious syncretism, but there are a number of social issues as well. Food was offered to idols in a variety of places and on numerous occasions. Immediately one thinks of food that has been offered to idols in the context of specific cultic activity within the temple, but sacrifice was also offered to civic and other deities on the occasion of the celebration of the public games, weddings, funerals, and the festive dinners of a number of private associations. These celebrations took place in the appropriate venues.

Food offered to idols could be consumed in various locales: in the temple precincts, in the dining areas attached to temples or located in nearby edifices, in private homes. Food that had been offered to idols was available in the public market; it could be served during a dinner at which a person was only an invited guest. What does one do with regard to weddings, funerals, and other celebrations when food offered to idols is to be served? A willingness to eat of this food is a matter of social participation. What does one do when one is an invited guest at a dinner during which such food will be served?

Another dimension of social issues involved in the matter of food offered to idols is the situation of the poorer members of the community. The poor had relatively little opportunity to eat meat. One of the rare occasions when they had access to meat was on the completion of the rituals attendant upon the celebration of the public games and other major civic festivities. These events typically included an element of sacrifice to one or another deity with the result that some meat was available for distribution to or purchase by the poor. Should the poor be deprived of meat because, practically speaking, the only meat that was available to them had been sacrificed to idols?

The variety of social concerns facing Christians in Corinth suggests that the issues addressed in this third rhetorical demonstration are not necessarily those Paul discusses in Romans 14. The situations are really distinct from one another. For whom was the issue addressed by Paul in 1 Corinthians 8–10 a matter of concern? Paul writes about the weak (8:9) and identifies himself with them (9:22), but his letter gives no indication that the weak had registered a complaint with him nor is there any real indication that there existed in Corinth any identifiable group of "weak" as such. "Weak" might have been a derogatory characterization of some within the community by others who looked down upon them because they did not act with sufficient "freedom" in this matter. Perhaps it was only Paul who was troubled by their conduct. His Hellenistic Jewish contemporary, Philo of Alexandria, considered that participation in the meals of religious associations entailed both a violation of Jewish dietary laws and eating forbidden and idolatrous food (cf. *Dreams* 2.123; *Joseph* 154; *Life of Moses* 1.31, 241, 278, 298; 2.167, 270; *Special Laws* 3.126; *Rewards* 98; *Flaccus* 14, 50). It may be that Paul's preaching of the *Shema* (Deut 6:4) provided an opportunity for some Corinthians to exploit the reality of monotheism in a way that was truly harmful to other members of the community.

Paul offers his reflections on food offered to idols in a three-part exposition, a palistrophe, a literary pattern in which the final element, following an A-B-A' schema, reflects the first element. The triadic exposition is typical of Paul's style of writing but was not exclusive to Paul. The style is found in many classical letters, that is, as distinct from the more personal letters found among Hellenistic papyri. The style of writing is akin to a feature of Aristotelian logic that cites a major premise and a minor premise before arriving at a conclusion. From the perspective of the structure of the text Paul's argument builds up to ch. 10, with the command of v. 14, "my beloved, flee from idolatry." Throughout the three-chapter demonstration Paul's argumentation is characterized by *logos*, the quasi-logical type of appeal known to ancient rhetors.

The argument of the first element of the palistrophe, ch. 8, is carefully constructed. It consists of three movements of thought. In a first subunit (vv. 1-3) the topic, *food* offered to idols *(eidōlothytos)*, is identified but the discussion focuses on knowledge. In the second subunit (vv. 4-6) the topic is more specifically identified as the *eating* of food. Paul continues the discussion of knowledge, describing its content and specifying that the ultimate content of knowledge is the one God. In the third subunit (vv. 7-13) the consequences of this knowledge, which all do not share in the same way, are examined. The discussion raises issues as to the proper use of freedom. As it comes to closure the apostle insinuates that the precise issue at hand is eating meat that has been offered to idols (v. 13).

An abrupt transition between chs. 8 and 9 has led some authors to suggest that Paul's disquisition on his own apostolic freedom is something of a *corpus extraneum.* The rhetorical digression *(parekbasis)* is, however, one of a number of such digressions in 1 Corinthians. Its ethos argument contrasts with the quasi-logical argument of the encompassing chapters. Paul uses the rhetorical device of digression to establish a basis for reflection. He can then come to a consideration of the specifics of the issue. The result is the familiar A-B-A' pattern of argument. The digression in ch. 9 focuses on the issue of the Corinthians' rights *(exousia,* 8:9). Paul offers himself as an example, identifying himself as an apostle and reflecting on the fashion in which he has chosen to exercise his rights *(exousia,* 9:4, 5, 6, 12, 18) when the salvation of others is at issue. The way that philosophical writings contemporary with Paul treat the independence of the sage is part of the background of Paul's appeal to the Corinthians.

The unity of the rhetorical demonstration is also questioned by some authors who suggest that all the material in the three-chapter unit did not come from a single letter. The section in 10:14-22 seems to recommend that the Corinthians cease and desist from any kind of eating that would imply their participation in idol worship, while 8:1-13 and 10:23–11:1 appear to suggest an accommodation according to which the eating of food offered to idols is to be avoided to the extent that it proves offensive to a member of the Corinthian community who has a delicate conscience. Some scholars assign the different approaches to two different letters (see above, pp. 10–14). Lamar Cope takes a still more radical approach. He claims that 10:1-22 is an interpolation added by an editor who wanted to make Paul's view consistent with the views of the later Church, which abhorred idolatry in all its forms. Cope argues that the radical approach of 10:1-22 is not found in Paul's other letters. The flow of thought in chs. 8–10 and the passage's terminology and midrashic use of the Scriptures, he claims, make it likely that the passage was not composed by Paul. Cope's radical view finds no support in the manuscript tradition. It would, moreover, require of Paul a kind of epistolary consistency that is not his style.

FOR REFERENCE AND FURTHER STUDY

Borgen, Peder. "'Yes,' 'No,' 'How Far?': The Participation of Jews and Christians in Pagan Cults" in Troels Engberg-Pedersen, ed., *Paul in His Hellenistic Context*. Minneapolis: Fortress, 1995, 30–59.

Brunt, John C. "Rejected, Ignored, or Misunderstood? The Fate of Paul's Approach to the Problem of Food Offered to Idols in Early Christianity," *NTS* 31 (1985) 113–124.

Cope, Lamar. "First Corinthians 8–10: Continuity or Contradiction?" ATR.S 11 (1990) 114–123.

Davis, James A. "The Interaction Between Individual Ethical Conscience and Community Ethical Consciousness in 1 Corinthians," *HBT* 10 (1988) 1–18.

Delobel, Joël. "Coherence and Relevance of 1 Cor 8–10," *CorC* 177–190.

Fee, Gordon D. "*Eidōlothyta* Once Again: An Interpretation of 1 Corinthians 8–10," *Bib.* 61 (1980) 172–197.

Fichter, H.-F. "Anstössige Freiheit in Korinth. Zur Literarkritik der Korintherbriefe (1 Kor 8,1-3 und 11,2-16)," *CorC* 561–575.

Fisk, Bruce N. "Eating Meat Offered to Idols: Corinthian Behavior and Pauline Response in 1 Corinthians 8–10 (A Response to Gordon Fee)," *TrJ* 10 (1989) 49–70.

Gooch, Paul W. "'Conscience' in 1 Corinthians 8 and 10," *NTS* 33 (1987) 244–254.

Gooch, Peter D. *Dangerous Food: 1 Corinthians 8–10 in Its Context*. Studies in Christianity and Judaism 5. Waterloo: Wilfrid Laurier University Press, 1993.

Heil, Christoph. *Die Ablehnung der Speisegebote durch Paulus. Zur Frage nach der Stellung des Apostels zum Gesetz*. BBB 96. Weinheim: Beltz Athenäum, 1994.

Horrell, David G. "Theological Principle or Christological Praxis? Pauline Ethics in 1 Corinthians 8.1–11.1," *JSNT* 67 (1997) 83–114.

Lambrecht, Jan. "Universalism in 1 Cor 8:1–11:1?" *Greg* 77 (1996) 333–339.

Lorenzi, Lorenzo De, ed. *Freedom and Love: The Guide for Christian Life (1 Co 8–10; Rom 14–15)*. Monographic Series of "Benedictina," Biblical-Ecumenical Section 6. Rome: St. Paul's Abbey, 1981.

Malherbe, Abraham J. "Determinism and Free Will in Paul: The Argument of 1 Corinthians 8 and 9" in Troels Engberg-Pedersen, ed., *Paul in His Hellenistic Context*. Minneapolis: Fortress, 1995, 231–255.

Meggitt, Justin J. "Meat Consumption and Social Conflict in Corinth," *JThS* 45 (1994) 137–141.

Murphy-O'Connor, Jerome. "Freedom or the Ghetto (I Cor., VIII, 1-13; X, 23–XI,1)," *RB* 85 (1978) 543–574.

_____. *St. Paul's Corinth* 161–167.

Nasuti, Harry P. "The Woes of the Prophets and the Rights of the Apostle: the Internal Dynamics of 1 Corinthians 9," *CBQ* 50 (1988) 246–264.

Richter, Hans-Friedemann "Anstössige Freiheit in Korinth. Zur Literarkritik der Korintherbriefe (1 Kor 8,1-3 und 11,2-16)," *CorC* 561–575.

Sibinga, Joost Smit. "The Composition of 1 Cor. 9 and its Context," *NovT* 40 (1998) 136–163.

Smit, Joop F. M. "'Do Not Be Idolaters.' Paul's Rhetoric in First Corinthians 10:1-22," *NovT* 39 (1997) 40–53.

_____. "The Rhetorical Disposition of First Corinthians 8:7–9:27," *CBQ* 59 (1997) 511–527.

_____. "Paulus 'over de afgodsoffers': De kerk tussen joden en grieken (1 Kor. 8,1–11,1)," *TvT* 37 (1997) 228–242.

Söding, Thomas. "Starke und Schwache. Der Götzenopferstreit in 1 Kor 8–10 als Paradigma paulinischer Ethik," *ZNW* 85 (1994) 69–92.

Spawforth, Antony J. S. "The Achaean Cult Part I: Pseudo-Julian Letters 198," *TynB* 46 (1995) 151–168.

Tomson, Peter J. *Paul and the Jewish Law* 150–220.

Willis, Wendell Lee. *Idol Meat in Corinth: The Pauline Argument in 1 Corinthians 8 and 10*. SBLDS 68. Chico: Scholars, 1985.

Winter, Bruce W. *Seek the Welfare of the City* 165–178.

_____. "In Public and in Private: Early Christian Interactions with Religious Pluralism" in A. D. Clarke and Bruce W. Winter, eds., *One God, One Lord in a World of Religious Pluralism*. Cambridge: Tyndale, 1961, 112–134.

_____. "The Achaean Federal Imperial Cult II: The Corinthian Church," *TynB* 46 (1995) 169–178.

_____. "Theological and Ethical Responses to Religious Pluralism in 1 Corinthians 8–10," *TynB* 41 (1990) 208–226.

Witherington, Ben W. III. "Why Not Idol Meat? Is It What You Eat or Where You Eat It?" *Bible Review* 10 (1994) 38–43, 54–55.

1. *Food Offered to Idols* (8:1-3)

1. Concerning food that has been offered to idols, we know that we all have knowledge. Knowledge puffs us, but love builds up. 2. If anyone thinks that he or she knows something, that one does not yet know as he or she ought to know. 3. If someone loves God, that person is known by him.

INTERPRETATION

Paul introduces the topic at hand, namely food that had been offered to idols, with a formal "concerning" *(peri de)*. This abrupt shift of thought from sexual abstinence to food offered to idols and the topical "concerning" suggest that food offered to idols might be a subject about which some Corinthians had voiced concern in their letter to Paul (7:1). Food offered to idols could be consumed in temple precincts (8:10). It could be purchased in the market (10:25). It might be served at a dinner to which one had been invited (10:27).

Eating food offered to idols is the problem (see 8:4), but Paul defines the real issue as one of knowledge. He seems to have understood that it was the claims of some to be knowledgeable that led them to eat food offered to idols. Although those who wrote to Paul were concerned about the eating of the food, Paul's first remarks deal with the quality of knowledge.

Everybody Knows. Paul begins his disquisition on the topic of food offered to idols with a bold statement, "we know that we all have knowledge." As is his custom, Paul makes a concession to those with whom he would take issue before beginning his pastoral reflection. Some commentators have held that Paul is quoting from the Corinthians' letter (so, J. J. Wettstein, J. S. Semler, J. S. Howson, C.F.G. Heinrici, Johannes Weiss, etc.). "We have knowledge" is arguably a Corinthian buzz word, but the intrusive "all" suggests that "we all have knowledge" is Paul's own expression. The "all" is to be explained by the fact that some within the Corinthian community were laying exclusive claim to knowledge. The "we know that" formula is similar to the familiar "do you not know that . . . ?" punctuating the letter. This disclosure formula introduces a point of departure for the following exposition.

Letters that reply to earlier correspondence typically reflect the language of the query to which a reply is being given. In ch. 8 Paul responds to a concern about which the Corinthians had written. That his response should not only have identified the matter of their concern but also some aspects of the problem is only to be expected. From this point of view "we have knowledge" may well reflect an important aspect of the food-offered-to-idols problem. Some may have claimed the right to eat food offered to idols because they were "knowledgeable."

Paul responds to this bold assertion by affirming that knowledge is not limited to any single group among the Christians of Corinth. "Knowledge" *(gnōsis)* is not the exclusive possession of one or another group: all *(pantes)* the Corinthian Christians have knowledge. For Paul the real issue is not who has knowledge; it is the kind of knowledge one has. There is "knowledge" and then there is knowledge. In 8:1-3 Paul brings four critical remarks to bear on the Corinthians' claim to be "knowledgeable" with regard to food offered to idols. The first is that not some but all Christians have knowledge (v. 1b). The second is that knowledge is to be distinguished from love (v. 1c). The third is that those who think that they know something, the know-it-alls, really do not have a correct kind of knowledge (v. 2). The fourth is that knowledge of God is reciprocal and this seems to be something the Corinthians have not understood (v. 3).

Affirming that there is knowledge that is not as it ought to be (v. 2), Paul indicates that he is about to correct the sloganeers' understanding of "knowledge." By correcting their language and affirming that knowledge is the possession of all within the community Paul offers a pointed corrective to the stand of the exclusivist Corinthians. He offers the language of love to counter the language of knowledge. In 12:1-3 Paul takes a similar tack. In ch. 12 the problematic situation to which Paul offers his response is that of spiritual gifts (*pneumatika*, v. 1). Paul will modify the language by introducing the terminology of gifts (*charismata*, v. 4). Having done so he affirms that the possession of such gifts is not the exclusive province of a limited number of Corinthians. All enjoy the spiritual gifts the Spirit imparts to them (see 1 Cor 12:6, 7, 11). A similar kind of argumentation is employed in 8:1 as Paul both corrects the language of the troublemakers at Corinth and affirms that their vaunted possession is the possession of everyone within the community.

Knowledge Puffs Up. The distinction between two kinds of knowledge is summed up in the phrase "knowledge puffs up, but love builds up." The phrase incorporates three motifs that echo throughout the letter, "knowledge," "puffing up," and "love." Paul's terse phrase is arguably one of the least controversial—and surely one of the most quotable— affirmations in the entire letter. Paul's words may appear to imply a distinction between knowledge and love, as if there were an antithetical relationship between the two, but it is preferable to read them as if they describe two kinds of knowledge, a purely intellectual knowledge and one that is accompanied by—and proceeds from—love.

Paul is not opposed to knowledge. Having knowledge is a reason for giving thanks (1:5; cf. Rom 15:14; 2 Cor 8:7). He does, however, contrast a purely Hellenistic notion of knowledge, an intellectual exercise, with a biblical notion of knowledge (*yādaʿ*). The latter is experiential and, in the case of the knowledge of another person or of God, a mutual experience. When Paul writes about love building up he is preparing the way for v. 3, in which he affirms that anyone who loves God will be known by God.

The contrast between experiential knowledge and the knowledge that is not as it ought to be, that is, not accompanied by love, confirms the idea that "we have knowledge" (v. 1) reflects a Corinthian slogan, a sort of rallying-cry of the Corinthian hybrists.

Being Known by God. Paul's understanding of knowledge is deeply rooted in his biblical tradition, complemented by his conviction that Jesus is Lord. Knowledge of God is experiential and salvific. The knowledge of God implies an experience of God in which the one who truly knows experiences God and is experienced (known) by God (v. 3; cf. 13:12). There is some mutuality in the knowledge of God (cf. 14:38; Gal 4:9). To be known by God is to be acknowledged by God. In effect Paul affirms that those who love God are the object of divine election.

Theocentric love, people's love for God, is not often a focal point of Paul's reflection and exhortation on love. It is, nonetheless, a commonplace of his Jewish tradition and is reflected in the scriptural citation in 2:9 as well as in Rom 8:28. Paul introduces the traditional motif of humans' love for God in 8:3 to counter the Corinthians' claim with respect to their knowledge of God. For Paul what is important is that the Corinthians love God and that they be known by God.

Effectively the apostle has turned the tables on the Corinthians, and he has done so twice. He has turned the discussion on human conduct to a discussion on love. He has turned the discussion on knowledge to a matter of being known rather than knowing.

NOTES

1. *Concerning food that has been offered to idols:* "Food offered to idols" (*eidōlothytōn*), unattested before 1 Corinthians, may have been a derisive neologism coined in Pauline circles. Because of the term's etymology (from *thyō*, "to slaughter"), Paul's strongly rhetorical "I will not eat meat" (8:13), and later first-century usage many commentators assume that the specific topic was eating meat that had been offered to idols. The term may, however, have been used in the general sense of food offered to idols. Such an interpretation would be consistent with the use of a generic word for "food" (*brōseōs*) in v. 4, there in apposition to "food offered to idols." Literature of the period provides clear evidence that not only meat but also grain was sometimes offered to deities.

   we know that we all have knowledge: There may be a touch of irony in Paul's statement, "we know that we all know," with its use of two different expressions meaning "to know" (*oidamen, gnōsin echomen*). "We know that" (*oidamen hoti*) suggests some common experience shared by Paul and those to whom he was writing (cf. BAGD 556.1e). Many authors (Archibald Robertson and Alfred Plummer, E. B. Allo, C. K. Barrett, John Calvin, etc.) think that "we all have knowledge" is one of the slogans voiced by those who were disturbing the unity of the Corinthian community. Voiced by an elitist group in Corinth, the slogan suggests that knowledge was the esoteric possession of a few privileged individuals, members of an in-group all of whom had knowledge. The pervasive dualism of a gnosticizing understanding of knowledge (*gnōsis*) would have contributed to such exclusivism.

That Paul's letter might have reflected the language used by the trouble-makers does not necessarily imply that he was quoting the slogans verbatim. Those who were listening to the reading of the letter would nonetheless have caught the allusion to the popular saying. They would also have noted Paul's use of an emphatic—and corrective—"all" *(pantes)*. Knowledge is not the precious possession of a few privileged individuals.

Knowledge puffs up, but love builds up: Using a rhetorical contrast Paul introduces a second critique of the know-it-alls' claim to have knowledge. Knowledge is contrasted with love; puffing up *(physioi,* see "Interpretation" on 4:6) with building up. The kind of knowledge to which some Corinthians lay claim gives them swelled heads, as it were. Paul's contrast puts the emphasis on love (see ch. 13). This is, however, the only Pauline text explicitly linking "love" *(agapē)* and "building up." For Paul "to build up" *(oikodomeō)* and the related noun, "building" *(oikodomē),* have an ecclesial sense. See the use of the verb in 8:1, 10; 10:23; 14:4, 17; cf. Rom 15:20; Gal 2:18; and of the noun in 3:9; 14:3, 5, 12, 26; cf. Rom 14:19; 15:2; 2 Cor 5:1; 10:8; 12:19; 13:10).

2. *If anyone thinks that he or she knows something, that one does not yet know as he or she ought to know:* The conditional sentence (cf. 3:17; 14:37) offers a third critique of those who claim knowledge. The "knowledgeable" may think that they know something, but they really do not know properly. The manuscript tradition shows much variation with regard to the phraseology, but for the most part the variants have to do with the Greek particles and do not substantially change the meaning of the text.

3. *If someone loves God, that person is known by God:* The text of v. 3 appears in virtually the same form in almost all of the ancient manuscripts, with the exception of the oldest manuscript, 𝔓⁴⁶, which offers a simple version of the text, omitting the direct object of the conditional clause and the qualifying prepositional phrase of the apodosis. Elements of this shorter reading are found in various Fathers (Tertullian, Ambrosiaster, Clement, Ephraem), but no patristic witness has the text just as it appears in 𝔓⁴⁶, thereby making the papyrus the sole consistent witness to the shorter reading. The overwhelming weight of the manuscript tradition militates against the authenticity of its more fluid reading.

FOR REFERENCE AND FURTHER STUDY

Horsley, Richard A. "Gnosis in Corinth: I Corinthians 8.1-6," *NTS* 27 (1980) 125–127.

Smit, Joop F. M. "1 Cor 8,1-6: A Rhetorical *Partitio.* A Contribution to the Coherence of 1 Cor 8,1–11,1," *CorC* 577–591.

Wischmeyer, Oda. "*Theon agapan* bei Paulus. Eine traditionsgeschichtliche Miszelle," *ZNW* 78 (1987) 141–144.

Witherington, Ben III. "Not So Idle Thoughts about *eidōlothytōn,*" *TynB* 44 (1993) 237–294.

2. *The Monotheistic Confession of Faith* (8:4-6)

4. Concerning, then, eating food that has been offered to idols, we know that "in the world an idol is nothing" and that "there is no God but one." 5. For if it is true that there are so-called gods in heaven or on earth— even as there are many gods and many lords—6. yet for us there is one God, the Father, from whom are all things and for whom we exist, and there is one Lord, Jesus Christ, by whom all things exist and by whom we exist.

Interpretation

With v. 4 Paul returns to the subject at hand, indicating that he will deal with the eating of food, specifically food that has been offered to idols. In his consideration of the topic Paul begins with what is known, not treating knowledge generically as he did in vv. 1-3 but citing two bits of knowledge that are pertinent to the topic at hand: Idols do not really exist; there is only one God.

Paul's argument is hardly a syllogism in the strict sense of the term, but it is a form of reasoning akin to the syllogism. Verse 4 represents the major premise, the axiom; v. 5 the minor, Paul's explanation; and v. 6 the conclusion. Just as the earlier argument (vv. 1-3) had ended on a note with soteriological implications (election by God), so the argument of vv. 4-6 concludes on a soteriological note, the eschatological role of Jesus as Lord. Verse 6 sums up the theological basis of Paul's entire argument: there is only one God. The traditional confession of faith is, however, to be understood within a soteriological perspective. Within a hymnic structure Paul declares the theological perspective against which the whole issue of eating food that had been offered to idols must be considered. The framework is that God is one but Jesus alone is Lord. The lordship of Jesus is the dominant referent in the determination of what is appropriate conduct for Christians.

The Slogans. Paul's language is not so much that of reasoned reflection as of popular slogans. The first of these, "idols do not exist in this world," has a polemical thrust. The second, "there is no God but one," has almost the aura of a confession of faith. The ideology of these slogans is similar to that found in some currents of Hellenistic Judaism (e.g., Philo and the book of Wisdom). The affirmation that idols do not have any real existence contrasts with the proclamation of the one God who does have existence. This kind of polemical contrast reflects Paul's biblical background (see Psalm 115) and echoes the apologetic discourse of Hellenistic Judaism (e.g., Acts 17:24-29). Paul's own polemical attitude toward both the worship of idols and the divinization of creatures is similar to that found in the book of Wisdom, whose author takes to task both those who assume that natural elements are god (Wis 13:1-9) and those who construct idols (Wis 13:10-19). Wisdom 13 was known to Paul and used by him in Rom 1:21-23.

Some Corinthians may have deliberately misconstrued or simply misunderstood Paul's teaching. With some sort of naïve simplicity they found grounds for the affirmation of the nonexistence of idols in a Jewish monotheistic confession of faith (Deut 6:4; cf. Rom 3:30; Eph 4:5; 1 Tim 2:5) that was used polemically as a slogan. This naïve assumption led to a blasé attitude toward the eating of food offered to idols and an apparent disdain for those who did not eat this food. Paul confronts this simplistic attitude in the following verses with both a reality factor (v. 5) and the Christian confession of faith (v. 6).

So-called Gods and Many Lords. Having affirmed the existence of the one God and the nonexistence of idols in the real world Paul offers a reflection on the real state of affairs in Corinth (note the explanatory *gar* ["for"] at the beginning of v. 5). He appeals to the Corinthians' own experience. In the cosmopolitan world in which they lived—otherwise the issue of eating food that had been offered to idols would not have arisen in the first place!—a variety of artifacts, temples, statues, monumental and numismatic inscriptions provided tangible evidence of the popular conviction that there were indeed various gods and lords. A second-century description of Corinth mentions Chronos, Poseidon, the Sun, the Calm, the Sea, Aphrodite, Artemis, Isis, Dionysius, a tree (to be worshiped equally with the god), Fortune, Apollo, Hermes, Zeus, Asklepios, Bunaea, and many other deities (Pausanias, *Description of Greece* 1–5). Sanctuaries in honor of these deities and images of several of them had been erected on the Corinthian agora prior to Pausanias' visit ca. 165 C.E.

Paul speaks about "so-called gods" and "many gods and many lords." His language is judgmental ("so-called," *legomenoi*) and comprehensive ("in heaven or on earth," *eite en ouranǭ eite epi gēs*). He makes a distinction between the "so-called gods" existing either in heaven or on earth and the "many gods and many lords." The former are likely to have been natural realities such as the stars, sun, fire, sea, or wind, which various segments of the population worshiped as gods (cf. Wis 13:2-3). The latter would have been divinized humans, most probably emperors such as Julius Caesar and Caesar Augustus, whose apotheosis was acknowledged on the coinage and statuary of Paul's day. Various Fathers of the Church distinguished the gods in heaven from the gods on earth. Chrysostom and Theophylact consider the gods in heaven to be the sun, moon, and stars, the gods on earth to be demons and divinized humans. For Theodoret the heavenly deities are Zeus, Apollo, Hera, and Athena, while the earthly deities are Streams, Rivers, the Nymphs, Heracles, Dionysus, Asklepios, and so forth.

It is difficult to determine exactly what it is that Paul is referring to when he makes reference to "many gods and many lords" *(theoi polloi kai kyrioi polloi)*. The phrase is crucial to his rhetorical argument. "Many gods and many lords" creates a contrast with the "one God and one Lord" of the Christian confession to follow (v. 6). Are these "many gods" the so-called "gods in heaven" and the "many lords" the so-called "gods on earth"? Or does "many gods and many lords" refer comprehensively to the "so-called gods"?

One God, One Lord. In contrast with the so-called gods recognized by elements of the Corinthian population, their many gods and lords, Paul places the one God of his biblical tradition (cf. Deut 6:4). The contrast functions on two levels. There is a contrast between the anonymous persons to whom allusion is made in Paul's "so-called" of v. 5 and the "us" of v. 6. There is also a contrast between the many gods and many lords of popular perception and the one God and one Lord of the Christian confession.

The hymnic confession of faith in v. 6 is an expansion on the commonly held conviction that there is but one God (v. 4). For Christians there is but one God who is not only Father but also the origin and end of all creation. The affirmation that God was the creator of all things, a commonplace in Hellenistic Judaism, served a polemical purpose insofar as it placed natural elements in proper perspective, in a position subordinate to the God who had created them (Wis 13:3; Rom 1:20, 25). Paul's mention of God the Father evokes a mention of Jesus Christ the Lord (cf. 1:3). Paul's understanding of God was affected by his understanding of Christ. In his letters he often complements his "god-talk," especially when God is identified as Father, with language that speaks of Christ. The title "Lord," used in the biblical tradition of God himself, suggests Jesus' participation in the work of God. In the passage at hand Paul affirms that Jesus has a role in the protological and eschatological work of God. In both Jesus is God's agent.

Larry Hurtado sees in this hymnic passage an expression of the early Christian mutation of the Jewish monotheistic tradition (see Hurtado, *One God, One Lord* 97–99). Fully committed to Jewish monotheism— hence the allusion to the *Shema* in v. 6a—early Christians associated Jesus, in an exclusive manner, with the one God of the Jewish tradition. Jesus is God's agent in the work of eschatological salvation but also in the work of creation. Because Jesus is seen as the exclusive agent of God Christians hold him in an exalted position, second only to that of God. They attribute to him titles and other qualifications that are similar to those used of God. Of these the title "Lord" is the most striking since this title was used of God himself in the Greek Bible (see above, p. 96). At the root of the present usage, suggests Hurtado, is an older Jewish category of divine agency in which the patriarchs and the angels functioned as the agents of God in fulfilling the divine will.

Among exegetes there is some discussion as to whether the hymnic construction is the work of Paul or whether it is a pre-Pauline tradition appropriated by the apostle. The hymn says much that is not otherwise attested in the Pauline letters, specifically with regard to the mediating role of Christ in creation and to the use of "Father" as a designation of the Creator. The formula seems, in any case, not to have been composed in the course of his writing this letter. It introduces motifs that exceed Paul's rhetorical exigence.

God the Father. In the biblical tradition God is frequently described as Father. God's paternity was revealed in his redemption of Israel (see Isa 63:16, etc.). Various significant figures in the history of Israel, angels, and Israel itself (Hos 11:1) are described as God's sons. Fatherhood is, moreover, an appropriate metaphor for God insofar as God is the creator (Isa 64:8, etc.). A tendency toward universality in the use of the paternal metaphor with reference to God as creator is evident in the biblical tradition (see Deut 32:6; Isa 64:8; etc.). Jewish texts of the second and first centuries B.C.E. commonly describe God as Father. See Wis 14:3; cf. 2:16; Jdt 9:12; Tob 13:4; Sir 23:1, 4; 51:10; cf. 4:10; 3 Macc 2:21; 5:7; 6:3, 8; cf. 7:6; 4 Ezra 1:28-29 (somewhat later than the others).

Jewish authors of the first century C.E. are heir to this tradition. Philo writes about God as father in a variety of ways, particularly in respect to creation. There is "one Father," he writes, "the maker of the universe" (*Decalogue* 64; cf. *Creation* 84, 89; *Special Laws* 1.96; 2.6, 30-31; 3.189; *Drunkenness* 81). Philo goes so far as to describe the universe *(to pan)* as the Father's son (*Special Laws* 1.96; *Drunkenness* 30; *Life of Moses* 2.134). Josephus identifies God as "the Father and origin of all things" (*Ant.* 7.380). Paul, too, writes about God as Father in a variety of ways. Only in 1 Cor 8:6, however, does Paul describe God as Father with creation as his point of reference.

Paternity is, nevertheless, the most frequently mentioned attribute of God in the Pauline correspondence. Paul calls to mind the oracular utterance of 2 Sam 7:14, "I will be a father to him, and he shall be a son to me," as he writes in 2 Cor 6:18 "I will be your father, and you shall be my sons and daughters, says the Lord Almighty." Indeed, the attribution of fatherhood to God is so commonplace in Paul's writings that H. J. Holtzmann maintained that Paul had but a single concept of God, namely that of God-Father (see his *Lehrbuch der neutestamentlichen Theologie* [2nd. ed. Tübingen: Mohr, 1911] 2:103). Paul typically identifies God as father in the salutations of his letters: "God our Father and the Lord Jesus Christ"

(1:3; Rom 1:7; 2 Cor 1:2; Gal 1:3; Phil 1:2; Phlm 3). He writes about "our God and Father" (Gal 1:4; Phil 4:20; 1 Thess 1:3; 3:11, 13), "God the Father" (1 Cor 8:6; 15:24), and simply "the Father" (Rom 6:4). The "Abba, Father" invocation of Rom 8:15 and Gal 4:6 recalls the *abba* prayer of Jesus and the prayer of early Aramaic-speaking Christians. The description of God as father calls attention to God's children. Father and child are correlative terms, as the oracular formula cited by Paul in 2 Cor 6:18 clearly indicates. The fatherhood of God is evoked in those Pauline passages that speak of the children of God (Rom 8:14-15; 9:26 [citing Hos 1:10]; 2 Cor 6:18; Gal 3:26).

Paul's mention of "Father" often calls for a mention of Jesus. This is the case not only in 1 Cor 8:6 but also in the opening greeting of each of the authentic letters with the exception of 1 Thessalonians. The first of Paul's extant letters has a shorter salutation, the simple "grace to you and peace" (1 Thess 1:1). The epistolary opening of the first letter nonetheless links the paternity of God with Jesus. Paul describes the assembly of the Thessalonians as being "in God the Father and the Lord Jesus Christ" (1 Thess 1:1).

In not a few instances Paul specifically associates the paternity of God with the lordship of Jesus. God's fatherhood implies that Jesus is Lord. The motif is found in Paul's customary epistolary salutation, but it is echoed in many other passages of his correspondence. In Rom 15:6 and 2 Cor 1:3 appears a formulaic "God and Father of our Lord Jesus Christ." The conclusion of the christological hymn in Phil 2:6-11 closely links the lordship of Jesus and the fatherhood of God: "Jesus Christ is Lord, to the glory of God the Father" (Phil 2:11). Jesus' lordship is directed to the glory of God the Father. It leads to the praise of God as Father. "It actually," writes P. T. O'Brien, "reveals him as Father, in particular as the Father of Christ" (*The Epistle to the Philippians: A Commentary on the Greek Text.* NIGTC [Grand Rapids: Eerdmans, 1991] 251). In Paul's writings the christological title of Lord is principally associated with Jesus insofar as he has been raised by the Father. It is also associated with his role at the parousia. Each of these correlative realities reveals God as Father.

A wish prayer in 1 Thess 3:11-13 closely links the action of Jesus and the Father—it is in fact a single action (note the verb *kateuthynai*, "to direct," in the singular)—and places both the lordship of Jesus and the fatherhood of God in an eschatological context: "Now may our God and Father himself and our Lord Jesus direct our way to you. . . . And may he so strengthen your hearts in holiness that you may be blameless before our God and Father at the coming of our Lord Jesus with all his saints." Earlier, in the letter to the Thessalonians, Paul had identified Jesus as Son in a passage that makes reference to both the resurrection and the eschaton (1 Thess 1:10). The reality of Jesus as Son obviously implies the reality of

God as Father. The confessional material in the extended greeting of the letter to the Romans also links the sonship of Jesus with his resurrection (Rom 1:4). In the opening verse of his letter to the Galatians Paul writes about his own commission as an apostle "through Jesus Christ and God the Father" (Gal 1:1), but he immediately identifies the Father as the one who raised Jesus from the dead.

The resurrection of Jesus is the inauguration of the eschatological sequence and the revelation of God as Father, a revelation of God's paternity that is brought to completion in the eschaton. The hymnic confession of 1 Cor 8:6 alludes to the eschatological revelation of the paternity of God and its relationship to the lordship of Jesus. The midrashic use of Pss 8:7 and 110:1 in 1 Cor 15:20-28 provides Paul with an opportunity to focus on the eschaton. The passage highlights the relationship between God the Father and Jesus as the eschatological Lord, but it does not exploit the *Kyrios* title.

NOTES

4. *Concerning, then, eating food that has been offered to idols:* After his almost parenthetical remarks on the larger issue of knowledge Paul returns to the matter of eating food that has been offered to idols *(tēs brōseōs tōn eidōlothytōn)* with a resumptive *oun,* "then." In his earlier identification of the topic under consideration Paul had indicated that it was food offered to idols *(tōn eidōlothytōn);* now he specifies that the issue is eating *(tēs brōseōs)* food that has been offered. In fact there are two issues, the cognitive issue of what one thinks about food offered to idols and the behavioral issue of how one acts as a result of one's knowledge. Paul's resumptive identification of the issue at hand moves the discussion to the behavioral plane. "Eating" *(brōsis)* is hapax in 1 Corinthians (cf. Rom 14:17; 2 Cor 9:10). Verse 13 seems to suggest that the food offered to idols under discussion was, in fact, meat.

   we know: The knowledge of the Corinthians is a major issue in 1 Corinthians. Paul frequently challenges the Corinthians with a rhetorical "do you not know?" *(ouk oidate hoti;* see 3:16, etc.). Only in 8:1 and 8:4 does he say "we know" *(oidamen).* At first sight v. 4 seems to take up the formulation of v. 1. Paul, however, offers a correction to the thought of the Corinthians. "We know," said they, "that all have knowledge." What we (really) know, says Paul, is "that an idol in the world is nothing and that there is no God but one." The verb in the first person plural establishes a bond between Paul and his addressees, but Paul moves the discussion from the topic of idols to the reality of the one God.

   that "in the world an idol is nothing" and that "there is no God but one": The knowledge shared by Paul and the Corinthians can be summed up in these two slogans. Since Paul has appealed to what they know, the slogans were probably familiar to the members of the Corinthian community. From the time of C.F.G. Heinrici (1887) commentators have echoed the patristic view that the first slogan is a quotation from the Corinthians' letter to Paul (see Chrysostom, *On the First Epistle to the Corinthians, Homily* 20.2; *PG* 61, 162-163; Theodoret, *Interpretatio* 214; *PG* 82, 288). They opine that "no idol in the world" is one of the liberating slogans bandied about in Corinth. Support for this understanding of the text is found in Paul's use of the formulaic "that" *(hoti)*, followed by "and that" *(kai hoti;* cf. 15:3-5a).

Some authors (including, e.g., Johannes Weiss) are of the opinion that the second slogan was composed on the model of the first. In Greek the parallel slogans are characterized by paronomasia, *hoti ouden . . . hoti oudeis.* Neither slogan has a verb. Literally translated, Paul's words are "that no idol in the world and that no God but one." Given the parallelism between the phrases it is most likely that the verb to be understood is the verb "to be" *(einai),* used not as a copulative but as an affirmation of existence. The second slogan echoes the *Shema,* the confession of faith, with its proclamation of the uniqueness of the Lord God of Israel (cf. Deut 6:4), uttered three times a day by devout Jews.

Of itself the term "idol" *(eidōlon)* simply denotes an image, even an image in one's imagination. In Jewish and Christian literature, however, the term was specifically used of physical representations of deities, especially those designated for cultic use. This is the first mention of an idol in 1 Corinthians. The *eidōlo-* word group provides a common refrain in 1 Corinthians 8–10: idol *(eidōlon)* in 8:4, 7; 10:19; food offered to idols *(eidōlothytos)* in 8:1, 4, 7, 10; 10:19; idolatry *(eidōlolatria)* in 10:14; idolator *(eidōlolatrēs)* in 10:7; temple of an idol *(eidōlion)* in 8:10.

5. *For if it is true that there are so-called gods in heaven or on earth:* Having affirmed that idols do not really exist, Paul turns his attention to the perception of deity. He argues that some humans recognize as god either the powers of nature or powerful human beings (divinized emperors, etc.). His use of "so-called" *(legomenoi)* is derogatory. Similar usage of "so-called" is found in Xenophon. Theodoret held that vv. 5-6 are Paul's expansion on the argument of the Corinthians of which a summary is found in v. 4.

even as there are many gods and many lords: Paul's aside, a concessive (cf. BDF 454.2), "even as there are many gods and many lords," confronts the Corinthians' naïve proclamation of the reality of idols (v. 4b). The summarizing aside is important for Paul's rhetorical argument. It sets up a contrast with the one God and one Lord of the Christian confession of faith (v. 6).

6. *yet for us there is one God, the Father, from whom are all things and for whom we exist:* The popular perception of the reality of many gods and lords is countered "for us" in a Christian hymn (note the parallelism and the absence of any verb). Paul's use of the pronoun "we," echoed in each of the hymn's two stichs, provides a strong experiential reference for his rhetoric. The hymn provides the core content of what "we" really know (see vv. 1b, 4b). It proclaims a monotheistic faith (cf. Philo, *Special Laws* 1.208-209; Josephus, *Ant.* 4.201; *Ap.* 2.167; Acts 17:24-28) from the Christian standpoint that God is Father and Jesus is Lord (cf. Eph 4:5-6; 1 Tim 2:5-6). In contrast to the many gods and

many lords recognized by the Corinthian populace there is but one God and one Lord. Paul's protology implies an eschatology; understanding the first times implies an understanding of the final times (cf. 15:45-50). His understanding of God includes a christological element, a notion of creation, and an inkling of salvation.

and there is one Lord, Jesus Christ, by whom all things exist and by whom we exist: As did the first stich, the second stich of the hymn speaks of all things *(panta)* and of human beings *(hēmeis).* As is his custom Paul twice uses the preposition "by" *(dia,* 26x in the extant correspondence) to speak of the intermediary role of Christ. In talking about God Paul had used the preposition "from" *(ex)* in reference to creation and the preposition "for" *(eis)* in reference to human finality. Both of these prepositions appear in the four-part doxology of Rom 11:36 with its stress on the uniqueness of God. In 1 Cor 8:6 Paul's emphasis lies on the uniqueness of God and of his Christ. Notwithstanding Neil Richardson's arguments (see *Paul's Language* 297), it is unnecessary to take the "all things" of the second stich as referring exclusively to God's salvific work through Christ. "One Lord, Jesus Christ, by whom all things exist and by whom we exist" is a formula in which, as Bultmann (*Theology of the New Testament* 1.132) noted, "the cosmological and soteriological roles of Christ are combined."

Verse 6 is the only passage in the extant letters in which Paul clearly attributes a mediating function in creation to Christ. It is, moreover, the oldest extant literary expression of the conviction that Christ, perhaps as divine wisdom (see Prov 3:19; 8:30; Wis 7:22; 9:2-4; cf. 1 Cor 1:30), has participated in the work of creation. As such the text seems to presuppose the preexistence of Christ and in this respect is similar to a small number of other New Testament texts, especially Col 1:15-20 and Heb 1:3. The idea of Christ's preexistence and his role in creation may depend on a model according to which eschatology and protology parallel one another. It is in any case certain that Paul understood the final times to be a new creation (see 1 Corinthians 15) and that Christ had a significant role to play in the new creation (see 2 Cor 5:17; Gal 6:15).

Gregory of Nyssa and a few relatively late Greek manuscripts (55, 72, etc.) have appended a third stich to Paul's two-part hymn. This third stich speaks of the Spirit, "and one Holy Spirit, in *(en)* whom all things exist and in whom we exist." This is clearly an addition, a Trinitarian "corrective" to the earlier tradition.

FOR REFERENCE AND FURTHER STUDY

Davis, Carl J. *The Name and Way of the Lord: Old Testament Themes, New Testament Christology.* JSNT.S 129. Sheffield: Sheffield Academic Press, 1996, 141–155.

DeLacey, D. R. "'One Lord' in Pauline Christology" in Harold H. Rowdon, ed., *Christ the Lord: Studies in Christology Presented to Donald Guthrie.* Leicester and Downers Grove: Inter-Varsity, 1982, 191–203.

Denaux, Adelbert. "Theology and Christology in 1 Cor 8,4-6. A Contextual-Redactional Reading," *CorC* 593–606.

Hurtado, Larry W. *One God, One Lord: Early Christian Devotion and Ancient Jewish Monotheism.* Philadelphia: Fortress, 1988.

Murphy-O'Connor, Jerome. "1 Cor VIII.6: Cosmology or Soteriology?" *RB* 85 (1978) 253–267.

Richardson, Neil. *Paul's Language about God.* JSNT.S 99. Sheffield: Sheffield Academic Press, 1994, 296–304.

3. *Eating and Freedom* (8:7-13)

7. There is not, however, knowledge in everyone. Some who have been accustomed to idols up until now eat as of food offered to idols, and their consciousness, being weak, is defiled. 8. But food will not put us in the presence of God. We are not inferior if we do not eat, nor are we superior if we eat. 9. Watch out lest this very right of yours become a stumbling block for the weak. 10. For if someone sees you, a knowledgeable person, reclining in the temple of an idol, will not that person's consciousness, being weak, be encouraged to eat food offered to idols? 11. So by reason of your knowledge the weak person is destroyed—a brother or sister for whose sake Christ has died. 12. Sinning thus against your brothers and sisters and wounding their weak consciousness you sin against Christ. 13. Therefore if food causes my brother or sister to stumble I will not eat meat until the age (to come), so that I do not cause my brother or sister to stumble.

INTERPRETATION

Having affirmed the uniqueness of God within a christological and soteriological perspective and having acknowledged that nonetheless there are "gods" and "lords" in the real world of the Corinthians' everyday experience, Paul begins to focus on the topic at hand with some practical suggestions. His concern is that someone with a weak consciousness might be led into idolatry as a result of the blasé attitude of those who are convinced that idols are unreal.

His words are addressed to those who claim that everyone is "in the know" (v. 1). Paul's first rejoinder (v. 7) is an affirmation that the claim is simply not true, as they themselves should realize. Within the community there are people who are not knowledgeable. These are those whose consciousness, that is, their self-awareness, is weak and delicate. Most likely the knowledgeable folks themselves had characterized these members of the community as weak. Paul's words echo the demeaning jargon used by those who made a claim to the possession of knowledge.

Paul's second rejoinder (v. 8) serves to confront the haughtiness of those in the know. He reminds them that the eating of food offered to idols does not assure them of access to God. Eating food is morally neutral: it does not improve one's relationship with God nor is it to be construed as some sort of dramatic gesture prophetically proclaiming that there is but one God and one Lord. Eating food that has been offered to idols creates no warrant for a claim to superiority. Conversely, it provides no excuse for considering others inferior.

Paul's third remark (vv. 9-13) is a minatory exhortation, a warning addressed to those "knowledgeable" persons who cause others to fall. These others appear to be recent converts from paganism. Until just before the time of Paul's letter they had been accustomed to participation in idol worship. So inured, they would continue to be inclined to think that the eating of food that had been offered to idols was participation in the worship of idols.

The Idol's Temple. For the first and only time in his letter Paul mentions a temple of an idol in v. 10. Archaeological excavations have unearthed the remains of the temple of Asklepios, one among the many temples of Hellenistic Corinth (see James Wiseman, "Corinth & Rome I" 487–489). Originally constructed in the fourth century B.C.E., it was destroyed during the sack of the city (146 B.C.E.) and restored during the period of Roman colonization. Three dining rooms, in which at least some cooking was done, were situated on the eastern side of the temple courtyard. The presence of seven small tables allowed for the placement of several couches so that eleven persons could recline "at table" during a meal. The temple's dining facilities were used for meals of religious associations and for meals with some religious overtones such as those offered to celebrate births, marriages, and cures (the trove of many ex-votos attests to the number of such cures associated with the worship of Asklepios). Occasionally the dining facilities were used for merely social events. The god himself was specifically mentioned in some formal invitations that have been found. For example, "Chaeremon asks you to dine in the room of the Serapheion [= the temple of Asklepios] at a banquet of the Lord Serapis tomorrow the 15th from the ninth hour" (*P. Oxyrhynchus* 110).

Remains of the sanctuary of Demeter and Kore on the ancient road to Acrocorinth, the fortified acropolis above Corinth, have also been found. At least forty dining rooms existed within the precincts of the sanctuary. The dining rooms were located on the lowest level, close to the entrance. They were not, however, restored during the Roman period.

A Warning. The presence of Corinthian Christians at social events such as those that took place in the temple of Asklepios created a situation in which a neophyte Christian could observe a "knowledgeable" Christian eating food that had been offered to idols. The knowledgeable members of the community might well assume that they had a right *(exousia)* to eat in this fashion. Those whom the knowledgeable disdained as being weak might be truly scandalized by their behavior. They might be moved to emulate the example of those who were eating food in the temple precincts. Their previous pagan practices would have led them to assume that this "right behavior" was a matter of eating food that really was offered to idols. For these people to eat food offered to idols was participation in idol worship.

With rights come responsibilities. Should the conduct of Christians "in the know" lead others within the community to participate in what they considered to be idol worship, their conduct would endanger the salvation of those they considered weak. Their very existence as Christians was at risk. Should the knowledgeable act in this fashion, leading one or another of their weak brothers or sisters astray, they would not only offend their siblings but they would also sin against Christ. In effect there is a double offense, that against a member of the Christian family and another against Christ. The one who is destroyed as a result of the disdain of a "knowledgeable" person is someone for whom Christ has died (v. 11). Leading people astray in this fashion is an affront to Christ who died for them.

In vv. 11b-13 Paul's rhetoric highlights the kinship language he has used to describe the bonds that ought to exist within the community. Four times he calls the one who might be led astray a "brother or sister" *(adelphos)*. The repeated use of kinship language underscores the egregiousness of the behavior of those in the know. They sin against the members of their own family. Paul's rhetoric also exploits the Christ title of the Christian creed (v. 11). The twofold reference to Christ (vv. 11, 12) evokes the soteriological and eschatological christology of the hymn Paul had cited in v. 6. For Christians there can be no understanding of God that does not include an appreciation of his Christ. "Knowledgeable" Christians, who proclaim that there is one God, sin when they disrupt the redemptive work of Christ. Indeed, they do not follow the example of Christ who gave his life for the sake of the weak.

Paul brings the warning to a conclusion by citing his own conduct as an example for the Corinthians. He tells them (v. 13) that he would willingly forego the eating of meat rather than let one member of the community fall because of his personal behavior. His description of causing another to stumble *(skandalizō)* picks up on the image of the stumbling block *(proskomma, v. 9)* with which Paul had begun his warning to the hybrists. The image forms an *inclusio* around Paul's appeal and provides literary unity for his argument. The conclusion to Paul's argument (v. 13) is a powerful rhetorical utterance. Paul's ethos appeal shifts the argument from the discursive plane to the exemplary. The apostle would rather refrain from eating meat until the eschaton than cause a Christian to stumble and fall into idolatry. The forceful remark of v. 13 preserves the eschatological teleology of the hymn in v. 6.

What is at stake is the salvation of a member of the Christian family. A sibling must not be lost. Paul's dramatic conclusion maintains the thrust of the *ethos* appeal, characteristic of the argument throughout the letter. This rhetorical blast introduces the rhetorical digression that is to come, a long disquisition on Paul's willingness to forego the use of his rights (9:1-27).

NOTES

7. *There is not, however, knowledge in everyone:* Paul's phrase obviously means that not everyone has knowledge. The wording recalls and qualifies what he has stated in his concessive rephrasing of the Corinthians' slogan (v. 1). "Everyone" *(pasin)* reprises the "all" *(pantes)* of v. 1. Although all possess knowledge, not everyone has fully integrated this particular knowledge, the secure knowledge that an idol is really nothing and that there is but one God (v. 4).

Some who have been accustomed to idols up until now eat as of food offered to idols: Paul writes about those who are accustomed (*synētheia,* "custom") to idols. Some manuscripts (D, G, many minuscules and Latin Fathers, as well as an early corrector of ℵ) read the text as if it were about those who were aware *(syneidēsis)* of idols. The relatively rare use of "custom" by Paul and the weight of the manuscript evidence suggest that Paul was indeed writing about those who had practiced idol worship. "As" *(hōs)* serves to stress the quality of what it was that some were eating (cf. BAGD 898.3.1.a). Having been accustomed to eating food offered to idols as part of their cult prior to their becoming Christian, they now eat food as if it were offered to real idols.

and their consciousness, being weak, is defiled: Popular philosophical writings contemporary with Paul presented those who had difficulties in conforming to the demands of the virtuous life as weak. The Stoics in particular considered that such people were prone to false judgments (*SVF* 1.67; 3.177; Plutarch, "Reply to Colotes," *Moralia* 1122C; Cicero, *Tusculan Disputations* 4.15). They are people, says Cicero, who "regard a thing that need not be shunned as though it ought to be shunned" (*Tusculan Disputations* 4.26). Corinthians who prided themselves in their knowledge (8:1) probably caricatured others in the community as weak.

Consciousness (*syneidēsis,* vv. 10b, 12) arises from knowledge (*syn-eidenai*). The term "consciousness" first appeared in the papyri as of 59 C.E. Paul probably took the term over from its use in popular philosophy. As used by Paul it retains its traditional meaning of self-awareness. There is no need to see in Paul's use of the term the modern notion of moral conscience.

Those with a weak consciousness were not in harmony with the knowledgeable. Their old habits had left a residue on their self-awareness such that it was not governed by their present Christian beliefs. Their self-awareness would be defiled (*molynetai*, hapax in Paul) were they to eat food they considered to have been offered to idols.

8. *But food will not put us in the presence of God. We are not inferior if we do not eat, nor are we superior if we eat:* Although the textual apparatus of *GNT*[4] does not indicate any problem with regard to the reading of the Greek text, the manuscript tradition shows evidence of three significantly different readings. The reading adopted by *GNT*[4] is found in the Codex Vaticanus and $\mathfrak{P}^{46}$, while D, F, G, and various patristic witnesses read "neither are we superior if we eat, nor are we inferior if we do not eat." The original reading of Codex Alexandrinus, "neither are we superior if we do not eat, nor are we inferior if we do eat," is supported by Jerome Murphy-O'Connor ("Food and Spiritual Gifts in 1 Cor 8:8"). Murphy-O'Connor argues that 8:8 is a Corinthian slogan. Claiming that food is morally neutral in God's eyes (cf. 6:13), the hybrists would have claimed that food will not bring us before the judgment seat of God. People are not better off for not eating nor are they worse off for eating. On balance the weight of the external evidence ($\mathfrak{P}^{46}$, ℵ, A, B, P, Ψ, etc.) and internal considerations favor the reading adopted in *GNT*[4] (see Joël Delobel, "Textual Criticism and Exegesis: Siamese Twins?" in Barbara Aland and Joël Delobel, eds., *New Testament Textual Criticism, Exegesis and Church History: A Discussion of Methods.* CBET 7 [Kampen: Kok Pharos, 1994] 98–117, especially 104–107). The reading is consistent with an understanding of v. 8 that takes it to be a statement formulated by Paul in the development of his argument.

Verse 8 is part of Paul's argument, but the language is ambiguous. The three verbs have a physical sense; Paul uses them in a figurative sense. Even on a figurative reading of the text the referent is not entirely clear. Is Paul stating that those who do not eat should have no less standing in the community than those who do? Or is he affirming that those who do not eat have no spiritual advantage over those who do and vice versa? Given the reference to God in 8:8a and the fact that Paul generally uses the verb "to be superior" *(perisseuō)* with regard to spiritual goods, the latter would seem to be the case.

9. *Watch out lest this very right of yours become a stumbling block for the weak:* Paul's exhortation urges the Corinthians to be wary lest their "right" (*exousia*, alternatively, "power" or "authority") be exercised in such a way that one or another person stumble (*proskomma*, "stumbling block," hapax in 1 Corinthians; cf. Rom 9:32, 33; 14:13, 20). His words are a warning (*blepete*; cf. 3:10; 10:12; 16:10; comp. 1:26) addressed to those who proclaim that "all things are lawful" (*panta exestin*, 6:12; 10:23). Commentators typically call these people "strong." Calling them strong reflects the language of the letter to the Romans, but it is not the language of the letter to the Corinthians. In Romans 14 Paul treats an issue of food, but the rhetorical situation and the issues in Romans are different from those of 1 Corinthians. Within the compass of the "Jewish question" the issue in Romans is the eating of unclean food (cf. Gal 2:11-14). The "weak" are those who are weak in faith whereas the "strong" (Rom 15:1) are those who are strong in faith. In contrast, "the strong" of 1 Cor 1:26 are those who are socially and politically powerful.

10. *For if someone sees you, a knowledgeable person, reclining in the temple of an idol, will not that person's consciousness, being weak, be encouraged to eat food offered to idols?* With an explanatory *gar* Paul offers an explanation of what he has said. Typically he uses the verb *oikodomeō* in the positive sense of "build up" or "edify"; only here does he use it to suggest a negative example. The knowledgeable person is literally "one who has knowledge," a reference to the self-characterization of some Corinthians (cf. 8:1). It is likely that these used "weak" to deride those without knowledge. Typically Paul uses an adjective to designate the weak *(asthenēs)*; only in vv. 11 and 12 does he use a participial form of the verb "to be weak" *(astheneō)* for this purpose.

The use of the second person singular in the rhetorical question sharpens the thrust of Paul's rhetorical appeal. How is it that the weak might fall? By following the example of those in the know. Those who are weak would be led to idolatry because of the knowledgeable person's indiscriminate eating in temple precincts. They would eat food offered to idols as if it were truly dedicated to one or another idol (cf. 8:7).

11. *So by reason of your knowledge the weak person is destroyed:* The discursive reasoning process continues. In 1:18, 19 Paul used "to destroy" in the sense of the loss of salvation; here the verb is used in the passive, suggesting the punitive action of God (cf. 10:9, 10). This confirms that those who are disdained as weak will, in fact, be lead into idolatry by reason of the haughty example of those who would insist on eating food offered to idols because of their conviction that idols did not truly exist (8:4).

a brother or sister for whose sake Christ has died: Allusion to the creed (cf. 15:3; 1 Thess 5:10) provides a christological focus for Paul's argument. A christological and soteriological perspective was introduced into the discussion in 8:6. Now Paul exploits that perspective to sharpen the scandal of the one who offends a fellow Christian by reason of haughty knowledge. Food may be neutral but the issue at hand must be considered in light of the redemption effected by Christ (cf. Rom 14:15). The destruction of the weak and delicate person is the loss of his or her Christian condition. Their salvation (cf. 8:6) is lost because they have been led to engage in what they considered to be idol worship. Such is the drastic result of the actions of the "knowledgeable" who eat food that had been offered to idols without consideration of the impact of such behavior on others, specifically their fellow Christians.

Paul's use of the preposition *dia* with accusative to express the vicarious character of Christ's death is exceptional. Normally he uses *hyper* with the genitive (cf. 1:13; 15:3; Rom 5:8; 8:32; 14:15, etc.). Christ is cited with the *Christos* title that specifically evokes the memory of his death. The reference to the death of Christ serves an important function in Paul's rhetoric. The example *(paradeigma)* of Christ is offered to the Corinthians. Christ has given his life for the sake of the weak members of the community. How much more should the Corinthians do the same. They should at least forego the eating of meat, to which they were entitled.

12. *Sinning thus against your brothers and sisters and wounding their weak consciousness:* "Weak" *(asthenousan)*, omitted by $\mathfrak{P}^{46}$ and Clement, is broadly attested in

the manuscript tradition (‭א‬, A, B, D, G, K, P, Ψ, etc.). "Injuring their weak consciousness" explains (the *kai* is epexegetical; BDF 442.9) the sin of the knowledgeable. The knowledgeable inflict harm (*typtontes,* hapax in Paul) on the weak by leading them to eat food as if it were dedicated to idols. Such conduct is a violation of sibling love (see Rom 14:15) and a sin. Refraining from sin in this regard is not so much a matter of the knowledgeable changing their own judgments as it is a matter of being sensitive to the plight of the weak.

you sin against Christ: Such behavior is not only a sin against one's brother or sister, it is also an offense against Christ. Indiscriminate conduct justified on the grounds that "all things are lawful" (6:12; 10:23) flies in the face of the death and resurrection of Christ *(Christon).* With this reference to Christ Paul intimates that his understanding of love has a christological/soteriological foundation.

13. *Therefore if food causes my brother or sister to stumble I will not eat meat until the age (to come), so that I do not cause my brother or sister to stumble:* Paul's "therefore" *(dioper)* introduces a powerful rhetorical conclusion to this phase of his argument. Paul's abrupt introduction of his own person into the argument provides a focus against which the following digression (1 Corinthians 9) must be read. The refusal to exercise one's rights for the sake of another is not a limitation of freedom; it is the very foundation of freedom.

For Reference and Further Study

Dawes, Gregory W. "The Danger of Idolatry: First Corinthians 8:7-13," *CBQ* 58 (1996) 82–98.

Gooch, Paul W. "'Conscience' in the New Testament," *NTS* 33 (1987) 244–254.

Murphy-O'Connor, Jerome. "Food and Spiritual Gifts in 1 Cor 8:8," *CBQ* 41 (1979) 292–298.

4. *Apostolic Rights* (9:1-14)

1. Am I not free? Am I not an apostle? Have I not seen Jesus our Lord? Are not you the result of my work in the Lord? 2. If I am not an apostle to others I am certainly at least an apostle to you. For you are the seal of my apostleship in the Lord. 3. To those who question me my defense is this. 4. Don't we have the right to eat and drink? 5. Don't we have the right to take along a Christian wife as do the other apostles, the brothers of the Lord, and Cephas? 6. Or is it only I and Barnabas who do not enjoy the right not to work? 7. Who ever serves as a soldier at his own expense? Who plants the vine and does not eat its fruit? Or who shepherds the flock and does not eat of the milk of the flock? 8. I do not say

this on human authority, do I? Does not the law also say this? 9. Yes, it is written in the Law of Moses, "Do not muzzle the ox that is threshing." It is not oxen who are of concern to God, is it? 10. Doesn't he really speak for our sake? Yes, it is for our sake that it is written that "whoever plows should plow in hope and whoever threshes should have a hope of sharing in the crop." 11. If we sow spiritual things among you, is it too much that we reap material things from you? 12. If others share this right over you, how much more should we? However, we do not use this right; we endure all things in order not to create any obstacle for the gospel of Christ.

13. Do you not know that those who perform sacred works eat things from the temple; those who serve at the altar partake of the altar? 14. Similarly the Lord arranged that those who proclaim the gospel live from the gospel.

INTERPRETATION

Paul introduces his *apologia pro vita sua* (see v. 3) with a series of four rhetorical questions. The technique is that of the Hellenistic diatribe. The rhetorical impact of the questions is increased by their brevity, creating an almost staccato effect as Paul sets forth his questions using alliteration and paronomasia. The negative form of each of the four questions calls for a positive answer on the part of the putative respondent. The rhetorical setting of Paul's dramatic appeal is that of a mock courtroom in which a lawyer pleads for the defense. In this case Paul is acting in his own defense, but it is all a ploy—a rhetorical strategy to make a point.

The series of initial questions serves to identify Paul and his work. Effectively it is a kind of rhetorical *diēgēsis* that Paul uses to formally introduce his "defense," his *apologia,* a term taken from the vocabulary of classical rhetoric where it designates a speech that is given in defense. Its proper locale is the courtroom. The communication that follows upon Paul's opening statement is replete with the kinds of oratorical devices characteristic of a courtroom defense, particularly the plethora of rhetorical questions. These questions are addressed to the Corinthian community, cast in the role of a fictive jury.

Paul's communication is not so much a defense of his apostolate as it is a clever rhetorical ploy that enables him to present his own life conduct in such a way as to serve as an example to the community. Ancient literature, including the Bible, offers several examples of authors' making creative use of a literary form in a situation other than its natural setting *(Sitz im Leben)*. In Isa 14:4-21, for example, a text that has the form of a dirge is used not to mourn the death of someone beloved but to mock and announce the premature death of a foreign king. Paul does something similar in ch. 9. His "defense" is used to encourage the Corinthians to make a judgment with respect to the case at hand, namely the matter of food that had been offered to idols. The rhetorical digression of ch. 9 serves Paul's purpose well as he argues why the knowledgeable members of the Corinthian community should forego their right to eat food offered to idols. One who listens carefully to Paul's defense will surely notice how often the matter of food appears on the lips of the defendant (see the notes on vv. 4, 7, 9, 10, 13).

Paul's Freedom. Christians living in Corinth certainly knew the difference between slavery and freedom. The descendants of the Roman colonists were free. The population of Corinth included some who were free as a result of manumission (see the allusion in 7:22-23). On the other hand perhaps one third of the population lived in slavery (see S. Scott Bartchy, *First Century Slavery* 58). The city, a major commercial center in Paul's day, may also have been a center of slave trade.

In Paul's Hellenistic world political freedom was a two-pronged reality. Freedom *(eleutheria)* was both freedom from and freedom for. Hundreds of inscriptions dealing with the manumission of slaves and dating from 200 B.C.E. to 75 C.E. clearly attest to this double dimension of freedom. As his or her own master a freedman or freedwoman had no need to have his or her activity approved and supported by another. He or she was no longer to be treated like chattel. On the other hand, the freedman or freedwoman was allowed to earn such livelihood as he or she desired. Freed persons were free to move about and to live where they wanted (see W. L. Westermann, "Two Studies in Athenian Manumission," *JNES* 5 [1946] 92–104, especially 92–93).

As a Roman citizen (cf. Acts 25:10-11, 12, 21, 25; 26:32) Paul was a free man. He enjoyed the freedom of movement afforded by his political situation. Indeed, he used this freedom effectively in his apostolate. Paul does not, however, appeal to his status as a Roman citizen and the freedom it entailed in any of his extant letters. In his so-called apology Paul talks about his freedom in terms of his rights (vv. 4, 5, 6, 12, 18; cf. 8:9). In the Hellenistic world the exercise of one's rights was concomitant with freedom. "Freedom" *(eleutheria)* and "right/s" *(exousia)* belong to the same semantic domain. They are almost correlative terms. Paul relates his freedom to his call as an apostle rather than to his status as a Roman citizen.

Paul's Apostolate. With the opening salvo of rhetorical questions, all of which call for a response in the affirmative (vv. 1-2), Paul shows that he grounds the exercise of his freedom in his apostleship. An apostle is a free person, albeit paradoxically so (see vv. 15-18). Paul's vision of the Lord Jesus (cf. 15:8-10) is the foundational warrant for his apostleship and the freedom it entails.

In Paul's vocabulary "apostle" *(apostolos)* denotes a function rather than a title (cf. 9:5). An apostle is someone who has been sent (see note on 1:1). To be an apostle is a matter of being sent on a mission. Hence apostleship always includes, at least implicitly, a reference to those to whom the apostle is sent. In that sense apostleship is community-specific. Paul's mission as he proclaims it in this letter is to the church of God at Corinth (1:1-2).

There can be no doubt that Paul's mission was effective. The community Paul had evangelized is the church of God. The very existence of the community at Corinth is the seal of Paul's apostolate. Paul's mention of the "seal" *(sphragis)* evokes the sphere of legality. So, too, does the mention of his rights *(exousia)*. As an apostle Paul enjoys a certain *exousia*, the rights and authority delegated to him by the one who has sent him. Paul's Lord, the one who sent him, is the Lord Jesus (v. 1).

The Right to Eat. The first rhetorical question in the body of Paul's so-called defense concerns his right to subsistence (v. 3). The question is a not-so-subtle allusion to the issue at hand. Paul speaks about eating and about his rights. The two motifs take up the matters addressed in ch. 8, eating in 8:8 and 10, rights in 8:9. This double motif will dominate the exposition of Paul's self-styled defense.

Paul develops the notion of a right to eat by means of a number of examples, the *paradeigmata* that are so important in Hellenistic rhetoric. The idea of eating is explicit in Paul's references to the vintner and the shepherd (v. 7), and is implicit in his reference to the sustenance of the soldier (v. 7) and in his use of the agricultural imagery of v. 9. The latter recalls the biblical injunction of Deut 25:4 that an ox tethered to a mill should not be muzzled. Muzzling the animal would prevent it from eating as the mill was being turned. In his reference to the sacerdotal caste that habitually eats of the offerings brought for sacrifice (v. 13) Paul takes up the idea of eating in yet another way. By means of these different examples he rehearses the idea of his own right to eat. If, as the Law attests, even an animal has a right to eat, how much more does an apostle have a right to eat? The question is posed not so much to establish the fact that Paul has a right to eat as it is to establish a premise for his argument. He has a right to eat. As he willingly foregoes the exercise of that right (9:12b, 15), so the Corinthians ought to do likewise.

The Rights of an Apostle. Paul's reference to his own rights capitalizes on the idea that some Corinthians have exploited their rights to the detriment of others (8:9); Paul will forego the use of his rights for the gospel's sake. The burden of his defense is that he has willingly foregone the use of his rights (see vv. 5, 6, 12, 18; cf. v. 15), especially his right to be provided for. As an apostle Paul had a right to receive financial support from the community to which he was sent.

Paul's willingness to forego the exercise of this right sets him apart from other evangelists (v. 6) with whom the Corinthians are familiar. Among these Paul generically refers to other apostles—for him a group larger than the twelve disciples of Jesus' Galilean ministry—and the brothers of the Lord. Two of those who preached the gospel are specifically identified, Simon Peter and Joseph Barnabas. In keeping with Paul's customary usage each of these other apostles is identified by his nickname, respectively "Cephas" ("Rock," 1:12; 3:22; 15:5) and "Barnabas" ("Son of Encouragement," cf. Gal 2:1, 9, 13). Peter was well known in the early Christian tradition as someone who was married (see Matt 8:14-15; Mark 1:29-31; Luke 4:38-39). Barnabas was Paul's sometime companion in the apostolate (Gal 2:1, 9, 13; cf. Col 4:10), but he is mentioned only here in 1 Corinthians. It may be that Paul and Barnabas had adopted the practice of supporting themselves as they exercised their apostolate at some point early on in their common missionary ventures.

The practice of exercising his trade not only allowed Paul to support himself during his missionary journeys; it also gave him opportunities for evangelization. Installed in a leatherworker's shop on the agora, Paul had ample opportunity to speak the good news to customers and passersby alike (see 1 Thess 2:9). Along with the synagogue and the home of a sympathizer or believer, the artisan's workshop was a place where Paul could and did proclaim the gospel.

By exercising a trade as he did Paul was following a tradition whereby it was considered most appropriate for rabbis to support themselves (cf. *m. ʾAbot* 2:2; 4:5; *t. Qidd.* 1:11; *b. Qidd.* 29a). To be sure, Paul, who lived in the Hellenistic world, might have chosen to provide for his livelihood in the way that most Hellenistic philosophers did, that is, by securing a patron to take care of their sustenance, by charging students with fees, or by begging, as did some of the philosophers of his day. Other philosophers, particularly among the Stoics and Cynics (e.g., Cleanthes, Dio Chrysostom, Musonius Rufus), chose to be self-supporting. Paul's choice was like that of this latter group and the rabbis.

The practice of his trade provided Paul with independence and an opportunity for preaching, but it was not always easy (4:12; 9:19; 1 Thess 2:9; 2 Cor 11:7). It was a burden he bore for the sake of the gospel. Paul's exercise of a trade to support himself as he evangelized seems to have been exceptional in the early Christian movement. His practice was not always appreciated and may even have merited for Paul the accusation that he had demeaned himself to the level of a slave (1 Cor 9:19).

Paul's Rhetoric. The reference to the other apostles, the brothers of the Lord, Cephas, and Barnabas in the rhetorical questions of vv. 5-6 is an example of the well-known rhetorical technique of *sygkrisis*, comparison. In comparing himself to other apostles Paul follows a pattern he uses on other occasions when he compares other apostles to himself (cf. 15:5-11; Gal 1:18–2:14). He first mentions a situation that seems to imply his own inferiority (v. 4). Then he argues for his parity (vv. 5-6). He concludes with a claim to the superiority of his own ministry, generally on the basis of his "boldness" *(parrhēsia)* in proclaiming the gospel (vv. 10-12). In this particular instance Paul concludes his argument (v. 12) with an appeal *a minore ad majus,* an example of the *qal wa-ḥomer* type of argumentation often used in rabbinic literature.

The use of rhetorical questions is a feature not only of Paul's letter to the Corinthians. It is also characteristic of the Hellenistic diatribe. Paul begins the body of his "defense" with a series of three rhetorical questions (vv. 4-6). The use of triads is a feature of Paul's literary style, seen not only in the composition of 1 Corinthians but in his other letters as well. Paul's predilection for threes is evident in the chiastic pattern of many of his arguments but it is also apparent in the series of three words or phrases that punctuates, with excellent rhetorical effect, so much of his correspondence. The three rhetorical questions of vv. 4-6 highlight three rights whose exercise Paul has willingly sacrificed for the sake of the gospel. These apostolic rights are the right to sustenance and support from the community (v. 4), the right to the companionship of one's wife (v. 5), and the right not to work (v. 6).

Another group of three rhetorical questions (v. 7) introduces three examples that Paul uses to bolster his arguments. The examples cited by Paul are classic: the soldier, the vinedresser, and the shepherd. The use of examples *(paradeigmata)* is a classic feature of Hellenistic rhetoric. Throughout his letter to the Corinthians Paul demonstrates his skill in the judicious use of examples.

A final weapon in Paul's rhetorical arsenal is an argument from authority. Hellenistic rhetors would typically cite philosophers and sages. Paul cites the Jewish Scriptures, which he here describes in somewhat untypical style as the law of Moses. Paul's Scripture is a pastiche of two texts linked with one another by means of the verb "thresh" in accordance with the *gezera shawah* principle of biblical interpretation (see note on 3:19). The first text is Deut 25:4, a principle of agricultural law. To this is joined a saying of unknown origin that may derive from oral *halakah.* Recognition of the uncertain origin of this second "Scripture" (cf. 2:9) underscores the importance that Paul, teacher that he was, attaches to scriptural argumentation. Both passages are cited as what has been written, that is, as Scripture, the preferred source of Paul's arguments from authority.

Paul typically uses Scripture to reflect on his own mission or to provide authentic Christian praxis with a supportive authority. Both of these purposes are satisfied in the argument of vv. 8-10. The argument functions on two levels. On one level Paul wishes to establish that apostolic labors merit due recompense. That pragmatic goal is subordinate to Paul's ultimate purpose, to exhort the Corinthians to forego, as he did, the exercise of their rights *(exousia)* and an otherwise legitimate use of their freedom *(eleutheria)* for the sake of others within the community.

Paul's surface argument reaches a conclusion, albeit somewhat provisional, with a brace of *a fortiori* arguments in the form of rhetorical questions (vv. 11-12a). Paul claims that he and Barnabas had a right to material support from the Corinthians and that they had a right to this support even more so than did some of those to whom the Corinthians had accorded such support, probably those in the community who had succeeded Paul and Barnabas in community leadership.

That Paul's argument, a literary piece in the form of a judicial defense, should employ as many rhetorical devices as it does is hardly surprising. In the rhetorical schools the teaching of judicial rhetoric was more firmly established and better systematized than was the teaching of other forms of rhetoric. The rhetorical skill employed by Paul in 9:1-12a shows him well versed in the communication skills of Hellenistic culture even though he is well rooted in the Jewish and Christian traditions.

Denouement. The final words of Paul's appeal (vv. 12b-14) enjoy something of the character of a rhetorical epilogue, the peroration *(epilogos)*. The appeal summarizes and explicates the argument that had been developed in the barrage of rhetorical questions, sixteen in all. It is set off as a discrete literary and rhetorical unit by the *inclusio,* which features the expression "did not use" (vv. 12b, 15a), with Paul's rights being identified as what he did not use. The purpose of the entire argument had been to demonstrate that he enjoyed various apostolic rights. In his denouement Paul reveals that he has chosen not to exercise those rights. For the sake of the gospel he has not done so. He would place no obstacle in the path of the gospel, let alone his legitimate claims to the free exercise of his rights. With his bold statement the argument from his personal *ethos* is clearly expressed (v. 12b).

The conclusion to Paul's judicial argument introduces yet another rhetorical question (v. 13). Paul uses an example taken from the religious sphere. With a pointed "Don't you know that . . .?" he evokes the experience of the Corinthians. The apostle reminds them that religious functionaries, priests and those who work in the temple customarily are sustained by gifts that are offered in sacrifice. Paul's argument is fairly subtle. He evokes the example *(paradeigma)* of those who perform sacred works and serve at the altar. They earn their food as a result of their religious activity. Paul himself is willing to forego the food that is rightly his as a result of his religious activity (the proclamation of the gospel). In similar fashion the Corinthians ought to forego their right to eat for the

sake of all that the gospel implies, including the salvation of those presumed to be weak.

The final argument in Paul's demonstration is a command of the Lord.
Verse 14 is one of the relatively rare examples of an argument of this type
in the entire Pauline correspondence. The idea that those who proclaim
the gospel should live from the gospel is echoed in Matt 10:10; Luke 10:7;
and 1 Tim 5:18. Despite the fact that the Lord *(Kyrios),* whose authority
continues to reign over the community, has arranged *(dietaxen)* things in
this fashion, Paul remains steadfast in his determination not to exercise
his rights. The Lord's arrangement establishes a right whose exercise
Paul would willingly forego.

NOTES

1. *Am I not free?* Some Western and Byzantine manuscripts (D, F, G, Ψ, the majority of the Byzantine mss., along with the Ambrosiaster and Pelagius) invert
   the first two questions. The reading found in *GNT*[4] is, however, supported by
   some of the oldest and best manuscripts ($\mathfrak{P}^{46}$, ℵ, A, B, P) and is to be preferred.
   This reading places the rhetorical question on freedom in a focal position. The
   question is the defense lawyer's opening gambit. By identifying the issue as
   he does Paul has forged a contextual link with the encompassing passages
   that deal with the responsible use of freedom.

   Am I not an apostle? The obvious answer to Paul's second rhetorical question
   is that he is an apostle. At the very outset of his letter he had identified himself as one "called apostle of Jesus Christ through the will of God" (1:1). His
   status as an apostle grounds his freedom; his apostolate is grounded in his
   having seen the Lord.

   Have I not seen Jesus our Lord? Paul's question recalls the early Christian confessional tradition in which the verb "to see" *(horaō)* in the passive form *(ōphthē,*
   as an intransitive) was used to identify visionary experiences of the risen
   Lord (see 1 Cor 15:5, 6, 7, 8; Luke 24:34). The verb clearly makes reference to
   the event to which Paul alludes in 15:8. Its perfect tense *(heōraka,* "I have
   seen") points to the impact of the vision on Paul, the subject of the vision.

   Some ancient manuscripts and some of the ancient Eastern versions (syr,
   cop, arm, geo) identify the object of Paul's visionary experience by means of
   the full christological designation, "Jesus Christ our Lord." This textual phenomenon may simply be the result of a scribal tendency to multiply the honorific titles of Jesus, but it cannot be excluded that the fuller designation was
   the result of a conscious effort to thwart Gnostic tendencies to separate
   "Jesus" from "the Christ." On the other hand the weight of the manuscript
   evidence strongly favors a simpler "Jesus our Lord," as does the rhetorical
   context. The title identifies Jesus as the one raised by God (cf. Rom 1:4; 10:9;
   Phil 2:11).

That Paul has seen the Lord is what has permanently established him as an apostle. His opening gambit mentions "the Lord" *(Kyrios)* three times. The term evokes someone in authority. In context the term suggests that Paul, although free, has a Lord. Although free, he has a master, the Lord Jesus. What he does, although done willingly, is in conformity with the will of his master. By implication the Corinthians should be responsive to the same Lord Jesus. For Paul the risen Jesus is not *my* Lord; he is *our* Lord.

Are not you the result of my work in the Lord? Although Paul often uses words derived from th˧ root *erg-* ("work") to refer to his and his coworkers' apostolic labors, this is the sole instance in which he refers to the product of his labor as an *ergon,* a work. The implication is that the Corinthian Christian community exists as the church of God because of Paul's apostolic labor among them.

2. *If I am not an apostle to others, I am certainly at least an apostle to you:* Paul's protestation that he is not the universal apostle underscores the reality that he had been sent as an apostle to the Corinthians. He has indeed been sent to them (note the emphatic *ge,* BDF 439.2). It is on this basis (cf. 1:1) that he can make his appeal to them.

For you are the seal of my apostleship in the Lord: Paul occasionally (cf. 1 Thess 2:4) employs official ambassadorial language to describe the preaching of the gospel in his exercise of the apostolate. The reference to the seal (elsewhere in Paul only in Rom 4:11) suggests that Paul is legally mandated. The Corinthians are the proof of his apostolate and stand under that apostolate.

3. *To those who question me, my defense is this:* Paul returns to the use of juridical language, previously employed in 4:1-5, where the verb "to question" *(anakrinō)* had appeared three times (4:3[2x], 4; cf. 2:14, 15; 10:25, 27; 14:24). Paul's "defense" is an *apologia,* a technical term used to describe a juridical defense. The language adopted by Paul suggests an adversarial situation but the evocation of this rhetorical situation would appear to be a stratagem on the part of Paul.

4. *Don't we have the right to eat and drink?* Paul's reference to his own eating constitutes yet another link between his digressive apology and the context to which it relates. The Corinthians' right *(exousia)* to the eating of food is the source of the situation that imperils the salvation of the weak members of the community. The Corinthians' claim to exercise this right is a particular instance of their claim to universal rights. Universal rights are rights that Paul also enjoys *(panta mou exestin,* 6:12). With respect to the advantageous use of rights the issue for Paul is how he exercises the rights that are his. He begins with his right to eat and drink. Given the negative form of Paul's rhetorical question this is a right the Corinthians should acknowledge. When Paul brings the discussion on eating to a close (10:29b-30) a short series of rhetorical questions will again bring to the fore the exemplary nature of Paul's own dining habits. Here, as throughout the letter, Paul presents himself to his correspondents as a paradigm of the kind of conduct he wants them to adopt.

5. *Don't we have the right to take along a Christian wife:* It is likely that Paul is here revindicating the right of the traveling evangelist to be accompanied by a wife, like Aquila and his wife, Prisca, who were Paul's coworkers in the task of evangelization (16:19; cf. Rom 16:3). "A Christian wife" is literally "a sister" *(adelphēn)*. In Hellenistic papyrus letters spouses were customarily called brother or sister. In Christian circles, gathering in homes, the language of brother and sister was commonly used to refer to a fellow Christian. Thus it could be that Paul is referring to a right to be accompanied by a female missionary, but in context this is an unlikely reading of the text. In the Mediterranean world a woman who traveled with a man would enjoy his protection but if she were not his wife she would have been considered a prostitute.

as do the other apostles, the brothers of the Lord: It is impossible to determine with certainty who are the "other apostles and brothers of the Lord" to whom Paul makes reference. Paul, unlike Luke and the other synoptists, does not restrict the use of the term "apostle" to the Twelve. For Paul the nomenclature is functional. The term can aptly be applied not only to Paul and Barnabas, as here, but also to Silvanus and Timothy (1 Thess 2:7), Epaphroditus (Phil 2:25), Andronicus and Junia (the latter apparently a woman; see Rom 16:7). He also writes about all the apostles (15:7), superapostles (2 Cor 11:5), and false apostles (2 Cor 11:13). In 9:5 the anonymous other apostles are compared to Paul; they are "the other" *(hoi loipoi)* apostles. Paul's experience of his own apostolate (1:1) is the norm according to which others may be called apostle.

With his reference to the brothers of the Lord and Cephas, Paul harkens back to the Jerusalem community. The brothers of the Lord *(hoi adelphoi tou Kyriou)* are a well-known group in early Christian tradition. Referenced in the gospels (Matt 12:46-49; 13:55; 28:10; Mark 3:31-34; Luke 8:19-21; John 2:12; 7:3-10; 20:17), their presence continued to be recognized in the church of Jerusalem in the period after Jesus' resurrection (see Acts 1:14). Paul recognizes James, the leader of the church in Jerusalem, as a brother of the Lord (Gal 1:19; cf. 1 Cor 15:7), but he does not otherwise make reference to a group of brothers of the Lord in his extant correspondence.

The negative form of Paul's rhetorical question demands a positive response. Paul's question implies not only that the other apostles and the brothers of the Lord were married but also that they were accompanied by their spouses as they exercised their missionary functions. The reference to wives, as well as the traditional nature of the expression, suggests that *adelphoi* should be rendered in the masculine plural (thus "brothers"), rather than inclusively, "brothers and sisters," the more appropriate translation for *adelphoi* in its other occurrences in 1 Corinthians.

and Cephas: The list of those with whom Paul compares himself in 9:5 is shorter than the comparable list in 15:5-7. The name of Cephas stands out on both lists. That Peter ("Cephas"; cf. 1:12; 3:22; 15:5) was married is attested in the synoptic tradition that tells of Jesus' cure of Peter's mother-in-law (Matt 8:14-15; Mark 1:29-31; Luke 4:38-39). Neither the gospel narratives nor Paul, however, tell us the name of Peter's wife. Later Christian tradition confirms Paul's intimation that Peter's wife was a Christian. Citing a story from

Clement's *Stromata* (7.11.47-50; *PG* 9, 488), Eusebius tells the tale of an encounter between Peter and his wife while she was being led out to martyrdom (*Ecclesiastical History* 3.30.2; *PG* 20, 277).

6. *Or is it only I and Barnabas:* "Barnabas" is a nickname ("son of encouragement") used in Christian circles for a Cypriot Levite whose given name was Joseph (Acts 4:36). He was a leader of the church in Antioch before Paul became a Christian. Luke describes Barnabas as the one who introduced Paul to the leaders of the Christian community in Jerusalem, a community that had been reluctant to welcome this neophyte (Acts 9:27). Together Barnabas and Paul formed a missionary team and were delegated by the church at Jerusalem to gather a collection for famine relief (11:27-30). According to the account in the Acts of the Apostles Barnabas appears initially to have been the leading figure in their partnership in evangelization. By the time of their visit to Paphos Paul seems to have assumed leadership of the missionary group (Acts 13:8-13). Later the two missionaries had a falling out (Acts 15:38-40). To some extent this may have been due to their difference of opinion with regard to table fellowship, Paul believing that Barnabas had been led astray in this regard. See Gal 2:1-14, the only other passage in the extant correspondence in which Paul writes about Barnabas.

In v. 6 Paul writes empathetically of Barnabas, his fellow apostle, implying that among the apostles only the two of them supported their missionary endeavors by exercising a trade. Luke records the story of Barnabas' having given to the Jerusalem apostles the proceeds of the sale of a field he owned (Acts 4:37), but neither Luke in Acts nor Paul in his letters gives any indication as to the trade exercised by Barnabas. Luke's account does not mention that Barnabas had visited Corinth. Paul's benign reference to Barnabas in 9:6 not only suggests that any rift that might have existed between the two had been healed but also that Barnabas was a figure known to the Corinthians, if only by reputation.

who do not enjoy the right not to work? The double negative, an instance of classical usage, is employed by Paul only in 9:6 and 12:15 (BDF 431.1). That Paul worked for a living is well documented in the NT, beginning with his own affirmation in 1 Thess 2:9 that he and his companions "worked night and day." Paul does not specify the nature of his "labor and toil." In Acts 18:3, however, Luke indicates that Paul's trade was that of the leatherworker, a trade he exercised in Corinth together with his patrons, Aquila and Prisca (see 16:19; Acts 18:3; Rom 16:3-5). While rabbis typically plied a trade, philosophers in the Hellenistic world generally did not do so. Cleanthes, the Stoic, a gardener and miller, Menedemus and Asclepiades, Platonists who worked as millers, Dio Chrysostom, the Cynic who worked as a gardener and at various odd jobs, Demetrius of Sunium, the Cynic employed as a porter, and Musonius Rufus, the Stoic who worked a farm, were well-known exceptions (see Ronald Hock, *Social Context* 46). Other philosophers derived their support from fees charged to students, the gifts of their patrons, or begging.

Not only did Paul work for a living; he steadfastly refused the support of others, occasional support from his beloved Philippians being the only documented exception to his general rule (see Phil 4:16), and that may have been due to the insistence of Paul's female coworkers in Philippi (see F. X. Malinowski, "The Brave Women of Philippi," *BTB* 15 [1985] 60–64).

7. *Who ever serves as a soldier at his own expense? Who plants the vine and does not eat its fruit? Or who shepherds the flock and does not eat of the milk of the flock?* Paul cites the vinedresser and the shepherd, as he will cite the ox and the priest, as those who have a right to eat. It may be that Paul was also thinking of a soldier who receives his rations as a result of his soldiering. "Expense" *(opsōniois)* was commonly used to designate pay for services rendered, but the etymology of the term (from *opson*, cooked fish, and *ōneomai*, to buy) and its first use in the papyri suggest that it connotes the supplying of provisions (see *TLNT* 2:600–603).

The soldier, vinedresser, and shepherd are typical examples in Hellenistic rhetoric. In 2 Tim 2:4-6 the soldier, the athlete (cf. 9:24-27; 15:32), and the farmer who is cited as one who has a right to receive a share of the crops are mentioned in a reflection on Paul's ministry. The use of examples *(paradeigmata)* in the development of an argument is typical of Hellenistic rhetoric.

8. *I do not say this on human authority, do I? Does not the law also say this?* "This" is actually a demonstrative plural *(tauta,* literally, "these things") used to refer to Paul's total argument thus far. The formula "on human authority" *(kata anthrōpon)* recurs with a similar connotation in Rom 3:5 and Gal 1:11 (cf. 1 Cor 3:3; 15:32; Gal 3:15).

Having invited the Corinthians to think about the rights that he as an apostle had a right to exercise (vv. 4-6), and after a short lesson in which he makes use of well-known examples of three types of people who were able to eat as a result of their work, Paul turns from a rational argument to an argument from authority. This two-step mode of reasoning, like the argument from examples that preceded it, is similar to the scholarly exposition of Hellenistic rhetoric that first advances rational arguments and then an argument from authority (cf. Pliny, *Epistles* 2.20.9; Quintilian, *Training of an Orator* 4.5.3). Paul adapts this twofold approach as he demonstrates for his putative audience that he has a right to receive support from the Corinthian community. In Hellenistic rhetoric the dicta of philosophers and sages were typically cited in pursuit of an argument that was being developed. Paul appeals to the authority of the Jewish Scriptures, "the law of Moses." "The law" *(ho nomos)* is contrasted with "human authority" *(anthrōpon),* thereby implying that the law is an expression of God's authority.

Paul's scriptural citation is introduced by a rhetorical question, actually a double question. The first part of the disjunctive rhetorical question awaits a negative response, "certainly not." The second expects a positive response, "surely" (BDF 427.2; 440.1), but Paul then answers his own question. Yes (on this use of postpositive *gar* see BDF 452), he answers (v. 9), the Law does imply that one has a right to exercise one's rights, "for it is written in the Law of Moses, 'you shall not muzzle an ox while it is treading out the grain.'" This is the first time in his interrogatory appeal that Paul gives the answer to his own rhetorical question (see v. 10b). Although he expected that his audience would mentally respond to the questions of v. 8 with a respective "no" and "yes" he offers an answer so as to assure that they have the correct answer.

9. *Yes, it is written in the Law of Moses, "Do not muzzle the ox that is threshing":* Having already argued from reason (vv. 4-7) for the legitimacy of exercising one's rights, Paul claims that the Scriptures themselves provide a warrant for his legitimate exercise of rights. He introduces the pertinent Scripture with a classic introductory lemma, "it is written in the Law of Moses." Although hapax in Paul's letters, the formula is a textual equivalent of a rabbinic formula (see *b. Yoma* 35b, 66a). Early Christian authors likewise use the expression "Law of Moses" to refer to the Jewish Scriptures (Luke 2:22; 24:44; John 7:23; Acts 13:39; 15:5; 28:23; Heb 10:28). The Scripture adduced by Paul is Deut 25:4, a fragment of agricultural law: "Do not muzzle *(kēmōseis)* the ox that is threshing." Paul's four-word quotation (in Greek) of the text conforms to the LXX except for the verb. A more literary term, *phimōseis*, appears in the LXX and in many manuscript copies of 1 Cor 9:9 ($\mathfrak{P}^{46}$, ℵ, A, D, most minuscules, etc.). Despite the strong manuscript evidence for this reading it is probable that Paul's own citation differed slightly from that of the standard Greek Bible. Scribes have a tendency not only to make stylistic improvements but also to make NT manuscripts conform to the standard Bible.

Paul's use of Deut 25:4 is often cited as an example of his noncontextual use of the Scriptures. He has taken a bit of agricultural law and applied it, by means of an *a fortiori* kind of argument, to his own situation. His usage is, however, not altogether out of keeping with contemporary practice. He used another agricultural image to describe his apostolic work in 3:5-9. The argument from the minor premise to the major, from the lesser to the greater, the *qal wa-ḥomer,* was a well-known principle of biblical interpretation. Traditionally ascribed to Hillel, it is cited as the first of R. Ishmael's hermeneutical principles. It was, moreover, customary for rabbis to compare farmhands and other servants with domestic animals in *halakah* pertaining to agriculture and tort (e.g., *b. B. Meṣ.* 87a-91b; *m. Yad.* 4:7; Philo, *Virtues* 145). Deuteronomy 25:4 is quoted with similar purpose in 1 Tim 5:18, where the biblical text is cited with the words used in the LXX (cf. *Did.* 13:1). The appearance of Deut 25:4 in this deutero-Pauline text may be an indication of its author's familiarity with 1 Corinthians. Some (such as P. J. Tomson) claim that the halakhic midrash on wages is an element of apostolic *halakah* derived from the Jewish church.

Notwithstanding the alleged contrast between the type of arguments adduced, the scriptural citation of v. 9 is part of Paul's logical argument. In his quasi-syllogistic reasoning v. 9a serves as the major premise of his argument, while the rhetorical questions of vv. 9b-10 serve as the minor premise (see Wilhelm Wuellner, "Paul as Pastor," 68).

It is not oxen who are of concern to God, is it? Paul uses a double rhetorical question—in Greek a single disjunctive rhetorical question (vv. 9c-10a)—as an introduction to his own hermeneutical reflection on the significance of the Scripture. As was the case in 9:8a-b the first part of the double question expects a negative response while the second part awaits a positive response. Although calling for a tacit negative response to the first part of his question

Paul does not intend to deny God's providential care of animals. Rather he is arguing that the Law is not concerned with trivia (cf. Philo, *Dreams* 1.93; *Ep. Arist.*144), a notion that is akin to the modern legal principle *de minimis non curat lex.*

10. *Doesn't he really speak for our sake?* Much depends on how the *pantōs* ("really") is understood. If the adverb is to be rendered "entirely" *(NRSV, RSV, NJB;* cf. *REB)* Paul is virtually rejecting the literal sense of the text. If the word is to be rendered "really," "surely," or "certainly" *(RNAB, NIV, JB)* Paul has retained the literal sense of the biblical passage but has subordinated the agricultural norm to its hortatory value. This is the case in 9:9-10. Paul's rhetoric suggests that it is not so much animals who benefit from Deut 25:4 as it is humans who profit from the legal prescription. On a somewhat superficial level it can be argued that humans benefit from the Law insofar as they obey it. The thrust of Paul's argument goes beyond this. Using the *gezera shawah* principle to link traditional *halakah* with the biblical precept and exploiting the full rhetorical force of his *qal wa-ḥomer* argumentation, Paul claims that if animals are to receive a just reward for their labors, *a fortiori* humans are entitled to a just recompense for theirs.

Yes, it is for our sake that it is written that "whoever plows should plow in hope and whoever threshes should have a hope of sharing in the crop": Once again Paul answers his own question, using the particle *gar* ("yes") to suggest the positive response (see BDF 452). As in v. 9, Paul introduces a Scripture into his argument. This is one of two passages (cf. 15:54) in 1 Corinthians in which Paul uses *graphō* to refer to a specific scriptural passage without using *gegraptai* in the perfect passive. Paul's words clearly state his conviction that the Scriptures continue to be relevant for his audience. This conviction is echoed in 15:54, where a striking lemma, "then the saying that is written will be fulfilled," introduces the final scriptural citation in 1 Corinthians.

A parallelism exists between 8a-9b and 9c-10d. Each unit offers a response to a similarly structured disjunctive rhetorical question *(mē . . . ē . . . legei).* The responses are introduced by a rhetorical *gar,* use a formulaic form of *graphō,* and give a scriptural citation that contains "thresh" *(aloaō),* a catchword linking the two "Scriptures" with one another. Despite the parallelism, the *hoti* ("that") of v. 10 appears to be recitative rather than causal (thus "for" in the *NRSV).*

It is clear that v. 9b is a citation of Deut 25:4. The source of v. 10cd is less clear even though v. 10c may be an allusion to Sir 6:19. The balanced structure of the "Scripture" (note the lemma, *egraphē,* "it is written") and its non-Pauline language *(arotriaō, arotria, aloaō)* suggest that it is an element of traditional lore. Paul's source may be a well-known saying, later incorporated into the Mishnah:

These may eat [of the fruits among which they labor] by virtue of what is enjoined in the Law: he that labors on what is still growing after the work is finished, and he that labors on what is already gathered before the work is finished; [this applies only] to what grows from the soil (*m. B. Meṣ.* 7:2).

The somewhat uncertain origin of Paul's version of the adage may have contributed to the ambiguity found in the manuscript tradition of v. 10. Some scribes understood "share" *(metechein)* to be the object of "it is fitting" *(opheilei)* and modified the text to read *tēs elpidos autou metechein,* "to share hope" (D, F, G, etc.). Later scribes, including the correctors of ℵ and D, further "improved" the text by repeating "hope." Thus "he that thresheth in hope should be a partaker of his hope" *(AV,* reflecting the Textus Receptus). Following 𝔓⁴⁶, ℵ, B, C, and many of the ancient versions I read *ep' elpidi tou metechein* and presume *aloan* as the object of "whoever threshes" *(ho aloōn [aloan],* parallel with the preceding *ho arotriōn arotrian).* See Metzger, *Textual Commentary* 492.

11. *If we sow spiritual things among you, is it too much that we reap material things from you?* Paul's rhetorical questions (vv. 11-12a) in support of his contention that those who preach the gospel have a right to receive their livelihood therefrom employ a *qal wa-ḥomer* kind of reasoning, from the greater to the lesser. The argument is typical of rabbinic disputation, particularly in the interpretation of the Scriptures, but it is also a kind of argument that Paul uses effectively throughout his correspondence. An emphatic "we" *(hēmeis)* appears in both the protasis and the apodosis of the first question. This first question makes effective use of the antithesis between "spiritual" *(pneumatika)* and "material" *(sarkika),* adjectives derived from a classic and Pauline antithesis between *pneuma* and *sarx* (literally "body"). If Paul has a right to expect spiritual benefits from the community, how much more should he be able to demand material support (cf. 1 Thess 2:6-7; Phil 4:15)? In Gal 6:6 Paul urges that those who receive oral instruction share their material resources *(agatha)* with those who have instructed them (cf. 1 Tim 5:17). For the use of the agricultural metaphor to describe his work see 3:5-9.

12. *If others share this right over you, how much more should we?* The rhetorical question of v. 12 is linked to the rhetorical question of v. 11. "Others" *(alloi),* which may be a reference to the workers in the community who came after Paul (cf. 3:10), contrasts with the "we" of the apodosis as well as with the repeated "we" in v. 11. "More" *(mallon,* v. 12) corresponds to the "too much" *(mega,* literally "great") of v. 11.

However, we do not use this right; we endure all things in order not to create any obstacle for the gospel of Christ: In v. 12 Paul returns to the issue of his rights (cf. 9:4-6; compare 8:9). Although he and his companions might make legitimate demands on the Corinthians as their God-appointed apostles, they willingly forego their right to the financial support of the community for the sake of the gospel. Rather than exercising their right to all things (cf. 6:12) they endure all things. Among NT authors Paul is alone in using the verb "endure" *(stegō;* cf. 13:7; 1 Thess 3:1, 5), but the term is well attested in classical and Hellenistic literature (cf. P. Oxyrhynchus 1775.10). Hapax in the NT, "obstacle" *(egkopēn; ekkopēn* in ℵ, D*, L, Ψ, etc.) was used by such authors as Heraclitus and Diodorus Siculus.

Some Stoics refused to receive financial remuneration for their philosophical endeavors (see note on 9:6). Paul was adamant in his determination that the gospel be preached free of charge (9:15; cf. 1 Thess 2:9). As one who endures all things for the sake of the gospel he is a man motivated by the love of God (see 13:7). As a slave (see 9:19-23) he does not enjoy the right to act as a freedman; he puts up with many things—hard work, the difficulties of the apostolate, and opposition—for the sake of the gospel (cf. 1 Thess 2:2, 9).

13. *Do you not know that those who perform sacred works eat things from the temple, those who serve at the altar partake of the altar?* While Paul's mention of rights harks back to 9:4-6, thus forming a kind of *inclusio,* and although v. 12 anticipates the presentation of Paul as the slave of Christ (9:19-23), vv. 13-14 should not be separated from the preceding discussion (*e contrario* Harry Nasuti, "Woes and Rights," 249–250). Verse 13 picks up the motif of eating from the fruits of one's labor (9:7) and harks back to the idea of Paul having a right to food and drink (9:4).

The cultic motif with the idea of eating echoes the problematic situation outlined in 8:7-13, the response to which has prompted Paul's rhetorical digression in ch. 9. That priests have a right to a portion of the animals and grain offered in sacrifice is well attested in biblical and extra-biblical tradition (cf. Lev 2:10; 5:13; 6:9-11, 18, 22-23; 7:6-10, 14, 30-34; 10:12-13; Josephus, *Ant.* 3.224-236). Paul's distinction between those who perform and those who serve may reflect the two classes of temple service within the Jewish tradition, that is, priests and Levites.

In the specificity of his rhetorical argument, directed to knowledgeable Corinthians, the temple (*hieron,* different from the *eidōleion* of 8:10) is the place where those in the know eat food that had been offered to idols. An implication of Paul's argument may be that those who eat of food sacrificed to idols are like those who serve at the idol's altar (cf. 10:18-22).

14. *Similarly, the Lord arranged that those who proclaim the gospel live from the gospel:* 1 Corinthians 9:14 and 7:10 are the surest references to the Lord's sayings in the extant Pauline correspondence. They are the only two such references in 1 Corinthians. Verse 14 is, however, no more an exact citation of a saying of Jesus found in the synoptic tradition (a Q logion, Luke 10:7 *par.* Matt 10:10) than is 7:10. A similar saying, likewise linked with Deut 25:4, is used in support of a double payment for those elders who are involved in a ministry of preaching and teaching in 1 Tim 5:18, apparently under the influence of 1 Cor 9:9-14.

Despite his use of *dietaxen* ("arranged"), ordinarily translated as "commanded," Paul seems not to consider the tradition as having the force of a command of the eschatological Lord. For Victor Furnish (*Jesus According to Paul: Understanding Jesus Today* [Cambridge: Cambridge University Press, 1993] 51) Paul reinterprets the "decree as a 'right' that, for the sake of the gospel, he is free to give up."

FOR REFERENCE AND FURTHER STUDY

Brewer, David I. "1 Corinthians 9.9-11: A Literal Interpretation of 'Do not Muzzle the Ox,'" *NTS* 38 (1992) 554–565.

Caragounis, Chrys C. "*Opsōnion:* A Reconsideration of Its Meaning," *NovT* 16 (1974) 35–57.

Collins, Raymond F. "'It was indeed written for our sake' (1 Cor 9,10): Paul's Use of Scripture in the First Letter to the Corinthians," SNTU 20 (1995) 151–170.

Dungan, David L. *The Sayings of Jesus in the Churches of Paul: The Use of the Synoptic Tradition in the Regulation of Early Church Life.* Philadelphia: Fortress, 1971, 3–80.

Furnish, Victor P. *Jesus According to Paul. Understanding Jesus Today.* Cambridge: Cambridge University Press, 1993, 40–65.

Gordon, J. Dorcas. *Sister or Wife? 1 Corinthians 7 and Cultural Anthropology.* JSNT.S 149. Sheffield: Sheffield Academic Press, 1997.

Hock, Ronald F. *The Social Context of Paul's Ministry: Tentmaking and Apostleship.* Philadelphia: Fortress, 1980.

Horrell, David G. "'The Lord Commanded . . . But I have not Used. . . .' Exegetical and Hermeneutical Reflections on 1 Cor 9.14-15," *NTS* 43 (1997) 587–603.

Lee, G. M. "Studies in Texts: 1 Corinthians 9.9-10," *Theology* 71 (1968) 122–123.

Noonan, John T., Jr. "The Muzzled Ox," *JQR* 70 (1980) 172–175.

Plag, Christoph. "Paulus und die *Gezera schawa:* Zur Übernahme rabbinischer Auslegungskunst," *Judaica* 50 (1994) 135–140.

Willis, Wendell L. "An Apostolic Apologia? The Form and Function of 1 Corinthians," *JSNT* 24 (1985) 33–40.

Wuellner, Wilhelm. "Greek Rhetoric and Pauline Argumentation" in W. R. Schoedel and R. L. Wilken, eds., *Early Christian Literature and the Classical Tradition: in honorem Robert M. Grant.* Paris: Beauchesne, 1979, 177–188.

Zimmermann, M. and R. "Zitation, Kontradiktion oder Applikation? Die Jesuslogien in 1 Kor 7,10f. und 9,14: Traditionsgeschichtliche Verankerung und paulinische Interpretation," *ZNW* 87 (1996) 83–100.

5. *Christ's Slave* (9:15-18)

15. I have not made use of any of these. I am not writing this in order that something similar happen to me. I would rather die than . . . ! No one will make my boasting null and void! 16. If I proclaim the gospel, that is not my boast. Constraint presses upon me. Woe to me if I do not proclaim the gospel! 17. If I do this of my own free will, I have a reward; if unwillingly, I have been given a task. 18. What then is my reward? That in preaching the gospel I make the gospel free of charge, not using the rights that are mine in proclaiming the gospel.

INTERPRETATION

In the development of his "defense" Paul directed rhetorical question after rhetorical question to the Corinthians. His defense essentially consisted of sixteen such questions interlaced with various examples, an appeal to authority (both to the Law and to the Lord), and an appeal to the Corinthians' own experience.

With 9:15 the manner of Paul's appeal changes, but it is no less passionate. With an emphatic *egō* Paul begins to write about himself in the first person singular. The opening volley of his defense consisted of a series of rhetorical questions in the first person singular (9:1-2). After announcing that he would take up his defense (9:3) Paul switched to the first person plural, departing from this usage only in 9:6 when he wrote about himself and Barnabas. The emphatic *egō* marks a return to the first person singular. Paul will continue in this vein until the end of the chapter.

Paul's opening statement, "I have not made use of any of these," brings the peroration to closure, its negative particle and verb forming an *inclusio* with v. 12b. The substantivized demonstrative "these" is a clear reference to the apostolic rights Paul had spelled out in his defense: the right to sustenance, the right to being accompanied by a believing wife, and the right not to work. As Paul affirms that he has made use of none of these rights, he particularizes the general statement of 9:12b. His doing so prepares the reader for the exposition of the reason why Paul had not made use of his rights despite his more than legitimate claim to enjoy such rights (9:12a).

Before setting forth the reason why he had not made use of the rights that were his Paul takes a moment to set the record straight. He tells the Corinthians that his reason in writing to them about his rights as he did was not to cajole them into providing for his financial and material support. That was far from Paul's purpose. He had other reasons for writing to them, as he explained in 4:14 (cf. 5:9). His reason for writing in his own "defense" was not to obtain some kind of personal gain; it was to set forth an example, that of his own apostolic *egō*. Paul's presentation of himself is an important feature of the *ethos* appeal of his rhetoric.

The Apostolic "I." Paul presents himself as one who has not exercised his apostolic rights in a series of interlocking explanations. Five times he uses an explanatory *gar* (vv. 15, 16 [3x], 17) as he develops his thought in a kind of logical exposition. Paul's presentation of himself is not lacking in passion. Having uttered a mild oath, he breaks off his thought in midstream: he "would rather die than . . ." (v. 15). He writes about his own boasting (vv. 15d-16a). A rare "woe is me!" appears on his lips (v. 16c). He fears lest the Corinthians misconstrue his intentions in writing to them and that someone will nullify his solitary boast.

Although the pieces of Paul's thought are held together by means of the fivefold *gar*, his argument does not have the form of syllogistic reasoning. To capture somewhat the passion of Paul's appeal I have chosen not to translate the particle. Each of the points highlights the fact that

Paul considers himself to be a slave of Christ. His explanation is replete with language that describes the condition of a slave: constraint, anxiety about the assigned task not being done, the inability to exercise free will, and responsibility for household management, typically a slave's task.

The language Paul uses to describe his task in life as that of a slave is rather unusual for him (see notes). Paul's vocabulary is nonetheless similar to that used by his contemporary, Philo of Alexandria, as he describes the good man (see above, pp. 300–301). The good man is free:

> He who always acts sensibly . . . will have the power *(exousian)* to do anything *(panta)* and to live as he wishes, and he who has this power *(hō de taut' exestin)* must be free *(eleutheros)*. But the good man always acts sensibly, and, therefore, he alone is free *(eleutheros)*. Again, one who cannot be compelled *(anagkasai)* to do anything or prevented from doing anything, cannot be a slave *(doulos)*. But the good man cannot be compelled *(anagkasai)* or prevented: the good man, therefore, cannot be a slave *(doulos)*. That he is not compelled *(anagkazetai)* nor prevented is evident. One is prevented when he does not get what he desires, but the wise man desires things that have their origin in virtue, and these, being what he is, he cannot fail to obtain. Further, if one is compelled *(anagkazetai)* he clearly acts against his will *(akōn)*. But where there are actions, they are either righteous actions born of virtue or wrong actions born of vice or neutral and indifferent. The virtuous actions he performs not under constraint but willingly *(ekōn)*, since all that he does are what he holds to be desirable. (*Every Good Man is Free* 59-61)

The way in which Paul describes himself as a slave in 9:15-18 clearly contrasts with Philo's portrayal of the good and free man. Paul's final statement (v. 18), which creates a literary *inclusio* with v. 15, is an affirmation of his desire to act as a slave. He will not make use of the rights of a freedman.

Earlier in this letter to the Corinthians Paul appealed to the Corinthians to remain in the condition in which they had been called (7:17-24). He wrote about the paradox of slavery and freedom. The slave is a freed person of the Lord; the one who is free is a slave of Christ (7:22). In vv. 15-18 Paul applies this paradox in self-referential fashion. Having affirmed his freedom (9:1) and having set forth a defense of his rights in the hearing of the community (9:3-14), Paul alludes to his situation as a slave of Christ. He may be free but he acts in a way that is fitting for a slave of Christ. Because he is a slave of Christ he is not to be paid for the proclamation of the gospel. He is one to whom a task *(oikonomia*, literally "the task of household management," 9:17; cf. 4:1-2) has been assigned. Paul must do his duty. Woe to him if he does not fulfill the task that has been entrusted to him!

Paul's Boast. "Boasting" is a major theme in 1 Corinthians (see above, pp. 99–101), but it is only in 9:15-16 that Paul writes about his own boasting (cf. 2 Cor 9:3). To describe his boasting he uses the term *kauchēma,* an expression that properly denotes the content of one's boast rather than the act of boasting *(kauchēsis).* The object of Paul's boasting is not the preaching of the gospel (9:16). He cannot take pride in the fact that he preaches the gospel. The object of his boasting is that, as the Lord's slave, he preaches the gospel free of charge. Paul expresses the wish that no one may deprive him of the possibility of such a boast, that no one will make his solitary boast null and void.

Paul's boast is that he has not made use of the rights to which he is entitled. Typically Hellenistic philosophers and sages gained their livelihood from begging, receiving pay for teaching their students, or having the support of a patron, but Paul chose, as did many philosophers in the Stoic-Cynic tradition, to support himself by doing manual labor (4:12). Musonius Rufus, the Stoic philosopher and occasional farmer, opined that supporting oneself as one pursued philosophy was beneficial in a variety of ways. "Pupils," he wrote, "would seem to me benefitted by seeing him [the philosopher] at work in the fields, demonstrating by his own labor the lessons that philosophy inculcates—that one should endure hardships, and suffer the pains of labor with his own body, rather than depend upon another for sustenance" (Musonius, frag. 11).

That Paul chose to support himself by the work of his own hands might have been a source of contention among the Corinthians. Peter Marshall (*Enmity in Corinth* 217) opines that Paul's refusal of the Corinthians' financial support lies behind the mock defense of ch. 9. Those people in Corinth who overestimated human freedom (6:12; 10:23) and who placed undue value on knowledge (8:1) may well have considered Paul's manual labor to be demeaning for an apostle. Some of these Corinthians may even have taken umbrage at Paul's refusal to allow them to function as patrons in his regard. Certainly some within the community were capable of serving as Paul's benefactors if he had allowed them to do so (cf. 1:11, 16).

Paul, however, boasted of the fact that he was able to preach the gospel free of charge (cf. Phil 4:15). In his eyes, working to support himself as he preached the gospel gave him reason to boast and set him apart from other preachers (9:6; cf. 2 Cor 11:5-12).

NOTES

15. *I have not made use of any of these. I am not writing this in order that something similar happen to me:* 1 Corinthians 9:15 is one of four passages in the letter in

which Paul talks about his purpose in writing (see 4:14; 5:11; 14:37). These other passages clearly indicate that Paul has written to exhort the Corinthians, not to acquire any benefit for himself. In 9:15 Paul states his desire that the Corinthians not get the wrong idea from the letter he is writing. He does not want them to think that his writing of the letter is a subtle plea for financial support.

"None of these" (*oudeni toutōn*) obviously has "rights" (*exousia*, v. 12b) as its immediate referent, but the broader reference is to the three apostolic rights cited in the triad of rhetorical questions in 9:4-6. Paul has not taken advantage of any of his rights, nor does he intend to do so. In what is tantamount to an aside in his argument he tells the Corinthians that his purpose in writing was not to gain their financial support. He did not intend that his sustenance should be provided for in a way similar (*houtōs*) to the way in which all of those cited in 9:5-12 expected to receive sustenance as a reward for their work.

I would rather die than. . . . : Paul's expletive remains forever uncompleted. It is an instance of abrupt interruption of the flow of rhetoric as a result of strong feelings (aposiopesis). In Paul's rhetoric the unfinished expletive has a function similar to that of the occasional oaths that punctuate his thought (Rom 1:9; 1 Thess 2:5; cf. 1 Thess 2:10). What it is that he would rather die than not do is left to the imagination. It is not immediately evident. Paul's writing a letter in order to beg for financial support for himself comes immediately to mind, but Paul may well have had the same passion about foregoing all of his apostolic rights.

No one will make my boasting null and void! An elliptical "no one will make null my boasting" (*to kauchēma oudeis kenōsei*), after he had broken off the train of thought in midsentence, is the source of a well-attested textual problem. Scribes who did not recognize that Paul had broken off his thought have "corrected" the text so as to make sense of his words. The principal variant is that some manuscripts (ℵ^c, C, D^c, Ψ, supported in BDF 369.2; 393.2) read *hina tis* rather than *oudeis*, as if Paul's words had the form of a purpose clause, "I should rather die so that someone might deprive me of my boasting." With some hesitation the editors of *GNT*^{4} have opted for the reading "no one will deprive" (*oudeis kenōsei*, found in 𝔓^{46}, ℵ, B, D, several ancient versions and some Latin Fathers). This reading, attested by the oldest manuscripts, is to be preferred on the basis of the *lectio difficilior* principle.

Some of the many variants in the textual tradition pertain to the reading of the verb, *kenoō*, "to make empty," "to render null and void." The verb is otherwise used by Paul in this letter only at 1:17, where it refers to the cross of Christ. It is a powerful word in Paul's lexicon (cf. Rom 4:14; Phil 2:7). Second Corinthians 9:3 contains another reference to Paul's boasting being rendered null and void. In that instance the reference is to Paul's boasting about the Corinthians themselves.

16. *If I proclaim the gospel, that is not my boast. Constraint presses upon me:* Paul had previously used the word *anagkē*, literally "force, constraint, necessity" (see 7:37) to describe the penultimate situation in which Christians live (7:26).

Some authors therefore suggest that Paul has the impending eschaton in mind in 9:16. However, 9:15-18 is a passage in the letter in which Paul writes about his servile condition. Hence the term should be taken in its ordinary meaning. It describes the conditions under which slaves toil, occasionally indicating the pain or torture to which they were subject. As a slave Paul is without rights. He is entirely subject to another's will. He is constrained to preach the gospel and woe to him if he does not.

Woe to me if I do not proclaim the gospel! Paul's solitary woe expresses the depth of his feeling with regard to his need to preach the gospel. Unlike Jeremiah (Jer 4:13, 31; 6:4; cf. Isa 24:16; Ps 120:5), whose example often served Paul as a paradigm of prophetic existence (cf. Gal 1:15; 1 Thess 2:4, etc.), Paul does not bemoan his constrained situation. Rather he embraces it, as he will explain in vv. 17-18. The substantival interjection, "woe" *(ouai),* is hapax in the Pauline literature. It may be a Semitism (cf. BDF 58).

17. *If I do this of my own free will, I have a reward; if unwillingly, I have been given a task:* Paul explains that although he may be constrained to preach the gospel he nonetheless does so willingly. Were things otherwise, he would still have to preach. He is but a slave. He has a task to do, a task from which he cannot escape.

Paul phrases his argument in a pair of antithetical conditional sentences. He first describes the situation of a free man who is paid for doing what he does. Then (the antithetical *de* in the elliptical protasis is best left untranslated) Paul describes the condition of a slave who can only say that he has fulfilled the task that has been assigned (cf. Luke 17:10). The choice of vocabulary is striking and exceptional. In the NT the adjective *hekōn,* "of one's own free will," is used only by Paul, here and in Rom 8:20. The contrasting expression, *akōn,* "unwillingly," is a rare Attic contraction, the contrary of *hekōn* and hapax in the NT. According to Epictetus the free man is a friend of God, but obeys God willingly *(hekōn; Discourses* 4.3.9).

Paul ordinarily uses the verb *pisteuō* in the active voice with the meaning "to believe." His use of it in the passive with the meaning "to be entrusted with" is rare. See 1 Thess 2:4, where he also uses this construction of the verb to refer to his own ministry, albeit evoking the image of the public official rather than that of the slave.

"To be given a task," *oikonomian pepisteumai,* is literally "to be entrusted with the task of household management." Paul's language harks back to 4:1-2, where he stated that he was a steward *(oikonomos)* of the mysteries of God and that the first quality required of a steward is that he be found trustworthy *(pistos,* 4:2; cf. 7:25). The task of household management was usually entrusted to a trustworthy slave (cf. Luke 12:42; Josephus, *Ant.* 12.199-200; compare Demosthenes, *Private Orations* 36.43-44; Xenophon, *Memorabilia* 2.5.2). Epictetus, in his discourse on the ideal Cynic *(Discourses* 3.22.3-4), uses the image of the *oikonomos* to describe the role of humans, subservient to God, in the world.

As a slave entrusted with a task Paul is constrained to preach the gospel. Despite being a slave he is nonetheless free (cf. 7:22; 9:1). In somewhat similar fashion, albeit from a rather different perspective, Seneca wrote that freedom, happiness, and even a divine quality affect the one who desires what is necessary (cf. *Epistles* 54.7; 61.3).

18. *What then is my reward? That in preaching the gospel I make the gospel free of charge, not using the rights that are mine in proclaiming the gospel:* The passage began with an emphatic *egō* (v. 15) and a reference to Paul's rights. It concludes with a twofold mention of Paul's *egō*. The opening rhetorical question is explanatory. It picks up the theme of the reward Paul receives for his work. The infinitive clause, "not using the rights," is epexegetical (BDF 394). Its verb, *katachrēsasthai*, used elsewhere by Paul only at 7:31, means taking advantage of, using to the utmost even to the point of abusing.

Ironically Paul's reward for preaching the gospel is that he preach it free of charge, thereby not laying a burden on the Corinthians (cf. 2 Cor 11:7-12; 12:14-15). Preaching the gospel is its own reward. Paul's reference to the reward or pay (*misthos,* vv. 17-18) that he did not accept contrasts with the reward that others who labor in the Lord's house can expect to receive (3:8, 14; cf. 9:12a). That Paul did not receive or accept any material reward for preaching the gospel may well have been a bone of contention and a source of division among the Corinthians. See note on v. 16 and the discussion in Marshall, *Enmity in Corinth.* The situation is to be understood within a Hellenistic context in which philosophers were typically supported by a patron or were paid for their teaching.

FOR REFERENCE AND FURTHER STUDY

Marshall, Peter. *Enmity in Corinth: Social Conventions in Paul's Relations with the Corinthians.* WUNT 2d. ser. 23. Tübingen: Mohr, 1987.

6. *For the Sake of the Gospel* (9:19-23)

19. For, being free from all, I have made myself a servant to all so that I might win over even many more. 20. For the Jews I have become as a Jew so that I might win over Jews; for those under the law as one under the law, even though I am not under the law, so that I might win over those under the law; 21. for those outside the law as one outside the law, even though I am not outside the law of God, but subject to the law of Christ, so that I might win over those outside the law. 22. For the weak I have become weak so that I might win over the weak; to all people I have become all things so that I might surely save some. 23. All these things I do for the sake of the gospel, so that I might share in it.

The burden of Paul's mock defense fell on an affirmation of his rights (9:1-14). This was followed by the reasons why Paul had not made use of the rights that were legitimately his (9:15-18). He had not taken advantage of his rights because he considered himself a slave. In 9:19-23 he continues to explain himself. Note the explanatory *gar*, "for," with which the pericope begins. Paul begins by explaining that despite being free he has indentured himself. The phrase clearly sums up what he had obliquely stated in the preceding pericope. The allusion to his freedom, however, harks back to 9:1, where Paul's opening statement to the Corinthian jury asked them to consider him a free man. Paul will not be enslaved by anyone or anything (6:12c-d), yet he will make himself a slave. The norm of his freedom is the advantage that accrues to others (6:12a-b). Ultimately the freedom Paul enjoys is paradoxical (cf. 7:22). Although free, he has indentured himself. To what purpose?

The Rhetorical Unit. Paul's explanatory excursus is defined by an *inclusio* that circumscribes the literary unit. The unit has a common literary structure as well as a central and unifying theme. The inclusion features the double use of "all" in vv. 19a *(pantōn pasin)* and 22b *(pasin . . . panta)*. The purpose clause of v. 19b, "so that I might win over many more" is parallel with and elucidated by the purpose clause of v. 22b, "so that I might surely save some." The final verse of the pericope mentions the gospel. This creates a verbal link with the immediately preceding pericopes (cf. vv. 14, 18) and provides a broader *inclusio* defining the unit as consisting of vv. 19-23, despite the tightly knit structure of vv. 20-22.

Grammatically the unit is characterized by seven purpose clauses with a similar *hina* construction, six of which are parallel with one another:

> . . . to all,
> > so that I might win over many more
> for the Jews I have become as a Jew
> > so that I might win over Jews
> for those under the law as one under the law [. . .]
> > so that I might win over those under the law
> for those outside the law as one outside the law [. . .]
> > so that I might win over those outside the law.
> for the weak I have become weak
> > so that I might win over the weak
> to all people I have become all things
> > so that I might surely save some.

The first of these clauses explains why it is that Paul has become an indentured servant. The next four represent a rhetorical division of the first clause; various segments of the "all" whom Paul would win over are identified, namely Jews, those under the law, those outside the law, and the weak. "I have become" (*egenomēn,* in the aorist) appears in the second clause, is absent from the third and fourth clauses, but recurs in the fifth and sixth clauses. The *inclusio* helps to form the second through the fifth clauses as a literary unit, pointing to the fifth clause as the climax and suggesting that the sixth clause is a summary of the four preceding clauses ("for the Jews . . . for the weak").

Thematic Unity and Emphasis. It is on the fifth clause, "for the weak I have become weak," that Paul's emphasis lies. It contains a principal verb (*egenomēn*) that looks back to the second clause. Unlike clauses 2-4, this fifth clause omits the comparative particle "as" (*hōs*). Whereas Paul compares himself with Jews, those under the law, and those outside the law, he identifies with the weak. In a culture where shame and honor are dominant factors Paul has portrayed himself as being in an unfavorable situation by identifying with the weak. It is particularly this group for whom Paul has enslaved himself. Identifying with the weak, Paul confounds the Corinthian hybrists who would disdain the weak and be unconcerned about their salvation. Verses 8:11 and 9:22b clearly express the contrasting attitudes of Paul and these hybrists.

The parallelism of Paul's balanced structure is interrupted by two parenthetical expressions. Each of them speaks of Paul's relationship to "the law": "even though I am not under the law" (v. 20) and "even though I am not outside the law of God, but subject to the law of Christ" (v. 21). These parenthetical remarks begin with a similar "even though I am not" (*mē ōn*). Paul rarely writes about his own relationship to the law. The idea of the law, nonetheless, provides a central theme and major focus for 9:19-23.

Nomos ("law") is a sound that resonates throughout the unit. Nine times within the space of a few verses the sound is heard. The word itself occurs four times (v. 20), and compounds of *nomos* five times (*anomos,* "outside the law," four times; *ennomos,* "under the law," once). Paul's emphasis on *nomos* is all the more striking in that most of these occurrences are to be found in parenthetical remarks. The second parenthesis features a play on words in which Paul contrasts *ennomos* ("under the law") with *anomos* ("outside the law"). The play on words is possible only because Paul imparts his own meanings to *anomos* and *ennomos.* In ordinary Greek the terms simply mean "illegal" and "legal." Paul uses the terms to describe a way of life, one in which the law is not the norm of life, the other in which the law is indeed the norm of life.

The concentration of legal language in vv. 20-21, to which the concentric pattern of vv. 19-23 points, may suggest the real reason why Paul has added parenthetical expressions in vv. 20 and 21. In light of the Corinthians' baneful exploitation of the "everything is lawful" slogan Paul may have wanted to focus on the notion of obligation in the context of Christian freedom and rights. He is developing an *ethos* argument. In comparison with Jews he is not under the law (v. 20d, with an emphatic *autos*). In comparison with Gentiles he is not under the law (v. 21b). In neither of the social worlds in which he lives is Paul under the law. In principle everything is permissible for him (6:12). There is, however, a caveat. Although Paul is not under the law he is not beyond the pale of the law. He is under the law of Christ (v. 21; cf. Gal 6:2), which is the law of love. The reference to "Christ" evokes the memory of his death and resurrection. Christ has died for the weak members of the community (8:11). In turn (cf. 11:1) Paul has indentured himself for the sake of the weak. Dare the hybrists do otherwise?

Pauline Populism. Paul's argument reflects a rhetorical and political *topos* that portrays populist leaders as enslaving themselves to the people they are to lead. Such leaders lower themselves socially. They even change their appearance in order to win the support of the masses. Paul's *pasin panta*, "all things to all people," echoes the populist appeal. He uses a verb in the perfect tense *(gegona)* to draw attention to the lasting effect of what he has done. The populist appeal serves Paul's rhetorical purpose well. It is in keeping with the deliberative intent of his composition, which is to urge the community to be unified.

Paul's overriding motivation is surely the gospel. He concludes his paradoxical excursus on his use of freedom with a mention of the gospel (cf. vv. 14, 18). The mention of the gospel recalls the reward he claimed to be his, namely the preaching of the gospel free of charge (v. 18). The Christian paradox of slavery and freedom must be seen in the light of the gospel and all that the gospel entails. Paul has adopted his style of life, that of a slave of Christ and a slave to all, because it allows him to share in the proclamation of the gospel. Some may deem his way of life to be shameful, others may accuse him of being a chameleon, but Paul does what he does for the sake of the gospel.

NOTES

19. *For, being free from all, I have made myself a servant to all so that I might win over even many more:* With an explanatory "for" *(gar)* Paul clarifies the ideas on slavery that he had been developing. With utter simplicity he proclaims, "I have made myself a servant to all." Although Paul occasionally calls himself a "servant of Jesus Christ" (e.g., Phil 1:1), 9:19 is unique in its description of Paul as one who has indentured himself *(emauton edoulōsa)*. The expression has a strong antithetical ring: Paul begins with an affirmation of his absolute freedom—he is free from everything. Notwithstanding his freedom, he has taken a bold course of action so that he "might win over many more." On the

translation of *pleionas* see BDF 244.3. The verb "win over" *(kerdainō)*, used by Paul only here and in Phil 3:8), belongs to the semantic domain of "advantage," an argument used with great profit in deliberative rhetoric.

Hellenistic moralists frequently observed that true freedom could be characterized negatively and positively (see the note on 9:1), as freedom from and freedom for. Paul describes his own as a radical freedom. He is free from every constraint, free from all involuntary servitude. "From all" *(ek pantōn,* in the plural) could have a personal or more general reference. The latter seems to be the case in 9:19. *Pantōn* is the opposite pole of *panta* (v. 22). Moreover, Paul's entire discussion of freedom and rights takes place with the Corinthians' slogan "everything is lawful" *(panta exestin,* 6:12) echoing in the background. As to the positive purpose of his exercise of freedom, Paul affirms that his self-enslavement is not without purpose. This general statement is the first in a series of seven purpose clauses in which Paul spells out why he, a free man, has willingly enslaved himself. That he has done so purposely continues to be reaffirmed as he cites different categories of people to whom he has enslaved himself: Jews, those under the law, those not under the law, and the weak.

Commentators frequently note that Paul's explanation for his self-enslavement is verbally similar to thoughts attributed to Jesus by each of the synoptics (Matt 20:26-27; Mark 10:43-45; Luke 22:25-27), albeit in different ways. Three features of these passages are particularly striking: (1) the theme of "serving" (with the Greek root *doul-*); (2) the idea that the disciples are to be like Jesus in their service; (3) the Semitic "for many" *(anti pollōn,* Mark 10:45). The study of the tradition history of these synoptic logia is fairly complex, but scholars generally agree that there is a genuine logion of Jesus at the origin of the tradition and that the tradition did not originally include an idea of following Jesus in the self-oblation of his death as a way of following him in service.

20. *For the Jews I have become as a Jew so that I might win over Jews:* "For the Jews" *(tois Ioudaiois,* a dative of advantage) is Paul's only use of an arthrous *Ioudaioi,* a term he uses not so much to identify an extant social group as to underscore a distinctive quality of this group (see BDF 262.1). Paul's social world was simply organized. There were Jews and there were Gentiles. To emphasize that he has made himself a servant to all Paul divides the question, speaking about Jews and Gentiles. He first speaks about his subservience to the Jews. This is in keeping with the Jew-then-Gentile schema he often uses in his exposition.

for those under the law as one under the law: As Paul divides his argument it is easy to read the reference to those under the law as pertaining to Jews, thus parallel to v. 20a, and v. 21 as pertaining to Gentiles. On this reading Paul specifies that the Jews are under the law and sets the stage for the contrast made in vv. 20b-21. This facile reading of the text is supported by Robert Estienne's sixteenth-century versification, which divides v. 21 from v. 20 and suggests to readers that "those under the law" is a phrase in apposition to "the Jews."

"Under the law" *(hypo nomon)* is a technical expression to describe Jews (cf. Rom 6:14, 15; Gal 4:5, 21; 5:18). The law separates two social worlds from one another; it serves to delineate two communities. It may be that Paul was thinking specifically of Jewish Christians, particularly those at Corinth, as distinct from the Gentile Christians to whom reference is made in v. 21.

Why did Paul not allude to the division between Jew and Gentile more simply, as he does in 1:22-24; 10:32; and 12:13? He could easily have omitted v. 20b. Alternatively, if Paul wanted a mention of the law to serve as the focus of his Jew-Gentile distinction, why did he not place before the words of v. 21 an appositional statement, "for the Gentiles," in parallel fashion with v. 20a?

Why did Paul introduce a mention of the law *(nomos)* and dwell on it as extensively as he seems to have done when the law seems not to have been as divisive an issue at Corinth as it was in Rome and the Galatian region? Paul plays with the idea of the law in this excursus on his freedom, but his reflections on the law do not suppose the sophistication that is to be found in his letters to the Romans and the Galatians. The problems and controversies that occasioned those letters were seemingly far from Paul's ken when he wrote about the law in 1 Cor 9:19-23. In this pericope the "law" is not so much the Jewish law *per se* as it is the law in general. Paul's emphasis lies on his paradoxical use of freedom in regard to the law, whatever that law might be.

even though I am not under the law, so that I might win over those under the law: "Even though I am not under the law" is a phrase well attested in the manuscript tradition (‭א‬, A, B, C, D, F, G, P, along with various minuscules, ancient versions, and Patristic writings), but it does violence to the parallelism between the two parts of v. 20. An alternate reading found in Ψ, Byzantine ecclesiastical manuscripts, and the Textus Receptus (cf. *AV*) omits the parenthetical phrase. The disputed phrase breaks the parallelism, but it is well attested in the manuscript tradition ($\mathfrak{P}^{46}$, ‭א‬, A, B, C, D, F, and many of the early versions) and seems to have provided Paul with a vehicle for developing his thought in antithetical fashion. The phrase breaks the parallelism with v. 20a but establishes the basis for the parallelism with v. 21. Its omission in some of the manuscripts probably results from parablepsis, the scribe's inadvertent movement of the eye from one "under the law" to the next occurrence of this phrase.

As a Christian and as an apostle Paul is not under the law. Christian existence is not existence "under the law"; it is existence "under grace" (Rom 6:14-15). This in no wise means, nor does Paul ever say, that Jews and Jewish Christians should not observe the Jewish law. Although they may observe the law, Jewish Christians are no longer under the law. The Jewish law is no longer the norm according to which they are to pattern their lives.

21. *for those outside the law as one outside the law, even though I am not outside the law of God, but subject to the law of Christ, so that I might win over those outside the law:* With its parenthetical expression this verse is clearly parallel with v. 20b. "Those outside the law" *(anomois)* contrasts with "those under the law" *(tois hypo nomon)*. The expressions are, however, not directly contradictory. *Anomos* suggests independence of the law. Commonly used of those who violate the

law (so "lawless," cf. 2 Thess 2:8; 1 Tim 1:9; 2 Pet 2:8), it is also used of those who are without the law in the sense that they do not fall under the jurisdiction of a particular law. For the Jews, Gentiles are *anomoi* insofar as the law was not given to them (cf. Acts 2:23). As a consequence Gentiles are not bound by the law.

Verse 21 contains an alternate subjunctive form of the verb "to gain" *(kerdanō)*. Another form of the verb, *kerdēsō* (see vv. 20, 21[2x]) appears in $\mathfrak{P}^{46}$, Ψ, the Byzantine text, and $\aleph^c$. *Kerdanō* is well attested in the ancient manuscripts (א, A, B, C, F, G, etc.). *Kerdēsō* is a scribal correction for the sake of stylistic conformity.

In his parenthesis Paul offers himself as an example (really an example within an example) to explain what it means for Gentile Christians not to be under the law. Paul's pun, the playful contrast between *anomos* ("outside the law") and *ennomos* ("subject to the Law"), in which the root *nomos* controls the respective genitives *theou* ("of God") and *Christou* ("of Christ"), seems to be of his own coinage. In classical and Hellenistic Greek the antithetical terms simply mean "illegal" and "legal."

Paul's hapax use of *ennomos* (cf. Acts 19:39) seems to suggest that there is a law of Christ in contrast to the law of God, the Jewish law. There is, of course, no law of Christ as such. The "law of Christ" *(ho nomos tou Christou,* hapax in Paul at Gal 6:2; cf. Rom 8:2) is the law of love. It leads Christians to bear one another's burdens. Those who love their neighbor have fulfilled "the law" (see Rom 13:8-10). Paul's thought is that Gentile Christians, subject to Christ whom they recognize as Lord, fulfill and must fulfill the demands of the law of God. Several other passages in Paul's correspondence deal with the issue of Gentile Christians observing a moral norm (e.g., Rom 1:18-23; 2:24; 1 Thess 2:12; 4:1-8). Doing such does not place them "under the law." Gentile Christians continue to be outside the law *(anomos)* insofar as the Jewish law does not define the parameters of their existence.

22. *For the weak I have become weak so that I might win over the weak:* Paul had compared himself with Jews, with those under the law, and with those outside the law (note the threefold use of "as" in vv. 20-21; an "as" *[hōs]* appears in some mss., $\aleph^c$, C, D, F, G, Ψ, etc., at v. 22, but this is probably due to scribal error), but he identifies with the weak. Despite the observations made by D. A. Black ("A Note on 'the Weak' in 1 Corinthians 9,22," *Bib.* 64 [1983] 240–242) there is little reason to suggest that the weak are Gentiles who are unable to obtain salvation by dint of their own efforts.

to all people I have become all things so that I might surely save some: "Being all things to all people" may have been an accusation that some in the Corinthian community had directed against Paul, accusing him of being something of a chameleon, with inconsistent behavior (thus Marshall, *Enmity in Corinth* 156). In the Hellenistic world people were expected to remain true to their own character throughout the various circumstances of their lives. Paul's behavior is clearly marked as countercultural—for the sake of the gospel! (v. 23). Having become a slave to all (v. 19), Paul has become everyone's factotum. His cipher "to all people" *(tois pasin)* sums up the various contrasting groups enumerated in vv. 20-21. Paul did not become all things for all people so as to become a crowd pleaser (cf. Gal 1:10); he has done so in order that some people, from among Jews and Gentiles alike, might be saved (cf. 1:18-31). The reference to salvation, in a sixth purpose clause parallel to the previous five, paraphrases and explains what it is for Paul to win over various groups of people.

23. *All these things I do for the sake of the gospel, so that I might share in it:* Some interpreters, generally from among those who think that 1 Corinthians is a composite text, arguing that vv. 19-22 are a self-consistent unit and that the idea and language of the purpose clause is unique in Paul, hold that v. 23 is a post-Pauline editorial gloss. Their position has no support in the manuscript tradition. Verse 23 functions somewhat as an epilogue to the *apologia*. The "gospel" has been an important motif in Paul's *apologia* (vv. 12, 14[2x], 18[2x]). Typically the epilogue recapitulates the previous argument. Accordingly it is to be expected that Paul would make reference to the gospel in his closing argument. "All these things" (*panta;* some later mss. have the demonstrative *touto,* this) summarizes Paul's rehearsal (vv. 19-22) and forms an *inclusio* with the "all" of v. 19. The gospel Paul preached is the gospel of Christ (9:12); that is, it is the good news about the Christ who died for us (8:11).

What does Paul mean by "sharing in the gospel" *(hina sygkoinōnos autou genōmai)*? Since the gospel is the proclamation of the death and resurrection of Christ (cf. 15:3-4), the ground of believers' hope for eschatological salvation, commentators frequently assume that Paul is expressing the hope that he might share in eschatological salvation: thus the *NRSV*'s "so that I might share in its blessings." This notion is, however, foreign to the ideas that Paul expresses in 1 Corinthians (hence the suggestion by some that v. 23 is an interpolation!). On the other hand, Paul has expressed the idea that preaching the gospel is its own reward (9:18). He has a predilection for compounds of *syn,* some of which he has apparently coined himself. These compounds express various forms of solidarity in Christian existence. Here the substantivized adjective is *sygkoinōnos* (Rom 11:17; Phil 1:7), a "fellow sharer." Paul expresses the idea that by becoming all things to all people he himself shares in the preaching of the gospel (cf. 3:5, 9).

For Reference and Further Study

Barton, Stephen C. "'All Things to All People': Paul and the Law in the Light of 1 Corinthians 9:19-23" in James D. G. Dunn, ed., *Paul and the Mosaic Law.* WUNT 89. Tübingen: Mohr/Siebeck, 1996, 271–285.

Bornkamm, Günther. "The Missionary Stance of Paul in I Corinthians 9 and in Acts" in Leander E. Keck and J. Louis Martyn, eds., *Studies in Luke-Acts.* London: S.P.C.K., 1968, 194–207.

Chadwick, Henry. "'All Things to All Men' (1 Cor. IX.22)," *NTS* 1 (1955) 261–277.

Hall, Barbara. "All Things To All People: A Study of 1 Corinthians 9:19-23" in Robert T. Fortna and Beverly Roberts Gaventa, eds., *The Conversation Continues: Studies in Paul & John.* Nashville: Abingdon, 1990, 137–157.

Hooker, Morna D. "A Partner in His Gospel: Paul's Understanding of His Ministry" in Eugene H. Lovering, Jr., and Jerry L. Sumney, eds., *Theology and Ethics in Paul and His Interpreters. Essays in Honor of Victor Paul Furnish.* Nashville: Abingdon, 1996, 83–100.

Theobald, Michael. "'Allen bin ich alles geworden . . .' (1 Kor 9, 22b). Paulus und das Problem der Inkulturation des Glaubens," *ThQ* 176 (1996) 1–6.

7. The Games (9:24-27)

24. Don't you know that in a race all the runners run, but only one receives the prize? Run in such a way as to get it. 25. Every competitor exercises self-discipline in all ways—they to receive a perishable crown, we, however, to receive an imperishable one. 26. So I run accordingly, without hesitation. I box in the same way, not as someone flailing at the air, 27. but I bruise my body and I subjugate it lest, having preached to others, I myself fail to qualify.

INTERPRETATION

Paul concludes his rhetorical digression (ch. 9) by evoking the image of the athlete, specifically the runner and the boxer. The image of the athlete, the *agōn* motif, is one of the oldest in extant Hellenistic literature. With roots in the Homeric writings, the motif appears in Isocrates' fourth letter, written about the middle of the fourth century B.C.E. Variants of the athletic metaphor are found in Stoic and Cynic literature, in which the *agōn* motif (cf. Phil 1:30; 1 Thess 2:2) was used as a metaphor for the struggle on behalf of truth and virtue. The imagery suggests a public contest in which the competitors vie for the attention and allegiance of the spectators in order to win them over to the truth. Among Paul's contemporaries the *agōn* motif was variously exploited by the moralists, Epictetus, Plutarch, and Seneca. For example:

> Now God says to you, "Come at length to the contest, show us what you have learned, how you have trained yourself. How long will you exercise alone? Now the time has come for you to discover whether you are one of the athletes who deserve victory, or belong to the number of those who travel about the world and are everywhere defeated. (Epictetus, *Discourses* 4.4.30)

> Most of all must we consider whether the spirit of contention and quar-
> relling over debatable questions has been put down, and whether we
> have ceased to equip ourselves with arguments, as with boxing-gloves
> or brass knuckles, with which to contend against one another, and to
> take more delight in scoring a hit or a knockout than in learning and im-
> parting something. (Plutarch, "Progress in Virtue," *Moralia* 80B)

The Agōn Motif in Paul. Paul writes about his preaching of the gospel
in a way that is analogous to the way the Stoics talked about the struggle
for truth (1 Cor 15:32; Phil 2:16; 3:13-14; cf. 1 Thess 2:2; 1 Tim [1:18]; 4:7; 2
Tim 2:5; 4:7), but he also uses the athletic imagery to exhort the Corinthians to lead an appropriate Christian life. That he is using a classic topos
in 9:24-27 is indicated not only by its subject matter but by the plethora of
terms that occur but rarely in the undisputed correspondence. Several of
these terms are found only once in his writings. Many of them do not appear elsewhere in the NT. Within the particular jargon of this pericope are
such expressions as "prize" *(brabeios)*, "competitor" *(agōnizomenos)*, "exercise self-discipline" *(egkrateuomai)*, "crown" *(stephanos)*, "without hesitation" *(adēlōs)*, "box" *(pykteuō)*, "flail at the air" *(derō aera)*, "bruise"
(hypōpiazō), "subjugate" *(doulagōgeō)*, and "failing to qualify" *(adokimos)*.

First Corinthians 9:24-27 is the most extensive use of the *agōn* motif in
the extant Pauline correspondence (cf. 15:32). The image of the runner is
also featured in the letter to the Philippians (Phil 2:16; 3:13-14), but 1 Cor
9:26-27 is the only instance in which Paul uses the image of the boxer.
Both images are present in the deutero-Pauline Pastoral Epistles (1 Tim
1:18; 4:7-8; 6:12; 2 Tim 4:7; cf. Heb 12:1, Jude 3). The Paulinist author of 2
Timothy allegorizes the athletic imagery in an extended reflection on the
life and significance of the apostle (2 Tim 4:7-8). Paul himself uses the imagery more in keeping with the fashion in which it was used in Hellenistic rhetoric, in reference to his own preaching of the gospel and to
Christians striving to lead a Christian life.

Using another image, Paul describes himself in 1 Thess 2:4 as having
been found qualified by God *(dedokimasmetha hypo tou theou;* cf. *adokimos,*
"unqualified," in 9:27). God was never far removed from either Paul's or
the Hellenists' use of the *agōn* motif. Civic games were always celebrated
under the patronage of the local gods. The moral discourses of Epictetus
bear witness to this theological dimension of the motif:

> When a difficulty befalls, remember that God, like a physical trainer, has
> matched you with a rugged young man *(Discourses* 1.24.1).

> Great is the struggle, divine the task; the prize is a kingdom, freedom,
> serenity, peace. Remember God; call upon Him to help you and stand by
> your side, just as voyagers, in a storm, call upon the Dioscuri *(Discourses*
> 2.18.28-29).

The Agōn Motif in 9:24-27. Paul's use of the *agōn* motif in 9:24-27 is characterized by a deft use of pronominal references in the first, second, and third persons. This is in keeping with his paraenetic purpose, in which he makes use of examples and develops an *ethos* argument. The initial rhetorical question appeals to the audience's experience and engages them. Paul's metaphor speaks about racing in the Hellenistic world, where women and children also took part in athletic events. Almost immediately after engaging his addressees Paul makes a direct hortatory appeal to them. His terse formula in the present imperative might well be rendered "keep running so that you get the prize."

Thereupon Paul shifts to the third person as he develops the image of the athlete in training. He allows the minds of his addressees to focus on the picture placed before them. Immediately thereafter comes a shift to the first person, marked by Paul's characteristic "we, however" *(hēmeis de)*. Having thus identified with the Corinthians, Paul offers himself as one who has striven with a purpose. Mention of his own example is reinforced by an emphatic introductory "I, moreover" *(egō toinyn*, a Pauline hapax) and an emphatic "myself" *(autos)* in the expression of apprehension with which his exposition of the *agōn* motif is brought to a close.

Two hortatory motifs stand out in Paul's use of the *agōn* topos. One emerges from his use of the image of the runner with its reference to the prize and the victor's wreath. The focus is on the victory to be won. The Corinthians should do what they have to do in order to win. Then, having challenged the Corinthians with the idea that only one runner obtains the prize, Paul suggests that the victor's wreath is to be the common reward of all Christians. The irony is striking. It provides Paul's exhortation with strong rhetorical force and confronts the individualism of those Corinthians who so glibly proclaimed "everything is lawful for me" (6:12) to the detriment of the weak and delicate among them (8:8).

With the contrast between a perishable victory wreath and an imperishable one Paul maintains the eschatological perspective against which the conduct of the knowledgeable Corinthians is to be judged (cf. 8:6, 11; 9:10, 23). The reference to the eschatological calling of Christians gives a particular Pauline twist to the classic topos. Although Hellenistic moralists were not disinclined to note the ephemeral quality of the victors, the contrast they set forth was with virtues and values (peace, serenity, etc.).

Another paraenetic emphasis emerges, particularly from the image of the boxer. In the Hellenistic world the athlete's training *(askēsis)* was legendary. Seneca wrote, "No prize-fighter can go with high spirits into the strife if he has never been beaten black and blue" *(Epistles* 13.1). Dio Chrysostom wrote of the boxer Melancomas, ". . . beautiful as he was, he was even more remarkable for his self-control and moderation . . . and he had trained so rigorously and went so far beyond others in toilsome exercising that he was able to remain for two whole days in succession with his hands up, and nobody could catch him letting them down or taking a rest, as athletes usually do" (*Discourses* 28.6-7). Paul refers to the discipline of the athlete's training. He mentions the self-discipline (*egkrateia*) of the runner and the physical hardship (sparring?) that the boxer must undergo in order to be successful in competition. The image of the athlete who embraces *askēsis* for the sake of victory reminds the Corinthians of what they must forego in order that victory be theirs, a point to be made in the rhetorical appeal of chs. 8–10.

The Isthmian Games. "Don't you know that . . .," the rhetorical formula used to introduce the topos, is a commonplace of Paul's first letter to the Corinthians. The first direct appeal to the Corinthians since 9:13, the rhetorical question appeals to the Corinthians' own experience. Paul's use of the *agōn* motif is particularly apropos in a letter to Corinth, a city renowned for the biennial Isthmian Games. L. Castricius Regulus had reestablished these traditional games, held just outside the city, sometime between 7 B.C.E. and 3 C.E. His deed merited for him the title of *agonothete,* "leader of the games," the highest local honor to be conferred upon a Corinthian. Juvencus, a younger contemporary of Regulus, introduced the Caesarean Games, in honor of the emperor, as a prelude to the Isthmian Games. At the time of Paul's Corinthian correspondence Tiberius Claudius Dinippus was the *agonothete* of the Caesarean and Isthmian games (ca. 55 C.E.).

The athletes who competed in the games were often professionals (*athlētēs* as distinct from the *idiōtēs,* an amateur). They competed for monetary prizes, either a sum of money or a reduction of taxes. Some of the same athletes who participated in the games at Olympia joined in the Isthmian Games in Corinth. In the Oxyrhynchos games (2nd or 3rd c. C.E.) prizes amounting to four hundred drachmas were awarded to the winners. Sometimes the reward for a victorious race came from the winner's home town, honored as it was by the fame and glory that resulted from the victory.

Paul demonstrates a fair amount of awareness of athleticism. He mentions two athletic contests, running and boxing. He notes the importance of training so as to be able to win. He is aware of the possibilities of failing to qualify and being disqualified (cf. 2 Tim 2:5). He knows full well that there is only one winner in a race (Phil 3:14; cf. 2 Tim 2:5) and that it is really necessary to press forward in order to win (Phil 3:14). He knows about the prizes (*brabeios*) and the crown (*stephanos*) of victory. At Olympia the crown was an olive wreath; in the Isthmian Games it was a pine wreath. Paul disparagingly compares the victor's wreath to the imperishable crown won by Christians, but even the ancients were aware of the garland's lack of real value (cf. Lucian, *Anacharsis* 9–10).

NOTES

24. *Don't you know that in a race all the runners run, but only one receives the prize?*
Having made a passionate appeal in his own defense (vv. 15-23), Paul again
engages his imaginary interlocutors with a rhetorical question. Throughout
his apology Paul has used the rhetorical question (17x thus far), but not the
apostrophic vocative—strikingly absent from ch. 9!—to engage his audience.
The rhetorical question introduces an *agōn* motif (vv. 24-27), a classic rhetorical topos. Paul's question is addressed to the whole community.

Paul's specific image is that of the runner (see Phil 2:16; 3:13-14; cf. 2 Tim
4:7 Heb 12:1) whose mind is focused on winning. The image is sharpened by
means of a contrast between the pack of runners (*pantes;* cf. *pas* in v. 25) and
the single runner *(heis)* who receives the prize. In a race there is only one winner, only one who receives the crown of victory. The prize (*brabeios,* in the NT
only here and Phil 3:14) is the victor's wreath (v. 25b), but there may be other
prizes as well. In Phil 3:13-14 Paul also uses the image of the runner, not so
much to underscore that there is a single prize to be won as to highlight the
image of the runner straining to cross the finish line.

Run in such a way as to get it: Having engaged his audience and focused the
metaphor, Paul makes a paraenetic appeal to his addressees in the form of a
continuing metaphor. The present imperative *(trechete)* suggests continuing
effort. Paul urges the audience to run so as to obtain the prize. His language
is elliptical; the object of the verb (*katalabēte,* "get") must be inferred from the
immediately preceding rhetorical question. Paul's exhortation appeals to the
Corinthians to make the effort to win the prize. In the following verse he will
explain that there is a condition to be fulfilled in order to obtain the prize, and
that the prize is a special one.

25. *Every competitor exercises self-discipline in all ways:* A postpositive *de* links
Paul's exhortation to a third-person description that allows for his further
exploitation of the athletic metaphor. The aphorism, that every competitor
exercises self-discipline in every way, employs language that is not characteristic of Paul's vocabulary. "Competitor," the participle *agōnizomenos,* cognate with *agōn* (cf. Phil 1:30; 1 Thess 2:2), is hapax in his writings. Among NT
authors Paul alone uses the verb "to exercise self-discipline," *egkrateuomai,*
whose cognate noun, hapax in Paul, appears in a catalogue of virtues (Gal
5:23). His other use of the verb describes control of the sexual drive (1 Cor
7:9), a usage that Paul shares with other Hellenistic writers.

they to receive a perishable crown, we, however, to receive an imperishable one: Paul's
comment on the aphorism draws a contrast *(men . . . de)* between "them" and
"us," between athletes and Christians committed to the gospel. His customary "we, however" (*hēmeis de;* cf. 1:23; 2:12, 16; 4:10[2x]; 9:25) enhances the
contrast between athletes with their crowns and Christians with their imperishable crowns. The resumptive *men oun* with which the contrast is introduced indicates that the contrast is not real; it is merely fictive. The metaphor,
however, is imperfect. Only one athlete can receive the prize (9:24); all Christians are to gain the prize that is theirs.

The motif of the crown, the victor's wreath (*stephanos;* cf. 4 Macc 17:15), is part of the literary topos. Elsewhere in Paul "crown" is used in a merely metaphorical sense (see Phil 4:1; 1 Thess 2:19). On the contrast between perishable and imperishable (*phtharton–aphtharton*) see 15:50. The privative alpha of *aphtharton* creates a sharp antithesis.

26–27. *So I run accordingly, without hesitation:* Having engaged his audience with the direct appeal of v. 24 and having explained the point that he was making (v. 25), Paul again offers himself as an example in vv. 26 and 27. In his *ethos* appeal the image Paul continues to evoke is that of the runner (cf. 2 Tim 4:7) running the race with only one goal in mind, namely to come in first and win the victor's wreath. Paul uses contrast to make his point. He runs with determination so as to win; he does not run in haphazard and indifferent fashion. *Adēlōs,* "without hesitation," is hapax in the NT (cf. Paul's use of the related adjective in 14:8).

I box in the same way: Paul continues the *agōn* motif with another image, that of the boxer. This is the only time in his extant correspondence that he employs this image (cf. 1 Tim 6:12; 2 Tim 4:7). It was, however, a classic topos used, among others, by Paul's contemporaries, the moralists Plutarch and Seneca. See Plutarch, "Advice about Keeping Well," *Moralia* 133E; "Table Talk," Moralia 624B, 638D-640A; Seneca, *Epistles* 80.1-3. Boxing, says Plutarch, is "first among the gymnastic sports." He cites Homer as his authority for this. See "Self Praise," *Moralia* 539B; "Table Talk," *Moralia* 640A.

not as someone flailing at the air, but I bruise my body and I subjugate it: Again Paul uses contrast (this time with *alla*) to make his point. His unusual vocabulary comes from the world of boxing. "Box" (*pykteuō*), "flail at the air" (*derō aera*), and "subjugate" (*doulagōgeō*) are hapax in the NT. "Bruise" (*hypōpiazō*) appears elsewhere only in Luke 18:5, where it is a metaphor. The image is that of serious sparring. Paul is not like a shadow-boxer sparring with the air. Rather he is like the boxer who is bruised and bloodied in the rough-and-tumble of the fight. His unusual jargon comes from the boxing world.

lest, having preached to others, I myself fail to qualify: Paul's preaching of the gospel is like a contest in which he is vying for people's attention and allegiance, but his final word expresses some apprehension (*mē pōs*). Paul has preached to others. That is his role in life (1:17). To speak of his preaching Paul uses *kēryssō* ("to proclaim," cf. 1:23; 15:11, 12), with emphasis on the public character of the announcement rather than *euaggelizomai,* "to announce the good news," which points to the content of the announcement. As the philosophers proclaimed their teaching in the public forum, so Paul has proclaimed the gospel to others.

Paul's fear is that despite having proclaimed the gospel he might (note the emphatic *autos*) still fail to make the grade. Within Paul's athletic metaphor *adokimos,* "failing the testing process," suggests a failure to qualify. Hapax in 1 Corinthians (cf. Rom 1:28; 2 Cor 13:5, 6, 7), the adjective belongs to a word group that Paul often employs. In 1 Thess 2:4 he used its cognate *dokimazō* to speak of himself as having been found qualified to be entrusted with the mission of preaching in the gospel. In that passage it is God who passes judgment on Paul's qualifications. Had he not acted as he did, Paul might have failed to participate in the *agōn* of preaching the gospel (cf. 9:23). Paul's words reflect the Stoics' use of the *agōn* motif, in which the image of the athletic contest is used to describe the struggle for the truth. In this regard the Stoics and Cynics spoke of Hercules as a model to be followed.

FOR REFERENCE AND FURTHER STUDY

Deidun, T. J. "Linford Christi?" *Month* 29 (1996) 340–344.
Garrison, Roman. "Paul's Use of the Athlete Metaphor in 1 Corinthians 9," *SR* 22 (1993) 209–217. Reprinted in idem, *The Graeco-Roman Context of Early Christian Literature.* JSNT.S 137. Sheffield: Sheffield Academic Press, 1997, 95–104.
Papathomas, Amphilochios. "Das agonistische Motif 1 Kor 9.24ff. im Spiegel zeitgenössischer dokumentarisher Quellen," *NTS* 43 (1997) 223–241.
Pfitzner, Victor C. *Paul and the Agōn Motif: Traditional Athletic Imagery in the Pauline Literature.* NovT.S 16. Leiden: Brill, 1967.
Schwankl, Otto. "'Lauft so, dass ihr gewinnt'. Zur Wettkampfmetaphorik in 1 Kor 9," *BZ* 41 (1997) 174–191.

8. *Learning from Scripture* (10:1-13)

1. Brothers and sisters, I don't want you not to know that all our ancestors were under the cloud and all passed through the sea 2. and all were baptized into Moses in the cloud and in the sea 3. and all ate the same spiritual food 4. and all drank the same spiritual drink; for they drank of the spiritual rock, which was following, and the rock was Christ. 5. But God was not pleased with most of them. They were put to death in the wilderness. 6. These things became examples for us so that we might not crave for evil, as they craved. 7. Do not become idolaters as some of them did, as it is written, "the people sat down to eat and drink and rose to play." 8. Let us not engage in sexual misconduct as some of them engaged in sexual misconduct, and twenty-three thousand fell in one day. 9. Let us not tempt Christ as some of them tempted, and were destroyed by serpents. 10. Do not grumble as some of them grumbled, and were killed by the Destroyer. 11. These things happened to them by way of example. They were written for our admonition, we on whom the ends of the ages have arrived. 12. And so let the one who thinks that he or she is standing watch out lest he or she fall. 13. No temptation has taken hold of you except a very human one. God is faithful. He will not allow you to be tempted beyond your capacity. With the temptation God will also create a way out, so that you can survive.

Having completed his digression Paul captures the attention of his addressees with an apostrophic "brothers and sisters," a form of address last used in 7:29. A formal disclosure formula is used to introduce an extended reflection on Israel's Exodus experience (1 Cor 10:1-13).

A Midrash on Numbers. Rhetorically Paul's reflection on the events in the wilderness is an argument from authority. The tale Paul develops in 10:1-13 is consistent with the use of examples *(paradeigmata)* in Hellenistic rhetoric and Judaism's use of Scripture. In the *Art of Rhetoric* Aristotle states that there are two kind kinds of examples. One consists in relating things that had happened in history *(pragmata progegenēmena);* the other consists of comparisons and fables (see *Art of Rhetoric* 2.20.2-4). Within Judaism midrash is essentially the written explanation of a written text. The present passage abounds in allusions to the story of the Exodus as it is appears in the book of Numbers. Numbers is the text chosen by Paul in his rhetorical *heurēsis.* For the most part the passages in Numbers to which allusion is made are those that deal with eating and drinking. Thus the choice of scriptural passages is well adapted to Paul's rhetorical argument.

First Corinthians 10:1-13 is a sustained midrashic exposition, the first and longest of such expositions in the letter. Paul's use of the Exodus account bears similarity to rabbinic *haggadah* (the story) and *halakah* (the behavioral imperative). In the midrashic exposition of a text rabbis often had recourse to other scriptural passages. Within Paul's midrash an explicit citation of Exod 32:6 (LXX) is to be found in 10:7. This is the only text cited verbatim in the passage. The citation serves as a warrant for Paul's exhortation to the Corinthians that they avoid idolatry. Paul's use of the Scripture in this fashion is consistent with the way Hellenistic rhetors cited the words of philosophers and sages.

Paul's exposition uses a number of exceptional expressions, many of them hapax legomena in 1 Corinthians. Some are hapax in the Pauline correspondence or even in the entire NT. Since many of the hapax also occur in Numbers their presence in 10:1-13 serves to confirm the midrashic nature of Paul's exposition. That so much of the vocabulary is not otherwise found in Paul's writings suggests that Paul's midrash has its roots in a pre-Pauline, perhaps even a pre-Christian, tradition. G. D. Collier opines that the epistolary unit is a midrash on Numbers 11's *epithymia* ("craving") motif in the tradition of Psalms 78 and 106.

The Rock Was Christ. In the development of his argument Paul interfaces the wilderness experience with the experience of the Corinthians. He interprets the guidance of the people by the cloud and their passage through the sea as "being baptized" in Moses. Christian language, speaking of a redemptive experience, is used to describe the Israelites' experience during the Exodus. For the Corinthians' benefit Paul has rehearsed the story of the Exodus in the light of the Corinthians' own experience. He interprets the manna and the water provided at Meribah (Exod 17:6; Num 20:7-11) as "spiritual food and drink." The allusion to the Eucharist is easily recognized. Paul will develop the allusion in the following pericope (10:14-22).

Paul makes it easy for the Corinthians to grasp his message by introducing Christ into his rehearsal of the wilderness events. The rock at Meribah is allegorically identified as the Christ (v. 4). The name of Christ recurs in Paul's negative exhortations. The Corinthians are urged not to "tempt Christ" (v. 9), an allusion to the people of Israel who tested the Lord (Exod 17:7) when they complained against Moses because they had no water for themselves, their children, and their livestock.

The summary rehearsal of the Exodus events with which Paul begins his exposition (vv. 1-5) sets the stage for what proves to be an actualizing interpretation of the biblical narrative. In the next pericope, when Paul invites the Corinthians to reflect on their eucharistic experience of eating and drinking (10:14-22) he will again use the name of Christ (10:16). Again he will urge the Corinthians to learn from the experience of Israel (10:18). The events of the past have not been rehearsed so that the past can be understood; they have been retold so that the present can be understood (10:11).

Paul develops his exposition of the Scriptures in such a way that they are pertinent to the life of the Christians at Corinth. This is important since of themselves the Jewish Scriptures are for the most part alien to the largely Gentile Christian community at Corinth. Notwithstanding their ethnicity Paul has virtually coöpted the Gentile Christians of Corinth into the Jewish community. He begins his exposition with a mention of "all our ancestors." The Israelites of the generation in the wilderness are the ancestors of the Corinthian Christians.

Midrashic Exhortation. Paul's scripturally-based exposition begins with a narrative of events (vv. 1-5) on which Paul reflects and from which he educes pertinent paraenesis (10:6-13). Thereupon he draws a strong inference from the midrash he has developed. "Wherefore, my beloved," he says, "flee from idolatry" (10:14). The command echoes 10:7 in which Paul urges the Corinthians not to become idolaters, "Do not become idolaters as some of them were, as it is written, 'the people sat down to eat and drink and rose to play.'" The first imperative of his paraenetic exhortation is interpreted by means of a scriptural citation, Exod 32:6. Reinforced both by this argument from authority and by the inferential command of 10:14, the exhortation provides a focus for Paul's hortatory remarks.

Part of the force of Paul's exhortation derives from the negative example of the wilderness generation of Israelites. Paul uses their example in five loosely parallel statements (10:6-10), each of which employs a negative and is couched in language that evokes the experience of some Israelites during the time of the Exodus. The five negative statements contrast sharply with the five positive statements (10:1-4) in the opening rehearsal of events, "all our ancestors were under the cloud and all passed through the sea and all were baptized into Moses in the cloud and in the sea and all ate the same spiritual food and all drank the same spiritual drink." With their repeated (5x) "all" *(pantes)* the five positive statements speak of the experience of the wilderness generation in terms that evoke salvation, albeit from a Christian perspective.

The five negative statements are characterized by the use of a negative particle *(mē* once, *mēde* four times) and a construction that makes use of simile *(kathōs* four times, *kathaper* once), ". . . not crave for evil, as they craved. Do not become idolaters as some of them did. . . . Let us not engage in sexual misconduct as some of them engaged in sexual misconduct, and twenty-three thousand fell in one day. Let us not tempt Christ as some of them tempted, and were destroyed by serpents. Do not grumble as some of them grumbled, and were killed by the Destroyer." The last four exhortations talk about "some of them" *(tines autōn),* an expression that contrasts sharply with the fivefold "all" *(pantes)* of vv. 1-4.

In vv. 9-11 Paul specifies the biblical allusion by describing what happened to "some of them." They fell . . . were destroyed . . . were killed. The fate of some who had shared in the common experience of salvation should serve as a warning to the Corinthians who themselves share a common experience of salvation. The message could not be lost on the Corinthians. A salvific experience does not guarantee that some will not perish. Paul first makes his point in v. 5. He then spells it out in graphic detail with references to those who participated in the worship of Baal at Peor (Num 25:1-9), those who grumbled against the Lord and Moses (Num 21:5-6), and those who had murmured against Moses and Aaron (Num 14:2; cf. Exod 16:2-3).

The negative injunctions are characterized not only by their parallelism but also by the fact that they have been incorporated into a literary unit delimited by the encompassing notion of "example" *(tauta de typoi,* v. 6; *tauta de typikōs,* v. 11). The *inclusio* defines vv. 6-11 as a discrete subunit within Paul's scriptural exposition. The definition is all the more striking insofar as *typikōs* is hapax in the NT and *typos* is hapax in 1 Corinthians. Elucidating the nature of the events in the wilderness, Paul states that these past events "became examples for us so that we might not crave for evil" (v. 6). As he brings the subunit to closure he affirms that "these things happened to them by way of example; they were written for our admonition" (v. 11). The intervening injunctions flesh out what these things and their consequences are.

In his terse reference to the events at Kibroth-hattaavah (Num 11:34-35) Paul does not say that the events took place only so that there might be examples for the Corinthians. His point is that once an account of these events had been written it served a paraenetic function. The Corinthians are not to replicate the experience of the Israelites in the wilderness. They are to avoid idolatry and all its consequences. Basking in the experience of "all" of them (10:1-4), they must shun the conduct of "some of them."

Paul's first mention of "some of them" is clarified by the citation of Exod 32:1-6, an obvious reference to the incident of the golden calf. With Moses as a notable exception, that only "some" participated in the idolatrous worship is obvious. The reference is particularly apposite in Paul's letter to the Corinthians. The Corinthians themselves were grappling with idolatry, at least in the question of what to do about food that had been offered to idols. Citing Exod 32:6, Paul evokes the memory of idolatrous worship during the Exodus, Israel's salvific experience par excellence.

In its biblical context Exod 32:6 refers to the gala festivities of the Israelites who were celebrating the completion of the golden calf. In Paul's account the same Scripture is used to fulfill important rhetorical and literary functions. It provides a transition between his narrative account of events that have become examples (v. 6) and his paraenetic exhortation that exploits the example of the Israelites (v. 11). Rhetorically the Scripture functions as a *partitio*. Its first part with reference to eating and drinking sums up the narrative account and points to the eating and drinking of the Corinthians (vv. 2-4). Its second part with reference to child's play (cf. 3:1-4; 4:14-21) sums up the kind of immorality that devolves from idolatry, the kind of evil the Corinthians are urged to shun (vv. 8-10).

The use of Exod 32:6 is a clever pun that serves as the turning point in Paul's scriptural argument. It represents a kind of irony whose point cannot be missed. Eating and drinking as they did, the Israelites could not have been more audacious in their idolatrous behavior, or more egregious. The hybrist Corinthians are in much the same situation.

NOTES

1. *Brothers and sisters, I don't want you not to know:* Paul's words are akin to language that is commonly used today, "I want you to know that." The use of the "disclosure formula" is typical of his epistolary style (10:1; 11:2; 12:1; cf. Rom 1:13; 11:25; 2 Cor 1:8; 1 Thess 4:13). As used in Hellenistic Greek the classic formula consisted of the verb *thelō*, "to wish," the identification of the person addressed, a verb of knowledge in the infinitive, (sometimes) a formula

of direct address, and a *hoti* clause that contains the information. All five elements of the literary form are found in 10:1 (see T. Y. Mullins, "Disclosure").

With the use of a double negative (not . . . not to know, *agnoein*, literally "not-know") additional emphasis is achieved. Paul uses two variants of the classic disclosure formula, one with a double negative as here *(ou . . . agnoein)*, the other in a positive form. He uses the positive form when he supposes that the information is already known to his addressees (11:2; cf. 12:3; 15:1; Gal 1:11). The form with the double negative is used to impart new information (12:1; Rom 1:13; 11:25; 2 Cor 1:8). The use of the disclosure formula is singularly important as Paul moves from the digression on his apostolic rights to the topic at hand, eating food offered to idols. Paul had opened his discussion of this subject by affirming that the heart of the matter was knowledge and the use to which knowledge is put (8:1-3).

that all our ancestors were under the cloud and all passed through the sea: The reference to the cloud and the sea derive from traditional lore about the Exodus (see Exod 14:19-22). Although the community at Corinth was for the most part composed of Gentile Christians, Paul addresses the community as if they were Israelites, the covenanted and holy people of God (cf. 1:2; 5:13; 12:2). This, however, is the only instance in this letter in which he will refer to the Exodus generation of Israelites as the ancestors *(pateres)* of the Corinthian Christians. In 2 Corinthians Paul will also share elements of the story with them (see 2 Corinthians 3–4). In this account Paul emphasizes that the experience of the Israelites was a common and universal experience. Twice he mentions that all of them *(pantes)* shared the experience. This pronominal adjective is used as the subject for each of the verbs in vv. 2-4a (v. 4b is a midrashic comment). The use of the rhetorical device of paronomasia sets the stage for the paraenesis to come.

2. *and all were baptized into Moses in the cloud and in the sea:* Paul writes about the baptism of the Israelites in terms that recall Christian baptism (see Rom 6:3; Gal 3:27). The phraseology *(ebaptisthēsan* in א, A, C, D, G, Ψ, various minuscules and the Eastern Fathers) recalls the language used for Christian baptism (see 1:13, 15, etc.). Some ancient manuscripts read *ebaptisanto* (B, K, L, P), apparently to distinguish "baptism into Moses" from "baptism into Christ." That there was such a corrective dynamic operating in the textual tradition is confirmed by 𝔓⁴⁶ in which *ebaptisanto* appears as a correction of the manuscript. Virtually no evidence exists to support the contention of some scholars that late Judaism occasionally described the Israelites' passage through the Reed Sea as a baptism. Verse 1 is intended to compare the experience of the Israelites and the experience of the Corinthians. This enables Paul to draw a hortatory example from the Exodus experience. In a similarly free fashion the anonymous author of the Wisdom of Solomon used the motif of the passage through the Reed Sea to describe wisdom (cf. Wis 10:17-18; cf. 19:7).

3–4. *and all ate the same spiritual food and all drank the same spiritual drink:* In his midrash on the Exodus story Paul affirms that the manna eaten by the Israelites during the Exodus (Exod 16:4-36; Num 11:6-9), the water they drank, and the rock from which it flowed (Exod 17:1-7; Num 20:1-13) were "spiritual."

Since Paul explains that these events serve as examples for us and that they happened to provide an example (vv. 6, 11) Myles Bourke has suggested that one of the meanings of "spiritual" is "figurative." Paul uses spirit-language when he is reading biblical texts in an actualized, Christian manner (cf. 2 Cor 3:17), but to take "spiritual" in vv. 3-4 as simply meaning allegorical is to limit the range of Paul's thought. In the NT "spiritual" *(pneumatikos)* is a Pauline term (15x in 1 Corinthians; cf. Rom 1:11; 7:14; 15:27; Gal 6:1; Eph 1:3; 5:19; 6:12; Col 1:9; 3:16; 1 Pet 2:5[2x]). It describes reality that is thoroughly influenced by the Spirit, the creative and salvific power of God. In the context of Paul's midrash the description of the manna as spiritual food suggests a contrast between the food craved by the Israelites and the food given by God.

The aorist tense of the verbs "eat" *(ephagon)* and "drink" *(epion)* draw the reader's attention to the highlighted event. In the biblical tradition God's provision of drink for the people was exploited in a fashion somewhat independently of the narrative of the provision of food (cf. Num 20:7-11; Ps 78:15-16). Paul does something similar in 10:4 in order to evoke the presence of Christ (cf. 8:11-12; 9:12, 21) with the Corinthian community. The mention of food *(brōma)* recalls the food Paul was willing to forego (8:13) and the topic at hand (8:1, 4).

For they drank of the spiritual rock, which was following, and the rock was Christ: In Paul's view the rock must have followed the Israelites because Moses was able to strike it more than once (Num 20:11). The hitherto echoing "all" *(pantes)* is absent from this explanatory comment *(gar)* in which echoes of Christ as the wisdom of God can be discerned. Philo, Paul's Hellenistic Jewish contemporary, personified the rock (Exod 17:6), suggesting that it accompanied Israel on the salvific journey through the wilderness. In Philo's view the rock was the wisdom of God (see *Allegorical Interpretation* 2.86; Pseudo-Philo, *Biblical Antiquities* 10:7). Wisdom 11:4-8 speaks of the intervention of God's wisdom in the history of Israel, specifically in providing water from a rock for the people of Israel.

5. *But God was not pleased with most of them. They were put to death in the wilderness:* The punitive decree, "they shall die in the wilderness" (Num 26:65), is seen as a sign of God's displeasure (note the explanatory *gar*) with the Israelites. According to the biblical tradition only two of the Israelites who entered the wilderness, Caleb son of Jephunneh and Joshua son of Nun, were spared from God's punitive judgment (Num 14:29-30; 26:65).

6. *These things became examples for us:* Only here does Paul use "example" *(typos,* hapax in 1 Corinthians) in the plural (cf. Rom 5:14; 6:17; Phil 3:17; 1 Thess 1:7; cf. 2 Thess 3:9; 1 Tim 4:12; Titus 2:7). The term anticipates the *typikōs* of v. 11, creating the *inclusio* that identifies 10:6-11 as a discrete literary unit. In classical Greek "example" *(typos)* denotes the impression formed by the use of a mold or die or left as a result of a blow. In Phil 3:17 and 1 Thess 1:7 Paul uses the term in reference to himself, as an example to be imitated. The *typos* of Rom 6:17 may have an analogous sense, but more likely it means "compendium" (cf. Plato, *Republic* 414A, 491C).

Some of the Apostolic Fathers (*Barn.* 7:3, 7, 10, 11; 12:2, 5, 6, 10; 13:5; Justin, *Dialogue with Trypho* 42:4) used *typos* in reference to the prefiguration of events related to salvation history in Jesus Christ. Along with Rom 5:14, 1 Cor 10:6, 11 is often cited as a NT warrant for a typological reading of the Bible. Paul, however, is not to be seen as a proponent of patristic hermeneutics. He uses *typos* to present a model, the *paradeigma* of Hellenistic rhetoric, from which the Corinthians are to learn.

so that we might not crave for evil, as they craved: The purpose clause explicates the exemplary character of the Exodus events, specifically the events at Kibroth-hattaavah described in Numbers 11 (see especially Num 11:4, 34-35). The biblical narrative describes the Israelites' inordinate desire for meat and for the food of Egypt (Num 11:4-6) rather than for the manna provided by YHWH. This inordinate craving led to their death (Num 11:33-34). The Israelites craved for "meat" (*krea*, 11:4, 13[2x], 18[3x], 21, 33 [LXX]). In his discussion on food offered to idols Paul emphatically referred to "meat," *krea*, which he would gladly forgo for the sake of his brothers and sisters (8:13). "Crave" (*epithymeō*) suggests a strong desire to satisfy a felt need, often in excessive fashion. Paul's use of the same verb in reference to both the Israelites and the Corinthians suggests that their experiences are comparable. In the paraenesis to follow (vv. 7-10) Paul will repeatedly compare and, by means of the expected positive response to the exhortation, contrast the experience of the Israelites and the behavior of the Corinthians: do not become idolaters . . . let us not engage in sexual misconduct . . . let us not tempt . . . do not grumble.

7. *Do not become idolaters as some of them did:* Paul begins his exhortation with the mention of idolatry in order to define the matter at hand. The real issue in Paul's discussion about food offered to idols is idolatry. Above all else the Corinthians must flee idolatry (10:14), for there is only one God (8:6). Although Paul's first exhortation directs the Corinthians not to be idolaters, idolatry is not mentioned in Numbers' account of the events at Kibroth-hattaavah. The Israelites who had craved for meat and the food of Egypt were, however, idolaters, as the story of the golden calf illustrates so well (Exod 32:1-6).

Paul's language is elliptical; "as some of them did" is literally "as some of them" (*kathōs tines autōn*). His exhortation consists of a noun (*eidōlolatrai*) and a verb. Only in 1 Corinthians does Paul use the noun "idolater." Paul had previously employed the noun in two catalogues of vices (5:10-11; 6:10) as he was urging the community to avoid sexual immorality (cf. 10:8).

as it is written, "the people sat down to eat and drink and rose to play": Exodus 32:6 is the only scriptural verse actually cited by Paul in his midrash on the Exodus. The Scripture, formally introduced by means of the classic lemma "as it is written" (*hōsper gegraptai*), is quoted verbatim according to the Septuagint, *ekathisen ho laos phagein kai pein kai anestēsan paizein.* The verse functions as the leitmotif of Paul's exposition, providing a structural basis for a midrashic reflection. Its first part sums up the events described in vv. 1-5; the second part provides a point of departure for the exhortation to follow. Thus it serves as a transition between the rehearsal of events and its paraenetic application.

In Paul's midrash the citation of Exod 32:6 is singular not only because of its form and function but also because Paul's narrative otherwise alludes to the Book of Numbers' account of the wilderness events. R. B. Hays (*Echoes of Scripture* 92) sees references to Num 14:26-35; 25:1-9; 26:62; 21:5-9, and 16:41-50 in the midrashic exposition. The editors of N-A[27] identify Num 20:7-11 (v.4); 14:16 (v. 5); 11:4 (v. 6), 34 (v. 6); 25:1 (v. 8), 9 (v. 8); 21:5-6 (v. 9); 14:2 (v. 10), 36 (v. 10); 16:11-35 (v. 10) as passages to which Paul has made allusion.

Paul apparently considers sexual immorality, testing, and complaining (vv. 8-10) as so much "child's play." A key idea in rabbinic anthropology is the notion of the presence of two inclinations, one evil (*yēṣer hāraꜥ*), one good (*yēṣer haṭṭôb*), in a human being. The evil inclination was generally considered to have been created at birth (cf. *Qoh. Rab* 4:13, 1). More or less equivalent to self-serving sensuality, the evil inclination is also the source of vanity, anger, and so forth. The good inclination makes its appearance when one takes on the yoke of the Torah at the age of adolescence (hence *bar mitzvah*, literally "son of the commandment"). Children are those who have not received or accepted the yoke of the law.

Exodus 32:6 is introduced into the narrative with no little irony on Paul's part. The "eating and drinking" of Exod 32:6 refers to the feasting that accompanied the idolatrous worship of the golden calf. Paul uses the verse to recall the Israelites' eating the food (the manna) and drinking the water (from the rock) that God had provided for them. Their idolatry was all the more egregious after their experience of God's graciousness to them. The rhetorical effect created by Paul's referential transference is powerful. "The slap-in-the-face audacity of the people's idolatry," says Hays (*Echoes* 92) "is underscored by Paul's device of reading the eating and drinking as a reminiscence of the earlier narrative of God's gracious provision." The baptismal language of v. 1 similarly establishes the Corinthians as people favored by God.

8. *Let us not engage in sexual misconduct as some of them engaged in sexual misconduct, and twenty-three thousand fell in one day:* The incident at Peor to which Paul refers (Num 25:1-2) describes the Israelites having sexual relations with the women of Moab and participating in idolatrous worship. Probably the lewd conduct and the idolatry were associated with one another. Numbers 25:9 recounts that twenty-four thousand died by the plague as a result. Paul's reference to the twenty-three thousand who fell is a reminiscence of Num 26:62. In vv. 7-8 Paul capitalizes on the Jewish tradition (and prejudice) according to which idolatry is the root cause of sexual immorality (see note on v. 7; cf. Rom 1:26-31; 1 Thess 4:5). His exhortation, with both the negative plea and the historical example making use of the same verb, is in the first person plural subjunctive. In this respect it is unlike the paraenetic injunction of v. 7 but similar to the paraenesis of v. 9.

9. *Let us not tempt Christ as some of them tempted, and were destroyed by serpents:* In place of the unusual phrase "let us not tempt Christ" many ancient manuscripts have the biblical phrase "let us not tempt the Lord" (so ℵ, B, C, and the Textus Receptus; see Deut 6:16; cf. Exod 17:7), while a few others (A, 81) read "God." Chrysostom, perhaps the most influential of the Eastern patristic

commentators on the Scriptures, sometimes has "Christ" and sometimes "the Lord." The difficulty inherent in the idea that the Israelites tempted Christ makes "Christ" the *lectio difficilior* and serves as a warrant for its acceptance in *GNT*[4]. It could, however, be argued that the presence of "Christ" is the result of a scribal tendency to christianize the Jewish Scriptures. In fact orthodox Christians used 1 Cor 10:9 with "Christ" as its reading as a proof text against Paul of Samosata, the third-century heretical bishop of Antioch. For the proponents of orthodoxy 1 Cor 10:9 affirmed that Christ was not simply human. Christ was, so the argument went, divine and already active in biblical times.

Paul's comparative clause is elliptical; "tempted" lacks a direct object. The incident to which he refers is described in Num 21:5-6 (cf. Ps 78:18). Because of their lack of food and drink people complained against God and Moses (Num 21:5). As punishment poisonous snakes were sent among the people and many of them died. The event led to Moses' erecting a bronze image of a poisonous snake on a pole so that those who looked on it might live (cf. John 3:14-15).

10. *Do not grumble as some of them grumbled, and were killed by the Destroyer:* Instead of the imperative form of the verb (A, B, C, K, P, Ψ, various minuscules and Fathers) some manuscripts have a hortatory "let us not grumble" (ℵ, D, Origen, Augustine, etc.). The exhortative form probably comes from the influence of the previous exhortation (v. 9). The first and fourth of Paul's parallel exhortations (vv. 7, 10), in which he uses the wilderness generation of Israelites as a negative example, are in the imperative; the second and third (vv. 8-9) employ a hortatory subjunctive.

Israel's complaint against Moses and Aaron is mentioned in Num 14:2 (cf. Exod 16:2-3; Num 16:11-35). Only here does Paul use the verb "to grumble" (*goggyzō*, 2x). His use of "Destroyer" is hapax in the NT. The biblical narrative employs an onomatopoeic *diagoggyzō* (cf. *goggyzete . . . egoggysan* in 10:10). The Destroyer (*ho olothreutēs*) was the avenging Lord (Num 14:15-16; cf. Exod 16:3). In Exod 12:23 the Angel of Death is described as the destroyer (*ho olethreuōn*).

11. *These things happened to them by way of example. They were written for our admonition:* "These things happened to them" is found in some of the most important majuscules (A, B) and the writings of many Fathers. The Byzantine text type, along with a significant number of ancient manuscripts and some important Fathers, has a version of the text that incorporates a stylistic qualification, "all" (*panta*), sometimes preceding (ℵ, D, F, G), sometimes following the demonstrative (C, Ψ). Its mobility and the fact that it brings stylistic improvement to the text suggest that it is a scribal emendation.

"Admonition" (*nouthesian*) is hapax in Paul (cf. Eph 6:4; Titus 3:10). Etymologically the term suggests something that is put into a person's mind. Hence it has the meaning of instruction (cf. *TLNT* 2:548–551). Frequently, however, the connotation is that of admonition, particularly parental admonition (see Paul's use of the cognate *nouthetōn* in 4:14). The motif of divine admonition was well known in Hellenistic Judaism. God corrects his people with great consideration (*Ep. Arist.* 207) in order not to have to punish them (Philo, *Life of Moses* 1.110). Paul's suggestion that the biblical narrative was written to admonish the Corinthians is ironic. Many of them, the know-it-alls, considered themselves to be fully mature adults, all that they could be (cf. 2:6).

we on whom the ends of the ages have arrived: The relative clause modifies the qualifying pronoun "of us" [*our* admonition]. Paul's epistolary "we" includes himself, the Corinthians, and Sosthenes. In describing the group as those on whom the ends of ages (*ta telē tōn aiōnōn,* hapax in the NT) have arrived, Paul identifies himself and his correspondents as eschatological people, people upon whom the final events have begun to dawn (cf. 2:6-16). This eschatological identification of those for whose sake the Scriptures were written suggests that in Paul's vision the Scriptures themselves have eschatological significance.

12. *And so let the one who thinks that he or she is standing watch out lest he or she fall:* A strong inferential "and so" (*hōste*) is used to introduce the final exhortation. The exhortation is a warning. "To see" (*blepō*) is always used metaphorically, most often in a hortatory and sometimes a minatory sense (1:26; 3:10; 8:9; 10:12, 18; 12:10; 13:12) in 1 Corinthians. It can be rendered "watch out." With a contrast between standing and falling, Paul's exhortation is ironically phrased. Those who think that they are standing straight will soon fall. "To fall" (*piptō*) is commonly used to describe death on a battlefield (10:8; cf. Num 14:3), but here it is used metaphorically. Those who think they are standing must pay heed lest they die. The verbal forms in the singular call each member of the community to individual responsibility.

13. *No temptation has taken hold of you except a very human one:* In Greek v. 13 is a single, fairly long periodic sentence. To capture its rhetorical force as the peroration of Paul's argument it seems preferable to render the sentence in (three) shorter English sentences. Paul's verb in the perfect expresses a reality that occurred in the past with implications and force for the present. The adjective "human" (*anthrōpinos*) contrasts the human and the divine, a contrast that is explicit in Paul's text. It connotes the merely human (2:13; 4:3; cf. Rom 6:19).

God is faithful: That God is faithful is a commonplace confession in Paul's writings (1:9; 2 Cor 1:18; 1 Thess 5:24; cf. 2 Thess 3:3; 2 Tim 2:13). The affirmation reflects the biblical confession in which fidelity appears as one of YHWH's defining traits (see note on 1:10).

He will not allow you to be tempted beyond your capacity: In Paul's Greek "God" is the relative pronoun, "who" (*hos*). The relative clause is an affirmation of God's providential care for his people. God's care for the people is an expression of his fidelity to them. Paul's use of a pronoun in the plural contrasts with his use of the singular in the warning of v. 12. "Allow" (*easei*) is hapax in his writings.

With the temptation God will also create a way out, so that you can survive: Paul's relative clause continues with a strong adversative "but" (*alla,* not translated).

The parallel is heightened by the use of "temptation" *(peirasthēnai. . . peirasmǭ;* cf. v. 13a) and "can" *(dynasthe . . . dynasthai)* in each of the juxtaposed clauses. "Way out" *(ekbasin)* and "survive" *(hypenegkein)* are hapax in Paul. The latter is used in an infinitive construction that has a consecutive sense (BDF 400.2). The imagery of exit and escape continues the motif of the Exodus experience, written for the benefit of the Corinthians.

For Reference and Further Study

Bandstra, Andrew J. "Interpretation in 1 Corinthians 10:1-11," *CTJ* 6 (1971) 5–21.

Burchard, Christoph. "The Importance of Joseph and Aseneth for the Study of the New Testament: A General Survey and a Fresh Look at the Lord's Supper," *NTS* 33 (1987) 102–134, especially 121–123.

Collier, Gary D. "'That We Might Not Crave Evil': The Structure and Argument of 1 Corinthians 10.1-13," *JSNT* 55 (1994) 55–75.

Ehrman, Bart D. *The Orthodox Corruption of Scripture: The Effect of Early Christological Controversies on the Text of the New Testament.* New York: Oxford University Press, 1993, 90–91.

Enns, Peter E. "The 'Moveable Well' in 1 Cor 10:4: An Extrabiblical Tradition in an Apostolic Text," *BBR* 6 (1996) 23–38.

Feuillet, André. *Le Christ Sagesse de Dieu* 87–111.

Hahn, Ferdinand. "Teilhabe am Heil und Gefahr des Abfalls. Eine Auslegung von 1 Ko 10:1-22" in Lorenzo De Lorenzi, ed., *Freedom and Love* 149–171.

Hays, Richard B. *Echoes of Scripture in the Letters of Paul.* New Haven and London: Yale University Press, 1989.

Jervis, L. Ann. "'But I Want You to Know . . .': Paul's Midrashic Intertextual Response to the Corinthian Worshipers (1 Cor 11:2-16)," *JBL* 112 (1993) 231–246.

Koet, Bart J. "The Old Testament Background to 1 Cor 10,7-8," *CorC* 607–615.

Kreitzer, Larry. "1 Corinthians 10:4 and Philo's Flinty Rock," *CV* 35 (1993) 109–126.

Marks, Herbert. "Pauline Typology and Revisionary Criticism," *JAAR* 52 (1984) 71–92.

Meeks, Wayne A. "'And Rose Up to Play': Midrash and Paraenesis in 1 Corinthians 10:1-22," *JSNT* 16 (1982) 64–78. Reprinted in Stanley E. Porter and Craig A. Evans, eds., *The Pauline Writings. A Sheffield Reader.* Sheffield: Sheffield Academic Press, 1995, 124–136.

Mullins, Terence Y. "Disclosure. A Literary Form in the New Testament," *NovT* 7 (1964) 44–50.

Osburn, Carroll D. "The Text of 1 Corinthians 10:9" in Gordon D. Fee and Eldon J. Epp, eds., *New Testament Textual Criticism: Its Significance for Exegesis. Essays in Honour of Bruce M. Metzger.* Oxford: Clarendon Press, 1981, 201–212.

Perrot, Charles. "Les examples du désert (1 Cor 10:6-11)," *NTS* 29 (1983) 437–452.

Smit, Joop F. M. "'Do Not Be Idolaters.' Paul's Rhetoric in First Corinthians 10:1-22," *NovT* 39 (1997) 40–53.

9. *Avoid Idolatry* (10:14-22)

14. Wherefore, my beloved, flee from idolatry. 15. I speak as to sensible people. Judge what I say. 16. The cup of blessing that we bless, is it not communion in the blood of Christ? The bread that we break, is it not communion in the body of Christ? 17. Because there is one bread we, the many, are one body, for we all share in one and the same bread. 18. Look at Israel according to the flesh. Don't those who eat the offerings share in the altar? 19. What then am I saying? That food offered to idols is something? Or that an idol is something? 20. Rather, what they offer, they offer to demons and not to God. I don't want you to be associated with demons. 21. You cannot drink the cup of the Lord and the cup of demons; you cannot share the table of the Lord and the table of demons. 22. Are we making the Lord jealous? Are we stronger than he?

INTERPRETATION

In this passage Paul continues to reflect on Israel's Exodus experience. The strong inference he draws in v. 14 ("wherefore") and his exhortation to recall the historical experience of Israel in v. 18 ("look at Israel according to the flesh") show that Israel's desert experience is very much on his mind. These verses (vv. 14, 18) link Paul's exhortation to the argument he had developed in 10:1-13. The main thrust of his argumentation is nonetheless drawn from the Corinthians' own experience, their communion in the blood and body of Christ.

The Experience of Eucharist. In 1 Corinthians Paul does not so much teach about the Eucharist as he draws rhetorical arguments (the argument from *pathos*) from the Corinthians' experience of it. This he does with good effect in 10:14-22. He alludes to the eucharistic ritual in references to the cup of blessing and the bread that is broken (10:16). The cup-bread sequence, different from the bread-cup sequence of 11:23-26, appears in another document of early Christianity, *The Teaching of the Twelve Apostles,* whose language and motifs are similar to those used by Paul in 10:14-22. *Didache* 9:2-4 mentions a cup-bread sequence and highlights the motifs of blessing, breaking the bread, and the unity of the community.

Paul's words with regard to the cup *(potērion)* appear to be repetitive. He twice mentions the blessing, "the cup of blessing that we bless" *(tēs eulogias ho eulogoumen).* This does not mean that there are two rituals of blessing; rather it suggests that the cup is twice blessed, once by God and once by the celebrating community. Offered to God by the Corinthian community, the eucharistic cup is similar to the cup of salvation offered by one who calls on the name of the Lord (cf. Ps 116:13). The eucharistic cup (v. 16b), an anamnesis of the cup drunk by Jesus (11:25-26; cf. Matt 26:27; Mark 14:23; Luke 22:17, 20), is a cup in which the Corinthians experience the blessing of God.

With regard to the one bread (*heis artos*, v. 17) Paul refers to a ritual of breaking the bread (v. 16). Early Christian tradition used the language of "breaking of the bread" to describe and designate the eucharistic celebration (Luke 24:35; Acts 2:42; *Did.* 14:1; Ign. *Eph.* 20:2). At the beginning of the Jewish meal there was a ritual of breaking bread. The householder would say a blessing such as "Blessed are you, Lord, our God, King of the world, who has brought forth bread from the earth." After the blessing the householder would break the bread and distribute it to those reclining at table. The bread, broken and shared, was a symbolic mediation of the blessing. The early Christian practice of the Eucharist retained this ritual. Using the language of *koinōnia,* "communion," Paul states that sharing the cup and sharing the bread are participation in the death of Christ (v. 16; cf. 11:24-25). Mention of "Christ" evokes the memory of his death and resurrection.

Sharing the Lord's table through cup and bread creates a situation of radical incompatibility with sharing the table of demons, that is, participating in the ritual meals of idol worship. An idol may be nothing (8:4; 10:19), but participation in such cultic practice can be described as sharing the table of demons. No more than an individual Christian should share the table of demons should he or she be instrumental in leading a sibling, for whom Christ died, to recline at the table of demons.

Paul's Rhetoric. Paul's *lexis,* his chosen vocabulary, expresses the significance of the Christian Eucharist in a way that would be meaningful to Corinthians familiar with Hellenistic mystery religions. In that environment the language of "communion," *koinōnia* and its cognates, was commonly used with regard to cultic meals (cf. 8:10; 9:13; 10:20-21). Paul uses the abstract noun in 10:16 (cf. 1:9) and the related subjective noun *koinōnoi,* "participants," in 10:16, 20. The terminology belongs to the same body of language as "mystery," "knowledge," "power," "consciousness," and "food," other terms used by Paul that reflect the language of the socio-religious world in which the Corinthian Christians were living.

The "sharing" word group (*metechō* [vv. 17, 21, 30], *metochē, metochos*) is virtually synonymous with the "communion" word group (*koinōneō, koinōnia, koinōnos*). Similar types of semantic questions can be raised with regard to both these word groups. Does the terminology highlight the subjective dimension, the *association* of the participants, or the objective dimension, their sharing in a *common endeavor* or reality? Like the *koinōn*-word group, the sharing word group was used in the Hellenistic world to describe various cultic phenomena. Hosea 4:17 and 1 *Enoch* 104:6 speak of Ephraim being an associate (*metochos*) of idols. A second-century epigram of Serenos speaks of participation in libations and sacrifices: "It was for libations and sacrifices that we came here [Philae], desiring to participate *(metaschein)* in them" *(Sammelbuch griechischer Urkunden aus Ägypten* 8681.8).

Paul's rhetoric is marked by the strong inference of his opening remarks, "Wherefore, flee from idolatry." The inference *(dioper,* "wherefore") is drawn from the historical example of Israel whose wilderness story Paul had developed at length in 10:1-13. The rhetorical paradigm of Israel is again exploited in 10:18 when Paul urges the Corinthians to look at historical Israel.

The wording of Paul's direct address, "beloved" (cf. 4:14; 15:58; 16:24), is unusual. Typically Paul appeals to the Corinthians as to members of his family, his "brothers and sisters." Called beloved by the apostle, the Corinthians are characterized as sensible people. The designation is a form of *captatio benevolentiae* and may reflect terminology the "wise" Corinthians used of themselves. The language functions as an argument from *pathos*. An emphatic *hymeis* (a "you" that has not been translated) urges the Corinthians to make a judgment for themselves. Paul appeals to them as reasonable people. He asks them to judge the merits of the argument he is developing. Three pairs of rhetorical questions, among others, engage the audience and ask its members to make a judgment about what Paul is saying.

Paul's argument makes effective use of comparison and contrast. The Corinthians' eating food offered to idols is juxtaposed with Israelite priests' eating food offered in sacrifice. The Lord is contrasted with demons and the cup of the Lord with a cup offered to demons. With its synthetically parallel references to the cup and the bread v. 16 serves as a kind of major and minor premise in the argumentation. Paul's line of reasoning is virtually that of a syllogism from which he draws the conclusion, "because there is one bread we, the many, are one body" (v. 17). Paul brings a community focus to bear in a statement that sets forth a clear contrast between the one and the many ("all") as Paul appeals to the unity of the community (cf. 12:12-26) in urging that idolatry be avoided.

The Unity of 1 Corinthians. Verse 14 draws a pointed conclusion from Paul's reflections on Israel's Exodus experience: "flee from idolatry." Some Corinthian Christians had been so liberated by their experience of Christian freedom that they experienced no discomfort in participating in temple meals. Paul's attitude to such behavior takes a hard line. He affirms that it is radically incompatible with participation in the table of the Lord. His rigorous approach seems to contrast with the openness expressed in ch. 8. There a tolerance for eating food that has been offered to idols is restricted only by concern for the "weak" members of the community. The contrast between 8:1-13 and 10:14-22 is so sharp (compare

10:19 and 8:4) as to lead some commentators to opine that 1 Corinthians 8–10 is not a single composition. They claim that 10:1-22 (or at least 10:14-22) must have come from one letter and 8:1-13 from another.

The argument over the relationship between 10:14-22 and 10:23–11:1, with 8:1-13, is of major importance in the discussion of the unity of 1 Corinthians. H.-J. Klauck, for example, suggests that 1 Cor 10:1-22, together with 9:1-18, 24-27 and 11:2-34, comes from an early letter in which Paul proclaimed that Christians were not to participate in sacrificial offerings to pagans. Confronted by those Corinthians who claimed that he had not given sufficient reflection to the importance of Christian freedom or to such practical considerations as accepting dinner invitations and buying food in the marketplace, Paul would have written a second letter in which he offered latitude in this regard (10:23–11:1, together with 8:1-13 and 9:19-23, Klauck's "letter B"). Lamar Cope has gone a bit further, claiming that 10:1-22 is a post-Pauline interpolation into the text.

This commentary has adopted the stance (see Introduction) that 1 Corinthians as it has come down to us is a single letter. Paul's use of the A-B-A' chiastic pattern of exposition is one in which the A' element is generally more pointed than the A element. This is the case with regard to the relationship between chs. 8 and 10. Chapter 8 argues more generally, ch. 10 more specifically. It is unnecessary to consider 8:1-13; 10:23-33 as relating to one situation, eating food that had previously been offered to idols, and 10:14-22 as relating to another kind of situation, actual participation in idolatrous worship, since 10:14-22 gets to the heart of the issue by warning the Christians of Corinth to avoid idolatry.

Paul's imperative is more than a merely personal directive. Given the solidarity that exists among the members of the community, effectively symbolized by their sharing a common cup and the common loaf, it is imperative that the hybrists not lead into idolatry the weaker members of the community for whom Christ died (8:11).

Notes

14. *Wherefore, my beloved, flee from idolatry:* The use of the word "wherefore" *(dioper)* clearly indicates that Paul intends to draw an inference from the reflections he has just developed (see v. 18). In his extant correspondence Paul uses this Greek particle, "wherefore," only twice. Both instances occur in 1 Corinthians 8–10 (8:13; 10:14) as Paul grounds his exhortation on the basis of the argument he has developed. He would have it that the Christians of Corinth not offend their Christian siblings and that they flee from idolatry. Paul's injunction points to idolatry as being the root issue in the whole discussion. The present tense of the imperative (cf. 6:18) indicates that the Corin-

thians must constantly strive to avoid idolatry. In making his strong appeal Paul uses a form of address that recalls his love for the Corinthians (cf. 4:14; 15:58; 16:24). Rather than his customary "brothers and sisters" he appeals to them as his "beloved" (*agapētoi*). This form of address appears in 1 Corinthians only here (cf. Rom 12:19; 2 Cor 7:1; 12:19; Phil 2:12 [with *mou*, "my"]) and in 15:58, where "beloved" qualifies "brothers and sisters" (cf. Phil 4:1, again with *mou*).

15. *I speak as to sensible people. Judge what I say:* The *captatio benevolentiae* of v. 14 is continued as Paul describes the Corinthians as prudent folk (cf. 4:10, "prudent in Christ"). Having appealed to their intelligence, he directs them to make a judgment on the considerations he is placing before them. Each of the two short sentences used to expand the apostrophe of v. 14 includes a striking word that emphasizes what Paul has to say, *hōs*, "as" ("how sensible are the people to whom I speak") and *hymeis*, "you" ("judge for yourselves").

16. *The cup of blessing that we bless:* In the biblical tradition the cup (*potērion*; in Paul only in 10:14-22; 11:23-26) is a symbol of salvation (Pss 16:5; 23:5; 116:13), sometimes in contrast with the cup that is a symbol of divine wrath (Pss 11:6; 75:8). Jewish tradition knows of "the cup of your blessing" (*kôs šel běrākâ* that is, of God's blessing. See the prayer of Joseph in *Joseph and Aseneth* where the cup of blessing is mentioned (*potērion eulogias, JosAs* 8:9; cf. 19:15). The cup of blessing was not merely a Passover ritual nor was it a custom reserved to a solemn festival. The cup of blessing was drunk as often as wine was drunk at a meal. The Jerusalem Talmud recalls that after a common meal "R. Jacob took the cup and recited the blessing" (*y. Ber.* 7.3).

   is it not communion in the blood of Christ? The christological title used by Paul is "Christ," nomenclature that in Pauline usage alludes to the death of Jesus. His words recall the beginning of the letter when he reminded the Corinthian Christians that they were called to fellowship (*koinōnia*, 1:9; cf. 2 Cor 6:14; 8:4; 9:13; 13:13) with Jesus Christ our Lord. Now he specifies that fellowship with the Lord is realized through participation in his blood and body. Despite Wendell Lee Willis's disclaimer (see *Idol Meat* 167–222), sharing the cup of blessing (see v. 21) is presented as a participation in the death of Christ. Paul's reference to the death of Christ (cf. 11:23-26) may serve to counter Corinthian claims that the meal they ate was a spiritual meal (cf. 10:3-4). Eating the meal is participation in the death of Christ who died for the weak members of the community (8:11).

   the bread that we break, is it not communion in the body of Christ? Bread (*ton arton*) is in the accusative case by inverse attraction (BDF 295). "We break" (*klōmen*, used by Paul only in reference to the Eucharist; cf. 11:24) highlights the action itself. The broken bread, like the shared cup, is a participation in the death of Christ.

17. *Because there is one bread we, the many, are one body, for we all share in one and the same bread:* Paul draws a lesson from the eucharistic experience of the Corinthians, to whom he had appealed in the parallel rhetorical questions of v. 16. The repeated "one" (*heis . . . hen . . . henos*) not only provides emphasis

(BAGD 231.2) but also contrasts with "many" and "all" (*hoi polloi . . . pantes;* cf. the similar use of *pantes* in 10:2-4). Paul's strong emphasis on the unity of the community is a rejoinder to those within the community whose disdain for the "weak" led some of these to think of food as if it had really been offered to idols (8:7).

Paul takes up the motif of the one body and its many members again in 12:12-26 (cf. 12:12; Rom 12:5). There he uses a classic rhetorical *topos* rather than an appeal to the cultic experience of the Corinthians as he develops his argument.

18. *Look at Israel according to the flesh:* "Look at Israel" (*blepete ton Israēl*) recapitulates the motif developed at length in 10:1-13. *Blepete,* "look at," is not, however, as minatory as is the *blepetō* of v. 12. "According to the flesh" (*kata sarka*) is used to designate Israel as it actually existed, in this case historical Israel (cf. Rom 9:5). Given the experience of some of the Israelites during the wandering through the desert (10:6-11), some negativity may be implied in Paul's use of this term to describe historical Israel.

    Don't those who eat the offerings share in the altar? Paul returns to a familiar style of argumentation as he directs the first of a pair of rhetorical questions to the Corinthians. "Offerings" (*tas thysias,* the sacrificial meal, hapax in 1 Corinthians), is different from "food offered to idols," *eidōlothyta,* the subject under discussion (8:1, 4; cf. 10:19). In the example Paul offers for the Corinthians to consider "offerings" probably designates the portion of sacrificed food that was eaten by Israelite priests, cf. 9:13). By eating sacrificial food Israelite priests were associated with the altar of sacrifice (*koinōnoi tou thysiastēriou*) and its Lord (cf. Lev 7:5-8; Deut 18:1-5).

19. *What then am I saying? That food offered to idols is something? Or that an idol is something?* Paul's rhetorical question "what then am I saying?" represents his attempt to explain himself. His analogy is deficient. Food offered on the Israelite altar is offered to the one God of Israel (cf. 8:4-6). Idols have no real existence (8:4). Paul's strong urging of the Corinthians to shun idol worship and to avoid eating food offered to idols does not imply a parity of situation between sacrificial food offered to God and food offered to idols. The form of the disjunctive rhetorical questions suggests that the Corinthians will concur that idols are nothing (cf. 8:4) and that food offered to idols has not really been offered to idols.

20. *Rather, what they offer, they offer to demons and not to God:* A strong adversative (*alla*) introduces Paul's response to his rhetorical questions (cf. 9:12, for the technique). Even if idols are in reality nothing, food offered to idols is not without taint. It is not offered to God; it is offered to demons.

    Only in 1 Cor 10:20-21 does Paul speak about demons (*daimonia*). In the popular Hellenistic mentality of his time nature was a complex of various demonic forces that humans would attempt to control with various rites and magical rituals. Paul considers that although idols may be nothing (8:4), those who participate in idol worship commonly believe that they are attempting to wrest control of nature from the demons who control it. All reality, however, belongs to the one God who has entrusted sovereignty over all things to the one Lord (8:6; 15:27) raised from the dead. To participate in idol worship is, implicitly, to deny the sovereignty of the Lord Jesus. Hence there is radical incompatibility between the worship of idols and sharing the table of the Lord.

The textual tradition of v. 20 admits of considerable variation. With but few exceptions (e.g., Tertullian, Ambrosiaster), the textual witnesses include the antithetical phrase "to demons and not to God," albeit sometimes in inverted sequence. To qualify the indeterminate third person plural form of the verb some manuscripts (including $\mathfrak{P}^{46}$ and $\aleph$) add a clarifying "the Gentiles" *(ta ethnē)*. The wording of this clarification is not consistent throughout the manuscript tradition. Because of this variety, and since the insertion of this clarification is more intelligible than its omission, text critics generally hold that the clarification was not part of the earliest textual tradition.

I don't want you to be associated with demons: Christians, who are called to fellowship *(koinōnia)* with the Lord Jesus Christ (1:9), should not be associated *(koinōnous)* with demons. Eating food offered to idols makes them partners with demons (see the similar use of *koinōnoi* in 10:18). That is something that Paul does not want for his beloved Corinthians. There is but one Lord (8:6). This one Lord is even now in the process of destroying the powers that are hostile to him (15:24-26).

21. *You cannot drink the cup of the Lord and the cup of demons; you cannot share the table of the Lord and the table of demons:* A brace of parallel statements expresses a radical incompatibility between fellowship with the Lord and fellowship with demons. Neither "Lord" nor "demons" is qualified by the article (BDF 259.3). The anarthrous use of the nouns highlights the respective qualities of the cup and table.

"Cup of the Lord" *(potērion kyriou)* and "table of the Lord" *(trapezēs kyriou)* are hapax in the NT (cf. v. 16, "the cup of blessing . . . the bread that we break"). The "cup of the Lord" is undoubtedly the "cup of blessing" (v. 16). In the eucharistic tradition of the early Church that cup is associated with the cup that the Lord Jesus took and blessed. Note the repeated use of *Kyrios* (four times in 11:21-26) to identify Jesus. "Share" continues to have the cultic connotation that it had in 10:17.

22. *Are we making the Lord jealous?* In the biblical tradition God's jealousy is associated with idol worship (Exod 20:5; 34:14; Deut 5:9; 1 Kings 14:22; Ezek 8:3, etc.). Jealousy leads God to judge the people severely when they abandon him for some god or goddess (Deut 6:14-15; Josh 24:19-20; Ps 78:58-64; Zeph 1:14; Nah 1:2; etc.). In light of the vengeance typically associated with divine jealousy Paul's rhetorical question implies the threat of divine vengeance.

Are we stronger than he? The import of this rhetorical question is somewhat puzzling. As a followup to the rhetorical question of v. 22a and calling for a negative response (note the initial *mē*), it suggests the absurdity of trying to overcome God's judgment. References to God's strength are legion in the Hebrew Scriptures (Deut 32:30, 31, 37; Wis 6:7-8; 12:16-18, etc.). The targums, especially the Targum of Deuteronomy 32, sometimes present idolatry as a contest of strength with YHWH. For Paul it is futile to expect to escape the vengeance of the jealous God.

FOR REFERENCE AND FURTHER STUDY

Audet, Jean-Paul. *La Didachè: Instructions des Apôtres.* EtB. Paris: Gabalda, 1958, 372–433, especially 398–410.

Baumert, Norbert. "*Koinōnia tou haimatos tou Christou* (1 Cor 10,14-22)," *CorC* 617–622.

Cope, Lamar. "First Corinthians 8–10: Continuity or Contradiction?" *ATR.S* 11 (1990) 114–123.

Klauck, Hans-Josef. *Herrenmahl und hellenisticher Kult. Eine religionsgeschichtliche Untersuchung zum ersten Korintherbrief.* NTA n.s. 15. Münster: Aschendorff, 1982.

Panikulam, George. *Koinōnia in the New Testament* 17–30.

Rosner, Brian S. *Paul, Scripture and Ethics* 195–203.

Sebothoma, Wilfred. "*Koinōnia* in 1 Corinthians 10:16," *Neotest.* 24 (1990) 63–69.

———. "*Koinōnia* in 1 Cor. 10,16: Its Significance for Liturgy and Sacrament," *Questions liturgiques* 70 (1989) 243–250.

Söding, Thomas. "Eucharistie und Mysterien. Urchristliche Herrensmahltheologie und antike Mysterienreligiosität im Spiegel von 1 Kor 10," *BiKi* 45 (1990) 140–145.

10. *Summing Up* (10:23–11:1)

23. All things are lawful, but not everything is advantageous; all things are lawful, but not everything builds up. 24. Let no one seek his or her own advantage; rather let each one seek the advantage of the other. 25. Eat everything sold in the market not questioning for the sake of consciousness. 26. For "the earth is the Lord's and all that is in it." 27. If a nonbeliever invites you and you wish to go, eat everything placed before you not questioning for the sake of consciousness. 28. If, however, someone says to you, this is food that has been offered in sacrifice, do not eat for the sake of the one who has made the disclosure and for the sake of consciousness. 29. I mean not your own consciousness, but the other's. For why should my freedom be judged by another's consciousness? 30. If, as of course I do, I partake with gratitude, why am I reviled because of that for which I give thanks? 31. So whether you eat or drink or whatever else you do, do all for the glory of God. 32. Give no offense

to Jews and to Hellenes, nor to the church of God, 33. just as I myself aim to please everyone in every way, not seeking my own advantage but that of the majority, in order that they be saved. 1. Be imitators of me as I myself am of Christ.

INTERPRETATION

A characteristic feature of the deliberative mode of Hellenistic rhetoric is the argument from advantage. Seeking to change the audience's pattern of behavior, the rhetor tells them that it is to their advantage (*sympherein*) to follow the pattern of conduct he is urging. In exploiting the argument from advantage in 10:23–11:1 Paul returns to the slogan he had first criticized in 6:12. He deals with it in similar fashion. Everything may be permissible, but not everything is advantageous. He concedes the truth of the slogan and then adds a qualifying "but."

Social Realities. Before dealing with the "but" Paul addresses two realities in the everyday life of first-century Corinthian Christians: going to the market and being invited to dinner. Paul's mention of these two situations reflects his awareness of the real conditions of life of those to whom he was writing. It is also consistent with the kind of casuistry that pervades the letter. Repeatedly Paul interrupts the flow of his more theoretical discourse so as to address a variety of real situations that the Corinthians might face.

The first situation is going to market. Two inscriptions from the time of Augustus indicate that the market at Corinth had been a gift of the city's elite to the populace (cf. Jerome Murphy-O'Connor, *St. Paul's Corinth* 32). After the games or other major civic events meat was often sold in the market at prices that made it available for purchase by those of limited financial means. The sacrifices that had been offered to the local gods on the occasion of these celebrations provided the source of this windfall. Purchasing such food would then have been a possibility for the artisans of limited means (cf. 16:1-4) who made up a significant part of the Corinthian church.

Another fact of life was that the Christians of Corinth lived neither in a Christian quarter nor in a ghetto. They lived in a social situation in which they had a variety of contacts with those who were not members of the church. Some of these contacts are mentioned in 1 Corinthians, where nonbelievers (*apistoi*) are mentioned in 6:6; 7:12-15; 14:22-24, in addition to 10:27. In such circumstances the possibility could arise of a Christian being invited to dinner by a nonbeliever. The nonbelievers might even have been the Christian's "in-laws" (cf. 7:12-15). It is likely that well-to-do Corinthian Christians were those who might receive dinner invitations from social acquaintances who did not belong to the community of believers. Paul does not specifically mention that the invitation was to dine in someone's home. Sometimes dining halls were located within temple precincts (see above, p. 322). The locales were sometimes used by members of religious associations, but at times they were used for merely social purposes, much as a church hall might be used at the present time. Paul's advice to the Corinthians with respect to both the situations he has set before them is the same: "eat whatever." Eat whatever you purchase in the market. Eat whatever is placed before you when you recline at table. Should you accept a dinner invitation, follow the normal rules of etiquette and eat everything that is served by the host.

It may have been that some within the community were disinclined to eat the food available for purchase in the public market. Paul argues the case by introducing a citation of Scripture, but without the customary formal introduction, "it is written." His scriptural warrant is Ps 24:1, cited according to the Septuagint. The scriptural verse articulates a motif previously expressed in the monotheistic confession of faith with which Paul began his exposition on the matter of food offered to idols (8:4-6).

The situation of the dinner invitation changes when someone indicates that the food has been sacrificed in the temple precincts. Paul does not specify who that "someone" *(tis)* is. It could be a fellow guest, perhaps a pagan, who speaks out of concern for the Christian. Or it might be a Christian, perhaps a slave serving the dinner, who is one of the "weak" members of the community. The unusual use of "food offered in sacrifice" (v. 28) and the reference to Hellenes (v. 32) might incline the reader to think that Paul had a pagan guest in mind; his reference to the consciousness of the other (cf. v. 24) might incline one to think of a Christian. Despite the ambiguity of Paul's "someone," his advice is clear. One must forego the food for the sake of that person's consciousness.

To some extent Paul's wrestling with these practical issues is similar to the way rabbis of his and subsequent generations wrestled with the reality of idolatry in a cosmopolitan environment. Jews were involved in a variety of situations, civic, commercial, and social, in which they had contacts with Gentiles. They were even encouraged, at least by the disciples of Hillel, to be on good terms with Gentiles. Idolatry was, however, abhorrent to Jews. Their monotheism precluded any service of idols whatsoever. The issue in their real, cosmopolitan world was how to define and prohibit exactly those forms of behavior that were truly idolatrous.

A Kind of Peroration. The way in which Paul concludes his reflection (vv. 31-33) has the character of the peroration in a deliberative rhetorical appeal. The purpose of a rhetorical epilogue is to sum up the argument that has been developed. Frequently, and especially in pieces of deliberative rhetoric, the epilogue includes an exhortation. First Corinthians

10:31–11:1 is a threefold exhortation that summarizes the argument Paul developed in chs. 8–10.

The first exhortation (v. 31) specifically addresses itself to the issue of food, the subject of the discussion in chs. 8 and 10. In these chapters Paul had clearly identified the one God (cf. 8:6) as the overarching reality in the light of which all eating of food was to be considered. Another aspect of the discussion was consideration for others. Such concern was especially voiced in 8:4-15 and 10:23-30. This concern is the object of Paul's second hortatory remark, supported by a reference to himself (vv. 32-33). Throughout the letter and in the immediately preceding discussion Paul had exploited an *ethos* appeal. That genre of appeal served as the central argument (ch. 9) in Paul's chiastic structure. The argument, introduced in v. 33, is dramatically summarized in Paul's third exhortation. He urges the Corinthians to be imitators of him, just as he is of Christ (11:1). Paul's reference to Christ recalls the christological complement to the monotheistic confession of faith in 8:6 as well as the anamnesis of the Eucharist evoked in 10:14-22. Christ is the ultimate example of service rendered to others (cf. Rom 15:1-7; Gal 6:2; Phil 2:5-11).

Paul's epilogue urges a singularity of purpose among the Corinthians. It refers to cultural and ethnic factors that might divide them from one another. It speaks of "advantage," one of the most important arguments in deliberative rhetoric. The threefold reference to "all" in the final verse underscores the unity of the community, which is the primary object of the appeal of the entire letter. It is not inconceivable that Paul actually turned the argument of those who criticized him for being a social chameleon, acting as a Jew with Jews and as a Greek with Greeks (cf. 9:20-21), against them. With a bit of rhetorical hyperbole he says that he "pleases" (*areskei*, in the present tense) everyone in every way. Absent from the community, Paul could hardly be sure that he has actually pleased all the members of the community in everything he did. The sense of his affirmation is that he aims to please everyone. The choice of vocabulary may be dictated by Paul's rhetoric. As the argument from advantage (cf. vv. 23-24, 33) is typical of deliberative rhetoric (cf. v. 24), so the verb "to please" belonged to the semantic domain of political rhetoric (e.g., Herodotus). Like the Latin *placet* it was especially used to express the agreement of a public body. Paul does what he does so as to obtain the acquiescence of people, whether Jews or Hellenes, to win them over to the gospel so that they might be saved.

The force of Paul's rhetoric is seen more clearly when what he says here is compared with what he otherwise says about pleasing people. Elsewhere in 1 Corinthians he speaks only of a man pleasing his wife and a wife pleasing her husband (7:32-34), but in Rom 15:1-3 Paul says that pleasing one's neighbor is something that a Christian ought to do in imitation of Christ. On the other hand Paul often affirms that Christians should strive to please God rather than humans (Rom 8:8; 1 Thess 2:4; 4:1; cf. 1 Thess 2:15 and 1 Cor 7:32-34) and disavows his own attempt to please people (Gal 1:10).

NOTES

23. *All things are lawful, but not everything is advantageous; all things are lawful, but not everything builds up:* Under the influence of 6:12 many ancient manuscripts and some correctors (e.g., ℵ, C) have added "for me" *(moi)* to the slogan "all things are lawful." While 6:12 suggests that the slogan was used to justify sexual impropriety, now it is seen to have been used to justify a radical individualism that is indifferent to the harm that one's own conduct (eating meat offered to idols) can cause another. For Paul such radical individualism is not advantageous. What is advantageous is what builds up the community. In Paul the verb *oikodomeō*, "to build up," "to edify," usually has a specifically ecclesial reference. It is a matter of building up the church (cf. 8:1). In the way that Paul deals with the Corinthians' libertarian slogan he shows that he considers a proper ethical attitude to be a necessary and integral element in the building up of the church.

24. *Let no one seek his or her own advantage; rather let each one seek the advantage of the other:* With this antithesis Paul turns the argument from advantage on its face. He exhorts the Corinthians to seek the advantage not of themselves, but of others in the community. Paul's terse phrase is elliptical in Greek; it supposes a "let each one seek" in the antithetical clause (BDF 479.1). Paul's rhetorical appeal is an alternative expression of his appeal for love (cf. 13:5b; Rom 15:1-2; Phil 2:4). See also Paul's critique of another Corinthian slogan in 8:1 when he reminds the Corinthians that it is love, rather than knowledge, that builds up the community.

25. *Eat everything sold in the market not questioning for the sake of consciousness:* Paul's reference to the market *(makellō,* hapax in the NT) is another indication of his awareness of the real-life circumstances of Corinthian Christians. Although they must be concerned for the salvation of the weak within the community, not leading them into the sin of idolatry, other members of the community need not be scrupulous. They need not avoid buying what is available for purchase in the market. In the following verse Paul will explain why this is so. With his mention of consciousness *(syneidēsin)* Paul returns to a subject he had raised in the first section of his lengthy chiastic consideration on food offered to idols. There he had considered the consciousness (8:7, 10, 12) of those considered to be weak in the community. The connection suggests that the "other" of 10:24 is, in fact, a "weak" member of the community. Cicero wrote about people who "regard a thing that need not be shunned as though it ought to be shunned" *(Tusculan Disputations* 4.26). These are the weak.

26. *For "the earth is the Lord's and all that is in it":* As a warrant for his contention that one need not be overly scrupulous in making purchases in the market Paul cites the Scriptures. The citation of Ps 24:1 (23:1 LXX) is from a psalm of David, traditionally used in a liturgical procession. In 1 Corinthians Paul typically identifies scriptural citations by means of a formal introductory lemma, but that is not always the case (cf. Isa 40:13 in 2:16; Deut 17:7 in 5:13; Isa 45:14 in 14:25; Ps 110:1 in 15:25; and Isa 22:13 in 15:32). The use of the explanatory, postpositive *gar,* "for," in 10:26 (cf. 2:16; 15:25) suggests that Paul is citing the Scripture as if it were a well-known adage. In the enthymemes of his quasi-syllogistic reasoning Paul uses the words of Scripture rather than the words of sages as premises for his arguments. Since everything that exists in the world belongs to the Lord, there is no need for the Corinthians to avoid making purchases when they go to the market.

27. *If a nonbeliever invites you and you wish to go:* Elsewhere in 1 Corinthians Paul uses the verb *kaleō* in reference to the Christian's being called by God (1:9; 7:15, 17, 18[2x], 20, 21, 22[2x], 24; 15:9). Here he uses the verb, in the active voice, of a dinner invitation. In fact some few of the manuscripts have added *eis deipnon,* "to dinner." The usage is classic.

    As is his wont in 1 Corinthians Paul uses a conditional clause in order to address one or another real-life situation faced by the Corinthians. The conditional clause (with *ei* and the present indicative) underscores the reality of Paul's assumption. The "nonbeliever" is literally "anyone from among the non-believers" *(tis . . . tōn apistōn).*

    eat everything placed before you not questioning for the sake of consciousness: The wording of Paul's advice is similar to his advice with regard to food purchased in the market (v. 25), "eat everything . . . not questioning for the sake of consciousness."

28. *If, however, someone says to you, this is food that has been offered in sacrifice:* Paul's conditional clause (with *ean* and the subjunctive) suggests that given the circumstances of the dinner invitation it is to be expected that someone might note that the food had been offered in sacrifice. Should this prove to be the case—another instance of Paul's casuistry!—the situation changes.

    This is the only time that Paul writes about "food offered in sacrifice" *(hierothyton).* Elsewhere he writes of food that has been offered to idols *(ei-dōlothyton,* the reading found at 10:28 in C, D, F, G, Ψ, and other mss.). The terminology of 10:28 suggests something that has been sacrificed *(thyō)* in the precincts of a temple *(hieron).* Paul may have had in mind a situation like the one he mentioned in 8:10, where he also used *ean* with the subjunctive to describe a situation that might arise.

    do not eat for the sake of the one who has made the disclosure and for the sake of consciousness: In the specific situation he has just described Paul gives a different sort of advice. The changed situation requires a different kind of behavior. Should it be asserted that the food to be eaten had been offered in sacrifice (to a pagan god), a Christian should not eat the food. In this situation Christian freedom (see v. 23) does not permit the believer to consume the food with impunity. Concern for the upbuilding of the church requires that he or she take into consideration the one who has provided the information (*ton mēnysanta,* hapax in Paul) and that person's self-consciousness.

Some manuscripts, including the majority of medieval texts, again (cf. v. 26) cite Ps 24:1 at the end of this verse. The paean of praise is, however, absent from most of the major majuscules (א, A, B, C, D, etc.). Its presence in some manuscripts is most likely the result of scribal parablepsis, the eye of the scribe wandering from "consciousness" at the end of v. 28 to "consciousness" at the end of v. 26, his hand then repeating the psalm verse. The weight of the manuscript tradition and the possibility of scribal error coalesce in leading to the judgment that a citation of Ps 24:1 was originally not to be found in v. 28.

29-30. *I mean not your own consciousness, but the other's:* As in 10:19 Paul uses a verb "to speak" (there *phēmi,* here *legō*) to explain what he means. His explanation reverts back to his initial exhortation, namely that each one must pursue the advantage of the other (v. 24). One's own advantage is not the decisive factor in decisions made as to the eating of food. As was customary in Hellenistic Greek, a reflexive pronoun *(heautou)* appears in place of the simple personal pronoun.

For why should my freedom be judged by another's consciousness? If, as of course I do, I partake with gratitude, why am I reviled because of that for which I give thanks? Paul uses a pair of rhetorical questions to support (note the explanatory *gar*) his position. The questions concern freedom, the attitude that lies behind the claim that all things are lawful (10:23). The first question (v. 29b) is more or less equivalent to "why should my freedom be limited because someone else is scrupulous?" Both questions are phrased in the first person singular, a classic construction in which the "I" is used to illustrate something universal (BDF 281). Use of the first person in this way is especially characteristic of the diatribe.

To speak of his own gratitude to God Paul uses the term *charis* (see 15:57; 2 Cor 2:14; 8:16; 9:15; Rom 6:17; 7:25; cf. 1 Tim 1:12; 2 Tim 1:3), a term commonly used in his correspondence to denote the favor God has bestowed on the community (cf. 1:3, 4). "Partaking" links this passage with the immediately preceding pericope (cf. 10:17, 21). The indicative mood of the verb in the conditional clause suggests the reality of the condition (BDF 372.2c). Paul partakes with gratitude. His language is consistent with the argument from his own prestige *(ethos)* used throughout the letter and particularly exploited in chs. 8–10. In dealing with the issue of food offered to idols he cited himself as an example in 8:13. He devoted a lengthy excursus to how he had made use of the rights that were his (ch. 9). The topical unit concludes with a kind of peroration in which Paul urges the Corinthians to imitate him as he imitated Christ.

31. *So whether you eat or drink or whatever else you do, do all for the glory of God:* An epistolary "so" *(oun)* marks the transition from the presentation of background material to the appeal (cf. 4:16; 16:18). The "whether . . . or" construction is Pauline (BDF 454.3). Paul's theological use of *doxa,* "glory," reflects

the biblical *kābôd*. The terminology expresses the reality of God especially insofar as this is manifest in revelation. In writing about God's glory Paul often stresses the salvific nature of God's self-revelation. In matters of eating or drinking—indeed, says Paul, with regard to whatever else one does (*ti*, with *allo* omitted, meaning "whatever else," is a classic Greek construction; cf. BDF 480)—all that is done ought to be done for the glory of God (*eis*, "for," expresses purpose). Effectively the norm of one's conduct in matters of eating and drinking ought to be concern for the salvation of others (cf. 8:11-13).

32. *Give no offense to Jews and to Hellenes:* Paul's theological exhortation is supported by an expressed concern for the welfare of all people and the church. As he occasionally does, Paul reinforces his ideas with a kind of synonymous parallelism that features negative (v. 32) and positive (v. 31) statements in tandem. The exhortation of v. 32, coming at the end of a long disquisition on food offered to idols, shows that Paul's understanding of a Christian's moral responsibility includes a consideration of the impact of one's behavior on others. His moral exhortation is driven by social concern.

The loose parallelism between v. 32 and v. 33 suggests that "give no offense" (*aproskopoi . . . ginesthe*) is virtually synonymous with "please" (*areskein*). *Aproskopos*, "not stumbling," "giving no offense," is cognate with "stumbling block" (*proskomma*) in 8:9. The adjective appears elsewhere in Paul only in Phil 1:10, where it clearly has an eschatological reference. On the day of the Lord Christians should be found to have given no offense.

Jews and Hellenes (see note on 1:22) comprise the two parts of Paul's social world (cf. 1:22, 24). As he himself was concerned for Jews and Gentiles (9:20-21), so he urges the Corinthians to consider the impact of their behavior on the salvation of Jews and Gentiles. For Jews it was simply out of the question to eat the flesh of animals who had not been slaughtered according to the prescriptions of the Torah. Participation in events that took place within the precincts of a pagan sanctuary was likewise to be shunned. Paul is concerned lest the conduct of the Corinthian hybrists impede the access of Jews to the gospel. He is likewise concerned that such conduct might scandalize Gentiles. The danger is that they might consider such behavior tacit acceptance of the reality of the so-called gods and the legitimacy of their cult (cf. vv. 27-29).

nor to the church of God: Paul adds a third element to his exhortation, "the church of God." To some extent Paul's entire letter is devoted to the question of what it means for the Corinthian community to be the church of God (cf. 1:2). The venerable title, used of Israel of old, had been appropriated as a description of the Christian church. It echoes the language used in Deuteronomy to describe Israel during the Exodus, Israel as the *qĕhal-yhwh*. In 10:1-13 Paul forcefully told the Corinthians that the experience of that original church of God, whose story Paul briefly rehearsed, had been written to admonish the Corinthians.

The term "church" normally designates a specific Christian gathering, a "local church," and it is most likely in this sense that the term is to be understood in the present context. It is on this that Paul's emphasis lies. Paul urges the Corinthians to be mindful of the upbuilding of the church of God, their local Christian assembly. Christians are not to give offense to the brother or sister for whom Christ died (8:11). The danger is that some members of the community, disdained as weak, might be so influenced by the conduct of some hybrists that they revert to what they think to be idol worship (8:7-13).

33. *just as I myself aim to please everyone in every way:* In urging the Corinthians to be concerned for the salvation of all Paul reverts once again to an argument from his own prestige (note the emphatic *kagō*, "and I myself," with which the verse begins). He had previously done so when he considered the matter of food offered to idols (8:13). He himself had become a slave to all so that all people might be saved (9:19-23). "Aim to please" is a verb *(areskō)* originally used with a legal sense, "to establish a relationship," especially one that had been broken. In Paul's usage the verb sometimes suggests subservience and obedience (cf. Gal 1:10; 1 Thess 2:4).

Paul's "everyone in every way," with a double use of the universal *(panta pasin)*, is similar to the usage found in that earlier discussion (9:19, *ek pantōn pasin*; 9:22, *tois pasin . . . panta*). An emphasis on everyone and everything has, in fact, dominated the entire discussion on food offered to idols. "All" *(pas,* in various forms) appears twenty-eight times in chs. 8–10.

not seeking my own advantage but that of the majority, in order that they be saved: A participial clause explains Paul's point. He takes up the motif of advantage with which the pericope had begun (vv. 23-24) and offers himself as an example of how the Christian should seek advantage. The contrast between his own advantage and the advantage of the majority emphasizes his point. Paul seeks the advantage of the majority. His purpose clause explains what he understands their advantage to be.

Linguistically the phrase "my own advantage" *(to emautou symphoron)* contains the only example of *emautou* with a substantive in the entire NT. "Majority" is an instance of the use of the positive *(pollōn)* for the comparative (BDF 245.1), but it may reflect Semitic usage where "many" often means "all" (cf. Matt 26:28; Mark 14:24). On text-critical grounds *symphoron* (cf. 7:35), found in $\mathfrak{P}^{46}$, $\aleph$, A, B, and C, is preferable to the *sympheron* found in most minuscules, D, F, G, Ψ, and a correction to $\aleph$. *Sympheron* is endorsed by BDF 413.3, but it is not the choice of the editors of GNT^4.

1. *Be imitators of me as I myself am of Christ:* Stephen Langton's thirteenth-century division of the NT into its now-familiar chapters does not always respect the literary conventions of the NT authors. His separation of 11:1 from ch. 10 divides Paul's final and forceful conclusion—in fact, the conclusion to the entire discussion on the eating of food offered to idols!—from the preceding discussion. That it belongs with the preceding material rather than with what follows is to be seen in the semantic and syntactic ties between 11:1 and 10:33. This is confirmed by "I commend you" *(epainō de)* in 11:2. The introductory formula begins a new section of Paul's letter.

From the opening salutation of this letter Paul has offered himself as an example *(paradeigma)* to the Corinthians. His personal example is one of the most constant and forceful arguments in his rhetorical arsenal. What distinguishes vv. 10:33–11:1 from Paul's earlier use of his own example is that there is nothing subtle about it. He has set himself out as an example in v. 33 with a blatant and emphatic comparison *(kathōs kagō)*. Thereafter he minces no words as he says "be imitators of me." Finally he affirms that he is doing nothing other than imitating Christ himself. Paul's final exhortation suggests a kind of chain reaction: the Corinthians are to imitate Paul as Paul has imitated Christ (cf. 1 Thess 1:6).

In his paraenesis Paul typically identifies Jesus as Lord *(Kyrios)*. That is not the case here, where Jesus is called "Christ." Use of this title harks back to 10:14-22 where Paul used the Corinthians' participation in the Eucharist in his argument. Anamnesis of the Lord's Supper typically calls for use of the Christ title with its suggestion of the death of Christ. In what sense can Paul say that he imitates Christ? Some authors see Paul's imitation of Christ in his resolute dedication to the gospel, but it is more likely that it is in his "being for others" (cf. 11:24) that the emulation lies. Christ gave himself in death for even the weak members of the community (8:11). The Corinthians' celebration of the Eucharist should remind them of that fact (cf. 11:24).

For Reference and Further Study

Fiore, Benjamin. *The Function of Personal Example in the Socratic and Pastoral Epistles.* AnBib 105. Rome: Pontifical Biblical Institute, 1986.

Getty, Mary Ann. "The Imitation of Paul in the Letters to the Thessalonians" in Raymond F. Collins, ed., *The Thessalonian Correspondence.* BEThL 87. Leuven: University Press/Peeters, 1990, 277–283.

Gill, David W. J. "The Meat-Market at Corinth (1 Corinthians 10:25)," *TynB* 43 (1992) 389–393.

Sanders, Boykin. "Imitating Paul: 1 Cor 4:16," *HThR* 74 (1981) 353–363.

Schütz, John Howard. *Paul and the Anatomy of Apostolic Authority.* MSSNTS 26. Cambridge: Cambridge University Press, 1975.

Stanley, David M. "'Become Imitators of Me.' The Pauline Conception of Apostolic Tradition," *Bib.* 40 (1959) 859–877. Reprinted in idem, *The Apostolic Church in the New Testament.* Westminster, Md.: Newman, 1967, 371–389.

Waele, Ferdinand-Joseph de. "The Roman Market North of the Temple at Corinth," *AJA* 34 (1930) 432–454.

Watson, Duane F. "1 Corinthians 10:23–11:1 in the Light of Greco Roman Rhetoric: The Role of Rhetorical Questions," *JBL* 108 (1989) 301–318.

E. FOURTH RHETORICAL DEMONSTRATION (11:2-34)

Saying "I commend you" (11:2), Paul moves from his consideration of the complex issue of the Corinthians' eating food offered to idols to a new topic. Ostensibly the issue is the traditions the Corinthians had received from Paul (11:2). The discussion, however, focuses on two issues, proper hairstyle for men and women (11:2-16) and eating the fellowship meal (11:17-34). Each of the two issues relates to tradition (vv. 2, 23), and they concern the way Christians ought to behave when they come together. What is at issue in the discussion is the behavior of the assembly at Corinth (see v. 16).

Because the community's practice is under consideration in chs. 11 and 14 it is tempting to consider 1 Corinthians 11–14 as a single rhetorical demonstration. The two chapters dealing with the practice of the church form an *inclusio* around chs. 12 and 13, thus establishing an A-B-B'-A' structure. While this approach has some merit it is not entirely clear that chs. 12 and 13 should be considered as analogous units.

Chapters 12–14 are clearly arranged in a chiastic pattern. Both ch. 12 and ch. 14 deal with spiritual gifts. The tightly knit structure of chs. 12–14 suggests that these chapters are a distinct rhetorical demonstration by themselves. Chapter 11 must then be identified as a rhetorical demonstration sandwiched between longer units on food offered to idols (chs. 8–11:1) and on spiritual gifts (chs. 12–14). Paul's letter to the Corinthians is, after all, a letter. It is not a literary piece that has been crafted and then revised for publication.

For Reference and Further Study

Klauck, Hans-Josef. *Herrenmahl und hellenistischer Kult. Eine religionsgeschichtliche Untersuchung zum ersten Korintherbrief.* NTA n.s. 15. Münster: Aschendorf, 1982.

Lampe, Peter. "Das korinthische Herrenmahl im Schnittpunkt hellenistisch-römischer Mahlpraxis und paulinisher *Theologia Crucis* (1 Cor 11,17-34)," *ZNW* 82 (1991) 183–213.

_____. "The Corinthian Eucharistic Dinner Party: Exegesis of a Cultural Context (1 Cor. 11:17-34)," *Affirmation* 4 (1991) 1–15.

Ringe, Sharon H. "Hospitality, Justice, and Community: Paul's Teaching on the Eucharist in 1 Corinthians 11:17-34," *Prism* 1 (1986) 59–68.

Schüssler Fiorenza, Elisabeth. "Tablesharing and the Celebration of the Eucharist," *Concilium* 152 (1982) 3–12.

Swanston, Hamish F. G. "Liturgy as Paradise and as Parousia," *SJTh* 36 (1983) 505–519.

1. *Let Men Be Men and Women Be Women* (11:2-16)

2. I commend you because you remember me in every way and you have retained the traditions just as I have handed them on to you. 3. I want you to understand that the head of every man is Christ, the head of a woman is man, and the head of Christ is God. 4. Every man who prays or prophesies having something on his head disgraces his head. 5. And every woman who prays or prophesies with her head uncovered disgraces her head; for it is one and the same thing as if she were a shaved woman. 6. For if a woman does not cover herself, let her hair be cut; if, however, it is shameful for a woman to have her hair cut off or be shaved, she should be covered. 7. For a man should not cover his head, since he is the image and glory of God, and woman is the glory of man. 8. For man is not from woman; rather woman is from man. 9. For man was not created for the sake of woman, rather woman was created for the sake of man. 10. Wherefore a woman ought to have authority over her head because of the angels. 11. On the other hand, neither is woman different from man nor man different from woman in the Lord; 12. for just as woman exists from man, so also it is through woman that man exists; and it is from God that all things exist.

13. Judge these things for yourselves; is it fitting for a woman to pray to the Lord with her head uncovered? 14. Does not nature itself teach you that if a man has a hairdo it is a disgrace to himself, 15. but if a woman has a hairdo it is to her glory? Hair is given to her for a covering. 16. If anyone is determined to be contentious, neither we ourselves nor the churches of God have this custom.

INTERPRETATION

For contemporary readers 11:2-16 is one of the most difficult passages in the entire letter. With its allusions to a specific situation within the Corinthian church and to the biblical stories about creation, the passage is somewhat confusing and difficult to understand. For many contemporary readers the passage is also difficult to accept. On first reading it appears to advance a Pauline claim that women are inferior and subordinate to men.

A Radical Suggestion. The passage is so problematic and employs so much vocabulary that is not used elsewhere in Paul's undisputed letters that various scholars in the modern history of the interpretation of the text have suggested that the passage was not written by Paul. They theorize that it is a post-Pauline gloss. A pair of radical French critics, Henri Delafosse (= Joseph Turmel, 1926) and Alfred Loisy (1933), were among the earlier proponents of this suggestion. Taking up where they left off, William O. Walker advanced the claim that this section of the text is a post-Pauline interpolation (1975). For Walker the passage comes from three small units of non-Pauline material (vv. 3, 8-9, 11-12; vv. 4-7, 10, 13, 16; vv. 14-15) that have been integrated into a literary unit by a post-Pauline editor. A somewhat different tack was taken by H. F. Richter who claims that 11:2-22, 27-34 was originally an independent letter of Paul to the Corinthians. With its own appropriate epistolary opening and closing, it would have been a short response to some specific issues that had arisen within the community.

Walker's suggestion has been pursued by Lamar Cope (1978) and G. W. Trompf (1980). These authors admit the literary unity of the disputed passage but claim that its linguistic and thematic characteristics demonstrate its non-Pauline character. The passage, says Cope, is "suspect *in any context* in a Pauline letter." Additional arguments for the interpolation hypothesis are found in the idea that v. 17 can easily follow after v. 1 and that the manuscript variants of v. 17 point to the existence of some confusion in the transmission of the text.

Apart from the fact that the textual tradition does not furnish any manuscripts that lack the passage, Jerome Murphy-O'Connor, Joël Delobel, and Caroline Vander Stichele have shown the coherent nature of the passage. They provide different but reasonable explanations of it as a text that comes from the apostle's pen.

The Epistolary Context. On first reading the pericope appears to deal with an issue quite unrelated to the one Paul has just treated, the matter of food that had been offered to idols. A new topic is formally introduced with words of praise (11:2; cf. 11:17). It begins with a kind of *captatio benevolentiae* and is brought to conclusion with reference to a practice recognized by Paul and the churches (v. 16). The verses delineating the pericope appear to be only loosely connected with the topic. On a closer reading the concluding verse (11:16) coheres with the thesis of the entire letter (1:10). Paul was urging the community to avoid contentiousness. His arguments are those from *ethos* and *paradeigma*, the example of himself and the churches, so typical of Paul's appeal in the letter.

What is the topic? What was it that divided the community? What was it over which contentiousness might have arisen? The opening verse commends the Corinthians, but it is quickly followed by a forceful disclosure formula (v. 3). The contrast is such that Paul appears to be commending the Corinthians for following the traditions he had passed along to them but then wants them to know that there is something that stands in need of correction. That something has to do with the gathering of the community, specifically its gathering together for worship (vv. 4, 5, 10, 13). This links the passage to its immediate context. Previously Paul had addressed the issue of common meals (chs. 8–10), a topic to which he returns under another guise in 11:17-34. Thereafter he will treat of the various gifts that have been given to the community, a discussion that is oriented toward the use of these gifts in the liturgical assembly (ch. 14).

Paul's first words have the form of a *captatio benevolentiae* designed to elicit the good will of his audience in preparation for the case he is about to make. These words serve as an acknowledgement that the difficult situation Paul hopes to clarify arose from the Corinthians' naïve adherence to Paul's teachings and the traditions he had shared with them. It may even be that there is a touch of irony in Paul's commendation of the Corinthians, if indeed the situation he seeks to redress arose from a deliberate distortion of the meaning of his message. That this may be the case is suggested by Paul's use of the verb "commend" *(epaineō)*, a verb he does not use very often. It is to be found only in 1 Corinthians 11 (vv. 2, 17, 22; and Rom 15:11, where it occurs in a quotation of Ps 117:1).

Tradition. The *captatio benevolentiae* recalls that the Corinthians remembered Paul and continue to hold on to the traditions the apostle had delivered to them. The reference to tradition in 11:2 prepares for the reference to common church practice (v. 16) with which it forms a kind of *inclusio.* Given the contrast between v. 2 and v. 17, Elisabeth Schüssler Fiorenza *(In Memory of Her* 226) opines that Paul is not referring to any particular abuse in this pericope, but that he is introducing regulations and customs that were observed in other Christian communities (11:16; 14:33).

Verse 2 speaks of "traditions" *(paradoseis),* the first and only mention of traditions in the letter. This is the only time that Paul uses the term "tradition" of Christian tradition (cf. Gal 1:14). He does, however, use the jargon of tradition, "to hand on" *(paradidōmi,* cognate with *paradosis,* "tradition"), in reference to the cultic tradition of the Lord's Supper (11:23) and to the credal tradition (15:3). The reference to traditions and the use of "handed down" *(paredōka)* evoke the situation of rabbinical schools in which rabbis passed along (Hebrew *māsar)* the tradition as lore to a new generation of pupils. The students in turn "received" *(qibbēl)* the tradition (cf. *m.* ʾ*Abot.* 1:1; Josephus, *Ant.* 13.297; compare Mark 7:3-5, 13). The process was one characterized by authoritative source and faithful transmission. The language of the rabbinic schools, which Paul echoes in 11:2 and again in 11:23 and 15:2-3, is similar to language used in Hellenistic circles of the transmission of the rites and rituals of the mystery celebrations from a cultic leader to the devotees (cf. Cicero, *Tusculan Disputations* 1.29; compare Wis 14:15; Plato, *Theaetetus* 198B).

Are there specific traditions to which Paul is referring in v. 2? Marco Adinolfi and Peter J. Tomson suggest that "the traditions" specifically refer to the Palestinian Jewish custom of women being veiled in public. For Tomson this is one of five apostolic *halakhot* explicitly mentioned in 1 Corinthians. The others are the Lord's prohibition of divorce (7:10), the

Lord's command on apostolic support (9:14), the tradition of the Eucharist (11:23-26), and the custom of women's silence in the assembly (14:33b-36). G. Bouwman is of the opinion that in 11:2 Paul makes reference to the idea that Christ is the head of the freedman. It may be, however, that Paul is referring to the baptismal tradition that proclaims the radical equality of men and women (cf. Gal 3:28). Implicit reference to the baptismal formula, with its allusion to Gen 1:27, would explain why Paul exploits this Scripture in midrashic fashion and why he focuses on men and women as he does.

A Difficult Passage. Robin Scroggs describes 11:2-16 as a passage in which "the logic is obscure at best and contradictory at worst" ("Paul and the Eschatological Woman," 297). Various aspects of Paul's language contribute to the obscurity of the passage and make it difficult for the modern reader to understand. Part of the difficulty in understanding what Paul has said and why he has said it is that Paul's discussion employs a number of terms that are not otherwise found in his correspondence: "uncovered" (*akatalyptos,* twice, in vv. 5, 13), "to have long hair" (*katakalyptomai,* three times in vv. 6, 7), "to shave" (*xyraomai,* twice, vv. 5, 6), "to cut [hair]" (*keirō,* twice in v. 6). Some of these terms are not used elsewhere in the NT (e.g., "uncovered" and "to have long hair"). In addition Paul seems to have deliberately used words that are polyvalent, notably "head" (*kephalē*), "authority" (*exousia*), and "glory" (*doxa*). These terms are key to Paul's argument, "head" occurring nine times (vv. 3, 4, 5, 7, 10), "authority" once in v. 11, and "glory" three times (vv. 7[2x], 15). There is also the problematic reference to angels in v. 10.

Paul's rhetorical argument is constructed on the basis of a pun. He plays on the multiple meanings of "head." The pun is all the more striking in that Paul does not often write about the "head." Apart from 12:21, where "head" appears in his allegory on the body, he uses the word only in Rom 12:20, where it appears in a citation of Prov 25:22.

There is also a problem with the internal consistency of Paul's argument. Having used the language of "head" and introduced a reference to Christ in his statement of principle in v. 3, Paul adopts iconic imagery in v. 7 but omits any christological reflection. In addition, there is some tension between his description of the relationship between man and woman in vv. 3 and 7, a description that seems to suggest that women are inferior to men, and vv. 8 and 11-12, where he apparently affirms the complementarity of men and women.

Contemporary Discussion. A big issue in Paul's day was the way people wore their hair. Archaeological evidence indicates that even emperors' wives, Livia and Octavia, for example, wore their hair in a simple bun, while other women wore elaborate hair styles (see Diana E. E. Kleiner and Susan B. Matheson, eds., *I Claudia: Women in Ancient Rome* [New

Haven: Yale University Art Gallery, 1996] 36–39, 53, 124–125). The coiffure suggested an elite status in society. Only the upper class had the leisure time necessary for such care of the hair and the economic position that allowed for the use of a hairdresser slave to do the work.

The entire twenty-seventh fragment of the Stoic philosopher Musonius Rufus is on cutting the hair *(ek tou peri koupas)*. He argues from nature *(physis)* and from the authority of Zeno, the philosopher, who said that it is quite as natural to cut the hair as it is to let it grow long. Hair might be cut so that a person is not burdened by too much of it or hampered for any activity. In the words of Musonius:

> the hair should be cut only to get rid of too much of it and not for looks, as some think they must, who shave their cheeks and imitate the beardless or, would you believe it, boys who are just beginning to grow a beard, and the hair on the head they do not cut all in the same way, but differently in front and behind. In fact that which seems to them good-looking is quite the opposite and does not differ from the efforts of women to make themselves beautiful. For they, you know, plait some parts of their hair, some they let fall free, and some they arrange in some other way in order to appear more beautiful. So men who cut their hair are obviously doing it out of a desire to appear handsome to those whom they wish to please, and so some of their hair they cut off completely, some they arrange so as to be most pleasing to the women and boys by whom they want to be admired. Nowadays there are even men who cut their hair to free themselves of the weight of it and they also shave their cheeks. Clearly such men have become slaves of luxurious living and are completely enervated, men who can endure being seen as womanish creatures, hermaphrodites *(androgynoi kai gynaikōdeis)*, something which real men would avoid at all costs (frag. 21).

The geographer Strabo also wrote about men looking like women because of the way they wore their hair. He went on to say that "speaking generally, the art of caring for the hair consists both in its nurture and in the way it is cut, and both are given special attention by girls and youths" *(Geography* 10.3.8). Similarly Epictetus wrote about the way people wore their hair:

> Young man, whom do you wish to make beautiful? First learn who you are, and then, in the light of that knowledge, adorn yourself. You are a human being; that is, a mortal animal gifted with the ability to use impressions rationally. And what is "rationally"? In accordance with nature and perfectly *(physei homologoumenō kai teleōs)*. What element of superiority, then, do you possess? The animal in you? No. Your mortality? No. Your ability to use impressions? No. Your reason is the element of superiority which you possess; adorn and beautify that; but leave your hair to Him who fashioned it as He willed. Come, what other

designations apply to you? Are you a man or a woman?—A man.—Very well then, adorn a man, not a woman. Woman is born smooth and dainty by nature, and if she is very hairy she is a prodigy, and is exhibited at Rome among the prodigies. But for a man not to be hairy is the same thing, and if by nature he has no hair he is a prodigy, but if he cuts it out and plucks it out of himself, what shall we make of him? Where shall we exhibit him and what notice shall we post? "I will show you," we say to the audience, "a man who wishes to be a woman rather than a man." What a dreadful spectacle! No one but will be amazed at the notice; by Zeus, I fancy that even the men who pluck out their own hairs do what they do without realizing what it means. Man, what reason have you to complain against your nature *(ti echeis egkalesai ou tē physei)?* Because it brought you in the world as a man? What then? Ought it to have brought all persons into the world as women? And if that had been the case, what good would you be getting of your self-adornment? For whom would you be adorning yourself, if all were women? Your paltry body doesn't please you, eh? Make a clean sweep of the whole matter; eradicate your—what shall I call it?—the cause of your hairiness; make yourself a woman all over, so as not to deceive us, not half-man and half-woman. Whom do you wish to please? Frail womankind? Please them as a man. "Yes, but they like smooth men." Oh, go hang! And if they liked sexual perverts *(kinaidois),* would you have become such a pervert? Is this your business in life, is this what you were born for, that licentious women should take pleasure in you? Shall we make a man like you a citizen of Corinth *(politēn Korinthiōn),* and perchance a warden of the city, or superintendent of *ephebi,* or general, or superintendent of the games *(agōnothetēn)?* Well, and when you have married are you going to pluck out your hairs? For whom and to what end? And when you have begotten boys, are you going to introduce them into the body of citizens as plucked creatures too? A fine citizen and senator and orator! Is this the kind of young men we ought to pray to have born and brought up for us? By the gods, young man, may such not be your fate! *(Discourses* 3.1.24-36; see also 3.1.14, 42-45; 3.22.10, 30; 4.1.116; Frag. 18).

The scribe Arrian recounts that these were not so much the words of Epictetus as they were of "some kindly god or other speaking through him" *(Discourses* 3.1.36). Occasionally Epictetus writes about how the philosopher should wear his hair *(komē) (Discourses* 4.8.5-6; 4.11.25-29). Apropos the impious man *(asebestate anthrōpe)* he says:

> But you are publishing the Mysteries abroad and vulgarizing them, out of time, out of place, without sacrifices, without purification; you do not have the dress which the hierophant ought to wear, you do not have the proper head or hair, nor head-band *(ou komēn, ou strophion oion dei),* nor voice, nor age; you have not kept yourself pure as he has, but you have picked up only the words which he utters, and recite them. Have the words a sacred force all by themselves? *(Discourses* 3.21.15-16)

Like the philosophers, so Hellenistic Jewish writers of Paul's day had something to say about the appropriate way to wear one's hair. The *Sentences of Pseudo-Phocylides* 210-212, for example, say, "If a child is a boy do not let locks grow on his head. Do not braid his crown nor the cross knots at the top of his head. Long hair is not fit for boys, but for voluptuous women." Stronger still are the words of Philo. Speaking of pederasty *(paiderastein)*, he writes,

> Mark how conspicuously they braid and adorn the hair of their heads *(tas tēs kephalēs trichas anaplekomenoi)* and how they scrub and paint their faces with cosmetics and pigments and the like, and smother themselves with fragrant unguents. . . . In fact the transformation of the male nature *(tēn arrena physin)* to the female is practiced by them as an art and does not raise a blush. These persons are rightly judged worthy of death by those who obey the law, which ordains that the man-woman who debases the sterling coin of nature *(to physeōs gomisma)* should perish unavenged, suffered not to live for a day or even an hour, as a disgrace *(oneidos)* to himself, his house, his native land and the whole human race. *(Special Laws* 3.37-38)

What Paul has written in 11:2-16 is to be seen in the light of this contemporary discussion. With Epictetus he shares the diatribal style and its rhetorical questions. With Musonius Rufus he cites authoritative dicta (for Paul these are the words of Scripture). With philosophers like Philo he writes about nature. The philosophers appeal to the gods and speak about the way humans are born. That kind of discourse leads a Jewish Christian author like Paul to speak of creation. That men should be men and women should be women, and should look like what they are, is something important to all the authors. Their fear is homosexuality and pederasty.

Creation. Paul's teaching on the radical equality of men and women had apparently been misunderstood. Only such a misunderstanding would seem to explain adequately the forceful use of "I want you to understand" as he begins to take up the issue of men and women in the assembly (v. 3). This disclosure formula introduces a statement of principle on the basis of which Paul formulates a limited dress code (vv. 4-5). The essence of the principle is that there is a divinely ordained descending hierarchy in creation: God, Christ, man, woman. Paul's essential understanding of creation is formulated in Jewish Hellenistic fashion in a series of three relational statements: Christ is the head of man, man is the head of woman, God is the head of Christ. Each unit of the triad is so phrased so as to emphasize the element that is the "head" *(kephalē)*, obviously used in a metaphorical sense.

The triad offers a synthetic formulation of a Christian theology of creation. In keeping with 8:6 Paul first affirms that Christ is the head of the man. Summing up the Yahwist's etiology of human gender (Gen 2:18-25), a theme to which he will return in v. 8, Paul affirms that man is the head of woman. His theocratic and Jewish understanding of God finally leads him to affirm that God is the head of Christ (cf. 3:23; 8:6; 11:12; 15:28).

The third link in Paul's chain of relationships, "the head of Christ is God," is somewhat different from other examples of the chain formulation in Hellenistic literature. Paul affirms that creation cannot be understood without reference to the death and resurrection of Jesus. See further 15:45-48 where Paul's midrashic interpretation of Gen 2:7 offers his version of Hellenistic Judaism's topos on the first and second creation.

A Dress Code. On the basis of his statement of principle in v. 3 Paul articulates a short dress code for men and women at worship in vv. 4-5. The promulgation of this code is obviously related to the situation at Corinth, but it is difficult to determine with full certainty exactly what that was. It is probable that the situation was one that resulted from the attitude of "anything goes" (see 6:12; 10:23). But does it have to do with men wearing or not wearing something on their head, or the style of their haircut? Did it have to do with women wearing or not wearing veils? Did it have to do with the way Corinthian women wore their hair when they were present in the Christian assembly? Is Paul suggesting that women follow the Jewish custom and men the Hellenistic practice?

One must also ask whether Paul is really dealing with men and women or whether the underlying issue is the behavior of a few problematic women at Corinth. As it did in the earlier discussions on sexuality and marriage in ch. 7 (vv. 4, 5; 7a, 7b; 10; 11a, 11b; 12a, 12b; 14, 15), the principle of mutuality dominates Paul's discussion, but it would appear that the real issue is the attire of women. The formulation of the dress code in vv. 4-5a is balanced, that is, until Paul begins to formulate a rationale for a practice he exhorts women to observe (vv. 5b-6).

Dressed for Worship. In the Hellenistic world an issue related to coiffure was what is to be worn on the head when one comes to worship. Archaeological evidence, especially numismatic and statuary finds from imperial times, gives ample evidence of men wearing a headdress while at prayer. The Augustan Altar of Peace and the somewhat later Column of Trajan attest to the practice. None of the evidence comes from Corinth itself, but it is not unlikely that the Roman practice was also customary in imperial Corinth. Plutarch gave some attention to the matter. He suggests that a covered head has symbolic value. The covered head suggests humility and symbolizes the concealment of the soul by the body. In his discussion of headdress Plutarch cites Castor as an authority. He identifies praying and prophesying as forms of cultic activity:

> But if there is anything else to be said, consider whether it be not true that there is only one matter that needs investigation: why men cover

their heads when they worship the gods *(tous theous proskynountes epika-lyptontai);* and the other follows from this. For they uncover their heads *(apokalyptontai)* in the presence of men more influential than they: it is not to invest these men with additional honor, but rather to avert from them the jealousy of the gods, that these men may not seem to demand the same honors as the gods, nor to tolerate an attention like that bestowed on the gods, nor to rejoice therein. But they thus worshiped the gods, either humbling themselves by concealing the head, or rather by pulling the toga over their ears as a precaution lest any ill-omened and baleful sound from without should reach them while they were praying *(euchomenois).* That they were mightily vigilant in this matter is obvious from the fact that when they went forth for purposes of divination *(epi manteian),* they surrounded themselves with the clashing of bronze.

Or, as Castor states when he is trying to bring Roman customs into relation with Pythagorean doctrines: the Spirit within us entreats and supplicates the gods without, and thus he symbolizes by the covering of the head the covering and concealment of the soul by the body.

Why do they sacrifice to Saturn with the head uncovered? . . . ("The Roman Questions," *Moralia* 266C-E).

Jewish tradition required that men, and certainly priests, pray with heads covered during worship services (Exod 28:36-40; Ezek 44:18-20). The Roman and the Jewish practice was that men should pray with their heads covered; the traditional Greek custom was that men pray with heads uncovered. Within this context it may be a clash of customs that is the real issue in 11:2-16. Unlike Plutarch, who speaks of the use of the toga *(to himation)* to cover one's head, Paul does not identify any object actually placed on the head. On the other hand, he does talk about cutting and shaving the hair (vv. 5-6) and about the hairdo (vv. 14-15). It is more probable that Paul is talking about hair styles than about wearing a veil or covering one's head with the toga.

The matter of how to wear one's hair in the assembly may also reflect some of the social tensions that existed within the Corinthian community itself. Pottery of the times shows Hellenistic women with jewelry, ribbons, and veils on their heads. Some artifacts indicate that women wore fairly elaborate coiffures, with the hair piled on the head and fastened with jeweled decorated pins. The women who are so depicted are urban woman of the upper classes. Not many of the Christian community belonged to the higher class (cf. 1:26). Poorer women may have worn braided hair, perhaps wrapped in some sort of bun.

Praying and Prophesying. The man *(anēr,* v. 4), like the woman *(gynē,* v. 5), is described as praying or prophesying. "Praying" *(proseuchomenos)* is the most common word for prayer in the NT. It suggests some sort of verbal activity directed *(pros-)* to God who is invoked (see 11:13). The term connotes worship or uttering prayers. Praying often includes an element of intercession. Paul returns to the subject of praying and prophesying in ch. 14 (cf. 14:13-15). There prayer is further specified as praying in tongues, and prophesying is presented as the more important gift. Both praying and prophesying are charismatic activities.

Prophesying *(prophēteuōn),* a verb Paul uses only in 1 Corinthians (11:4, 5; 13:9; 14:1, 3, 4, 5, 24, 31, 39), is speaking on behalf of God. In secular Greek the term connotes the activity of interpreting the will of the gods; in the NT it generally suggests speaking or preaching under the influence of the gift of the Spirit. Paul's description of men and women praying and prophesying suggests that he has in mind a situation of the Christian community gathered together for worship.

Rationale for the Dress Code. To explain and justify what he presents as a normative dress code Paul offers a first argument based on the order of creation as known from Scripture (vv. 7-12), a second based on nature in Stoic fashion (vv. 13-15), and a third based on the custom of the churches (v. 16). In his so-called apology Paul developed a similar three-part argument based on Scripture, nature, and Christian practice (9:3-12).

The argument developed in vv. 7-16 appears to confirm that it was women's appearance that was problematic. The second argument, drawn from "nature" (vv. 13-15), refers principally to women. The focus on women's coiffure may be continued in the final argument drawn from the practice of the churches (v. 16). Paul mentions women in phrases that relate women to men, but men are not described solely in relationship to women. Moreover, Paul affirms that Christ is the head of the man (v. 3) and that the man is the image and glory of God (v. 7). Each of these is a pregnant theological affirmation, but nothing similar is said about women.

In proclaiming the dress code in vv. 4-5a Paul initially treats men and women in similar fashion as he generally does in this letter (cf. 7:1-16). Both men and women pray and prophesy in the Christian assembly (cf. 14:33b-36). As he is wont to do Paul begins with the men, but his emphasis seems to lie on the women. The rhetorical appeal of vv. 5b-6 confirms that this is the case. The scriptural argument Paul adduces (vv. 7-9) highlights the situation of women, seemingly urging their subordination. Paul alludes to each of the Genesis creation stories. In v. 7 he evokes the Priestly author's summary statement on the creation of humanity, Gen 1:27, a verse to which the baptismal formula of Gal 3:28 refers. Paul uses the language of "glory" rather than the Torah's "likeness" in his paraphrase. Alluding to Genesis 2 with its story of the creation of woman in vv. 8-9, Paul draws the inference that woman is the glory of man. Because God has created the human genders in different ways a distinction is to be maintained when the community assembles for worship.

All this seems to imply the subordination of woman to man, but Paul offers a corrective in the final development of his scriptural argument

(vv. 11-12). The problem may have been principally gender-specific, but Paul's overall view of creation and the new order in the Lord is comprehensive and egalitarian. His use of a forceful "on the other hand" *(plēn)* shows that he intends to nuance somewhat the one-sided emphasis on woman's secondary place that has hitherto dominated his discussion.

Verses 11-12 seem to be a corrective aside, as it were. Verse 11 contains a carefully balanced statement of principle formulated in a pair of parallel statements: woman is not different from man; man is not different from woman. The parallelism of the verse echoes the parallelism Paul had employed in ch. 7 when he discussed issues of sexuality and marriage. From a Christian perspective, "in the Lord," there is similarity between woman and man. Verse 12 functions as an explanation of v. 11. It harks back to the book of Genesis' etiological narrative of the origin of the sexes (Gen 2:18-25) and recalls the simple biological fact that each man is born of a woman. Ultimately there is no radical difference between women and men because woman is from man and men are from women. In philosophical terms they share a common nature. Having made his point, Paul brings his comprehensive view of gender to closure with a theological adage: all things are from God (cf. 8:6; 10:26).

Verses 11-12 are presented in such a way as to present an interpretive nuance to Paul's reflections. They also provide an important commentary on v. 3. Verse 3 had introduced the idea of the relationship between the sexes along with the notion that creation must be understood within a Christian and theological perspective. These ideas are reprised in vv. 11 and 12 with their respective "in the Lord" and "all from God." Paul's explanatory aside proclaims that from the standpoint of a Christian understanding of creation there is radical equality between men and women. Having put matters into this theological perspective, Paul moves on to his second argument, the argument from nature. He urges the males within the community to look like men and the females in the community to look like women when they gather for their common worship. His slogan might well have been "Vive la différence." Epictetus would say "leave the man a man, and the woman a woman" (*Discourses* 3.1.39). Men should look like men; women should look like women. Paul appeals to the good sense of the community. His argument from public propriety takes the form of a rhetorical question (v. 13).

After this convoluted toying with the Scriptures to support the contention that men and women should be customarily and distinctively coiffed and attired while the assembly is in session, Paul presents a social argument in vv. 14-15. His manner of reasoning, drawn from "nature" *(physis),* is akin to that of Hellenistic moralists, especially the Stoics. Paul argues that men naturally have short hair and that they should act accordingly; women have naturally long hair, and they, too, should act accordingly. In the elaboration of this argument Paul appeals to the Corinthians' sense of shame and honor, significant realities indeed in the social world of first-century Mediterranean culture. The purpose of his argument is not to reaffirm gender differences, nor is it to affirm the subordination of women to men. Rather Paul seeks to promote the good order of the Christian assembly at worship and to ensure that the meaning of this assembly is not wantonly misconstrued by outsiders and unbelievers (see 14:23-24).

Paul's third and final argument is an appeal from his own example and that of the churches. It is not at all certain that Paul is suggesting that all the churches have the same dress code that Paul has urged upon the Corinthians. What is certain is that Paul is urging the Corinthians to avoid contentiousness over the matter of dressing one's hair (see 1:10). The Corinthians should be no more contentious about this matter than were Paul and the churches of God (cf. 1:2; 10:32).

The section in 11:2-16 deals with a particular issue, but it deals with it as a matter that is divisive for the community, as does the following pericope (cf. 11:18). Paul's response to the issue is appropriate in a piece of deliberative rhetoric that uses political language to appeal for the unity of the community (cf. 1:10).

NOTES

2. *I commend you:* This verse should be taken as an introduction to what will follow rather than as a kind of epilogue to the exhortation Paul has just concluded. Some manuscripts (D, F, G, K, L, Ψ, 33, supported by many of the early translations including the Old Latin and the Vulgate, along with early Syriac, Gothic, and Ethiopian versions) insert "brothers and sisters" after "I commend you." Although Paul frequently uses this formula of direct address in the letter, its absence from the oldest Greek manuscripts ($\mathfrak{P}^{46}$, A, B, C) and from some of the early translations makes it highly unlikely that Paul would have used "brothers and sisters" at this point in his letter. "Brothers and sisters" is, moreover, a form of address that evokes the warm positive regard Paul has for the Corinthian community. Its absence from passages in which he is taking the community to task is noteworthy (cf. 5:1).

That the apostrophic address is absent from 11:2 suggests that the matter to which Paul is about to turn his attention, namely, the covering of the head, is a continuation of the earlier discussion on participation in the eucharistic assembly. See the references to the bread, cup, and table in 10:14-22.

because you remember me in every way: Assonance (*mimētai . . . memnēsthe*) links this phrase with the exhortation in 11:1. This is the only passage in 1 Corinthians in which Paul mentions the fact that the Corinthians remember anything, let alone remember him. Paul's words lack the warmth of the way he writes about the Thessalonians having remembered him (1 Thess 3:6). "In every way" (*panta;* cf. 10:33) adds emphasis to Paul's *captatio benevolentiae.* To the extent that Paul's words are ironic the adverb heightens the irony.

and you have retained the traditions just as I have handed them on to you: The Corinthians' remembrance of Paul is an active memory. They have maintained the traditions Paul passed along to them just as Paul had handed them down. "Just as" *(kathōs)* suggests a faithful reception of the traditions by the Corinthians. Faithful transmission of the oral law from one generation to the next was a hallmark of teaching within the rabbinic tradition.

3. *I want you to understand that the head of every man is Christ:* Paul uses a disclosure formula (cf. 10:1; 12:1) to make his point. His view on creation, inspired by the biblical tradition and his own Christian perspective, is expressed in a series of relationships. The formulation with its focus on the male-female relationship and its reference to Christ is Paul's own expression. The form, however, is typical of Hellenistic-Jewish literature (cf. Isa 7:8-9). The *Corpus Hermeticum,* for example, says, "Eternity, therefore, is an image of God, the cosmos is an image of eternity, and the sun is an image of the cosmos. The human is an image of the sun" (*Corp Herm* 11:15). Philo's triad is God, reason, and human, in which reason or word *(logos)* is the image of God, and human *(anthrōpos)* is the cast of the divine image (*Heir* 230-231). The language of the image of God focuses these chains as it does Paul's own reflection (11:7; cf. Gen 1:27). Comparable Hellenistic triads used to provide a schema for creation are God-world-human (*Corp Herm* 8:5) and One-mind-world (Plotinus, *Enneades* 2.9).

   Paul's triad lacks a consistent descending or ascending relationship. He has not used the classic rhetorical device of *klimax (gradatio).* He has, however, used the device of *paronomasia.* "*Kephalē*" (head) is the recurrent sound in the three members of the chain. Many commentators take "head" in the sense of "authority" or "leadership." As an argument in support of their position they cite the biblical "head" *(rōʾš).* The argument is fallacious. The LXX, which uses *kephalē* to translate *rōʾš* some 281 times, tends not to use *kephalē* as a translation when *rōʾš* has the metaphorical meaning of "authority" (exceptions being Judg 10:18; 11:8, 9, 11 [ms. A only]; 1 Kings 21:12 [ms. A*]; 2 Sam 22:44; Isa 7:8-9; Jer 31:7 [38:7 LXX]). To render *rōʾš* with the metaphorical connotation of authority or leadership the Greek Bible generally translates the Hebrew with a cognate of *archē,* "beginning" (especially *archōn, archēgos;* cf. Robin Scroggs, "Paul and the Eschatological Woman," 298 n. 41; Jerome Murphy-O'Connor, "Sex and Logic," 492; Caroline Vander Stichele, "Authenticiteit," 290–304). Josephus uses *kratos* to speak of the authority given to humans by God (*Ap.* 2.201). On the other hand, classical Greek often uses *kephalē* with the metaphorical sense of "source" or "origin" and that appears to be the meaning of the term in v. 3 (cf. C. K. Barrett and F. F. Bruce).

   Jerome Murphy-O'Connor interprets Christ's headship soteriologically ("Sex and Logic," 493–494, with references to 2 Cor 5:17 and 1 Cor 1:30). It is preferable, however, to take the affirmation as a reference to the role of Christ in creation (8:6). Support for this interpretation can be found not only in

Paul's adoption of the three-part chain, a form used of creation in Hellenistic Judaism, but also in the fact that Paul's somewhat convoluted reference to the adornment of the head in the following verses is a tapestry woven against the background of the Genesis stories of creation. Jewish tradition has, moreover, described the wisdom of God present at creation as God's glory (Wis 7:26; 9:9-11; *b. B. Batra* 58a; *Gen. Rab.* 8:1, 10; 12:6; *Pirqe R. El.* 4:4; *Qoh. Rab.* 8:1-5; *Pesiq. R.* 4:36a-38). In 1:24 Paul identifies Christ with the wisdom of God.

the head of a woman is man: This may be an oblique reference to the creation narrative of Gen 2:18-25, to which Paul alludes in v. 8 and perhaps even in v. 7. "It is hard," writes David Wenham, "to avoid the conclusion that Paul believed the husband to have a position of God-given leadership in the family" (*Paul: Follower of Jesus or Founder of Christianity?* [Grand Rapids: Eerdmans, 1995] 238 n. 54).

and the head of Christ is God: The notion that Christ is dependent on God appears in the Pauline writings almost exclusively in 1 Corinthians. The use of "Christ" without the name "Jesus" or the title "Lord" is also characteristic of 1 Corinthians, where the usage occurs forty-one times, of which twenty-nine are anarthrous. The soteriological implications of the title are apparent. Paul uses the title in his reflections on the crucified Christ (cf. 1:10-25), on Christ who has been raised (cf. 15:1-28), and in the soteriological formula "in Christ." Soteriological in its connotation, the title focuses on the human Jesus who is the object of God's saving activity.

4. *Every man who prays or prophesies:* In dealing with issues relating to gender Paul generally offers a balanced opinion. He first addresses the issue as it relates to men, then as it relates to women. Many scholars are convinced that the problem at Corinth is that of women's appearance. Paul adds something about men because of his commitment to gender equality.

having something on his head: "Having something on his head" (*kata kephalēs echōn*, literally "to have down from the head") is difficult to interpret. "To have" is a transitive verb that normally requires a direct object (in the accusative case) but Paul does not use a direct object. Many modern translations render Paul's elliptical expression along the lines of "having something on the head" (*NRSV*; cf. BDF 225, "hanging down from the head," "on the head"). To preserve the sense of downward motion (*kata* with the genitive), Archibald Robertson and Alfred Plummer and C. K. Barrett suggest that Paul is thinking of men wearing a veil on their heads, in effect being attired as a woman. John Chrysostom, on the other hand, suggested that the "hairdo" (*koma*) of v. 14 is what Paul had in mind when using his elliptical expression (Chrysostom, *On the First Epistle to the Corinthians, Homily* 26.3-4; *PG* 61, 217). The idea that Paul was talking about men with long hair and elaborate hairdos is supported by Abel Isaksson, W. J. Martin, J. B. Hurley, and Jerome Murphy-O'Connor. Like Chrysostom these authors construe "hairdo" to be the missing object of the verb. It is certainly the case that Paul speaks of the shame that a man brings upon himself by wearing some form of elaborate coiffure in v. 14. If Paul's "having something on the head" is a reference to a long hairdo, some balance is achieved with v. 5.

disgraces his head: Paul's affirmation that a man who prays or prophesies with long hair disgraces his head is likewise problematic. What does it mean for a person to "disgrace his head?" More specifically, what is the meaning of "his head?" What is the meaning of Paul's figure of speech? Is it metaphor? Or is it metonymy? In the immediately preceding verse Paul has identified Christ as the head of the man. If "head" is a metaphor and Christ is Paul's referent, what does it mean for a man with long hair to disgrace Christ? Isaksson suggests that it is a matter of a Christian prophet refusing to serve Christ by not following the haircut regulations pertinent to the new temple (cf. Ezek 44:20; see *Marriage and Ministry* 167–168). Given the thrust of Paul's argument in v. 14 it is more likely that "head" represents the whole person. A man who prays or prophesies with long hair disgraces himself.

What then is the problem? Why is a man with long hair a disgrace to himself? Paul's assumption is that men should wear short-cropped hair as was customary in the Hellenistic world. A major part of his argument is that men should look like men and women should look like women. Beyond this Paul's affirmation may be reflecting the cultural bias that men who wore long hair, particularly if it were stylized, were effeminate and, perhaps, homosexual.

5. *And every woman who prays or prophesies with her head uncovered disgraces her head:* Given the parallelism between vv. 5 and 6 "her head" must refer to the woman herself. A woman who appears in the assembly with unkempt hair brings shame upon herself. Some commentators, however, conjecture that the reference to the head goes back to v. 3 and that it is the woman's husband whom she has disgraced by wearing her hair down. Her flowing hair would be a sign that she wanted to be independent of her husband, an infringement of her husband's rights. Were this the correct interpretation Paul would have been strongly urging the subordination of Christian wives to their husbands.

Commentators disagree in their assessment of the practice that Paul had in mind. 1. Annie Jaubert ("Le voile des femmes [1 Cor xi.2-16]," *NTS* 18 [1972] 419–430), Robin Scroggs ("Paul and the Eschatological Woman," *JAAR* 40 [1972] 283–303), Marco Adinolfi, Wayne Meeks, André Feuillet ("La dignité et le rôle de la femme d'après quelques textes pauliniens," *NTS* 21 [1975] 157–191), Robert Jewett ("The Sexual Liberation of the Apostle Paul," *JAAR-Sup* 47/1 [1979] 55–87) and some others hold that some Corinthian women resisted Paul's attempt to introduce Jewish customs, specifically the practice of women wearing veils, by not wearing veils on their heads as they prayed. Just before his discussion of men's and women's costume Paul had made reference to cultural distinctions in the community (10:32). Heinrich Weinel suggested that while Jewish veils covered the nose and mouth some Corinthian women wanted to remove the veils in order to pray and prophesy in the Christian assembly (*Paulus. Der Mensch und sein Werk. Die Anfänge des Christentums, der Kirche und des Dogmas.* Lebensfragen 3 [2nd. ed. Tübingen: Mohr-Siebeck, 1915] 202).

2. A more common opinion is that the Corinthian women rejected the use of the veil, a symbol of woman's subjection to man, because of their conviction that men and women were equal in Christ. According to some scholars the

rejection of the veil was the result of Corinthian women taking Paul at his word and putting the Christian gospel of freedom and equality into practice (e.g., John Meier, "Veiling of Hermeneutics," 217). For others the root of the problem is an ideology that had begun to make inroads into the Christian community, an exaggerated "realized eschatology" that blurred the distinction between the sexes (Wayne Meeks, "Image of the Androgyne," 202; Jerome Murphy-O'Connor, "Sex and Logic," 490) or an early gnostic demand for the liberation and equality of women (Else Kähler, *Frau* 50; Walter Schmithals, *Gnosticism in Corinth* 239).

More radically, Dennis R. MacDonald has suggested *(There is no Male and Female)* that some Corinthians, pushing the meaning of Christian baptism to an extreme (cf. Gal 3:28), celebrated the ritual as a transvestite ceremony in which the participants put off the old body so as to return to humanity's original androgynous state. MacDonald opines that Gal 3:28 is related to a logion with older origins. This older logion appeared in the Gospel of the Egyptians. It is preserved in a citation by Clement of Alexandria (*Stromata* 3.13.1; *PG* 8, 1193; cf. 2 *Clem.* 12:2; *PG* 1, 345). The saying is: "When you tread on the garment of shame and when the two become one, the male with the female neither male nor female. . . ." According to MacDonald "treading" refers to a subjection of the body in order that perfection be achieved, "becoming one" refers to the androgynous state, and "male with the female" refers to the effect of this state, namely sexual abstinence. Indeed a kind of asexuality, symbolized by a form of Christian nudism, was highly valued in some early Gnostic literature (cf. *Gos. Thom.* 21, 22, 37). The unveiling of women, to which Paul reacts, would be an expression of this asexual state. Paul responds by affirming the indispensability of women (vv. 11-12) and providing a scriptural warrant (Gen 2:22-23; cf. v. 8) for their subordinate social status.

3. Another view is that Paul was referring to hairstyles, not to the wearing of veils. Richard and Catherine Kroeger and Elisabeth Schüssler Fiorenza (*In Memory of Her* 227–228) suggest that some Corinthian women, caught up in their ecstatic-pneumatic worship, adopted the custom of the devotees of Dionysus, Cybele, and Isis (similarly the cult of the Pythia at Delphi) who let their free flowing hair hang down in efforts to produce effective magical incantation. A variant on the idea that the real issue is the influence of pagan cult has been expressed by Stephan Lösch ("Christliche Frauen in Korinth [1 Cor 11,2-16]. Ein neuer Lösungsversuch," *ThQ* 127 [1947] 216–261). On the basis of two Peloponnesian epigraphs Lösch argued that some Greek cults forbade women to participate in religious processions with their hair braided or their heads veiled, either of which was considered a sign of pretentiousness. Neophyte Christians, formerly of this observance, maintained the religious practice when they joined the Christian assembly.

Another approach to the idea that hairstyle is the issue derives from the fact that for Jewish women who took considerable care of their coiffure (cf. Isa 3:24; Jdt 10:3; 16:8), loose hair was a sign of uncleanness (cf. Lev 13:45; Num 5:18). Paul uses the adjective "uncovered" *(akatalyptǭ)* to describe the condition of the woman's head. His choice of language may reflect the idiom of the

LXX where similar wording *(hē kephalē autou akatalyptos,* Lev 13:45; cf. Num 5:18) is used to render a Hebrew expression *(wĕrōʾšô yihyeh pārûaʿ)* describing someone with disheveled hair. The adjective "uncovered" is a rare word, occurring in the New Testament only in 1 Cor 11:5, 13 (cf. Philo, *Special Laws* 3.60).

for it is one and the same thing as if she were a shaved woman: Paul's sarcastic remark is offered as an explanation of his dress code for women. His way of referring to "a shaved woman" *(hē exyrēmenē)* implies the existence of a specific class of women who were shorn. Vestal virgins and adolescent Greek girls shaved their heads on reaching puberty. The sarcasm of Paul's remark might then be tantamount to his saying that if a woman prays or prophesies with short hair she might as well adopt other pagan customs.

6. *For if a woman does not cover herself, let her hair be cut:* Similar parenthetical remarks dealing with particular situations are common in 1 Corinthians (see the similarly terse phrases in 7:15, 21). The conditional clause with a verb in the present tense suggests a condition of reality (BDF 372, 2a). "To shave," "to cut [hair]," and "to cover oneself" [= "to wear long hair"], "to uncover" are used by Paul only in 1 Cor 11:5b-7a, with the exception of the latter verb which is also found in v. 13. Paul's words refer to a particular situation, most likely that of the neophyte woman whose hair was not long. In such a case the woman is enjoined to let her hair remain cropped. Abel Isaksson had suggested that the possibility of a Christian woman's cutting her hair was an alternative to the rule Paul had set out. The situation he envisioned is that of the female Christian Nazarite who with her husband's permission shaved her head.

if, however, it is shameful for a woman to have her hair cut off or be shaved, she should be covered: Verse 6b presents the norm; the present imperative pertains to ordinary circumstances. Paul's conditional clause appeals to women's sense of shame. Its use of the substantivized infinitives "to have her hair cut off or be shaved" is loosely anaphoric, referring back both to the situation mentioned by Paul in v. 5 and to his sarcastic remark.

7. *For a man should not cover his head, since he is the image and glory of God:* In contrast with women, a man should not be covered. In urging women's coiffure Paul appealed to the sense of shame. In urging men to wear their hair as he does he advances a theological argument. His words are clearly an echo of Gen 1:26. Paul's appeal to biblical anthropology makes it likely that the situation to which he responds in 11:2-16 derives from a perverted understanding of the new creation in Christ.

Paul's use of "image" recalls the creation stories of Genesis (cf. 15:49; Rom 1:23; 8:29). He uses a binomial expression, but not the biblical pair "image and likeness" (Gen 1:26). Had Paul simply written of the man as "the image of God" he would have evoked—at least to his Jewish readers—the idea of sinful humanity (cf. Sir 17:1-13; *Apoc. Mos.* 10:3; 12:2). Reference to glory, the glory that humans lost through sin (cf. Rom 1:23; *Apoc. Mos.* 20:1-2; 21:6), evokes the image of the human as intended by the creator God. Paul himself associates the notions of image and glory in Rom 1:23 and 2 Cor 3:18; 4:4. For Paul it is Christ who is the image of God *par excellence.* As the image of God, Christ possesses glory (see 2 Cor 4:4).

and woman is the glory of man: Since "glory" evokes the biblical stories of creation, Paul's reference to woman as "the glory of man" recalls the etiological narrative of Gen 2:18-22 (cf. 11:3b). That story evokes the image of a prototypical man and woman who cling to one another in marital union. In v. 7 Paul is writing about the relationship between a woman and her husband.

Paul does not say that the female gender is the glory of masculinity; rather he is commenting on the role of woman in a society in which honor and shame were dominant factors. In the Hellenistic world a woman was considered to be the glory of her husband, as appears on a Greek epitaph on a Jewish tomb in Rome, "Lucilla, the blessed glory of Sophronius" (Hermann Vogelstein and Paul Rieger, *Geschichte der Juden in Rom.* 2 vols. [Berlin: Mayer & Müller, 1895–1896] 1:65, 466). Within Judaism the Jerusalem Talmud tells the story of R. Jose the Galilean being advised to divorce his wife because she was not "his glory." "The wife of R. Jose, the Galilean, caused him much annoyance. R. La'azar went up to see him. He said to her: 'Rabbi, divorce her for she is not thy glory'" (*y. Ketub.* 11:3).

8. *For man is not from woman; rather woman is from man:* Paul continues his explanation (note the *gar*) with a reference to the story of the creation of the prototypical woman that describes her as being made of the rib of the man (Gen 2:21-23).

9. *For man was not created for the sake of woman; rather woman was created for the sake of man:* An untranslated *kai* links this explanation to the immediately preceding one. As Paul continues his explanation he alludes to the fact that the woman was created as the helper and partner of the man (Gen 2:18, 20, 24 [cf. 6:16]. Sociality and the complementarity of the sexes belong to the human condition as created by God. "Was created" (*ektisthē*) is a theological passive. Paul's phrasing is elliptical; the verb is not repeated in the antithetical clause.

10. *Wherefore a woman ought to have authority over her head:* Paul is clearly drawing an inference ("wherefore," *dia touto*) from the creation narrative. The idea that women should have authority (*exousia*) over their heads has, nonetheless, long puzzled commentators. What did Paul mean by *exousia?*

The problem is an old one. The word is to be found in almost all the Greek manuscripts of 11:10, but many of the ancient translations (the Coptic, the Ethiopian, some manuscripts of the Vulgate, and perhaps the Armenian) interpreted the word metaphorically, as if it meant "veil" (*kalymma*), as did many of the Greek and Latin Fathers, including both Chrysostom and Augustine. A Latin translation of Origen (*PG* 13, 119B) resolves the difficulty with a text that reads "a veil and authority." This is clearly a secondary reading; the wording of the ancient text was *exousia,* literally "authority."

What does this mean? Since Jewish women were required to wear veils in public, but not at home, some commentators assume that the veil is a symbol of the authority to which a wife submits, namely that of her husband. The problem with this approach is that *exousia* is presumed to connote the authority to which one is subject, rather than the authority one exercises oneself—a meaning of *exousia* not otherwise attested in Greek literature!

Stephan Lösch ("Christliche Frauen") considers that "authority" was Paul's way of referring to a hair ornament *(spleggis)* that women wore as a sign of submission to their husbands. In an analogous argument Gerhard Kittel (1920) pointed out that an Aramaic word for veil or hair ornament is *šlṭwnyh*, whose consonantal root is the same as that of an Aramaic verb meaning "to have dominion." Following a similar line of thought, Günther Schwarz ("*Exousian echein epi tēs kephalēs?* [1 Korinther 11:10]," *ZNW* [1979] 249) has suggested that the underlying Aramaic word may be *ḥûmrāʾ*, which means both "power" and "head covering."

Morna Hooker ("Authority"), followed by some commentators (e.g., C. K. Barrett, F. F. Bruce, J. A. Walther), opines that Christian women exercise authority over their heads by wearing veils. A wife is the glory of her husband (v. 7). Were she to wear nothing on her head during worship she would be reflecting the glory of the man. Covering herself (the man's glory) during worship allows God alone to be glorified and permits a woman to participate in the prayer and prophesying of the assembly. In effect the wearing of the veil expresses the equality of Christians at worship. The veil is a symbol of their new power in the Christian assembly.

The natural meaning of Paul's phrase is that a woman has authority or power over her head. She presumably exercises [proper] control over her head when she wears her hair appropriately, that is, as is fitting in the context of worship. It may be, however, that the words imply something more. Women who pray and prophesy in a worship setting are the concern of 11:2-16. The inferential "wherefore" of v. 10 introduces a change in the development of the argument. The focus may be on woman's authority over their physical heads. The head contains the organ of speech. It is the locus of revelatory dreams and prophetic inspiration (Daniel 2; Philo, *Heir* 258–266). Since Paul is concerned with order in the assembly (14:26-32) and with rationality (14:19), the thought expressed in v. 10 may be that it is appropriate for women to take responsibility when they pray and prophesy during worship (cf. 14:32b).

However, does "head" *(kephalē)* denote a woman's physical head? Elisabeth Schüssler Fiorenza (*In Memory of Her* 228) suggests that in v. 10 "head" is a *double entendre*. It means both the woman's physical head and the man, described as head of the woman in v. 3. Because of the angels who, according to Jewish and Christian tradition, mediate prophetic utterances, women have authority to adorn their heads as they wish. In the Christian egalitarian community women have as much power over men as men do over women.

because of the angels: A reference to angels is cryptically introduced into the discussion and is difficult to understand. That the passage is indeed a crux is indicated by the variants in its textual tradition and the patristic exegesis that interprets the phrase metaphorically as a reference to priests or bishops.

Assuming that 11:10 is the conclusion (*dia touto*, "wherefore") to Paul's re-flections on creation, some commentators take the phrase to be a reference to the role of angels as witnesses to creation (cf. Philo, *Dreams* 1.140; *Jub.* 4:6; *1 Enoch* 19:3). Others believe that it is a reference to the role of the angels as me-diators of revelation (Gal 1:8; 3:19; cf. 1 Cor 13:1). Still others believe that the reference is to the evil forces who are repelled by something a woman wears on her head as a kind of talisman.

It is more likely that the phrase is a reference to the presence of angels in the assembly. The Qumran literature includes a number of passages that allude to the presence of angels when the community gathers. For example, "And no-one stupid or deranged should enter; and anyone feeble-minded or insane, and those with sightless eyes, the lame or one who stumbles, or a deaf person, or an under-age boy, none of these should enter the congregation, since the holy angels are in its midst" (4QDᵉ 10:11; cf. 1QM 7:4-6; 1QSa 2:3-11; 4QMᵃ). Passages such as this affirm that the presence in the assembly of those who are not ritually pure gives affront to the angels. Paul's reference may be to angelic spirits (cf. 13:1) who inspire (female) prophets. Joël Delobel ("1 Cor 11,2-16," 386) adds, "the behavior of women in worship has to respect the order of creation symbolized by the angels who are indeed present in wor-ship and watching the observance of this order."

11. *On the other hand, neither is woman different from man nor man different from woman in the Lord:* With an interpretive aside (vv. 11-12), Paul offers a per-spective from which his audience is to construe his commentary on the crea-tion myth. The aside begins with an adversative conjunction (*plēn*; cf. Phil 1:18; 3:16; 4:14). It makes parallel statements about woman and man and af-firms that one gender is not different (*oute . . . chōris*) from the other in the Lord. The verse lacks a verb; the verb "to be" with the connotation "exist" or "come into existence" must be supplied. "Different" (*chōris*) is a preposition that most commonly means "apart from" or "without." Using Gen 26:1 as a major argument, Josef Kürzinger has shown that the word is better translated "different from."

"In the Lord" (*en Kyriǭ*) is an important Pauline formula, occurring some forty-four times in his letters. Its range of usage runs the gamut from a con-notation approximating that of the adjective "Christian" to one that points to an almost mystical union between a believer and Christ. Many commentators find in v. 11 an allusion to the egalitarian baptismal formula of Gal 3:27-28, but in context the phrase evokes the similar reference in v. 3. It suggests that the creation of humanity be understood from a Christian perspective, one that incorporates the role of Christ in creation. The fact that Paul has need not only to assert the basic social distinction of the sexes and their equality im-plies that "both sorts of statements were required . . . to address specific dis-agreements that had arisen with regard to the activities of women in the Corinthian church" (Christopher D. Stanley, *Paul and the Language of Scripture* 230).

12. *for just as woman exists from man, so also it is through woman that man exists:* With a postpositive *gar*, "for," v. 12 explains Paul's affirmation that woman is not

different from man nor is man different from woman. The explanatory comment shows that Paul "does not want to deny the creational interdependence
and mutuality of men and women" (Schüssler Fiorenza, *In Memory of Her*
229). In explaining himself Paul makes use of the Yahwist's story of creation
(Gen 2:18-25; cf. v. 7), to which he had already alluded in vv. 8-9. He summarizes the etiological narrative in Genesis by affirming that woman is created
from man (v. 12a).

The continuation of the sentence is motivated by Paul's desire to affirm
the mutuality of the sexes. His affirmation is contrapuntal not only to v. 12a,
with which it is juxtaposed, but also to vv. 8-9, tersely summarized in v. 12a.
He counterbalances the statement that woman has been created from man
with an affirmation that (every) man is born of woman. As does the epilogue
to the creation story (Gen 2:24), Paul's reflection speaks of the physical nature
of the relationship between man and woman. He affirms the biological fact
that man is born of woman, perhaps reflecting the encomium of Gen 4:1.

and it is from God that all things exist: The aside concludes with the theological
affirmation that all things come from God (cf. 8:6; comp. 3:21-23). Even the
biological condition of men being born from women is the result of divine
ordinance. This concluding statement provides a kind of transition to the
argument from human logic, specifically the argument from nature that he
will introduce in v. 14 (see 9:8, where the first rhetorical question provides a
transition between two different types of arguments pertaining to one and the
same debatable point).

13. *Judge these things for yourselves; is it fitting for a woman to pray to the Lord with
her head uncovered?* Paul urges the Corinthians to use their own judgment in
this matter (cf. 10:15b). Earlier he had introduced the subject of women at
prayer (v. 5). Common sense (*prepon estin,* "it is fitting," hapax in Paul) should
dictate how women should adorn their heads when they gather with others
in the liturgical assembly.

14–15. *Does not nature itself teach you that if a man has a hairdo it is a disgrace to himself, but if a woman has a hairdo it is to her glory?* Paul's rhetorical question
achieves gender balance by means of two parallel phrases, distinguished
from one another by man/woman, disgrace/glory. Paul's argument hits
home in a society where shame (cf. 11:6) and honor are potent motivating
forces. His argument from nature is similar to that employed by the Stoics
Musonius Rufus and Epictetus. Nature, they observe, provides features for
the distinction between men and women. Plutarch held that nature was the
best of teachers ("Brotherly Love," *Moralia* 478D-479).

Hair is given to her for a covering: An untranslated *hoti* introduces the reason
why Paul considers a woman's hairdo to be her glory. "To her" (*autē*) is absent from some manuscripts (including $\mathfrak{P}^{46}$, D, F, G, Ψ, the Byzantine texts,
and many ancient translations), but the weight of the manuscript evidence is
sufficient to suggest that the reading "to her" was part of the original text. In
the manuscript tradition "to her" is sometimes found before the verb (C and
several minuscules) and sometimes after (ℵ, A, B, with support in many of the
translations).

"Covering" *(peribolaion)* is hapax in Paul. Its only other NT usage is in Heb 1:12, where it appears in a citation of Ps 102:26. Because it has the connotation of a covering that is thrown "around" *(peri)* someone or something that is covered, Jerome Murphy-O'Connor has suggested that Paul is making reference to a bun of hair on a woman's head and consequently interprets the "uncovered head" of v. 4 as "untended hair" ("Sex and Logic," 488).

16. *If anyone is determined to be contentious, neither we ourselves nor the churches of God have this custom:* To what custom *(synētheian;* cf. 8:7) does Paul refer? Recent commentators tend to take the expression as a reference to a customary hairdo; earlier commentators were wont to take it as a reference to contentiousness itself. The earlier commentators are probably correct. Neither Paul nor the churches of God (cf. 1:2) are inclined to be contentious *(philoneikos,* "strife-loving," hapax in the NT).

Paul's argument ends on an appeal to his prestige (the *ethos* argument) and the example *(paradeigma)* of the churches of God (cf. 10:32). An underlying motif throughout Paul's exposition is: what does it mean for the Corinthians to live as God's holy people, the church of God (cf. 1:2)?

FOR REFERENCE AND FURTHER STUDY

Adinolfi, Marco. "Il velo della donna e la rilettura paolina di 1 Cor. 11,2-16," *RivBib* 23 (1975) 147–173.

Amjad-Ali, Christine. "The Equality of Women: Form or Substance (1 Corinthians 11.2-16)" in Rasich S. Sugirtharajah, ed., *Voices from the Margin: Interpreting the Bible in the Third World.* Maryknoll, N. Y.: Orbis, 1991, 205–213.

Bouwman, Gijs. "'Het hoofd van de man is de vrouw': Een retorische analyse van 1 Kor 11,2-6," *TvT* 21 (1981) 28–36.

Chakkalakal, Pauline. "Paul and Women: A Critical Reflection," *Jeevadhara* 27 (1997) 188–203.

Cope, Lamar. "1 Cor 11:2-16: One Step Further," *JBL* 97 (1978) 435–436.

Corrington, Gail P. "The 'Headless Woman': Paul and the Language of the Body in 1 Cor 11:2-16," *PRS* 18 (1991) 223–231.

Delobel, Joël. "1 Cor 11,2-16: Towards a Coherent Interpretation" in Albert Vanhoye, ed., *L'Apôtre Paul: Personalité, style et conception du ministère.* BEThL 73. Louvain: Louvain University Press/Peeters, 1986, 369–389.

Engberg-Pedersen, Troels. "1 Corinthians 11:16 and the Character of Pauline Exhortation," *JBL* 110 (1991) 679–689.

Fitzmyer, Joseph A. "A Feature of Qumran Angelology and the Angels of I Cor. xi. 10," *NTS* 4 (1957–1958) 48–58. Reprinted in Jerome Murphy-O'Connor, ed., *Paul and Qumran.* London: Chapman, 1968, 31–47; and in Joseph A. Fitzmyer, *Essays on the Semitic Background of the New Testament.* London: Chapman, 1971, and Missoula: Scholars, 1974, 187–204.

_____. "Another Look at *kephalē* in 1 Corinthians 11.3," *NTS* 35 (1989) 503–511.

_____. "*Kephalē* in I Corinthians 11:3," *Interp.* 47 (1993) 52–59.

Gill, David W. J. "The Importance of Roman Portraiture for Head-coverings in 1 Corinthians 11,2-16," *TynB* 41 (1990) 245–260.

Grudem, Wayne A. "Does *kephalē* ('Head') mean 'Source' or 'Authority Over' in Greek Literature? A Survey of 2,336 Examples," *TrJ* 6 (1985) 38–59.

Hall, David R. "A Problem of Authority," *ExpT* 102 (1990) 39–42.

Holmyard, Harold R. "Does 1 Corinthians 11:2-16 Refer to Women Praying and Prophesying in Church?" *BSac* 154 (1997) 461–472.

Hooker, Morna D. "Authority on Her Head: An Examination of I Cor. xi. 10," *NTS* (1963–1964) 410–416.

Isaksson, Abel. *Marriage and Ministry in the New Temple: A Study with Special Reference to Mt. 19.13-12 [sic] and 1. Cor. 11.3-16.* ASNU 24. Lund: Gleerup, 1965.

Jervis, L. Ann. "'But I Want You to Know . . .': Paul's Midrashic Intertextual Response to the Corinthian Worshipers (1 Cor 11:2-16)," *JBL* 112 (1993) 231– 246.

Kähler, Else. *Die Frau in den paulinischen Briefen. Unter besonderer Berücksichtigung des Begriffes der Unterordnung.* Zürich and Frankfort: Gotthelf-Verlag, 1960.

Kroeger, Richard Clark, and Catherine Clark Kroeger. "An Inquiry into Evidence of Maenadism in the Corinthian Congregation," SBL.SP 1978, 2, 331–338.

Lowery, David K. "The Head Covering and the Lord's Supper in 1 Corinthians 11:2-34," *BSac* 143 (1986) 155–163.

MacDonald, Dennis R. *There is No Male and Female: The Fate of a Dominical Saying in Paul and Gnosticism.* HDR 20. Philadelphia: Fortress, 1987.

Martin, William J. "1 Corinthians 11:2-16: An Interpretation" in W. Ward Gasque and R. P. Martin, eds., *Apostolic History and the Gospel: Biblical and Historical Essays presented to F. F. Bruce on his 60th Birthday.* Grand Rapids: Eerdmans, 1970, 231–241.

Meeks, Wayne A. "The Image of the Androgyne: Some Uses of a Symbol in Earliest Christianity," *HR* 13 (1974) 165–208.

Meier, John P. "On the Veiling of Hermeneutics (1 Cor 11:2-16)," *CBQ* 40 (1978) 212–226.

Mercadante, Linda A. *From Hierarchy to Equality: A Comparison of Past and Present Interpretations of 1 Cor 11:2-16 in Relation to the Changing Status of Women in Society.* Vancouver: G-M-H Books, 1978.

Murphy-O'Connor, Jerome. "The Non-Pauline Character of 1 Corinthians 11:2-16?" *JBL* 95 (1976) 615–621.

————. "Sex and Logic in 1 Corinthians 11:2-16," *CBQ* 42 (1980) 482–500.

Oster, Richard E., Jr. "When Men Wore Veils to Worship: The Historical Context of 1 Corinthians 11:4," *NTS* 34 (1988) 481–505.

————. "Use, Misuses and Neglect of Archaeological Evidence in Some Modern Works on 1 Corinthians (1 Cor 7,1-5; 8, 10; 11,2-16; 12,14-26)," *ZNW* 83 (1992) 52–73.

Padgett, Alan. "'Authority Over Her Head.' Toward a Feminist Reading of St. Paul," *Daughters of Sarah* 13 (1986) 5–9.

————. "Paul on Women in the Church: The Contradictions of Coiffure in 1 Corinthians 11.2-16," *JSNT* 20 (1984) 69–86.

Pella, G. "Voile et soumission? Essai d'interprétation de deux textes pauliniens concernant le statut de l'homme et de la femme," *Hokhma* 30 (1985) 3–20.

Pérez Gordo, Alfonso. "¿Es el velo en 1 Co 11,2-16 símbolo de libertad o de sumisión?" *Burgense* 29 (1988) 337–366.

Richter, Hans-Friedemann. "Anstössige Freiheit in Korinth. Zur Literarkritik der Korintherbriefe (1 Kor 8,1-11 und 11,2-16)," *CorC* 561–575.

Scroggs, Robin. "Paul and the Eschatological Woman," *JAAR* 40 (1972) 283–303.

Shoemaker, Thomas P. "Unveiling of Equality: 1 Corinthians 11:2-16," *BTB* 17 (1987) 60–63.

Thompson, Cynthia L. "Hairstyles, Head-coverings, and St. Paul: Portraits from Roman Corinth," *BA* 51 (1988) 99–115.

Tomson, Peter J. *Paul and the Jewish Law* 131–139.

Trompf, G. W. "On Attitudes Toward Women in Paul and Paulinist Literature: 1 Corinthians 11:3-16 and Its Context," *CBQ* 42 (1980) 196–215.

Vander Stichele, Caroline. "Authenticiteit en integriteit van 1 Kor 11,2-16. Een bijdrage tot de discussie omtrent Paulus' visie op de vrouw." Catholic University of Leuven S. T. D. dissertation, 1992.

Walker, William O. "The Vocabulary of 1 Corinthians 11.3-16: Pauline or Non-Pauline?" *JSNT* 35 (1989) 75–88.

———. "1 Corinthians 11:2-16 and Paul's Views Regarding Women," *JBL* 94 (1975) 94–110.

Williams, Ritva. "Lifting the Veil: A Social-Science Interpretation of 1 Corinthians 11:2-16," *Consensus* 23 (1997) 53–60.

Wilson, Kenneth T. "Should Women Wear Headcoverings?" *BSac* 148 (1991) 442–462.

Winandy, Jacques. "Un curieux casus pendens: 1 Corinthiens 11.10 et son interprétation," *NTS* 38 (1992) 621–629.

Wire, Antoinette C. *The Corinthian Women Prophets* 116–134, 226–228.

2. The Lord's Supper? (11:17-22)

17. Saying this, I do not commend you because you come together not for the better, but for the worse. 18. First of all, when you do come together in the gathering, I hear that there are divisions among you, and I partially believe it. 19. For it must be that there are factions among you so that those among you who are truly genuine might be recognized. 20. When, however, you come together in the same place it is not to eat the supper of the Lord. 21. For in eating each one by preference takes his or her own meal; and one goes hungry while another gets drunk. 22. Don't you have houses for eating and drinking? Do you despise the church of God and dishonor those who have not? What shall I tell you? Shall I commend you? In this I do not commend you.

INTERPRETATION

Paul's refusal to commend the Corinthians, repeated in vv. 17 and 22, makes a literary unit of the following section by means of the device of *inclusio.* "I do not commend you" *(ouk epainō)* is the phrase that brackets Paul's discussion. This phrase contrasts with the "I commend you" *(epainō de hymas)* with which the previous pericope had begun (11:2). The contrast links this section with the preceding unit (11:2-16). It also underscores the importance of the matter Paul treats in vv. 17-22 and the severity of his judgment on the conduct of the Corinthians.

The Rhetoric. The importance of the matter treated in this rhetorical unit is underscored by Paul's declaration that he wants to speak of the issue "first of all" *(prōton men,* v. 18) and by the fact of his willingness to delay the consideration of other issues until his arrival (v. 34). The issue of social discrimination in the eucharistic community is one that could not wait. Paul is blunt in affirming, twice, that the conduct of the Corinthians in this regard is not commendable (vv. 17, 22). The contrast employed in v. 17, "you come together not for the better but for the worse," is a rhetorical device that emphasizes Paul's strong negative judgment on the behavior of the Corinthians. Other contrasts in the pericope are that between the Lord's supper *(kyriakon deipnon,* v. 20) and "your own" supper *(to idion deipnon,* v. 21), being hungry and getting drunk (v. 21), having houses and having nothing (v. 22).

The rhetoric of the pericope is reinforced by the series of rhetorical questions with which it closes. Each of them is powerful, inviting the Corinthians to make a judgment about their behavior. Paul responds to the final question with his own answer. He does not find their behavior commendable. The intensity and severity of his judgment are underscored by the fact that he will return to this issue in the summary exhortation of vv. 33-34. He wants to disabuse the Corinthians of the notion that a meal in which the social divisions of the community are manifest can properly be construed as the Lord's supper.

The Lord's Supper. Hans-Josef Klauck has shown that the Christian celebration of the Lord's supper *(kyriakon deipnon)* was in some ways similar to the fellowship meals in the Hellenistic world, where heads of large households sometimes functioned as patrons of voluntary associations. These voluntary associations frequently met for a formal dinner party either in the sanctuary of a god or in the home of the patron. The dinner consisted of the meal *(deipnon),* a libation of wine offered to the god—frequently considered to have been invited to the meal or as serving as the host—and a symposium, a round of drinking during which various activities took place. The pattern is not unlike that of contemporary banquets where there is a meal followed by ritual (the toast) and speeches.

The meal taken on the occasion of some celebration or the gathering of an association was often one in which each participant contributed his or her own share. Such potluck dinners *(eranoi)* were traditional in the

Hellenistic world. Centuries before Paul the Athenian dramatist Aristophanes gave the wording of an invitation to such a dinner: "Come at once to dinner and bring your pitcher and your supper chest" (*Acharnians* 1085). Rules of etiquette for these social events are preserved in the writings of Plato (*Symposium* 174A) and Martial (*Epigrams* 10.48; 11.52).

In the metropolitan center of Corinth there were probably several house churches under the respective patronage of Stephanas (1:16; cf. 16:17-18), perhaps Chloe (see note on 1:11), Gaius (Rom 16:23), and others as well. Paul's double use of "come together" (*synerchomai*, vv. 17, 18, 20; cf. v. 33) suggests that the various house churches came together under one roof, as it were, on at least some occasions. The purpose of these gatherings was a communal meal (11:33; cf. vv. 20-21). Following the customary pattern of the Hellenistic dinner, the Christian gathering consisted of a meal, the Lord's supper, and a service of the word.

Although the Christian assembly was in many respects similar to the gatherings of Hellenistic voluntary and religious associations, there were several differences between the Christian assembly and these associations. One was that the latter were usually recognized by civic authorities. Another was that the Christian assembly came together under the patronage of the Lord rather than that of one or another deity (Serapis, Dionysius, etc.). Another difference was that the Christian community was not socially homogeneous. It consisted of men and women, slaves and free, Jews and Gentiles, rich and poor. In Roman society men and women dined together. In Greek families men and women dined apart (cf. Plato, *Symposium* 176E). The church of Corinth, where there were families with a Latin culture (see the Latin names of Gaius in 1:14, Fortunatus and Achaicus in 16:17, Gaius, Erastus, and Quartus in Rom 16:23), may have followed the Latin custom. Only free men reclined at table; women, children, and such slaves as might be present sat during the meal.

When the Christians of Corinth came together for their common meal the social divisions among them were manifest. The celebration proved to be divisive for the Corinthians. Those who came early to the meal owned their own houses (v. 22). The "haves" were able to come early because their socioeconomic condition allowed them more control of their own time. Slaves and day laborers, beholden to their masters and employers, would not have been free to come as early to the common meal as were the well-to-do householders. As a result these latter were prone to eating and drinking in excess, while the slaves and day laborers went hungry. They could eat only the leftovers, if anything.

It might also be the case that physical space contributed to the problem. The first guests, presumably those served by slaves, could join the host in the *triclinium,* the dining room proper. Latecomers would be rele-

gated to the hall *(atrium)* or the courtyard *(peristylum)*. The physical location of the latecomers attested to their social location within the community and underscored the social division that rent the community at
Corinth.

The Christians at Corinth who went ahead eating their own meal before the arrival of others may have believed that they were eating the
Lord's supper. It is this belief that Paul challenges as he brings judgment
to bear on their divisive conduct. In the following pericope (11:23-26)
Paul explains why it is that Christians' coming together to eat can be considered the Lord's supper. What was happening at Corinth was not in his
judgment the Lord's supper. People were eating their own meals; others
were without anything to eat (v. 21). For Paul this is all the more outrageous in that it provides evidence that the community is not subservient
to the Lord (cf. 11:20). The first-century C.E. statutes of an Egyptian religious association, the "Gild" of Zeus Hypsistos, cite "making factions"
(schismata synistasthai) as an activity that is incompatible with the
monthly banquet in the sanctuary of Zeus. In somewhat similar fashion
Plutarch complained that when the conversation in the after-dinner part
of a gathering is not one in which all share, "gone is the aim and end of
the good fellowship *(koinōnias to telos)* of the party and Dionysius is out-
raged" ("Table-Talk," *Moralia* 615A).

Social divisions within a community may well be inevitable (v. 19).
Paul speaks of their inevitability in another fashion as he brings judgment to bear on a situation in which community divisions are apparent.
The inevitability of division is a sign of the impending eschaton. The conflicts within the community as well as the way in which their gifts are
used for building up the community (3:12-16) are part of the eschatological testing of the community. They reveal who it is that is approved by
God.

A Breach of Etiquette. The contrast (v. 22) between the "haves" and the
"have nots" is a classic topos in Greco-Roman rhetoric. There is a difference between the rich and the powerful, the poor and the powerless.
Even in fellowship meals it was not unknown for poorer food and wine
to be served to the ordinary clients of the patron while better food and
fine wine were offered to the host and his well-placed friends. Pliny, for
example, describes the dining habits of "a person who, in his own opinion, lives in splendor combined with economy":

> Some very elegant dishes were served up to himself and a few more of
> the company, while those that were placed before the rest were cheap
> and paltry. He had apportioned in small flagons three different sorts of
> wine; but you are not to suppose it was that the guests might take their
> choice: on the contrary, that they might not choose at all. One was for
> himself and me; the next for his friends of a lower order (for you must

> know, he measures out his friendship according to the degrees of qual-
> ity); and the third for his own freedmen and mine. (*Epistles* 2.6)

In Pliny's opinion dining in this fashion was a matter of dining in "a sor-
did manner." Similar practices were satirized by such classic authors as
Martial (*Epigrams* 1.20; 3.49, 60; 4.85; 6.11) and Juvenal (*Satires* 5.24-25,
152-155). Juvenal describes the treating of guests in this fashion as pure
maliciousness. In one of his satires he wrote: "You may perhaps suppose
that Virro grudges the expense; not a bit of it! His object is to give you
pain. For what comedy, what mime, is so amusing as a disappointed
belly? His one object, let me tell you is to compel you to pour out your
wrath in tears, and to keep gnashing your molars against each other. . . .
In treating you thus, the great man shows his wisdom" (*Satires* 5.156).

In contrast, Plutarch stressed that equality among all present (*he isotēs
tois andrasi,* "Table Talk," *Moralia* 613F) ought to be a feature of the common meal. Centuries before Plutarch, Pliny, and Paul the historian Xenophon described what should happen when people come together for a
meal. He wrote:

> Whenever some of those who came together for dinner brought more
> meat and fish than others Socrates would tell the waiter either to put the
> small contributions into the common stock or to portion them out
> equally among the diners. So the ones who brought a lot felt obliged not
> only to take their share of the pool, but to pool their own supplies in re-
> turn; and so they put their own food also into the common stock. Thus,
> they got no more than those who brought little with them. (*Memorabilia*
> 3.14.1)

Socrates urged that the *eranos* be truly a communal meal. The philosophic moralists of Paul's era show that this was not always the case.
Plutarch complained about the danger of disorder during the meal (cf.
"Table Talk," *Moralia* 615E, 618C). Some associations developed a code of
conduct for appropriate behavior during fellowship meals. There was to
be no quarreling or fighting; nor was one to speak out of turn without
permission (see D. E. Smith, "Meals and Morality," 323). In similar fashion Sir 31:12–32:13 sets forth a number of exhortations with regard to
food, wine, and banquets. The host is to take care of others first; only then
should he sit down (Sir 32:1-2). The one who is generous with food is
blessed (Sir 31:23-24). Those in attendance at a banquet are urged not to
help themselves before others are able to eat (Sir 31:18).

Drunkenness (cf. 11:21) was a common disturbance during Hellenistic banquets (see Lucian, *Carousal [Symposium] or the Lapiths* 17; Athenaeus, *Deipnosophists* 2.36; Sir 31:29-31). Intoxication was so common that
the potluck dinner was once banned in Sparta and Crete; some hosts tried
to bring the meal to a timely end so as to avoid the problem (see D. E.

Aune, "Septem sapientium convivium," 73). The situation that developed when the Christians of Corinth came together for what they presumed to be the Lord's supper (11:20) seems not to have been so different from the situation of other Hellenistic groups of people who came together for a potluck dinner.

NOTES

17. *Saying this, I do not commend you because you come together not for the better, but for the worse:* The opening clause, for which there are some textual variants in the manuscript tradition, picks up on the formulation of 11:2 and links this passage to what Paul has just said. Both passages deal with the Christian community at worship. "Saying" (*paraggellōn;* cf. 7:10; 1 Thess 4:11) generally connotes "giving a message" or "giving orders," but "saying this" seems a better epistolary translation. "Not commend" (*ouk epainō*) is reprised in v. 22, thereby forming an epistolary unit under the rubric of non-commendation. The situation Paul will describe is simply scandalous. The contrast between better and worse underscores the abnormality of the situation.

18. *First of all, when you do come together in the gathering:* "First of all" (*prōton men*) is emphatic rather than enumerative (cf. Rom 1:8; BDF 447.4 suggests that "from the outset" might be an appropriate translation). Other matters will be treated when Paul arrives (11:34). "Gathering" is *ekklēsia,* elsewhere rendered as "church." The Greek term means "assembly" or "gathering." That nuance should not be lost when Paul writes about "coming together" (*synerchomenōn*). The outrageousness of the Corinthians coming together in a way that is inconsistent with their being the "church of God" (11:16, 22) must not, however, be overlooked.

    I hear that there are divisions among you, and I partially believe it: "And I partially believe it" underscores Paul's acceptance of what he had heard. "I hear" (*akouō* of the Greek) actually means "I have heard," just as it does in English. Presumably news of the divisions that were manifest in the assembly of Christians was conveyed orally to Paul, rather than being mentioned in the letter he had received (7:1). Chloe's people had delivered an oral report on the divisions within the community at Corinth (1:11).

    The terms used by Paul in 11:17-22 "divisions" (*schismata;* cf. 1:10) and "factions" (*haireseis,* v. 19), indicate social division. Walter Schmithals, Hans-Martin Schenke, and a few other commentators think that the "divisions" of 11:18 are different from the "divisions" of 1:10 and that therefore the passages in which these expressions are found come from two different letters. It is more likely that the divisions within the community that Paul had criticized in the earlier part of his letter were particularly apparent when the community gathered together. The social stratification of the community was manifest in the conduct of the gathered community. Hence the intensity and severity of Paul's criticism.

19. *For it must be that there are factions among you:* "Factions" *(haireseis)* appears elsewhere in Paul only in Gal 5:20, where it is cited in a section of a catalogue of vices dealing with social divisiveness. That factions are inevitable *(dei)* bespeaks their eschatological necessity. Early Christians were convinced that divisions were not only necessary; they were also a penultimate reality. As a harbinger of the eschaton they proclaimed the imminence of judgment and the revelation of those who are faithful (cf. 3:13-14). See Matt 10:34-36; Luke 12:51-53; cf. Matt 24:5, 21; Mark 13:6-8; 12; Luke 21:8, 16; Justin, *Dialogue with Trypho* 35.3 *(PG* 6, 549); *Pseudo-Clementine Homilies* 16.21.4 *(PG* 2, 382); *Didascalia Apostolorum* 23.

    so that those among you who are truly genuine might be recognized: The divisions within the community are revelatory. Paul typically uses the adjectival noun "the genuine" *(hoi dokimoi)* in the context of commendation (2 Cor 10:18; 13:7; cf. Rom 14:18). The word is highlighted by Paul's use of *kai,* loosely rendered as "truly." The "genuine" are those who have been proven themselves and who are, in consequence, recognized by others for who they are and what they have done (cf. *TLNT* 1:353–361, at 358–360). The conduct of the Corinthians as they gather together for their memorial meal reveals who genuine people really are (cf. 3:13). Again there may be a touch of irony in Paul's words. It is not impossible that the hybrists considered themselves the ones who were "for real" *(hoi dokimoi)* within the community.

20. *When, however, you come together in the same place:* "In the same place" *(eis to auto),* reinforcing the *syn,* "together," of Paul's "come together" *(synerchomenōn),* may suggest that the general assembly of the Christians in Corinth was not the most usual form of Christians coming together.

    it is not to eat the supper of the Lord: "Lord's," *kyriakon* (cf. Rev. 1:10), following a classic construction (cf. BDF 113.2), is an adjective formed from the noun *Kyrios,* "Lord." Apparently the Christians of Corinth thought that their common meal, no matter the divisions that were manifest, was the Lord's supper. For Paul, however, when Christians come together in an assembly marked by factions and divisions the meal they share is not the Lord's supper.

21. *For in eating each one by preference takes his or her own meal; and one goes hungry while another gets drunk:* One feature that would have differentiated the Christian community from other Hellenistic religious associations, besides its adherence to the Lord rather than to idols (cf. 10:14-22), was that they were not socially homogeneous (cf. 1:26).

    "Takes by preference" *(prolambanei)* may mean starting to eat before the others do. This, in fact, is the common interpretation of the verb, drawing attention to the temporal aspect of the prepositional prefix *pro.* Paul, however, does not stress the temporal aspect of the verb on the only other occasion that he uses it (Gal 6:1). The verb can simply mean to partake of food, as it does on a stele in the sanctuary of Asclepius in Epidaurus (see Rudolf Herzog, *Die Wunderheilungen von Epidauros,* PhilSup 22/3 [Leipzig: Dieterich'sche Verlagsbuchhandlung, 1931] 43–45; cf. MM 542) or to take by preference, as it does in Sophocles.

Paul's description of the outrageous conduct of those Christians who have come together for a meal highlights two features of their dining habits. Different timetables and different tables bear witness to the divisions within the community. First of all, some (*hekastos*, literally each one, but see 14:26) get off to a head start *(pro-)* without waiting for the others. They cannot wait. Second, each one takes his or her own meal *(to idion deipnon).* The sharing of food that is appropriate for Christians when they come together does not happen. "His or her own" *(idion)* provides a sharp antithesis with "the Lord's" *(kyriakon)* in v. 20. Rather than eating the Lord's supper some of the Corinthian Christians prefer to eat their own supper. The result of some getting a head start and going ahead with their own meals is that some go hungry while others have so much to drink that they get drunk (note the distributive *hos . . . hos,* "one . . . another"). Paul's opinion on the isolating meal of the Christians at Corinth resonates with that of Plutarch's Hagias, who is reported to have said "but where each guest has his own private portion, companionship fails" *(all' hopou to idio estin, apollytai to koinon,* "Table-Talk," *Moralia* 644C).

22. *Don't you have houses for eating and drinking?* The staccato series of five rhetorical questions in v. 22 (the second and third are joined by *kai,* "and") creates a strong rhetorical appeal. The questions are addressed to those who have their own houses and set these people over and against the have-nots. This suggests that it is the behavior of the well-to-do within the community that is problematic. The impact of the first questions is heightened by Paul's use of emphatic particles, *gar* in the first question (cf. BAGD 152.1.f) and *ē* in the second, neither of which has been specifically translated.

Paul's first question contains a double negative and calls for a positive response: "Of course you do" (BDF 427.2). The question implies that the Corinthians had come from their own homes to someone else's home for their gathering. There is "something special" about the meal that is eaten when the community comes together.

Do you despise the church of God and dishonor those who have not? Paul's second question identifies the Corinthians as the church of God (see 1:2). The expression evokes the reality of the Corinthian church as a group (cf. v. 18) that has been assembled by God. It also calls to mind the memory of Israel during the Exodus (cf. 10:1-13), when it was assembled as "the church of God." "Despise" *(kataphroneite;* cf. Rom 2:4), a strong verb used by Paul, connotes disdain. Directed against God who has called together a people, the verb suggests impiety (see *TLNT* 2:280–284), a virtual rejection of God.

Paul's third question is equally forceful. Implicitly it contrasts the behavior of the "haves" who despise *(kataischynete)* the "have-nots" *(tous mē echontas)* with the behavior of God who has chosen the have-nots to put the haves to shame (1:26-29, with a repeated *kataischynē* in v. 27).

What shall I tell you? Shall I commend you? In this I do not commend you: The fourth and fifth rhetorical questions in the staccato series evoke the relationship between Paul and the community. Their rhetorical force lies in their expression of an authority figure's frustration. As he has done earlier in the letter (cf. 9:8, 10, 15), Paul answers his own question. He brings the unit to closure (cf. v. 17) by affirming that although he may commend the Corinthians for preserving the traditions he had handed on to them (11:2), in no way does he commend them for the way they eat when they come together.

For Reference and Further Study

Aune, David E. "Septem sapientium convivium" in Hans Dieter Betz, ed., *Plutarch's Ethical Writings and Early Christian Literature*. SCHNT 4. Leiden: Brill, 1978, 51–105.

Blue, Bradley B. "The House Church at Corinth and the Lord's Supper: Famine, Food Supply, and the Present Distress," *CTR* 5 (1991) 221–239.

Boccaccini, Gabriele. "Il valore memoriale dell'atto eucaristico alla luce della tradizione giudaica." *Vita Monastica* 36 (1984) 107–117.

Campbell, R. Alastair. "Does Paul Acquiesce in Divisions at the Lord's Supper?" *NovT* 33 (1991) 61–70.

Coutsoumpos, Panayotis. "Paul's Teaching of the Lord's Supper: A Socio-Historical Study of the Pauline Account of the Last Supper and Its Graeco-Roman Background." Ph.D. thesis, University of Sheffield, 1996.

Hahn, Ferdinand. "Herrengedächtnis und Herrenmahl bei Paulus," *Liturgisches Jahrbuch* 32 (1982) 166–177.

Hofius, Otfried. "The Lord's Supper and the Lord's Supper Tradition: Reflections on 1 Corinthians 11:23b-25" in Otto Knoch, et al., *One Loaf, One Cup* 75–115. In German: "Herrenmahl und Herrenmahlsparadosis. Erwägungen zu 1 Kor 11,23b-25," *ZThK* 85 (1988) 371–408.

Lampe, Peter. "The Eucharist. Identifying with Christ on the Cross," *Interp.* 48 (1994) 36–49.

Paulsen, Henning. "Schisma und Häresie. Untersuchungen zu 1 Kor 11, 18.19," *ZThK* 79 (1982) 180–211.

Rakotoharintsifa, A. "Historiographie et Lecture socio-historique de 1 Corinthians," *Foi et Vie* 96 (1997) 115–123.

Roberts, Colin H., Arthur Darby Nock, and Theodore C. Skeat. "The Gild of Zeus Hypsistos," *HThR* 29 (1936) 37–90.

Schrage, Wolfgang. "Einige Hauptprobleme der Diskussion des Herrenmahls im 1. Korintherbrief," *CorC* 191–198.

Smith, Dennis E. "Meals and Morality in Paul and His World," *SBL.SP* 1981, 319–339.

———. "Social Obligation in the Context of Communal Meals: A Study of the Christian Meal in 1 Corinthians in Comparison with Graeco-Roman Communal Meals." Ph.D. dissertation, Harvard University, 1980.

Theissen, Gerd. *The Social Setting of Pauline Christianity* 145–174.

Therrien, Gérard. *Le Discernement dans les écrits pauliniens*. EtB. Paris: Gabalda, 1973, 218–259.

3. *The Lord's Supper* (11:23-26)

23. For I received from the Lord what I have also handed on to you, that the Lord Jesus on the night he was handed over took bread 24. and having given thanks broke it and said, "this is my body that is for your sake. Do this in reminiscence of me." 25. Similarly he took the cup after the meal saying, "this cup is the new covenant in my blood. As often as you drink, do this in reminiscence of me." 26. For as often as you eat this bread and drink the cup you announce the death of the Lord until he comes.

INTERPRETATION

To explain (note the postpositive *gar*) what he means by the Lord's supper and why the Corinthians' individual meals are not the Lord's supper (11:20) Paul cites an early Christian tradition. Tensions within the community, manifest in their dining, dress, and speaking, are the epistolary *stasis* that has called for Paul's rehearsal of the tradition. In Paul's rhetoric the narration functions as a cultic etiology. It simultaneously refers to the origin of Christian eucharistic practices and provides a basis for reflection on the Corinthians' actual practice.

Citing the origin of what the Corinthians presume to celebrate, the tradition evokes its normativity. Paul had previously written about the eucharist in 10:16-21 with a reference to the cup of blessing and the bread that is broken (10:16). He wrote obliquely about the eucharist in 10:1-13 with a reference to spiritual food and drink (10:3-4). Some commentators consider that what Paul writes about the eucharist in 11:23-26, to which the rhetorical inference of vv. 27-34 is appended, is the focal point of a macro-chiasm encompassing all of chs. 11–14. From this perspective what Paul writes is at the heart of a rhetorical structure in which he addresses the practical issues of appropriate dress and proper etiquette during the assembly, the eucharist, and practical issues pertaining to the use of charismatic gifts in the assembly.

Tradition. 1 Corinthians 11:23-26 contains the oldest literary account of the Last Supper. The account antedates the letter. Paul's introduction (11:23a) reminds the Corinthians that the account is something he had previously shared with them, presumably at the time of his visit to them in the middle of the first century C.E. The tradition is older than that. Paul's introductory formula tells his correspondents that the account he passed along circa 51 C.E. was a tradition that he himself had received and that he had faithfully (*ho kai,* v. 23) passed on to them.

Paul explicitly states that he is rehearsing a Christian tradition. His language, in which the verbs "received" (*parelabon*) and "handed on" *(paredōka)* seem to call for one another, echoes the language of Hellenistic philosophers and that of the ancient rabbis. As used by the rabbis the equivalent Hebrew verbs *qibbēl*, "to receive" and *māsar*, "to deliver" had virtually a technical meaning. Principally used in reference to the tradition of the *halakoth*, the terminology implied that received teaching was faithfully and authoritatively handed on from one generation to the next. Use of this terminology implied the relevance of what was handed on for those to whom it was given. What was at issue when these verbs were used was a living tradition, firmly rooted in the memory of the past and fully applicable to the lives of those to whom it was being transmitted.

As a good father (note the emphatic *egō* with which the pericope begins), Paul had passed the tradition on to his children, the Corinthians. Paul is not catechizing the Corinthians for the first time with regard to the eucharist. Rather he is recalling a tradition they have already received, but of whose significance they may have lost sight. He uses the tradition to recall why it was that what the Corinthians were doing when they came together and individualistically ate their own meals was not a celebration of the Lord's supper (11:20-21).

An Independent Narrative. Paul's rather abrupt transition to the brief narrative, coupled with the use of the technical language of tradition and the recitative *hoti,* suggest that the unit had a life of its own prior to its incorporation into Paul's letter. Contemporary literary analysis of the synoptic gospels holds to the view that the material out of which Mark wove his passion narrative had previously been handed down in the form of independent units of oral tradition. The supper narrative is absent from the Fourth Gospel, but there is some allusion to the tradition in the Johannine discourse on the bread of life (see especially John 6:51-58). The tradition that Paul recalls in 11:23-26 is similar to but older than the narrative versions that appear in the synoptic gospels (Matt 26:26-28; Mark 14:22-24; Luke 22:19-20).

Paul's version of the Lord's supper tradition is closer to the Lukan account than it is to the narratives found in Mark and Matthew. With regard to the bread Luke, like Paul, makes reference to Jesus' having given thanks *(eucharistēsas).* Both authors provide a clarifying "that is for your sake" *(to hyper hymōn).* Only Paul and Luke have the anamnesis formula, "do this in reminiscence of me" *(touto poieite eis tēn emēn anamnēsin).* With regard to the cup Luke, like Paul, makes reference to the "the new covenant in my blood" *(hē kainē diathēkē en tǭ emǭ haimati).* He also places the cup "similarly . . . after the meal" *(hōsautōs . . . meta to deipnēsai).* None of these five traits is to be found in the Markan-Matthean account of the supper.

That Paul's version of the narrative is the oldest literary attestation to the tradition of the institution of the eucharist does not mean that every detail in his narrative is traditional. Still less does it imply that the pre-Pauline tradition used by Paul was innocent of some shaping by the community. The community's cultic practice influenced the tradition as it was handed down in the first Christian decades. In the version used by Paul the balance achieved by the repeated "in reminiscence of me" (vv. 24, 25) is most probably due to the liturgical use of the tradition. On the other hand, some features of Paul's account show that the narrative has its roots in a historical event. Telltale signs of the essential historicity of the narrative are the lack of perfect balance between the ritual of the bread and the narrative of the cup, the fact that the narrative of the cup is not ritualized, and that the drinking of the cup is said to have come after the meal. These features of Paul's account coalesce to support the view that the tradition is more than mere stylized ritual. Its origins are rooted in historical memory.

Paul has taken the tradition over for his own rhetorical purpose and formulated it to serve that purpose. The identification of Jesus as Lord (*Kyrios*), an epithet that reprises Paul's favorite christological title, may well be Paul's own interpretive addition to the tradition. In context the nomenclature is striking. The narrative speaks of events attendant upon Jesus' being handed over. With the *Kyrios* title Paul subtly reminds his audience that Jesus was subsequently raised as Lord. His death anticipates the parousia, as does the eucharist (v. 26). The *Kyrios* title identifies Jesus as one having ultimate authority. In the following exhortation (vv. 27-34) Paul continues to identify Jesus as Lord (vv. 27, 32). The Lord is the authority on the basis of which Paul makes his plea to the community. By introducing the title of Lord into the rehearsal of the traditional cult legend Paul provides a basis for his paraenesis.

The short story of the Lord's supper, told ever so briefly, recalls the beginning and the end of a meal. Prior to his final meal with the disciples Jesus performed a thanksgiving ritual (the Jewish *bĕrākâ*) over the bread. The disciples are identified in the narrative as "you" (*to hyper hymōn*, "for you"). The use of the pronoun in the second person invites the Corinthians to participate in the account of the narrated events. Jesus' words at the conclusion of the meal interpret the cup as one that recalls the new covenant announced by Jeremiah (Jer 31:31). This interpretive word over the cup suggests that the supper is to be remembered as a covenantal meal, one that joins people together and links them with their God. Calling the covenant the "new" covenant (Jer 31:31), Jesus identifies the covenant of which he speaks as the eschatological covenant. With this designation the meal and Jesus' death are given ultimate, eschatological significance.

Cultic Reminiscence. Paul's anamnesis command, "do this in reminiscence of me" (vv. 24, 25), is found with exactly the same wording in Luke

22:19. Unlike Paul, Luke does not repeat the anamnesis command in regard to the cup (cf. Justin, *First Apology* 66.3).

Hans Lietzmann (*An die Korinther* 56–57; *Messe und Herrenmahl* 223) and Hans-Josef Klauck (*Herrenmahl* 76–88) interpret the anamnesis formula in the light of a common practice in Hellenistic religious associations. Various associations regularly held dinners in memory of their founder and patron. An ancient text tells about a Roman widow who established a cultic association, with a venue, so that meals in honor of Jupiter could regularly be held "in memory of Anicus Priscus, her husband" (*ILS* 3081). Epicurus' will prescribed that a memorial meal be held on the twentieth of each month "in our memory and in memory of Metrodorus" (Diogenes Laertius, *Lives* 10.18). Such meals easily developed into a kind of hero worship that would partially explain the openness of Hellenists, such as those Christians in Corinth, to the practice of the Lord's supper.

Paul's account of the Lord's supper is, nonetheless, a cultic aetiology with Palestinian roots. His anamnesis formula must be seen in the light of the Jewish tradition of remembrance. The tradition is characterized by its use of the verb *zākar*, "to remember." "In reminiscence of" (*eis tēn anamnēsin*) is a formula that appears four times in the Greek Bible, the Septuagint (Lev 24:7, Wis 16:6, and the titles of Pss 37 and 69, each time without the definite article). The Greek formula, similar to Paul's formula in vv. 24-25, is parallel with the Hebrew *lĕzikkārôn*. To remember God's saving events in the past was to remember God himself. To remember God was to remind God about something. Reminding God about something past makes prior salvific events foundational for salvation in the present and enables those who participate in a cultic activity to share in the effects of the salvific events that are remembered. In Jewish tradition the annual celebration of Passover was a reminiscence event (cf. Exod 12:14; 13:3, 9; Deut 16:3; *Jub.* 49:7-23; Josephus, *Ant.* 2.317; *m. Pesaḥ.* 10:5; *y. Pesaḥ.* 10:35). So, too, were the Sabbath *qiddush* and daily prayer.

Reminiscence, as a motif of the Passover celebration, was particularly significant. In the celebration of Passover a Jewish family not only recalled the saving events of the Exodus experience but also reminded God of those events and themselves became participants in the salvific experience of their ancestors. In Paul's narrative salvific events are evoked in various ways: the use of the title "Lord," the reference to the night of Jesus' being handed over, and the interpretive word over the bread, "this, my body, for you." Salvation effected through the death and resurrection of Jesus is specifically alluded to in v. 26b. Paul's words explain and have a meaning similar to his anamnesis formula.

Although 11:23-26 contains an etiological narrative, its rhetorical significance in 1 Corinthians must not be overlooked. Paul offers a recitation of the cultic narrative as an example of Jesus' self-donation (cf. 8:11).

What Jesus did on the night he was handed over is an example *(paradeigma)* of the historical sort (cf. Aristotle, *Art of Rhetoric* 2.20.3). At the beginning of the chapter Paul had urged the Corinthians to follow his example even as he followed the example of Christ (11:1).

Announcing the Death of the Lord. In the biblical tradition reminiscence and proclamation are often associated with one another. In remembering one proclaims; in proclaiming one remembers (cf. Ps 71:15-17 [NB. the Hebrew *('azkîr)* and Greek *(mnēsthēsomai)* texts of Ps 71:16b have the verb "to remember" (see also the Latin Vulgate, and *JB*) translated as "I will praise your righteousness" *(NRSV)*]; Ps 105:1, 5). Commenting on the Passover ritual, Rabbi Gamaliel is reputed to have said, "we are bound to give thanks, to praise, to glorify, to honor, to exalt, to extol, and to bless him who wrought all these wonders for our ancestors and for us. He brought us out from bondage to freedom, from sorrow to gladness, and from mourning to a Festival-day" *(m. Pesaḥ.* 10:5).

Proclamation often means preaching, but it is not restricted to the formal activity of preaching. Paul sometimes uses the terminology, for example *kataggellete,* "announce," of v. 26, in a more expansive fashion. The ritual is a speaking word, a sign (Heb. *'ôt*) that proclaims a revelatory message. The celebration of eucharist is gospel, the proclamation of good news. Proclamation takes place not only through the spoken word but also through the speaking word of a symbolic gesture, though not through the gesture alone. The verb "to announce" always implies the spoken word.

In the rhetoric of 1 Corinthians Paul's reference to an announcement of the Lord's death anticipates his extensive discussion on the Lord's death and resurrection in ch. 15. The eucharistic celebration proclaims the salvific event of Jesus' death *(ton thanaton tou kyriou,* cf. 2:8). The salvific events include the resurrection, hence the use of the *Kyrios* title and the reference to the parousia (cf. 16:22). The Syriac Peshiṭta's translation of v. 26b implies that Paul is writing about a remembrance of the death of the Lord. According to Paul Jesus died for the weak within the community (8:11). Accordingly the Corinthians' meal can hardly be the Lord's supper. Their meal is one in which social divisions are manifest. Their practice is irreconcilable with the tradition of the eucharist.

A Historical Note. Paul used language that had been adopted by Hellenistic philosophers and Jewish rabbis to affirm that he was faithfully passing along the received teaching. Nonetheless, scholars of various stripes contend that Paul's narrative does not faithfully reflect a tradition that derives from the historical Jesus. In the early part of the twentieth century, some scholars, especially German academics from the history-of-religions and radical form-critical schools of interpretation (e.g., Hans Lietzmann, Rudolf Bultmann, Herbert Braun, Alfred Loisy) adopted a skeptical attitude toward the historicity of the event. More recently members of the so-called Jesus Seminar have denied that Jesus' last meal was significant in any way other than that it happened to be his last meal (e.g., Dominic Crossan). Following upon the work of Loisy and Lietzmann, Hyam Maccoby, far from denying that Paul has evoked the memory of the eucharist for hortatory purposes, claims that Paul is the originator of the tradition insofar as he received a personal vision from the Lord. On the basis of that personal vision Paul taught the Corinthians about the Lord's supper with its interpretive words over bread and wine.

A strict application of the criteria for historicity generally accepted by proponents of the historical-critical method of biblical interpretation points, however, to the basic historicity of the narrative that Paul has recounted for the Corinthians. Synoptic criticism clearly shows that Matthew's account is secondary to that of Mark. There is no evidence that Luke was dependent on Paul; most probably both Luke and Paul represent different versions of a like tradition. All four narratives connect the eucharist with a supper and the time of Jesus' death. Paul's account alone refers to the night of Jesus' being handed over, but Paul does not give an account of Jesus' being handed over. His letters contain no Passion narrative. Nor does Paul make an attempt to cast the Last Supper as a Passover meal.

With regard to the bread all four NT accounts provide a recitation with four elements: the ritual gesture of taking bread, thanksgiving (a blessing in Matthew and Mark), the gesture of breaking bread, and the interpretive word. To these the synoptics add a fifth element, the actual giving of the bread to the disciples. The first three elements are typical of the beginning of a Jewish meal, with a blessing and breaking of bread. As in *JosAs* 16:14, Jesus' interpretive word does more than simply clarify the meaning of his gesture. Jesus' word is also a word of bestowal. His word over the bread invites the disciples, past and present, to relate the bread to Jesus' death that is on their behalf. It conveys oneness in Christ (cf. 10:17) and invites them into communion with one another in a remembering community, the church. The cup provides a share in the new covenant.

The Sequence of Events. In Paul's Hellenistic culture the "meal" (*deipnon*; cf. 11:20) was a formal meal. It was often followed by a round of drinking (*symposium*), introduced by a libation to the gods. Sometimes the drinking was accompanied by entertainment. As various satirists indicate, the entertainment was almost bawdy at times. At other times the meal was followed by serious philosophical discussion, of which Plato's *Symposium* is the classic example (cf. 1 Esdr 4:13-41; Luke 22:24-38; John 15–17).

Some commentators, Otfried Hofius for example, take Paul's "after the meal" as an indication that the cup ritual took place after the formal meal, inferring from this reference that the bread ritual took place during the blessing of bread with which the typical Jewish meal began (cf. 10:16). On this reading the scandalous meal enjoyed by some of the Corinthians would have taken place between the bread ritual and the cup ritual. It is, however, more likely that the Christians of Corinth had come together for a festive meal, at the end of which they celebrated a ritual recalling what the Lord Jesus had done on the night before he died, and then proceeded to a more general worship service in which hymns, psalms, speaking in tongues, and prophecies took place (cf. 1 Corinthians 14). This sequence would have corresponded to the normal sequence followed in the gatherings of Hellenistic associations, that is, the formal meal, a libation offered to the gods, and the round of drinking accompanied by conversations. Plutarch describes a series of rules of etiquette that ought to be in force during the after dinner *(meta deipnon)* conversation, when philosophical talk *(philosophein)* took place (see "Table Talk," *Moralia* 612F).

That both the bread ritual and the cup ritual took place together and that both occurred after the formal meal had been completed also seems to be suggested by Paul's "similarly" *(hōsautōs)* and by the fact that he suggests that some went ahead and began the meal before others arrived (vv. 21, 33). If the bread ritual took place at the beginning of the meal the latecomers would have been excluded from the bread ritual altogether. That is unlikely in itself and contrary to Paul's argument in 10:16-17.

NOTES

23–24. *For I received from the Lord what I have also handed on to you:* Paul's language *(parelabon . . . paredōka)* reflects the technical language of Jewish rabbinic tradition, where it bespeaks the authoritative and accurate handing on of *halakah*. The language is akin to that used in rabbinic writings and in some Hellenistic circles (see above, pp. 425–426). Paul normally uses "Lord" to denote the Risen One, but the appearance of this title in v. 23 does not imply that Paul had received a vision of the Risen Lord. The tradition is one that goes back to the Christian community in Jerusalem. The Risen Lord is the one who guarantees its accuracy and imparts to it its authority. The latter element is particularly significant in 1 Corinthians, as Paul explains (note his explanatory *gar*) why it is that the supper they were eating was not the Lord's supper (v. 20).

that the Lord Jesus on the night he was handed over: Among the four NT accounts of the Lord's supper, Paul's alone explicitly indicates that the "Lord Jesus" performed the ritual (cf. Matt 26:26). Paul situates the event on the night when Jesus was handed over. The passive voice of the verb *(paredideto)* might be a divine passive, suggesting that God was the principal agent in Jesus' passion (cf. Rom 4:25; 8:32). Paul's use of the title and the reference to the night of the handing over, perhaps a reflection of pre-Pauline tradition, indicate that Paul wants to situate the origin of the Lord's supper in the context of decisive salvific events. The apostle does not, however, interpret the Last Supper as a Passover meal (cf. 5:7).

took bread and having given thanks broke it and said: The ritual sequence of taking bread, giving thanks (offering praise in Matthew and Mark), breaking the bread, and saying is found in all four NT accounts (Matt 26:26; Mark 14:22; Luke 22:19; 1 Cor 11:23-24). The ritual is typically found at the beginning of a Jewish meal, when the presider would pronounce a blessing over a loaf of bread. The sharing of the blessed and broken bread would symbolize that those who partook of the meal shared in the blessing. See notes and interpretation of 10:16-17.

this is my body that is for your sake. Do this in reminiscence of me: All four NT accounts have the interpretive phrase "this is my body" *(touto estin to sōma mou),* but only Luke 22:19 has "that is for your sake" and "do this in reminiscence of me." A Johannine account (see John 6:51, 54-55) makes it likely that Jesus' words were closer to "this is my flesh" (cf. Ign. *Rom.* 7:3; *Phld.* 4:1). The Aramaic *biśrāʾ* (Heb. *bāśār*), meaning "flesh," can be translated into Greek either by *sarx* (flesh) or *sōma* (body). As he was speaking a Semitic tongue, Jesus' own words would have lacked a copula (thus "this, my body"). Biblical texts such as Lev 5:8 and Deut 28:23 suggest that Jesus' entire phrase, including "for your sake" *(to hyper hymōn),* derives from a Semitic formulation.

In cultic language *hyper* ("for [your] sake") specifies the beneficiaries of the sacrifice or dedication. More than thirty NT texts use the preposition in reference to Jesus' death (cf. 1:13; 15:3). The interpretive phrase "that is for your sake" is absent from the Markan-Matthean narrative (Matt 26:26; Mark 14:22), but it undoubtedly belonged to pre-Pauline tradition. For Jesus to have identified the bread with his body without some interpretive remark such as that succinctly summarized in Paul's "for your sake" would have been virtually unintelligible in a Jewish context. It would have been all the more difficult to interpret if the cup, with its own interpretive word, was not shared until much later in the meal, as Paul indicates that it was.

The manuscript tradition shows that the terse qualifying phrase "for your sake," at least in its Greek formulation, demands an explanation. The underlying Aramaic tradition of the bread word is more readily explicable than is its rendition in Greek. The Codex Athous Lavrensis (Ψ) and correctors of such important majuscules as ℵ, C, and D read the text with a clarifying "broken" *(klōmenon),* D with "broken in pieces" *(thryptomenon),* and the Coptic version with "given" *(didomenon;* cf. Luke 22:19). "Broken" is well attested in Syria and the East during the fourth century and is found in the great majority of Greek manuscripts. Jean Duplacy thinks that "broken" best explains the other variants and suggests that it may have been omitted by some scribes who found the notion of eating pieces of Jesus' fragmented body altogether harsh. A shorter reading appears, however, in the older manuscripts ($\mathfrak{P}^{46}$, ℵ, A, B, C). These manuscripts are predominantly of Egyptian provenance. Their shorter reading seems best able to explain a later appearance of the various participles, each of which seems to be a scribal clarification.

In the textual tradition of v. 24 some manuscripts (C³, K, L, P, most of the medieval texts, and several ancient versions) have "take and eat" *(labete phagete)* after "said" *(eipen)*. Given the ecclesial prominence accorded to Matthew in the early centuries, this variant undoubtedly reflects the influence of Matt 26:26.

25. *Similarly he took the cup after the meal:* Rudolf Pesch and Peter Stuhlmacher take the phrase "the cup after the meal" *(to potērion meta to deipnēsai)* as a reference to the third Passover cup, construing "after the meal" to be a prepositional attributive modifying "the cup." Both grammatical and referential difficulties exist with regard to this interpretation. From a grammatical point of view the prepositional phrase is not introduced by an article, as it should be were it to modify the noun. From a referential point of view Paul's narrative does not suggest that the tradition was that of a Passover meal celebrated by the Lord Jesus. Along with the "you" of v. 24, "after the meal" probably should be taken as an element of historical reminiscence (cf. Mark 14:22-25; Luke 22:20).

saying, this cup is the new covenant in my blood: The interpretive saying over the cup includes a reference to the blood of the covenant (cf. Exod 24:3-8). Unlike Matthew and Mark, neither Paul nor Luke identifies the contents of the cup with Jesus' blood. The shared cup is a covenant ritual. The covenant banquet is widely attested in Ancient Near Eastern texts, including some within the biblical tradition (cf. Gen 14:18, 24; 26:26-33; 31:43-54; Exod 24:9-11; Josh 9:3-16). "In my blood" has a Semitic ring. "In" reflects the Semitic *bĕ* and creates an instrumental or causal clause (thus Joachim Jeremias). The eucharistic cup expresses the covenant, of which Jesus' blood is a symbol and a mediation (cf. Exod 24:8). Pre-Pauline tradition (cf. Luke 22:19-20) added the specification of "new" to the covenant reference, undoubtedly under the influence of Jer 31:31 and the community's awareness of the eschatological nature of the Christ event.

Hans-Josef Klauck's analysis of the history of tradition leads him to conclude that after his symbolic reference to the bread Jesus made reference to his impending death and the eschaton (cf. Matt 26:29; Mark 14:25; Luke 22:18). The post-Easter tradition created a saying over the cup analogous to the saying over the bread, hence Paul's "similarly" *(hōsautōs).* The parallelism between the two and the emphasis on the elements *per se* allowed for the separation between the cup and the bread, that is, for the "liturgical order" presupposed by Paul in 11:23-26. The parallelism is, however, not exact (cf. Mark 14:22, 24). Thus it is more likely that the shared cup (cf. 10:16, "the cup of blessing;" 10:21, "the cup of the Lord"), interpreted covenantally, came at the end of the meal.

As often as you drink, do this in reminiscence of me: Given the importance of *zkr*, "to remember," in the Hebrew cultic tradition, it is likely that the two exhortations to remember (vv. 24, 25) derive from the early church's liturgical tradition. The verb is in the present imperative. Its connotation is "keep on doing this in memory of me." Among the four NT narratives of the Last Supper, Paul's is the only account that repeats the exhortation to remember, with its clause "as often as you drink" after the interpretive cup word.

26. *For as often as you eat this bread and drink the cup you announce the death of the Lord until he comes:* "As often as you drink" (v. 25) serves as a lemma that Paul expands with a reference to the bread and for which he provides an eschatological interpretation. Paul's joining together the eating of the bread and the drinking of the cup suggests that they constitute a single liturgical gesture in two parts. The compound conditional clause is not perfectly balanced. A demonstrative, "this" *(touton)*, qualifies "bread," but "cup" (despite 𝔓⁴⁶, "corrections" of ℵ, C, and D, etc.) is unqualified. That there is no demonstrative with "cup" is owing to Paul's reprise of the words of v. 25. The double reference, to bread and to cup, is echoed in the following exhortation that three times speaks of eating and drinking (11:27, 28, 29).

Paul's explanation (see the explanatory *gar*, "for") suggests that Paul knew of the traditional eschatological saying that made a link between the eucharistic cup and the eschatological banquet (Matt 26:29; Mark 14:25). His words confront what might be the Corinthians' overly realized eschatology and prepare for the theme of judgment that he will exploit in the ensuing paraenetic exhortation. Paul would have the Corinthians know that the end has not yet come.

FOR REFERENCE AND FURTHER STUDY

Burchard, Christoph. "The Importance of Joseph and Aseneth for the Study of the New Testament: A General Survey and Fresh Look at the Lord's Supper," *NTS* 33 (1987) 102–134.

Cangh, Jean-Marie van. "Peut-on reconstituer le texte primitif de la Cène? (1 Co 11,23-26 par. Mc 14,22-26," *CorC* 623–637.

Chenderlin, Fritz. *"Do This as My Memorial." The Semantic and Conceptual Background and Value of Anamnēsis in 1 Corinthians 11:24-25.* AnBib 99. Rome: Pontifical Biblical Institute, 1982.

Chrupcalla, Leslaw D. "Chi mangia indegnamente il corpo del Signore (1 Cor 11,27)," *SBFLA* 46 (1996) 53–86.

Clancy, Robert A. D. "The Old Testament Roots of Remembrance in the Lord's Supper," *CJ* 19 (1993) 35–50.

Duplacy, Jean. "A propos d'un lieu variant de 1 Co 11,24: Voici mon corps (–, rompu, donné, etc.) pour vous" in Joël Delobel, ed., *Etudes de critique textuelle du Nouveau Testament.* BEThL 88. Louvain: Louvain University Press, 1987, 329–346.

Farmer, William R. "Peter and Paul, and the Tradition concerning 'The Lord's Supper' in 1 Corinthians 11:23-26" in Otto Knoch, et al, eds., *One Loaf, One Cup* 35–55.

Garlatti, Guillermo J. "La eucaristía como memoria y proclamación de la muerte del Señor (Aspectos de la celebración de la cena del Señor según San Pablo)," *RevB* 46 (1984) 321–341; 47 (1985) 1–25.

Gaventa, Beverly Roberts. "'You Proclaim the Lord's Death': 1 Corinthians 11:26 and Paul's Understanding of Worship," *RExp* 80 (1983) 377–387.

Hofius, Otfried. *"To sōma to hyper hymōn 1 Kor 11,24,"* *ZNW* 80 (1989) 80–88.

Huser, Thierry. "Les récits de l'institution de la Cène. Dissemblances et traditions," *Hokhma* 21 (1982) 28–50.

Jeremias, Joachim. *The Eucharistic Words of Jesus*. New York: Scribner's, 1966.

Karrer, Martin. "Der Kelch des neuen Bundes. Erwägungen zum Verständnis des Herrenmahls nach 1 Kor 11,23b-25," *BZ* 34 (1990) 198–221.

King, Fergus J. "Eating in Corinth: Full Meal or Token Meal?" *IBS* 19 (1997) 161–173.

Lietzmann, Hans. *Messe und Herrenmahl. Eine Studie zur Geschichte der Liturgie.* AKG 8. Bonn: Marcus & Weber, 1926. English: *Mass and Lord's Supper: A Study in the History of the Liturgy.* Leiden: Brill, 1979.

Luke, K. "'The Night in which He was Delivered up' (1 Cor 11:23)," *BibBH* 10 (1984) 261–279.

Maccoby, Hyam. "Paul and the Eucharist," *NTS* 37 (1991) 247–267.

Magne, Jean. "Les paroles sur la coupe," *Cahiers du Cercle Ernest-Renan* 32 (1984) 241–248.

Meier, John P. "The Eucharist at the Last Supper: Did it Happen?" *TD* 42 (1995) 335–352.

Passakos, Demetrius C. "Eucharist in First Corinthians: A Sociological Study," *RB* 104 (1997) 192–210.

Smith, Barry D. "The More Original Form of the Words of Institution," *ZNW* 83 (1992) 166–186.

4. *Judgment* (11:27-34)

27. Therefore the one who eats the bread or drinks the cup of the Lord unworthily is answerable for the body and blood of the Lord. 28. Let a person scrutinize him- or herself and so eat of the bread and drink of the cup. 29. For the one who eats and drinks, not recognizing the body, eats and drinks judgment upon him- or herself. 30. Hence there are many weak and sick among you and some have died. 31. If we really judge ourselves, then we should not be judged; 32. we who are judged by the Lord are chastised so that we might not be condemned with the world. 33. Wherefore, my brothers and sisters, when you come together to eat, wait for one another. 34. If anyone is hungry, let that one eat at home so that you do not come together unto judgment. As for the rest, I will give instructions when I come.

INTERPRETATION

Throughout the pericope Paul writes about eating and drinking (vv. 27, 28, 29), that is, the bread and the cup (v. 27, 28), the body and the blood (v. 27). His emphasis on both elements of the eucharistic celebration is consistent with what he has previously written (10:3-4, 16-17, 31; 11:21, 22, 23-25, 26).

Judgment. The inference Paul draws from his reminder about the eucharist is replete with judicial language. "Unworthily" (*anaxiōs*, v. 27; cf. 6:2), "answerable" (*enochos*, v. 27), "scrutinize" (*dokimazō*, v. 28), "judgment" (*krima*, vv. 29, 34; cf. 6:7), "judge" (*diakrinō*, vv. 29, 31; *krinō*, vv. 31, 32), "chastise" (*paideuō*, v. 32), and "condemn" (*katakrinō*, v. 32) all belong to the semantic domain of the law and the courtroom. The literary device of paronomasia, that is, the repetition of the same word stem in close proximity, enhances the judicial atmosphere. Six words derived from the root *krin- (krima, diakrinōn, diekrinomen, ekrinometha, krinomenoi, and katakrithōmen)* appear in vv. 29-32. Paul's use of this word group, whose radical connotation is judgment, means that there can be no doubt about the principal theme of the pericope. Paul's reflections recall the rhetorical topos of judgment, the *iudicatio*, in which judgment is made by the gods, men of repute, or judges (see [Aristotle], *Rhet. ad Alex.* 1422a.25-28). Eating the bread and drinking the cup is the action to be judged. In fact there are two judgments, one by those who eat and drink, the other by the Lord. Those who eat and drink are invited to scrutinize themselves, to really judge themselves (vv. 28, 31). The basis for their judgment should be what it means for the community to be the body of the Lord (v. 29). The alternative to judging oneself is being judged by the Lord.

The christology that emerges from Paul's exhortation features the parousiac Lord. Paul continues to maintain the eschatological perspective introduced in v. 26. That eating the bread and drinking the cup is a matter of ultimate concern is suggested in various ways. Paul begins his strongly worded paraenesis with a sentence of holy law (v. 27), a kind of eschatological *quid pro quo.* Then, using the rhetorical device of *gradatio*, climax, he speaks of death as a form of chastisement (v. 30). Finally he mentions the condemnation of the world (v. 32). Paul's intention is that those at Corinth should be spared ultimate condemnation. To make his point clearly he adds to the paraenesis of vv. 27-32 a second, summarizing inference (vv. 33-34). When the Corinthians come together they should wait for one another. Otherwise they eat and drink judgment upon themselves. Lest the errant Corinthians fall victim to final judgment, God has chastised them. Chastisement is not condemnation (cf. 5:5). A well-known biblical proverb proclaims that the Lord chastises those whom he loves (Prov 3:12; Heb 12:6).

Apparently Paul considers sickness, weakness, and even death to be forms of chastisement. Paul's premise is that inappropriate behavior in the eucharistic context can lead to sickness and death. His words reflect the popular Jewish notion that sickness and death are forms of punishment for sin (cf. Mark 2:9, par.; John 9:2, and the legendary account of Job in the OT). The experience of sickness, weakness, and death should help Christians avoid condemnation, but many members of the community are weak and sick; some have even died. "Weak" *(astheneis)* and "sick" *(arrōstoi,* hapax in Paul) are essentially synonymous terms, but given Paul's rhetorical crescendo "weak" surely indicates a less serious situation than does "sick." Those who are weak previously figured in Paul's digression on eating food offered to idols. Those who have died will again be mentioned in 15:6. Verse 30 contains the only mention of the sick at Corinth. That some have died (cf. 10:8-10) does not mean that they have received the ultimate, eschatological penalty (see note on 15:6). Their death is, nonetheless, a matter of concern for the community. Hence Paul's extensive exposition on the resurrection of those who have died in ch. 15 of this letter.

Structure and Authority of Paul's Argument. The final exhortation of ch. 11 (vv. 33-34) concerns the lack of eucharistic manners about which Paul had written in vv. 17-22. The exhortation uses the very language that had been used to describe the situation, "come together," "eat," "hungry," "home," and "wait" (loosely antithetical to "take first"). This choice of language enables Paul to establish his point by means of a chiastic A-B-A' exposition in which he first addresses the scandalous behavior of the community (vv. 17-22), then reflects upon the eucharist (vv. 23-32), and finally offers a specific behavioral exhortation (vv. 33-34).

The central unit of the exposition is made up of vv. 23-32, composed of two-subsections, the etiological narrative of vv. 23-26 and the paraenetic inference of vv. 27-32. The leitmotif of both units is "the Lord." "The Lord" *(Kyrios)* appears three times in each unit, twice in the opening sentence (vv. 23, 27) and once in the closing sentence (vv. 26, 32). "The Lord" forms an *inclusio* for each of the units, identifying each of them as a distinct subunit in Paul's argument. The first subunit explains (the explanatory *gar*) what the Lord's supper is, thereby clarifying why it is that what the Corinthians are doing is not eating the Lord's supper (11:20). The second subunit (with its inferential *hōste*) explains what subservience to the Lord should mean for a community that gathers in such a way that it does not celebrate the Lord's supper. Subservience to the Lord should give the Corinthians pause to think (vv. 28, 31). Failing that, they are liable to judgment.

The authority and the example of the Lord provide the principal argument in Paul's rhetoric. To this Paul adds the authority that derives from his presence as an apostle and an argument based on his own familial relationship with the Corinthians. The apostrophic vocative of v. 33 is characteristic of the paraenesis of 1 Corinthians. It is, however, unique insofar as he calls the Corinthians "my" *(mou)* brothers and sisters, thereby strengthening the rhetorical force of the kinship bonds that the formula evokes. The Lord's example *(paradeigma)* and his own personal relationships *(ethos)* are the arguments Paul employs in order to persuade the Corinthians to abandon their less-than-Christian pattern of behavior.

The pronoun "my" in v. 33 also serves to characterize the meal more clearly as a family meal from which the latecomer would be excluded if the others did not wait. Excluding the latecomer is a matter for judgment. As in earlier passages of the letter (cf. 6:5-8, with regard to lawsuits; 8:11-13, with regard to food offered to idols), Paul implies that socially discriminatory conduct is all the more egregious in that it is directed against members of the family.

NOTES

27. *Therefore the one who eats the bread or drinks the cup of the Lord unworthily is answerable for the body and blood of the Lord:* Paul's wording is sharp, the language judicial. An inferential *hōste*, "therefore," (cf. v. 33) draws a conclusion from what he wrote about the eucharist in vv. 23-26. Anyone who partakes of the eucharist in an unseemly and unworthy manner merits the Lord's judgment and punishment (vv. 29, 34).

Paul's wording may be another example of a sentence of holy law (cf. 3:17) used to condemn conduct that is inimical to the well-being of the community. The correspondence between the harmful practice and the expected eschatological punishment is not expressed in unequivocal verbal parallelism as it has been in his previous uses of the literary form and will be in his use of the form in later correspondence. In 11:27 there is, nonetheless, similarity of thought between the relative clause and the main clause, the use of judicial language (*anaxiōs*, "unworthily"; *enochos*, "answerable"), and an eschatological context (see v. 26).

"Answerable" (*enochos*, hapax in Paul), is primarily a judicial term, used in reference to the court, the punishment, the crime, or the person against whom the crime is committed, as here (see BAGD, 268.2bγ, "sin against the body and blood;" cf. 8:12). "Unworthily" (*anaxiōs*) is not necessarily a legal term, but Paul uses it in reference to court cases in 6:2. The genitive "of the Lord" (*tou kyriou*) qualifies the bread as well as the cup, the body as well as the blood.

28. *Let a person scrutinize him- or herself and so eat of the bread and drink of the cup:* Paul's gender-inclusive *anthrōpos*, "a person," suggests a contrast between the human and the divine (cf. 2:11-16). In the following verses (vv. 27-32) he speaks about divine judgment. Here he urges the Corinthians to an exercise in self-scrutiny (cf. v. 31) before eating the bread and drinking the cup. The self-scrutiny he encourages is a matter of the recognition of the body (v. 29). It is not so much a matter of moral introspection as of concern for the community. Use of this text by various Fathers of the Church shows that ecclesial unity and charity are at the heart of Paul's concern.

29. *For the one who eats and drinks, not recognizing the body, eats and drinks judgment upon him- or herself:* Paul explains (note the explanatory *gar*) why self-scrutiny is necessary: the alternative is (divine) judgment. Failure to recognize the body of the Lord brings judgment upon oneself. An inherent system of justice is at work (cf. v. 30). The [Lord's] body has as its referent the eucharistic body, but Paul also alludes to the community (cf. 12:12-26) as the body of Christ. People who do not recognize the community as the body of the Lord but dare to eat the bread and drink the cup bring judgment upon themselves. Paul's language is crisp and cryptic. It may reflect some of the ideas associated with the ordeal of bitter waters described in Num 5:11-31 (cf. *m. Soṭa* 3:1-5).

    To elucidate Paul's terse phraseology, some "intelligent scribes," including those who transcribed D, F, G, Ψ, and other majuscules and some of the correctors of the Sinaiticus and Ephraemi Rescriptus codices (א², C³), have added a qualifying "unworthily" (*anaxiōs*, cf. v. 27) after the first reference to eating and drinking. They have also added an interpretive "of the Lord" *(tou kyriou)* to "the body." Both additions are widely attested in the medieval textual tradition (cf. *AV*) but are absent from the most important witnesses ($\mathfrak{P}^{46}$, א, B).

30. *Hence there are many weak and sick among you and some have died:* This verse relates the situation of those who are weak, those who are sick, and those who have died to the eucharist. Paul's premise is that behavior that is inappropriate in a eucharistic context can lead to sickness and death. Using the rhetorical figure of *klimax (gradatio)*, Paul has arranged the three afflictions in an order of increasing intensity. The first two conditions are essentially synonymous, but given the crescendo "weak" *(astheneis)* surely indicates a less serious situation than does "sick" *(arrōstoi*, hapax in Paul). Those who are weak previously figured in Paul's digression on eating food offered to idols. Those who have died will again be mentioned in 15:6. Although v. 30 contains the only explicit mention of the sick at Corinth, the charism of healing given as a gift to some members of the community (12:9, 28, 30) implies that some of them had been sick.

31. *If we really judge ourselves, then we should not be judged:* The indicative mood of Paul's subordinate clause suggests an unreal condition (BDF 360.4). The intensive "really judge" *(diekrinomen)* implies a process of discrimination, making the necessary distinctions. The apodosis has a verb in the passive voice, implying that judgment will come at the hands of a divine judge. The passive is a divine passive. The apodosis speaks of ultimate eschatological judgment (cf. vv. 31, 26). Verse 32 specifies that the judge is the Lord.

32. *we who are judged by the Lord are chastised so that we might not be condemned with the world:* A negative judgment by the Lord leads to the chastisement of those who neglect the community. The chastisement about which Paul writes is quite distinct from condemnation (*katakrithōmen*, hapax in 1 Corinthians; cf. 2 Cor 6:9). Paul does not often write about chastisement. His notion of cosmic condemnation derives from an apocalyptic worldview.

33. *Wherefore, my brothers and sisters, when you come together to eat, wait for one another:* This final exhortation addresses itself to the issue of the lack of eucharistic manners that Paul had broached in vv. 17-34. It echoes the language of that pericope. Paul's initial "wherefore" harks back to v. 27, where Paul began to draw an inference after having recalled the origin and significance of the eucharist. His apostrophic vocative is characteristic of the paraenesis of 1 Corinthians, but it is distinctive insofar as Paul uses the pronoun "my" (*mou*, literally, "of me") brothers and sisters. The pronoun emphasizes the kinship bonds evoked by Paul's vocative. The pronoun also serves to characterize the meal more clearly as a family meal, from which the latecomer would be excluded if the others did not wait. Notwithstanding the observations of Hofius ("The Lord's Supper," 93–94), the verb *ekdechesthe* has the simple meaning "wait for" (*TDNT* 1:407).

34. *If anyone is hungry, let that one eat at home, so that you do not come together unto judgment:* As is his wont, Paul incorporates casuistry (*ei*, "if," see above, p. 263) into his exhortation. His conditional clause is an element of parenthetical casuistry similar to that found in 7:15, 21. Should there prove to be some within the community who are hungry, the proper thing for them to do is to eat at home before the assembly comes together (cf. v. 22). Otherwise they are not eating the Lord's supper (v. 20). If they do not share the meal in inclusive fashion they are not eating the Lord's supper; rather they are eating and drinking judgment on themselves (v. 29).

As for the rest, I will give instructions when I come: The *ethos* of Paul's exhortation is initially grounded in the ties of kinship that bind him to the community (cf. "my brothers and sisters," v. 33), but kinship is not the only source of his authority. Paul's final words remind the community that he has authority to give them instructions. When he does come (cf. 4:19; 16:5-7) he will instruct them on other matters as well. He does not specify what the other matters are. "When," *hōs an* instead of *hotan*, is Pauline usage (BDF 455.2).

For Reference and Further Study

Clancy, Robert A. D. "The Old Testament Roots of Remembrance in the Lord's Supper," *CJ* 19 (1993) 35–50.

Gundry-Volf, Judith. "Punishment of the Disobedient: To 'Eat' and 'Drink' Judgment" in eadem, *Paul and Perseverance*. WUNT 37, 2. Tübingen: Mohr, 1990, 99–113.

Klauck, Hans-Josef. "Der Gottesdienst in der Gemeinde von Korinth," *Pastoralblatt* 36 (1984) 11–20.

Murphy-O'Connor, Jerome. "House Churches and the Eucharist," *TBT* 22 (1984) 32–38.

Perrot, Charles. "'C'est pourquoi il y a parmi vous beaucoup de malades' (1 Co 11,30)," *Supplément* 170 (1989) 45–53.

Pesce, Mauro. "Mangare e bere il proprio giudizio. Una concezione culturale commune a 1Cor e a Sota?" *RivBib* 38 (1990) 495–513.

Sánchez Caro, José Manuel. "'Probet autem seipsum homo' (1 Cor 11, 28). Influjo de la praxis penitencial eclesiástica en la interpretación de un texto bíblico," *Salm* 32 (1985) 293–334.

Schneider, Sebastian. "Glaubensmängel in Korinth. Eine neue Deutung der 'Schwachen, Kranken, Schlafenden' in 1 Kor 11,30," *FNT* 9 (1996) 3–19.

F. FIFTH RHETORICAL DEMONSTRATION (12:1–14:40)

In this demonstration Paul takes up the topic of the "spiritual gifts" *(pneumatika)* with which the members of the Corinthian community had been abundantly enriched (1:5-7). The use of "concerning" *(peri de)* to identify the topic for discussion may indicate that spiritual gifts were one of the troubling issues about which the Corinthians had written to Paul (7:1). As he is wont to do, Paul develops his reflections in a three-part argument. The paean on love (ch. 13) serves as the focal point.

The chiastic structure of the demonstration is similar to that of chs. 8–10. In both cases the discussion of the topic at hand begins with a formulaic use of *peri de* to indicate the matter for discussion. In each case the identification of the topic is expanded by the use of popular slogans, by Paul's reference to what is known, and by his critique of the slogans (cf. 8:1-3 and 12:1-3). The third unit of each chiastic pattern reprises the theme of the first unit, treating it almost casuistically in reference to the immediate situation at Corinth. The intervening unit in each case is a rhetorical digression featuring Paul's personal example. Each digression is characterized by a marked shift from the imperatives of the first part of the chiastic unit to a series of concrete examples that are allusively and ever so succinctly cited.

The first part of the argument in the fifth rhetorical demonstration focuses on the spiritual gifts. Paul prefers to call these gifts "charisms," thereby accentuating their character as gift (12:4). Without giving an exhaustive list of all the gifts that had been given to the members of the community Paul offers an overview of the various gifts given to the Corinthians (12:4-11). His argument is highlighted by his use of the body image (12:12-26), a traditional rhetorical topos that Paul adroitly uses to his own advantage. The image allows the apostle to focus on the unity of the community and the diversity of its gifts. Then he returns to a consideration of the gifts (12:27-31a). He offers two lists that differ somewhat from the first one. The list in 12:28 seems to stress the idea that some gifts are more important than others, while the list in 12:29-30 consists of a series of rhetorical questions the purport of which is to suggest that no member of the community has all the gifts and that none of the gifts is given to all members of the community. Thus ch. 12 is chiastically arranged, A: gifts (vv. 1-11), B: body (vv. 12-26), A': gifts (vv. 27-31a).

Paul's first listing of the gifts (12:8-10) is encompassed within a theological framework (12:4-7, 11) that circumscribes the epistolary unit and provides a point of view from which the several gifts are to be considered. Charisms are gifts of the Spirit given for the benefit of the community. Paul's list of the individual gifts focuses on those of speech (vv. 8, 10). The relative importance of the gift of tongues and of the gift of prophecy seems to have been problematic for the Corinthians. The gift of tongues may have been a status symbol within the community. If so the problem of the relative importance of the spiritual gifts would be a further indication of the extent to which socioeconomic status contributed to the divided situation of the community.

Paul's overview of the gifts identifies one that is complementary to the gift of prophecy, namely the gift of discernment of spirits, and one that is complementary to the gift of tongues, namely the gift of the interpretation of tongues. A more detailed reflection on these two gifts is given in ch. 14, a chapter devoted exclusively to the gifts of tongues and prophecy.

The use of chiasmus is the most significant structural feature of Paul's fifth rhetorical demonstration. Use of the structure allows him to affirm the importance of the community as the experiential criterion for the evaluation of individual gifts. His interpretive digression on the body of Christ (12:12-26) brings a community focus to bear on the gifts. In ch. 14 Paul's frequent recourse to the theme of "upbuilding" (the verb in vv. 4[2x], 17; the noun in vv. 3, 5, 12, 26) identifies the motif in the light of which the gift of prophecy is to be esteemed over and against the gift of tongues.

At the heart of the macro-chiasm is ch. 13, Paul's encomium on love. The unit is defined by an *inclusio*, "avidly desire" the gifts (12:31; 14:1). In an opening exhortation Paul says that it is the greater gifts that are to be sought and that he will be helpful to the Corinthians insofar as he will show the way that surpasses all others. He urges the community to pursue the way he had identified. "Strive for love," he writes in 14:1. Then, having exhorted the community to seek after spiritual gifts, Paul identifies prophecy as a gift to be especially pursued (14:1c). Although verbal identity is lacking, the elements of superior gifts/prophecy and surpassing way/love are part of the *inclusio* that formally sets 12:31–14:1 apart as the central element in Paul's chiasm. The theme of the central section is "love," *agapē*. This noun occurs ten times in 12:31–14:1, but it is not present in either of the encompassing units. These have spiritual gifts (ch. 12) and upbuilding (ch. 14) as their respective leitmotifs.

Structurally ch. 13 has the form of an encomium. The rhetorical pattern (cf. Plato, *Symposium* 197A-E; 1 Esdr 4:34-40) consists of a prologue, a recitation of acts, a comparison, and an epilogue. When the encomium praises a person the prologue is followed by an account of the person's birth and upbringing. The rhetorical pattern is evident in ch. 13. The verses in 12:31–13:3 function as the prologue, 13:4-7 as the *acta,* 13:8-12 as the comparison, and 13:13–14:1 as the epilogue. The literary form of the encomium enhances Paul's personification of love in vv. 4-8, the central unit within a chapter that is itself chiastically structured.

Some commentators, especially proponents of some of the partition theories of composition (Johannes Weiss, Walter Schmithals, Wolfgang Schenk, Hans-Martin Schenke and Karl Martin Fischer; see above, Introduction, pp. 10–14), are of the opinion that the encomium on love is a secondary addition to Paul's letter. Others opine that the piece may have had a pre-Pauline origin. These opinions cannot be satisfactorily substantiated. The entire chapter reflects Paul's way of argumentation, his vocabulary, and his ideas. In the form of an encomium the chapter serves the deliberative purpose of Paul's letter much as the rhetorical digression of ch. 9, in the form of a judicial apology, served the paraenetic purpose of the letter's third rhetorical demonstration (chs. 8–10). The closing exhortation of ch. 13, "strive for love," and the exhortation that contributes to the *inclusio,* "avidly desire the spiritual gifts," bespeak the paraenetic purpose of the chapter. Forming the core of a chiastic pattern, the chapter is a rhetorical digression *(parekbasis)* that provides a foundation for the specific argumentation to be developed in ch. 14.

The heart of Paul's ground-laying digression is the manifold description of love in vv. 4-7. Rehearsing the *acta* of love, this unit constitutes the theological and ethical core of the entire reflection. Then, in vv. 8-11, Paul compares the permanence of love with the ephemeral charisms. The first of the charisms to be cited is the gift of prophecy. Its emphatic position gives it a place of prominence over and against the gifts of tongues and knowledge, phenomena that had been so highly valued among the Corinthians. The love of which Paul writes in 1 Corinthians 13 is the love of one's neighbor, but Paul considers this in the light of the Christian's love of God and his or her love of Christ. His perspective is theological rather than ethical. For Paul love is the eschatological power of God at work.

FOR REFERENCE AND FURTHER STUDY

Callan, Terrance. "Prophecy and Ecstasy in Greco-Roman Religion and in 1 Corinthians." *NovT* 27 (1985) 125–140.

Carson, Donald A. *Showing the Spirit: A Theological Exposition of 1 Corinthians 12–14*. Grand Rapids: Baker Book House, 1987.

Dautzenberg, Gerhard. *Urchristliche Prophetie. Ihre Erforschung, ihre Voraussetzungen im Judentum und ihre Struktur im ersten Korintherbrief*. BWANT 104. Stuttgart: Kohlhammer, 1975.

Focant, Camille. "1 Corinthians 13. Analyse rhétorique et analyse de structures," *CorC* 199–245.

Forbes, Christopher. *Prophecy and Inspired Speech: in Early Christianity and its Hellenistic Environment*. WUNT 2nd ser. 75. Tübingen: J.C.B. Mohr (Paul Siebeck) 1995; Peabody, Mass.: Hendrickson, 1997.

Gardner, Paul Douglas. *The Gifts of God and the Authentication of a Christian: An Exegetical Study of 1 Corinthians 8–11:1*. Lanham, Md.: University Press of America, 1994.

Heckel, Ulrich. "Paulus und die Charismatiker. Zur theologischen Einordnung der Geistesgaben in 1 Kor 12-14," *ThBeitr* 23 (1992) 117–138.

Holladay, Carl R. "1 Corinthians 13: Paul as Apostolic Paradigm" in David L. Balch et al., eds., *Greeks, Romans, and Christians. Essays in Honor of Abraham J. Malherbe*. Minneapolis: Fortress, 1990, 80–98.

House, H. Wayne. "Tongues and the Mystery Religions at Corinth," *BSac* 140 (1983) 134–150.

Johnson, Luke T. "Norms for True and False Prophecy in First Corinthians," *ABR* 22 (1971) 29–45.

Lampe, Peter. "The Corinthian Worship Services in Corinth and the Corinthians' Enthusiasm (1 Cor. 12–14)," *Affirmation* 4 (1991) 17–25.

Martin, Dale B. "Tongues of Angels and Other Status Indicators," *JAAR* 59 (1991) 547–589.

Parmentier, Martin. "Das Zungenreden bei den Kirchenvätern," *Bijdr* 55 (1994) 376–398.

Perrot, Charles. "Charisme et institution chez Saint Paul," *RSR* 71 (1983) 81–91.

Sabbe, Maurits. "De Weg van de Liefde (1 Cor. 13)," *CBG* 10 (1964) 494–511; 11 (1965) 433–480. Reprinted in idem, *Studia Neotestamentica: Collected Essays*. BEThL 98. Leuven: University Press/Peeters, 1991, 261–328.

Schneider, Sebastian. "Glaubensmängel in Korinth. Eine neue Deutung der 'Schwachen, Kranken, Schlafenden' in 1 Kor 11,30," *FNT* 9 (1996) 3–19.

Sigountos, James G. "The Genre of 1 Corinthians 13," *NTS* 40 (1994) 246–260.

Smit, Joop F. M. "The Genre of 1 Corinthians 13 in the Light of Classical Rhetoric," *NovT* 33 (1991) 193–216.

Suurmond, Jean-Jacques. "A Fresh Look at Spirit-Baptism and the Charisms," *ExpT* 109 (1998) 10–106.

Talbert, Charles H. "Paul's Understanding of the Holy Spirit: The Evidence of 1 Corinthians 12–14," *PRS* 11 (1984) 95–108.

Wischmeyer, Oda. *Der höchste Weg. Das 13. Kapitel des 1. Korintherbriefes*. SNT 13. Gütersloh: Mohn, 1981.

Zerhusen, Robert. "The Problem of Tongues in 1 Cor 14: A Reexamination," *BTB* 27 (1997) 139–152.

1. *A Matter of Principle* (12:1-3)

1. Concerning spiritual realities, brothers and sisters, I don't want you to be ignorant. 2. You know that as Gentiles you were marched away to mute idols, however you were led. 3. For this reason I want you to know that no one speaking by the Spirit of God says "Jesus is Anathema," and that no one can say "Jesus is Lord," except by the Holy Spirit.

INTERPRETATION

The opening verse (12:1) contains three typical Pauline expressions, all of which indicate a transition in his thought. These are the textual marker "concerning," the apostrophic "brothers and sisters," and the disclosure formula, "I don't want you to be ignorant." The verse says that Paul is taking up the consideration of a new subject, "the things of the spirit." His enumerative formula, "concerning," may suggest that the issue of spiritual realities was a topic broached in the Corinthians' letter to Paul (cf. 7:1).

That Paul uses a disclosure formula with a double negative, an example of the rhetorical device of litotes, to introduce his discussion of the issue implies that he intends to give the Corinthians new information (see note on 10:1 and contrast with 11:2, 23). Johannes Vos suggests that Paul's opening remarks follow the classic rhetorical model of *proemium* (v. 1), *diēgēsis* (v. 2), and *prothesis* (v. 3), but it is not necessary to make such a precise analysis of Paul's words in order to grasp his point. He affirms that the confessional acclamation, "Jesus is Lord," serves as an authenticating criterion of the true charismatic. All the baptized are pneumatics. Paul rejects pneumatic elitism out of hand by affirming that all who utter the baptismal confession have the Holy Spirit.

Paul's insistence that all speech that people claim to come from the Spirit be tested for its content suggests that such testing had not been the practice at Corinth. In his letters to the Thessalonians (1 Thess 5:19-22) and to the Romans (Rom 12:1-2) Paul exhorts those to whom he was writing to judge charismatic activity (cf. 12:10) within the context of the community's experience. The community is charged with responsibility for discerning authentic charismatic experience (cf. 5:1-5).

Contrasts. Antithesis was a device well known to ancient rhetoricians. "This kind of style," said Aristotle, "is pleasing, because contraries are easily understood and even more so when placed side by side, and also because antithesis resembles a syllogism; for refutation is a bringing together of contraries" (*Art of Rhetoric* 3.9.8). The device serves Paul's argument well in 12:1-3. These verses speak of a contrast between ignorance and knowledge. The Corinthians' prior experience is (implicitly) contrasted with their present experience, dumb idols with the Holy Spirit, not speaking by the Spirit with speaking by the Spirit, and cursing Jesus with a confessional acclamation of Jesus. The use of contrast pervades Paul's exposition of spiritual realities. Pneumatic experiences are contrasted with charismatic gifts (12:1, 4), diversity with unity (12:4-6), and irrational religious experience with community concern and moral sensitivity (12:2; 14:19, 26-32). In his considered treatment of the real issue at hand the gift of speaking in tongues is regularly contrasted with the gift of prophecy.

The Slogans. "Jesus is Anathema" and "Jesus is Lord," each only two words in Greek *(Anathema Iēsous; Kyrios Iēsous)*, are contrasting slogans. The competing slogans not only provide a criterion of social division between nonbelievers and believers; they also provide a proof of the fact that believers, that is, all who profess Jesus as Lord, are empowered by the Holy Spirit.

"Jesus is Lord" is a confessional acclamation that may derive from the baptismal liturgy of the early church (cf. Rom 10:9; Phil 2:11). As a confessional acclamation it proclaims that Jesus has been raised from among the dead. Simultaneously it is a proclamation of loyalty to the one acclaimed as Lord, to whom Christians are servants. As a commonly uttered confessional acclamation it is a unifying element among all baptized Christians.

What is the meaning of "Jesus is Anathema," the curse that Paul contrasts with the acclamation of faith? During the second century Roman persecutors forced Christians to revile the name of Christ (Pliny, *Epistles* 10.96.5). It is, however, anachronistic to suggest that some first-century Christians suffered under similar duress. Walter Schmithals (*Gnosticism* 124–130), Ulrich Wilckens (*Weisheit* 121 n. 1), and James D. G. Dunn (*Jesus and the Spirit: A Study of the Religious and Charismatic Experience of Jesus and the First Christians as Reflected in the New Testament* [Philadelphia: Westminster, 1975] 234–235; *Unity and Diversity* 278), along with many others, think that the curse expresses the denigration of the earthly Jesus by gnosticizing Christians who valued only an experience of the Spirit. More likely the phrase is one that had been spoken by non-Christians in Corinth, perhaps even by the pre-Christian Paul or by some Corinthians who later became Christians. The Christian presumption is that such a curse was uttered under demonic influence (see v. 2). In no way could it be attributed to the Spirit of God.

NOTES

1. *Concerning spiritual realities, brothers and sisters, I don't want you to be ignorant:* "Spiritual realities" renders *tōn pneumatikōn,* in the genitive plural. The Greek

words can be masculine, feminine, or neuter. Most English language translations take *pneumatikōn* to be neuter. The expression designates the phenomena, the spiritual gifts that Paul discusses in chs. 12–14. The principal
argument in favor of this understanding of the topic is the parallel expression,
charismata, in v. 4. This term offers a terminological critique of the notion of
spiritual phenomena. D.W.B. Robinson suggests nonetheless that the term
does not so much identify spiritual gifts in general as it does the specific
phenomenon of speaking in the spirit (cf. 12:3; 14:1; see D.W.B. Robinson,
"Charismata versus Pneumatika: Paul's Method of Discussion," *RTR* 31
[1972] 49–55, especially 51). A small number of commentators prefer to identify *pneumatikōn* with a personal referent (especially Johannes Weiss, F. F.
Bruce, John C. Hurd, Birger Pearson, T. W. Gillespie), especially on the basis
that the pericope with which the rhetorical demonstration closes (see 14:37)
uses *pneumatikos*, in the singular, of a personal subject. The parallelism with
12:4 and 14:1 suggests that it is preferable to take *pneumatikōn* as connoting
spiritual phenomena. The difference between the two understandings is relatively minor. People of the Spirit participate in spiritual phenomena.

2. *You know that as Gentiles you were marched away to mute idols, however you were*
   led: Paul begins his treatment of the issue with an appeal to the Corinthians'
   own experience (12:2). Elsewhere in 1 Corinthians Paul uses the recollection
   formula as a negative rhetorical question ("Don't you know that?"; cf. 3:16).
   Only here does he use the formula positively and affirmatively. Paul's recollection reveals that many, and probably most of the Christians at Corinth had
   been pagans. As in 5:1 Gentiles serve as a negative reference group for standards of Christian behavior (cf. 1 Thess 4:5).

   Jews of Paul's day considered idolatry to be the characteristic practice of
   Gentiles (cf. Rom 1:23; 1 Thess 1:9). In their earlier lives the Gentile Christians
   of Corinth had been devotees of idols (cf. 8:7). Idols are incapable of speech.
   Accordingly they were mocked in Jewish literature and apology (Ps 115:5, 7,
   etc.). *Joseph and Aseneth* describes idols as "deaf and dumb" (*kōpha*, *JosAs* 8:3;
   11:8; 12:5; 13:11). Aseneth's conversion is symbolized by her recognition of
   that fact (*JosAs* 13:11). Paul's own description of the idols as mute (*aphōna*,
   elsewhere in Paul only in 10:14) contributes to his focus on patterns of speech
   in 1 Corinthians 12–14.

   When he used the participle "being marched away" (*apagomenoi*), hapax
   in his writings, Paul may have had in mind the procession (*pompē*) prior to the
   religious events that inaugurated civic celebrations (cf. Terence Paige, "1
   Corinthians 12.2: A Pagan *Pompē?*" *JSNT* 44 [1991] 57–65). His parenthetical
   "however you were led" (*hōs an ēgesthe*) employs a cognate verb. It implies
   that the Corinthians had been "driven" by dumb idols (so Udo Borse, *EDNT*
   1:25; cf. 1:114). Carried away as they had been, they were in a state of ecstasy.
   The Corinthians' Greco-Roman culture widely assumed that religious experience was involuntary and irrational. Ecstatic experience was a matter beyond
   human control; it was a matter of being driven by a divine force.

3. *For this reason I want you to know:* The disclosure formula, phrased positively
   (cf. 15:1) rather than with the double negative (cf. v. 1), suggests a link

between v. 3 and Paul's opening statement. The inferential "for this reason" *(dio)* indicates a close link between this verse and the previous ones. Most commentators assume the link to be one of contrast between the conduct of those who are led astray to dumb idols (v. 2) and those who are led by the Spirit to confess "Jesus is Lord." Jouette Bassler, however, argues that an analogy exists between the two verses insofar as one under the influence of the spirit, whether the spirit be a demon or the Holy Spirit (cf. Rom 8:15-16, 26), has no control over his or her actions.

that no one speaking by the Spirit of God says "Jesus is Anathema," and that no one can say "Jesus is Lord," except by the Holy Spirit: Contrasted with the confession of Jesus as Lord is the curse "Jesus is Anathema." "Anathema" (16:22) was sometimes used of votive offerings, but it was also used to translate the Hebrew *ḥērem* ("ban") and thus functioned as a curse (cf. Deut 7:26 [LXX]).

The two prepositional phrases, with the instrumental *en* ("in"), respectively speak of the Spirit as the Spirit of God and as the Holy Spirit. In 1 Corinthians the more usual terminology is "the Spirit of God" (2:11, [12], 14; 3:16; 6:11; 7:40; 12:3; cf. 2:10). Paul speaks of the Holy Spirit only in 6:19 and 12:3. A nuance of significance is to be attributed to the terminology of 12:3. "The Spirit of God" is the Spirit that comes from God. No one who has the Spirit given by God can curse Jesus. Utterance of the curse, "Jesus is Anathema," identifies a person as someone who is not moved by God's Spirit. "The Holy Spirit," on the other hand, is the Spirit of God insofar as it is sanctifying power (cf. 1:2). Given to and active among Christians, it prompts them to utter the confessional acclamation, "Jesus is Lord."

FOR REFERENCE AND FURTHER STUDY

Bassler, Jouette M. "1 Cor 12:3—Curse and Confession in Context," *JBL* 101 (1982) 415–418.

Brox, Norbert. "*ANATHEMA IESOUS* (1 Kor. 12,3)," *BZ* 12 (1968) 103–111.

Derrett, J. Duncan M. "Cursing Jesus (1 Corinthians XII.3): The Jews as Religious 'Persecutors,'" *NTS* 21 (1974) 544–554.

Kramer, Werner R. *Christ, Lord, Son of God.* Translated by Brian Hardy. SBT 50. Naperville, Ill.: Allenson, 1966.

Pearson, Birger A. "Did the Gnostics Curse Jesus?" *JBL* 86 (1967) 301–305.

2. *Allotment of Gifts* (12:4-11)

4. There are allotments of gifts, but the same Spirit; 5. and there are allotments of services, but the same Lord; 6. and there are allotments of activities, but the same God who works all things in all. 7. To each is given the manifestation of the Spirit for the common good. 8. For to one is

given the word of wisdom through the Spirit, to another the word of knowledge according to the same Spirit, 9. to someone else faith in the same Spirit, to another gifts of healings in the one Spirit, 10. to another the activities of working miracles, to another prophecy, to another the discernment of spirits, to someone else different kinds of tongues, to another the interpretation of tongues. 11. One and the same Spirit activates all of these, allotting to each one, as he wills, his or her own gifts.

INTERPRETATION

Having introduced spiritual phenomena as a point to be considered (12:1), Paul begins his reflection in a section of the letter that has the Spirit as its unifying and dominant theme. "The same Spirit" is the phrase that holds the unit together by way of ring construction (vv. 4, 11). "Spirit" is the dominant word in the unit. Repeated eight times, it echoes throughout the pericope, linking it with Paul's general introduction (12:1-3), which speaks of spiritual gifts and the Holy Spirit.

With the exception of the participial clause defining the divine activity in v. 6b the ideas expressed in vv. 4-6 are presented in parallel fashion, a construction that recalls the Semitic penchant for parallelism in which the thought expressed in a second colon is sharper than that expressed in the first. The thought progresses as the parallelism unfolds. Paul's parallel descriptions of the same realities underscore the idea that the gifts have been distributed, that they have been given for the service of the community, and that through these gifts God is at work in believers. Paul's three parallel statements speak of the Spirit, the Lord, and God respectively, but the text should no more be construed as an expression of Trinitarian theology than are the other so-called "Trinitarian formulae" in the Pauline writings (2 Cor 1:21-22; 13:13; Gal 4:6; Rom 8:11; 15:15-16, 30). Trinitarian theology is a later theological development.

The three verses constitute a rhetorical *partitio*, that is, a division of the argument. Mention of the spiritual gifts (v. 4) anticipates the discussion of these gifts in vv. 7-11. Mention of the single Lord prepares for the discussion of the body of Christ in vv. 12-26. Finally the working of God prepares for the third section of the chapter, where the charisms are identified as coming from God (vv. 28-32). The identification of the gifts as "gifts" (*charismata*) in v. 4 foreshadows a mention of gifts in v. 31. The *inclusio* ("*charismata*" + list of gifts; list of gifts + "*charismata*") suggests that Paul expressed his thought in a chiastic pattern, as he is wont to do. By means of the *inclusio* the entire chapter is formed into a literary unit, introduced by 12:1-3.

Critical Reflection. In the introduction (12:1-3) Paul invited the Corinthians to reflect critically on the authentic manifestation of the Spirit. He introduced the idea that utterances that come from peoples' lips distinguish those who possess the Spirit of God from those who do not. All those who proclaim that Jesus is Lord possess the Holy Spirit. Their acclamation identifies them as people moved by the Spirit of God. The choice of "gifts" *(charismata)* in v. 4 as a term to identify spiritual realities functions as a theological corrective to "spiritual phenomena" *(pneumatika,* v. 1), a term that highlights the ecstatic and the extraordinary. One of Paul's basic strategies is "redefinition" (R. A. Humphries, "Paul's Rhetoric of Argumentation in 1 Cor. 1–4," G.T.U. Ph.D. thesis, Berkeley, Cal., 1980, 75). In 12:4 he employs the strategy with great advantage, underscoring the idea that authentic spiritual phenomena are gifts, charisms.

With this emphasis Paul puts the hybrists, those who consider themselves to be people of the Spirit (cf. 14:37), in their place. Anyone within the community who disdains the gifts given to any member disdains the work of the Spirit. The one God (cf. 8:6), working through the Spirit, is the common source of all the gifts. These gifts are, Paul says, services and activities. The exercise of the gifts that have been given is the way in which each Christian serves one and the same Lord. Present in the Christian these gifts are the means by which God acts within the community.

Paul identifies nine gifts that have been given to various members of the community. His encompassing remarks (vv. 7, 11) identify two criteria to be used in evaluating charisms. They are "for the common good" (v. 7) and "to each his or her own" (v. 11). The authenticity of spiritual phenomena can be gleaned from the use to which these phenomena are put. Gifts are given to individual members of the community not for their personal enhancement, but for the common good. Paul stresses the idea that charisms are given for the sake of the common good in the classic terms of deliberative rhetoric *(sympheron).* The post-Pauline author of Ephesians expresses a similar idea but with an ecclesiological formulation: the gifts are given "for building up the body of Christ" *(eis oikodomēn tou sōmatos tou Christou,* Eph 4:12). An idea similar to that expressed in 12:4-11 is reflected in the paraenesis of 1 Pet 4:10, "Like good stewards of the manifold grace of God, serve one another with whatever gift each of you has received."

Another criterion for judging charisms derives from the fact that these gifts are distributed by the Spirit to all members of the community, to each his or her own, as the Spirit wills. The juxtaposition of "to each" and "in all" *(pasin hekastō)* in vv. 6–7 provides a frame of reference for understanding what Paul says. He envelops the list of nine gifts by mentioning "to each" at the beginning and at the end of the list (vv. 7, 11). Verse 11 resumes and highlights the point by noting that the distribution of gifts to each one is "as the Spirit wills." The Spirit freely gives his gifts as he wills.

"To each one's own" is a criterion of discernment of authentic spiritual phenomena. All the members of the community are charismatic. They each possess at least one charism, but no one has all the charismata. With this principle Paul counters any claim to the exclusive possession of the Spirit. Paul himself is richly graced. He has been given many different charisms, wisdom, faith, healing, and tongues among those on his list of nine, but not even Paul has all the gifts.

A Diversity of Charisms. The list of nine gifts cited by Paul is different from each of the lists found at the end of ch. 12 (12:28, 29-30). It is also different from other Pauline (Rom 12:6-8) and post-Pauline (Eph 4:11-12; 1 Pet 4:10-11) lists. The listing of nine charisms in 12:8-10 is not all-inclusive. It contains a number of gifts used to illustrate the giftedness of the church (cf. 1:4-5). The gifts that Paul has chosen to mention on this first list are probably arranged in descending order of importance according to his evaluation of the gifts.

Aware that Paul frequently organizes his thought in patterns of three, such classic commentators on 1 Corinthians as Johannes Weiss and Ernest-Bernard Allo thought that Paul's list was a triad of triads. Paul's own use of language, however, indicates a different pattern of organization, 2 + 5 + 2, in an A-B-A' arrangement. Paul begins with two gifts of the word (v. 8). "To someone else" *(heterọ)* introduces a series of five charisms (vv. 9-10c). Another "to someone else" introduces the final pair. The first two charisms have to do with wisdom and knowledge, a Pauline understanding of which was developed in chs. 1–4. The last two charisms have to do with talking in tongues, another matter of Pauline concern (see ch. 14).

It is sometimes difficult to distinguish the gifts on Paul's list from one another. Two of the charisms are gifts of speech (wisdom and knowledge); three suggest miraculous powers (faith, healing, working miracles). It is not easy to determine precisely what Paul means by the discernment of spirits and speaking in tongues. The difficulty in understanding the precise nature of each of the gifts is compounded by the fact that the gifts appear on a list. No adequate distinguishing characteristics are cited. Paul only mentions that various charisms have been given to some within the community but not to others. As mere items on a list the various charisms are occasionally as difficult to distinguish one from the other as are the various vices in Paul's catalogues of vices, used with similar rhetorical purpose as is the list of charisms in 12:4-11.

It is, in fact, the list itself that is important in vv. 8-10. The relatively lengthy list, the longest of any list of charisms in the NT, is characterized by the rhetorical device of *repetitio*, used for emphasis' sake. The accumulation of several gifts serves to illustrate and highlight the rich giftedness of the community. Awareness of this fact is more important than is the determination of the precise nature of any single gift. The chiastic structure of ch. 12 must also be brought into consideration. When dealing with macro-chiasms Paul customarily addresses the issues in general or in principle (A), then after a pertinent rhetorical digression (B), returns to the matter at hand, addressing the matter again, but this time in specific and detailed consideration (A'). In ch. 14 Paul will pay particular attention to the relative importance of the gifts of prophecy and speaking in tongues. In passing he also says something about the gift of the interpretation of tongues.

NOTES

4. *There are allotments of gifts, but the same Spirit:* Exploiting the theme of the one and the many, Paul focuses on the one Spirit of God and the allotments of spiritual gifts. Johannes Weiss and D. A. Carson (*Korintherbrief* 297; *Showing the Spirit* 32; cf. *EDNT* 1:302) take "allotments" (*diaireseis;* in the NT only in vv. 4, 5, 6; cf. *diairoun* in v. 11) not only as an allusion to the diversity of gifts, nine of which will be mentioned in the immediate context, but also to the distribution of the gifts (cf. 12:11). The term helps to frame 12:4-11 as a literary unit.

   Paul's choice of "gifts" (*charismata;* cf. 1:7; 7:7; 12:4, 9, 28, 30, 31) to describe the spiritual phenomena (*pneumatika*) about which he will write is jarring. The new term provides a theological corrective to the popular Corinthian notion of spiritual phenomena. Instead of accentuating the ecstatic nature of the phenomena Paul draws attention to the fact that authentic spiritual realities are gifts. The Spirit (cf. 12:2-3), the power of God at work, is the source of these gifts. The relatively new term "charism" (see note on 1:7) is one to which Paul provides his own personal nuance, that is, a charism is a gift of the Spirit to someone within the community for the sake of building up the community as the body of Christ.

5. *and there are allotments of services, but the same Lord:* Most authors consider that this clause is parallel with vv. 5 and 6, opining that a rhetorical need of emphasis has led Paul to a kind of repetition. Repetition is a classic literary device used for the sake of emphasis. J. N. Collins, however, demurs from the *opinio communis*. He holds that "charismata" is the genus, and that services and activities are different species of charismata. Activities (*energēmata,* v. 6) are gifts like those listed in vv. 8-10, while "services" (*diakoniai*) denotes the ministry of proclamation, received as a commission from the Lord. The description of the gifts as services is correlative to the affirmation that there is one and the same Lord (cf. 8:6b). While services benefit one another within the community of believers, they are ultimately services to the Lord.

6. *and there are allotments of activities, but the same God who works all things in all:* Paul indicates that the various charismata receive expression in a corresponding field of activity (cf. 12:29; Rom 12:6b-8). "Activities" (*energēmatōn;* in the NT only in 12:6, 10) connotes the actualization of power. Paul's terminology evokes the image of God, active in creation and thereafter. Paul's under-

lying idea is that God empowers those to whom he gives his gifts so that God in fact works in and through charismatically endowed persons.

The notion that it is the one God who gives all the gifts is an expression of Paul's Jewish monotheism (cf. 8:6). The contrast between one and all provides additional force for his argument. The first "all" refers to the totality of charismatic activity; the second "all" refers to charismatics themselves. Paul affirms that all Christians are charismatics. Romans 12:6b-8 expresses the idea that the gift of God entails on the part of the one who is gifted a corresponding responsibility to exercise the gift.

7. *To each is given the manifestation of the Spirit for the common good: Pace* Gordon Fee (*First Corinthians* 589), the distributive "each" confirms that each and every one receives a charism (see v. 11). Paul's polemic is directed to those who claim an exclusive privilege of being pneumatic (cf. 3:1). His language underscores the fact that these charisms are gifts gratuitously given (cf. v. 4). They are expressions (*phanerōsis,* hapax in the NT) of the power of God, the Spirit. Their purpose is the common good, the "advantage" of the community, *sympheron,* a neuter participle (cf. the use of the substantivized adjective *symphoron* in 7:35; 10:33). Charisms are given in order that the community might be "built up" (cf. 1 Cor 14:3-5, 12, 26; 2 Cor 12:19; 13:10; Eph 4:12, 16), not so that some one individual within the community might be puffed up (cf. 8:1).

8. *For to one is given the word of wisdom through the Spirit:* With an explanatory *gar* Paul begins to tease out the idea that charisms, through which the Spirit is revealed, are given to each person. The first gift cited by Paul is the expression of wisdom (*logos sophias;* cf. 2:1-5). Mention of this gift at the head of the list recalls Paul's lengthy discussion on word and wisdom (1:18–4:21) and serves as an argument in favor of the unity of the letter. Verse 8 cannot be separated from the totality of Paul's rhetorical argument thus far. As a charism the "word of wisdom" describes a gift given to Paul who speaks the wisdom of God hidden in mystery in the demonstrative proof of the spirit and power (2:4). First Corinthians 2:6-16 is Paul's own commentary on the charism of the word of wisdom that had been given to him and his fellow missionaries (cf. Eph 3:10-11; Col 1:9).

to another the word of knowledge according to the same Spirit: Having used "through" *(dia)* to relate the charismatic gift of the word of wisdom to the Spirit, Paul now uses another preposition, "according to" *(kata).* A third preposition appears in v. 9, where "in" *(en)* appears twice. No substantial difference in meaning appears to result from Paul's use of different prepositions. In the popular *koinē* Greek of his time prepositions tended to lose their specific meaning and were readily interchangeable with one another. The various prepositions in Paul's list of charisms provide the list with stylistic variation.

It is difficult to determine exactly what Paul means by "the word of knowledge" and how it is distinct from the word of wisdom. Wisdom and knowledge appear together among the basic elements of the spirit of the children of light in 1QS 4:3-4. The Qumran text lists them at the end whereas Paul places wisdom and knowledge at the beginning of the list. Walter Schmithals suggests that the characterization of the charism of knowledge may reflect a Gnostic expression that Paul uses alongside an expression ("wisdom") derived from the synagogue (*EDNT* 1:250). Schmithals's idea may contain a kernel of truth insofar as the Corinthian hybrists vaunted their possession of knowledge (cf. 8:1-7a). It may be that Paul cites "the word of knowledge" among the gifts of the Spirit to counter the hybrists' claims to knowledge (cf. 8:1).

9. *to someone else faith in the same Spirit:* T. W. Gillespie (*First Theologians* 113) takes faith *(pistis)* in the sense of *sola fide* and opines that faith is "the ground, anthropologically speaking, of all other activities of the Spirit," but the charismatic faith of which Paul writes is something different from the faith that characterizes all believers. Charismatic faith is to be understood as a kind of miraculous faith, if not necessarily the faith that can move mountains (13:2; cf. Matt 17:20; 21:21) at least the faith that provides occasion for a faith healing. The idea of *sola fide* faith is based on what Paul says about faith in Romans and Galatians, letters that reflect the controversy on justification. There is no indication that a controversy over justification took place in mid-first-century Corinth.

to another gifts of healings in the one Spirit: Codices A and B, along with various witnesses to the Latin tradition of the Scriptures, read "the one Spirit." 𝔓⁴⁶ reads "the Spirit." Codices ℵ, D, F, G, and the medieval Byzantine tradition read "the same Spirit." "The one Spirit," which does not appear elsewhere in the context (cf. v. 11), is the *lectio difficilior.* "The same Spirit" is a reading derived by attraction to vv. 8 and 9a.

In the NT the expression "gifts of healings" *(charismata iamatōn)* appears only in 12:9, 28, 30. Among the nine gifts on the list of charisms in vv. 8-10 only this gift and the gift of working miracles are in the plural, that is, both the principal noun and the qualifying genitive (an epexegetical genitive in both instances). The plural suggests that Paul considers each exercise of the gift as a charism. Some members of the community had experienced sickness. In 11:30 Paul writes about sickness in terms of its being a chastisement for disordered behavior in the eucharistic assembly. Paul does not claim for himself the gift of healing (cf. 2 Cor 12:12) as he does for the gift of tongues and prophecy. Luke, however, narrates accounts of various healings by Paul (Acts 14:8-10; 19:11-12; 20:7-20; 28:8-9; cf. Acts 16:18).

An important sanctuary dedicated to Asklepios, the Greek god of healing, was located in Corinth (see below, p. 462). Asklepios was the most popular deity in the Hellenistic world. More than two hundred Asklepieia, shrines in honor of the god, are known to have existed. Virtually every major settlement had its Asklepieion. Records of the cures *(iamata)* show that ritual baths and healing dreams were associated with cures. Paul's exposition of the gifts given to the members of the church at Corinth invites comparison with the experience of nonbelievers (12:2; 14:22-23). In his exposition he also mentions the ritual bath of baptism (12:13). It may be that the existence of the Asklepieion at Corinth provided the occasion for Paul's mention of the gift of healings. The gift is not exploited in 1 Corinthians 12–14—it is merely mentioned in 12:28 and 30—nor does it appear on the list of charisms in Rom 12:6-

8. Paul's concern for the cures associated with the cult of Asklepios may have prompted him to emphasize that gifts of healing take place by the power of the one Spirit. Departing from the previous language, which spoke of the same Spirit (vv. 8b-9a), he indicates that there is only one Spirit.

10. *to another the activities of working miracles:* "Working miracles" (*dynameōn*, literally, "of powers"; cf. Rom 15:19; 2 Cor 12:12) is a term used in the synoptics and in Hellenistic literature to denote miraculous powers (e.g., Mark 5:30 *par.*) and miraculous events (e.g., Mark 6:2). The activity of working miracles is juxtaposed with gifts of healings, but there may be no adequate distinction between the two. Some commentators, nonetheless, attempt to see in "healings" physical cures and in "miraculous activities" nature miracles. Others hold that this charism has been added to include the gift of exorcism since possession would not have been classified as a sickness (cf. *EDNT* 1:357).

to another prophecy: Six of the nineteen NT occurrences of the noun (*prophēteia*) occur in Paul (cf. 1 Tim 1:18; 2 Tim 4:14), all but two of them (Rom 12:6; 1 Thess 5:20) in 1 Corinthians. All ten of Paul's uses of the related verb (*prophēteuō*) are in 1 Corinthians, especially in 1 Corinthians 14 where Paul treats the issue of prophetic activity at length. The noun can designate either the charism of prophecy, as it does here (cf. 13:2, 8; Rom 12:6; 1 Thess 5:20), or a prophetic utterance (1 Cor 14:6, 22). Prophecy is a gift given for building up the church (14:3; cf. 14:31). It is a gift enjoyed by Paul (13:2; cf. 14:6) and by several people within the community (cf. 14:30-31). In the enumerated list of charisms in 12:28 and in the following series of rhetorical questions (12:29) it is cited in second place. Only the gifts of prophecy, speaking in tongues, and healing appear on all three of the Pauline lists in ch. 12. Among these three only the gift of prophecy also appears on the list of charisms in Rom 12:6-8. There it is listed first.

to another the discernment of spirits: Helmut Merklein and Gerhard Dautzenberg ("Der Prophet," 418–419; "Zum religionsgeschichtlichen Hintergrund der *diakrisis pneumatōn* [1 Kor 12,10]," *BZ* 15 [1971] 93-104) explain the discernment of spirits as a charism of interpreting prophetic utterance. This charism is complementary to the occasional use of the charism of prophecy. More likely this charism is the gift of discernment, the ability to distinguish true prophets from false prophets and authentic prophetic utterance from that which is not (cf. 14:29; Rom 12:1-2; 1 Thess 5:19-22). Discernment is the gift of charismatic judgment rather than that of explanatory prophecy.

to someone else different kinds of tongues: Paul's use of another pronominal adjective (*heterō*, a dual pronominal adjective used more broadly by Paul with the meaning of "another"—here "someone else"—to distinguish the adjective from *allō*) indicates some shift in emphasis. Arguing from the technical use of "tongue," *glōssa*, to mean language, some commentators have suggested that Paul's reference is to some sort of self-serving demonstration of an ability to speak a foreign language (Robert Gundry, J. G. Davies, Charles Hodge, J. Massyngberde Ford, Gerhard Dautzenberg [*EDNT* 1:253]). Admittedly Paul compares speaking in different tongues to speaking a foreign language (14:10-11), but he also compares speaking in tongues with the inarticulate sounds of musical instruments (14:8). The gift of tongues mentioned in 1 Corinthians 12–14 is different from the disciples' experience at Pentecost (Acts 2:5-13), which reversed the legendary experience of the Tower of Babel (Gen 11:1-9). It is likely that Paul is referring to sounds expressed in ecstatic worship, an angelic "dialect" used in the praise of God and communication with God (1 Cor 13:1; cf. *T.Job* 48-50; Rom 8:26). Paul speaks about praying in tongues (14:14) as a "word" that is not intelligible (14:9). The gift of tongues, glossolalia, was apparently considered the highest gift by the Corinthians. It was a gift enjoyed by Paul, so much so in fact that he could use the prestige of his own exercise of the gift in his rhetorical argument (13:1; 14:6, 14, 18).

to another the interpretation of tongues: The gift of the interpretation of tongues is complementary to the gift of tongues (cf. 12:30; 14:13, 26). Since words built on the root *hermēneu-*, "interpret," suggest putting something into words, the gift of the interpretation of tongues must be the ability to articulate the meaning of the experience of tongues for the benefit of others in the community. See Anthony C. Thiselton, "The 'Interpretation' of Tongues: A New Suggestion in the Light of Greek Usage in Philo and Josephus," *JTS* 30 (1979) 15–36. Some interpreters, nonetheless, use the fact that many of the uses of the *hermēneu-* word group in the LXX and the NT (by some counts eighteen out of twenty-one) have something to do with translation (cf. *TLNT* 3:312–317) as an argument in favor of the idea that the gift of tongues is the ability to speak a foreign language.

11. *One and the same Spirit activates all of these, allotting to each one, as he wills, his or her own gifts:* By means of an *inclusio* with v. 4 this resumptive sentence brings closure to Paul's exposition on the distribution of gifts. "The same Spirit" *(to auto pneuma)* and "allotting" *(diairoun,* hapax in Paul) are the encompassing elements. Rhetorically the sentence underscores the point of the exposition with a resumptive "all" *(panta)* and the attribution of "one" *(to en)* to the Spirit. "Activates" *(energei)* recalls the "activities" of v. 6. The verb and the noun are derived from the same root, *energ-*. Thus the Spirit is seen as God's power at work, not as a distinct person of the Trinity.

The Spirit works through the gifts that are given to each member of the community. The freedom of the Spirit in allocating the charisms is emphasized by the clause "as he wills" *(kathōs bouletai).* The free Spirit apportions gifts as the free Spirit wills. The Spirit wills that gifts be given to each and every one. "His or her own" *(idią,* absent from $\mathfrak{P}^{46}$, F, and G, and deleted from the original of D) is used adverbially, recalling that the charisms properly belong to the Spirit but that they are given individually to each member of the community. Each person within the community has gifts that the Spirit has given to him or her. One person has some gifts; another has other gifts. No one has them all.

For Reference and Further Study

Collins, John N. *Diakonia: Re-interpreting the Ancient Sources.* New York and Oxford: Oxford University Press, 1990.

_____. "God's Gifts to Congregations," *Worship* 68 (1994) 242–249.

_____. "Ministry as a Distinct Category among Charismata (1 Corinthians 12:4-7)," *Neotest.* 27 (1993) 79–91.

Grudem, Wayne A. "A Response to Gerhard Dautzenberg on 1 Cor. 12:10," *BZ* 22 (1978) 253–270.

Käsemann, Ernst. "Ministry and Community in the New Testament" in idem, *Essays on New Testament Themes.* SBT 41. Naperville, Ill.: Allenson, 1960, 63–69.

Maleparampil, Joseph. *The "Trinitarian" Formulae in St. Paul: An Exegetical Investigation into the Meaning and Function of Those Pauline Sayings which Compositely Make Mention of God, Christ, and the Holy Spirit.* European University Studies Series 23; Theology 546. Frankfurt: Peter Lang, 1995.

Schatzmann, Siegfried S. *A Pauline Theology of Charismata.* Peabody, Mass.: Hendrickson, 1987.

Talbert, Charles H. "Paul's Understanding of the Holy Spirit: The Evidence of 1 Corinthians 12–14" in idem, ed., *Perspectives on the New Testament: Essays in Honor of Frank Stagg.* Macon, Ga.: Mercer University Press, 1985, 95–108.

3. *The Body* (12:12-26)

12. For just as the body is one and has many members and all the members of the body, although many, are one body, so also is Christ. 13. For we all were baptized into one body in the one Spirit, whether Jews or Gentiles, slaves or free, and we all drank the one Spirit. 14. For indeed the body is not a single member but many members. 15. If the foot says, "because I am not a hand, I am not of the body," is it for this reason less a part of the body? 16. And if the ear says, "because I am not an eye, I am not of the body," is it for this reason less a part of the body? 17. If the eye is the whole body, where is the hearing? If the hearing is the whole body, where is the sense of smell? 18. Now then God has arranged the members in the body, each one of them according as he willed. 19. If all were a single member, where would the body be? 20. Now there are many members, but one body. 21. The eye cannot say to the hand, "I don't need you" nor the head to the feet, "I don't need you." 22. To the contrary, the members that are thought to be weaker are all the more necessary, 23. and on those members of the body we consider to be less honorable we confer greater honor, and our shameful members have greater modesty; 24. but our modest members do not need this. In contrast God has formed the body together, giving all the more honor to the least member 25. so that there is no bodily rupture and members are mutually concerned about one another. 26. If one member suffers, all the members suffer; if one member is honored, all the members rejoice.

INTERPRETATION

Verses 12-13 provide a transition between Paul's listing of the gifts of the Spirit (12:4-11) and his exploitation of the body metaphor in vv. 14-26. The body (*sōma*, 3x in 12:12) is a classic topos in Hellenistic rhetoric. Paul intends to speak both of the unity of the body and of the diversity of its several members as well as of the interrelationship between the one and the many. Reference to the one Spirit in v. 13 links the image of the body with the exposition of the gifts of the Spirit.

These transitional verses provide a two-tier explanation (note the explanatory particles, *kathaper* and *gar*) as to how there can be unity in diversity and diversity in unity. The first level of explanation is Paul's use of a topos classically employed to speak of the unity of the body politic (v. 12). His second level of explanation is the reality of Christian baptism and the celebration of eucharist (v. 13). When Paul speaks of these Christian rituals as unifying realities in the Corinthians' own experience, his language provides the linguistic links for his argument. Baptism "into one body" links the Christian experience to the rhetorical topos of the body politic. A twofold reference to the "one Spirit" links baptism and eucharist to the charisms about which he had written in 12:4-11 (see vv. 9, 11).

The Body. The human body has always been used as a literary image for society (cf. Mary Douglas, *Natural Symbols* [2nd ed. London: Barrie & Jenkins, 1973] 98). As a metaphor for a social or political group the body was a classic topos in ancient literature. It was, in fact, the most common topos for unity. Dio Chrysostom affirms that Aesop used the metaphor (*Discourses* 33.16). It is well attested in Plato's *Republic* and was used by Cicero (*On Duties* 3.5.22-23; 3.6.26-27).

The philosophic moralists who were Paul's contemporaries used the body image extensively. Seneca, for example, wrote:

> What if the hands should desire to harm the feet, or the eyes the hands? As all the members of the body are in harmony one with another because it is to the advantage of the whole that the individual members be unharmed, so mankind should spare the individual man, because all are born for a life of fellowship, and society can be kept unharmed only by the mutual protection and love of its parts. (*Anger* 2.31.7)

Dio Chrysostom used the metaphor in his speeches on concord so often in his writings that it sometimes seems to be overworked (*Discourses* 9.2; 33.44; 34.32; 39.5; 40.21; 41.9; 50.3). In addition, he speaks about the body when he speaks about friends. For Dio friends are even more useful than the members of one's own body because they can move around (see *Discourses* 3.104-107; cf. 1.31-32).

One of the best-known examples of the use of the body image in the Hellenistic world is a fable attributed to the Roman senator Menenius Agrippa. In a speech urging the Roman populace to abandon sedition and work together for harmony Menenius is reputed to have told the story of hands, mouth, and teeth revolting against the belly, with the result that the whole body is impaired (see Livy, *History of Rome* 2.32.7-33.1). Aelius Aristides compared political unrest to a disease like consumption, to a tearing apart of the body, and to the folly of cutting off one's own feet (*Orations* 17.9; 23.31; 24.18, 38-39; 26.43).

In deliberative speeches intended to deter the assembly from political unrest the orator's use of the body image commonly implied the subordination of some members of the body to others (cf. Eph 4:1-16; Col 2:8-19). In Menenius's famous speech, for example, the belly represents the ruling classes of society. Use of the body image is also found in literature that speaks of the different gifts of the members of the community and of how these gifts can be utilized for the advantage of the entire community. Epictetus (ca. 55 C.E.–ca. 135 C.E.), for example, wrote, "What, then, is the profession of a citizen? To treat nothing as a matter of private profit, not to plan about anything as though he were a detached unit, but to act like the foot or the hand, which, if they had the faculty of reason to understand the constitution of nature, would never exercise choice or desire in any other way but by reference to the whole" (*Discourses* 2.10.4-5; cf. Dionysius of Halicarnassus [ca. 20 B.C.E.], *Roman Antiquities* 6.86.4). Regarding the variety of the members of the body Plutarch commented that nature teaches that the various members are "for mutual preservation and assistance, not for variance and strife" ("On Brotherly Love," *Moralia* 478D). Earlier Plato had written about human diversity without, however, using the body image. "Our several natures," he wrote, "are not all alike but different. One man is naturally fitted for one task, and another for another" (*Republic* 370A-B). From this observation Plato concluded that things are better when each man acts according to his nature.

Use of the image of the body in Greco-Roman literature continued well into the second century C.E. It was also used by Hellenistic Jewish authors. Josephus, for example, wrote: "As in the body when inflammation attacks the principal member all the members catch the infection, so the sedition and disorder in the capital gave the scoundrels in the country free license to plunder" (*Bell.* 4.406-407; cf. 1.507; 2.264; 5.277-279). Philo wrote about the high priest who offers prayers and asks for blessings in order "that every age and every part of the nation regarded as a single body *(henos sōmatos)* may be united in one and the same fellowship *(koinōnian)*, making peace and good order their aim" (*Special Laws* 3.131; cf. *Dreams* 1.27-28).

Paul's Use of the Metaphor. Paul's exhortation to the Christian assembly at Corinth is the classic Christian use of the metaphor of the body as a symbol of social unity (cf. Rom 12:4-5; cf. Eph 1:23; 2:16; 3:6; 4:1-16; Col 1:18-24; 2:17-19; 3:15). The topos of the human body was commonplace among the rhetoricians, philosophers, moralists, and historians contemporary with Paul. It was used by Dionysius, Epictetus, Josephus, Philo, and Plutarch. Paul was a rhetorician in their mold. He used the traditional topos in the context of an extended plea for unity within the assembled community (1 Corinthians 12–14). His use of the image is remarkably similar to that of ancient rhetors. Paul writes about the hands and the feet, the eyes and the ears (vv. 16-17, 21). These members are precisely those cited by Plutarch, who also writes about the nostrils ("On Brotherly Love," *Moralia* 478D; "Old Men in Public Affairs," *Moralia* 797E), and by Dio Chrysostom, who adds the tongue (*Discourses* 3.104-107). Paul speaks about the necessary parts of the body (v. 22). Plutarch speaks of the necessary parts of the body, most of which, in his estimation, are double like the hands and feet, eyes and ears. In vv. 15-16 and 21 Paul dramatizes his argument by personifying the foot, the ear, the eye, and the head. Dionysius of Halicarnassus (*Roman Antiquities* 6.86.2) and other ancient authors similarly personified the members of the body.

Paul's use of the body image was, nonetheless, different from that of the classical topos insofar as Paul attributes the diversity of the various members of the body and the order among them to God (*theos,* vv. 18, 24) rather than to nature *(physis).* Another difference is that Paul used the metaphor to urge all members to utilize their gifts for the common good (12:7; cf. Rom 12:3-8) rather than to urge the subordination of some members to others for the good of the whole. He employed the image to advocate the interdependence of all bodily members (vv. 21, 25-26). He states that it is the supposedly weaker (and presumably less honorable) members of the body that are to be honored and that this is in accordance with the divine ordinance in arranging the body (vv. 22-25).

In his use of the body metaphor Paul underscored both the unity and the diversity of the body. A carefully crafted opening sentence clearly states, "for just as the body is one and has many members, and all the members of the body, although many, are one body, so also is Christ." The two parts in his summary description of the body indicate that he intends to stress both its diversity, its "many members," and its unity; it is "one body." Paul's "just as . . . so also" indicates that he was self-consciously using a metaphor. Developing the metaphor, Paul first picks up on the many members of the body, only to conclude that the body is one body (vv. 15-20). Thereupon, even as he continues the personification of the body with its members imaginatively talking with one another, Paul underscores the unity of the body (vv. 20-26). Rhetorician that he was, Paul divided the question, treating first the diversity of the body, then its unity. Both points needed to be emphasized in his communication to the Christians of Corinth.

Paul's subsequent discussion (see especially ch. 14) makes it clear that speaking in tongues was the spiritual phenomenon that was especially esteemed among the Corinthians. Some considered glossolalia to be the spiritual reality *par excellence,* almost to the point of being the sole gift that was recognized by the Corinthians. When Paul brings his chiasm to closure in ch. 14 he lays stress on speaking in tongues and demonstrates that this phenomenon was the real issue with regard to spiritual gifts in Corinth. Because of the Corinthians' undue emphasis on this single gift Paul was constrained to underscore the diversity of gifts within the community. Hence his first glance at the body emphasized its diversity (vv. 14-20); later he turns his attention to the unity of the body (vv. 20-26). His overarching concern is for the church, which is to be built up (cf. 14:4, 5, 12).

Paul initially put the gift of speaking in tongues in its place by citing the gift of glossolalia toward the end or at the very end of the list of gifts (12:10, 28, 30), and relativized the value of this gift by putting the interpretation of tongues, a gift correlative to speaking in tongues, next on his list (vv. 10, 30). After exploiting the body metaphor Paul returns to the gift of tongues as a point of departure for his encomium on love, the gift *par excellence.* Chapter 14 shows the relatively greater importance of the gift of prophecy in building up the church. Despite his many-pronged attempt to put the gift of glossolalia in its place within the community, Paul recognizes that it is nonetheless a gift of the Spirit. Hence he urges at the very end of his discourse that those who have this gift not be restrained from speaking in the assembly. His one caveat is that there should be propriety and order (14:39b-40).

Time. Following the example of Paul, the authors of the deutero-Pauline epistles to the Colossians and to the Ephesians (see especially Eph 4:1-16; Col 1:18-24), Clement of Rome, John Chrysostom (*On the First Epistle to the Corinthians, Homily* 32.1 [*PG* 61, 263]), and various other Fathers of the Church used the body image to advantage in appealing for unity within the community. A few decades after Paul wrote to the Corinthians Clement used the image of the body in an appeal for harmony within the Christian community at Corinth. Two generations after Paul's death the community was still troubled by discord, so Clement wrote, "Let us take our body as an example. The head without the feet is nothing; so likewise the feet without the head are nothing: even the smallest limbs of our body are necessary and useful for the whole body; but all the members conspire and unite in subjection, that the whole body may be saved" (*1 Clem.* 37; *PG* 1, 284).

And Space. Paul has embodied his use of the topos of the body in a passage dealing with the gifts given to the members of the community (see 12:1). He recalls the Corinthians' own experience when they were still pagans (12:2). He also writes about the impression that the exercise of the charisms makes upon unbelievers (14:22-24). From this perspective Paul's use of the body topos in a letter to Corinthians was particularly apropos. Archaeological excavations in Corinth have unearthed terracotta ex-votos of various body parts at the site of the temple of Asklepios, the ancient Greek god of healing. The trove is one of the largest extant collections of life-size representations in terracotta of the members of the human body cured by the god.

One interesting feature of the extant Corinthian collection is that it includes eighteen complete examples of male genitalia. The presence of these artifacts in the collection is occasionally cited as an item of archaeological evidence pointing to Corinthian licentiousness, as if the offerings were made in an effort to petition Asklepios for a cure of some venereal disease. In fact, it is more likely that these votive offerings were thank offerings, placed in the sanctuary as an expression of gratitude for the cure of impotence. In this respect the bodily artifacts found in the Corinthian shrine are not unlike the collections of crutches and prostheses found at Lourdes and other Christian shrines.

Even if Paul had not seen bodily votive offerings in this Corinthian temple, he could have seen similar artifacts in other parts of the Mediterranean world. The cult of Asklepios was celebrated in various sanctuaries throughout the Greco-Roman world. More than seventy stories of healings attributable to Asklepios are associated with the god's sanctuaries in Epidaurus, Kos, and an island in the Tiber at Rome.

NOTES

12. *For just as the body is one and has many members and all the members of the body, although many, are one body, so also is Christ:* Paul's use of two comparative particles, "for just . . . so also" (*kathaper . . . houtōs*) indicates that he intends to use a metaphor to explain how the various gifts cohere with one another. Paul uses the metaphor of "Christ"; he does not speak of the church as such (cf. Col 1:18). Much of the thought of this verse, with the same language, is reprised in Rom 12:4-5. The passage in Romans is shorter than 12:12-26, but like 12:12-26 it occurs as the B element in an A-B-A' exposition on gifts (Rom 12:3-8).

13. *For we all were baptized into one body in the one Spirit:* Paul continues to unfold the theological underpinnings of Christian unity despite the diversity of the membership of the church. His "for" (*kai gar*) really means "for also" (cf. BDF 452.3). Given the parallelism between v. 13a and v. 13c T. W. Gillespie (*First Theologians* 120), like J.D.G. Dunn (*Baptism in the Holy Spirit.* London: S.C.M., 1970, 129) and Gordon Fee (*First Corinthians* 603–606), takes "baptism" in a metaphorical sense, as a simple reference to the common experience of the

Spirit among believers. Paul's normal usage and the use of a baptismal formula in v. 13b suggest, however, that Paul is making reference to Spirit-inspired ritual baptism as the act of incorporation into the one body (see note on 12:9). In baptism the power of the Spirit is at work.

whether Jews or Gentiles, slaves or free: The baptismal unity of Christians in Christ transcends ethnic and social differences. "Whether . . . or" *(eite . . . eite)* is a vintage Pauline expression. His language recalls the baptismal formula of Gal 3:28 from which it differs by omitting any reference to sexual differentiation. In Gal 3:28 the reference to the gender difference transcended in baptism echoes the story of creation (Gen 1:27). Paul may have omitted a potential "whether male or female" from 12:13 (cf. Col 3:11) because of the Corinthians' misunderstanding of the nature of human sexuality now that they are "in Christ" (see 1 Corinthians 5, 7). The passage in 7:17-24 offers a corrective to that misunderstanding by arguing from the situation of Jews and Gentiles, slaves and free.

and we all drank the one Spirit: Despite G. J. Cuming's argument that this is a reference to baptism by affusion, the clear meaning of the verb is "made to drink." References in the Hebrew Scriptures might suggest that the metaphor refers to the experience of the Spirit of God. The phrase is nevertheless difficult to understand. The textual tradition indicates that various scribes attempted to clarify Paul's words. Some manuscripts read "we all were made to drink one drink." The Codex Alexandrinus reads "we all are one body."

With its reference to "all," "drink," and "Spirit" 12:13a echoes 10:4. It refers to the eucharistic cup (11:25). Drinking of the cup marked the transition from the meal to the activities of the liturgical assembly in a fashion similar to the way in which a libation of wine offered to the gods marked the transition between the dinner and the symposium in the formal dinner parties of the Hellenistic world, particularly those sponsored by various associations (see D. E. Smith, "Meals and Morality," 326, 331; and see Plutarch's remarks quoted above, pp. 419, 423).

14. *For indeed the body is not a single member but many members:* After the theological explanation of v. 13, a resumptive v. 14 presents the body metaphor in the way that Paul intends to exploit it. It is a kind of *prothesis,* an opening statement in which Paul says that his attention will focus on the diversity of the (social) body.

15–16. *If the foot says, "because I am not a hand, I am not of the body," is it for this reason less a part of the body? And if the ear says, "because I am not an eye, I am not of the body," is it for this reason less a part of the body?* Verses 15-16 represent a rare Pauline instance of the classical rhetorical device of personification. He compares one bodily extremity with another, one sense organ with another. The two rhetorical questions are completely parallel. They each use a double negative, canceling one another out (elsewhere in the NT only in Acts 4:20; cf. BDF 431.1). Notwithstanding its difference from the hand, the foot still belongs to the body. Similarly, despite its difference from the eye, the ear still belongs to the body (cf. BDF 236.5). Difference does not create independence.

17. *If the eye is the whole body, where is the hearing? If the hearing is the whole body, where is the sense of smell?* Another pair of parallel rhetorical questions further exploits the sense organs mentioned in v. 16. Like Plutarch, Paul speaks of the members that belong to the body in pairs. The list could be extended. Paul has established the first two links in a chain, eye/hearing, hearing/smell, smell/ . . . . Were any single member to be the whole body, the body would be deficient. It would lack something that is necessary for it to function properly.

18. *Now then God has arranged the members in the body, each one of them according as he willed:* In the traditional Hellenistic use of the body image each member has its place. The harmonious order of the whole is a given. The order derives from nature *(physis).* Paul asserts that God has arranged the structured unity of the diverse members of the human body, according as he willed *(kathōs ēthelēsen;* cf. 12:11).

19. *If all were a single member, where would the body be?* One of the rare unreal periods in Paul's letters (cf. 2:8; 11:31; Gal 1:20; 3:21; 4:15), v. 19 reprises the thought of v. 17. If there were only one member there would be no body (v. 17). Were there only one member there would be no body as created by God (v. 18).

20. *Now there are many members, but one body:* Verse 20a sums up the argumentation of vv. 14-19. The fact is that a body has many members. That having been said, Paul can move on to the second point he wants to develop on the basis of the body image, the unity of the body as seen in the interdependence of its several parts.

21. *The eye cannot say to the hand, "I don't need you" nor the head to the feet, "I don't need you":* Paul continues to employ personification as he portrays an imaginary dialogue between various members of the body, the eye, hand, and feet having appeared in vv. 15-16. In Paul's biblical tradition "feet" may be a euphemism for the sexual organ, and given the situation of the shrine of Asklepios in Corinth and Paul's reference to the necessary and less honorable members of the body in the following verses it is possible that Paul intends his audience to understand by "feet" the body's sexual organs. His general point is that the body needs each of its members and that the several members are interdependent. They need one another.

22–24. *To the contrary, the members that are thought to be weaker are all the more necessary, and on those members of the body we consider to be less honorable we confer greater honor, and our shameful members have greater modesty; but our modest members do not need this:* "To the contrary" suggests a denial of what is implied by the putative utterance of the eye and the head in v. 21. "All the more" is *pollǭ mallon,* literally "how much more." "Confer" *(perithithemen)* and "less honorable" *(aschēmona,* in context meaning "unpresentable") are hapax in Paul.

Repetition makes Paul's point all the more clear. His contrasts were telling in a society where shame and honor were values and forces such as they are not in contemporary Western society. Playing with words, Paul points to the simultaneous lower and higher status of the weaker, less honorable, and more shameful members of our body. Human beings, driven by shame and honor, readily cover the less seemly portions of the body. The irony of this, as Paul's concluding statement makes clear, is that the more seemly parts of the human body receive no such beautifying treatment.

Paul's writing sometimes derives its power from what Mikhail Bakhtin has called "heteroglossia," that is, polyvalent vocabulary (see *Speech Genres and Other Late Essays* [Austin: University of Texas Press, 1986]). He occasionally uses expressions with more than one meaning. Here the apostle may be referring to those weaker organs and members that are necessary *(anagkaia);* on the other hand "the necessary member" was sometimes a euphemism for the male organ in the Hellenistic world (e.g., Artemidorus, *Dream Handbook* 1.45, 79, 80).

24–25. *In contrast God has formed the body together, giving all the more honor to the least member so that there is no bodily rupture and members are mutually concerned about one another:* Paul's language continues to be characterized by heteroglossia. As in the first part of the argument drawn from the topos of the body (v. 18), he notes that it is God who has formed the body together *(synekerasen,* hapax in Paul who has a predilection for compound verbs with *syn)* and united it so that there is no bodily rupture *(mē ē̦ schisma en tō̦ sōmati).*

The result of God's activity in creating the body is a reprise of Paul's statement of purpose in writing to the Corinthians (1:10, where *schisma* appears in the plural; cf. 11:18). Paul's strategic use of the term is an indication of the careful rhetorical composition of his letter. *Schisma* in the sense of a rupture in the body politic is generally unknown in the literature of the time. The only known use of the noun in an injunction against religious factions is to be found in documentation pertaining to the guild of Zeus Hypsistos (P.London 2710.13).

The compound *hina* clause (with *alla*) emphasizes what it means for there to be no rupture in the social body. In place of division there should exist mutual concern *(to auto hyper allēlōn merimnōsin)* of the members for one another. The kind of care and concern about which Paul speaks is comparable to the care and concern that spouses are presumed to have for one another (note the use of *merimnaō* in 7:32-34). God's choice of "the least" members is illustrated in 1:27-28.

26. *If one member suffers, all the members suffer; if one member is honored, all the members rejoice:* This classic case of parallel construction is loosely linked to the preceding sentence by *kai.* The parallel clauses are alike in every respect but the verbs. The language is Pauline. The clauses are joined together by *eite . . . eite,* "if . . . if." The verbs in the two protases are compounds with *syn (sympaschei, sygchairei;* cf. *synekerasen* in v. 24): suffering with, rejoicing with. Paul's observation that if one member of the body suffers all suffer (cf. 2 Cor 11:29) is consistent with his use of the body image. The pain of a toothache is hardly confined to a single tooth. Using the body image as a symbol of society Dio Chrysostom *(Discourses* 34.17; 38.14; 39.5) and Plutarch ("On Brotherly Love," *Moralia* 478D-479B) also talked about the health of the body. The mutual

experience of suffering represents a Pauline emphasis as does the mutual experience of rejoicing (cf. Rom 12:15). With other NT authors Paul uses "to
honor" of humans' homage to God (6:20; cf. Rom 1:21; 15:6, 9; 2 Cor 9:13; Gal
1:24), but he also uses it of glorification given by God to humans (Rom 8:30;
2 Cor 3:10). In 12:26 the verb *(doxazetai)* is probably to be taken in the ordinary
secular sense of being honored, but the passive voice (a divine passive?)
might possibly suggest that Christians are to rejoice with one another because
of the gifts God gives to any single member of the group.

For Reference and Further Study

Garner, G. G. "The Temple of Asklepius at Corinth and Paul's Teaching," *Buried
History* 18 (1982) 52–58.

Hill, Andrew E. "The Temple of Asclepius: An Alternative Source of Paul's Body
Theology," *JBL* 99 (1980) 437–439.

Käsemann, Ernst. "The Theological Problem Presented by the Motif of the Body
of Christ" in idem, *Perspectives on Paul*. NTL. Philadelphia: Fortress, 1971,
102–121.

Knoch, Otto. "'Do This in Memory of Me!' (Luke 22:20; 1 Corinthians 11:24ff.):
The Celebration of the Eucharist in the Primitive Christian Communities"
in Otto Knoch, et al, eds., *One Loaf, One Cup* 1–10.

Martin, Dale B. *The Corinthian Body* 94–96.

Nestle, Wilhelm. "Die Fabel des Meneius Agrippa," *Klio* 21 (1927) 350–360.

Neyrey, Jerome H. "Body Language in 1 Corinthians: The Use of Anthropological
Models for Understanding Paul and His Opponents," *Semeia* 35 (1986)
129–170.

Roebuck, Carl A. *The Asklepieion and Lerna: based on the excavations and preliminary
studies of F. J. de Waele*. ASCS (Athens), Corinth 14. Princeton: American
School of Classical Studies in Athens, 1951.

Rogers, E. R. "*Epotisthēmen* Again," *NTS* 29 (1983) 139–142.

4. *Christ's Body* (12:27-31a)

27. And you are the body of Christ, each member for his or her own part
28. whom God has arranged in the church; first, apostles, second, prophets, third, teachers, then powers, gifts of healings, helpers, leaders, a difference of tongues. 29. Are all apostles? Are all prophets? Are all
teachers? Are all powers? 30. Do all have the gifts of healings? Do all
speak in tongues? Do all interpret? 31. Avidly desire the greater gifts.

The core of this epistolary unit consists of two lists of charisms. The first (v. 28) has the form of a list. It enumerates eight charisms, citing them as first, second, third, then, then. . . . The second list (vv. 29-30) is in the form of a series of seven rhetorical questions. The first five questions concern the first five gifts on the enumerated list, that is, the five that are introduced by adverbs in v. 28. The last two questions pertain to the final gift on the enumerated list, the gift of tongues. One rhetorical question asks whether all within the community possess this gift. The other asks whether all within the community possess the correlative gift of the interpretation of tongues, a gift that was not cited on the enumerated list.

The Epistolary Unit. Identifying the core of the epistolary unit is easy. It is not as easy to identify the extent of the unit. This was not a problem for Paul. The exposition of his ideas flowed freely from his lips as the scribe wrote them down. The problem is one for the modern interpreter who must deal with Paul's letters one unit at a time. The problem of identifying the extent of this epistolary unit was not as clear to Stephen Langton (d. 1228) and Robert Estienne (d. 1559), who respectively divided the NT into chapters and verses. As a result of their work 1 Cor 12:31 reads, "Avidly desire the greater gifts. And I will show you the way that surpasses all others."

Today the printing of most editions of the NT seems to suggest that the first part of 12:31 (12:31a) really belongs with the material in ch. 12, while the second part of 12:31 (12:31b) introduces the material of ch. 13. The second half-verse, 12:31b, is in the first person singular, as is the material in 13:1-3, while 12:31a is in the second person plural, as is 12:27. The list of charisms in v. 28 is in the third person as the literary form requires. The list leads to a series of rhetorical questions, directly addressed to a (fictive) audience. The negative response expected for each question confirms that all members of the community do not possess all the gifts. By means of the questions Paul leads the Corinthians to acknowledge, at least implicitly, what he has affirmed in v. 11, namely that the Spirit has allotted different gifts to the various members of the community.

The unit in 12:27-31, identified as a workable epistolary unit by the use of the second person in vv. 27 and 31a, is closely connected with both the preceding material and the material that follows. The opening verse links this new exposition on the gifts to the motif of the body, which had been developed at length in 12:12-26 (cf. 12:12-13 and its interpretation, p. 458). "Body of Christ" in v. 27 is virtually a title for the entire metaphor (see 12:12). "Each member for his or her own part" gives a referent for the extended metaphor. The catchword "member" appeared ten times in the exposition of the metaphor (vv. 12[2x], 14, 18, 19, 20, 22, 25, 26[2x]).

The Enumerated List. The list of eight charisms in v. 28 is the only enumerated list of charisms in the NT (cf. Rom 12:6-8; Eph 4:11; 1 Pet 4:11). There is some difference between the list of eight in v. 28 and the nine cited in 12:8-10. There is also some difference between the list of eight and the seven rhetorical questions in vv. 29-30. The enumeration of "apostles," "prophets," and "teachers" highlights the importance of these functions in the Christian assembly.

The enumeration draws attention to the role of the apostle as one who preaches the gospel and thereby brings the community into being as a community of believers. Earlier in the letter Paul had identified himself as an apostle (1:1; cf. 9:5). Thereafter he used a variety of metaphors to speak about his foundational role with regard to the community at Corinth: mother (3:1-2), father (4:15), one who plants (3:6), one who lays a foundation (3:10).

Placing the apostolate as the first of the charisms in 12:28 does not suggest that those who have this role have superior status within the community. As a matter of fact Paul frequently uses terms denoting a lower status (servants, workers, assistants, stewards) to describe the function of himself and his coworkers. He recalls that they, himself in particular, are of low esteem in the eyes of the world (1:20; 2:6; 9:16-19). He himself is the least of the apostles (15:9). By placing the gift of tongues last on the enumerated list Paul puts glossolalia in its place with respect to the other gifts. The place on the list occupied by speaking in tongues suggests the radical relativization of the gift of glossolalia in the eyes of Paul.

Various Gifts. The enumerated list cites eight charisms: apostles, prophets, teachers, powers, gifts of healings, helpers, leaders, tongues. To this list the rhetorical question of v. 30 adds a ninth charism, the interpretation of tongues. Four other gifts appeared among the charisms cited in vv. 8-10: the word of wisdom, the word of knowledge, faith, the discernment of spirits. All told, thirteen gifts appear on the three lists. No single list contains them all.

Moreover, some functions exercised within the Corinthian community seem not to be specifically identified on any of the lists in 1 Corinthians 12. Someone must have organized the Lord's supper to which Paul makes reference in 1 Corinthians 11, yet the apostle does not identify any host or presider. Someone must have baptized the neophyte Christians at Corinth, but Paul does not identify either the role or the person other than to say that he himself occasionally, and exceptionally, fulfilled that role (1 Cor 1:14-17). A collection is to be made at Corinth for the benefit of the saints (1 Cor 16:1), but Paul does not at that point provide a titular rubric for those who were responsible for organizing the collection (see below, pp. 585–588).

The nature of many of the gifts is reasonably clear, but for some of them it is not (see notes on 12:8-10). C. K. Barrett (*Paul: An Introduction to His Thought* [Louisville: Westminster/John Knox, 1994] 123) singles out helpers and leaders as two roles that are particularly difficult to specify. The terms appear only in the enumerated list of v. 28 and are not otherwise employed by Paul. "Helpers" seems to suggest that those so designated fulfill a role of service within the community, but it is strange that Paul does not employ the term servant *(diakonos)*, which he does use elsewhere (Rom 16:1; Phil 1:1; cf. 1 Cor 3:5) and that later came into common usage in the church. "Leaders" *(kybernēseis)* suggests some kind of directive activity, but again Paul does not employ terms that are otherwise familiar to him, overseer *(episkopos,* Phil 1:1) or presider (from the verb *proistēmi;* cf. Rom 12:8; 1 Thess 5:12). Could it be that "helpers" was the term used by the Corinthians to designate those who were involved with taking up the collection on behalf of the saints in Jerusalem and that "leaders" was used of the patrons of house churches and/or those who presided at eucharist?

One might even suggest that some ambiguity attaches to "apostles," cited in the first instance on Paul's list of functions within the church. "Apostles" *per se* might simply connote delegates who are sent on a mission (cf. 1 Cor 16:3-4). Paul's use of the term with reference to himself (Apollos and Barnabas), along with his extensive reflection on his foundational role with respect to the church of God at Corinth, supports the idea that in 12:28 "apostle" has, nonetheless, more or less the meaning that Christians generally assign to it. The term was not so narrowly restricted as to designate only the Twelve and Paul, but its presence at the head of the list and its specific enumeration seem to identify it as a most significant, that is, a foundational function. Those who are apostles in this sense are those who, having preached the gospel, are involved in the foundation of a Christian community.

The third gift on the enumerated list and the subject of the third rhetorical question is "teacher" *(didaskalos),* a term used by Paul only in 12:28-29 and Rom 2:20. The term appears as a charism in Eph 4:11. This gift is distinct from the apostolate, preaching, and prophesying. The teacher is one who instructs with regards to God's will, whether in catechesis (cf. 14:9) or as an interpreter of the Scriptures. In the early church the latter would be a particularly important function insofar as the Scriptures were applied to the Christian experience (9:9-10) and provided a hermeneutical tool for understanding Jesus (15:3-4). Teaching was a function that Paul exercised in each of the communities he had evangelized (14:6). The post-Pauline 1 Tim 2:7 and 2 Tim 1:11 describe Paul as a teacher of the Gentiles, a function that is juxtaposed with that of herald and apostle. In Rom 12:7 Paul exhorts the one who has the gift to use it for instruction *(didaskalia),* apparently for the teaching of doctrine.

27. *And you are the body of Christ, each member for his or her own part:* The transitional verse continues the image of the body. Using a distributional expression (*melē ek merous,* cf. BDF 212), Paul describes Christians as members of the one body of Christ. In similar fashion Seneca stated, "we are the parts of one great body" (*membra sumus corporis magni*). He continued, "Nature produced us related to one another, since she created us from the same source and to the same end. She engendered in us mutual affection (*haec nobis amorem indidit mutuum*) . . ." (*Epistles* 95.52). In similar fashion Paul will move from his disquisition on the body to a consideration on love (1 Corinthians 13). Before doing so he explains his use of the metaphor of the body.

28. *whom God has arranged in the church:* With an epexegetical *kai* (BDF 442.9; the *kai* has not been translated) as a connective Paul indicates that he is about to explain the metaphor. The relative pronoun, "whom," refers back to "members" (*melē* in the plural) in v. 27. "God has arranged" reprises the language of 12:18 (cf. 12:24). The same words are used. "Members" is the true direct object of the verb in each instance. "Church" (*ekklēsia*) is the local community whose unity and diversity Paul has sought to clarify by means of the body metaphor.

    first, apostles, second, prophets, third, teachers, then powers, gifts of healings, helpers, leaders, a difference of tongues: This is the only time in the NT when charismatic gifts are enumerated as first, second, third, then, then (*prōton, deuteron, triton, epeita, epeita*). Four of the eight gifts on the enumerated list appear among the nine cited in 12:8-10. These are the gifts of prophecy, powers, healing, and tongues, each of which is reprised in the rhetorical questions that follow. The relative sequence of the four gifts in 12:28 is different from what it was in 12:8-10. There the order was healings . . . powers, prophecy . . . tongues. Two of the gifts appear in v. 28 with nomenclature that is slightly different from the terminology of 12:8-10. Paul speaks of "prophets" (*prophētai*) instead of "prophecy" (*prophēteia*), of "powers" (*dynameis*) instead of "activities of powers" (*energēmata dynameōn*). The four gifts that do not appear on the earlier list are apostles (*apostolous*), teachers (*didaskalous*), helpers (*antilēmpseis,* hapax in the NT), and leaders (*kybernēseis,* hapax in the NT; a cognate appears in Acts 27:11; Rev 18:17). "Leaders" may be a nautical metaphor, a striking term for leadership in the maritime community of Corinth (see the note on "assistants" in 4:1).

29–30. *Are all apostles? Are all prophets? Are all teachers? Are all powers? Do all have the gifts of healings? Do all speak in tongues? Do all interpret?* A negative response is expected for each of these seven rhetorical questions. The series reprises six of the eight charisms of v. 28, including the four that first appeared in 12:8-10. No questions are asked with regard to the gifts of helpers and leaders. On the other hand, v. 30 includes a rhetorical question about "interpretation" (*diermēneuousin;* cf. 14:5, 13, 27), presumably the interpretation of tongues (*hermēneia glōssōn;* cf. 12:10). Mention of the correlative gift of the interpretation of tongues serves Paul's rhetorical purpose insofar as Paul is trying to order a community some of whose members desire to have and to exercise, in disordered fashion, the gift of tongues. No literature earlier than Paul's own letter to the Corinthians uses the phrase "to speak in tongues" as Paul does. In ancient literature similar phraseology was used of a person who could speak more than one language.

31. *Avidly desire the greater gifts:* Given the literary function of v. 31 (the first part of an *inclusio*) and the parallelism with 14:1, most commentators take the verb *zēloute,* "avidly desire," as an imperative. The phrase may be taken as an indicative, in which case it would introduce ch. 13 along with v. 31b, but the thrust of Paul's argument seems to demand that it be taken as an imperative. An imperative brings the needed closure to Paul's exposition on the gifts. In 14:39 (cf. 14:12), moreover, Paul urges the Corinthians to desire the gift of prophecy, which he deems superior to that of speaking in tongues (14:5).

For Reference and Further Study

Roberts, P. "Seers or Overseers?" *ExpT* 108 (1997) 301–305.

5. *Not to Have Love (12:31b–13:3)*

31b. I will show you an extraordinary way. 1. If I speak in the tongues of humans and even of angels, and do not have love, I have become sounding brass rather than a resounding cymbal. 2. And if I have the gift of prophecy and know all mysteries and all knowledge and if I have all faith such that mountains are moved, and do not have love, I am good for nothing. 3. And if I give away all my possessions and if I hand over my body so that I burn, and do not have love, it is not to my advantage.

Interpretation

Chapter 13 is a digression in Paul's rhetorical argument, element B in the A-B-A' structure of chs. 12–14. The digression is closely linked with its proximate context. The gift of tongues cited in v. 1 takes up a motif cited in 12:28, 30 (cf. 14:2, 4, 5); the gift of prophecy in v. 2 recalls the charismatic gift of prophecy cited in 12:28, 29 (cf. 14:1, 3, 4, 5). These two gifts, speaking in tongues and prophesying, provide the focal point of Paul's discussion in ch. 14. Embedded between two chapters with an ecclesiological perspective, ch. 13 is anthropological and theological. What Paul has written in this chapter underscores the essential quality of the Christian life. Love, *agapē,* is the *sine qua non* of the Christian life.

Structure. Like ch. 12, ch. 13 is structured in chiastic fashion. Virtually all commentators draw attention to its three parts: vv. 1-3 (A), 4-7 (B), and 8-13 (A'). Verses 1-3 affirm that without love charismatic gifts have no real value. Verses 4-7 offer a panorama on love, featuring both its positive and negative qualities, that is, what love does and what love does not do. Verses 8-13 contrast love with the spiritual gifts, affirming that love never ends. Essentially elements A and A' of Paul's chiastic structure affirm that love is God's gift *par excellence.* The last verse (13:13) sums up Paul's argument, providing a conclusion to the encomium on love.

Each of the three parts of ch. 13 develops Paul's argument in a threefold movement of thought. The prologue (13:1-3) contains three parallel arguments. Each argument has the same threefold pattern: one or more conditional clauses, the phrase "and do not have love," and an apodosis that affirms the nothingness of a gift without love. The protasis of each of the parallel arguments is doubled. In v. 1 the duplication occurs in the reference to two kinds of languages. The duplication in vv. 2 and 3 has the form of a compound conditional clause.

The rhetorical device of gradation *(klimax)* characterizes the entire argument. The protases of the three verses are arranged in an order of ascending intensity. Paul "ups the ante" as he develops his point. He first writes of gifts he can use for the benefit of others. He begins with the lesser gift of speaking in tongues, then continues with the greater gift of prophecy. Finally he speaks of the ultimate gift, the gift of self-sacrifice for the benefit of others. Paul employs the rhetorical device of hyperbole, but his point is clear. If he did not have love even the gift of self-sacrifice would not accrue to his personal advantage. Not even that kind of ultimate self-giving would be profitable *(ouden ōpheloumai).* J. H. Petzer describes this as an example of the phenomenon of defamiliarization, that is, presenting the familiar in an unfamiliar way (breaking the ordinary rules).

The Ethos Argument. Paul uses the first person singular in each clause of his three-part argument in both the protasis and the apodosis of the sentence. Although some interpret Paul's words in a general sense as if "I" meant the generic human being, the natural sense of the words suggests that Paul is referring to himself in his first-person statements. When he writes "if I speak in tongues . . ." and so on he is talking about himself.

The structural parallelism of chs. 12–14 with chs. 8–10 confirms the autobiographical and self-referential character of the first subunit in Paul's digression (vv. 1-3). In ch. 13, as in ch. 9, Paul writes about himself as did Epictetus *(Discourses* 1.18.15-16). Both offer themselves as examples of what they are talking about. A true first-person reading of 13:1-3 is consistent with Paul's use of the first person singular in the rest of the letter.

His deliberative style prompts the use of autobiographical example as a rhetorical argument. There may even be a touch of irony in the challenge Paul addresses to the Corinthians. They pursue spiritual gifts, but Paul will show a more excellent way. His encomium on love is prompted by the fact that in their pursuit of spiritual gifts the Corinthians follow a hierarchy he cannot accept.

By speaking of himself as he does Paul develops an *ethos* appeal. Even the reference to his boasting can be seen as an almost disparaging reference to his rhetorical success as he employs the deliberative style to advantage. Paul returns to the use of the first person in vv. 11-12, thereby reinforcing the *ethos* appeal and forming a loose *inclusio* with vv. 2-3. This inclusion is a feature of the chiastic structure of ch. 13, whose theological core is to be found in vv. 4-7.

Metaphor. Along with the rhetorical devices of gradation Paul's argument profits from the use of metaphor, including hyperbole, which is a kind of metaphor (cf. Aristotle, *Art of Rhetoric* 3.11.15), and comparison. Verse 1 uses the striking metaphors of angelic speech and sounding brass to speak of the gift of tongues, a charism Paul himself enjoyed. When he writes about this charism in 1 Cor 14:6, 14, 18 Paul intimates that he himself might have spoken in tongues while he was among the Corinthians. In 13:1 he suggests that cacophonous musical sounds are an apt metaphor for any inordinate use of the charism. Sound is the element of comparison between even disharmonious music and a gift of speaking *(lalō)*.

"Angels" are mentioned elsewhere in 1 Corinthians (4:9; 6:3; 11:10) but this is the only place in the letter where Paul describes the phenomenon of glossolalia as angelic speech. With an idea of angels similar to that of early Christian thought the Hellenistic *Testament of Job* (first century B.C.E.–first century C.E.) speaks of the daughters of Job who are given the gift of ecstatic speech as a form of compensation for their not being heir to their father's property. The ecstatic speech of these daughters of Job is described as the language of angels (*T. Job* 48:3), archons (*T. Job* 49:2), and cherubim (*T. Job* 50:2).

For a striking contrast with angelic speech Paul draws upon the experience of the Corinthians whose economy was to a significant degree dependent upon the manufacture and trading of bronze items. In Paul's day echo chambers, generally made of bronze, were strategically placed in niches around amphitheaters, where they served as effective acoustical devices (cf. Vitruvius, *Architecture* 5.3.8 [ca. 30 B.C.E.]). A loveless Paul and those speaking in tongues without love are comparable to pieces of bronze. They echo sound but they do not resonate the tone of a fine musical instrument (cf. 14:7-8). "I have become sounding brass" (v. 1) is parallel with "I am good for nothing" (v. 2) and "it is not to my advantage" (v. 3).

Each of the latter clauses, "I am good for nothing" and "it is not to my advantage" is a pithy expression in Greek *(outhen eimi; ouden ōpheloumai)*. In v. 2 the rhetorical force of the argument is strengthened by the contrast between the thrice-repeated "all" and Paul's single "nothing" *(outhen)*. The contrast between all and nothing continues in v. 3, where Paul adopts the language of deliberative rhetoric as he speaks about what is advantageous *(ōpheloumai)*.

Notes

31b. *I will show you an extraordinary way:* Paul's use of "and" *(kai)* and the comparative *eti* (not translated) underscore the superlative quality of the way that Paul will show. Joop F. M. Smit ("The Genre") suggests that Paul's use of the verb "to show" *(deiknymi,* hapax in Paul) indicates that he is about to engage in an exercise of epideictic or demonstrative rhetoric. *E contrario* it should be argued that Paul's encomium on love serves a deliberative purpose. His disquisition on love is a critique of the Corinthians' pursuit of the gifts of tongues and knowledge. Paul demonstrates a more excellent way to seek after spiritual gifts. The demonstrative force of Paul's choice of vocabulary, his *lexis,* must not be overlooked. The verb "to show" was used by moralists such as Epictetus and Lucian. Like Paul, Epictetus uses the expression "to show the way" *(Discourses* 1.4.29; cf. 10, 32). Paul's showing the way *(hodon deiknymi)* is more than merely teaching about love. The way that he puts before the Corinthians is the way of his own life. Paul not only teaches about love. He offers himself as an example of love. His personification of love allows its distinctive qualities to be appreciated. Verses 1-3 are thoroughly self-referential. Using himself as an example in a rhetorical digression is similar to what he did in ch. 9.

The prepositional phrase *(eti kath' hyperbolēn,* "extraordinary" in this translation) literally means "beyond excess" (cf. Rom 7:13; 2 Cor 1:8; 4:17; Gal 1:13). It connotes the idea of a way *sans pareil.* The phrase suggests that the way Paul will demonstrate is beyond compare. The phrase is normally used adverbially and W. C. van Unnik ("The Meaning of 1 Corinthians 12:31," *NovT* 35 [1993] 142–159) argues that the phrase has an adverbial sense in 12:31 and that it modifies the verb "avidly seek" *(zēloute).* In Isocrates, although with another referent, the phrase means "extravagantly." Van Unnik argues that Paul's phrase modifies "avidly seek spiritual gifts" with the result that the verb "avidly seek" has both a direct object and an adverbial qualifier joined together with an "and" *(kai).* On his reading, 12:31a means "practice the spiritual gifts zealously"; 12:31b then becomes an independent sentence with the meaning, "I will show you the way."

Paul's prepositional phrase is, however, at some distance removed from "avidly seek." In Greek six words come between the prepositional phrase and the verb "to seek avidly." Accordingly it is preferable to take the phrase as an attributive qualification of the verb "to show" *(deiknymi).* Its technical rhetorical meaning is "in hyperbole" (Isocrates, *Letters* 4.88; Aristotle, *Art of Rhetoric* 3.11.15-16; Demetrius, *On Style* 52; Strabo, *Geography* 1.2.33; 3.2.9). Aristotle says that there is something youthful about metaphors, "for they show vehemence. Those who are in a passion most frequently make use of them" (*Art of Rhetoric* 3.11.16). The metaphorical sense of Paul's rhetorical expression must not be overlooked. His allusive description of himself (vv. 1-3) is characterized by hyperbole.

1. *If I speak in the tongues of humans and even of angels, and do not have love:* Paul begins his digression on love with a reference to ordinary speech and speaking in tongues. Speaking (cf. ch. 14) is the counterpoint of what he will have to say about love. The gift of speaking in tongues was quite visible and highly esteemed among the Corinthians. Paul claimed that he had the ability to speak in tongues even more than the Corinthians did (14:6, 18). J. G. Sigountos ("Genre," 252) takes "and of angels" as a hyperbolic expression, but Paul's phrase appears to designate the phenomenon of speaking in tongues. Parallels in the *Testament of Job* confirm that this is the connotation of Paul's phrase. His mode of expression follows a kind of "from the lesser to the greater" rhetorical construction in the form of gradation. His use of the rhetorical device of *klimax* emphasizes the gift of speaking in tongues.

I have become sounding brass rather than a resounding cymbal: The language is metaphorical (cf. 9:24-27; 14:7-8). Tiberius called Apion, Josephus' foil, "the world's cymbal," but it is unlikely that Paul is here referring to rhetors, nor is he referring to pagan worship in which cymbals were used. His choice of metaphor stands in its own right. There is no need to see in it a self-conscious polemical expression against those who make self-serving use of their oratorical skills or against those who participate in pagan rituals. The image of harmonious sound as a metaphor for a community whose members are in harmony with one another was well known to ancient authors (cf. 4 Macc 13:8; Plutarch, "On Brotherly Love," *Moralia* 478D-479B). In the Hellenistic world as well as in Paul's biblical tradition cymbals were considered to be fine musical instruments. In contrast, sounding brass is merely an echoing device. Were Paul not to have love he would be comparable (his *ē* is comparative, not disjunctive) to an echo chamber rather than to a fine instrument that produces melodious sounds.

2. *And if I have the gift of prophecy and know all mysteries and all knowledge:* In 14:6 Paul describes himself as bringing to the Corinthians not only teaching *(didachē)*, but also revelation *(apocalypsei)*, knowledge *(gnōsei)*, and prophecy *(prophēteią)*. "Knowledge" must be taken in its Semitic connotation where it refers to experiential and practical knowledge. In 8:1-3 Paul had written about knowledge, contrasting it with love that builds up. The compound object of the verb "know" *(eidō)* in 13:2 shows that the gift of knowledge (cf. 12:8) is something other than the knowledge of esoteric mysteries, whether those exalted in the mystery religions or those proclaimed in apocalyptic discourse. The content of Paul's preaching is the "mystery of God" (*to mysterion tou theou*, 2:1), an apocalyptic idea.

and if I have all faith such that mountains are moved, and do not have love, I am good for nothing: On the faith (cf. 12:9) that moves mountains see Matt 17:20; 21:21. In 14:6 (cf. 7:40) Paul admits to having the gifts of prophecy and knowledge. Elsewhere he confesses having miraculous powers. "The signs of the apostle" *(sēmeia tou apostolou)* were among the "signs and wonders and mighty works" *(sēmeiois te kai terasis kai dynamesin)* done among the Corinthians (2 Cor 12:12; cf. Rom 15:19). That Paul was a worker of miracles is an important feature of the *Paulusbild* developed by Luke in Acts (14:3; 16:16-24; 19:11; 28:3-6). Paul's "I am good for nothing" *(ouden ōpheloumai;* cf. 15:32) is echoed by the "even though I am nothing" *(ei kai ouden eimi)* of 2 Cor 12:11. The latter occurs in a context that rhetorically denigrates the importance of Paul's thaumaturgical activity.

3. *And if I give away all my possessions and if I hand over my body so that I burn, and do not have love:* There is a major textual problem with regard to the reading "so that I burn" *(hina kauthēsōmai,* of which three or four variants are attested in the manuscript tradition). "Burning" is found in various majuscules, including C, D, F, G, L, and most medieval manuscripts, and is reflected in some of the ancient versions. This reading was incorporated into the Textus Receptus (cf. *AV, NIV*) and is accepted by many modern critics, including J. K. Elliott, René Kieffer, J. G. Sigountos ["Genre," 253–255]), and C. C. Caragounis. "So that I might boast" *(hina kauchēsōmai)* is found in the older and generally preferable manuscripts (including, 𝔓⁴⁶, ℵ, A, B) and the writings of Jerome. It is reflected in the Coptic version. This reading has been adopted by the editors of *GNT*⁴. It is accepted by Bruce Metzger and J. H. Petzer.

In Greek the sight and sound of the two expressions are not vastly different from one another. Thus either reading could be the result of scribal error. On intrinsic grounds "boasting" appears to have the greater claim to authenticity. "To boast" *(kauchaomai)* is a common Pauline term, occurring some thirty-five times in the letters. To be sure, Paul generally takes a disparaging view of boasting (especially in 1 Corinthians 1–4), but he is not one who is above taking pride in his ministry (2 Cor 8:24; Phil 2:16; 1 Thess 2:19). On the other hand, the fact that there are three or four grammatical versions of "burning" weakens the case for this reading. It could further be argued that although sacrificial self-immolation was not a common Christian practice, pious scribes, for whom martyrdom was virtuous, may have found boasting on the part of a saint reprehensible and substituted an act of virtue for something they considered to be wrong.

Nonetheless, the various "burning" readings are explicable (see C. C. Caragounis, "Crux"). These readings, taken in the totality of their manuscript evidence, provide strong external evidence for "burning" and constitute a claim for its originality. "To hand over" is a verb of incomplete predication. In order for it to make sense it must be complemented by another clause or phrase. "So that I burn" appears to be such a complementary clause. It is hyperbolic (cf. Sigountos, "Genre") but corresponds to the argument in 12:31b–13:3, which is admittedly hyperbolic (12:31b) and makes thoroughgoing use of the rhetorical device of *klimax*. Paul's choice of phrase might have been an allusion to the martyrdom of the three young men in Daniel 3.

On balance "burning" appears to be the preferable reading. In 13:3 Paul's argument comes to its climax. He pushes his argument to the limit, and beyond human control. Cf. *1 Enoch* 108:8, "Those who love God have loved neither gold nor silver, nor all the good things that are in the world, but have given over their bodies to suffering. . . ." The context speaks of burning, of mountains, and of angels who speak (*1 Enoch* 108:4-11). Paul's argument may also reflect the language of the Last Supper tradition (11:23-24; cf. 11:1). There is a similarity of expression between the second part of Paul's protasis and the traditional institution narrative, which includes the motifs of "handing over" and "the body" (cf. Mark 14:18-25).

it is not to my advantage: If Paul were to give away all his possessions and even his very self (cf. 1 Thess 2:8; 2 Cor 7:15) to the point of giving up his own life but did not have love it would profit him not at all. Paul's argument is couched in the language of the rhetorical argument from advantage (cf. 14:6). "Advantage" (*ōpheleia*) is equated with "advantage" (*ton sympheron*) by Dionysius of Halicarnassus (*Roman Antiquities* 8.44.2). Paul has previously urged the Corinthians to consider what is to their own advantage (6:12; 7:35; 10:23, 33; 12:7). Now he offers himself as an example of one who has considered what is to his own advantage and has come to the conclusion that there is no advantage whatsoever that would accrue to himself if he does not have love.

For Reference and Further Study

Caragounis, Chrys C. "'To Boast' or 'To Be Burned'? The Crux of 1 Cor 13:3," *SEÅ* 60 (1995) 115–127.

Elliott, John K. "In Favour of *kauthēsomai* at I Corinthians 13³," *ZNW* 62 (1971) 297–298.

Harris, William V. "'Sounding Brass' and Hellenistic Technology," *BARev* 8 (1982) 38–41.

Kieffer, René. "'Afin que je sois brûlé' ou bien 'Afin que j'en tire orgueil'? (1 Cor. xiii. 3)," *NTS* 22 (1975) 95–97.

Klein, William W. "Noisy Gong or Acoustic Vase? Note on 1 Corinthians 13.1," *NTS* 32 (1986) 286–289.

Louw, Johannes P. "The Function of Discourse in a Sociosemiotic Theory of Translation Illustrated by the Translation of *zēloute* in 1 Corinthians," *BiTr* 39 (1988) 329–335.

Petzer, J. H. "Contextual Evidence in Favour of *kauchēsōmai* in 1 Corinthians 13.3," *NTS* 35 (1989) 229–253.

Sanders, Todd K. "A New Approach to 1 Corinthians 13.1," *NTS* 36 (1990) 614–618.

Smit, Joop F. M. "Two Puzzles: 1 Corinthians 12.31 and 13.3: A Rhetorical Solution," *NTS* 39 (1993) 246–264.

Standaert, Benoît. "1 Corinthians 13" in Lorenzo De Lorenzi, ed., *Charisma und Agape (1 Ko 12-14)*. Benedictina 7. Rome: St. Paul's Abbey, 1983, 127–147.

6. *Love's Rhythm* (13:4-7)

4. Love waits patiently, it is kind; love is not jealous, love is not conceited, nor is it inflated; 5. it does not behave improperly, nor does it seek its own interests; it does not get carried away in anger, nor does it calculate evil; 6. it does not rejoice in lawlessness, but rejoices together in truth; 7. it bears everything, believes everything, hopes everything, endures everything.

INTERPRETATION

The central section of Paul's rhetorical digression on love focuses on the qualities of love. This exclusive concentration distinguishes the central unit from its enveloping context (vv. 1-3; 8-13). The encompassing sections contain sentences with a complex grammatical structure, but those in Paul's central section are short and simple. In Plato's encomium on love (*erōs* rather than Paul's *agapē*), Eros' deeds are similarly set forth in a series of short sentences with Eros as the subject (*Symposium* 197A-E). Plato's words in praise of love are characterized by comparison (*sygkrisis*; cf. 13:1-3) and a series of attributes. After Plato the literary topos of the paean on love was generally associated with the *symposium* (cf. Plutarch, "Table Talk", *Moralia* 622C-623A). Paul's praise of love is likewise situated in the context of an after-dinner reflection (cf. 11:17-34). Like the words of Plato, Paul's words are characterized by comparison and a rehearsal of the attributes of love.

Structure and Rhetoric. Paul begins with two positive affirmations about love (v. 4a), follows with a series of eight clauses that state what love does not do (vv. 4b-6), and concludes with four affirmations of the universal embrace of love (v. 7). The last of the eight negative clauses is highlighted by a contrast focusing on the absence and presence of joy. Here, then, we have yet another example of Paul's use of chiasm: positive affirmations (v. 4a-b), negative statements (vv. 4c-6a), positive affirmations (vv. 6b-7). All told, including the contrast in v. 6, there are seven positive descriptions of love and eight negations about love.

Throughout the pericope Paul's language is crisp. The eight negations follow rapidly one after another so as to give a staccato effect. The final four statements also come in rapid succession. Each consists of but two words, the first of which in Greek is "all things" *(panta)*. Paul's four-fold use of *panta* introduces a universal dimension into the praise of love and furnishes the encomium with a clear theological perspective. The literary device of paronomasia, a specific form of *repetitio*, provides the finale of the passage with the emphasis it deserves.

The rhetorical device of *sygkrisis*, comparison, was an important tool of ancient rhetoric. Paul uses the device to link together the series of negative and positive states by describing a circumstance in which love does not rejoice and a circumstance in which it does rejoice (v. 6). The sound of rejoicing *(chairei)* links the two parts of v. 6 together, providing a transition between the negative and positive statements. This is an effective use of the literary device of paronomasia.

Contrast, so effectively used by Plato in his paean on love, also characterizes Paul's encomium on love. Not only does contrast link together the two clauses that speak of rejoicing; Paul's series of eight negatives, the core of his chiastic structure, is in fact an extended comparison (cf. 1 Thess 5:14-15). Moreover, the encompassing units, elements A and A' in the chiastic structure of ch. 13, use comparison very effectively. The first unit (12:31b–13:3) is a highly evocative piece on the absence of love; it is characterized by a variety of rich metaphors. The second unit (13:8-12+13) compares love with some of the charisms enjoyed by members of the community; it makes an effective use of simile and metaphor (vv. 11-12).

Love is the real subject of all fifteen verbs in this highly evocative unit. The word love, *hē agapē* (cf. v. 8), is expressed as the subject of the first positive affirmation. It recurs twice at the start of the series of negative statements. Thereafter it is absent from the unit. The use of ellipsis allows Paul to highlight the qualities of love, both negative and positive. It provides emphasis and verve for his words of praise. The negative qualities illustrate the attitude and conduct of the Corinthians. Personified, they present a behavioral pattern to be avoided. The positive qualities typify Paul's personal behavior. Paul is to be imitated (11:1). These qualities offer a pattern of behavior to be put into practice.

Theology. In this focal point of his praise of love Paul personifies it, as Plato did in the *Symposium.* Love is a model to be emulated. In content, but not in form, much of what Paul says about love in 13:4-7 is paralleled and concretized in Rom 12:9-21. In 1 Corinthians this description of love serves a critical function. Having cited himself as an example of a richly endowed charismatic, one who has enjoyed the gift of tongues (13:1; 12:10), the gift of prophecy (13:2; 12:10), the gift of knowledge (13:2; 12:8), and the gift of faith (13:2; 12:9), Paul proclaims the supremacy of love and then spells out the characteristics of love in such a way that it can be recognized for what it is. Much of what he says about love can be applied to

God. In this respect there is some parallel between Paul and Plato, who treats Eros as a deity. Some of what Paul says about love has, in fact, been said about God in his tradition. This serves to confirm that, for Paul, love is the power of God (cf. 13:13; Rom 5:5). Love is neither a human virtue, nor is it simply one of the charisms. It is the charism par excellence, the very power of God at work. Paul talks about the love of neighbor, writes Thomas Söding, with a reference that stands in a Spirit-constituted creative unity [*Spannungseinheit*] with the love of God and of Jesus Christ. In the love of neighbor the Christian confirms [*bejaht*] what God said to humankind in Jesus Christ (*Das Liebesgebot* 142).

NOTES

4. *Love waits patiently; it is kind:* Paul begins his encomiastic praise of love by putting "love" (*hē agapē*, cf. vv. 1, 2, 3) in the forefront of his discussion. Personified love is described as waiting patiently (*makrothymei*; elsewhere in Paul only in 1 Thess 5:14) and being kind (*chrēsteuetai*, hapax in the NT). The qualities of love, about which Paul writes, are qualities generally attributed to God. Patience (*makrothymia*) and kindness (*chrēstos*) appear together as divine attributes in Rom 2:4. Patience is especially characteristic of God, suggesting God's forbearance of sinners. As a Christian virtue patience frequently appears within the NT's catalogue of virtues, where it is often joined with kindness (2 Cor 6:6; Gal 5:22; Col 3:12) and other social qualities (Eph 4:2; Col 1:11; 2 Tim 3:10).

   love is not jealous, love is not conceited, nor is it inflated: The series of eight negative statements about love begins by highlighting love itself (*hē agapē*). "Love" is repeated again as the subject of "is not conceited." The presence of an explicit subject breaks the rhythm and sentence structure of Paul's thought. "Love" is absent from many manuscripts (including B), but it is present in most of the older manuscripts (ℵ, A, C, D, Ψ, etc., cf. 𝔓[46]) and the majority of medieval manuscripts, and must be considered to be part of Paul's text.

   That love is not jealous (*ou zēloi*) is particularly important in a community where jealousy and rivalry are present (3:3). "Is conceited" (*perpereuetai*) is not otherwise used in the NT, but its use in other literature suggests that it connotes ostentatious bragging (cf. *TDNT* 6:93–95). In the writings of Polybius the related adjective *perperos* means vainglorious or braggart. Paul's third negation bears directly upon the situation of those Corinthians who are "inflated" (5:2; cf. 4:6, 18, 19; 8:1). Unlike knowledge, love does not inflate nor is it inflated. On the contrary, love builds up the community (8:2). Passages in Paul's other letters illustrate what he implies in his negative description of love (cf. 2 Cor 2:7-8, Gal 6:1, and 1 Thess 5:15).

5. *it does not behave improperly, nor does it seek its own interests:* That love does not behave improperly (*ouk aschēmonei*, cf. 7:36; Rom 1:27) suggests radical incompatibility between love and those who take "all things are lawful" (6:12;

cf. 10:23) as the normless norm of their behavior. Behaving improperly connotes behavior that departs from customary mores. It is conduct that is shameful because it offends against custom. Paul may specifically have had in mind behavior that did not correspond to the standards of the Christian community with regard to sexual behavior (cf. 7:36; 12:23). The scribe who produced 𝔓⁴⁶, the oldest textual witness to 1 Corinthians, unaccountably wrote *ouk euschēmonoi*, "does not behave with decorum," and placed it after "is not conceited" (v. 4).

That love does not seek its own interests *(ou zētei ta heautēs)* echoes an earlier exhortation (10:24; cf. Phil 2:4) that Paul had supported with an appeal to his own prestige (10:33). Accentuating this aspect of love is particularly important in a community whose members boast of their own gifts at the expense of others (chs. 12, 14).

it does not get carried away in anger, nor does it calculate evil: That love does not get carried away in anger *(ou paroxynetai,* hapax in Paul; used of God in the LXX, cf. Deut 1:34; Hos 8:5; Zech 10:3) suggests that the one who has love does not succumb to any sort of irate self-justification. Noting the use of the verb in the LXX, some commentators suggest that Paul may have in mind a kind of anger that leads to murmuring against God (cf. Num 14:11; 16:30; 20:24; Deut 9:7, 8; 31:20; Ps 9:25). If so, this negative qualification might evoke the Exodus experience exploited by Paul in 10:1-13.

The statement that love does not calculate evil *(ou logizetai;* cf. Prov 25:21-22) makes use of a commercial term sometimes used in political discourse. Following on the mention of being carried away in anger it may be a subtle reminder that vengeance belongs to the Lord alone (cf. Rom 12:19 with its citation of Deut 32:35; 1 Thess 4:6 with its allusion to Ps 94:1).

6. *it does not rejoice in lawlessness, but rejoices together in truth:* Paul's eighth and final disavowal is emphasized by means of a contrast, "rejoices in truth," that leads the positive characterization of love in v. 7. The antithetical structure of v. 6 together with the parallelism of the following verse suggests that v. 6b is to be read with v. 6a. The antithesis focuses on lawlessness and truth.

Lawlessness *(adikia)* is a major theme in Paul's letter to the Romans (1:18, 29; 2:8; 3:5; 6:13; 9:14), but it is not otherwise mentioned in 1 Corinthians. This letter has much to say about knowledge but little about truth *(alētheia).* "Truth" must be taken in the biblical sense of fidelity. That love does not rejoice in lawlessness introduces into the encomium on love the idea of justice. Paul's paean on love suggests that love implies the biblical notion of "justice," right relationships with God and other people. Love implies a commitment to justice. Love finds its joy in the fidelity of God.

For the importance of joy in Pauline paraenesis see Rom 12:12; Phil 2:1-2; 1 Thess 3:9; 5:16. There is the suggestion of celebration or at least of intense joy in Paul's call for rejoicing in the truth. The compound *(synchairei,* a compound with *syn-,* cf. 12:26) implies mutual joy and a more intense experience than a simple rejoicing (cf. Phil 2:17-18).

7. *it bears everything:* The final affirmations are characterized by their rhythm and paronomasia (the fourfold occurrence of *panta,* "all;" cf. vv. 2-3). Rarely

found in literary Greek, the verb *stegō* ("bears") can have different meanings. Some would have it that Paul intends to affirm that love protects all (so Camille Focant) or that love hides everything in the sense of covering evil with silence (see *TLNT* 3:290), but the verb also means to "bear with," "endure" (cf. 1 Thess 3:1, 5). Paul is an example of someone who bears everything (see 9:12). This is neither masochism nor mere passivity. It is a matter of being ready to put up with difficulties and even evil (cf. 6:7) for the sake of the gospel and the good of God's people. The idea that love bears everything represents to some extent Paul's version of the love of enemies (cf. Rom 12:20-21).

believes everything: The mention of faith and hope in v. 7 anticipates the summarizing conclusion of v. 13. Before affirming the superiority of love over faith and hope Paul speaks of the relationship between love and faith and hope, the traditional characteristics of an authentic Christian life. That love believes everything in no wise implies a naïve credulity; neither does the affirmation that love hopes everything imply a naïve optimism.

Faith and hope are to be seen in the light of Paul's rich theological understanding of these terms. He frequently links love with faith (Gal 5:6; 1 Thess 3:6; 5:8; Phlm 5). Sometimes it is linked with hope as well (13:13; cf. 1 Thess 1:3; 5:8). Faith is always cited in the first place, since faith is the ground of love. Conversely, says Paul in v. 7b, real love implies total faith.

Both faith and love are extolled in the tradition of Hellenistic Judaism (e.g., *Jub.* 17:18; *2 Enoch* 66:6), but Paul's understanding of these qualities differs significantly from that of Hellenistic Judaism. Relating them to one another, Paul has given each a novel and specific configuration. Faith is not only faith in the creed, although it is that (see 15:3-5); it is not only faith in the power of God to accomplish the extraordinary, although it is that (see 12:9; 13:2). Faith is a total acceptance of and orientation to God. In the context of 1 Corinthians faith is a matter of finding one's self-definition in the saving power of God, which is revealed in the cross of Christ (see 1:18-25). The exposition of this understanding of faith has polemical undertones in 1 Corinthians insofar as Paul takes issue with those who are puffed up because of their knowledge *(gnōsis).*

hopes everything: Hope is the eschatological complement of faith. It looks to the fulfillment of salvation in the parousia and the coming of the kingdom. In 1 Corinthians Paul's expression of hope relates argumentatively to those who deem the Spirit to be fully operative in the gifts they presently enjoy, to the denigration of the gifts enjoyed by others. This is the burden of chs. 12–14, for which the paean on love provides a theological orientation. With its focus on the parousia and the resurrection of the dead (ch. 15) hope confronts those who deny the resurrection of the dead (15:12).

Love, faith, and hope form a triad that defines authentic Christian existence. Love is the expression of faith and hope. According to Söding love confirms in its reference to God, Christ, and humankind everything that faith and hope recognize and confess as the ground of their obedient confidence (*Das Liebesgebot* 141).

endures everything: The last of the "all" series complements the first; semantically it is similar to the third. Not only does love imply a readiness to endure evil for the sake of the gospel; it actually entails real suffering. Endurance implies perseverance even in the midst of the tribulations of the final times (cf. Rom 12:12; 1 Thess 1:3). Love provides the power to endure this suffering.

7. A Unique Gift (13:8–14:1a)

8. Love never comes to an end; but prophecies will pass away; tongues will cease; knowledge will pass away. 9. For we know in part and we prophesy in part. 10. When the end comes the partial will pass away. 11. When I was a child I spoke as a child, I thought as a child, I counted as a child. When I became a man I abandoned childish ways. 12. For now we see by means of a mirror with a dim picture; then we will see face to face. Now I know in part; then I will know just as I have been known. 13. Now then there remain faith, hope, and love, these three. The greatest of these is love. 14:1. Strive for love.

INTERPRETATION

Mention of love at the outset of v. 8 and at the conclusion of v. 13 and in 14:1 serves as an *inclusio* that defines the pericope as a literary unit with love as its topic. The unit completes the chiastic structure of ch. 13; vv. 8-13 correspond to vv. 1-3. Both units reflect on the value of the charisms in comparison with love. They proclaim the singular importance of love as God's gift par excellence.

The use of contrast is a significant feature of the framing units. Paul's antithetical comparison of love with the gifts of prophecy, tongues, and knowledge reminds us of the ancients' use of *priamel,* a literary form in which something that is of most value is measured against things of lesser value. In the Hellenistic literary encomium, of which 1 Corinthians 13 is a good example, the use of comparison *(sygkrisis)* is a common stylistic feature. The stages of human development and the reflection in a mirror are striking similes employed by Paul to provide the kind of verve that the rhetoricians of old achieved in their encomia by means of comparison.

Love. Paul's vision of love is rooted in the tradition of Hellenistic Judaism. That Paul typically uses the noun *agapē* rather than the verb *agapan* in his discourse on love places him within the tradition of Hellenistic

Judaism (see Philo, 4 Maccabees; cf. the Qumran scrolls). Paul's understanding of love is, however, different from Hellenistic Judaism's notion of it. Within Hellenistic Judaism love appears in catalogues of virtues, often in the form of sibling love or friendship love (see Siegfried Wibbing, *Die Tugend- und Lasterkataloge*). In Hellenistic Judaism love is an ethical and religious reality understood within the context of Hellenistic psychology and ethics. For Paul love is not so much a virtue as it is eschatological power, the gift of God poured out into the very depths of one's being (Rom 5:5).

In this respect Paul's notion of love is also quite different from the synoptists' understanding of love. In the synoptic tradition "love" is typically a verb *(agapan)* whose meaning is ethical. In the synoptics "love" is often explained in reference to Lev 19:18. The synoptic discourse on love is halakhic in nature rather than theological. The synoptic pericope on the great commandment (Matt 22:34-40; Mark 12:28-34; Luke 10:25-28) situates the twofold commandment of love within the context of a discourse on the *halakah.* Jesus' logion on love is a response to a question about the meaning of the Torah. Similarly legal in tone are those passages in which the tradition preserves a memory of Jesus talking about those whom his disciples should love (Matt 5:38-48; Luke 6:27-36; 10:29-37).

Paul's discourse on love is theological. He does not list love within a series of virtues; he separates love from the other gifts of God. He does not define love with regard to one or another commandment of the Law. He does not digress on the object of love; rather he uses a striking series of contrasts (permanence/transitoriness, partial/full reality, infancy/ adulthood, oblique/direct vision) to underscore the eschatological character of *agapē.* Four times Paul writes about "the partial" *(to ek merous,* vv. 9-10, 12), which he contrasts with fullness *(to teleion,* v. 10).

In 1 Cor 13:8-13 Paul underscores the eschatological character of love. The preceding section (vv. 4-7), with a characterization of love in language otherwise used of God, emphasized the divine quality of love. The love of which Paul writes in 1 Corinthians 13 is a gift beyond compare (13:13) because it is the Spirit of God at work. Paul's placing love at the heart of a rhetorical digression within a macro-chiasm that speaks of the life of the church indicates that for him the primary locus of love is the common life of the church. It is love that makes the life of the church possible.

Faith, Hope, and Love. Christian tradition has taken hold of 1 Cor 13:13 in such a way as to make "faith, hope, and love" its classic description of the Christian life. Roman Catholic theology considers faith, hope, and love to be the three theological virtues. The triad appears in the NT in this sequence only in 1 Cor 13:13. The classic triad is, in fact, unique. The sequence of the three elements has been organized by Paul in such a way as to place love in the emphatic final position. The rhetorical "these three" makes it clear that 1 Cor 13:13 is an *ad hoc* composition.

The three elements of the triad, faith, hope, and love, appear together in only one other NT writing, namely, in 1 Thessalonians (see 1 Thess 1:3; 5:8). In both 1 Thess 1:3 and 1 Thess 5:8 "hope" appears in the emphatic and final position. Hope was the reality that Paul needed to emphasize in writing to the Thessalonians who had been shaken by the death of some of their number. The needs of the Corinthians were different. They were a community torn by a spirit of factionalism and the disdain of some by others within the community. So Paul writes to them about love, whose proper object, if one need be specified, is other members of the Christian assembly (cf. 1 Thess 3:12; 4:9-10).

The triad of faith, hope, and love adequately describes Christian existence. The way Paul deals with the imagery of military armor in 1 Thess 5:8 (cf. Isa 59:17) shows that both forms of the triad, that is, the sequence of 1 Thessalonians as well as the sequence of 1 Corinthians, are Pauline constructions suited to the respective rhetorical purposes of each of the letters.

Among the three elements of the triad there is a particularly close relationship between faith and love. The essential description of the Christian life, the breastplate in Paul's panoply, is "faith and love." With regard to existence in Christ Jesus faith working through love is the defining reality (Gal 5:6). The Christian's relationship with God expresses itself and is realized in his or her relationships with other members of the community, ultimately with all humankind.

NOTES

8. *Love never comes to an end; but prophecies will pass away; tongues will cease; knowledge will pass away:* Having previously used the verb *piptō,* "comes to an end," (literally "falls") in the metaphorical sense of "to die" (10:8), Paul brings his (positive) description of love to closure with a brief characterization that concludes his personified description of love. Love does not die. In similar fashion 1 Esdras' encomium on truth professes the permanence of truth (1 Esdr 4:38). The trait of immortality introduces Paul's evocative description of the eschatological quality of love and recalls the eternity of God (cf. 4 Ezra 7:33-34) whose traits provide the horizon against which vv. 4-7 were to be read.

The temporal transcendence of love contrasts with the temporality of the gifts of prophecy, tongues, and knowledge, charisms enjoyed by Paul but powers of little worth if love is not present (13:1-2). Even the charism of prophecy, a gift superior to the gift of speaking in tongues (14:5) and one worth striving for (14:1), will pass away. The charism of speaking in tongues will cease (*pausontai,* hapax in Paul). These gifts stand under an eschatological reservation; they will pass away (*katargēthēsontai, katargēthēsetai;* cf. 1:28,

2:6; 6:13; 15:24, 26). The four occurrences of "pass away," *katargeō,* in the pericope (vv. 8[2x], 10, 11) place the charisms within the perspective of the impending eschaton.

9. *For we know in part and we prophesy in part:* Another characteristic of charisms
is that they are given and exercised by each charismatic only partially (*ek merous,* "in part"). No one fully possesses any of the charismatic gifts, given as
the Spirit wills (12:11). Four times Paul uses the verb "to pass away" to stress
the temporary character of the charisms; he uses *ek merous* four times (vv.
9[2x], 10, 12) to underscore their limited character. On knowledge as a partial
reality see also 8:2, where Paul similarly relativizes knowledge with respect
to love.

10. *When the end comes the partial will pass away:* The ideas of being only partial
and being limited in time come together in Paul's principal clause, "the partial will pass away" *(to ek merous katargēthēsetai).* Some textual witnesses (D,
the medieval manuscripts, and the Syriac versions) accentuate the contrast
between this limited situation and ultimate finality by putting "then" *(tote)*
before the principal clause. Even without the additional adverb the contrast
is clear. *To teleion* provides a sharp contrast with *to ek merous,* "the partial." In
English *to teleion* can be rendered as "the end" or "the perfect." Given the
eschatological thrust of the pericope, it seems useful to render the Greek by
"the end." It is clearly a reference to the eschaton.

11. *When I was a child I spoke as a child, I thought as a child, I counted as a child. When
I became a man I abandoned childish ways:* As so often in 1 Corinthians Paul appeals to an *ethos* argument to make his point. Paul is an adult. His adult behavior contrasts with his behavior as a child whether in speaking, thinking,
or doing his sums. The fivefold use of "child" *(nēpios)* provides a vivid contrast with his state as an adult male *(anēr).* The gender-specific "man" denotes
a mature human male; the "child" is only an infant. Etymologically the Greek
term suggests someone who is not yet able to speak.

In classical and Hellenistic Greek "child" was often used metaphorically
to describe someone who is childish, silly, or foolish. This is not Paul's meaning; he simply wants to capture the partial human development of someone
(himself in his *ethos* appeal) who is only beginning to speak, think, and enu-
merate. Paul describes himself as a child in 1 Thess 2:7 (with a textual problem); more commonly he describes himself as a father (cf. 4:14-16). The
Corinthians, on the other hand, who think of themselves as fully mature (2:6)
are really just infants when it comes to the things of Christ (3:1).

"Abandoned" *(katērgēka,* in the aorist) reprises the verb *katargeō,* previously used to affirm that the use of charisms was "passing away" (vv. 8, 10).
"Childish ways" *(ta tou nepiou)* are literally "the things of the child." Paul is
writing about activities, not objects, hence "childish ways."

12. *For now we see by means of a mirror with a dim picture; then we will see face to face:*
Plutarch ("Isis and Osiris," *Moralia* 382A-C) and other ancients used the metaphor of a mirror and the image on it in a way that is similar to Paul's. They
used the metaphor to express the difficulties encountered by humans who try

to understand the deity. Paul's language, like Plutarch's, may reflect a kind of popular philosophical agnosticism. For Paul the somewhat indistinct image on the mirror contrasts with a face-to-face encounter with God. "Mirror" (*esoptrou*; cf. Jas 1:23) and "dim picture" (*ainigmati*) are hapax in Paul. Paul's imagery is similar to the language of the midrash on Num 12:8. The midrash speaks of speaking clearly (*stoma kata stoma*, "mouth toward mouth"). Speaking clearly is contrasted with speaking "in riddles" (*en ainigmati*). Paul makes effective use of the rhetorical device of contrast. His "face to face" contrasts with "a mirror with a dim picture"; his "then" to "now." His phrasing is elliptical; "we see" (*blepomen*) is not repeated in the second clause.

Now I know in part; then I will know just as I have been known: Repeating the now-then (*arti-tote*) contrast of v. 12a, Paul spells out the implication of his use of the metaphor of the mirror. Paul had previously written about the relative value of partial knowledge in comparison with loving and being known by God in 8:1-3. Now he returns to the theme of knowledge possessed by human beings, including himself (13:2; 14:6). The gift of knowledge is limited in time (12:8; 13:8); it is not possessed by everyone (8:7; cf. 12:11); it is not full knowledge. It is only partial (*ek merous*, 13:9, 12). This partial knowledge contrasts with the knowledge of the eschatological future. In the *tote* clause that speaks of that future "Paul compares his eschatological future with his having been known by God before the foundation of the world and, equally, at the time of his historical call" (Jan Lambrecht, *Pauline Studies* 101). The passive "have been known" (*epegnōsthēn*) is clearly a divine passive. To be known by God, to have the divinely-initiated experience of God is paramount in the religious experience of any charismatically gifted person (cf. 12:6).

13. *Now then there remain faith, hope, and love, these three:* With a rhetorical flourish Paul brings his encomium to its conclusion (cf. 1 Esdr 4:41, where truth is proclaimed as great). Instead of the contrasting "now-then" (*arti-tote*, 2x in v. 12), Paul uses a rhetorical "now then" (*nyni de*). Now is the present moment (cf. LSJ *s. v.*). Faith, hope, and love are the abiding realities of the present moment of salvation (cf. Rom 8:24; 2 Cor 5:7). The triad of faith, hope, and love defines authentic Christian existence.

The triad recalls the conclusion of the previous pericope (13:7), where Paul spoke of the relationship between love and faith and the relationship between love and hope. Faith implies recognition of the lordship of Jesus and God's saving power present in the resurrection. Hope looks to the coming of the kingdom and eschatological fulfillment. Love suggests the dynamism of one's relationship with God, Christ, and other humans. These three elements do not so much indicate different temporal referents for Christian existence (past, future, present) as they define Christian existence in its totality.

Paul's language specifies neither the relationship between love and faith nor that between love and hope. It simply highlights the importance of love. In writing to the Thessalonians (1 Thess 1:3; 5:8) Paul also wrote about faith, hope, and love, but "hope" was in the final and emphatic position in his triad. In 13:13 Paul places the stress on "love." "Love" is placed in the final position (cf. 16:14). Paul underscores his emphasis by adding "these three" (*ta tria tauta).* This rhetorical formula is universally attested in the manuscript tradition, but a few early witnesses ($\mathfrak{P}^{46}$, Clement, Augustine; cf. the Syriac Peshitta) place the formula in a grammatically preferable position before "faith, hope, and love." The formula indicates that Paul is not rehearsing a tradition that spoke of faith, hope, and love, but that he has structured his argument in such a way as to emphasize love (note the anaphoric use of the article in *hē agapē;* BDF 258, 1). Love is the primary focus of his paraenesis (cf. 16:14).

The greatest of these is love: In 12:31 Paul had made reference to the "the greater *(ta meizona)* spiritual gifts"; now he identifies love as "the greatest" *(meizōn,* used as a superlative; cf. BDF 244). Love is a gift of the Spirit, but it is unlike any of the other gifts. It is the greatest of gifts because it is the very power of God at work. In some texts of late Judaism love is described as a gift of God's Spirit *(T. Gad* 4:7). It could be included among God's gifts to his people (1QS 4:5). Paul appears to be heir to this tradition, but he has given it a specific configuration insofar as he has made love the gift of God *par excellence.*

14:1. *Strive for love:* With this exhortation Paul concludes the epilogue to his encomium on love. In antiquity a rhetorical epilogue was expected to summarize the argument that had been developed. Encomia frequently end on a note that urges the imitation of the person or virtue that is praised in the encomium. Paul's exhortation to love summarizes the encomium and serves to articulate its paraenetic purpose. As such it anticipates the letter's final exhortation (16:14), which confirms the deliberative purpose (1:10) of the entire letter. Apart from ch. 13 Paul rarely writes about love in 1 Corinthians. Nonetheless, his paraenetic encomium on love contributes greatly to the exposition of his argument. The exhortation to love confronts those who are puffed up with knowledge (8:1).

FOR REFERENCE AND FURTHER STUDY

Downing, Francis G. "Reflecting the First Century: 1 Corinthians 13:12," *ExpT* 95 (1984) 176–177.

Fishbane, Michael. "Through the Looking Glass: Reflections on Ezek 43:3, Num 12:8 and 1 Cor 13," *HAR* 10 (1986) 63–75.

Gill, David H. "Through a Glass Darkly: A Note on 1 Corinthians 13.12," *CBQ* 25 (1963) 427–429.

Houghton, Myron J. "A Reexamination of 1 Corinthians 13:8-13," *BSac* 153 (1996) 344–356.

Neirynck, Frans. "De Grote Drie. Bij een nieuwe vertaling van I Cor., XIII, 13," *EThL* 39 (1963) 595–615.

Söding, Thomas. *Die Trias Glaube, Hoffnung, Liebe bei Paulus: eine exegetische Studie.* SBS 150. Stuttgart: Katholisches Bibelwerk, 1992.

Weiss, Wolfgang. "Glaube—Liebe—Hoffnung. Zu der Trias bei Paulus," *ZNW* 84 (1993) 196–217.

Wischmeyer, Oda. "Traditionsgeschichtliche Untersuchung der paulinischen Aussagen über die Liebe *(agapē),*" *ZNW* 74 (1983) 222–236.

8. *The Greater Gift of Prophecy* (14:1b-5)

1b. Avidly desire spiritual realities, especially that you might prophesy. 2. For the one who speaks in a tongue speaks not to human beings, but to God. Nobody understands. The one who speaks in a tongue utters mysterious realities by the Spirit. 3. The one who prophesies utters edification, exhortation, and encouragement for people. 4. One who speaks in a tongue builds up the self. The one who prophesies builds up the church. 5. I wish that all of you would speak in tongues, but much more that you might prophesy. One who prophesies is greater than the one who speaks in tongues, except if someone interprets so that the church be built up.

INTERPRETATION

Picking up where he had left off before his digression on love, Paul returns to the topic of the spiritual gifts. The exposition on spiritual gifts in ch. 12 culminated in a final exhortation, "avidly desire the greater gifts" (12:31). The greatest of God's gifts is love, the gift *par excellence,* as Paul demonstrates in ch. 13. Now, in ch. 14, Paul returns to the quest for the greater gifts, explaining to the Corinthians that among the various charisms it is the gift of prophecy that they should particularly seek to have.

The Development of the Argument. Paul's argument is developed according to the customary chiastic pattern in which element A' (ch. 14) corresponds to element A (ch. 12). Chapter 12 discussed the charisms in general. In ch. 14 Paul turns his attention specifically to two gifts of speech. These are the gift of prophecy and the gift of tongues. Between his two treatments of spiritual gifts is sandwiched the rhetorical digression of ch. 13, neatly delineated by an external *inclusio.* The final exhortation of ch. 12 (12:31a) corresponds to the opening exhortation of ch. 14 (14:1b).

The argument Paul systematically develops in ch. 14 is built on what he has previously written. Using a different verb ("avidly desire," *zēloute,* 14:1b) from the one he had used with regard to love ("strive for," *diōkete,* 14:1a), Paul distinguishes the pursuit of love from the pursuit of spiritual realities *(pneumatika).* Love is of a different order from spiritual realities.

Paul's opening exhortation, "avidly desire spiritual realities" *(zēloute de ta pneumatika)* brings the reader back to the subject matter of ch. 12, namely spiritual realities *(pneumatika,* 12:1; cf. 2:13). It likewise recalls the closing exhortation of the chapter, "avidly desire spiritual gifts" *(zēloute de ta charismata,* 12:31a). In ch. 12 Paul developed a theological critique of the notion of spiritual realities by affirming that authentic spiritual realities were, in fact, gifts (12:4, 31). As the apostle returns to the subject of spiritual realities in 14:1 he uses spirit language (*pneuma-*; cf. 14:1, 2, 14, 15[2x], 16, 32, 37; compare 12:1) rather than gift language (*charisma-*, 5x in ch. 12, but absent from ch. 14). The double exhortation of 14:1b-c, "avidly desire spiritual realities, especially that you might prophesy," continues the personal focus of the third list of gifts (12:29-30). That prophesying is a gift for which one should especially strive echoes the notion of a hierarchy of gifts that was present in the second list (12:28).

In the first inventory of charisms (12:8-10) Paul indicated that he was principally concerned with ways of speaking by the gifts of speech at the head of his list (cf. *logos*, "word," 12:8). In ch. 14 the two gifts with which Paul is concerned, prophecy and the gift of tongues, are clearly identified as patterns of speech (see vv. 3 and 2), different ways of speaking. The chapter focuses on ways of speaking. Twenty-four times Paul uses the verb "to speak" *(lalein)*. As Paul begins his exposition (14:3), the verb occurs three times. The entire chapter is a discourse on speech.

The gift of tongues was highly esteemed and avidly desired by the Corinthians. Paul adopts a discursive mode as he explains (note the *gar* in 14:2) why prophecy is a gift superior to the gift of tongues. The criterion for judging the value of spiritual realities is the edification of the church (14:4-5). Paul's imagery is significant. The building motif (*oikodomē* and its cognates) occurs seven times in the chapter, four times in the opening pericope (cf. 14:12, 17, 26). This motif recalls the theme of the church as God's building developed in 3:9-17. As an apostle (12:28) Paul laid the foundation of the church (3:10). His concern is communitarian. He wants the entire community of believers to be built up. In an evaluation of the relative value of the gift of prophecy vis-à-vis the gift of speaking in tongues, building up the church is the primary criterion.

Prophecy. The gift of prophecy is identified as a gift distinct from the gift of speaking in tongues (see note on 12:8) by means of three contrasts. The gift of tongues is God-directed speech; the gift of prophecy is human-directed speech. The one who speaks in tongues utters mysteries; the one who prophesies utters words of encouragement and upbuilding. The one who speaks in tongues builds up the ego; the one who prophesies builds up the church.

Paul urges his addressees to strive for prophecy. His choice of vocabulary is important. In the Greco-Roman world "prophecy" was a highly esteemed mantic experience characterized by trances and other ecstatic phenomena. Paul, however, carefully distinguishes prophecy from the gift of tongues. He may have done so in order to distinguish Christian prophecy from the ecstatic speech forms known throughout the Hellenistic world (cf. 14:22-24), where what Paul describes as speaking in tongues would have been subsumed within the category of prophecy.

For Paul prophecy is a gift of the Spirit that is integral to the life of the church (12:28). It is the only gift that is cited in all four of his lists of charisms (12:10, 28, 29; Rom 12:6). It is the only gift of the Spirit that is cited in 1 Thess 5:19-20. In Paul's enumerated list of charisms (12:28) prophecy is found in second place, after the apostolate and before teaching. Prophecy seems to be a gift without which the church cannot exist (cf. 14:22).

Prophecy is a gift that Paul himself possessed (14:6). He frequently describes himself in terms that recall the biblical prophets. Jeremiah and Deutero-Isaiah seem to have particularly shaped his articulated vision of himself, as the allusions to Isa 52:15 in Rom 15:21; to Isa 49:1 in Gal 1:15; and to Jer 11:20 in 1 Thess 2:4 seem clearly to indicate. In the development of his *ethos* argument in 1 Corinthians Paul does not particularly exploit the model of the biblical prophets. In this letter Paul prefers to use cultural models and his exposition of what it means to be an apostle when he makes an argument based on his own prestige. It may be that scriptural allusions would not have been a particularly effective device to illustrate the stature of the apostle for a community that was largely Hellenistic.

Prophecy, as the etymology indicates, is a matter of speaking on behalf of God, functioning in a sense as God's spokesperson. In 14:3 Paul emphatically identifies exhortation as the characteristic function of prophecy. Two virtual synonyms, "exhortation" and "encouragement," have in Greek an initial "p" sound that links them to one another and to "prophecy." Paul speaks about exhortation and encouragement as the way in which the community is built up. In writing to the Thessalonians he had previously linked exhortation to the building up of the community (1 Thess 5:11; cf. 1 Thess 4:18). In 14:3 he identifies the building up of the community as the purpose to which prophecy is directed. Prophesying builds up the community insofar as the members of the community are "edified," that is, exhorted and encouraged. Paul returns to this idea in 14:31-32 when he urges prophets to speak in turn and listen to one another.

NOTES

1b. *Avidly desire spiritual realities, especially that you might prophesy:* The particle *de* ("and") connects this exhortation with the final words of the encomium on love (14:1a). Parallel with 12:31a, the exhortation completes the *inclusio* that isolates ch. 13 as a single rhetorical unit, thereby confirming the paracletic thrust of the encomium. The exhortation also serves a transitional purpose. It allows Paul to return to the specific issue at hand, namely the exercise of spiritual gifts *(pneumatika)* within the community. Among the spiritual gifts Paul focuses on the gift of prophecy. The comparisons that follow suggest that the expression of a preference for prophecy (note Paul's use of *mallon*, "especially") is in relationship to the Corinthians' desire for the gift of tongues. Avid desire *(zēloute)* for spiritual gifts, of which love is the foundation, should confront the jealousy *(zēlos*, 3:3; cf. 1:10-12; 11:18) that is a source of division within the community.

2. *For the one who speaks in a tongue speaks not to human beings, but to God:* A postpositive *gar* introduces Paul's explanation of why Christians should want to prophesy rather than pursue some other spiritual gift. The rhetorical device of antithesis is used to emphasize that speaking in tongues is speech that is addressed to God rather than to human beings. With regard to speech Paul uses the verb *laleō* as he does throughout the chapter (vv. 2[3x], 3, 4, 5[2x], 6[2x], 9[2x], 11[2x], 13, 18, 19, 21, 23, 27, 28, 29, 34, 35, 39)—twenty-four times in all, beginning with its three occurrences in v. 2. This verb properly means "to talk, chat, prattle, or babble," in contrast with the verb *legō*, "to speak," which would have conveyed the idea that what is spoken is an intelligible communication.

Nobody understands. The one who speaks in a tongue utters mysterious realities by the Spirit: Paul offers this reflection as an explanation (the clause contains an explanatory *gar*) of the idea that the one who speaks in tongues speaks only to God. From the time of Homer and Plato the verb "understands," *(akouei,* literally "to hear") implied hearing with understanding, really listening. Paul's phrasing is elliptical. The implied subject of the verb "utters" *(lalei*, literally "speaks") is "the one who speaks in tongues" (v. 2a), but the subject is not expressed. "Mysterious realities" is the direct object of "utters"; it is the unexpressed but implied object of "understands" *(akouei).*

The reason why other members of the assembly are not able to understand is that the one speaking in tongues utters mysterious realities *(mystēria;* cf. 2:1-16). Notwithstanding their lack of intelligibility Paul places these utterances in a most favorable light. They are mysterious things in the Spirit (cf. 2:1, 7; 13:2; 15:51). Paul's explanatory comment is almost an aside that prepares for the idea developed in the following verse, namely that the one who prophesies speaks for edification's sake.

3. *The one who prophesies utters edification, exhortation, and encouragement for people:* An adversative *de* ("but") introduces a statement that is in contrasting parallelism with v. 2a. Paul reprises the language of speaking to people *(anthrōpois lalei)* from the earlier verse. The use of this formulaic expression results in a sentence that might be more literally rendered "the one who prophesies speaks to people edification, exhortation, and encouragement." The repetition is for emphasis' sake. Edification, exhortation, and encouragement are set over and against the mysterious realities spoken by one who has the gift of tongues. With emphasis, paraenesis is identified as the characteristic function of prophecy (cf. 14:31; see Ulrich B. Müller, *Prophetie und Predigt* 24).

"Exhortation" *(paraklēsin)* and "encouragement" *(paramythian)* are virtual synonyms, linked to "edification" *(oikodomēn)* by means of a paratactic *kai*. Exhortation-encouragement (the second *kai* is epexegetical) is the way in which prophecy builds up the community. The initial "p" of both *paraklēsin* and *paramythian* creates assonance with "one who prophesies" *(ho prophēteuōn)*. Gerhard Dautzenberg (*Urchristliche Prophetie* 298) has opined that the up-building of the community and exhortation are the result, but not the object or purpose of prophecy.

4. *One who speaks in a tongue builds up the self. The one who prophesies builds up the church:* The third contrast between speaking in tongues and prophesying highlights the motif of edification, building up the church, a theme Paul picks up from the previous verse. Developing his thoughts on the importance of prophecy, he exploits the idea of edification (the noun in vv. 5, 12; the cognate verb *oikodomeō* in vv. 4, 17). The imagery is significant. All but five of Paul's uses of the words formed from the root *oikodomē-* occur in the Corinthian correspondence (cf. Eph 2:21; 4:12, 16, 29). "Edification" can be taken in a metaphorical sense, but the metaphor must not be overlooked. The image is that of a building, an image that Paul used of the church at Corinth in 3:9-15. Just as the foundational gift of love builds up the church (8:1), so the exercise of the individual charisms, the active expressions of love, builds up the church. Among the charisms the exercise of the gift of prophecy particularly contributes to the building up of the church. An authentic charism, prophecy is a manifestation of the Spirit that builds up the church. In 14:4 the church stands in contrast with the self *(heauton).*

5. *I wish that all of you would speak in tongues, but much more that you might prophesy:* Paul echoes v. 1 ("that you might prophesy," *hina prophēteuēte*). He explains that his preference for the exercise of the gift of prophecy does not imply that he disdains the gift of speaking in tongues (*glōssais,* in the plural; compare with the use of the singular in vv. 2, 4). The gift of tongues is exercised in the power of the Spirit (v. 2c). No one should disdain the Spirit of God (cf. 1 Thess 4:8). The situation is not one of either-or. The gift of tongues is a desirable gift, but the gift of prophecy is more advantageous to the church. More than one spiritual gift could be given to an individual, as they were to Paul (13:1-2; 14:6, 14). No single person, however, enjoys all the charisms (cf. 12:7-11).

One who prophesies is greater than the one who speaks in tongues: Having introduced the idea of a hierarchy among the charisms in 12:28-29, 31, Paul now says that the one who exercises the gift of prophecy is greater than the one who exercises the gift of tongues. This is his specific concern. Having explained in vv. 2-4 why he wants the Corinthians to strive for the gift of prophecy, Paul offers as his concluding and summarizing remark that the exercise of the gift of prophesying is superior to speaking in tongues.

Speaking in tongues is, relatively speaking, an inferior gift. Its lesser status vis-à-vis the gift of prophecy had already been intimated in the three lists of charisms in ch. 12. On all three lists the gift of prophecy was placed before the gift of speaking in tongues (12:10, 28, 29). On the second list the gift of prophecy is cited as second *(deuteron)* among the gifts, while the gift of tongues is last on the list. The gift of tongues is not even cited in the list found in Rom 12:6-8, but this may be due to the situation of that church or to Paul's unfamiliarity with the Roman community.

except if someone interprets so that the church be built up: The criterion by which spiritual gifts are to be judged is the building up of the church. The exercise of the gift of speaking in tongues contributes to the upbuilding of the church only if that gift is accompanied by another gift, the gift of the interpretation of tongues. The correlation between these two gifts is another indication of the inferiority of the gift of tongues, but that is not Paul's point here. Here he mentions that the gift of tongues is conducive to the upbuilding of the church if one condition be met, namely that there be an interpreter available. Of itself the gift of tongues does not build up the church. Speaking in tongues serves the church only to the extent that it is exercised in the presence of someone who has the gift of the interpretation of tongues (12:10, 30).

The verb "interprets" (*diermēneuē*) has an indeterminate subject, expressed only in the inflection of the verb. It may be that in some cases the interpreter was the person who spoke in tongues. Grammatically that would seem to be the better reading of Paul's text, but the principle of the allocation of gifts (12:4-11) implies that the interpreter would ordinarily be someone other than the one who speaks in tongues (cf. 14:27). In any case Paul's "except" clause indicates that the mysterious sayings uttered by those who spoke in tongues were not always interpreted (v. 28). Only if these sayings are interpreted do they edify.

FOR REFERENCE AND FURTHER STUDY

Aune, David E. *Prophecy in Early Christianity and the Ancient Mediterranean World.* Grand Rapids: Eerdmans, 1983.

Engelbrecht, Edward A. "'To Speak in a Tongue': The Old Testament and Early Rabbinic Background of a Pauline Expression," *CJ* 22 (1996) 295–302.

Grudem, Wayne A. *The Gift of Prophecy in the New Testament and Today.* Eastbourne: Kingsway, 1988.

_____. *The Gift of Prophecy in 1 Corinthians.* Lanham, Md.: University Press of America, 1982.

Murphy-O'Connor, Jerome. *Paul on Preaching.* London: Sheed and Ward, 1964, 104–145.

9. A Trilogy of Cultural Analogies (14:6-12)

6. Now then, brothers and sisters, if I come to you speaking in tongues how do I benefit you if I do not speak to you with a revelation, knowledge, prophecy, or teaching? 7. If lifeless instruments, whether the flute or the harp, emit a sound that is not distinct, how can the sound of the

flute or the sound of the harp be appreciated? 8. And if the trumpet emits an uncertain sound, who will prepare for war? 9. Similarly with you, if you do not utter a clear word with your tongue, how can what is spoken be understood? You are speaking in the air. 10. There may be, for example, a wide variety of languages in the world, and no one of them is not heard. 11. If I do not really know the meaning of a phoneme I am a foreigner to the one who is speaking, and the one who is speaking is a foreigner as far as I am concerned. 12. Similarly with you, seeing that you are zealous for spiritual realities, strive to excel in the building up of the church.

INTERPRETATION

Verses 6-12 make up the central element in this chiastically structured unit of 1 Corinthians (14:1-19). With its reference to musical instruments and to the gifts of revelation, knowledge, and prophecy the pericope recalls the opening words of Paul's digression on love (13:1-2). In typical fashion Paul offers three examples to demonstrate why it is that sounds must be sufficiently heard and properly distinguished if they are to be of benefit to people. The analogies are the flute and the harp, the trumpet, and foreign languages. In appealing to musical instruments Paul makes use of a motif found in the classical rhetorical treatment of inspiration. He urges the Corinthians to reflect on their own previous experience when they had engaged in idol worship. They had raised questions about spiritual phenomena (12:1). Among them speaking in tongues was one of the most important. In describing this kind of cultic experience, in which religious frenzy had a role (cf. 12:3), Paul's contemporaries also wrote about the sounds of the flute, the harp, and the trumpet.

A Musical Interlude. Paul himself does not often talk about music and musical instruments. He does so, however, in 1 Corinthians 13–14. The context of his discussion is the Christian assembly, presumably gathered for a kind of symposium after the celebration of eucharist (11:17-26). Judaism had restricted the use of public music on the sabbath (cf. *m. Beṣa* 5:2) and the public use of music was further limited in imperial times, but music was used in the synagogue. The sounds of music appealed to the affect of those gathered and contributed to a holistic learning experience in the synagogue. Early Christians most likely profited from this Jewish experience (14:15, 26; cf. Matt 26:30; Mark 14:26; Acts 16:25; Eph 5:19; Col 3:16). That the book of Revelation exploits liturgical motifs as it does, with hymns and music (Rev 5:8; 14:2; 15:2), suggests that music and song were also part of the experience of Christians who gathered for worship.

Under the empire, with the demise of levitical musical guilds similar to those in other Near Eastern cultures, the use of musical instruments was banned from the synagogue. This may explain Paul's reference to "lifeless instruments." The flute and the harp were well known. Paul's biblical tradition was aware that the music of these instruments could be instrumental in effecting an ecstatic experience of prophetic trance (1 Sam 10:5; 2 Kgs 3:15). The silence of the harp signified guilt and punishment (Isa 24:8; Ezek 26:13). The mighty angel in the Book of Revelation pronounces a curse on Babylon, that "the sound of harpists and minstrels and of flutists and trumpeters will be heard in you no more" (Rev 18:22). The sound of the pipes was, on the other hand, a sign of joy (Matt 11:17; Luke 7:32). The absence of musical sound was a sign of the impending eschaton.

Whether all this would be known to Paul's Hellenistic correspondents cannot be known for certain, but some suggestion to the effect that Paul's reflection has eschatological overtones might be gleaned from his reference to the trumpet. The trumpet is the only musical instrument that Paul mentions more than once. It is an instrument he associates with the coming of the eschaton (15:52, where both the noun and the related verb appear, and 1 Thess 4:16; cf. Rev 1:10; 4:1; 8:2, 6, 13; 9:14). In the biblical tradition the sound of the trumpet was an invitation to battle (Num 10:9; Josh 6:4-20; Judg 3:27; 6:34; 1 Sam 13:3; Isa 18:3; 27:13; 58:1; Jer 4:5, 19, 21; 51:27).

When dealing with mantic inspiration Hellenistic authors contemporary with Paul referred to the sound of music. Music and musical instruments are a feature of the classical rhetorical topos on "inspiration." Music was an important element in the rhetorical *heurēsis* of those who wrote and spoke about this topic. The philosopher Plutarch wrote about the lyre, the flute, the trumpet, and the harp ("Oracles at Delphi," *Moralia* 404F). The geographer Strabo writes at length about the role of music and the importance of the flute in symposia and those religious rites in which enthusiastic inspiration has a role to play (see *Geography* 10.3.9-19). For Strabo music puts us in touch with the divine:

> Music, which includes dancing as well as rhythm and melody, at the same time, by its artistic beauty, brings us in touch with the divine, and this for the following reason; for although it has been well said that human beings then act most like the gods when they are doing good to others, yet one might better say, when they are happy; and such happiness consists of rejoicing, celebrating festivals, pursuing philosophy, and engaging in music. (*Geography* 10.3.9)

Apart from whatever intertextual allusions may be inferred from the set of musical instruments cited by Paul, the analogy is meaningful. Indistinct sounds, whether coming from fine musical instruments like the flute or the harp or from a pedestrian instrument like the trumpet, do not affect those who hear them. Neither sympathetic vibration nor a rallying to the battle cry is effected when the sounds of the instruments are muffled. So it is with the sounds produced by those speaking in tongues. Not understood, they do not produce an effect in those who hear them. As far as others are concerned those who speak in tongues might as well be speaking into thin air.

A Polyglot Culture. Hellenistic rhetors valued the use of the literary device of comparison *(sygkrisis)* as a way of making their point. Having used the comparison of musical instruments to make his point about the relative lack of value of the gift of tongues, Paul uses the analogy of the different languages spoken in the world to make a similar point. The analogy was apropos to the social situation in Corinth. In Paul's day the city was a provincial capital, under the influence of Hellenistic culture and Roman politics. It was located on the intersection of two major trade routes, one going north and south, the other going east and west. The presence of various sanctuaries in the city underscores the influence of a wide range of cultures on metropolitan Corinth. Transient merchants, some of whom may have had to winter in Corinth (cf. 16:6), exposed the city's population to a variety of languages. The Greek and Latin tongues would have been known to various segments of the population. Paul himself was a bit of a linguist. He wrote in Greek, read Hebrew, and probably spoke some Aramaic.

In Paul's use of the experience of different languages to make a point about the gift of tongues there is a trace of an appeal to Hellenistic hybris. Paul speaks of the experience of different languages in the world, *en kosmō,* implying not so much cosmopolitan culture as properly structured and well-ordered society. The "foreigner" *(barbaros)* of whom Paul speaks was one whose tongue betrayed him or her as such. The onomatopoeia of the word suggests stumbling and stammering in speech. It was used to describe one who could not speak Greek properly, hence the "foreigner" (see Strabo, *Geography* 14.2.28; Herodotus, *Persian Wars* 2.158; etc.). "Foreigners" were deemed to be uneducated and uncultured. Some Hellenistic Jewish writings use *barbaros* as an expression of disdain (e.g., 2 Macc 2:21; *Ep. Arist.* 122), not to mention the English language derivative, "barbarian."

NOTES

6. *Now then, brothers and sisters, if I come to you speaking in tongues how do I benefit you if I do not speak to you with a revelation, knowledge, prophecy, or teaching?* Paul begins a new moment in his appeal with a rhetorical "now then" *(nyn de)* and the vocative "brothers and sisters." The direct appeal suggests that his remarks are addressed to the community as a whole, not merely to the hybrists

and/or those who had a disordered desire for the gift of tongues. That Paul was sent to the Corinthians is a given (9:2). That he came to the Corinthians as a tongue speaker is not so readily apparent, but Paul thrice (13:1; 14:6, 18) affirms that speaking in tongues was characteristic of his mode of presence among the Corinthians. While with the Corinthians he was one of the tongue-speakers; hence he was well qualified to speak to them as his brothers and sisters.

Paul, in fact, could more readily speak in tongues than could some of the other glossolalists (14:18). Using himself as an example he was able to reaffirm the merely relative value of the gift of tongues. His presence among the Corinthians was advantageous to them not because he was a glossolalist but because he could offer them revelation, knowledge, prophecy, or teaching. Paul's argument with its *ethos* appeal and the argument from advantage (*ōphelēsō*; cf. 13:3) is cast in the mode of deliberative rhetoric.

On revelation, knowledge, and prophecy see the notes on 13:1-3. To these three Paul adds teaching, repeating the conjunction "or" (*ē*) three times (polysyndeton). Of itself "teaching" (*didachē*) can be active (the act of teaching) or passive (what is taught, the content of teaching). Here the sense is passive even though "teaching" is the result of charismatic activity. Teaching does not appear on Paul's first list of charisms (12:8-10), but it is on both the enumerated list (12:28) and the personal list of charisms (12:29-30). As the third of the enumerated charisms teaching was very important in the life of the church (cf. Rom 12:6; Eph 4:11). Distinct from prophecy, teaching involved a new interpretation of the word of God, whether in catechesis or in the explanation of Scripture (cf. J.D.G. Dunn, *Jesus and the Spirit; A Study of the Religious and Charismatic Experience of Jesus and the First Christians as Reflected in the New Testament* [Philadelphia: Westminster, 1975] 237–238). Apart from 14:6 (cf. 4:17) Paul does not claim for himself the charism of teaching, but he was revered as a teacher by later Christian tradition (cf. Col 1:28; 3:16; 1 Tim 2:7; 2 Tim 4:11). Certainly he exposited the Scriptures, especially for the benefit of the Corinthians (9:10; 10:11). In this light it may be that Paul is here alluding to his work of scriptural interpretation among the Corinthians.

7–8. *If lifeless instruments, whether the flute or the harp, emit a sound that is not distinct, how can the sound of the flute or the sound of the harp be appreciated? And if the trumpet emits an uncertain sound, who will prepare for war?* Paul uses a rare adversative conjunction, *homōs* (cf. Gal 3:15; John 12:42), to introduce his metaphor. His language is unusual. "Lifeless" (*apsycha*) is hapax in the NT. "Flute," "play the flute," "harp," and "play the harp" are hapax in Paul and rare in the NT. In discussing the phenomenon of ecstatic inspiration Plutarch also talks about these instruments, as well as the trumpet and the lyre (cf. 14:15b), to wit, "Wherefore it is not possible . . . to make a cylinder in motion behave in the manner of a sphere or a cube, nor a lyre like a flute, nor a trumpet like a harp. No, the use of each thing artistically is apparently no other than its natural use" ("Oracles at Delphi," *Moralia* 404F). When compared with Plutarch, Paul's metaphor seems to bear upon the different sounds of each of the instruments. "The sound that is distinct" is literally "a distinction in sounds" *(diastolēn tois phthoggois).* "Be appreciated" is *gnōsthēsetai,* literally "be known." "Uncertain" *(adēlos)* is hapax in Paul, as is "prepare for battle" *(paraskeuasetai eis polemon).*

9. *Similarly with you, if you do not utter a clear word with your tongue, how can what is spoken be understood? You are speaking in the air:* Paul clarifies the referent of his metaphors, making sure that the Corinthians understand that the metaphors refer to them, that is, to those among them who speak in tongues. His language reflects the language of his metaphor. "Utter" is *dōte* ("give"), rendered as "emit" in v. 7; "understood" is *gnōsthēsetai* ("be known"), rendered as "be appreciated" in v. 7. The tongue (with an instrumental *dia*) is compared with a sound-producing instrument; "what is spoken," with a passive form of the verb *(to laloumenon),* is parallel with "sound of the flute" and "sound of the harp," similarly expressed in the form of passive participles. Paul's use of "tongue" provides a point of reference for the understanding of his metaphor. He answers his rhetorical question strikingly. If what is said cannot be understood it might as well be said into the air, where no one can hear. In 9:16 Paul had used sparring in the air as a metaphor for futility; speaking in the air is of the same order. "Clear" *(eusēmos)* is hapax in the NT.

10-11. *There may be, for example, a wide variety of languages in the world, and no one of them is not heard. If I do not really know the meaning of a phoneme I am a foreigner to the one who is speaking, and the one who is speaking is a foreigner as far as I am concerned:* Paul plays with the meaning of "sound," *phōnē* in this passage. The word *phōnē* essentially means "sound," but one of its meanings is language or dialect (so, Aeschylus, Thucydides). That would seem to be the meaning of the term in Paul's use. "Not heard" *(aphōnon)* is literally "without sound" *(a-phōnon;* cf. 12:2). Rendering the term as "not heard" seems most apropos to the cultural situation of Paul's letter. The "meaning of a phoneme" is literally the "power of sound."

"Power" *(dynamis)* was used by Plato and others to describe the meaning of a word. "Phoneme" seems the preferable rendering of *tēs phōnēs* since it evokes a sound byte. Paul's use of "if . . . really" *(ean oun)* suggests that he was well aware that he could not speak and understand all languages. His inability to understand another's language erects a barrier, at least of communication, between the two. With regard to social differences, whether they be of gender, class, or ethnicity, as here, Paul shows himself to be an egalitarian as he does throughout the letter (cf. 1:20-24; 7:1-40).

12. *Similarly with you, seeing that you are zealous for spiritual realities, strive to excel in the building up of the church:* Again Paul draws the inference from his own example (cf. v. 9). The *captatio benevolentiae* leads him to acknowledge the zeal of the Corinthians for spiritual realities. Earlier he had urged them to strive after the more important gift of prophecy (14:2); now he urges them to pursue spiritual realities in keeping with the standard by which all spiritual gifts must be measured, namely the building up of the church. "To excel" is *hina perisseuēte,* "to abound," "to have an advantage."

10. *Praying with Full Participation* (14:13-19)

13. Wherefore let the one who speaks in a tongue pray that he or she might interpret. 14. For if I pray in a tongue my spirit prays and my mind is useless. 15.What then? I will pray in the spirit, and I will pray in mind. I will sing praise in the spirit, and I will sing praise in mind. 16. Otherwise, if you utter a blessing in the spirit how would the one who occupies the place of an outsider say "Amen" to your thanksgiving? He or she does not know what you are saying. 17. You may make a good thanksgiving, but the other person is not built up. 18. I give thanks to God; more than all of you I speak in tongues. 19. But in the assembly I prefer to utter five words with my mind so that I instruct others rather than utter an untold number of words in a tongue.

In this reflection on the gift of tongues Paul clearly has in mind the use of the charism when the community comes together for worship. Several features of the discourse point to the liturgical setting. Paul writes about songs of praise (v. 15), using language that does not appear in any other passage of this or any other of his letters. He writes of the possibility of another saying "Amen" to a blessing that he considers to be a prayer of thanksgiving (v. 16). He writes about catechizing others when the community gathers together (v. 19). The three forms of prayer that Paul mentions—intercessory prayer, songs of praise, and thanksgiving—indicate some of the various expressions of worship used in early Christian liturgical assemblies. Joined with catechetical activity, they suggest that the Christian symposium was rather like the Jewish synagogue service. When Paul writes about the various forms of liturgical prayer his paramount concern is that it take place with a speech act that allows for full participation of the assembly.

Self-Reflection. From his cultural analogies Paul draws a strong inference, namely that the Corinthians should pray for the gift of the interpretation of tongues. The point is so important that Paul develops a different kind of argument in support of it. His argument is based on a kind of discursive reasoning process in which he features himself as an example—again the *ethos* appeal!

Paul reflects on the modality of his own speech (14:14-19). He insists that he has the gift of tongues and the ability to speak in tongues. The conditional clause of v. 14 is an acknowledgment that Paul can speak in tongues. The apostle uses this gift more than any of the Corinthians do (14:18). There is, nonetheless, something more important than speaking in tongues. That is instructing the people (14:19). A numerical contrast graphically highlights Paul's convictions about the relative value of the gift of tongues and the charism of teaching.

The Corinthians considered the gift of tongues to be highly desirable. Paul does not consider it insignificant. It is a gift of God and an important one (14:2, 5a, 14a), but the criterion for evaluating the use of this gift is its utility for the church. Like all spiritual gifts the gift of tongues should be useful for the church (12:7). If it is to be beneficial it must be accompanied by the gift of the interpretation of tongues (cf. 14:5).

Spirit and Mind. As Paul argues the point that the gift of tongues is useful for the upbuilding of the church if what is spoken in tongues is interpreted, he develops an anthropological reflection. Paul often had the occasion to present aspects of his anthropology in order to counter various excesses within the community (cf. 2:11-15, etc.). In 14:13-19 Paul employs a contrast between "spirit" *(pneuma)* and "mind" *(nous)*. The contrast was well known in the Hellenistic world, where "spirit" was considered to be a faculty superior to that of mind. In the Platonic view of inspiration the mind is somehow displaced or inactive, virtually asleep, when inspiration occurs.

For Paul, unlike the Platonists, such inactivity is problematic. He does not so much argue for the use of reason against the spirit *(pneuma)*, understood as a higher source of knowledge, as he pleads that the spirit and the mind work together. His plea is for the complementarity of spirit and mind in prayer. Ultimately his anthropology is holistic. Its descriptive terminology does not allow for the division of the human person into component principles; rather each of its principal terms speaks of the whole human with respect to one or another aspect of its humanity. In this case Paul underscores the "mind," that is, the human being as a locus of communication with others, as he talks about the one praying in tongues.

Praying in tongues is directed to God (14:2), and that is good. Good Jew that he is, Paul cannot dissociate the relationship to God from the relationship with other human beings. Praying to God in its various liturgical modalities must incorporate or be accompanied by communication with others so that the prayer of the liturgical assembly may be fully meaningful and participatory.

NOTES

13. *Wherefore let the one who speaks in a tongue pray that he or she might interpret:* A strong inferential "wherefore" *(dio)* introduces the paraenesis that Paul draws from his three images. Those who speak in tongues should themselves pray that they might have the power to interpret what has been said in tongues (cf. 14:5b). Paul uses the verb "to pray" *(proseuchesthō)*. As the etymology suggests, this verb connotes prayer directed to God. It generally refers to prayer

in which the name of God is invoked. Often, as here, "to pray" is to make intercessory prayer. True prayer proceeds from the power of the Spirit (cf. Rom 8:23). One need not be particularly concerned about its wording.

Paul has the welfare of the community in mind (cf. vv. 16-17, 19). Therefore he urges that one who prays in a tongue pray that the prayer in tongues be interpreted (for the benefit of the community). According to Iamblicus (ca. 300 C.E.) one who is caught up in the enthusiasm of prophetic inspiration cannot even understand what he or she is saying, so much is he or she enraptured by the power of the predominating deity (cf. *On the Mysteries*, 3.8). This is unacceptable to Paul.

14. *For if I pray in a tongue my spirit prays and my mind is useless:* Paul appears to adopt the language of Hellenism as he establishes a contrast between spirit *(pneuma)* and mind *(nous)*. In popular Hellenistic understanding the spirit was superior to the mind. The spirit is the faculty by which one is in communion with the deity. The mind is an organ of thought that allows for ordinary communication among human beings.

Paul's words imply that praying in tongues is a matter of being somehow enraptured so that the one who prays is taken hold of by an outside force. This external force produces a kind of "enthusiasm" (from *enthousiazō*, "to be possessed by or inspired by the god") that enables anyone who has been taken hold of in this fashion to pray. Since Paul writes of "my spirit" *(to pneuma mou)* and "my mind" *(ho nous mou)*, the opposition is not *(pace* Johannes Weiss, *Der erste Korintherbrief* 327–328, for whom the "spirit" is the apportioned spirit of God) between the divine and the human, but concerns something that is going on within the human. Should Paul pray only in tongues, his mind would be idle. Lest the mind be idle one should pray for the gift of interpreting the prayer in tongues.

15. *What then? I will pray in the spirit, and I will pray in mind. I will sing praise in the spirit, and I will sing praise in mind:* The parallelism between praying in the spirit and praying in the mind corresponds to the mention of the two charisms of v. 13, praying in tongues and the interpretation of tongues. Rather than praying only in the spirit Paul would pray in mind as well. There is a "horizontal" dimension to his prayer as well as a "vertical" dimension. Communal prayer should be such that others can understand.

Apart from the citation of Ps 17:50 [LXX] in Rom 15:9 this is the only time in his correspondence that Paul writes about singing praise (cf. 14:26; comp. Eph 5:19). Etymologically the verb *(psallō)* means "to play the harp." Paul is referring to singing praises to God aloud. In the *Testament of Job* the daughter called Hemera is described as having "spoken ecstatically in the angelic dialect, sending up a hymn to God in accord with the hymnic style of the angels" (*T. Job* 48:3). Sung praise of God, a form of communal prayer, was a feature of the Jewish synagogal service. It seems to have been characteristic of the Christian symposium as well.

16. *Otherwise, if you utter a blessing in the spirit how would the one who occupies the place of an outsider say "Amen" to your thanksgiving? He or she does not know what you are saying:* Additional terms from Paul's liturgical glossary appear in this

verse, namely blessing, thanksgiving, and Amen. "Utter a blessing" (*eulogēs;* cf. 10:16) reflects traditional Jewish usage in which the verb *brk* was especially used of the table blessing. Even within Hellenistic Judaism it seems to have been interchangeable with "give thanks" (cf. Josephus, *Ant.* 8.111; compare *Corp Herm* 1:26, 27), as it is here. The words suggests praise and thanksgiving. "Amen" is a liturgical concluding formula found in the OT (first in Neh 8:6) and Jewish sources (e.g., *m. Ber.* 8:8).

"Occupy the place of" (*anaplēroō ton topon tinos;* cf. BAGD 59.4) is an idiom to Plato, Diodorus Siculus, and Epictetus. Outsiders were not totally excluded from the Christian assembly (cf. vv. 23-24). They would not be able to associate with the prayer of blessing-thanksgiving were it uttered only in tongues. They would not be able to say "Amen," says Paul, because (*epeidē*) they would not understand what is being said (cf. 14:2).

17. *You may make a good thanksgiving, but the other person is not built up:* As Paul continues the theme of thanksgiving (cf. vv. 16, 18) he notes that one may address one's thanksgiving to God well enough (*kalōs eucharisteis*), but that is not the only thing of importance in the Christian assembly. When the Christian community comes together it and its members ought to be built up. Thanksgiving that is addressed to God in the form of an utterance in tongues does not contribute to the building up of others. Neither, one might conclude, does it contribute to the up building of the church.

18. *I give thanks to God; more than all of you I speak in tongues:* The Greek text of this verse is well attested in the manuscript tradition, but the tradition attests to a variety of clarifying emendations. Several majuscules add "my" (*mou*) to "God" (K, L, 326, etc.). Others add a *hoti* as if Paul were giving thanks for his ability to speak in tongues (F, G, and the tradition of the Vetus Latina). 𝔓⁴⁶ adds *hyper,* as if Paul were giving thanks for "all of you." Some manuscripts have "tongues" in the singular (*glōssē*), apparently an accommodation to vv. 13-14, 19, and suggesting that Paul would only speak in one tongue at a time (א, A, D, F, etc.). The majority of medieval manuscripts read the verb "speak" as a participle (*lalōn*), interpreting the text clearly to mean that Paul is talking about his giving thanks in tongues. Stylistically that is acceptable, but this medieval reading would appear to be the result of scribal emendation.

Verses 16-17 speak of someone giving thanks to God while speaking in tongues. The more difficult reading of v. 18, with a second principal verb, is found in א, B, D, F, G, P, and Ψ. As the text is read in these old manuscripts, Paul presents himself not only as one who gives thanks in the assembly (cf. 1:4) but also as one who can speak in tongues (cf. 13:1; 14:6). Indeed, more than others he has received the charismatic gift that allows him to speak in tongues. The self-referential description is a feature of his *ethos* appeal. A peristatic catalogue (4:10-13) indicated that Paul had suffered for the sake of Christ. The argument from his defense presented him as one who was an apostle to the Corinthians (9:2). Now a similar argument presents Paul as someone who, with regard to tongues at least, is even more gifted than the abundantly gifted Corinthians (1:4-7; 4:8).

19. *But in the assembly I prefer to utter five words with my mind so that I instruct others rather than utter an untold number of words in a tongue:* On the whole Paul's
phraseology is at least inelegant. Paul's "prefer" is in Greek "I wish" *(thelō)*,
but "rather" *(mallon)* has been elliptically omitted (BDF 480.4). In the course
of the textual transmission of this verse various scribes tried to clarify Paul's
wording. The preposition "in" *(en)* appears in 𝔓⁴⁶; "by means of" *(dia)* is in the
medieval manuscripts. Some patristic witnesses (Marcion, Pelagius, Ambrosiaster) read *dia ton nomon,* "for the sake of the law," rather than "with my
mind" *(tǭ noi mou),* but reference to the law *(nomos)* is not found in the ancient
Greek manuscripts. The textual variations probably arose on the part of
scribes who read "mind" as a part of the human person rather than as that
element in Paul's holistic anthropology that looks to the person as one who
has a capacity for social communication.

Paul wants to speak as a social being so that he might catechize others.
The "assembly" *(ekklēsia)* is clearly the liturgical assembly, the church gathered for worship. Paul rarely uses the verb "to give oral instruction" *(katēcheō;*
cf. Rom 2:18; Gal 6:6), but here he uses the expression to contrast his speaking in tongues with his didactic activity among the Corinthians (cf. "teaching" in 14:6; compare 12:28, 29). What benefits the community is all-important
as a criterion for his own action (cf. 9:19-22). That there is didactic activity in
the liturgical assembly suggests that there existed some similarity between
the Christian "assembly" and the Jewish "synagogue."

The numerical contrast between a handful of words ("five," *pente*) and an
untold number of words *(myrious;* cf. 4:15) and the presence of ellipsis—the
verb "to speak" *(lalēsai)* is not repeated—underscore the relatively lesser
value Paul ascribes to an exercise of speaking in tongues, even for the sake of
praying or giving thanks to God (cf. vv. 14, 16-17), vis-à-vis the exercise of the
charism of teaching. In his view all charisms are to be judged on the basis of
their ability to contribute to the upbuilding of the church.

FOR REFERENCE AND FURTHER STUDY

Martin, Dale B. *The Corinthian Body* 96–102.
Roberson, C. H. "The Meaning and Use of *Psallō,*" *ResQ* 6 (1962) 19–31, 57–66.

11. *Outsiders and Unbelievers* (14:20-25)

20. Brothers and sisters, do not be children in your thoughts. Be childish
in evil; be adults with your thoughts. 21. In the law it is written, "In foreign tongues and with the lips of aliens I will speak to this people and
even then they will not listen to me, says the Lord." 22. So tongues are a
sign not for believers, but for unbelievers; prophecy is a sign not for un-

believers, but for believers. 23. If, then, the whole church comes together as one and all are speaking in tongues, and if outsiders and unbelievers enter, wouldn't they say that you are mad? 24. If, however, all were prophesying and an unbeliever or outsider entered, that one would be corrected by everyone, would be judged by everyone, 25. and the hidden things of the heart would be made manifest so, falling on the face, that one will worship God proclaiming, "God is really in your midst."

INTERPRETATION

After his long explanation (14:2-19) of the reasons why Christians should strive after the gift of prophecy over and above other charismatic gifts, especially over and above the gift of speaking in tongues, Paul returns to the topic at hand with a renewed exhortation. He addresses himself to the community at Corinth as to his brothers and sisters, as he customarily does in the letter. Although he calls the Corinthians his siblings, he speaks to them in fatherly fashion (v. 20; cf. 3:1-3; 4:14-21). Phrased in this way Paul's words are an admonition addressed to the Corinthians.

A People Set Apart. The argument of 14:2-19 was directed to the members of the community. Concern for the building up of the church was the overarching principle in Paul's evaluation of prophecy and speaking in tongues. In 14:20-25 Paul continues to compare these two charisms, but the focus of his attention is on the impact the exercise of these gifts has on those outside the community (cf. 14:16). From the beginning of the letter Paul had identified the group of Christians at Corinth as the church of God, God's holy people. This identified them as a people set apart. Verses 20-25 treat the issue of prophecy and speaking in tongues from this perspective. What does the exercise of these gifts mean for a community that is set apart from others? What does the exercise of these gifts mean to those others from whom the Christians of Corinth have been set apart?

Two scriptural allusions set the tone for the pericope and frame the explanatory exposition appended to Paul's paternal admonition (14:20). The first is a citation of Isa 28:11-12; the second Isa 45:14. In both its biblical setting and its use by Paul Isa 28:11-12 is an oracle of judgment. Speaking to the people in a foreign tongue will not lead them to fidelity, says the Lord. The speech may come from the Lord but it does not build up the people as God's own people. In Isaiah these words were addressed to the ruling classes in Jerusalem. In Paul they are addressed to glossolalists that pride themselves in the gift that is theirs.

In contrast with speaking in tongues the exercise of the gift of prophecy in the community is a revelatory experience, not only for the members of the community, for whom prophecy is a sign, but also for outsiders and nonbelievers. The exercise of the gift of prophecy convinces outsiders of their lack of belief and reveals the secrets of their inmost being. This is the beginning of their conversion. Having heard prophetic utterance among the Corinthians they are led to acknowledge that God is with them (Isa 45:14). Their gesture of adoration, prostration in the presence of God whom they acknowledge to be present among the Corinthians, signifies their acceptance of the God of Israel, the God of the Christians at Corinth. The gift of prophecy is a sign for believers not only because prophetic utterance is meaningful (a sign, *sēmeion*) in itself, but also because it leads to the conversion of some outsiders and the proclamation that God is present in the Corinthian community.

Outsiders and Unbelievers. The Christian community at Corinth was a new community trying to find its way in the midst of a cosmopolitan and largely pagan society. Although it was a community set apart, the church did not exist in isolation from nonbelievers (cf. 1:18-25; 5:1; 6:1-11; 7:12-16; 8–10; 10:27; 12:2). Legal structures, social situations, and even marriage created a situation in which Christians interacted with non-Christians. A Christian symposium held in a house large enough for all of the smaller Christian communities to come together in a single assembly (14:23) provided occasion for non-Christians to experience the various forms of "speech" uttered by Christians (cf. 10:27). Christians who had a well-founded hope for the conversion of their non-Christian spouses (7:16), already partially coopted into the people set apart (7:14), might have brought these non-Christian spouses to the general assembly with its symposium. In 7:12-15 these non-Christian spouses are described as *apistoi*, nonbelievers, the language used by Paul in vv. 22-24. The householders' servants, or perhaps even some invited guests (cf. 10:27), may have been among the non-Christians who witnessed the church symposium.

These non-Christians may not have been unfamiliar with people speaking in tongues (cf. 12:2). Tongues are not proper to believers; they are known to unbelievers. Prophecy was, on the other hand, a gift that is given to believers. At least in the sense in which Paul understands prophecy it is unknown among nonbelievers. Paul may have been the first to make a careful distinction between speaking in tongues and uttering prophecy. Nonbelievers would have described the kind of ecstatic speaking that Paul identifies as speaking in tongues as "prophecy." For Paul prophecy is something different from that. Only one who confesses with the lips (Rom 10:9) Jesus as Lord truly speaks as a Spirit-inspired Christian (cf. 12:2-3).

Non-Christians who experience a Christian symposium in which there is speaking in tongues—all the more so if everyone is speaking in tongues! (v. 23a)—would think that Christians were simply being carried away in some sort of mantic frenzy (v. 23b). They would remain bystanders to the situation, outside observers, as it were. If, however, the situation were different, if all were uttering intelligible statements about God, then the outsiders would have a different experience. They would no longer remain outsiders; they would become insiders as they came to recognize the presence of the one God (8:6) among the Corinthian Christians.

The conduct of the assembly, says Paul, is a powerful force in evangelization. Should unbelievers witness the Christian gathering they should be impressed by the exercise of the gift of prophesy so as to see their false ways and turn to the worship of the living and true God (1 Thess 1:9). That outsiders had the occasion to witness a Christian symposium is another indication of the importance of the Christian household in evangelization. Not only did the household provide hospitality to evangelists during the course of their missionary trips; the exercise of the gift of prophecy in the symposium that took place in a Christian household was a powerful witness to the power of the gospel.

NOTES

20. *Brothers and sisters, do not be children in your thoughts. Be childish in evil; be adults with your thoughts:* The verb *nēpiazō*, "to act childishly," is hapax in the NT. Paul has, however, used the image of little children *(nēpioi)* to describe the Corinthians in 3:1. Apart from its two occurrences in v. 20 the noun *phresin,* "thoughts," does not occur in the NT. As used by Homer (*Iliad* 1.193) and Aristotle (*Posterior Analytics* 3.10.672b) the term connotes reflection and insight as opposed to indistinct emotions.

Within Paul's complex three-part antithesis a first part contrasts a child's thoughts with the evil in which a child was deemed to be involved. With regard to the evil inclination to which children were subject *(yēṣer hāraʿ)* see note on 10:7. A second antithesis contrasts childish involvement in evil with the reflection and insight of the mature adult. The point is that just as the bad behavior of the child is different from the maturity of the adult, so ecstatic speaking in tongues is different from the rationality of prophecy. The Christians of Corinth are to strive after prophecy (14:1); they are to be mature in their thinking. Previously (13:11) Paul had given himself as an example of someone who on attaining maturity abandoned childish behavior.

21. *In the law it is written, "In foreign tongues and with the lips of aliens I will speak to this people and even then they will not listen to me, says the Lord":* As adapted by Paul the text of Isa 28:11-12 is an oracle of judgment on those who speak in uninterpreted tongues. Paul has omitted from the citation of Isaiah "to whom he has said, 'This is rest; give rest to the weary; and this is repose'" (Isa 28:12ab). These words express God's salvific will in counterpoint to the prophetic oracle of judgment (Isa 28:11). Paul's use of the first person singular "I will speak," *lalēsō,* in place of the Bible's "he will speak" increases the

rhetorical force of the citation, which is further accentuated by Paul's use of a future "they will not hear" *(oud'. . . eisakousontai)* instead of the biblical "they would not hear." The reformulated phrase then stands in sharp contrast with "I will speak": "I will speak and they will not hear." Paul further emphasizes the force of his citation by adding an oracular "thus says the Lord" (cf. Rom 12:19; compare Isa 28:12a).

There is a touch of irony in Paul's use of a scripture directed against confused priests and prophets (see Isa 28:7). The Corinthians' disarray is no less than the confusion suffered by those priests and prophets. W. A. Grudem suggests that Paul has used Isa 28:7 to show that uninterpreted tongues are a sign of divine displeasure and impending judgment. To the extent that this suggestion has merit it implies the coming of the eschaton, a perspective that is never far removed from Paul's evaluation of charismatic gifts (cf. 13:8-13; 14:8).

22. *So tongues are a sign not for believers, but for unbelievers; prophecy is a sign not for unbelievers, but for believers:* Paul makes his point with a clever use of rhetorical devices. The entire sentence has an antithetical structure; within each of its parts there is a further antithesis. The phrase is elliptical; "sign" *(sēmeion;* cf. 1:22) appears in the first part of the verse but not in the second. The whole comes together in a chiastic pattern in which believers are designated by means of a participle (see note on 1:21) and unbelievers by means of a substantivized adjective *(apistoi;* cf. 6:6; 7:12-15; 10:27).

The contrast between believers and unbelievers may suggest that Paul has in mind a distinction between prophecy as it was understood within his biblical tradition and prophecy as it was commonly understood in the Greco-Roman world. In the Hellenistic world "prophecy" connoted ecstatic utterance, sounds expressed by someone in a trance. In the biblical tradition the prophet (the Hebrew *nābîʾ)* spoke an intelligible utterance.

Nonbelievers may be impressed by those who utter unintelligible sounds, but believers are edified by those who prophesy. The exercise of the gift of tongues can be a sign for nonbelievers insofar as language that is not understood is a sign of judgment (Isa 28:11). On the other hand, prophecy is a sign for believers not only in the sense that it is intelligible communication but also insofar as it is an instrument of conversion of the nonbeliever (see v. 25).

23. *If, then, the whole church comes together as one and all are speaking in tongues, and if outsiders and unbelievers enter:* Only in 14:23 does Paul speak about "the whole church" *(hē ekklēsia holē)* coming together as a single body. With its double qualification of "coming together" (11:17, 20, 33; 14:26) "whole" *(holē;* cf. Rom 16:23; Acts 15:22), "as one" *(epi to auto),* Paul seems to suggest that the coming together of the entire body of Corinthian Christians in a single assembly was a somewhat exceptional happening. When Christians came together as an entire community they celebrated the eucharist (11:17-34) and had a kind of symposium. The symposium featured speaking in tongues and prophecy. Paul does not indicate where it was that this larger assembly of Christians took place. His only other mention of the "whole church" is in Rom 16:23, where he mentions Gaius, host to himself and "to the whole

church." It is not impossible that it was in the home of Gaius, Paul's patron and one of the richer members of the Corinthian community, that the "whole church" of Corinth came together in the kind of assembly about which Paul writes in 14:23. Since Gaius was a prominent Corinthian it is not unlikely that his home would be visited by members of the populace who were not Christian (cf. 10:27, with regard to social contacts between Christians and non-Christians).

That all would be speaking in tongues flies in the face of both the Pauline principle that the Spirit distributes to individuals such gifts as he wills (12:4-11) and the analogy of the body (12:12-26). That all would be speaking in tongues points to the "desirablility" of this particular gift in the Corinthians' popular estimation.

It is not imperative that a truly adequate distinction be made between the "outsiders" (*idiōtai*; cf. 14:16, 24) and unbelievers. In Greek the most common connotation of "outsider" is a private individual, someone who was not a public official. With respect to religious guilds the term can designate the uninitiated. With regard to the professions and the exercise of particular skills it suggests the beginner, the untutored (even a lay person in distinction to a priest). Ceslas Spicq renders the term used in 14:23 as "uninitiated persons" (*TLNT* 2:212–214, at 214). Some of Paul's "outsiders" may well have been on their way to becoming Christians.

wouldn't they say that you are mad? This is Paul's only known use of the verb "to be mad" (*mainesthe*, all five NT uses of which have negative overtones; cf. John 10:20; Acts 12:15; 26:24, 25). In Greek the term was often used in reference to cultic frenzy. Herodotus (*Persian Wars* 4.79) uses it to speak of one driven mad by a god. Homer in the *Iliad* and Sophocles use it of Dionysiac frenzy. Female devotees of Dionysius, whose cult was celebrated in Corinth, were known as "mad women" (*mainades).* Paul seems to be suggesting that speaking in tongues gone awry in the Christian assembly might lead to outsiders' equating Christian worship with a kind of bacchanalia. Drunkenness was common in the cult of Dionysus, but the verb "to be mad" was sometimes simply used in the sense of being deranged as a result of overindulgence in wine (thus Homer in the *Odyssey*). Earlier in his letter Paul had indicated that the drunkenness of some Corinthians contributed to their problematic situation (11:21).

24–25. *If, however, all were prophesying and an unbeliever or outsider entered:* Comparing the gift of prophecy with the gift of speaking in tongues, Paul envisions a scenario other than the one described in v. 23. The new scenario is that all are prophesying (highly unlikely in light of the principle of the allotment of charisms). The unity of all these prophets (note the use of *pan-*, "all," three times in v. 24) contrasts with the cacophony of sounds emitted by those speaking in tongues. Their unified activity can also be brought to bear on the single *(tis)* unbeliever or outsider who enters the assembly.

that one would be corrected by everyone, would be judged by everyone, and the hidden things of the heart would be made manifest: With "corrected" (*elegchetai*) and "judged" (*anakrinetai*) Paul returns to the use of juridical language, which had been a feature of earlier sections of his letter. "Corrected" is hapax in the extant Pauline correspondence; "judged" was used in 2:14, 15; 4:3[2x], 4; 9:3; 10:25, 27. Together the two terms indicate a kind of prophetic behavior in which, at least in Paul's hypothesis, all would take part. Paul is thinking of the corrective and admonitory efforts of those members of the community who have the gift of prophecy.

The clauses are joined asyndetically, without a connective. The key words of the third clause (hidden, heart, made manifest) recall 4:5 where, in a context that speaks of judgment, Paul writes of the Lord who sheds light upon things hidden in darkness and makes manifest the intentions of hearts. The description of the Christian prophet doing something similar to what the Lord does intimates that the prophet is inspired by God. By the power and Spirit of God with which he or she is endowed the prophet performs a function properly performed by God.

so, falling on the face, that one will worship God proclaiming, "God is really in your midst": Paul's description of one whose heart has been touched by the prophets' insight as falling down on his or her face echoes language that is found in 1 Kings 18:39. To fall on one's face in the presence of the deity is a gesture of profound awe. The language of "worship" (*proskynēsei*) is common in the NT, but Paul uses it only in 14:25. In the NT "to worship" is frequently accompanied by the verb "to fall" (*piptō;* cf. Matt 2:11; 4:9; 18:26; Acts 10:25; Rev 4:10; 5:14; 7:11; 11:16; 19:4, 10a; 22:8). Worship is expressed gesticularly. Prostration is a form of worship that bespeaks the complete awe of the worshiper in the presence of God. Paul may be using the language metaphorically, but there is no reason to believe that he did not consider prostration to be a symbolic gesture of the acceptance of the monotheistic God of Israel.

The convert's gesture of adoration is accompanied by a simple confession of faith. The confession reprises the language of Isa 45:14. In Isaiah and in Zech 8:23, where a similar phrase is found (with the preposition *meta*, rather than *en* as in Isaiah), the declaration that God is among us is spoken by foreigners. The foreigners are Egyptians in Isaiah and "ten men from nations of every language" in Kings. Zechariah 8:23 explicitly mentions language. It has the prophetic formula "says the Lord" (*legei kyrios,* cf. 14:21). These expressions in Zechariah may be the verbal links that allow Paul to express his reflections on the impact of the exercise of the gift of tongues on outsiders with a brace of biblical allusions that speak of the relationship between the God of Israel and non-Israelites.

For Reference and Further Study

Grudem, Wayne A. "1 Corinthians 14.20-25: Prophecy and Tongues as Signs of God's Attitude," *WThJ* 41 (1979) 381–396.

Rebell, Walter. "Gemeinde als Missionsfaktor im Urchristentum. I Kor 14,24f. als Schlüsselsituation," *ThZ* 44 (1988) 117–134.

Sandnes, Karl Olav. "Prophecy—A Sign for Believers (1 Cor 14,20-25)," *Bib.* 77 (1996) 1–15.

Smit, Joop F. M. "Tongues and Prophecy: Deciphering 1 Cor 14,22," *Bib* 75 (1994) 175–190.

12. *Order in the Assembly* (14:26-40)

26. What then, brothers and sisters? When you come together each has a song of praise, a teaching, a revelation, a tongue, an interpretation. Let all things be done for the sake of upbuilding. 27. If anyone speaks in a tongue, two or at most three, one at a time. Let there be someone to interpret. 28. If there be no interpreter let that one be silent during the gathering. Let him or her speak to the self and to God. 29. Let two or three prophets speak; let the others judge. 30. If there is a revelation to someone else who is seated, let the first person be silent. 31. You can all prophesy in turn, so that everyone might learn and everyone be encouraged. 32. And the spirits of the prophets are subject to the prophets. 33. For God is not of disorder, but of peace.

As in all the assemblies of the saints, 34. let women be silent in the assembly. For it is not permitted for them to speak. Let them be subject, even as the law says. 35. If they want to learn, let them inquire of their own husbands at home. For it is shameful for a woman to speak in the assembly. 36. Can it be that the word of God originated with you? Did it reach only you?

37. If anyone thinks that he or she is a prophet or a spiritual person, understand that what I am writing to you is a command of the Lord. 38. If anyone does not acknowledge this, that person is not acknowledged.

39. Wherefore, my brothers and sisters, strive to prophesy and do not forbid speaking in tongues. 40. Let everything be done with propriety and in orderly fashion.

INTERPRETATION

This pericope brings to closure not only Paul's reflections on the relative importance of the gifts of prophecy and tongues but also the entire macro-unit on spiritual gifts (chs. 12–14). Verse 39 with its reference to striving, prophecy, and tongues forms an *inclusio* with 14:1-2, thereby forming ch. 14 into a discrete literary unit, element A' in the chiastic structure of Paul's reflection on spiritual realities. Verse 40 with its summary exhortation, "let all things be done" *(panta ginesthō)*, harks back to the summary exhortation of v. 26 and establishes vv. 26-40 as a distinct unit within the letter. The unit speaks, in practical terms, about the building up of the community. Its forceful introduction, "what then, brothers and sisters?" indicates that Paul is going to bring his discursive reflections on the gifts to a practical conclusion.

Order in the Assembly. The chapter's final exhortation calls for propriety and order in the assembly (v. 40). Paul's thought is that the eucharistic assembly should reflect the nature of the church as the body of Christ. In the body there are several members, each contributing its respective function. When the several members of the community gather each is to exercise his or her respective charism. It is the charisms of speech that could prove most detrimental to the order of the community. Accordingly Paul sets out specific guidelines for those who would exercise the gifts of speech in the assembly, specifically tongues and prophecy.

The order in the assembly for which Paul calls is necessary for the upbuilding of the community as it gathers together. The similar form of vv. 26 and 40 brings together the ideas of order and upbuilding. Coming together, the community manifests itself as a social body. Various members of the community are so charismatically endowed that they can make a speech act during the assembly. These speech acts are of various sorts. Paul identifies five kinds: songs of praise, teaching, revelation, speaking in tongues, the interpretation of tongues (v. 26). Lest the symposium degenerate into a disorderly cacophony of sounds, Paul sets forth specific directives for those who would speak in tongues and for those who would prophesy. His overarching principle is that everything that is done be done for the sake of building up the community (v. 26). A theological understanding undergirds this principle (v. 33). Cacophony is to be excluded because God is not a God of disorder and confusion. Upbuilding the community is necessary because God is a God of peace. The God of the covenant wills the well-being of his people.

Paul does not offer any particular directives for the use of songs of praise in the assembly, perhaps because these could be communal activities (see notes). He does, however, have something to say about tongues and the interpretation of tongues. Three rules are set forth for the exercise of speaking in tongues. First, that there be a limited number of such utterances, no more than two or three. Second, that those who speak in tongues speak in turn. Third, that the utterances be interpreted. The latter condition is a *sine qua non.* If there is no one to interpret what is being said in tongues it should not be said aloud. Speaking in tongues is the praise of God. If other members of the assembly cannot understand what is being said and if they cannot join in with an "Amen" (14:2, 16) the prayer should be directed to God and God alone.

The exercise of gifts of prophecy is more beneficial to the community than is the exercise of the gifts of tongues. Paul's language implies that prophecy was a common feature of the Christian symposium. Nevertheless, even the gift of prophecy must be used in orderly fashion if it is to benefit the community (v. 26). As Paul speaks of prophecy he appears to identify revelation and teaching (vv. 26, 30, 31) as forms of prophecy even though prophecy and teaching are presented as seemingly different gifts in 12:28-29.

Three rules for the exercise of the gift of prophecy are set forth. These parallel the rules for tongue-speakers. First, no more than two or three prophets should speak in the assembly, but Paul presumes that the prophets will speak. Second, those who prophesy should speak in turn. This is a particularly important point, which Paul underscores by noting the importance of a prophet yielding the floor to another prophet who has received a revelation. Even prophets are expected to be subject to the Spirit of prophecy. This requires that they be silent when others are speaking. All within the community must be able to profit from prophetic utterance, whether that be didactic or paraenetic. Third, others must judge what the prophets say. Not every utterance of a prophet is a prophetic utterance. As he did in his first letter, Paul urges the Corinthians to judge the quality of the prophets' speech (cf. 1 Thess 5:19-20).

Womens' Silence. The exhortation that women be silent is problematic both from a modern perspective and from the perspective of the letter itself. The discussion of this matter is somewhat complicated by the issue of social location. Three times Paul speaks about the assembly (vv. 33, 34, 35); he also mentions a common practice, a rule that would forbid women's speaking in the assembly and observes that for a woman to speak publicly is shameful.

Christian assemblies took place on a rather small scale. They occurred in the homes of Christians. At home, and particularly in Greco-Roman society, women took a more active role than they did in public civic life. Some commentators (Stephen Barton, Caroline Vander Stichele, etc.) suggest that there may have been some blurring of the distinction between domestic and community roles among the Christian women of Corinth, women assuming a role in the assembly that was normally theirs as wife and mother simply because the assembly took place at home. If this were the situation, Paul would be reminding the Christians at Corinth that their gathering really enjoyed the character of a public assembly. Roles that were appropriate at home should not be indiscriminately brought into a Christian assembly, exception always to be made for the kind of privileged communication between God and human, and vice-versa, that can be appropriately called prophecy and prayer as in 11:5. What is appropriate at home is not necessarily appropriate in a Christian assembly (cf. 11:22).

On another reading of the sub-unit on women's role in the assembly the situation Paul had in mind was disorderly chattering *(lalein)*, perhaps under the guise of prophecy or speaking in tongues. Some women may have been speaking in a frenzied fashion similar to that experienced in the cult of Dionysus. Since Paul focuses on their questions in v. 35 it might be that he had in mind women raising questions in the assembly or, following a Delphic model, female prophets responding to questions, often about one's personal life, that other people had asked. Other commentators suggest that the situation might be that of an early Gnostic woman's liberation movement in which some women wanted to speak their mind in the presence of the Christian assembly. Paul would have considered such interventions as these as being "out of order." One difficulty with this line of reasoning is that Paul's "rule" seems to be general and not specific to the situation at Corinth (see, however, note on v. 33b).

Since v. 35 speaks about women getting information from their husbands at home some commentators (Elisabeth Schüssler Fiorenza, etc.) are of the opinion that Paul is not talking about women in general, but only about married women. It would have been on married women that the injunction to be silent falls. As a sign of their subordination they should remain silent in the assembly. If they need to know something they should speak to their husbands at home. To this one could object that 11:2-16 speaks of the appearance of women who pray and prophesy in the assembly, presumably married women as well (cf. 11:3). For Antoinette Wire the discussion on women's appearance in 11:2-16 is a concession on the part of the apostle. His real goal is to obtain the silence of women in the Christian assembly. As such Paul would be urging a kind of social conservatism that would anticipate the discipline of the churches of later generations (1 Tim 2:11-12; cf. Eph 5:22; Col 3:18; 1 Pet 3:1). Paul has, however, such favorable things to say about women, many of whom he looks upon as his coworkers (1:11; 16:19; Rom 16:1-16; Phil 4:2-3; Phlm 2; cf. Acts 16:11-40; 17:34; 18:2-26; Col 4:15; 2 Tim 4:21), that Wire's opinion seems quite implausible.

It may be that Paul is not at all encouraging women to be silent in the assembly, at least no more than he enjoined men to be silent. It may be that in vv. 33b-36 Paul is dealing with men who wanted to maintain their own patriarchal status and so require women to be silent in public and subservient to their husbands at home. The argument of these men took the form of an appeal to accepted *halakah* and the practice of the synagogue (vv. 33b-34). To this would have been added an argument from shame (v. 35b), so important in the social circumstances of first-century Mediterranean culture. For women to speak in an assembly dishonors, these people might have claimed, the women themselves as well as their husbands. On this view vv. 33b-35 represent the position of some people at Corinth, much in the fashion of the "slogans" summarizing positions with which Paul was constrained to take issue. Some of these slogans appear to have been buzzwords circulating among the Corinthians (6:12, 13; 7:1; 10:23), but others may have been Paul's own formulation (1:12), as could be the case here.

Having summarized their argument in this casuistic section of this letter, the apostle rejects it out of hand. His double rhetorical question is a quick dismissal. To those who would appeal to traditional *halakah* in an effort to silence female prophets Paul offers a blunt reminder that the word of God did not originate from them; neither do they enjoy some sort of an exclusive claim on the word of God. If the Spirit wills (12:11), the gift of prophecy can be allotted to women. Gender is not a qualification for the gift of prophecy, which is given for the benefit of the whole community (see 14:29). To prevent a woman who was so endowed from speaking within the assembly is an obstacle to God's working within the community.

An Interpolation? For more than a century various scholars have been convinced that 1 Cor 14:33b-36 has been interpolated into Paul's text by someone other than Paul at a relatively early stage in the history of the tradition of the manuscript. On this view the verses are an expression of the social and ecclesial discipline represented by such NT passages as Eph 5:22-24; Col 3:18; 1 Tim 2:11-15; and 1 Pet 3:1-6.

Scholars who favor the interpolation theory include Christian Holsten (1880), Daniel Völter (1889), Alfred Loisy (1922), Walter Schmithals (1956), Robert Jewett (1978), Gerhard Sellin (1987), Eduardo de la Serna (1991), Jouette Bassler (1992), J. H. Petzer (1993), Richard Hays (1997) and, especially, Winsome Munro. In a series of articles (1973, 1988, 1990) Munro claimed that the interpolation consists of a somewhat larger segment containing vv. 32-38. In the *NRSV* and some other recent translations of 1 Corinthians vv. 33b-36 are printed in parentheses or brackets, an editorial procedure that betrays the editors' hesitancy as to the authenticity of the verses.

Those who doubt the authenticity of these verses argue that they break Paul's line of thought. The other side of this argument is that v. 37 seems easily to follow v. 33a. In addition, some of the language is non-Pauline, especially the phrase "the law says," used as a cipher for a substantive argument in a discussion. Paul generally expresses a somewhat negative view of the law (*ho nomos*; cf. 15:56). When he wants to develop a scriptural argument he cites the pertinent passages of Scripture (cf. 9:9; 14:21), rather than making a merely general reference under the rubric of "the law." A final argument in favor of the inauthentic character of vv. 33b-35 is that the silence of women in the Christian assembly conflicts with 11:5. That verse establishes a kind of dress code for women who pray and prophesy during the assembly. To these various internal arguments against the authenticity of 14:33b-36 one can add that the idea of the subjection of women expressed in 14:34 goes contrary to Paul's view of women as his coworkers (14:19, see note; Phil 4:2-3; Rom 16:1-5) and Paul's idea that the Christian is not enslaved to anyone (cf. 6:12).

That some majuscules (D, F, G) and some Western witnesses to the Latin text type (including some Old Latin manuscripts and Ambrosiaster) place the verses at the end of ch. 14 (after 14:40) adds an external argument in favor of the hypothesis of interpolation. Such "movement" of a passage from one location to another within text is often an indication of the weak hold that it has on the claim that it belongs to the text. The phenomenon is not unknown in the history of the manuscript tradition of the NT (cf. John 7:53–8:11), but instances of it in the Pauline corpus are relatively rare. P. B. Payne (1995, 1998) introduced into the discussion of the state of the text the evidence of a Latin manuscript (Codex Fuldensis, 546 or 547 C.E.) and the scribal sigla in B. He cites Bishop Victor of Capua, under whose authority the Codex Fuldensis was produced, as an ancient witness to the idea that the passage is an interpolation.

There are, indeed, various reasons to consider vv. 33b-36 as a later interpolation into Paul's text. The arguments are, however, not weighty. The manuscripts where the passage wanders to the end of ch. 14 are few in number and closely related. They belong almost entirely to the Western type of text. The oldest manuscripts ($\mathfrak{P}^{46}$, $\aleph$, A, B) along with Ψ and the Byzantine tradition read the letter with the problematic verses in their canonical location.

There are, moreover, substantial internal arguments that confirm the Pauline character of the text. These bear principally upon its vocabulary and syntax. The disputed passage's references to speaking, being silent, being subject, and the assembly link these verses to what Paul has said in the immediately preceding paragraph. It may be argued that Paul's vocabulary is somewhat unusual, but six key expressions occur in 1 Corinthians in an immediately adjacent or similar context: "to be silent" (*sigaō*) in 14:28, 30; "to be subject" (*hypotassō*) in 14:32 (cf. 15:27-28 [6x]; 16:16); "the law says" (*ho nomos legei*) in 9:8; "to learn" (*manthanō*) in 14:31 (cf. 4:6); "their own husbands" (*idioi andres*) in 7:2 (in the singular); "shameful" (*aischros*) in 11:6. Verses 33b-36 are, moreover, structured in a way that is similar to Paul's exhortations to prophets and those speaking in tongues. In each instance the instruction is followed by a conditional clause and with regard to women and to prophets there is a final motivation (vv. 34b; 35b).

To the extent that some of the phraseology and some of the content of 14:33b-35 has a non-Pauline sense this may be due to Paul's summarizing not his own thought, but the argument of another. In any case the argument for 14:33b-36 as an interpolation into Paul's text does not have sufficient merit. These verses belong to the letter and must be explained in context. Verses 33b-36 represent a conservative argument that Paul rebuts by means of the double rhetorical question in v. 36. To demand the silence of women in the Christian assembly is to claim for oneself a monopoly on the word of God. Such a monopoly no one can claim.

The Double Exhortation. The double exhortation in vv. 37-40 brings Paul's reflection on the gifts of prophecy and tongues to conclusion. The first exhortation (vv. 37-38) makes use of two conditional sentences. With the first Paul appeals to those who think themselves prophetic types and/or spiritual persons. He confronts them in their self-inflation by re-inforcing his apostolic *ethos*. What Paul has conveyed in his letter apro-pos the exercise of charismatic gifts comes from the Lord. It is, to use Paul's words, "a command of the Lord." Paul adds weight to his argu-ment in the second conditional sentence. He has done a fair amount of case study in the letter, particularly in 14:26-36. Now he adds an element of case law in the form of a sentence of holy law. If anyone does not ac-knowledge what Paul says to have come from the Lord, that person will not be acknowledged by the Lord. He or she will not be known by the Lord. Paul's warning is a warning of eschatological disaster.

The second exhortation (vv. 39-40) is positively phrased. Paul appeals to his brothers and sisters. This is a truly unusual appeal in this letter since it includes the adjective "my." Paul urges them to pursue eagerly the gift of prophecy, but not, he warns them, to the neglect of the gift of tongues. The gift of prophecy may be of more importance for building up the community. The gift of speaking in tongues has, nonetheless, its role to play in the life of the community. What is imperative is that when the community comes together for worship, the order in the assembly should reflect the order that exists within the body of Christ. Everything is to be done with propriety and in order.

NOTES

26. *What then, brothers and sisters?* The resumptive "then" *(oun)* and the direct ap-peal to the members of the community indicate that Paul is pulling his argu-ment together. After his theoretical observations he is about to provide some practical directives for order in the assembly.

    When you come together each has a song of praise, a teaching, a revelation, a tongue, an interpretation: "Coming together" probably indicates that the various forms of speech took place during the symposium after the meal (cf. 11:18, 20, 33; 14:23). No more than in 11:21 does Paul's "each" *(hekastos)* necessarily suggest that each and every Christian had something to say during the symposium. Paul presumes that every Christian has his or her own gift, but some of these gifts are not gifts of speech (12:4-11).

On teaching and revelation see the notes on 14:6 and 13:2 respectively. On tongues and the interpretation of tongues see the notes on 12:10. In the NT Luke-Acts uses "songs of praise" as a reference to the book of Psalms (see Luke 20:42; 24:44; Acts 1:20; 13:33), but the song of praise of 14:26 *(psalmon)* is probably a Christian composition used when Christians came together for worship. This is Paul's only reference to the use of songs of praise in Christian worship (cf. 14:15b). It may be that he had in mind someone spontaneously bursting forth in song under the inspiration of the Spirit. Whether the "song of praise" had a christological content (Phil 2:5-11; cf. Col 1:15-20; Rev 4:8, 11; 5:9-10; 14:3-4, etc.) is uncertain. The NT's deutero-Pauline epistles make reference to the use of songs of praise, hymns *(hymnos)*, and songs *(ōdē)* in Christian prayer (Col 3:16; Eph 5:19).

Let all things be done for the sake of upbuilding: This summary exhortation (cf. 14:40; 16:14) provides a transition to the practical directives of vv. 27-33. Exhorting the community to make the upbuilding of the community the norm and purpose of their charismatic activity, Paul echoes a motif he had articulated in 14:5, 12.

27. *If anyone speaks in a tongue, two or at most three, one at a time. Let there be someone to interpret:* The first century C.E. statutes of the Guild of Zeus Hypsistos indicate that disorderly conversation ("chattering," line 6) was incompatible with the nature of the cultic assembly. Paul likewise was concerned that the Christian assembly not be reduced to a cacophony of sound. Three norms are set forth to regulate the use of the gift of tongues in the assembly: (1) The number of those who speak should be limited to two or three; (2) they must speak in turn; and (3) there must be someone to interpret. "At most" *(to pleiston;* BDF 60.2) seems to imply that those endowed with the gift of speaking in tongues were eager to demonstrate their charismatic prowess in the midst of the assembly. In reaction Paul would limit the number of those who were allowed to speak.

Paul's sentence is expressed in the form of a simple condition. Its emphasis lies on the apodosis, which is introduced by an explicative *kai* (cf. BDF 442.9) and has "someone" *(heis,* literally "one") as its subject. There may be two or three members of the assembly speaking in tongues but only one interpreter. Paul's language seems to suggest that it is one of those who speaks in tongues who provides the interpretation for the two or three (cf. 14:13).

28. *If there be no interpreter let that one be silent during the gathering. Let him or her speak to the self and to God:* A casuistic aside of a sort found throughout the letter (cf. 7:11, 21) allows Paul to reiterate the emphasis of the apodosis of the preceding sentence. What is uttered in tongues must be interpreted if it is to contribute to the upbuilding of the church (14:4-5, 6, 13, 22). Since the upbuilding of the church is the normative principle for the use of charismatic gifts (14:26), should there be no one present to interpret what is spoken in tongues the tongue-speaker should remain silent. If the one who speaks in tongues does not have the gift of the interpretation of tongues (14:13), that one should remain silent in the presence of the assembly *(ekklēsia),* directing his or her prayer to God (14:2) in the form of a soliloquy (cf. BDF 188.2).

29. *Let two or three prophets speak; let the others judge:* The norms Paul sets out for prophets are similar to those stipulated for those who speak in tongues: (1) No more than three prophets should speak; (2) they should speak in turn (see v. 31); (3) others should be involved in turning the exercise of the charismatic gift to the benefit of those who have gathered. This second set of rules is joined to the first by an untranslated *de*. That there is no exception to the exercise of the gift of prophecy (cf. v. 28) points to the greater importance of prophecy in the Christian assembly. In recommending that only two or three prophets speak to the assembly Paul suggests that this is a maximum number (cf. v. 27), but the apostle is not as forceful in limiting the number of speakers as he had been in setting down a rule for those who spoke in tongues.

    As he was accustomed to do (cf. 1 Thess 5:19-22; Rom 12:1-2), Paul calls upon all members of the community (*hoi alloi*, "the others," introduced by a *kai*, "and," in Paul's Greek) to discern authentic charismatic experience, in this case to make a judgment as to the kind of prophecy that would build up the community (W. A. Grudem, *Prophecy in 1 Corinthians* 63, 105–106; *Prophecy in the New Testament* 75, 104–105; D. E. Aune, *Prophecy in Early Christianity* 47). Paul's verb, *diakrinetōsan*, suggests the idea of discrimination, judging among several possibilities. The notion that it is necessary not only to distinguish true prophets from false prophets but also to distinguish authentic prophetic utterance from what is not authentic prophetic utterance, even if spoken by one who has the gift of prophecy, is rooted in Paul's biblical tradition (cf. Deut 18:22).

30. *If there is a revelation to someone else who is seated, let the first person be silent:* Having spoken of tongues and their interpretation and of prophecy, Paul turns his attention to the revelation of mysteries (see v. 26). His reference is to a particular mode of prophetic discourse. He encourages one who has been prophesying to give way to the one to whom a revelation comes. Those who prophesy, as he explains in the following verse, should do so in turn. "To be seated" (*kathēmenō*) is hapax in the Pauline letters. It suggests the context of the symposium during which guests would continue to be seated.

31. *You can all prophesy in turn, so that everyone might learn and everyone be encouraged:* Paul offers this reflection by way of summative commentary (note the postpositive *gar*) on his directives relative to prophets speaking in the assembly. He reiterates the purpose of prophecy, echoing ideas expressed in 14:3, 6, but from the perspective of the impact that prophecy has on the members of the community. His threefold use of "all/everyone" (*pantes*) indicates that the exercise of the gift of prophecy affects the entire community. Prophecy serves to build up the community. That Christians both learn from and are encouraged by prophetic utterance seems to indicate that there is not a truly adequate distinction between the gift of teaching and the gift of prophecy.

32. *And the spirits of the prophets are subject to the prophets:* This, too, is a rule for order in the assembly. "The spirits of the prophets" may be a reference to angelic spirits present to the cultic assembly, the source of prophetic inspiration (cf. 13:1; Gal 1:8; 3:19). It is, however, more likely that the reference is to the

prophets' own spirits. Prophets speak forth inspired utterances, but not irrationally. One prophet must cede to another.

33. *For God is not of disorder, but of peace:* By way of conclusion to his directives for order in the assembly Paul appeals to the authority of God. He contrasts the God of peace with a god of disorder and confusion (cf. 2 Cor 6:5; 12:20). The contrast between peace and *akatastasia* (note the privative alpha), a term used of unsettled conditions and political insurrection, is particularly apropos in a letter whose primary purpose is exhortation to social harmony within the community. The good order that should reign in the gathered assembly is a response to the God of peace. It is a sign of the peace that should reign in the community. The eucharistic gathering with its symposium is a dramatic sign and symbol of the community.

Paul frequently mentions the "God of peace" (cf. 7:15) toward the conclusion of his letters. Typically mention of the God of peace appears as a significant element in Paul's final benediction (Rom 15:33; 2 Cor 13:11; Gal 6:16; Phil 4:9; 1 Thess 5:23), but there is no such blessing in 1 Corinthians. "Peace" is not simply a matter of good order. The God of peace is the God of the biblical *shalom.* The word summarizes the well-being of the entire community. It is the commonweal, as willed by God and fostered in God's covenant relationship with the people.

As in all the assemblies of the saints: Along with a few modern translations Richard Hays (*Moral Vision* 59, n. 82; cf. *First Corinthians* 244) considers this phrase to be the conclusion of the preceding sentence on the grounds of its redundancy and Paul's rhetorical practice in which the example of the churches is cited as a final argument (cf. 11:16). It seems, however, preferable to take the phrase as part of the argument that women are to be silent in the assembly. Alfred Loisy considered this phrase, along with similar phrases in 1:2; 4:17; 7:17; 11:16 and 14:33, as an ecclesiastical addition to Paul's text. According to Loisy the phrase was inserted into 1 Corinthians at the time when the letter became part of a collection of Pauline letters intended for circulation among the churches. The manuscript tradition does not, however, provide any indication that the text of 1 Corinthians ever existed without this clause.

A question can be raised whether "assemblies of the saints" *(tais ekklēsiais tōn hagiōn)* refers to Christian gatherings. It may be that the groups of saints to whom reference is being made are not Christian gatherings, but Jewish synagogues, where women were not permitted to speak. Paul uses *ekklēsia* of the Christian assembly (cf. 1:2), and he uses the noun in the plural when he wants to refer to more than one local gathering of Christians (cf. 16:1, 19). He also uses the substantivized adjective *hoi hagioi,* "the saints" to designate Christians, God's holy people (1:2). Nonetheless, "in all the assemblies of the saints" *(en pasais tais ekklēsiais tōn hagiōn)* has a formulaic ring. The phrase is, moreover, hapax in Paul's letters. When Paul wants to qualify the Christian assembly as belonging to God, he typically uses the biblical expression "the church of God" *(hē ekklēsia tou theou),* as he does in 1:2. On balance it would seem that the practice of Jewish assemblies is being cited as a frame of reference for the practice that has been urged at Corinth. The norm of behavior cited in v. 34 and the supporting arguments that are adduced appear to be more at home in a Jewish community than they do in the Gentile Christian community at Corinth.

34. *let women be silent in the assembly:* Ostensibly women, along with those who have the gift of tongues but no interpreter and prophets who must remain quiet while someone who has a revelation speaks (14:28, 30), are a third category of people who are to be silent in the Christian assembly (*en tais ekklēsiais,* in the plural). The injunction that women be silent occurs nowhere else in the NT. Unlike Paul's directives to prophets and those who have the gift of tongues no conditions are stipulated as to when silence is desired. The injunction appears to have a general import, underscored by the explanation that follows.

For it is not permitted for them to speak: The norm that has been cited in v. 34a is explained (note the postpositive *gar*) by means of an antithetical statement in which the negative, "it is not permitted for them to speak," comes before the positive, "let them be subject," so that the emphasis falls on the latter (cf. v. 33). Often in the letter Paul uses the rhetorical device of antithesis for the sake of emphasis. "To permit," here in a divine passive, suggests a decision by someone in authority (cf. 16:7, Paul's only other use of the verb *epitrepō,* "to permit"). In the deutero-Pauline 1 Timothy a directive is set forth, perhaps under the influence of 14:34 (if this is not an interpolation!), to the effect that it is not permitted for women to teach (*didaskein gynaiki ouk epitrepō,* 1 Tim 2:12).

Let them be subject: Second- and first-century B.C.E. marriage contracts provide evidence of the duties incumbent upon a wife in the Hellenistic world. First among these duties was that she should be subject to her husband (cf. P.Giessen 21; P.Tebtunis I, 104; Claude Vatin, *Recherches sur le mariage et la condition de la femme mariée à l'époque hellénistique* [Paris: de Boccard, 1970] 200–201). The subjection of a woman to her husband is enjoined by the late-first-century deutero- and trito-Pauline texts (Eph 5:22-24; Col 3:18; 1 Tim 2:11-15; 1 Pet 3:1-6). That practice is to be explained by the social circumstances of late-first-century Christian communities. These communities sought to achieve social acceptance.

Paul's clause begins with a strong adversative, *alla,* "but." The rhetorical force of the argument is better preserved in English by omitting the conjunction and beginning a new sentence. A fifth-century codex (A) adds a clarifying *tois andrasin,* "to their husbands," literally "to the men" (with the definite article but without an explanatory *idioi;* cf. v. 35) to Paul's "let them be subject" (*hypotassesthōsan).*

even as the law says: To the argument from the practice of Jewish communities is added a second "Jewish" argument, namely the law. No particular scripture is, however, cited in support of the practice that is being urged on the Corinthian community.

35. *If they want to learn, let them inquire of their own husbands at home:* The exhortation expresses patriarchal authority within the household, not only insofar as reference is made to the women's own husbands (*tous idious andras*) but also

insofar as the conduct that is enjoined (questioning instead of speaking) expresses dependence and subservience. In the Hellenistic world one of the responsibilities of husbands was the instruction of their wives (cf. Xenophon, *Oeconomicus* 7.4-9.19). This was assumed to contribute to the good order of the household. In Judaism children were expected to ask their fathers questions pertaining to the religious, cultural, and historical traditions of their nation (cf. Deut 32:7; cf. Eph 6:4).

For it is shameful for a woman to speak in the assembly: "In the assembly" (*en ekklēsią*; cf. v. 28) contrasts with "at home" (*en oikǫ*, v. 35a). In Mediterranean culture shame and honor were among the most important social values. Marriage contracts of the second and first pre-Christian centuries stipulated that a wife must not do anything that would shame her husband.

36. *Can it be that the word of God originated with you? Did it reach only you?* The double question, in fact two questions linked by the conjunction "or" (*ē*), is a classic construction that Paul employs from time to time (cf. 1:13b-c; 11:22). The particle *ē*, used to introduce the first rhetorical question, is exclamatory ("Can it be that . . .?"). This is in keeping with NT and classical usage (MM 2228).

Paul's rhetorical rejoinder might be construed as having been addressed to those who speak in tongues and to prophets as well (cf. vv. 27-33a), but it is more likely that the double rhetorical question challenges those who would limit Christian women's right to speak. It is addressed to males; "only you" *(eis hymas monous)* is in the masculine plural. Paul addresses his rejoinder to those men who object to women speaking in the assembly. Bluntly and forcefully he asks them, "do you presume to have an exclusive claim on the word of God?"

37. *If anyone thinks that he or she is a prophet or a spiritual person, understand that what I am writing to you is a command of the Lord:* Paul's words reprise a formula, "if any one thinks" *(ei tis dokei),* that had appeared in 3:18 and 8:2. The hybrists within the community think themselves wise, knowledgeable, and spiritual. Paul calls them up short with "if anyone thinks." The truly spiritual person should recognize the gifts of the Spirit (see 2:12-16).

In what sense has Paul written a "command of the Lord"? Peter J. Tomson ("Document de la tradition apostolique") takes the reference to the command of the Lord with some seriousness, suggesting that although it is without parallel in the canonical gospels the restriction on women in vv. 33-37 substantially represents an unwritten tradition, an *agraphon,* coming from Jesus. This is unlikely. Some manuscripts (D, G) and some Fathers of the Church (Origen, Ambrosiaster, Hilary, Pelagius) have resolved the question by removing the reference to a commandment. They read "what I have written is of the Lord." By and large, however, the textual tradition retains the reference to a commandment, albeit in different forms and sometimes in the plural ("what I have written to you, that they are commandments of the Lord"). The editors of the *GNT*[4] have opted for the reading in the singular ($\mathfrak{P}^{46}$, A, B, and the "corrected" ℵ). With this formula Paul underscores the authoritative nature of his directives to the community, highlighting thereby the need for good order in the liturgical assembly.

38. *If anyone does not acknowledge this, that person is not acknowledged:* Variations in the textual tradition read Paul's words as if they expressed an exhortation to a specific kind of social behavior, either in the form of a passive imperative, "let that person not be acknowledged" (𝔓⁴⁶, B, K, Ψ, the weight of the Byzantine tradition and correctors to ℵ, A and D), or in the form of a second person plural imperative, "do not acknowledge that one" (D). An imperative form would be consistent with the context of ch. 14, in which Paul is constantly exhorting the Corinthians to adopt appropriate behavior when they come together. The present passive (ℵ, A; cf. Origen, Ephraem, Jerome) is the *lectio difficilior* and enjoys the greater likelihood of being the authentic reading. A reading in the present passive (see 8:2-3, where active and passive forms of the same verb occur) is more forceful. The verb *agnoeō*, literally "not to know" is generally used of things, but it is occasionally used of persons (cf. MM 50).

    With the passive form of the verb Paul's words are an expression of "holy law," a literary formula used by Paul in order to speak about the eschatological retribution of human conduct (cf. 3:17). Characteristic of the formula, a kind of eschatological law of talion, is the use of the same language to describe the offense and its punishment. In 14:38 the passive is a divine passive. The idea of divine action is suggested without God's name being cited. In this fashion a sense of the transcendence of God is maintained. Paul's use of this sentence of holy law provides a strong reinforcement of the idea evoked in v. 37. If anyone does not acknowledge the command of the Lord that person will not be acknowledged by the Lord. If anyone does not know, in the sense of accepting and living by the command of the Lord, that one will not be known *(a- gnoeitai)* by the Lord (cf. 8:3; comp. 13:12). Only if love (see ch. 13, the directive rhetorical digression for 1 Corinthians 12–14) moves a person to recognize and accept the gifts of one another within the community will that one be known and acknowledged by the Lord.

39. *Wherefore, my brothers and sisters, strive to prophesy and do not forbid speaking in tongues:* A strong inferential "wherefore" introduces the conclusion to Paul's extended exhortation on prophecy and tongues. The injunction is given additional force by the apostrophic "my brothers and sisters," reinforced by "my" *(mou)*, which does not occur in any of the other vocative uses of "brothers and sisters" in 1 Corinthians (cf. 15:58). As a final exhortation on the importance of charismatic gifts Paul's counsel recalls the letter to the Thessalonians, "do not quench the Spirit; do not despise the words of prophets" (1 Thess 5:19-20). "Striving," "prophesying," and "speaking in tongues" are three expressions that form an *inclusio* with 14:1-2, thereby constituting ch. 14 as a discrete literary unit within the letter.

    The manuscript tradition witnesses to some textual variance that, however, does not significantly affect the meaning of Paul's exhortation. Some manuscripts (including 𝔓⁴⁶, D, F, etc.) omit "my." The expression "do not forbid speaking in tongues" appears in a variety of stylistic forms (order of words, use or lack of the article and preposition).

40. *Let everything be done with propriety and in orderly fashion:* Paul's long exposition on the spiritual gifts, which began in 12:1, is brought to conclusion with

a final exhortation, "let everything be in order" (*kata taxin ginesthō*; cf. 14:26; 16:14). This is Paul's only known use of the word *taxis* with its connotations of political and social order. The term is properly at home in a rhetorical appeal whose purpose is the unity and harmony of the body politic, as is Paul's first letter to the Corinthians. Its emphatic position in Paul's exposition reveals that the good order of the community is of primary importance to Paul in the entire exposition. The good order of the assembly should reflect the good order of the body politic, identified in 12:12-26 as the body of Christ.

For Reference and Further Study

Allison, Robert W. "Let Women be Silent in the Churches (1 Cor. 14.33b-36): What did Paul Really Say, and What did it Mean?" *JSNT* 32 (1988) 27–60.

Arichea, Daniel C. "The Silence of Women in the Church: Theology and Translation of 1 Corinthians 14.33b-36," *BiTr* 46 (1995) 101–112.

Barton, Stephen C. "Paul's Sense of Place: An Anthropological Approach to Community Formation in Corinth," *NTS* 32 (1986) 225–246.

Blampied, Anne B. "Paul and Silence for 'the Women' in 1 Corinthians 14:34-35," *StBT* 13 (1983) 143–165.

Bryce, David W. "'As in All the Churches of the Saints.' A Text-Critical Study of 1 Corinthians 14:34, 35," *LTJ* 31 (1997) 31–39.

Collins, Raymond F. *The Birth of the New Testament: The Origin and Development of the First Christian Generation.* New York: Crossroad, 1993, 97–104.

Ellis, E. Earle. "The Silenced Wives of Corinth (1 Cor 14. 34-5)" in Eldon J. Epp and Gordon D. Fee, eds., *New Testament Textual Criticism: Its Significance for Exegesis.* Oxford: Clarendon, 1981, 213–220.

Flanagan, Neal M., and E. H. Snyder, "Did Paul Put Down Women in 1 Cor 14:34-36?" *BTB* 11 (1981) 10–12.

Hasitschka, Martin. "'Die Frauen in den Gemeinden sollen schweigen.' 1 Kor 14,33b-36—Anweisung des Paulus zur rechten Ordnung im Gottesdienst," *SNTU* 22 (1997) 47–56.

Jervis, L. Ann. "1 Corinthians 14.34-35: A Reconsideration of Paul's Limitation of the Free Speech of Some Corinthian Women," *JSNT* 58 (1995) 51–74.

Kroeger, Richard C., and Catherine Kroeger. "Strange Tongues or Plain Talk?" *Daughters of Sarah* 12 (1986) 10–13.

Maier, Walter A. "An Exegetical Study of 1 Corinthians 14:33b-38," *CTQ* 55 (1991) 81–104.

Manus, Chris U. "The Subordination of the Women in the Church. 1 Cor 14:33b-36 Reconsidered," *RAT* 8 (1984) 183–195.

Munro, Winsome. "Interpolation in the Epistles: Weighing Probability," *NTS* 36 (1990) 431–443.

_____. "Patriarchy and Charismatic Community in Paul" in *Women and Religion: 1972 AAR Proceedings.* Missoula: Scholars, 1973, 141–159.

_____. "Women, Text and the Canon: The Strange Case of 1 Corinthians 14:33-35," *BTB* 18 (1988) 26–31.

Murphy-O'Connor, Jerome. "Interpolations in 1 Corinthians," *CBQ* 48 (1986) 81–94.

Nadeau, Denis J. "Le problème des femmes en 1 Co 14/33b-35," *EThR* 69 (1994) 63–65.

Nuccum, Curt. "The Voice of the Manuscripts on the Silence of Women: The External Evidence for 1 Cor 14.34-5," *NTS* 43 (1997) 242–255.

Odell-Scott, David W. "Let the Women Speak in Church. An Egalitarian Interpretation of 1 Cor 14:33b-36," *BTB* 13 (1983) 90–93.

_____. "In Defense of an Egalitarian Interpretation of 1 Cor 14:34-36. A Reply to Murphy-O'Connor's Critique," *BTB* 17 (1987) 100–103.

Payne, Philip B. "Fuldensis, Sigla for Variants in Vaticanus, and 1 Cor 14.34-5," *NTS* 41 (1995) 240–262.

_____. "MS. 88 as Evidence for a Text without 1 Cor 14.34-5," *NTS* 44 (1988) 152–158.

Petzer, J. H. "Reconsidering the Silent Women of Corinth—a Note on 1 Corinthians 14:34-35," *Theologia Evangelica* 26 (1993) 132–138.

Richardson, William. "Liturgical Order and Glossolalia in 1 Corinthians 14.26c-33a," *NTS* 32 (1986) 144–153.

Rowe, Arthur. "Silence and the Christian Women at Corinth. An Examination of 1 Corinthians 14:33b-36," *CV* 33 (1990) 41–84.

Schüssler Fiorenza, Elisabeth. *In Memory of Her: A Feminist Theological Reconstruction of Christian Origins.* New York: Crossroad, 1983, 230–233.

Vander Stichele, Caroline. "Is Silence Golden? Paul and Women's Speech in Corinth," *LS* 20 (1995) 241–253.

Wire, Antoinette C. *Corinthian Women Prophets* 135–158.

G. SIXTH RHETORICAL DEMONSTRATION (15:1-58)

Thomas W. Gillespie (*First Theologians* 235) considers ch. 15 an "instance of prophetic utterance" with intertextual links to the discussion on prophecy in ch. 14. As an instance of prophetic utterance it consists of the interpretation of the apostolic kerygma (vv. 3b-8) in the light of a revelation (vv. 50-58). Its use of illustrative scripture and its critique of a so-called prophetic utterance (v. 12b) confirms its being an instance of prophetic utterance. For Gillespie the additional transitional formulae found in vv. 12, 20, 35, 50, and 58 neatly divide ch. 15, whose primary focus is death, into six units, vv. 1-11, 12-19, 20-34, 35-49, 50-57, 58. In the demonstration Paul seeks to respond to those who deny that there is a resurrection of the dead.

In his response to those who doubted, Paul first proclaims that the gospel he preached is the common gospel of all believers. He makes his point by affirming that he simply handed on what he himself had received. The gospel he has preached is the gospel that others have preached. There is but one and the same gospel across time and space. Some of those who denied the resurrection of the dead may also have denied the resurrection of Jesus. That Paul devotes as much attention as he does to the appearances of the risen Christ—he cites six witnesses in all—can be taken as an indication that the reality of the resurrection of Christ might have been doubted and/or contested in some Corinthian quarters. The rehearsal of witnesses to the risen Christ provides prima facie evidence that Paul was much concerned with the reality of the resurrection, a singular event to be understood soteriologically.

A crucial question in the interpretation of ch. 15 is the relationship between vv. 1-11 and the rest of the chapter. Some authors—Peter von der Osten-Sacken, for example—claim that Paul was under attack at Corinth. He had to defend himself before he could treat the real issue at hand, namely, the denial of the resurrection of the body. On this reading of Paul's letter the rehearsal of the creed is Paul's defense. Having established his apostolic authority on the basis of his experience of the risen Lord, Paul can then spell out the implications of the traditional kerygma and confront those who deny bodily resurrection.

Another way to read 15:1-11 is to pay due attention to its rhetorical function. Verses 1-2 serve as the introduction to Paul's argument (the *exordium* or *proemium*). Paul's citation of the credal formula (vv. 3b-5) serves the argument as a kind of *narratio* or *diēgēsis*, a rehearsal of the facts that can then serve as a ground for his subsequent argumentation. The appeal to the common and traditional faith of the church is consistent with Paul's initial description of the Christian community in Corinth. In 1:2 he had reminded them that they were called to be holy. In this they were not alone, for they were called "together with all those in every place who invoke the name of the Lord Jesus Christ." The rehearsal of facts continues until Paul brings it to closure with an affirmation of the Corinthians' belief in the gospel that is believed by all (v. 11; cf. vv. 1-2).

Verse 12, although phrased in the form of a rhetorical question, "how can some among you say that there is no resurrection of the dead?" functions as a statement of the case, the *prothesis* of Paul's demonstration. Some deny the resurrection of the dead. Arguing that there is a resurrection of the dead, Paul makes his point in two movements of thought. He first deals with the reality of the resurrection of the dead (vv. 12-34); then he takes up the issue of how it is possible for the dead to be raised (vv.

35-57). Rhetorically the two units function as proofs *(pisteis)* of Paul's demonstration. The argument is brought to closure with the peroration of v. 58.

The exposition of the first proof is set forth in the familiar chiastic pattern: A (vv. 12-19), B (vv. 20-28), A' (vv. 29-34). Elements A and A' presume that the resurrection of Jesus is related to the resurrection of those who believe in him. If there is no resurrection from the dead, then Christ has not been raised. If Christ has not been raised there is little meaning to what Paul and the Corinthians have been doing. Futility would have been the hallmark of their existence.

Element B (vv. 20-28) seeks to explain the link between the resurrection of Christ and the resurrection of those who believe in him. Christ is "the first fruits of those who have died" (15:20). The resurrection of Christ, though singular, is not a reality that affected Christ alone (see 1 Thess 4:14, 16). As a Jew of the Pharisaic persuasion (Phil 3:5) Paul held that the resurrection of the dead is God's ultimate salvific act. The resurrection of Christ from the dead is the inaugural event in the resurrection of the dead. The resurrection of Christ stands or falls with the possibility of the resurrection of all believers. If Christ has been raised it is possible for all believers to be raised; if resurrection from the dead is, in principle, an impossibility, then Christ has not been raised.

Throughout the discussion Paul identifies Jesus as "Christ." This title alone is used as a designation for Jesus. In Pauline usage this honorific epithet is used of Jesus insofar as he has died and has been raised. The use of the title without mention of the name of Jesus or the title "Lord" is striking. Paul normally used "Lord," his favorite christological title, when writing about the resurrection. "Lord" recalls the resurrection and looks ahead to the revelation of Jesus as the parousiac Lord. The use of the "Christ" title is more appropriate in 15:12-34. It calls to mind the death and resurrection of Jesus. The title allows Christ to serve as an effective paradigm for the Corinthians who will die but who will also be raised from the dead.

In the second proof (vv. 35-57) Paul addressed the issue of how it is possible for the dead to be raised. In his exposition he rejoins a Pharisaic discussion on the nature of the resurrection body. A kind of midrashic exposition on the creation narratives of Genesis 1–2 allows Paul to affirm that God provides appropriate bodies for all he creates (vv. 35-44a). He goes on to say that the first Adam has only a natural body whereas the second Adam has an inspirited body (vv. 44b-49). The creation stories continue to focus Paul's exposition as he urges Christians to put on the image of the heavenly one, the inspirited second Adam.

The apocalyptic scenario of vv. 50-57 provides Paul with the language to answer the question of his imaginary interlocutor (v. 35). With what kind of body will those come who are raised from the dead? Paul responds that they will come with a transformed body, a body that is imperishable and immortal. God makes all that possible through our Lord Jesus Christ. Therefore, says Paul, remain steadfast in the gospel.

FOR REFERENCE AND FURTHER STUDY

Barth, Gerhard. "Zur Frage nach der in 1Korinther 15 bekämpften Auferstehungsleugnung," *ZNW* 83 (1992) 187–201.
Boer, Martinus C. de. *The Defeat of Death: Apocalyptic Eschatology in 1 Corinthians 15 and Romans 5.* JSNT.S 22. Sheffield: JSOT Press, 1988.
Frutiger, Simone. "La mort, et puis . . . avant? 1 Corinthiens 15," *EThR* 55 (1980) 199–229.
Hasler, Victor. "Credo und Auferstehung in Korinth. Erwägungen zu I Kor 15," *ThZ* 40 (1984) 12–33.
Holleman, Joost. *Resurrection and Parousia: A Traditio-Historical Study of Paul's Eschatology in 1 Corinthians 15.* NovT.S 84. Leiden: Brill, 1996.
Lindemann, Andreas. "Paulus und die korinthische Eschatologie. Zur These von einer 'Entwicklung' im paulinischen Denken," *NTS* 37 (1991) 373–399.
Lorenzi, Lorenzo De, ed. *Résurrection du Christ et des Chrétiens. 1 Co 15.* Série Monographique de Benedictina 8. Rome: Abbaye de S. Paul, 1985.
Pérez Gordo, Alfonso. "¿Es 1 Co 15 una homilía?" *Burgense* 27 (1986) 9–98.
Plank, Karl A. "Resurrection Theology: the Corinthian Controversy Reexamined," *PRS* 8 (1981) 41–54.
Plevnik, Joseph. *Paul and the Parousia: An Exegetical and Theological Investigation.* Peabody, Mass.: Hendrickson, 1997.
Saw, Insawn. *Paul's Rhetoric in 1 Corinthians 15: An Analysis Utilizing the Theories of Classical Rhetoric.* Lewiston: Mellen Biblical Press, 1995.
Stenger, Werner. "Beobachtungen zur Argumentationsstruktur von 1 Kor 15," *LB* 45 (1979) 71–128.
Vorster, J. N. "Resurrection Faith in 1 Corinthians 15," *Neotest.* 23 (1989) 287–307.
Wagner, Günter. ". . . encore 1 Corinthiens 15. Si les chrétiens refusent d'agir, alors Christ n'est pas ressuscité," *EThR* 56 (1981) 599–607. English translation in *IBS* 6 (1984) 27–39.

1. *The Creed* (15:1-11)

1. I want you to know, brothers and sisters, the gospel I have proclaimed to you, which you received, and in which you stand firm, 2. through which you are saved, if you hold fast to the word I proclaimed to you— unless you have believed in vain. 3. For in the first instance I delivered

to you what I had also received, that Christ died for our sins according to the scriptures 4. and that he was buried and that he was raised on the third day according to the scriptures 5. and that he appeared to Cephas, then to the twelve; 6. then he appeared at one time to more than five hundred brothers and sisters, many of whom remain until now, but some have died; 7. then he appeared to James, indeed to all the apostles; 8. last of all he appeared also to me, as to a miscarriage. 9. For I am the least of the apostles, one who is not worthy to be called an apostle, because I persecuted the church of God. 10. Yet by the grace of God I am what I am and his grace in me was not in vain. On the contrary I have toiled more than all of them, not I but the grace of God that is with me. 11. Whether I or they, so we have proclaimed and thus you have believed.

INTERPRETATION

A traditional credal formula is set forth in order to remind the Christians of Corinth of the key elements of the gospel, what it means for them to acknowledge Jesus as Lord. At bottom there is the confession that "Christ"—one of Paul's favorite christological epithets!—has died and has been raised (vv. 3-4). Each part of the traditional two-part formula is expanded by a clause that underscores the reality of the salvific events highlighted in the creed. The burial points to the death of Christ, the appearances to his resurrection. Each part of the credal formula is qualified by a brief expression that serves to indicate how the reality is to be understood: Christ died for our sins and was raised on the third day. A third qualifying expression, "according to the scriptures," found in each part of the twofold formula, provides a kind of hermeneutical key for the elements of the gospel cited in the creed. The message is to be understood in the light of the Scriptures.

Throughout the letter Paul has appealed to the Corinthians to overcome the things that have divided the community. He often cites himself as an example for their consideration. Verses 1-11 serve Paul's argument insofar as the subunit presents him as someone who has accepted the traditional kerygma. He is someone who has experienced the risen Lord and who has, by the grace of God, allowed that experience to change his life. What seems to be an apology is really a feature of his *ethos* appeal (cf. ch. 9).

The Credal Formula. The confessional formula found in vv. 3b-5 is the longest of the credal formulas cited by Paul (cf. 1 Thess 1:10; 4:14; 5:10). The formula is neatly balanced. Each member of the bipartite creed consists of four elements strictly parallel with one another: (1) an affirmation about Christ (death, burial); (2) a qualifying prepositional phrase; (3) the formulaic "according to the scriptures;" (4) a second affirmation that substantiates the first affirmation. The death and resurrection of Christ are clearly seen as correlative realities: his death is the condition for his resurrection; his resurrection fulfills his death.

The creed speaks of Christ, a christological title that dominates ch. 15 (vv. 3, 12, 13, 14, 15, 16, 17, 18, 19, 20, 22, 23[2x]). In this chapter the title is used without further qualification more often than not. The designation of Jesus as "Christ" evokes the memory of his death and resurrection. Paul presents Christ as the object of the creed. This is different from the creed of 1 Thess 4:14, which focuses on "Jesus." The use of the Christ title in 15:1-11 is consistent with the usage throughout 1 Corinthians, where the Christ title is highlighted from the first mention of the gospel (1:17). Used in the creed, the title allows Paul to focus on the reality of the death of the mortal Christ and on the reality of the resurrection, an act of God.

The first element in the two-part creed is the simple affirmation that Christ died and was raised. No mention is made of the cross (cf. 1:13, 17, 18, 23; 2:2, 8), nor is there mention of "from the dead" (cf. 15:12, 20; Rom 1:4; 4:24; 6:4, 9; 7:4; 8:11[2x], 34; 10:7, 9; Gal 1:1). The creed's affirmation that Jesus was raised *(egēgertai)* is in the perfect passive, a passive that suggests divine agency in the resurrection (v. 15). The resurrection of Christ is the act of God. Its perfect tense contrasts with the preceding aorists, "died . . . was buried" *(apethanen . . . etaphē)*. The aorists indicate that the events took place at a given moment in human history; the perfect tense evokes the continuing effect of Jesus' resurrection. One of these effects is that Christ has appeared to Paul (v. 9); another is that the resurrection of Jesus serves as the ground of Christian hope.

The second element in the credal formula consists of a pair of qualifying prepositional phrases, "for our sins" and "on the third day." These phrases of the creed must be understood in the light of the Scriptures. "According to the scriptures" *(kata tas graphas)* provides the hermeneutical key by means of which believers can understand and interpret the death and resurrection of Christ. The phrase is not a fulfillment formula; it is an interpretive formula. The death and resurrection of Jesus are to be understood by means of biblical categories. The interpretive formula is generic, but commentators generally point to Isa 53:3-5 as a passage of Scripture that is particularly helpful for understanding the death and resurrection of Jesus.

The prepositional phrases that serve as the parallel parts of the second element in the confessional formula, "for our sins" and "on the third day," point the direction in which the scriptural interpreter must go if he or she is to understand the death and resurrection of Christ. "For our sins" elucidates the meaning of Christ's death. The words evoke Isa 53:5 (see the Masoretic text and *Tg. Isa* 53; compare Rom 4:25) and suggest the expiatory nature of Jesus' death. "On the third day" interprets the resurrection. The formula may be an allusion to Hos 6:2 (LXX). In any case it situates the resurrection on the first day of the week. The temporal reference may provide a hermeneutical clue to the understanding of the resurrection as a new creation, God's act (see vv. 20-22, 38-41, 42-50; cf. 2 Cor 5:17; Gal 6:15).

The parts of the fourth element in the balanced formula, "was buried" and "appeared," are introduced by "and that" *(kai hoti)*. The fourth element is the reality factor in the confessional formula. The burial of Christ points to the reality of his death; the appearances of Christ witness to the reality of his resurrection. Paul does not otherwise affirm that Christ was buried. That the verb "was buried" *(etaphē)* does not appear elsewhere in his letters is a sign of the traditional nature of the credal formula the apostle cites in vv. 3-5. The verb "appeared" serves as another indication of the traditional nature of Paul's creed. This expression was used in early Christian confessional material to describe the appearances of the risen Jesus to his disciples (Luke 24:34; Acts 13:31; cf. Matt 17:3; Mark 9:4).

The formulaic introduction to the credal formula, "I delivered to you what I also received" (15:3), suggests—and its non-Pauline vocabulary confirms—that the creed of 15:3b-5 is a traditional formulation. Some scholars, especially Philipp Vielhauer and Hans Conzelmann, have argued that the confessional formula arose in Hellenistic Christian circles, but most scholars (e.g., Joachim Jeremias, John Kloppenborg) are convinced that it originated in a Palestinian context. Every element of the confession derives its meaning from Jewish apocalyptic thought: Christ, sins, scripture, resurrection, and the symbolic "Twelve" (v. 5). An anarthrous "Christ," the Aramaic "Cephas" (v. 5), and the *parallelismus membrorum* point to its Palestinian origins. The formulation of the creed may have been modified in the Hellenistic church. The expressions "according to the scriptures" *(kata tas graphas)* and "appeared" *(ōphthē)* and the Septuagintal allusions suggest a final Hellenistic form. Within the Hellenistic church the credal formula may have been used in a baptismal setting (cf. Rom 6:3-4; Col 2:12). Paul himself may have added some emphasis to the creed by repeating "and that" *(kai hoti)*. The second appearance of these words (v. 4) emphasizes "he appeared" *(ōphthē)*, a verb form that Paul repeats four times in a sequence leading to the appearance of Christ to Paul himself (v. 8). The three additional uses of "he appeared" probably come from the hand of Paul. They climax with an appearance of Christ to Paul (the rhetorical device of *klimax* or *gradatio*). The serial arrangement (then . . . then . . . last of all . . .) is characteristic of Paul's literary style.

In the LXX the verb "to appear" *(ōphthē)* is used of the appearances of God (Gen 12:7; 26:24; 35:9; 48:3; Exod 6:3; 1 Kgs 3:5; 9:2; 2 Chr 1:7; 3:1;

7:12) and the manifestation of God's glory (Exod 16:10; Lev 9:23; Num 14:10; 16:19; 17:7; 20:6). Given the Septuagint's tendency to use this expression of the manifestation of God during the great eras of Israel's salvation (the patriarchs, the Exodus, David and Solomon), the use of this verb form in the credal formula indicates that the appearance of Jesus inaugurates a new era of salvation.

Paul. Paul is concerned that his apostolate be considered as similar to that of those who were among the earliest witnesses to the resurrection, the leaders of the Jerusalem community, Cephas and James, and the Twelve of earliest Christian memory. He also wants his proclamation of the gospel to be considered as of no less importance than that of other apostles. To establish the content of his preaching on an authoritative basis he not only states that his gospel reflects the common creed of the church, but also focuses on his apostolate. He returns once again (see especially ch. 9) to a motif announced in the opening words of the letter where Paul described himself as one called an apostle by God (1:1).

In his reflection on his own apostolate Paul makes good use of the rhetorical device of *sygkrisis,* comparison (cf. 9:5-6). Use of the device enhances Paul's *ethos.* The comparison with Cephas (cf. Gal 1:18-24; 2:6-14), cited first and in such a way that the other witnesses are an addendum to the mention of Cephas, is particularly important. Throughout the letter Paul has presented his own apostolate in contrapuntal fashion to that of Cephas (see 1:12; 3:22; 9:5). In 15:1-11 his argument is that he may be the least of the apostles but he is no less an apostle, because he has seen the risen Christ and has been called. He may have been unworthy to be an apostle, but he has been called and established as an apostle by a gracious God who freely does what he does. Paul has responded faithfully to his call, working harder, thanks to God's grace, than any of the other apostles.

Finally, Paul would have his readers know that his apostolate is effective. Their own belief is a sign of the effectiveness of his preaching (cf. 9:2). Three times in his reflection on the apostolate (v. 10) Paul mentions the grace of God, just as he does in Gal 1:11-15 (cf. 2:9). The grace of God, the gracious gift of God, is the source of Paul's call; it is the power of his preaching; it is the source of that preaching's effectiveness. Verses 9 and 10 form a virtual aside, a kind of apologetic digression. In thought and phraseology the verses are similar to Gal 1:11-15. Both passages speak of the apostle, the call, grace, and the persecution of the church of God. In both 1 Corinthians and the letter to the Galatians Paul underscores both his apostolic authority as one who has been called according to the will of God and the veracity of his message.

From another perspective vv. 10-11 provide a kind of *inclusio* with vv. 1-2, reprising, albeit with different words, the themes of preaching, belief, acting "in vain," and emphasizing Paul's own mission as in the introduction to this epistolary unit. With this construction Paul circumscribes vv. 1-11 as a self-contained literary unit that highlights the traditional kerygma as the core of his proclamation. Taken in its entirety the unit emphasizes Paul's apostolic mandate and focuses on the resurrection of Jesus. Thereafter Paul is able to address the issue at hand, the claim by some members of the community that there is no resurrection from the dead (15:12).

NOTES

1. *I want you to know, brothers and sisters, the gospel I have proclaimed to you:* Paul's use of a disclosure formula (cf. 12:3; 2 Cor 8:1; Gal 1:11) establishes the transition (cf. "concerning" in 7:1, 25; 8:1; 12:1) from the previous discussion on spiritual realities. The formula itself suggests that Paul is going to talk about something the community already knows. "The gospel I have proclaimed to you" (cf. 9:2) is what the community has already experienced. The proclamation of the gospel is the task that characterizes Paul as an apostle (9:1-23; 15:9; cf. 1 Thess 2:4). Preaching the gospel is his mission in life. Fulfillment of that task enables Paul to have a paternal role with respect to the Corinthians (4:15).

   which you received, and in which you stand firm: The gospel Paul has preached is a gospel the Corinthians had "received" (cf. 1 Thess 2:13). Paul's choice of language is technical. "Receive" *(parelabete)* reflects the Hebrew *qibbēl*, describing the process in which students learned from their rabbinic masters (see above, p. 426). Paul's words sound almost as if their function is that of a *captatio benevolentiae.* Not only have the Corinthians received the gospel, they are also steadfast in maintaining their faith in it. In Hellenistic Judaism the verb "to stand fast" *(histēmi)* was used to describe steadfast faithfulness to the law and covenant (1 Kings 6:12; 2 Kings 23:3; Sir 11:20; 43:10; *T. Dan.* 5:4; *T. Jos.* 1:3; Pseudo-Philo, *Biblical Antiquities* 9:4).

2. *through which you are saved, if you hold fast to the word I proclaimed to you—unless you have believed in vain:* Here, as elsewhere in Paul's correspondence, "word" *(logō)* is a synonym for "gospel" (cf. 1:18). The expression accentuates the source and content of the word. Paul's word is the word of God, the word from God, the word about God. Reference to the saving power of the word of God rehearses a theme with which Paul had begun his letter (cf. 1:18, 21). God saves through the word that Paul preaches (cf. 9:22; 10:33).

   There is, nonetheless, a proviso. Those to whom the gospel is preached are saved under the condition that they hold fast to what they have heard. "To hold fast" is an expression similar to the vocabulary Paul employed in 11:2. There he had also used the technical language for handing on tradition. There he praised the Corinthians for holding fast to the traditions he had delivered to them. Now, however, Paul's rhetoric is phrased in a conditional clause. This suggests that some in the community have not retained the gospel he had preached (cf. 15:34). Their belief, like his preaching, would have been in vain (cf. 15:14; 1 Thess 2:1). Conditional clauses abound in 1 Corinthians as Paul accommodates his words to the real situation of those to whom he is writing.

3. *For in the first instance I delivered to you what I had also received:* Paul's explanatory words (note the explanatory "for") interpret the "gospel" that Paul had proclaimed and the Corinthians had "received" (v. 1). Paul presents himself as someone who has also received the tradition; in this regard he is no different from the Corinthians themselves. Throughout the letter he had proposed his own conduct as an example for the Corinthians. Now, for the last time, he offers his own acceptance of the kerygma as an example for them.

The words "deliver/receive" recall the technical terminology of the rabbinic schools, in which "deliver *(māsar)*/receive *(qibbēl)*" was the preferred language to designate the faithful handing on of the tradition that had been received from one's teachers (see above, pp. 425–426). That Paul uses the language of tradition as adeptly as he does suggests that he had formal rabbinic training prior to becoming a Christian. In 15:1-2 he appeals to the common and traditional faith of the church as he lays ground for a response to those who would deny the resurrection (15:12).

"In the first instance" has neither chronological nor logical significance. Rather it points to the kerygma, expressed in the creed, as the focal point of Paul's gospel. The good news can be and is summarized in the creed Paul had received. His acceptance of the kerygma underscores his fidelity to the tradition and undergirds the authority on which he was able to address a command of the Lord to the Corinthians (14:37).

3b-4. *that Christ died for our sins according to the scriptures and that he was buried and that he was raised on the third day according to the scriptures:* A simpler form of the creed in 1 Thess 4:14 simply affirms the death and resurrection of Jesus without further qualification. That formula, too, is traditional, but it uses a different verb, "to rise up" *(anestē),* in reference to the resurrection.

The early church used several biblical texts in its scriptural reflection on the death and resurrection of Christ (cf. Acts 2–3, with its references to Ps 16:8-11 and Ps 110:1, the scripture most frequently cited in the New Testament), but scholars find the most useful texts in the fourth Isaian Servant of YHWH canticle (Isaiah 53). Some interesting parallels can be found in the targum on Isaiah 53. Daniel Patte has, however, observed that the kerygma about Christ itself functioned as a kind of oral scripture for early Christians (*Paul's Faith and the Power of the Gospel* [Philadelphia: Fortress, 1983] 213, 227).

The formulae used by Paul to qualify the resurrection are striking. His use of the phrase "for our sins" confirms the traditional nature of this credal formula. Apart from biblical citations (Rom 4:7-8) and traditional formulae (cf. Gal 1:4; Col 1:14) Paul rarely uses sin *(hamartia)* in the plural. The notion of "taking away sins" is generally absent from his theology (cf. 15:17; comp. Eph 2:1). As for Christ's being raised "on the third day," Jens Christensen thinks the phrase specifically refers to the third day of creation on which, according to some interpreters contemporary with Paul, the garden of Eden with its tree of life was created.

5. *and that he appeared:* "He appeared" (*ōphthē*) is in a verbal form that may be understood as a verb in the passive voice with the sense of "was seen by" or, in an intransitive sense, "appeared" (BDF 313; cf. Luke 1:11 [22:43]; Acts 7:2, 26, 30 and 16:9; Rev 12:1, 3). The traditional Jewish understanding of divine transcendence, particularly strong at the time of Paul, suggests that the use of this traditional language with regard to a manifestation of the divine did not imply physical sight. In the biblical accounts of a manifestation of the divine, auditory elements predominate.

to Cephas: Paul's mention of resurrection appearances to Cephas (on the name see note on 1:12) and the Twelve in v. 5 is the oldest extant literary attestation to the resurrection appearances of Jesus. The tradition that Peter was the first to have seen the risen Lord is echoed in Luke 24:34 (cf. Mark 16:7). Luke also tells of Peter's visit to the empty tomb. See Luke 24:12, a verse that on text-critical grounds some scholars believe not to have been part of the original text. Having previously given the verse a D rating, "high degree of doubt," but including it in their critical edition of the gospel, the editors of *GNT*[4] now assign it a B rating, "some degree of doubt." The Fourth Evangelist, who also tells about Peter's visit to the empty tomb (John 20:2-10) and adds to the risen Jesus dossier a tale of an appearance of the risen Jesus to seven disciples places Peter first on the list (John 21:1-19). The narrative includes a dialogue, contrapuntal to Peter's threefold denial of Jesus (John 18:15-18; 25-27), between the risen Jesus and Peter.

then to the twelve: Apart from the expanded confessional formula of 15:3-7 the Twelve are not otherwise mentioned by Paul. The number "twelve" is symbolic, alluding to the twelve tribes of Israel. Jesus' choice of twelve from among his disciples then has eschatological significance, symbolizing a new/renewed people of God. Memory of Jesus' appearance to the Twelve also belongs to the tradition of the early church. See Matt 28:16-20; Luke 24:36-53; cf. Mark 16:14-18).

6. *then he appeared at one time to more than five hundred brothers and sisters, many of whom remain until now:* "Then" (*epeita*) is a Pauline term; ten of its sixteen NT occurrences are in Paul. The use of "then" to string together different elements is a Pauline literary technique (cf. 1 Cor 12:28; Gal 1:18–2:1), as is the use of a triad, a series of three parallel expressions. The conjunction marks the transition between the traditional kerygma synopsized in the credal formula and Paul's exploitation of the traditional kerygma. In vv. 6-8 the words are Paul's own: "then he appeared . . . then he appeared . . . finally he appeared. . . ." In Gal 1:18–2:1 a series also concludes with reference to Paul's own experience.

Rhetorically the series of "then" clauses assures the readers that nothing has been left out. As the inaugural event of the new creation the resurrection of Christ is an eschatological event. It has an abiding effect (see the use of the perfect, "he was raised," v. 4). The string of Christ's appearances has been made possible by his resurrection. The sequential pattern recalls the apocalyptic view of end-time reality, characterized globally by a periodic view of history. In God's plan of salvation everything falls into place.

The appearance of the risen Christ to five hundred believers is otherwise unattested in the New Testament. Some authors (e.g., Gerd Lüdemann and Alf Özen, in *What Really Happened to Jesus: A Historical Approach to the Resurrection* [London: SCM, 1995]) opine that the reference is to the Pentecost event (Acts 2:1-13). "At one time" (*ephapax*, cf. Rom 6:10) normally indicates a singular event. The reference to the five hundred appears, however, to be Paul's attempt to sum up the appearances of the Risen One to all believers. He seeks to provide some verification of the resurrection. Christ appeared to many people. The experience of the Risen One was not a subjective hallucination; it was shared by a good number of people. Some of these are still alive and can attest to their experience.

Only with the inclusive *adelphoi*, "brothers and sisters," does Paul make any allusion to the appearance of Jesus to women. He makes no mention of the appearance of the Risen One to the Galilean women (Matt 28:9-10; Luke 24:10-11; John 20:14-18; cf. Mark 16:9-11). According to the prevalent Jewish understanding of the law in his time women could not be cited as witnesses.

but some have died: The metaphorical use of *koimaomai*, "to die" (literally "to fall asleep") is in tandem with Paul's preferential use of *egeirō* (literally "to awaken") as a cipher for resurrection. Paul uses the verb in reference to those who have died and will be raised from among the dead. See 7:39; 11:30; 15:6, 18, 20, 51; cf. 1 Thess 4:13, 14, 15. The metaphor, signifying death but without further qualification, was used in extra-biblical literature as early as the fifth century B.C.E. (Sophocles, *Electra* 509). Paul commonly employed the verb in this figurative sense, especially when writing about the resurrection of the dead.

That some have died (cf. 11:30) introduces the issue of the death of some believers, the reality that may have triggered the contentious affirmation that there is no resurrection from the dead (v. 12; cf. 1 Thess 4:13-17). The affirmation is not without rhetorical significance in Paul's argument. The creed of the early community grounds Paul's affirmation of the resurrection. The early Christian community's experience of death did not confound that community's holding fast to the creed Paul has handed on to the Corinthians. Similarly the experience of death should not deter the Corinthians from believing in the resurrection.

7. *then he appeared to James:* The only apostles Paul cites by name in his rehearsal of witnesses to the risen Christ are Cephas and James. He met them on the occasion of his first visit to Jerusalem as a Christian (Gal 1:18-19). Other than Cephas and James, Paul names only John as one of the Jerusalem apostles (see Gal 2:9). That the apostle cites the names of Cephas and James as witnesses to the Risen One suggests that he expects his readers to be familiar with them. They were the successive leaders of the Christian community in Jerusalem, a community with which the Christians at Corinth had some contact (16:3).

On the basis of the parallelism between v. 7 and v. 5 Jacob Kremer (*Das älteste Zeugnis von der Auferstehung Christi* [Stuttgart: Katholisches Bibelwerk, 1967] 28) has argued that this verse also represents a pre-Pauline tradition. The reference to the appearance to James may be a cipher for an otherwise unattested appearance of Jesus to his "brothers and sisters" (cf. Matt 28:10). Paul seems, however, to make no qualitative distinction between the resurrection appearance to Cephas *(ōphthē Kēphą)* and the appearance to James *(ōpthē Iakōbǭ).*

indeed to all the apostles: For Paul the "apostles" are a group larger than the Twelve, who constituted the intimate circle of Jesus' disciples (see note on 1:1). The reference to *all* the apostles provides a transition to a presentation of himself as one called (to be) an apostle. The "all" *(pasin)* is probably a Pauline gloss on the tradition inserted for his own argumentative purpose; it adds emphasis to the word "apostles" (BDF 275.5).

8. *last of all he appeared also to me, as to a miscarriage:* "Last of all" *(eschaton de pantōn)* does not necessarily have a chronological sense. It can bring the series to completion, indicating that nothing has been omitted, or it can indicate the least item in a series. The latter is the meaning of the expression as Paul uses it (cf. 4:9). His simile *(hōsperei,* "as") makes use of an image that is hapax in the NT. Paul compares himself to an unborn child *(ektrōma).* His metaphor reminds the modern reader of Shakespeare's "from my mother's womb untimely ripped."

Use of the simile highlights the reality of Paul's having been chosen from birth as were the biblical prophets (Isa 49:1; Jer 1:5; cf. Gal 1:15), as well as the fact that at the time of the Damascus experience he was ill-prepared for the role that was his (cf. v. 9b). The theme of prophetic unpreparedness is commonplace in the OT, particularly in narratives that portray the prophetic call (Isa 6:5; Jer 1:6; cf. Exod 3:11; 4:10, 13; 1 Sam 9:21; see also the Lukan accounts of the call of the prophet Paul in Acts 9:1-9; 22:6-16; 26:12-18).

It is likely that Paul himself first used the description to characterize his coming to faith in Christ and his being chosen as an apostle by means of the Damascus event. Throughout 1 Corinthians he has shown himself to be a master of the metaphor, particularly when describing himself. *Ektrōma* is a well-attested, albeit infrequent expression used metaphorically to describe someone whose situation is deplorable. It appears in the LXX (Num 12:12; Job 3:16; Qoh 6:3), other biblical translations (Aquila, Theodotion, and Symmachus, collectively known as The Three), and in some Jewish literature. Ezekiel's oracle against Jerusalem includes a graphic description of an untimely birth followed by the exposure of the female child (Ezek 16:3-5), but Markus Schaefer suggests that *ektrōma* has a meaning similar to the "unwise son" of Hos 13:13.

Some commentators, including C. K. Barrett, believe that the expression *(ektrōma)* has its origin in a derisive epithet hurled at Paul by his opponents, perhaps mocking his claim that he, like the prophets of old (see Isa 49:1; Jer 1:5), had been chosen by God from his mother's womb (Gal 1:5). These interpreters render *ektrōma* as "monster" or "horrible thing."

9. *For I am the least of the apostles, one who is not worthy to be called an apostle, because I persecuted the church of God:* Paul's explanation of the simile uses the rhetorical device of litotes, understatement for effect. Although he professes that he is unworthy to be called an apostle (cf. 2 Cor 3:5), he has been called an apostle (1:1) and is, in fact, an apostle to the Corinthians (9:1). His unworthi-

ness lies in the fact that he had persecuted the church of God (see note on 1:2). That it was the church *of God* (cf. Gal 1:13) that Paul persecuted served to exacerbate the offense. The NT's post-Pauline tradition capitalized on the tradition of Paul's having persecuted the church (cf. Acts 9:1-9; 22:3-11; 26:9-18; 1 Tim 1:13).

10. *Yet by the grace of God I am what I am and his grace in me was not in vain:* In the opening of the letter Paul had affirmed that his apostolate derived from the will of God; now he affirms that it comes from the grace of God. "Grace" *(charis)* is to be taken in the sense of gift. Paul had not been qualified to be an apostle; it was only by the gratuitous gift of God that he became an apostle. The appearance of Christ to him was God's free gift.

    Throughout his letters Paul expresses a concern that his apostolate not be in vain *(ou kenē;* cf. 15:14, 58; 2 Cor 6:1; Gal 2:2; Phil 2:16[2x]; 1 Thess 2:1; 3:5). Now he affirms that God's gift to him was not useless (cf. 2 Cor 6:1; comp. Gal 2:21). It was put to good use; it was operative and effective. Paul preached the gospel. That gospel was received by the Corinthians who came to believe as a result of Paul's preaching (cf. vv. 1-2, 11).

    On the contrary I have toiled more than all of them: As Paul's affirmation that he was the least of all the apostles was a rhetorical ploy (hence the use of litotes), so his affirmation that he toiled more than all the other apostles is rhetorical hyperbole employed to underscore his own apostolic endeavor. Those to whom Paul compares himself are the other apostles, not exclusively the Twelve. The verb "to toil" *(ekopiasa)* can mean "to work hard" (cf. 4:12), but it is part of the jargon Paul uses to describe apostolic labors (cf. 16:16; Rom 16:6, 12[2x]; Gal 4:11; Phil 2:16; 1 Thess 5:12), often in contexts where he alludes to the possibility of apostolic endeavors having no positive result.

    Not I, but the grace of God that is with me: As elsewhere in the letter Paul gets carried away with his own rhetoric and so must introduce a necessary corrective (cf. 1:16; 7:10). Having drawn attention to the extent of his apostolic labors, he recognizes that their effectiveness derives not from the intensity of his effort but from the very gift of God. The effectiveness of his proclamation, evidenced in the faith of the Corinthians (v. 11), derives from the gift of God (cf. 2:3-5).

    Paul affirms that grace is the gift "that is with me" *(hē syn emoi,* with the article *hē).* The article is found in some major majuscules (A, K, P, Ψ), some corrected manuscripts (ℵ, D), and most of the Byzantine manuscripts, but it is lacking in B. Since the use of the article with a qualifying phrase is a feature of Pauline style (e.g. 1 Thess 1:8) its presence may be reasonably presumed in v. 10. An alternate reading, "in me" *(hē eis eme),* is found in 𝔓⁴⁶ and some of the ancient versions (Syriac, Gothic), but it is poorly attested in the manuscript tradition.

11. *Whether I or they, so we have proclaimed and thus you have believed:* Paul brings his rehearsal of facts to closure with a forceful resumptive statement that forms an *inclusio* with vv. 1-2. The entire pericope, 15:1-11, deals with preaching and belief. Paul used the credal formula to present the essential content

of belief. His elaboration of the various witnesses to the resurrection, of whom he considers himself to be the last, speaks of those who are qualified to preach the good news. His "I or they" recalls the fact that he has an apostolic function along with Cephas and the Twelve. There is but one gospel (cf. Gal 1:6; Phil 1:15-18). It has been preached by Cephas, the Twelve, and the other apostles. Paul, too, has proclaimed the common kerygma (vv. 3b-5). As a result the Corinthians believe. They have "received" the common kerygma (see v. 3). That the Corinthians are presented as those who believe in the gospel prepares for the exposition on the resurrection that occupies the rest of ch. 15.

For Reference and Further Study

Bartsch, Hans-Werner. "Inhalt und Funktion des urchristlichen Osterglaubens," *NTS* 26 (1980) 180–196.

Christensen, Jens. "And that He Rose on the Third Day According to the Scriptures," *SJOT* 4 (1990) 101–113.

Collins, Raymond F. "Paul's Damascus Experience: Reflections on the Lukan Account," *LouvSt* 11 (1986) 99–118.

Conzelmann, Hans. "On the Analysis of the Confessional Formula in I Corinthians 15:3-5," *Interp.* 20 (1966) 15–25.

Hollander, Harm W., and Gijsbert E. Van der Hout. "The Apostle Paul Calling Himself an Abortion: 1 Cor. 15:8 within the Context of 1 Cor. 15:8-10," *NovT* 38 (1996) 224–236.

Jeremias, Joachim. *Eucharistic Words* 101–105.

_____. "Artikelloses Christos. Zur ursprache von I Cor. 15:3b-5," *ZNW* 57 (1966) 211–215.

Jones, Peter R. "1 Corinthians 15:8: Paul the Last Apostle," *TynB* 36 (1985) 3–34.

Kearney, Peter J. "He appeared to 500 Brothers (I Cor. xv 6)," *NovT* 22 (1980) 264–284.

Kloppenborg, John. "An Analysis of the Pre-Pauline formula in 1 Cor 15:3b-5 in Light of Some Recent Literature," *CBQ* 40 (1978) 351–367.

Margerie, Bertrand de. "Le troisième jour, selon les Ecritures, il est ressucité. Importance théologique d'une recherche exégétique," *RevScR* 60 (1986) 158–188.

Matera, Frank J. *Galatians.* SP 9. Collegeville: The Liturgical Press, 1992, 52–65.

Meier, John P. "The Circle of the Twelve: Did It Exist During Jesus' Public Ministry?" *JBL* 116 (1997) 635–672.

Murphy-O'Connor, Jerome. "Tradition and Redaction in 1 Cor 15:3-7," *CBQ* 43 (1981) 582–589.

Nickelsburg, George W. E. "An *Ektroma,* Though Appointed from the Womb: Paul's Apostolic Self-Description in 1 Corinthians 15 and Galatians 1," *HThR* 79 (1986) 198–205.

Osten-Sacken, Peter von der. "Die Apologie des paulinischen Apostolats in 1 Kor 15:1-11," *ZNW* 64 (1973) 245–262.

Pastor-Ramos, Federico. "'Murió por nuestros pecados' (1 Cor 15,3; Gal 1,4). Observaciones sobre el origen de esta fórmula en Is 53," *EstEcl* 61 (1986) 385–393.

Plevnik, Joseph. "Paul's Appeals to His Damascus Experience and 1 Cor. 15:3-7: Are They Legitimations?" *TJT* 4 (1988) 101–111.

Radl, Walter. "Der Sinn von *gnōrizō* in 1 Kor 15,1," *BZ* 28 (1984) 243–245.

Satake, Akira. "1 Kr 15,3 und das Verhalten von Paulus des Jerusalemern gegenüber," *AnJBI* 16 (1990) 100–111.

Schaefer, Markus. "Paulus, 'Fehlgeburt' oder 'unvernüftiges Kind'? Ein Interpretationvorschlag zu 1 Kor 15,8," *ZNW* 85 (1994) 207–217.

Webber, Randall C. "A Note on 1 Corinthians 15:3-5," *JETS* 26 (1983) 265–269.

2. *If Christ Has Not Been Raised* (15:12-19)

12. And if Christ is proclaimed, that he has been raised from the dead, how can some among you say that there is no resurrection of the dead? 13. If there is no resurrection of the dead, neither has Christ been raised; 14. and if Christ has not been raised, then not only is our preaching in vain but also your faith is in vain. 15. We are even found to be false witnesses to God, because we testified against God that he raised Christ, whom he did not raise if, as they say, the dead are not raised. 16. For if the dead are not raised, neither has Christ been raised. 17. And if Christ has not been raised your faith is worthless since you are still in your sins. 18. Then even those who have fallen asleep in Christ have perished. 19. If in this life we have only hoped in Christ we are the most pitiable of human beings.

INTERPRETATION

In 15:4 Paul had affirmed that Christ has been raised, but he did not specifically state that Christ had been raised from among the dead as he customarily does. He introduces this section on his preaching by stating that he had preached Christ as one who had been raised "from among the dead" *(ek nekrōn)*. The traditional formula, "raised from the dead," puts Jesus as one who has been raised from the dead in solidarity with all those who have died.

The opening statement (v. 12) of this pericope twice mentions the dead, those who have died. The paronomasia links the resurrection of Christ to the fate of human beings who die. It is likely that some discussion of the fate of the dead had taken place in Corinth, much as it had in

Thessalonica (cf. 1 Thess 4:13-18). Archaeological finds suggest that concern for the dead was important for the people of Corinth (see Carl W. Blegen, Hazel Palmer, and Rodney S. Young, *Corinth, 13: The North Cemetery* [Princeton, NJ: ASCS at Athens, 1964] 79; cf. R. E. DeMaris, "Corinthian Religion and Baptism for the Dead [1 Corinthians 15:29]" 663–671). Paul's Corinthian Christians shared this concern. In 15:6 Paul observed that some of the earliest witnesses to the resurrection of Jesus had already died. In 11:30 he mentioned that some Corinthian Christians had died. The strange practice of the baptism of the dead (15:29) shows that concern for the dead was an issue in the community, and a divisive one. Some members of the community denied that there was a resurrection of the dead. Paul addresses the matter in vv. 12-19.

The Denial of the Resurrection. The denial of the resurrection appears to be a refusal to accept the possibility of bodily resurrection (note the importance of "body" language in 15:35-44a). Jewish apocalyptic hope included an expectation of bodily resurrection. Some Corinthian Christians, however, apparently believed that they were already fully sharing in the benefits of the reign of God, with nothing more to come (cf. 4:8).

It has sometimes been claimed that the Corinthians' denial of the resurrection derives from a misinterpretation of Paul's teaching, a bold and radical interpretation of Paul's teaching on baptism (Rom 6:1-14; cf. Col 2:11-13) as an anticipation of the resurrection (cf. 2 Tim 2:18; 2 Thess 2:2). Ramón Trevijano Etcheverría, however, suggests that it is not Paul's teaching on baptism that has been misconstrued by the Corinthians; rather, the cause of the problem was Paul's ethical teaching, which promoted the notion of the destruction of the "flesh" (*sarx;* cf. 5:5). Paul certainly taught that by baptism the Christian is related to the death and resurrection of Jesus (Rom 6:1-14; cf. Eph 2:6; Col 2:12; 2 Tim 2:11). He also taught that existence in the spirit is antithetical to existence in the flesh (see 3:1-3). There is, however, no clear textual evidence that either Paul's teaching on baptism or his ethical exhortation was so misconstrued as to lead to the denial of a future bodily resurrection.

The history of religions does not provide any clear indication that the Corinthians' denial of the resurrection might derive from their own previous involvement in mystery religions or other pagan cults (cf. 12:2). It is more likely that those who claimed to be spiritual (3:1) and to be all that they could be (2:6) denied a future bodily resurrection. Future bodily resurrection would be the antithesis of their liberation from bodily reality as they perceived it. It would constitute a threat to their immortality (cf. 6:13) and would seem to entail the loss of their present relationship with Wisdom, the source of their perfection.

The Argument. Paul's argument on the resurrection of the body is a carefully reasoned piece. He begins with a short *diēgēsis* (v. 12a), recapitulating

the creed that he and all the other apostles had preached, all the while reminding the Corinthians that Christ had been raised from among the
dead. There follows a statement of Paul's thesis in the form of a rhetorical question, "how can some among you say that there is no resurrection
of the dead?" (v. 12b). Having set forth the grounds for his argumentation
with reference to the accepted kerygma (v. 11), Paul identifies the issue,
namely the denial by some *(tines)* within the community of the resurrection from the dead.

The argument is developed in a logical, almost syllogistic fashion, beginning with the words of the creed, "Christ has been raised" (*Christos
. . . egēgertai*, v. 12). In his recitation of the credal formula (15:4) Paul had
emphasized "has been raised" by adding "that" *(hoti)* to the traditional
formulation. He further highlighted the reality of Christ's resurrection by
citing a series of six witnesses, including himself. The phrase "has been
raised" occurs in v. 12 and is repeated an additional four times in the pericope (vv. 13, 14, 16, 17). With his constant reference to this credal formula
Paul demonstrates that he intends to draw out the implications of the
heart of the Christian kerygma.

The crux of his argument is expressed in a series of conditional sentences (vv. 12, 13, 14, 15, 16, 17, 19). The first of the seven conditional
clauses relates the topic at hand to the kerygma, "if Christ is proclaimed,
that he has been raised from the dead, how can some among you say that
there is no resurrection of the dead?" (v. 12). The issue is "the resurrection
of the dead" *(anastasis nekrōn)*; the core of Christian faith is that "Christ
has been raised" *(Christos egēgertai)*, that is, raised from among the dead
(ek tōn nekrōn, v. 12b).

The second conditional sentence (v. 13) draws as a logical conclusion
from the denial of the resurrection of the dead the denial that Christ himself has been raised (cf. v. 16). Thereupon Paul divides the question in the
terms with which he had concluded the rehearsal of events in the *diēgēsis*
of v. 12. He first presents the implications of the denial of the resurrection
of the dead for his preaching (vv. 14-15), using a pair of conditional
clauses to reinforce the argument. Then he considers the implications of
such a denial for the faith of the Corinthians (vv. 16-19). Three conditional
sentences are used to drive the argument home to the audience.

With regard to the preaching of the gospel, if Christ has not been raised
from the dead preachers and believers alike are the most pitiable of human
beings. Those who preached that Christ had been raised from the dead
have not only preached in vain; they have also affronted God by bearing
false witness to him. If Christ has not been raised, preachers have affirmed that God has done something he has not done. Moreover, if Christ
has not been raised the Corinthians themselves are also to be pitied. Their
faith is useless; it has no purpose. Those who are alive remain captive in

sin. Those who have died have not merely fallen asleep *(koimēthentes)*. They have perished.

The metaphor of falling asleep links together Christ (v. 20) as the first-fruits of those who have fallen asleep, those early Christians who had witnessed the risen Christ and who have fallen asleep (v. 6), and the Corinthians who have fallen asleep (v. 18). All share a similar fate. If Christ has not been raised, neither will the Corinthians who have "fallen asleep" be raised. Their death is ultimate reality. They have perished!

NOTES

12. *And if Christ is proclaimed, that he has been raised from the dead:* Before presuming to set forth the point he is about to argue Paul summarizes the *narratio* contained in 15:1-11. Doing so, he echoes the early Christian kerygma and his own proclamation (Rom 4:24; 6:4, 9; 7:4; 8:11[2x], 34; 10:7, 9; Gal 1:1; 1 Thess 1:10). The use of the passive voice *(kēryssetai,* "is proclaimed") calls attention to the fact that what has been proclaimed is proclaimed by all (see v. 11).

    Paul's use of the credal formula in v. 4 did not include the expression "from the dead" *(ek nekrōn).* The qualifying phrase, with "dead" in the plural *(nekrōn),* is classic in the early kerygma and NT credal formulae (cf. Acts 3:15; 4:2, 10; 10:41, 42; 13:30, 34; 17:3, 31 (cf. v. 32); Rom 4:24; 6:4, 9, 13; 7:4; 8:11[2x], 34; 10:7, 9; 11:15; 14:9; 1 Cor 15:20; Gal 1:1; Eph 1:20; 5:14; Phil 3:11; Col 1:18; 2:12; 2 Tim 2:8; 1 Pet 1:3, 21). "From the dead" indicates that by dying Christ had entered into the realm of the dead. The plural suggests that the dead as a whole are the true horizon against which the resurrection of Christ must be considered. The traditional formula's passive voice, "raised *(egēgertai)* from the dead" intimates divine agency in the resurrection of Christ.

    how can some among you say that there is no resurrection of the dead? Jean-Noel Aletti ("La *disposition* rhétorique dans les épîtres pauliniens: proposition de méthode," *NTS* 38 (1992) 385–401, especially 396) makes the pertinent observation that the recognition that this rhetorical question functions as a statement of Paul's thesis allows us to realize that the issue at Corinth was not a denial that Jesus had been raised from the dead. The issue was the denial that Christians will be raised from the dead. Paul does not set out to prove that Jesus has been raised from the dead. That Jesus has been raised is the basis on which he builds his argument.

    Crucial to an understanding of Paul's argument is the interpretation of the phrase "resurrection of the dead" *(anastasis nekrōn,* vv. 12-13; 21, 42; cf. Rom 1:4). In context this phrase indicates not so much the general resurrection of the dead as the possibility of rising from the dead. The expression signifies "leaving the realm of the dead" (see Michael Bachmann, "Zur Gedanken-führung in 1. Kor. 15, 12ff," *ThZ* 34 [1978] 265–276). The possibility of the dead leaving the realm of the dead is the issue under discussion.

13. *If there is no resurrection of the dead, neither has Christ been raised:* Verse 13 forms the crux of the argument, the premise on which Paul will develop the argu-

ment of vv. 14-15 and 17-18. "If" *(ei)* is used with the indicative in an exercise of logical reasoning (BDF 372.2b). If resurrection from the dead is impossible, then Christ has not been raised. This is the crucial premise in Paul's argument. To deny the resurrection of the dead is to deny the resurrection of Christ from the dead, the core of the Christian gospel.

14. *and if Christ has not been raised, then not only is our preaching in vain, but also your faith is in vain:* Paul's quasi-syllogistic reasoning draws two inferences from the suggestion that Christ has not been raised. The one pertains to preaching, the other to faith ("your faith" is widely attested in the manuscript tradition and appears to be the reading required by the context, but some ancient manuscripts, including B and D, read "our faith"). The motifs of proclamation and belief were the key elements in the *inclusio* within which Paul had contained his rehearsal of events in vv. 1-11 (cf. vv. 1-2, 11).

   Rhetorically v. 14 divides the question. The implications of preaching in vain will be spelled out in v. 15; the implications of believing in vain are given in vv. 17-18. Paul is developing an argument that is contrary to fact. At the conclusion of the rehearsal of facts in 15:1-11 Paul had affirmed that, rather than being in vain God's grace in him was effective (15:10). He had entertained the possibility that the Corinthians believed in vain (15:2), but describes them as believers (15:11; cf. 1:21; 3:5; 14:22).

15. *We are even found to be false witnesses to God, because we testified against God that he raised Christ, whom he did not raise:* Paul returns to the language of the courtroom (cf. 9:1) as he makes his point. He speaks of false witnesses *(pseudomartyres)* and of witnessing *(emartyrēsamen).* "False witness" is a technical term used by Demosthenes and other Hellenistic authors (cf. Matt 26:60). Both technical terms are hapax in 1 Corinthians. The juridical language ups the ante of Paul's rhetoric. If Christ has not been raised, Paul's preaching is perjured testimony with regard to God. He would have testified that God had raised Christ from the dead, but God would not have done so. A weak *de* ("and") connects this statement with v. 14; the *kai* ("even") is emphatic.

   if, as they say, the dead are not raised: With a concluding conditional clause *(eiper ara* adds a further condition; cf. BDF 454.2) Paul precludes the possibility that his words might be so construed as to deny the resurrection. The verb is in the passive voice, suggesting divine agency as the source of resurrection.

   "If, as they say" is not found in some Western witnesses and is not often used in Paul's letters. Some scholars infer then that the entire clause results from scribal clarification of Paul's letter. The clause is, however, a paraphrase of the protasis of v. 13. It renders the abstract "if there is no resurrection of the dead" (vv. 12, 13) in personal terms. It uses the verb *egerein,* literally "to raise up" (cf. 15:40). Paul prefers to use "to raise up" rather than "to arise" *(anistēmi,* cognate with *anastasis,* "resurrection") when talking about the resurrection. The presence of this paraphrasing interpretive aside with its use of Paul's verb of choice suggests that the "resurrection of the dead" formula in vv. 12-13 is language used by the Corinthians and that the aside interprets their formula in Paul's own words.

16–17. *For if the dead are not raised, neither has Christ been raised; and if Christ has not been raised your faith is worthless:* In vv. 16-17 Paul repeats, for emphasis' sake, the line of reasoning he had employed in vv. 13-14, namely that the denial of the resurrection has as its logical consequence a denial that Christ has been raised from the dead. The denial that Christ has been raised has as *its* consequence that the faith of the Corinthians is in vain. The structure of 15:16-17a is similar to that of 15:13-14. Both units contain a conditional clause, the apodosis, a conditional clause drawn from this apodosis, and a new apodosis. Verses 16-17a do not, however, merely repeat the words of 13-14. Rather than repeat the adjective "in vain" (*kenē,* which he typically uses in reference to his own ministry), Paul uses the adjective "worthless" (*mataia,* hapax in Paul except for the quotation of Ps 93:11 [LXX] at 3:20) to describe the quality of the Corinthians' faith if Christ is not raised.

since you are still in your sins: Having moved the discussion to the personal level, Paul writes about the living (v. 17) and the dead (v. 18). For the Corinthians who are still alive the consequence of Christ not having been raised is that they remain in their sins. Had Christ not been raised, his death as a death for our sins (15:3) would have been invalidated. The vicarious effect of his death would have been nil. The resurrection of Christ is the condition that allows his death to have its salvific effect.

In 1 Corinthians it is only in ch. 15 that Paul entertains a specific discussion on sin. In the peroration of the first proof (v. 34) Paul exhorts the Corinthians to turn from their sins and set their minds straight. In v. 56 (see note) Paul states that there is a relationship between death, sin, and law. Sin is the sting of death. If sin remains, death is not overcome.

18. *Then even those who have fallen asleep in Christ have perished:* The consequence of sin remaining is that death also remains (see v. 56). If sin remains even those who have died in Christ have perished. On the expression "those who have died in Christ" see 1 Thess 4:16, which has a similar expression but uses the substantivized adjective *nekroi,* "the dead," rather than the metaphorical verb, "to fall asleep." This metaphor is, however, used in 1 Thess 4:13-18. "The dead" and "those who have fallen asleep" are synonymous expressions.

19. *If in this life we have only hoped in Christ, we are the most pitiable of human beings:* Appealing to *pathos,* Paul draws a final conclusion from a denial of the resurrection of the dead. The Apocalypse of Baruch (early 2nd c.) echoes Paul's words: "For if only this life exists which everyone possesses here, nothing could be more bitter than this" (*2 Apoc. Bar.* 21:13).

Grammatically one may ask whether "only" modifies the participial form "we have hoped" (that is, "we have only hoped in Christ") or whether it modifies the entire clause (that is, "we have only hoped"; we haven't believed or loved). In either case Paul seems to be taking issue with those Corinthians who deny the possibility of the resurrection of the dead. For Paul Christians enjoy during their lives a hope grounded on him who has died and has been raised. If Christ has not been raised, believing Christians are a most pitiable lot.

FOR REFERENCE AND FURTHER STUDY

Bachmann, Michael. "Noch einmal: 1 Kor 15,12 ff und Logik," *LB* 59 (1987) 100–104.

_____. "Rezeption von 1. Kor. 15 (V. 12ff.) unter logischem und unter philologischem Aspekt," *LB* 51 (1982) 79–103.

_____. "Zur Gedankenführung in 1. Kor. 15,21 ff," *ThZ* 34 (1978) 265–276.

Binder, Hermann. "Zum geschichtlichen Hintergrund von I Kor 15,12," *ThZ* 46 (1990) 193–201.

Bucher, Theodor G. "Allgemeine Überlegungen zur Logik im Zusammenhang mit 1 Cor 15,12-20," *LB* 53 (1983) 70–98.

DeMaris, Richard E. "Corinthian Religion and Baptism for the Dead (1 Corinthians 15:29): Insights from Archaeology and Anthropology," *JBL* 114 (1995) 661–682.

Horsley, Richard A. "'How can some of you say that there is no resurrection of the dead?' Spiritual Elitism in Corinth," *NovT* 20 (1978) 203–231.

Plank, Karl A. "Resurrection Theology: The Corinthian Controversy Reexamined," *PRS* 8 (1981) 41–54.

Sellin, Gerhard. "'Die Auferstehung ist schon geschehen'. Zur Spiritualisierung apokalyptischer Terminologie im Neuen Testament," *NovT* 25 (1983) 220–237.

_____. *Der Streit um die Auferstehung der Toten. Eine religionsgeschichtliche und exegetische Untersuchung von 1. Korinther 15.* FRLANT 138. Göttingen: Vandenhoeck & Ruprecht, 1986.

Trevijano Etcheverría, Ramón M. "Los que dicen que no hay resurrección (1 Cor 15,12)," *Salm* 33 (1986) 275–302.

Tuckett, Christopher M. "The Corinthians Who Say 'There is no resurrection of the dead' (1 Cor 15,12)," *CorC* 247–275.

Wedderburn, A.J.M. "The Problem of the Denial of the Resurrection in I Corinthians xv," *NovT* 23 (1981) 229–241.

3. *Ultimate Victory* (15:20-28)

20. Now then, Christ has been raised from the dead, the firstfruits of those who have fallen asleep. 21. For since death comes through a human being, resurrection of the dead also comes through a human. 22. For as all die in Adam, so all will be made alive in Christ, 23. each in proper order: the firstfruits, Christ, then, at his parousia, those who belong to Christ.

24. Then is the end, when he will hand over the kingdom to God and Father, when he will destroy every sovereignty and every authority and power. 25. For he must reign until he has put all enemies under his feet. 26. Death is the last enemy destroyed. 27. For he has placed all things

under his feet. When it says that all things are subject to him, it is evident that [this means] everything except the one who subjects all things to himself. 28. When all things are subject to him, then also the Son himself will be subject to the one who subjects all things to himself, so that God might be everything to everyone.

INTERPRETATION

If Christ had not been raised from the dead, Paul's preaching and the faith of the Corinthians would have been futile (15:14). In fact neither Paul's preaching nor the faith of the Corinthians was futile (15:10-11). God's grace had been active in Paul's preaching as it had been in the faith of the Corinthians. Hence Paul is able to affirm the truth of the kerygma as he moves his argument forward. There can be no doubt that Christ has been raised from the dead. Christ has been seen by a whole host of witnesses (15:5-8). Moreover, the proclamation of Christ's resurrection from the dead has been guaranteed by God (15:10-11).

In 15:20-28 Paul turns his attention to the implications of the kerygma. The line of reasoning follows the familiar chiastic A-B-A' pattern. Having discussed the content of his preaching and the implications of that preaching for the Corinthians (15:12-19), Paul digresses substantively upon the resurrection and its consequences (vv. 20-28) and then returns to the situation of the Corinthians and his own apostolic endeavors (vv. 29-34).

Firstfruits. Verses 20-28 constitute the nub of Paul's argument. Having proclaimed again that Christ has been raised (v. 20a), he sets out to explain how the resurrection of Christ has implications for those who have died in Christ (cf. 1 Thess 4:13-18). The declarative statement with which his argument begins (v. 20) contrasts sharply with the conditional statements that open the rhetorical units enveloping Paul's central argument. Element A in his rhetorical schema had begun with a condition (v. 12); so, too, does element A' (v. 29). The central point in Paul's development of the three-part argument begins with a strong declarative statement, "Now then Christ has been raised from the dead" (v. 20).

Key to Paul's explanation of the resurrection is the idea that the risen Christ is "the firstfruits" *(aparchē)* of those who have fallen asleep (vv. 20, 23). Within the pericope 15:20-23 constitutes a subunit with firstfruits as its leitmotif. Paul initially uses the term in explanatory apposition to "Christ," who has been raised. His reasoning is almost syllogistic as he articulates an explanation (with an explanatory *gar*) in v. 21 and clarifies his explanation (with an additional *gar*) in vv. 22-23.

"Firstfruits" is, literally, the first portion of an agricultural harvest, the thing that precedes the rest of the harvest. As such it is a harbinger of things to come. The idea of firstfruits implies that other fruits will be harvested at a later time. The notion implies not only temporal sequence but also some sort of relationship between the firstfruits and the later harvest: the harvest of firstfruits serves almost as a guarantee of the later harvest(s). It suggests, but does not actually prove, that a later harvest will take place. The image of the harvest is only implicit in Paul's description. The image of the harvest is, however, exploited in the NT's synoptic tradition as a metaphor for the realities of the final times (cf. Matt 13:30, 39-43).

In Paul's biblical tradition the term "firstfruits" was most often used to designate that portion of fruit and grain, deemed to be the choicest portion, that was to be offered to the Lord in accordance with the sacrificial prescriptions of Exodus, Leviticus, and Deuteronomy. The cultic nuance is absent from Paul's use of the metaphor; he uses the term simply to suggest that Christ—a christological title that points to the humanity and death of Jesus—who has been raised is the harbinger of things to come.

To show that the resurrection of Christ does more than merely suggest the resurrection of those who have died in Christ Paul exploits the example of Adam, the prototypical human. The comparison and contrast between Christ and Adam form a significant part of Paul's christological exposition not only here in 1 Corinthians but also in his letters to the Romans and to the Philippians (Rom 5:12-21; Phil 2:6-11).

In Paul's exposition of the Adam-Christ figure vv. 21 and 22 are set in synonymous parallelism. As such they mutually interpret one another. Adam is the source of death for human beings (cf. Rom 5:14, 15, 17); Christ is the source of life (cf. Rom 5:17-18). In Rom 5:17 Paul explains how much more significant is what happened through Christ than what happened through Adam. By means of Christ (*en Christō*, v. 22) all will be made alive. This, says Paul, will take place at the parousia, a technical term he uses to describe the ultimate appearance of Christ as eschatological Lord. That Paul uses the metaphor of falling asleep to refer to those who have died suggests that death is a transitional state prior to final restoration to life.

The End. The parousia of Christ is the end. The end encompasses the destruction of all Christ's enemies, including death, and the establishment of God's dominion over all. Paul uses the image of the destruction of one's enemies and a brace of scriptural allusions to make his point. Military metaphors and scriptural allusions are classic features of Jewish apocalyptic's description of the end times.

The scriptural allusions are introduced as a clarifying remark (note the explanatory *gar*, "for" in v. 25). Paul's scriptural midrash features Ps 110:1 and Ps 8:7. This classic pair of scriptural verses was often used in early Christian apologetic (see Eph 1:20-23; 1 Pet 3:22; Heb 1:13; 2:6-9; cf.

Mark 12:36; Matt 22:44). The combination apparently predated Paul, but he offers the oldest documentary evidence of the christological use of these psalms. Paul uses the biblical texts for his own purposes and adapts them to suit those purposes just as later authors would do. For his Hellenistic readers Sacred Scripture is like an oracle that Paul can use, as he does here, in a variety of contentious circumstances.

The presence of a variety of apocalyptic motifs—the predetermined order, the presence of evil powers, the end-time confrontation, the victory of God's designated agent—and the cosmic perspective show that Paul has drawn upon classic apocalyptic traditions. The series of four temporal clauses (see the fourfold use of *hotan*, "when," in vv. 24, 27, 28) suggests that Paul is concerned with a series of interrelated events. In vv. 25 (Ps 110:1) and 27 (Ps 8:7) his aim is to present a biblical warrant for the apocalyptic scenario he had briefly outlined in vv. 23-24.

Despite the parenthetical comment of v. 27c Paul's argument constitutes a well-structured whole. Indeed, the neat structure suggests that there may be some truth to Walter Schmithals's claim that underlying Paul's argument is an older credal or instructional formula (vv. 24b-25, 28). Paul uses a kind of ring construction in which the two temporal clauses of v. 28 (when, then) correspond inversely to the two temporal clauses of v. 24 (then, when). The construction molds the various elements of the argument within a single literary unit. At the heart of the argument is the scriptural reflection. Paul's "must" (*dei*, v. 25) bespeaks the apocalyptic inevitability of the events he is describing. These events simply have to happen. It is God's will that such be the case.

To establish that the sequence he is describing is in keeping with God's plan—and ultimately fulfills that plan (v. 28c)—Paul alludes to the Scriptures. However, he does not quote them. In v. 25 he does not cite the Greek text of Ps 110:1 exactly, nor does he cite the biblical text of Ps 8:7 in v. 27. Neither scriptural reference is introduced with "as it is written" or some other classic introduction to a passage of Scripture. The allusive character of his scriptural references is consistent with the way in which apocalyptic literature makes use of the Scriptures. Apocalyptic literature does not cite Scripture directly so much as it evokes Scripture to provide color and authority for the scene that is unfolded.

Paul freely paraphrases the Scriptures so as to paint and provide warrant for his apocalyptic scene. In the process the biblical texts undergo a christological and eschatological transformation. Introducing a non-scriptural "all" (*pantas*) into his citation of Ps 110:1 in v. 25, Paul provides a universal and cosmic dimension consistent with his apocalyptic imagery. A substitution of "reign" for the biblical image of sitting at the right hand of Yhwh (Ps 110:1) enables Paul to use the Scripture in an apocalyptic and soteriological fashion.

By using the expression "under his feet" in his version of both psalm verses (*hypo tous podas autou* in place of two different Greek and Hebrew expressions) Paul relates Ps 110:1 to Ps 8:7. The use of such a "hook-word" technique to link individual scriptures together is commonplace in Paul's letters (cf. 9:9-10). The hermeneutical principle known as *gezera shawah*, the comparison of similar expressions, legitimized the use of one biblical passage to clarify another if the same expression occurs in both passages. Reformulating the texts as he does, Paul is able to use Psalm 8 to elucidate the meaning of Psalm 110.

Having used his scriptural midrash to explain Christ's reign, Paul comes to the climax of his argument. When Christ's dominion is complete, as it will be at "the end," everything will be turned over to the Father (v. 24) so that God might be everything for everyone. Christ's lordship will be complete and the kingdom of God will have reached its perfection. It will be all that it can be.

Paul employs kinship language to symbolize the new state of the relationship between Christ and God. He calls Christ "Son" (v. 28) and God "Father" (v. 24). From a literary standpoint the use of this relational language helps to tie vv. 24-28 together as a literary unit. From a theological standpoint the use of kinship language articulates the unique relationship between God and his Christ. Paul commonly describes God as Father, but he rarely calls Christ the Son (cf. 1:9). The language is, however, tradition in the early church. It derives from Jesus' calling God "Abba" (cf. Rom 8:15; Gal 4:6). Paul uses the filial title of Jesus beginning with the resurrection (Rom 1:4). The title points to the unique relationship between Jesus and God and to God's unique act in raising Jesus from the dead, an act that inaugurates the eschatological scenario that culminates in Christ's handing all things over to God. At this moment when the kingdom is consummated the unique relationship between Christ and God is fully apparent. Christ will have completed the Father's work. The "Son" title not only refers to the uniqueness of the relationship between the Father and the Son. It also expresses the idea that the Son has done the Father's work and states the relative subordination of the Son to the Father.

The consummation of redemption includes all of creation; nothing is beyond the pale of God's redemptive activity in Christ. "Everything to everyone" (*panta en pasin*) encapsulates the idea of the kingdom of God without using kingdom terminology. In this passage of Paul's letter kingdom language is used of Christ's dominion (v. 25).

NOTES

20. *Now then Christ has been raised from the dead, the first fruits of those who have fallen asleep:* Paul reprises the kerygma in its explicated form, namely that Christ

has been raised *from the dead*. "Firstfruits of those who have fallen asleep" is placed in apposition to "Christ," the subject of the credal formula. This phrase succinctly articulates the relationship between Christ and others who have died. They are identified not as those who are dead (*nekroi*, cf. 15:20a), nor as those who have died (*apothnēskousin*, cf. 15:22), but as those who have fallen asleep (*kekoimēmenōn*), a metaphorical expression that suggests the possibility of resurrection (see note on 15:6). As elsewhere in this letter Paul uses the strategy of redefinition, a terminological corrective, to make his point (cf. 3:1; 12:1, 4).

The term "firstfruits" (*aparchē*) was often used in the Bible (Exod 23:16 [*prōtogenēma*], 19a; Lev 23:10-14; Num 18:8-13; Deut 18:4; 26:2, 10; 2 Chr 31:5; Neh 10:37). With the exception of Jer 2:3 (which reads *archē genēmatōn*) it was always used in a literal, agricultural sense. In the NT the term appears almost exclusively in the Pauline corpus (cf. Jas 1:18; Rev 14:4; cf. *1 Clem.* 24:1; 42:4), but it is always used in a metaphorical, figurative sense. In 9:9 a passage of agricultural law (Deut 25:4) was similarly used in reference to humans. Like Philo and the rabbis Paul uses the expression "firstfruits" not so much to highlight the aspect of an offering to God as to underscore the relationship between the firstfruits and the entire harvest (see *TLNT* 1:145–152). Firstfruits are the harbinger of the harvest to come.

21. *For since death comes through a human being, resurrection of the dead also comes through a human:* Paul's language is elliptical; neither of the balanced phrases has a verb. "Death" (*thanatos*) is objectified and contrasted with "resurrection of the dead" (*anastasis nekrōn;* cf. v. 12). Both are said to have come through a human being (*di' anthrōpou*, with an instrumental *dia*).

22. *For as all die in Adam, so all will be made alive in Christ:* Paul uses a double contrast to explain (*gar*) what he has said in v. 22. The first contrast is between dying (*apothnēskousin*, in the present active) and being made alive (*zōopoiē-thēsontai*, in the future passive, here the divine passive). In the NT the verb "to make alive" is always used in a soteriological sense, principally with the meaning of God's raising of the dead (cf. John 5:21). "Making alive" calls to mind the original creation. It suggests that resurrection from the dead is to be understood as a new creation (cf. 15:45-49).

The second contrast is between "Adam" and "Christ." Prepositional phrases with "in" (*en*, reflecting the Semitic *bĕ*) provide clarification for the repeated "through a human being" of v. 21. To summarize Paul's use of the Adam motif in christological exposition various authors commonly speak of Jesus as a new Adam. Paul, however, never actually uses the expression "new Adam." In Phil 2:6-11 he does not cite Adam's "name," but the Adamic allusion is clear. See Jerome H. Neyrey, *Christ is Community: The Christologies of the New Testament.* GNS 13 (Wilmington: Michael Glazier, 1985) 214–236.

23. *Each in proper order: the firstfruits, Christ, then, at his parousia, those who belong to Christ:* "Each" (*hekastos*) represents a commentary on the "all" (*pantes*) of v. 22. "Order" (*tagmati*) is hapax in the NT. In classical and Hellenistic Greek it was often used of military order. Its use by Paul suggests an ordered scenario of

the end-time events. A periodic view of history, particularly of its final denouement, is typical of apocalyptic thought (cf. 1 Thess 4:15-17). "Parousia" (*parousia,* literally "presence" or "arrival") is a technical term used in the early church to describe the end-time presence of the Lord to his elect. Apart from its occurrence here Paul uses the term in its technical sense only in his earlier letter to the Thessalonians (2:19; 3:13; 4:15; 5:23).

In its ordinary sense the term evokes the notion of presence in contrast with absence. Its connotation is often that of arrival (hence the popular use of "second coming" to refer to the parousia of Christ at the end of time). Paul uses *parousia* in its ordinary sense to describe his own presence (2 Cor 10:10; Phil 1:26; 2:12) or that of someone else (16:17; 2 Cor 7:6, 7). In 16:17 he expresses his joy at the arrival *(parousia)* of Stephanas, Fortunatus, and Achaicus. Evoking presence as contrasted with a situation of absence, and sometimes suggesting a person's arrival, the term *parousia* and its cognates, especially the verb *pareimi* (5:3) belong to Hellenistic epistolary jargon. In Paul's letters his own presence, whether in person or by letter, is of relatively minor importance compared to The Presence, which is that of Jesus, the eschatological Lord.

First Thessalonians 4:15 gives imaginative expression to the parousia of the Lord by evoking the image of the victory procession of an emperor or a conquering general. Use of the term to evoke the image of the definitive presence of the eschatological Lord has been exploited by the author of 2 Thessalonians, a thoroughgoing apocalyptic composition (2 Thess 2:1, 8). Otherwise *parousia* is used in this technical, eschatological sense in a wide range of late NT literature, but only by Matthew among the evangelists (Matt 24:3, 27, 37, 39; Jas 5:7, 8; 2 Pet 1:16; 3:4, 12; 1 John 2:28).

Paul does not explain who those are who belong to Christ *(hoi tou Christou).* Presumably they are those who are related to Christ by having been baptized in his name (cf. 1:13; 3:23).

24. *Then is the end, when he will hand over the kingdom to God and Father:* "Then" *(eita)* is problematic. Does it introduce a third element in a sequence, the firstfruits, those who belong to Christ, the end (see the sequential use of *eita* in 15:5, 7), or is it merely interpretive? The latter would seem to be the case. Grammatical and theological considerations preclude an interpretation of the verse that suggests an interregnum between the parousia and the end. Notwithstanding Hans Lietzmann's attempt to offer a revisionist reading of this verse (see *Korinther* 80), no known Greek usage allows "the end" *(to telos)* to be construed as the rest (of those to be raised). Despite L. J. Kreitzer, who argues for the existence of a temporary messianic kingdom between the parousia and "the end" (see Jesus and God, 131–164, especially 142–145), C. E. Hill ("Paul's Understanding") has convincingly argued that the kingdom of Christ is Christ's present lordship, exercised from heaven between the parousia and "the end." With the resurrection of believers at the parousia the temporary messianic kingdom has reached its completion.

The risen Christ is the plenipotentiary agent of God between the time of the resurrection when he was constituted as Lord and Son (cf. Rom 1:4) and the parousia. Verses 24-28 constitute a unit that belongs together as an interpretation of the parousiac event. Its militaristic overtones evoke Paul's and apocalyptic use of military metaphors to describe the end-time events (cf. "order" in v. 23). Jewish apocalyptic literature frequently used military images in its "description" of end-time events. On the eschatological revelation of God as Father see above, pp. 316–318.

when he will destroy every sovereignty and every authority and power: The three terms (cf. Rom 8:38) clearly refer to hostile powers. An accumulation of cosmic powers over whom Christ reigns is attested in the deutero-Pauline literature (cf. Eph 1:21; 6:12; Col 1:16; 2:10; 1 Pet 3:22). "Sovereignty" *(archēn)* is hapax in 1 Corinthians, but the term is cognate with "the rulers *(archontes)* of this age" who are part of the eschatological drama according to 2:6-7.

The accumulation of powers hostile to God in the great eschatological show-down is part of the drama in Jewish apocalyptic literature. At the end all hostile powers are to be destroyed (cf. 1 Enoch 1:5; 6:1–10:17; 21:1-10; cf. Isa 24:21-22). Paul's verb *(katargēsē)* has a future perfect sense: Christ will hand over the kingdom when he will have destroyed all his enemies (including death; see v. 26).

25. *For he must reign until he has put all enemies under his feet:* Paul's explanation of the apocalyptic scenario evokes biblical imagery, as does much apocalyptic writing, Pauline and otherwise. "He has put all enemies under his feet" are words taken from Ps 110:1, the biblical verse most often quoted in the NT (see Matt 22:44; Mark 12:36; Luke 20:42-43; Acts 2:34-35; Heb 1:3, 13, with not a few additional allusions in these and other books). The words "he must reign" *(dei gar auton basileuein)* are a paraphrase of Ps 110:1's reference to the king's sitting at the right hand of God. Paul's use of Ps 110:1 in 1 Cor 15:25 is the oldest christological use of this important psalm verse.

His citation of the biblical text reflects the Greek text of the Bible, the Septuagint, much more than it does the Hebrew text. Paul has, however, modified the Greek text so that it has a clear christological reference by substituting the third person singular for the biblical text's second person singular. In the psalm the verse is part of YHWH's direct address to the king, hence, the second person singular. Paul has also modified the biblical text by adding an interpretive "all." The addition allows death to be included among the enemies to be destroyed; the psalm verse makes reference only to political enemies. The addition also establishes a correlation with Ps 8:7, which Paul will introduce in v. 27. He has introduced the biblical quotation into his running text instead of identifying it by means of "it is written." It serves, therefore, as an implicit rather than an explicit warrant for his argument. Incorporating the psalm verse into his text has required Paul to transpose the verb into a third person singular.

Who is it that will put enemies underfoot? In Ps 110:1 God is the subject of "put" *(thō, Ps 109:1 LXX)*. God is likewise the subject of "made subject" *(hypotaxas)* in Ps 8:7, cited by Paul in v. 27. Many authors and the editors of the NRSV take God to be the implied subject of the verb "made subject" in 15:27. Some (e.g., Tashio Aono) then argue for theocentric consistency between vv. 25 and 27. The language of v. 25 does not point to God so clearly as does that of v. 27. Moreover, the reference to God in v. 27 is not as clear as some commentators think (cf. *NRSV*). On the other hand Paul frequently appropriates biblical texts that deal with God to speak about Christ as Lord, particularly with reference to the parousia. The grammar of v. 25 seems to suggest that it is Christ who puts all enemies under his feet. (For a discussion of the issues and the arguments favoring a christological reading of this verse see Lambrecht, *Pauline Studies* 134–140).

26. *Death is the last enemy destroyed:* The verb in the present tense *(katargeitai)* effectively establishes the destruction of death as a fait accompli. Paul has personified death. In the apocalyptic scenario he envisions, death is the ultimate enemy. Christ must rule until death is conquered. In Paul's militaristic scene death is the final enemy, the last in the series of those who are to be made subject to and destroyed by Christ. Death is destroyed by resurrection.

   In his midrashic exposition of Ps 110:1 Paul had suggested that the enemies who were made subject to Christ were *all* his enemies (v. 25). Their subjection implies their destruction (v. 24b). The note of universality, "all enemies," is introduced into the discussion by inference from Ps 8:7, used according to the *gezera shawah* principle to interpret Ps 110:1.

27. *For he has placed all things under his feet:* This citation of Ps 8:7 serves as a biblical warrant for Paul's discourse on the destruction of death. Paul departs from the typical Jewish way of understanding Psalm 8. Rather than reading the psalm as one that celebrates the creation of humanity by YHWH, Paul reads v. 7 in an individualized and eschatological way, such that his personal targum proclaimed that Christ will subject all things under his feet. "All things" *(panta)* are the universe (BDF 275.7).

   So as to facilitate its christological application Paul has somewhat modified the biblical text. The Psalter's "you have put all things under their feet" is in the form of direct address to God (see a similar use of Ps 62:12b in Rom 2:6). In the Pauline narrative the words appear in the third person singular. Paul has also changed the Greek form of the expression "under his feet" *(hypokatō tōn podōn autou* in the LXX; *hypo tous podas autou* in 15:27) so as to make it the same as the form he had employed in the citation of Ps 110:1 in v. 25. This modification enables Paul to apply the *gezera shawah* principle in his hermeneutical endeavor. The use of the "hook-word" technique to link individual scriptures together is commonplace in Paul's letters (cf. 15:54-55; Rom 2:27-29; 3:10-18; 9:33; 11:8-10; 2 Cor 6:16-18, etc.).

   Paul makes another christological use of Ps 8:7 in Phil 3:21. His use of Ps 8:7 in conjunction with Ps 110:1 is echoed by Eph 1:20-22 in blatant dependence on 1 Corinthians (see Otto Michel, *Paulus und seine Bibel* [Gütersloh: Bertelsmann, 1929] 193). Psalm 110:1 is similarly linked with Psalm 8 in the epistle to the Hebrews (Heb 1:13–2:8).

   When it says that all things are subject to him, it is evident that [this means] everything except the one who subjects all things to himself: Paul's midrash on Ps 8:7 requires an explanatory note. "When it says" *(hotan de eipē)* is a loose formula that equivalently identifies v. 27a as scriptural. Paul's anacoluthon forms an interpretive aside. He does not use an appropriate grammatical construction to introduce his explanation. His explanation is that God is the one who subjects all things to himself (cf. v. 28b). Clearly God is not subject to Christ.

28. *When all things are subject to him, then also the Son himself will be subject to the one who subjects all things to himself:* After his apologetic aside Paul returns to the main line of thought. The "end" (v. 24) is when all things are subject to Christ. Paul's cosmic perspective is consistent with his notion of Christ's universal role in human salvation (see 3:21-23; 8:6; 11:3, 11-12). Nowhere does Paul elaborate upon the universal role of Christ as such; rather, he uses his universalistic conviction as part of his rhetorical argument in response to a particular concern that arose in the community at Corinth. Paul's cosmic perspective (cf. Rom 8:19-25) is beautifully echoed in the deutero-Pauline epistles to the Colossians (Col 1:15-20) and Ephesians (cf. Eph 1:20-23).

so that God might be everything to everyone: The ultimate purpose of the entire eschatological scenario is expressed in Paul's final purpose clause. The goal of Christ's dominion is the kingdom of God. Paul's resounding finale equivalently states that the kingdom of God is the purpose of the lordship of Christ and the reason for his conquest of all enemies, including death (cf. 3:21-23; 8:6). For Paul the resurrection of the dead is in function of the fulfillment of the kingdom of God.

For Reference and Further Study

Aono, Tashio. "Exkurs: 'Theozentrik in 1 Kor 15,24-28," *Die Entwicklung des paulinischen Gerichtsgedankens bei den Apostolischen Vätern.* Europäische Hochschulschriften 23, 137. Bern: Peter Lang, 1979, 26–28.

Boer, Martinus C. de. "Paul's Use of a Resurrection Tradition in 1 Cor 15,20-28," *CorC* 639–651.

Hay, David M. *Glory at the Right Hand: Psalm 110 in Early Christianity.* SBL.MS 18. Nashville and New York: Abingdon, 1973.

Heil, Uta. "Theo-logische Interpretation von 1 Kor 15,23-28," *ZNW* 84 (1993) 27–35.

Hill, Charles E. "Paul's Understanding of Christ's Kingdom in I Corinthians 15:20-28," *NovT* 30 (1988) 297–320.

Holleman, Joost. "Jesus' Resurrection as the Beginning of the Eschatological Resurrection (1 Cor 15,20)," *CorC* 653–660.

Jansen, John Frederick. "I Cor. 15. 24-28 and the Future of Jesus Christ," *SCJT* 40 (1987) 543–570.

Johnson, Andy. "Firstfruits and Death's Defeat: Metaphor in Paul's Rhetorical Strategy in 1 Cor 15:20-28," *Word & World* 16 (1996) 456–464.

Kreitzer, L. Joseph. *Jesus and God in Paul's Eschatology.* JSNT.S 19. Sheffield: JSOT Press, 1987, 131–164.

Lambrecht, Jan. "Paul's Christological Use of Scripture in 1 Cor. 15.20-28," *NTS* 28 (1982) 502–527. Reprinted in idem, *Pauline Studies* 125–149.

_____. "Structure and Line of Thought in 1 Cor. 15:23-28," *NovT* 32 (1990) 143–151. Reprinted in idem, *Pauline Studies* 151–160.

Lindemann, Andreas. "Parusie Christi und Herrschaft Gottes. Zur Exegese von 1 Kor 15,23-28," *WuD* 19 (1987) 87–107.

Plevnik, Joseph. *Paul and the Parousia* 122–144.

Schmithals, Walter. "The Pre-Pauline Tradition in 1 Corinthians 15:20-28," *PRS* 20 (1993) 357–380.

Templeton, Douglas A. "Paul the Parasite: Notes on the Imagery of 1 Corinthians 15:20-28," *HeyJ* 26 (1985) 1–4.

Zimmer, Christoph. "Das argumentum resurrectionis 1 Kor 15,12-20," *LB* 65 (1991) 25–36.

4. *An Exhortation* (15:29-34)

29. Otherwise what do those do who are baptized for the sake of the dead? If those who are really dead are not raised, why at all are they baptized for their sake? 30. And why are we in danger at every hour? 31. I die every day.

Brothers and sisters, you indeed are the object of my boasting in Christ Jesus our Lord. 32. If, humanly speaking, I fought with wild beasts in Ephesus, what good does it do me? If the dead are not raised, "let's eat and drink, for tomorrow we die."

33. Don't go astray! "Bad company corrupts good morals." 34. Wake up properly from your drunken slumber and do not sin. Some do not know God. I say this to shame you.

Interpretation

The interpretation of 15:29-34 is difficult. Paul makes reference to the experience of the Corinthians and to his own experience in language that is specific but enigmatic. What does Paul mean by baptism for the dead? What happened to him at Ephesus?

Baptism for the Sake of the Dead. 1 Corinthians 15:29 is the NT's only reference to baptism for the sake of the dead *(hyper tōn nekrōn)*. Most interpreters take the phrase as a reference to some sort of baptismal ritual on behalf of relatives or friends who had recently died. There was, as R. E. DeMaris indicates, a general concern for the dead among the Corinthian population. The practice of baptizing the living as a vicarious rite of passage to benefit the dead might have been a Christian response to this general concern. The intended beneficiaries would have been members of their families or catechumens who had not yet been baptized at the time of their deaths.

Apart from the enigmatic reference in 15:29 there is little evidence that the practice existed in the early church (cf. Chrysostom, *On the First Epistle to the Corinthians, Homily* 40; *PG* 61, 347). It is likely that the practice took place only in first-century Corinth, where religious syncretism was a fact of life even for Corinthian Christians. Paul's unusual use of the third person plural in a rhetorical question suggests that the practice may not have been widespread among the Corinthian Christians. Only a few of them may have practiced vicarious baptism on behalf of the dead.

Some recent commentators have taken a different approach to the interpretation of this enigmatic reference. J. C. O'Neill ("1 Corinthians 15:29") understands "the dead" to be the moribund. In his interpretation Paul's rhetorical questions refer to the baptism of deathbed converts or dying infants. What is the use of baptizing the bodies of those who are about to die, says Paul, if there is no resurrection of the body?

Jerome Murphy-O'Connor ("Baptized for the Dead") believes that Paul's reference derives from a gibe directed against him. "The dead" (v. 29a) are those who lack wisdom. The "really dead" (v. 29b) are those who have actually died. "To be baptized" is a metaphor for "to be destroyed" (cf. Mark 10:38; Luke 12:50). Paul's rhetorical questions are part of his diatribal defense against those who have undermined his apostolic ministry (vv. 29-32). Why, Paul asks, are preachers being harassed, why are they destroyed, for the sake of those who lack wisdom? Why are they being ruined if there is to be no resurrection of those who have died? Murphy-O'Connor's suggestion requires that Paul's words be understood in a way that is not at all usual. The obvious meaning of Paul's words in the Greek text is that some Christians at Corinth practiced a kind of vicarious baptism.

Fighting with Wild Beasts. Dennis R. MacDonald reads v. 32 as if it were a denial by Paul of a tale about his having fought with wild beast in Ephesus. This interpretation is found in some of the older commentaries (Johannes Weiss, Jean Héring, Hans Conzelmann), but apart from this enigmatic reference the NT provides no indication that Paul ever fought with wild beasts. Is the reference to be taken literally or figuratively? The verb "to fight with wild beasts" *(ethēriomachēsa)* is hapax in the NT. If it is to be taken literally, Paul's reference is to some kind of gladiatorial struggle that he had with wild animals in the public arena in Ephesus. If it is to be taken as a metaphor, the reference is consistent with his use of the Hellenistic *agōn* motif (cf. Ps 35:17). Paul, like the moralists, used images taken from athletic combat to describe a speaker's efforts on behalf of virtue.

The use of the diatribal style, similar to the one Paul adopts in 15:29-34, is a feature of Hellenistic moral discourse, particularly that of the Cynics and Stoics, who used the *agōn* motif to good effect. Like the philosophers

Paul has used the *agōn* motif in pictorial descriptions of his preaching of the gospel. Earlier in this letter (9:24-27), at the end of his self-styled apology, he exploited the motif with good rhetorical effect (see above, pp. 357–363; cf. 1 Thess 2:2). He does so again here as he describes his apostolic work in Ephesus. Paul was in Ephesus as he was writing to the Corinthians (16:8). The use of the formulaic "humanly speaking" (*kata anthrōpon;* cf. 3:3; 9:8), the moralistic language of v. 33, and Paul's diatribal style coalesce to suggest that it is philosophical moral discourse that provides the rhetorical *heurēsis* of v. 32a.

The possibility of Paul's having experienced some real danger at Ephesus is, however, not to be dismissed out of hand. Romans 16:3-4 refers to Prisca and Aquila as having saved Paul's neck. They were Paul's coworkers in Ephesus (16:19), and Acts 19:21-41 describes a riot occasioned by Paul's visit to Ephesus.

The Structure and Rhetorical Force of Paul's Argument. After the apocalyptic interlude of vv. 20-28 the mode of Paul's argument takes a sharp turn. With a series of three rhetorical questions he returns to the kind of direct appeal that had previously characterized his approach to the Corinthians.

The conditional clause of v. 29b, "if those who are really dead are not raised," echoes the conditional clauses of vv. 15c and 16a. The presence of these conditional clauses helps to define vv. 20-28 as the B element in the chiastically structured argument appended to Paul's rehearsal of the kerygma (15:3-5). Verses 20-28 are characterized by the quasi-syllogistic form of their argument. This is a rhetorical argument from *logos* for which the Scriptures provide an authority. In 15:29-34 Paul's argument takes a personal turn. As of v. 30 its verbs, like those in 15:12-19, are in the first and second person. The *ad hominem* argument of v. 29 is an expression of a *pathos* form of rhetorical argument, as is the paraenesis in vv. 33-34. The intervenient argument (vv. 30-32) from Paul's own experience has the force of a rhetorical *ethos* argument. If there is no resurrection from the dead why does Paul bother to do what he does in order to preach the gospel?

Enigmatic on first reading, 15:29-34 is a carefully crafted rhetorical unit. Its four rhetorical questions are in the diatribal style. Its use of climax (vv. 30-31) and contrast (v. 33) provide rhetorical force. Two popular sayings (vv. 32, 33) embody the authority of popular wisdom. Metaphor (vv. 32, 34) enhances the argument. Two references to the possibility of the dead not being raised (vv. 29, 32) hark back to the opening section of the rhetorical proof (15:12-19).

The unit concludes with an exhortation, phrased in classic paraenetic language, urging the community as a whole to be mindful of their status as God's holy people. That some within their midst deny the resurrection is contrary to their experience of God in whom they believe as one who has raised Christ from the dead. That some deny the resurrection can be but a source of shame for the community. In a culture where honor and shame are motivating values the shame that the Corinthians experience should provide motivation for their changing the situation. "Bad company corrupts good morals."

NOTES

29. *Otherwise what do those do who are baptized for the sake of the dead? If those who are really dead are not raised, why at all are they baptized for their sake?* "Otherwise" (*epei*; see 14:16) is a classical construction after a question. "On behalf of" (*hyper*) suggests some sort of transferred application of benefits, a vicarious effect (cf. 11:24). Given the enigmatic nature of the practice, some commentators interpret the prepositional phrase as if it were a reference to being baptized in the presence of the dead (a graveyard), with death in front of them, or in a symbolic sense as if Paul were stating that some people were being baptized in light of future death and resurrection. J. D. Reaume takes the preposition to mean "because of" and suggests that Paul is stating that Christian neophytes were baptized because of the influence of deceased Christians. Such interpretations would require a meaning of *hyper* that departs from Pauline usage of the preposition. On *kai* = still, see BDF 442.14.

30-31a. *And why are we in danger at every hour? I die every day:* Paul's argument is full of *pathos*. The rhetorical questions appeal to the Corinthians. The juxtaposition of two temporal elements (hour, day) and the movement from danger to death are an example of Paul's use of the rhetorical device of *klimax* (*gradatio*) and contribute to the strength of his argument. Building up the climax of his appeal, Paul moves from the first person plural to the first person singular, but he does not provide any specific information as to the source of the danger to him or to what he means by "dying" (*apothnēskō*). Elsewhere in 1 Corinthians (8:11; 9:15; 15:3, 22, 32, 36) the verb implies real death. Here it seems to indicate an experience of mortal danger (cf. *EDNT* 2:130-131).

"To be in danger" (*kindyneuomen*) is hapax in Paul, but the cognate noun is used eight times in the peristatic catalogue of 2 Cor 11:26. The list of sufferings in the so-called "fool's speech" of 2 Corinthians has a strong rhetorical force. It expresses the lengths to which Paul would go, the extent of hardships (cf. 4:10-13, also with a temporal referent) he would endure in order that his ministry might be effective. In the fool's speech he contrasts his hardships with his boast, as he does in 15:30-31. Acts 19:21-41 twice (vv. 27, 40) uses the verb "to be in danger" in its description of the perils that might ensue from the riot at Ephesus.

31b. *Brothers and sisters:* "Brothers and sisters" is absent from some important manuscripts ($\mathfrak{P}^{46}$, D, F, G, L, Ψ), but the apostrophic use of "brothers and sisters" (*adelphoi*) is a common feature of Pauline style and is frequently found in 1 Corinthians. For stylistic reasons some ancient versions qualify Paul's use of the absolute vocative with a modifying pronoun, "my" (Syriac and Coptic) or "our" (Ethiopian).

You indeed are the object of my boasting in Christ Jesus our Lord: Paul's words may be taken to mean "you are my pride and joy in Christ Jesus our Lord." His use of the strong affirmative particle, *nē* (see BDF 107), is singular in the New Testament. It adds to the *pathos* of his argument, as Paul contrasts his hardships with what brings him joy. Christ Jesus our Lord—the full christological title (cf. 1:2, 8, 9, 10; 5:4; 9:1; 15:57)—is the ground of Paul's boasting in the Corinthians. Through Christ the Corinthians have come to faith; through Christ they will be raised from the dead and participate in the fully realized kingdom of God (cf. v. 28).

Paul's words are "I have pride in you *(tēn hymeteran kauchēsin)* that is in Christ Jesus our Lord." Ceslas Spicq renders these words as "Great is the pride that I have in you" *(EDNT* 2:301, n. 28). On "boasting" as a word group see above, pp. 99–101 "The object of boasting" *(kauchēsis)* is a word that generally has a positive connotation.

Despite the unanimous manuscript evidence D. R. MacDonald ("Conjectural Emendation") is of the opinion that the relative clause is a scribal interpolation intended to harmonize this text with 2 Tim 4:17. The suggestion is unwarranted.

32. *If, humanly speaking, I fought wild beasts in Ephesus, what good does it do me?* Using an image from the *agōn* motif to describe his preaching in Ephesus, Paul again places before the Corinthians the suggestion of what is advantageous (see note on 6:12). This is an important point in the argument of his deliberative rhetoric in which he offers himself as an example to the Corinthians. "Good" *(ophelos)* is hapax in Paul (cf. Jas 2:14, 16); his construction is classical (cf. Plato, Aristotle). His rhetorical question asks, in effect, "what do I gain from preaching as I do if there is no resurrection of the dead?"

If the dead are not raised, "let's eat and drink, for tomorrow we die": Paul's protasis echoes 15:15, 16, 29, as he draws yet another consequence from the idea that there might not be a resurrection from the dead. He cites Isa 22:13 with the exact wording of the LXX. The present tense of the citation's "we die" *(apothnēskomen)* has a future sense (BDF 323.1). In Isaiah the words belong to an oracle of doom (Isa 22:1-14). The people's failure to do the will of YHWH necessarily leads to disaster. In Paul the words function almost as a *bon mot* with an Epicurean ring. If there is no resurrection from the dead then he, and the Corinthians with him, might just as well abandon ministry to pursue the pleasures of this life.

33. *Don't go astray! "Bad company corrupts good morals":* The hortatory subjunctives of the biblical citations provide a transition to the paraenesis of vv. 33-34. The exhortation "don't go astray" is a classic formula of moral exhortation (see note on 6:9). The language of "going astray" *(planaō* and its cognates) is characteristic of the discourse of Hellenistic moralists. The exhortation concludes the first proof of ch. 15 (vv. 12-34).

To the exhortation Paul adds a popular slogan that appears in Menander's comedy, *Thais* (Fragment 187). First Corinthians 15:33 is the only citation of a pagan author that appears in the authentic Pauline corpus (cf. Titus 1:12; Acts 17:28[2x]). Menander (d. 292 B.C.E.) was a comic dramatist (cf. 4:9 for Paul's use of the image of the theater) known for his bawdy portrayals of private life. It is likely that Paul cites the slogan not as a literary quotation but as a *bon mot* in popular currency. "Morals" *(ēthē)* and "company" *(homiliai)* are hapax in the NT; "good" *(chrēsta)* is hapax in 1 Corinthians.

Paul's version of the slogan does not make use of the elision that the aphorism requires. He has *chrēsta homiliai* instead of the *chrēsth' homiliai* demanded by its meter (see BDF 17). The slogan functions well because of the contrast between "bad" and "good." For Paul the well-being of the community (1:2) demands its radical separation from evil (cf. 5:5, 6, 9, 13).

34. *Wake up properly from your drunken slumber and do not sin. Some do not know God. I say this to shame you:* The verse functions as a peroration to Paul's first section of proof on the resurrection. "Wake up from your drunken slumber" *(eknēpsate)* is hapax in the NT. However, both the language of "waking" and a metaphorical use of drunkenness are characteristic of Paul's moral exhortation (cf. Rom 13:11-13; 1 Thess 5:5-8). His exhortation is an appeal to the Corinthians to get back on the right track and abandon their wayward behavior. "Do not sin" *(mē hamartanete)* clarifies the metaphor. It is a communitarian and theological parallel to the "don't go astray" of philosophical discourse (v. 33).

That "some do not know God" is offered as an explanatory commentary (see the postpositive *gar*) on Paul's exhortation to the community. Paul shares the Jewish view that idolatry and the failure to acknowledge the one God lead to immoral behavior (cf. 6:9-10; Rom 1:20-31; 1 Thess 4:5). "Some" *(tines)* recalls the "some of you" *(en hymin tines)* with which the rhetorical proof began (15:12). Paul's remarks are clearly directed to some within the community (cf. v. 29), but they are of importance to all members of the community who bear some responsibility for the presence of evil in their midst (cf. 5:1-13). The some who do not know God are those who deny the resurrection. The God who is known and experienced by his people is one who has raised Christ from the dead and promises resurrection to those who believe the kerygma. Those who deny the resurrection can be equated with people who have not experienced God (1 Thess 4:5), the living God who has raised Jesus from the dead.

That people such as these exist within the community is a matter of some shame. "I say this to shame you" reprises with a different verb (*lalō* instead of *legō*) the formula of 6:5. Called to be God's holy people, the Corinthians have not yet reached a stage where they are cleansed from sin within (5:1-13; 15:34) and define their relationship with unjust outsiders (6:12).

FOR REFERENCE AND FURTHER STUDY

Deer, Donald S. "Whose Pride/Rejoicing/Glory(ing) in I Corinthians 15.31?" *BT* 38 (1987) 126–128.

DeMaris, Richard E. "Corinthian Religion and Baptism for the Dead (1 Corinthians 15:29): Insights from Archaeology and Anthropology." *JBL* 114 (1995) 661–682.

_____. "Demeter in Roman Corinth: Local Development in a Mediterranean Religion," *Numen* 42 (1995) 105–117.

Downey, James. "1 Cor 15:29 and the Theology of Baptism," *Euntes docete* 38 (1985) 23–35.

MacDonald, Dennis R. "A Conjectural Emendation of 1 Cor 15:31-32: Or the Case of the Misplaced Lion Fight," *HThR* 73 (1980) 265–276.

Malherbe, Abraham J. "The Beasts of Ephesus (1 Cor 15:32)," *JBL* 87 (1968) 71–80.

Murphy-O'Connor, Jerome. "'Baptized for the Dead' (I Cor., XV, 29). A Corinthian Slogan?" *RevB* 88 (1981) 532–543.

O'Neill, John C. "1 Corinthians 15:29," *ExpT* 91 (1980) 310–311.

Reaume, John D. "Another Look at 1 Corinthians 15:29, 'Baptized for the Dead,'" *BSac* 152 (1995) 457–475.

Rissi, Mathias. *Die Taufe für die Toten. Ein Beitrag zur paulinischen Tauflehre.* AThANT 42. Zurich: Zwingli, 1962.

White, Joel R. "'Baptized on account of the Dead': The Meaning of 1 Corinthians 15:29 in its Context," *JBL* 116 (1997) 487–499.

5. *How Can the Dead Be Raised?* (15:35-44a)

35. But someone will say, how can the dead be raised? With what kind of body do they come? 36. You fool! What you yourself sow does not come to life unless it dies. 37. As for what you sow, you sow not the body that will be, but only a naked seed, for example wheat or something else. 38. And God gives a body to it such as he wills, to each of the seeds its own body. 39. Not all flesh is identical flesh. Some is the flesh of humans, other the flesh of beasts, other the flesh of birds, and other the flesh of fish. 40. And there are heavenly bodies and earthly bodies; but the glory of heavenly bodies is one thing, the glory of earthly bodies another. 41. One thing is the glory of the sun, another the glory of the moon, and another the glory of the stars; for star differs from star in glory. 42. So also is the resurrection of the dead. It is sown in mortality; it is raised in immortality. 43. It is sown in dishonor; it is raised in glory. It is sown in weakness; it is raised in power. 44. A natural body is sown; an inspirited body is raised.

INTERPRETATION

Verse 35 marks a new beginning in the development of Paul's argument. "If the dead are not raised" (vv. 15, 16, 29, 32) was the leitmotif of the previous argument. Now the question is "how are the dead raised?" This is a different question from the issue treated in 15:12-34. "But someone will say" serves as a terse introductory phrase to get the discussion of this second issue underway. Paul's "someone" *(tis)* is the orator's imaginary interlocutor. The dialogue with the imaginary interlocutor continues in the direct address of v. 36. Paul calls his rhetorical foil a fool and addresses him in the second person singular.

What Kind of Body? The idea of bodily resurrection is one that derives from a Jewish apocalyptic understanding. At best Hellenistic thinkers would have thought in terms of the immortality of the soul. Not so Paul and those Jews who espoused the notion of bodily resurrection. Belief in corporeal resurrection readily leads to speculation as to the kind of body that will appear at the resurrection of the dead. Rabbis raised questions as to whether the bodies of those who are raised from the dead will be perfect bodies or the imperfect bodies of ordinary humans. Will the raised bodies have clothes or will they be naked? How will the bodies of those pious Jews who have died in the Diaspora travel to the land of Israel? Speculation on questions such as these appear in *b. Ketub.* 11a; *b. Sanh.* 90b; *y. Kil.* 9:3; *y. Ketub.* 12:3; *Qoh. Rab.* 1:4; *2 Apoc. Bar.* 49; and elsewhere.

Paul spoke to this issue by using the rhetorical ploy of the imaginary interlocutor. Paul, the speaker, appears to engage in direct conversation with this hypothetical figure. In the argument of Hellenistic rhetoric metaphors are singularly important providing they are "neither strange nor superficial," says Aristotle (*Art of Rhetoric* 3.10.6). Aristotle went on to say that "smart sayings" are derived from metaphor (*Art of Rhetoric* 3.11.1, 6). "It becomes evident to him [the hearer]," says Aristotle, "that he has learnt something, when the conclusion turns out contrary to his expectation, and the mind seems to say, 'How true it is! but I missed it'" (*Art of Rhetoric* 3.11.6).

To meet Jewish speculation as to the nature of the resurrected body for the benefit of a Hellenistic community, some of whose members denied the possibility of resurrection from the dead, Paul uses analogies drawn from the world of everyday experience. These were neither strange nor superficial. The first set of analogies is agricultural (vv. 36-38), the second zoological (v. 39), the third astronomical (vv. 40-41). The analogies speak to the unspeakable (see 2:9).

In its reflection on the end time Jewish apocalyptic frequently appealed to biblical images. The analogies used by Paul reflect the biblical tradition. The living beings cited in the second analogy (v. 39) are divided into categories that reflect God's work of creation on the fifth and sixth days (Gen 1:20-28). The three categories of celestial bodies cited in the third analogy (vv. 40-41) reflect the work of the fourth day of creation

(Gen 1:14-19). Since the second and third analogies so clearly reflect the Priestly author's story of creation it is not unlikely that Paul's agricultural analogy alludes to the creation of seeds and plant life on the third day of creation (Gen 1:11-13). The biblical story of God's creation of agriculture uses the verb "to sow" (*speirein*, "yielding" in the *NRSV* translation of Gen 1:11) and "seed" (*sperma*), two of the key words in Paul's agricultural metaphor (cf. vv. 42-45).

That Paul uses the creation story to provide analogies for the resurrection of the body suggests that resurrection might be considered a "new creation." In 1 Corinthians Paul does not actually use the terminology of "new creation" (cf. 2 Cor 5:17; Gal 6:15) when he writes about the resurrection of the body. There is, nonetheless, an analogy between the resurrection of the body and creation in that God, who gives bodies as he wills (v. 38), creates both the living body and the resurrected body.

The analogies Paul presents to his presumed interlocutor do not simply mirror the biblical story of creation. The presentation of the metaphor includes language that reflects Paul's concern to say something about bodily resurrection. He uses *sōma*/body (7x) and *sarx*/flesh (4x). In laying out the agricultural metaphor Paul speaks of seed that cannot come to life unless it has died (v. 36). He speaks of the future "body" (*sōma*, vv. 37, 38) rather than the future plant. He speaks of God giving the body (v. 38). The presence of these motifs betrays Paul's true interests.

Something is to be learned (cf. Aristotle, *Art of Rhetoric* 3.11.6) from Paul's rehearsal of the three metaphors. The "smart saying" he draws from the analogies is contained in v. 42, "so also is the resurrection of the dead." What is to be learned concerns the resurrection of the dead. Paul's real concern is with bodily resurrection. With what kind of body do they come? is the topical question in v. 35. The response is that they come with an inspirited body. This response appears in v. 44, the climax of a series of rhetorical antitheses.

The Structure of the Passage. "Body" and "raised" are the key terms in vv. 35 and 44. The literary device of *inclusio* thus allows 15:35-44a to be identified as a distinct literary unit within Paul's letter. The unity of the passage is ensured by Paul's inappropriate language. Rather than speak of a plant arising from seed that has been sown, he speaks of the body that emerges (v. 37). The human body that is raised has previously been sown (vv. 42-44). In effect the language of the smart saying has entered into the exposition of the metaphor and the language of the metaphor has entered into the exposition of the smart saying.

The agricultural metaphor is situated on a time axis. The contrast is between what has gone before and what comes after, and what God does to bring that about. The zoological and astronomical metaphors are situated as it were on a space axis. They contrast one kind of body with another. With G. D. Fee (*First Corinthians* 783) it is possible to analyze Paul's exposition of the latter metaphors by means of a chiastic structure: A-B-C-C'-B'-A', in which "not all flesh is identical" corresponds to "star differs from star," the kinds of flesh to the kinds of heavenly glory, and heavenly and earthly bodies to Paul's statements about their respective glory (elements C and C', v. 40). The paired central element is the focal point of the chiasm. Its contrast anticipates the smart word of vv. 42-44a and prepares for the contrast between the first and the last Adam in 15:44b-49.

Verses 42-44a consist of a series of four antithetical statements characterized by their parallel structure. Apropos the use of contrast Aristotle remarked that "the more concisely and antithetically they [sayings] are expressed, the greater is their popularity. The reason is that antithesis is more instructive and conciseness gives knowledge more rapidly" (*Art of Rhetoric* 3.11.9). Paul's four antitheses are characterized by their terseness. Each consists of only six words in Greek, three in each part of the antithesis. Each unit is characterized by its balanced structure, but the structure of the fourth unit is different from that of the first three (see note on v. 44a). The four antitheses are arranged in a kind of crescendo, culminating with the finale, "an inspirited body is raised." This is not only the climax of the series, it is also the answer to the question Paul had raised in v. 35. As he builds up to this response Paul's antitheses allow him to identify the qualities of the risen body: immortality, glory, and power.

NOTES

35. *But someone will say, how can the dead be raised? With what kind of body do they come?* The rhetorical "but someone will say" marks a shift in Paul's argumentation. The first rhetorical question recalls the proposition he set forth in v. 12, but it turns the argument away from a discussion of the reality or facticity of the resurrection to its possibility and modality. The second question indicates that the resurrection of the dead is a resurrection of the body. This, in fact, is a new element in the discussion. For the first time in this context Paul speaks of the "body" (*sōma*). If there is to be a bodily resurrection, with what kind of body will the dead rise? That is the question Paul may have considered to be a veiled argument against the possibility of resurrection (cf. Matt 22:23-33; Mark 12:18-27; Luke 20:27-40). Insawn Saw (*Paul's Rhetoric* 223–225) claims that what begins in v. 35 is a kind of *refutatio* that follows upon the threefold proof of 15:12-34.

36–37. *You fool! What you yourself sow does not come to life unless it dies. As for what you sow, you sow not the body that will be, but only a naked seed, for example wheat or something else:* The vocative "you fool" (*aphrōn*, hapax in 1 Corinthians) is reminiscent of the style of the Hellenistic Stoic-Cynic diatribe (see Rudolf Bultmann, *Der Stil der paulinischen Predigt und die kynisch-stoische Diatribe.*

FRALNT 13 [Göttingen: Vandenhoeck & Ruprecht, 1910] 14, 66). Paul's emphatic *sy*, "yourself," helps to provide the argument with the allure of a direct response. This response comes from the world of agriculture, contrasting the seed (*kokkon*, hapax in Paul) that is sown with the plant (*sōma*, "body"; the Greek term properly designates the human body) that will arise. The sower sows nothing but (*alla*) a seed. What emerges is not the seed, for that must die, nor is it another seed of the same kind. What emerges is a body that corresponds to the specific kind of seed. In sum, the body is the body that God will give (v. 38).

The ideas that the seed must die if it is to give rise to life and that different kinds of seed are sown in the field are not foreign to Paul's perspective in his use of the agricultural metaphor. Earlier in the letter he had used the image of the field to describe the Corinthian community (3:9). John 12:24 likewise speaks of the seed dying before rising to new life.

38. *And God gives a body to it such as he wills, to each of the seeds its own body:* "God" contrasts with the rhetorical "you yourself" of v. 37. That verse's suggestion to the effect that there are different kinds of seed anticipates the idea that there are different kinds of plants ("bodies"). In using the agricultural metaphor in 3:7 Paul had affirmed that God provides for agricultural growth. The truism recurs here, but it is so phrased as to focus on the individual plant. The emphasis is on God's will and the different bodies/plants that are God's gifts (cf. 12:11, "to each as he wills"). For the sake of emphasis and to underscore the diversity Paul uses an emphatic *kai* (BDF 442.9) before "each" (*hekastō*), but the *kai* has not been translated. "Seeds" (the generic *spermatōn*, cf. Gen 1:12) is hapax in 1 Corinthians and different from the "seed" in v. 37 (*kokkon*, a word that designates seed of a specific kind, mustard seed in Matt 13:31, wheat in Diogenes Laertius, *Lives* 6.88, etc.).

39. *Not all flesh is identical flesh. Some is the flesh of humans, other the flesh of beasts, other the flesh of birds, and other the flesh of fish:* On the Septuagintal phrase "all flesh" (*pasa sarx*) see the note on 1:29. Flesh (*sarx*) entails the solidarity of humans with all animate creatures. Paul's *men . . . de* construction contrasts the flesh of human beings with the flesh of other kinds of animate creatures. A serial *allē* [4x], "some . . . other . . . other . . . other," divides "flesh" into four kinds. The division recalls the Priestly author's story of the fifth and sixth days of creation (Gen 1:20-25). Fish, birds, and animals are distinguished from one another. These three are further distinguished from the human being who was also created on the sixth day (Gen 1:26-28).

40–41. *And there are heavenly bodies and earthly bodies; but the glory of heavenly bodies is one thing, the glory of earthly bodies another. One thing is the glory of the sun, another the glory of the moon, and another the glory of the stars; for star differs from star in glory:* As he speaks of the distinction between heavenly bodies and earthly bodies Paul continues to hark back to the Priestly author's creation narrative. "Earthly bodies" (*sōmata epigeia*) summarizes the four types of fleshy existence that Paul listed in v. 39. "Glory" (*doxa*) had been a feature of Paul's discourse on creation in 11:7, 15 (see notes). In a way similar to that in which different seeds produce different plant-bodies (vv. 36-37), so heavenly bodies have a glory that is different from the glory enjoyed by earthly bodies. Paul's phraseology is elliptical; both clauses in v. 40 lack a verb.

The story of the fourth day of creation (Gen 1:14-19, v. 16) distinguishes among kinds of heavenly bodies, the sun, the moon, and the stars, just as Paul does in v. 41. To distinguish between the glory of heavenly and of earthly bodies he uses a "one thing . . . another thing" *(hetera . . . hetera)* construction; to distinguish among the glories of the three sorts of heavenly bodies he uses a serial *allē* construction as he does in v. 39.

42–44a. *So also is the resurrection of the dead. It is sown in mortality; it is raised in immortality. It is sown in dishonor; it is raised in glory. It is sown in weakness; it is raised in power. A natural body is sown; an inspirited body is raised:* Paul returns to the topic at hand, the resurrection of the dead *(hē anastasis tōn nekrōn)* as he draws a conclusion from the two sets of analogies. A series of four contrasts, a "model example of parallelism" (BDF 490), is used to describe the resurrected body. The fourfold use of "is sown" *(speiretai)* links these contrasts to the first set of analogies (vv. 36-38). There the emphasis was on different states of existence, the latter dependent on God. Here the resurrected body is characterized as immortal, glorious, powerful, and inspirited.

The plethora of unusual contrasts led Richard A. Horsley ("Spiritual Elitism at Corinth," 206) to the conviction that Paul has appropriated the language of the Corinthians to whom he was writing. The first three contrasts are in a staccato sequence. "Being sown" and "being raised" are each qualified by a prepositional phrase. The first prepositional phrase relates to death, looking back to v. 36. The resurrected body has immortality *(en aphtharsią)*. The second phrase recalls vv. 40-41, alluding to the biblical story of creation and humanity's loss of God's shared glory (Rom 3:23; cf. 11:7). The resurrected body is glorious *(en doxą)*. The third phrase picks up the characteristic of weakness that has echoed throughout the letter, beginning in 1:28. In contrast with weakness the resurrected body is power *(en dynamei)*. The motifs of glory and weakness also appear in 4 Ezra's scenario of the end time (see 4 Ezra 7:112-115).

Paul's emphasis lies on the fourth contrast, between the natural body *(sōma psychikon;* cf. 2:14) and the inspirited body *(sōma pneumatikon)*. The grammatical structure of the fourth contrast is different from that of the first three. Instead of a verb modified by a prepositional phrase, Paul uses the same verbs, "is sown," "is raised," but supplies the subject that could only have been supposed up to this point. All along Paul has been talking about a physical body and a spiritual body; what has hitherto been implicit becomes explicit in the fourth antithesis. The natural body is vitalized only by a vital force *(psychē)*. The inspirited body is the human insofar as he or she is energized by the Spirit of the living God *(pneuma)*.

Paul has used the rhetorical devices of antitheses and *klimax* to focus on the inspirited body, which is where his emphasis lies. In v. 35 the imaginary interlocutor has asked "with what kind of body do they come?" Paul answers in v. 44ab, "they come with an inspirited body." The inspirited body then becomes the focus of the following pericope (cf. v. 46).

FOR REFERENCE AND FURTHER STUDY

Bonneau, Normand. "The Logic of Paul's Argument on the Resurrection Body in 1 Cor 15:35-44a," *ScEs* 45 (1993) 79–92.
Burchard, Christoph. "1 Korinther 15:39-41," *ZNW* 75 (1984) 233–258.
Horsley, Richard A. "Pneumatikos vs. Psychikos: Distinctions of Spiritual Status among the Corinthians," *HThR* 69 (1976) 269–288.
Jewett, Robert. *Paul's Anthropological Terms* 265–267.
Jucci, Elio. "Terreno, psichico, pneumatico nel capitolo 15 della prima epistola ai Corinzi," *Henoch* 5 (1983) 323–341.
Martin, Dale B. *The Corinthian Body* 117–136.
Pamment, Margaret. "Raised a Spiritual Body: Bodily Resurrection according to Paul," *NBl* 66 (1985) 372–378.

6. *The Last Adam* (15:44b-49)

44b. If there is a natural body there is also an inspirited body. 45. And thus it is written, "The first person Adam was made into a living creature"; the last Adam is made into a lifegiving spirit. 46. But it is not the inspirited one that is first, but the natural; then the inspirited one. 47. The first person is of dust from the earth; the second person is from heaven. 48. As the one of dust, so those of dust, and as the heavenly one, so those who are heavenly. 49. And as we have borne the image of the one of dust, let us also bear the image of the heavenly one.

INTERPRETATION

Verses 44b-49 form a unit that interprets the idea of the inspirited body *(sōma pneumatikon)* introduced in v. 44a. Verse 44b states Paul's thesis: "if there is a natural body there is also an inspirited body."

The First and the Last. Authority for the affirmation that the inspirited body exists is to be found in the Scriptures. Paul cites Gen 2:7, "and the person became a living being," as the basis for his argument. The person is identified as Adam, specified as the "first" person. Paul's language is generic. "Adam" is not the male *(anēr)* but a human being *(ho anthrōpos)*. The numerical adjective "first" *(prōtos)* suggests that there will be other human beings. Paul does not describe a series of human beings; rather he goes directly to the last Adam *(ho eschatos Adam)*.

The last Adam is not identified by name. Paul's interest is in establishing an eschatological paradigm. He does so by placing a contrast between the first and the last. His protological statement calls for an eschatological statement. Eschatological existence is to be contrasted with ordinary human existence, the "order of creation" of which theologians speak. Paul's last *(eschatos)* means not so much "last in a sequence"—it certainly does not mean that!—as "final," "ultimate." Since the man Jesus Christ is not the last human being, it is appropriate for Paul to have avoided his name as he pushes the frontiers of his anthropological reflection to either end of the temporal spectrum. There is a beginning and an end (cf. 15:26-28), a first and a last.

A consistent use of antithesis throughout the pericope, seven times in all, allows Paul to maintain the contrast between the initial state of human existence and the eschatological state. The initial state is "natural" (see note) and dusty (see note); the final state is spiritual and heavenly.

Adam. The Scriptures are the interpretive tool whereby the death and resurrection of Christ can be understood (15:3b-5). They provide a warrant for Paul's affirmation that there will be a spiritual body. At the same time they provide some insight into the death and resurrection of Christians.

In 15:35-44a Paul had clearly alluded to the story of the third, fourth, fifth, and sixth days of creation as narrated in Genesis 1. The biblical narrative, coming from the Priestly tradition, is a dramatic account that features the power of the Spirit in the ordering of the universe (Gen 1:2). The Spirit-moved transformation of the universe from chaos to cosmos culminates in the creation of the human (Gen 1:26-29). Paul reads the Genesis story of creation in a naïve fashion. Without the insights of modern biblical scholarship, he does not distinguish the Priestly author's narrative in ch. 1 from the Yahwist's narrative in ch. 2. For Paul the story of the creation of Adam and Eve (Gen 2:4b and following) continues the story of the creation of the universe. The garden story features a narrative account, in mythical language, of the creation of the first human: Adam, formed from the dust of the earth *(choun apo tēs gēs)*, into whom God breathed the breath *(pnoēn)* of life, so that this first human became a living being *(eis psychēn zōsan,* Gen 2:7).

His reading of the Scripture allows Paul to develop an Adam-Christ typology by means of antithetical parallelism. Whereas the first human became a living being, the last Adam is a lifegiving spirit *(eis pneuma zōopoioun)*. Whereas the first received life, the last gives life *(zōsan* as contrasted with *zōopoioun)*. Whereas the first is natural *(psychēn)*, the last is spiritual *(pneuma)*. Whereas the first is formed of dust of the earth *(ek gēs choikos)*, the last is from heaven *(ex ouranou)*. The contrast between the two is clear. It is no less clear that Paul chooses the language of his contrast on the basis of the language found in the biblical narrative.

The Image of the Heavenly One. Paul brings the midrash on Gen 2:7 to a close in vv. 48-49, as he draws out the implications of his Adamic

christology. A first implication is that living human beings are in conformity with the first person; like the first person they are of dust. In contrast, those who are in conformity with the last person are heavenly. To
establish a sharp contrast between earthly and heavenly existence Paul
apparently coined an adjective "of dust," "dusty" *(choikos)*. His neologism recalls Gen 2:7. Used as a substantivized adjective it contrasts "those
of dust" *(hoi choikoi)* with "those of heaven" *(hoi epouranioi)*.

The Genesis stories of creation continue to dominate the imagery of
Paul's concluding exhortation. Living human beings who are "of dust"
bear the image of the one of dust. Paul conflates the imagery of Gen 2:7
(dust) with that of Gen 1:26-27 (image) in order to create the contrasting
image of the heavenly one. This is the image Christians should strive to
bear. The last Adam, the unnamed Christ (cf. 15:57), must be the paradigm of their existence.

<h2 style="text-align:center">NOTES</h2>

44b. *If there is a natural body there is also an inspirited body:* Paul's fourth contrast distinguished the natural body from the inspirited body. In v. 44b the distinction
is reprised in the form of a conditional clause that serves as a thesis for the
argument Paul develops in vv. 45-49. His thesis is not that because there is a
natural person there must be an inspirited person, but rather that just as the
natural body exists, so too the inspirited body exists.

45. *And thus it is written, "The first person Adam was made into a living creature":* To
make his point Paul cites a passage from the Bible's creation narratives, to
which he had alluded in vv. 39-41. Paul would have been unaware of contemporary scholarship's judgment that a first creation account, Gen 1:1–2:4a,
to which the allusions of 15:39-41 refer, derives from a later, Priestly source,
and that the second creation account, Gen 2:4b-24, from which the Scripture
cited in 15:45 comes, derives from an earlier, Yahwist source.

The scriptural text (Gen 2:7) is cited as an authority on the basis of which
Paul affirms the existence of the inspirited body. An introductory lemma
identifies the text as Scripture *(gegraptai;* see above, p. 95). Rather than an explanatory *gar* ("for"), an epexegetical *kai* ("and") is used to link the scriptural
citation to Paul's thematic statement. The Scripture is the point of departure
for a midrashic reflection on the inspirited person. The inspirited person is
distinct from the natural person.

Paul's version of Gen 2:7 differs from the LXX by the addition of "first"
(prōtos) and the presence of the word "Adam." "Adam" appears in both
Theodotion and Symmachus, so it may be that "Adam" also appeared in the
Greek Bible Paul was citing at this point. On the other hand, "first" is manifestly a Pauline addition to the text. The word underscores the contrast between the first and the last Adam. The enhancement it brings contributes to
the rhetorical force of Paul's protology-eschatology schema.

Hapax in 1 Corinthians, *psychēn* (literally "soul," but here "creature"), is one of a group of anthropological terms in the Pauline corpus that, rather than designating component parts of the human person, indicate the whole person under one or another aspect. *Psychē* identifies the human being as a vital, living creature (see Graham J. Warne, *Hebrew Perspectives on the Human Person in the Hellenistic Era: Philo and Paul.* Mellen Biblical Press Series 35 [Lewiston: Edwin Mellen, 1995]).

the last Adam is made into a lifegiving spirit: The statement parallels the wording of the scriptural text. A contrast is drawn between first and last, between the living creature and the lifegiving spirit *(pneuma zōopoioun;* cf. 15:22, 36). An anonymous last Adam is the inspirited one. Inspirited, the last Adam is life-giving.

46. *But it is not the inspirited one that is first, but the natural; then the inspirited one:* The contrast between the inspirited and the physical recalls 2:14-15. Introduced by the strong contrasting particle *alla,* "but," Paul's words clarify the meaning of v. 45. Extant Hellenistic Jewish texts—for example, those of Philo—distinguished between two types of humanity, heavenly or earthly (cf. v. 47), immortal or mortal (cf. v. 53). They did not, however, employ the inspirited-natural *(pneumatikos-psychikos)* contrast in their interpretation of Gen 2:7.

47. *The first person is of dust from the earth:* Paul's language is elliptical; it lacks a verb. The phrase "of dust from the earth" *(ek gēs choikos)* is an obvious allusion to the text of Gen 2:7, cited by Paul in v. 45. Unable to render the Hebrew pun adequately, "human being *(ʾādām)* from the dust of the earth *(ʾădāmâ),*" the LXX describes the prototypical human as "human being from the dust of the ground" *(anthrōpon choun apo tēs gēs).* The Hebrew text underscores the close link between humanity and its environment. Paul's own description of the first human is a paraphrase of the biblical text. In doing so he seems to have coined an adjective, "dusty" *(choikos),* not found in Hellenistic literature prior to 1 Corinthians. The new adjective occurs four times in 1 Cor 15:47-49. It creates and highlights a contrast between "dusty" and "heavenly," that is, of dust and from the heavens.

the second person is from heaven: Like the parallel phrase in v. 47a this phrase is elliptical; it lacks a verb. There is also a textual problem. In some manuscripts (A, K, P, Ψ and correctors of ℵ and D) "the Lord" *(ho kyrios)* is found in apposition to "second person" *(ho deuteros anthrōpos).* In 𝔓⁴⁶ "second person" is qualified by the addition of "spiritual" *(pneumatikos).* According to the general principles of textual criticism the reading is to be preferred that best explains the origin of all others. Accordingly the simple "second person" *(ho deuteros anthrōpos),* widely attested in the manuscript tradition, is the preferred reading in 15:47.

48. *As the one of dust, so those of dust, and as the heavenly one, so those who are heavenly:* An elliptical phrase without a verb enunciates a statement of principle. Marked by its clear parallelism (BDF 490), it compares human beings with the first person and humans with the heavenly one. To describe the heavenly one

Paul employs the adjective *epouranios* (used by him only in 1 Cor 15:40[2x], 48[2x], 49) rather than the prepositional phrase "from heaven" *(ex ouranou)* employed in v. 47.

49. *and as we have borne the image of the one of dust, let us also bear the image of the heavenly one:* As he did in v. 34, Paul concludes his rhetorical proof with an exhortation. The exhortation harks back to the biblical tradition according to which the descendants of Adam bear his image (Gen 5:3). This is combined with the notion that humans are created in the image of God (Gen 1:27). Paul's words express a christological and eschatological transformation of the image-motif. For Paul the normative image is that of Christ, but it is an image we must strive to bear even if it is a gift of God. Ultimately there is to be conformity between human beings and the heavenly one.

A question arises as to the mood of the verb. The hortatory aorist subjunctive tense *(phoresōmen)*, for which there is "greatly preponderant external evidence" (Archibald Robertson and Alfred Plummer), is found in $\mathfrak{P}^{46}$, ℵ, A, C, D, Ψ, and a variety of other important manuscripts (cf. Homily "On the Paschal Mystery" by an unknown ancient author, *Sermo* 35.4.6; *PL* 17, 674). *GNT*[4] opts for a reading in the future tense ("we shall bear," *phoresomen*), to which B, several other ancient manuscripts and a variety of Fathers, including Chrysostom and Jerome, attest on the basis of its "intrinsic probability." The context, notes Bruce Metzger, is didactic (see *Textual Commentary* 502). The easiest reading of the text requires a future; by comparison the hortatory subjunctive is the *lectio difficilior.* The rhetorical analysis of ch. 15 shows, moreover, that Paul concludes each of his proofs (vv. 34, 49) and his peroration (v. 58) with an exhortation. Hence, on the basis of the "greatly preponderant external evidence" and the character of Paul's rhetoric, the subjunctive reading is to be preferred. (Cf. S. P. Botha, "1 Korintiërs 15:49b: 'n Hortatief- of futurumlesing? *Hervormde teologiese studies* (Pretoria) 49 [1993] 760–774).

For Reference and Further Study

Brodeur, Scott. *The Holy Spirit's Agency in the Resurrection of the Dead: An Exegetical Study of 1 Corinthians 15,44b-49 and Romans 8,9-13.* Tesi Gregoriana, Serie Teologia 14. Rome: Pontifical Gregorian University, 1996.

Horsley, Richard A. "Pneumatikos vs. Psychikos: Distinctions of Spiritual Status among the Corinthians," *HThR* 69 (1976) 269–288.

Jucci, Elio. "Terreno, psichico, pneumatico nel capitolo 15 della prima epistola ai Corinzi," *Henoch* 5 (1983) 323–341.

Pamment, Margaret. "Raised a Spiritual Body: Bodily Resurrection according to Paul," *NBl* 66 (1985) 372–378.

Sterling, Gregory E. "'Wisdom among the perfect': Creation Traditions in Alexandrian Judaism and Corinthian Christianity," *NovT* 37 (1995) 355–384.

7. *Victory over Death* (15:50-58)

50. This I say, brothers and sisters: Flesh and blood cannot inherit the kingdom of God, nor does the perishable inherit imperishability. 51. See there! I am telling you a mystery. Not all of us will fall asleep, but all will be transformed, 52. in an instant, in the blinking of an eye, with the last trumpet. For the trumpet will sound and the dead shall rise imperishable and we shall be transformed. 53. For it is necessary for this perishable being to put on imperishability and this mortal being to put on immortality. 54. When this perishable being puts on imperishability and this mortal being puts on immortality, then will come to pass the word that has been written, "Death has been swallowed up in victory. 55. Where, O death, is your victory? Where, O death, is your sting?" 56. The sting of death is sin and the power of sin is the law.

57. Thanks be to God who gives us victory through our Lord Jesus Christ. 58. Therefore, my beloved brothers and sisters, be firm, be steadfast, always exceeding in the work of the Lord, knowing that in the Lord your labor is not in vain.

Interpretation

With "this I say, brothers and sisters" Paul appeals again to the attention of the Corinthians. The apostrophic vocative marks the beginning of a new unit. The unit, vv. 50-58, concludes the body of the letter. From a rhetorical perspective it functions more specifically as the conclusion to Paul's demonstrative argument on the resurrection (15:1-49). Insawn Saw (*Paul's Rhetoric* 238) has suggested that this discrete and relatively short unit has its proper rhetorical structure with an *exordium* (vv. 50-51a), *narratio* (vv. 51b-52), *probatio* (vv. 53-55), *refutatio* (vv. 56-57), and *peroratio* (v. 58).

The Line of Thought. Beginning with a direct appeal to the Corinthians, designated as Paul's kin, the unit brings to closure Paul's extensive disquisition on the resurrection of the dead. The language, images, and ideas are taken from Jewish apocalyptic, but Paul makes efforts to "translate" the Semitic concepts into language that can be understood by a Hellenistic audience. "Flesh and blood" is perishable (v. 50). "Perishable" is mortal (v. 53).

The pericope, 15:50-58, essentially consists of two parts, vv. 50-53 and vv. 54-57, with a general conclusion, v. 58. The language of the first part shows that it is organized in a chiastic pattern (vv. 50, 51-52, 52-53). This subunit affirms a radical incompatibility between the present condition of human existence and the resurrected condition. It is imperative (note the *dei*, "it is necessary," in v. 53) that the perishable assume imperishability, that the mortal assume immortality. Transformation is necessary. In affirming that all will be transformed Paul has recourse to apocalyptic categories. Organized as it is, the subunit proclaims that from an anthropological perspective the parousia entails the transformation of the living and the dead. From a theological perspective the source and force of the transformation is the kingdom of God.

References to the Scriptures are rife in Jewish and Christian apocalyptic literature. In the second part of the exposition (vv. 54-57) Paul uses a pair of scriptural texts (Isa 25:8; Hos 13:14) offered as a single citation. In interpreting these texts he continues to exercise his prophetic function (see above, pp. 94–96). Paul uses the Scriptures to present the transformation of the human from the perishable/mortal state to the imperishable/immortal state as a victory over death. Death is infectious because of sin and the law—not necessarily the Jewish Law, but any law. Victory over death is achieved through our Lord Jesus Christ, who had been raised from the dead. His resurrection looks forward to his parousia, when victory over death will be brought to completion.

The image of the transformation of the resurrected body as a victory over death evokes a military metaphor, which recalls the description of the parousia in 15:23-26. Military images—of which Rev 16:14-16 is but one example—abound in apocalyptic literature, where the final times are often portrayed as God's conquest of evil in all its forms. In Paul's scenario the final enemy, the last evidence of evil to be destroyed, is death (vv. 26, 56).

Exultation in victory over death gives rise to the glorious doxology of v. 58, "thanks be to God who gives us victory through our Lord Jesus Christ." This is a song of triumph that with gratitude proclaims the victory of God over death achieved through his agent, Jesus Christ our Lord. With "Christ," the epithet that appeared so frequently in vv. 12-28, the full christological title evokes the death and resurrection of Jesus (cf. 15:3). With "Lord" it evokes the resurrection and parousia of Christ, when his lordship will be truly manifest (vv. 24-28). That Jesus Christ is identified as "our" Lord evokes not so much his sovereignty over Christians as the fact that he is their supreme benefactor. In the Greco-Roman world, of which first-century Corinth was a part, the benefactor system was an important part of life and its social fabric. Those acknowledged as Lord were celebrated for the benefaction they bestowed on those over whom they exercised their lordship. As a benefactor of the Christian community Jesus Christ won victory over death on their behalf (cf. 8:6).

Intertextuality. The central element in the first part of Paul's exposition (vv. 51-52) shares several stylistic and thematic similarities with what he had written in 1 Thess 4:15-18. In both cases he begins with a dangling "this" ("this I tell you, brothers and sisters"). He highlights the theme by means of a focus word. In 1 Corinthians the focus is on the "mystery" (v. 51); in 1 Thessalonians it is on the "word of the Lord" (1 Thess 4:15). In both cases Paul's exposition makes abundant use of traditional apocalyptic imagery. The parallel presentations articulate a belief in the resurrection and the expectation that (some of) the living will experience the parousia.

The similarities between 1 Cor 15:51-52 and 1 Thess 4:13-18 are striking, but there are significant differences between the two texts. One notable difference is their focus, a difference derived to a large degree from the circumstances that prompted the respective letters. 1 Thessalonians was written to a community stricken by surprise and grief that some of their number had died, perhaps at the hands of violent people in the city, before the parousia had taken place. First Corinthians was written to a community some of whose members denied bodily resurrection. It does not express an expectation of the imminence of the parousia as does 1 Thessalonians. In fact, although Paul clearly expected to be alive at the parousia when he wrote 1 Thessalonians, that expectation is not so obvious in 1 Corinthians. Indeed, although both 1 Thessalonians and 1 Corinthians speak of the living and the dead at the parousia, the tenor of 1 Thessalonians is such as to suggest that the dead are expected to be the exception at that moment. The tenor of 1 Corinthians suggests almost the opposite.

If 1 Thess 4:13-18, written before 1 Corinthians, is a significant parallel with 1 Cor 15:51-52, 2 Cor 5:1-5 is another important parallel. The language of this text employs different metaphors from those used in 15:51-52 and 1 Thess 4:13-18. Its images of dwelling and clothing go poorly together with one another, but both are to be found in Jewish apocalyptic speculation. The heavenly dwelling recalls the eschatological temple (*2 Apoc. Bar.* 4:3; 4 Ezra 10:40-57). Clothing brings to mind rabbinic speculation about the clothes to be worn by the dead at their rising. Despite its difference of imagery from 1 Cor 15:50-57 and its mention of the Spirit (2 Cor 5:5, but absent from 1 Cor 15:50-57), an intertextual reading of 2 Cor 5:1-5 is important for a fuller understanding of 1 Cor 15:50-57. Both texts speak of the transformation of the body and the ultimate agency of God in the eschatological scenario. In fact the apocalyptic-eschatological ideas developed by Paul in 2 Cor 4:7–6:2 are essentially those of 1 Corinthians 15, due attention being made to some modification in the situation of the addressees.

Apocalyptic Categories. Verses 50-53 affirm the contrast between the present condition of the human body and the condition of the resurrected body (cf. 15:42-49). The contrast is maintained in v. 54 as Paul seeks to interpret by means of a scriptural reference the meaning of the transformation of the human body. Verses 50-51 affirm that a transformation is to take place and offer some suggestion as to the nature of the transformation.

Paul's affirmation of the radical incompatibility between the present state of the human condition and the resurrected state is a theme he shares with Jewish apocalyptic literature. Baruch, for example, says in a farewell discourse:

> For that which is now is nothing. But that which is in the future will be very great. For everything will pass away that is corruptible, and everything that dies will go away, and all present time will be forgotten, and there will be no remembrance of the present time which is polluted by evils. . . . For that which will be in the future, that is what one will look for, and that which comes later, that is what we shall hope for. For there is a time that does not pass away. And that period is coming which will remain forever; and there is the new world which does not carry back to corruption those who enter into its beginning. . . . For those are the ones who will inherit this time of which it is spoken, and to these is the heritage of the promised time. (*2 Apoc. Bar.* 44:8-13)

Baruch's speech expresses the radical incompatibility between the state of future existence and the present state of existence in language used by Paul in 15:50-55. See also *2 Apoc. Bar.* 74:2, "For that time is the end of that which is corruptible and the beginning of that which is incorruptible."

The Fourth Book of Ezra, after speaking of the temporary messianic kingdom of the Son (cf. 15:24-28), refers to the death of all human beings. The text continues:

> And the world shall be turned back to primeval silence for seven days, as it was at the first beginnings; so that no one shall be left. And after seven days the world, which is not yet awake, shall be roused, and that which is corruptible shall perish. And the earth shall give up those who are asleep in it; and the chambers shall give up the souls which have been committed to them" (4 Ezra 7:29-32).

In this passage 4 Ezra, like Paul, uses the metaphor of sleep to describe death. Elsewhere it uses the motifs of inheritance and immortality (4 Ezra 7:96; 8:54) and glory (4 Ezra 7:112) to describe the human condition to come. These are motifs that Paul also employs.

In 15:50-53 Paul's point is that all will be changed; all will be transformed. How can this be? To explain the inexplicable Paul has recourse to apocalyptic motifs. Jewish apocalyptic literature also talked about a transformation of the human condition at the end time. Thus 4 Ezra 8:53-54, "The root of evil is sealed up from you, illness is banished from you, and death is hidden; hell has fled and corruption has been forgotten; sorrows have passed away, and in the end the treasure of immortality is made manifest." See also *2 Apoc. Bar.* 49–50, which presents a dialogue in which the seer asks God, "In which shape will the living live in your day? Or how will remain their splendor which will be after that? Will they, perhaps, take again this present form . . .? Or will you perhaps change these things which have been in the world?" The question is not unlike the one with which Paul had begun his reflection on bodily resurrection, "With what kind of body do they come?" (v. 35). *First Enoch* 90:37-38 offers an analogy of animals transformed in the end time. Daniel 12:3 says of those who have fallen asleep and who awaken to everlasting life that they shall shine like the stars forever and ever. The motif of an end-time transformation is common in apocalyptic literature, but none of this literature talks about transformation into the image of the Messiah. This, however, is precisely Paul's point (15:49).

A Short Midrash. The apocalyptic genre, whether used by Jewish or Christian authors, is characterized by its use of Scripture. Sometimes the Scripture is quoted directly; sometimes there are only allusions to scriptural passages and motifs. In 15:50-58 Paul has recourse to the language of apocalyptic as he explains the relationship between the human condition as it now is and the human condition as it will be at the moment of bodily resurrection.

Adopting the patterns of the apocalyptic genre, Paul continues his reflection on the resurrection in vv. 54-55 with the help of a pair of biblical quotations, Isa 25:8 and Hos 13:14, which he cites directly. According to the *gezera shawah* principle of rabbinic hermeneutics the presence of the same expression in more than one text implies that one of them can be interpreted in the light of the others. In vv. 54-55 "death" is the catchword that allows Paul to join Isa 25:8 and Hos 13:14 together in a single scriptural unit with the two texts interpreting one another. Paul cites the two verses almost as if they were one. There is only one introductory lemma for both, and they run on as if one continued the other. The technique strengthens the rhetorical force of Paul's scriptural argumentation. It is found elsewhere in his letters as he sometimes conflates quotations of scripture (cf. Rom 9:25-26; 11:26-27; 2 Cor 6:16-18).

Neither Isa 25:8 nor Hos 13:14 is cited by Paul exactly as it is found in the Greek Bible [LXX]. The Hebrew text of Isa 25:8 is generally rendered "he will swallow up death forever." Instead of "forever" Paul's Greek text reads "in victory" *(eis nikos)*. This reading represents one of the traditional understandings of the prophetic text; the Greek versions of Aquila and Theodotion, but not the LXX, read "in victory." Victory is important for Paul's argument since "victory" *(nikos)* is a catchword that, along with "death," links Isa 25:8 with Hos 13:14. The idea of victory (cf. 15:25-26) serves to provide a thrust for the exultant doxology of v. 57.

Paul's version of Hos 13:14 also differs from that of the LXX. "Victory," the catchword, does not appear in Hos 13:14 [LXX]. The manuscript tradition of this verse in the Greek Bible offers various readings, among which "judgment" *(dikē)* seems preferable, thus "Where, O death, is your judgment?" (Hos 13:14). Paul's personification of death in 15:54-55 has been borrowed from Hos 13:14. The apostle is not disinclined to use personification as a literary and rhetorical device (cf. 12:15-16, 21).

E. Earle Ellis (*Paul's Use of the Old Testament* [Edinburgh: Oliver & Boyd, and Grand Rapids: Eerdmans, 1957]) and others suggest that the form of the conflated texts that appears in 15:54-55 has a pre-Pauline origin. Christopher D. Stanley (*Paul and the Language of Scripture* 215), however, correctly maintains that "the fundamentally Pauline origin of this carefully structured rhetorical unity can hardly be doubted." Paul has adapted the texts so that they might be read together and be mutually interpretive. Paul's way of dealing with the texts, in the form of near-citations and with application to the situation at hand, is akin to the way in which the Scriptures were used in rabbinic commentaries, in the Targums, and in the Qumran midrashim.

M. Gertner ("Midrashim in the NT," *JSSt* 7 [1962] 267–272) claimed that 15:55-56 is one of only three NT passages that properly has the form of a biblical midrash. The other two would be Mark 4:1-20 and Luke 1:67-79. There can be little doubt, however, that 15:54b-57 has the characteristics of a midrash. It is an applied commentary on a specific passage of Scripture. Moreover, Paul's use of midrashic techniques can hardly be limited to 15:54b-57. In 1 Corinthians, 1:18–2:16; 10:1-13; and 15:20-28 clearly contain elements that show the midrashic technique at work.

The Final Exhortation. Paul's explanation is brought to closure with an exhortation (v. 58) similar in function to the exhortation of 1 Thess 4:18. The language of this final exhortation in 15:58 is unusual (see note). Particularly striking is the way in which it is introduced, "therefore, my beloved brothers and sisters." The strongly inferential "therefore" *(hōste)* shows that Paul is really bringing things to a conclusion. He urges the community to be steadfast and adhere to the gospel.

The community is addressed as "my beloved brothers and sisters." This is the fullest form of address in Paul's sporadic appeals to the community. As such it provides for the conclusion not only of 15:50-57, nor only of ch. 15, but of the entire letter. Paul solemnly addresses the Corinthians, appealing to their kinship relationship with him and his love for them, in this final paraenesis.

From a rhetorical standpoint v. 58 functions as the peroration of the entire letter. To be sure, the letter will continue with Paul directing his concern to a number of practical matters and then bringing the letter to full closure with a variety of closing epistolary conventions (16:13-24). These epistolary features are present because Paul's rhetorical appeal has been conveyed in the form of a letter. From the standpoint of epistolary criticism v. 58 concludes the body of the letter, which had begun with Paul's statement of principle in 1:10.

The rhetorical and epistolary functions of v. 58 are such that Paul introduces his final exhortation in the way that he does. The exhortation serves as yet another, and a final, appeal to the community for harmony. It evokes the bonds of kinship that exist among them and between them and Paul. Its expression of the apostle's love for the community anticipates his last word (16:24). The exhortation to the community to stand fast anticipates the epistolary closing of 16:13 (see note).

NOTES

50. *This I say, brothers and sisters:* Paul marks a turning point in his exposition with an apostrophic "brothers and sisters." He begins the exposition with a dangling demonstrative (the cataphoric *touto*; cf. 1 Thess 4:15).

    Flesh and blood cannot inherit the kingdom of God, nor does the perishable inherit imperishability: Paul's words are obviously structured in the form of *parallelismus membrorum*. Crucial to their understanding is an appreciation of the parallelism. Is it synthetic parallelism, so that the second clause complements the first? Or is it synonymous parallelism, so that the second clause is a paraphrase of the first? Joachim Jeremias has argued the former, claiming that "flesh and blood," a Semitic metaphor for the merely human (cf. Sir 14:18; 17:31; Matt 16:17; Gal 1:16; Eph 6:12; Heb 2:14) refers to those who would be living at the time of the parousia; "the perishable" refers to those who would have died before the parousia. On Jeremias' reading of the text Paul writes as he does in v. 50 as an introduction to his response to the first of the questions raised in v. 35, namely how the dead are to be raised. As in 1 Thess 4:13-18, Paul's answer is couched in apocalyptic imagery.

    Paul's parallelism is better understood as a form of synonymous parallelism, a kind of rhetorical *repetitio* in Semitic fashion. "Perishable"—which can hardly mean "the dead," as Jeremias suggests—is a Hellenistic form of expression, synonymous with the Semitic "flesh and blood." With his parallelism Paul has shifted from the language of Jewish apocalyptic to the language of Hellenistic philosophy and rhetoric.

    "Kingdom of God" is an expression that occurs only seven times in Paul's letters, but five of the occurrences are in 1 Corinthians (4:20; 6:9, 10; 15:24; cf. Rom 14:17; Gal 5:21; compare 1 Thess 2:12). The phrase is a cipher for God's ultimate reign. In the NT "to inherit" (*klēronomeō*) is frequently used with eschatological connotations (cf. Matt 19:29; Mark 10:17; Luke 10:25; 18:18; Heb 1:14; 6:12; 12:17). Its cognate nouns, "inheritance" (*klēronomia*, cf. Gal 3:18) and "heir" (*klēronomos*, cf. Rom 8:17; Gal 3:29; 4:7) are also used with an eschatological nuance. Paul combines the two eschatological notions in the phrase "to inherit the kingdom of God" (cf. 6:9, 10; Gal 5:21; cf. 2 *Apoc. Bar.* 44:13; 4 Ezra 7:17; compare 7:9, 96). Rather than moral fault excluding someone from the kingdom (6:9-10; Gal 5:21) it is one's present physical condition that constitutes the barrier.

51. *See there! I am telling you a mystery:* With these words Paul reprises the "this I say" of v. 50. The imperative "see there" *(idou),* hapax in 1 Corinthians (cf. Rom 9:33; 2 Cor 5:17; 6:2, 9; 7:11; 12:14; Gal 1:20), is a call for attention. The "mystery" *(mystērion)* is the end-time scenario. Paul's words, "I am telling you a mystery" *(idou mystērion hymin legō)* are similar to the enigmatic "this we declare to you by the word of the Lord" *(touto . . . hymin legomen en logō kyriou)* with which he introduced the apocalyptic scenario of 1 Thess 4:15-17.

Not all of us will fall asleep, but all will be transformed: On the basis of the available manuscript evidence and the widely attested patristic tradition the editors of the *GNT*[4] consider that the reading "not all of us will fall asleep, but all will be transformed" is preferable to the other readings found in the manuscript tradition. This reading best explains the origin of the different readings in that tradition.

𝔓[46] has a negative in both parts of the phrase. Other manuscripts have a negative in the second part but not in the first, thus "all of us will fall asleep, but not all of us will be transformed." The problem to which the various readings point may well lie in the fact that death is the obvious fate not only of all Christians but also of all human beings. This reality led "intelligent" scribes, living long after Paul and his correspondents at Corinth had died, to transpose the negative to the second part of the phrase. This modified text expressed a truism, but the correction did not take into account Paul's expectation of an imminent parousia, such that some of those to whom he wrote were expected to be alive at the time of the appearance of Jesus as Lord (see 1 Thess 4:17).

Helmut Merklein ("Der Prophet," 416–418) considers Paul's teaching to be a prophetic utterance with an explanatory function. It explains the mystery Paul has set forth. Paul's anaphoric use of "all" *(pantes)* suggests that he continues to have the unity of the community in mind as he approaches the end of his letter. What he is about to say concerns not some but all members. The notion that all will be transformed (see 15:36-38, 42-44a, 49) suggests both continuity and discontinuity. By urging both of these ideas Paul maintains the identity of the human person, the difference between earthly and heavenly existence, and the preeminence of God's ultimate reign, the new creation.

52. *in an instant, in the blinking of an eye, with the last trumpet:* Paul uses the rhetorical device of *repetitio* to good effect as he leads up to an apocalyptic motif. "In an instant" *(en atomō)* is hapax in the NT. "In the blinking of an eye" is a phrase drawn from popular parlance. "The trumpet" is a standard feature in apocalyptic literature, where it is the signal of a new beginning (cf. 1 Thess 4:16; Rev 11:15). "Last" may not suggest so much last in a series (cf. Rev 8:2; 11:15), as the source of the final, eschatological trumpet sound. With the sound of the trumpet comes the passing of the present order of reality and the beginning of the kingdom of God.

For the trumpet will sound and the dead shall rise imperishable and we shall be transformed: The three clauses reprise the motifs Paul has already introduced in his presentation of the eschatological drama, the trumpet of v. 52a, the imperishability of v. 50, and the universal human change of v. 51. The sound of the last trumpet sets the stage for the final events. Having prepared the scene for the eschatological scenario in apocalyptic terms, Paul affirms that at the end there will be a fundamental equality between the lot of those who have died and the lot of those who are still alive at the eschaton. The resurrection of the dead is the condition for the realization of this equality. The dead shall rise. They are dead no more; they rise imperishable (*aphthartoi;* cf. 9:25). Equal, all will be transformed.

This passage shares several similarities with 1 Thess 4:15-18. There are, however, differences in emphasis. From Paul's earlier letter it appears that only a few members of the community had died; the emphasis is on the translation of the dead. Here the presumption is that only a few will be alive at the parousia; the emphasis is on the transformation of the body. First Thessalonians 4:17 clearly implies that Paul expects to be alive at the time of the parousia, but it is not entirely clear that 1 Cor 15:52 intimates the same thing.

53. *For it is necessary for this perishable being to put on imperishability and this mortal being to put on immortality:* The parallelism that marked v. 50, when Paul spoke of the radical incompatibility between present existence and future existence, continues in vv. 53 and 54. As before, the first member of the parallel construction is phrased in language that has a Semitic ring while the second is plainly Hellenistic. Paul appears to be attempting to translate Jewish apocalyptic thought for his Hellenistic audience.

The perishable/mortal being *(to phtharton touto, to thnēton touto)* to whom Paul refers is not himself, but the human being insofar as the human, in its present condition, is perishable and mortal. "It is necessary" *(dei)* bespeaks the eschatological certainty of what Paul is about to describe. The imperishability *(aphtharsian)* of those who have been raised is a quality of the risen body (cf. vv. 42, 50). In similar fashion 4 Ezra and the Syriac *Apocalypse of Baruch* speak of corruption and incorruption. In the NT "mortal" *(thnētos)* is a Pauline term (15:54; Rom 6:12; 8:11; 2 Cor 4:11; 5:4). "Immortality" *(athanasian,* 15:54; 1 Tim 6:16), on the other hand, is clearly a Hellenistic concept.

The qualities the risen body must attain are emphasized in the pair of contrasts. That the qualities of imperishability and immortality are indicated by Greek terms that begin with a privative alpha suggests that these are not qualities that belong to the perishable and mortal being. Deprived of imperishability and immortality, the risen body must receive these qualities as a gift.

54. *When this perishable being puts on imperishability and this mortal being puts on immortality:* The parallelism of v. 53 is continued in v. 54. Paul's repetitious phrasing has, nonetheless, proven to be problematic in the textual tradition. Some manuscripts (A and a few others) invert the two parts of the parallelism; others ($\mathfrak{P}^{46}$, $\aleph$) contain but the second part; still others have a variety of stylistic modifications, be they as simple as the use of the article with each

of the abstract nouns (33). The preponderant weight of the tradition, with such ancient majuscules as B, C, D, K, P, and Ψ and a variety of Fathers, including Origen, Chrysostom and Augustine, make "when this perishable being puts on imperishability and this mortal being puts on immortality" the preferable textual reading. Having spoken of the inevitability of the transformation in v. 53, Paul now talks about the inevitable reality coming to pass.

then will come to pass the word that has been written: The unusual introductory lemma—Paul typically uses a perfect passive form of the verb to write, *gegraptai,* in a formulaic "it is written," sometimes incorporating a postpositive *gar;* cf. 1:19, 31; 2:9; 3:19; 9:9; 10:7; 14:21; 15:45—underscores the dynamic reality of God's word: Then the word will come to pass *(genēsetai ho logos).*

54c–55. *"Death has been swallowed up in victory. Where, O death, is your victory? Where, O death, is your sting?"* The editors of *GNT*[4] have determined that "Where, O death, is your victory? Where, O death, is your sting?" is the most accurate reading of Paul's citation of Hos 13:14. The manuscript tradition offers many different versions. There are essentially three units of variation, different combinations of which are attested by the textual tradition. The first variable concerns the placement of "victory" and "sting." Some manuscripts (D, Ψ, etc.) have "sting" in v. 54b and "victory" in v. 55. A second variable concerns the word "victory" itself *(nikos).* In a classic case of itacism many manuscripts (𝔓[46], B, D, etc.) read the alternative form *neikos.* The third variable pertains to the vocative, "O death," in v. 55. Some manuscripts (Ψ, the "corrected" ℵ, etc.) and a variety of Fathers, including Origen and Chrysostom, read "O Hades" in place of "O death." This is obviously a scribal correction intended to make Paul's text conform to the LXX's wording of Hos 13:14.

56. *The sting of death is sin and the power of sin is the law:* Despite Friedrich W. Horn's idea ("1 Korinther 15,56—ein exegetischer Stachel," *ZNW* 82 [1991] 88–105) that 15:56 may be a gloss, albeit representing a fair appraisal of Pauline theology, the verse is part of Paul's text. The remark is not incidental to his argument. It is his commentary on the pair of scriptural passages that he has woven into a single scripture, which speaks of a victory over death.

In two distinct movements of thought, his two rhetorical proofs, Paul has argued for the resurrection of the dead. He is, however, convinced that death itself is the result of sin. This thought, which will be explicitly elaborated in his later letters (Romans, Galatians, Philippians), is a key element in his anthropology, derived from Judaism. Philo *(Creation* 134–169; *Questions on Genesis* 1.51) and Jewish apocalyptic (4 Ezra 3:7; *2 Apoc. Bar.* 17:2-3) were at one in considering that the death of Adam was the result of his transgression. Since then humankind has existed in a state of some degeneracy leading to death. Paul's thoughts in this regard resonate with some ideas current in Hellenistic popular philosophy (especially its Cynic current) but he expresses them in the powerful scriptural metaphor that likens death to the sting of a lethal insect.

It is tempting to take "law" as referring to Jewish Law with the connotation it will acquire in the polemic of Romans and Galatians, but it may be that "law" refers generically to all human law. The Cynics, particularly, espoused an antithesis between nature, of which they held a somewhat optimistic view, and law, which they deemed to have been promulgated because of human degeneration and further compromised because it is promulgated by degenerate humans (see Harm W. Hollander and Joost Holleman, "Death, Sin, and Law").

57. *Thanks be to God who gives us victory through our Lord Jesus Christ:* Unlike the prayer reports that use the verb *eucharistō* to express Paul's thanksgiving, this is a genuine prayer of thanksgiving. Its principal clause, lacking a verb, uses the noun *charis* to express Paul's thanks (see the note on 10:30). As is customary for Paul, thanksgiving is directed to God. The occasion for the thanksgiving is God's future gift of victory. The victory is God's, but Jesus Christ is God's agent *(dia)* in bringing victory about (cf. 15:24-28). Death, the last enemy (15:26), has been defeated by Jesus Christ. Christians share in the victory over death. The victory belongs to Christians because they belong to Christ who is "our Lord" *(hēmin . . . hēmōn).*

58. *Therefore, my beloved brothers and sisters:* As in 1 Thess 4:18, Paul concludes his apocalyptic discourse with an exhortation. The apostrophic "my beloved brothers and sisters" forms an *inclusio* with the "brothers and sisters" of v. 50. The vocative expression in v. 58 is exceptional both by reason of its function (at the end of a pericope) and its form (only here does "my beloved"—see 16:24—modify "brothers and sisters"). The exceptional character of this formula of direct address indicates that the exhortation provides a conclusion not only for the pericope and the chapter but also for the entire letter. It is a final exhortation to unity (cf. 1:10).

be firm, be steadfast, always exceeding in the work of the Lord, knowing that in the Lord your labor is not in vain: Repetition enhances the rhetorical force of Paul's final exhortation. He voices eschatological exhortations in Rom 13:12-14 and 1 Thess 5:6, but the phraseology of 15:58 is striking. "Firm" *(hedraioi)* occurs elsewhere in the NT only in 7:37 and Col 1:23. "Steadfast" *(ametakinētoi)* is hapax in the NT. The qualifying phrases, a pair of participial clauses, underscore the exhortation, stressing not so much its urgency but its breadth of scope and certainty of outcome. Reference to the parousia is highlighted by a twofold use of *kyrios,* which designates Jesus as the eschatological Lord. Specifically, Paul is exhorting the community to stand fast in the work of proclaiming the gospel (cf. 15:1).

In Paul's rhetorical lexis "work" *(ergō;* cf. 16:10; Phil 1:22; 2:30; see note on 9:1) and "toil" *(kopos;* cf. 3:8; 2 Cor 10:15; 11:23; 1 Thess 2:9; 3:5) are almost technical terms used to describe the work of evangelization. On the "work" of the Corinthians see 3:10-17. It is a work of building up the community as the temple of God, in which the Spirit dwells.

Although Paul had earlier expressed some fear that his own work of evangelization might be in vain (1 Thess 3:5; cf. Phil 2:16), he is confident that the Corinthians' evangelization will not be without success. His reference to preaching the gospel brings the audience back to the beginning of his long disquisition on the resurrection of the body (15:1-2). He had begun with a reference to his preaching of the gospel, whose core content was that Christ had been raised from the dead. He had intimated that his preaching was not in vain (*ektos ei mē eikē*, v. 2) and had affirmed that God's grace working in him was not in vain (*ou kenē*, v. 10). Now, as he is about to conclude his letter to the Corinthians, who are expected to continue his work of evangelization (3:10), he expresses the conviction, to be shared by the Corinthians, that their work of proclaiming the gospel will likewise not be in vain. This is the motif that encompasses Paul's entire discourse on the resurrection of the body.

For Reference and Further Study

Becker, Jürgen. *Auferstehung der Toten im Urchristentum.* SBS 82. Stuttgart: Katholisches Bibelwerk, 1976, 96–105.

Gillman, John. "Transformation in 1 Cor 15,50-53." *EThL* 58 (1982) 309–333.

_____. "A Thematic Comparison: 1 Cor 15:50-57 and 2 Cor 5:1-5," *JBL* 107 (1988) 439–454.

Hollander, Harm W., and Joost Holleman. "The Relationship of Death, Sin, and Law in 1 Cor 15:56," *NovT* 35 (1993) 270–291.

Jeremias, Joachim. "Flesh and Blood Cannot Inherit the Kingdom of God (1 Cor 15.50)," *NTS* 2 (1955–1956) 151–159.

Lüdemann, Gerd. "The Hope of the Early Paul: From the Foundation-preaching at Thessalonika to 1 Cor. 15:51-57," *PRS* 7 (1980) 195–201.

Merklein, Helmut. "Der Theologe als Prophet. Zur Funktion prophetischen Redens im theologischen Diskurs des Paulus," *NTS* 38 (1992) 402–429.

Müller, Karlheinz. "Die Leiblichkeit des Heils 1 Kor 15,25-58" in Lorenzo De Lorenzi, ed., *Résurrection du Christ.* Rome: Abbaye de S. Paul, 1985, 171–281.

Perriman, A. C. "Paul and the Parousia: I Corinthians 15.50-7 and 2 Corinthians 5.1-5," *NTS* 35 (1989) 512–521.

Pitta, Antonio. *Sinossi Paolina.* Milan: San Paolo, 1994, 99–117.

Plevnik, Joseph. *Paul and the Parousia* 145–169.

Schneider, Sebastian. "1 Kor 15,51-52. Ein neuer Lösungvorschlag zu einer alten Schwierigkeit," *CorC* 661–669.

Söding, Thomas. "'Die Kraft der Sünde ist das Gesetz' (1Kor 15,56). Anmerkungen zum Hintergrund und zur Pointe einer gesetzeskritischen Sentenz des Apostels Paulus," *ZNW* 83 (1992) 74–84.

Vicuña, Maximo. "I Corintios 15:54b-57, un canto anticipado de victoria sobre la muerte. Un Midrash en el NT," *Theologika biblia* 3 (1988) 2–19.

CLOSING (16:1-24)

1. *Collection for the Holy Ones* (16:1-4)

1. Concerning the collection for the holy ones, as I have ordered the churches of Galatia, so you should do likewise. 2. On the first day of the week let each one of you put aside and save whatever he or she has gained, so that the collections don't take place when I come. 3. When I do come I will send those whom you hold in high regard, with letters, to take your gift to Jerusalem. 4. If it is fitting for me too to go, they will go with me.

INTERPRETATION

In 16:1 Paul turns his attention to a new topic, identified as the collection for the holy ones. In his letter he has used the pronomial adjective "holy ones" *(hoi hagioi)* to describe the Christians of Corinth (1:2; 6:1-2). Of itself the adjective is a cultic term, one that the NT frequently associates with Jerusalem, particularly with the cult that was celebrated there (cf. 3:17). Paul uses the plural form of the term to designate various groups of Christians (Rom 8:27; 16:2, 15; 2 Cor 1:1; 13:12; Phil 1:1; 4:22; Phlm 5), but the term appropriately designates the Christian community in Jerusalem (Rom 15:25, 26, 31; 2 Cor 8:4; 9:1, 12), as it does in 16:1. Use of the adjective to describe other Christian communities implicitly evokes the bonds that tie these other communities to the early Christian community in Jerusalem.

Each of Paul's longer letters makes reference to a collection made on behalf of the Christians in Jerusalem (1 Cor 16:1-4; Rom 15:25-28; 2 Corinthians 8–9; Gal 2:10). The collection was taken up in various churches in Achaia, Macedonia, and Galatia to help the poor among the Christians of Jerusalem. Paul describes it as a matter of sharing resources "with the poor among the holy ones of Jerusalem" (Rom 15:26; cf. Gal 2:10). In a later motivational address to the Corinthians Paul will write about Christ becoming poor for our sakes (2 Cor 8:9).

The collection was made so that the "needs of the holy ones" *(ta hysterēmata tōn hagiōn,* 2 Cor 9:12) might be met, but it was more than a humanitarian gesture. Paul describes it as a "proof of love" *(tēn endeixin tēs agapēs,* 2 Cor 8:24), about which he could boast. He writes at length about the collection in 2 Corinthians 8–9. There he describes it as service to the holy ones *(tēs diakonias tēs eis tous hagious,* 2 Cor 8:4; 9:1). For motivational purposes he cites the example of the churches of Macedonia (a rhetorical *paradeigma*). Conversely he had boasted about the generosity of the Corinthians in his appeal to the Macedonians (2 Cor 9:2). Titus is designated as chief agent for the collection (2 Cor 8:1-6, 16-23).

Beyond the merely human motivation of keeping up with the Macedonians Paul offers the generosity of Christ and the manifold gifts of God as reasons why the Corinthian Christians should be generous in giving to the collection for Jerusalem. As Christ became poor for our sakes, so it is fitting for the Corinthians to share their possessions with those less fortunate (2 Cor 8:9). God has shared with us an abundance of gifts. Sharing generously with those in need not only meets their needs, it is also an act of thanksgiving to God (2 Cor 9:12).

The collection for the holy ones in Jerusalem was also a profound ecclesial gesture, a concrete expression of communion among the churches (cf. 1:2). Beyond that it was an expression of the debt of gratitude that the churches of the Pauline mission owed to the mother church in Jerusalem (Rom 15:27; cf. 1 Cor 15:3-7), the church from which they took the name of "the holy ones." The financial support Paul's churches provided for the poor of the community in Jerusalem was offered as a material gift in gratitude for the many spiritual benefits they had received (Rom 15:25-27; cf. 1 Cor 9:11). The ecclesial aspect of the collection is particularly important in a letter written to urge the Christians of Corinth to behave as God's holy people (1:2). Paul reminded them of their union with other Christians (1:2) and urged them to learn from the lesson of their ancestors, the Israelites (10:1-13).

Verses 1-4 offer several insights into how the collection took place and how it was sent to Jerusalem. The collection was to be taken regularly on Sundays, a day on which Christians gathered together, but only until Paul's arrival. The typical members of Paul's churches, free artisans, small traders, slaves (see W. A. Meeks, *The First Urban Christians* 63–72), would have very limited incomes. They would be able to contribute only a little at a time to the collection for the saints in Jerusalem. So Paul urges regular saving as a strategy for a successful collection. He expects each member (*hekastos*) of the community to participate in a way similar to that in which each member of the community had his or her particular charism with concomitant responsibility to work for the common good of the local church (12:7). Similarly, all members of the church are to be aware of their relationship to the larger church and their spiritual indebtedness to the community at Jerusalem. Financial participation in the collection bespeaks this awareness.

Paul also addresses the issue of how much the members of the community were expected to contribute, but his language is a bit difficult for moderns to understand (v. 2). In his later correspondence with the Corinthians he will state that "the gift is acceptable according to what one has *(katho ean echē euprosdektos)*—not according to what one does not have. I do not mean," says he, "that there should be relief for others and pressure on you, but it is a question of a fair balance between your present abundance and their need" (2 Cor 8:12-14). Just before writing these words Paul praised the Macedonian Christians: "for during a severe ordeal of affliction their abundant joy and their extreme poverty have overflowed in a wealth of generosity on their part . . . they voluntarily gave according to their means *(kata dynamin)* and even beyond their means" (2 Cor 8:2-3). Acts 11:29-30 describes the role of Paul and Barnabas in the relief collection taken up in the Galatian city of Antioch on behalf of beleaguered Christians in Jerusalem. On that occasion each member of the community was expected to participate according to his or her ability *(kathōs euporeito tis,* Acts 11:29).

The monies collected on Sundays were to be saved for later delivery to Jerusalem. Paul himself wanted to be involved in the delivery of the funds (16:3), if only by means of letters of recommendation written on behalf of those who would carry the monies to Jerusalem. Accompanied by Barnabas, Paul himself had taken to Jerusalem the proceeds of the collection in Antioch of Pisidia (Acts 11:30). In 16:1-4 (cf. v. 4) he suggests his willingness to modify his travel plans so as to be able to lead those who would take the collection to Jerusalem. In Rom 15:25, 28, he describes himself as being on the way to Jerusalem to deliver the monies that had been raised in Achaia and Macedonia. Orchestrating the collection was something that Paul was eager to do (Gal 2:10). Later he would engage the services of Titus to oversee the collection in Corinth, but he was quick to describe Titus as someone who was closely associated with himself. Titus, he would write, was "my partner and coworker in your service" *(koinōnos emos kai eis hymas synergos,* 2 Cor 8:23).

Despite Paul's desire to be responsible for the organization of a collection in Corinth and for its delivery to Jerusalem, he was nonetheless attentive to local involvement in the project. The delegation from the Corinthian community itself was to take the collection to Jerusalem, even if its members were eventually to accompany Paul to Jerusalem for this purpose. A decision had not yet been taken as to whether the delegates would go by themselves or in the company of Paul (v. 4).

In 16:15 Paul describes the members of Stephanas' household as assigning themselves to the service of the holy ones *(eis diakonian tois hagiois).* He commends them for this involvement. The phrase used to describe their activity evokes the formal description of the collection, "the service to the holy ones" *(tēs diakonias tēs eis tous hagious,* "ministry to the saints" [NRSV]) in 2 Cor 8:4 and 9:1. That they "assigned themselves" *(etaxan heautous)* might suggest another aspect of the organization of the collection in addition to the procedures Paul outlines in v. 3, which indicates that the collection should be taken up regularly on Sundays and be saved up for delivery to Jerusalem on a single occasion. Verse 15 might well imply that Stephanas' people had put themselves in charge of gathering the monies to be collected for the church in Jerusalem.

NOTES

1. *Concerning the collection for the holy ones:* The matter of the collection is formally introduced by means of the formulaic expression "concerning" (*peri de;* cf. 7:1, 25; 8:1, 4; 12:1; 16:12). In each of his letters Paul addresses financial matters. Most often these concern his own support (see ch. 9) and the "collection for the holy ones." In 16:1-2 he uses the technical term *logia,* "collection" (cf. the verb *logizomai,* "to count," "to calculate") to designate the "collection." Elsewhere he speaks about the "service" (*diakonia*) of the holy ones (see 2 Cor 8:4; 9:1; Rom 15:25; cf. Heb 6:10). Paul's longest discourse on the collection is to be found in 2 Corinthians 8–9. These chapters of the second letter to the Corinthians may originally have been two separate "administrative letters" that Paul sent to Corinth in support of the collection for the saints (thus H. D. Betz, *2 Corinthians 8 and 9*).

    as I have ordered the churches of Galatia, so you should do likewise: As he often does in 1 Corinthians, Paul cites other Christian churches as an example to be followed by the Corinthians (9:14; 14:33b; cf. 1 Thess 1:8; 2:14). This is in keeping with his common use of examples (*paradeigmata*) as a rhetorical argument. A question must be raised as to the location of these churches. Does Paul mean by "Galatia" the old Galatian kingdom? Or does he mean the Roman province of Galatia? The latter hypothesis is the more likely so that "the churches of Galatia" include Pauline foundations in Antioch of Pisidia, Iconium, Lystra, and Derbe, churches established by Paul during the first missionary voyage (Acts 13–14). See the discussion of this issue in F. J. Matera, *Galatians*. SP 9 (Collegeville: The Liturgical Press, 1992) 19–24.

    That Paul ordered the churches in Galatia to take up a collection for Jerusalem is a sign of the universality of his appeal on behalf of Jerusalem Christians. For Paul the appeal is not an incidental matter. Participation in the appeal is something that he ordered (*diatassō,* a verb that connotes authority, cf. 7:17; 9:14; 11:34) the churches in Galatia to do. The use of the imperative "do" (*poiēsate*) in addressing the Corinthians is evidence not only of Paul's authority; it also suggests the mandatory nature of his appeal on behalf of the Jerusalem community.

    The NT does not otherwise indicate that Paul had given such an order to the churches in Galatia (for the plural, see Gal 1:2). The letter to the Galatians does, however, mention that James, Cephas, and John had urged Paul and Barnabas "to remember the poor" (Gal 2:10). Paul had assured the Galatians that that was something he was eager to do, apparently appealing to their own experience of the collection.

2. *On the first day of the week:* In the extant correspondence it is only here that Paul mentions the first day of the week (*kata mian sabbatou*, cf. Acts 20:7; *sabbaton*, hapax in Paul, can mean week as well as sabbath), Sunday, as being a special day for Christians. Presumably this was a day on which they would gather (cf. 11:20). "On" *(kata)* implies that Paul is enjoining a regular practice on the part of the Corinthians.

let each one of you put aside and save whatever he or she has gained: It is difficult to translate Paul's Greek *(ho ti ean euodōtai)* exactly. The verb *euodoō* (cf. Rom 1:10) literally means "to go along a good road," hence metaphorically "to get along well" or "prosper." Sometimes when used of financial matters the verb means "to profit." BAGD 323 translates Paul's relative clause "as much as he gains." Paul is hardly demanding that the Corinthians regularly hand over an entire week's wages for the support of the church in Jerusalem, not even for the limited time remaining before his arrival (16:5). He is, however, certainly asking the Corinthians to do something more than make a modest contribution from whatever surplus they might have.

so that the collections don't take place when I come: Paul does not give any indication why he prefers that the collection not continue (cf. v. 2) during the time that he will be with the Corinthians. That he doesn't want the collection to be taken up during that time is all the more surprising insofar as he intends to spend some time with them (v. 5). Perhaps his intention is that the collection not be deferred until the last minute. If the collection were to be deferred it might yield a lesser amount. If Paul is expecting to spend the winter with the Corinthians it may be that he anticipated sending the delegation (v. 3) to Jerusalem almost immediately upon his arrival in Corinth.

3. *When I do come I will send those whom you hold in high regard, with letters, to take your gift to Jerusalem:* Paul intends to visit the Corinthians after having passed through Macedonia (16:5). The infinitive *apenegkein* is used to clarify the purpose of the delegates' mission (BDF 351.1). In the absence of any formal postal service and given the precariousness of sending monetary gifts by means of a passing traveler, the Corinthians are to choose some well-esteemed members of their community for the task of bringing the collection to Jerusalem. The letters were most probably letters of introduction, Pseudo-Demetrius' commendatory type *(typos systatikos).* This type of letter, writes Pseudo-Libanius, is one "in which we commend someone to someone. It is also called the introductory style *(kai parathetikē kaleitai)*" (Malherbe, *Ancient Epistolary Theorists,* 68–69). Pseudo-Demetrius' textbook example of a commendatory letter suggests that the letter of recommendation often included a request that hospitality be offered to the letter carrier. Paul himself was the beneficiary of such letters when, as a persecutor of the church, he went to Damascus with letters of credence in his possession (Acts 9:2; 22:5). Acts 15:22-23 (cf. Acts 13:2-3) describes Paul and Barnabas having been sent on a mission by the Jerusalem community, letter in hand.

4. *If it is fitting for me too to go, they will go with me:* Paul's language indicates that a considered decision will have to be made as to whether he should lead the

delegation of those who would be taking the collection to Jerusalem. Even if he were to take the collection to Jerusalem he is to be accompanied by delegates representing the Corinthian community. Early Christians traveled together (see 16:11, 12, 17). There seems to be something more in Paul's words than merely an expression of his desire not to travel alone. It was important that Christians from Corinth bring the collection to Jerusalem and that they be properly introduced to that community (v. 3). Their presence in Jerusalem would be a sign of the family ties that bind the two communities together. Paul himself was eager to commit himself to the work of supporting the poor among the saints in Jerusalem (Gal 2:10). In Rom 15:25-28 he describes the rationale for the collection taken up in Achaia and Macedonia. He writes about how pleased the Achaians and Macedonians were to participate in the collection and about his own plans to take the collection to Jerusalem. As he now writes to the Corinthians he describes his travel plans for the immediate future in 16:5-9.

FOR REFERENCE AND FURTHER STUDY

Betz, Hans Dieter. *2 Corinthians 8 and 9: A Commentary on Two Administrative Letters of the Apostle Paul.* Hermeneia. Philadelphia: Fortress, 1985.
Funk, Robert W. "The Apostolic Presence: Paul" in idem, *Parables and Presence* 81–102.
Georgi, Dieter. *Remembering the Poor: The History of Paul's Collection for Jerusalem.* Nashville: Abingdon, 1992. [German original 1965]
Nickle, Keith F. *The Collection: A Study in Paul's Strategy.* SBT 48. London: SCM, and Geneva, Ala.: Allenson, 1966.

2. *Travel Plans* (16:5-9)

5. I will come to you when I pass through Macedonia, for I will be passing through Macedonia. 6. Possibly I will stay with you or even spend the winter so that you might send me on my way. 7. For I do not want to see you now just in passing. If the Lord permits, I hope to remain with you for some time. 8. I will stay in Ephesus until Pentecost. 9. A wide and effective door has been opened for me, and many are opposed.

INTERPRETATION

Letters, written by people physically separated from those to whom they are writing, often express a desire on the part of the letter writer to be with the addressee(s) once again. This was as true of the Hellenistic letter as it is of the letters written in our day. Like other Hellenistic letter writers Paul writes about his upcoming travel plans, specifically his plans to visit those to whom he is writing.

Apostolic Travels. "Travelogue" is a term frequently used to label those sections of Paul's letters in which he describes his future travels. Typically the travel plans occur toward the end of the letters (here and Rom 15:22-32; 2 Cor 12:14–13:1, 10; Phlm 22; cf. 1 Thess 2:17-20; 3:11-13). Two features of Paul's description of his travels are particularly noteworthy. The first is that he does not simply write about his travels as such; rather he is writing about his desire to visit those to whom he is writing. His letter is a means of extended presence. With his future visit Paul intends to replace his absence *(apousia)* with his presence *(parousia)*. From this point of view the "travelogue" has an epistolary function.

A second feature of Paul's writing about his travel plans is that it focuses on his preaching of the gospel and other aspects of the apostolic ministry. Accordingly Paul's description of his travels is sometimes called "the apostolic parousia." What he writes about his travel is expressed in terms that speak about his apostolic ministry. This is clearly the case in 16:5-9. The pericope follows Paul's appeal on behalf of the collection for God's people in Jerusalem (16:1-4). Paul had virtually volunteered to accompany the delegation that would take the donation to Jerusalem (16:4). His mention of being sent on his way by the Corinthians (v. 6) is to be seen in that light.

Three geographic areas are mentioned in this pericope. Paul has worked in each of them. Macedonia was the Roman province in which the cities of Philippi and Thessalonica were located. These were cities with which Paul maintained close relationships even after he expanded his missionary horizons (cf. Phil 4:14-18). Corinth was the city where the recipients of the letter were actually living. While Paul gave every indication that he had to pass through the city to get where he was going, presumably from Macedonia to Jerusalem, he seems almost anxious to assure the Corinthians that his visit to them will be something more than a convenient stop on the way. He emphatically states that he intends to spend some time with them (v. 7). He looks forward to their support as they send him on his way (v. 6). Finally there is Ephesus (vv. 8-9), the Asian metropolis. If Paul does not immediately leave Ephesus in order soon to get to Corinth it is because he has an apostolic mission to accomplish in the Asian city. The work there has begun successfully but there is more to be done. The apostle has also encountered some opposition, so he intends to tarry awhile in Ephesus to continue his work.

The Topos. The literary topos, distinct from the rest of the letter, is characterized by its particular vocabulary. A number of *hapax legomena* and words otherwise rarely used by Paul are to be found in 16:5-9. For the most part they emerge from the unit's literary genre. They include references to place and time ("Macedonia," "passageway," "Ephesus," "Pentecost") and expressions that are appropriate to descriptions of one's travels ("pass through," "stay," "spend the winter," "on my way," "remain with you"). The details cited by Paul indicate that he used the major trade routes. They also suggest his attentiveness to weather-watchful "travel advisories."

The inclusion of some details of Paul's intended travel plans in this letter provides clues to the letter's place and date of composition. Intending to stay in Ephesus (v. 8), Paul has clearly written the letter from that Asian metropolis. That he intends to stay until Pentecost is an indication that the letter was written in early spring, perhaps as early as the spring of 53 C.E.

NOTES

5. *I will come to you when I pass through Macedonia, for I will be passing through Macedonia:* Paul generally designates geographical areas according to the name of the Roman province. The cities of Philippi and Thessalonica, where Paul had established communities of Christians that were extremely loyal and supportive to him, were located in Macedonia (cf. 2 Cor 7:5-7; 8:1-5; 11:9; Phil 4:14-18). The province of Achaia, of which Corinth was the capital, lay to the south. Second Corinthians 1:16 describes Paul's intention to piggyback visits to Corinth onto his visit to Macedonia.

   The explanatory clause expresses Paul's firm intention to visit Macedonia. The verb *dierchomai* in the present has a futuristic sense, "will be passing." The construction, following the verb "to come," is classic (cf. BDF 323.1).

6. *Possibly I will stay with you or even spend the winter, so that you might send me on my way:* Paul's verb, *paramenō*, "will stay with" is found in $\mathfrak{P}^{46}$, $\aleph$, A, C, D, Ψ, and the medieval manuscripts. An alternate reading, *katamenō*, with the meaning "stay behind" is found in $\mathfrak{P}^{34}$, B, some other manuscripts, and the Textus Receptus. Were *katamenō* the preferred reading it would be hapax in Paul. *Paramenō*, however, better fits the context and is used by Paul in Phil 1:25, where it describes Paul's intended stay in the Macedonian city of Philippi. "Spend the winter" (*paracheimasō*) is hapax in Paul. Winter travel was more difficult than travel during other seasons of the year. Often ships put up in port for the winter months.

   "On my way" is literally "wherever I shall go" (*hou ean poreuōmai*). In 2 Cor 1:16 with a construction similar to that of 16:6 Paul affirms that he intends to visit Judea after his post-Macedonian stay in Corinth. This is consistent with the idea that the collection (16:1-4) might be brought to Jerusalem by Paul. The nearby port of Cenchreae (cf. Rom 16:1-2) would have been a likely point of departure for a sea voyage to the East.

7. *For I do not want to see you now just in passing. If the Lord permits, I hope to remain with you for some time:* "In passing" (*en parodō,* hapax in the NT) has a local sense. Its literal meaning is "in a passageway." Paul is explaining to the Corinthians that he does not intend to make Corinth merely a stopover on his way to wherever it was that he was going. His affection for the Corinthians (10:14; 16:24) would not permit such a short visit. To underscore his point Paul reiterates positively what he had first stated negatively. "To remain" (*epimenō,* generally with some indication of time and/or place) is a verb that occurs frequently in travel reports and travel plans. Paul's travel plans are, of course, dependent on the Lord. His phrase, a conventional formula (cf. Heb 6:3; compare Acts 18:21; Jas 4:15), is similar to the contemporary "God willing," but highlights Paul's subservience to the Lord.

8. *I will stay in Ephesus until Pentecost:* Ephesus was the principal city and capital of the province of Asia (cf. 15:32). "Pentecost" (*pentēkostē),* literally the "fiftieth" day, is hapax in Paul, but see Acts 2:1; 20:16; Philo, *Decalogue* 160; Josephus, *Ant.* 3.252; and so forth. It is the Hellenistic Jewish designation for the traditional Jewish feast of Weeks. The fiftieth day was originally counted from the beginning of harvest, but in late Judaism it was counted from the feast of Passover.

Paul's note about Ephesus lets us know that his letter was written from Ephesus. The mention of Pentecost suggests that he intended to stay in Ephesus until the middle of spring, but does not necessarily imply that he intended to celebrate the feast in Ephesus (cf. Acts 20:16). Much as people today might say that they will remain abroad until Christmas without actually meaning that they intend to "celebrate" Christmas abroad, so Paul could say that he intended to stay in Ephesus until Pentecost. "Pentecost" might simply indicate a time rather than the feast *per se.* The Christian community in Ephesus was largely comprised of Gentile Christians.

9. *A wide and effective door has been opened for me, and many are opposed:* With their explanatory *gar* these words explain the reason for Paul's stated desire to remain in Ephesus for some additional time. The image of the open door is used to describe the proclamation of the gospel in Ephesus. The metaphor recurs in 2 Cor 2:12, where Paul writes about his preaching opportunities in Troas. There he indicates that the Lord opened the door for him; here the divine passive evokes a similar understanding. Paul describes the door as "wide and effective." The first adjective evokes the extent of Paul's missionary field. The second mixes the metaphor. Apart from Phlm 6 "effective" (*energēs)* is hapax in Paul. It belongs to a word group (*ergon, ergazomai, energeia, energeō, energēma)* commonly used by Paul to describe his proclamation of the gospel. As used in 16:9 it suggests that Paul's mission in Ephesus has been successful.

Although Paul's preaching in Ephesus met with success (see 16:19), there was also some opposition (15:32), as there always is (cf. Phil 1:28 [with *antikeimai,* "to oppose"]; 1 Thess 2:2). In any case there is more work for Paul to do in Ephesus. Acts 19 gives Luke's stylized description of Paul's apostolic success in Ephesus and the opposition he encountered there.

3. *Timothy and Apollos* (16:10-12)

10. If Timothy comes, see to it that he is free from fear while he is among you, for he does the Lord's work just as I do. 11. So let no one treat him with contempt. Send him on his way in peace so that he might come to me. I am waiting for him, along with the brothers and sisters. 12. Concerning Apollos, our brother, I have frequently urged him to come to you accompanied by brothers and sisters, and yet in no way does he want to come now. He will come when he finds time.

INTERPRETATION

Paul's use of "concerning" *(peri de)*, an epistolary marker, in v. 12 might suggest that the reader should separate his remarks about Apollos from his words about Timothy. There are, however, good reasons for treating Paul's words about the two emissaries together. The remarks are relatively brief. The epistolary situation is such that a series of brief and somewhat disjointed notations appears at the end of this letter (cf. 2 Cor 13:11-13; Gal 6:16-18; Phil 4:20-23; 1 Thess 5:12-24; Phlm 19-25) as it does at the end of many other Hellenistic letters. Paul has, moreover, previously mentioned Timothy and Apollos together (see ch. 4, his previous mention of Timothy). There are also topical reasons for considering the two sets of remarks together. Both concern a close associate of Paul who is being sent by him to the Corinthians. Both speak of Paul's concern for the one he has sent. Both mention the early Christian practice of having missionaries travel in the company of other Christians. Both intimate something about the relationship between the emissaries and the Christians at Corinth.

Letter of Recommendation. Compared with other Hellenistic correspondence Paul's letter to the Corinthians is a long letter. It is a single letter with an overarching purpose (1:10), but that purpose is achieved in a variety of ways. Paul's letter of recommendation suggests that the unity of the community at Corinth will be served well if the Corinthians heed the emissaries who have come to them from Paul.

Paul had admonished the Corinthians in an earlier passage of the letter (4:14-21). That pericope had the characteristics of a letter of admonition. The letter of admonition, Pseudo-Demetrius' *typos nouthetētikos*, is a sub-genre within the epistolary genre of the letter as a whole. The letter of recommendation *(typos systatikos)* was another kind of letter identified by Pseudo-Demetrius, who listed it second among his twenty-one epistolary types. He described the letter of recommendation as one "which we write on behalf of one person to another, mixing in praise, at the same time also speaking of those who had previously been unacquainted as though they were now acquainted." To give a textbook example Pseudo-Demetrius writes:

> "So-and-so, who is conveying this letter to you, has been tested by us and is loved on account of his trustworthiness. You will do well if you deem him worthy of hospitality both for my sake and his, and indeed for your own. For you will not be sorry if you entrust to him, in any matter you wish, either words or deeds of a confidential nature. Indeed, you, too, will praise him to others when you see how useful he can be in everything" (Malherbe, *Ancient Epistolary Theorists* 33).

C.-H. Kim's analysis of the Hellenistic letter of recommendation, based on a study of eighty-three ancient letters, identifies five distinct features of the letter of recommendation: the epistolary salutation, presentation of the background of the one who is recommended (often in the form of an *intitulatio*), a request to the recipient of the letter from the sender, an expression of appreciation, and an epistolary closing. As often as not the expression of appreciation is omitted. Paul was familiar with the letter of recommendation as an epistolary genre. In 16:3 he speaks of such a letter, and his letter to Philemon is clearly a letter of recommendation. In 1 Corinthians, 16:10-11, 4:17, and 16:15-16 are crafted in a style that recalls the features of the genre. Incorporated into a longer letter, these passages lack the typical epistolary salutation and the epistolary closing that would be characteristic of a self-standing letter of recommendation.

The letter of recommendation was frequently used in the Hellenistic world to introduce and commend the letter carrier. The recipients were typically urged to offer hospitality to the bearer. Since 4:17 and 16:10-11 are recommendations of Timothy, many commentators are of the opinion that it is Timothy who actually carried Paul's letter to the Corinthians. On the other hand, a similar case might be made with regard to Stephanas, Fortunatus, and Achaicus (16:15-16). I am inclined to the view that it was this group that served as Paul's postal service.

Timothy. The Corinthians are instructed about how they should act in regard to Timothy, whom Paul has sent to them (4:17). Paul's threefold instruction that Timothy be given no reason to fear, that he not be disdained, and that he be sent on his way "in peace" suggests that Paul might have had some concern about the way the Corinthians might treat Timothy. His urging them to see to it that Timothy have no reason to fear seems to imply that they might previously have caused him some difficulty. That Paul urges them not to look down on Timothy suggests that they had not previously looked favorably on him. That Paul urges them to send Timothy on his way in peace seems to imply that Timothy might previously have been allowed to depart without support, perhaps after some hostility or tension.

If the Corinthians were negatively disposed toward Timothy, this may have been because of Timothy's association with Paul. Timothy may have been a victim by transference; he may have been presumed "guilty" by association. By the time that Paul wrote his "second" letter to the Corinthians Timothy was well known to the community. In 2 Cor 1:1 he is described as "[our] brother."

Apollos. Apollos was a figure well known to the Corinthian Christians. Paul wrote about him at length in the first part of his letter (chs. 1–4). He proposed the working relationship between himself and Apollos as one from which the Corinthians might learn. The way Paul writes about Apollos in v. 12 seems to suggest that some among the Corinthians wanted Apollos to visit them. Paul's brief remark provides no clue as to why they wanted Apollos to come to them, nor does it give any indication as to why Apollos was so firm in his decision not to go to the Corinthians at that time. His decision was not rooted in hostility to the Corinthians. Paul tells them that Apollos will visit at an opportune moment (note Paul's "the Lord willing," v. 7). Whether Apollos was actually in the company of Paul at the time when he wrote 1 Corinthians is also something that cannot be determined with certainty.

NOTES

10. *If Timothy comes: Ean,* literally "if," used with the subjunctive denotes what is expected to occur. At times the meaning of the conjunction approaches that of "whenever" or "when," but the construction implies a trace of uncertainty as to whether Timothy had actually arrived. Hence the translation "if." Paul had sent Timothy to the Corinthians, but he seems not to have any knowledge of Timothy's having arrived. The purpose of Timothy's mission is described in 4:17-21 (see above, pp. 195–203).

    see to it that he is free from fear while he is among you: Blepete is hortatory ("see to it") rather than minatory ("watch out," cf. 10:12). "Free from fear" (*aphobōs genētai;* cf. Phil 1:14) can be taken either subjectively or objectively. If the former ("that you put him at ease," *RSV*) it would imply that Timothy is a timid personality who needs to be put at ease by the Corinthians. If the latter ("that he has nothing to fear among you," *NRSV*) it would imply that Timothy's anxiety is grounded in reality and that the Corinthians need to do something about the things that might provoke anxiety on the part of Timothy. The remarks in 4:18 and 16:10c-11a seem to imply that some Corinthians might not have taken well to Timothy's visit. "While he is among you" *(pros hymas)* is literally "among you."

    for he does the Lord's work just as I do: "Work" *(ergon)* is a term Paul characteristically chooses to describe his own work of evangelization. The "Lord's work" is an expression he uses to describe Christian ministry (15:58; Rom

14:20 [with *tou theou*]; Phil 2:30 [with *Christou;* with *Kyriou* in **ℵ**, A, P, Ψ]). Throughout the letter Paul has emphasized that his work, although singular (see 4:16; 9:2), is not solitary. The opening of ch. 3, vv. 1-15, is a particularly strong affirmation of this conviction. Timothy's work is Paul's work. Timothy is to remind the Corinthians about Paul's ways in Christ (cf. 4:17).

11. *So let no one treat him with contempt:* Some of the Corinthian hybrists treated other members of the community with disdain. Paul asks each of them (cf. 10:12 for the construction) not to subject Timothy, his chief lieutenant and "faithful son," to such treatment.

    Send him on his way in peace so that he might come to me: That Paul is unsure about Timothy's arrival and yet asks the Corinthians to send him on a return trip to Paul suggests that Timothy was a man on a mission. He had a particular task to fulfill; once it was accomplished he was to return to Paul. The task is described in 4:17. With a somewhat different task Timothy had been previously sent on a mission to Thessalonica (1 Thess 3:2-3). On its completion he returned to Paul with a report on his visit (1 Thess 3:6). The situation is somewhat similar in Corinth. Paul asks the Corinthians to send Timothy on the return journey to Paul "in peace." The formula suggests that Timothy should depart Corinth, with the Corinthians bidding him to go in peace. "Shalom" (*eirēnē* in Greek) was the common greeting among Semites, both as a welcome and as a farewell (cf. Acts 15:33). The reference to "peace," which typically evokes physical and social well-being, might suggest that Paul expects the Corinthians to provide supplies for Timothy's return journey. Whether Paul expected to meet Timothy in Ephesus or whether he expected that they would meet later in Macedonia is unclear.

    I am waiting for him, along with the brothers and sisters: While not necessarily anxious about Timothy's return, Paul offers a word to suggest that the Corinthians might send Timothy on his way because (note the explanatory *gar*) Paul is expecting him. "Along with the brothers and sisters" suggests that other Christians are expected to be with Timothy when he returns to Paul. Rarely did people travel alone in Paul's day (cf. 9:5). Paul will welcome them as he welcomes Timothy. Chloe's people were one group that came from Corinth to Paul (1:11); Stephanas, Fortunatus, and Achaicus were another such group (16:17). Paul's mention of each of these groups suggests the ease of travel during the time of the imperial peace. That they traveled as a group reflects the social circumstances of the times.

12. *Concerning Apollos, our brother:* The name of Apollos is introduced into Paul's closing remarks by means of the *peri de,* "concerning," formula. Use of the formula (cf. 7:1, 25; 8:1; 12:1; 16:1; cf. 8:4) might possibly suggest that Paul had learned that some of the Corinthians were anxious to have Apollos visit them. On the other hand it may simply be that Paul uses the formula to mark the next item on his agenda as he is finishing up his letter. Apollos was mentioned several times in the first part of the letter (1:12; 3:4, 5, 6, 22; 4:6), but this is the first time that Paul mentions him since he reminded the Corinthians that he had written about Apollos and himself for their benefit in 4:6. Apollos

is identified as "brother" *(adelphou)* without any qualifying adjective. "Our" is added in this translation because it captures the sense of Paul's appellation (cf. 1:1). Previously Paul had described him as a servant (3:5), God's coworker (3:9), Christ's assistant, and a steward of the mysteries of God (4:1). In 4:9 Paul suggests that Apollos is to be considered an apostle (4:9).

I have frequently urged him to come to you accompanied by brothers and sisters: At the beginning of the phrase the Clementine Vulgate reads *notum nobis facio,* "I report to you." This introduction echoes a few majuscules (‭א‬, D, F, G), but it is not otherwise strongly supported in the Greek manuscript tradition.

Throughout the letter Paul has urged *(parakalō)* the Corinthians to respond to his appeal (1:10; 4:13, 16; 16:15). Now he tells them that he has urged Apollos to do something, the only time that he mentions that he urged a particular individual to do something specific. If some Corinthians wanted Apollos to visit them Paul's remark about his having repeatedly *(polla,* used adverbially) urged Apollos to go to the Corinthians may affect an apologetic tone. It was Paul's intention that Apollos be accompanied by a group of other Christians. It was common for Christian missionaries to travel together (see v. 11). Paul's desire that Apollos travel in the company of other Christians may also reflect a concern for Apollos' safety *en route.*

and yet in no way does he want to come now. He will come when he finds time: Paul's "and yet" *(kai;* cf. BAGD, 392, 2g; cf. also 1 Cor 5:2; 2 Cor 6:9) expresses his surprise at Apollos' reluctance to visit the Corinthians. Paul does not explain the reasons for Apollos' wholehearted *(pantōs)* decision *(ouk ēn thelēma,* "it is not his will") not to go to Corinth at that time *(nyn),* but it is clear that his firm decision was not final. The "now" and "he will come when he finds time" suggest that Apollos considers the present moment to be inopportune for a visit to Corinth. He intends to visit the Corinthians on some future occasion. "When he finds time" *(eukairēsē,* hapax in Paul) is an expression found almost exclusively in the private letters of the Hellenistic period. Its presence in 1 Corinthians is another example of Paul's familiarity with Hellenistic epistolary style.

For Reference and Further Study

Kim, Chan-Hie. *Form and Structure of the Familiar Greek Letter of Recommendation.* SBL.DS 4. Missoula: Scholars, 1972.

4. *Goodbye* (16:13-14)

13. Be alert! Stand fast in the faith! Be brave! Be strong! 14. Let everything you do be done in love.

INTERPRETATION

Verse 13 begins the formal closing of Paul's letter. Paul's contemporaries generally ended their letters with *errōso* or *errōsthe*, the singular or the plural form of the verb *rōnnymi*, "farewell" (literally "be made strong"), but Hellenistic writers occasionally used *eutychei*, "prosper" as their farewell greeting. As the opening greeting of 1 Corinthians (1:3) is akin to the classic epistolary salutation, but distinctively Christian in its content and Pauline in its formulation, so Paul's farewell wishes are distinctively Christian in their content and Pauline in their formulation, albeit similar in function and inspiration to the final greeting of the Hellenistic letter.

Paul brings his letter to closure with words that express his own formulation and a Christian perspective. The final words demonstrate a marked similarity with the closing features of many Hellenistic letters. Among the common epistolary conventions found at the end of Paul's letter are the expression of joy (vv. 17-18), the greetings, with the names of appropriate individuals (vv. 19-20), the Pauline autograph (v. 21), the farewell (v. 23), and a postscript (v. 24). Each of these standard epistolary conventions is used in such a way that it applies specifically to the correspondence between Paul and the Corinthian community with a particular emphasis on love.

Paul's Letter-closing. The series of terse exhortations that begins in v. 16 is typical of Paul's style. A series of short exhortations is found at the end of several of his letters (cf. Rom 16:17-19; 2 Cor 13:11; Phil 4:8-9; 1 Thess 5:12-22). In 1 Corinthians there are five such exhortations (vv. 13-14), just as there are in 2 Cor 13:11. The five *seriatim* imperatives are in the present tense, calling for a continuous response. The sequence of the first four is characterized by rhetorical *repetitio*, which provides additional emphasis to the final exhortations in the letter.

The first two exhortations, "Be alert!" "Stand fast in the faith!" provide an eschatological orientation to the conclusion of Paul's letter. The perspective of the coming age had been placed before the assembly at the conclusion of the opening thanksgiving (1:8-9). The curse and invocation of 16:22 confirm the eschatological perspective with which Paul brings his letter to its final conclusion in the pointed paraenesis of v. 13.

The classic farewell greeting, "farewell," or "prosper," does not appear in any of Paul's extant letters (cf. Acts 15:29 and, in some manuscripts,

Acts 23:30). The conclusion of 1 Corinthians does, however, have a pair of expressions that are virtually synonymous with the classic greeting. Paul's words are "Be brave! Be strong!" *(andrizesthe, krataiousthe)*. Despite their semantic similarity with the Hellenistic epistolary farewell these greetings do not appear elsewhere in Paul's letters. "Be brave" does, however, occur as a farewell greeting in some ancient literature.

Emphasis on Love. The four second-person-plural imperatives in the staccato paraenesis of v. 13 are unqualified except for the expression "in the faith" *(en tē pistei)*, which modifies the exhortation to steadfastness, the second imperative. In v. 14 Paul adds a fifth imperative, in the passive voice, which features a formulaic "in love" *(en agapē)*. With the two qualifying phrases Paul has crafted a unique expression of his binomial characterization of the Christian life. That life is a life in faith and in love (cf. 1 Thess 1:3; 5:8; Gal 5:6).

Paul emphasized the importance of the love command by placing it in the final, emphatic position in this series of closing exhortations. The postscript of v. 24, unusual in a Pauline letter, assures the entire community of the apostle's love for them. In this way the love motif forms an *inclusio* encompassing Paul's final remarks. Among them the curse of v. 22a anathematizes those who do not love the Lord. This threefold rehearsal of the importance of love at the end of a letter (vv. 14, 22, 24) is unique in the Pauline correspondence. Paul's emphasis on love is, however, a reprise of the major theme of 1 Corinthians, announced in the programmatic statement of 1:10, "that all of you be in agreement and that there be no divisions among you."

Each of Paul's final statements about love is singularly formulated. At the end of a string of five *seriatim* imperatives (vv. 13-14), the exhortation to love is in the position (v. 14) where it receives the greatest emphasis. Longer than the preceding exhortations, the exhortation to love is set off from them by reason of its length and its syntax. The earlier exhortations are in the second person plural; the exhortation to love is in the third person. It expresses the apostle's wish that all that is done within the community be done with love. In this context v. 14 has something of the character of a rhetorical recapitulation.

The wording of the curse (v. 22) is also unique. Paul's letters offer only one other example of an anathema, namely in Gal 1:8-9 where Paul anathematizes anyone who proclaims a gospel other than that proclaimed by him and received by the Galatians. Except in 16:22 Paul does not write about Christians' love for the Lord (cf. Rom 8:28). Normally he speaks of the love that Christians should have for one another.

Finally, Paul's postscript is likewise unique. Only in the letter to the Romans does he add anything to the grace benediction (Rom 16:20; compare 1 Cor 16:24) that serves as the typical signoff in his letters. Nowhere else in his correspondence does Paul assure the community of his love in a fashion as solemn as he does in 1 Corinthians. Paul expresses his love for individuals within the community (Rom 16:5, 8, 9, 12; 1 Cor 4:17; Phlm 1, 16), but he generally assures the community of his love only by means of an apostrophic "my beloved" (Rom 12:19; 1 Cor 10:14; 15:58; 2 Cor 7:1; 12:19; Phil 2:12; 4:1; 1 Thess 2:8). In 1 Corinthians, however, Paul assures the community of his paternal love (4:14-15). He concludes his letter with an emphatic postscript that assures the entire community of his love for them.

NOTES

13. *Be alert! Stand fast in the faith! Be brave! Be strong!* Other than in 16:13 Paul uses the verb "to be alert" only in 1 Thess 5:6, 10, where it clearly has the connotation of eschatological alert (cf. Matt 24:42-43; 25:13 [26:38-41]; Mark 13:34-38 [14:34-38]; Luke 12:37-39). "Stand fast" appears six times in the Pauline correspondence, generally with the connotation of steadfastness in a situation of eschatological expectation (see Gal 5:1; Phil 4:1; 1 Thess 3:8; [2 Thess 2:15]; cf. Rom 14:4; Phil 1:27).

   "Be brave" (*andrizesthe,* literally "act like a man") and "be strong" (*krataiousthe*) are hapax in Paul. Despite their semantic kinship with *errōso* (*errōsthe*) they do not appear as farewell greetings in other Pauline letters. The former is hapax in the NT; the latter is occasionally used in the NT as a transitive verb, "to hold." As a formula of farewell "be brave" occurs in Mattathias' parting exhortation (1 Macc 2:64). See also *Herm. Vis.* 1.4.3, "She smiled as she departed and, as she was going, she said to me, 'Be brave, Hermas' (*andrizou Herma*)."

14. *Let everything you do be done in love:* Literally this reads "let all things of yours be done in love" (cf. 14:26). Emphatically placed, the exhortation serves as a summary of Paul's paraenesis (see especially chs. 8–10, 12–14). Together with the postscript to the letter (16:24), it constitutes a minor *inclusio* encompassing Paul's closing of the letter. The *inclusio* highlights the motif of love. Love is the dominant factor in the relationship between Paul and the Corinthians; love should characterize all that the Corinthians do.

FOR REFERENCE AND FURTHER STUDY

Weima, Jeffrey A. D. *Neglected Endings: The Significance of the Pauline Letter Closings.* JSNT.S 101. Sheffield: JSOT Press, 1994.

5. *Commendation of Stephanas* (16:15-18)

15. Brothers and sisters, you know the household of Stephanas, that they are the firstfruits of Asia and that they have assigned themselves to the service of the holy ones. 16. I exhort you to be subject to such as them and to every coworker and laborer. 17. I rejoice at the coming of Stephanas and Fortunatus and Achaicus because they have made up for your absence; 18. they have given comfort to my spirit and to yours. Acknowledge people such as these.

INTERPRETATION

As Paul continues to bring his long letter to closure, his style and choice of expression reflect those of other letter writers in the Hellenistic era. The epistolographic features of 16:15-18 are striking. The passage has several features akin to the letter of recommendation *(typos systatikos)* described by Pseudo-Demetrius (see above, pp. 594–595). For Pseudo-Libanius "the commending style *(systatikē)* is that in which we commend someone to someone."

In the Hellenistic letter of recommendation the sender is generally identified in a sentence that (1) gives the name of the person to be recommended; (2) identifies the person by means of a participial clause; (3) uses the verb "to be" with the recommended one as the subject; (4) has a predicate that stipulates the relationship between the one recommended and the sender (C.-H. Kim, *Form and Structure* 38). These elements are present in the commendation of the household of Stephanas (1). Paul uses the verb "to be" (3) in order to identify them as his first converts in Asia, his firstfruits (4). In the typical Hellenistic letter of recommendation the one who is recommended is often unknown, the letter itself serving to introduce the letter-carrier. Since the household of Stephanas was well known to the Corinthians, Paul reminds them of their acquaintance (2).

In the Hellenistic letter of recommendation the request made of those to whom the letter is addressed typically consists of three elements: (1) a request clause; (2) a circumstantial or conditional clause; (3) a purpose clause (Kim, *Form and Structure* 64). Although the request clause commonly uses some form of the verb "to ask" *(erōtō)*, four of the extant papyrus letters studied by Kim (pp. 71, 195, 196, 202, 213) use, as does Paul in 16:15, a *parakalō* construction to make the request. To state the purpose of the request Hellenistic letters used either a *hopōs* or a *hina* clause. Paul uses the latter construction when he tells the Corinthians "I encourage *(parakalō)* you . . . to be subject *(hina kai hymeis hypotassēsthe)* to such as them and to every coworker and laborer."

In the Hellenistic letters the circumstantial clause generally has the form of "if he has need of anything from you" or "for whatever matter he comes to you." Paul's recommendation of the household of Stephanas does not include a conditional clause as such. He does, however, describe the members of the household of Stephanas as having been devoted to the service of the holy ones. This note may be construed to be an indication of the kind of leadership exercised by members of the household of Stephanas and the warrant for the appeal Paul is making to the Corinthians. Paul's entire letter is an expression of concern for the well-being of the community. Apparently the household of Stephanas, whom Paul proudly proclaims to be his firstfruits, had taken that concern to heart.

Most of the extant Hellenistic letters of recommendation are relatively short and serve as self-contained, single-purpose letters of recommendation. Paul's letter to Philemon is an example of a such self-contained letter. Paul has inserted the recommendation of Stephanas into this much longer composition. He was not alone in incorporating a passage of recommendation into a longer letter. At least three other examples of the phenomenon are to be found in the extant papyrus letters (see Kim, *Form and Structure* 5, 198, 203, 209).

When Paul inserts a recommendation into a longer letter he customarily places the commendation toward the end of his missive, that is, after he has reflected on the coming eschaton, as he does in 15:20-58 (cf. Rom 16:1-2; Phil 2:29-30; 4:2-3; 1 Thess 5:12-13a). In 16:15-18 Paul has expanded his commendation of the household of Stephanas. Not only does he mention the latter's devoted service to the community at Corinth; he also makes reference to a visit of Stephanas, accompanied by Fortunatus and Achaicus, to Paul. Mention of this visit, which brought comfort to Paul, is further attestation of the relationship between Stephanas and Paul. It provides an additional warrant for the request that Paul makes of the Corinthians. The joy of which Paul writes and his mention of the arrival *(parousia)* of his visitors reflect familiar Hellenistic epistolary motifs.

Stephanas, Fortunatus, and Achaicus. Nothing definite is known about the relationship among Stephanas, Fortunatus, and Achaicus. Stephanas is undoubtedly the one who, along with his household, had been baptized by Paul (1:16), but Fortunatus and Achaicus receive no other mention in the NT. Since they have Latin names it is likely that they came from families who belonged to the group of Roman colonists in Corinth. The name of Achaicus is derived from the province of Achaia, in which Corinth is located. "Achaicus" may have been a nickname originally attributed to someone who had lived in the province and then returned to Italy. That Achaicus and Fortunatus were able to travel to Ephesus from Corinth is an indication that they had financial resources at their disposition. The money may not have been their own. They may possibly have enjoyed the patronage of Stephanas, a man who was certainly a patron of the church at Corinth.

It is likely that Paul intended the trio to bring the letter he had written to the Corinthians. The emperor Augustus (27 B.C.E.–14 C.E.) had instituted a kind of postal system consisting of a series of relay stations, but use of the system was restricted to the imperial mails (cf. Suetonius, *Augustus* 49). People who did not have slaves to carry their correspondence to its destination generally had to rely on passing travelers to carry mail for them. Often these passersby were barely known by those who gave them mail to deliver, so the system was hardly secure.

Letters of recommendation, on the other hand, frequently accompanied trusted letter carriers. The hearty recommendation of the household of Stephanas in 16:15-18 may indicate that Paul intended that his letter be brought to the Corinthians through their good graces. Other authors, both ancient and modern, hold that it was Timothy who delivered the letter to Corinth. It is likely that the letter carrier, whoever he or she might have been, was expected to read the letter to the congregation.

NOTES

15. *Brothers and sisters:* Paul's recommendation of the household of Stephanas begins with a *parakalō de hymas adelphoi* formula. *Parakalō,* followed by a *hina* purpose clause, is an epistolary convention used in Hellenistic letters of recommendation. Since 16:15-18 has the characteristic traits of an epistolary recommendation, Paul's use of *parakalō* in 16:15 should be seen as a feature typical of requests made in such letters. The literary form of the passage suggests that *parakalō* be translated in conjunction with the purpose clause to which it is related (see v. 16, "I exhort you").

Paul's *parakalō* formula, literally "I exhort you, brothers and sisters," recalls the opening of his letter where a similar formula appeals explicitly to the authority of Jesus Christ, "in the name of our Lord Jesus Christ." In 1:10 the formula implicitly appeals to Paul's own apostolic authority (cf. 4:16). Paul's apostrophic use of "brothers and sisters" as a formula of direct address is a constant feature of his letter.

you know the household of Stephanas, that they are the firstfruits of Asia: Paul seems to have had fond memories of those who were among the first in a geographic area to embrace Christ (see Rom 16:5, where Epaenetus is designated as the firstfruits of Asia). The firstfruits (*aparchē,* cf. 15:20, 23) are a harbinger of things to come. They are a sign of hope. In this instance the embrace of the gospel of Jesus Christ by Stephanas' household and their subsequent baptism (1:16) gave promise of the success of Paul's mission of evangelization in Asia. They provided hope for the continuing success of his apostolate in that Roman province (cf. Acts 13:13–16:10). Paul tends to use the term *aparchē* in a metaphorical sense (see above, p. 547), but his usage of the expression is, nonetheless, dependent on the biblical tradition (see the reference to Num 15:17-21 in Rom 11:16) and retains something of its cultic nuance. As "firstfruits" the household of Stephanas is dedicated, in this case, to Christ (cf. Rom 16:5).

Paul's verb is in the singular *(estin)* but must be rendered in the plural. In English when the subject of a sentence is a collective noun with a distributive sense it calls for a verb in the plural. In Greek the so-called *constructio ad sensum* allows a collective noun to be used with a singular verb (BDF 134.1) even when the plural sense of the collective noun appears later, as it does in 16:16 ("be subject to such as them," *tois toioutois*). In Greek a change in number in cases such as this does not cause offense.

In Rom 16:5 Epaenetus, otherwise unknown except in the later legend that tells of his becoming bishop of Carthage, is characterized as the firstfruit of Asia for Christ. It is likely that Epaenetus was Paul's first individual convert in the Roman province of Asia; similarly the household of Stephanas was the first group in Achaia to have embraced the gospel preached by Paul. Paul's work of evangelization took place in the major population centers but he was convinced that the good news of the gospel would echo beyond the immediate locale in which it was preached (cf 1 Thess 1:8).

and that they have assigned themselves to the service of the holy ones: Paul uses the verb "assign" *(tassō)* only here and in Rom 13:1. In both instances the verb is found in a passage that deals with "leadership" within the community and with the responsibility of some in the community to be subject *(hypotassō,* cognate with *tassō)* to those in leadership positions. From the outset of his letter Paul had designated the Christian community at Corinth as the holy ones (1:2), but the designation aptly describes Christians in Jerusalem (16:1; cf. 2 Cor 8:4; 9:1) on behalf of whom the collection was made. Although it is not to be excluded that the household of Stephanas had some role in the collection (see above, p. 587), it is likely that Paul is commending the household of Stephanas for the service *(diakonia,* see 12:5) it had rendered to the Christian community at Corinth.

16. *I exhort you to be subject to such as them and to every coworker and laborer:* As he did in his earlier letter to the Thessalonians (1 Thess 5:12-13) Paul urges his addressees to be subject to those who lead the community. There, as here, the activity of the leaders is described in terms of "work" and "toil." Although both these terms are occasionally used by Paul in the straightforward sense of physical labor, they are also used metaphorically of Christian activity. The first is virtually a technical term for the work of evangelization. The second suggests Christian activity or work in general, but with a nuance that suggests the difficulty of this work (cf. Phil 2:16; Gal 4:11; Rom 16:6, 12; 1 Thess 3:5).

Paul's lexis shows a marked predilection for compounds formed with *"syn-," "with."* These are frequently best rendered in English by compound nouns and verbs beginning with "co-" (from the Latin *cum*). Particularly noteworthy is Paul's use of the term "coworker" to describe those who share with him a common ministry of evangelization (in participial form here and 2 Cor

6:1; more generally as a noun, Rom 16:3, 9, 21; 2 Cor 1:24; 8:23; Phil 2:25; 4:3; Phlm 1, 24; cf. 1 Cor 3:9; 1 Thess 3:2). He normally employs the term in contexts that suggest the commendation of those who are described as his coworkers (Rom 16:3, 9; Phil 2:25; 4:3; 2 Cor 8:23; 1 Thess 3:2; Phlm 24).

17. *I rejoice:* The writers of Hellenistic letters typically mentioned how happy they were as they were writing their letters. The classic expression consisted of the verb "rejoice," an adverb expressing the intensity of their joy (e.g., *echarēn lian*), and a clause citing the reason for their joy. As he comes to the end of his letter (cf. Rom 16:19; Phil 4:10-20) Paul, like other Hellenistic letter writers, mentions his joy.

at the coming of Stephanas and Fortunatus and Achaicus: Paul's joy is occasioned by the arrival of Stephanas, Fortunatus, and Achaicus. In the context of a recommendation passage the joy and comfort provided by these three is to be seen as an epistolary feature that describes the relationship between those who are recommended and the sender of the letter. That Stephanas and his companions visited Paul provides additional warrant for their commendation.

because they have made up for your absence: The presence/absence motif (*parousia/hysterēma*) is a typical feature of Hellenistic letters, as it is of modern letters (cf. 5:3; 2 Cor 10:11; 13:2). Rather than the classic *apousia* Paul has used *hysterēma*, a word that suggests want, lack, or need. Apropos of this Ceslas Spicq comments, "On the level of emotions . . . the apostle was—if we may put it so—'in a state of lack'" (*TLNT* 3:430-431). This Pauline word is hapax in 1 Corinthians, but see 2 Cor 8:14[2x], 9:12; 11:9; Phil 2:30; 1 Thess 3:10 (cf. Col 1:24; Luke 21:4).

18. *they have given comfort to my spirit and to yours:* The clause explains (see the explanatory *gar*) how it is that the visitors have compensated for the absence of the Corinthians. Paul also uses the verb "to comfort" (*anapauō*) in 2 Cor 7:13 (with reference to "spirit," *to pneuma*) and in Phlm 7, 20 (with reference to *ta splagchna*, "the heart" [*NRSV*]). In all four instances he joins the motif of his having been comforted with his joy. Generally he suggests that others share in his joy and comfort as he does in theirs (here as well as 2 Cor 7:13; Phlm 7). In Paul's anthropological lexicon "my spirit" (*to emon pneuma*) is a way of identifying his very self. His anthropological terms typically designate the whole person, albeit under one or another aspect. Paul uses an emphatic genitive (*emou*) to underscore the support the Corinthian delegation had given him. In his writings he does not use the emphatic *emou* except in conjunction with another genitive. A similar example of correlative genitives is to be found in 1:2, "their Lord and ours." The complex construction of 16:18 doubly underscores that Paul was indeed invigorated by the visit of Stephanas and his companions.

Acknowledge people such as these: Paul concludes his recommendation with a summary exhortation (note the inferential, but not translated *oun*). The verb *epiginōskete*, "acknowledge," is rarely used by Paul (cf. 13:12[2x]; 14:37; Rom 1:32; 2 Cor 1:13, 14; 6:9; 13:5). Connoting a kind of knowledge that is particularly profound, the verb implies recognition and appreciation. Although the verb is not otherwise used by Paul in this sense, the apostle's thought repeats the idea expressed in v. 16a *(tois toioutois; tous toioutous)* and echoes similar sentiments expressed in 1 Thess 5:12-13.

FOR REFERENCE AND FURTHER STUDY

Kim, Chan-Hie. *Form and Structure of the Familiar Greek Letter of Recommendation.* SBL.DS 4. Missoula: Scholars, 1972.

6. *Greetings* (16:19-21)

19. The churches of Asia greet you. Aquila and Prisca, together with the church in their house, send you warm greetings in the Lord. 20. All the brothers and sisters greet you. Greet one another with a holy kiss. 21. A greeting in my own hand, the hand of Paul.

INTERPRETATION

From the mid-first century onwards it was customary for letter writers to convey personal greetings to those who might listen to the reading of their letters. When Paul wrote letters he often sent greetings on behalf of others (see Rom 16:16, 21, 23; 2 Cor 13:12; Phil 4:21; Phlm 23; cf. Col 4:10-14; 2 Tim 4:21). Only in his correspondence with the Galatians and with the Thessalonians does he fail to do so. The list of people who are named in Rom 16:3-15 is longer than the number of persons who are individually named in 1 Cor 16:19-21. Only two individuals, Aquila and Prisca, are mentioned in 16:19-21, but the greetings in 1 Corinthians are the most complex series of final greetings in all of Paul's letters. Unlike the conclusion to the letter to the Romans, which has greetings only in the second (Rom 16:3-15) and third persons (Rom 16:16b), 1 Corinthians has greetings in the first person (v. 21), the second person (v. 20b), and the third person (vv. 19-20a).

The third-person greetings are particularly complex. Paul extends greetings from the churches of Asia, from Aquila, Prisca, and the church that gathers in their house, and from all believers. The abundance of greetings serves to enhance the philophronetic function of Paul's letter; it expresses the affection that Paul, his companions, and his acquaintances have for the Christians of Corinth. The many greetings also have a theological function; they underscore Paul's description of the church of Corinth as one that is in communion with other gatherings of Christians who call on the name of the Lord Jesus Christ (1:2).

Paul's various words of greetings function as do similar words found at the end of letters we write today. Personal letters often end with the letter writer conveying greetings on behalf of a third party ("X asked me to say hello"). Similarly, letter writers frequently ask those to whom they write to convey their greetings to others: "Give the kids a hug," for example. Finally, a handwritten note of personal greeting is often added to a letter that has been typed or printed.

Aquila and Prisca. Mentioned five other times in the NT, Aquila and Prisca, whom Luke prefers to call "Little Prisca" (Priscilla), are among the most famous of early Christian couples (Acts 18:2, 18, 26; Rom 16:3; 2 Tim 4:19). Epigraphical evidence suggests that neither of the couples' names was ordinarily used for slaves, leading to the conviction that both Aquila and Prisca were freeborn. The names are Roman, but it was not uncommon for Jews (see Acts 18:2) living in the Diaspora to have Roman names. When dealing with his Hellenistic world Saul, the writer of this letter, used the name of Paul, the name of an Aemelian family.

Aquila, a Jew from Pontus on the Black Sea, and Prisca were among the first Christians in Rome. There the couple continued to participate in synagogal gatherings. During the reign of Claudius (49 C.E.; see Suetonius, *Claudius* 25.4; Orosonius, *Historiorum libri septem* 7.6.15-16; *PL* 31, 1075B) the proclamation of the gospel led to civic unrest in the capital of the empire. Those presumed to be involved, including Prisca and Aquila, were expelled from the city. From Rome Aquila and Prisca went to Corinth, where they established their trade and were able to provide Paul with a base of operations, a place of lodging, and a shop where he carried on the task of evangelization for about eighteen months (Acts 18:11).

According to Luke, Aquila and Prisca accompanied Paul when he left Corinth after the attack on him during the (pro)consulate of Gallio (Acts 18:18). They established themselves in Ephesus, where their home served as a home for the Christian church. Memory of their activity in Corinth remained sufficiently alive to warrant Paul's conveying to the Corinthian Christians a greeting from the couple and from the church that gathered in their house. After Paul wrote his letter to the Corinthians Aquila and Prisca apparently returned to Rome. Once again a community of Christians gathered in their home. Aquila and Prisca, Paul's coworkers in Christ Jesus, were the first of the Roman Christians to be greeted by Paul in the letter to the Romans (Rom 16:3-5).

Aquila and Prisca traveled a great deal. They were able to provide lodging and a means of livelihood for Paul (Acts 18:2-3; see note on 16:19).

Thus the suggestion is often made that the couple was fairly well off. Since the name of Prisca, the feminine equivalent of a *cognomen*, appears before that of her husband in four of the six NT references (Acts 18:18, 26; Rom 16:3; 2 Tim 4:19), it has been suggested that Prisca came from greater wealth and higher social status than did Aquila. Her role appears to be that of the *matrona* in a Roman household. On this hypothesis Aquila would have married into the family business.

Luke identifies the trade of Prisca and Aquila as that of leather worker (Acts 18:3). A leather worker was a small artisan who would probably set up shop on the agora and hang out an appropriate sign of the trade. Artisans such as these, although self-sufficient, could hardly be qualified as affluent. That Prisca's name appears before that of Aquila might, nonetheless, be an indication of her superior social status. Otherwise it might be a reflection of her greater role in the Christian mission, as many have suggested, or of the desire of Paul and Luke alike to underscore the role of women in the early Christian mission.

The New Testament does not provide any evidence as to how the couple came to embrace the Christian faith. It does not appear that they had been baptized by Paul (cf 1:14-16). This may be an indication that the couple had not been evangelized by Paul. In Acts 18:24-28 Luke tells the story of an important interaction between Apollos and this early Christian couple. Scholars are, however, hesitant to affirm the historicity of the events, at least in the form in which they are presented in the Lukan narrative.

The Kiss. Toward the end of four of his letters Paul exhorts those who have listened to its reading to greet one another with a holy kiss (Rom 16:16; 1 Cor 16:20; 2 Cor 13:12; 1 Thess 5:26; cf. Phil 4:21). Greeting people with an embrace, a kiss, was the common practice in the ancient Near East. Both the OT and the NT mention the practice. See, for example, Gen 29:11; Mark 14:45; Acts 20:37; cf. *T. Reub.* 1:5; *T. Sim.* 1:2. Paul's "holy kiss" is undoubtedly equivalent to the "kiss of love" of 1 Pet 5:14 (*en philēmati agapēs*). "Holiness" is a quality of Christian existence (see note on 1:2). "Love" characterizes Christian activity (cf. Gal 5:6). So it would seem that the holy kiss is a form of greeting appropriate to Christians. It would have been distinct from the ordinary kiss of welcome exchanged among nonbelievers insofar as it expressed the bonds of love and kinship that united Christians with one another. An exhortation to exchange this symbolic and specifically Christian gesture is particularly appropriate in a letter directed to a community that had experienced tensions and divisions (cf. 1:10).

Should one understand the "holy kiss" to be some sort of liturgical gesture? Patristic texts of the second and third centuries clearly indicate that a kiss of peace was part of the Christian eucharistic ritual. See, for example, Justin, *First Apology* 65.2; *PG* 6, 428; Hippolytus, *Apostolic Tradition* 4.1; 22.3; Tertullian, *Orations* 18; *PL* 1, 1176–1181; Cyprian, *Unity of the Catholic Church* 9; *PL* 4, 506–507; Origen, *Commentary on Romans* 10.33; *PG* 14, 1282–1283; Cyril, *Catecheses* 23.2; *PG* 33, 1109. These later texts do not provide sufficient evidence to warrant the conclusion that Paul's "holy kiss" was a liturgical gesture. Paul's second-person greetings are an epistolary formula. As such they are somewhat akin to language found in contemporary personal letters as, for instance, when a letter writer says "say hello to your wife for me."

Paul's Signature. In the Hellenistic world letters were generally dictated to professional scribes, but sometimes the author, the "letter writer," appended a personal greeting in his or her own hand if he or she were literate. In several of the extant papyri letters variations in calligraphy show the difference between the main part of the letter, written by the scribe (amanuensis), and the final words of greeting appended by the author (cf. Gal 6:11). Paul has personalized his letter to the Corinthians by adding a handwritten greeting, a "greeting in my own hand," at the end of the letter. This greeting served as an expression of Paul's affection for the Corinthian community (16:24).

Appending his own name added authority to Paul's communiqué. In his day the practice of "signing" a letter was not yet a feature of letter writing. Apart from legal documents (cf. Phlm 19) it was rare for a letter writer to actually sign his or her name at the end of the letter. The author's name had already been given in the salutation. Sometimes it had also appeared on the outside of the rolled-up scroll.

That Paul added a personal greeting at the end of the letter is a clear indication that he used the services of a scribe for its transcription (cf. Rom 16:22). Differences in the calligraphy between the body of the letter, the work of the scribe, and Paul's handwritten greeting would not have been apparent to the Corinthians, who had listened to the reading of the text. This may have been a contributing factor in Paul's not only "signing" the letter but also stating that he had signed the letter.

NOTES

19. *The churches of Asia greet you:* Churches are gatherings of believers (see note on 1:1). "Asia," mentioned elsewhere by Paul only in Rom 16:5 and 2 Cor 1:8, was the Roman province of Asia, situated in the western part of Asia Minor (the western part of modern Asian Turkey). From the time of Augustus its capital was Ephesus (16:8). Apparently Christians gathered in several of the cities of Asia, as they did in the province of Galatia (16:1; cf. Gal 1:2). Among the Asian cities mentioned in the NT are Colossae and Laodicaea, along with Pergamum, the ancient capital, and Smyrna, Thyatira, Sardis, Philadelphia,

Hierapolis, Assos, and Adramyttium (cf. Rev 1:11; 2:1–3:22; Acts 20:13-14; see also the epistle to the Colossians, especially 4:16, and Acts 19:10, 22). Several of these later references suggest Pauline influence on early Asian Christianity. That Paul can speak in 1 Corinthians not only for the churches of Asia (v. 19a) but also for all the brothers and sisters (v. 20a) is a sure sign of his sensitivity to his role and his authority in the early Christian church.

Aquila and Prisca: The diminutive "Priscilla" is found in many of the ancient manuscripts (C, D, F, G, Ψ, and most minuscules) but "Prisca" is the preferred reading. It is found in the oldest of the manuscripts ($\mathfrak{P}^{46}$, ℵ, B) and is the name by which Paul calls the lady in Rom 16:3, his only other mention of her. It is likely that "Priscilla" has entered into the textual tradition of 16:19 under the influence of Acts, where "Priscilla" is found in Acts 18:2, 18, 26.

Since the name of Aquila, the husband (Acts 18:2), follows that of Prisc[ill]a, his wife, in Acts 18:18, 26 and Rom 16:3, many commentators opine that Prisca's family was more affluent and that Aquila married into her status. The ambiguity of the data notwithstanding, Robert Jewett has suggested that Aquila was a Jewish handworker with a slave background and that Prisca was a Latin noblewoman ("To All of God's Beloved in Rome: New Discoveries About the Recipients of Paul's Letter," a lecture on the occasion of his installation in the Harry R. Kendall Chair at Garrett-Evangelical Theological Seminary, March 24, 1988).

together with the church in their house: "With whom I am also being housed" is found as an addendum to this description in some few manuscripts, chief among them being F, G, and the scribally corrected D. In the NT the formulaic expression "the church in someone's house" (*hē kat' oikon [tinos] ekklēsia*) is found in epistolary openings and closings (Rom 16:5; 1 Cor 16:19; Phlm 2; cf. Col 4:15). The formula recalls that the usual venue for Christian gatherings in first-century Corinth was the home of one of their number (see above, p. 74). The name of the householder was the name by which the local assembly was known. On the church in the house of Aquila and Prisca see also Rom 16:5.

send you warm greetings in the Lord: The adverb *polla* (literally "many") is typical of the greetings found in many Hellenistic letters. It adds a note of personal warmth to the letter writer's expression of greetings. "In the Lord" (*en kyriǭ*) may modify "you" (*hymas*), so as to describe the Christians at Corinth as being in the Lord. It is, however, more probable that the expression qualifies the verb "to greet" with the result that Paul intends to convey some form of Christian greetings to the Corinthians. Such an interpretation is consistent with the "holy kiss" of the following verse. The greetings would then at least implicitly include the Christian wishes of peace (*shalom;* cf. 1:3; 16:11) and grace (1:3; 16:23).

20. *All the brothers and sisters greet you:* Jerome Murphy-O'Connor (*Paul the Letter-Writer* 105) opines that Paul had probably at first intended merely to convey greetings from the churches of Asia, but that Aquila and/or Prisca had asked that their personal greetings also be sent to the Corinthians. This, in turn, would have prompted Paul to add that "everybody sends their greetings"— that is, at least the entire group of Christians that was with Paul.

Greet one another with a holy kiss: Paul's second-person greetings are typically expressed in succinct fashion. A notable exception is the letter to the Romans, in which Paul requests that his greetings be extended to a large number of individually named persons (Romans 16). The list in Romans is so exceptional that many commentators hold that Romans 16 was originally an independent letter of greetings, intended to be sent to the church in Ephesus.

Mentioned in Luke 7:45; 22:48 (cf. Luke 22:47, *par.* Matt 26:49; Mark 14:45), the kiss of greeting appears as a "holy kiss" *(en philēmati hagiǭ)* at the conclusion of this and other Pauline letters (Rom 16:16; 2 Cor 13:12; 1 Thess 5:26; cf. 1 Pet 5:14). A Hellenistic Jewish text roughly contemporary with Paul, *Joseph and Aseneth* (1st c. B.C.E.–2nd c. C.E.), tells a tale that illustrates the role of the kiss within a community of believers. Joseph, the hero of the tale, at first refused to kiss the priestess Aseneth because it was not fitting for a man who worships God to do so *(JosAs* 8:5-7). After her conversion his kiss imparts to her the spirit of life, the spirit of wisdom, and the spirit of truth *(JosAs* 19:11).

21. *A greeting in my own hand, the hand of Paul:* The frequent appearance of the name of Paul in 1 Corinthians (1:1, 12, 13; 3:4, 5, 22; 16:21) is a rarity in letters of the Hellenistic era. In Hellenistic letters the name of the author is not very often found after the opening salutation. When it does appear the presence of the name imparts particular authority to the letter. Apart from 1 Corinthians the name of Paul appears after the initial salutation only in 2 Cor 10:1; Gal 5:2; 1 Thess 2:18; and Phlm 9, 19. On the other hand, the name of the apostle occurs with some frequency in the deutero-Pauline correspondence (Eph 3:1; Col 1:23; 4:18; 2 Thess 3:17). The "signed" greeting of Col 4:18 and 2 Thess 3:17 reprises the formula of 16:21. Its appearance in these later epistles may be an attempt to provide epistolary verisimilitude for a pseudepigraphal text.

Mention of his name adds authoritative emphasis to Paul's plea in 2 Cor 10:1; Gal 5:2; and Phlm 9. As in 16:21, the use of his own name in 1 Thess 2:18 underscores his affection for the community (cf. Chariton, *Chaereas and Callirhoe* 8.4.5-6; Gregory Nazianzen, *Epistles* 64.5; 93; *PG* 37, 125–128, 168). References to Paul's own hand are to be found at the end of his letters to the Galatians (6:11) and to Philemon (v. 19), but only the latter includes Paul's signature.

FOR REFERENCE AND FURTHER STUDY

Benko, Stephen. "The Kiss" in idem, *Pagan Rome and the Early Christians.* Bloomington: Indiana University Press, 1984, 79–102.

Cotter, Wendy. "Women's Authority Roles in Paul's Churches: Countercultural or Conventional?" *NovT* 36 (1994) 350–372.

Donfried, Karl P. "Paul as *Scēnopoios* and the Use of the Codex in Early Christianity" in Karl Kertelge, Traugott Holtz, and Claus-Peter März, eds., *Christus bezeugen: Festschrift für Wolfgang Trilling zum 65. Geburtstag,* 1. ETS 59. Leipzig: St. Benno, 1989, 249–256.

Gielen, Marlis. "Zur Interpretation der paulinischen Formel *hē kat' oikon ekklēsia,*" *ZNW* 77 (1986) 109–205.

Gillman, Florence M. *Women Who Knew Paul* 49–58.

Hock, Ronald F. *The Social Context of Paul's Ministry: Tentmaking and Apostleship.* Philadelphia: Fortress, 1980.

Klassen, William. "The Sacred Kiss in the New Testament," *NTS* 39 (1993) 122–135.

Klauck, Hans-Josef. *Herrenmahl und hellenistischer Kult* 352–356.

Richards, E. Randolph. *The Secretary in the Letters of Paul.* Tübingen: Mohr, 1991.

Thraede, Klaus. "Ursprünge und Formen des 'Heiligen Kusses' im Frühen Christentum," *JAC* 11/12 (1968–69) 124–180.

Weima, Jeffrey A. D. *Neglected Endings* 104–117.

White, John Lee. "The Improved Status of Greek Women in the Hellenistic Period," *BR* 39 (1994) 62–79.

7. *Solemn Farewell* (16:22-24)

22. If anyone does not love the Lord, let that one be anathema. Maranatha. 23. The grace of the Lord Jesus be with you. 24. My love for all of you in Christ Jesus.

INTERPRETATION

The solemnity of the formulation of v. 22 suggests that a new section of the letter begins in that verse, even though the handwritten note begins in v. 21. Verse 21 is part of a complex series of greetings and so is appropriately considered together with the other greetings (vv. 19-21). A kind of postscript brings the letter to a close in vv. 22-24. After Paul's signature come a curse, a blessing, and an expression of love for the Christians of Corinth. The handwritten note gives a personal tone to what Paul has written, much in the fashion in which a contemporary business person might add a personal postscript to a letter that has been dictated or computer-produced.

Paul's final expression of love, unusual in his letters, further conveys his desire to maintain a friendly relationship with the Corinthian community. Nonetheless, his formulation of a curse immediately after he has signed the letter serves to confirm that he views his relationship with the community, albeit friendly, as an authoritative one (see note and interpretation of Paul's use of his name in v. 21). He is, as he stated in the personal identification with which he began to write (1:1), an apostle of Christ Jesus by the will of God.

Come, Lord Jesus! At the conclusion of its description of the eucharist
the *Didache,* a Syrian text probably dating from the beginning of the second century, has a prayer for the coming of the eschaton followed by a
pertinent exhortation: "May grace come and may this world pass away.
Hosanna to the God of David. Should anyone be holy, let that person
come. Should anyone be not [holy], let that person repent. Maranatha.
Amen" (*Did.* 10:6). The "Amen" suggests that the liturgical formula—
perhaps spoken before the actual reception of the eucharistic bread—was
originally part of a dialogue.

Jean-Paul Audet is of the opinion that within the eucharistic context
of early Christianity *"maranatha"* is both a prayer for the coming of the
eschatological Lord, the parousia, and an affirmation of the presence of
the Lord in the liturgical celebration. *"Maranatha"* is a transliteration into
Greek of an Aramaic expression. The Aramaic may be *māranā> tā>,* "may
our Lord come!" or *māran >ătā>,* "our Lord comes." Since there was no
separation between the letters in the majuscule manuscripts the Greek
letters of *māranā> tā>* adequately render one or the other, but not both, of
these Aramaic expressions. "Come, Lord Jesus," in the Greek text of Rev
22:20, a book whose dependence on the Pauline literature is generally acknowledged, suggests that the better verbalization of *"maranatha"* in 1
Cor 16:22 is *marana tha,* "may our Lord come."

The eschatological wish-prayer points to the antiquity and Palestinian
origin of the tradition that designated Jesus as Lord. It confounds the
claims of those who hold that the christological title of Lord is a cultic formula that Hellenistic Christians adopted from their Hellenistic world.
This was a classic view of several early-twentieth-century scholars who
belong to the history-of-religions school of the interpretation of Paul's letters (see especially Wilhelm Bousset, *Kyrios Christos: A History of the Belief
in Christ from the Beginnings of Christianity to Irenaeus* [Nashville: Abingdon, 1970; German original 1913]). That the christological title did not
originate in the Hellenistic world does not mean that Hellenistic Christians were loath to use the title of Lord when they gathered for eucharist.
Quite the contrary (cf. 11:23). Since the title alludes to Jesus' role as eschatological Lord, its use as a eucharistic formula confirms the eschatological orientation of the early Christian celebration of eucharist.

The presence of this Aramaic formula in 1 Corinthians is an indication
not only of Paul's reliance upon early Christian traditions in his composition of the letter but also of the generally conservative character of liturgical and prayer formulae (see also the *abba* formula in Rom 8:15 and Gal 4:6).
Its presence at the end of Paul's letter confirms the eschatological expectations of the Corinthian Christians to whom Paul was writing (cf. 1:7-9).

Christian Liturgy. Can one draw from the fact that the *maranatha* formula has a eucharistic setting in the *Didache* and in Justin's *Apology* and

that the discriminatory exhortation of 1 Cor 16:22 is similar to the formulae in *Did.* 10:6 and *First Apology* 66, the idea that 16:22 is a formula used in early Christian liturgy and that Paul expected his letter to be read just prior to the eucharistic synaxis?

K. Luke suggests that 16:22 was a kind of dismissal formula pronounced as the community gathered for the eucharistic celebration. In fact it has been often claimed that the finale of Paul's letter, beginning with his mention of the holy kiss in v. 20, served as a transition between the reading of the letter and the celebration of eucharist. The autograph of 16:21 is certainly an epistolary formula. The holy kiss, the formulae of inclusion and exclusion, and a grace benediction are, however, similar to phenomena found in the liturgy of the early church.

G. J. Cuming has argued that a pre-eucharistic situation is the most plausible situation for the reading of Paul's letters. One must, however, not hastily conclude that Paul intended the reading of his letter to be followed by a liturgical celebration. It may well be that later Christian liturgy was influenced by the community's reading of Paul's letters. That formulae similar to those used by Paul were appropriated by later Christians for their eucharistic gatherings does not necessarily imply that Paul's intended epistolary stasis was a eucharistic gathering.

Paul's experience of eucharist was such that he could employ liturgical formulae in the composition of his letters. His letter to the Corinthians clearly alludes to Christian liturgical formulae in 1:13 and 11:23-25. Other liturgical allusions are scattered here and there throughout the text. The manifold references to the eucharist throughout the letter clearly portray the Corinthian community as a eucharistic community.

From an epistolary point of view, one of the functions of the conclusions of Paul's letters (as of the rhetorical *epilogos/peroratio*) is to summarize and highlight Paul's argument. The grace benediction of 16:23 forms an *inclusio* with the wish of grace and peace in the salutation of the letter (1:3), thereby constituting the whole as a literary unit. The formula used in 1:3 may well derive from earlier liturgical use. Something similar might be said of Paul's penultimate salutation.

The Postscript. Paul does not usually add anything to the grace benediction with which he concludes his letters. He has, however, added a kind of postscript to this letter to the Corinthians. Hellenistic and Jewish letters of his time frequently contained a brief remark after the customary farewell, but it was not Paul's custom to do so. Only in the letter to the Romans does anything follow the grace benediction (Rom 16:21-27).

The final words of 1 Corinthians are an emphatic expression of Paul's love for the entire body of Corinthian Christians. That Paul assures the entire community of his love echoes some of the dominant themes of the letter. Exhorting the community to put aside its divisions (1:10) and addressing the issues that were a source of division within the community, Paul frequently had occasion to talk about his own relationship with the community. Some sections of his letter had taken members of the community to task. His salutation assures all members of the community of his love (cf. 4:14-15). His final words again tell them that he loves them all.

Apart from 1 Corinthians a reference to love appears in the closing of a Pauline letter only in 2 Cor 13:13. That reference has a function somewhat different from the farewell of 16:24. In 1 Corinthians Paul's last word to the community reprises the theme of love that had pervaded much of the letter (see 4:21; 8:1; 13:1-3, 13; 14:1; 16:14, 24). The motif of universal love provides an *inclusio* for Paul's final greetings (16:13-24). "All" and "love" appear in both v. 14 *(panta . . . agapē)* and v. 24 *(agapē . . . pantōn)*. Verse 14 emphasizes the comprehensive nature of universal Christian love; v. 24 expresses its personal nature. As Paul extends his love to all members of the community his words serve as a final reminder that there should be no divisions within that community. Paul's parting words are the ultimate expression of the ethos appeal of his argument.

NOTES

22. *If anyone does not love the Lord:* Paul writes of those who "love God" *(agapōsin ton theon)* in Rom 8:28, but the expression "love the Lord" *(philei ton kyrion)* is not otherwise found in his writings. The formula nonetheless echoes a biblical idea found in the Decalogue (Exod 20:6; Deut 5:10) and elsewhere in the OT (Deut 6:5; 7:9; 10:12; Ps 31:23; 97:10; Sir 1:10; 2:15-16; 47:22; cf. Jas 1:12; *1 Enoch* 108:8; and, in the form of "love him," *Pss Sol* 4:25; 6:6; 10:3; 14:1). In 16:22 "Lord" *(kyrion,* see the *mār* of *maranatha)* would seem to designate the risen Lord Jesus. The verb "to love" *(phileō)* is hapax in Paul's extant correspondence.

let that person be anathema. Maranatha: "Maranatha" is an Aramaic expression written in Greek letters. The discussion as to its interpretation is reflected in the manuscript tradition. G (apparently), K, L, Ψ, and editorial additions to B and D separate *māran* from *ʾătāʾ,* thereby indicating that the Aramaic wording is to be understood as an acclamation (see Interpretation). Other ancient manuscripts (including F and the majority of minuscules, where words are separated from one another in the Greek text), read all nine letters as if they constituted a single word. The older majuscules did not separate letters and words from one another. Their lack of evidence (see 𝔓⁴⁶, ℵ, A, B, C, D, etc.) makes their witness moot as far as this issue is concerned.

Of itself anathema *(anathema)* can connote something that is consecrated to God or something that is handed over to the divine wrath. In Paul's writings the word is used in the latter sense (12:3; Rom 9:3; Gal 1:8, 9). Galatians 1:8-9 pronounces an anathema upon a deviant member of the community.

Ernst Käsemann ("Sentences of Holy Law," 68–70) considers the curse of Gal 1:8-9 to be similar in form to 1 Cor 16:22. In Rom 9:3 Paul uses the language of anathema only to emphasize his profound longing that his Jewish kin become Christian (Rom 9:3). In 12:3 he recalled that some people at Corinth had pronounced a curse on "Jesus" even as they claimed to speak in the spirit.

Hans Lietzmann and Günther Bornkamm consider v. 22 to be a liturgical formula used at the beginning of the eucharistic celebration when the community was being called to self-examination. K. Luke interprets it as a formula of exclusion, perhaps a dismissal formula, used at the beginning of the eucharistic celebration.

23. *The grace of the Lord Jesus be with you:* A scribal "Christ," the result of some scribes' tendency to expand sacred names, is found in many of the ancient manuscripts (A, C, D, F, G, Ψ, most minuscules, and the corrected ℵ). Absent from ℵ, B, and some other majuscules, it was probably added to the text under the influence of the other Pauline grace benedictions (2 Cor 13:13; Gal 6:18; Phil 4:23; 1 Thess 5:28; Phlm 25; cf. Rom 16:24; 2 Thess 3:18) and the attraction of v. 24.

Earlier commentators, notably Ernst Lohmeyer, focused on the possible liturgical provenance of Paul's grace benediction and drew attention to the fact that Paul's letters were read to a Christian assembly, perhaps just before the celebration of eucharist. C.F.D. Moule (*Worship in the New Testament.* Lutterworth Studies in Worship 9 [London: Lutterworth, 1961] 43–44) and Philipp Vielhauer (*Geschichte der urchristlichen Literatur* [Berlin: de Gruyter, 1975] 37–39) are among those who have argued for the liturgical setting of the final verses in Paul's letter.

In contrast recent authors tend to focus on the idea that Paul's wish is an epistolary greeting. The grace benediction, found in all of Paul's authentic letters (also the canonical pseudepigrapha), substitutes for the final "farewell" (*errōsthe*) of the Hellenistic papyri. The grace wish forms an *inclusio* with the opening salutation (1:3). The identification of the Lord Jesus as the source of grace is typical of the Pauline grace benediction, but it is otherwise a rare motif in Paul's correspondence.

24. *My love for all of you in Christ Jesus:* Postscripts are rare in the Pauline correspondence (cf. Rom 16:21-27), but they were far from unknown in Hellenistic letters. With its use of "love" (*agap-*) and "all" (*pan-*), Paul's affirmation of love for all the members of the Corinthian community echoes 16:14. An *inclusio* has been formed that emphasizes the comprehensive nature of Christian love. Paul's expression of love for all the members of the community is particularly apropos in a letter to a group of people who are torn by tension and division. There may even have been tension between some members of the community and Paul himself, hence the particularly appropriate formula of Paul's expression of love for the entire community.

Paul's formulation reflects the wording of v. 23, especially in its elliptical construction (there is no verb), the reference to Jesus, and the formula "with you" (*meth' hymōn*). That "all" (*pantōn*) appears in v. 24 and not in v. 23 underscores the emphasis that Paul wants to attain in expressing his affection for the community. The use of the "Christ" title in Paul's love wish echoes the frequent use of "Christ" throughout the letter. It reflects the connotation of his earlier use of the title. Verse 24 lacks a verb, as does v. 23. The verb "to be" may be supplied, but contemporary epistolary style often includes a love wish without any verb "to be," hence this translation. On Paul's love for the Corinthians see 4:14; 10:14; 15:58; cf. 2 Cor 8:7 (*GNT*[4], *NRSV*, following 𝔓[46], B, etc.); 12:15.

Some ancient manuscripts (including ℵ, A, C, D, K, P, Ψ, and most of the Byzantine manuscripts) have an "Amen" at the end of Paul's letter. This is reflected in the Textus Receptus, *AV, RSV, NIV,* and various other modern translations of the text. On the other hand, the Codex Vaticanus and not a few other manuscripts bring the text to a close with the final prepositional phrase, "in Christ Jesus." Since many scribes tended to add liturgical formulae in their transcription of NT texts, modern text critics readily identify the final "Amen" as a scribal flourish.

FOR REFERENCE AND FURTHER STUDY

Audet, Jean-Paul. *La Didachè* 411–424.

Bornkamm, Günther. "Das Anathema in der urchristlichen Abendmahlsliturgie," *TLZ* 75 (1950) 227–230.

Cuming, Geoffrey J. "Service-Endings in the Epistles," *NTS* 22 (1975–76) 110–113.

Gibbs, James M. "Canon Cuming's 'Service-Endings in the Epistles.' A Rejoinder," *NTS* 24 (1977–78) 545–547.

Lietzmann, Hans. *Mass and Lord's Supper: A Study in the History of the Liturgy.* Leiden: Brill, 1979.

Luke, K. "Maranatha (1 Cor 16:22)," *BibBH* 10 (1984) 54–73.

Richards, E. Randolph. *The Secretary in the Letters of Paul.* Tübingen: Mohr, 1991.

Robinson, John A. T. "Traces of a Liturgical Sequence in 1 Cor. 16.20-24," *JTS* 54 (1953) 38–41.

INDEXES

INDEX OF SCRIPTURE REFERENCES

Biblical Books and Apocrypha

The commentary occasionally employs citations that depend upon the versification of the LXX. These are so noted in the index.

Gen		2:22-23	408
1–2	25, 527	2:24	7, 94, 243, 247, 248, 254,
1	569		267, 301, 410, 413
1:1–2:4	570	4:1	413
1:2	569	4:26	53
1:11-13	564	5:1-32	53
1:11	564	5:3	572
1:12	566	9:2	119
1:14-19	564, 567	9:6	154
1:16	567	11:1-9	456
1:20-28	563	12:7	531
1:20-25	566	12:8	53
1:26-29	569	13:4	53
1:26-28	566	14:18	433
1:26-27	570	14:24	433
1:26	409	20:6	258
1:27	396, 402, 405, 463, 572	21:33	53
1:28	254	26:1	412
2	142, 402, 569	26:24	531
2:4-24	570	26:25	53
2:4	569	26:26-33	433
2:7	7, 94, 400, 568, 569, 570, 571	29:11	609
2:18-25	399, 403, 406, 413	31:43-54	433
2:18-22	410	35:9	531
2:18	410	39	248
2:20	410	40:8	135
2:21-23	410	40:16	135

40:22	135	31:6	151
48:3	531	32:1-6	367, 370
49:4	209	32:6	7, 95, 364, 365, 367, 370, 371
		34:14	381
Exod		35:30–36:1	151
3:11	537	35:32-33	150
4:10	537		
4:13	537	*Lev*	
6:3	531	2:10	342
9:16	102, 246	5:1	173
12:14-20	214	5:8	432
12:14	428	5:13	342
12:15	214	6:9-11	342
12:21	214	6:18	266, 342
12:23	372	6:22-23	342
13:3	428	7:5-8	380
13:7	214	7:6-10	342
13:9	428	7:14	342
14:19-22	368	7:30-34	342
15:16	119	9:23	532
16:2-3	366, 372	10:12-13	342
16:3	187, 372	11:44	52
16:4-36	368	13:45	408, 409
16:10	532	18:3	209
17:1-7	368	18:7-8	209
17:6	96, 365, 369	18:8	209, 210
17:7	365, 371	18:22	236
18:21-27	228	18:27	209
18:21	228	18:29	209
19:15	256	19:2	52
20:5	381	19:18	484
20:6	616	20:11	209
20:14-15	230	20:13	236
21:6	232	20:26	52
21:7-11	299	23:10-14	551
21:10	259	24:7	428
21:23-25	154	24:20	154
23:16	551		
23:19	551	*Num*	
24:3-8	433	5:11-31	439
24:8	433	5:18	408, 409
24:9-11	433	6:24-26	47
25:3-7	150	10:9	496
28:36-40	401	11	25, 364, 370
29:37	266	11:4-6	370
31:1-5	151	11:4	370, 371
31:4-5	150	11:6-9	368

11:13	370
11:18	370
11:21	370
11:33-34	370
11:33	370
11:34-35	367, 370
11:34	371
12:8	487, 488
12:12	537
14:2	187, 366, 371, 372
14:3	373
14:10	532
14:11	481
14:15-16	372
14:16	371
14:26-35	371
14:29-30	369
14:36	371
15:17-21	605
16:11-35	371, 372
16:19	532
16:30	481
16:41-50	371
17:7	532
18:8-13	551
20:1-13	368
20:3	187
20:6	532
20:7-11	365, 369, 371
20:11	369
20:24	481
21:5-9	371
21:5-6	96, 366, 371, 372
21:5	372
24:17	53
25:1-9	366, 371
25:1-2	371
25:1	371
25:9	371
26:62	371
26:65	369
31:22-23	157
Deut	
1:16	234
1:34	481
2:25	119

3:24	102
4:10	52
4:37	132
5:9	381
5:10	616
5:18-19	230
6:4	132, 305, 314, 315, 319
6:5	616
6:14-15	381
6:16	371
7:3	265, 303
7:8	132
7:9	65, 66, 616
7:26	448
9:7	481
9:8	481
9:10	52
10:12	616
10:21	100
11:25	119
16:3	428
17:7	7, 95, 208, 212, 218, 223, 387
18:1-5	380
18:4	551
18:16	52
18:22	519
19:19	218, 223
19:21	154
20:5-6	147
21:21	218, 223
21:22-23	92
22:21	218, 223
22:30	
[23:1 MT]	209, 210
23:1-8	52
24:4	270
24:7	218, 223
24:3-4	264
25:4	7, 95, 330, 332, 339, 340, 342, 551
25:5-10	299
26:2	551
26:10	551
27:20	209
28:23	432
29:2-4	132
30:6	132

30:15-16	200
30:20	132
31:20	481
32	52, 382
32:4	65, 66
32:6	316
32:7	522
32:21	96
32:30	381
32:31	381
32:35	481
32:37	381

Josh
4:24	102
6:4-20	496
7:25	154
9:3-16	433
24:15	200
24:19-20	381

Judg
3:27	496
6:34	496
10:18	405
11:8	405
11:9	405
11:11	405
20:2	52

1 Sam
2:10	99
9:21	537
10:5	496
13:3	496
15:26	154
17:36	284

2 Sam
7:14	316
16:21-22	264
20:3	264
22:44	405

1 Kings
3:5	531
6:12	533

8:14	52
9:2	531
14:22	381
18:39	510
20:11	101
21:9	210
21:12	210, 405

2 Kings
3:15	496
23:3	533

Isa
3:3	155
3:24	408
5:1-7	142
6:5	537
6:9-10	125
6:10	132
7:8-9	405
8:14	107
10:20	158
13:6	65, 158
13:9	65, 158
14:4-21	328
18:3	496
19:12	103
19:16	119
22:1-14	560
22:13	7, 94, 387, 560
24:8	496
24:16	348
24:21-22	553
25:8	7, 94, 125, 574, 577
27:13	496
28:7	508
28:11-12	7, 94, 505, 507
28:11	507, 508
28:12	507, 508
29:14	7, 91, 93, 94, 96, 103, 151, 162, 165
29:16	103
29:18	103
29:24	103
31:8	234
33:18	103
40:13	7, 94, 96, 122, 125, 387

42:6	66
45:14	7, 94, 387, 505, 506, 510
46:10	66
48:12	66
49:1	491, 537
49:7	65, 66
52:11	258, 271
52:15	94, 131, 491
53	534, 540
53:3-5	530
53:5	530
55:10-11	101
58:1	496
58:3-6	210
59:17	485
61:1	132
63:16	316
64:4 [64:3 LXX]	94, 131, 132, 138
64:8	316

Jer

1:5	537
1:6	537
1:10	147
2:3	551
4:5	496
4:13	348
4:19	496
4:21	496
4:31	348
5:21-23	132
6:4	348
9:22-23 [LXX]	7, 91, 95, 96, 99, 100, 114
9:23 [9:22 LXX]	90, 94, 99, 113
9:24 [9:23 LXX]	91, 112
9:26	284
11:20	174, 491
14:12	210
16:21	102
17:10	159
18:7-10	147
21:8-14	200
24:6	147

25:33 [32:33 LXX]	65
31:7 [38:7 LXX]	405
31:28	147
31:31	427, 433
36:1-32	93
42:10	147
43:1-7	93
51:27	496

Ezek

7:10	65
8:3	132, 381
13:5	65
16:3-5	537
22:10-11	209
22:18-22	157
26:13	496
43:3	488
44:18-20	401
44:20	407

Hos

1:10	317
3:1-3	250
4:17	376
6:2	531
8:5	481
11:1	316
13:13	537
13:14	7, 95, 125, 574, 577, 578, 582

Joel

1:14	210
2:1	65
2:3	159
2:30	159
2:32 [3:5 LXX]	53, 65
3:14 [4:14 LXX]	65

Amos

5:18-20	65
5:18	65

5:20	65		31:17	111
9:11	158		31:20	131
			31:23	616
Obad			35:4	111
1:15	65		35:17	557
			35:26-27	111
Nah			37 [LXX]	428
1:2	381		40:13	137
			46:2	102
Zeph			52:1	101
1:7	65		54:6 [LXX]	119
1:14-16	158		59:17	102
1:14	65, 381		62:5 [LXX]	237
1:18	158		62:12 [61:13	
2:3	158		LXX]	159, 554
			66:10	157
Zech			69 [LXX]	428
8:23	510		69	107
10:3	481		69:23-24	107
12:3-4	158		71:15-17	429
13:9	157		71:16	429
			75:8	379
Mal			78	364
1:7	96		78:15-16	369
3	162		78:18	96, 372
3:2-3	157, 160		78:58-64	381
3:5	259		94:1 [93:1	
4:1-6	158		LXX]	173, 481
4:1 [3:19			94:4	101
LXX]	65, 159		94:10 [93:10	
			LXX]	165
Pss			94:11 [93:11	
6:10	111		LXX]	7, 94, 163, 165, 545
8	550, 554		97:10	616
8:7 [LXX]	7, 94, 318, 548, 549, 550,		99:6	53
	553, 554		101	217
9:25 [LXX]	481		102:26	414
11:6	379		104:3 [LXX]	237
12:7	157		105:1	53, 429
16:5	379		105:5	429
16:8-11	534		106	364
17:50 [LXX]	502		110	550, 555
21:2	102		110:1 [109:1	
21:14	102		LXX]	7, 94, 318, 387, 534, 548,
23:5	379			549, 550, 553, 554
24:1 [23:1			115	313
LXX]	7, 94, 96, 384, 387, 388		115:5	447

115:7	447
116:13	375, 379
117:1	395
120:5	348
128:8	
[LXX]	237
145:13 [144:13	
LXX]	65, 66
Job	
2:6	212
3:16	537
5:12-13	94
5:12	7, 95
5:13	163, 165
9:4	165
22:25	157
27:6	173
Prov	
3:12	436
3:19	320
5:3	248
5:15	258
5:18	258
6:23–7:27	248
6:25-28	248
6:29	258
8:10-11	157
8:19	157
8:30	320
10:13	202
13:24	202
22:15	202
23:13-14	202
25:14	101
25:21-22	481
25:22	396
26:3	202
27:1	101
Qoh	
6:3	537
7:10	227
Lam	
3:45	191

Esth	
4:16	210
Dan	
1:20	119
2	125, 128, 411
2:20	108
3	477
3:50 [LXX]	160
3:94 [LXX]	160
4	125
5	125
5:7	135
7	125
7:9	159
7:21-22	231
8	125
10–12	125
10:2	210
11:38	157
12:3	577
Ezra	
2:64	52
7–10	207
7:26	207
8:21	210
9:2	303
10:6	210
10:8	207
10:44	207
Neh	
1:4	210
1:10	102
8:6	503
8:9	210
10:37	551
13:25	265
1 Chr	
22:14-16	150
29:2	150
31:5	551
2 Chr	
1:7	531
3:1	531

3:6	150
7:12	532
20:3	210
32:27	157

Apocrypha

Bar

3:9–4:4	93, 129
3:16	129
3:23	129
3:27-28	94
3:27	130
3:28	129
3:29	94
4:1	94
4:7	94

1 Esdr

4:13-41	430
4:34-40	443
4:41	487
4:38	485
8:72 [8:69 LXX]	210
9:2	210

4 Ezra

1:28-29	316
2:34	295
3:7	582
4:26	295
7:9	579
7:17	579
7:29-32	576
7:33-34	485
7:91-101	131
7:96	576, 579
7:112-115	567
7:112	576
8:53-54	576
8:54	576
10:40-57	575
16:42-45	291

Jdt

2:28	119
9:12	316
10:3	408
16:8	408

1 Macc

1:15	284
2:64	601

2 Macc

2:21	497

3 Macc

2:21	316
5:7	316
6:3	316
6:8	316
7:6	316

4 Macc

4:10	119
13:8	475
13:25	71
17:15	362

Sir

1:10	616
2:15-16	616
4:1	259
4:10	316
4:11	231
4:15	231
6:19	7, 95, 340
9:6	248
11:20	533
11:27	159
14:18	579
15:11-17	200
17:1-13	409
17:6	132
17:31	579
19:2	248
23:1	316
23:4	316

23:16	269		
28:11	79		
31:12–32:13	420		
31:18	420		
31:23-24	420		
31:29-31	420		
32:1-2	420		
34:21-22	259		
38:24–39:11	104		
39:6	119		
40:5	79		
40:9	79		
43:10	533		
47:22	616		
49:7	147		
51:10	316		

Tob

4:12	258
13:4	316

Wis

2:16	316
3:4-6	157
3:7-8	231
3:8	231
6:7-8	381
6:21	187
7:22	320
7:26	406
9:2-4	320
9:9-18	128
9:9-11	406
10:17-18	368
11:4-8	369
12:16-18	381
12:24	221
13	314
13:1-9	314
13:2-3	314
13:3	315
13:10-19	314
14:3	316
14:15	395
16:6	428
19:7	368

New Testament

Matt

2:11	510
3:10	159
3:11	153, 159
3:12	159
4:9	510
5:8	296
5:9	50
5:22	159
5:32	264, 269, 270
5:34	209
5:38-48	484
5:38	154
5:48	129
7:1	173
8:14-15	331, 336
10:2	80
10:10	334, 342
10:28	159
10:34-36	422
11:17	496
12:12	302
12:46-49	336
13:1-23	125
13:3-9	142
13:24-30	125, 142, 223
13:30	548
13:31	566
13:36-43	125, 223
13:39-43	548
13:40	159
13:42	159
13:50	159
13:55	336
15:8-9	103
15:17	245
16:17	579
16:18	80
17:3	531
17:20	454, 476
18:8	159
18:9	159
18:15-18	208, 215
18:26	510
19:3-12	415

19:9	264, 269, 270
19:17	284
19:29	235, 579
20:8	159
20:26-27	353
21:21	454, 476
22:23-33	299, 565
22:34-40	484
22:44	549, 553
24:3	552
24:5	422
24:21	422
24:27	552
24:37	552
24:39	552
24:42-43	601
24:43	230
25:13	601
25:34	235
25:41	159
26:26-28	426
26:26	431, 432, 433
26:27	376
26:28	390
26:29	433, 434
26:30	495
26:38-41	601
26:49	612
26:60	544
28:9-10	536
28:10	336, 537
28:16-20	535
28:19	82

Mark

1:13	260
1:15	235
1:29-31	331, 336
2:9	436
2:26	153
3:16	80
3:31-34	336
4:1-20	125, 578
4:2-9	142
4:10-12	102
4:12	125
4:26-32	142

5:30	455
6:2	455
7:3-5	395
7:6-7	103
7:9	245
7:13	395
7:37	302
8:38	154
9:4	531
9:43	159
9:45	159
9:47	159
10:11-12	264, 269, 270
10:17	235, 579
10:19	259
10:38	557
10:43-45	353
10:45	353
12:18-27	299, 565
12:28-34	484
12:36	549, 553
13:6-8	422
13:12	422
13:34-38	601
14:12	214
14:18-25	477
14:22-26	434
14:22-25	433
14:22-24	426
14:22	432, 433
14:23	376
14:24	390, 433
14:25	433, 434
14:26	495
14:34-38	601
14:45	609, 612
16:7	535
16:9-11	536
16:14-18	535

Luke

1:11	535
1:67-79	578
2:22	339
2:32	64
2:37	259
3:6	111

3:9	159		22:48	612
3:16	153, 159		24:10-11	536
3:17	159		24:12	535
4:20	172		24:34	334, 531, 535
4:38-39	331, 336		24:35	376
6:27-36	484		24:36-53	535
6:27	302		24:44	339, 518
6:37	173			
7:32	496		*John*	
7:45	612		1:42	80
8:1-15	125		2:12	336
8:5-8	142		3:14-15	372
8:19-21	336		5:21	551
10:7	159, 334, 342		6:51-58	426
10:25-28	484		6:51	432
10:25	235, 579		6:54-55	432
10:29-37	484		7:3-10	336
12:37-39	601		7:23	339
12:39	230		7:53–8:11	516
12:42	168, 172, 348		9:2	436
12:49	159		10:20	509
12:50	557		12:24	566
12:51-53	422		12:42	498
15:2	222		14:15	284
16:1-8	168		14:21	284
16:18	264, 269, 270		14:24	284
17:10	348		15–17	430
17:28	147		15:10	284
18:5	362		17:2	111
18:18	235, 579		18:15-18	535
20:27-40	299, 565		18:25-27	535
20:34-35	294		20:2-10	535
20:42-43	553		20:14-18	536
20:42	518		20:17	336
21:4	606		21:1-19	535
21:8	422			
21:16	422		*Acts*	
22:7	214		1:8	120
22:17	376		1:14	336
22:18	433		1:20	518
22:19-20	426, 433		1:21-22	50
22:19	428, 432		2–3	534
22:20	376, 433, 466		2:1-13	536
22:24-38	430		2:1	593
22:25-27	353		2:5-13	456
22:43	535		2:17	111
22:47	612		2:21	53

2:23	355	15:1-2	284
2:34-35	553	15:5	339
2:38	82, 237	15:22-23	589
2:42	376	15:22	508
3:6	212	15:23	47
3:15	543	15:29	599
4:2	543	15:33	597
4:10	543	15:38-40	337
4:20	463	16:2-3	196
4:36	337	16:9	535
4:37	337	16:11-40	514
6:1	268	16:15	75, 78
7:2	535	16:16-24	476
7:26	535	16:18	454
7:30	535	16:21-23	183
8:16	82	16:25	495
9:1-9	537, 538	16:33	75
9:2	79, 589	17:3	543
9:27	337	17:17	116
9:39-41	268	17:22-31	106
10:25	510	17:24-29	313
10:33	302	17:24-28	319
10:41	222, 543	17:28	561
10:42	543	17:31	543
10:48	82, 237	17:32	543
11:3	222	17:34	514
11:26	51, 200	18	24
11:27-30	337	18:1-18	23, 33, 37, 44
11:29-30	587	18:1-17	52
11:29	587	18:1-3	185
11:30	587	18:2-26	514
12:15	509	18:2-3	608
13–14	588	18:2	23, 24, 608, 611
13:1	52	18:3	74, 337, 609
13:2-3	589	18:4	22, 23
13:8-13	337	18:7	84
13:13–16:10	604	18:8	83, 98
13:16-31	106	18:11	24, 608
13:30	543	18:12	23
13:31	531	18:17	42, 51
13:33	518	18:18	51, 608, 609, 611
13:34	543	18:21	593
13:39	339	18:24–19:1	79
14:3	476	18:24-28	72, 609
14:8-10	454	18:26	608, 609, 611
14:14	50	18:27	79
14:23	259	19	593

19:5	82	1:10	56, 57, 589
19:10	106, 611	1:11	369
19:11-12	454	1:13	367, 368
19:11	476	1:14-27	209
19:21-41	558, 559	1:14	106
19:22	23, 611	1:16–3:20	107
19:27	559	1:16	102, 105, 106
19:39	355	1:18-32	105
19:40	559	1:18-23	355
20:3	77	1:18	481
20:7-20	454	1:19-32	221
20:7	589	1:20-31	561
20:13-14	611	1:20	315
20:16	593	1:21-23	314
20:21	106	1:21	249, 466
20:37	609	1:22	104
22:3-11	538	1:23	409, 410, 447
22:5	589	1:24-27	217, 230, 236
22:6-16	537	1:25	286, 315
22:16	237	1:26-31	371
23:26	41	1:27	480
23:30	600	1:28	362
24	278	1:29-31	218, 230
25:10-11	329	1:29	481
25:12	329	1:32	606
25:21	329	2–4	284
25:25	329	2:4	423, 480
26:9-18	538	2:5	64
26:12-18	537	2:6	554
26:24	509	2:8	481
26:25	509	2:9-10	106
26:32	329	2:16	173
27:11	470	2:18	504
28:3-6	476	2:20	143, 469
28:8-9	454	2:21-22	230
28:23	339	2:21	230
		2:24	355
Rom		2:25-29	284
1:1	43, 51, 172	2:27-29	554
1:3-4	92	3:1-2	284
1:4	48, 60, 108, 212, 246, 318,	3:3	223
	334, 530, 543, 550, 552	3:4	247
1:5	76	3:5	338, 481
1:7	47, 51, 52, 53, 317	3:6	247
1:8	55, 56, 57, 58, 421	3:9	106
1:9-10	57	3:10-18	554
1:9	347	3:20	112

3:22	105	6:22	113, 271
3:23-26	113	7:2	271, 303
3:23	567	7:4	530, 543
3:24	113	7:5	236
3:27–4:12	284	7:6	286
3:30	314	7:7	247
3:31	247	7:11	164
4:4	159	7:13-20	284
4:5	105	7:13	247, 474
4:7-8	534	7:14	136, 143, 369
4:7	303	7:25	388
4:8	303	8:2	113, 355
4:11	105, 335	8:4	144
4:14	347	8:8	386
4:24	530, 543	8:9-13	572
4:25	92, 237, 431, 530	8:11	449, 530, 543, 581
5	528	8:14-15	317
5:2-5	111	8:15-16	448
5:5	480, 484	8:15	48, 317, 550, 614
5:6-9	232	8:17	579
5:8-11	236	8:19-25	555
5:8	82, 326	8:19	63, 64
5:10	232	8:20	348
5:12-21	548	8:23	63, 113, 502
5:14	369, 370, 548	8:24	487
5:15	548	8:25	63
5:17-18	548	8:26	448, 456
5:17	548	8:27	133, 585
6:1-14	541	8:28	311, 600, 616
6:1-11	82	8:29-30	60, 130
6:2	247	8:29	409
6:3-4	531	8:30	466
6:3	82, 368	8:32	82, 232, 326, 431
6:4-8	188	8:33	65
6:4	48, 317, 530, 543	8:34	92, 530, 543
6:6	91	8:35	183
6:9	530, 543	8:38	129, 553
6:10	536	9–11	107
6:12	581	9:3	616, 617
6:13	481, 543	9:4-5	284
6:14-15	354	9:5	380
6:14	354	9:6	101
6:15-23	236	9:14	247, 481
6:15	247, 354	9:17	246
6:17	369, 388	9:25-26	577
6:18	113, 271	9:26	317
6:19	373	9:32	325

9:33	107, 325, 554, 580		12:15	212, 295, 466
10:4	105		12:19	379, 481, 508, 601
10:6-8	94		12:20-21	482
10:7	530, 543		12:20	396
10:8-9	92		13:1	605
10:9	334, 446, 506, 530, 543		13:3-4	175
10:12	106, 186		13:5	293
10:13	53, 76		13:7	258
10:14-15	105		13:8-10	355
11:1-10	107		13:9	178, 223, 230, 284
11:1	247		13:11-13	561
11:8-10	554		13:11-12	291
11:9	107		13:12-14	583
11:11-24	106		13:12	158
11:11-12	107		13:13	79, 144, 218, 230
11:11	247		14–15	307
11:12	234		14	305, 325
11:15	543		14:3	111
11:16	266, 605		14:4	601
11:17	356		14:9	543
11:25-36	137		14:10	111
11:25	115, 367, 368		14:11	223
11:26-27	577		14:13	325
11:29	109, 285		14:15	82, 326, 327
11:30-32	236		14:17	202, 318, 579
11:32	232		14:18	286, 422
11:33-34	133		14:19	312
11:34	133, 137		14:20	325, 597, 597
11:36	320		14:21	290, 294
12–15	249		14:22	112, 303
12:1-2	445, 455, 519		15:1-7	385
12:1	5, 76, 249		15:1-3	385
12:3-8	462		15:1-2	386
12:3	177		15:1	110, 325
12:4-5	460, 462		15:2	312
12:5	380		15:6	48, 249, 317, 466
12:6-8	158, 451, 452, 453, 454, 455, 468, 494		15:9	249, 466, 502
12:6	455, 491, 498		15:11	395
12:7	469		15:14	310
12:8	469		15:15-16	449
12:9-21	479		15:15	174
12:9	247		15:16	172
12:11	286		15:19	63, 455, 476
12:12	481, 483		15:20	149, 156, 222, 312
12:13	4		15:21	491
12:14	190		15:22-32	591
			15:25-28	585, 590

15:25-27	586
15:25	585, 587, 588
15:26	585
15:27	143, 369, 586
15:28	587
15:30	5, 76, 449
15:31	585
15:32	201
15:33	520
16	612
16:1-16	514
16:1-5	516
16:1-2	74, 98, 197, 198, 253, 592
16:1	44, 172, 469
16:2	200, 303, 585
16:3-16	74
16:3-15	607
16:3-5	74, 337, 608
16:3-4	558
16:3	146, 336, 606, 608, 609, 611
16:5	73, 601, 604, 605, 610, 611
16:6	538, 605
16:7	51, 336
16:8	601
16:9	146, 200, 601, 606
16:10-11	78
16:11	200
16:12	200, 538, 601, 605
16:13	200
16:15	585
16:16	607, 609, 612
16:17-19	599
16:17	5
16:18	164, 286
16:19	606
16:20	600
16:21-27	615, 617
16:21	146, 196, 606, 607
16:22	3, 42, 200, 610
16:23	23, 52, 70, 74, 79, 84, 98, 168, 418, 508, 607
16:24	617
16:25	64, 105, 115, 119, 125
16:26	260, 289

1 Cor (see p. 643)

2 Cor	
1:1	43, 51, 52, 53, 196, 197, 585, 596
1:2	47, 53, 317
1:3	48, 317
1:8	367, 368, 474, 610
1:11	63
1:12	62, 100, 143, 215
1:13	606
1:14	65, 100, 606
1:16	592
1:18	101, 373
1:19	60, 196
1:21-22	449
1:21	63
1:24	146, 606
2:3-4	4, 13
2:4	216
2:5	211
2:7-8	480
2:8	5
2:9	4, 13, 216
2:10	118
2:12	63, 593
2:14	388
2:17	101, 215
3–4	368
3:1-2	197
3:1	9
3:3	136, 143
3:5	537
3:6	172
3:10	466
3:17	369
3:18	410
4:1	293
4:2	101, 112
4:4	104, 129, 271, 410
4:5	172
4:7–6:2	575
4:7-12	190
4:8-9	183, 190
4:9	190
4:10-11	191
4:11	581
4:17	474
5:1-5	575, 584

5:1	73, 312		8:8	260, 289
5:3	190		8:9	186, 585, 586
5:4	581		8:10	244, 293
5:5	575		8:12-14	587
5:7	487		8:14	606
5:10	65, 174		8:15	223
5:12	100		8:16-23	586
5:14-15	82		8:16	388
5:17	320, 405, 531, 564, 580		8:18	198
5:19	101		8:21	112
6:1	5, 538, 606		8:22	198
6:2	580		8:23	51, 146, 587, 606
6:4-5	183		8:24	100, 476, 585
6:4	172, 293		9:1	585, 587, 588, 605
6:5	520		9:2-4	111
6:6-7	219		9:2	100, 586
6:6	480		9:3	100, 198, 346, 347
6:8-10	183		9:7	293
6:8	190		9:9	223
6:9	439, 580, 598, 606		9:10	318
6:10	62		9:11	62
6:13	194		9:12	585, 586, 606
6:14–7:1	11, 12		9:13	63, 249, 379, 466
6:14	271, 379		9:15	388
6:15	271		10:1–13:13	12
6:16-18	554, 577		10:1-2	202
6:16	160		10:1	5, 50, 202, 612
6:17	118, 253, 258, 271		10:4	143
6:18	316, 317		10:7	81, 171
7:1	194, 379, 601		10:8	100, 312
7:2	161		10:10-11	206
7:4	100		10:10	109, 111, 232, 552
7:5-7	592		10:11	171, 606
7:6	552		10:12	135
7:7	552		10:13	100, 107, 178
7:11	580		10:14	63
7:12	112, 211		10:15	100, 583
7:13	606		10:16	100
7:14	100, 111		10:17	99, 100, 113
7:15	119, 477		10:18	422
8–9	585, 588, 590		11:1–12:10	100
8:1-6	586		11:1	190
8:1-5	592		11:2	293
8:1	533		11:3	161, 164
8:2-3	587		11:4	190
8:4	379, 585, 587, 588, 605		11:5-12	346
8:7	62, 194, 310, 618		11:5	336

11:6	62, 120		13:4	91, 92, 102, 246
11:7-15	185		13:5	362, 606
11:7-12	349		13:6	362
11:7	244, 331		13:7	362, 422
11:9	592, 606		13:9	110
11:10	100		13:10	202, 312, 453, 591
11:12	100		13:11-13	594
11:13	51, 179, 336		13:11	54, 77, 295, 520, 599
11:14	179		13:12	585, 607, 609, 612
11:15	172, 179		13:13	379, 449, 616, 617
11:16-29	116			
11:16	100, 118		*Gal*	
11:17	100		1	539
11:18	100, 118		1:1	43, 51, 318, 530, 543
11:19-20	186		1:2	588, 610
11:19	190		1:3-4	48, 92
11:20	190		1:3	47, 317
11:21–12:20	189		1:4	82, 104, 113, 129, 130, 221, 317, 534, 540
11:21	118		1:6	539
11:22	118		1:7	63
11:23-29	183		1:8-9	600, 616, 617
11:23	172, 583		1:8	412, 519, 616
11:25	183		1:9	616
11:26	559		1:10	130, 356, 386, 390
11:27	185		1:11-15	532
11:29	269, 465		1:11	338, 368, 533
11:30	100		1:12	64
12:1	64, 100, 132, 244		1:13-17	236
12:5	100		1:13	46, 51, 190, 474, 538
12:6	100		1:14	395
12:7	64, 132, 183, 212		1:15	348, 491, 537
12:9	100, 119, 212		1:16	579
12:10	110, 293		1:18–2:14	332
12:11	111, 476		1:18–2:1	535
12:12	106, 454, 455, 476		1:18-24	532
12:13-18	185		1:18-19	536
12:14–13:1	591		1:18	80
12:14-15	349		1:19	336
12:14	194, 201, 580		1:20	112, 464, 580
12:15	194, 618		1:23	190, 236
12:17	198		1:24	249, 466
12:19	194, 312, 379, 453, 601		2:1-14	337
12:20-21	218		2:1	331
12:20	79, 118, 144, 230, 520		2:2	64, 538
12:21	209, 210, 221, 230		2:6-14	532
13:1	201		2:7-8	80
13:2	206, 606			

2:7	149	5:5	63
2:9	80, 331, 532, 536	5:6	284, 482, 485, 600, 609
2:10	585, 587, 588, 590	5:9	213, 214
2:11-14	325	5:11	91, 92
2:11	80	5:14	178
2:12	222	5:16	283
2:13	331	5:18	354
2:14	80	5:19-23	219
2:16	111	5:19-21	218, 219, 230
2:17	247	5:19	209, 221
2:18	312	5:20	79, 144, 230, 422
2:19	91	5:21	202, 229, 235, 579, 580
2:21	538	5:22-23	219
3:1	91, 92	5:22	480
3:9	270	5:23	202, 260, 361
3:10-14	92	5:24	92
3:13-14	422	6:1	369, 422, 480
3:13	91, 113, 286	6:2	352, 355, 385
3:15	338, 498	6:6	101, 341, 504
3:18	579	6:7	235
3:19	412, 519	6:9	178
3:21	130, 247, 464	6:11	2, 610, 612
3:24-25	195	6:12	91, 92
3:26	317	6:14	91, 92, 100, 247
3:27-28	412	6:15	284, 320, 531, 564
3:27	82, 368	6:16-18	594
3:28	106, 278, 287, 396, 402, 408, 463	6:16	520
		6:17	191
3:29	579	6:18	617
4:1-7	60		
4:1	143	*Eph*	
4:2	168	1:1	50
4:3-10	236	1:2	47
4:3	143, 271	1:3	369
4:5	113, 286, 354	1:17	64, 131
4:6	48, 317, 449, 550, 614	1:19	246
4:7	579	1:20-23	548, 555
4:9	311	1:20-22	554
4:11	538, 605	1:20	543
4:14	111	1:21	553
4:15	130, 464	1:23	460
4:18	290, 294	2:1-10	236
4:19	141, 194	2:1	534
4:21	354	2:6	541
4:28	107	2:9	100
5:1	601	2:16	460
5:2	50, 284, 612	2:20-21	161

2:20	155, 156
2:21	493
3:1	82, 612
3:3-5	132
3:3	64
3:4-5	125
3:6	460
3:10-11	453
3:13	82
4:1-16	459, 460, 461
4:1	275
4:2-3	219
4:2	480
4:5-6	319
4:5	314
4:11-12	451
4:11	158, 468, 469, 498
4:12	450, 453, 493
4:16	453, 493
4:17-24	236
4:29	493
4:31	218
4:32–5:2	219
5:3-5	218
5:5	221, 230
5:8	236
5:9	219
5:14	543
5:19	369, 495, 502, 518
5:20	237
5:21	259
5:22-24	515, 521
5:22	514
6:4	372, 522
6:5	119
6:12	369, 553, 579

Phil

1:1	43, 50, 172, 196, 352, 469, 585
1:2	47, 54, 317
1:3-11	56, 59
1:3-4	57
1:3	56, 57
1:4	56, 57, 58
1:6	65
1:7	63, 356

1:10-11	59
1:10	59, 65, 389
1:14	596
1:15-18	539
1:18	223, 412
1:22	583
1:25	592
1:26	552
1:27	63, 138, 601
1:28	174, 593
1:30	357, 361
2:1-2	481
2:4	386, 481
2:5-11	92, 127, 385, 518
2:5	138
2:6-11	317, 548, 551
2:7	295, 347
2:8	91, 92
2:9-10	76
2:10	237
2:11	48, 317, 334, 446
2:12	119, 379, 552, 601
2:16	65, 158, 358, 361, 476, 538, 583, 605
2:17-18	481
2:17	191
2:19-24	197
2:19	198
2:20	196
2:22	196, 197
2:23	198
2:25	51, 146, 198, 336, 606
2:28	198
2:29-30	603
2:30	583, 597, 606
3:3	100
3:5	50, 527
3:6	190
3:8	353
3:10	108, 246
3:11	543
3:13-14	358, 361
3:14	109, 285, 360, 361
3:16	212, 412
3:17	193, 369
3:18	91, 92
3:20	63

3:21	179, 554
4:1	362, 379, 601
4:2-3	514, 516, 603
4:2	5
4:3	146, 606
4:8-9	599
4:8	219
4:9	520
4:10-20	606
4:10	3
4:12	183
4:14-18	591, 592
4:14	302, 412
4:15	341, 346
4:16	338
4:18	3
4:20-23	594
4:20	48, 317
4:21	607, 609
4:22	73, 585
4:23	617
Col	
1:1	50, 51, 196
1:2	47
1:3	57
1:9	369, 453
1:11	480
1:14	534
1:15-20	320, 518, 555
1:16	553
1:18-24	460, 461
1:18	462, 543
1:21-22	236
1:22	65
1:23	583, 612
1:24	82, 606
1:26-27	125
1:28	498
2:1	82
2:7	156
2:8-19	459
2:10	553
2:11-13	541
2:12	531, 541, 543
2:13	236
2:17-19	460

2:18	100, 177, 181
2:23	177
3:5-9	236
3:5	218, 230
3:8	218
3:11	463
3:12	219, 480
3:15	460
3:16	369, 495, 498, 518
3:17	237
3:18	514, 515, 521
4:5	223
4:8	198
4:10-14	607
4:10	331
4:15	78, 514, 611
4:16	611
4:18	2, 612
1 Thess	
1:1	44, 196, 317
1:2–2:12	59
1:2-10	56
1:2-3	57
1:2	56, 57, 58
1:3	317, 482, 483, 485, 487, 600
1:5	116, 120
1:6	193, 391
1:7	105, 369
1:8	101, 538, 588, 605
1:9	286, 447, 507
1:10	59, 60, 64, 92, 102, 113, 246, 317, 529, 543
2	175
2:1-12	170
2:1	534, 538
2:2	183, 190, 342, 357, 358, 361, 558, 593
2:3	219
2:4	172, 174, 335, 348, 358, 362, 386, 390, 491, 533
2:5	83, 347
2:6-7	341
2:6	51
2:7-8	141
2:7	141, 143, 194, 336, 486
2:8	477, 601

2:9-12	235	4:14	92, 527, 529, 530, 534, 536
2:9	23, 185, 331, 337, 342, 583	4:15-18	574, 581
2:10-12	201	4:15-17	552, 580
2:10	105, 347	4:15	64, 264, 536, 552, 575, 579
2:11-12	141, 192	4:16-17	188
2:11	141, 194	4:16	496, 527, 545, 580
2:12	59, 202, 283, 355, 579	4:17	580, 581
2:13	101, 105, 533	4:18	491, 578, 583
2:14	51, 588	5:1-11	59, 291
2:15	130, 386	5:2	65, 230
2:16	65	5:3	212
2:17-20	591	5:4	158, 230
2:17	107, 206	5:5-8	561
2:18	50, 129, 612	5:6-8	236
2:19	64, 362, 476, 552	5:6	583, 601
3:1-6	197	5:8	107, 482, 485, 487, 600
3:1	196, 341, 482	5:9-10	102
3:2-3	597	5:10	92, 326, 529, 601
3:2	63, 146, 196, 198, 606	5:11	155, 491
3:5	341, 482, 538, 583, 605	5:12-24	594
3:6	405, 482, 597	5:12-22	599
3:7	293	5:12-13	603, 605, 607
3:8	303, 601	5:12	229, 469, 538
3:9	481	5:13	158
3:10	606	5:14-15	479
3:11-13	59, 317, 591	5:14	5, 480
3:11	48, 201, 317	5:15	480
3:12	485	5:16	481
3:13	48, 60, 64, 65, 317, 552	5:19-22	445, 455, 519
4:1-8	355	5:19-20	491, 513, 523
4:1	5, 283, 386	5:20	111, 455
4:3-8	261	5:23	60, 64, 65, 520, 552
4:3-6	253	5:24	66, 373
4:3	221	5:26	609, 612
4:5	209, 217, 223, 236, 248, 277, 371, 447, 561	5:27	3, 18
		5:28	617
4:6	481		
4:8	493	*2 Thess*	
4:9-10	485	1:1	196
4:10-12	278	1:2	47
4:10	5	1:3	57
4:11	264, 421	1:6-10	59
4:12	223	1:7	64
4:13-18	59, 541, 545, 547, 575, 579	1:8	159
4:13-17	536	2:1	552
4:13	367, 536	2:2	541
4:14-16	246	2:8	355, 552

2:15	601
3:3	373
3:8	185
3:9	369
3:14	194, 217
3:17	2, 612
3:18	617

1 Tim

1:1	50, 51
1:2	196, 197
1:9-10	218
1:9	355
1:10	236, 238
1:12-17	236
1:12	388
1:13	293, 538
1:16	293
1:18-20	208
1:18	358, 455
1:20	208, 212
2:5-6	319
2:5	314
2:7	107, 469, 498
2:11-15	515, 521
2:11-12	514
2:12	521
3:1	138
3:2-4	219
3:6-7	223
3:8-10	219
3:10	65
3:11-12	219
4:7-8	358
4:7	358
4:12	219, 369
4:14	63
5:3-16	268
5:17	341
5:18	334, 339, 342
6:2	285
6:4-5	218
6:5	259
6:11	219
6:12	358, 362
6:14	284

6:16	581
6:18	219

2 Tim

1:1	50, 51
1:2	196, 197, 200
1:3	388
1:6	63
1:9-10	125
1:11	107, 469
2:4-6	338
2:5	358, 360
2:8	543
2:11	541
2:13	373
2:18	541
2:22-25	219
3:2-5	218
3:3	260
3:10	219, 480
4:7-8	358
4:7	358, 361, 362
4:11	498
4:14	455
4:17	560
4:19	608, 609
4:20	23
4:21	514, 607

Titus

1:1	50
1:2-3	125
1:4	197
1:6	65
1:7	65, 168, 218
1:8	219
1:12	561
2:2-10	219
2:7	369
2:8	194
3:3	218, 236
3:10	372
3:13	80

Phlm

1	43, 50, 51, 196, 601, 606
2	52, 73, 514, 611

3	47, 54, 317	1:27	268
4–7	56	2:1	131
4	56, 57	2:8	302
5	482, 585	2:14	560
6	593	2:16	560
7	606	2:19	302
9	5, 50, 612	3:6	159
10	141, 192, 193, 195, 196, 199	3:14	100
11	236	4:15	593
14	293	5:7	552
16	199, 601	5:8	552
19–25	594		
19	2, 50, 610, 612	*1 Pet*	
20	606	1:2	54
22	201, 591	1:3	543
23	607	1:7	64, 157, 159
24	146, 606	1:13	64
25	617	1:20-21	125
		1:21	543
Heb		1:24	111
1:3	320, 553	2:1	218
1:12	414	2:2	143
1:13–2:8	554	2:4-5	161
1:13	548, 553	2:5	369
1:14	579	2:10	236
2:6-9	548	2:25	236
2:14	579	3:1-6	515, 521
5:12-13	143	3:1	514
6:3	593	3:20	63
6:10	588	3:22	548, 553
6:12	579	4:1-4	236
7:26	219	4:3	218, 230
9:28	63	4:10-11	158, 451
10:28	339	4:10	63, 168, 450
12:1	358, 361	4:11	468
12:5-11	202	4:12-19	160
12:6	436	4:12	157
12:17	579	4:13	64
12:29	159	4:15	218, 230
13:2	4	5:2	3
		5:14	609, 612
Jas			
1:1	47	*2 Pet*	
1:9	100	1:2	54
1:12	616	1:6	260,
1:18	551	1:16	552
1:23	487	1:19	302

2:4	232
2:8	355
3:4	552
3:10	159
3:12	159, 552
3:16	53

1 John

1:1-3	125
2:3	284
2:4	284
2:28	552
3:22	284
3:24	284

2 John

3	54

3 John

2	55
6	302

Jude

3	358
6	232

Rev

1:1	64
1:4	47, 54
1:5	129
1:10	422, 496
1:11	611
2:1–3:22	611
2:23	133
3:18	157
4:1	496
4:8	518
4:10	510
4:11	518
5:8	495
5:9-10	518
5:14	510
7:11	510
8:2	496, 580
8:6	496
8:13	496
9:14	496

9:20	230
11:15	580
11:16	510
12:1	535
12:3	535
12:17	284
14:2	495
14:3-4	518
14:4	293, 551
14:12	284
15:2	495
16:14-16	574
17:13	77
17:17	77
18:12	157
18:17	470
18:22	496
19:4	510
19:10	510
21:8	218
21:18-19	150
22:8	510
22:15	218, 230
22:20	614

First Corinthians

1 Cor

1–10	167
1–7	39
1–6	35
1–4	14, 34, 39, 76, 88, 89, 117, 121, 181, 232, 450, 451, 476, 596
1–3	88, 89
1:1–6:11	11, 12, 40
1:1–5:8	12
1:1–4:21	12
1:1-9	29, 41, 48, 282
1:1-3	5, 29, 41, 49, 64
1:1-2	330
1:1	3, 5, 7, 49–51, 55, 56, 68, 85, 101, 108, 109, 115, 145, 155, 156, 172, 197, 274, 275, 330, 334, 335, 336, 468, 532, 537, 598, 610, 612, 613
1:2-3	1

1:2	1, 8, 11, 17, 21, 25, 26, 45, 46, 49, 50, 51–53, 60, 64, 65, 66, 68, 76, 77, 108, 109, 151, 152, 153, 154, 160, 161, 167, 201, 206, 211, 213, 214, 217, 222, 227, 231, 232, 237, 238, 264, 267, 271, 274, 275, 283, 368, 389, 404, 414, 423, 448, 520, 526, 538, 560, 561, 585, 586, 605, 606, 608, 609
1:3-9	58
1:3-4	134
1:3	53–54, 55, 56, 61, 64, 267, 315, 317, 388, 599, 611, 615, 617
1:4–4:21	88
1:4-9	6, 20, 29, 55, 170
1:4-7	503
1:4-5	124, 451
1:4	47, 57, 58, 61–62, 83, 134, 155, 388, 503
1:5-7	26, 441
1:5	58, 59, 61, 62, 63, 84, 101, 186, 201, 234, 310
1:6	58, 59, 62–63, 81, 118
1:7-9	60, 614
1:7-8	60, 151, 153, 174
1:7	27, 58, 59, 63–65, 148, 171, 182, 186, 249, 261, 452
1:8-9	599
1:8	58, 59, 63, 64, 65, 96, 213, 560
1:9	45, 50, 58, 60, 61, 65–66, 108, 274, 275, 373, 376, 379, 381, 387, 550, 560
1:10–15:58	30, 67
1:10–4:21	88, 146, 185, 196
1:10–4:16	63, 179, 192, 195
1:10–4:5	176, 179
1:10–3:23	14, 162
1:10–3:4	89
1:10–2:16	162–163
1:10–2:5	15
1:10-25	406
1:10-17	30, 67, 87, 140
1:10-12	492
1:10-11	45, 176
1:10	5, 6, 8, 9, 13, 14, 17, 19, 20, 21, 27, 45, 47, 51, 64, 65, 69, 70, 75, 76–78, 82, 84, 87, 109, 124, 127, 153, 163, 167, 169, 170, 173, 179, 185, 191, 195, 206, 209, 211, 222, 237, 293, 373, 394, 404, 421, 465, 488, 560, 579, 583, 594, 598, 600, 604, 609, 615
1:11-17	87
1:11-12	16, 170
1:11	5, 9, 16, 24, 51, 76, 78–79, 98, 140, 199, 206, 209, 264, 346, 418, 421, 514, 597,
1:12	18, 50, 71, 73, 74, 75, 78, 79–81, 84, 124, 138, 140, 142, 144, 145, 162, 164, 166, 170, 176, 180, 190, 251, 331, 336, 515, 532, 535, 597, 612
1:13-17	27, 139
1:13	50, 75, 77, 81–83, 84, 85, 91, 92, 124, 222, 237, 326, 368, 432, 522, 530, 552, 612, 615
1:14-17	83, 107, 468
1:14-16	609
1:14	51, 79, 81, 83–84, 85, 98, 418
1:15	84, 85, 124, 222, 368
1:16	73, 74, 84–85, 98, 346, 418, 538, 603, 604
1:17–4:21	80
1:17–4:20	89
1:17–3:3	89
1:17-18	115
1:17	18, 51, 75, 83, 85, 91, 92, 96, 97, 101, 102, 103, 107, 115, 116, 117, 118, 119, 120, 128, 149, 156, 201, 281, 347, 362, 530
1:18–4:21	30, 59, 86, 87, 90, 150, 155, 170, 220, 453
1:18–4:5	142
1:18–3:23	83, 87, 94, 149
1:18–3:20	88
1:18–2:16	85, 163, 578
1:18-31	30, 42, 87, 89, 98, 99, 103, 114, 117, 122, 123, 356
1:18-25	91, 98, 114, 482, 506

1:18-24	90		1:30	26, 94, 103, 112–113, 123,
1:18-23	26			128, 164, 174, 208, 249, 320,
1:18-19	87			405
1:18	9, 27, 59, 85, 88, 90, 91, 92,		1:31	7, 90, 91, 94, 95, 96, 99, 100,
	93, 94, 101–103, 106, 107,			103, 112, 113, 166, 206, 213,
	109, 111, 116, 119, 128, 129,			218, 582
	136, 171, 201, 212, 246, 326,		2:1-16	492
	530, 533		2:1-5	6, 30, 62, 63, 85, 87, 104,
1:19-25	93			115, 116, 117, 118, 121, 123,
1:19	7, 91, 93, 94, 95, 96, 103,			128, 139, 167, 188, 202, 453
	113, 151, 162, 165, 218, 326,		2:1-4	7, 185
	582		2:1	9, 51, 62, 76, 85, 116,
1:20-24	499			117–118, 119, 122, 123, 139,
1:20	93, 96, 103–105, 111, 114,			142, 172, 185, 201, 475, 492
	129, 133, 163, 177, 201, 468		2:2	63, 91, 92, 102, 116,
1:21-25	104			118–119, 149, 156, 530
1:21	21, 93, 103, 104, 105, 107,		2:3-5	538
	111, 115, 119, 123, 130, 133,		2:3	116, 118, 119, 185
	134, 163, 508, 533, 544		2:4-5	119, 201
1:22-24	92, 106, 276, 354		2:4	85, 105, 116, 119–120, 128,
1:22	93, 97, 104, 105–107, 112,			132, 185, 201, 453
	389, 508		2:5	116, 119, 120–121, 201
1:23-24	103, 128, 136		2:6–3:23	143
1:23	91, 92, 107–108, 134, 361,		2:6-16	15, 26, 30, 42, 87, 121, 122,
	362, 530			123, 124, 125, 126, 127, 128,
1:24	45, 50, 90, 94, 102, 103, 106,			135, 136, 137, 138, 139, 140,
	107, 108, 112, 114, 123, 128,			142, 143, 144, 145, 153, 155,
	201, 206, 275, 389, 406			160, 165, 167, 171, 174, 202,
1:25-29	108			241, 373, 453
1:25	90, 108–109, 110, 134		2:6-13	186
1:26-31	90, 91, 93, 104, 109, 114		2:6-9	125
1:26-29	423		2:6-7	184, 553
1:26-28	90, 114, 184, 189		2:6	103, 104, 105, 106, 122, 123,
1:26	9, 23, 24, 25, 45, 50, 51, 76,			124, 125, 126, 128–129, 130,
	79, 83, 91, 99, 109–110, 111,			135, 138, 139, 143, 163, 170,
	112, 113, 114, 156, 163, 164,			245, 373, 468, 486, 541
	186, 190, 201, 228, 231, 233,		2:7-10	125, 132
	235, 275, 280, 285, 325, 373,		2:7	105, 116, 122, 123, 124,
	401, 422			129–130, 132, 137, 172, 492
1:27-29	110		2:8	91, 92, 104, 124, 127,
1:27-28	94, 165, 189, 465			130–131, 137, 138, 246, 429,
1:27	100, 109, 110–111, 114, 119,			464, 530
	130, 134, 163, 423		2:9	7, 17, 25, 94, 95, 122, 123,
1:28	111, 163, 232, 245, 485, 567			125, 129, 131–132, 135, 138,
1:29-31	181			139, 174, 218, 311, 332, 563,
1:29	100, 106, 109, 111–112, 113,			582
	127, 140, 166, 170, 206, 566		2:10-16	125, 132

2:10-11	133, 134
2:10	103, 122, 123, 124, 127, 128, 132–133, 134, 137, 151, 448
2:11-16	27, 438
2:11-15	501
2:11	123, 124, 126, 127, 133, 136, 137, 448
2:12-16	522
2:12	103, 107, 122, 123, 124, 125, 134, 135, 163, 361, 448
2:13-15	212
2:13	116, 122, 128, 134–135, 136, 201, 373, 489
2:14-16	125, 127, 153, 212
2:14-15	126, 127, 136, 571
2:14	103, 124, 127, 128, 135–136, 137, 335, 448, 510, 567
2:15	103, 117, 124, 127, 129, 135, 136–137, 172, 220, 335, 510
2:16	7, 70, 77, 94, 96, 100, 107, 122, 123, 125, 127, 132, 137–138, 139, 361, 387
3	147, 597
3:1-23	15
3:1-17	87, 163, 275
3:1-15	597
3:1-9	30, 123, 139, 141, 167
3:1-4	71, 140, 143, 367
3:1-3	144, 505, 541
3:1-2	8, 142, 147, 178, 194, 202, 468
3:1	9, 26, 51, 76, 118, 136, 139, 140, 142–143, 151, 153, 163, 170, 179, 194, 199, 215, 453, 486, 507, 541, 551
3:2	141, 143, 146, 147, 186
3:3-4	140, 170
3:3	79, 140, 141, 143–144, 283, 286, 338, 492, 558
3:4-17	143
3:4-9	176
3:4	50, 80, 140, 141, 142, 145, 166, 597, 612
3:5–4:5	88, 170, 179
3:5-9	148, 178, 186, 261, 339, 341
3:5	50, 80, 141, 142, 145, 148, 155, 172, 280, 281, 356, 469, 544, 597, 598, 612
3:6-9	8, 150
3:6-8	148
3:6	80, 104, 141, 142, 145–146, 149, 156, 181, 468, 597
3:7	141, 146, 149, 156, 167, 566
3:8	141, 145, 146, 148, 149, 150, 159, 190, 349, 583
3:9-17	490
3:9-15	493
3:9	20, 25, 141, 142, 146–147, 148, 149, 153, 154, 155, 156, 161, 167, 312, 356, 566, 598, 606
3:10-17	8, 30, 148, 151, 152, 154, 161, 163, 583
3:10-15	16, 147, 148, 152, 153, 156, 159, 160, 161, 162
3:10-13	170, 261
3:10	61, 144, 145, 148, 149, 150, 151, 155–156, 157, 164, 167, 181, 195, 325, 341, 373, 468, 490, 584
3:11	148, 149, 150, 156
3:12-16	419
3:12-15	146, 150
3:12	150, 151, 156, 157, 158, 160
3:13-17	27
3:13-15	150, 171, 207, 211, 223
3:13-14	145, 159
3:13	59, 145, 148, 149, 150, 151, 153, 157, 158–159, 161, 162, 170, 173, 174, 206, 213, 422
3:14-17	170
3:14	149, 150, 152, 156, 159, 160, 349
3:15	102, 148, 149, 150, 152, 153, 154, 156, 159, 160, 161, 213
3:16-17	25, 147, 148, 152, 153, 161, 208, 241
3:16	82, 148, 149, 150, 153, 154, 160–161, 235, 249, 318, 349, 447, 448
3:17	146, 149, 150, 151, 153, 154, 160, 161, 202, 220, 223, 312, 438, 523, 585
3:18-23	30, 162, 163
3:18-20	87

3:18 — 93, 104, 139, 155, 163, 164–165, 181, 522

3:19-20 — 87, 162, 165

3:19 — 7, 94, 95, 134, 163, 165, 181, 218, 332, 582

3:20 — 7, 94, 103, 165, 545

3:21-23 — 62, 182, 413, 555

3:21-22 — 186

3:21 — 99, 100, 164, 166, 206

3:22 — 50, 80, 145, 163, 164, 166, 170, 172, 176, 331, 336, 532, 597, 612

3:23 — 26, 122, 166–167, 171, 249, 400, 552

4 — 195, 594

4:1-5 — 27, 30, 167, 169, 170, 171, 181, 335

4:1-4 — 170

4:1-2 — 168, 170, 345, 348

4:1 — 8, 116, 145, 170, 171–172, 186, 281, 470, 598

4:2 — 167, 172, 181, 293, 348

4:3-5 — 169, 170, 178, 181, 207, 211

4:3 — 59, 137, 167, 169, 170, 171, 172–173, 181, 189, 207, 220, 335, 373, 510

4:4-5 — 171, 173, 220

4:4 — 137, 167, 169, 171, 172, 173, 335, 510

4:5 — 59, 122, 146, 150, 159, 167, 169, 170, 173–174, 179, 181, 202, 223, 302, 510

4:6-21 — 87

4:6-7 — 30, 175

4:6 — 9, 51, 76, 79, 80, 100, 142, 145, 170, 176, 178, 179–181, 182, 193, 201, 206, 210, 213, 232, 312, 480, 516, 597

4:7-8 — 179

4:7 — 100, 112, 178, 181, 182, 188, 202, 206, 213

4:8-13 — 30, 182

4:8 — 26, 171, 178, 179, 181, 182, 183, 186–188, 191, 202, 235, 243, 503, 541

4:9-13 — 178, 179, 182

4:9 — 24, 179, 182, 188, 189, 191, 473, 537, 561, 598

4:10-13 — 183, 190, 503, 559

4:10 — 107, 109, 110, 179, 184, 185, 188–189, 190, 361, 379

4:11-12 — 184, 185, 189–191

4:11 — 183, 184, 186, 191

4:12-13 — 184

4:12 — 185, 190, 331, 346, 538

4:13 — 182, 183, 184, 185, 190, 191, 598

4:14-21 — 10, 71, 141, 184, 191, 195, 206, 367, 505, 594

4:14-17 — 8

4:14-16 — 30, 87, 192, 196, 216, 486

4:14-15 — 194, 601, 616

4:14 — 1, 3, 9, 10, 17, 71, 95, 141, 194, 202, 344, 347, 372, 377, 379, 618

4:15 — 9, 142, 194–195, 196, 199, 200, 202, 235, 468, 504, 533

4:16 — 5, 7, 27, 49, 76, 141, 169, 170, 176, 179, 185, 191, 193, 195, 388, 391, 597, 598, 604

4:17-21 — 24, 30, 194, 195, 198, 216, 596

4:17 — 3, 9, 11, 35, 47, 52, 53, 71, 172, 191, 194, 197, 199–201, 202, 216, 283, 498, 520, 595, 597, 601

4:18 — 100, 106, 177, 190, 197, 201, 206, 210, 480, 596

4:19-21 — 3

4:19 — 100, 106, 176, 177, 201, 206, 210, 440, 480

4:20 — 201–202, 235, 579

4:21 — 192, 202, 616

5–16 — 14

5–7 — 14, 16, 38, 181, 204, 219

5–6 — 33, 204, 205, 226

5 — 15, 203, 205, 215, 216, 220, 224, 225, 463

5:1–7:40 — 30, 203, 205

5:1–6:11 — 220

5:1-13 — 45, 96, 154, 177, 561

5:1-8	12, 13, 26, 30, 205, 206, 215, 216, 220, 225, 226, 245	6:1-8	169, 238
		6:1-6	171, 173, 227, 235
5:1-5	215, 445	6:1-3	229
5:1	16, 19, 21, 118, 209–210, 214, 217, 221, 225, 258, 404, 447, 506	6:1-2	585
		6:1	21, 169, 220, 225, 226, 227, 230, 231
5:2	100, 106, 176, 177, 181, 206, 210–211, 213, 220, 480, 598	6:2-4	27
		6:2	82, 160, 188, 220, 225, 228, 231–232, 436, 438
5:3-5	27, 169		
5:3-4	204, 220	6:3-4	227
5:3	3, 9, 70, 169, 206, 211, 220, 233, 552, 606	6:3	7, 82, 160, 220, 225, 231, 232, 235, 473
5:4-5	211, 220	6:4	21, 111, 225, 232, 234, 238
5:4	47, 65, 68, 76, 206, 207, 211–212, 213, 237, 560	6:5-8	438
		6:5	18, 51, 181, 225, 228, 233–234, 561
5:5	9, 59, 102, 158, 206, 207, 208, 211, 212–213, 215, 436, 541, 561	6:6	21, 51, 71, 118, 220, 225, 227, 231, 233, 234, 271, 341, 383, 508
5:6-8	208		
5:6	6, 82, 100, 160, 206, 210, 213–214, 222, 235, 294, 561	6:7-8	227, 259
		6:7	203, 209, 225, 228, 234, 235, 436, 482
5:7-8	214		
5:7	63, 214, 220, 432	6:8	51, 71, 118, 227, 231, 233, 235
5:8	214–215		
5:9-13	12, 30, 208, 216, 220, 229	6:9-20	250
5:9-10	222	6:9-11	227, 238
5:9	1, 4, 11, 12, 13, 21, 45, 95, 192, 216, 219, 220–221, 223, 241, 251, 344, 561	6:9-10	218, 225, 230, 232, 235–236, 561, 580
		6:9	82, 160, 202, 221, 222, 228, 229, 235, 236, 238, 240, 560, 579
5:10-11	220, 230, 370		
5:10	217, 218, 219, 221–222, 223, 229, 230, 240	6:10-11	219
		6:10	202, 219, 221, 222, 236, 370, 579
5:11	1, 13, 17, 45, 51, 95, 217, 218, 219, 221, 222–223, 230, 240, 241, 251, 347	6:11	47, 76, 118, 122, 211, 219, 222, 229, 236–238, 281, 292, 448
5:12-13	225	6:12–11:16	40
5:12	21, 206, 209, 217, 220, 223	6:12–10:23	271, 291, 300
5:13	7, 21, 94, 95, 207, 208, 212, 214, 217, 218, 219, 220, 223–224, 225, 230, 368, 387, 561	6:12–7:40	204
		6:12-20	11, 12, 26, 30, 225, 230, 239, 240, 241, 250, 251, 254, 262, 292, 301
6	15, 160, 203, 204, 224, 238, 246	6:12-14	239
6:1-20	13	6:12-13	13
6:1-11	12, 21, 30, 59, 62, 96, 98, 177, 189, 203, 219, 220, 224, 225, 226, 227, 231, 233, 234, 238, 239, 506	6:12	19, 134, 166, 187, 203, 239, 241, 243–244, 245, 248, 249,

	250, 253, 254, 255, 259, 271, 272, 281, 325, 327, 335, 341, 346, 350, 352, 353, 359, 383, 386, 400, 477, 480, 515, 516, 560, 561
6:13-20	249
6:13-16	246
6:13-14	241, 242
6:13	186, 187, 221, 239, 240, 244–246, 248, 253, 292, 325, 486, 515, 541
6:14	64, 212, 241, 246, 292
6:15-18	266
6:15-17	239
6:15-16	247
6:15	82, 160, 235, 239, 240, 242, 247
6:16	7, 25, 82, 94, 160, 224, 235, 239, 240, 242, 247–248, 250, 258, 267, 294, 301, 410
6:17	247, 248, 250, 292
6:18-20	239
6:18	221, 224, 239, 240, 241, 248–249, 250, 294, 378
6:19-20	242, 250
6:19	82, 160, 161, 174, 235, 240, 241, 242, 243, 247, 248, 249, 281, 448
6:20	26, 164, 240, 243, 248, 249–250, 286, 466
7–14	252
7	15, 16, 45, 59, 98, 204, 205, 240, 241, 249, 254, 255, 261, 264, 273, 276, 277, 290, 291, 295, 298, 302, 343, 400, 403, 463
7:1–16:12	13
7:1–9:23	12
7:1–8:13	11, 12
7:1-40	12, 204, 499
7:1-17	275
7:1-16	15, 16, 254, 258, 274, 276, 288, 289, 298, 402
7:1-7	30, 251, 252, 253, 255, 260, 261
7:1-6	295
7:1-5	33, 415
7:1	4, 5, 10, 13, 16, 134, 203, 204, 216, 221, 240, 244, 252, 253, 257–258, 261, 265, 289, 290, 294, 298, 300, 301, 304, 309, 421, 441, 445, 515, 533, 588, 597
7:2-7	262, 263, 298
7:2-6	268
7:2-4	255, 262, 289, 294
7:2	221, 241, 252, 254, 256, 258, 263, 290, 293, 294, 302, 516
7:3-4	296
7:3	256, 258–259
7:4	241, 244, 256, 258, 259, 271, 400
7:5-7	261, 268
7:5	212, 256, 258, 259–260, 268, 400
7:6-7	261
7:6	18, 252, 256, 259, 260, 261, 289
7:7	145, 149, 252, 256, 260–261, 263, 268, 295, 400, 452
7:8-24	261
7:8-16	30, 262
7:8-14	294
7:8-9	262, 290, 300
7:8	8, 18, 118, 193, 252, 256, 258, 260, 263, 264, 268, 270, 294, 296, 415
7:9	252, 260, 263, 265, 268–269, 290, 293, 294, 301, 302, 361
7:10-24	272, 290
7:10-11	70, 262, 270, 289, 300
7:10	6, 8, 132, 204, 260, 264, 265, 269, 270, 272, 273, 289, 290, 292, 342, 343, 395, 400, 415, 421, 538
7:11	263, 264, 268, 269–270, 271, 281, 294, 400, 518
7:12-16	262, 265, 275, 506
7:12-15	21, 383, 506, 508
7:12-14	263, 290
7:12-13	262, 264, 270–271
7:12	7, 8, 18, 51, 234, 260, 263, 264, 267, 268, 269, 270, 271, 289, 290, 292, 400

7:13	234, 263, 268, 269, 270, 271, 272	7:25-26	298, 299
7:14-15	154	7:25	5, 7, 13, 70, 77, 172, 204, 251, 253, 260, 288, 289, 290, 293, 294, 297, 299, 304, 348, 533, 588, 597
7:14	51, 234, 259, 265, 266, 267, 271, 272, 273, 292, 400, 506		
7:15-16	263, 268, 272	7:26	253, 289, 290, 292, 293–294, 295, 298, 299, 302, 347
7:15	45, 50, 51, 234, 263, 264, 268, 269, 270, 271–272, 275, 277, 281, 294, 387, 400, 409, 440, 520	7:27-31	298
		7:27-28	293, 299
7:16	265, 272, 290, 506	7:27	263, 271, 290, 294, 298, 299, 301
7:17-24	15, 25, 30, 91, 204, 261, 262, 271, 273, 274, 276, 277, 280, 281, 287, 288, 345, 463	7:28	263, 288, 290, 293, 294, 295, 301, 303
7:17-18	285	7:29-31	27, 288, 291, 292, 295, 297
7:17	11, 45, 47, 50, 52, 53, 145, 201, 274, 275, 276, 277, 282–283, 284, 286, 287, 290, 301, 387, 520, 588	7:29	9, 18, 51, 76, 171, 291, 293, 294–295, 364
		7:30-31	295
		7:31	59, 292, 295, 349
7:18–8:4	297	7:32-35	260, 288, 294, 297
7:18-19	276, 279	7:32-34	290, 385, 386, 465
7:18	45, 50, 275, 279, 281, 282, 283–284, 285, 294, 387	7:32	268, 289, 290, 291, 292, 295–296, 297
7:19	277, 278, 279, 283, 284, 286	7:33-34	292, 296
7:20	45, 50, 109, 145, 274, 275, 276, 285, 286, 287, 290, 301, 387	7:33	289, 296
		7:34	268, 288, 289, 290, 292, 293, 296, 297, 299, 300
7:21-24	254	7:35	18, 19, 244, 288, 290, 292, 293, 297, 298, 390, 453, 477
7:21-23	276, 279		
7:21-22	287	7:36-40	30, 298
7:21	45, 50, 269, 271, 275, 280, 281, 283, 285–286, 287, 294, 301, 387, 409, 440, 518	7:36-38	298, 299, 301, 304
		7:36	263, 288, 293, 299, 300, 301–302, 303, 480, 481
7:22-23	249, 280, 329	7:37	288, 293, 299, 300, 301, 302, 347, 583
7:22	45, 50, 165, 172, 200, 244, 275, 279, 280, 286, 290, 301, 345, 348, 350, 387	7:38-39	290
		7:38	263, 288, 293, 299, 300, 302–303
7:23	26, 113, 164, 249, 280, 281, 284, 286, 287	7:39-40	298
7:24	9, 45, 50, 51, 76, 145, 274, 275, 276, 277, 278, 286–287, 290, 301, 387	7:39	200, 204, 263, 265, 266, 270, 271, 290, 292, 300, 301, 303, 304, 536
7:25-40	15, 16, 254, 274, 288, 289, 293, 297, 298, 299, 303	7:40	7, 70, 77, 118, 149, 153, 172, 204, 245, 270, 288, 289, 299, 300, 301, 303–304, 448, 476
7:25-38	276, 298		
7:25-35	30, 287, 288, 292, 294	8–16	40
7:25-28	288	8–14	46

8–10	14, 15, 34, 181, 219, 305, 307, 308, 319, 360, 378, 382, 385, 388, 390, 394, 441, 443, 451, 472, 506, 601
8	15, 25, 34, 45, 98, 186, 306, 307, 308, 309, 330, 377, 378, 385
8:1–11:1	30, 244, 304, 307, 308, 312, 392, 444
8:1–9:27	12
8:1-13	13, 306, 308, 377, 378
8:1-11	416
8:1-7	454
8:1-6	312
8:1-3	30, 306, 307, 308, 309, 313, 368, 441, 475, 487
8:1	5, 13, 19, 59, 100, 106, 155, 177, 244, 252, 253, 288, 310, 311–312, 318, 319, 321, 324, 326, 346, 369, 380, 386, 453, 454, 480, 488, 493, 533, 588, 597, 616
8:2-3	132, 523
8:2	163, 165, 310, 312, 480, 486, 522
8:3	5, 310, 311, 312, 523
8:4-15	385
8:4-6	30, 306, 313, 320, 380, 384
8:4	252, 253, 309, 311, 313, 315, 318–319, 324, 326, 369, 376, 378, 380, 588, 597
8:5-6	319
8:5	24, 25, 313, 314, 315, 319
8:6	25, 26, 62, 112, 167, 313, 314, 315, 316, 317, 318, 319–320, 321, 323, 324, 326, 359, 370, 381, 385, 399, 400, 403, 405, 413, 450, 452, 453, 507, 555, 574
8:7–9:27	308
8:7-13	30, 306, 321, 327, 342, 390
8:7	59, 244, 319, 321, 324–325, 326, 380, 386, 414, 447, 487
8:8	244, 253, 322, 325, 327, 330, 359
8:9-13	322
8:9	109, 156, 243, 305, 306, 323, 325, 329, 330, 341, 373, 389
8:10	19, 24, 33, 59, 155, 304, 309, 312, 319, 322, 324, 326, 330, 342, 376, 386, 387
8:11-13	323, 389, 438
8:11-12	369
8:11	51, 59, 82, 323, 326, 351, 352, 356, 359, 378, 379, 390, 391, 428, 429, 559
8:12	51, 323, 324, 326–327, 386, 438
8:13–9:1	13
8:13	7, 51, 306, 311, 318, 323, 324, 327, 369, 370, 378, 388, 390
9	62, 167, 193, 244, 306, 308, 327, 329, 342, 346, 356, 357, 361, 363, 385, 388, 443, 472, 474, 529, 532, 588
9:1–10:13	15
9:1-27	7, 324
9:1-23	11, 533
9:1-18	12, 378
9:1-14	30, 327, 350
9:1-12	333
9:1-2	44, 329, 344
9:1	65, 82, 117, 200, 244, 330, 334–335, 345, 348, 350, 353, 537, 544, 560, 583
9:2	16, 50, 116, 200, 335, 498, 503, 532, 533, 597
9:3-14	169, 345
9:3-12	402
9:3	10, 137, 167, 169, 328, 330, 335, 344, 510
9:4-7	339
9:4-6	332, 338, 341, 342, 347
9:4	306, 329, 332, 335, 342
9:5-12	347
9:5-6	331, 332, 532
9:5	51, 80, 244, 260, 306, 329, 330, 332, 336–337, 468, 532, 597
9:6	244, 306, 329, 330, 331, 332, 337–338, 344, 346

9:7	143, 244, 329, 330, 332, 338, 342
9:8-10	8, 223, 332
9:8-9	340
9:8	18, 338–339, 413, 423, 516, 558
9:9-14	342
9:9-11	342
9:9-10	339, 340, 343, 469, 550
9:9	7, 94, 95, 218, 223, 285, 329, 330, 338, 339–340, 515, 551, 582
9:10-12	332
9:10	7, 35, 94, 95, 329, 338, 340–341, 343, 359, 423, 498
9:11-12	333, 341
9:11	143, 341, 586
9:12-14	333
9:12	63, 306, 329, 330, 332, 333, 341–342, 344, 347, 349, 356, 369, 380, 482
9:13-14	342
9:13	82, 160, 235, 329, 330, 333, 342, 360, 376, 380
9:14-15	343
9:14	6, 273, 283, 334, 342, 343, 350, 352, 356, 396, 588
9:15-23	361
9:15-18	30, 116, 280, 281, 329, 343, 345, 348, 350
9:15-16	344, 346
9:15	1, 17, 95, 100, 192, 213, 294, 330, 333, 342, 344, 345, 346–347, 349, 423, 559
9:16-19	468
9:16-18	85, 185, 244
9:16	100, 213, 293, 344, 346, 347–348, 499
9:17-18	348, 349
9:17	159, 344, 345, 348–349
9:18	19, 74, 159, 306, 329, 330, 345, 349, 350, 352, 356
9:19-23	12, 30, 190, 233, 342, 349, 350, 351, 354, 356, 357, 378, 390
9:19-22	244, 356, 504
9:19	185, 244, 271, 331, 350, 352–353, 355, 356, 390
9:20-22	350
9:20-21	351, 353, 355, 356, 385, 389
9:20	19, 106, 351, 352, 353–354, 355
9:21	351, 352, 353, 354–355, 369
9:22-23	244
9:22	9, 185, 186, 189, 305, 350, 351, 353, 355–356, 357, 390, 533
9:23-24	13
9:23	355, 356, 359, 363
9:24–10:22	12, 13
9:24-27	8, 11, 24, 30, 110, 338, 357, 358, 359, 361, 378, 475, 558
9:24	82, 160, 235, 361, 362, 363
9:25	107, 361–362, 581
9:26-27	358, 362–363
9:26	362
9:27	107, 358, 362
10	25, 34, 45, 186, 306, 307, 308, 378, 382, 385, 390
10:1–11:34	12
10:1-23	11
10:1-22	307, 308, 374, 378
10:1-13	7, 25, 30, 46, 363, 364, 374, 375, 377, 380, 389, 423, 425, 481, 578, 586
10:1-12	208
10:1-11	374
10:1-5	27, 365, 370
10:1-4	366, 367
10:1	9, 51, 58, 76, 295, 367–368, 371, 405, 445
10:2-4	367, 368, 380
10:2	82, 368
10:3-4	368–369, 379, 425, 436
10:4	96, 100, 365, 368, 369, 374, 463
10:5-14	222
10:5	366, 369
10:6-13	365
10:6-11	366, 369, 374, 380
10:6-10	366
10:6-7	222
10:6	95, 366, 367, 369–370

10:7-10	370
10:7-8	371, 374
10:7	7, 25, 94, 95, 143, 186, 218, 232, 319, 364, 365, 370–371, 372, 507, 582
10:8-10	367, 371, 437
10:8	370, 371, 372, 373, 485
10:9-11	366
10:9	96, 100, 326, 365, 371–372, 374
10:10	326, 372
10:11	46, 59, 65, 95, 188, 365, 366, 367, 369, 370, 372–373, 498
10:12	156, 163, 325, 373, 380, 596, 597
10:13	65, 66, 177, 373–374
10:14–11:1	15
10:14-22	13, 27, 30, 306, 365, 375, 377, 378, 379, 382, 385, 391, 404, 422
10:14-21	304
10:14	3, 21, 25, 194, 248, 306, 319, 365, 370, 375, 377, 378–379, 447, 593, 601, 618
10:15	8, 18, 189, 379, 413
10:16-21	425
10:16-17	66, 431, 432, 436
10:16	365, 375, 376, 377, 379, 381, 382, 425, 431, 433, 503
10:17	376, 377, 379–380, 381, 388, 430
10:18-22	342
10:18	156, 365, 373, 375, 377, 378, 380, 381
10:19	18, 319, 376, 378, 380, 388
10:20-21	376, 380
10:20	21, 94, 214, 295, 376, 380–381
10:21	96, 100, 376, 379, 381, 388, 433
10:22-23	13
10:22	96, 100, 109, 381–382
10:23–11:1	12, 13, 30, 244, 306, 308, 378, 382, 383, 391
10:23-33	378
10:23-30	385
10:23-24	244, 385, 390
10:23	19, 134, 155, 166, 187, 241, 242, 243, 244, 253, 254, 312, 325, 327, 346, 386, 387, 388, 400, 477, 481, 515
10:24–11:1	11
10:24	384, 385, 386, 388, 481
10:25-26	304
10:25	24, 137, 309, 335, 386, 387, 391, 510
10:26	7, 94, 96, 100, 387, 388, 403
10:27-31	304
10:27-29	389
10:27	21, 24, 50, 137, 234, 271, 275, 309, 335, 383, 387, 506, 508, 509, 510
10:28	384, 387–388
10:29-30	11, 335, 388
10:29	18, 388
10:30	376, 583
10:31–11:1	385
10:31-33	384
10:31-32	233
10:31	5, 195, 385, 388–389, 436
10:32-33	385
10:32	46, 51, 106, 354, 384, 389–390, 404, 407, 414
10:33–11:1	390
10:33	9, 19, 118, 244, 297, 385, 389, 390, 391, 405, 453, 477, 481, 533
11–14	392, 425
11	45, 112, 392, 395, 437, 468
11:1	7, 27, 49, 118, 170, 193, 202, 352, 385, 390–391, 394, 404, 429, 477, 479
11:2-34	11, 12, 13, 30, 378, 392, 415
11:2-22	394
11:2-16	15, 30, 33, 70, 276, 285, 307, 308, 374, 392, 393, 396, 399, 401, 404, 407, 408, 409, 411, 412, 414, 415, 416, 417, 514
11:2-6	414
11:2	367, 368, 390, 392, 394, 395, 396, 404–405, 417, 421, 424, 445, 533
11:3-16	415, 416
11:3-15	6, 204

11:3	167, 295, 394, 396, 399, 400, 402, 403, 405–406, 407, 410, 411, 412, 414, 514, 555
11:4-7	394
11:4-5	399, 400, 402
11:4	394, 396, 401, 402, 406–407, 414, 415
11:5-7	409
11:5-6	400, 401, 402
11:5	394, 396, 401, 402, 406, 407–409, 413, 513, 515
11:6	396, 407, 409, 413, 516
11:7-16	402
11:7-12	402
11:7-9	25, 402
11:7	130, 396, 402, 405, 406, 409–410, 411, 413, 566, 567
11:8-9	394, 402, 413
11:8	396, 400, 406, 408, 410
11:9	410
11:10	394, 396, 410–412, 414, 415, 416, 473
11:11-12	11, 26, 287, 394, 396, 403, 408, 412, 555
11:11	200, 396, 403, 412
11:12	400, 403, 412–413
11:13-15	402
11:13	394, 396, 401, 403, 409, 413
11:14-15	394, 401, 403, 413–414
11:14	406, 407, 413
11:15	396, 566
11:16	11, 46, 47, 51, 53, 163, 165, 201, 283, 392, 394, 395, 402, 414, 421, 520
11:17-34	15, 392, 394, 440, 478, 508
11:17-26	495
11:17-22	30, 46, 98, 416, 417, 421, 437
11:17-20	52
11:17	264, 269, 394, 395, 416, 417, 418, 421, 424, 508
11:18-22	74
11:18-19	69
11:18	46, 51, 74, 77, 404, 417, 418, 421, 423, 424, 465, 492, 517
11:19	176, 419, 421, 422, 424
11:20-21	24, 186, 418, 426
11:20	26, 417, 418, 419, 421, 422, 423, 425, 430, 431, 437, 440, 508, 517, 589
11:21-26	381
11:21-22	189, 280
11:21	13, 222, 417, 419, 420, 422–423, 431, 436, 509, 517
11:22	46, 51, 73, 220, 395, 416, 417, 418, 419, 421, 423–424, 436, 440, 513, 522
11:23-32	437
11:23-26	7, 26, 27, 30, 264, 375, 379, 396, 419, 425, 426, 428, 433, 434, 437, 438
11:23-25	424, 435, 436, 615
11:23-24	431–433, 477
11:23	392, 395, 425, 431, 435, 437, 445, 614
11:24-25	264, 376, 428, 434
11:24	82, 379, 391, 427, 433, 434, 466, 559
11:25-26	376
11:25	427, 433, 434, 463
11:26	174, 427, 428, 429, 434, 436, 437, 438, 439
11:27-34	27, 30, 394, 425, 427, 435
11:27-32	148, 207, 211, 212, 436, 437, 438
11:27	232, 427, 434, 435, 436, 437, 438, 439, 440
11:28	171, 434, 435, 436, 437, 438, 441
11:29-32	436
11:29	434, 435, 436, 438, 439, 440
11:30	303, 436, 437, 439, 440, 441, 444, 454, 536, 541
11:31	130, 436, 437, 438, 439, 464
11:32	427, 436, 437, 439
11:33-34	417, 436, 437
11:33	9, 51, 52, 76, 418, 431, 437, 438, 440, 508, 517
11:34	3, 24, 73, 283, 417, 421, 436, 438, 440, 588
12–14	14, 15, 58, 60, 63, 84, 181, 194, 241, 392, 444, 447, 454, 456, 457, 460, 471, 472, 478, 482, 511, 523

12	11, 15, 46, 62, 149, 151, 256, 310, 392, 442, 451, 452, 455, 467, 468, 472, 481, 489, 490, 493, 601	12:10	373, 442, 445, 452, 455–456, 457, 461, 470, 479, 491, 493, 494, 518
12:1–16:24	12	12:11	26, 62, 145, 310, 442, 449, 450, 452, 453, 454, 456, 458, 464, 467, 486, 487, 515, 566
12:1–14:40	12, 30, 441		
12:1-31	12	12:12-31	247
12:1-11	15, 442	12:12-26	8, 15, 20, 26, 31, 62, 69, 79, 81, 241, 247, 377, 380, 439, 441, 442, 449, 457, 462, 467, 509, 524
12:1-3	30, 310, 441, 445, 449		
12:1	5, 9, 13, 51, 63, 76, 187, 252, 253, 295, 310, 367, 368, 405, 445, 446–447, 449, 450, 462, 489, 490, 495, 523, 533, 551, 588, 597		
		12:12-13	458, 467
		12:12	20, 380, 442, 458, 462, 467, 468
12:2-3	452, 506	12:13	106, 354, 454, 458, 462–463
12:2	21, 24, 25, 212, 368, 445, 446, 447, 448, 454, 462, 499, 506, 541	12:14-26	33, 415, 458
		12:14-20	461
		12:14-19	464
12:3-8	460	12:14	463, 468
12:3	249, 368, 442, 445, 447–448, 495, 533, 616, 617	12:15-20	460
		12:15-16	460, 463, 464, 578
12:4-26	275	12:15	79, 337
12:4-13	238	12:16-17	460
12:4-11	30, 261, 441, 448, 450, 451, 452, 458, 494, 509, 517	12:16	79, 464
		12:17	442, 464
12:4-7	442, 457	12:18	145, 460, 464, 465, 468, 470
12:4-6	446, 449	12:19	130, 464, 468
12:4	26, 63, 310, 441, 442, 446, 447, 449, 450, 452, 453, 456, 490, 551	12:20-26	460
		12:20	464, 468
		12:21	79, 396, 460, 464, 578
12:5	81, 442, 452, 605	12:22-25	460
12:6-7	450	12:22-24	464–465
12:6	25, 62, 158, 310, 449, 452–453, 456, 487	12:22	460, 468
		12:23	189, 302, 481
12:7-11	449, 493	12:24-25	465
12:7-10	158	12:24	297, 460, 465, 470
12:7	19, 26, 61, 62, 145, 244, 304, 310, 450, 453, 460, 477, 501, 586	12:25-26	460
		12:25	69, 77, 468
		12:26	210, 442, 465–466, 468, 481
12:8-10	442, 451, 452, 454, 468, 469, 470, 490, 498	12:27-31	15, 31, 441, 442, 466, 467
		12:27	20, 247, 467, 470
12:8-9	455	12:28-32	449
12:8	59, 61, 62, 442, 451, 453–454, 475, 479, 487, 490	12:28-29	469, 493, 513
		12:28	8, 44, 148, 155, 158, 439, 441, 451, 452, 454, 455, 461, 467, 468, 469, 470, 471, 490, 491, 493, 498, 504, 535
12:9-10	451		
12:9	439, 452, 453, 454–455, 458, 463, 476, 479, 482		

12:29-30	158, 442, 451, 467, 468, 470–471, 490, 498	13:9	402, 486, 487
		13:10	245, 484, 486
12:29	44, 452, 455, 471, 491, 493, 504	13:11-12	473, 479
		13:11	143, 245, 486, 507
12:30	439, 452, 454, 456, 461, 468, 470, 471, 494	13:12	156, 311, 373, 484, 486–487, 488, 523, 606
12:31–14:1	442	13:13–14:1	443
12:31–13:13	12	13:13	472, 479, 480, 482, 483, 484,
12:31–13:3	31, 443, 471, 476, 479		485, 487–488, 616
12:31	200, 442, 449, 452, 467, 471, 474–475, 476, 477, 488, 489, 490, 491, 493	14	15, 26, 123, 132, 392, 395, 402, 431, 442, 443, 451, 452, 455, 461, 471, 475, 481, 489, 490, 511, 516, 523, 525
13–14	495		
13	11, 15, 27, 312, 392, 441, 442, 443, 444, 467, 470, 471, 472, 473, 478, 479, 483, 484, 488, 489, 491, 523	14:1–16:7	11
		14:1-40	12
		14:1-19	495
		14:1-5	31, 489
13:1-3	7, 49, 194, 467, 472, 474, 475, 478, 483, 498, 616	14:1-2	511, 523
		14:1	26, 402, 442, 447, 471, 483, 485, 488, 489, 490, 491–492, 493, 507, 616
13:1-2	62, 485, 493, 495		
13:1	8, 102, 188, 412, 456, 471, 472, 473, 475, 477, 479, 480, 498, 503, 519	14:2-19	505
		14:2-4	493
		14:2	116, 172, 471, 490, 492, 493, 499, 501, 503, 512, 518
13:2-3	473, 481		
13:2	26, 59, 106, 116, 253, 454, 455, 472, 473, 474, 475–476, 479, 480, 482, 487, 492, 518	14:3-5	453
		14:3	20, 155, 312, 402, 455, 471, 490, 491, 492–493, 519
		14:4-5	490, 518
13:3	19, 100, 472, 473, 474, 476–477, 480, 498	14:4	20, 155, 312, 402, 461, 471, 492, 493
13:4-13	27	14:5	20, 26, 155, 295, 312, 402, 461, 470, 471, 485, 492, 493–494, 501, 518
13:4-8	443		
13:4-7	31, 443, 472, 473, 478, 479, 484, 485		
		14:6-12	31 494, 495
13:4-6	478	14:6	9, 19, 26, 51, 59, 64, 76, 106, 132, 194, 455, 456, 469, 473, 475, 476, 477, 487, 491, 492, 493, 497–498, 503, 504, 518, 519
13:4	100, 106, 177, 181, 478, 480, 481		
13:5	302, 386, 480–481		
13:6-7	478		
13:6	215, 479, 481	14:7-8	8, 473, 475, 498–499
13:7	341, 342, 478, 481–483, 487	14:7	499
13:8–14:1	31, 483	14:8	362, 456, 508
13:8-13	472, 478, 483, 484, 488, 508	14:9	59, 456, 469, 492, 499
13:8-12	443, 479	14:10-11	455, 499
13:8-11	443	14:11	492
13:8	59, 245, 455, 479, 483, 485–486, 487		
13:9-10	484		

14:12	20, 155, 312, 453, 461, 471, 490, 493, 499, 518	14:27	470, 492, 494, 518, 519
14:13-19	31, 500, 501	14:28	492, 494, 516, 518, 519, 521, 522
14:13-15	402	14:29	455, 492, 515, 519
14:13-14	503	14:30-31	455
14:13	456, 470, 492, 501–502, 518, 518	14:30	513, 516, 519, 521
		14:31-32	491
14:14-19	500	14:31	402, 455, 492, 513, 516, 519
14:14-15	194,	14:32-38	515
14:14	77, 456, 473, 490, 493, 500, 501, 502, 504	14:32	411, 490, 516, 519–520
		14:33-38	524
14:15	10, 77, 490, 495, 498, 500, 502, 518	14:33-37	522
		14:33-36	396, 402, 514, 515, 516, 517, 524, 525
14:16-17	502, 503, 504	14:33-35	514, 515, 516, 524, 525
14:16	490, 500, 502–503, 505, 509, 512, 559	14:33-34	514
14:17	20, 155, 312, 490, 493, 503	14:33	47, 53, 201, 267, 283, 395, 512, 513, 514, 515, 520–521, 588
14:18-19	26		
14:18	106, 456, 473, 475, 492, 498, 500, 503	14:34-38	13
		14:34-36	524, 525
14:19	59, 77, 195, 411, 446, 492, 500, 502, 503, 504, 516	14:34-35	11, 524, 525
		14:34	244, 492, 513, 516, 521, 524
14:20-25	31, 504, 505, 510, 511	14:35	73, 492, 513, 514, 516, 521–522, 524
14:20	9, 51, 76, 215, 505, 507		
14:21	7, 94, 95, 218, 492, 507–508, 510, 515, 582	14:36	517, 522
		14:37-40	517
14:22-25	209	14:37-38	517
14:22-24	21, 383, 462, 490, 506	14:37	1, 5, 17, 95, 153, 163, 165, 192, 264, 312, 347, 447, 450, 490, 515, 522, 523, 534, 606
14:22-23	454		
14:22	105, 106, 234, 271, 455, 491, 508, 510, 518, 544	14:38	154, 311, 523
		14:39-40	461, 517
14:23-24	404, 503	14:39	9, 51, 76, 402, 471, 492, 511, 523
14:23	234, 271, 492, 506, 507, 508–509, 517		
		14:40	511, 512, 516, 518, 523–524
14:24-25	509–510	15	12, 13, 60, 112, 241, 320, 429, 437, 482, 525, 526, 528, 530, 539, 545, 546, 560, 568, 572, 575, 578
14:24	137, 234, 271, 335, 402, 509, 510		
14:25	7, 94, 174, 387, 508, 510		
14:26-40	31, 511		
14:26-36	517	15:1-58	12, 31, 525
14:26-33	525	15:1-49	573
14:26-32	411, 446	15:1-28	406
14:26	9, 20, 51, 64, 76, 155, 312, 423, 453, 456, 490, 495, 502, 508, 511, 512, 513, 517–518, 519, 524, 601	15:1-11	31, 44, 525, 526, 528, 529, 530, 532, 533, 538, 539, 543, 544
14:27-33	518, 522	15:1-3	82

15:1-2	16, 52, 526, 532, 534, 538, 544, 583
15:1	9, 51, 76, 368, 447, 533, 534, 540, 583
15:2-3	395
15:2	9, 533–534, 544, 584
15:3-8	525
15:3-7	535, 539, 540, 586
15:3-5	27, 92, 319, 482, 526, 529, 531, 539, 540, 558, 569
15:3-4	137, 356, 469, 529, 534
15:3	82, 326, 395, 432, 530, 531, 534, 539, 540, 545, 559, 574
15:4	246, 531, 535, 540, 542, 543
15:5-11	332
15:5-8	547
15:5-7	336
15:5	50, 80, 331, 334, 336, 531, 535, 536, 552
15:6-8	535
15:6	51, 303, 334, 437, 439, 535–536, 539, 541, 543, 551
15:7	50, 334, 336, 536–537, 552
15:8-10	51, 329, 539
15:8-9	188
15:8	118, 188, 334, 531, 537, 539, 540
15:9	5, 45, 46, 50, 51, 60, 190, 275, 387, 468, 530, 532, 533, 537–538
15:10-11	532, 547
15:10	61, 149, 532, 538, 544, 584
15:11-12	107
15:11	362, 526, 538–539, 542, 543, 544
15:12-57	59
15:12-34	526, 527, 560, 563, 565
15:12-28	574
15:12-20	546, 556
15:12-19	31, 525, 527, 540, 541, 547, 558
15:12-13	543, 544
15:12	13, 18, 27, 187, 241, 245, 246, 253, 362, 482, 525, 526, 530, 533, 534, 536, 540, 541, 542, 543, 544, 546, 547, 551, 561, 565
15:13-19	6
15:13-14	545
15:13	530, 542, 543–544
15:14-15	542, 544
15:14	105, 119, 530, 534, 538, 542, 544, 547
15:15	530, 542, 544, 558, 560, 562
15:16-19	542
15:16-17	545
15:16	10, 530, 542, 558, 560, 562
15:17-18	544
15:17	530, 534, 542, 545
15:18	3, 303, 530, 536, 543, 545
15:19	530, 542, 545
15:20-58	603
15:20-34	525
15:20-28	31, 59, 64, 318, 527, 546, 547, 555, 558, 578
15:20-23	547
15:20-22	531
15:20	246, 303, 525, 527, 530, 536, 543, 547, 550–551, 555, 604
15:21-24	27
15:21	543, 546, 547, 548, 551
15:22-23	547
15:22	530, 548, 551, 559, 571
15:23-28	555, 556
15:23-26	574
15:23-24	549
15:23	64, 530, 547, 551–552, 553, 604
15:24-28	550, 553, 555, 574, 576, 583
15:24-26	129, 130, 381
15:24-25	549
15:24	26, 59, 65, 129, 202, 245, 317, 486, 549, 550, 552–553, 554, 555, 579
15:25-58	584
15:25-26	577
15:25	7, 94, 291, 387, 548, 549, 550, 553–554
15:26-28	569
15:26	245, 486, 553, 554, 574, 583
15:27-28	167, 516
15:27	7, 94, 381, 549, 553, 554–555

15:28	60, 167, 400, 549, 550, 555, 560
15:29-34	31, 527, 547, 556, 557, 558
15:29-32	27, 557
15:29	22, 209, 541, 546, 547, 556, 557, 558, 559, 560, 561, 562
15:30-32	558
15:30-31	558, 559
15:30	558
15:31-32	562
15:31	9, 51, 65, 76, 100, 191, 559–560, 561
15:32	7, 14, 19, 94, 338, 358, 387, 476, 557, 558, 559, 560, 562, 593
15:33-34	558, 560
15:33	6, 94, 161, 235, 558, 560–561
15:34	18, 233, 534, 545, 558, 561, 572
15:35-57	27, 527
15:35-50	25
15:35-49	27, 246, 525
15:35-44	31, 527, 541, 562, 564, 568, 569
15:35	27, 242, 525, 527, 562, 564, 565, 567, 577, 579
15:36-41	8, 141
15:36-38	563, 567, 580
15:36-37	565–566, 567
15:36	559, 563, 564, 567, 571
15:37	564, 566
15:38-41	531
15:38	62, 564, 566
15:39-41	568, 570
15:39	563, 566, 567
15:40-41	130, 563, 566–567
15:40	544, 565, 567, 572
15:41	567
15:42-50	531
15:42-49	575
15:42-45	564
15:42-44	564, 565, 567, 580
15:42	543, 564, 581
15:43	130
15:44-49	31, 527, 565, 568, 572
15:44-46	136
15:44	564, 565, 567, 568, 570

15:45-50	320
15:45-49	551, 570
15:45-48	400
15:45	7, 94, 95, 218, 570–571, 582
15:46	567, 571
15:47-49	571
15:47	571, 572
15:48-49	569
15:48	571–572
15:49	409, 572, 577, 580
15:50-58	31, 59, 525, 573, 577
15:50-57	125, 525, 527, 575, 578, 584
15:50-55	576
15:50-53	573, 575, 576, 584
15:50-51	573, 575
15:50	9, 18, 51, 76, 202, 235, 294, 362, 525, 573, 579–580, 581, 583, 584
15:51-57	584
15:51-52	246, 573, 574, 575, 584
15:51	116, 172, 303, 492, 536, 575, 580, 581
15:52-53	573
15:52	8, 496, 580–581
15:53-55	573
15:53	571, 573, 581, 582
15:54-57	573, 574, 578, 584
15:54-55	94, 554, 577, 578, 582
15:54	7, 94, 125, 340, 575, 581–582
15:55-56	578
15:55	7, 95, 582
15:56-57	573
15:56	515, 545, 574, 582–583, 584
15:57-58	20
15:57	59, 61, 62, 65, 388, 560, 570, 577, 583
15:58	9, 19, 51, 76, 146, 194, 200, 377, 379, 523, 525, 527, 538, 572, 573, 574, 578, 579, 583–584, 596, 601, 618
16:1-24	12, 31
16:1-12	12, 24
16:1-4	31, 383, 585, 586, 587, 591, 592
16:1-2	588, 603

16:1	5, 13, 47, 53, 252, 253, 283, 468, 520, 585, 588, 597, 605, 610
16:2	586, 589
16:3-4	3, 469
16:3	1, 9, 197, 198, 536, 587, 589, 590, 595
16:4	118, 587, 589–590, 591
16:5-9	3, 31, 590, 591, 592
16:5-7	440
16:5	589, 592
16:6	497, 591, 592
16:7-9	11
16:7	3, 295, 521, 591, 593, 596
16:8-9	591
16:8	11, 14, 24, 208, 558, 592, 593, 610
16:9	593
16:10-24	11
16:10-14	11
16:10-12	31, 594
16:10-11	3, 9, 196, 197, 595, 596
16:10	109, 118, 146, 156, 197, 325, 583, 596–597
16:11	111, 232, 590, 597, 598, 611
16:12	5, 13, 51, 80, 252, 253, 588, 590, 594, 596, 597–598
16:13-24	2, 12, 48, 578, 616
16:13-14	31, 599, 600
16:13	579, 599, 600, 601
16:14	487, 488, 518, 524, 600, 601, 616, 617
16:15-20	11
16:15-19	11
16:15-18	4, 5, 9, 31, 84, 98, 197, 602, 603, 604
16:15-16	251, 595
16:15	9, 51, 73, 76, 84, 587, 588, 598, 602, 604–605
16:16	4, 516, 538, 599, 605–606, 607
16:17-18	3, 4, 24, 418, 599
16:17	5, 16, 84, 251, 264, 418, 552, 590, 597, 606
16:18	4, 5, 195, 388, 606–607
16:19-21	31, 607, 613
16:19-20	2, 98, 599, 607
16:19	23, 47, 51, 52, 53, 70, 73, 74, 185, 336, 337, 514, 520, 558, 593, 608, 610–611
16:20-24	618
16:20-21	11
16:20	2, 45, 51, 607, 609, 611–612, 615
16:21-24	3, 11
16:21	2, 50, 599, 607, 612, 613, 615
16:22-24	11, 31, 613
16:22	174, 429, 448, 599, 600, 613, 614, 615, 616–617, 618
16:23	2, 61, 62, 599, 611, 615, 617, 618
16:24	2, 9, 194, 202, 377, 379, 579, 583, 593, 599, 600, 601, 610, 616, 617–618

INDEX OF CLASSICAL, JEWISH,
AND PATRISTIC SOURCES

Classical Literature

Aelius Aristides, *Orations*
17.9   459
23.31   459
24.18   459
24.37   78
24.38-39   459
26.43   459

Andocides, *Orations*
1.17   212

Antipater, *On Marriage*
SVF 3.255.12-18   255
SVF 3.255.5-6   254
SVF 3.255.22-23   296
SVF 3.256.32-33   255

Antiphon, *Prosecution for Poisoning*
20   212

Appian, *Civil Wars*
1.1   81

Aristophanes, *Acharnians*
1085   418

Aristotle, *Art of Rhetoric*
1.1   119, 120
1.1.11   120, 133
1.1.14   120

2.7   155
2.20.2-4   364
2.20.3   429
2.21.14   166
3.2.10   141
3.2.13   141
3.9.8   445
3.10.6   563
3.11.1   563
3.11.6   563, 564
3.11.9   565
3.11.15-16 475
3.11.15   473
3.11.16   475
3.13.1-2   69
3.13.3   86
3.13.4   20
3.16.11   20

Aristotle, *Nicomachean Ethics*
6.7   155

Aristotle, *Politics*
7.12   258

Aristotle, *Posterior Analytics*
3.10.672b   507

[Aristotle] *Rhet. ad Alex.*
1422a.25-28 436
1430b.1-25 289
1431b.9-15 289

Arrian, *History of Alexander and Indica*
7.10.2   183

Artemidorus, *Dream Handbook*
1.45   465
1.79   465
1.80   465

Athenaeus, *Deipnosophists*
2.36   420

Celsus, *Medicine*
7.25.1   284

Chariton, *Chaereas and Callirhoe*
8.4.5-6   612

Cicero, *Academia*
2.44.136-
  167   187

Cicero, *De finibus*
3.22.75-76 187
3.22.75   166
4.27.74   166

Cicero, *De inventione*
1.9.12   206
1.19.27   14
1.22.32   87

Cicero, *De oratore*
1.11.47   75
2.19.80   14

Cicero, *Letters to his Friends*
7.14-15   44
14.14   42
14.18   42
16.1   42
16.3   42
16.4   42
16.5   42
16.6   42

Cicero, *On Duties*
3.5.22-23   458
3.6.26-27   458

Cicero, *Orations against Verres*
2.5.165   92
2.5.168   92

Cicero, *Pro Murena*
29.61   187

[Cicero] *Rhetorica ad Herennium*
1.14.21   206

Cicero, *Tusculan Disputations*
1.29   395
4.15   324
4.26   324, 386

Corpus Hermeticum
1:26   503
1:27   503
8:5   405
11:15   405

Crates, *Greek Anthology*
9.497   297

Demetrius, *On Style*
52   475
223–224   18
227   206
229   198

Demosthenes, *Against Neaera*
59.97   177

Demosthenes, *On the Embassy*
19.314   177

Demosthenes, *Private Orations*
36.43-44   348
45.61   212
49.9   212
51.8   212

Dio Cassius, *Roman History*
57.14.5   23

Dio Chrysostom, *Discourses*
1.31-32   458
3.10   187, 243

3.40	187
3.44	187
3.104-107	458, 460
7.136-140	240
9.2	458
13.32	221
14.13-16	243
14.14	240
14.17	189
17.22	221
28.6-7	360
33.16	458
33.44	458
34.17	465
34.32	458
35.5	133
38.14	465
39.3	77
39.5	458, 465
39.8	78
40.21	458
41.9	458
50.3	458
71.5	147

Diodorus Siculus, *Library of History*
12.66.2	77
20.65.1	157

Diogenes Laertius, *Lives*
6.37	166
6.72	166
6.88	566
7.125	166
10.18	428

[Dionysius of Halicarnassus]
  Ars rhetorica
2.1-2	255

Dionysius of Halicarnassus,
  Roman Antiquities
6.86.2	460
6.86.4	459
8.44.2	477

Empedocles (fragments)
1.2	131

Epictetus, *Discourses*
1.4.10	474
1.4.18	289
1.4.20	289
1.4.29	474
1.4.32	474
1.18.15-16	472
1.24.1	358
2.2.16	104
2.10.4-5	459
2.14.13	289
2.16.39	143
2.18.15-26	240
2.18.15	187
2.18.28-29	358
2.19.24	184
2.22.26-27	289
2.22.29-30	289
3.1.14	398
3.1.24-36	398
3.1.36	398
3.1.39	403
3.1.42-45	398
3.7.21	240
3.10.17	104
3.20.5	289
3.21.15-16	398
3.22.3-4	172, 348
3.22.3	168
3.22.10	398
3.22.13	240
3.22.30	398
3.22.47-48	255
3.22.55-56	229
3.22.69	291
3.22.76	302
3.22.95	240
3.23.15	171
3.23.18	289
3.24.9	143
4.1.1	243
4.1.37	279
4.1.116	398
4.1.133	289
4.1.143	240
4.3.9	348
4.4.30	357

4.6.23   236
4.8.5-6   398
4.9.17   289
4.11.25-29 398
4.13.17-24 289

Epictetus, *Encheiridion*
33.8   240

Epictetus, (fragments)
18   398

Epiphanius, *Treatise on Weights and*
   Measures
16   284

Euripides, *Alcestis*
348   155

Euripides (fragment preserved in
   Stobaeus' *Anthology*)
ISA 4.525.16-526.1   303

Florentinus, *Digest*
1.5.4   279

Gaius, *Institutes*
1.63   209

Hermogenes, *Progymnasmata*
11   255

Herodotus, *Persian Wars*
2.158   497
4.79   509
5.28   77
7.219   77

Hierocles, (fragments)
52.26-27   255
53.3   255
53.11   255
54.14-27   255

Homer, *Iliad*
1.193   507

Iamblicus, *On the Mysteries*
3.8   502

Isocrates, *Letters*
4.88   475

Isocrates, *Nicocles, or The Cyprians*
45   76

Isocrates, *Orations*
17.15   212

JosAs
4:9   293
8:1   293
8:3   447
8:5-7   612
8:9   379
11:8   447
12:5   447
13:11   447
16:14   430
19:11   612
19:15   379

Josephus, *Ap.*
2.167   319
2.201   405

Josephus, *Ant.*
1.163   258
1.183   146
2.317   428
3.224-236 342
3.252   593
4.201   319
7.380   316
8.111   503
8.114   161
12.241   284
12.199-200 348
13.297   395
14.235   227
18.309   146

Josephus, *Bell.*
1.507   459
2.151-153 183

2.264 459
4.165 184
4.406-407 459
5.277-279 459
6.300-309 130
7.203 92

Juvenal, *Satires*
5.24-25 420
5.152-155 420
5.156 420
6.535-537 253

Letter to Kleareta
116.4-12 296

Livy, *History of Rome*
2.32.7-33.1 459

Longinus, *On the Sublime*
11.1 120

Lucian, *Anacharsis*
9–10 360

Lucian, *Carousal [Symposium] or the Lapiths*
17 420

Lucian, *The Downward Journey*
13 158
23–27 158

Lucian, *Philosophies for Sale*
24 146, 159

Lucias Annaeus Seneca, *Controversiae*
10.1.2 226

Lysias, *Orations*
14.17 212

Martial, *Epigrams*
1.20 420
3.49 420
3.60 420
4.16 209

4.85 420
6.11 420
7.35 284
7.82 284
10.48 418
11.52 418

Maximus Tyrius, *Dissertations*
6.4 155

Menander (fragments)
3K 303

Menander (fragment preserved in Stobaeus' *Anthology*)
ISA 3.10.3 221

Menander, *Thais*
Fragment 187 560

Musonius Rufus (fragments)
3.38.30 258
3.38.31 258
4.48.9 221
6.52.18 221
8.60.6-10 257
8.62.17 221
10.15-23 229
11 185, 346
12.84.32-86.1 240
12.86.6-8 240
12.86.10-15 240
12.88.6 240
16 258
21 397

Orosonius, *Historiorum libri septem*
7.6.15-16 608

Ovid, *Amores*
1.8.74 253

Pausanias, *Description of Greece*
1–5 314
2.2 22

Petronius, *Satyricon*
57.4   286

Philo, *Allegorical Interpretation*
1.66-67   189
2.29   186
2.70   186
2.86   369
3.8   221
3.48   147
3.228   66

Philo, *Cherubim*
100–102   147

Philo, *Creation*
84   316
89   316
134–169   582
169   186

Philo, *Decalogue*
48   157
64   316
160   593

Philo, *Dreams*
1.27-28   459
1.93   340
1.140   412
2.8   155
2.10   143
2.123   305

Philo, *Drunkenness*
30   316
81   316

Philo, *Every Good Man is Free*
59–61   300, 345
59   189
160   143

Philo, *Flaccus*
14   305
50   305
91   186

Philo, *Gaius*
69   177
86   177
154   177
281   23

Philo, *Heir*
93   66
230–231   405
258–266   411

Philo, *Husbandry*
9   141, 143
32   186
48   186

Philo, *Joseph*
37   168
38–39   168
154   305

Philo, *Life of Moses*
1.31   305
1.110   373
1.241   305
1.278   305
1.298   305
2.13   186
2.134   316
2.164   186
2.167   305
2.270   305

Philo, *Migration of Abraham*
29   143
69   221
228   186

Philo, *Names*
205   221

Philo, *Posterity*
50   172
98   186
145   186

Philo, *Preliminary Studies*
19   143

Philo, *Questions on Genesis*
1.51   582

Philo, *Rewards*
98   305
116   260

Philo, *Sacrifices*
44   172
80   157
93   66

Philo, *Special Laws*
1.96   316
1.208-209   319
1.311   100
2.6   316
2.30-31   316
3.20-28   210
3.20   210
3.37-38   399
3.43   186
3.60   409
3.126   305
3.131   459
3.189   316

Philo, *Virtues*
145   339
162   186

Philo, *The Worse Attacks the Better*
39   134
44   134
133   134

Philostratus, *Lives of the Sophists*
1.25.2   233

Pindar, *Nemean Odes*
7.25   155

Plato, *Gorgias*
509C   229

Plato, *Laws*
1.643B   147
8.840A   258

Plato, *Phaedrus*
272E   75
273B–273C   75
275B   177

Plato, *Republic*
414A   369
491C   369
370A-B   459

Plato, *Sophist*
230B   177
231B   177

Plato, *Symposium*
174A   418
176E   418
197A-E   443, 478

Plato, *Theaetetus*
198B   395

Pliny, *Epistles*
2.6   420
2.20.9   338
10.96.5   446

Plotinus, *Enneades*
2.9   405

Plutarch, *Alexander*
21.5   258

Plutarch, *Moralia*
"Progress in Virtue"
80B   358

"Advice about Keeping Well"
133E   362

"Advice to the Bride and Groom"
140D   265

"Sayings of Kings and Commanders"
183D   146

"The Roman Questions"
266C-E   401

"On the Fortune or the Virtue of
   Alexander"
326D-E   183
327A-C   183

"Isis and Osiris"
382A-C   486

"The E at Delphi"
387A   120

"Oracles at Delphi"
404F   496, 498

"On Brotherly Love"
478D-479   413
478D-479B 71, 465, 475
478D   459, 460
480A-D   200
481B-E   71
481B   234
481E–482C 229

"On Inoffensive Self-Praise"
539B   362
544D-E   7
544F   7

"Table Talk"
612F   431
613F   420
615A   419
615E   420
618C   420
622C–623A 478
624B   362
638D–640A 362
640A   362
644C   423

"Old Men in Public Affairs"
797E   460

"Precepts of Statecraft"
814E–816A 229

"The Stoics and the Poets"
1058B   187

"Reply to Colotes"
1122C   324

Polybius, *Histories*
8.21.9   81

Propertius, *Elegies*
4.5.28-34   253

Pseudo-Demetrius, *Elocution*
287   176
292–294   176

Pseudo-Demetrius, *Epistolary Types*
7   192

Pseudo-Plato, *Alcibiades II*
145E   177

Quintilian, *Training of an Orator*
1.2.3   19
2.15.3-4   120
3.6.9   206
3.6.12   206
3.6.21   206
3.6.83   206
3.8.6   19
4.3.15   14
4.5.3   338
7.4   206

Seneca, *Anger*
2.31.7   458

Seneca, *Benefits*
4.1.3   159
4.33.3   159
5.13.3   190
7.2.5   166, 187
7.3.2-3   166
7.3.2   187
7.4.1   166
7.8.1   166
7.10.6   166

Seneca, *Epistles*
1.69	240
1.71	240
7.11	7
12.10	7
12.11	7
13.1-3	8, 141
13.1	359
13.9	6
14.10	6
14.12-13	7
22.11-12	6
24.6-8	7
24.9	7
24.26	7
26.8	7
29.12	7
40.2	7
40.4	6
41.2	7
42.7	6
44.4	7
45.11	6
47.19	6
54.7	349
59.6	7, 8, 141
61.3	349
65.4	7
66.18	7
66.45-48	7
67.7	7
71.8	7
76.10	6
77.15	6
78.5	7
78.7	7
78.15	7
78.16	8, 141
80.1-3	362
80.1	7
80.7	7
83.13	7
85.4	7
85.18	7
85.19-20	6
85.19	7
85.24	6

86.1-2	7
90.20	7
94.27	7
95.52	8, 229, 470
95.65-66	7
95.70	7
104.1	24
104.21	7
105.11	7
105.33	7
105.53	7
105.68	7
108.24	7
108.25	7
109.1	166
119.14	7

Seneca, *Mercy*
1.8.5	187

Sophocles, *Electra*
509	536

Strabo, *Geography*
1.2.33	475
3.2.9	475
8.2.1-3	22
8.4.8	22
8.6.2	52
8.6.20-23	22
10.3.8	397
10.3.9-19	496
10.3.9	496
14.2.28	497

Suetonius, *Augustus*
49	604

Suetonius, *Claudius*
25	23
25.4	608

Thucydides, *History of the Peloponnesian War*
5.31.6	77

Vitruvius, *Architecture*
5.3.8	473

Xenophon, *Memorabilia*
1.2.25   177
2.5.2   348
3.14.1   420

Xenophon, *Oeconomicus*
7.4-9.19   522

Pseudepigrapha

2 Apoc. Bar.
4:3   575
17:2-3   582
21:13   545
44:8-13   576
44:13   579
49-50   576
49   563
51:10   131
74:2   576

Apoc. Moses
10:3   409
12:2   409
20:1-2   409
21:6   409

1 Enoch
1:5   553
1:9   231
6:1–10:17   553
10:11-14   232
14:9-10   157
19:3   412
21:1-10   553
22:14   131
25:3   131
25:7   131
27:3   131
27:5   131
38:1   231
38:5   231
45:3   158
51:2   158

60:6   158
62:13   158
62:15   131
63:2   131
67-68   232
90:37-38   577
91:15   232
95:3   231
96:1   231
98:12   231
104:6   376
108:4-11   477
108:8   477, 616
108:12   231

2 Enoch
30:15   200
66:6   183, 482

Ep. Arist.
122   497
144   340
207   373

Gos. Thom.
3   17
11   17
17   17, 131
18   17
21   408
22   17, 408
24   17
28   17
36–37   17
37   408
51   17
63   17
64   17
76   17
81   17
85   17
95   17
106   17
109   17
110   17
113   17
114   17

Jub.

4:6	412
17:18	482
24:29	231
33:10-13	210
49:7-23	428

Pseudo-Philo, *Biblical Antiquities*

6:16-18	160
9:4	533
10:7	369
26:13	131
38:3-4	160

Pseudo-Phocylides

53	99
210–212	399

Pss Sol

4:25	616
6:6	616
10:3	616
14:1	616

Sib. Or.

2.73	236
3.55	158
3.741	158
3.764-766	230

T. Abr.

13:11-14	159

T. Asher

1:3-5	200
1:6–5:4	200

T. Dan

5:4	533

T. Gad

3:1	236
4:7	488

T. Job

48–50	456
48:3	473, 502

49:2	473
50:2	473

T. Jos.

1:3	533
1:4-7	184
8:5	248
10:1-3	248

T. Judah

13:2	99

T. Levi

9:9-10	254, 258
9:9	248
18:11	221

T. Mos.

8:3	284

T. Naph.

8:8	254, 257

T. Reub.

1:5	609
1:10	210
3:5	258
5:5	224, 248

T. Simeon

1:2	609

Qumran and Related Literature

CD

2:14-16	256
5:6-11	210

1QH

4:26-27	231

1 QM

7:4-6	412

1QpHab

5:4-5	231

1 QS
1:6   256
3:13–4:26   200
4:3-4   453
4:5   488
4:9-11   218
6:8-10   207, 212
8:5-9   161
8:5   147
11:5   147
11:21   256

1 QSa
1:25-26   257
2:3-11   412

4 QD^e
10:11   412

4 QM^a   412

4 QpNah
1:7-8   92

11 Q Temple
64:6-13   92
66:11-12   210

Mishnaic and Related Literature

Babylonian Talmud

b. B. Batra
58a   406

b. B. Meṣ.
87a–91b   339

b. ʿErub.
100b   259

b. Ketub.
11a   563

b. Mena
43b   277

b. Qidd.
22a   193
29a   185, 331
68b   265

b. Sanh.
19b   193
90b   563
99a   131

b. Yebam.
45a   265
62b–64a   260

b. Yoma
35b   339
66a   339

Mishna

m. ʾAbot
1:1   395
2:2   185, 331
2:7   104
4:1   189
4:5   185, 331

m. B. Meṣ.
7:2   340

m. B. Qam.
1:1   183
1:4   183

m. Ber.
8:8   503

m. Beṣa
5:2   495

m. Giṭ.
9:2   303
9:3   303

m. Ker.
1:1   210

m. Ketub.
4:4   267
5:6   257

m. Ned.
4:11   284

m. Pesaḥ.
10:5   183, 428, 429

m. Qidd.
1:2   267

m. Sanh.
7:4   210

m. Soṭa
3:1-5   439

m. Yad.
4:7   339

m. Yebam.
6:6   260

Tosepta

t. Ber.
7:18   277

t. Ned.
5:6   257

t. Qidd.
1:11   185, 331

t. Šabb.
15:9   284

t. Sanh.
10:1   210

Jerusalem Talmud

y. Ber.
7:3   379
9:1   277

y. Ketub.
11:3   410
12:3   563

y. Kil.
9:3   563

y. Pesaḥ.
10:3-5 428

Other Jewish Literature

Gen. Rab.
8:1   406
8:10   406
9:7   258
12:6   406

Pesiq. R.
4:36a-38   406

Pirqe R. El.
4:4   406

Qoh. Rab.
1:4   563
4:13, 1 371
8:1-5   406

Sipre Deut.
17:8-9 227

Tg. Isa.
53   530, 534

Early Patristic Literature

Apostolic Fathers
Barn.
7:3   370
7:7   370
7:10   370
7:11   370
12:2   370

12:5	370		Ign. *Magn.*	
12:6	370		6:1	125
12:10	370		8:2	125
13:5	370			
18-20	200		Ign. *Phld.*	
			4:1	432
1 Clem.				
3:2	236		Ign. *Pol.*	
24:1	551		4:3	282
30:1	236		6:1	172
37	461			
42:4	551		Ign. *Rom.*	
46:5	77, 79		7:3	432
47:3	80			
55:2	286		*Mart. Pol.*	
			15:2	157
2 Clem.				
12:2	408		Patristic Writers	
			[Anonymous] "On the Paschal Mystery"	
Did.			35.4.6	572
1	200			
1:2–2:7	218		*Apocalypse of Pseudo-Methodius*	
5–6	200		11:14	157
5:1-2	218			
9:2-4	375		*Apostolic Constitutions*	
10:6	614, 615		7:1	200
13:1	339			
14:1	376		Clement of Alexandria, *Stromata*	
16:5	157		3.10.22-23	259
			3.13.1	408
Herm. Man.			3.15.18	259
4.1.8	270		3.18.68-70	259
			5.5.60-61	200
Herm. Sim.			7.11.47-50	337
4.2-4	174			
9.10-11	301		Cyprian, *Unity of the Catholic Church*	
9.12.2-3	125		9	610
9.13	301			
9.15	301		Cyril, *Catecheses*	
			23.2	610
Herm. Vis.				
1.4.3	601		*Didascalia Apostolorum*	
4.3.4	157		23	422
Ign. *Eph.*			Eusebius, *Ecclesiastical History*	
19:1-2	125		3.4.5	197
20:2	376		3.30.2	337

Gregory Nazianzen, *Epistles*
64.5   612
93   612

Hippolytos, *Apostolic Tradition*
4.1   610
22.3   610

John Chrysostom,
    On the First Epistle to the Corinthians
Homily 3.1   80
Homily 12.1   179
Homily 17.1   19
Homily 20.2   319
Homily 26.3-4   406
Homily 32.1   461
Homily 40   557

Justin, *Dialogue with Trypho*
35:3   422
42.4   370

Justin, *First Apology*
65.2   610
66   615
66.3   428

Origen, *Commentary on Romans*
10.33   610

Origen, *Contra Celsum*
3.44   98
3.48   98

Pseudo-Clementine Homilies
1.18   236
15.7   200
16.21.4   422

Tertullian, *Orations*
18   610

Theodoret, *Interpretatio*
164   197
214   319

INDEX OF MODERN AUTHORS

Achelis, Hans, 301
Adamo, David, 87
Adinolfi, Marco, 395, 407, 414
Aland, Barbara, 325
Aland, Kurt, 75
Aletti, Jean-Noel, 87, 117, 128, 543
Allcock, P. J., 39
Allison, Robert W., 524
Allo, Ernest-Bernard, xiv, 38, 311, 451
Amjad-Ali, Christine, 414
Anderson, R. Dean, Jr., 34
Aono, Tashio, 553, 555
Arichea, Daniel C., 524
Audet, Jean-Paul, 382, 614, 618
Aune, David E., 421, 424, 494, 519

Baarda, Tijtze, 138
Bachmann, Michael, 543, 546
Bailey, Kenneth E., 35, 199, 250
Baird, William, 34
Bakhtin, Mikhail, 465
Balch, David L., 35, 37, 54, 89, 204, 297, 444
Baljon, J. M. S., 180
Bammel, Ernst, 114, 215
Bandstra, Andrew J., 374
Barbaglio, Giuseppe, 39
Barclay, William, 39
Barrett, Charles Kingsley, xiv, 38, 39, 120, 160, 169, 244, 311, 405, 406, 411, 469, 537
Bartchy, S. Scott, 279, 286, 287, 329
Barth, Gerhard, 528
Barton, Stephen C., 35, 356, 513, 524

Bartsch, Hans-Werner, 539
Basevi, Claudio, 204
Bassler, Jouette M., 202, 448, 515
Baudraz, François, 39
Bauer, Johannes B., 303
Baumann Rolf, 72, 83, 87
Baumert, Norbert, 12, 204, 221, 287, 304, 382
Baur, Ferdinand Christian, 71, 80
Beare, Francis Wright, 86
Beatrice, Pier Franco, 87
Becker, Jürgen, 70, 584
Beker, Johan Christiaan, 138, 202
Belleville, Linda L., 31, 197
Benanti, O., 287
Bender, Wilhelm, 113
Bengel, Johann Albrecht, 199
Benko, Stephen, 612
Berger, Klaus, 35, 138, 154, 161
Best, Ernest, 273
Betz, Hans Dieter, 424, 588, 590
Bieringer, Reimund, xv, 35
Binder, Hermann, 546
Bjerkelund, Carl J., 68, 86
Black, David Alan, 355
Blampied, Anne B., 524
Blank, Josef, 273
Blegen, Carl W., 541
Blue, Bradley B., 293, 424
Boccaccini, Gabriele, 424
Boer, Martinus C. de, 13, 14, 32, 528, 555
Bonneau, Normand, 568
Borgen, Peder, 307

Borghi, Ernesto, 88
Boring, M. Eugene, 35
Bornkamm, Günther, 12, 356, 617, 618
Borse, Udo, 31, 447
Botha, S. P., 572
Boucher, Madeleine, 287
Bouwman, Gijs, 396, 414
Bourke, Myles, 369
Bousset, Wilhelm, 614
Bowersock, Glenn, 234
Branick, Vincent P., 87, 88
Braun, Herbert, 429
Brewer, David I., 342
Brodeur, Scott, 572
Broneer, Oscar, 33
Brown, Alexandra R., 88, 97
Brox, Norbert, 448
Bruce, Frederick Fyvie, 39, 266, 405,
    411, 415, 447
Brunt, John C., 307
Bryce, David W., 524
Bucher, Theodor G., 546
Buck, Carl Darling, 149
Bullmore, Michael, 121
Bultmann, Rudolf, 97, 126, 138, 304,
    320, 429, 565
Bünker, Michael, 6, 34, 169, 194
Burchard, Christoph, 374, 434, 568
Burgos Núñez, Miguel de, 12, 32
Byrne, Brendan, 147, 250

Cadbury, Henry J., 169, 174
Calef, Susan, xv
Callan, Terrance, 443
Calvin, John, 311
Cambier, Jules, 215
Campbell, Alastair R., 424
Campbell, Barth, 215
Caragounis, Chrys C., xv, 261, 343, 476,
    477
Carroll, John T., 37
Carson, Donald A., 444, 452
Carter, Timothy L., 35
Castelli, Elizabeth A., 195
Cerfaux, Lucien, 96
Chadwick, Henry, 356
Chakkalakal, Pauline, 414

Charlesworth, James H., xvii, 159, 160
Chenderlin, Fritz, 434
Chmiel, Jerzy, 297
Chow, John K., 35, 210
Christensen, Jens, 534, 539
Chrupcalla, Leslaw D., 434
Church, F. Forrester, 54
Cipriani, Settimio, 88
Clancy, Robert A. D., 434, 440
Clark, Gillian, 35
Clarke, Andrew D., 35, 210, 308
Claudel, Gerard, 204
Clemen, Carl, 11, 32
Colella, Pasquale, 214
Collier, Gary D., 374
Collins, Adela Yarbro, 215
Collins, John J., 31, 304
Collins, John N., 452, 456, 457
Collins, Raymond F., 32, 35, 54, 261,
    273, 276, 343, 391, 524, 539
Colpe, Carsten, 35
Conzelmann, Hans, xiv, 39, 96, 158,
    531, 539, 557
Cope, Lamar, 307, 378, 382, 394, 414
Corrington, Gail P., 414
Cosgrove, Charles H., 37
Cotter, Wendy, 86, 612
Coutsoumpos, Panayotis, xv, 424
Crofts, Marjorie, 35
Cross, Frank Leslie, 36
Crossan, John Dominic, 17, 72, 430
Cuming, Geoffrey J., 463, 615, 618

Dahl, Nils A., 88, 125, 138, 169, 251
Dahood, Mitchell, 15
Daube, David, 114, 273
Dautzenberg, Gerhard, 444, 455, 457,
    493
Davies, J. G., 455
Davis, Carl J., 320
Davis, James A., 88, 96, 307
Dawes, Gregory W., 287, 327
Deer, Donald S., 561
Deidun, T. J., 363
DeLacey, D. R., 320
Delafosse, Henri, 393
Delcor, Mathias, 238

Delling, Gerhard, 86, 273
Delobel, Joël, 285, 307, 325, 394, 412, 414, 434
DeMaris, Richard E., 541, 546, 556, 562
Deming, Will, xv, 204, 226, 270, 281, 287
Denaux, Adelbert, 320
Derrett, J. Duncan M., 162, 238, 250, 448
deSilva, David A., 113
Dewey, Joanna, 35
Dick, Jack, xv
Dinkler, Erich, 12, 238
Dodd, Brian J., 250
Dodd, C. H., 140, 141
Dolfe, K. G. E., 297
Donfried, Karl P., 36, 612
Douglas, Mary, 458
Downey, James, 562
Downing, Francis G., 488
Dungan, David L., 36, 343
Dunn, James D. G., 36, 205, 356, 446, 462, 498
Duplacy, Jean, 432, 434
Duplessis, Johannes, 128
Dupont, Jacques, 96
Durken, Daniel, 215

Ebner, Martin, 178
Ehrenberg, Victor, 226
Ehrman, Bart D., 374
Ellingworth, Paul, 39
Elliott, John K., 476, 477
Elliott, Neil, 88
Ellis, E. Earle, 36, 87, 88, 138, 175, 524, 578
Eltester, Walther, 138
Engberg-Pedersen, Troels, 35, 307, 308, 414
Engelbrecht, Edward A., 494
Enns, Peter E., 374
Epp, Eldon J., 374, 524
Eriksson, Anders, 34
Estienne, Robert, 353, 467
Evans, Craig A., 374
Evans, Ernest, 39

Falk, Ze'ev Wilhelm, 201
Farmer, William R., 88, 203, 434
Fascher, Erich, 39
Fauconnet, Jean-Jacques, 204
Fee, Gordon D., xiv, 36, 39, 79, 120, 138, 158, 212, 258, 307, 374, 453, 462, 524, 565
Ferguson, Everett, 35, 37, 251
Feuillet, André, 36, 96, 374, 407
Fichter, H.-F., 307
Fiore, Benjamin, 34, 178, 181, 204, 391
Fischer, James A., 287
Fischer, Karl Martin, 12, 443
Fishbane, Michael, 488
Fisk, Bruce N., 250, 307
Fitzgerald, John T., 88, 178, 191, 215
Fitzmyer, Joseph A., 108, 114, 414
Flanagan, Neal M., 524
Focant, Camille, 444, 482
Forbes, Christopher, 444
Ford, J. Massyngberde, 293, 455
Forkman, Göran, 215
Fortna, Robert T., 34, 357
Francis, James, 147
Frankovic, Joseph, 261
Fredrickson, David E., 36
Friedrich, Georg, 70
Frutiger, Simone, 528
Funk, Robert W., 138, 197, 203, 590
Furnish, Victor P., 36, 147, 342, 343, 357

García Martínez, Florentino, xvii
Gardner, Paul Douglas, 444
Garland, David E., 261
Garlatti, Guillermo J., 434
Garner, G. G., 466
Garrison, Roman, 363
Gasque, W. Ward, 415
Gaventa, Beverly Roberts, 34, 147, 357, 434
Gavrock, M., 204
Geneste, Olivette, 36, 114
Genton, Philippe, 297
George, Timothy, 54
Georgi, Dieter, 590
Gertner, M., 578
Getty, Mary Ann, 391

Gibbs, James M., 618
Gibbs, Jeffrey A., 191
Gielen, Marlis, 612
Gill, David H., 488
Gill, David W. J., 35, 391, 414
Gillman, Florence M., 79, 86, 174, 613
Gillman, John, 584
Gillespie, Thomas W., 36, 447, 454, 462, 525
Glenny, W. Edward, 297
Gnilka, Joachim, 114, 153
Goguel, Maurice, 12
Gooch, Paul W., 88, 128, 307, 327
Gooch, Peter D., 307
Gordon, J. Dorcas, 343
Goulder, Michael D., 88
Gräfe, Eduard, 301
Gramaglia, Pier Angelo, 298
Grant, Robert M., 34, 89, 154, 162
Grässer, Erich, 175
Grayston, Kenneth, 86
Greeven, Heinrich, 32
Gregory, C. R., 38
Groh, Dennis E., 162
Grosheide, Frederik Willem, 39
Grosvenor, Mary, 285
Grudem, Wayne A., 415, 457, 494, 508, 510, 519
Grundmann, Walter, 147
Guerra, Manuel, 53
Gundry, Robert, 455
Gundry-Volf, Judith, 204, 440
Guthrie, Donald, 320
Gutierrez, Pedro, 195

Hadidian, Dikran Y., 273
Hagge, H., 11, 33
Hahn, Ferdinand, 67, 374, 424
Hall, Barbara, 357
Hall, David R., 181, 415
Hanges, James C., 181
Hanson, Anthony T., 191
Harding, Mark, 33
Hardy, Brian, 448
Harnack, Adolf, 38
Harrill, James A., 287
Harrington, Daniel, xv

Harris, Gerald, 215
Harris, William V., 477
Harrisville, Roy A., 39
Hartman, Lars, 86
Harvey, Anthony Ernest, 36
Hasitschka, Martin, 524
Hasler, Victor, 528
Hatton, Howard A., 39
Hauck, Friedrich, 191
Havener, Ivan, 215
Hay, David M., 36, 555
Hays, Richard B., 36, 39, 371, 374, 515, 520
Healey, Joseph P., 267
Heathcote, A. W., 39
Heckel, Ulrich, 444
Hegel, Georg Wilhelm Friedrich, 71
Heil, Christoph, 307
Heil, Uta, 555
Heinrici, Carl Friedrich Georg, 39, 80, 309, 319
Hengel, Martin, 114
Hense, Otto, 221
Héring, Jean, 12, 39, 244, 557
Herzog, Rudolf, 422
Hester, James, 34
Hill, Andrew E., 466
Hill, Charles E., 552, 555
Hock, Ronald F., 192, 337, 343, 613
Hodge, Charles, 455
Hodgson, Robert, Jr., 192
Hofius, Otfried, 424, 430, 434, 440
Holladay, Carl R., 444
Hollander, Harm W., 36, 159, 162, 539, 583, 584
Holleman, Joost, 528, 555, 583, 584
Holmyard, Harold R., 415
Holsten, Christian, 515
Holtz, Traugott, 36, 612
Holtzmann, H. J., 316
Hooker, Morna D., 38, 147, 357, 411, 415
Horbury, William, 215
Horn, Friedrich W., 582
Horrell, David G., 307, 343
Horsley, Richard A., 35, 88, 96, 121, 312, 546, 567, 568, 572

Houghton, Myron J., 488
House, H. Wayne, 444
Howson, J. S., 309
Hübner, Hans, 36, 114
Humphries, Raymond A., 88, 99, 450
Hunt, Allen Rhea, 136
Hurd, John C., 13, 33, 86, 169, 447
Hurley, J. B., 245, 406
Hurtado, Larry, 315, 316, 321
Huser, Thierry, 435
Hyldahl, Niels, 88

Isaksson, Abel, 406, 409, 415

Jansen, John Frederick, 555
Jaubert, Annie, 407
Jenkins, Claude, 195, 252
Jeremias, Joachim, 32, 75, 260, 433, 435, 531, 539, 579, 584
Jervis, L. Ann, 33, 374, 415, 524
Jewett, Robert, 12, 36, 135, 162, 302, 407, 515, 568, 611
Johnson, Andy, 555
Johnson, E. Elizabeth, 37
Johnson, Luke T., 444
Jones, Arnold Hugh Martin, 226
Jones, F. Stanley, 287
Jones, Peter R., 539
Jucci, Elio, 568, 572
Judge, Edwin Arthur, 114

Kähler, Else, 408, 415
Karrer, Martin, 435
Käsemann, Ernst, 152, 154, 162, 457, 466, 617
Kautzsch, A. F., 95
Kearney, Peter J., 539
Keck, Leander E., 114, 356
Kent, John Harvey, 33
Kertelge, Karl, 36, 612
Kieffer, René, 476, 477
Kim, Chan-Hie, 595, 598, 602, 603, 607
King, Fergus J., 435
Kinman, Brent R., 238
Kirchhoff, Renate, 250
Kittel, Gerhard, 411
Klassen, William, 613

Klauck, Hans-Josef, 12, 33, 35, 86, 378, 382, 392, 417, 428, 433, 440, 613
Klein, George L., 250
Klein, William W., 54, 477
Kleiner, Diana E. E., 396
Kloppenborg, John, 531, 539
Klijn, A. F. J., 138
Knoch, Otto, 424, 434, 466
Knopf, Rudolf, 11
Knox, John, 88, 203
Koester, Helmut, 17, 36, 37, 54, 72
Koet, Bart J., 37, 374
Koperski, Veronica, 121
Koskenniemi, Heikki, 3, 32, 55
Kovacs, Judith, 138
Kramer, Werner R., 448
Kraus, Wolfgang, 37
Kreitzer, Larry, 374
Kreitzer, L. Joseph, 552, 555
Kremer, Jacob, 39, 536
Krentz, Edgar, 37
Kroeger, Catherine Clark, 408, 415, 524
Kroeger, Richard Clark, 408, 415, 524
Kruse, Colin G., 211
Kuck, David W., 88, 158, 159, 173, 175, 178
Kümmel, Werner Georg, 53, 175, 304
Kürzinger, Josef, 412

Lambrecht, Jan, xiv, 37, 39, 307, 487, 554, 555
Lampe, Peter, 88, 392, 424, 444
Lanci, John R., 162
Laney, J. Carl, 273
Lang, Friedrich, 39, 73, 88, 269
Lang, Mabel L., 33
Langton, Stephen, 390, 467
Lassen, Eva Maria, 195
Laughery, G. J., 204
Lausberg, Heinrich, 15
Lautenschlager, Markus, 114
Lee, G. M., 343
Leitch, James W., 39
Lewis, Lemoine G., 251
Lietzmann, Hans, xiv, 39, 119, 428, 429, 430, 435, 552, 617, 618
Lieu, Judith M., 54

Lim, Timothy H., 121
Lindemann, Andreas, 273, 528, 556
Lisle, Robert, 33
Litfin, A. Duane, 88, 121
Lohmeyer, Ernst, 54, 617
Loisy, Alfred, 12, 393, 429, 430, 515, 520
Longenecker, Richard N., 33
Lorenzi, Lorenzo De, 307, 374, 478, 528, 584
Lösch, Stephan, 408, 411
Louw, Johannes P., 477
Lovering, Eugene H., Jr., 147, 357
Lowery, David K., 415
Lüdemann, Gerd, 12, 24, 37, 536, 584
Lührmann, Dieter, 13, 32
Luke, K., 435, 615, 617, 618
Lütgert, Wilhelm, 72, 97, 187

Maccoby, Hyam, 430, 435
MacDonald, Dennis R., 295, 408, 415, 557, 560, 562
MacDonald, Margaret Y., 261, 298
Magne, Jean, 435
Maier, Walter A., 524
Malan, François S., 37, 66
Maleparampil, Joseph, 457
Malherbe, Abraham J., xiv, 32, 35, 54, 68, 89, 170, 175, 204, 247, 308, 444, 562, 589, 595
Malick, David E., 238
Malinowski, Francis X., 338
Mangan, Céline, 114
Manus, Chris U., 524
Marcus, Joel, 138
Margerie, Bertrand de, 539
Marks, Herbert, 223, 374
Marshall, Peter, 35, 160, 177, 181, 186, 187, 192, 346, 349, 355
Martens, M. P., 273
Martin, Dale B., 37, 47, 287, 444, 466, 504, 568
Martin, Ralph P., 37, 415
Martin, William J., 406, 415
Martyn, J. Louis, 37, 138, 356
Marxsen, Willi, 12
März, Claus-Peter, 36, 612
Matera, Frank, J., 214, 215, 235, 539, 588

Matheson, Susan B., 396
Mearns, Christopher L., 37
Meeks, Wayne A., 35, 37, 78, 84, 147, 169, 224, 374, 407, 408, 415, 586
Meggitt, Justin J., 23, 308
Meier, John P., 215, 408, 415, 435, 539
Mercadante, Linda A., 415
Merklein, Helmut, 13, 33, 39, 114, 273, 455, 580, 584
Metzger, Bruce, 180, 296, 341, 374, 476, 572
Meyer, Heinrich August Wilhelm, 39
Michel, Otto, 554
Miller, Donald G., 273
Miller, J. I., 250
Minear, Paul S., 205
Miranda, Americo, 37
Mitchell, Alan C., 227, 231, 233, 234, 238
Mitchell, Margaret M., xiv, 13, 32, 34, 203, 244
Moffatt, James, 39
Moiser, Jeremy, 273, 298
Montagnini, Felice, 114
Morris, Leon, 40
Moule, Charles Francis Digby, 88, 180, 203, 617
Müller, Karlheinz, 584
Müller, Paul-Gerhard, 224
Müller, Ulrich B., 37, 492
Müller-Bardoff, Johannes, 12
Mullins, Terence Y., 58, 368, 374
Munck, Johannes, 73
Munro, Winsome, 515, 524
Murphy-O'Connor, Jerome, xiv, 32, 33, 37, 40, 42, 52, 54, 169, 180, 238, 245, 250, 273, 308, 321, 325, 327, 383, 394, 405, 406, 408, 414, 415, 440, 494, 525, 539, 557, 562, 611
Mussner, Franz, 224

Nadeau, Denis J., 525
Nasuti, Harry P., 308, 342
Navarro Puerto, Mercedes, 298
Neirynck, Frans, 273, 488
Nejsum, Peter, 205
Nestle, Wilhelm, 466

Newman, Carey C., 138
Neyrey, Jerome H., 466, 551
Nickelsburg, George W. E., 539
Nickle, Keith F., 590
Niebuhr, Richard R., 88, 203
Nock, Arthur Darby, 424
Noonan, John T., 343
North, J. Lionel, 138
Nuccum, Curt, 525

O'Brien, Peter T., 66, 317
O'Day, Gail R., 110, 114
Odell-Scott, David W., 525
Olbricht, Thomas H., 43, 54
O'Mahony, Kieran, 33
Omanson, Roger L., 37
O'Neill, John C., 557, 562
Orge, Manuel, 205, 285
Orr, William F., 40
Osburn, Carroll D., 374
Osten-Sacken, Peter von der, 526, 539
Oster, Richard E., Jr., 33, 415
Özen, Alf, 536

Pack, Frank, 114
Padgett, Alan, 415
Paige, Terence, 37, 447
Palliparambil, Jacob, 54
Palmer, Hazel, 541
Pamment, Margaret, 568, 572
Panikulam, George, 66, 382
Papadopoulos, Konstantinos Nicolaou,
    260, 304
Papathomas, Amphilochios, 363
Parmentier, Martin, 444
Pascuzzi, Maria, 205
Passakos, Demetrius C., 435
Pastor-Ramos, Federico, 540
Patte, Daniel, 534
Patterson, Stephen J., 17, 37, 72
Paulsen, Henning, 424
Payne, Philip B., 516, 525
Pearson, Birger A., 37, 96, 447, 448
Pella, G., 415
Penna, Romano, 37, 114
Perdelwitz, Emil R., 81
Pérez-Gordo, Alfonso, 415, 528

Perkins, Pheme, 86
Perriman, Andrew C., 584
Perrot, Charles, 374, 440, 444
Pesce, Mauro, 138, 440
Pesch, Rudolf, 12, 33, 169, 433
Petersen, William L., 238
Peterson, Erik, 87, 88
Petzer, J. H., 472, 476, 477, 515, 525
Pfitzner, Victor C., 37, 210, 215, 363
Phipps, William E., 261
Pickett, Raymond, 37
Pitta, Antonio, 584
Plag, Christoph, 167, 343
Plank, Karl A., 169, 181, 528, 546
Plevnik, Joseph, 528, 540, 556, 584
Plummer, Alfred, xiv, 40, 158, 311, 406,
    572
Pogoloff, Stephen M., 85, 88, 120, 180
Poirier, John C., 261
Ponsot, Hervé, 138
Popkes, Wiard, 208
Porter, Stanley E., 250, 374
Pöttner, Martin, 88
Prior, Michael, 42
Probst, Hermann, 34
Proctor, John, 162

Quinn, Jerome D., 53

Radcliffe, Timothy, 250
Radl, Walter, 540
Rakotoharintsifa, A., 424
Ramsaran, Rollin A., 167, 298
Ratzinger, Joseph, 224
Reaume, John D., 559, 562
Rebell, Walter, 510
Reese, James M., 89
Reiling, J., 133, 138
Reinmuth, Eckart, 34
Reitzenstein, Richard, 137
Reumann, John H., 175
Richard, Earl J., 120
Richards, E. Randolph, 32, 42, 613, 618
Richardson, Neil, 37, 173, 320, 321
Richardson, Peter, 33, 80, 86, 226, 238
Richardson, William, 525
Richter, Hans-Friedemann, 308, 394, 416

Rieger, Paul, 410
Rigaux, Béda, 54, 108
Ringe, Sharon H., 392
Rissi, Mathias, 136, 562
Roberson, C. H., 504
Roberts, Colin H., 424
Roberts, J. H., 67
Roberts, P., 471
Robertson, Archibald, xiv, 40, 158, 311, 406, 572
Robinson, D. W. B., 447
Robinson, John A. T., 618
Roebuck, Carl A., 466
Roepe, Georgius, 95
Rogers, E. R., 466
Roloff, Jürgen, 145
Rosner, Brian S., 38, 207, 215, 223, 224, 238, 247, 382
Rossman, Heribert, 224
Rowdon, Harold H., 320
Rowe, Arthur, 525
Ruef, John S., 40
Russell, Kenneth C., 273
Ryan, Thomas J., 224

Sabbe, Maurits, 444
Sánchez Bosch, Jorge, 114
Sánchez Caro, José Manuel, 441
Sanders, Boykin, 195, 391
Sanders, E. P., 159
Sanders, Jack T., 35
Sanders, Todd K., 477
Sandnes, Karl Olav, 511
Sänger, Dieter, 114
Satake, Akira, 540
Saunders, Ernest W., 162
Saw, Insawn, 528, 565, 573
Schaefer, Markus, 537, 540
Schatzmann, Siegfried S., 457
Schenk, Wolfgang, 12, 203, 443
Schenke, Hans-Martin, 12, 421, 443
Schenke, Ludger, 86
Schlier, Heinrich, 178
Schmithals, Walter, 11, 12, 13, 38, 72, 97, 408, 421, 443, 446, 453, 454, 515, 549, 556
Schnackenburg, Rudolph, 67, 114

Schneider, Johannes, 212
Schneider, Sebastian, 441, 444, 584
Schnelle, Udo, 246
Schnider, Franz, 32, 52
Schoedel, William R., 34, 89, 343
Schökel, L. Alonso, 180
Schrage, Wolfgang, xiv, 32, 40, 261, 424
Schreiner, Josef, 114
Schubert, Paul, 67
Schüssler Fiorenza, Elisabeth, 38, 78, 392, 395, 408, 411, 413, 514, 525
Schütz, John Howard, 391
Schwankl, Otto, 363
Schwarz, Eberhard, 89
Schwarz, Günther, 411
Scott, James M., 223
Scroggs, Robin, 97, 128, 238, 261, 396, 405, 407, 416
Sebometha, Wilfred, xv, 382
Sellin, Gerhard, 12, 13, 33, 38, 72, 89, 515, 546
Semler, J. S., 309
Senft, Christophe, 12, 40, 169
Serna, Eduardo de la, 13, 14, 33, 515
Sevrin, Jean-Marie, 89
Shanor, Jay Y., 162
Shoemaker, Thomas P., 416
Sibinga, Joost Smit, 308
Sigountos, James G., 444, 475, 476
Skeat, Theodore C., 424
Slingerland, Dixon, 24, 33
Smit, Joop F. M., 308, 312, 374, 444, 474, 477, 510
Smith, Barry D., 435
Smith, Dennis E., 420, 424, 463
Snyder, Edwina H., 524
Soards, Marion, 138
Söding, Thomas, 38, 89, 114, 308, 382, 480, 482, 488, 584
South, James T., 215
Spawforth, Anthony J. S., 308
Spicq, Ceslas, 509, 560, 606
Spilly, Alphonse P., 38
Stagg, Frank, 457
Stählin, Gustav, 191
Standaert, Benoît, 478
Stanley, Christopher D., 38, 95, 412, 578

Stanley, David M., 391

Steely, John E., 38, 138

Stenger, Werner, 32, 52, 224, 528

Sterling, Gregory E., 38, 139, 572

Steyn, Gert J., 54

Stowers, Stanley K., 32, 89, 96, 128, 239, 244, 251, 261

Stuhlmacher, Peter, 139, 433

Sugirtharajah, Rasich S., 414

Suhl, Alfred, 12

Sumney, Jerry L., 147, 357

Suurmond, Jean-Jacques, 444

Swanston, Hamish F. G., 392

Talbert, Charles H., 15, 40, 444, 457

Templeton, Douglas A., 556

Terry, Ralph Bruce, 32, 34

Therrien, Gérard, 424

Thomson, Ian H. , 15

Theissen, Gerd, 35, 78, 169, 173, 175, 424

Theobald, Michael, 357

Thielman, Frank, 287

Thiselton, Anthony C., 215, 456

Thompson, Cynthia L., 416

Thraede, Klaus, 8, 32, 613

Thrall, Margaret E., 40

Thurston, Bonnie B., 268

Tischendorf, Constantin von, 180

Tomson, Peter J., 38, 205, 308, 339, 395, 416, 522

Trevijano Etcheverría, Ramón M., 89, 205, 541, 546

Trilling, Wolfgang, 36, 612

Trompf, Garry W., 394, 416

Trublet, Jacques, 87

Tuckett, Christopher M., 546

Turmel, Joseph, 393

Unnik, Willem C. van, 175, 474

Vadakkedom, J., 89

van Belle, Gilbert, xv

van Cangh, Jean-Marie , 434

Vander Broek, Lyle D., 216

Van der Hout, Gijsbert, 539

Vander Stichele, Caroline, 394, 405, 416, 513, 525

Vanhoye, Albert, 34, 414

Van Segbroeck, F., 273

Vatin, Claude, 521

Verheyden, Joseph, 139

Verhoef, Eduard, 54

Vicuña, Maximo, 584

Vielhauer, Philipp, 12, 89, 531, 617

Vogelstein, Hermann, 410

Vogler, Werner, 86

Völter, Daniel, 515

von Rad, Gerhard, 101, 267

Vorster, J. N., 528

Vos, Craig Stephen De, 216

Vos, Johannes Sijko, 89, 179, 181, 445

Wachsmuth, Curt, 221

Waele, Ferdinand-Joseph de, 391, 466

Wagenhammer, Hans, 224

Wagner, Günter, 528

Wagner, J. Ross, 181

Wahl, Thomas P., 37

Wainwright, Elaine, xv

Walker, William O., 393, 416

Walther, James A., 40, 411

Ward, Richard F., 38

Ward, Roy Bowen, 261, 269

Warne, Graham J., 571

Watson, Duane F., 391

Watson, Nigel M., 40

Watson, Patricia A., 209

Webber, Randall C., 540

Wedderburn, A. J. M., 546

Weigandt, Peter, 86

Weima, Jeffrey A. D., 601, 613

Weinel, Heinrich, 407

Weiss, D. Bernard, 38

Weiss, Johannes, xiv, 11, 12, 13, 38, 40, 52, 80, 120, 158, 169, 309, 319, 443, 447, 451, 452, 502, 557

Weiss, Wolfgang, 488

Welborn, L. L., 89, 178, 182

Weizsäcker, Karl Heinrich von, 301

Wendland, Heinz-Dietrich, 40

Wenham, David, 38, 406

Wenham, Gordon J., 53

West, Allen Brown, 168

Westermann, W. L., 329
Wettstein, J. J., 309
White, Joel R., 562
White, John Lee, 32, 44, 56, 613
White, L. Michael, 147
Wibbing, Siegfried, 216, 484
Widmann, Martin, 12, 122
Widmer, Gabriel-Philippe, 89
Wilckens, Ulrich, 17, 89, 97, 135, 446
Wilken, Robert L., 34, 89, 343
Wilkins, Michael J., 37
Williams, George Hunston, 54
Williams, Ritva, 416
Willis, Wendell Lee, 139, 308, 343, 379
Wilson, Kenneth T., 416
Wilson, Robert McLachlan, 38
Wilson, Stephen G., 38
Winandy, Jacques, 416
Windisch, Hans, 96
Winstedt, Eric Otto, 285
Winter, Bruce W., 38, 97, 182, 232, 233, 238, 251, 261, 287, 298, 308
Wire, Antoinette C., 38, 416, 514, 525

Wischmeyer, Oda, 312, 444, 488
Wiseman, James, 24, 33, 34, 322
Witherington, Ben, III, xiv, 40, 308, 312
Wolff, Christian, 40
Wright, David F., 238
Wuellner, Wilhelm, xiv, 34, 87, 89, 110, 114, 339, 343

Yarbrough, O. Larry, 147, 261, 293, 297, 302
Yeo, Khiok-Khng, 12, 34
Yinger, Kent L., 182
Young, Norman H., 203
Young, Rodney S., 541

Zaas, Peter S., 224, 238
Zerhusen, Robert, 444
Zerwick, Max, 285
Zimmer, Christoph, 556
Zimmerman, M., 273, 343
Zimmerman, R., 273, 343
Zuntz, Günther, 120

INDEX OF TOPICS

Absence of Paul, 205–206, 211
Achaicus, 603, 606
Adam, 548, 551, 568–572
Admonition, 372–373
Adscriptio, 43
Advantage, argument from, 19, 22, 244, 292–293, 297, 383, 385, 386, 390, 453, 477
Affliction, 294
Age
   this, 93, 104, 124, 129, 165, 223
   age to come, 104, 115
Agōn motif, 357–360, 363, 557–558
Agriculture, 141–142, 146, 147, 148, 339, 547–548, 550, 564
Allegiance, 71–72
"All things are lawful," 187, 231, 241, 243–244, 351–352, 353, 386
"All things are yours," 164, 166
Altar, 333, 342, 380
Amanuensis (*see* Scribes)
Amen, 618
Amphitheater, 182, 188
Anamnesis, 427–428
Anathema, 446, 448, 600, 616–617
Ancestors, 368
Angels, 232, 411–412, 473, 496, 502, 519
Animals, 330
Anthropology, 13, 77, 126–127, 139, 144, 213, 241–242, 245, 247, 249–250, 254–255, 259, 292, 300, 302, 371, 409, 569, 571, 606
Antipater, 253–254, 255

Antithesis (*see* contrast)
Apocalypse of Elijah, 122, 131–132
Apocalyptic, 17, 116, 124–126, 129–130, 151, 160, 202, 218, 528–529, 535, 549, 551, 563, 573–574, 575–577
Apollos, 79–80, 142, 145–147, 150, 162, 163, 164, 166, 176, 179, 182, 194, 594, 596, 597–598, 609
Apology, 167, 328–329
Apostle, apostolate, 44–45, 50–51, 115, 155, 329–330, 334, 335, 468, 532–533, 537–538
Apostolic letter, 43
Apostolic "I," 7, 344–345
Appearances of the risen Jesus, 526, 531–531, 535–538
Aquila and Prisca, 23, 73–74, 79, 98, 336, 607, 608–609, 611
Arbitrator, arbitration, 228, 233
Archaeology, 22–23, 33–34, 322, 462, 541
Aristotle, 7, 18, 20, 69, 86–87, 120, 133, 140, 364, 445, 475, 563
Asceticism, 251–253, 258
Asia, 610–611
Asklepios (*see* Serapis)
Assembly, 3, 51–52, 211, 412, 413, 419, 421, 500, 504, 507, 508, 511–525, 618
   order of, 511–525
   of saints, 520–521
Assistants, 172
Associations, 226
Athlete, 338, 357, 360

Audience, 8
Authority
  of men and women, 259, 410–411
  of Paul, 5–6, 7, 68, 270, 290, 612
Avarice, 220

Baptism, 27, 73–75, 77, 82, 83–85, 237,
  368, 408, 458, 462–463, 541
  baptismal formula, 237, 278, 396,
  463
  for the dead, 556–557, 559
Barnabas, 50, 331, 334
Baruch, book of, 93, 129
Believers, 103, 105
Benefactor, 574
Betrothed, 299, 301–302
Blessed, 303
Boasting, 99–101, 166, 206, 213, 346–
  348, 476–477, 560
Body, 20–21, 79, 81, 126, 140, 239–251,
  291, 432, 439, 457–466, 527–528, 563,
  535, 567, 570
  of Christ, 20, 241, 379–380, 436, 449,
  466–471
  resurrection of, 562–568
  transformation of, 575–577
Boldness, 332
Boxing, 359–360, 362
Brachylogy, 285
Bread, breaking of, 375–376, 379–380,
  432
Brothers and Sisters, 9, 21, 45, 51, 68,
  70–71, 76, 78, 109, 139, 142, 217,
  233–235, 270, 271, 278, 286, 294–295,
  323, 326, 367, 378–379, 437–439, 440,
  445, 523, 533, 536, 560, 583, 604, 611
Brothers of the Lord, 336
Builder, building, 148–151, 155
Building materials, 150–151, 157
Burial of Jesus, 531
Burning, 158–159, 160, 476–477

Call, calling, 50, 60, 66, 108, 109, 267,
  272, 273–285
Captatio benevolentiae, 58, 182, 377, 394–
  395, 499
Carnal people, 140, 142, 144

Celsus, 98
Cephas, 72, 80, 162, 164, 166, 331, 336–
  337, 532, 535, 536–637
Charism(s), 26–27, 63, 441–445, 447,
  448–457, 467, 485–486
  diversity of, 451–452
Chester Beatty papyrus (P⁴⁶), 10–11
Chiasms, 14–16, 10, 184, 189, 244, 274,
  276, 286, 378, 392, 437, 441, 442, 472,
  527, 547, 563
Child, children, 70–71, 136, 143, 178,
  194, 196–197, 199, 201, 202, 258–259,
  267, 271, 371, 486, 507, 537
Chloe, 78–79, 98, 418
Christ, 48, 80–82, 91–92, 405–406
Christ party, 71–72
Christology, 60, 64–65
Christolological titles
  Christ, 64, 107, 137, 214, 247, 323,
  527, 530, 617–618
  Jesus Christ, 156
  Lord, 64–65, 96, 173, 245, 280, 290,
  334–335, 391, 427, 431, 437, 574,
  614, 617
  Lord Jesus Christ, 64, 206
Chrysostom, 179, 197
Church, 43, 45–46, 49, 51–52, 73–75,
  389–390, 470, 490, 493, 498, 508, 610
  of God, 46, 51–52, 389–390, 414, 423,
  538–539
Cicero, 42, 75, 92, 324, 386
Circumcision, 283–284
City manager, 168
Claudius, 23–24
Clement of Alexandria, 258–259
Climax *(gradatio),* 436–437, 439, 472
Collection for the holy ones, 468–469,
  585–590, 605
Command of the Lord, 1, 264–265, 289,
  334
Commandment of God, 284
Commendation, 171, 174, 392, 416–417,
  421
Community of Corinth, 20–21
Conceit, 201, 206, 210
"Concerning," 5, 251–252, 257, 288,
  304, 594, 597

Consciousness, 321, 324, 326, 386, 387, 388

Construction, 145, 147, 148–162, 163

Contradictio, 83, 85, 102

Contrast, 102, 134, 190, 201, 215, 289, 445–446, 479, 483, 565, 569

Corinth
city, 43–44
history, 21–24, 33–34
location, 43–44

Corinthian community, 97

Court, 167, 169–170, 178, 203, 207, 224–238

Covenant, 61, 266, 267, 284, 427, 433

Covert allusion, 176, 179, 193

Coworker, 146–147, 605–606

Creation, 25, 112, 130, 142, 242, 320, 393, 399–400, 402, 409, 410, 412–413, 563–564, 566–567

Creed, credal formula, 92, 326, 526, 528–540, 542, 549

Crispus, 83, 98

Cross, crucifixion, 81–82, 85, 91–92, 101, 107–108, 118, 130–131, 137

Crown, 360, 361–362

Cultic formula, 82

Cup
of blessing, 375–376, 379
of demons, 381
of the Lord, 381, 438

Curse, 212

Customs, 400–401, 418

Cynics, 291, 337

Daniel, book of, 125, 128

Day of the Lord, 65, 96, 151, 158, 206, 213

Death of Christ, 323, 326, 430, 429, 434, 529, 530–531, 534

Death, the dead, 188, 371–372, 373, 436–437, 536, 540–541, 543–545, 551, 554, 556–557, 559, 567, 579, 581, 582

Decalogue, 230

Demetrius, 18, 198, 206

Demons, 380–381

Demonstrative proof *(apodeixis),* 117, 133

Destroyer, 372

Deuteronomy, book of, 223, 339

Diatribe, 75, 91, 144, 236, 243, 247, 267, 271, 557, 558, 565

Digression, 14–15, 39, 152, 276, 278, 306, 441, 471, 532

Dining, 222–223, 322, 383–384, 387, 423

Dio Chrysostom, 116, 240, 359–360, 458

Discernment of spirits, 442, 455

Disclosure formula, 152, 160, 367–368, 445, 533

Distinction, 181

Divisions, 26–27, 69, 421, 617

Divorce, 254, 263–265, 269–270, 303, 410

"Don't you know," 235, 333

Drinking, 335, 368–369, 370–371, 388–389, 423, 434, 438–439

Drunkenness, 220, 222, 236, 417, 420–421, 509, 561

Dust, 569, 571–572

Eating, 186, 193, 330, 335, 368–369, 370–371, 377–378, 388–389, 417–419, 423, 434, 438–439

Ecclesial Letter, 43

Ecclesiastical argument, 47, 201, 283

Ecclesiology *(see* church)

Edification, 155, 492–493

Eloquence, 116–117

Emissaries, 198

Encomium, 443, 478, 488

End, the, 65, 373, 549–550, 552–553

Endogamy, 265–267, 303

Entertainment, 188

Enthusiasm, 187, 502

"Enthusiasts," 72

Enthymeme, 6, 91, 133, 243, 387

Epaenetus, 605

Ephesus, 79–80, 84, 557–558, 560, 591, 593, 608

Epictetus, 143, 240, 255, 289, 302, 348, 357, 358, 397–399, 403, 459

Epispasm, 284

Epistolary aorist, 199, 216–217, 222

Epistolary formulas, 5, 195, 206, 251–252, 257, 552, 599–600, 603, 604

Epistolary function, 41–45, 55–58, 607

Erastus, 23, 98, 168–169

Eschatology, 27–28, 25, 59–60, 65, 82, 92–93, 101–102, 107, 115–116, 152, 153, 187–188, 211, 245, 289, 291, 293, 295, 320, 359, 373, 422, 427, 434, 484, 485–488, 523, 535, 601

Eschaton, 65, 151, 154, 171, 289, 433, 486, 614

Ethnicity, 91, 92–93, 97, 277, 463

Ethos, 49, 82–83, 139, 149, 170–171, 194, 268, 289, 323–324, 344, 388, 390, 472–473, 503, 529, 532, 558

Eucharist, 27, 74, 375–376, 425, 435–436, 458, 469, 614–615

Evangelization, 74, 85, 141, 146, 583–584

Examples, 7, 49, 176, 178, 244, 252, 263, 323, 330, 333, 359, 364, 366–367, 369–370, 372–373, 391, 404, 438, 474, 585, 588

Exclusionary formula, 207, 218, 223

Excommunication, 208, 212–213

Exhortation, 1, 68, 76, 517, 556–562, 578–578

Exodus, 7, 363–374, 389, 428
book of, 364, 367, 370–371

Factionalism, 16, 71–73

Faith, 120–121, 234, 454, 476, 482, 484–485, 487–488, 538, 542, 544–545

Father
God as, 48, 54, 108, 316–318, 550
Paul as, 70–71, 141, 192–193, 195, 202, 235, 425
role of, 193, 194

Fear and trembling, 119

Feet, 460, 461, 463, 464, 554

Fellowship, 60, 66, 274

Fellowship meals, 392, 417–419

Field, 146, 147

Fire, 151–152, 153, 157, 158–159, 160

First Thessalonians, 574–575, 581

First Corinthians
contemporaneity of, 28–29
purpose of, 1, 194, 222, 233, 346–347
structure of, 29–31
theology of, 25–29
unity of, 10–14, 198, 203, 377–378

First day of the week (*see* Sunday)

Firstfruits, 547–548, 551, 604–605

Flesh, 111–112, 140, 143–144, 212, 247–248, 566

Food, 244–245
offered to idols, 304–327, 380

Fool's speech, 100

Foolish, foolishness, 91, 93, 101, 104–105, 110–111, 136, 163
of God, 108–109

Fools, 188–189, 565–566

Foreign language, 455, 497, 499, 507

Forensic language (*see* judicial language)

Fortunatus, 603, 606

Foundation, 148–149, 155, 156–157

Freedmen, 279, 280

Freedom, 239, 244, 249, 255, 271–272, 279–281, 285, 291, 300–301, 305, 329, 334, 350, 352–353, 388

Gaius, 74, 83–84, 98, 418, 508–509

Galatia, 588

Galatians, letter to, 61

Gallio, 23–24, 608

Games, 110, 305, 357–363

Genesis, book of, 247, 248, 402–403, 409, 413, 568–570, 572

Gentiles, 82, 97, 102, 107–108, 209, 284, 353–354, 447, 463

Gentleness, 202

Gezera shawah principle, 165, 332, 554

Gifts, 26, 62–63, 148–149, 181, 256, 261, 441–445, 448–457, 586–587

Gladiators, 188

Glorifying God, 249–250

Glory, 130–131, 388–389, 409–410, 413, 565, 566–567

Glossolalia (*see* tongues, gift of)

Gnosticism, 16–17, 72, 96–97, 138, 334

God, 48, 56–57, 61, 65–66, 83, 110–112, 123–124, 133, 145, 146–147, 148, 156, 181, 237, 245, 274–277, 311, 313, 315–318, 324, 358, 369, 373–374, 380–382, 385, 388–389, 413, 449, 452–453, 465, 470, 479–480, 510, 520, 523, 544, 555, 561, 583

Gods, 314–315, 319, 358
Gold, 157
Gospel, 90, 195, 341–342, 347–349, 352, 356, 526, 533
Gospel of Thomas, 17
Grace, 47–48, 54, 61–62, 148–149, 155, 532, 538, 615, 617
Greetings, 607–613
Guilds (religious associations), 168, 383, 418–419, 420, 428, 463, 518

Hairstyles, 392, 396–399
Hardship list, 183–184, 189–191
"Have-nots," 111, 418–419, 423
Head, 396, 399, 405–407, 410–411
Healing, 454–455, 462
Heart, 174, 301, 302
Hellenes, 106–108, 389
Hellenistic Judaism, 218, 313, 483–484
Hellenistic moralists, 6–8, 176, 200, 210, 221, 248, 270, 560
Heuresis (inventio), 62, 128, 205, 206, 214, 496, 558
Hillel, 104, 165
Holy, holiness, 21, 25, 45–46, 52, 112, 153, 154, 159, 167, 203, 217, 231–232, 238, 266–267, 291, 296, 609
Holy law, sentence of, 154, 436, 438, 523
Homosexuality, 230, 236
Hope, 482, 484–485, 487–488, 545
Hosea, book of 125, 577–578, 582
House, household, 73–75, 78, 84, 338, 345, 348, 418, 423, 469, 604–605, 608, 609, 611
Human authority, 338
Humanity, humans, 108–109, 123, 126, 127, 133, 143, 171, 465
Hungry, the, 440
Husband(s), 258–259, 263–264, 269–273, 296, 303, 514, 521–522
Hybris, 178, 219–220
Hybrists, 187, 351, 422, 450
Hymn, 313, 315–316, 319–320
Hyperbole, 63, 232, 383, 472, 475

Idolatry, 25, 219, 221–222, 230, 304, 365–367, 370, 371, 375–382, 384, 447

Idols, 313–314, 318–319, 447
Image, 572
of God, 409–410
Imagery, 20–21, 182
Imitation, 7, 27, 193–194, 195, 390–391
Immortality, 574, 581–582
Imperishability, 573, 581–582
"In the Lord," 200, 265, 303, 412, 611
Incest, 203, 205–216
Inclusio, 90, 154, 165, 166, 174, 204, 228, 241, 274, 286, 299, 369, 392, 511, 600, 601, 615, 617
Indentured servant, 352–353
Indicative-imperative schema, 232
Infants, 141, 143, 194
Inscription, 23, 149, 157, 161
Insiders, 217, 220, 223
Interpolation, 52–53, 122, 393–394, 443, 515–517
Intitulatio, 42–43, 49, 85, 115
Irony, 110, 116–117, 139, 143, 184–185, 186, 201
Isaiah, book of, 94, 103, 125, 137, 505, 507–508, 530, 534, 577
Isis, 253, 408
"It is written," 7, 96, 113, 131, 224, 370, 384

James, 536–537
Jealous, jealousy, 144, 381
Jeremiah, book of, 99–100, 113, 427
Jerome, 132
Jerusalem, 586–587, 589
Jesus Christ, 26, 62, 112, 118, 149, 315–318
as rock, 364–365
as Son, 60, 317–381, 550, 555
Jews, 82, 102, 105–107, 227, 233, 276, 284, 353, 463, 563
Job, book of, 165
Josephus, 130, 459
Joy, 295, 606
Judgment, 65, 101, 125, 136–137, 146, 150, 170–171, 173–174, 206, 207–209, 211, 220, 223, 225, 231–232, 435–441, 509–510
Judicial language, 167, 169, 225, 436, 438, 544

Justice, administration of, 226–227
Justification, 112–113, 236–237
Juvenal, 420

Kerygma, 103, 104, 106, 116, 123, 535, 539, 547, 550
Kingdom, 187–188, 201–202, 229, 235–236, 552–553, 555, 579–580
Kings, 178, 187, 243
Kinship language (*see* "Brothers and Sisters")
Kiss, 609–610, 612
Knowledge, 62, 134, 309–312, 318, 322, 324, 326, 453, 475, 485
Knowledgeable, the, 322–323, 326
Koinōnia (*see* Fellowship)

Law, 351–352, 353–355, 515, 582
    of Christ, 355
    of Moses, 338, 339
Lawlessness, 481
Lectio brevior principle, 199
Letter to Paul, 4, 5, 251, 257
Letters to the Corinthians
    delivery, 3–4, 604
    number of, 4
Letters, xiii–xiv, 1–8
    apostolic, 43
    of admonition, 10, 71, 192–195, 216, 594
    of advice, 244, 252, 297
    of apology, 10, 11
    closing of, 599–600
    diplomatic, 68
    friendly, 8–9, 11, 68
    Hellenistic, xiii, 1–3, 9, 11, 41–42, 44, 49–50, 55–56, 67, 68–69, 201, 612, 615
    purpose of, 3, 9, 21
    of recommendation, 4, 9, 197–198, 200, 216, 589, 594–595, 602–603
    of response, 10
Letters of Paul
    collection of, 53
    features of, 1–6
Litotes, 63, 108, 445

Liturgy, 27, 500, 502–503, 609–610, 614–615
Logos, argument from (logic), 117, 123, 127, 141, 243, 265, 306
Lord, 145, 173, 200, 201, 248, 269, 282–283, 290, 292, 293, 315–316, 335, 418, 422, 427, 452, 583, 593, 596, 616
Lord's Supper, 7, 391, 416–424, 425–435, 437, 439, 468
Lords, 314–315
Lost letter, 216
Love, 26–27, 202, 310, 442–443, 471–488, 493, 585, 600–601, 609, 616
Lowly birth, 111
Luke, 79, 106, 426

Macedonia, 586–587, 590, 592
Manumission, 249, 280–282, 286
"Maranatha," 174, 614, 616
Market, 383, 386
Marriage, 252, 262–273, 290, 294, 298–304
    in the Lord, 265, 303
Maxims, 178, 213–214, 289–290
Meal, 392, 417–419, 427, 430
Meat, 311, 370
Men, 393–416
Menander, 6, 94, 560–561
Menenius Agrippa, 459
Metaphors, 8, 140, 148, 151, 155, 460–461, 473, 551, 553
Midrash, 25, 87, 95–96, 122, 214, 222, 364–365, 365–367, 528, 548, 577–578
Military, 338, 553, 574
Milk, 140, 141, 143
Mind, 501, 502
Mind of Christ, 127, 137–138
Miracles, 106–107, 212, 455, 476
Mirror, 486
Miscarriage, 537
Mishnah, 210, 257, 340
Mission
    of Paul, 106, 115–116, 117–118, 330
Mixed marriages, 265–268
Monotheism, 146, 153, 311–321, 384, 453

Moralists, 146
Moses, 339, 366–367, 368
Mother, 141
Mourning, 210
Music, 473, 475, 495–497, 498–499
Musonius Rufus, 185, 229, 240,
    257–258, 346, 397
Mystery, 115–116, 118, 124–125, 129–
    130, 132, 172, 475, 580
Mystery religions, 138, 376

Nakedness, 189–190
Name
    of brother or sister, 222
    of Lord, 47, 53, 68, 76–77, 82, 206,
        211, 237
Natural persons, 135–136
Nature, 403, 413, 459, 460, 464, 470, 582
Noble birth, 109
Numbers, book of, 364–365, 366–367,
    370, 371

Onesimus, 199
Opinion (*gnōmē*), 77–78, 288, 289–290,
    292
Origen, 98, 122, 132
Outsiders, 217, 220, 223, 503, 506–507,
    509
Oxen, 339–340

Pagans, 206
Papyri, 2, 10–11, 41
Paradox, 279–281, 286, 345
Paraenesis, 150, 151, 170, 191, 214,
    291
Parakalō formula, 68, 195, 604
Parallelism, 90, 101–102, 103, 108, 262,
    270, 289, 319, 449, 579
Paratactical style, 166
Paronomasia, 289, 296, 319, 405, 436,
    479, 481
Parousia, 63–64, 65, 293, 436, 548,
    551–552, 553
Partitio, 90, 367, 449
Passover, 208, 214, 428, 433
Pastoral care, 141, 143

Pastoral Epistles, 208, 358
Pathos, argument from, 71, 265, 377,
    559
Patience, 480
Patron, patronage, 74, 226
Paul
    as slave, 343–349
    charismatic, 497–498
    condition of, 116–117
    mission of, 115–116, 117–118, 293
    name of, 49–50, 82, 83, 608
    rhetoric of, 17–20, 85, 120, 178, 229–
        231, 242–243, 331–333
    trade of, 23, 185–186, 190, 331, 337,
        609
    work of, 139–147, 148–149, 155–156,
        337–338, 538, 583, 596–597
Pay, paymaster, 146, 152, 159, 342
Peace, 47–48, 54, 267, 272, 520, 597, 611,
    615
Pentecost, 593
Perfect, the, 128–129
Peristatic catalog (*see* hardship list)
Peroration, 162
Personification, 463, 474, 479
Philippi, 591
Philo, 80, 96, 99–100, 134, 141, 143, 155,
    210, 300, 305, 318, 345, 369, 399, 459
Planting, 141–142, 146
Plato, 7, 75, 177, 430, 443, 459, 478
Pliny, 419–420
Plutarch, 71, 228, 265, 268, 358, 362,
    400–401, 431, 459, 464
Pneumatists, 136, 140, 152
Political language, 69, 76, 77, 79, 82,
    352, 383
Polysyndeton, 236
Poor, 189, 305, 419, 586, 587
Populism, 352
Postscript, 600–601, 613, 615–616
Power
    of God, 92–93, 102–103, 109, 143,
        202, 246
    of Lord Jesus Christ, 212
Powerful, the, 109
Prayer, praying, 259–260, 401–402,
    405–406, 413, 500–504, 611

Preaching, 103, 105, 108, 149, 362–363, 429, 544
Presence,
  in letter, 3, 43, 192, 196, 202, 206, 211, 212, 606
  of God, 111–112
Prestige (*see Ethos*)
Priests, 342
Proclamation, 107, 116, 429, 538, 543
Prophecy, prophetic language, 26, 125, 401–402, 406–407, 442, 455, 461, 470, 485–486, 489–494, 505–506, 512–513, 519–520, 525–526, 580
Propositio (prothesis), 69–70, 86
Prostitute(s), 204, 240, 247, 336
Prudence, 189
Psalm(s) 94, 165, 384, 387, 388, 548–550, 553–554
Pseudo-Demetrius, 8–10, 68, 192, 197, 252, 589, 595–596
Puffed up, 100, 176–177, 180–181, 210, 310, 312
Purgatory, 153
Purity of the community, 208–209

Quality control, 150
Quarrels, 79
Quietism, 278
Quintilian, 14, 19, 120–121
Qumran, 147, 161, 200, 207, 210, 212, 256–257
Quotations,
  in letter, 6–7, 94

Rabbinic argument, 133, 332, 339, 340, 341
Redefinition, 99, 166, 450
Redemption, 112–113, 249
Refuse, 191
Remember, reminiscence, 404–405, 427–429
Repetition, 103–104
Reports, as a source of information, 78–79, 209, 421
Resurrection
  denial of, 245, 541
  of humans, 246, 526, 542, 562–568

  of Jesus, 81–82, 246, 318, 400, 526, 529, 530–531, 540–546, 548, 550–551
  of the body, 562–568
Revelation, 132, 520
  of the Lord, 64
  schema, 125, 132
Rhetoric, xiii–xiv, 17–20, 48–49, 75–76, 86–87, 91, 117
  deliberative, 16, 17–20, 49, 127, 147, 169, 244, 385
  demonstrative, 19
  forensic, 20, 169
  philosophic, 111
Rhetorical comparison (*sygkrisis*), 108, 135, 532
Rhetorical function, 48–49, 58–59, 69–70, 526–528, 578–579
Rhetorical proof (*pistis*), 20, 121, 128
Rhetorical questions, 75, 81, 103–104, 178, 181, 227–228, 247, 267, 281, 285, 331–333, 361, 388, 423–424, 526
Righteousness (*see* justification)
Rights, 244, 306, 323, 335
  apostolic, 327–343
Ritual, 27
Rivalry, 144
Rock, Christ as, 364–365
Romans, letter to, 61, 83–84, 612, 615
Rulers of this age, 124, 129
Running, 359, 361–362

Sacrifice, 342, 387
Salutation, 1, 5, 41–54, 153
Salvation, 93, 102–103, 104, 107, 532, 533–534
Sanhedrin, 207, 211
Satan, 207, 208, 212
Scribes, 2–3, 104, 610
Scripture, 6–7, 25–26, 87, 90–91, 94–96, 107, 113, 125, 131–132, 137, 163–164, 165, 218, 223–224, 246–247, 332, 338, 340, 363–374, 384, 469, 505, 525, 530, 548–549, 574
Seed, 566
Self-control, 260, 268–269

Self-discipline, 360, 361
Self-praise, 7
Seneca, 6–8, 14, 159, 359, 362, 458, 470
Serapis, 55–56, 168, 322, 454–455, 462, 464
Servants, 145, 172
Sex, sexuality, 15, 26, 204, 208, 243, 251–252
Sexual abstinence, 256–257, 259, 260, 408
Sexual equality, 254, 255–256, 258, 262, 267, 294, 403
Sexual Immorality *(porneia)*, 21, 205, 210, 215, 219, 220–221, 230, 239–240, 245, 254, 371
Sexual tabu, 209–210
Shame, 111, 189, 194, 233, 404, 409, 521, 558
Sharing, 376–377, 380
Shema, 315
Siblings, 233–235
Sick, sickness, 436–437, 439
Signature, 2–3, 610
Signs, 105–107, 508
Silence, 513–517, 518, 521
Similes, 8, 141
Sin, 247–248, 294, 299, 323, 326–327, 436, 530–531, 534, 545, 561, 582
Singing, song, 502, 512, 518
Slave, slavery, 168, 172, 244, 271, 278–282, 286, 343–349, 350, 418, 463
Sleep, 303, 543, 551, 580
Slogans, 71, 73, 79, 140, 145, 162–167, 203–204, 239, 241, 242–243, 252–254, 258, 290, 294, 312, 313–314, 386, 446, 561
Social concerns, 217–218
Social status, 98, 109–111, 223, 274, 276–277, 279–281
Socialization, 193
Socrates, 170
Soldier, 338
Sosthenes, 42, 45, 51, 107
Speech, 85, 119
Spirit, 26, 120, 123, 125, 128, 132–134, 145, 153, 160–161, 237, 249, 251, 304, 369, 446, 448, 449–450, 452–455, 456, 484, 492, 500, 569, 571

Spiritual gifts, 15, 441–445, 448–457, 474, 492
Spiritual marriage, 299, 301
Spiritual persons, 26, 135–136, 142, 522
Spiritual realities, 135, 341, 446–447, 489–490, 491–492, 498
Stasis (status), 58, 205, 239–240, 240, 425
Stephanas, 3–4, 9, 73–75, 83–84, 98, 197, 251, 418, 586–587, 602–607
Stewards, 168–169, 172, 345, 348
Stoics, 190, 218, 239–240, 254–255, 267, 291, 296, 324, 331, 337, 341, 346
Stones, precious, 157
Strabo, 22, 496
Strong, the, 99, 110–111
Stumbling block, 107, 323, 325, 389
Style, 14
Sunday, 586, 589
Syllogism, 6, 133, 339, 542, 558
Symposium, 417, 431, 500, 517
Synagogue, 22–23, 495, 500, 520

Table fellowship, 217, 222–223
Talion, law of, 154
Teacher, teaching, 469, 498
Temple, 148, 149, 152, 153–154, 160–161, 249, 304–305, 342
Tempt, temptation, 371–372, 373–375
Testimony, 62–63
Thanksgiving, 55–67, 83, 388, 432, 503
Then-now schema, 236
Theology, 25–29, 34–38
Thievery, 230
Time, 104, 294–295
Timothy, 9, 195–203, 594, 595–597, 604
Titus, 586, 587
Tongues
  gift of, 26–27, 442, 455, 461, 468, 475, 485, 490, 493–494, 497–498, 500–501, 502, 506–507, 518
  interpretation of, 456, 470–471, 494, 501–502, 518
Tradition, 392, 395–396, 405, 425–426, 431, 530, 533–534
Travel, 201, 417, 440, 589–593
Travelogue, 591

Triads, 184, 188–189, 332, 451, 484–485, 487–488
Tribunal, 169–170, 173
Trumpet, 496–497, 580–581
Tutors, 192–193, 195
Twelve, the, 535

Unbeliever, 234, 270–271, 506–507
Unity
　of First Corinthians, 10–14, 198, 203, 306–307, 377–378
　of the church at Corinth, xiv, 14, 20, 27, 69–70, 77–78, 458, 460, 462–463
Unleavened bread, 214–215
Unmarried, 287–298

Veils, 407–408, 410–411
Vices, catalogue of, 144, 215, 219–220, 222, 225, 229–231, 240
Victory, 359, 361–362, 546–556, 573–584
Virgin, 292, 293, 296
Virtues, catalogue of, 215, 220, 480, 484

Wages, 149, 159
"Walking," 144, 283
Watering, 141–142, 146
Ways, two, 200
Weak, weakness
　of God, 108
　of humans, 110–111, 305, 324–327, 386, 436–437, 439
　of Paul, 119, 351, 355–356

Widow, widower, 263, 268–269, 300
Wife, wives, 258–259, 265, 269–273, 294, 295, 303
Wild beasts, 557–558, 560
Will of God, 51
Wisdom
　divine, 72, 80, 89–114, 121–139
　gift of, 453
　human, 119, 134–135, 163
　Jesus Christ, as, 112
　of Paul, 122–123, 128
　of world, 96–97
Wise, the, 109, 110, 233
Wish prayer, 317–318, 614
Woe, 344, 348
Women, 292, 338, 393–416, 536
　domestic role, 513
　silence of, 513–517, 521
Word
　gift of, 62
　of God, 522, 533
　of the Lord, 267, 269
Work, 146, 149, 158, 160, 583
World, 104–105, 218, 221, 231, 295
Worship, 400–401, 402, 456, 510
Writing, 216

Xenophon, 420

Yeast, 213–214